EXCHANGE ARRANGEMENTS

AND

EXCHANGE RESTRICTIONS

ANNUAL REPORT 1997

Library of Congress Cataloging-in-Publication Data

International Monetary Fund.
  Annual report on exchange arrangements and exchange restrictions.
1979—

Continues: International Monetary Fund. Annual report on exchange
restrictions, 1950–1978
  1. Foreign exchange — Law and legislation — Periodicals. 2. Foreign
exchange — Control — Periodicals. I. Title.
K4440.A13 I57 [date] 341.7'51 79-644506
ISSN 0250-7366
ISBN 1-55775-666-X

Price: US$76.00
(US$38.00 to full-time university faculty members and students)

Please send orders to:
International Monetary Fund, Publication Services
700 19th Street, N.W., Washington, D.C. 20431, U.S.A.
Tel.: (202) 623-7430   Telefax: (202) 623-7201
E-mail: publications@imf.org
Internet: http://www.imf.org

recycled paper

Letter of Transmittal to Members
and Governors of the Fund

August 8, 1997

Dear Sir:

I have the honor to transmit to you a copy of the International Monetary Fund's *Annual Report on Exchange Arrangements and Exchange Restrictions, 1997*, which has been prepared in accordance with the provisions of Article XIV, Section 3 of the Articles of Agreement.

On behalf of the Executive Board, I should like to express our appreciation of the cooperation of the countries in the preparation of the Report.

Sincerely yours,

Michel Camdessus
*Chairman of the Executive Board
and Managing Director*

CONTENTS

CONTENTS

Note: The term "country," as used in this publication, does not in all cases refer to a territorial entity that is a state as understood by international law and practice; the term also covers some territorial entities that are not states but for which statistical data are maintained and provided internationally on a separate and independent basis.

PREFACE

The Annual Report on Exchange Arrangements and Exchange Restrictions has been published annually by the IMF since 1950. It draws on information available to the IMF from a number of sources, including that provided in the course of official visits to member countries, and it has been prepared in close consultation with national authorities. This report presents the information in a new tabular format and expands the coverage on the regulations on capital transactions.

This project was coordinated in the Monetary and Exchange Affairs Department by a staff team directed by R. Barry Johnston and coordinated by Susana Crossa de Sosa, comprising Alexander Kyei, Dmitri Menchikov, Virgilio A. Sandoval, Fabienne Piccinni, and Gregory S. Taft. It draws on the specialized contribution of that department (for specific countries), with assistance from staff members of the IMF's six area departments, together with staff of other departments. The report was edited by Gail Berre and Martha Bonilla of the External Relations Department, and was produced by Ms. Piccinni and the IMF Graphics Section.

DEFINITION OF ACRONYMS

Note: This list does not include acronyms of purely national institutions mentioned in the country chapters.

ACP	Atlantic, Caribbean, and Pacific countries
ACU	Asian Clearing Union (integrated by Bangladesh, India, the Islamic Republic of Iran, Myanmar, Nepal, Pakistan, and Sri Lanka)
AFTA	ASEAN free trade area (see ASEAN, below)
AMU	Asian monetary unit
ANZCERTA	Australia-New Zealand Closer Economic Relations and Trade Agreement
ASEAN	Association of South East Asian Nations (integrated by Brunei, Indonesia, Malaysia, Philippines, Singapore, and Thailand)
ATC	Agreement of Textiles and Clothing
BCEAO	Central Bank of West African States (Banque centrale des états de l'Afrique de l'ouest). (The West African States are Benin, Burkina Faso, Côte d'Ivoire, Mali, Niger, Senegal, and Togo.)
BEAC	Bank of Central African States (Banque des états de l'Afrique centrale). (The Central African States are Cameroon, Central African Republic, Chad, the Republic of Congo, Equatorial Guinea, and Gabon.)
BLEU	Belgian-Luxembourg Economic Union
CACM	Central American Common Market (integrated by Costa Rica, El Salvador, Guatemala, Honduras, and Nicaragua)
CAP	Common agricultural policy (of the EU)
CARICOM	Caribbean Common Market (integrated by Antigua and Barbuda, The Bahamas, Barbados, Belize, Dominica, Grenada, Guyana, Jamaica, Monster, St. Kitts and Nevis, St. Lucia, St. Vincent and the Grenadines, and Trinidad and Tobago)
CEEAC	Economic Community of Central African States
CEFTA	Central European free trade area
CEPGL	Economic Community of the Great Lakes Countries
CEPT	Common effective preferential tariff of the ASEAN free trade zone
CET	Common external tariff
CFA	Communauté financière africaine
CIS	Commonwealth of Independent States
CMA	Common monetary area (a single exchange control territory comprising Lesotho, Namibia, South Africa, and Swaziland)
CMCF	Carribean Multilateral Clearing Facility
CMEA	Council for Mutual Economic Assistance (dissolved) (Bulgaria, Cuba, Czechoslovakia, Hungary, Mongolia, Poland, Romania, U.S.S.R., and Vietnam)
COCOM	Coordinating Committee for Multilateral Export Controls
COMESA	Common market for Eastern and Southern Pacific
CPI	Consumer Price Index
ECCB	Eastern Caribbean Central Bank (Anguilla, Antigua and Barbuda, Dominica, Grenada, Montserrat, St. Kitts and Nevis, St. Lucia, and St. Vincent and the Grenadines)
ECLAC	Economic Commission for Latin America and the Caribbean
ECOWAS	Economic Community of West African States (Cedeao)
ECSC	European Coal and Steel Community
ECU	European currency unit
EEA	European economic area
EFTA	European Free Trade Association
EMS	European monetary system
ERM	Exchange rate mechanism (of the EMS)
EU	European Union (formerly European Community), (integrated by Austria, Belgium, Denmark, Finland, France, Germany, Greece, Ireland, Luxembourg, Netherlands, Portugal, Spain, Sweden, and United Kingdom)
FSU	Former Soviet Union
GATT	General Agreement on Tariffs and Trade
GCC	Gulf Cooperation Council (Cooperation Council for the Arab States of the Gulf) (Bahrain, Oman, Qatar, Saudi Arabia, and the United Arab Emirates)
GSP	Generalized system of preferences
HCDCS	Harmonized commodity description and coding system
IBEC	International Bank for Economic Cooperation
LAIA	Latin American Integration Association (integrated by Argentina, Bolivia, Brazil, Chile, Colombia, Ecuador, Mexico, Paraguay, Peru, Uruguay, and Venezuela)

LIBOR	London interbank offered rate
MERCOSUR	Southern Cone Common Market (integrated by Argentina, Brazil, Paraguay, and Uruguay)
MFA	Multifiber Arrangement
MFN	Most favored nation
MTN	Multilateral trade negotiations
NAFTA	North American Free Trade Agreement
NATO	North Atlantic Treaty Organization
OECD	Organization for Economic Cooperation and Development
OECS	Organization of Eastern Caribbean States (integrated by Antigua and Barbuda, Dominica, Grenada, Montserrat, St. Kitts and Nevis, St. Lucia, and St. Vincent and the Grenadines)
OGL	Open general license
OPEC	Organization of the Petroleum Exporting Countries
PTA	Preferential trade area for Eastern and Southern African states
SACU	Southern African Customs Union (integrated by Botswana, Lesotho, Namibia, South Africa, and Swaziland)
SADC	Southern Africa Development Community (integrated by Angola, Botswana, Lesotho, Malawi, Mauritius, Mozambique, Namibia, South Africa, Swaziland, Tanzania, Zambia, and Zimbabwe)
SDR	Special drawing rights
SIBOR	Singapore Interbank Offered Rate
SPARTECA	South Pacific Regional Trade and Economic Cooperation Agreement (signed by Australia, Cook Islands, Fiji, Kiribati, Nauru, New Zealand, Niue, Papua New Guinea, Solomon Islands, Tonga, Tuvalu, Vanuatu, and Western Samoa)
UAPTA	Union of account of the PTA
UDEAC	Central African Customs and Economic Union
UN	United Nations
UNITA	National Union for the Total Independence of Angola
VAT	Value-added tax
WACH	West African Clearing House
WAEC	West African Economic Community (CEAO) (dissolved)
WAEMU	West African Economic and Monetary Union (formerly WAMU, integrated by Benin, Burkina Faso, Côte d'Ivoire, Mali, Niger, Senegal, and Togo)
WTO	World Trade Organization (supersedes GATT)

INTRODUCTION

The report provides a detailed description of the exchange arrangements and exchange restrictions of individual member countries, including Hong Kong, China, for which the United Kingdom had accepted the IMF Articles of Agreement,[1] and Aruba and the Netherlands Antilles, for which the Kingdom of the Netherlands has accepted the IMF Articles of Agreement. In general, the description relates to the exchange and trade systems as of the end of 1996, but in appropriate cases, reference is made to significant developments that took place in early 1997.

The description of the exchange and trade system is not necessarily confined to those aspects involving exchange restrictions or exchange controls. As in previous reports, questions of definition and jurisdiction have not been raised, and an attempt has been made to describe exchange and trade systems in their entirety, except for the tariff structure and, in most cases, direct taxes on imports and exports.

Following a standardized approach, the description of each system is broken down into similar headings, and the coverage for each country includes a final section that lists chronologically the more significant changes during 1996 and early 1997.

The report is presented in a new tabular format that enhances transparency and the uniformity of treatment of the information among countries and also expands the coverage on the regulatory framework for capital movements. The information is drawn from a new exchange arrangements and exchange restrictions database established by the IMF. The following country tables present an abstract of the relevant information available to the IMF. The table on Summary Features of Exchange Arrangements and Regulatory Frameworks for Current and Capital Transactions in Members Countries (Appendix I) provides an overview of the characteristics of the exchange and trade systems of IMF member countries. A country table matrix (Appendix II) provides a listing of the possible entries in this database. In cases where the information in an entire section is not available at the time of publication, this is noted by "n.a." When information in a particular category within a section is not available at the time of publication, the category is not included in the table. When information is available on all but a particular item or items within a category, these are displayed with a note to that effect (i.e., n.a.).

The tabular presentation is organized as follows:

Status Under IMF Articles of Agreement indicates whether the member country has accepted the obligations of Article VIII, Sections 2, 3, and 4 of the IMF's Articles of Agreement or whether the country continues to avail itself of the transitional arrangements of Article XIV, Section 2.

Exchange Arrangement provides the description of the exchange arrangement that a member country has furnished to the IMF under Article IV, Section 2(*a*), including the exchange rate structure (i.e., whether there are one, two, or multiple exchange rates); the classification of the exchange arrangement on the basis of how the exchange rate is determined in the main market when there is more than one market; the existence of exchange taxes or subsidies; and the features of forward exchange markets, if any. Official coverage of forward operations refers to the case where an official entity (the central bank or the government) assumes the exchange risk of a certain foreign exchange transaction.

Arrangements for Payments and Receipts provides a description, where appropriate, of the prescription of currency requirements, the nature of payment arrangements, the administration of exchange control, international security restrictions, the nature of payments arrears, and controls on the trading of gold and domestic and foreign banknotes. Under this section, *Prescription of currency requirements* describes the requirements affecting the selection of the currency and the method of settlement for transactions with other countries. When a country has concluded payment agreements with other countries, the terms of these agreements often lead to a prescription of the currency for specified categories of payments to and from the countries concerned. *Administration of control* gives some indication of the authorities' responsibility for policy and the administration of controls, and of the extent to which their powers are delegated for working purposes. *International security restrictions* identifies restrictions on payments and transfers for current international transactions imposed by member countries for reasons of national or international security. IMF Executive Board Decision No. 144-(52/51) establishes the obligation of members to notify the IMF before imposing such restrictions, or, if circumstances preclude advance notification, members should notify the IMF as promptly as possible, but ordinarily no later than 30 days after imposing the restrictions.

Resident Accounts and *Nonresident Accounts* describe the manner in which the country treats accounts, if any, that are maintained in the national currency or in foreign currency, locally or abroad, by resident or nonresident account holders, and the facilities and limitations attached to such accounts. When there are more than one type of resident/nonresident account, the nature and operation of the various types are also described.

Imports and Import Payments describes the nature and extent of exchange and trade restrictions on imports and includes information on the existence of a foreign exchange budget (i.e., a priori allocation of a certain amount of foreign exchange, usually on an annual basis, for the importation of specific types of goods, sometimes indicating amounts for specified registered importers); on financing requirements for imports (minimum financing and advance payment requirements, and the existence of advance deposits); and on

---

[1] During the 1996/97 financial year, Hong Kong was administered by the United Kingdom. It was returned to the People's Republic of China as of July 1, 1997, and became a special administrative region of China.

documentation requirements for the release of foreign exchange for the payment of imports, such as the obligation to domicile the transactions with a specified financial institution, a preshipment inspection aimed at establishing the veracity of the import transaction in terms of volume, quality, and price, the obligation to pay by means of a letter of credit, and the need to submit an import license to obtain the foreign exchange. *Import licenses and other nontariff measures* uses the following terms to describe the licensing system, if any: (1) *Positive list* refers to a list in which goods that can be imported are listed; (2) *Negative list* refers to a list in which goods whose importation is prohibited are listed; (3) *Open general licenses* indicates arrangements whereby certain imports or other international transactions are exempt from the restrictive application of licensing requirements; (4) *Licenses with quotas* refers to cases where a license for the importation of a certain good is granted, but a specific limit is imposed on the amount to be imported; and (5) *Other nontariff measures* may include the prohibition to import a certain good or all goods from a certain country. Also, this section provides a brief description of the import tax/tariff system, specifying these revenues are collected through the exchange system, and providing information on whether state monopolies for the importation of certain goods exist.

Exports and Export Proceeds identifies restrictions on the use of export proceeds, as well as regulations on exports such as financing and documentation requirements (including letters of credit, the provision of guarantees, domiciliation, preshipment inspection, licensing requirements, and taxes levied—in particular through the exchange system—on exports). *Repatriation requirements* refers to the obligation of exporters to bring into the country export proceeds either by selling them in the foreign exchange market or depositing them in authorized accounts. *Surrender requirements* refers to regulations requiring the recipient of export proceeds to sell any foreign exchange proceeds in return for local currency, sometimes at a specified exchange rate, to the central bank, commercial banks, or exchange dealers authorized for this purpose.

Payments for Invisible Transactions and Current Transfers describes the procedures for effecting payments abroad for current transactions in invisibles with reference to prior approval requirements, the existence of quantitative and indicative limits, and/or bona fide tests. Detailed information on the most common categories of transactions is provided when regulations differ for the various categories. *Indicative limit* establishes maximum amounts up to which the purchase of foreign exchange is allowed upon declaration of the purpose of the transaction, mainly for statistical purposes. Amounts above those limits are granted if the bona fide nature of the transaction is established by the presentation of appropriate documentation. Bona fide tests also may be applied for transactions for which quantitative limits have not been established.

Proceeds from Invisible Transactions and Current Transfers gives all regulations governing exchange receipts derived from transactions in invisibles as well as a description of any limitations on the conversion into domestic currency and the use of those receipts. The concepts of repatriation and surrender requirements are similar to those applied to export proceeds. *Restrictions on use of funds* refers mainly to the limitations imposed on the use of receipts previously deposited in certain bank accounts.

Capital Transactions describes regulations influencing capital movements. The concepts of controls and capital transactions are interpreted broadly. Thus, controls on capital movements include prohibitions; need for prior approvals, authorizations, and notifications; multiple currency practices; discriminatory taxes; and reserve requirements or interest penalties imposed by the authorities that regulate the conclusion or execution of transactions or transfers with respect to both inward and outward capital flows or the holding of assets at home by nonresidents and abroad by residents. The coverage of the regulations would apply to receipts as well as payments and to actions initiated by nonresidents and residents. Moreover, because of their close association with capital movements, information is also provided on local financial operations conducted in foreign currency.

Under capital transactions, *Capital and money market instruments* refers to the public offering or private placement on a primary market or listing for offering on a secondary market. *Capital market securities* refers to shares and other securities of a participatory nature, and bonds and other securities with original maturity above one year. *Money market instruments* refers to securities of an original maturity of one year or less and includes short-term instruments such as treasury bills, certificates of deposit, and bills of exchange.

Collective investment securities includes share certificates and registry entries or other evidence of investor interest in an institution for collective investment, such as mutual funds, and unit and investment trusts.

Derivatives and other instruments refers to operations in other negotiable instruments and nonsecuritized claims not covered under the above subsections. These may include operations in rights; warrants; financial options and futures; secondary market operations in other financial claims (including sovereign loans, mortgage loans, commercial credits, negotiable instruments originating as loans, receivables, and discounted bills of trade); forward operations (including those in foreign exchange); swaps of bonds and other debt securities; credits and loans; and other swaps (interest rate, debt/equity, equity/debt, foreign currency, as well as swaps of any of the instruments listed above).

Credit operations is subdivided into *commercial credits* covering operations directly linked with international trade transactions or with the rendering of international services; *financial credits*, which are credits other than commercial credits; *guarantees and sureties*, including securities pledged for payment or performance of a contract, such as warrants or avals, performance bonds, and stand-by letters of credit;

and *financial backup facilities*, which cover credit facilities used as a guarantee for independent financial operations.

Direct investment refers to investment for the purpose of establishing lasting economic relations, essentially for the purpose of producing goods and services, and, in particular, investments that allow investor participation in their management. It includes the creation or extension of a wholly owned enterprise, subsidiary, or branch and the acquisition of full or partial ownership of a new or existing enterprise that results in effective influence over the operations of this enterprise. *Liquidation of direct investment* refers to the transfer of principal, including the initial capital and capital gains, of a direct investment as defined above.

Real estate transactions refers to the acquisition of real estate not associated with direct investment. It would include, for example, investments of a purely financial nature

in real estate or the acquisition of real estate for personal use.

Provisions specific to commercial banks and other credit institutions describes regulations that are specific to these institutions, such as monetary and prudential controls, including reserve requirements; liquid asset requirements; interest rate regulations; credit controls; and open foreign exchange position limits. *Provisions specific to institutional investors* describes controls specific to institutions such as insurance companies and pension funds, and may include, for example, controls on the proportion of the institutions' portfolios that may be held in local or foreign assets. *Other controls imposed by securities laws* refers to additional regulations on capital movements imposed by those laws, such as restrictions on the listing of foreign securities on local security markets.

ISLAMIC STATE OF AFGHANISTAN

(Position as of December 31, 1994)

Status Under IMF Articles of Agreement

Article XIV	Yes.

Exchange Arrangement

Currency

The currency of the Islamic State of Afghanistan is the Afghani. Two types of Afghanis are in circulation; that which circulates in the north is illegal in Kabul and other areas under Taliban control.

Exchange rate structure

Multiple

The Da Afghanistan Bank (DAB) (the central bank) maintains an official rate defined in terms of the U.S. dollar. The official rate is applied to no more than 10% of convertible currency transactions including a few transactions of the central government (mainly debt-service payments) and certain foreign currency income earned in the Islamic State of Afghanistan. Almost all other official transactions are conducted at a commercial rate set by the government. A free market, in the form of a money bazaar, is also operative. In the north, the free market exchange rate is about Af 75,000 per $1, and in other areas, it is about Af 25,000 per $1. The exchange rate applied to transactions of international organizations is set at 80% of the level of the commercial exchange rate.

Classification

Independent floating

Most convertible currency transactions are effected at the floating commercial market rate. The DAB posts rates for deutsche mark, French francs, Indian rupees, Pakistani rupees, pounds sterling, and Swiss francs.

Forward exchange market

No.

Arrangements for Payments and Receipts

Prescription of currency requirements

Settlements with countries with which the Islamic State of Afghanistan maintains bilateral payments agreements are made in bilateral accounting dollars in accordance with the procedures set forth in these agreements. Exchange rates for trade under bilateral payments agreements are determined under each agreement. The proceeds from exports of karakul to all countries must be obtained in convertible currencies. There are no other prescription of currency requirements.

Payment arrangements

Bilateral arrangements

The Islamic State of Afghanistan maintains bilateral payments agreements with Bulgaria, China, the Czech Republic, Hungary, Russia, and the Slovak Republic. Some of these have been inactive for several years and others are being phased out.

Operative	Yes.
Inoperative	Yes.
Regional arrangements	n.a.
Clearing agreements	n.a.
Barter agreements and open accounts	n.a.

Administration of control

Exchange control authorities

Foreign exchange transactions are controlled by the government through the DAB. No restrictions apply to transactions in the free exchange market.

Controls on trade in gold (coins and/or bullion)

Controls on external trade

Imports and reexports of gold are permitted, subject to regulations. Exports of gold bullion, silver, and jewelry require permission from the DAB and the Ministry of Finance. Commercial exports of gold and silver jewelry and other articles containing minor quantities of gold or silver do not require a license. Customs duties are payable on imports and exports of silver in any form, unless the transaction is made by or on behalf of the monetary authorities.

Controls on exports and imports of banknotes

On exports

Domestic currency

Travelers may take out up to Af 2,000 in domestic banknotes and Af 50 in coins.

Foreign currency

n.a.

On imports

Domestic currency

Travelers may bring in up to Af 2,000 in domestic banknotes and Af 50 in coins.

Foreign currency

Travelers entering the Islamic State of Afghanistan are required to spend a minimum of the equivalent of $26 a day in foreign exchange. They may bring in any amount of foreign currency but must declare it when entering the country if they intend to take out any unspent amount on departure, subject to the above minimum conversion requirement.

Resident Accounts

n.a.

Nonresident Accounts

n.a.

Imports and Import Payments

Foreign exchange budget

An annual import program drawn up by the Ministry of Commerce covers both public and private sector imports. Adjustments in the public sector import plan are made as circumstances change. The import plan for the private sector, drawn up on the basis of proposals submitted by the Chamber of Commerce, is indicative.

Documentation requirements for release of foreign exchange for imports

Domiciliation requirements

n.a.

Preshipment inspection

n.a.

Letters of credit

Payments for imports through the banking system to countries with which the Islamic State of Afghanistan has payments agreements may usually be made only under letters of credit. Payments to other countries may be made under letters of credit, against bills for collection, or against an undertaking by the importer to import goods of at least equivalent value to the payment made through the banking system. Except for public sector imports under the government budget, all importers are required to lodge minimum import deposits with banks when they open letters of credit. The deposit ratios, based on the c.i.f. value of imports, are 20% for essential products and range from 30% to 60% for other products.

Import licenses used as exchange licenses	n.a.
Import licenses and other nontariff measures	Imports are not subject to license, but import transactions must be registered before orders are placed abroad.
Positive list	Most bilateral agreements, however, specify quantities (and sometimes prices) for commodities to be traded.
Negative list	The importation of certain drugs, liquor, arms, and ammunition is prohibited on grounds of public policy or for security reasons; in some instances, however, special permission to import these goods may be granted. The importation of a few textiles and selected nonessential consumer goods is also prohibited.
Open general licenses	n.a.
Licenses with quotas	There are no quantitative restrictions on most imports, but tariff rates on most consumer items range from 30% to 50%.
Import taxes and/or tariffs	No.
State import monopoly	No.

Exports and Export Proceeds

Repatriation requirements	Export proceeds from bilateral accounts may be retained in bilateral clearing dollar accounts with the DAB. These retained proceeds may either be used directly by the original exporter or sold to other importers. In either case, the retained proceeds are converted at the clearing rate applicable to that particular bilateral arrangement. In the case of exports to countries trading in convertible currencies, export proceeds may be retained abroad for 3, 6, or 12 months, depending on the country of destination. During the relevant period, the exporter may use these funds to import any goods not included on the list of prohibited goods. Alternatively, at the end of the relevant holding period limit, foreign exchange holdings abroad must be repatriated and held in a foreign currency account with a bank in the Islamic State of Afghanistan or sold at the commercial exchange rate.
Surrender requirements	Proceeds from exports of raisins, fresh fruits, animal casings, skins, licorice roots, medicinal herbs, and wool must be surrendered immediately at the commercial exchange rate.
Export licenses	Export transactions must be registered. The exportation of opium and museum pieces is prohibited. Otherwise, control is exercised only over exports to bilateral agreement countries.
Without quotas	Yes.

Payments for Invisible Transactions and Current Transfers

Controls on these payments	Foreign exchange for most private purposes may be acquired in the money bazaar.
Payments for travel	The DAB levies a charge of Af 0.75 per $1 and 1% of hard currency for permits that approve the exportation of convertible currency by authorized travelers.
Prior approval	Yes.
Quantitative limits	The limit for tourist travel is $1,000, except for private travel to India, for which the limit is the equivalent of $700. The limit for business travel is $15,000.
Indicative limits/bona fide test	n.a.
Medical costs	For medical treatment, the central bank levies a commission of Af 0.75 per $1.
Prior approval	Yes.
Quantitative limits	Normally, the DAB grants $2,500 for medical treatment.

Indicative limits/bona fide test	n.a.
Foreign workers' wages	Foreign employees working in the Afghan public and private sectors must convert 60% of their foreign currency salaries into Afghanis at the official rate.
Prior approval	n.a.
Quantitative limits	Yes.
Indicative limits/bona fide test	n.a.

Proceeds from Invisible Transactions and Current Transfers

n.a.

Capital Transactions

Controls on direct investment

Outward direct investment	n.a.
Inward direct investment	Investments require prior approval and are administered by the Investment Committee. The law stipulates that foreign investment in the Islamic State of Afghanistan can take place only through joint ventures, with foreign participation not exceeding 49%, and that an investment approved by the Investment Committee shall require no further license in order to operate in the Islamic State of Afghanistan. The Foreign and Domestic Private Investment Law No. 1353 (1974) includes the following provisions:

(1) income tax exemption for 4 years (6 years outside Kabul province), beginning with the date of the first sale of products resulting from the new investment;

(2) exemption from import duties on essential imports (mainly of capital goods);

(3) exemption from taxes on dividends for 4 years after the first distribution of dividends, but not more than 7 years after the approval of the investment;

(4) exemption from personal income and corporate taxes on interest on foreign loans that constitute part of an approved investment;

(5) exemption from export duties, provided that the products are not among the prohibited exports; and

(6) mandatory procurement by government agencies and departments from enterprises established under the law as long as the prices are not more than 15% higher than those of foreign suppliers.

Controls on liquidation of direct investment

Capital may be repatriated after 5 years at an annual rate not exceeding 20% of the total registered capital.

Changes During 1995–96

[The IMF has not received from the authorities the information required for a description of the exchange and trade system as of December 1995 and December 1996.]

ALBANIA

(Position as of December 31, 1996)

Status Under IMF Articles of Agreement

Article XIV	Yes.

Exchange Arrangement

Currency

The currency of Albania is the lek.

Other legal tender

In special cases and with prior approval from the Bank of Albania (BOA), foreign exchange may serve as a means of payment.

Exchange rate structure

Unitary.

Classification

Independent floating

The exchange rate of the lek is determined on the basis of supply and demand for foreign exchange. The BOA calculates and announces the daily average exchange rates for the U.S. dollar and 22 other major currencies. No margins are set between buying and selling rates for the official exchange rate. Government transactions are conducted at market rates. However, the commercial banks charge commissions ranging from 0.2% to 2%, depending on the amount, for cashing traveler's checks.

Exchange tax

No.

Exchange subsidy

No.

Arrangements for Payments and Receipts

Prescription of currency requirements

Payment for all merchandise trade is made in convertible currencies. All transactions under bilateral payment agreements were suspended in 1992, and the settlement of clearing accounts is pending the outcome of negotiations.

Payment arrangements

Bilateral arrangements

Inoperative

Albania maintains bilateral payment agreements in nonconvertible currencies with Bulgaria, Cuba, the Czech Republic, Germany, Hungary, the Democratic People's Republic of Korea, Poland, Romania, and Vietnam. Albania also maintains bilateral payment agreements in convertible currencies with Algeria, Bulgaria, China, Cuba, the Czech Republic, Egypt, Greece, the Democratic People's Republic of Korea, Romania, the Slovak Republic, Turkey, Vietnam, and the Federal Republic of Yugoslavia (Serbia/Montenegro).

Regional arrangements

Yes.

Barter agreements and open accounts

Albania maintains a clearing agreement with Malaysia.

Administration of control

Exchange control authorities

The BOA is vested with the powers to administer exchange controls. The BOA may (1) authorize foreign exchange operations and allow securities banks to conduct foreign exchange operations; (2) define the limits of their activities; and (3) supervise foreign exchange operations to prevent any participant from dominating the market. It monitors licensed banks and foreign exchange bureaus and dealers to ensure that their operations comply with foreign exchange regulations. There is a reporting requirement on banks and exchange dealers for transactions above $15,000 or its equivalent at the exchange rate prevailing on the date the transaction is effected.

Payment arrears

Official

Albania has arrears on debts with China, Turkey, Greece, and with a number of commercial creditors.

Controls on trade in gold (coins and/or bullion)

Controls on domestic ownership and/or trade

Yes.

Controls on external trade

Yes.

Controls on exports and imports of banknotes

On exports

  Domestic currency

Natural and juridical persons are allowed to take out up to lek 100,000 a person in banknotes and coins. The BOA may authorize larger amounts.

  Foreign currency

Foreign visitors may take abroad in cash or traveler's checks foreign exchange in an amount equal to the amount brought into the country. Natural or juridical persons are not allowed to export amounts larger than $15,000 or its equivalent.

On imports

  Domestic currency

Natural and juridical persons are allowed to import up to lek 100,000 in domestic banknotes and coins. The BOA may authorize larger amounts.

  Foreign currency

Natural and juridical persons are allowed to import foreign currency up to $15,000 or its equivalent in any other currency.

Resident Accounts

Eligibility to hold accounts

Juridical and natural persons are eligible.

Foreign exchange accounts permitted

Yes.

Held domestically

Yes.

Held abroad

Approval is required, but a commercial bank may, on its own account or on behalf of a third party, open and hold balances with other banks as well as other financial institutions abroad without prior approval from the BOA.

Accounts in domestic currency convertible into foreign currency

No.

Nonresident Accounts

Eligibility to hold accounts

Juridical and natural persons are eligible.

Foreign exchange accounts permitted

Yes.

Domestic currency accounts

Yes.

Convertible into foreign currency

Yes.

Blocked accounts

No.

Imports and Import Payments

Foreign exchange budget	No.
Financing requirements for imports	No.
Documentation requirements for release of foreign exchange for imports	
Letters of credit	Letters of credit should be used for the payment of imports in excess of $200,000 or its equivalent.
Import licenses used as exchange licenses	Licenses are required for payments of imports equal to or larger than $5,000.
Import licenses and other nontariff measures	No.
Import taxes and/or tariffs	There are five tariff rates: zero, 5%, 10%, 20%, and 30%, which are applied to the c.i.f. value.
Taxes collected through the exchange system	No.
State import monopoly	No.

Exports and Export Proceeds

Repatriation requirements	Yes.
Surrender requirements	No.
Financing requirements	No.
Documentation requirements	No.
Export licenses	There are export bans on unprocessed wood and metal scrap.
Export taxes	No.

Payments for Invisible Transactions and Current Transfers

Controls on these payments	There are no controls on these payments, but supporting documents for transactions exceeding $5,000 are required.

Proceeds from Invisible Transactions and Current Transfers

Repatriation requirements	Yes.
Surrender requirements	No.

Capital Transactions

Controls on capital and money market instruments	Purchases of these instruments abroad by residents require prior approval of the BOA.
On capital market securities	
Sale or issue locally by nonresidents	n.a.

Purchase abroad by residents	Purchases are subject to the prior approval of the BOA.
Sale or issue abroad by residents	n.a.

On money market instruments

Sale or issue locally by nonresidents	n.a.
Purchase abroad by residents	Purchases are subject to the prior approval of the BOA.
Sale or issue abroad by residents	n.a.

On collective investment securities

Sale or issue locally by nonresidents	n.a.
Purchase abroad by residents	Purchases are subject to the prior approval of the BOA.
Sale or issue abroad by residents	n.a.

Controls on credit operations

Commercial credits	Commercial banks may not, without prior approval of the BOA, extend credit to non-residents, except banks and other financial institutions.
By residents to nonresidents	Yes.

Financial credits

By residents to nonresidents	Yes.

Guarantees, sureties, and financial backup facilities

By residents to nonresidents	Yes.

Controls on direct investment

Outward direct investment	Yes.

Controls on liquidation of direct investment	No.

Controls on real estate transactions

Purchase abroad by residents	Purchases are subject to prior approval of the BOA.

Provisions specific to commercial banks and other credit institutions

Lending to nonresidents (financial or commercial credits)	Commercial banks may not, without prior approval of the BOA, extend credit to non-residents, except to banks and other financial institutions.
Differential treatment of nonresident deposit accounts and/or deposit accounts in foreign exchange	
Liquid asset requirements	Authorized banks must maintain 90% cover on the foreign deposits placed with them.
Open foreign exchange position limits	The limit is 8% of the banks' capital.

Changes During 1996

No significant changes occurred in the exchange and trade system.

ALGERIA

(Position as of December 31, 1996)

Status Under IMF Articles of Agreement

Article XIV	Yes.

Exchange Arrangement

Currency	The currency of Algeria is the Algerian dinar.
Exchange rate structure	Unitary.
Classification	
Managed floating	The external value of the dinar is set at the interbank foreign exchange market. No margin limits are imposed on buying and selling exchange rates in the interbank foreign exchange market. However, a margin of DA 0.017 has been established between the buying and selling rates of the Bank of Algeria (BOA) for the dinar against the U.S. dollar.
Exchange tax	No.
Exchange subsidy	No.
Forward exchange market	Authorized banks may provide forward cover to residents, but this has not taken place.
Official cover of forward operations	No.

Arrangements for Payments and Receipts

Prescription of currency requirements	Settlements with countries with which no payments agreements are in force are made in convertible currencies. Payments under foreign supply contracts can be made in either the currency in use at the headquarters of the supplier or that of the country of origin of the merchandise, except that transactions with Morocco can be effected in U.S. dollars through special clearing accounts maintained at the central banks of the respective countries.
Payment arrangements	
Clearing agreements	Specified noncommercial settlements with Morocco and Tunisia are made through a dirham account at the Bank of Morocco and a Tunisian dinar account at the Bank of Tunisia.
Administration of control	
Exchange control authorities	The BOA has general jurisdiction over exchange controls. Authority for a number of exchange control procedures has been delegated to 7 commercial banks and the Postal Administration.
International security restrictions	No.
Payment arrears	No.
Controls on trade in gold (coins and/or bullion)	
Controls on domestic ownership and/or trade	Residents may purchase, hold, and sell gold coins in Algeria for numismatic purposes. Unworked gold for industrial and professional use is distributed by the Agence nationale pour la distribution et la transformation de l'or et des autres métaux précieux (AGENOR); this agency is also authorized to purchase gold in Algeria and to hold, process, and distribute any other precious metals.

Controls on external trade	AGENOR is authorized to import and export any precious metals, including gold. Gold used by dentists and goldsmiths is imported by AGENOR. Gold and other precious metals are included on the list of items importable by concessionaires.
Controls on exports and imports of banknotes	
On exports	
Domestic currency	Resident travelers may take out up to DA 200 a person.
Foreign currency	Foreign nonresident travelers may reexport any foreign currency they declared upon entry. Resident travelers can export foreign currency withdrawn from their foreign currency accounts up to the equivalent of F 50,000 a trip. (The number of trips a year is unlimited.)
On imports	
Domestic currency	Resident travelers may reimport up to DA 200 a person. Nonresidents are not permitted to bring in Algerian dinar banknotes.
Foreign currency	There are no restrictions on the importation of foreign banknotes, but residents and nonresidents must declare them when they enter Algeria.

Resident Accounts

Eligibility to hold accounts	Juridical and natural persons are eligible.
Foreign exchange accounts permitted	Yes.
Held domestically	These accounts may be freely credited with book transfers of convertible currencies from abroad using either postal or banking facilities, imported convertible foreign currencies that were declared at the time of the account holder's entry into the country, and domestic bank-to-bank book transfers between accounts held by individuals. These accounts may be debited freely for book transfers abroad but only through the banking system. They may also be debited for purchases of dinars, for book transfers in dinars, and for purchases of convertible foreign currencies to be physically exported by the account holder. The interest rate payable on deposits in these accounts is fixed quarterly by the BOA.
	Economic entities are also allowed to open foreign currency accounts for receiving and making foreign currency transfers, including the retained proportion of their export proceeds. They may transfer funds in these accounts to other foreign currency accounts or use them to make payments in Algeria or to make foreign currency payments for goods and services pertaining to their business.
Held abroad	No.
Accounts in domestic currency convertible into foreign currency	These accounts are permitted in certain cases, e.g., embassies.

Nonresident Accounts

Eligibility to hold accounts	Juridical and natural persons are eligible.
Foreign exchange accounts permitted	These accounts may be credited with foreign currency banknotes and other means of payment denominated in foreign currency, as well as other dinar-denominated funds that meet all requirements for transfers abroad. They may be debited without restrictions to make transfers abroad, to export through withdrawals of foreign banknotes, and to make dinar payments in Algeria. These accounts pay interest and may not show a net debit position.

Domestic currency accounts	Final departure accounts may be opened, without prior authorization, in the name of any natural person residing in Algeria who is not of Algerian nationality, and who intends to leave Algeria to return to his or her country of origin. These accounts may be credited with an amount equivalent to the holdings as of October 20, 1963, of the person concerned; the proceeds from sales of real estate by the account holder, provided that the funds are paid directly by a ministerial officer; the proceeds of the sale of securities through a bank; and any other payments, up to DA 2,000. These accounts may be debited without prior approval for certain payments in Algeria on behalf of the account holder.
Convertible into foreign currency	Outward transfers require individual approval.
Blocked accounts	Individual suspense accounts may be opened without authorization and may be credited with payments from any country.

Imports and Import Payments

Foreign exchange budget	No.
Financing requirements for imports	Payments for imports of gold, other precious metals, and precious stones must be made from foreign currency accounts. External borrowing by importers for import financing purposes must be arranged through the authorized intermediary banks.
Advance payment requirements	Except otherwise indicated by the BOA, down payments for imports may not exceed 15% of the total value of imports. When a public agency, public enterprise, or ministry incurs expenditures for imports deemed to be urgent or exceptional, the bank may effect payment before exchange and trade control formalities have been completed.
Advance import deposits	Although not an official regulation, domiciled banks may require from the importer, as part of their normal commercial operations, a deposit in dinars up to the full value of the imports.
Documentation requirements for release of foreign exchange for imports	Imports must be insured by Algerian insurers.
Domiciliation requirements	All imports are subject to obligatory domiciliation at an authorized intermediary bank, which an importer must establish by submitting a commercial contract or pro forma invoice. Import payments may be made freely but only through the domiciled bank, which effects payments in foreign exchange and debits the importer's account with corresponding amounts in dinars valued at the official exchange rate.
Import licenses and other nontariff measures	Any juridical or natural person registered under the Commercial Register (including concessionaires and wholesalers) may import goods without prior authorization; no license is needed.
Negative list	There are no legal restrictions against Israel, but there are no imports from Israel in practice. A small number of imports are prohibited for religious or security reasons.
Import taxes and/or tariffs	No.
State import monopoly	No.

Exports and Export Proceeds

Repatriation requirements	Proceeds must be repatriated within 120 days. Petroleum companies are subject to the same rule, but proceeds may be deposited in a guaranteed account with a foreign correspondent bank of the BOA.
Surrender requirements	All export proceeds from crude and refined hydrocarbons, by-products from gas, and mineral products must be surrendered to the BOA. Exporters of other products must surrender 50% of the proceeds to the interbank market; the remaining portion may be retained in a foreign currency account. Exporters may use the funds in these accounts

for imports or other payments pertaining to their business, or they may transfer the funds to another foreign currency account. Proceeds from exports of nonhydrocarbons, and nonminerals may be surrendered to commercial banks and other authorized participants in the interbank foreign exchange market.

Financing requirements	No.
Documentation requirements	The requirements are not enforced in practice.
Letters of credit	Yes.
Guarantees	Yes.
Domiciliation	Yes.
Preshipment inspection	Yes.
Export licenses	All exports to Israel are prohibited, and certain exports are prohibited for social or cultural reasons regardless of destination.
Export taxes	No.

Payments for Invisible Transactions and Current Transfers

Controls on these payments	All trade-related payments for approved trade transactions are free; there are no controls on payments for freight and insurance, unloading and storage costs, administrative expenses, commissions, credit card use abroad, and on interest payments.
Profit/dividends	
Prior approval	Profit remittances are permitted, provided tax obligations have been met.
Payments for travel	Foreign exchange allocation for tourism by Algerian residents was suspended in October 1986. Pilgrims traveling to Saudi Arabia receive an allowance in Saudi Arabian riyals. The amount is fixed for each pilgrimage and may be provided in the form of checks that may be cashed on arrival for those traveling by air or by sea. Travel tickets purchased by nonresidents for travel abroad must be paid for with imported foreign exchange.
Prior approval	Yes.
Quantitative limits	The limits range between DA 300,000 and DA 1,800,000 for official or business travel depending on (1) annual revenues, (2) capital base, and (3) financial statements of the company in question. Commercial banks (not BOA) are responsible for determining limits within ceilings.
Indicative limits/bona fide test	n.a.
Medical costs	
Prior approval	Approval is required for amounts over DA 120,000.
Quantitative limits	The limit is DA 120,000 a year.
Indicative limits/bona fide test	Yes.
Study abroad costs	Banks and the Postal Administration may provide foreign exchange up to the established limit.
Prior approval	Approval is required for amounts over DA 7,500.
Quantitative limits	The limit is DA 7,500 a month, for a school year.
Indicative limits/bona fide test	Yes.
Subscriptions and membership fees	
Prior approval	Approval of the BOA is required.

Indicative limits/bona fide test	Yes.
Consulting/legal fees	
Prior approval	Approval of the BOA is required.
Indicative limits/bona fide test	Yes.
Foreign workers' wages	
Quantitative limits	Residents of other countries working in Algeria under technical cooperation programs for public enterprises and agencies or for certain mixed companies may transfer abroad up to 100% of their salaries.
Indicative limits/bona fide test	Yes.
Pensions	
Prior approval	Approval of the BOA is required.
Indicative limits/bona fide test	Yes.
Family maintenance/alimony	
Prior approval	The BOA must authorize the granting of foreign exchange.
Quantitative limits	Limits are set on a case-by-case basis.
Indicative limits/bona fide test	n.a.

Proceeds from Invisible Transactions and Current Transfers

Repatriation requirements	Yes.
Surrender requirements	Fifty percent of the receipts must be surrendered to the banks.
Restrictions on use of funds	No.

Capital Transactions

Controls on capital and money market instruments	Capital transfers to any destination abroad are subject to individual approval by the BOA.
On capital market securities	
Purchase locally by nonresidents	n.a.
Sale or issue locally by nonresidents	n.a.
Purchase abroad by residents	Yes.
Sale or issue abroad by residents	n.a.
On money market instruments	
Sale or issue locally by nonresidents	n.a.
Purchase abroad by residents	Yes.
Sale or issue abroad by residents	n.a.
On collective investment securities	
Purchase locally by nonresidents	n.a.
Sale or issue locally by nonresidents	n.a.

Purchase abroad by residents	Yes.
Sale or issue abroad by residents	n.a.
Controls on derivatives and other instruments	
Purchase locally by nonresidents	n.a.
Sale or issue locally by nonresidents	n.a.
Purchase abroad by residents	Yes.
Sale or issue abroad by residents	n.a.
Controls on credit operations	
Commercial credits	
By residents to nonresidents	Yes.
To residents from nonresidents	n.a.
Financial credits	
By residents to nonresidents	Yes.
To residents from nonresidents	n.a.
Guarantees, sureties, and financial backup facilities	
By residents to nonresidents	Yes.
To residents from nonresidents	n.a.
Controls on direct investment	
Outward direct investment	Yes.
Inward direct investment	Foreign direct investment is freely permitted, except in certain specified sectors, provided that it conforms to the laws and regulations governing regulated activities and that prior declaration is made to the authorities.
Controls on liquidation of direct investment	No.
Controls on real estate transactions	
Purchase abroad by residents	Yes.
Purchase locally by nonresidents	n.a.
Sale locally by nonresidents	n.a.
Provisions specific to commercial banks and other credit institutions	
Borrowing abroad	Banks and financial institutions can borrow from abroad for their own needs or for those of their clients.
Lending to nonresidents (financial or commercial credits)	n.a.
Lending locally in foreign exchange	These transactions are restricted; however, banks and financial institutions can on-lend foreign funds borrowed abroad.
Purchase of locally issued securities denominated in foreign exchange	n.a.

Differential treatment of nonresident deposit accounts and/or deposit accounts in foreign exchange

   Interest rate controls

The interest rates applicable to foreign currency accounts are determined quarterly by the BOA.

Open foreign exchange position limits

Banks and financial institutions are required to meet the following cover:

(1) a maximum spread of 10% between their position (short or long) in each currency and the amount of their counterpart funds in domestic currency; and

(2) a maximum spread of 30% between total exposure (short and long positions, whichever is highest) for all foreign currencies and domestic currency resources.

Provisions specific to institutional investors

No.

Changes During 1996

Exchange arrangements

January 2. The BOA established an interbank foreign exchange market.

December 18. The BOA authorized the establishment of foreign exchange bureaus.

Arrangements for payments and receipts

December 19. The BOA delegated to commercial banks the authority to carry out foreign exchange transactions up to specific ceilings for health and education spending abroad, as well as for business expenses.

ANGOLA

(Position as of December 31, 1996)

Status Under IMF Articles of Agreement

Article XIV	Yes.

Exchange Arrangement

Currency	The currency of Angola is the adjusted kwanza (KZR).
Exchange rate structure	Unitary.
Classification	
Pegged	Through June 1996, the official exchange rate of the adjusted kwanza was fixed by the National Bank of Angola (BNA) and applied to sales of foreign exchange to commercial banks on the basis of allocations that were administratively set at fixing sessions held from time to time. On July 1, 1996, the authorities pegged the official exchange rate to the U.S. dollar and mandated that all transactions take place at the official exchange rate. Exchange houses were no longer allowed to deal at market-determined rates but instead were obliged to deal at rates set for commercial banks. The BNA applies a spread of 1% to its buying and selling exchange rates (primary official), and commercial banks apply a spread of 6.1% to their buying and selling rates (secondary official). An illegal parallel rate also exists as a result, inter alia, of restrictions on official rate foreign exchange transactions. The premium as of end-1996 was 20%–25% and the spread about 7%–8%.
Exchange tax	No.
Exchange subsidy	No.
Forward exchange market	No.

Arrangements for Payments and Receipts

Prescription of currency requirements	The BNA prescribes the currency to be used in import and export transactions, which is either that of the country of origin of imports or the country of destination of exports, or the U.S. dollar.
Payment arrangements	
Barter agreements and open accounts	Bilateral settlement arrangements, which do not contain bilateral payment features, are maintained with Brazil, Portugal, and Spain.
Administration of control	
Exchange control authorities	According to the new exchange law approved in early 1997, the BNA is the exchange authority; it has the authority to delegate its powers pertaining to specific activities to other entities. The BNA has authorized commercial banks and exchange houses to carry out transactions in the foreign exchange market. Foreign exchange dealers licensed to operate in foreign exchange may deal only in banknotes and traveler's checks. The BNA has delegated authority to banks to license and execute permitted invisible and capital foreign exchange transactions.
International security restrictions	No.
Payment arrears	
Official	Yes.
Private	Yes.

Controls on trade in gold (coins and/or bullion)	
Controls on domestic ownership and/or trade	Residents are permitted to hold and trade gold only in the form of jewelry.
Controls on external trade	Imports and exports of gold are the monopoly of the BNA.
Controls on exports and imports of banknotes	
On exports	
Domestic currency	Exports of domestic currency are prohibited.
Foreign currency	Residents are permitted to take out more than $5,000 in foreign exchange only if they present exchange purchase documents. Nonresidents must present such documents when the amount exceeds $10,000. When departing Angola, nonresidents visiting the country for purposes of tourism or business are permitted, upon presentation of the corresponding sales vouchers, to repurchase up to 50% of the foreign exchange they sold to institutions accredited to deal in foreign exchange.
On imports	
Domestic currency	Reimports of domestic currency are prohibited.
Foreign currency	There are no limits on the amount of foreign banknotes or traveler's checks that a person may bring into the country, but any amount exceeding the equivalent of $10,000 must be declared upon arrival.

Resident Accounts

Eligibility to hold accounts	Juridical and natural persons are eligible.
Foreign exchange accounts permitted	Yes.
Held domestically	Checkbooks may not be issued against personal accounts. These accounts may be credited with retained export earnings, foreign currency transferred from abroad, cash, traveler's checks, foreign payment orders, and interest accrued. They may be debited with sales against domestic currency, but, as of July 1996, they may not be used in settlement of imports of goods and invisibles or capital payments. Transfers between these accounts are prohibited.
Held abroad	n.a.

Nonresident Accounts

Eligibility to hold accounts	Juridical and natural persons are eligible.
Foreign exchange accounts permitted	Prior approval is required to open these accounts; they may be credited with foreign exchange transferred from abroad or the deposit of proceeds from the account holder's activities in Angola. They may be debited with the sale of foreign exchange or the repatriation of all or part of the existing deposit.
Domestic currency accounts	Accounts in adjusted kwanzas may be opened or held by former residents, but the funds in such accounts may only be withdrawn to cover expenses incurred during their stay in Angola.
Convertible into foreign currency	No.
Approval required	n.a.

Imports and Import Payments

Foreign exchange budget   Yes.

Documentation requirements for release of foreign exchange for imports

Domiciliation requirements   n.a.

Preshipment inspection   Yes.

Letters of credit   Yes.

Import licenses and other nontariff measures

Positive list

All imports are subject to licensing according to a positive list and the foreign exchange budget. The issuance of import licenses for transactions paid with foreign exchange purchased from the banking system is subject to the availability of foreign exchange. The corresponding positive list assigns priority to particular transactions, which are periodically announced by the BNA. Import licenses are also required for statistical purposes even if, exceptionally, the foreign exchange is not purchased from the banking system. These licenses are issued upon application. Licenses for imports requiring foreign exchange from the banking system are granted only to importers registered with the Ministry of Commerce and require a pro forma invoice from the supplier valid for 90 days that includes the price and shipment cost, as well as a bank guarantee of payment of the local currency counterpart. Prior to shipment, products must be submitted for inspection to ascertain compliance with market-competitive pricing by the Société générale de surveillance. Import licenses are valid for 180 days after issuance and may be extended once for an additional 180 days. A license fee of 0.1% of the import value is levied. The importation of goods using the importer's own funds requires the prior sale of foreign currency to a commercial bank in an amount equal to the value of the operation in question. It is also possible to import under the bonded warehouse system, in which case the importer applies to the commercial bank for the requisite authorization, presenting the required documentation. Merchandise imports involving credit from the exporter are subject to analysis by the BNA as a means of ensuring optimal and sound management of external financial resources and guaranteeing compliance with, and maintenance of, a sustainable level of indebtedness. Accordingly, in submitting the import documentation to the commercial bank, importers must attach the terms and conditions of credit with respect to the goods to be imported, and must then follow the same procedures that apply to other arrangements.

Import taxes and/or tariffs   Yes.

Taxes collected through the exchange system   No.

State import monopoly

There is a state import monopoly on petroleum.

Exports and Export Proceeds

Repatriation requirements   Yes.

Surrender requirements

Except for foreign oil companies, all export proceeds must be surrendered to the BNA or the commercial bank through which exports were carried out. The BNA may authorize exporters of goods and services to retain a certain proportion of foreign exchange earnings to be deposited in accounts at local banks. Proceeds from exports must be collected and surrendered within 30 days of shipment. Some Angolan firms may receive a portion of their export earnings in foreign exchange in accounts opened abroad for that purpose. The decision to grant eligibility for this special arrangement is based on the role that such accounts play in generating revenue for Angola. However, the amounts involved are determined on a case-by-case basis.

Export licenses

Without quotas

Except for exports of the foreign oil companies, all exports of goods and services are subject to licensing. Exports of arms and ammunition, ethnological collections, ships, ostrich products, cattle, and ivory products are prohibited. Special export regimes apply to aircraft, animals and animal products, historical objects, minerals and mineral products, toxic substances, cotton, rice, pork, coffee, cereals, wood and wood products, tobacco, and petroleum. Reexports of goods other than capital goods and personal belongings are also prohibited. Restrictions apply to the export of products that are in short domestic supply.

Export taxes

Yes.

Taxes collected through the exchange system

No.

Payments for Invisible Transactions and Current Transfers

Controls on these payments

All payments require prior approval. Information on the application of bona fide tests is not available.

Freight/insurance

Service contracts with nonresidents are subject to licensing. Preferential treatment given to domestic air and sea transportation companies, and imports not insured domestically are approved only in exceptional cases.

Quantitative limits

n.a.

Unloading/storage costs

Quantitative limits

n.a.

Administrative expenses

Quantitative limits

n.a.

Commissions

Quantitative limits

n.a.

Interest payments

Quantitative limits

n.a.

Profit/dividends

Quantitative limits

Foreign investors may remit dividends provided the investment in the resident company exceeds $250,000. In this case, an authorization from the Ministry of Finance (MOF) is required only as a formality.

Payments for travel

Quantitative limits

Resident nationals may, upon presentation of their passports and airline tickets, purchase foreign exchange from financial institutions as follows: (1) children up to the age of 16 years, up to $500 a person a trip to neighboring countries and up to $1,000 a trip to other countries; and (2) individuals over 16 years, up to $1,500 a person a trip to neighboring countries and up to $3,000 a trip to other countries. Companies may purchase foreign exchange from financial institutions to cover their employees' travel expenses abroad on trips of up to 30 days for business, service, or training, with the following daily limits: (1) president or equivalent, $350; (2) vice-president or equivalent, $300; and (3) department director or equivalent, $200. If a person returns to Angola earlier than planned, the remaining foreign exchange must be resold to a financial institution.

Medical costs

Prior approval

Foreign exchange is provided through the National Health Board on a case-by-case basis at the official rate.

Quantitative limits	The limit is $5,000.
Study abroad costs	
Quantitative limits	Education travel expenses are normally expected to be covered by scholarships, but an additional foreign exchange amount may be granted: up to $2,500 a month is granted to residents who spend up to 90 days abroad for educational, scientific, or cultural purposes.
Subscriptions and membership fees	
Quantitative limits	n.a.
Consulting/legal fees	
Quantitative limits	n.a.
Foreign workers' wages	
Quantitative limits	n.a.
Pensions	
Quantitative limits	n.a.
Gambling/prize earnings	
Quantitative limits	n.a.
Family maintenance/alimony	
Quantitative limits	Up to the equivalent of $1,500 a month may be granted to Angolans or foreigners residing abroad who are direct ascendants or descendants of, and financially dependent on, residents in Angola, provided that (1) they are minor descendants under 18 years or, if of legal age, demonstrate that they are students or are incapable of working; or (2) they are ascendants over 60 years or, if younger, demonstrate they are incapable of working.
Credit card use abroad	n.a.

Proceeds from Invisible Transactions and Current Transfers

Repatriation requirements	Yes.
Surrender requirements	Service earnings must be surrendered to the BNA or to the commercial banks within 30 days of receipt, unless the provider is authorized by the BNA to retain a certain proportion of the proceeds.
Restrictions on use of funds	Yes.

Capital Transactions

Controls on capital and money market instruments	Foreign investment activities (i.e., the setting up of new companies or branches, but also acquisition of equity, total or partial takeover of operations, and lending related to profit sharing) are subject to the provisions of the Foreign Investment Law (1994) as well as the provisions of foreign exchange legislation and regulations. Implementation is the responsibility of the Foreign Investment Bureau under the Ministry of Planning and Economic Coordination. Foreign investments in the areas of petroleum production, diamond mining, and financial institutions are governed by separate legislation. All capital transfers are subject to licensing by the BNA, which has delegated certain authority to the commercial banks.
On capital market securities	Yes.
On money market instruments	Yes.
On collective investment securities	Yes.

Controls on derivatives and other instruments	There are no such instruments in Angola, but, in principle, transactions are covered by foreign exchange and foreign investment legislation.
Controls on credit operations	
Commercial credits	Resident foreign companies must obtain prior authorization from the MOF and, above certain limits, from the BNA to borrow abroad.
By residents to nonresidents	Yes.
To residents from nonresidents	Yes.
Financial credits	Yes.
Controls on direct investment	
Outward direct investment	Yes.
Inward direct investment	Foreign investment is prohibited in the following areas: (1) defense, internal public order, and state security; (2) central banking and currency issue; and (3) other areas reserved for the state (education, health, utilities, communications, and transportation infrastructure). Direct investments in the oil sector are encouraged.
Controls on liquidation of direct investment	Foreign investors are guaranteed the right to transfer abroad the proceeds of the sale of investments, including gains and amounts owed to them after payments of taxes due, but prior approval of the MOF is required.
Controls on real estate transactions	
Purchase abroad by residents	Yes.
Purchase locally by nonresidents	Yes.
Sale locally by nonresidents	Yes.
Provisions specific to commercial banks and other credit institutions	
Borrowing abroad	n.a.
Maintenance of accounts abroad	n.a.
Lending to nonresidents (financial or commercial credits)	n.a.
Lending locally in foreign exchange	n.a.
Purchase of locally issued securities denominated in foreign exchange	n.a.
Differential treatment of nonresident deposit accounts and/or deposit accounts in foreign exchange	
Reserve requirements	Reserve requirements are on local currency deposits only.
Open foreign exchange position limits	n.a.

Changes During 1996

Exchange arrangements	*June 12.* Exchange houses were prohibited from selling foreign currency notes and limited to $5,000 in traveler's checks a client.
	July 1. Following successive devaluations, the official exchange rate was fixed at a level close to the parallel rate, to be maintained in real terms and adjusted to market conditions. Exchange houses were obliged to deal at the secondary official rate rather than the (market-determined) parallel rate.

Arrangements for payments and receipts	*September 30.* A foreign exchange budget was reintroduced.
Resident accounts	*July 1.* The use of foreign currency accounts "own exchange" for settlement of import invisibles was suspended.
	July 26. The use of "own exchange" by the productive sectors (agriculture, industry, transport, etc.) was again permitted, subject to strict criteria and prior approval.
	July 29. The requirement of prior BNA approval was withdrawn for banks to open foreign currency demand and time deposits for residents (and nonresidents), and approved types of transactions were specified, including payment for imports.
Nonresident accounts	*July 29.* The requirement of prior BNA approval for foreign currency accounts was withdrawn (as above).
Imports and import payments	*July 1.* The use of foreign currency accounts at local banks for settlement of imports was suspended until July 26, when it was again permitted under tight restrictions.
	July 1. Imports were restricted to goods deemed essential in order to increase their supply; the restriction was eased gradually in subsequent months.
Payments for invisible transactions and current transfers	*July 1.* The availability of foreign exchange for invisibles was suspended.
	September 30. Allowances for invisibles (travel, medical treatments, education, etc.) were reinstated.

ANTIGUA AND BARBUDA

(Position as of December 31, 1996)

Status Under IMF Articles of Agreement

Article VIII	Date of acceptance: November 22, 1983.

Exchange Arrangement

Currency	The currency of Antigua and Barbuda is the Eastern Caribbean dollar issued by the ECCB.
Exchange rate structure	Unitary.
Classification	
Pegged	The Eastern Caribbean dollar is pegged to the U.S. dollar, the intervention currency, at EC$2.70 per US$1. The ECCB also quotes daily rates for the Canadian dollar and the pound sterling.
Forward exchange market	No.

Arrangements for Payments and Receipts

Prescription of currency requirements	Settlements with residents of member countries of the CARICOM must be made either in the currency of the country concerned or in Eastern Caribbean dollars. Exports to Jamaica are settled in U.S. dollars. Settlements with residents of other countries may be made in any foreign currency or in Eastern Caribbean dollars.
Administration of control	
Exchange control authorities	The Ministry of Finance (MOF) applies exchange control to all currencies.
International security restrictions	No.
Payment arrears	Yes.
Official	n.a.
Private	n.a.
Controls on trade in gold (coins and/or bullion)	No.
Controls on exports and imports of banknotes	
On exports	
Foreign currency	n.a.
On imports	
Foreign currency	Checks and drafts in U.S. and Canadian currency can be tendered up to US$1,000 without restriction; for amounts over US$1,000, approval from the MOF must be obtained.

Resident Accounts

Eligibility to hold accounts	Juridical and natural persons are eligible.
Foreign exchange accounts permitted	External accounts may be opened, especially in tourist-oriented industries or export trade, whose receipts are primarily in foreign currency and a large number of inputs are imported or financed in foreign currency.

Held domestically

Commercial banks are required to report external accounts operations to the MOF on a monthly basis.

Held abroad

n.a.

Nonresident Accounts

Eligibility to hold accounts

Juridical and natural persons are eligible.

Foreign exchange accounts permitted

External accounts may be maintained in any currency and can be credited with receipts from sales of merchandise (whether from export-oriented or local production) or from remittances. Commercial banks are required to report external accounts operations to the MOF on a monthly basis.

Imports and Import Payments

Documentation requirements for release of foreign exchange for imports

Payments for authorized imports are permitted upon application and submission of documentary evidence.

Domiciliation requirements

n.a.

Preshipment inspection

n.a.

Letters of credit

n.a.

Import licenses used as exchange licenses

n.a.

Import licenses and other nontariff measures

Certain commodities require individual licenses, unless imported from CARICOM countries. Antigua and Barbuda follows the CARICOM rules of origin adopted in June 1981. Payments for authorized imports are permitted upon application and submission of documentary evidence.

Positive list

n.a.

Negative list

n.a.

Open general licenses

Most goods may be freely imported under open general licenses granted by the MOF and the Ministries of Industry and Commerce.

Licenses with quotas

n.a.

Import taxes and/or tariffs

Antigua and Barbuda applies the CARICOM's common external tariff. Tariff rates range from zero to 35% for nearly all items. Tariff rates on a number of items, including milk and poultry, are zero. Exemptions from import duties exist for some goods, including basic foods and agricultural goods. Other exemptions for machinery, equipment, and raw materials are granted on a case-by-case basis.

Exports and Export Proceeds

Surrender requirements

No.

Export licenses

No.

Export taxes

Reexports are not subject to any tax if transactions take place within the bonded area.

Taxes collected through the exchange system

n.a.

Payments for Invisible Transactions and Current Transfers

Controls on these payments

Payments for freight, insurance, unloading, and storage are not restricted.

Administrative expenses

    Prior approval   n.a.

    Indicative limits/bona fide test   n.a.

Commissions

    Prior approval   n.a.

    Indicative limits/bona fide test   n.a.

Interest payments

    Prior approval   n.a.

    Indicative limits/bona fide test   n.a.

Profit/dividends   Profits may be remitted in full after compliance with corporate income tax payments.

Payments for travel   Upon presentation of supporting documents and with the authorization of the MOF, residents may purchase foreign exchange, including CARICOM traveler's checks (which are denominated in Trinidad and Tobago dollars) for each trip outside the ECCB area.

    Prior approval   Approval on a case-by-case basis is required.

    Quantitative limits   n.a.

    Indicative limits/bona fide test   Yes.

Medical costs

    Prior approval   Approval on a case-by-case basis is required.

    Quantitative limits   n.a.

    Indicative limits/bona fide test   n.a.

Study abroad costs

    Prior approval   Approval on a case-by-case basis is required.

    Quantitative limits   n.a.

    Indicative limits/bona fide test   n.a.

Foreign workers' wages

    Prior approval   Approval on a case-by-case basis is required.

    Quantitative limits   n.a.

    Indicative limits/bona fide test   n.a.

Family maintenance/alimony

    Prior approval   Approval on a case-by-case basis is required.

    Quantitative limits   n.a.

    Indicative limits/bona fide test   n.a.

Proceeds from Invisible Transactions and Current Transfers

n.a.

Capital Transactions

Controls on capital and money market instruments   No.

Controls on derivatives and other instruments	No.
Controls on credit operations	No.
Controls on direct investment	
Outward direct investment	Large transfers abroad for investment purposes can be phased over time by the Financial Secretary.
Controls on liquidation of direct investment	No.
Controls on real estate transactions	No.

Changes During 1996

No significant changes occurred in the exchange and trade system.

ARGENTINA

(Position as of December 31, 1996)

Status Under IMF Articles of Agreement

Article VIII	Date of acceptance: May 14, 1968.

Exchange Arrangement

Currency	The currency of Argentina is the Argentinian peso.
Other legal tender	Transactions in convertible currencies are permitted, and contracts in these currencies are legally enforceable, although the currencies are not legal tender.
Exchange rate structure	Unitary.
Classification	
Pegged	The external value of the peso is pegged to the U.S. dollar under a currency board type of arrangement. Exchange rates of other currencies are based on the buying and selling rates for the U.S. dollar in markets abroad.
Exchange tax	No.
Exchange subsidy	No.
Forward exchange market	Swap transactions and forward exchange operations are permitted in any currency, and the rates may be freely negotiated.
Official cover of forward operations	No.

Arrangements for Payments and Receipts

Prescription of currency requirements	Transactions with countries with which there are no payments agreements must be settled in freely convertible currencies.
Payment arrangements	
Regional arrangements	Within the framework of the multilateral clearing system of the LAIA, payments between Argentina and Brazil, Chile, Colombia, Ecuador, Mexico, Paraguay, Peru, Uruguay, and Venezuela are settled voluntarily through payment agreements and a reciprocal credit mechanism. All payments between Argentina and Bolivia and the Dominican Republic must be made through the accounts specified in the agreements.
	Argentina has agreements with Bulgaria, Cuba, Hungary, Malaysia, and Russia. Payments between Argentina and these countries are settled on a voluntary basis through accounts opened with the Central Bank of Argentina (BCRA) and the other central banks concerned, with the exception of Bulgaria and Cuba, where settlement through the accounts specified in the agreements is obligatory.
Administration of control	
Exchange control authorities	All exchange transactions are carried out through entities authorized expressly for this purpose with no restrictions on the purchase or sale of foreign exchange at market prices. These authorized entities include banks, exchange agencies, exchange houses, exchange offices, and financial companies. Each type of institution is subject to separate regulations. Credit funds and mortgage savings and loan companies may also make certain foreign exchange transactions on the condition that they meet certain additional capital requirements.
International security restrictions	
In accordance with UN sanctions	Restrictions on current payments with respect to Iraq, Libya, and the Federal Republic of Yugoslavia (Serbia/Montenegro) were imposed.

Payment arrears	No.
Controls on trade in gold (coins and/or bullion)	
Controls on domestic ownership and/or trade	Residents may hold gold coins and gold in any other form in Argentina or abroad. Financial institutions, exchange houses, and exchange agencies may buy or sell gold in the form of coins or good delivery bars among themselves, and may buy such gold from their clients, as well as other precious metals the market value of which is based on the daily list prices of major transactions.
Controls on external trade	The importation of gold coins and good delivery bars is not restricted. Gold exports must be paid for in convertible currencies. Imports of gold by industrial users are subject to a statistical duty of 3%, as well as a sales tax. Institutions may carry out arbitrage operations with their clients in gold coins or good delivery gold bars against foreign banknotes. Authorized institutions may export gold to entities abroad.
Controls on exports and imports of banknotes	No.

Resident Accounts

Eligibility to hold accounts	Juridical and natural persons are eligible. Authorized banks may open accounts in pesos or in foreign exchange provided that identification requirements aimed, inter alia, at preventing money laundering have been met.
Foreign exchange accounts permitted	Foreign exchange accounts must be denominated in convertible currencies and may be credited only with cash or with remittances in the following currencies: U.S. dollars for current accounts, savings, and fixed-term deposits; and other currencies that the BCRA explicitly authorizes at the request of financial institutions for deposits in savings and fixed-term accounts. Credit balances may be used freely in Argentina or abroad. Transfers between accounts may be made freely. The use of checking accounts denominated in U.S. dollars is allowed for domestic transactions.
Held domestically	Yes.
Held abroad	Yes.
Accounts in domestic currency convertible into foreign currency	Yes.

Nonresident Accounts

Eligibility to hold accounts	Same regulations as for resident accounts apply.
Foreign exchange accounts permitted	Yes.
Domestic currency accounts	Yes.
Convertible into foreign currency	Yes.
Blocked accounts	No.

Imports and Import Payments

Foreign exchange budget	No.
Financing requirements for imports	No.
Documentation requirements for release of foreign exchange for imports	No.

Import licenses and other nontariff measures

Negative list	Restrictions are in force solely for security, hygiene, and public health reasons.
Licenses with quotas	Quantitative restrictions are applied to the automobile sector and to some paper products.
Other nontariff measures	There are no nontariff barriers on intra-MERCOSUR trade. However, Argentina applies a special regime to automobile and sugar imports with the authorization of MERCOSUR, pending agreement on a common regime for these sectors. Quantitative restrictions are applied to the automobile sector and to some clothes, freezers, furniture, paper, plastics, tires, and iron and steel products.
Import taxes and/or tariffs	A substantial portion of intra-MERCOSUR trade is conducted at a zero tariff rate, but member countries may maintain tariffs for some items. Argentina applies tariffs to certain textiles, paper, and iron and steel products. This regime will be in force until the end of 1998, at which time tariffs will be reduced to zero.
	Argentina and the MERCOSUR countries apply a common external tariff (CET) to imports from the rest of the world that encompasses all products, with certain exceptions (Argentina has 300 exceptions) that are subject to a transitional regime until 2001 and 2006. CET rates currently range up to 20%. At the end of the transitional period in 2001, the CET will be 14% for capital goods, and in 2006, the CET will be 16% for computer and telecommunications equipment.
	A statistical tax of 3% is applied to imports from all countries, except those from MERCOSUR countries, Chile, and Bolivia. This tax is waived for capital goods, fuel, and sensitive goods from the paper, computer, and telecommunications sectors.
Taxes collected through the exchange system	No.
State import monopoly	No.

Exports and Export Proceeds

Repatriation requirements	No.
Surrender requirements	No.
Financing requirements	No.
Documentation requirements	No.
Export licenses	Licenses are required only for goods subject to quantitative restrictions.
With quotas	Quantitative restrictions on exports are maintained only on arms, sensitive goods and war materials, narcotics, and protected animal species.
Export taxes	A 15% export duty is applied to untanned, pickled aplite, and wet blue leathers, and a 3.5% duty is applied to soybeans, groundnuts, flax, turnips, sunflower seeds, and cotton.
Taxes collected through the exchange system	No.

Payments for Invisible Transactions and Current Transfers

Controls on these payments	No.

Proceeds from Invisible Transactions and Current Transfers

Repatriation requirements	No.

Surrender requirements	No.
Restrictions on use of funds	No.

Capital Transactions

Controls on capital and money market instruments

On capital market securities

Sale or issue locally by nonresidents

Under the regulations of the National Securities Commission (CNV), foreign investors must meet the same requirements as those applicable to Argentine investors to make a public offering of securities in Argentina. In each case, they must establish a permanent representative office and a domicile in Argentina to receive notices. They must state whether the securities are also being offered to the public in their country of origin, and specify the initial and periodic information requirements to which they are subject. If the CNV believes that the regulations in the country of origin properly protect local investors and guarantee an adequate flow of information, the CNV may lower the requirements for these investors. The CNV may authorize foreign investors on a case-by-case basis to submit only such information as they would periodically submit to the corresponding authority in their jurisdiction of origin.

On collective investment securities

Sale or issue locally by nonresidents

Yes.

Controls on derivatives and other instruments

No.

Controls on credit operations

No.

Controls on direct investment

Inward direct investment

Foreign companies are allowed to invest in Argentina without prior government approval on an equal footing with domestic firms and may enter into any area of economic activity on their own, because no law or regulation forces them to be associated with local partners. This principle applies even in cases where a foreign investment results in full foreign ownership of a domestic company. Some restrictions apply on investment in sensitive sectors, including air transport, fishing, insurance, nuclear plants, and shipyards.

Controls on liquidation of direct investment

Foreign investors are entitled to freely repatriate their investment, including earnings, at any time, and also have unrestricted access to the foreign exchange market. These rights assisting foreign investors have been further established under international law by means of over 30 investment promotion and protection agreements, with the following countries: Canada, France, Germany, Italy, Spain, Sweden, Switzerland, the United Kingdom, and the United States. Argentina is a member of the Multilateral Investment Guarantee Agency and the International Center for the Settlement of Investment Disputes, and maintains a valid and active agreement with the Overseas Private Investment Corporation.

Controls on real estate transactions

Purchase locally by nonresidents

For purchases of real estate in border areas, a foreign investor must seek prior approval for the project from the Border Superintendency of the Ministry of Defense. This limitation exists for national security reasons.

Provisions specific to commercial banks and other credit institutions

Lending to nonresidents (financial or commercial credits)

In the case of credit extended by financial intermediaries, the funds must be used in the country.

Provisions specific to institutional investors

Limits (max.) on portfolio invested abroad

There is a 25% limit of the investment trust portfolio, but this limit does not apply to MERCOSUR. For security reasons, and according to Law No. 24.241 (Pension Funds Reform), no more than 10% of pension funds may be invested in securities issued by a foreign country, or in securities of foreign corporations.

Limits (min.) on portfolio invested locally

In the event that the trust's assets consist of the securities, tender offer should be made in Argentina or abroad with a minimum of 75% of the investment being made in assets issued and traded in Argentina.

Other controls imposed by securities laws

No.

Changes During 1996

No significant changes occurred in the exchange and trade system.

ARMENIA

(Position as of December 31, 1996)

Status Under IMF Articles of Agreement

Article XIV	Yes.

Exchange Arrangement

Currency	The currency of Armenia is the dram.
Exchange rate structure	Unitary.
Classification	
Independent floating	The exchange rate of the dram against the U.S. dollar is determined on the basis of exchange rates in the interbank market and at foreign exchange auctions held 5 times a week in the Yerevan Stock Exchange (YSE) and twice a week in the Gjumry Stock Exchange (GSE). Banks and financial dealers holding licenses from the Central Bank of Armenia (CBA) may participate in the auctions. Anyone may buy and sell at the auction through banks. However, since late 1996, foreign exchange transactions have taken place predominantly in the interbank market in which the CBA also participates. The CBA quotes official rates in terms of U.S. dollars daily on the basis of the weighted average rate in the interbank market and at the foreign exchange auctions on the previous trading day. This rate is used for accounting valuation of all foreign exchange transactions of all economic agents, including the Ministry of Finance. Exchange rates for other major currencies are calculated either on the basis of quotations on the YSE, when applicable, or solely on the basis of quotations for the U.S. dollar in major international interbank markets against the currencies concerned. Foreign exchange is also freely bought and sold by enterprises and persons without restrictions through authorized banks and licensed exchange bureaus that conduct cash transactions.
Exchange tax	No.
Exchange subsidy	No.
Forward exchange market	There are no restrictions for forward cover against exchange rate risk operating in the official or the commercial banking sectors.
Official cover of forward operations	Yes.

Arrangements for Payments and Receipts

Prescription of currency requirements	Settlements with other countries are made through correspondent accounts maintained by the commercial banks, which may be opened freely without notifying the CBA. The settlements can also be effected through the correspondent accounts of the CBA. Settlements with countries with which Armenia maintains bilateral payments agreements are effected in accordance with the terms of the agreements. Settlements with all other countries may be made in any currency.
Payment arrangements	
Bilateral arrangements	
Inoperative	Armenia maintains agreements with Russia and Turkmenistan.
Regional arrangements	Armenia is a signatory of the 1993 Treaty of Economic Union (with Azerbaijan, Belarus, Kazakhstan, Kyrgyz Republic, Moldova, Russia, Tajikistan, and Uzbekistan), which provides for the eventual establishment of a customs union, a payments union, cooperation on investment, industrial development, and customs procedures. On October 21, 1994, Armenia joined the Agreement on the Establishment of Payments Union of CIS member countries. Armenia is a member of the Black Sea Economic

Cooperation (BSEC) organization (with Albania, Azerbaijan, Bulgaria, Georgia, Greece, Moldova, Romania, Russia, Turkey, and Ukraine). Bilateral free trade agreements (FTAs) have been signed with the Kyrgyz Republic, Moldova, Russia, Tajikistan, and Ukraine, though only the agreement with Russia is in operation.

Clearing agreements	There is an arrangement with Turkmenistan for the importation of natural gas. In addition, bilateral clearing agreements with the Baltic countries and the other countries of the FSU exist, but all have become largely inoperative.

Administration of control

Exchange control authorities	The CBA has overall responsibility for regulating financial relations between Armenia and other countries in close collaboration with the Ministry of Finance (MOF). Banks are granted two types of foreign exchange licenses. A general license gives a bank authority to conduct any type of foreign exchange transaction, including those with nonresidents abroad and gold transactions that require an additional license. Banks with a full license may offer a full range of currency transactions, including those in gold. A second, more restricted form of license allows banks operating in Armenia to buy and sell foreign exchange only on behalf of their clients.
Payment arrears	There are commercial arrears vis-à-vis Russia and overdue obligations to the EU.
Official	Yes.
Private	Yes.
Controls on trade in gold (coins and/or bullion)	A license is required for trading.
Controls on domestic ownership and/or trade	There are no specific regulations governing domestic trade in gold.
Controls on external trade	Yes.
Controls on exports and imports of banknotes	
On exports	
Foreign currency	Yes.
On imports	
Foreign currency	A declaration is required for amounts exceeding the equivalent of $500.

Resident Accounts

Eligibility to hold accounts	Juridical and natural persons are eligible.
Foreign exchange accounts permitted	Yes.
Held domestically	Residents may open, maintain, and use foreign currency accounts at licensed banks in Armenia. There are no limits on the amount of foreign currency banknotes that can be purchased with drams from banks or exchange bureaus, and banknotes can be deposited in a foreign exchange account or used for transactions with nonresidents. However, residents may not transfer balances in these accounts to other residents in order to make payments for goods and services.
Held abroad	Resident natural and juridical persons may open, maintain, and use accounts in banks abroad. Prior approval is required.

Nonresident Accounts

Eligibility to hold accounts	Juridical and natural persons are eligible.

Foreign exchange accounts permitted	Nonresident natural and juridical persons may freely open and use foreign exchange accounts with licensed domestic banks. They are also free to make withdrawals to make current transactions. Balances in these accounts may be transferred abroad or sold to licensed domestic banks for drams.
Domestic currency accounts	Foreign governments and international institutions may freely open dram accounts with banks in Armenia without prior authorization from the CBA. Prior approval is required.
Convertible into foreign currency	These accounts are permitted, but prior approval is required.
Blocked accounts	No.

Imports and Import Payments

Foreign exchange budget	No.
Documentation requirements for release of foreign exchange for imports	
Domiciliation requirements	n.a.
Preshipment inspection	n.a.
Letters of credit	Yes.
Import licenses and other nontariff measures	
Positive list	Yes.
Negative list	Import licenses from the Ministry of Agriculture and the Ministry of Health are required and granted on a case-by-case basis to import medicinal preparations and pesticides. Imports of weapons, military equipment and parts, and explosives require special authorization from the government.
Import taxes and/or tariffs	There are two rates of customs duties: zero and 10%; most imports are zero rated. Products imported from countries in the CIS are exempted.
Taxes collected through the exchange system	No.

Exports and Export Proceeds

Repatriation requirements	Proceeds should be repatriated within 30 days of receipt.
Surrender requirements	No.
Export licenses	Export licenses are required for medicines, wild animals and plants, and textile products exported to the EU. In addition, special government permission is required for the export of nuclear technology, nuclear waste, related nonnuclear products, and technology with direct military applications. Minimum threshold prices for the export of ferrous and nonferrous metals and the reexport of foreign-produced goods thereof, remain in force.
Without quotas	Yes.
Export taxes	No.

Payments for Invisible Transactions and Current Transfers

Controls on these payments	No.

Proceeds from Invisible Transactions and Current Transfers

Repatriation requirements	Proceeds must be repatriated within 30 days, except those from cultural activities performed abroad.
Surrender requirements	No.

Capital Transactions

Controls on capital and money market instruments	No.
Controls on derivatives and other instruments	No.
Controls on credit operations	No.
Controls on direct investment	No.
Controls on liquidation of direct investment	No.
Controls on real estate transactions	No.
Provisions specific to commercial banks and other credit institutions	No.
Provisions specific to institutional investors	No.
Other controls imposed by securities laws	No.

Changes During 1996

No significant changes occurred in the exchange and trade system.

ARUBA

(Position as of January 31, 1997)

Status Under IMF Articles of Agreement

Article VIII   Date of acceptance: February 15, 1961.

Exchange Arrangement

Currency   The currency of Aruba is the florin (Af.).

Other legal tender   No.

Exchange rate structure   Unitary.

Classification

Pegged   The florin is pegged to the U.S. dollar at Af. 1.79 per $1. The Centrale Bank van Aruba (CBA), the central bank, deals with local commercial banks within margins of 0.002795% on either side of parity. A foreign exchange commission of 1.3% is levied on all payments to nonresidents, except when settled in Netherland Antillean guilders.

Exchange tax   No.

Exchange subsidy   No.

Forward exchange market   No.

Arrangements for Payments and Receipts

Prescription of currency requirements   No.

Payment arrangements   No.

Administration of control

Exchange control authorities   The CBA administers foreign exchange control.

International security restrictions   No.

Payments arrears   No.

Controls on trade in gold (coins and/or bullion)   No.

Controls on exports and imports of banknotes

On exports

   Domestic currency   The exportation of domestic banknotes is prohibited.

   Foreign currency   The exportation of foreign banknotes requires a license, except for traveling purposes.

Resident Accounts

Eligibility to hold accounts   Natural and juridical persons may hold accounts.

Foreign exchange accounts permitted   Yes.

Held domestically   Yes.

Held abroad   These accounts are permitted, but prior approval is required.

Accounts in domestic currency convertible into foreign currency	These accounts are not allowed.

Nonresident Accounts

Eligibility to hold accounts	Natural and juridical persons may hold accounts. The opening of a nonresident account should be reported in writing to the CBA.
Foreign exchange accounts permitted	No.
Domestic currency accounts	Yes.
Convertible into foreign currency	Balances up to Af. 200,000 are convertible.
Blocked accounts	No.

Imports and Import Payments

Foreign exchange budget	No.
Financing requirements for imports	No.
Documentation requirements for release of foreign exchange for imports	No.
Import licenses and other nontariff measures	
Licenses with quotas	The importation of eggs may be subject to quotas depending on the domestic supply situation.
Import taxes and/or tariffs	No.
State import monopoly	No.

Exports and Export Proceeds

Repatriation requirements	Yes.
Surrender requirements	Unless specifically exempted, export proceeds must be converted into local currency within 8 working days and credited to a foreign currency account with a local foreign exchange bank or deposited in a foreign bank account approved by the CBA.
Financing requirements	No.
Documentation requirements	No.
Export licenses	No.
Export taxes	n.a.
Taxes collected through the exchange system	No.

Payments for Invisible Transactions and Current Transfers

Controls on these payments	Approval was required for payments of unloading/storage costs, administrative expenses, commissions, subscriptions and membership fees, consulting/legal fees, foreign workers' wages, pensions, and gambling and prize earnings in excess of Af. 50,000 and of medical costs, study abroad costs, and family maintenance/alimony in excess of Af. 10,000 a calendar quarter; approval was granted for bona fide requests. Also, a license was required for payment of interest and profits and dividends. As of January 1, 1997, all restrictions were eliminated.

Proceeds from Invisible Transactions and Current Transfers

Repatriation requirements	Yes.
Surrender requirements	Unless specifically exempted, proceeds must be converted into local currency within 8 working days and credited to a foreign currency account with a local foreign exchange bank or deposited in a foreign bank account approved by the CBA.
Restrictions on use of funds	No.

Capital Transactions

Controls on capital and money market instruments	A CBA license is required for transactions exceeding Af. 200,000 a year. Purchases of these instruments in the country by nonresidents require a CBA license.
Controls on derivatives and other instruments	A CBA license is required for transactions exceeding Af. 200,000 a year.
Controls on credit operations	A license is required for credits exceeding Af. 200,000 a year.
Controls on direct investment	
Outward direct investment	There is an annual limit of Af. 500,000 for companies and Af. 200,000 for natural persons. The CBA may require divestment, repatriation, and surrender of proceeds to the CBA.
Inward direct investment	Yes.
Controls on liquidation of direct investment	A CBA license is required.
Controls on real estate transactions	A CBA license is required.
Purchase abroad by residents	A license is required if the amount of the transaction exceeds Af. 200,000 a year.
Purchase locally by nonresidents	Yes.
Sale locally by nonresidents	Yes.
Provisions specific to commercial banks and other credit institutions	No.
Provisions specific to institutional investors	
Limits (max.) on portfolio invested abroad	Yes.
Limits (min.) on portfolio invested locally	The limits are 40% of the first Af. 10 million of outstanding liabilities; 50% of the second Af. 10 million; and 60% of the remaining liabilities.

Changes During 1996

No significant changes occurred in the exchange and trade system.

Changes During 1997

Imports and import payments	*January 1.* All restrictions on payments for imports were removed.
Payments for invisible transactions and current transfers	*January 1.* All restrictions on payments and transfers were removed.
Capital transactions	*January 1.* The requirement of a special license for foreign investments of less than Af. 500,000 a year by resident entities (excluding commercial banks and institutional investors) was eliminated.

AUSTRALIA

(Position as of December 31, 1996)

Status Under IMF Articles of Agreement

Article VIII	Date of acceptance: July 1, 1965.

Exchange Arrangement

Currency

The currency of Australia is the Australian dollar. It also circulates in several other countries, including Kiribati, Nauru, and Tuvalu.

Exchange rate structure

Unitary.

Classification

Independent floating

The exchange rate of the Australian dollar is market determined. Authorized foreign exchange dealers may deal among themselves, with their customers, and with overseas counterparties at mutually negotiated rates for both spot and forward transactions in any currency with regard to trade- and nontrade-related transactions. But the Reserve Bank of Australia (RBA) retains discretionary power to intervene in the foreign exchange market. There is no official exchange rate for the Australian dollar. The RBA publishes an indicative rate for the Australian dollar based on market observation at 4 p.m. daily.

Exchange tax

No.

Exchange subsidy

No.

Forward exchange market

Active trading takes place in forward and futures contracts.

Official cover of forward operations

No.

Arrangements for Payments and Receipts

Prescription of currency requirements

No.

Payment arrangements

No.

Administration of control

Exchange control authorities

The RBA supervises authorized dealers and regulates open foreign exchange positions. The Australian Transaction Reports and Analysis Center (AUSTRAC), a law enforcement agency, receives information on international transactions including those in cash, which it can pass on to a number of other enforcement and governmental agencies.

International security restrictions

In accordance with UN sanctions

The only restrictions on external payments and transfers are those to give effect to UN Security Council resolutions imposing sanctions against Iraq, Libya, and the Federal Republic of Yugoslavia (Serbia/Montenegro).

Payments arrears

No.

Controls on trade in gold (coins and/or bullion)

No.

Controls on exports and imports of banknotes

Exportation or importation of notes and coins totaling $A 5,000 or more must be reported to AUSTRAC. Residents must purchase foreign currency from an authorized dealer. Nonresident travelers may take out any foreign currency they brought into Australia.

Resident Accounts

Eligibility to hold accounts	Juridical and natural persons are eligible.
Foreign exchange accounts permitted	Yes.
Held domestically	Local purchases and sales of foreign currency must be through an authorized dealer.
Held abroad	Yes.
Accounts in domestic currency convertible into foreign currency	Conversion must be effected through an authorized foreign exchange dealer.

Nonresident Accounts

Eligibility to hold accounts	Juridical and natural persons are eligible.
Foreign exchange accounts permitted	Local purchases and sales of foreign currency must be through an authorized dealer.
Domestic currency accounts	Yes.
Convertible into foreign currency	Conversion must be effected through an authorized foreign exchange dealer.
Blocked accounts	Only those accounts affected by UN sanctions are blocked.

Imports and Import Payments

Foreign exchange budget	No.
Financing requirements for imports	No.
Documentation requirements for release of foreign exchange for imports	No.
Import licenses and other nontariff measures	There are no import-licensing requirements or quotas on imports other than the tariff quota, which applies to certain cheeses and curd.
Negative list	For some products, imports are allowed only if written authorization is obtained from the relevant authorities or if certain regulations are complied with. Among the goods subject to control are narcotic, psychotropic, and therapeutic substances, firearms and certain weapons, certain chemicals and primary commodities, some glazed ceramic ware, and various dangerous goods. These controls are maintained mainly to meet health and safety requirements; to meet certain requirements for labeling, packaging, or technical specifications; and to satisfy certain obligations arising from Australia's membership in international commodity agreements.
Licenses with quotas	n.a.
Import taxes and/or tariffs	Most tariff rates had been reduced to a maximum of 5% through July 1996. Tariffs on passenger automobiles will decline to 15% from 35%, while tariffs on textiles, footwear, and clothing will decline to a maximum of 25% by the year 2000.
	The ANZCERTA establishes free trade in goods. The SPARTECA provides nonreciprocal, duty-free access to most markets in Australia and New Zealand for other members. Trade between Papua New Guinea and Australia is covered by the Agreement on Trade and Commercial Relations between Australia and Papua New Guinea.
	Developing countries receive tariff preferences on exports to Australia under the Australian System of Tariff Preferences for Developing Countries, with a uniform preferential margin of 5%. Preferences have been eliminated on imports of certain industries such as textiles, clothing and footwear, chemicals, vegetable and fruit preparations, tuna,

and sugar, except from the least-developed countries and South Pacific Island Territories.

Taxes collected through the exchange system	No.

Exports and Export Proceeds

Repatriation requirements	No.
Surrender requirements	No.
Financing requirements	No.
Documentation requirements	No.
Export licenses	Export prohibitions and restrictions in effect are designed to ensure quality control, administer trade embargoes, and meet obligations under international arrangements. These prohibitions are also set up to restrict the exportation of certain defense materials; regulate the exportation of goods that involve high technology and have dual civilian and military applications; maintain adequate measures of control over designated cultural property, resources, flora, and fauna; secure conservation objectives; and respond to specific market distortions abroad. Remaining controls on primary products apply mainly to food and agricultural products.

Approval must be obtained from the government to export coal, liquid natural gas, bauxite, alumina, and mineral sands. Export controls apply to uranium to ensure compliance with the government's nonproliferation policy obligations. Restrictions also apply to certain other nuclear and related materials. Licenses are required for exports of unprocessed wood, including wood chips. The Australian Dairy Corporation administers export control powers in relation to prescribed dairy products under the provisions of the Dairy Produce Act. All exporters of controlled dairy products must be licensed. This system allows the control of exports to markets where quantitative restrictions apply and ensures that export prices do not fall below minimum prices agreed to under the WTO for these products.

Exports of red meat and livestock can be made only by persons or firms licensed by the Australian Meat and Livestock Corporation (AMLC). The AMLC has the power to engage in export trading in its own right and may introduce arrangements to control Australian exports to observe quantitative restrictions in any particular market. Other Commonwealth statutory marketing authorities that have export control powers are the Australian Horticultural Corporation, the Australian Honey Board, the Australian Wheat Board, and the Australian Wine and Brandy Corporation. The Australian Wheat Board's powers make it the sole exporter of Australian wheat.

Without quotas	n.a.
With quotas	n.a.
Export taxes	n.a.
Taxes collected through the exchange system	No.

Payments for Invisible Transactions and Current Transfers

Controls on these payments	No.

Proceeds from Invisible Transactions and Current Transfers

Repatriation requirements	No.

Surrender requirements	No.
Restrictions on use of funds	No.

Capital Transactions

Controls on capital and money market instruments

The purchase of shares and other securities of a participatory nature, which may be affected by laws on inward direct investment, is restricted. Foreign governments, their agencies, and international organizations are not permitted to issue bearer bonds and, when borrowing in the Australian capital market, must advise the Australian authorities of the details of each borrowing after its completion. Subject to certain disclosure requirements, overseas banks may issue securities in the wholesale capital market in amounts of $A 500,000 or more.

On capital market securities

    Purchase locally by nonresidents   Yes.

    Sale or issue locally by nonresidents   Yes.

On money market instruments

    Sale or issue locally by nonresidents   Yes.

Controls on derivatives and other instruments

Sale or issue locally by nonresidents   Yes.

Controls on credit operations   No.

Controls on direct investment

Inward direct investment

Prior authorization is required for (1) proposals by foreign interests that would result in the ownership of a shareholding of 15% or more by a single foreign interest or associates, or 40% or more by two or more unrelated foreign interests in an Australian corporation; however, foreign investment in businesses other than the restricted sectors, with total assets of less than $A 5 million (less than $A 3 million for rural properties) is exempt from examination and notification; (2) all investments in the banking, civil aviation, shipping, media, and telecommunication sectors are subject to special restrictions; and (3) proposals to establish new businesses in other than the restricted sectors of the economy where the total amount of the investment is $A 10 million or more.

Controls on liquidation of direct investment   No.

Controls on real estate transactions

Purchase locally by nonresidents

All acquisitions of real estate must be notified, unless exempt by regulation. Acquisitions of nonresidential commercial real estate for development are normally approved as are acquisitions of developed nonresidential commercial real estate. Acquisition of developed nonresidential commercial real estate is exempt where the total value of the property is less than $A 5 million.

Approval is also normally granted for residential land for development and for the acquisitions of dwellings (including condominiums), direct from a developer, either "off the plan," while under construction, or completed but never occupied, provided that no more than 50% of the total number of dwellings are sold to foreign investors.

Foreign acquisitions of established residential real estate are not normally approved except in cases involving temporary residents who require accommodation for a period in excess of 12 months, subject to resale of the property upon departure. Foreign persons who are entitled to reside permanently in Australia are not required to seek approval to acquire any form of residential real estate. Foreign acquisition of residential real estate (including condominiums) within a designated integrated tourist resort is exempt from authorization.

Sale locally by nonresidents

n.a.

Provisions specific to commercial banks and other credit institutions

Banks are subject to prudential requirements, e.g., liquidity management, credit concentration, and open foreign exchange position limits.

Open foreign exchange position limits

Yes.

Other controls imposed by securities laws

The rules of the Australian Stock Exchange require that, to be a stockbroker, a majority of the directors of the stockholding entity must be Australian residents. This rule does not prohibit foreigners from owning a stockbroking entity.

Changes During 1996

Arrangements for payments and receipts

April 11. Sanctions against the Republic of Bosnia and Herzegovina were suspended in accordance with UN Security Council resolutions.

Capital transactions

September 25. The rules to allow foreign domiciled banks to issue, in their own name, securities on the wholesale capital market were liberalized. Such securities must be in amounts of not less than $A 500,000, and must indicate that they are being issued by a bank that is not authorized under the Banking Act.

AUSTRIA

(Position as of December 31, 1996)

Status Under IMF Articles of Agreement

Article VIII
Date of acceptance: August 1, 1962.

Exchange Arrangement

Currency
The currency of Austria is the Austrian schilling.

Exchange rate structure
Unitary.

Classification

Cooperative arrangement
Austria participates in the ERM of the EMS. In accordance with this agreement, Austria maintains the spot exchange rates between the schilling and the currencies of the other participants within margins of ±15% around the cross rates based on the central rates expressed in ECUs. At the same time, it continues to keep the schilling's external value constant against the deutsche mark. However, to ensure a proper functioning of the system, the Austrian National Bank (ANB) intervenes in concert with the other EMS members to smooth out fluctuations in exchange rates; the intervention currencies are the currencies of participant countries and the U.S. dollar.

Exchange tax
No.

Exchange subsidy
No.

Forward exchange market
Yes.

Official cover of forward operations
No.

Arrangements for Payments and Receipts

Prescription of currency requirements
Settlements with all countries may be made either in foreign currencies or through free schilling accounts.

Payment arrangements

Bilateral arrangements

Operative
There are no bilateral payment agreements; however, several bilateral agreements exist for the promotion and protection of investments, which include provisions on transfers between the signatories.

Administration of control

Exchange control authorities
Most exchange transactions are effected through Austrian banks authorized by the central bank.

International security restrictions

In accordance with UN sanctions
Regulation No. 241/94 of the EU Council regarding the further discontinuation of the economic and financial relations between the EU and the areas of Bosnia and Herzegovina under the control of Bosnian Serb forces has been in force since January 1, 1995. Restrictions are imposed on certain current payments and transfers to Libya in accordance with UN Security Council Resolution No. 833 (1993). Certain restrictions on payments and transfers for current international transactions to the government of Iraq are still in force.

Payment arrears
No.

Controls on trade in gold (coins and/or bullion)
No.

Controls on exports and imports of banknotes	No.

Resident Accounts

Eligibility to hold accounts	Juridical and natural persons are eligible.
Foreign exchange accounts permitted	Yes.
Held domestically	Yes.
Held abroad	Yes.
Accounts in domestic currency convertible into foreign currency	Yes.

Nonresident Accounts

Eligibility to hold accounts	Juridical and natural persons are eligible.
Foreign exchange accounts permitted	Yes.
Domestic currency accounts	Yes.
Convertible into foreign currency	Yes.
Blocked accounts	These are accounts affected by UN sanctions.

Imports and Import Payments

Foreign exchange budget	No.
Financing requirements for imports	No.
Documentation requirements for release of foreign exchange for imports	No.
Import licenses and other nontariff measures	Export and import licenses must be issued by the Federal Ministry for Economic Affairs for industrial products and by the Federal Ministry of Agriculture and Forestry for agricultural products. As a member of the EU, Austria applies all import regulations based on the common commercial policy (Art. 113 EEC), i.e., for industrial product import restrictions in the textile and clothing sectors and statistical surveillance for products falling under the scope of the ECSC Treaty. There are also regulations vis-à-vis China for imports of some consumer products based on current EC law.
Positive list	Yes.
Licenses with quotas	Yes.
Import taxes and/or tariffs	Austria applies the Common Import Regime of the EU.
Taxes collected through the exchange system	No.
State import monopoly	No.

Exports and Export Proceeds

Repatriation requirements	No.

Surrender requirements	No.
Financing requirements	No.
Documentation requirements	No.
Export licenses	Licenses for exports must be obtained from the relevant ministry or at the time of clearance from the customs authorities. For most exports, licenses are not required. Export licenses are issued with due consideration for the provisions of relevant EU trade agreements and the fulfillment of quotas established in accordance with such agreements, and the needs of the Austrian economy.
Without quotas	Yes.
With quotas	Yes.
Export taxes	No.

Payments for Invisible Transactions and Current Transfers

Controls on these payments	No.

Proceeds from Invisible Transactions and Current Transfers

Repatriation requirements	No.
Surrender requirements	No.
Restrictions on use of funds	No.

Capital Transactions

Controls on capital and money market instruments	No.
Controls on derivatives and other instruments	No.
Controls on credit operations	No.
Controls on direct investment	
Outward direct investment	Investments exceeding S100,000 must be reported to the ANB.
Inward direct investment	In the auditing and legal professions, the transport sector, and the electric power generation sector certain restrictions apply for investments by nonresidents and Austrian residents who are not nationals of one of the countries of the EEA.
Controls on liquidation of direct investment	No.
Controls on real estate transactions	
Purchase locally by nonresidents	The acquisition of real estate is subject to approval by local authorities.
Provisions specific to commercial banks and other credit institutions	A reporting requirement exists.
Borrowing abroad	n.a.
Maintenance of accounts abroad	n.a.
Lending to nonresidents (financial or commercial credits)	n.a.

Lending locally in foreign exchange	n.a.
Purchase of locally issued securities denominated in foreign exchange	n.a.
Open foreign exchange position limits	An open position must not exceed 30% of own funds at the end of any business day; the total sum of all open positions must not exceed 50% of own funds.
Provisions specific to institutional investors	A reporting requirement exists.
Currency matching regulations on assets/liabilities composition	Yes.
Other controls imposed by securities laws	A reporting requirement exists.

Changes During 1996

No significant changes occurred in the exchange and trade system.

AZERBAIJAN

(Position as of January 31, 1997)

Status Under IMF Articles of Agreement

Article XIV   Yes.

Exchange Arrangement

Currency   The currency of Azerbaijan is the Azerbaijan manat.

Exchange rate structure   Unitary.

Classification

Independent floating   The external value of the manat for noncash operations is determined in daily auctions held at the Baku Interbank Currency Exchange (BICEX). Participation in the auctions is restricted to the commercial banks that are licensed to deal in foreign exchange bidding on behalf of their customers. Authorized banks are free to set rates for cash transactions, which are published weekly by the International Bank. The Azerbaijan National Bank (ANB) determines the official exchange rate against the U.S. dollar daily, which is equal to the auction rate prevailing in the BICEX. The official rate is used for all official foreign exchange transactions, including transactions by state-owned enterprises, and for the valuation of foreign assets.

An official rate against the ECU and the Russian ruble is also posted. No commission is assessed on purchases of foreign exchange by the International Bank, but a commission of about 0.3% is added for sales of foreign exchange.

Exchange tax   No.

Exchange subsidy   No.

Forward exchange market   No.

Arrangements for Payments and Receipts

Prescription of currency   Settlements with the Baltic countries, Russia, and the other countries of the FSU are
requirements   effected through correspondent accounts of the commercial banks in these states or through correspondent accounts of the respective central banks.

Payment arrangements

Bilateral arrangements   n.a.

Barter agreements and open accounts Yes.

Administration of control

Exchange control authorities   The ANB regulates foreign exchange transactions, conducts foreign currency operations, and administers gold and convertible currency reserve holdings. The ANB also has overall responsibility for issuing licenses to deal in foreign exchange and to open foreign exchange accounts abroad; for regulating foreign exchange operations, including implementing and monitoring compliance with the law; and for establishing prudential rules governing foreign exchange operations. The Ministry of Foreign Economic Relations regulates foreign trade, while the Customs Service Law regulates the organization and operation of customs.

International security restrictions   No.

Controls on trade in gold (coins
and/or bullion)

Controls on external trade   A license is required to conduct international trade in gold.

51

Controls on exports and imports of banknotes	The exportation and importation of foreign banknotes are regulated by the ANB and the Ministry of Finance, in conformity with customs regulations.
On exports	
Foreign currency	Yes.
On imports	
Foreign currency	Yes.

Resident Accounts

Eligibility to hold accounts	Juridical and natural persons are eligible.
Foreign exchange accounts permitted	Yes.
Held domestically	Prior approval is required to open these accounts. No declaration of the origin of foreign exchange is required for individuals, who may transfer freely foreign exchange held in these accounts up to $5,000 and, upon authorization, larger amounts to their bank account abroad or may freely convert it into domestic currency.
Held abroad	Resident persons or enterprises may open and use foreign exchange bank accounts at banks abroad, subject to authorization by the ANB. Enterprises are obliged to repatriate the foreign exchange held in accounts abroad (except the amount used to pay for imports).

Nonresident Accounts

Eligibility to hold accounts	Juridical and natural persons are eligible.
Foreign exchange accounts permitted	Prior approval is required to open these accounts. Foreign exchange in these accounts may be transferred abroad or sold to the banks for manats.
Domestic currency accounts	Nonresident enterprises may also open and operate accounts in manats and use them for domestic transactions, in accordance with instructions issued by the ANB. Foreign governments and international institutions may open and operate manat accounts with specific authorization from the ANB.
Convertible into foreign currency	These accounts are permitted, but prior approval is required.

Imports and Import Payments

Foreign exchange budget	No.
Financing requirements for imports	
Advance payment requirements	Advance import payments of more than 60 or 180 days prior to the delivery of goods are not allowed for state-owned enterprises or private enterprises. Prepayments by bank transfers for import contracts of goods and services are limited to the equivalent of $10,000.
Documentation requirements for release of foreign exchange for imports	
Domiciliation requirements	n.a.
Preshipment inspection	n.a.
Letters of credit	Prepayments by bank transfers in excess of $10,000 require either a letter of credit or the authorization of the ANB.

Import licenses and other nontariff measures	No.
Import taxes and/or tariffs	During 1996, most import duties ranged from 10% to 20%. In January 1997, tariffs were unified at 15% for all goods and for imports from all countries. A customs fee of 0.15% is levied on imports from all sources.
Taxes collected through the exchange system	No.
State import monopoly	No.

Exports and Export Proceeds

Repatriation requirements	Residents are required to repatriate all proceeds from exports within 3 months and transfer them to a licensed bank in Azerbaijan within 10 days of receipt, unless specifically exempted by the government. Expenses, commissions, and taxes paid abroad relating to economic activities may be deducted from the proceeds prior to transfer to a licensed bank.
Surrender requirements	Since June 1996, exporters are no longer required to sell 30% of their earnings at the BICEX auctions.
Export licenses	No.
Export taxes	Exports of strategic goods whose domestic prices have been significantly below world market levels, notably oil products and cotton, are subject to export duties that tax away 70% of the difference between the domestic and the export price.
Taxes collected through the exchange system	No.

Payments for Invisible Transactions and Current Transfers

Controls on these payments	Access to the BICEX for payments for current international transactions by resident individuals acting in their personal capacity is denied. Individuals may not transfer abroad from their foreign exchange accounts in excess of $5,000 a transaction, unless they are transferring foreign exchange that had been previously sent to them. Information on indicative limits and bona fide tests was not available at the time of publication.
Interest payments	n.a.
Profit/dividends	n.a.
Payments for travel	
Quantitative limits	The limit is $5,000 a trip.
Medical costs	
Quantitative limits	The limit is $5,000 a transaction.
Study abroad costs	
Quantitative limits	The limit is $5,000 a transaction.
Foreign workers' wages	n.a.
Pensions	n.a.
Gambling/prize earnings	n.a.
Family maintenance/alimony	
Quantitative limits	The limit is $5,000 a transaction.

Credit card use abroad — n.a.

Proceeds from Invisible Transactions and Current Transfers

Repatriation requirements — Proceeds must be repatriated within 3 months and transferred to a licensed bank within 10 days of receipt.

Surrender requirements — No.

Capital Transactions

Controls on capital and money market instruments

On capital market securities

   Purchase locally by nonresidents — n.a.

   Sale or issue locally by nonresidents — n.a.

   Purchase abroad by residents — Residents are not allowed to buy foreign securities.

   Sale or issue abroad by residents — n.a.

On money market instruments

   Purchase locally by nonresidents — n.a.

   Sale or issue locally by nonresidents — n.a.

   Purchase abroad by residents — Residents are not allowed to buy money market instruments abroad.

   Sale or issue abroad by residents — n.a.

On collective investment securities — n.a.

Controls on direct investment

Outward direct investment — n.a.

Inward direct investment — Profits may be reinvested in local currency held in Azerbaijan or converted into foreign currency and transferred without restriction. Foreign investors are granted certain privileges: enterprises or joint ventures with foreign equity capital ownership of more than 30% are entitled to a 2-year holiday on profit taxes, imports and exports of goods and services may be undertaken without licenses, and exporters of manufactured goods are allowed to retain 100% of their foreign exchange earnings.

Changes During 1996

Exchange arrangements — *November 1.* Foreign exchange auctions were increased to 5 times a week, from 3 times a week.

Exports and export proceeds — *June 1.* The requirement to sell 30% of export proceeds at the BICEX auctions was eliminated.

Changes During 1997

Imports and import payments — *January 1.* Tariffs were unified at 15% for all goods imported from all countries.

THE BAHAMAS

(Position as of February 28, 1997)

Status Under IMF Articles of Agreement

Article VIII	Date of acceptance: December 5, 1973.

Exchange Arrangement

Currency	The currency of The Bahamas is the Bahamian dollar.
Other legal tender	Commemorative coins in denominations of B$10, B$20, B$50, B$100, B$150, B$200, B$250, B$1,000, and B$2,500 in gold, and B$10 and B$25 in silver are legal tender but do not circulate. The U.S. dollar circulates concurrently with the Bahamian dollar.
Exchange rate structure	
Dual	In addition to the official exchange market, there is a market in which investment currency may be negotiated between residents through the Central Bank of The Bahamas (CBB); the current premium bid and offer rates are 20% and 25%, respectively. The use of investment currency is prescribed for the purchase of foreign currency securities from nonresidents and direct investments outside The Bahamas. In certain circumstances, the CBB may also permit residents to retain and use foreign currency from other sources to make such outward investments.
Classification	
Pegged	The Bahamian dollar is pegged to the U.S. dollar, the intervention currency, at B$1 per $1. Buying and selling rates for the pound sterling are also officially quoted, with the buying rate based on the rate in the New York market; the selling rate is 0.5% above the buying rate. The CBB deals only with commercial banks. For transactions with the public, commercial banks are authorized to charge a commission of 0.50% buying and 0.75% selling per $1, and 0.50% buying or selling per £1.
Exchange tax	A stamp tax of 1.5% is applied to all outward remittances.
Exchange subsidy	No.
Forward exchange market	Commercial banks may provide forward cover for residents who are due to receive or must pay foreign currency under a contractual commitment. Commercial banks may not, however, sell foreign currency spot to be held on account in cover of future requirements without the CBB's permission. Authorized dealers may deal in foreign currency forward with nonresidents without prior approval from the CBB. Commercial banks may deal forward among themselves at market rates and must ensure when carrying out all forward cover arrangements that their open spot or forward position does not exceed the equivalent of B$500,000 long or short.
Official cover of forward operations	No.

Arrangements for Payments and Receipts

Prescription of currency requirements	The exchange control system of The Bahamas makes no distinction between foreign territories. Settlements with residents of foreign countries may be made in any foreign currency or in Bahamian dollars through an external account. Foreign currencies comprise all currencies other than the Bahamian dollar.
Payment arrangements	No.
Administration of control	
Exchange control authorities	Exchange control is administered by the CBB, which delegates to authorized dealers the authority to approve allocations of foreign exchange for certain current payments,

including payments for imports up to B$100,000; approval authority for cash gifts is not delegated, except in the Family Islands.

International security restrictions	No.
Payment arrears	No.

Controls on trade in gold (coins and/or bullion)

Controls on domestic ownership and/or trade — Residents, other than authorized dealers, are not permitted to hold or deal in gold bullion. However, residents who are known users of gold for industrial purposes may, with the approval of the CBB, meet their current industrial requirements. There is no restriction on residents' acquisition or retention of gold coins.

Controls on external trade — Authorized dealers are not required to obtain licenses for bullion or coins, and no import duty is imposed on these items. Commercial imports of gold jewelry do not require a license and are duty free, although a 10% stamp tax is required. A 1.5% stamp tax payable to customs is also required on commercial shipments of gold jewelry from any source.

Controls on exports and imports of banknotes

On exports

Domestic currency — A traveler could export banknotes up to B$70 until February 17, 1997, when the limit was raised to B$200.

Foreign currency — Bahamian travelers need CBB approval to export foreign banknotes.

On imports

Domestic currency — Importation is subject to CBB approval.

Resident Accounts

Eligibility to hold accounts	Juridical and natural persons are eligible.
Foreign exchange accounts permitted	Yes.
Held domestically	These accounts are permitted, but prior approval is required.
Held abroad	These accounts are permitted, but prior approval is required.
Accounts in domestic currency convertible into foreign currency	No.

Nonresident Accounts

Eligibility to hold accounts	Juridical and natural persons are eligible.
Foreign exchange accounts permitted	Yes.

Domestic currency accounts — With the prior approval of the CBB, authorized banks may also open external accounts in Bahamian dollars for nonresident companies that have local expenses in The Bahamas and for nonresident investors. Authorized banks may freely open external accounts denominated in Bahamian dollars for winter residents and for persons with residency permits who are not gainfully employed in The Bahamas. Persons of a foreign nationality who have been granted temporary resident status are treated in some respects as nonresidents but are not permitted to hold external accounts in Bahamian dollars. External accounts in Bahamian dollars are normally funded entirely from foreign currency originating outside The Bahamas, but income on registered investments may also be credited to these accounts with the approval of the CBB.

Convertible into foreign currency	These accounts are permitted, but prior approval is required.
Blocked accounts	The accounts of residents emigrating from The Bahamas and who are redesignated upon departure as nonresidents are blocked for amounts in excess of B$25,000 for a period of 4 years. Balances on blocked accounts are transferable through the official exchange market after that time or through the Investment Currency Market at any time; they may also be invested with the approval of the CBB in certain resident-held assets or they may be spent locally for any other purpose.

Imports and Import Payments

Foreign exchange budget	No.
Financing requirements for imports	No.
Documentation requirements for release of foreign exchange for imports	Prior approval from the CBB is required to make payments for imports exceeding B$100,000, irrespective of origin, except in the Family Islands, where this authority is delegated to clearing bank branches. This approval is normally given automatically upon submission of pro forma invoices or other relevant documents proving the existence of a purchase contract.
Import licenses and other nontariff measures	
Negative list	The importation of certain commodities is prohibited or controlled for social, humanitarian, or health reasons. For all imports of agricultural products, a permit must be obtained from the Ministry of Agriculture. All other goods may be imported without a license. Customs entries are subject to a stamp tax of 7%.
Import taxes and/or tariffs	Import duties vary from zero to 210%. The tariff rate on most goods is 42%, and the average tariff rate is 35%. Stamp duties on imports vary from 2% to 7%. There is no import duty on certain tourist-related goods but these goods attract stamp duty ranging from 8% to 20%.
Taxes collected through the exchange system	No.
State import monopoly	No.

Exports and Export Proceeds

Repatriation requirements	Yes.
Surrender requirements	The proceeds of exports must be offered for sale to an authorized dealer as soon as the goods have reached their destination or within 6 months of shipment; alternatively, export proceeds may be used in any manner acceptable to the CBB.
Financing requirements	No.
Documentation requirements	No.
Export licenses	
Without quotas	Export licenses are not required, except for crawfish, conch, and arms and ammunition.
Export taxes	Yes.
Taxes collected through the exchange system	No.

Payments for Invisible Transactions and Current Transfers

Controls on these payments	There are no restrictions on current payments. However, there are limits on the approval authority delegated to commercial banks by the CBB. Authorized dealers may make

payments to nonresidents on behalf of residents for certain services and other invisibles, such as commissions, royalties, education, and non-life-insurance premiums, within specified limits. CBB approval is required for payments in excess of those limits or for categories of payments not delegated.

Unloading/storage costs

Prior approval   CBB approval is required for transactions over B$3,000.

Commissions

Prior approval   CBB approval is required for transactions over B$6,000.

Profit/dividends

Prior approval   For all investments with approved status, permission is given upon application for the transfer.

Payments for travel

Prior approval   Yes.

Quantitative limits   Under delegated authority, the limits for tourist travel are B$1,000 a person above the age of 18 years and B$500 a person up to the age of 18 years a trip. For business or professional travel, the limit is B$10,000 a person a year. The allowance for tourist travel excludes the cost of fares and travel services, which are normally obtained against payment in Bahamian dollars to a travel agent in The Bahamas. Foreign exchange obtained for travel may not be retained abroad or used abroad for purposes other than travel; any unused balance must be surrendered within a week of issue or, if the traveler is still abroad, within 1 week of returning to The Bahamas.

Indicative limits/bona fide test   Yes.

Medical costs

Indicative limits/bona fide test   Apart from a B$1,000 cash allowance, authorized dealers may approve all medical payments to doctors or medical establishments.

Study abroad costs

Quantitative limits   Under delegated authority, residents are entitled to a foreign exchange allowance of B$3,000 a person a trip.

Indicative limits/bona fide test   Subject to adequate documentary evidence, an education allowance is granted by the CBB without a limit.

Subscriptions and membership fees

Quantitative limits   Under delegated authority, the limit is B$1,000.

Consulting/legal fees

Prior approval   Yes.

Quantitative limits   Under delegated authority, the limit is B$3,000.

Indicative limits/bona fide test   Yes.

Foreign workers' wages

Prior approval   Yes.

Quantitative limits   The limit is 50% of wages and salaries.

Indicative limits/bona fide test   If commitments outside The Bahamas are more than 50% of wages and salaries, additional amounts may be remitted. Temporary residents may also repatriate all of their accumulated savings resulting from their employment in The Bahamas.

Gambling/prize earnings   Residents are not allowed to remit funds for gaming purposes.

Prior approval   Yes.

Quantitative limits	Yes.
Indicative limits/bona fide test	Yes.
Credit card use abroad	
Prior approval	Approval is required for residents to hold an international credit card, which may not be used to pay for life insurance premiums and capital items.

Proceeds from Invisible Transactions and Current Transfers

Repatriation requirements	Residents are obliged to collect without delay all proceeds.
Surrender requirements	All foreign currency proceeds must be offered for sale to an authorized dealer without delay.
Restrictions on use of funds	No.

Capital Transactions

Controls on capital and money market instruments	All outward capital transfers require exchange control approval, and outflows of resident-owned capital are restricted. Inward transfers by nonresidents, which are encouraged, are required to go through the manual exchange control approval process, although the subsequent use of the funds in The Bahamas may require authorization. The same regulations as detailed below apply for money market instruments, collective investment securities, and derivatives.
On capital market securities	
Purchase locally by nonresidents	Nonresident buyers of Bahamian dollar-denominated securities must fund the acquisition of such securities from foreign currency sources. Interest, dividends, and capital payments on such securities may not be remitted outside The Bahamas, unless the holdings have been properly acquired by nonresidents. In principle, inward investment by nonresidents is unrestricted. However, the consent of the CBB is required for the issue or transfer of shares in a Bahamian company to a nonresident and for the transfer of control of a Bahamian company to a nonresident. The extent of such approvals generally reflects the government's economic and investment policy guidelines.
Sale or issue locally by nonresidents	Yes.
Purchase abroad by residents	Residents are not permitted to purchase foreign currency securities with official exchange, export proceeds, or other current earnings; payment must be made with investment currency. All purchases, sales, and swaps of foreign currency securities by Bahamian residents require permission from the CBB, and are normally transacted through authorized agents who are free to act on behalf of nonresidents in relation to such transactions without any further approval from the CBB. All foreign securities purchased by residents of The Bahamas must be held by, or to the order of, an authorized agent.
Sale or issue abroad by residents	Sale proceeds from such resident-held foreign currency securities, if registered at the CBB by December 31, 1972, are eligible for sale in the investment currency market. Unregistered securities may be offered for sale at the official rate of exchange.
Controls on credit operations	
Commercial credits	
By residents to nonresidents	A resident company wholly owned by nonresidents is not allowed to raise fixed capital in Bahamian dollars, although approval may be granted to obtain working capital in local currency. If the company is partly owned by residents, the amount of local currency borrowing for fixed capital purposes is determined in relation to the resident interest in the equity of the company. Banks and other lenders resident in The Bahamas

must have permission to extend loans in domestic currency to any corporate body (other than a bank) that is also resident in The Bahamas but is controlled by any means, whether directly or indirectly, by nonresidents. However, companies set up by nonresidents primarily to import and distribute products manufactured outside The Bahamas are not allowed to borrow Bahamian dollars from residents for either fixed or working capital. Instead, they must provide all their financing in foreign currency, and foreign currency loans are normally permitted on application.

To residents from nonresidents

Residents other than authorized banks must obtain permission to borrow foreign currency from nonresidents, and authorized dealers are subject to exchange control direction of their foreign currency loans to residents. Residents must also obtain permission to pay interest on, and to repay the principal of, foreign currency loans by conversion of Bahamian dollars. When permission is granted for residents to accept foreign currency loans, it is conditional upon the currency being offered for sale without delay to an authorized dealer unless the funds are required to meet payments to nonresidents for which permission has been specifically given.

Financial credits

Yes.

Guarantees, sureties, and financial backup facilities

Yes.

Controls on direct investment

Outward direct investment

The use of official exchange for direct investment abroad is limited to B$100,000 or 30% of the total cost of the investment (whichever is greater) for investments from which the additional benefits expected to accrue to the balance of payments from export receipts, profits, or other earnings within 18 months of the investment will at least equal the total amount of investment and will continue thereafter. Investments abroad that do not meet the above criteria may be financed by foreign currency borrowed on suitable terms subject to individual approval from the CBB, by foreign currency purchased in the investment currency market, or by the retained profits of foreign subsidiary companies. Permission is not given for investments that are likely to have adverse effects on the balance of payments.

Inward direct investment

CBB approval is required.

Controls on liquidation of direct investment

In the event of a sale or liquidation, nonresident investors are permitted to repatriate the proceeds, including any capital appreciation, through the official foreign exchange market.

Controls on real estate transactions

Purchase abroad by residents

Residents require the specific approval of the CBB to buy property outside The Bahamas; such purchases, if for personal use, may be made only with investment currency, and approval is limited to one property a family. Incidental expenses connected with the purchase of property for personal use may normally be met with investment currency. Expenditures necessary for the maintenance of the property or arising directly from its ownership may, with permission, be met with foreign currency bought at the current market rate in the official foreign exchange market.

Purchase locally by nonresidents

Foreigners intending to purchase land for commercial purposes or property larger than five acres in size must obtain a permit from the Investments Board. If such an application is approved, payment for the purchase may be made either in Bahamian dollars from an external source or in foreign currency. Nonresidents wishing to purchase property for residential purposes may do so without prior approval but are required to obtain a Certificate of Registration from the Foreign Investment Board on completion of the transaction.

Sale locally by nonresidents

Approval is required.

Provisions specific to commercial banks and other credit institutions

Borrowing abroad

Yes.

Lending locally in foreign exchange	Exchange control approval is required to make loans to residents.
Open foreign exchange position limits	The limit is B$500,000 for a long or short position.
Provisions specific to institutional investors	No.
Other controls imposed by securities laws	There is no securities legislation.

Changes During 1996

No significant changes occurred in the exchange and trade system.

Changes During 1997

Arrangements for payments and receipts	*February 17.* The limit on exports of banknotes by travelers was raised to B$200 from B$70.

BAHRAIN

(Position as of December 31, 1996)

Status Under IMF Articles of Agreement

Article VIII   Date of acceptance: March 20, 1973.

Exchange Arrangement

Currency   The currency of Bahrain is the Bahrain dinar.

Exchange rate structure   Unitary.

Classification

Pegged   The Bahrain dinar is pegged to the SDR at the rate of BD 0.47619 per SDR 1. The exchange rate of the Bahrain dinar in terms of the SDR may be set with margins of ±7.25% of this fixed relationship. In practice, however, the Bahrain dinar has maintained a stable relationship with the U.S. dollar, the intervention currency. The middle rate of the Bahrain dinar for the U.S. dollar is quoted by the Bahrain Monetary Agency (BMA) and has remained unchanged since December 1980. The BMA provides daily recommended rates to banks for amounts up to BD 1,000 in U.S. dollars, pounds sterling, and deutsche mark, based on the latest available U.S. dollar rates against those currencies. The BMA does not deal with the public. In their dealings with the public, commercial banks are required to use the BMA's rates for U.S. dollars, pounds sterling, and deutsche mark, but they are authorized to charge a commission of 2‰ (special rates of commission apply for transactions up to BD 1,000). The banks' rates for other currencies are based on the BMA's U.S. dollar rates and the New York market rates against the U.S. dollar.

Exchange tax   No.

Exchange subsidy   No.

Forward exchange market   The BMA monitors the forward exchange transactions of commercial banks through the open position of banks' monthly returns.

Official cover of forward operations   No.

Arrangements for Payments and Receipts

Prescription of currency requirements All settlements with Israel are prohibited. Otherwise, no requirements are imposed on exchange payments or receipts.

Payment arrangements   No.

Administration of control

Exchange control authorities   There is no exchange control legislation.

International security restrictions

In accordance with IMF Executive Board Decision No. 144-(52/51)   Yes.

In accordance with UN sanctions   Yes.

Payment arrears   No.

Controls on trade in gold (coins and/or bullion)   No.

Controls on external trade   Imports of gold jewelry are subject to a 10% customs duty, but gold ingots are exempt. Brokers doing business in gold and other commodities must obtain BMA approval before they can register with the Ministry of Commerce.

Controls on exports and imports of banknotes	No.

Resident Accounts

Eligibility to hold accounts	Juridical and natural persons are eligible.
Foreign exchange accounts permitted	Yes.
Held domestically	Yes.
Held abroad	Yes.
Accounts in domestic currency convertible into foreign currency	Yes.

Nonresident Accounts

Eligibility to hold accounts	Juridical and natural persons are eligible.
Foreign exchange accounts permitted	Yes.
Domestic currency accounts	Yes.
Convertible into foreign currency	Yes.
Blocked accounts	No.

Imports and Import Payments

Foreign exchange budget	No.
Financing requirements for imports	No.
Documentation requirements for release of foreign exchange for imports	
Domiciliation requirements	Importers must be registered with the commercial registry maintained by the Ministry of Commerce and must be members of the Bahrain Chamber of Commerce and Industry.
Import licenses and other nontariff measures	Mandatory government procurements give preference to goods produced in Bahrain and member countries of the Cooperation Council for the Arab States of the Gulf (GCC), provided that the quality and prices of these goods are within specified margins of the prices of imported substitutes (10% for goods produced in Bahrain and 5% for goods produced in member countries of the GCC).
Negative list	Licenses are required for imports of arms, ammunition, and alcoholic beverages. All imports from Israel are prohibited. Imports of a few commodities are prohibited from all sources for reasons of health, public policy, or security. Imports of cultured pearls are prohibited.
Import taxes and/or tariffs	The rates of customs tariffs range between 5% and 10% on most commodities but the rate is 20% on vehicles, a minimum of 50% of declared or estimated customs value of tobacco, and 125% on alcoholic beverages.
Taxes collected through the exchange system	No.
State import monopoly	In practice, rice is imported mainly by the Bahrain Import-Export Company.

Exports and Export Proceeds

Repatriation requirements	No.
Surrender requirements	No.
Financing requirements	No.
Documentation requirements	Exporters must be registered with the commercial registry maintained by the Ministry of Commerce and must be members of the Bahrain Chamber of Commerce and Industry.
Export licenses	All exports to Israel are prohibited.
Export taxes	No.

Payments for Invisible Transactions and Current Transfers

Controls on these payments	No.

Proceeds from Invisible Transactions and Current Transfers

Repatriation requirements	No.
Surrender requirements	No.
Restrictions on use of funds	Proceeds from invisibles from Israel are prohibited.

Capital Transactions

Controls on capital and money market instruments	No exchange control requirements are imposed on capital receipts or payments by residents or nonresidents, but payments may not be made to or received from Israel.
On capital market securities	
Purchase locally by nonresidents	There is a limit of 25% on holding of shares of public companies by nonnationals.
Controls on derivatives and other instruments	No.
Controls on credit operations	No.
Controls on direct investment	No.
Controls on liquidation of direct investment	No.
Controls on real estate transactions	No.
Provisions specific to commercial banks and other credit institutions	Banks are subject to special rules regarding the payment of dividends and the remittance of profits. Licensed offshore banking units may freely engage in transactions with nonresidents, although transactions with residents are not normally permitted.

Changes During 1996

Imports and import payments	*December 8.* The import tariff on tobacco and related products was set at a minimum of 50% of a declared or estimated customs value.

BANGLADESH

(Position as of January 31, 1997)

Status Under IMF Articles of Agreement

Article VIII   Date of acceptance: April 11, 1994.

Exchange Arrangement

Currency   The currency of Bangladesh is the Bangladesh taka.

Exchange rate structure   Unitary.

Classification

Pegged   The taka is pegged to a weighted currency basket of Bangladesh's major trading part-
                                           ners. The external value of the taka was adjusted on January 8, April 8, April 20,
                                           July 15, August 1, September 7, and September 23, 1996. Since January 1, 1996, the
                                           Bangladesh Bank (BB) ceased to deal in the currencies of the other ACU countries and
                                           deals with authorized domestic banks only in U.S. dollars, the intervention currency.
                                           Authorized banks are free to set their own buying and selling rates for the U.S. dollar
                                           and the rates for other currencies based on cross rates in international markets.

Exchange tax   No.

Exchange subsidy   No.

Forward exchange market   Forward contracts are available from authorized banks, covering periods of up to
                                           6 months for export proceeds and import payments and covering up to 3 months of
                                           remittances of surplus collection of foreign shipping companies and airlines. Authorized
                                           banks are permitted to retain working balances with their foreign correspondents. Cur-
                                           rency swaps and forward exchange transactions are permitted when they are effected
                                           against underlying approved commercial transactions.

Official cover of forward operations   The BB does not transact in the forward market, nor does it regulate transactions beyond
                                           the normal requirements of prudential supervision.

Arrangements for Payments and Receipts

Prescription of currency   Settlements normally take place in convertible currencies and, in some cases, through
requirements   nonresident taka accounts. Settlements with ACU member countries are required to be
                                           effected through the ACU in terms of the AMU (equivalent in value to the U.S. dollar,
                                           effective January 1, 1996). Settlements for trade under bilateral commodity exchange
                                           agreements are effected through special nonconvertible U.S. dollar accounts. Payments
                                           for imports may be made to any country (with the exception of countries from which
                                           importation is prohibited). They may be made (1) in taka for credit in Bangladesh to a
                                           nonresident bank account of the country concerned; (2) in the currency of the country
                                           concerned; or (3) in any freely convertible currency. Export proceeds must be received
                                           in freely convertible foreign exchange or in taka from a nonresident taka account.

Payment arrangements

Bilateral arrangements

   Inoperative   Bangladesh maintains commodity exchange agreements in nonconvertible U.S. dollars
                                           with Bulgaria, China, the Czech Republic, and Hungary.

Clearing agreements   The ACU was integrated by Bangladesh, India, the Islamic Republic of Iran, Myanmar,
                                           Nepal, Pakistan, and Sri Lanka.

Administration of control

Exchange control authorities

Exchange control is administered by the BB in accordance with general policy formulated in consultation with the Ministry of Finance. Commercial banks and specialized financial institutions are issued licenses as authorized dealers (authorized banks) in foreign exchange. The Chief Controller of Imports and Exports of the Ministry of Commerce is responsible for registering exporters and importers and for issuing the Import Policy Order (IPO). Registered importers can make their imports in terms of the IPO against letters of credit (LCs). LC authorization forms are issued by authorized dealers and do not require a separate import license.

International security restrictions

In accordance with UN sanctions

All settlements with Iraq and the Federal Republic of Yugoslavia (Serbia/Montenegro) are prohibited according to UN Security Council Resolution No. 757 (1992).

Payment arrears

No.

Controls on trade in gold (coins and/or bullion)

Controls on domestic ownership and/or trade

There are no restrictions on the internal sale, purchase, or possession of gold or silver ornaments (including coins) and jewelry, but there is a prohibition on the holding of gold and silver in all other forms except by licensed industrialists or dentists.

Controls on external trade

The importation and exportation of gold and silver require special permission. However, adult female travelers are free to bring in or take out any amount of gold jewelry without prior approval from the BB. Exports of gold jewelry and imports of gold and silver for exports/manufacturer of jewelry are allowed under the Jewelry Export Scheme.

Controls on exports and imports of banknotes

On exports

Domestic currency

Both Bangladesh and foreign nationals may take out up to Tk 500 in domestic currency.

Foreign currency

Nonresidents may take out the foreign currency and traveler's checks they declared on entry or up to $5,000 or the equivalent, brought in without declaration. They may also, without obtaining the approval of the BB, reconvert taka notes up to Tk 6,000 into convertible foreign currencies at the time of their departure. Residents may take out foreign currency and traveler's checks up to the amount of any travel allocation they are granted, and also up to $5,000 brought in without declaration upon return from a previous visit abroad.

On imports

Domestic currency

The importation of Bangladesh currency notes and coins exceeding Tk 500 is prohibited.

Foreign currency

Foreign currency traveler's checks and foreign currency notes may be brought in freely up to $5,000, but larger amounts should be declared to customs upon arrival in Bangladesh.

Resident Accounts

Eligibility to hold accounts

Juridical and natural persons are eligible.

Foreign exchange accounts permitted

Yes.

Held domestically

Bangladesh nationals and persons of Bangladesh origin who are working abroad are permitted to open foreign currency accounts denominated in deutsche mark, Japanese yen, pounds sterling, or U.S. dollars. These accounts may be credited with (1) remittances in convertible currencies received from abroad through normal banking and postal channels; (2) proceeds of convertible currencies (banknotes, traveler's checks, drafts, etc.) brought into Bangladesh by the account holders, provided that amounts exceeding $5,000 have been declared to customs upon arrival in Bangladesh; (3) transfers from other foreign currency accounts opened under the former Wage Earners' Scheme (WES); and (4) transfers from nonresident foreign currency deposit accounts. The accounts may be debited without restriction, subject to reporting to the BB.

Residents, when returning from abroad, may bring in any amount of foreign currency and may maintain a resident foreign currency deposit account with the foreign exchange brought in. However, proceeds of exports of goods and services from Bangladesh or commissions arising from business deals in Bangladesh are not allowed to be credited to such accounts. Balances in these accounts are freely transferable abroad and may be used for travel in the usual manner. These accounts may be opened in deutsche mark, Japanese yen, pounds sterling, and U.S. dollars. Exporters and local joint-venture firms executing projects financed by a foreign donor or international agency may open foreign currency accounts. Foreign currency accounts may also be opened in the names of diplomatic missions in Bangladesh, their expatriate personnel, and diplomatic bonded warehouses (duty-free shops). Prior approval is required.

Held abroad	Residents who had opened accounts abroad when previously residing abroad may maintain such accounts after returning to Bangladesh.
Accounts in domestic currency convertible into foreign currency	No.

Nonresident Accounts

Eligibility to hold accounts	Juridical and natural persons are eligible. All nonresident accounts are regarded for exchange control purposes as accounts related to the country in which the account holder is a permanent resident (the accounts of the United Nations and its agencies are treated as resident accounts).
Foreign exchange accounts permitted	Bangladesh nationals residing abroad; foreign nationals, companies, and firms registered or incorporated abroad; banks and other financial institutions, including institutional investors; officers and staff of Bangladesh missions and government institutions; autonomous bodies; and commercial banks may open interest-bearing nonresident foreign currency deposit accounts denominated in deutsche mark, Japanese yen, pounds sterling, or U.S. dollars. These accounts may be credited in initial minimum amounts of $1,000 or $500 ($25,000 for foreigners), with remittances in convertible currencies and transfers from existing foreign currency deposit accounts maintained by Bangladesh nationals abroad. The accounts bear interest if their terms range from 1 month to 1 year.

Bangladesh nationals may maintain a foreign currency account abroad while residing abroad and may continue to hold the account after returning to Bangladesh. The balance, including interest earned, may be transferred in foreign exchange by the account holder to any country or to any foreign currency deposit account maintained by Bangladesh nationals abroad. The balances in the accounts, which are freely convertible into taka, must be reported monthly by banks to the BB. Nonresident Bangladeshis who do not open or maintain a foreign currency deposit account while abroad may open a nonresident foreign currency deposit account with foreign exchange brought in from abroad within 6 months of the date of their return to take up permanent residence in Bangladesh. These accounts may be opened by authorized dealers without prior approval from the BB for Bangladesh nationals and foreign nationals who reside abroad and for foreign firms operating abroad. Specified debits and credits to these accounts may be made in the account holder's absence by authorized dealers without prior approval from the BB. Certain other debits and credits may be made without prior approval from the BB, but are subject to ex post recording.

Domestic currency accounts	Foreign missions and embassies, their expatriate personnel, foreign airline and shipping companies, and international nonprofit organizations in Bangladesh may open interest-bearing accounts, but the interest earned can be disbursed only in local currency.

Convertible into foreign currency	These accounts may be opened by all diplomatic missions operating in Bangladesh, their diplomatic officers, home-based members of the mission staffs, international nonprofit organizations (including charitable organizations functioning in Bangladesh and their respective personnel), foreign oil companies engaged in oil exploration in Bangladesh and their expatriate employees, UN organizations and other international organizations, foreign contractors and consultants engaged in specific projects, and foreign nationals residing in Bangladesh (regardless of their status). These accounts may be credited freely with the proceeds of inward remittances in convertible foreign exchange and may be debited freely at any time for local disbursements in taka, as well as for remittances abroad in convertible currencies. Transfers between convertible taka accounts are freely permitted. Prior approval is required.
Blocked accounts	Nonresident taka accounts of Bangladesh nationals can be blocked by the BB.

Imports and Import Payments

Foreign exchange budget	No.
Financing requirements for imports	
Advance payment requirements	Advance payments for imports require approval from the BB, which is normally given only for specialized or capital goods.
Documentation requirements for release of foreign exchange for imports	
Domiciliation requirements	Yes.
Preshipment inspection	An inspection is required for items prescribed in the IPO.
Letters of credit	Payment against imports is generally permissible only under cover of irrevocable LCs. Recognized export-oriented units operating under the bonded warehouse system may effect imports of up to 4 months' requirement of their raw and packing materials by establishing import LCs without reference to any export LC. They may also effect such imports by opening back-to-back LCs (either on a sight basis under the Export Development Fund, or up to a 180-day validity basis) against export LCs received by them. Public sector importers may import on a cash-against-documents basis, subject to authorization from the BB.
	Authorized dealers may establish LCs on an f.o.b. basis without the approval of the BB, subject to certain conditions. Foreign exchange for authorized imports is provided automatically by authorized dealers when payments are due.
Import licenses and other nontariff measures	All importers (including all government departments, with the exception of the Ministry of Defense) are required to obtain LC authorization forms (LCAFs) for all imports. Importers are allowed to effect imports against LCAFs issued by authorized dealer banks without an import license. Single-country LCAFs are issued for imports under bilateral trade or payment agreements and for imports under tied-aid programs. LCAFs are otherwise valid worldwide, except that imports from Israel and imports transported on flag vessels of Israel are prohibited. Goods must be shipped within 17 months of the date of issuance of LCAFs in the case of machinery and spare parts, and 9 months in the case of all other items.
Positive list	Items not specified in the control list of the IPO are freely importable, provided that the importer has a valid import registration certificate.
Negative list	The controlled list contains 110 items from about 1,400 categories at the 4-digit level of the Harmonized System Codes. The importation of these items is restricted or prohibited either for public safety, religious, environmental, and social reasons, or because similar items are produced locally. Up to 26 items are restricted purely for trade purposes (7 of which are banned and 19 are restricted). Imports from Israel are prohibited.

Open general licenses	All items not on the control list are freely importable by registered importers.
Licenses with quotas	Imports of specified raw materials and packing materials by industrial consumers are governed by an entitlement system, based on the requirements for various industries during each import program period established by the Board of Investment. Firms in the industrial sector are given an entitlement to import specified raw materials and packing materials, and LC authorization forms are issued on the basis of the entitlement. The entitlement system does not apply to raw materials and packing materials that are freely importable but does apply to items appearing on the controlled list. Separately, industrial consumers may be issued with LCAFs for parts and accessories of machinery. Goods imported against LCAFs issued to industrial consumers must be used in the industry concerned and must not be sold or transferred without prior approval.

Import taxes and/or tariffs	There are 7 tariff bands: zero, 2.5%, 7.5%, 15%, 22.5%, 30%, and 45%.
Taxes collected through the exchange system	No.
State import monopoly	No.

Exports and Export Proceeds

Repatriation requirements	Yes.
Surrender requirements	Proceeds from exports must be received within 4 months of shipment unless otherwise allowed by the BB. Exporters are permitted to retain 7.5% of the proceeds of exports of ready-made garments and 40% of the proceeds from other exports; they may use retained earnings for bona fide business purposes, such as business travel abroad, participation in trade fairs and seminars, and imports of raw materials, spare parts, and capital goods. These earnings may also be used to set up offices abroad without prior permission from the BB. Joint ventures, other than in the garment industry, located in export-processing zones (EPZs) are allowed to retain 80% of their export earnings in a foreign currency deposit account and place the remaining 20% in a bank account in domestic currency.
Documentation requirements	
Domiciliation	Yes.
Export licenses	Exports to Israel are prohibited. Exports of about 20 product categories are banned. Some of these are restricted for nontrade reasons, while others are restricted to ensure the supply of the domestic market. Export licenses are required for all banned or restricted items.
With quotas	Quotas are imposed on garment exports by the Chief Controller of Imports and Exports (since 1996) on the basis of the previous year's performance. The Export Promotion Bureau monitors quota use to be able to reallocate unfilled quotas.
Export taxes	Exports of jute are taxed.
Taxes collected through the exchange system	No.

Payments for Invisible Transactions and Current Transfers

Controls on these payments	Payments for invisibles related to authorized trade transactions are generally not restricted.
Unloading/storage costs	
Prior approval	Yes.

Administrative expenses

    Prior approval   No prior permission is required for the remittance of royalties and technical fees of up to 6% of sales, and of training and consulting fees of up to 1% of sales.

    Indicative limits/bona fide test   Yes.

Commissions

    Quantitative limits   Up to 5% of export receipts (up to 33.3% in the case of books) may be remitted abroad without prior approval from the BB.

Interest payments

    Prior approval   No approval is required if loan agreements are in conformity with Board of Investment (BOI) guidelines.

Profit/dividends   Authorized dealers are allowed to remit dividends to nonresident shareholders without the prior approval of the BB on receipt of applications from the companies concerned; applications must be supported by an audited balance sheet and profit-and-loss account, a board resolution declaring dividends out of profits derived from the normal business activities of the company, and an auditor's certificate that tax liabilities are covered. Authorized dealers may remit profits of foreign firms, banks, insurance companies, and other financial institutions operating in Bangladesh to their head office on receipt of applications supported by documentation. These remittances are, however, subject to ex post checking by the BB.

    Indicative limits/bona fide test   Yes.

Payments for travel

    Quantitative limits   The limit for personal travel by resident Bangladesh nationals to countries other than Bhutan, India, Maldives, Myanmar, Nepal, Pakistan, and Sri Lanka is $3,000 a year; the allowance for air travel to these 7 countries is $1,000 a person a year. For new exporters, the indicative limit for business travel is $6,000, while established exporters are permitted to utilize balances held under the export retention scheme (7.5% of exports of ready-made garments and 40% of other export proceeds). Manufacturers producing for the domestic market and importers are granted business travel allowances equivalent to 1% of turnover as declared in tax returns, and 1% of the value of imports, respectively. There is an annual ceiling of $5,000 in both cases.

    Indicative limits/bona fide test   Yes.

Medical costs

    Quantitative limits   Up to $10,000 can be obtained without prior approval. Larger amounts are subject to the approval of the BB.

    Indicative limits/bona fide test   Yes.

Study abroad costs   Foreign currency for education is made available up to the cost of tuition and living expenses, as estimated by the educational institution concerned. No prior permission is required for the remittance of fees for undergraduate, postgraduate, and some professional courses.

    Indicative limits/bona fide test   Applications for foreign exchange for study abroad are accepted upon verification of their bona fide nature.

Subscriptions and membership fees

    Indicative limits/bona fide test   Yes.

Consulting/legal fees

    Indicative limits/bona fide test   Industrial enterprises producing for local markets may remit up to 1% of sales receipts declared in the previous year's tax return.

Foreign workers' wages

Quantitative limits Foreign nationals may freely remit up to 50% of net salary in terms of service contracts approved by the government. The entire amount of their leave salaries and savings can also be freely remitted.

Pensions

Prior approval Yes.

Gambling/prize earnings Gambling is prohibited in Bangladesh.

Family maintenance/alimony Foreign exchange is available for the costs of dependents abroad, after production of a certificate from the Bangladesh embassy in the country concerned, up to a reasonable level based on prevailing prices.

Prior approval Applications for foreign exchange for family maintenance abroad are accepted upon verification of their bona fide nature.

Credit card use abroad

Prior approval General approval is given for exporters to use against the foreign exchange retention entitlement and for other residents to use for their travel allowance.

Quantitative limits Credit cards may be used up to the amounts authorized for travel allowances.

Proceeds from Invisible Transactions and Current Transfers

Repatriation requirements Yes.

Surrender requirements Exporters of services are permitted to retain 5% of the proceeds and to use retained earnings for bona fide business purposes. Bangladesh nationals working abroad may retain their earnings in foreign currency accounts or in nonresident foreign currency deposit accounts. Unless specifically exempted by the BB, all Bangladesh nationals who reside in Bangladesh must surrender any foreign exchange coming into their possession, whether held in Bangladesh or abroad, to an authorized dealer within 1 month of the date of acquisition. However, returning residents may keep, in foreign currency accounts opened in their names, foreign exchange brought in at the time of return from abroad, provided that the amount does not represent proceeds from exports from Bangladesh or commissions earned from business activities in Bangladesh. Residents may retain up to $5,000 brought into the country without declaration. Foreign nationals residing in Bangladesh continuously for more than 6 months are required to surrender within 1 month of the date of acquisition any foreign exchange representing their earnings with respect to business conducted in Bangladesh or services rendered while in Bangladesh.

Restrictions on use of funds Foreign exchange retainable as specified above may be used for travel abroad or bona fide business purposes.

Capital Transactions

Controls on capital and money market instruments

On capital market securities

Purchase locally by nonresidents Nonresidents may buy Bangladesh securities through stock exchanges against payment in freely convertible currency remitted from abroad through the banking channels.

Sale or issue locally by nonresidents Proceeds from sales, including capital gains and dividends earned on securities purchased in Bangladesh, may be remitted abroad in freely convertible currency. Nonresidents cannot issue securities in Bangladesh.

On money market instruments	These transactions are not allowed.
On collective investment securities	These transactions are not allowed.
Controls on derivatives and other instruments	
Sale or issue locally by nonresidents	These transactions are not allowed.
Purchase abroad by residents	Authorized dealer banks may obtain hedging abroad against exchange rate risks on underlying trade transactions.
Sale or issue abroad by residents	Yes.
Controls on credit operations	
Commercial credits	
By residents to nonresidents	Export payments deferred for more than 120 days require BB authorization.
To residents from nonresidents	Import payments deferred for up to 360 days in advance are permissible for capital machinery and for up to 180 days for industrial raw materials. Private industrial units may borrow funds from abroad without the approval of the Board of Investment if the interest rate does not exceed 4% above the LIBOR, the repayment period is more than 7 years, and the down payment is less than 10%. All other borrowing by industrial units requires prior BOI approval.
Financial credits	
By residents to nonresidents	Except in specific cases, credits are subject to prior BB approval.
To residents from nonresidents	Authorized dealers (i.e., commercial banks) may obtain short-term loans and overdrafts from overseas branches and correspondents for a period not exceeding 7 days at a time.
Guarantees, sureties, and financial backup facilities	
By residents to nonresidents	Banks may issue guarantees/sureties favoring nonresidents in relation to permissible current transactions on behalf of residents.
To residents from nonresidents	Receipt of guarantees/sureties by residents from abroad requires full disclosure of underlying transaction.
Controls on direct investment	
Outward direct investment	All outward transfers of capital require approval, which is sparingly granted for resident-owned capital.
Inward direct investment	Investments, except in the industrial sector, require approval. The Foreign Private Investment (Promotion and Protection) Act (1980) provides for the protection and equitable treatment of foreign private investment, indemnification, protection against expropriation and nationalization, and guarantee for repatriation of investment. There is no ceiling on private investment. Tax holidays are granted for periods of up to 9 years, depending on the location.
Controls on liquidation of direct investment	Requests for repatriation of the proceeds from liquidation of direct investment (in unlisted companies) are subject to prior scrutiny of the BB.
Controls on real estate transactions	
Purchase abroad by residents	Remittances of funds for these purchases are not permitted.
Purchase locally by nonresidents	Purchases of real estate by a nonresident with funds brought from abroad are allowed.
Sale locally by nonresidents	Repatriation of sales proceeds are subject to prior approval by the BB, which is not normally granted.

Provisions specific to commercial banks and other credit institutions

Borrowing abroad	Same regulations as for financial credits apply.
Maintenance of accounts abroad	The maintenance of these accounts is subject to notification to the BB.
Lending to nonresidents (financial or commercial credits)	Lending to nonresidents is not allowed, except with prior BB approval and in specific cases.
Lending locally in foreign exchange	Lending is subject to prior approval by the BB.
Purchase of locally issued securities denominated in foreign exchange	Purchases are subject to prior approval by the BB.
Differential treatment of nonresident deposit accounts and/or deposit accounts in foreign exchange	
Interest rate controls	Banks are required to maintain interest rates on foreign currency deposits in line with international market rates.
Open foreign exchange position limits	Since July 16, 1996, the BB has placed limits based on banks' paid-up capital and reserves. Beginning January 1997, the limits that the BB places on each authorized dealer's net open position were set at 12.5% of capital.

Provisions specific to institutional investors

Limits (max.) on portfolio invested abroad	Domestic institutional investors cannot acquire investment assets abroad.

Changes During 1996

Capital transactions	*July 16.* The BB set individual limits on the open exchange position for authorized dealers based on their paid-up capital and reserves.

Changes During 1997

Capital transactions	*January 1.* The BB set authorized dealers' net open positions at 12.5% of capital.

BARBADOS

(Position as of December 31, 1996)

Status Under IMF Articles of Agreement

Article VIII   Date of acceptance: November 3, 1993.

Exchange Arrangement

Currency   The currency of Barbados is the Barbabos dollar.

Other legal tender   Gold coins with face values of BDS$50, BDS$100, BDS$150, BDS$200, and BDS$500 are legal tender and are in limited circulation.

Exchange rate structure   Unitary.

Classification

Pegged   The Barbados dollar is pegged to the U.S. dollar, the intervention currency, at BDS$2 per US$1. Buying and selling rates for the Canadian dollar, the deutsche mark, and the pound sterling are also officially quoted on the basis of their cross-rate relationships to the U.S. dollar. The quoted rates include commission charges of 0.125% buying and 1.75% selling against the U.S. dollar, and 0.1875% buying and 1.8125% selling against the Canadian dollar, deutsche mark, and pound sterling.

Exchange tax   No.

Exchange subsidy   No.

Forward exchange market   The Central Bank of Barbados (CBB) periodically obtains forward cover in the international foreign exchange market to cover or hedge its own or the central government's exchange risks associated with foreign exchange loans that are not denominated in U.S. dollars. Commercial banks are allowed to obtain forward cover in the international markets. The CBB and commercial banks enter into swap transactions in U.S. dollars, while commercial banks freely switch between nonregional currencies.

Official cover of forward operations   No.

Arrangements for Payments and Receipts

Prescription of currency requirements   Settlements with residents of countries outside the CARICOM area may be made in any foreign currency or through an external account in Barbados dollars. Settlements with residents of CARICOM countries other than Guyana, Jamaica, Suriname, and Trinidad and Tobago may be made in the currency of the CARICOM country. Settlements with residents of these 4 countries should be made in U.S. dollars.

Payment arrangements

Bilateral arrangements   n.a.

Regional arrangements   Barbados is a member of the CARICOM.

Clearing agreements   Under clearing arrangements with regional monetary authorities, the CBB currently sells only 3 CARICOM country currencies: the Bahamian dollar, the Eastern Caribbean dollar, and the Belize dollar. The Trinidad and Tobago, Guyana, and Jamaica dollars now float against the U.S. dollar, and the CBB fixes daily selling rates based on rates supplied by the monetary authorities of these countries. These rates are applicable only to government transactions.

Barter agreements and open accounts   n.a.

Administration of control

Exchange control authorities   Exchange control applies to all countries and is administered by the CBB, which delegates to authorized dealers the authority to approve normal import payments and foreign

74

exchange for cash gifts. Trade controls are administered by the Ministry of Industry, Commerce, and Business Development (MICBD).

International security restrictions	No.
Payment arrears	No.

Controls on trade in gold (coins and/or bullion)

Controls on domestic ownership and/or trade

Residents other than the monetary authorities, authorized dealers, and industrial users are not permitted to hold or acquire gold in any form other than jewelry or coins for numismatic purposes. Any gold acquired in Barbados must be surrendered to an authorized dealer, unless exchange control approval is obtained for its retention.

Controls on external trade

The importation of gold by residents is permitted for industrial purposes and is subject to customs duties and charges. Licenses to import gold are issued by the MICBD. No license is required to export gold, but exchange control permission is required.

Controls on exports and imports of banknotes

On exports

Domestic currency

Travelers may take out up to BDS$200.

Foreign currency

Travelers may take out foreign currency notes and coins up to the value of BDS$500. Nonresident visitors may freely export any foreign currency they previously brought in.

Resident Accounts

Eligibility to hold accounts

Juridical and natural persons are eligible.

Foreign exchange accounts permitted

Yes.

Held domestically

Subject to specific conditions under delegated authority, authorized dealers may maintain foreign currency accounts in the names of individuals and companies resident in Barbados. Certain receipts and payments may be credited and debited to foreign currency accounts under conditions established at the time the account is opened. Other credits and debits require individual approval. However, where authority has not been delegated to authorized dealers, the permission of the CBB is required. Approval is given on the basis of the anticipated frequency of receipts and payments in foreign currency.

Held abroad

Permission of the CBB is required.

Nonresident Accounts

Eligibility to hold accounts

Juridical and natural persons are eligible.

Foreign exchange accounts permitted

Same regulations as for resident accounts apply.

Domestic currency accounts

These accounts may be credited with the proceeds from the sale of foreign currencies, with transfers from other external accounts, with bank interest, and with payments by residents for which the CBB has given general or specific permission. They may be debited for payments to residents of Barbados for the cost of foreign exchange required for travel or business purposes and for any other payment covered by delegated authority to authorized dealers. Other debits and any overdrafts require individual approval.

Convertible into foreign currency

Balances on external accounts are convertible. Approval is required.

Blocked accounts

The CBB may require certain payments in favor of nonresidents that are ineligible for transfer to be credited to blocked accounts. Balances in blocked accounts may not be withdrawn without approval, other than for the purchase of approved securities.

Imports and Import Payments

Foreign exchange budget	No.
Financing requirements for imports	
Minimum financing requirements	n.a.
Advance payment requirements	Authorized dealers may release foreign exchange up to the equivalent of BDS$100,000 (c.i.f.) for advance payments for imports into Barbados. Other advance payments require the prior approval of the CBB.
Advance import deposits	n.a.
Documentation requirements for release of foreign exchange for imports	Payments for authorized imports are permitted upon application and submission of documentary evidence (invoices and customs warrants) to authorized dealers; payments for imports of crude oil and its derivatives are subject to the approval of the CBB.
Domiciliation requirements	n.a.
Preshipment inspection	n.a.
Letters of credit	n.a.
Import licenses used as exchange licenses	n.a.
Import licenses and other nontariff measures	Certain imports require individual licenses. Some items on the import-licensing list may be freely imported throughout the year, while others are subject to temporary restrictions (particularly agricultural products, which tend to be subject to seasonal restrictions). Individual licenses are also required for imports of commodities that are subject to the provisions of the Oils and Fats Agreement between the governments of Barbados, Dominica, Grenada, Guyana, St. Lucia, St. Vincent, and Trinidad and Tobago whether the goods are being imported from CARICOM countries or from elsewhere. Special licensing arrangements have been made for the regulation of trade between Barbados and other CARICOM countries in 22 agricultural commodities.
Negative list	n.a.
Open general licenses	n.a.
Licenses with quotas	Not all goods that are subject to licensing are subject to quantitative restrictions or import surcharges.
Import taxes and/or tariffs	Customs duties correspond to the CET of CARICOM. Rates range from 5% to 30%. Import charges in the form of stamp duties, consumption taxes, and luxury taxes may attain 203%.
Taxes collected through the exchange system	No.

Exports and Export Proceeds

Repatriation requirements	Yes.
Surrender requirements	Yes.
Export licenses	Specific licenses are required for the exportation of certain goods to any country, including rice, sugarcane, rum, molasses, certain other food products, sewing machines, portland cement, and petroleum products. All other goods may be exported without license.
Without quotas	Yes.
With quotas	Exports of sugar to the United Kingdom and the United States are subject to bilateral export quotas, as are exports of rum to the EU.

Payments for Invisible Transactions and Current Transfers

Controls on these payments	Prior approval is required for payments above the established limits, which are also subject to indicative limits and/or bona fide tests. The established limits are (1) BDS$250,000 for payments for freight and insurance, unloading and storage costs, administrative expenses, commissions, consulting and legal fees; and (2) BDS$100,000 for interest payments and for remittances of profits and dividends. Other specific limits are listed below.
Payments for travel	
Quantitative limits	The limits are BDS$5,000 a person a calendar year for private travel and BDS$500 a day for business travel up to BDS$40,000 a person a calendar year.
Medical costs	
Quantitative limits	The limit is BDS$50,000 a person a year.
Study abroad costs	
Quantitative limits	The limit is BDS$40,000 a person a year.
Subscriptions and membership fees	
Quantitative limits	The limit is BDS$50,000 a person a year.
Foreign workers' wages	n.a.
Pensions	n.a.
Gambling/prize earnings	n.a.
Family maintenance/alimony	
Quantitative limits	The limits are BDS$1,000 for cash gifts and BDS$50,000 for alimony and other maintenance expenses.
Credit card use abroad	n.a.

Proceeds from Invisible Transactions and Current Transfers

Repatriation requirements	Yes.
Surrender requirements	Foreign currency proceeds from invisibles must be sold to authorized dealers.

Capital Transactions

Controls on capital and money market instruments	
On capital market securities	
Purchase locally by nonresidents	The issuance and transfer to nonresidents of securities registered in Barbados require exchange control approval, which is freely given provided that an adequate amount of foreign currency is brought in for their purchase.
Sale or issue locally by nonresidents	n.a.
Purchase abroad by residents	These purchases require exchange control approval, and certificates of title must be lodged with an authorized depository in Barbados. Earnings on these securities must be repatriated and surrendered to an authorized dealer.
Sale or issue abroad by residents	n.a.
On money market instruments	Same regulations as for capital market securities apply.
On collective investment securities	Same regulations as for capital market securities apply.

Controls on credit operations	The approval of the CBB is required for credit operations.
Controls on direct investment	Investments require exchange control approval.
Outward direct investment	Yes.
Inward direct investment	Yes.
Controls on liquidation of direct investment	Liquidation of proceeds is permitted, provided that evidence documenting the validity of the remittance is submitted, all liabilities related to the investment have been discharged, and the original investment was registered with the CBB.
Controls on real estate transactions	
Purchase abroad by residents	Purchases require exchange control approval.
Purchase locally by nonresidents	Nonresidents may acquire real estate in Barbados for private purposes with funds from foreign currency sources; local currency financing is not ordinarily permitted.
Sale locally by nonresidents	Proceeds from the realization of such investments equivalent to the amount of foreign currency brought in may be repatriated freely. Capital sums realized in excess of this amount may be repatriated freely on the basis of a calculated annual rate of return on the original foreign investment as follows: for the last 5 years, at 8%; for the 5 years immediately preceding the last 5 years, at 5%; and for any period preceding the last 10 years, at 4%. Amounts in excess of the sum so derived are restricted to remittances of BDS$30,000 a year.
Provisions specific to commercial banks and other credit institutions	
Borrowing abroad	Any borrowing abroad by authorized dealers to finance their domestic operations requires the approval of the CBB. Authorized dealers may assume short-term liability positions in foreign currencies for the financing of approved transfers in respect of both trade and nontrade transactions.
Maintenance of accounts abroad	n.a.
Lending to nonresidents (financial or commercial credits)	n.a.
Lending locally in foreign exchange	n.a.
Purchase of locally issued securities denominated in foreign exchange	n.a.
Differential treatment of nonresident deposit accounts and/or deposit accounts in foreign exchange	n.a.
Investment regulations	n.a.
Open foreign exchange position limits	n.a.
Provisions specific to institutional investors	A 6% tax is levied on portfolio investments of pension funds with foreign companies that are not registered with the Barbados Supervisor of Insurance.
Limits (max.) on portfolio invested abroad	n.a.
Limits (min.) on portfolio invested locally	n.a.
Currency matching regulations on assets/liabilities composition	n.a.

Changes During 1996

Arrangements for payments and receipts	*June 1.* Exchange control fees charged by the CBB were abolished.

BELARUS

(Position as of March 31, 1997)

Status Under IMF Articles of Agreement

Article XIV   Yes.

Exchange Arrangement

Currency

The currency of Belarus is the Belarussian rubel.

Exchange rate structure

Unitary. In September 1996, the National Bank of Belarus (NBB) allowed a 20% markup for cash and interbank transactions respectively over the official exchange rate established at the auction. In October 1996, the markup was raised to 30%. The rates were reunified on February 3, 1997.

Classification

Managed floating

A maximum transaction size for off-auction trading of $1,000 for dollars, DM 1,000 for deutsche mark, and Rub 100,000 for Russian rubles was in effect until October 1996, when the ceiling was raised to the equivalent of $30,000. In December 1996, the limit on off-auction interbank transactions was lifted. On April 11, 1996, the Minsk Interbank Currency Exchange (MICE) was nationalized and put under the direct control of the NBB. Also, the screening of bids in the auction was intensified, with all bids for purchases of foreign exchange for imports of "nonpriority" commodities summarily rejected.

The official exchange rate is set on the basis of the auction rate and used for accounting purposes, for all foreign exchange transactions of the government, for transactions related to exports and imports, and for most current transfers and capital account transactions. Banks can buy at the auction on their own account—subject to exposure limits defined by the NBB—as well as for confirmed import orders, and there are no restrictions on cash transactions at the auctions. After the reunification of the rates, the rate has been established on the basis of supply and demand and the inflation rate.

Exchange tax

Repatriation of profits in convertible currency is subject to a 15% tax payable in convertible currency.

Forward exchange market

The forward market is regulated by the same provisions as the spot market.

Official cover of forward operations

No.

Arrangements for Payments and Receipts

Prescription of currency requirements

In accordance with the Agreement on the Establishment of a Payment Union of Member Countries of the CIS (1994) and bilateral payment agreements between Belarus and the central banks of those countries, settlements between Belarus and CIS member countries are effected in the national currencies of the parties involved in the settlements, in the currencies of payment union member countries, and in freely convertible currencies, in accordance with legislation in effect on the territory of the country. Settlements between Belarus and CIS member countries and the Baltic countries are effected using noncash procedures via correspondent accounts of authorized banks and central banks.

In accordance with bilateral payment agreements between the NBB and the central banks of Armenia, Azerbaijan, the Kyrgyz Republic, Latvia, Lithuania, Moldova, Tajikistan, Uzbekistan, and Ukraine, only settlements for operations ensuing from the functions of central banks are effected via correspondent accounts of central banks. Settlements for all other accounts are effected via correspondent accounts of authorized banks.

In accordance with bilateral payment agreements between the NBB and the central banks of Estonia, Georgia, Kazakhstan, Russia, and Turkmenistan, settlements between economic agents of these countries may be effected both via correspondent accounts of authorized banks and via correspondent accounts of central banks.

Payment arrangements

Bilateral arrangements	Belarus maintains bilateral trade and/or payments agreements with 34 countries, including the CIS countries.
Operative	n.a.
Inoperative	n.a.
Regional arrangements	There are arrangements with Minsk, Moscow, and various regions in Russia.
Clearing agreements	There is an agreement with Uzbekistan calling for the exchange of cotton from Uzbekistan for strategic goods from Belarus on a balanced basis. There are also agreements with Moldova and Ukraine.
Barter agreements and open accounts	Barter trade of certain goods requires approval from the Commission of the Council of Ministers on the Issuance of Authorization to Engage in Commodity-Exchange Operations. Barter agreements are effected at the level of economic agents.

Administration of control

Exchange control authorities	The Parliament is responsible for legislating exchange control regulations and the NBB for administering them.

International security restrictions   No.

Payment arrears   Trade arrears on gas payments to Russia are maintained.

Official	Yes.
Private	n.a.

Controls on trade in gold (coins and/or bullion)

Controls on domestic ownership and/or trade	n.a.
Controls on external trade	A license is required for the exportation of gold.

Controls on exports and imports of banknotes

On exports

Domestic currency	Up to the rubel equivalent of 500 minimum wages may be taken abroad.
Foreign currency	Resident individuals are permitted to take abroad up to $500 a year. Larger amounts may be taken out with a customs declaration proving that they were brought into Belarus, or with a certificate from an authorized bank that they were exchanged legally.

On imports

Domestic currency	Up to the rubel equivalent of 500 minimum wages may be imported.

Resident Accounts

Eligibility to hold accounts	Juridical and natural persons are eligible.
Foreign exchange accounts permitted	Yes.
Held domestically	Without declaring the sources of their foreign exchange, residents may open foreign currency accounts at commercial banks in Belarus authorized to transact in foreign exchange.

Held abroad	These accounts are permitted, but approval of the NBB is required.
Accounts in domestic currency convertible into foreign currency	Balances may be converted for payments to import goods, labor, and services; payments for business trip expenditures and training abroad; and repayments of loans and interest. Nonbank financial organizations can convert balances to perform dealing operations, and insurance companies to establish insurance funds from net profits.

Nonresident Accounts

Eligibility to hold accounts	
Juridical persons	Yes.
Natural persons	n.a.
Foreign exchange accounts permitted	Nonresident juridical persons may maintain foreign exchange accounts with authorized banks in Belarus. The sources of the funds can be receipts from abroad; proceeds from the sales of goods and services in the territory of Belarus, including sales to residents; debt-service payment; interest earned on balances in the accounts; funds from other foreign exchange accounts of nonresidents in Belarus; and earnings from investments in the Baltic countries, Russia, and the other countries of the FSU. These accounts may be debited for purchases of goods and services and for investments in the Baltic countries, Russia, and the other countries of the FSU, as well as for payments to residents and nonresidents. Funds from these accounts may be freely repatriated or exchanged for rubels at the market exchange rate through authorized banks.
Approval required	n.a.
Domestic currency accounts	Until September 19, 1996, nonresident juridicial persons could open "L" accounts and "N" accounts at authorized commercial banks. On that date, these accounts were abolished and replaced by "I" (investment) and "T" (current) accounts. L accounts may be credited with the rubel counterpart of foreign exchange sold to the NBB or authorized banks, dividends from foreign-owned enterprises or joint ventures, returns on securities, and sales of such securities within Belarus. Funds from these accounts are freely usable in Belarus and may be converted into foreign currency at the market exchange rate. N accounts may be funded by proceeds from the sale of goods produced in Belarus or from the sale of goods directly imported from abroad. Balances in these accounts may be used only for business travel expenses, to purchase inputs used for the production of goods for export from Belarus, to purchase foreign exchange at the market exchange rate at auctions (up to the limit of nonresidents' initial investment plus proceeds from sales of their output in Belarus), for payment of wages, and for investment purposes as determined by the government with the permission of the Ministry of Foreign Economic Relations. Restrictions on the conversion of funds held in nonresident accounts were reintroduced in November 1995.
	As of April 1996, nonresidents are not allowed to use funds held in N accounts to purchase nonconvertible currencies, and are required to hold any Belarussian security purchased from funds held in the N account (which holds the nonresident proceeds from exports to Belarus) or from outside sources for at least 60 days in order to be able to transfer the proceeds from the sale of the securities to the L account (which holds the nonresident proceeds from investments in Belarussian securities and foreign exchange operations). If the security is held for less than 60 days, the sale proceeds will be returned to the N account.
	Since September 19, 1996, nonresident juridical persons may open I accounts and T accounts at authorized commercial banks. I accounts may be credited with the rubel counterpart of foreign exchange sales, dividends, resources from the realization of liquidated enterprises, and compensation in the event of the nationalization of enterprises. Resources from type I accounts may be used to purchase foreign currency, shares of enterprises, privatization checks, etc.

Type T accounts are used for the performance of current operations. Proceeds from the sale of foreign currencies and of goods and services, and resources from the placement of money in deposits and other debt obligations of banks, etc. are transferred into them. Resources from type T accounts may be used to purchase goods and services and bonds, and to pay for current expenditures.

Convertible into foreign currency	Only balances from I accounts are convertible. Approval is required.

Imports and Import Payments

Financing requirements for imports

Advance payment requirements — Approval is required for (1) down payments for goods or services exceeding $100,000; (2) payments for imports more than 60 days in advance of the receipt of the goods in Belarus, which require the special permission of the Ministry of Foreign Economic Relations (MFER) (for goods imported under barter or clearing arrangements, the period is 180 days); and (3) interest payments to nonresidents on returned down payments when an original contract is not fulfilled.

Documentation requirements for release of foreign exchange for imports

Domiciliation requirements — n.a.

Import licenses used as exchange licenses — Yes.

Import licenses and other nontariff measures

Positive list — Import licenses are required for importing certain pesticides, herbicides, and industrial wastes.

Negative list — The importing of radioactive or toxic wastes, as well as publications or videos that are against state morals, health, or security are prohibited.

Import taxes and/or tariffs — There are no customs barriers between Belarus and Russia, and a common trade policy toward third countries exists. The tariff structure consists of rates of 1% to 5% that apply to goods such as plants, seeds, foodstuffs, raw materials, ores, petroleum, and spare parts, and of rates of 40% to 100% that apply to goods such as weapons, ammunition, precious metal products, carpets, and motor vehicles. On March 18, 1997, certain custom duty rates were raised to harmonize them with those applied by Russia. For example, the following rates were raised: for apparel and clothing to 30% from 20%, for poultry to 30% from 25%, and the rate for refrigerators was raised by 5 percentage points. There are numerous exemptions. Regular import duty rates apply to countries with MFN status. Duties are applied at twice the MFN rate on imports from countries without MFN status. Duties on imports from developing countries covered by Russia's system of preferences are half the MFN rate or zero. On February 10, 1997, the list of goods to which a preferential regime does not apply was expanded.

Taxes collected through the exchange system — No.

State import monopoly — Imports of alcohol and tobacco products are effected by state monopolies.

Exports and Export Proceeds

Repatriation requirements — All proceeds must be repatriated within 120 days of shipping; special approval of the MFER is needed for longer periods of time. The period for goods exported under a barter or clearing contract is also 120 days.

Surrender requirements	There is a 50% surrender requirement. In October 1996, foreign exchange from export proceeds used to purchase raw materials and other inputs was exempted from the surrender requirement.
Documentation requirements	A transaction certificate is required.
Letters of credit	n.a.
Guarantees	n.a.
Domiciliation	n.a.
Preshipment inspection	n.a.
Export licenses	
Without quotas	Export bans exist for some medicinal herbs, art and antique collections, certain wild animals, and goods imported into Belarus on a humanitarian basis. Exports of certain goods, including amber, ores and concentrates, and precious metals and stones, require a license subject to the approval of the Precious Metals Committee of the Ministry of Finance.
With quotas	Mineral fertilizers and waste and scrap of ferrous and nonferrous metals are subject to export quotas and licensing requirements.
Export taxes	Customs duties for exports to non-CIS countries have been eliminated. VAT and excise taxes are collected on excisable goods that are exported to CIS countries.
Taxes collected through the exchange system	No.
Other export taxes	A rent payment for exported timber and products thereof applies.

Payments for Invisible Transactions and Current Transfers

Controls on these payments	
Freight/insurance	
Indicative limits/bona fide test	n.a.
Unloading/storage costs	
Indicative limits/bona fide test	n.a.
Administrative expenses	
Indicative limits/bona fide test	n.a.
Commissions	
Indicative limits/bona fide test	n.a.
Interest payments	
Indicative limits/bona fide test	n.a.
Profit/dividends	
Indicative limits/bona fide test	n.a.
Payments for travel	
Quantitative limits	Resident individuals are permitted to purchase up to $500 a year at the market exchange rate for tourist travel; however, persons who use their international credit cards for tourist travel expenses can purchase foreign exchange to settle the obligations on those cards. There are no restrictions on the purchase of foreign exchange for bona fide expenses related to business travel.

Indicative limits/bona fide test	n.a.
Medical costs	
Indicative limits/bona fide test	n.a.
Study abroad costs	
Indicative limits/bona fide test	n.a.
Subscriptions and membership fees	
Indicative limits/bona fide test	n.a.
Consulting/legal fees	
Indicative limits/bona fide test	n.a.
Foreign workers' wages	
Indicative limits/bona fide test	n.a.
Pensions	
Indicative limits/bona fide test	n.a.
Family maintenance/alimony	
Indicative limits/bona fide test	n.a.
Credit card use abroad	
Indicative limits/bona fide test	n.a.

Proceeds from Invisible Transactions and Current Transfers

Repatriation requirements	All service export proceeds must be repatriated after 120 days, unless special permission for longer period of repatriation has been granted by the MFER.
Surrender requirements	A requirement of 50% applies to receipts in freely convertible currencies and Russian rubles.

Capital Transactions

Controls on capital and money market instruments	The Ministry of Finance and the NBB establish procedures for transactions in securities.
Controls on credit operations	
Commercial credits	External borrowing by residents must be registered with the NBB.
By residents to nonresidents	n.a.
To residents from nonresidents	Yes.
Financial credits	
By residents to nonresidents	n.a.
To residents from nonresidents	Yes.
Controls on direct investment	
Outward direct investment	Yes.
Inward direct investment	Foreign investors are guaranteed full repatriation of their initial investment capital and profits earned in Belarus. Foreign investment must be registered at the MFER; in the case of financial institutions, also at the NBB. In the case of insurance institutions, it must also be registered at the State Insurance Oversight Committee. Certain activities

require special approval (license). When establishing an enterprise with foreign investments, the size of a foreign investor's share is not restricted, except for insurance organizations and banks, where it may not exceed 49%.

Controls on liquidation of direct investment	No.
Provisions specific to commercial banks and other credit institutions	
Borrowing abroad	n.a.
Maintenance of accounts abroad	The opening of bank accounts abroad requires approval from the NBB.
Lending to nonresidents (financial or commercial credits)	n.a.
Lending locally in foreign exchange	n.a.
Purchase of locally issued securities denominated in foreign exchange	n.a.
Differential treatment of nonresident deposit accounts and/or deposit accounts in foreign exchange	n.a.
Investment regulations	n.a.
Open foreign exchange position limits	n.a.

Changes During 1996

Exchange arrangements

September 6. The NBB allowed a 20% markup for cash and interbank transactions over the official exchange rate established at the auction.

October 6. The NBB allowed a 30% markup for cash and interbank transactions over the official exchange rate established at the auction.

October 21. The ceiling for a maximum transaction size for off-auction trading was raised to $30,000.

December 11. The limit on off-auction transactions was lifted.

Nonresident accounts

April 16. Nonresidents were prohibited to use funds held in N accounts to purchase nonconvertible currencies, and were required to hold any Belarussian security purchased from funds held in the N account (which holds the nonresident proceeds from exports to Belarus) or from outside sources, for at least 60 days to be able to transfer the proceeds from the sale of the securities to the L account (which holds the nonresident proceeds from investments in Belarussian securities and foreign exchange operations). If the security is held for less than 60 days, the sale proceeds must be returned to the N account.

September 19. L and N accounts were abolished and replaced by I and T accounts.

Changes During 1997

Exchange arrangements

February 3. The exchange rates were reunified under a managed floating system where the official exchange rate is set on the basis of supply and demand and the inflation rate.

Imports and import payments

February 10. The list of goods to which a preferential customs duty rate does not apply was expanded.

March 18. Certain customs duty rates were raised to harmonize them with those applied by Russia.

BELGIUM

(Position as of January 31, 1997)

Status Under IMF Articles of Agreement

Article VIII	Date of acceptance: February 15, 1961.

Exchange Arrangement

Currency	The currency of Belgium is the Belgian franc.
Other legal tender	The Luxembourg franc also circulates as legal tender.
Exchange rate structure	Unitary.
Classification	
Cooperative arrangement	Belgium and Luxembourg are linked in a monetary association, and the currencies are at par. Belgium participates in the ERM of the EMS. In accordance with this agreement, Belgium maintains spot exchange rates between their currencies and the currencies of the other participants within margins of 15% above or below the cross-rates derived from the central rates expressed in ECUs.
Exchange tax	No.
Exchange subsidy	No.
Forward exchange market	Banks are allowed to engage in spot and forward exchange transactions in any currency, and they may deal among themselves and with residents and nonresidents in foreign notes and coins.
Official cover of forward operations	No.

Arrangements for Payments and Receipts

Prescription of currency requirements	No.
Payment arrangements	No.
Administration of control	No.
International security restrictions	
In accordance with IMF Executive Board Decision No. 144-(52/51)	Belgium applies exchange restrictions against Iraq and Libya.
In accordance with UN sanctions	Yes.
Payment arrears	No.
Controls on trade in gold (coins and/or bullion)	No.
Controls on exports and imports of banknotes	No.

Resident Accounts

Eligibility to hold accounts	Juridical and natural persons are eligible.
Foreign exchange accounts permitted	Yes.

Held domestically	Yes.
Held abroad	Yes.
Accounts in domestic currency convertible into foreign currency	Yes.

Nonresident Accounts

Eligibility to hold accounts	Juridical and natural persons are eligible.
Foreign exchange accounts permitted	Yes.
Domestic currency accounts	Yes.
Convertible into foreign currency	Yes.
Blocked accounts	These are accounts affected by international security restrictions.

Imports and Import Payments

Foreign exchange budget	No.
Financing requirements for imports	No.
Documentation requirements for release of foreign exchange for imports	No.
Import licenses and other nontariff measures	
Positive list	Individual licenses are required for certain specified imports from all countries (most imports do not require an import license when imported from member countries of the EU), including many textile and steel products, diamonds, weapons, and nontextile products from China. All other commodities are free of license requirements.
Licenses with quotas	Along with other EU countries, the BLEU applies quotas on a number of textile products from non-EU countries in the framework of the MFA and also applies a system of minimum import prices to foreign steel products quotas on a number of steel products from Russia and Ukraine, and quotas on a number of products from China (toys, shoes, ceramic, porcelain, and glassware). On January 1, 1997, the quota on imports of steel products from Kazakhstan was eliminated.
Import taxes and/or tariffs	Belgium applies the Common Import Regime of the EU to imports of most other agricultural and livestock products from non-EU countries.
Taxes collected through the exchange system	No.
State import monopoly	No.

Exports and Export Proceeds

Repatriation requirements	No.
Surrender requirements	No.
Financing requirements	No.
Documentation requirements	No.

Export licenses	Export licenses are required only for a few products (mostly of a strategic character), for diamonds, and for some iron and steel products.
Without quotas	Yes.
Export taxes	No.

Payments for Invisible Transactions and Current Transfers

Controls on these payments	No.

Proceeds from Invisible Transactions and Current Transfers

Repatriation requirements	No.
Surrender requirements	No.
Restrictions on use of funds	No.

Capital Transactions

Controls on capital and money market instruments

On capital market securities

Sale or issue locally by nonresidents — The public issue or sale of debt securities that are not of EU origin is restricted.

On money market instruments

Sale or issue locally by nonresidents — The public issue or sale of money market securities and instruments that are not of EU origin is restricted.

On collective investment securities

Sale or issue locally by nonresidents — The public issue or sale of collective investment securities that are not of EU origin is restricted.

Controls on derivatives and other instruments

Sale or issue locally by nonresidents — The public issue or sale of instruments and claims that are not of EU origin is restricted.

Controls on credit operations — No.

Controls on direct investment

Inward direct investment — No authorization is required for inward direct investment in Belgium, except for a takeover by or on behalf of a person, company, or institution from a non-EU state, and the acquisition of Belgian flag vessels by shipping companies not having their principal office in Belgium.

Controls on liquidation of direct investment — No.

Controls on real estate transactions — No.

Provisions specific to commercial banks and other credit institutions — No.

Provisions specific to institutional investors

Currency matching regulations on assets/liabilities composition

Yes.

Other controls imposed by securities laws

No.

Changes During 1996

Arrangements for payments and receipts

October 2. Exchange restrictions against the Federal Republic of Yugoslavia (Serbia/Montenegro) and against the Republic of Bosnia and Herzegovina under the control of Serb forces were lifted.

Changes During 1997

Imports and import payments

January 1. Authorization for imports of certain preserved foodstuffs (tuna, bonito, and sardines) was abolished.

January 1. The quota on imports of steel products from Kazakhstan was lifted.

BELIZE

(Position as of April 30, 1997)

Status Under IMF Articles of Agreement

Article VIII	Date of acceptance: June 14, 1983.

Exchange Arrangement

Currency	The currency of Belize is the Belize dollar.
Exchange rate structure	Unitary.
Classification	
Pegged	The Belize dollar is pegged to the U.S. dollar at the rate of BZ$1 = US$0.50.
Exchange tax	A stamp duty of 1.25% is levied on all conversions from the Belize dollar to a foreign currency.
Exchange subsidy	No.
Forward exchange market	No.

Arrangements for Payments and Receipts

Prescription of currency requirements	The only prescription of currency requirement relates to a specific list of currencies in which authorized intermediaries are permitted to deal with the public. These currencies include Barbados dollars, Canadian dollars, Eastern Caribbean dollars, Guyana dollars, pounds sterling, Trinidad and Tobago dollars, and U.S. dollars. Payments to a CARICOM member country must be made in the currency of that country.
Payment arrangements	
Regional arrangements	Belize is a member of CARICOM.
Clearing agreements	Bilateral clearing between individual CARICOM members.
Administration of control	
Exchange control authorities	The Central Bank of Belize (CBB) is responsible for administering exchange control, which applies to all countries. Authority covering a wide range of operations is delegated to the commercial banks in their capacity as authorized dealers. Only in exceptional cases or in applications involving substantial amounts is reference made directly to the CBB. However, all applications for foreign exchange processed by authorized dealers are regularly forwarded to the CBB for audit and record keeping.
International security restrictions	No.
Payment arrears	No.
Controls on trade in gold (coins and/or bullion)	
Controls on domestic ownership and/or trade	Residents may not hold gold except with specific authorization from the CBB.
Controls on external trade	Gold may not be imported or exported without the approval of the CBB.
Controls on exports and imports of banknotes	
On exports	
Domestic currency	Each traveler may take abroad up to BZ$100. Amounts beyond these limits require the approval of the CBB, which is liberally granted when justified.

Foreign currency	Each traveler may take abroad up to the equivalent of BZ$400; visitors may take out up to the amount imported. Amounts beyond these limits require the approval of the CBB, which is liberally granted when justified.
On imports	
Domestic currency	Each traveler may bring in up to BZ$100.

Resident Accounts

Eligibility to hold accounts	Juridical and natural persons are eligible.
Foreign exchange accounts permitted	Foreign exchange accounts held domestically and abroad are permitted; prior approval is required.
Accounts in domestic currency convertible into foreign currency	No.

Nonresident Accounts

Eligibility to hold accounts	Juridical and natural persons are eligible.
Foreign exchange accounts permitted	Banks must have permission from the CBB to open external or foreign currency accounts.
Domestic currency accounts	These accounts may be credited with proceeds from the sale of foreign currency.
Convertible into foreign currency	Yes.
Blocked accounts	The CBB may stipulate that sums to be credited or paid to foreign residents be credited to a blocked account.

Imports and Import Payments

Foreign exchange budget	Yes.
Financing requirements for imports	No.
Documentation requirements for release of foreign exchange for imports	Prepayments for imports require authorization from the CBB; in most cases such authorization is delegated to the commercial banks. Since June 1995, the CBB began to ration its sales of foreign exchange to commercial banks on an ad hoc basis, except for a few essential import items such as fuel and pharmaceuticals.
Import licenses and other nontariff measures	
Negative list	For reasons of health, standardization, and protection of domestic industries, import licenses from the Ministry of Commerce and Industry are required for a number of goods—mostly food and agricultural products, and certain household and construction products; such licenses are liberally administered.
Import taxes and/or tariffs	Import tariff rates range from 5% to 30% with a number of items (particularly, agricultural inputs) entering duty free. Imports by most of the public sector and certain nonprofit entities, imports of an emergency or humanitarian nature, and goods for reexport are exempt from import duties; goods originating from the CARICOM area are also exempt. Some items are subject to revenue replacement duties ranging from 15% to 25%. Specific duties and surcharges apply to certain products. In November 1995, specific duties on beer, spirits, and tobacco were increased, and the import surcharge on fuel was increased by 25 cents a gallon. A 15% value-added tax was introduced on April 1, 1996, and the import tariff was reduced to 35% from a maximum of 45%. The stamp duty was also eliminated on that date. On April 1, 1997, the import tariff was further reduced to a maximum of 30%.

| Taxes collected through the exchange system | No. |
| **State import monopoly** | No. |

Exports and Export Proceeds

Repatriation requirements	Yes.
Surrender requirements	Export proceeds must be surrendered to authorized dealers not later than 6 months after the date of shipment, unless otherwise directed by the CBB. Since mid-1995, the CBB has resorted to direct purchases of sugar export proceeds, bypassing the traditional practice of purchasing from commercial banks.
Financing requirements	No.
Documentation requirements	No.
Export licenses	Export licenses are required for live animals, excluding pets; fish, crustaceans, and mollusks, excluding agricultural species; lumber and logs; beans; citrus fruits; and sugar.
Without quotas	Yes.
Export taxes	Exports of lobster, shrimp, conch, fish, turtles, mahogany, and wild animals are subject to an ad valorem export duty of 5%. A 2% tax is applied to sugar exports. On April 1, 1996, export duties were eliminated. Reexports and transshipments are subject to a 3% customs administration fee.
Taxes collected through the exchange system	No.

Payments for Invisible Transactions and Current Transfers

Controls on these payments	Since June 1995, the CBB has rationed its sale of foreign exchange for invisible payments to commercial banks on an ad hoc basis except for a few essential items such as insurance. There are no controls of payments for freight and insurance, unloading and storage, administrative expenses, and for the use of credit cards abroad.
Commissions	
Prior approval	Approval is granted by the CBB, subject to clearance by the Commissioner of Income Tax (CIT).
Interest payments	
Prior approval	Approval is granted by the CBB, subject to clearance by the CIT.
Profit/dividends	
Prior approval	Income statement and declaration of dividends must be presented along with clearance from the CIT.
Payments for travel	
Quantitative limits	The limits are (1) for nonbusiness travel by residents, up to BZ$5,000 a person a calendar year; (2) for business travel by residents, BZ$500 a person a day, up to a maximum of BZ$20,000 a year; (3) for business or nonbusiness travel by nonresidents, BZ$500 a person a year, unless payment is made from an external account or from proceeds of foreign currency. Resident travelers are required to sell their excess holdings of foreign currencies to an authorized dealer upon returning to Belize.
Indicative limits/bona fide test	Yes.
Medical costs	Payments are made directly to a doctor or hospital with original invoices or bills supporting the application.

Study abroad costs

   Indicative limits/bona fide test   Foreign exchange is provided by authorized dealers for payment of correspondence courses when applications are properly documented.

Subscriptions and membership fees

   Indicative limits/bona fide test   Similar requirements to those for study abroad apply.

Consulting/legal fees

   Prior approval   Approval is granted by the CBB, subject to clearance by the CIT.

Foreign workers' wages

   Prior approval   Approval is granted by the CBB, subject to clearance by the CIT.

Pensions

   Prior approval   Approval by the CBB is required.

   Quantitative limits   n.a.

   Indicative limits/bona fide test   n.a.

Family maintenance/alimony

   Prior approval   Approval by the CBB is required.

   Quantitative limits   The limit for gifts is BZ$100 a donor.

   Indicative limits/bona fide test   n.a.

Proceeds from Invisible Transactions and Current Transfers

Repatriation requirements   Yes.

Surrender requirements   Proceeds must be sold to an authorized dealer.

Restrictions on use of funds   No.

Capital Transactions

Controls on capital and money market instruments   All capital transfers require the approval of the CBB, but control is liberally administered.

Controls on derivatives and other instruments

Purchase locally by nonresidents   Yes.

Sale or issue locally by nonresidents   Yes.

Purchase abroad by residents   Yes.

Sale or issue abroad by residents   Yes.

Controls on credit operations

Commercial credits   Yes.

Financial credits   Yes.

Guarantees, sureties, and financial backup facilities   Yes.

Controls on direct investment

Outward direct investment   Yes.

Inward direct investment	It is advised that inward direct investment be registered with the CBB for future repatriation of profits.
Controls on liquidation of direct investment	Repatriation of proceeds requires clearance by the CIT.
Controls on real estate transactions	
Purchase abroad by residents	Yes.
Purchase locally by nonresidents	Yes.
Sale locally by nonresidents	Yes.
Provisions specific to commercial banks and other credit institutions	
Borrowing abroad	Yes.
Maintenance of accounts abroad	Yes.
Lending to nonresidents (financial or commercial credits)	Yes.
Lending locally in foreign exchange	Yes.
Purchase of locally issued securities denominated in foreign exchange	Yes.
Provisions specific to institutional investors	No.
Other controls imposed by securities laws	No.

Changes During 1996

Imports and import payments	*April 1.* A 15% value-added tax was introduced; the maximum import tariff was reduced to 35% from 45%, and the stamp duty on imports was eliminated.
Exports and export proceeds	*April 1.* Export duties were eliminated.

Changes During 1997

Imports and import payments	*April 1.* The maximum import tariff was reduced to 30% from 35%.

BENIN

(Position as of December 31, 1996)

Status Under IMF Articles of Agreement

Article VIII   Date of acceptance: June 1, 1996.

Exchange Arrangement

Currency   The currency of Benin is the CFA franc.

Exchange rate structure Unitary.

Classification

Pegged   The CFA franc is pegged to the French franc, the intervention currency, at the fixed rate of CFAF 1 per F 0.01. The official buying and selling rate is CFAF 100 per F 1. Exchange rates for other currencies are derived from the rate for the currency concerned in the Paris exchange market and the fixed rate between the French franc and the CFA franc. They include a bank commission of 2.5‰ on transfers to all countries outside the WAEMU, which must be surrendered to the Treasury.

Exchange tax   No.

Exchange subsidy   No.

Forward exchange market Forward exchange contracts may be arranged with prior authorization of the Ministry of Finance (MOF).

Official cover of forward operations   No.

Arrangements for Payments and Receipts

Prescription of currency requirements   Settlements with France, Monaco, and other countries linked to the French Treasury through an Operations Account are made in CFA francs, French francs, or the currency of any other Operations Account country.

Payment arrangements

Bilateral arrangements

   Inoperative   There is an arrangement with Hungary.

Clearing agreements   Current payments to or from The Gambia, Ghana, Guinea, Guinea-Bissau, Liberia, Mauritania, Nigeria, and Sierra Leone are normally made through the WACH.

Administration of control

Exchange control authorities   Exchange control is administered by the Directorate of Monetary and Banking Affairs in the MOF, in conjunction with the Directorate of External Commerce in the Ministry of Commerce and Tourism. The MOF, however, in collaboration with the BCEAO, draws up the exchange control regulations.

International security restrictions   No.

Payment arrears   No.

Controls on trade in gold (coins and/or bullion)

Controls on domestic ownership and/or trade   Authorization from the Directorate of External Commerce, issued after a favorable ruling by the Directorate of Monetary and Financial Affairs of the MOF, is required to hold, sell, import, export, or deal in raw diamonds and precious and semiprecious materials. In practice, residents are free to hold, acquire, and dispose of gold in any form in Benin.

Controls on external trade	Imports and exports of gold from or to any other country require prior authorization of the MOF, which is seldom granted.

Controls on exports and imports of banknotes

On exports

   Domestic currency

CFA franc banknotes may not be exported outside the territories of the CFA franc zone countries; BCEAO notes, up to a limit of CFAF 2 million, may be taken out for travel to BEAC countries and the Comoros.

   Foreign currency

The reexportation of foreign banknotes is allowed up to the equivalent of CFAF 250,000; the reexportation of foreign banknotes above these ceilings requires documentation demonstrating either the importation of the foreign banknotes or their purchase against other means of payment registered in the name of the traveler or through the use of nonresident deposits in local banks.

On imports

   Foreign currency

Nonresidents may bring in any amount of foreign banknotes and coins (except gold coins) of countries outside the Operations Account area. Residents bringing in foreign banknotes and foreign currency traveler's checks exceeding the equivalent of CFAF 25,000 must declare them to customs upon entry and sell them to an authorized intermediary bank within 8 days.

Resident Accounts

Eligibility to hold accounts	Juridical and natural persons are eligible.
Foreign exchange accounts permitted	Yes.
Held domestically	These accounts are permitted, but prior approval is required.
Held abroad	These accounts are permitted, but prior approval is required.
Accounts in domestic currency convertible into foreign currency	Yes.

Nonresident Accounts

Eligibility to hold accounts	Juridical and natural persons are eligible.
Foreign exchange accounts permitted	These accounts are permitted, but prior approval is required.
Domestic currency accounts	Because the BCEAO has suspended the repurchase of banknotes circulating outside the territories of the CFA franc zone, nonresident accounts may not be credited or debited with BCEAO banknotes. These accounts may not be overdrawn without prior authorization of the MOF. Transfers of funds between nonresident accounts are not restricted.
Convertible into foreign currency	Yes.
Blocked accounts	No.

Imports and Import Payments

Foreign exchange budget	No.
Financing requirements for imports	No.

Documentation requirements for release of foreign exchange for imports

Domiciliation requirements — All imports exceeding CFAF 500,000 are subject to the requirement.

Preshipment inspection — All imports exceeding CFAF 3 million are subject to inspection.

Letters of credit — Letters of credit are required for goods imported from outside the EU, Operations Account countries, and ACP countries.

Import licenses and other nontariff measures

Positive list — n.a.

Negative list — Certain imports, e.g., narcotics, are prohibited from all sources.

Open general licenses — All imports originating in non-ACP countries are subject to prior authorization.

Import taxes and/or tariffs — Customs duties consist of 4 bands: 5%, 10%, 15%, and 20%. A statistical tax of 3% is levied on the c.i.f. value of imports.

Taxes collected through the exchange system — No.

State import monopoly — Imports of petroleum products are made by a state company.

Exports and Export Proceeds

Repatriation requirements — Receipts must be collected within 180 days of the arrival of the shipment at its destination.

Surrender requirements — Proceeds must be repatriated through the BCEAO and sold to authorized banks within 30 days of the contractual due date.

Financing requirements — No.

Documentation requirements

Letters of credit — Yes.

Guarantees — n.a.

Domiciliation — Proceeds must be domiciled with an authorized intermediary bank when valued at more than CFAF 500,000.

Preshipment inspection — n.a.

Export licenses

Without quotas — Exports are permitted on the basis of a simple authorization from the Directorate of Foreign Trade. Exports of gold, diamonds, and all other precious metals, however, require prior authorization of the MOF, with the exception of articles with a small gold content, travelers' personal effects weighing less than 500 grams, and coins (fewer than 10 pieces, irrespective of their face value and denomination).

Export taxes — No.

Payments for Invisible Transactions and Current Transfers

Controls on these payments — Payments for invisibles to France, Monaco, and the Operations Account countries are permitted freely; those to other countries are subject to approval. Payments for invisibles related to trade are permitted by a general authorization when the basic trade transaction has been approved or does not require authorization. There are no controls on payments for freight and insurance, unloading and storage costs, administrative expenses, and commissions, and on interest payments and on remittances of profits and dividends. Payments for travel, medical costs, study abroad, subscription and membership fees, consulting and legal fees, pensions, and gambling and prize earnings are subject to indicative limits and/or bona fide tests.

Payments for travel	
Prior approval	Approval is required for travel outside the CFA franc zone.
Quantitative limits	The limits are CFAF 500,000 a trip for tourists and CFAF 75,000 a day for business travel. Allowances in excess of these limits must be authorized by the MOF or, by delegation, the BCEAO.
Medical costs	
Quantitative limits	The limits are the same as for tourist travel.
Study abroad costs	
Quantitative limits	The limits are the same as for tourist travel.
Foreign workers' wages	
Prior approval	Yes.
Quantitative limits	Upon presentation of an appropriate pay voucher, a residence permit, and documents indicating family situation, foreigners working in Benin may transfer up to 50% of their net salary abroad if they live with their family in Benin, or up to 80% if their family is living abroad.
Family maintenance/alimony	
Quantitative limits	Yes.
Credit card use abroad	
Quantitative limits	The same limits as for tourist and business travel apply.

Proceeds from Invisible Transactions and Current Transfers

Repatriation requirements	Yes.
Surrender requirements	Receipts from France, Monaco, and Operations Account countries are exempt from the requirement.
Restrictions on use of funds	No.

Capital Transactions

Controls on capital and money market instruments	Capital movements between Benin and France, Monaco, and countries linked to the French Treasury through an Operations Account are free of exchange control; most capital transfers to all other countries require prior approval of the MOF and are restricted, but capital receipts from such countries are permitted freely.
On capital market securities	
Sale or issue locally by nonresidents	Prior authorization of the MOF is required except for shares that are similar to, or may be substituted for, securities whose issuance or sale in Benin has already been authorized.
Purchase abroad by residents	Yes.
Sale or issue abroad by residents	Yes.
On money market instruments	
Sale or issue locally by nonresidents	Yes.
Purchase abroad by residents	Yes.

Sale or issue abroad by residents	Yes.
On collective investment securities	
Sale or issue locally by nonresidents	Yes.
Purchase abroad by residents	Yes.
Sale or issue abroad by residents	Yes.
Controls on credit operations	
Commercial credits	
By residents to nonresidents	Yes.
To residents from nonresidents	The following credits are exempt from MOF authorization: (1) loans constituting a direct investment, which are subject to prior declaration; (2) loans taken up by industrial firms to finance operations abroad, by international merchant and export-import firms (approved by the MOF) to finance transit trade, or by any type of firm to finance imports and exports; (3) loans contracted by authorized intermediary banks; and (4) subject to certain conditions, loans other than those mentioned above when the total amount outstanding of these loans, including the new borrowing, does not exceed CFAF 50 million for any one borrower. The repayment of the loan itself is subject to such approval, but is exempt if the loan was exempt from special authorization.
Financial credits	Yes.
Guarantees, sureties, and financial backup facilities	Yes.
Controls on direct investment	
Outward direct investment	At least 75% of the investments must be financed from foreign borrowing.
Inward direct investment	Yes.
Controls on liquidation of direct investment	The full or partial liquidation of investment requires declaration.
Controls on real estate transactions	Yes.
Provisions specific to commercial banks and other credit institutions	
Lending to nonresidents (financial or commercial credits)	Yes.
Lending locally in foreign exchange	Yes.
Purchase of locally issued securities denominated in foreign exchange	Yes.
Differential treatment of nonresident deposit accounts and/or deposit accounts in foreign exchange	
Credit controls	Yes.
Provisions specific to institutional investors	Yes.
Other controls imposed by securities laws	No.

Changes During 1996

Status under IMF Articles of Agreement	*June 1.* Benin accepted the obligations of Article VIII, Sections 2, 3, and 4 of the Fund Agreement.

BHUTAN

(Position as of December 31, 1996)

Status Under IMF Articles of Agreement

Article XIV	Yes.

Exchange Arrangement

Currency	The currency of Bhutan is the ngultrum.
Other legal tender	The Indian rupee is also legal tender.
Exchange rate structure	Unitary.
Classification	
Pegged	The ngultrum is pegged to the Indian rupee at a rate of Nu 1 per Re 1. The rates for currencies other than the Indian rupee are determined on the basis of the prevailing quotations by the Reserve Bank of India for those currencies.
Exchange tax	No.
Exchange subsidy	No.
Forward exchange market	No.

Arrangements for Payments and Receipts

Prescription of currency requirements	No.
Administration of control	
Exchange control authorities	The Ministry of Finance (MOF) controls external transactions and provides foreign exchange for most current and capital transactions. The MOF has delegated to the Royal Monetary Authority (RMA) the authority to release foreign exchange (other than Indian rupees) for current transactions. The RMA is charged with implementing the surrender requirements for proceeds from merchandise exports and approving the use of foreign exchange for imports.
International security restrictions	No.
Controls on trade in gold (coins and/or bullion)	No.
Controls on exports and imports of banknotes	No.

Resident Accounts

Eligibility to hold accounts	Yes.
Juridical persons	n.a.
Natural persons	n.a.
Foreign exchange accounts permitted	Yes.
Held domestically	Approval of the RMA is required to open these accounts.
Held abroad	n.a.

Nonresident Accounts

n.a.

Imports and Import Payments

Foreign exchange budget	An import license is required for the importation of capital and intermediate goods from countries other than India.
Financing requirements for imports	No.
Documentation requirements for release of foreign exchange for imports	
Domiciliation requirements	Yes.
Letters of credit	Yes.
Import licenses and other nontariff measures	The Ministry of Trade and Industries and the Division of Revenue and Customs have jointly introduced the "trade license for import" containing new rules and procedures for imports of goods from countries other than India. The rules and procedures were introduced to streamline the procurement system and further the process of trade liberalization.
Positive list	n.a.
Negative list	n.a.
Import taxes and/or tariffs	Imports from India are free from tariffs and are subject only to the Bhutan sales tax. Effective October 1, 1996, tax rates range from zero for essential commodities to 50% on tobacco products and alcoholic beverages.
	Imports from countries other than India are subject to tariffs. New customs rules and regulations and new tariff codes were introduced on September 1, 1996. The maximum tariff rate was lowered to 30% from 100%, with the exception of the rates for beer (50%), and for tobacco and other alcoholic beverages and spirits (100%).
Taxes collected through the exchange system	No.

Exports and Export Proceeds

Repatriation requirements	Yes.
Surrender requirements	Proceeds in currencies other than the Indian rupee must be surrendered to the RMA either directly or through the Bank of Bhutan within 90 days.
Export taxes	Export taxes are applied only to exports of unprocessed timber, apples, oranges, and cardamom. Exports to countries other than India receive a rebate at rates ranging from 5% to 20% of the c.i.f. value, with the lowest rate applying to unprocessed primary products and the highest rate applying to processed products.
Taxes collected through the exchange system	n.a.

Payments for Invisible Transactions and Current Transfers

Controls on these payments	Most invisible payments, other than those made in Indian rupees, must be approved by the RMA. Information on the existence of quantitative limits or the application of bona fide tests is not available.

Proceeds from Invisible Transactions and Current Transfers

Repatriation requirements	Yes.
Surrender requirements	All receipts from invisible transactions in currencies other than the Indian rupee must be surrendered to the RMA.

Capital Transactions

Controls on capital and money market instruments	All capital transactions must be approved by the RMA.
On capital market securities	Yes.
Purchase locally by nonresidents	n.a.
Sale or issue locally by nonresidents	n.a.
Purchase abroad by residents	n.a.
Sale or issue abroad by residents	n.a.
On money market instruments	Yes.
Purchase locally by nonresidents	n.a.
Sale or issue locally by nonresidents	n.a.
Purchase abroad by residents	n.a.
Sale or issue abroad by residents	n.a.
On collective investment securities	Yes.
Purchase locally by nonresidents	n.a.
Sale or issue locally by nonresidents	n.a.
Purchase abroad by residents	n.a.
Sale or issue abroad by residents	n.a.
Controls on derivatives and other instruments	Yes.
Purchase locally by nonresidents	n.a.
Sale or issue locally by nonresidents	n.a.
Purchase abroad by residents	n.a.
Sale or issue abroad by residents	n.a.
Controls on credit operations	
Commercial credits	Yes.
By residents to nonresidents	n.a.
To residents from nonresidents	n.a.
Financial credits	Yes.
By residents to nonresidents	n.a.
To residents from nonresidents	n.a.

Guarantees, sureties, and financial backup facilities	Yes.
By residents to nonresidents	n.a.
To residents from nonresidents	n.a.
Controls on direct investment	Yes.
Outward direct investment	n.a.
Inward direct investment	n.a.
Controls on liquidation of direct investment	Yes.

Changes During 1996

Imports and import payments	*September 1.* New customs rules and regulations and new tariff codes were introduced. The maximum tariff rate was lowered to 30% from 100%, with the exception of the rates for beer (50%), and for tobacco and other alcoholic beverages and spirits (100%).
	October 1. A new sales tax schedule ranging from zero for essential commodities to 50% on tobacco products and beverages was introduced.

BOLIVIA

(Position as of December 31, 1996)

Status Under IMF Articles of Agreement

Article VIII	Date of acceptance: June 5, 1967.

Exchange Arrangement

Currency

The currency of Bolivia is the boliviano.

Exchange rate structure

Unitary.

Classification

Independent floating

The official selling rate is determined at auctions held daily by the Central Bank of Bolivia (CBB). The official exchange rate is the average of the bid rates accepted in the latest auction and applies to all foreign exchange operations in Bolivia. The auctions are conducted by the Committee for Exchange and Reserves in the CBB. Before each auction, the Committee decides on the amount of foreign exchange to be auctioned and a floor price below which the CBB will not accept any bids. This floor price is the official exchange rate and is based on the exchange rates of the deutsche mark, Japanese yen, pound sterling, and U.S. dollar. The CBB is required to offer in all auctions unitary lots of $5,000 or multiples thereof; the minimum allowable bid is $5,000. Successful bidders are charged the exchange rate specified in their bid. In general, the spreads between the maximum and minimum bids have been less than 2%.

Except for the requirement to surrender the net proceeds from the exportation of goods and services, all banks, exchange houses, companies, and individuals may buy and sell foreign exchange freely. All public sector institutions, including public enterprises, must purchase foreign exchange for imports of goods and services through the CBB auction market. Sales of foreign exchange by the CBB to the public are subject to a commission of Bs 0.01 per $1 over its buying rate.

Exchange tax

No.

Exchange subsidy

No.

Forward exchange market

No.

Arrangements for Payments and Receipts

Prescription of currency requirements

No.

Payment arrangements

Regional arrangements

Payments between Bolivia and Argentina, Brazil, Chile, Colombia, Ecuador, Mexico, Paraguay, Peru, Uruguay, and Venezuela must be made through accounts maintained with each other by the CBB and the central bank of the country concerned, within the framework of the multilateral clearing system of the LAIA.

Clearing agreements

Yes.

Administration of control

Exchange control authorities

The CBB is in charge of operating the auction market for foreign exchange. It is also the enforcing agency for export surrender requirements as well as for other exchange control regulations. The Ministry of Finance (MOF), together with the CBB, is in charge of approving public sector purchases of foreign exchange for debt-service payments.

International security restrictions

No.

Payments arrears	No.
Controls on trade in gold (coins and/or bullion)	Gold may be traded freely, subject to a tax of 3% on the gross value of sale of gold bullion.
Controls on exports and imports of banknotes	No.

Resident Accounts

Eligibility to hold accounts	Juridical and natural persons are eligible.
Foreign exchange accounts permitted	Yes.
Held domestically	Yes.
Held abroad	Yes.

Nonresident Accounts

Eligibility to hold accounts	Juridical and natural persons are eligible.
Foreign exchange accounts permitted	Yes.
Held domestically	Yes.
Held abroad	Yes.
Domestic currency accounts	Yes.
Convertible into foreign currency	Yes.
Blocked accounts	No.

Imports and Import Payments

Foreign exchange budget	No.
Financing requirements for imports	No.
Documentation requirements for release of foreign exchange for imports	
Letters of credit	The letter of credit has to be opened at a bank in the Bolivian banking system.
Import licenses and other nontariff measures	
Negative list	Certain imports are controlled for reasons of public health or national security.
Import taxes and/or tariffs	Bolivia has a general uniform import tariff of 10%. A tariff of 5% is applied to capital goods, and a rate of 2% is applied to imports of books and printed matter. Donations of food, including wheat, are exempt from the import tariff.
Taxes collected through the exchange system	No.
State import monopoly	No.

Exports and Export Proceeds

Repatriation requirements	Yes.
Surrender requirements	All proceeds from exports of the public and private sectors must be sold to the CBB at the official exchange rate within 15 days of receipt, with the exception of reasonable amounts deducted for foreign exchange expenditures undertaken to effect the export transaction.
Financing requirements	No.
Documentation requirements	
Preshipment inspection	Exports other than hydrocarbons are subject to an inspection fee of 1.55% for nontraditional products and 1.6% for traditional products; these fees are paid by the government and not by the exporters.
Export licenses	No.
Export taxes	There are no export taxes. There is a system of tax rebates for indirect taxes and import duty paid on inputs of exported goods and services, including the duty component of depreciation of capital goods used. Exporters of small items whose value in Bolivia's annual exports is less than $3 million receive tax rebates of 2% or 4% of the f.o.b. export value under a simplified procedure, and other exporters receive tax and import duty rebates based on annually determined coefficients that reflect their documented cost structure.

Payments for Invisible Transactions and Current Transfers

Controls on these payments	
Interest payments	
Prior approval	Public sector purchases of foreign exchange for debt service must be approved by the MOF and the CBB.
Quantitative limits	No.
Indicative limits/bona fide test	No.
Profit/dividends	Profit remittances are subject to a 12.5% tax (which is computed as equivalent to the 25% income tax times the presumed net profit of 50% of the amount remitted).
Prior approval	No.
Quantitative limits	No.
Indicative limits/bona fide test	No.

Proceeds from Invisible Transactions and Current Transfers

Repatriation requirements	Yes.
Surrender requirements	Banks, exchange houses, hotels, and travel agencies may retain the proceeds from their foreign exchange purchases from invisible transactions, including those from tourism. They are required, however, to report daily their purchases on account of these transactions.
Restrictions on use of funds	No.

Capital Transactions

Controls on capital and money market instruments	No.

Controls on derivatives and other instruments	No.
Controls on credit operations	
Commercial credits	
To residents from nonresidents	All foreign credits, including suppliers' credits, to government agencies and autonomous entities, and credits to the private sector with official guarantees are subject to prior authorization by the MOF and to control by the CBB. All proceeds of borrowings from foreign public sector agencies must be surrendered to the CBB.
Financial credits	
To residents from nonresidents	Yes.
Controls on direct investment	No.
Controls on liquidation of direct investment	No.
Controls on real estate transactions	No.
Provisions specific to commercial banks and other credit institutions	
Borrowing abroad	Financial institutions may make loans in the form of credits denominated in foreign currency for imports of capital goods and inputs for the external sector with resources from international financial institutions, foreign government agencies, or external lines of credit.
Open foreign exchange position limits	The limit is the value of the banks' net worth minus their fixed assets.
Provisions specific to institutional investors	No.
Other controls imposed by securities laws	No.

Changes During 1996

No significant changes occurred in the exchange and trade system.

BOSNIA AND HERZEGOVINA

(Position as of December 31, 1996)

Status Under IMF Articles of Agreement

Article XIV   Yes.

Exchange Arrangement

Currency   The currency of Bosnia and Herzegovina is the Bosnian dinar.

Other legal tender   The deutsche mark circulates widely in all three regions of Bosnia: the Bosnian and Croatian majority areas (which together form the Federation) and the Serbian majority area, known as Republika Srpska. The Croatian kuna circulates widely in the Croatian majority area of Bosnia and Herzegovina, and the Yugoslav dinar circulates in the Republika Srpska.

Exchange rate structure   Unitary.

Classification

Pegged   The Bosnian dinar is pegged to the deutsche mark at BHD 100 per DM 1. The National Bank of Bosnia and Herzegovina (NBBH) communicates exchange rates to the commercial banks at least once a day. Commercial banks must charge the same rates for all transactions.

In the Republika Srpska, the National Bank of Republika Srpska (NBRS) receives each day from the National Bank of the Former Republic of Yugoslavia (NBFRY) a list of buying and selling rates for major currencies. These rates are communicated to the commercial banks for use the following day. Commercial banks must charge the same rates for all transactions. In both areas, commercial banks are free to buy and sell foreign exchange in the interbank market without restriction but must report all transactions on a regular and on a daily basis to the NBBH and NBRS, respectively.

Arrangements for Payments and Receipts

Administration of control

Exchange control authorities   The NBBH administers foreign exchange control regulations in the Federation with limited delegation to commercial banks. The NBRS oversees foreign exchange regulation in the Republika Srpska, although the commercial banks are responsible for implementing controls; the banks provide the NBRS with the documentation for all foreign exchange transactions on a regular basis. In addition, there is rationing of foreign exchange for imports and payments abroad for services in each area; the respective Ministries of Foreign Trade (MFT), Health, and Finance must approve requests for foreign exchange.

Controls on exports and imports of banknotes

On exports

   Domestic currency   n.a.

   Foreign currency   The NBBH imposes a limit of DM 2,000 on the amount of cash that can be taken across international borders in any one trip, but there is no limit on the frequency of trips. The NBRS imposes a limit of DM 1,000 and also does not impose any limits on the frequency of trips.

On imports   n.a.

Resident Accounts

Eligibility to hold accounts   Juridical and natural persons are eligible.

**Foreign exchange accounts
permitted**

Held domestically   Individuals and exporters can hold foreign exchange in accounts with commercial banks
and do not need to supply evidence of the source of these funds. Both the NBBH and
the NBRS allow foreign exchange accounts with no requirement for documentation of
the source of funds. Withdrawals for domestic transactions are unrestricted, but withdrawals for international transactions are restricted as described below. Foreign currency
deposits held prior to the dissolution of Yugoslavia and centralized at the NBFRY are
blocked.

Held abroad   n.a.

Nonresident Accounts

Eligibility to hold accounts   Juridical and natural persons are eligible.

**Foreign exchange accounts
permitted**   Yes.

Imports and Import Payments

Financing requirements for imports   No.

**Documentation requirements for
release of foreign exchange for
imports**   All importers in the Federation must be registered with a local court and the Ministry of
Foreign Trade (MFT). An importer can purchase foreign exchange to pay for foreign
goods and services without drawing on foreign exchange held in bank accounts. Foreign
exchange is rationed, with priority given to raw materials and essential items such as
drugs. Also, the MFT classifies goods into three regimes: free; subject to quotas (for the
protection of local industry); and banned (for health, environmental, or military reasons). In the Republika Srpska, importers must use all foreign exchange held in bank
accounts before they are entitled to purchase any further foreign exchange from a commercial bank or from the NBRS. Commercial banks ration foreign exchange, with priority given to raw materials and goods that meet basic human needs. Restrictions are
imposed on the importation of goods of which domestic production is significant.

Domiciliation requirements   n.a.

Preshipment inspection   n.a.

Letters of credit   n.a.

Import licenses used as exchange
licenses   n.a.

**Import licenses and other nontariff
measures**

Positive list   n.a.

Negative list   n.a.

Open general licenses   n.a.

Licenses with quotas   Yes.

Exports and Export Proceeds

Repatriation requirements   Yes.

Surrender requirements	The NBBH requires that 15% of proceeds be surrendered to the NBBH within 48 hours of repatriation in exchange for Bosnian dinars at the official exchange rate. Exports by companies that work abroad are subject to a surrender requirement of only 5%. In the Republika Srpska, 20% of the proceeds must be surrendered immediately upon repatriation.
Export licenses	Exporters in the Federation must be registered with the MFT and with a local court. Exporters in the Republika Srpska must be registered with the NBRS and a local court. The MFT imposes certain controls on the reimportation of some exports.
Export taxes	Yes.
Taxes collected through the exchange system	No.

Payments for Invisible Transactions and Current Transfers

Payments for travel

Prior approval	n.a.
Quantitative limits	The purchase of foreign exchange for business travel is unrestricted, subject to submission of the appropriate documentation to commercial banks in the Republika Srpska. The NBBH limits foreign exchange for individual trips abroad to DM 2,000 a trip including airfare, but there is no limit on the frequency of trips. The NBRS limit is DM 1,000 and, similarly, no limit on the frequency of trips applies.
Indicative limits/bona fide test	n.a.

Medical costs

Prior approval	Medical treatment abroad is on the priority list of foreign exchange for services but requires documentation from the Ministry of Health and from the Ministry of Finance (MOF) in the Federation. In the Republika Srpska, such treatment requires documentation from the Ministry of Health and a pro forma invoice from the provider of the medical services.
Quantitative limits	n.a.
Indicative limits/bona fide test	n.a.

Proceeds from Invisible Transactions and Current Transfers

Repatriation requirements	Yes.
Surrender requirements	Proceeds are subject to the same surrender requirements as proceeds from the export of goods.
Restrictions on use of funds	Payments of pensions from Germany were officially resumed in December 1995 following an agreement by which the NBBH provides documentation to Germany that the pensions are being paid by the commercial banks under its jurisdiction to the workers concerned.

Capital Transactions

Controls on capital and money market instruments	Portfolio investment abroad by Bosnian majority area residents requires permission from the NBBH.
On capital market securities	
Purchase abroad by residents	These transactions require MOF approval.

Sale or issue abroad by residents	These transactions require MOF approval, but the transfer of funds to service the securities issued is unrestricted.
On money market instruments	
Sale or issue locally by nonresidents	The transactions need to be intermediated by a bank.
Purchase abroad by residents	MOF approval is required.
Sale or issue abroad by residents	Notification to the MOF should be given.
On collective investment securities	
Purchase locally by nonresidents	MOF approval is required.
Sale or issue locally by nonresidents	n.a.
Purchase abroad by residents	n.a.
Sale or issue abroad by residents	Notification to the MOF should be given.
Controls on derivatives and other instruments	
Purchase abroad by residents	MOF approval is required.
Controls on credit operations	
Commercial credits	
By residents to nonresidents	Only juridical persons can receive these credits; credit for more than 3 months must be registered with the NBBH.
To residents from nonresidents	Credits with maturities longer than 3 months must be registered with the NBBH.
Financial credits	
By residents to nonresidents	Only juridical persons can receive these credits; credit for more than 3 months must be registered with the NBBH.
Guarantees, sureties, and financial backup facilities	
By residents to nonresidents	Only prudential regulations on banks apply.
Controls on direct investment	
Outward direct investment	MOF approval is required.
Inward direct investment	Investment abroad by Bosnian majority area residents requires permission from the NBBH.
Controls on liquidation of direct investment	Full repatriation of capital is permitted, after compliance with tax laws.
Controls on real estate transactions	
Purchase abroad by residents	MOF approval is required.
Purchase locally by nonresidents	n.a.
Sale locally by nonresidents	n.a.
Provisions specific to commercial banks and other credit institutions	
Borrowing abroad	Registration with the NBBH is required.
Maintenance of accounts abroad	Outstanding balances must be reported every 15 days to the NBBH.
Lending locally in foreign exchange	Lenders must use their own foreign exchange funds.

Purchase of locally issued securities   n.a.
denominated in foreign exchange

Differential treatment of nonresident   n.a.
deposit accounts and/or deposit accounts in foreign exchange

Investment regulations   n.a.

Open foreign exchange position limits   n.a.

Changes During 1996

No significant changes occurred in the exchange and trade system.

BOTSWANA

(Position as of December 31, 1996)

Status Under IMF Articles of Agreement

Article VIII	Date of acceptance: November 17, 1995.

Exchange Arrangement

Currency	The currency of Botswana is the pula.
Exchange rate structure	
Dual	The dual market arises from the operation of the foreign exchange risk-sharing scheme (FERSS), under which external loans undertaken by parastatals before October 1, 1990 (at end-1996, the scheme applied to 16 outstanding loans) are protected from exchange rate movements. Borrowers obtain foreign exchange to service those loans at exchange rates that result from applying the following scheme: risks associated with exchange rate fluctuations up to 4% are fully borne by the borrower, while the next 6% and the following 5% of fluctuations are shared between the borrower and the government on ratios of 50:50 and 25:75, respectively. Risks associated with exchange rate fluctuations in excess of 15% are fully borne by the government. The scheme is symmetrical in that the borrower and the government share any gains from an appreciation in the external value of the pula on the same basis.
Classification	
Pegged	The exchange rate of the pula is determined with reference to a weighted basket of currencies comprising the SDR and currencies of the country's major trading partners. The central bank deals in 4 currencies: the U.S. dollar, the South African rand, the deutsche mark, and the pound sterling.
Exchange tax	No.
Exchange subsidy	No.
Forward exchange market	Forward exchange cover is offered by the commercial banks, and may be given in respect of the foreign currency proceeds derived from the exportation of goods for up to 6 months.
Official cover of forward operations	Yes.

Arrangements for Payments and Receipts

Prescription of currency requirements	Payments to or from residents of foreign countries must normally be made or received in a foreign currency or through a nonresident-held pula account in Botswana.
Payment arrangements	
Bilateral arrangements	Botswana is a signatory to various bilateral trade agreements: China, Czechoslovakia, the Democratic People's Republic of Korea, Malawi, Romania, Russia, Yugoslavia, Zambia, and Zimbabwe.
Operative	Yes.
Inoperative	Yes.
Regional arrangements	Botswana is a member of the SACU, which allows for free import movements and, hence, has no restrictions on payments among the SACU countries.
Clearing agreements	n.a.
Barter agreements and open accounts	n.a.

Administration of control

Exchange control authorities	For practical/operational purposes, several administrative powers of the Bank of Botswana (BOB) have been delegated to commercial banks.
International security restrictions	No.
Payment arrears	No.
Controls on trade in gold (coins and/or bullion)	Only authorized dealers are permitted to deal in gold.
Controls on domestic ownership and/or trade	Yes.
Controls on external trade	Yes.

Controls on exports and imports of banknotes

On exports

Domestic currency	Residents are allowed to export up to P 5,000.
Foreign currency	Residents may take out up to the equivalent of P 5,000 a trip. Visitors may take out any foreign currency that they brought in with them.

Resident Accounts

Eligibility to hold accounts	Juridical and natural persons are eligible.
Foreign exchange accounts permitted	Yes.
Held domestically	Commercial banks are authorized to open foreign currency accounts for permanent and temporary residents. These accounts are set up to facilitate foreign receipts and payments for approved transactions, without having to convert foreign currency receipts into pula and vice versa, and to protect against fluctuations in exchange rates. Commercial banks are allowed to open foreign currency accounts in any currency at their discretion.
Approval required	n.a.
Held abroad	The BOB may authorize residents to maintain foreign currency accounts with banks abroad in cases where there is a proven legitimate commercial need for such facility, e.g., payment for imports.
Accounts in domestic currency convertible into foreign currency	Yes.

Nonresident Accounts

Eligibility to hold accounts	Juridical and natural persons are eligible.
Foreign exchange accounts permitted	Yes.
Domestic currency accounts	Yes.
Convertible into foreign currency	Yes.
Blocked accounts	No.

Imports and Import Payments

Foreign exchange budget	No.
Financing requirements for imports	
Advance payment requirements	Advance payments are permitted for a legitimate commercial need.
Documentation requirements for release of foreign exchange for imports	Payments for imports of value exceeding P 10,000 require supporting documentation before foreign exchange is released.
Import licenses and other nontariff measures	Imports of certain goods, including firearms, ammunition, fresh meat, and agricultural and horticultural products require permits regardless of the country of supply. Goods of domestic origin may move freely between Botswana and Zimbabwe, provided that they meet certain local value-added requirements and are not intended for reexport.
Negative list	Yes.
Open general licenses	n.a.
Licenses with quotas	n.a.
Import taxes and/or tariffs	As a member of the SACU, Botswana applies a common external tariff on imports from outside the SACU.
Taxes collected through the exchange system	No.
State import monopoly	No.

Exports and Export Proceeds

Repatriation requirements	Proceeds must be received in a foreign currency or from a nonresident pula account within 6 months of the date of exportation.
Surrender requirements	Retention of export proceeds for up to 1 year to finance certain transactions may be permitted by the BOB on a case-by-case basis.
Documentation requirements	No.
Export licenses	Certain exports are subject to licensing, mainly for revenue reasons. The exportation of a few items, such as precious and semiprecious stones, requires permits.
Without quotas	Yes.
Export taxes	No.

Payments for Invisible Transactions and Current Transfers

Controls on these payments	On February 15, 1996, indicative limits for current account transactions were abolished. However, authorized dealers must require documentary evidence for payments in excess of P 10,000 a transaction, to establish that the payment is for a legitimate purpose and a current account transaction.
Interest payments	Interest payments may not exceed a rate of 2% a month on import-related payment charges.
Profit/dividends	Authorized dealers may authorize remittances of interim dividends without reference to the BOB for companies listed in the Botswana Stock Exchange and may approve other remittances of dividends/profits without reference to the BOB subject to satisfactory supporting documentation.

Foreign workers' wages

　　Quantitative limits　　A temporary resident employed on a contractual basis may remit abroad, without reference to the BOB, his/her entire earnings net of tax. Self-employed temporary residents may remit their whole income net of tax.

Pensions

　　Prior approval　　Yes.

　　Indicative limits/bona fide test　　Yes.

Proceeds from Invisible Transactions and Current Transfers

Repatriation requirements　　Yes.

Surrender requirements　　The amount of unused foreign currency for travel that a resident may retain for future travel use is the equivalent of P 2,000 in currency or traveler's checks. Any excess amount must be surrendered within 6 months of the date of return.

Restrictions on use of funds　　No.

Capital Transactions

Controls on capital and money market instruments　　In the case of both inward and internal portfolio investments, a shareholder or his nominee may acquire an interest up to 5% of the company's paid-up stock. Total portfolio holdings by nonresidents, including nonresident-controlled companies, may not exceed 49% of the "free stock" (that is, total stock issued and paid up less stock held by nonresident direct investors) of a local company.

On capital market securities

　　Purchase locally by nonresidents　　Purchases should be financed by funds from nonresident sources. Nonresident-controlled companies may make internal portfolio investments, which need not be financed with funds from external sources.

　　Sale or issue locally by nonresidents　　n.a.

　　Purchase abroad by residents　　Individuals and business entities may invest abroad up to P 100,000 and P 1 million, respectively, in offshore securities.

　　Sale or issue abroad by residents　　n.a.

On money market instruments

　　Purchase locally by nonresidents　　Nonresidents are not permitted to buy the monetary instruments used by the BOB.

　　Sale or issue locally by nonresidents　　n.a.

　　Purchase abroad by residents　　Individuals and business entities may invest abroad up to P 100,000 and P 1 million, respectively, in offshore securities.

On collective investment securities

　　Purchase locally by nonresidents　　n.a.

　　Sale or issue locally by nonresidents　　n.a.

　　Purchase abroad by residents　　Individuals and business entities may invest abroad up to P 100,000 and P 1 million, respectively, in offshore securities.

　　Sale or issue abroad by residents　　n.a.

Controls on credit operations

Commercial credits

By residents to nonresidents

Nonresident-controlled companies (including branches of foreign companies) can borrow locally from all sources up to P 1 million. Banks and credit institutions in Botswana are permitted to grant loans and other credit facilities to nonresident-controlled entities up to 4:1 debt-to-equity ratio (after the initial tranche of P 1 million), without prior authorization from the BOB.

To residents from nonresidents

Authorized dealers are permitted to receive loan funds from nonresident sources on behalf of the permanent resident customers up to an equivalent of P 100,000 and P 1 million in respect of individuals and companies, respectively, without any prior reference to the BOB. Interest on these loans is restricted to 1% above the relevant LIBOR.

Financial credits

By residents to nonresidents

Nonresident-controlled companies (including branches of foreign companies) can borrow locally from all sources up to P 1 million. Banks and credit institutions in Botswana are permitted to grant loans and other credit facilities to nonresident-controlled entities up to 4:1 debt-to-equity ratio (after the initial tranche of P 1 million), without prior authorization from the BOB.

To residents from nonresidents

Authorized dealers are permitted to receive loan funds from nonresident sources on behalf of the permanent resident customers up to an equivalent of P 100,000 and P 1 million in respect of individuals and companies, respectively, without any prior reference to the BOB. Interest on these loans is restricted to 1% above the relevant LIBOR.

Guarantees, sureties, and financial backup facilities

By residents to nonresidents

The same regulations as for credits apply.

To residents from nonresidents

Yes.

Controls on direct investment

Outward direct investment

Authorized dealers may make foreign currency available to individuals and companies of amounts of up to P 100,000 and P 10 million, respectively, for either acquiring interest in existing business ventures or establishing new business. Companies must have been in operation for 2 years and registered with the Commissioner of Taxes.

Controls on liquidation of direct investment

Proceeds up to P 50 million may be repatriated immediately, but the excess of that amount may be repatriated in tranches to be agreed upon with the BOB.

Controls on real estate transactions

Purchase abroad by residents

Purchases limited to P 100,000 for individuals and P 10 million for business entities are allowed.

Purchase locally by nonresidents

n.a.

Sale locally by nonresidents

n.a.

Provisions specific to commercial banks and other credit institutions

Borrowing abroad

Borrowing is subject to prior approval by the BOB.

Maintenance of accounts abroad

These accounts may only be maintained by authorized dealers.

Lending to nonresidents (financial or commercial credits)

Yes.

Lending locally in foreign exchange

Authorized dealers are permitted to make these loans to any customer that operates foreign currency accounts.

Purchase of locally issued securities denominated in foreign exchange	A special dispensation has been made permitting dual listing of scripts of companies incorporated outside Botswana and listed in reputable international stock markets on an open register basis.
Open foreign exchange position limits	The limit is 10% of the core capital of a bank.
Provisions specific to institutional investors	
Limits (max.) on portfolio invested abroad	The limit is 70% of the investor's assets outside Botswana.
Limits (min.) on portfolio invested locally	n.a.
Currency matching regulations on assets/liabilities composition	n.a.

Changes During 1996

Payments for invisible transactions and current transfers	*February 15.* The indicative limits for these transactions were abolished. However, authorized dealers must require documentary evidence to support payments in excess of P 10,000 a transaction to establish that the payment is for a legitimate purpose or current account transaction.

BRAZIL

(Position as of May 31, 1997)

Status Under IMF Articles of Agreement

Article XIV	Yes.

Exchange Arrangement

Currency	The currency of Brazil is the real.
Exchange rate structure	Dual. There is an official rate (also identified as "free" or commercial) and a tourist (or floating) rate.
Classification	
Managed floating	In both exchange markets, the rates are freely negotiated between the authorized dealers and their clients. Banks make arbitrage operations between both markets; spot transactions must be settled within 2 working days. The Central Bank of Brazil (CBB) established an adjustable band for the external value of the real at R\$0.97–R\$1.06 per U.S. dollar on January 30, 1996. Since February 19, 1997, the band has been R\$1.05–R\$1.14. Rates for other currencies are based on the U.S. dollar rates in Brazil and the rates for specific currencies in the international market. Transactions in the exchange markets are carried out by banks, brokers, and tourist agencies authorized to deal in foreign exchange; the tourist agencies and brokers deal only in banknotes and traveler's checks.
Exchange tax	A tax on credit, foreign exchange operations, and insurance operations, or on transactions in financial instruments or securities (IOF) is levied on foreign exchange operations effected for the payment of imports of services at a 25% rate. (On May 2, 1997, this tax was eliminated with effect on June 1, 1997.) The IOF is also assessed on the equivalent in reais of foreign exchange entering Brazil generated by or earmarked for foreign exchange loans, investments in fixed-income funds and in financial instruments and securities, interbank operations between foreign financial institutions and banks authorized to conduct foreign exchange operations in Brazil, and holdings of short-term assets in Brazil by foreign residents. Exempt from this tax are settlements of foreign exchange operations contracted prior to August 10, 1995. On April 24, 1997, the rate of the IOF assessed on fixed-income funds was reduced to 2% from 7%; the rate on real property investment funds was reduced to zero from 5%. On the same date, the IOF ceased to be levied on foreign loans contracted by residents, including banks.
Exchange subsidy	No.
Forward exchange market	Banks are permitted to trade foreign exchange without restriction on a forward basis; such transactions must be settled within 360 days. Banks may pay their clients a premium, corresponding to the expected variation of the domestic currency in relation to the currency subject to negotiation, by reason of forward operations. In addition, when an exchange contract for forward settlement is concluded, banks can provide short-term financing to exporters by providing domestic currency in advance, before or after the shipment of goods.
Official cover of forward operations	No.

Arrangements for Payments and Receipts

Prescription of currency requirements	Prescription of currency is related to the country of origin of imports or the country of final destination of exports, unless otherwise prescribed or authorized. Settlements with Hungary are made in the terms specified in the bilateral agreement. Settlements with countries with which Brazil has no payment agreements and no special payment arrangements are made in U.S. dollars.

Payment arrangements

Bilateral arrangements

   Operative | Settlements with Hungary are made in U.S. dollars every 90 days, and interest rates payable on balances are based on those in the international capital market.

Clearing agreements | Payments between Brazil and Argentina, Bolivia, Chile, Colombia, the Dominican Republic, Ecuador, Mexico, Paraguay, Peru, Uruguay, and Venezuela can be made through special central bank accounts within the framework of the multilateral clearing system of the LAIA.

Administration of control

Exchange control authorities | The National Monetary Council is responsible for formulating overall foreign exchange policy. In accordance with the guidelines established by the Council, exchange control regulations affecting foreign capital and the management of international reserves are under the jurisdiction of the CBB. The Ministry of Planning and Budget enforces limits on foreign borrowing by the public sector. Foreign trade policy is formulated by the Ministry of Industry, Trade, and Tourism, implemented by the Secretariat of Foreign Trade (SECEX) and carried out by the Department of Foreign Trade Operations (DECEX). The Department of International Negotiations (DEINT) or the SECEX is responsible for formulating guidelines for tariff policy. The DEINT also decides on changes in customs duties under the provisions of existing legislation. The Ministry of Finance coordinates public sector import policy.

International security restrictions

In accordance with IMF Executive Board Decision No. 144-(52/51) | n.a.

In accordance with UN sanctions | There are restrictions imposed on Libya and Iraq.

Payment arrears

Private | Foreign exchange, for payments of principal and interest corresponding to medium- and long-term debt in arrears over 180 days, had to be obtained in the floating-rate exchange market until April 23, 1997, when it was required that foreign exchange for payments of debt in arrears be obtained in the same exchange market (free rate exchange market) through which the payments should have been made on due dates.

Controls on trade in gold (coins and/or bullion) | There are 2 separate markets for gold transactions: the financial and commercial markets. Over 50% of transactions occurs in the financial market, which is regulated by the CBB. The first domestic negotiation of newly mined gold on this market is subject to a 1% financial transactions tax. Rules regarding gold transactions for industrial purposes are defined separately by the federal states, which also establish different rates for the commercial tax levied on them. The CBB and authorized institutions are empowered to buy and sell gold on the domestic and international markets. Purchases of gold are made at current domestic and international prices; the international price is considered a target price.

Controls on domestic ownership and/or trade | Yes.

Controls on external trade | The CBB and authorized institutions may buy and sell gold for monetary use on the international market. Imports and exports of gold for nonmonetary use are subject to the same procedures as those that are applied through the SECEX in respect of other products.

Controls on exports and imports of banknotes | Travelers may take out or bring in domestic or foreign banknotes without restriction but must declare to customs any amount over the equivalent of US$10,000.

Resident Accounts

Eligibility to hold accounts | Juridical and natural persons are eligible.

Foreign exchange accounts permitted	Institutions authorized to operate in the floating-rate market, tourism agencies, the Brazilian mail, credit card companies, and the Brazilian Reinsurance Institute (IRB) may open these accounts.
Held domestically	Yes.
Held abroad	Yes.
Accounts in domestic currency convertible into foreign currency	No.

Nonresident Accounts

Eligibility to hold accounts	Juridical and natural persons are eligible.
Foreign exchange accounts permitted	Embassies, foreign delegations, and international organizations recognized by the Brazilian government; foreign companies of international transportation; foreign citizens in transit in the country; and Brazilian citizens living abroad may open these accounts.
Domestic currency accounts	Yes.
Convertible into foreign currency	Financial institutions, nonfinancial national institutions, and natural and juridical persons may hold these accounts. Deposits on these accounts are not convertible when the balance originated in a sale of foreign currency to a Brazilian bank.
Blocked accounts	No.

Imports and Import Payments

Financing requirements for imports	External financing for imports at terms in excess of 360 days must be registered in the "Financial Operations Registry," an electronic system. Financing is considered approved by the CBB if the registration is not refused by its Department of Foreign Capital (FIRCE) within 5 days. The time to finalize anticipatory settlements for critical imports is 30 days. Exchange contracts may be settled within 180 days. Payment for financed imports at terms of up to 360 days must be contracted for future liquidation 180 days in advance.
Documentation requirements for release of foreign exchange for imports	All importers must be registered in the SECEX Importer and Exporter Register. Goods may be imported only by registered firms or persons, except for imports by the public sector (federal, state, and municipal); imports by PETROBRAS (the Brazilian government oil enterprise) contracting or subcontracting firms for oil exploration through risk contracts; imports of medicine by persons up to US$5,000; imports of samples without commercial value, except for pharmaceutical products up to US$1,000; imports of products, except for those prohibited or under special control, by persons for personal consumption; and imports of goods considered as passengers' baggage for personal use. The import subsystem of the Integrated Foreign Trade System (SISCOMEX/IMPORT) was established on January 1, 1997. The subsystem allows importers, carriers, banks, and brokers to register the various stages of an import process directly through the interlinked computers of SECEX, customs, and the CBB. Imports are grouped into the following three broad categories: (1) imports that do not require prior administrative documentation, including samples without commercial value and certain educational materials; (2) imports that require prior import licenses issued by the SISCOMEX/IMPORT; and (3) prohibited imports. Importers are permitted to purchase foreign exchange in the exchange market within 360 days of the settlement date. There is also a limit on the direct importation and purchase on the domestic market of consumer goods by the public sector (the government, autonomous agencies, and public enterprises).
	Federal ministries and subordinate agencies and public enterprises are required to submit, for approval by the Ministry of Planning and Budget, an annual investment program specifying their expected import requirements.

Domiciliation requirements	Imports are not subject to any domiciliation requirement, with the exception of imports originating or proceeding from countries under restrictions determined by the Security Council of the United Nations and imports of bovines in any form originating or proceeding from the United Kingdom (Great Britain and North Ireland).
Letters of credit	The drafts or letters of credit must be settled on maturity against the presentation of the appropriate documents by the importer. Exchange contracts for imports financed under letters of credit must be closed on the date of settlement or 2 working days before the maturity date of the letters of credit.
Import licenses and other nontariff measures	Some imports require prior approval from the DECEX (i.e., an import license), which is usually given promptly to registered importers of nonprohibited items. As a rule, licenses are valid for 60 days except for imports of custom-made capital goods. The Secretariat of Federal Revenue (SRF) issues clearance certificates for certain groups of commodities to special bonded warehouse importers. Import licenses for a number of specified imports may be obtained after the commodities have been landed and customs clearance obtained. The importation of certain products requires approval of the Ministry of Science and Technology. For some products, eligibility for exemption from import duties may be precluded by the existence of a satisfactory domestic equivalent. Most imports are exempt from prior approval requirements.
Negative list	Imports of agrochemical products not authorized under Brazilian regulations, weapons, and certain drugs that are not licensed for reasons of security, health, morality, or industrial policy are prohibited.
Open general licenses	Open general import licenses are no longer issued by the SECEX. Issuance is restricted to their annexes, up to the existing remainder of issued open general licenses.
Licenses with quotas	In addition to imports under Brazilian concessions in the context of the LAIA agreement, goods imported into the Manaus and Tabatinga free zones are subject to an annual quota. Foreign goods up to the equivalent of US$2,000 imported into the Manaus free trade zone can be transferred to other parts of Brazil (as a passenger's baggage) free of import taxes. Since May 1996, in accordance with WTO rules, quotas were imposed on imports of textiles from China, Hong Kong, Korea, Panama, and Taiwan Province of China due to their effect on the domestic industry. In June 1996, the tariff rate on imports of toys was raised to 70% from 20%. In July 1996, with the inclusion of 18 items related to 8 products (such as rice, peaches, wine, and dye products), Brazil completed its exceptions list to the CET, which also included the increase to 65% from 30% for vehicles carrying more than 9 persons. Additionally in August 1996, other products, notably in the pulp and paper sector, were excluded from the exceptions list. For automobiles, transport vehicles, motorcycles, and bicycles, tariffs were raised in January 1996 to 70%, while the assemblers established in Brazil were favored with a special tariff of 35%. Later, in August 1996, a special tariff of 35% was established for imports from Japan, the EU, and South Korea for a period of 12 months and for a quota of 50,000 vehicles, distributed on a 3-monthly basis, according to the export performance of each country.
Import taxes and/or tariffs	The MERCOSUR customs union agreement stipulates a CET ranging from zero to 20% on about 85% of traded goods, and the remaining 15% of goods (including a list of national exceptions, capital goods, and computer goods) are subject to a schedule of adjustments designed to bring them into line with the CET within 5 or 6 years. The adjustment regime allows Brazil and Argentina to maintain tariffs on some intra-area trade until January 1, 1999, and Paraguay and Uruguay to maintain some intra-area tariffs until January 1, 2000. In April 1995, Brazil increased the number of goods on its list of national exceptions to MERCOSUR to 450 from 300.
Taxes collected through the exchange system	A financial transaction tax of 25% is levied on exchange operations effected for the payment of imports of services. The levy was abolished effective June 1, 1997.
State import monopoly	Imports of petroleum and derivatives are conducted by the state.

Exports and Export Proceeds

Repatriation requirements Yes.

Surrender requirements Yes.

Financing requirements Advances on foreign exchange contracts are allowed for operations with terms up to 360 days, and the time for anticipatory settlements is 180 days. Also, for products considered essential for the supply of the domestic market (fuel, mineral oils, chemical products, plastics, wood pastes, paper, cotton, linen and synthetic thread, flat steel, and aluminum) the maximum period is 180 days.

Documentation requirements Documentation includes invoices, international shipment notification, and export registration.

Preshipment inspection Inspection is required for commodities subject to standardization.

Export licenses Exports of wild animals and their hides, hair, plumes, or eggs in any form, jacaranda-da-Bahia wood, ipecacuanha plants, red and drab varieties of honey, and antiques of more than 100 years are prohibited. Exports of certain goods require prior approval of the SECEX, including those effected through bilateral accounts, exports without exchange cover, exports on consignment, reexports, commodities for which minimum export prices are fixed by the SECEX, and exports requiring prior authorization from government agencies. SISCOMEX integrates the activities related to the registration, monitoring, and control of foreign trade operations into a single computerized flow of information. The SISCOMEX comprises two subsystems (exports and imports). The exports subsystem allows exporters, carriers, banks, and brokers to register the various stages of an export process directly through the interlinked computers of the SECEX, customs, and the CBB. Exports of sawed or cleft pine woods, mahogany, Brazilian walnut, and virola are subject to quotas. Furthermore, for exports of ethyl alcohol and sugar in any form, including sugarcane syrup inappropriate for human consumption, to be eligible for exemption from the export tax of 40%, they must comply with the requirement that domestic needs be satisfied, as authorized by the Industry, Trade, and Tourism Minister and the Finance Minister.

Without quotas Exports of sawed or cleft pine woods, mahogany, Brazilian walnut, and virola are subject to quotas. For exports of ethyl alcohol and sugar in any form, including sugarcane syrup inappropriate for human consumption, the elegibility for exemption from the export tax of 40% is subject to quotas on the basis of an annual quantity exceeding domestic necessity authorized by the Industry, Trade, and Tourism Minister and the Finance Minister.

With quotas Besides imports under Brazilian concessions subject to quotas due to agreements in the LAIA member countries, goods imported into the Manaus and Tabatinga free zones are subject to an annual quota. Foreign goods up to the equivalent of US$2,000 imported into the Manaus free trade zone can be transferred to other parts of Brazil (as a passenger's baggage) free of import taxes.

Export taxes With the exception of exports of raw hides of cattle, horses, sheep, or any other raw hides, which are subject to an export duty of 9%, exports are free from export duty. Exports of coffee and cocoa are subject to a zero-rate duty. In September 1996, to promote exports the rules for the application of a value-added tax (VAT) by the states were amended, exempting exports of primary and semimanufactured products. Also, this exemption was extended to products used by companies to produce export goods.

Taxes collected through the exchange system No.

Payments for Invisible Transactions and Current Transfers

Controls on these payments Payments for current invisibles not covered by current regulations require approval from the CBB's Exchange Department (DECAM) or the FIRCE. Payments for freight and insurance, unloading and storage costs, administrative expenses, commissions, travel, medical treatment, study abroad, subscriptions and membership fees, consulting and legal fees, foreign workers' wages, pensions, family maintenance and alimony, the use of credit cards abroad, and remittances of profits and dividends are subject to indicative limits and/or bona fide test.

Freight/insurance	Insurance requires prior approval from the IRB.
Prior approval	Yes.
Unloading/storage costs	There are established rules and surveillance procedures related to the operations freely conducted in the commercial market.
Administrative expenses	
Indicative limits/bona fide test	Yes.
Interest payments	
Prior approval	Payments for medium- and long-term external debt are subject to prior approval by and registration with the CBB FIRCE, and the issue of a certificate of registration, which is the authorization to remit abroad the related interest, expenses, and fees, provided that due taxes are paid.
Quantitative limits	n.a.
Indicative limits/bona fide test	n.a.
Profit/dividends	In addition to certain restrictions on remittances stipulated in the Foreign Investment Law of 1962, limits on income tax deductions are placed on remittances of all royalties and technical assistance fees.
Prior approval	Yes.
Quantitative limits	Remittances are allowed only when the foreign capital concerned, including reinvestments, contracts for patents and trademarks, and for technical, scientific, and administrative assistance, are registered with the FIRCE. Profit remittances are exempt from withholding for income tax purposes. Amounts due as royalties for patents or for the use of trademarks, as well as for technical, scientific, and administrative assistance and the like, may be deducted from income tax liability to determine the taxable income, up to the limit of 5% of gross receipts in the first 5 years of the company's operation; amounts exceeding this limit are considered profits.
Gambling/prize earnings	Remittances for gambling are not permitted.
Prior approval	Yes.

Proceeds from Invisible Transactions and Current Transfers

Repatriation requirements	Yes.
Surrender requirements	Exchange proceeds from current invisibles must be sold to the authorized banks at the prevailing market rate.

Capital Transactions

Controls on capital and money market instruments

On capital market securities

Purchase locally by nonresidents — The direct purchase of shares of Brazilian companies by nonresidents basically occurs through direct investments and portfolio investments made by institutional investors through the managers of the respective portfolios. Depositary receipts (DRs) constitute another method of acquiring shares through stock exchanges. They provide a mechanism for the placement of shares of Brazilian enterprises in the international markets. DRs are certificates representing a certain number of shares of a given enterprise that confer upon their holders all of the rights inherent in said shares, including dividends, bonuses, splits, and market-quoted value. A Brazilian sponsoring enterprise places its shares in the custody of an institution headquartered in Brazil and authorized by the Securities Commission (CVM) to provide custody services for the specific purpose of DR issues (custodian institution). At the same time, an institution abroad (the depositary bank) issues the corresponding DRs based on the securities held in custody in Brazil. Investments effected through the DR mechanism are exempt from income tax on capital gains. The rate applicable to earnings obtained in Brazil is 10%, as these are investments in variable-income assets. In addition, there are specific regulations for investments in the MERCOSUR environment.

As for other securities, such as debentures and other fixed-income securities, the regulations do not provide for direct purchases by nonresidents, although they may be effected indirectly through investment funds. Resources of societies, portfolios, and investment funds established by Resolution No. 1289 (1987) were allowed to be applied in debentures convertible to equities. Securities portfolios held in the country by foreign institutional investors (i.e., pension funds, nonprofit institutions, and insurance companies) must be managed by an institution operating in the country and authorized by the CVM. The foreign investor has the option of applying for 2 types of registration for the portfolio: an "individual account" or an "omnibus account." The individual account registration allows the investor to operate in its own name only, while the omnibus account registration allows the account holder to operate only on behalf of third parties, known in the market as "passengers."

The management institution is responsible for the registration of foreign investment with the CBB, foreign exchange settlements, the collection of taxes, portfolio bookkeeping, and the safekeeping of documents related to the portfolio.

There is no limit or hold period for financial transfers resulting from inflows, flowbacks, and profits or dividends from capital duly registered with the CBB, provided that the accounting rules and tax laws are complied with. The transfers must be processed through banks authorized to conduct foreign exchange operations, with guaranteed access to the free foreign exchange market to purchase foreign currency.

To promote greater integration of the capital markets of the signatory countries of the Treaty of Asunción (MERCOSUR), an additional mechanism was established in 1992 to attract foreign resources targeting the Brazilian stock market. Natural and juridical persons resident or domiciled in Asunción Treaty countries may invest freely in Brazilian stock exchanges, without the necessity of trading through investment funds or portfolios. The Brazilian market may be accessed directly by contacting a member institution of the Brazilian securities distribution system, or indirectly through the intermediation of an institution in the securities distribution system of the investor's country.

The Brazilian intermediary institution, through which the foreign investor trades, represents the investor vis-à-vis the Brazilian authorities with respect to the operational, exchange, and tax aspects, and in providing information on the operations executed. These investments may be made in U.S. dollars, in the currency of the country of origin of the investment, or in reais. Operations involving the repatriation of capital are exempt from income tax withholding.

Earnings from variable-income investments are subject to a 10% income tax withholding and those from fixed-income investments to a 15% income tax withholding. Remittances of capital gains are subject to income tax at a rate of 15%.

Sale or issue locally by nonresidents

The sale of shares of foreign enterprises in Brazil is regulated essentially for the MERCOSUR environment through share custody certificates or directly. There is no regulation in force allowing the sale of other foreign securities in the country. Inward and outward remittances associated with investments must be processed through banks authorized to conduct foreign exchange operations in the floating exchange rate market. There are no limits, authorizations, or hold periods for the investments.

Purchase abroad by residents

Brazilian natural and juridical persons may make investments through the purchase on Brazilian stock exchanges of custody certificates representing shares issued by companies headquartered in Asunción Treaty countries. These securities may be purchased through foreign investment funds or through direct equity investments in enterprises abroad.

Sale or issue abroad by residents

In addition to the rules already mentioned governing the purchase of shares on stock exchanges by residents and the specific regulations for MERCOSUR, collective investments can be made through Brazilian investment companies and funds.

Issues of securities abroad by residents are accorded the same treatment as direct external borrowing operations. Thus, exchange contracts involving the entry of foreign currencies must be authorized in advance by the CBB. Fund transfers associated with issues of securities abroad are subject to the conditions of the respective certificates of registration issued by the CBB, the conditions of which are set forth in the contract between the debtor and the creditor.

On collective investment securities

Purchase locally by nonresidents

Portfolio investment by foreign investors in fixed-income instruments is restricted to 2 classes of fixed-income funds: the fixed-income funds that are subject to a transaction tax of 7% and the privatization funds that are subject to a transaction tax of 5%. As of April 24, 1997, the transaction tax for fixed-income funds was reduced to 2% and that for privatization funds was eliminated.

The regulated forms of collective investment in local shares by nonresidents are the investment companies, funds, and diversified stock portfolios. For collective investments in other securities, the forms provided for in the regulations are the foreign capital fixed-income funds, privatization funds, and, as of February 8, 1996, real estate investment funds and emerging enterprises investment funds. The IOF is assessed on the latter 2 types of investments at rates ranging from zero to 10%. Their establishment, as well as changes in their bylaws, must be authorized in advance by the CVM, except for the foreign capital fixed-income funds. The constitution of those funds must be announced in writing to the CBB within a maximum of 5 days. The CBB may determine changes in the regulations of the fixed-income funds. Funds entering the country are subject to registration with the CBB for purposes of controlling foreign capital and future remittances abroad of cash dividends or bonuses and capital gains realized in the sale of the company's shares.

Inward and outward remittances associated with investments must be processed through banks authorized to conduct foreign exchange operations, with guaranteed access to the free exchange rate market to purchase foreign currency.

Sale or issue locally by nonresidents

There are no regulations on these operations.

Purchase abroad by residents

There are no regulations on these operations.

Sale or issue abroad by residents

Foreign investment funds are organized in the form of open-end mutual funds. Participation is limited exclusively to natural and juridical persons and to funds and other collective investment entities resident, domiciled, or headquartered in Brazil. Foreign investment funds may be managed by a multipurpose bank, commercial bank, investment bank, brokerage firm, or securities distributor under the supervision and direct responsibility of the manager of the institution.

A minimum of 60% of the fund's investments must be in securities representative of the federal government's external debt and a maximum of 40% in other securities traded in the international market. These securities must be kept abroad in a custodian account in the fund's name. The fund is authorized to conduct operations in organized derivative markets abroad solely for the purpose of hedging the securities making up the respective portfolio.

Inward and outward transfers of resources through foreign investment funds are subject to registration with the CBB for purposes of monitoring and controlling Brazilian investment, as well as the respective income, investment repatriation, and capital gains. Transfers are processed in foreign currency through the free exchange rate market.

Earnings from the redemption of shares of foreign investment funds are subject to a 15% income tax to be withheld by the managing institution of the foreign investment funds on the date of the redemption payment or credit and paid within 3 working days of the 2-week period following the occurrence of the taxable event.

Controls on derivatives and other instruments

Purchase locally by nonresidents

Foreign capital fixed-income funds may conduct operations in organized derivative markets in the country, including futures operations carried out in markets managed by stock exchanges or commodities and futures exchanges. The resources of investors from Asunción Treaty countries may be invested in the domestic options and futures market. The use of funds entering the country for the purchase of fixed-income securities and in operations carried out in derivatives markets is prohibited. There are no restrictions on investments in derivatives operations in Brazil by recipients of direct investments.

Sale or issue locally by nonresidents

Yes.

Purchase abroad by residents

Private sector entities may engage in hedging operations with financial institutions or stock exchanges abroad to protect themselves against the risk of variations in interest rates, exchange rates, and commodity prices. The costs of such operations must conform to the parameters in force in the international market. The CBB may, at its sole discretion, require foreign exchange compensation sufficient to eliminate the effects of operations not in line with the established objective or executed outside those parameters, without prejudice to other sanctions that may apply. Payments and receipts in foreign currency scheduled or expected to occur in the future in connection with commercial or financial rights or obligations may also be protected by hedging. Hedging operations, however, are limited at any time (1) in interest rate and currency swaps, to the amount of the underlying commercial or financial rights and obligations remaining in foreign currency; and (2) in commodities swaps, open positions are limited to the physical volume of the commodity to be exported, imported, or traded in the domestic market.

Sale or issue abroad by residents

The same regulations as for purchases abroad by residents apply.

Controls on credit operations

Commercial credits

By residents to nonresidents

Only 2 forms of credits are permitted: (1) the Exporting Financing Program (PROEX), which is financed with national budget funds. PROEX resources may not be used to establish any facility for foreign public or private entities, insofar as financing is granted on a case-by-case basis, because credit may not be made available to nonresidents for use in several installments spread over a period of time; and (2) the Machinery and Equipment Export Financing Program (FINAMEX), which is operated through agent banks by the Special Agency for Industrial Financing (FINAME). It provides funds so that financial institutions (FINAME agents) can grant loans to national exporters at rates and on terms similar to those available to their foreign competitors.

To residents from nonresidents

Commercial credits with terms in excess of 360 days must be authorized by and registered with the FIRCE of the CBB.

Prepayment of exports must be authorized by the CBB prior to the entry of the foreign exchange into Brazil. Operations governed by these regulations have a 361-day minimum term and are exempt from income tax, and from the tax on credit, exchange, insurance operations, and securities operations. The CBB authorizes and registers external financing for imports of capital goods, intermediate goods, raw materials, and other goods and merchandise, regardless of the type of importer or the destination of the merchandise, if the operations have a term of at least 1 year.

In private sector import operations without the direct or indirect surety or guarantee of a public sector entity, the financing terms—interest rate, spread, down payment—are freely contracted by the parties. In the case of a public sector entity and in cases involving the direct or indirect surety or guarantee of a public sector entity, interest rates may not exceed the LIBOR rate for the reference period, plus specified maximum spreads.

Financial credits

By residents to nonresidents

Requests for authorization may be approved by the CBB, as there is no legal impediment to doing so.

To residents from nonresidents

The proceeds of financial credits granted to residents must be kept within the country, and the resources must be used for investment in economic activities. Exchange contracts involving the entry of foreign exchange in connection with borrowing are subject to prior approval by the CBB.

Remittances of loan, credit, or financing interest in excess of the interest rate indicated in the respective contract and registration are considered as principal payments. A 15% income tax rate is levied on remittances of interest and other income associated with foreign loan operations, except when bilateral agreements to avoid dual taxation specify another rate or when the borrower or lender is tax exempt.

The federal government, states, municipalities, the federal district, and their foundations and agencies, as well as multilateral organizations and foreign government agencies located abroad, are exempted.

Guarantees, sureties, and financial backup facilities

By residents to nonresidents

Guarantees by nonfinancial juridical persons in credit operations for their foreign subsidiaries are subject to prior authorization by the CBB.

Exchange operations involving financial transfers abroad in execution of bank sureties and guarantees in question are carried out exclusively through the floating exchange rate market when such guarantees relate or are linked to (1) imports and other foreign currency operations not covered by certificates issued by the CBB, or by a facility; and (2) repatriation of amounts entering the country as advance payment for exports, in the event of nonshipment of the goods.

Exchange operations involving financial transfers associated with the execution of payment guarantees for imports, loans, or external financing covered by certificates of authorization or registration issued by the CBB are processed through the free exchange rate market.

To residents from nonresidents

There are no restrictions on guarantees provided by nonresidents to residents in connection with foreign capital registered with the CBB, subject to the presentation of a formal statement by the foreign entity furnishing the guarantee. Data concerning the guarantee and the costs incurred in obtaining it are included in the Certificate of Authorization or Registration of the guaranteed operation. If costs are incurred in obtaining the guarantee, the credit operation must be authorized in advance by the CBB.

There are no specific regulations governing other operations. In the event of execution of a guarantee, the beneficiary must arrange for the entry of the corresponding foreign exchange directly through the banking system.

Controls on direct investment

Outward direct investment

Banks authorized to conduct foreign exchange operations may transfer up to US$5 million for each financial group, including all remittances in the last 12 months, and they are basically required to keep on file and make available to the CBB the documents mentioned in said regulations. Transfers exceeding the established limit must first be submitted to the CBB no less than 30 days in advance of the exchange contract, and, regardless of the amount, exchange operations in which the purchaser of the foreign exchange is an entity belonging to the direct or indirect public administration are subject to prior authorization by the CBB. In this case, remittances must be processed through the free exchange rate market.

Brazilian enterprises may invest in financial institutions abroad on the floating exchange rate market. However, such investments by nonfinancial enterprises require prior approval of the CBB and must meet some specified conditions. Investments abroad by institutions authorized to operate by the CBB must obtain the prior opinion of the CBB's Department of Financial System Organization and satisfy several conditions, especially with respect to paid-up capital, net assets, time in operation, fixed-asset ratio, and borrowing ceilings.

Inward direct investment

Applications for the registration of foreign direct investment and technology are not subject to prior authorization, except for foreign investments via the contribution of goods. Investments in commercial banks are limited to 30% of the voting capital, if there are restrictions on the operations of Brazilian banks in the markets where their main offices are located. The establishment in Brazil of new branches of financial institutions domiciled abroad is prohibited. Also, any increase in the percentage of equity participation in financial institutions headquartered in Brazil by natural or juridical persons resident or domiciled abroad is prohibited, except for authorizations resulting from international agreements, from reciprocity arrangements, or in the interest of the Brazilian government as expressed by presidential decree.

In the case of highway freight transportation, except for companies established before July 11, 1980, to which different rules apply, there are limitations on equity participation of up to one-fifth of the voting capital stock. In future capital increases by subscription, however, such entities are required to pay up to four-fifths of said increases in ordinary registered shares through national underwriters.

Foreign participation in journalistic and sound and image broadcasting enterprises is prohibited. Direct or indirect equity participation by foreign enterprises or capital in the health care sector in Brazil is also prohibited, except in special cases.

The registration of foreign investment through the verification of patent or trademark rights as a means of paying in capital is subject to prior recording of the deed of transfer or assignment of the rights to use the patent or trademark with the National Institute of Industrial Property, and is limited to the value stated in the latter. The investment is registered in the currency of the country where the beneficiary is domiciled or headquartered, and must be requested from the CBB by the party receiving the investment.

Foreign investments via the contribution of goods without exchange cover are subject to prior authorization by the CBB and the SECEX. The goods, machinery, or equipment must be used in the production of goods or the provision of services, must have a useful life of more than 5 years, and must be part of the enterprise's assets for at least 5 years.

Investments through currency transfers are not subject to prior authorization. This type of investment may take place through the free exchange rate market to pay up the subscribed capital of enterprises already operating in Brazil, to organize a new enterprise, or to acquire an interest in an existing Brazilian enterprise.

Branches of foreign companies may be opened, subject to the prior issuance of an authorizing decree by the president of the Republic. A branch is considered an office of a foreign enterprise. Enterprises established in Brazil with any degree of foreign equity participation are not covered by this restriction.

The entry of resources associated with the investment must be processed through a banking institution authorized to conduct foreign exchange operations.

Controls on liquidation of direct investment

Remittances of proceeds must be processed through banks authorized to conduct foreign exchange operations.

Controls on real estate transactions

Purchase abroad by residents

Transfers for the purchase of residential or commercial real estate abroad may be made through the floating exchange rate market.

Purchase locally by nonresidents

The purchase of real estate in Brazil is not restricted. Foreign investments in the capital of Brazilian enterprises (including resources to be used for investment in the capital of real estate enterprises) by parties resident, domiciled, or headquartered abroad are unrestricted and are not subject to prior authorization by the CBB. The exchange occurs on the free exchange rate market.

Provisions specific to commercial banks and other credit institutions

Borrowing abroad

Foreign borrowing for terms exceeding 360 days is subject to authorization and registration with the CBB. The CBB requires that banks authorized to conduct foreign exchange operations obtain facilities abroad for terms of up to 360 days to extend commercial credit in Brazil.

The National Bank for Economic and Social Development, private investment or development banks, commercial banks authorized to conduct foreign exchange operations, and multipurpose banks with a commercial portfolio (if authorized to conduct foreign exchange operations and holding an investment or development portfolio) are permitted to contract loans abroad to be onlent to enterprises in Brazil by issuing commercial paper. They may also borrow abroad by issuing floating-rate notes, fixed-rate notes, floating-rate certificates of deposit, fixed-rate certificates of deposit, government bonds, and private bonds.

Financial institutions in the National Rural Credit System may borrow abroad to finance costs, investment, or the marketing of agricultural and livestock production.

Banks may raise funds abroad to be onlent to natural or juridical persons to finance the construction or purchase of new real estate. Banks authorized to conduct foreign exchange operations may use facilities contracted for terms exceeding 360 days with banks abroad to finance imports by resident enterprises. The public sector may engage in external credit operations for the settlement of internal debt. In April 1997, the rate of the IOF applied to lending operations in foreign currency was reduced to zero from a range up to 3%.

Lending to nonresidents (financial or commercial credits)

There are no legal provisions authorizing banks or credit institutions headquartered in Brazil to grant financial loans to nonresidents or to purchase securities issued abroad for terms exceeding 360 days. This restriction does not apply to the foreign branches of Brazilian banks with regard to commercial credit.

Lending locally in foreign exchange

All contracts, securities, or other documents, as well as any obligations executable in Brazil that require payment in foreign currency, are null and void. Consequently, banks are prohibited from granting foreign currency loans within Brazil. However, this restriction does not apply to the onlending of external foreign currency loans.

Purchase of locally issued securities denominated in foreign exchange

Domestic operations in foreign currencies are prohibited.

Differential treatment of nonresident deposit accounts and/or deposit accounts in foreign exchange

n.a.

Investment regulations

n.a.

Open foreign exchange position limits

Limits differ according to the exchange market in which the transactions take place as follows: (1) banks authorized to conduct foreign exchange operations in the free exchange rate market may hold long positions of up to US$5 million, including all currencies and all of each bank's branches. Amounts exceeding this ceiling must be deposited with the CBB in U.S. dollars. The ceiling on banks' short exchange position is contingent upon each bank's adjusted net worth; and (2) on the floating exchange rate market, the following ceilings have been set:

(a) For licensed banks, the long exchange position is US$1 million (any amount in excess of this ceiling must be deposited with the CBB), and the short exchange position is contingent on the institution's adjusted net worth;

(b) For licensed dealers (brokerage firms; securities distributors; and credit, financing, and investment enterprises), the ceiling on the long exchange position is US$500,000 and no short exchange position is allowed;

(c) Licensed tourism agencies do not maintain exchange positions, but they are required to observe the daily operational ceiling (cash) of US$200,000; any surpluses must be sold to licensed banks or dealers; and

(d) Providers of tourist accommodations may have cash holdings in foreign currencies of up to US$50,000 to meet their operational needs; any surpluses must be sold to licensed banks or dealers.

Provisions specific to institutional investors

Limits (max.) on portfolio invested abroad

Institutional investors may invest up to 10% of their technical reserves in investment fund shares abroad. Private social security agencies may also invest up to 50% of their reserves, together with other investments up to the same ceiling, in shares of open companies, publicly issued convertible debentures, bonds for subscriptions to shares issued by open companies, and certificates of deposit for shares issued by companies headquartered in Asunción Treaty countries.

Currency matching regulations on assets/liabilities composition

n.a.

Changes During 1996

Exchange arrangements

January 30. The CBB set the adjustable band for the external value of the real at R$0.97–R$1.06 per U.S. dollar.

Nonresident accounts

April 1. Import duties were revised for several national exceptions: electronic products, bicycles, and motorcycles to 35% from 70%; white line products, 30%; footwear to 40% from 44%–56%; duties were eliminated on products considered important for industrial and technological development.

Imports and import payments

June 1. Quotas were imposed on imports of textiles originating from China, Hong Kong, Korea, Panama, and Taiwan Province of China.

Exports and export proceeds

September 13. Rules for application of the VAT by states were amended, exempting exports of primary and semimanufactured goods. This was extended to imports used by the export production companies.

Capital transactions

February 8. Collective investment by nonresidents in local shares was permitted for real estate investment funds and emerging enterprises investment funds. The IOF is assessed on these transactions at rates ranging from zero to 10%.

Changes During 1997

Exchange arrangements

February 19. The adjustable band for the external value of the real was revised to R$1.05–R$1.14 per U.S. dollar.

Arrangements for payments and receipts

April 23. Foreign exchange for payments of debt arrears must be obtained in the same exchange market (free rate exchange market) through which the payments should have been made on due dates.

Imports and import payments

January 1. An import subsystem, SISCOMEX/IMPORT, was introduced, which allows importers, carriers, banks, and brokers to register the various stages of an import process directly through the interlinked computers of SECEX, customs, and the CBB.

May 2. The application of the IOF, at a rate of 25%, to exchange operations effected for the payment of imports of services was discontinued.

Capital transactions

April 24. The IOF fixed-income fund was reduced to 2% from 7% and that for real property investment funds was eliminated. The IOF ceased to be levied on IOF loans contracted by residents, including banks.

BRUNEI DARUSSALAM
(Position as of December 31, 1996)

Status Under IMF Articles of Agreement

Article VIII

Date of acceptance: October 10, 1995.

Exchange Arrangement

Currency

The currency of Brunei Darussalam is the Brunei dollar.

Other legal tender

The Singapore dollar is also legal tender.

Exchange rate structure

Unitary.

Classification

Pegged

The Brunei dollar is issued by the Brunei Currency Board (BCB) only against payments in Singapore dollars and at par. Under the terms of a 1967 Currency Interchangeability Agreement (CIA) between the BCB and the Board of Commissioners of Currency of Singapore (BCCS), the Singapore dollar is customary tender in Brunei Darussalam and the Brunei dollar in Singapore. The BCB and BCCS have accepted each other's currency and have agreed to mutual exchange, at par and without charge. They have instructed their banks to do the same with their customers. Any excess currency is repatriated regularly, with the issuing institution bearing the costs, and settlements are made in the other country's currency. The BCB deals only in Singapore dollars and does not quote rates for other currencies. Banks, however, are free to deal in all currencies, with no restrictions on amount, maturity, or type of transaction.

The Brunei Association of Banks fixes daily buying and selling rates for electronic transfers and sight drafts in 17 other currencies on the basis of the interbank quotations for these currencies in relation to the Singapore dollar. Banks in Brunei must apply these rates for transactions with the general public for amounts up to B$100,000. Exchange rates for amounts exceeding B$100,000 are set competitively by each bank on the basis of the current interbank quotations for the Singapore dollar on the Singapore market.

Exchange tax

No.

Exchange subsidy

No.

Forward exchange market

There is no forward market for foreign exchange in Brunei Darussalam. However, as a result of the CIA, foreign exchange risk can be hedged in terms of Singapore dollars by resorting to facilities available in that country, including foreign currency futures and options traded on the Singapore International Monetary Exchange (SIMEX), over-the-counter forward transactions arranged by banks in Singapore, and short-term foreign exchange swap market operated among the banks in the Singapore money market.

Official cover of forward operations

No.

Arrangements for Payments and Receipts

Prescription of currency requirements

No.

Payment arrangements

No.

Administration of control

Exchange control authorities

There are no formal exchange controls, but the Ministry of Finance retains responsibility for exchange control matters.

132

International security restrictions	No.
Payment arrears	No.
Controls on trade in gold (coins and/or bullion)	
Controls on domestic ownership and/or trade	Only banks licensed to operate in Brunei Darussalam and gold dealers and jewelers specifically authorized by the Ministry of Finance may buy and sell gold bars. Gold bars are not subject to import duty, but a 10% import duty is levied on the importation of gold jewelry.
Controls on external trade	Yes.
Controls on exports and imports of banknotes	No.

Resident Accounts

Eligibility to hold accounts	Juridical and natural persons are eligible.
Foreign exchange accounts permitted	Yes.
Held domestically	Yes.
Held abroad	Yes.
Accounts in domestic currency convertible into foreign currency	Yes.

Nonresident Accounts

Eligibility to hold accounts	Juridical and natural persons are eligible. There is no distinction between accounts of residents and nonresidents of Brunei Darussalam.
Foreign exchange accounts permitted	Yes.
Domestic currency accounts	Yes.
Convertible into foreign currency	Yes.
Blocked accounts	No.

Imports and Import Payments

Foreign exchange budget	No.
Financing requirements for imports	No.
Documentation requirements for release of foreign exchange for imports	No.
Import licenses and other nontariff measures	
Negative list	A few imports are banned or restricted for nature conservation, health, safety, security, or religious reasons.
Import taxes and/or tariffs	Except for cigarettes and alcoholic beverages, most imports are subject to tariff rates of up to 200%. Some 70% of items (including basic foodstuffs, construction, and educational materials) are zero rated. Most other goods are subject to tariff rates of 5%, 15%,

or 20%. Fireworks are subject to a 30% duty, while automobiles are subject to duties ranging between 40% and 200%, depending on engine size. In accordance with the CEPT scheme for the AFTA, Brunei Darussalam will eliminate its tariffs on imports from other ASEAN members by 2003, with the exception of about 120 tariff lines that are permanently excluded from the plan.

Taxes collected through the exchange system	No.
State import monopoly	No.

Exports and Export Proceeds

Repatriation requirements	No.
Surrender requirements	No.
Documentation requirements	No.
Export licenses	Export licenses are required for alcoholic beverages, cigarettes, diesel, gasoline, kerosene, rice, salt, and sugar. There are no export taxes.
Without quotas	Yes.
With quotas	n.a.
Export taxes	No.

Payments for Invisible Transactions and Current Transfers

Controls on these payments	The provision of foreign exchange for these payments is subject to a bona fide test. Interest payments are subject to a 20% withholding tax.

Proceeds from Invisible Transactions and Current Transfers

Repatriation requirements	No.
Surrender requirements	No.
Restrictions on use of funds	No.

Capital Transactions

Controls on capital and money market instruments	No.
Controls on derivatives and other instruments	No.
Controls on direct investment	
Inward direct investment	There are no sectoral restrictions, but activities relating to national food security and those based on local resources require some degree of local participation. Industries producing for the local market that are not related to national food security and industries that solely export may be fully foreign owned. Joint ventures are particularly encouraged in export-import industries and activities supporting such industries. At least one-half of the directors of a company must be either Bruneian citizens or residents of Brunei Darussalam.
Controls on liquidation of direct investment	No.

Controls on real estate transactions

Purchase locally by nonresidents	Only Bruneian citizens are allowed to own land. However, foreign investors may lease land on a long-term basis, including sites destined for industry, agriculture, agroforestry, and aquaculture.
Sale locally by nonresidents	n.a.
Provisions specific to commercial banks and other credit institutions	No.
Provisions specific to institutional investors	No.
Other controls imposed by securities laws	No.

Changes During 1996

No significant changes occurred in the exchange and trade system.

BULGARIA

(Position as of December 31, 1996)

Status Under IMF Articles of Agreement

Article XIV	Yes.

Exchange Arrangement

Currency	The currency of Bulgaria is the lev.
Exchange rate structure	Unitary.
Classification	
Independent floating	The exchange rate of the lev is determined on the basis of a weighted average of transactions in the interbank market during the previous trading day.
Exchange tax	No.
Exchange subsidy	No.
Forward exchange market	No.

Arrangements for Payments and Receipts

Prescription of currency requirements	Payments to and from countries with which Bulgaria maintains bilateral agreements are made in the currencies and in accordance with the procedures set forth in those agreements. Transactions are generally settled through clearing accounts. Balances in these accounts (annual and multiyear) are generally to be settled in goods during the 6 months after the agreement has been terminated; thereafter, they are settled in convertible currencies.
Payment arrangements	
Bilateral arrangements	
Inoperative	There are arrangements with Bangladesh, Cambodia, China, Guinea, the Islamic Republic of Iran, the Lao People's Democratic Republic, and Syria. Bulgaria has outstanding transferable ruble accounts with Hungary, Mongolia, Poland, and Romania.
Barter agreements and open accounts	There are agreements with the Islamic State of Afghanistan, Bangladesh, Ethiopia, Ghana, Guyana, India, Mozambique, Nicaragua, Pakistan, Romania, and Tanzania.
Administration of control	
Exchange control authorities	Foreign exchange control is exercised by the Ministry of Finance (MOF), the Bulgarian National Bank (BNB), authorized banks, customs administration, border guards, and port offices.
International security restrictions	
In accordance with IMF Executive Board Decision No. 144-(52/51)	Yes.
Payment arrears	No.
Controls on trade in gold (coins and/or bullion)	
Controls on domestic ownership and/or trade	The MOF controls the acquisition, possession, processing, and disposal of gold, silver, and platinum. The BNB is the only institution entitled to purchase, sell, and hold gold. All domestic transactions for industrial purposes must be conducted at current prices through the BNB. Commercial banks are not authorized to deal or speculate (on their

own or on their customers' behalf) in precious metals, with the exception that the Bulgarian Foreign Trade Bank is licensed to deal in precious metals. Resident individuals may hold gold but may not trade or deal in it. However, in September 1996 the Constitutional Court declared the ban on trade unconstitutional.

Controls on external trade	The amount of gold and items of jewelry that residents may import is limited. Nonresidents are permitted to bring in and take out their jewelry but may not trade it. Nonresidents must have permission from the MOF, the BNB, and the Ministry of Industry and Commerce to buy gold, silver, and platinum products. The BNB is the only institution entitled to import or export gold.

Controls on exports and imports of banknotes

On exports

Domestic currency

Residents and nonresidents may take out banknotes and coins up to lev 10,000; permission from the BNB is required for larger amounts.

Foreign currency

Residents may take out up to the equivalent of $1,000 without restriction, from $1,000 to $10,000 upon presentation of a statement of account by a bank, and more than $10,000 with the permission of the BNB.

On imports

Domestic currency

Residents and nonresidents may bring in banknotes and coins up to lev 10,000; permission from the BNB is required to import larger amounts.

Foreign currency

The amount must be declared, and nonresidents may take out unspent foreign currency notes upon departure.

Resident Accounts

Eligibility to hold accounts	Juridical and natural persons are eligible.
Foreign exchange accounts permitted	Yes.
Held domestically	Residents may maintain these accounts in Bulgaria. Balances on these accounts earn interest at international market rates. The crediting and debiting of foreign currency accounts are not subject to any regulations. Transfers abroad may be made with permission from the MOF and the BNB.
Held abroad	These accounts are allowed, but prior permission from the BNB and MOF is required.
Accounts in domestic currency convertible into foreign currency	Transfers abroad from these accounts are free of restriction.

Nonresident Accounts

Eligibility to hold accounts	Juridical and natural persons are eligible.
Foreign exchange accounts permitted	The crediting and debiting of these accounts are not subject to any regulations.
Domestic currency accounts	Yes.
Convertible into foreign currency	n.a.
Approval required	n.a.
Blocked accounts	No.

Imports and Import Payments

Foreign exchange budget	No.
Financing requirements for imports	No.
Documentation requirements for release of foreign exchange for imports	No.
Import licenses and other nontariff measures	Imports of tobacco products, coal, petroleum, livestock and meat, dairy products, certain grains, textiles, ferrous metals and alloys, and flat glass must be registered. Imports of some sensitive goods are subject to registration at the Ministry of Trade.
Positive list	Special licenses are required for transactions under barter and clearing arrangements and for imports of military hardware and related technologies, endangered flora and fauna, radioactive and hazardous materials, crafts and antiques, pharmaceuticals, herbicides, pesticides, flour, unbottled alcohol, intellectual property, jewelry, and rare and precious metals. Licenses are normally granted within 2 working days.
Negative list	Imports of certain goods are restricted for health and security reasons.
Import taxes and/or tariffs	Import tariffs range from 5% to 55% and are calculated on a transaction-value basis in foreign currency and converted to leva. Certain energy products, pharmaceuticals, and facilities for environmental protection are exempt from customs duties or are subject to a reduced rate. An import surcharge of 5% was introduced in June 1996, which is to be gradually reduced and eliminated in 2000.
Taxes collected through the exchange system	No.
State import monopoly	No.

Exports and Export Proceeds

Repatriation requirements	Proceeds from exports must be repatriated within 1 month.
Surrender requirements	Proceeds do not have to be surrendered; they may be retained in foreign currencies or sold in the interbank exchange market.
Financing requirements	No.
Documentation requirements	Exports of tobacco products, coal, petroleum, livestock and meat, dairy products, certain grains, textiles, ferrous metals and alloys must be registered.
Export licenses	Special licenses are required for transactions under barter and clearing arrangements, for exports proceeds to be received in leva, exports of military hardware and related technologies, endangered flora and fauna, radioactive and hazardous materials, crafts and antiques, pharmaceuticals, herbicides, pesticides, flour, unbottled alcohol, intellectual property, jewelry, and rare and precious metals. Licenses are normally granted within 2 working days. Exports of metal scraps and wheat are prohibited, the latter until end-September 1997.
Without quotas	Yes.
With quotas	Exports under government credits and exports under voluntary export restraint agreements are subject to quotas. There are also quotas on exports of certain wheat products and metal scrap.
Export taxes	Export taxes are levied on certain types of timber, hides, wool, sunflower oil, grain, and certain copper products; taxes are quoted in U.S. dollars but paid in leva.
Taxes collected through the exchange system	No.

Payments for Invisible Transactions and Current Transfers

Controls on these payments	Payments for freight and insurance, unloading and storage costs, administrative expenses, commissions, travel, medical costs, subscriptions and membership fees, consulting and legal fees, and pensions are subject to indicative limits and/or bona fide tests.
Interest payments	
Indicative limits/bona fide test	Payments are processed by banks against authorization by the MOF, a credit contract, and documentation on the amount transferred.
Profit/dividends	No.
Payments for travel	Foreign exchange allowances for business travel are granted without restriction. Allowances for tourist travel are limited to the leva equivalent of $2,000 a person a year for people without foreign currency deposits but could be greater in all bona fide requests. Resident holders of foreign exchange deposits may use balances on these deposit accounts without restriction.
Quantitative limits	Yes.
Medical costs	
Prior approval	Approval of the MOF, in coordination with the Ministry of Health, is required.
Study abroad costs	
Quantitative limits	The limit is $10,000 a year. All amounts in excess of this limit require the permission of the MOF.
Indicative limits/bona fide test	n.a.
Subscriptions and membership fees	
Prior approval	Yes.
Quantitative limits	Yes.
Consulting/legal fees	
Quantitative limits	Yes.
Foreign workers' wages	These remittances are not explicitly regulated but have been treated implicitly as transfers abroad that are not related to merchandise imports, and therefore require prior permission from the BNB in consultation with the MOF.
Prior approval	Yes.
Pensions	
Prior approval	Yes.
Gambling/prize earnings	
Prior approval	Yes.
Family maintenance/alimony	These remittances are not explicitly regulated but have been treated implicitly as transfers abroad that are not related to merchandise imports, and therefore require prior permission from the BNB in consultation with the MOF.
Prior approval	Yes.
Credit card use abroad	No.

Proceeds from Invisible Transactions and Current Transfers

Repatriation requirements	Proceeds from invisibles must be repatriated within 1 month.
Surrender requirements	No.

Restrictions on use of funds	No.

Capital Transactions

Controls on capital and money market instruments

On capital market securities

    Purchase locally by nonresidents — Investments by nonresidents must be registered with the Securities and Stock Exchange Commission.

    Purchase abroad by residents — Prior permission of the BNB, in consultation with the MOF, is required.

Controls on derivatives and other instruments — No.

Controls on credit operations — Official credits extended to and received from abroad require permission of the BNB in consultation with the MOF.

Commercial credits — Yes.

Financial credits — Yes.

Controls on direct investment

Outward direct investment — Yes.

Inward direct investment — Investments must be registered with the MOF and require authorization only if they are undertaken in sectors that are considered sensitive. Foreign direct investments are guaranteed against expropriation, except for nationalization through legal process. Foreign firms are granted the same status as domestic firms.

Controls on liquidation of direct investment — No.

Controls on real estate transactions

Purchase abroad by residents — Purchases must be declared to the MOF.

Purchase locally by nonresidents — Prior permission of the MOF is required. Nonresidents may not purchase or own land. If they inherit land, they must dispose of it within a 3-year period.

Sale locally by nonresidents — Prior permission of the MOF is required.

Provisions specific to commercial banks and other credit institutions

Borrowing abroad — Licensed banks may borrow abroad without the authorization of the BNB. Licensed commercial banks, however, may borrow abroad only if they do not request a guarantee from the government of Bulgaria and if their borrowing complies with the prudential regulations set up by the BNB.

Provisions specific to institutional investors — No.

Other controls imposed by securities laws — No.

Changes During 1996

Arrangements for payments and receipts — *April 30.* The bilateral payment arrangement with Bangladesh became inoperative.

September 8. The regulations on the export and import of foreign exchange banknotes were liberalized.

Imports and import payments

June 4. A 5% import surcharge was imposed; it will be gradually reduced until eliminated in 2000.

Exports and export proceeds

October 15. The ban on wheat exports was extended through end-September 1997.

December 1. Bulgaria joined the WTO.

Capital transactions

December 12. The Law on Business Activity of Foreign Persons and Protection of Foreign Investments was passed.

BURKINA FASO

(Position as of December 31, 1996)

Status Under IMF Articles of Agreement

Article VIII   Date of acceptance: June 1, 1996.

Exchange Arrangement

Currency   The currency of Burkina Faso is the CFA franc.

Exchange rate structure   Unitary.

Classification

Pegged   The CFA franc is pegged to the French franc, the intervention currency, at the fixed rate of CFAF 1 per F 0.01. Exchange rates for other currencies are derived from the rate for the currency concerned in the Paris exchange market and the fixed rate between the French franc and the CFA franc. They include a bank commission of 2.5‰ on transfers to all countries outside the WAEMU, which must be surrendered in its entirety to the Treasury.

Exchange tax   No.

Exchange subsidy   No.

Forward exchange market   Forward exchange cover may be arranged only by residents for settlements with respect to imports of goods on certain lists. All contracts for forward exchange cover must be denominated in the currency of payment stipulated in the contract and are subject to prior authorization by the Ministry of Finance (MOF). Nonrenewable forward exchange contracts may be concluded for 1 month. For certain products, the maturity period of forward exchange cover may be renewed once for 3 months.

Official cover of forward operations   Yes.

Arrangements for Payments and Receipts

Prescription of currency requirements   Because Burkina Faso is linked to the French Treasury through an Operations Account, settlements with France, Monaco, and other Operations Account countries are made in CFA francs, French francs, or the currency of any other Operations Account country. Certain settlements are channeled through special accounts. Settlements with all other countries are usually effected either through correspondent banks in France or the country concerned in the currencies of those countries, or through foreign accounts in francs in French francs or other currencies of the Operations Account area.

Payment arrangements

Bilateral arrangements

Inoperative   Yes.

Clearing agreements   Current payments to or from The Gambia, Ghana, Guinea, Guinea-Bissau, Liberia, Mauritania, Nigeria, and Sierra Leone are normally made through the WACH.

Administration of control

Exchange control authorities   Exchange control is administered by the Directorate of the Treasury in the MOF. The approval authority for exchange control (except for imports and exports of gold, forward exchange cover, and the opening of external accounts in foreign currency) has been delegated to the BCEAO, which is also authorized to collect, either directly or through banks, financial institutions, the Postal Administration, or judicial agents, any information necessary to compile balance of payments statistics.

All exchange transactions relating to foreign countries must be effected through authorized banks, the Postal Administration, or the BCEAO. Settlements with a country outside the Operations Account area must be formally approved by the customs administration.

Import and export licenses were eliminated and replaced with preimport declarations (DPIs) issued for all import and export operations involving goods valued at CFAF 500,000 and over.

International security restrictions	No.
Payment arrears	
Official	Restructuring of arrears of debts to Libya, the Baltic countries, Russia, and the other countries of the FSU is in progress.
Private	n.a.

Controls on trade in gold (coins and/or bullion)

Controls on external trade

Imports of gold require prior MOF authorization, which is seldom granted. Exempt from this requirement are (1) imports by or on behalf of the Treasury or the BCEAO; (2) imports of manufactured articles containing minor quantities of gold (such as gold-filled or gold-plated articles); and (3) imports by travelers of gold objects up to a combined weight of 500 grams. Both licensed and exempt imports of gold are subject to customs declaration.

Exports of gold have been liberalized since May 1996. The monopoly granted to the Comptoir burkinabe des métaux précieux has been extended for a transitional period of 1 year from May 1996.

Controls on exports and imports of banknotes

On exports

Domestic currency

The exportation of CFA banknotes by nonresident travelers is not prohibited. However, repurchases by the BCEAO of exported banknotes are still suspended. In addition, shipments of BCEAO banknotes among authorized intermediaries and their correspondents situated outside the WAEMU are officially prohibited.

Foreign currency

The reexportation of foreign banknotes by nonresident travelers is allowed up to the equivalent of CFAF 500,000; the reexportation of foreign banknotes above these ceilings requires documentation demonstrating either the importation of the foreign banknotes or their purchase against other means of payment registered in the name of the traveler or through the use of nonresident deposits lodged in local banks.

On imports

Domestic currency

Yes.

Foreign currency

Residents and nonresidents may bring in any amount of foreign banknotes and coins (except gold coins) of countries outside the Operations Account area. Residents bringing in foreign banknotes and foreign currency traveler's checks exceeding the equivalent of CFAF 25,000 must declare them to customs upon entry and sell them to an authorized intermediary bank within 8 days.

Resident Accounts

Eligibility to hold accounts	Juridical and natural persons are eligible.
Foreign exchange accounts permitted	Yes.

Held domestically	The holding of these accounts is subject to prior approval by the MOF.
Held abroad	The holding of these accounts is not explicitly prohibited, but regulations prohibit any transfer tending to develop a resident's foreign holdings, unless approved by the MOF.
Accounts in domestic currency convertible into foreign currency	No.

Nonresident Accounts

Eligibility to hold accounts	Juridical and natural persons are eligible.
Foreign exchange accounts permitted	The holding of these accounts is not expressly covered by regulations. In practice, based on an interpretation of the regulations, such holdings require the prior approval of the MOF.
Domestic currency accounts	Because the BCEAO has suspended the repurchase of banknotes circulating outside the WAEMU territories, nonresident accounts may not be credited or debited with BCEAO banknotes. These accounts may not be overdrawn without the prior authorization of the MOF. Transfers of funds between nonresident accounts are not restricted.
Convertible into foreign currency	Foreign accounts denominated in CFA francs may be freely debited for the purpose of purchases by nonresidents of any foreign currencies on the official exchange market.
Blocked accounts	No.

Imports and Import Payments

Foreign exchange budget	No.
Financing requirements for imports	No.
Documentation requirements for release of foreign exchange for imports	
Domiciliation requirements	All imports exceeding CFAF 500,000 must be domiciled with an authorized bank.
Preshipment inspection	An inspection is required for quality and price.
Import licenses and other nontariff measures	A technical import visa (*certificat de conformité*) is required for sugar, insecticides, wheat and cereal flour, tires and inner tubes for motorcycles, vegetable oil, milk, electrical batteries, food preserves, and rice. The Ministry of Industry, Commerce, and Mines may, on the basis of criteria established by the MOF, waive the prescribed formalities for imports from countries with which Burkina Faso has concluded a customs union or free-trade-area agreement.
Positive list	Import licenses were eliminated and replaced with DPIs issued for all import operations valued at CFAF 500,000 and over.
Negative list	Imports of ivory and fishing nets with a mesh smaller than 3 square centimeters are restricted.
Import taxes and/or tariffs	Imports, with a few exceptions, are subject to customs duties of 5%; the rates on cereals range from 4% to 26%, plus a statistical tax of 4%.
	All imports from outside the ECOWAS are subject to a solidarity communal levy of 1%, and imports of certain goods that are also locally produced are subject to a protection tax ranging from 10% to 30%.
Taxes collected through the exchange system	No.
State import monopoly	No.

Exports and Export Proceeds

Repatriation requirements
Yes.

Surrender requirements
Export proceeds must be surrendered within 1 month of the date on which payments fall due. The authorized intermediary banks must then surrender such foreign exchange to the BCEAO via transfer through the bank of issue.

Financing requirements
No.

Documentation requirements

Letters of credit
n.a.

Guarantees
n.a.

Domiciliation
All export transactions of more than CFAF 500,000 must be domiciled with an authorized intermediary bank.

Export licenses
Export licenses were eliminated and replaced with preexport declarations (DPEs) issued for exports valued at CFAF 500,000 and over. Gold, diamonds, and all other precious metals are subject to MOF authorization. Exports of ivory are subject to special regulations.

Export taxes
Most exports are subject to a customs stamp tax of 6% and a statistical duty of 3%.

Taxes collected through the exchange system
No.

Payments for Invisible Transactions and Current Transfers

Controls on these payments
All payments are subject to indicative limits and/or bona fide tests.

Payments for travel

Prior approval
Prior approval is required only for those foreign exchange allowances in excess of the indicative limits. Such approval is granted after a bona fide test.

Quantitative limits
For travel outside the franc zone, the limits are the equivalent of CFAF 1 million a person a trip for tourist travel, with no limit on the number of trips or age distinctions, and the equivalent of CFAF 200,000 a person a day for business travel over a period of 1 month.

Medical costs

Prior approval
Yes.

Study abroad costs

Prior approval
Yes.

Quantitative limits
n.a.

Family maintenance/alimony

Prior approval
Yes.

Quantitative limits
n.a.

Credit card use abroad

Prior approval
Yes.

Quantitative limits
The limits are those applicable to tourist and business travel.

Indicative limits/bona fide test
n.a.

Proceeds from Invisible Transactions and Current Transfers

Repatriation requirements	Yes.
Surrender requirements	Resident travelers must declare to customs any foreign means of payment in excess of CFAF 50,000 that they bring in and must surrender these to an authorized bank within 8 days of their return.
Restrictions on use of funds	No.

Capital Transactions

Controls on capital and money market instruments	Capital movements between Burkina Faso and France, Monaco, and the Operations Account countries are free of exchange control. Capital transfers to all other countries require exchange control approval and are restricted, but capital receipts from such countries are permitted freely.
On capital market securities	
Sale or issue locally by nonresidents	Yes.
Purchase abroad by residents	Yes.
Sale or issue abroad by residents	Yes.
On money market instruments	
Sale or issue locally by nonresidents	Yes.
Purchase abroad by residents	Yes.
Sale or issue abroad by residents	Yes.
On collective investment securities	
Sale or issue locally by nonresidents	Yes.
Purchase abroad by residents	Yes.
Sale or issue abroad by residents	Yes.
Controls on derivatives and other instruments	
Sale or issue locally by nonresidents	n.a.
Purchase abroad by residents	Yes.
Sale or issue abroad by residents	n.a.
Controls on credit operations	
Commercial credits	
By residents to nonresidents	There are no restrictions on credits related to exports of goods, provided that the date on which payment falls due is not more than 180 days after the goods arrive at their destination. There are no restrictions on credits in connection with services rendered. In these cases, no deadline is set for the date on which payment falls due.
To residents from nonresidents	There are no restrictions, and repayments of commercial credits are generally approved, subject to the documentation requirement.
Financial credits	
By residents to nonresidents	These credits require prior approval from the MOF. Outward transfers necessary to service such facilities require an exchange authorization subject to the approval of the BCEAO, acting on behalf of the MOF, substantiated by documentation.

To residents from nonresidents	There are no restrictions on these credits, and the funds needed to service them must be transferred from the outside through an authorized intermediary bank. However, if such transactions take place between a direct investment company established in Burkina Faso and its parent company situated abroad, the transactions are regarded as direct investments and are therefore subject to prior declaration to the MOF.
Guarantees, sureties, and financial backup facilities	The same regulations as for financial credits apply.
By residents to nonresidents	Yes.
Controls on direct investment	
Outward direct investment	Yes.
Inward direct investment	Yes.
Controls on liquidation of direct investment	The liquidation is subject to MOF approval. After settlement, the liquidation or sale must be reported to the MOF and the BCEAO within 20 days following each operation.
Controls on real estate transactions	
Purchase abroad by residents	MOF prior approval is required.
Sale locally by nonresidents	The same regulations as for the liquidation of direct investment apply.
Provisions specific to commercial banks and other credit institutions	
Borrowing abroad	Yes.
Lending to nonresidents (financial or commercial credits)	MOF approval is required.
Lending locally in foreign exchange	Yes.
Purchase of locally issued securities denominated in foreign exchange	Yes.
Differential treatment of nonresident deposit accounts and/or deposit accounts in foreign exchange	Monetary regulations make no distinction between resident deposit accounts, nonresident deposit accounts, and foreign deposit accounts.
Investment regulations	Yes.
Other controls imposed by securities laws	No.

Changes During 1996

Status under IMF Articles of Agreement	*June 1.* Burkina Faso accepted the obligations of Article VIII, Sections 2, 3, and 4 of the Fund Articles of Agreement.
Arrangements for payments and receipts	*May 30.* Exports of gold were liberalized.
Imports and import payments	*May 30.* Import licenses were eliminated and replaced with DPIs for imports valued at CFAF 500,000 and over.
	September 25. The list of imports for which a technical import visa (*certificat de conformité*) is required was reduced.
Exports and export proceeds	*May 30.* Export licenses were eliminated and replaced with DPEs for exports valued at CFAF 500,000 and over.
Payments for invisible transactions and current transfers	*April 24.* Foreign exchange allowances for travel outside the franc zone were increased to CFAF 1 million for tourist travel and CFAF 200,000 for business travel.

BURUNDI

(Position as of December 31, 1996)

Status Under IMF Articles of Agreement

Article XIV	Yes.

Exchange Arrangement

Currency	The currency of Burundi is the Burundi franc.
Exchange rate structure	Unitary.
Classification	
Pegged	The Burundi franc is pegged to a basket of currencies of Burundi's main trading partners. Exchange rates for 18 currencies and for 2 units of account—the ECU and unit of account of the COMESA—are quoted by the Bank of the Republic of Burundi (BRB) on the basis of the Burundi franc-U.S. dollar rate and the transaction value of these currencies and units in terms of the U.S. dollar. Commercial banks are authorized to buy and sell foreign exchange on their own account and on behalf of their customers at rates within maximum margins of ±1% of the middle rate established by the BRB.
Exchange tax	No.
Exchange subsidy	No.
Forward exchange market	Commercial banks are allowed to borrow foreign exchange to hedge against exchange rate risks. Exporters of coffee are also allowed to borrow foreign exchange through their banks or from their customers for purposes of crop financing and hedging against exchange risks.
Official cover of forward operations	No.

Arrangements for Payments and Receipts

Prescription of currency requirements	Settlements relating to trade with the Democratic Republic of the Congo and Rwanda in products specified in the commercial agreements with these countries are effected through a clearing process, with balances paid in SDRs. Nonresidents staying in a hotel or guest house in Burundi must pay their hotel bills by selling convertible currencies or by using a credit card. Payment in Burundi francs is, however, acceptable in the case of guests for whom a resident company or individual has assumed responsibility with prior authorization from the BRB and in the case of nationals of the Democratic Republic of the Congo and Rwanda who produce declarations of means of payment issued under the auspices of the CEPGL.
Payment arrangements	
Bilateral arrangements	
Operative	There are trade agreements with the Democratic Republic of the Congo and Rwanda.
Regional arrangements	Regional agreements exist with eastern and southern African countries.
Clearing agreements	Clearing agreements exist with members of COMESA and CEPGL.
Administration of control	
Exchange control authorities	Control over foreign exchange transactions and foreign trade is vested in the BRB; authority to carry out some transactions is delegated to 6 authorized banks.
International security restrictions	No.

Payment arrears

Official

Yes.

Private

n.a.

Controls on trade in gold (coins and/or bullion)

Controls on domestic ownership and/or trade

Holders of gold mining permits issued by the ministers responsible for mining and customs may open purchasing houses for gold mined by artisans in Burundi. Gold produced by artisans may be sold only to approved houses.

Controls on external trade

Exports of gold must be declared in Burundi francs at the average daily rates communicated by the central bank. Gold exports are authorized jointly by the mining and customs departments.

Controls on exports and imports of banknotes

On exports

Domestic currency

All travelers may take out up to FBu 5,000.

Foreign currency

n.a.

On imports

Domestic currency

Travelers may bring in up to FBu 5,000.

Foreign currency

Travelers may bring in any amount of foreign currency quoted by the BRB in addition to traveler's checks.

Resident Accounts

Eligibility to hold accounts

Juridical and natural persons are eligible.

Foreign exchange accounts permitted

Exporters of nontraditional products and enterprises in free trade zones may hold foreign exchange accounts.

Held domestically

Authorized banks may freely open foreign exchange accounts but must forward copies of the relevant documents to the BRB.

Held abroad

Prior BRB authorization is required to open these accounts.

Accounts in domestic currency convertible into foreign currency

Yes.

Nonresident Accounts

Eligibility to hold accounts

Juridical and natural persons are eligible.

Foreign exchange accounts permitted

These accounts may be maintained by (1) natural and juridical persons of foreign nationality who reside abroad, (2) enterprises authorized to operate in the free trade zone, (3) exporters of nontraditional products who are authorized to retain 30% of their export proceeds, (4) Burundi nationals residing abroad, and (5) any other natural or juridical persons authorized by the BRB. These accounts may be credited freely with any convertible currency received from abroad. They may be debited freely for (1) conversion into Burundi francs for payments in Burundi; and (2) payments abroad for travel and representation or for the purchase of foreign goods, except for banknotes. These accounts must not be overdrawn. However, they may bear interest freely. The related bank charges and commissions must be settled in foreign exchange; and (3) up to FBu 20,000 may be withdrawn in banknotes upon presentation of travel documents. Withdrawals in excess of this amount are subject to the prior authorization of the central bank. If no deposits are made to the foreign account within 3 months of its opening, the account must be closed. Prior approval is required.

Domestic currency accounts	Yes.
Convertible into foreign currency	Accounts in convertible Burundi francs may be maintained by (1) natural persons of foreign nationality (such as staff of diplomatic missions) who are temporarily established in Burundi, (2) juridical persons of foreign nationality with special status (such as diplomatic missions and international organizations), and (3) any other natural or juridical persons authorized by the BRB. These accounts may be credited freely with any convertible currency, and they may be debited freely for withdrawals of Burundi francs or for conversion into foreign exchange. Up to FBu 20,000 in foreign currency may be withdrawn in banknotes upon presentation of travel documents (a passport and an airline ticket) for an unlimited number of trips. Withdrawals of banknotes in excess of this amount are subject to the prior authorization of the BRB. These accounts may bear interest freely and must not be overdrawn. Prior approval is required.

Imports and Import Payments

Foreign exchange budget	No.
Financing requirements for imports	No.
Documentation requirements for release of foreign exchange for imports	All goods imported into Burundi must be insured by approved Burundi insurers, and premiums must be paid in Burundi francs.
Preshipment inspection	All consignments of imports exceeding FBu 3 million in value (f.o.b.) may be subject to preshipment inspection with regard to quality, quantity, and price by an international supervising and oversight organization on behalf of the Burundi authorities.
Import licenses and other nontariff measures	
Negative list	The importation of a limited number of goods is restricted mainly for health or security reasons.
Import taxes and/or tariffs	Burundi is a member of the COMESA. There are 5 customs duty bands (10%, 12%, 15%, 40%, and 100%) applied to imports from countries not belonging to COMESA. Imports of petroleum products are subject to import duties ranging from 6% to 40%. A 6% service tax, which replaced the statistical tax, is levied on the c.i.f. value of imports, in addition to any applicable customs duties and fiscal duties.
Taxes collected through the exchange system	No.

Exports and Export Proceeds

Repatriation requirements	Export proceeds must be collected within 30 days of the date of export declaration at customs for shipment by air or within 90 days for all other shipments. Deadlines for the collection of proceeds from exports of nontraditional products are set by the bank carrying out the operation.
Surrender requirements	All proceeds from traditional exports must be surrendered to an authorized bank. Effective November 12, 1996, exporters of nontraditional products may retain up to 50% of proceeds, compared to 30% previously. Exporters operating in the free trade area are not required to surrender their export proceeds to an authorized bank.
Financing requirements	No.
Documentation requirements	No.
Export licenses	No.
Export taxes	Export taxes are levied on a range of exports. The generally applicable rate is 5%. For green coffee, the rate is set at each crop season.

Taxes collected through the exchange system	No.

Payments for Invisible Transactions and Current Transfers

Controls on these payments	All payments for invisibles require approval.
Freight/insurance	Shipping insurance on coffee exports normally must be taken out in Burundi francs with a Burundi insurer.
Indicative limits/bona fide test	Yes.
Unloading/storage costs	
Indicative limits/bona fide test	Limited to amounts indicated by invoice.
Administrative expenses	
Indicative limits/bona fide test	Yes.
Commissions	
Indicative limits/bona fide test	n.a.
Interest payments	
Indicative limits/bona fide test	n.a.
Profit/dividends	Private joint-stock companies may transfer 100% of the return on foreign capital and of the share allocated to foreign directors after payment of taxes. Airlines are authorized to transfer abroad 100% of their earnings after deduction of local expenses. Transfer of rental income is permitted (after payment of taxes and a deduction of 20% for maintenance expenses).
Indicative limits/bona fide test	Yes.
Payments for travel	
Quantitative limits	The foreign exchange allowance for business travel is $200 a person a day or its equivalent ($250 for exporters), subject to a maximum limit of 15 days a trip. There is no limit on the number of trips for each person.
Indicative limits/bona fide test	Yes.
Medical costs	
Quantitative limits	The limit is FBu 700,000.
Indicative limits/bona fide test	A supporting medical certificate is required.
Study abroad costs	
Quantitative limits	Limits depend on the type of student.
Indicative limits/bona fide test	An enrollment certificate is required.
Subscriptions and membership fees	
Quantitative limits	Limited to amounts indicated by invoices.
Indicative limits/bona fide test	n.a.
Consulting/legal fees	
Quantitative limits	Limited to amounts indicated by invoices.
Indicative limits/bona fide test	n.a.
Foreign workers' wages	
Quantitative limits	Upon presentation of evidence of payment of taxes, foreign nationals residing and working in Burundi are permitted to transfer abroad up to 70% of their net annual income (80% in the case of foreign nationals working for companies that export at least 50% of their production).

Indicative limits/bona fide test	A work contract is required.
Pensions	
Indicative limits/bona fide test	Applications must be submitted to the Social Security Institute.
Gambling/prize earnings	
Quantitative limits	n.a.
Indicative limits/bona fide test	n.a.
Family maintenance/alimony	
Quantitative limits	The limit is FBu 150,000 a year.
Indicative limits/bona fide test	n.a.
Credit card use abroad	The use of credit cards is not permitted.

Proceeds from Invisible Transactions and Current Transfers

Repatriation requirements	Yes.
Surrender requirements	Exchange receipts from invisibles must be surrendered to authorized banks.
Restrictions on use of funds	Yes.

Capital Transactions

Controls on capital and money market instruments	Capital transfers abroad by residents require individual authorization.
On capital market securities	
Purchase locally by nonresidents	n.a.
Sale or issue locally by nonresidents	n.a.
Purchase abroad by residents	Yes.
Sale or issue abroad by residents	n.a.
On money market instruments	
Purchase locally by nonresidents	n.a.
Sale or issue locally by nonresidents	n.a.
Purchase abroad by residents	Yes.
Sale or issue abroad by residents	n.a.
On collective investment securities	
Purchase locally by nonresidents	n.a.
Sale or issue locally by nonresidents	n.a.
Purchase abroad by residents	Yes.
Sale or issue abroad by residents	n.a.
Controls on derivatives and other instruments	
Purchase locally by nonresidents	n.a.

Sale or issue locally by nonresidents	n.a.
Purchase abroad by residents	Yes.
Sale or issue abroad by residents	n.a.

Controls on credit operations

Commercial credits

By residents to nonresidents	Yes.
To residents from nonresidents	n.a.

Financial credits

By residents to nonresidents	Yes.
To residents from nonresidents	n.a.

Guarantees, sureties, and financial backup facilities

By residents to nonresidents	Yes.
To residents from nonresidents	n.a.

Controls on direct investment

Outward direct investment	Yes.
Inward direct investment	Burundi guarantees foreign investors the right to invest in the country. Foreign investors are also assured an allocation of foreign exchange for the purchase of raw material abroad as well as for the repayment of loans taken out under the investment agreement.
Controls on liquidation of direct investment	Transfers of foreign capital on which a repatriation guarantee has been granted require individual authorization.

Controls on real estate transactions

Purchase abroad by residents	Purchase must be effected in foreign exchange.
Purchase locally by nonresidents	Yes.
Sale locally by nonresidents	n.a.

Provisions specific to commercial banks and other credit institutions

Borrowing abroad	Borrowing abroad must be effected through correspondent banks.
Maintenance of accounts abroad	Yes.
Lending to nonresidents (financial or commercial credits)	Yes.
Lending locally in foreign exchange	Yes.

Differential treatment of nonresident deposit accounts and/or deposit accounts in foreign exchange

Credit controls	Yes.
Investment regulations	Yes.
Provisions specific to institutional investors	No.

Changes During 1996

Exports and export proceeds	*November 12.* The portion of export proceeds from nontraditional products that may be retained was increased to 50% from 30%.

CAMBODIA

(Position as of December 31, 1996)

Status Under IMF Articles of Agreement

Article XIV	Yes.

Exchange Arrangement

Currency

The currency of Cambodia is the Cambodian riel.

Exchange rate structure

Dual

The exchange rate system comprises two rates: the official rate and the market rate. Adjustments to the official exchange rate are made daily by the National Bank of Cambodia (NBC) to limit the spread between the official and parallel market rates to less than 1%. In practice, the spread exceeds this range from time to time. The official exchange rate applies mainly to external transactions conducted by the government and state-owned enterprises.

Classification

Managed floating

The NBC quotes daily official rates, at which the Foreign Trade Bank of Cambodia (FTBC) and the Phnom Penh Municipal Bank (2 state-owned commercial banks) buy and sell foreign exchange. Other commercial banks are free to buy and sell foreign exchange at their own rates. Exchange transactions take place at the market rate. Foreign exchange dealers are permitted to buy and sell banknotes and traveler's checks at the market rate.

Exchange tax	No.
Exchange subsidy	No.
Forward exchange market	No.

Arrangements for Payments and Receipts

Prescription of currency requirements	No.

Payment arrangements

Barter agreements and open accounts	n.a.

Administration of control

Exchange control authorities

The responsibility for the management of foreign exchange rests with the Ministry of Economy and Finance and the NBC. The NBC is authorized to license commercial banks and other agents to engage in foreign exchange transactions and to regulate current and capital transactions. In practice, no restrictions apply. New foreign exchange laws that will align the de jure regime with current practice have been submitted to the National Assembly.

International security restrictions	No.
Payments arrears	No.

Controls on trade in gold (coins and/or bullion)

Controls on external trade	Restrictions on exports of gold and silver apply.

Controls on exports and imports of banknotes

On exports

   Domestic currency   n.a.

   Foreign currency   Exports are subject to prior notification to the NBC.

On imports

   Domestic currency   n.a.

   Foreign currency   There are no limits, but imports must be declared on entry.

Resident Accounts

Eligibility to hold accounts   Juridical and natural persons are eligible.

Foreign exchange accounts permitted   Yes.

Held domestically   There are no limits on the balances of these accounts, and the funds may be used to settle domestic obligations, and all transactions can be settled in foreign currency.

Held abroad   No.

Accounts in domestic currency convertible into foreign currency   No.

Nonresident Accounts

Eligibility to hold accounts   Juridical and natural persons are eligible.

Foreign exchange accounts permitted   Regulations applied to residents also apply to nonresidents.

Domestic currency accounts   No.

Imports and Import Payments

Documentation requirements for release of foreign exchange for imports

Domiciliation requirements   n.a.

Preshipment inspection   Preshipment import inspection is required for most goods.

Letters of credit   n.a.

Import licenses and other nontariff measures

Negative list   Imports of certain products are subject to control or are prohibited for reasons of national security, health, environmental well-being, or public morality.

Import taxes and/or tariffs   Import duties are levied, and an excise tax of 10% applies to selected imports.

Taxes collected through the exchange system   No.

State import monopoly   No.

Exports and Export Proceeds

Repatriation requirements	All proceeds from exports by state-owned enterprises must be sold to or deposited with the FTBC; private sector entities must hold export proceeds in accounts with resident commercial banks.
Surrender requirements	Yes.
Financing requirements	No.
Export licenses	
Without quotas	Exports of a limited list of goods by both state-owned and private sector entities must be licensed by the Ministry of Commerce. Export licenses are required for sawed timber, logs, and rice.
With quotas	Exports of rice, gems, and sawed timber are subject to a quota. Exports of antiques are restricted.
Export taxes	An excise tax of 10% of the estimated market value applies to exports of timber and other selected exports.
Taxes collected through the exchange system	No.

Payments for Invisible Transactions and Current Transfers

Controls on these payments	Payments for invisibles related to trade are not restricted, but are regulated by the Investment Law.
Payments for travel	
Prior approval	Yes.
Quantitative limits	An exchange allowance of $10,000 a person is granted at the official rate for all types of travel, irrespective of the length of stay; amounts in excess of this limit must be approved by the NBC. In practice, however, there are no limits.

Proceeds from Invisible Transactions and Current Transfers

Repatriation requirements	The requirement applies only to state-owned enterprises.
Surrender requirements	Only proceeds from invisibles earned by state-owned enterprises must be surrendered.

Capital Transactions

Controls on capital and money market instruments	There are no specific laws on capital market securities, and there is no issue of securities in national currency.
On capital market securities	
Purchase locally by nonresidents	Purchases are subject to approval by the Cambodia Investment Board.
Sale or issue locally by nonresidents	n.a.
Purchase abroad by residents	Approval of the government of Cambodia is required.
Sale or issue abroad by residents	Yes.
On money market instruments	Yes.
On collective investment securities	Yes.
Controls on derivatives and other instruments	There are no derivatives in national currency.
Purchase locally by nonresidents	Yes.

Sale or issue locally by nonresidents	Yes.
Purchase abroad by residents	Yes.
Sale or issue abroad by residents	Yes.
Controls on credit operations	
Commercial credits	
By residents to nonresidents	Interbank lending is free.
Financial credits	
By residents to nonresidents	In practice, there are no controls on these credits.
To residents from nonresidents	Borrowing abroad by public sector agencies is permitted only with the approval of the Ministry of Economy and Finance.
Guarantees, sureties, and financial backup facilities	In practice, there are no controls on these credits.
Controls on direct investment	
Outward direct investment	The requirement of government approval is not enforced.
Inward direct investment	Foreign investors are required to obtain approval from the Council for Development of Cambodia (CDC), but there are no foreign exchange restrictions.
Controls on liquidation of direct investment	Liquidation of foreign direct investment requires approval of the CDC or NBC, but in practice, this requirement is not enforced.
Controls on real estate transactions	
Purchase locally by nonresidents	Nonresidents may not own land in Cambodia.
Sale locally by nonresidents	n.a.
Provisions specific to commercial banks and other credit institutions	In practice, there are some controls.
Borrowing abroad	Yes.
Maintenance of accounts abroad	Yes.
Lending to nonresidents (financial or commercial credits)	Yes.
Lending locally in foreign exchange	Yes.
Purchase of locally issued securities denominated in foreign exchange	Yes.
Differential treatment of nonresident deposit accounts and/or deposit accounts in foreign exchange	
Credit controls	There are global and individual limits.
Open foreign exchange position limits	Banks are not allowed to exceed their short or long position in any single foreign currency by more than 5% and in all foreign currencies by more than 15% of the bank's net worth.
Provisions specific to institutional investors	There are no institutional investors in Cambodia.
Other controls imposed by securities laws	There are no securities laws.

Changes During 1996

No significant changes occurred in the exchange and trade system.

CAMEROON

(Position as of December 31, 1996)

Status Under IMF Articles of Agreement

Article VIII   Date of acceptance: June 1, 1996.

Exchange Arrangement

Currency   The currency of Cameroon is the CFA franc.

Exchange rate structure   Unitary.

Classification

Pegged   The CFA franc is pegged to the French franc at the fixed rate of CFAF 1 per F 0.01. Exchange transactions in French francs between the BEAC and commercial banks take place at the same rate. Buying and selling rates for certain other foreign currencies are also officially posted, with quotations based on the fixed rate for the French franc and the rates in the Paris exchange market for the currencies concerned. A commission of 0.25% is levied on transfers to countries that are not members of the BEAC, except transfers in respect of central and local government operations, payments for imports covered by a duly issued license and domiciled with a bank, scheduled repayments on loans properly obtained abroad, travel allowances and official representation expenses paid by the government and its agencies for official missions, and payments of reinsurance premiums.

Exchange tax   No.

Exchange subsidy   No.

Forward exchange market   Forward exchange cover requires the prior authorization of the exchange control authorities. It must be denominated in the currency of settlement prescribed in the contract, and the maturity period must be between 3 months and 9 months. Settlements must be effected within 8 days of the maturity date of the forward contract.

Official cover of forward operations   No.

Arrangements for Payments and Receipts

Prescription of currency requirements   Since Cameroon is an Operations Account country, settlements with France, Monaco, and the Operations Account countries are made in CFA francs, French francs, or the currency of any other Operations Account country. Settlements with all other countries are usually made through correspondent banks in France in any of the currencies of those countries or in French francs through foreign accounts in French francs.

Payment arrangements

Bilateral arrangements   n.a.

Regional arrangements   An Operations Account is maintained with the French Treasury.

Clearing agreements   n.a.

Barter agreements and open accounts   n.a.

Administration of control

Exchange control authorities   Exchange control is administered by the Directorate of Economic Controls and External Finance of the Ministry of Finance (MOF). Exchange transactions relating to all countries must be effected through authorized intermediaries (i.e., the Postal Administration and authorized banks). Import licenses for goods other than gold are issued by the Ministry of Commerce and Industry, and those for gold by the Ministry of Mines, Water, and Energy (MMWE). Export licenses are issued by the MOF.

Controls on trade in gold (coins and/or bullion)

Controls on domestic ownership and/or trade

Residents are free to hold, acquire, and dispose of gold jewelry in Cameroon. Approval of the MMWE is required to hold gold in any other form. Such approval is normally given only to industrial users, including jewelers. Newly mined gold must be declared to the MMWE, which authorizes either its exportation or its sale to domestic industrial users. Exports are made only to France. Both licensed and exempt imports of gold are subject to customs declaration.

Controls on external trade

Imports and exports of gold require prior authorization of the MMWE and the MOF, although such authorization is seldom granted for imports. Exempt from this requirement are (1) imports and exports by or on behalf of the monetary authorities, and (2) imports and exports of manufactured articles containing a small quantity of gold (such as gold-filled or gold-plated articles). Both licensed and exempt imports of gold are subject to customs declaration.

Controls on exports and imports of banknotes

On exports

Foreign currency

All resident travelers, regardless of destination, must declare in writing all means of payment at their disposal at the time of departure. The reexportation of foreign banknotes is allowed up to the equivalent of CFAF 250,000; reexportation above this ceiling requires documentation showing either the importation of foreign banknotes or their purchase against other means of payment registered in the name of the traveler or through the use of deposits lodged in local banks.

Resident Accounts

Eligibility to hold accounts

These accounts are not permitted.

Nonresident Accounts

Eligibility to hold accounts

Juridical and natural persons are eligible.

Foreign exchange accounts permitted

Yes.

Approval required

n.a.

Domestic currency accounts

The regulations pertaining to nonresident accounts are based on those applied in France. Since the BEAC has suspended the repurchase of BEAC banknotes circulating outside its zone of issue, BEAC banknotes received by the foreign correspondents of authorized banks and mailed to the BEAC agency in Yaoundé (capital of Cameroon) may not be credited to foreign accounts in CFA francs.

Nonresidents are allowed to maintain bank accounts in convertible francs. These accounts, held mainly by diplomatic missions, international institutions, and their nonresident employees, may be credited only with (1) proceeds of spot or forward sales of foreign currencies transferred from abroad by account owners; (2) transfers from other nonresident convertible franc accounts; and (3) payments by residents in accordance with exchange regulations. These accounts may be debited only for (1) purchases of foreign currencies; (2) transfers to other nonresident convertible franc accounts; and (3) payments to residents in accordance with exchange regulations. Nonresidents may not maintain accounts in CFA francs abroad or accounts in foreign currency in Cameroon.

Convertible into foreign currency

These accounts are permitted, but prior approval is required.

Imports and Import Payments

Financing requirements for imports   Advance import deposits are permitted if underlying contracts stipulate them.

Documentation requirements for release of foreign exchange for imports

Domiciliation requirements   All import transactions valued at more than CFAF 500,000 must be domiciled with an authorized bank if the goods are not considered in transit. Transactions involving goods in transit must be domiciled with a foreign bank.

Preshipment inspection   Imports from all countries are subject to inspection by the SGS (Société Générale de Surveillance).

Letters of credit   Letters of credit are allowed but are optional.

Import licenses used as exchange licenses   n.a.

Import licenses and other nontariff measures   In general, licenses have been replaced by simple declarations to the banks, but imports of certain products are still subject to licensing.

Positive list   n.a.

Negative list   Certain imports are prohibited for ecological, health, or safety reasons.

Open general licenses   n.a.

Licenses with quotas   n.a.

Import taxes and/or tariffs   Import tariffs range from 5% to 30%. Duties on products from members of the UDEAC are 20% of the rates applicable to nonmembers. Import surcharges apply to imports from countries outside the UDEAC. An import surcharge of 20% is applied to maize meal while a 10% surcharge is applied to imports of cement. Surcharges apply to imports from countries outside the UDEAC and to imports of maize meal and cement.

Taxes collected through the exchange system   Yes.

State import monopoly   There is a state import monopoly only for imports relating to sovereign expenditure (defense, security, etc.).

Exports and Export Proceeds

Repatriation requirements   Proceeds from exports to all countries must be repatriated within 30 days of the payment date stipulated in the sales contract.

Surrender requirements   Proceeds received in currencies other than those of France or an Operations Account country must be surrendered within 1 month of collection.

Financing requirements   No.

Documentation requirements

Letters of credit   Letters of credit are optional.

Domiciliation   Exports to all countries are subject to domiciliation requirements for the appropriate documents. Export transactions valued at CFAF 500,000 or more must be domiciled with an authorized bank.

Preshipment inspection   Exports to all countries are subject to inspection by the SGS.

Export licenses   Licenses are required for all exports valued at the equivalent of at least CFAF 500,000.

Without quotas   Yes.

Export taxes	An export tax of 13.5% is levied on coffee, cocoa, cotton, rubber, sugar, and medicinal plants; a specific tax of CFAF 6,500 per ton is levied on bananas. An export tax of 25% is applied to timber, and rates ranging from 15% to 25% are applied to semiprocessed timber.
Taxes collected through the exchange system	No.

Payments for Invisible Transactions and Current Transfers

Controls on these payments	Payments in excess of CFAF 500,000 for invisibles to France, Monaco, and the Operations Account countries require prior declaration and are subject to presentation of relevant invoices. Payments for invisibles related to trade follow the same regime as basic trade transactions, as do transfers of income accruing to nonresidents in the form of profits, dividends, and royalties. All payments and transfers are subject to prior approval, indicative limits, and/or bona fide tests.
Freight/insurance	Except in the case of foreigners working in Cameroon temporarily who have been insured previously, residents and nonresidents are not allowed to contract insurance abroad when the same services are available in Cameroon. However, payments of premiums for authorized contracts are not restricted.
Payments for travel	
Quantitative limits	Residents traveling for tourism or business purposes to countries other than France, Monaco, and the Operations Account countries may be granted foreign exchange allowances subject to the following regulations: (1) for tourist travel, CFAF 100,000 a day, up to CFAF 2 million a trip; (2) for business travel, CFAF 250,000 a day, up to CFAF 5 million a trip; and (3) allowances in excess of these limits are subject to the authorization of the MOF or, by delegation, the BEAC.
	Returning resident travelers are required to declare all means of payment in their possession upon arrival at customs and to surrender within 8 days all means of payment exceeding the equivalent of CFAF 25,000.
Foreign workers wages	
Quantitative limits	The transfer of up to 50% of the salary of a foreigner working in Cameroon, depending on the number of dependents abroad, is permitted upon presentation of the appropriate pay voucher, provided that the transfer takes place within 1 month of the pay period concerned.
Credit card use abroad	
Prior approval	The use of credit cards, which must be issued by resident financial intermediaries and approved by the MOF, is limited to the ceilings indicated above for tourism and business travel.

Proceeds from Invisible Transactions and Current Transfers

Repatriation requirements	All receipts from services and all income earned abroad must be collected within 1 month of the due date.
Surrender requirements	Foreign currency receipts must be surrendered within 1 month of collection. Returning resident travelers are required to declare all means of payment in their possession upon arrival at customs and to surrender within 8 days all means of payment exceeding the equivalent of CFAF 25,000.
Restrictions on use of funds	No.

Capital Transactions

Controls on capital and money market instruments	Capital transactions between Cameroon and France, Monaco, and the Operations Account countries are free of exchange control. Outward capital transfers to all other countries require exchange control approval and are restricted. Inward capital transfers are free of restrictions, except for foreign direct investments and borrowing, which are subject to registration and authorization.

On capital market securities

Sale or issue locally by nonresidents	Yes.
Purchase abroad by residents	The issuing, advertising, or offering for sale of foreign securities in Cameroon requires prior authorization of the MOF and must subsequently be reported to it. Exempt from authorization, however, and subject only to a report after the fact, are operations in connection with shares similar to securities, when their issuing, advertising, or offering for sale in Cameroon has already been authorized. All foreign securities and titles embodying claims on nonresidents must be deposited with an authorized intermediary and are classified as foreign, whether they belong to residents or nonresidents.
Sale or issue abroad by residents	Yes.

On money market instruments

Sale or issue locally by nonresidents	Yes.
Purchase abroad by residents	Yes.
Sale or issue abroad by residents	Yes.

On collective investment securities

Sale or issue locally by nonresidents	n.a.
Purchase abroad by residents	Yes.
Sale or issue abroad by residents	Yes.

Controls on credit operations

Commercial credits

By residents to nonresidents	Lending abroad by natural and juridical persons, whether public or private, whose normal residence or registered office is in Cameroon, or by branches or subsidiaries in Cameroon of juridical persons whose registered office is abroad, requires prior authorization of the MOF and must subsequently be reported to it. The following are, however, exempt from prior authorization and require only a report: (1) loans constituting a direct investment abroad for which prior approval has been obtained, as indicated above; (2) loans directly connected with the rendering of services abroad by the persons or firms mentioned above, or with the financing of commercial transactions either between Cameroon and countries abroad or between foreign countries, in which these persons or firms take part; and (3) loans of up to CFAF 500,000, provided the maturity does not exceed 2 years and the rate of interest does not exceed 6% a year.
To residents from nonresidents	Borrowing abroad by natural and juridical persons, whether public or private, whose normal residence or registered office is in Cameroon, or by branches or subsidiaries in Cameroon of juridical persons whose registered office is abroad, requires prior authorization of the MOF and must subsequently be reported to it. The following are, however, exempt from this authorization and require only a report: (1) loans directly connected with the rendering of services abroad by the persons or firms mentioned above, or with the financing of commercial transactions either between Cameroon and countries abroad or between foreign countries, in which these persons or firms take part; (2) loans contracted by registered banks and credit institutions; and (3) loans backed by a guarantee from the government.

Financial credits	Yes.
Guarantees, sureties, and financial backup facilities	Yes.

Controls on direct investment

Outward direct investment	Direct investments abroad (including those made through foreign companies that are directly or indirectly controlled by persons in Cameroon and those made by branches or subsidiaries abroad of companies in Cameroon) require prior approval of the MOF, unless they take the form of a capital increase resulting from the reinvestment of undistributed profits or do not exceed 20% of the fair market value of the company being purchased.
Inward direct investment	Foreign direct investments in Cameroon (including those made by companies in Cameroon that are directly or indirectly under foreign control and those made by branches or subsidiaries of foreign companies in Cameroon) require prior declaration to the MOF, unless they take the form of a capital increase resulting from reinvestment of undistributed profits; the ministry has a period of 2 months from receipt of the declaration during which it may request postponement.

Controls on liquidation of direct investment	The full or partial liquidation of direct investments in Cameroon requires only a report to the MOF, unless the operation involves the relinquishing of a participation that had previously been approved as constituting a direct investment in Cameroon.

Controls on real estate transactions

Purchase abroad by residents	Yes.
Purchase locally by nonresidents	n.a.
Sale locally by nonresidents	n.a.

Provisions specific to commercial banks and other credit institutions	At least one-third of the share capital of banks must be owned by nationals. Banks with foreign majority participation must submit to the monetary authorities information on all current transactions abroad and obtain prior approval for any changes in the structure of their equity holdings. Foreign managers must be approved by the monetary authorities and reside in Cameroon.

Changes During 1996

Status under IMF Articles of Agreement	*June 1.* Cameroon accepted the obligations of Article VIII, Sections 2, 3, and 4 of the Fund Articles of Agreement.
Exports and export proceeds	*July 1.* The export tax rate on coffee, cocoa, cotton, rubber, palm oil, sugar, and medicinal plants was reduced to 13.5%, and the specific tax on bananas was reduced to CFAF 6,500 per ton. The export tax regime for timber was changed: an export tax rate of 25% is applied to timber, and rates between 15% and 25% are applied to semiprocessed timber.

CANADA

(Position as of December 31, 1996)

Status Under IMF Articles of Agreement

Article VIII

Date of acceptance: March 25, 1952.

Exchange Arrangement

Currency

The currency of Canada is the Canadian dollar.

Exchange rate structure

Unitary

The Canadian authorities do not maintain margins in respect of exchange transactions.

Classification

Independent floating

The exchange rate of the Canadian dollar is determined on the basis of supply and demand; however, the authorities intervene from time to time to maintain orderly conditions in the market.

Exchange tax

No.

Exchange subsidy

No.

Forward exchange market

Forward exchange rates are freely determined in the exchange market.

Official cover of forward operations

No.

Arrangements for Payments and Receipts

Prescription of currency requirements

No.

Payment arrangements

No.

Administration of control

Exchange control authorities

There are no exchange controls. The licensing of imports and exports, when required, is handled mostly by the Department of Foreign Affairs and International Trade, but other departments also issue licenses in specialized fields.

International security restrictions

In accordance with IMF Executive Board Decision No. 144-(52/51)

Canada notified the IMF on July 23, 1992 that in compliance with UN Security Council Resolution No. 757 (1992), certain restrictions had been imposed on the making of payments and transfers for current international transactions in respect of the Federal Republic of Yugoslavia (Serbia/Montenegro).

In accordance with UN sanctions

Canada imposed restrictions on financial transactions with Bosnia and Herzegovina in accordance with UN Security Council Resolution No. 942.

Payments arrears

No.

Controls on trade in gold (coins and/or bullion)

Controls on external trade

Reexports of gold of U.S. origin to all countries except the United States require a permit. Commercial imports of articles containing minor quantities of gold, such as watches, are unrestricted and free of license.

Controls on exports and imports of banknotes

No.

Resident Accounts

Eligibility to hold accounts	Juridical and natural persons are eligible.
Foreign exchange accounts permitted	Yes.
Held domestically	Yes.
Held abroad	n.a.
Accounts in domestic currency convertible into foreign currency	Yes.

Nonresident Accounts

Eligibility to hold accounts	Juridical and natural persons are eligible.
Foreign exchange accounts permitted	Yes.
Domestic currency accounts	Yes.
Convertible into foreign currency	Yes.
Blocked accounts	Certain assets connected to Iraq, Libya, and the Federal Republic of Yugoslavia (Serbia/Montenegro) are frozen, pursuant to resolutions of the UN Security Council.

Imports and Import Payments

Foreign exchange budget	No.
Financing requirements for imports	No.
Documentation requirements for release of foreign exchange for imports	No.
Import licenses and other nontariff measures	Measures consistent with international trade obligations (e.g., antidumping, countervailing duties, and safeguard provisions) are maintained.
Negative list	Import permits are required for only a few agricultural items, certain textile products and clothing, certain endangered species of fauna and flora, natural gas, and material and equipment for the production or use of atomic energy. In 1995, permits were required for the importation of controlled substances classified as dangerous drugs and certain military armaments. In addition, Health Canada does not permit the importation of drugs not registered with it. Commercial imports of used motor vehicles (less than 15 years old) have been generally prohibited. However, the prohibition of imports of used vehicles from the United States was eliminated in 1994. The prohibition on imports of used vehicles from Mexico will be phased out by January 1, 2019.
Open general licenses	Yes.
Licenses with quotas	Imports of some clothing and certain textile products, usually in the form of bilateral restraint agreements (Memoranda of Understanding) concluded under the MFA negotiated within the framework of the GATT, are also subject to quantitative restrictions. In accordance with the provisions of the Uruguay Round Agreement on textiles and clothing, Canada's system of import controls on textiles and clothing is being liberalized in stages over a ten-year period beginning January 1, 1995. As a result of the commitments made under the Uruguay Round Agreement, Canada has agreed to replace all agricultural import restrictions with tariff rate quotas and to ensure import access levels as negotiated in the Uruguay Round (or under the Canada–U.S. Free Trade Agreement).

| Import taxes and/or tariffs | No. |
| State import monopoly | Certain monopolies exist at the subfederal level. |

Exports and Export Proceeds

Repatriation requirements	No.
Surrender requirements	No.
Financing requirements	No.
Documentation requirements	No.

Export licenses

Without quotas — The Export Control List identifies all goods that are controlled in order to implement intergovernmental arrangements, maintain supplies, or ensure security. It includes all items identified in the International Munitions List, the International Industrial List, and the International Atomic Energy List. In addition, controls are maintained for supply reasons and for purposes of promoting further processing in Canada (e.g., logs, herring roe) and for nonproliferation purposes (chemical, biological, and nuclear weapons and their delivery systems). The Area Control List includes a limited number of countries to which all exports are controlled. At present, the following countries are on the Area Control List: Angola and Libya. Permits are required for the exportation of listed goods to all countries except, in most cases, the United States as well as for all goods destined to countries on the Area Control List.

| Export taxes | No. |

Payments for Invisible Transactions and Current Transfers

| Controls on these payments | No. |

Proceeds from Invisible Transactions and Current Transfers

Repatriation requirements	No.
Surrender requirements	No.
Restrictions on use of funds	No.

Capital Transactions

Controls on capital and money market instruments	No.
Controls on derivatives and other instruments	No.
Controls on credit operations	No.

Controls on direct investment

Inward direct investment — Specific restrictions exist on inward direct investments in the broadcasting, telecommunications, transportation, fishery, and energy sectors. In addition, under the provision of the Investment Canada Act, new foreign investments are in general subject to notification requirements but not to review requirements. As a result of the NAFTA, only direct acquisitions of businesses with assets exceeding Can$168 million were subject to review during 1996; the amount was raised to Can$172 million for 1997. Indirect acquisitions are no longer subject to review. These provisions were multilateralized as part of

Canada's implementation of the Uruguay Round results. Investments subject to review are required only to pass a test proving that they will yield a net benefit to Canada.

Different thresholds apply in the case of investments made by non-WTO investors and in culturally sensitive sectors. The direct acquisition of a business with assets greater than Can$5 million and the indirect acquisition of a business with assets greater than Can$5 million and Can$50 million, which represent more than 50% of the value of the total international transaction in question, is subject to review.

The establishment of a new business, the direct acquisition of a business with assets of less than Can$168 million in 1996 and Can $172 million in 1997, and the indirect acquisition of a business by investors from WTO members are not subject to review and need only be notified, except in cases when the Canadian business represents 50% or more of the value of the total assets acquired in the international acquisition. (The acquisition of a Canadian enterprise may be considered "direct" where it involves the acquisition of control of a corporation carrying on a Canadian business and "indirect" where it involves the transfer of control of a non-Canadian corporation, which then controls a Canadian corporation carrying on a Canadian business.)

The direct acquisition of a business whose assets exceed the above-mentioned limit is reviewed and assessed according to its net benefit to Canada, authorization being generally granted. All acquisitions or investments to establish a new business in cultural sectors such as book publishing, sound recording, and film are normally subject to review. Reviewable cases must be resolved within 75 days, unless the investor agrees to a longer time period. In practice, most cases are resolved within 45 days.

Controls on liquidation of direct investment	No.
Controls on real estate transactions	No.
Provisions specific to commercial banks and other credit institutions	No.
Provisions specific to institutional investors	No.
Other controls imposed by securities laws	No.

Changes During 1996

No significant changes occurred in the exchange and trade system.

CAPE VERDE

(Position as of December 31, 1996)

Status Under IMF Articles of Agreement

Article XIV	Yes.

Exchange Arrangement

Currency	The currency of Cape Verde is the Cape Verde escudo.
Exchange rate structure	Unitary.
Classification	
Pegged	The Cape Verde escudo is pegged to a weighted basket of the currencies of the most important suppliers of imports and sources of emigrant remittances, including the United States. The composition of the basket is revised annually; weights are determined using a formula giving a two-thirds weight to imports and a one-third weight to remittances. The exchange rate of the Cape Verde escudo is expressed in terms of the U.S. dollar, the intervention currency, and fixed daily on the basis of quotations for the U.S. dollar and the other currencies included in the basket.
Exchange tax	No.
Exchange subsidy	No.
Forward exchange market	No.

Arrangements for Payments and Receipts

Prescription of currency requirements	Most dealings in foreign exchange with the general public are conducted by the 2 commercial banks, Banca Commercial do Atlantico (BCA) and Caija Economia de Cabo Verde (CECV). Export proceeds from invisibles must be repatriated in convertible currencies.
Payment arrangements	
Bilateral arrangements	
Inoperative	There are agreements with Angola and São Tomé and Príncipe, under which Cape Verde is a net creditor.
Regional arrangements	n.a.
Clearing agreements	n.a.
Barter agreements and open accounts	n.a.
Administration of control	
Exchange control authorities	All foreign exchange transactions are under the control of the Bank of Cape Verde (BCV), the central bank.
International security restrictions	Yes.
In accordance with IMF Executive Board Decision No. 144-(52/51)	n.a.
In accordance with UN sanctions	n.a.
Other	n.a.
Payment arrears	Yes.

Official	n.a.
Private	n.a.

Controls on trade in gold (coins and/or bullion)

Controls on domestic ownership and/or trade	n.a.
Controls on external trade	Imports and exports of gold require prior licensing by the BCV.

Controls on exports and imports of banknotes

On exports

Domestic currency	The exportation of domestic currency by travelers is prohibited.
Foreign currency	Residents traveling abroad may take out the equivalent of C.V. Esc 100,000.

On imports

Domestic currency	The importation of domestic currency is prohibited.
Foreign currency	Foreign travelers may bring in any amount but may reexport only up to the amount they declared upon entry.

Resident Accounts

n.a.

Nonresident Accounts

Eligibility to hold accounts	Juridical and natural persons are eligible.
Foreign exchange accounts permitted	Foreign enterprises may maintain accounts in foreign currency. Three types of special interest-bearing deposit accounts are available for emigrants: (1) foreign exchange deposit accounts, (2) savings-credit deposit accounts, and (3) special accounts in Cape Verde escudos. These accounts may be credited only with convertible foreign currencies and allow holders of savings-credit deposit accounts to benefit from loans on special terms for financing small-scale projects. Interest on such accounts may be freely remitted abroad.
Domestic currency accounts	Nonresidents may open demand deposit accounts in local currency. These accounts may be credited only with the proceeds from the sale, or surrender of receipts, of convertible currencies and may be debited for payment of any obligations in Cape Verde. Outward transfers of balances from such accounts may be made freely. Embassies and foreign officials of embassies are required to open special accounts in local currency; such accounts must be replenished exclusively with foreign exchange.
Convertible into foreign currency	Yes.

Imports and Import Payments

Documentation requirements for release of foreign exchange for imports	Imports of goods exceeding C.V. Esc 100,000 and not involving payments from the country's foreign exchange resources are subject to the preregistration requirement.
Domiciliation requirements	n.a.
Preshipment inspection	n.a.

Letters of credit	n.a.
Import licenses used as exchange licenses	n.a.
Import licenses and other nontariff measures	Licenses, which are issued by the General Directorate of Commerce in the Ministry of Economy, Transportation, and Communications, require the endorsement of the BCV and are generally valid for 90 days; they are renewable. The provision of foreign exchange is guaranteed when the license has been previously certified by the BCV. Licenses are, in general, granted liberally for imports of medicines, capital goods, and other development-related equipment. Imports with a value of less than C.V. Esc 100,000 are exempt from the licensing requirement.
Positive list	Yes.
Negative list	n.a.
Open general licenses	n.a.
Licenses with quotas	Most locally produced food items and beverages (e.g., fish, bread, tomatoes, bananas, cereals, salt, beer, and soft drinks) are subject to a global annual import quota; some items (e.g., potatoes, onions, and poultry) are subject to seasonal quotas.
State import monopoly	The importation of maize, rice, sugar, and cooking oil is conducted by state monopolies.

Exports and Export Proceeds

Repatriation requirements	Export proceeds must be repatriated within 3 months, but this period may be extended.
Surrender requirements	Yes.
Financing requirements	No.
Documentation requirements	No.
Export licenses	No.

Payments for Invisible Transactions and Current Transfers

Controls on these payments	
Freight/insurance	
Prior approval	Yes.
Quantitative limits	Yes.
Indicative limits/bona fide test	n.a.
Unloading/storage costs	
Prior approval	Yes.
Quantitative limits	Yes.
Indicative limits/bona fide test	n.a.
Administrative expenses	
Prior approval	Yes.
Quantitative limits	Yes.
Indicative limits/bona fide test	n.a.
Commissions	
Prior approval	Yes.

Quantitative limits	Yes.
Indicative limits/bona fide test	n.a.
Payments for travel	For business travel, the foreign currency allowance varies according to the country of destination and the duration of each trip.
Prior approval	For amounts exceeding C.V. Esc 100,000, approval is required.
Quantitative limits	Yes.
Indicative limits/bona fide test	n.a.
Medical costs	
Prior approval	Yes.
Quantitative limits	The amount varies according to medical needs.
Indicative limits/bona fide test	n.a.
Study abroad costs	
Prior approval	For amounts exceeding C.V. Esc 100,000, approval is required.
Quantitative limits	The limit is C.V. Esc 100,000 on leaving the country; students who do not hold scholarships are, in addition, entitled to a monthly allowance that varies according to the country of destination.
Indicative limits/bona fide test	n.a.
Consulting/legal fees	
Prior approval	For amounts exceeding C.V. Esc 200,000, approval is required.
Quantitative limits	n.a.
Indicative limits/bona fide test	n.a.
Foreign workers' wages	Transfers by foreign technical assistance personnel working in Cape Verde are authorized within the limits specified in the individual contracts. These contracts, as well as other contracts involving foreign exchange expenditures, are subject to prior screening by the BCV. Requests by other foreigners are examined on a case-by-case basis.
Prior approval	Yes.
Quantitative limits	n.a.
Indicative limits/bona fide test	n.a.
Family maintenance/alimony	
Prior approval	For amounts exceeding C.V. Esc 50,000, approval is required.
Quantitative limits	n.a.
Indicative limits/bona fide test	n.a.

Proceeds from Invisible Transactions and Current Transfers

Repatriation requirements	Yes.
Surrender requirements	Yes.

Capital Transactions

Controls on capital and money market instruments	Capital transactions must be approved in advance by the BCV, but legally imported capital, including foreign direct investment, may be reexported without limitation. The exportation of resident-owned capital is not normally permitted.

On capital market securities

   Purchase locally by nonresidents   n.a.

   Sale or issue locally by nonresidents   n.a.

   Purchase abroad by residents   Yes.

   Sale or issue abroad by residents   n.a.

On money market instruments

   Purchase locally by nonresidents   n.a.

   Sale or issue locally by nonresidents   n.a.

   Purchase abroad by residents   Yes.

   Sale or issue abroad by residents   n.a.

On collective investment securities

   Purchase locally by nonresidents   n.a.

   Sale or issue locally by nonresidents   n.a.

   Purchase abroad by residents   Yes.

   Sale or issue abroad by residents   n.a.

Controls on derivatives and other instruments

Purchase locally by nonresidents   n.a.

Sale or issue locally by nonresidents   n.a.

Purchase abroad by residents   Yes.

Sale or issue abroad by residents   n.a.

Controls on credit operations

Commercial credits

   By residents to nonresidents   Yes.

   To residents from nonresidents   n.a.

Financial credits

   By residents to nonresidents   Yes.

   To residents from nonresidents   n.a.

Guarantees, sureties, and financial backup facilities

   By residents to nonresidents   Yes.

   To residents from nonresidents   n.a.

Controls on direct investment

Outward direct investment   Yes.

Inward direct investment   n.a.

Controls on liquidation of direct investment   No.

Controls on real estate transactions

Purchase abroad by residents	Yes.
Purchase locally by nonresidents	n.a.
Sale locally by nonresidents	n.a.

Provisions specific to commercial banks and other credit institutions

Borrowing abroad	n.a.
Maintenance of accounts abroad	n.a.
Lending to nonresidents (financial or commercial credits)	n.a.
Lending locally in foreign exchange	n.a.
Purchase of locally issued securities denominated in foreign exchange	n.a.
Differential treatment of nonresident deposit accounts and/or deposit accounts in foreign exchange	n.a.
Investment regulations	n.a.
Open foreign exchange position limits	The BCA and the CECV are allowed net foreign exchange positions of up to the equivalent of $1.5 million and $1 million, respectively.

Changes During 1996

No significant changes occurred in the exchange and trade system.

CENTRAL AFRICAN REPUBLIC

(Position as of December 31, 1996)

Status Under IMF Articles of Agreement

Article VIII   Date of acceptance: June 1, 1996.

Exchange Arrangement

Currency   The currency of the Central African Republic is the CFA franc.

Exchange rate structure   Unitary.

Classification

Pegged   The CFA franc is pegged to the French franc, the intervention currency, at the fixed rate of CFAF 1 per F 0.01. Exchange transactions in French francs between the BEAC and commercial banks take place at that rate, free of commission. Buying and selling rates for certain other foreign currencies are also officially posted, with quotations based on the fixed rate for the French franc and the rates in the Paris exchange market for the currencies concerned. A commission of 0.25% is levied on all capital transfers to countries that are not members of the BEAC, except those made for the account of the Treasury and for the expenses of students.

Exchange tax   No.

Exchange subsidy   No.

Forward exchange market   There are no forward exchange markets. However, allowed by the fixed peg with the French franc, exporters and importers can always cover their position on the Paris foreign exchange market.

Arrangements for Payments and Receipts

**Prescription of currency
requirements**   Settlements with France, Monaco, and the Operations Account countries are made in CFA francs, French francs, or the currency of any other institute of issue that maintains an Operations Account with the French Treasury. Settlements with all other countries are usually made in the currencies of those countries or in French francs through foreign accounts in francs.

Payment arrangements

Clearing agreements   An Operations Account is maintained with the French Treasury, linking Operations Account countries. All purchases or sales of foreign currencies or French francs against CFA francs are ultimately settled through a debit or credit to the Operations Account.

Administration of control

Exchange control authorities   All draft legislation, directives, correspondence, and contracts having a direct or indirect bearing on the finances of the state require the prior approval of the Ministry of Finance (MOF). The Autonomous Amortization Fund (CAADE) of the MOF supervises borrowing abroad. The Office of Foreign Financial Relations of the same ministry supervises lending abroad; the issuing, advertising, or offering for sale of foreign securities in the Central African Republic; and inward and outward direct investment. Exchange control is administered by the MOF, which has delegated some approval authority to the BEAC (control over the external position of the banks, granting of exceptional travel allocations in excess of the basic allowances, and control over the repatriation of net export proceeds), to authorized banks, and to the Postal Administration. All exchange transactions relating to foreign countries must be effected through authorized banks. Export declarations are to be made through the Directorate of Foreign Trade of the Ministry of Commerce and Industry, except those for gold, which are to be made through the BEAC.

Payment arrears	Yes.
Official	n.a.
Private	n.a.

Controls on trade in gold (coins and/or bullion)

Controls on external trade	Imports and exports of gold require a license, which is seldom granted. In practice, imports and exports are made by an authorized purchasing office. Exempt from prior authorization are (1) imports and exports by or on behalf of the Treasury, and (2) imports and exports of manufactured articles containing a small quantity of gold (such as gold-filled or gold-plated articles). Both licensed and exempt imports of gold are subject to customs declaration. Certain companies have been officially appointed as Offices for the Purchase, Import, and Export of Gold and Raw Diamonds.

Controls on exports and imports of banknotes

On exports

Domestic currency	There is no limit on the amount of banknotes that residents and nonresidents can export from one BEAC country to another. Exports of banknotes outside the BEAC zone are prohibited.
Foreign currency	All resident travelers, regardless of destination, must declare in writing all means of payment at their disposal at the time of departure. The reexportation of foreign banknotes is allowed up to the equivalent of CFAF 250,000; the reexportation of foreign banknotes above these ceilings requires documentation demonstrating either their importation or their purchase against other means of payment registered in the name of the traveler or through the use of nonresident deposits held in local banks.

On imports

Domestic currency	There is no limit on the amount of banknotes that residents and nonresidents can import from another BEAC country. Imports of banknotes from outside the BEAC zone are prohibited.

Resident Accounts

Eligibility to hold accounts	Yes.
Juridical persons	n.a.
Natural persons	n.a.
Foreign exchange accounts permitted	Yes.
Held domestically	n.a.
Held abroad	n.a.

Nonresident Accounts

Eligibility to hold accounts	Yes.
Juridical persons	n.a.
Natural persons	n.a.
Domestic currency accounts	The regulations pertaining to nonresident accounts are based on regulations applied in France. The principal nonresident accounts are foreign accounts in francs. As the BEAC has suspended the repurchase of BEAC banknotes circulating outside the territories of

its member countries, BEAC banknotes received by the foreign correspondents of authorized banks and mailed to the BEAC agency in Bangui may not be credited to foreign accounts in francs.

Convertible into foreign currency	n.a.

Imports and Import Payments

Financing requirements for imports	No.
Documentation requirements for release of foreign exchange for imports	
Domiciliation requirements	All import transactions relating to foreign countries must be domiciled with an authorized bank.
Preshipment inspection	n.a.
Letters of credit	n.a.
Import licenses used as exchange licenses	Import declarations are required for all imports, and the import license entitles importers to purchase the necessary exchange, provided that the shipping documents are submitted to the authorized bank.
Import licenses and other nontariff measures	
Negative list	Imports of firearms of any origin are prohibited.
Import taxes and/or tariffs	The UDEAC CET applies; there are 4 rates: 5% for essential commodities, 10% for capital goods and inputs, 20% for intermediate goods, and 30% for consumer goods. The intra-UDEAC tariff is 20% of the CET.
Taxes collected through the exchange system	n.a.

Exports and Export Proceeds

Repatriation requirements	Proceeds must be collected and repatriated within 1 month of the due date, which must not be later than 90 days after the arrival of the goods at their destination, unless special authorization is obtained.
Surrender requirements	Export proceeds received in currencies other than French francs or those of an Operations Account country must be surrendered.
Documentation requirements	
Letters of credit	n.a.
Guarantees	n.a.
Domiciliation	All export transactions must be domiciled with an authorized bank.
Preshipment inspection	n.a.
Export licenses	All exports require a declaration.
Without quotas	Yes.
With quotas	n.a.
Export taxes	n.a.
Taxes collected through the exchange system	No.

Payments for Invisible Transactions and Current Transfers

Controls on these payments
Payments for invisibles to France, Monaco, and the Operations Account countries are permitted freely; those to other countries are subject to approval. Approval authority for many types of payment has been delegated to authorized banks. Prior approval is required for payments for freight and insurance, unloading and storage costs, administrative expenses, interest, commissions, travel, medical costs, and use of credit cards abroad, as well as for remittances of profits and dividends. However, payments for invisibles related to trade are permitted freely when the basic trade transaction has been approved or does not require authorization.

Payments for travel

Quantitative limits
Residents traveling to other countries of the franc zone may obtain an unlimited allocation in French francs. Within the BEAC zone, BEAC banknotes can be exported without limit. The allowances for travel to countries outside the franc zone are subject to the following regulations: (1) for tourist travel, CFAF 100,000 a day, with a maximum of CFAF 2 million a trip; (2) for business travel, CFAF 250,000 a day, with a maximum of CFAF 5 million a trip; (3) allowances in excess of these limits are subject to the authorization of the MOF or, by delegation, the BEAC. Returning resident travelers are required to declare all means of payment in their possession upon arrival at customs and surrender within 8 days all means of payment exceeding the equivalent of CFAF 25,000.

All resident travelers, regardless of destination, must declare in writing all means of payment at their disposal at the time of departure. The reexportation by nonresident travelers of means of payment other than banknotes registered in their name and issued abroad is not restricted. However, documentation is required that such means of payment has been purchased with funds drawn from a foreign account in CFA francs or with other foreign exchange.

Indicative limits/bona fide test
Bona fide requests for allowances in excess of the limits are normally granted.

Medical costs

Quantitative limits
The allowance for sick persons traveling to countries outside the franc zone for medical reasons is CFAF 100,000 a day, with a maximum of CFAF 2,500,000.

Indicative limits/bona fide test
Yes.

Study abroad costs

Quantitative limits
The limit is CFAF 1,000,000.

Indicative limits/bona fide test
Yes.

Consulting/legal fees

Prior approval
n.a.

Foreign workers' wages

Prior approval
n.a.

Quantitative limits
Foreign nationals working in the BEAC zone are allowed to transfer 50% of their net salary upon presentation of their pay vouchers, provided that the transfers take place within 3 months of the pay period concerned.

Pensions

Prior approval
n.a.

Gambling/prize earnings

Prior approval
n.a.

Family maintenance/alimony

Prior approval
n.a.

Credit card use abroad

    Quantitative limits   The use of credit cards, which must be issued by resident financial intermediaries and approved by the MOF, is limited to the ceilings set for tourism and business travel.

    Indicative limits/bona fide test   Bona fide requests for allowances in excess of limits are normally granted.

Proceeds from Invisible Transactions and Current Transfers

Repatriation requirements   Proceeds from transactions in invisibles with France, Monaco, and the Operations Account countries may be retained. All amounts due from residents of other countries in respect of services, and all income earned in those countries from foreign assets, must be collected within 1 month of the due date.

Surrender requirements   If payment is received in foreign currency, it must be surrendered within 1 month of the date of receipt.

Capital Transactions

Controls on capital and money market instruments   Capital movements between the Central African Republic and France, Monaco, and the Operations Account countries are free of exchange control. Capital transfers to all other countries require exchange control approval and are restricted, but capital receipts from such countries are permitted freely.

On capital market securities

    Purchase locally by nonresidents   n.a.

    Sale or issue locally by nonresidents   The issuing, advertising, or offering for sale of foreign securities in the Central African Republic requires prior authorization from the MOF. Exempt from authorization, however, are operations in connection with (1) loans backed by a guarantee from the government; and (2) shares similar to securities, when issuing, advertising, or offering them for sale in the Central African Republic has previously been authorized.

    Purchase abroad by residents   Yes.

    Sale or issue abroad by residents   n.a.

On money market instruments

    Purchase locally by nonresidents   n.a.

    Sale or issue locally by nonresidents   n.a.

    Purchase abroad by residents   Yes.

    Sale or issue abroad by residents   n.a.

On collective investment securities

    Purchase locally by nonresidents   n.a.

    Sale or issue locally by nonresidents   n.a.

    Purchase abroad by residents   Yes.

    Sale or issue abroad by residents   n.a.

Controls on derivatives and other instruments

Purchase locally by nonresidents   n.a.

Sale or issue locally by nonresidents   n.a.

Purchase abroad by residents	Yes.
Sale or issue abroad by residents	n.a.

Controls on credit operations

Commercial credits

By residents to nonresidents

Lending abroad by residents or by branches or subsidiaries in the Central African Republic of juridical persons whose registered office is abroad, requires prior authorization from the MOF. Exempt from this authorization are (1) loans granted by registered banks, and (2) other loans when the total amount of loans outstanding does not exceed CFAF 50 million for any one lender. The contracting of loans that are exempt from authorization and each repayment must be reported to the Office of Foreign Financial Relations within 20 days of the operation, except when the amount of the loan granted abroad by the lender is less than CFAF 500,000.

To residents from nonresidents

Foreign borrowing by the government or its public and semipublic enterprises, as well as all foreign borrowing with a government guarantee, requires the prior approval of the Director of the Budget. Borrowing abroad by residents or by branches or subsidiaries in the Central African Republic and by juridical persons whose registered office is abroad requires prior authorization from the MOF. Exempt from this authorization are (1) loans constituting a direct investment abroad for which prior approval has been obtained, as indicated above; (2) loans directly connected with the rendering of services abroad by the persons or firms mentioned above, or with the financing of commercial transactions either between the Central African Republic and countries abroad, or between foreign countries in which those persons or firms take part; (3) loans contracted by registered banks; and (4) loans other than those mentioned above, when the total amount of loans outstanding does not exceed CFAF 50 million for any one borrower. Loans referred to under (4) and each repayment must be reported to the Office of Foreign Financial Relations within 20 days of the operation, unless the total outstanding amount of all loans contracted abroad by the borrower is less than CFAF 500,000.

Financial credits	Yes.
Guarantees, sureties, and financial backup facilities	Yes.

Controls on direct investment

Outward direct investment

Direct investments abroad, including those made through foreign companies that are directly or indirectly controlled by persons in the Central African Republic and those made by branches or subsidiaries abroad of companies in the Central African Republic, require the prior approval of the MOF, unless they take the form of a capital increase resulting from the reinvestment of undistributed profits.

Inward direct investment

Investments must be declared to the MOF, unless they take the form of a capital increase resulting from the reinvestment of undistributed profits; the MOF may request a postponement of up to 2 months from receipt of the declaration.

Controls on liquidation of direct investment

The liquidation of investments requires prior approval from the MOF, unless the operation involves the relinquishing of a participation that had previously been approved.

Changes During 1996

Exchange arrangements

June 1. The Central African Republic accepted the obligations of Article VIII, Sections 2, 3, and 4 of the Fund Agreement.

CHAD

(Position as of January 31, 1997)

Status Under IMF Articles of Agreement

Article VIII	Date of acceptance: June 1, 1996.

Exchange Arrangement

Currency

The currency of Chad is the CFA franc issued by the BEAC.

Exchange rate structure

Unitary.

Classification

Pegged

The CFA franc is pegged to the French franc, at the fixed rate of CFAF 1 per F 0.01. Exchange transactions in French francs between the BEAC and commercial banks take place at the rate of CFAF 1 per F 0.01, free of commission. Buying and selling rates for certain other foreign currencies are also officially posted with quotations based on the fixed rate for the French franc and the rates in the Paris exchange market for the currencies concerned. All transfers and exchange operations are subject to a commission levied by the Treasury. The commission rate amounts to 0.25% in the CFA franc zone and 0.5% outside the CFA franc zone.

Exchange tax

No.

Exchange subsidy

No.

Forward exchange market

Forward cover for imports is permitted only for specified commodities and requires the prior approval of the Office of the Ministry of Economy and Commerce.

Official cover of forward operations

n.a.

Arrangements for Payments and Receipts

Prescription of currency requirements

Since Chad is an Operations Account country, settlements with France, Monaco, and the Operations Account countries are made in CFA francs, French francs, or the currency of any other institute of issue that maintains an Operations Account with the French Treasury. Settlements with all other countries are usually made in the currencies of those countries or in French francs through foreign accounts in francs.

Payment arrangements

Regional arrangements

An Operations Account is maintained with the French Treasury.

Clearing agreements

Yes.

Administration of control

Exchange control authorities

Exchange control is administered by the Ministry of Finance (MOF), which has delegated approval authority in part to the External Finance and Exchange Control Subdirectorate, which issues instructions to the authorized banks. All exchange transactions relating to countries outside the Operations Account area must be made through authorized banks. The MOF supervises public and private sector borrowing and lending abroad; the issuing, advertising, or offering for sale of foreign securities in Chad; and inward and outward direct investment. It also issues import and export authorizations for gold.

International security restrictions

No.

Payment arrears

Official

Yes.

Private

n.a.

Controls on trade in gold (coins and/or bullion)

Controls on domestic ownership and/or trade

Residents who are not producers of gold may not hold unworked gold without specific authorization.

Controls on external trade

Imports and exports of gold require prior authorization from both the Ministry and the Directorate of Geological and Mining Research, as well as a visa from the External Finance Department. Exempt from this requirement are (1) imports and exports by or on behalf of the monetary authorities and (2) imports and exports of manufactured articles containing a small quantity of gold (such as gold-filled or gold-plated articles). Unworked gold may be exported only to France. Both licensed and exempt imports of gold are subject to customs declaration.

Controls on exports and imports of banknotes

On exports

Domestic currency

The exportation of banknotes issued by the BEAC to areas outside the BEAC area is prohibited. Nonresidents traveling from one BEAC member country to another may take with them an unlimited amount of CFA franc zone banknotes and coins.

Foreign currency

Residents visiting other CFA franc zone countries may obtain an unlimited allocation in French francs. This allocation can be provided in banknotes, traveler's checks, bank drafts, and bank or postal transfers, etc. For travel to countries outside the CFA franc zone, the exchange allocation shall depend on the type of travel and can be made in banknotes, traveler's checks, bank drafts, or postal transfers. Nonresident travelers may take out foreign exchange or other foreign means of payment up to the amount they declared on entry into the BEAC area. If they have made no declaration on entry into one of the BEAC countries, they may take out only up to the equivalent of CFAF 500,000.

On imports

Domestic currency

Resident and nonresident travelers may bring in any amount of banknotes and coins issued by the BEAC, the Bank of France, or any other bank of issue maintaining an Operations Account with the French Treasury. The importation of banknotes issued by the BEAC from areas outside the BEAC area is prohibited.

Foreign currency

Resident and nonresident travelers may bring in any amount of foreign banknotes and coins (except gold coins) of countries outside the Operations Account area.

Resident Accounts

n.a.

Nonresident Accounts

Eligibility to hold accounts

Yes.

Juridical persons

n.a.

Natural persons

n.a.

Foreign exchange accounts permitted

Principal nonresident accounts are foreign accounts in francs.

Approval required

n.a.

Domestic currency accounts

The regulations pertaining to nonresident accounts are based on regulations applied in France. As the BEAC has suspended the repurchase of BEAC banknotes circulating outside the territories of the CFA franc zone, BEAC banknotes received by the foreign correspondents of authorized banks and mailed to the BEAC agency in Chad by the Bank of France or the BCEAO may not be credited to foreign accounts in francs.

Convertible into foreign currency	n.a.
Approval required	n.a.

Imports and Import Payments

Financing requirements for imports	No.
Documentation requirements for release of foreign exchange for imports	
Domiciliation requirements	Imports in excess of CFAF 100,000 and relating to foreign countries must be domiciled with an authorized bank.
Preshipment inspection	n.a.
Letters of credit	n.a.
Import licenses and other nontariff measures	
Negative list	A special import authorization by the Ministry of Commerce and Industrial Promotion is required for imports of sulphur and other explosives.
Import taxes and/or tariffs	Import tariffs on products from countries that are not members of the UDEAC range from 5% to 30% with 4 tariff bands. Tariffs on imports from UDEAC members are 20% of MFN rates.
Taxes collected through the exchange system	No.
State import monopoly	The import monopoly on sugar was lifted on January 1, 1997.

Exports and Export Proceeds

Repatriation requirements	Export proceeds normally must be received within 180 days of the arrival of the commodities at their destination.
Surrender requirements	Export proceeds received in currencies other than those of France or of an Operations Account country must be surrendered. The proceeds must be collected and, if received in a foreign currency, surrendered within 1 month of the due date.
Documentation requirements	
Letters of credit	n.a.
Guarantees	n.a.
Domiciliation	Export transactions to foreign countries exceeding CFAF 50,000 must be domiciled with an authorized bank.
Preshipment inspection	n.a.
Export licenses	Exports of cotton are effected by the government-controlled monopoly of Cotontchad.

Payments for Invisible Transactions and Current Transfers

Controls on these payments	Payments for invisibles to France, Monaco, and the Operations Account countries are permitted freely. Payments for invisibles related to trade are permitted freely if the basic trade transaction has been approved or does not require authorization.

Some current payments, however, may be subject to delay. On a temporary basis, non-residents, except diplomatic missions and their staff, international organizations and their staff, agencies with equivalent status and their staff, as well as employees and self-employed members of the professions (professionally active in Operations Account area countries for less than a year) are not permitted to send transfers to countries that are not CFA franc zone members without prior authorization from the proper authorities. They may, however, receive transfers from abroad. A simple declaration is required for transfers to countries outside the BEAC area not exceeding CFAF 500,000 by residents; for transfers of more than CFAF 500,000, prior authorization must be obtained from the proper authorities. For many types of payment, approval authority has been delegated to authorized banks, which are required to execute promptly all duly documented transfer orders, and to dispatch cable transfers within 48 hours of receipt of the relevant request.

On a temporary basis, nonresidents, except diplomatic missions and their staff, international organizations and their staff, agencies with equivalent status and their staff, as well as employees and self-employed members of the professions (professionally active in Operations Account area countries for less than a year) are not permitted to send transfers to countries that are not CFA franc zone members without prior authorization from the competent authorities.

Payments for freight and insurance, unloading and storage costs, administrative expenses, commissions, interest, travel, medical treatment, study abroad, subscriptions and membership fees, consulting and legal fees, foreign workers' wages, pensions, family maintenance and alimony, as well as remittances of profits and dividends are subject to prior approval, quantitative limits, and indicative limits and/or bona fide test.

Freight/insurance	Insurance on all imports with f.o.b. values exceeding CFAF 500,000 must be arranged with local insurance companies by the importer.
Payments for travel	Travelers—civil servants on missions, students, persons on pilgrimage, etc.—must use the following payments instruments: foreign exchange, traveler's checks, bank drafts, bank and postal transfers, etc. Residents visiting other CFA franc zone countries may obtain an unlimited allocation in French francs. This allocation can be provided in banknotes, traveler's checks, bank drafts, bank or postal transfers, etc.
Prior approval	For travel to countries outside the CFA franc zone, the exchange allocation is subject to prior authorization from the relevant administrative authorities.
Quantitative limits	Residents traveling outside the CFA franc zone for tourism, sporting events, participation in expositions, organization of fairs, participation in seminars or international meetings of a personal capacity, pilgrimages, etc., may obtain an exchange allocation equivalent to CFAF 200,000 a day up to a maximum of CFAF 4 million a person a trip over 10 years of age; for children under 10, the allocation is reduced by one-half. Residents traveling to countries outside the CFA franc zone for business may obtain an exchange allocation equivalent to CFAF 500,000 a day, up to a maximum of CFAF 10 million a trip.
	Civil servants and government employees traveling on official business to countries outside the CFA franc zone may obtain the same exchange allocation as tourists, but only if their mission costs are less than a daily allocation of CFAF 200,000, up to a limit of CFAF 4 million.
Medical costs	
Quantitative limits	For countries outside the CFA franc zone, the exchange allocation is equivalent to CFAF 250,000 a day up to a limit of CFAF 5 million.
Study abroad costs	
Quantitative limits	The exchange allocation for countries outside the CFA franc zone is the equivalent to a 3-month scholarship plus expenses for supplies. However, a student, whether or not the holder of a scholarship, may obtain an exchange allocation not exceeding the equivalent of CFAF 2 million.

Proceeds from Invisible Transactions and Current Transfers

Repatriation requirements	Yes.
Surrender requirements	Proceeds from transactions in invisibles with France, Monaco, and Operations Account countries may be retained. All amounts due from residents of other countries in respect of services, and all income earned in those countries from foreign assets, must be collected and, if received in foreign currency, surrendered within 2 months of the due date.

Capital Transactions

Controls on capital and money market instruments	Capital movements between Chad and France, Monaco, and the Operations Account countries are free of exchange control; capital transfers to all other countries require exchange control approval and are restricted, but capital receipts from such countries are permitted freely. All foreign securities, foreign currencies, and titles embodying claims on foreign countries or nonresidents held by residents or nonresidents in Chad must be deposited with authorized banks in Chad.
	Additional special controls are maintained over borrowing and lending abroad; inward and outward direct investment; and the issuing, advertising, or offering for sale of foreign securities in Chad. These controls relate only to the transactions themselves, not to payments or receipts. With the exception of those controls over the sale or introduction of foreign securities in Chad, the measures do not apply to France, Monaco, and the Operations Account countries.
On capital market securities	
Sale or issue locally by nonresidents	The issuing, advertising, or offering for sale of foreign securities in Chad requires prior authorization from the MOF. Exempt from authorization, however, are operations in connection with loans backed by a guarantee from the Chadian government, and shares similar to securities, when issuing, advertising, or offering them for sale in Chad has already been authorized.
Purchase abroad by residents	Yes.
Sale or issue abroad by residents	n.a.
On money market instruments	
Sale or issue locally by nonresidents	Yes.
Purchase abroad by residents	Yes.
Sale or issue abroad by residents	n.a.
On collective investment securities	
Sale or issue locally by nonresidents	Yes.
Purchase abroad by residents	Yes.
Sale or issue abroad by residents	n.a.
Controls on derivatives and other instruments	
Sale or issue locally by nonresidents	Yes.
Purchase abroad by residents	Yes.
Sale or issue abroad by residents	n.a.

Controls on credit operations

Commercial credits

    By residents to nonresidents — Lending requires prior MOF authorization. The following are, however, exempt from this authorization: (1) loans directly connected with the rendering of services abroad by the persons or firms mentioned above, or with the financing of commercial transactions either between Chad and countries abroad or between foreign countries in which these persons or firms take part; and (2) other loans when the total amount of these loans outstanding does not exceed CFAF 5 million for any one lender. The making of loans referred to under (2) is free of authorization, and each repayment must be declared to the MOF within 30 days of the operation.

    To residents from nonresidents — Borrowing requires prior authorization from the MOF. The following are, however, exempt from this authorization: (1) loans constituting a direct investment abroad for which prior approval has been obtained, as indicated above; (2) loans directly connected with the rendering of services abroad by the persons or firms mentioned above, or with the financing of commercial transactions either between Chad and countries abroad or between foreign countries in which these persons or firms take part; and (3) loans other than those mentioned above when the total amount of the loan outstanding does not exceed CFAF 10 million for any one borrower, the interest rate is no higher than 7%, and the maturity is 2 years or less. The contracting of loans referred to under (3) is free of authorization, and each repayment must be declared to the MOF within 30 days of the operation.

Financial credits — The same regulations as for commercial credits apply.

Controls on direct investment

Outward direct investment — Investments require the prior approval of the MOF, regardless of the method of financing.

Inward direct investment — Investments require the prior approval of the MOF, unless they take the form of a mixed-economy enterprise.

Controls on liquidation of direct investment — The full or partial liquidation of direct investments in Chad must also be declared to the MOF within 30 days of each operation.

Controls on real estate transactions

Purchase abroad by residents — Yes.

Purchase locally by nonresidents — n.a.

Sale locally by nonresidents — n.a.

Provisions specific to commercial banks and other credit institutions

Borrowing abroad — Yes.

Maintenance of accounts abroad — n.a.

Lending to nonresidents (financial or commercial credits) — Yes.

Lending locally in foreign exchange — n.a.

Purchase of locally issued securities denominated in foreign exchange — n.a.

Differential treatment of nonresident deposit accounts and/or deposit accounts in foreign exchange

    Reserve requirements — n.a.

    Liquid asset requirements — Commercial banks must maintain a specified minimum amount of their assets in Chad.

Interest rate controls	n.a.
Credit controls	n.a.
Investment regulations	n.a.
Open foreign exchange position limits	n.a.

Changes During 1996

Exchange arrangements   *June 1.* Chad accepted the obligations of Article VIII, Sections 2, 3, and 4 of the Fund Agreement.

Changes During 1997

Imports and import payments   *January 1.* The import monopoly on sugar was lifted.

CHILE

(Position as of April 30, 1997)

Status Under IMF Articles of Agreement

Article VIII   Date of acceptance: July 27, 1977.

Exchange Arrangement

Currency   The currency of Chile is the Chilean peso.

Exchange rate structure   Unitary.

Dual   There are 2 foreign exchange markets: the official market, through which debt-service payments, remittances of dividends and profits, and authorized capital transactions, including loan receipts, must be transacted; and the informal market, through which all transactions not required to be channeled through the formal market take place. The formal foreign exchange market consists of commercial banks and exchange houses and other entities licensed by the Central Bank of Chile (CBC).

Classification

Managed floating   In both exchange markets, economic agents are free to negotiate rates; the CBC conducts transactions in the official exchange market within margins of 10% around the reference rate. The exchange rate of the Chilean peso is adjusted daily on the basis of changes in the value of a basket of currencies calculated from a set formula (0.45 U.S. dollar, 0.46 deutsche mark, and 24.6825 Japanese yen) and the differential between domestic and foreign rates of inflation, adjusted for the estimated differential in productivity growth between Chile and its trading partners (2% a year). In January 1997, the margin around the reference rate was increased to 12.5%, while the composition of the basket was modified to 0.8 U.S. dollar, 0.24435 deutsche mark, and 5.911 Japanese yen.

Exchange tax   No.

Exchange subsidy   The CBC provides a subsidy (in the form of notes indexed to inflation with a minimum maturity of 6 years and an interest rate of 3%) on the following service payments on some debts contracted before August 6, 1982 (the original amount of the debt was about US$8 billion): (1) payments to Chilean banks or financial companies whose debt is indexed to the official exchange rate, and (2) payments abroad on debt obligations registered with the CBC. As of end-1996, only debtors whose obligations were equal to or less than US$50,000 on June 30, 1985, have had access to the subsidy, but many of the affected debtors are bankrupt and unable to claim the subsidy. On December 31, 1996, the subsidized rate was the official reference rate.

Forward exchange market   Yes.

Official cover of forward operations   No.

Arrangements for Payments and Receipts

Prescription of currency requirements   No.

Payment arrangements

Regional arrangements   Settlements with Argentina, Bolivia, Brazil, Colombia, the Dominican Republic, Ecuador, Malaysia, Mexico, Paraguay, Peru, Uruguay, and Venezuela are made through accounts maintained with each other by the CBC and the central banks of each of the countries concerned within the framework of the multilateral clearing system of the LAIA.

Clearing agreements	Yes.
Administration of control	
Exchange control authorities	The CBC is responsible for enforcing regulations aimed at collecting balance of payments information. The Chilean Copper Commission is responsible for advising the CBC with respect to exports of copper and subproducts.
International security restrictions	No.
Payment arrears	No.
Controls on trade in gold (coins and/or bullion)	
Controls on domestic ownership and/or trade	Monetary gold may be traded only by authorized dealers, but ordinary transactions in gold between private individuals are unrestricted.
Controls on external trade	Trade is unrestricted, subject to normal export and import formalities, including registration with the CBC.
Controls on exports and imports of banknotes	No.

Resident Accounts

Eligibility to hold accounts	Juridical and natural persons are eligible.
Foreign exchange accounts permitted	
Held domestically	Both natural and juridical persons can hold foreign currency checking accounts. However, juridical persons must take into account legal restrictions on investments, given their commercial activities (i.e., pension fund administrators). In the case of checking accounts, the commercial banks must certify the domicile reported. The average balance is subject to legal reserve requirements.
Held abroad	Prior approval is not required; however, juridical persons subject to regulations on investment abroad (i.e., banks and pension funds) must abide by such regulations.
Accounts in domestic currency convertible into foreign currency	No.

Nonresident Accounts

Eligibility to hold accounts	Juridical and natural persons are eligible.
Foreign exchange accounts permitted	Checking accounts may not be held by nonresidents because holders must be domiciled in the country.
Domestic currency accounts	No.
Blocked accounts	No.

Imports and Import Payments

Foreign exchange budget	No.
Financing requirements for imports	No.
Documentation requirements for release of foreign exchange for imports	Payments through the official foreign exchange market require an import report (*informe de importación*) issued by the CBC, which must be obtained from, and processed through, the intermediary of a local commercial bank. Access to foreign exchange is available no later than 30 days after the obligation's expiration date as documented on the import report.

Domiciliation requirements	Only resident natural or juridical persons may engage in import activities.
Import licenses and other nontariff measures	Most imports require an *informe de importación* issued by the CBC. Imports of wheat, maize, edible oil, and sugar are subject to after-duty price margin limits. Antidumping and countervailing duty laws are applied.
Negative list	Imports of used motor vehicles are prohibited.
Import taxes and/or tariffs	Imports are subject to a uniform 11% tariff rate with a few exceptions (including on imports from LAIA countries and under a number of bilateral trade agreements).
Taxes collected through the exchange system	No.
State import monopoly	No.

Exports and Export Proceeds

Repatriation requirements	Receipts from copper exports of CODELCO (state copper company) must be deposited in the account of the Copper Stabilization Fund at the CBC; withdrawals are permitted only under prescribed circumstances. Debtors of internal credits recorded under Chapter VI of Title II of the Compendium of Rules on International Exchange (CEIR) are authorized to settle interest, commissions, and/or expenses corresponding to those operations effected directly abroad with export proceeds. The CBC must be informed of these settlements.
Surrender requirements	No.
Financing requirements	Exports can be financed with advances from foreign buyers or with external or internal credits, as agreed between the trading parties. Such advances must be channeled through the formal exchange market. Credits must be identified with shipments and paid immediately after proceeds are received.
Documentation requirements	The exporter must submit an export report to the CBC through a banking company, establishing the exporter's identity and the terms of the operation.
Letters of credit	The commercial bank that receives the letter prior to payment of the foreign exchange will demand from the exporter the shipping documents of the merchandise and the additional requirements established in the letter of credit.
Domiciliation	Yes.
Preshipment inspection	Inspections are done by customs agents, who perform the role of "customs ministers of faith"; subsequently, a shipment order is issued, which is subject to customs control.
Export licenses	No.
Export taxes	No.

Payments for Invisible Transactions and Current Transfers

Controls on these payments	Most current payments are free of controls; remittances of profits and dividends require prior approval by the CBC, and there is a maximum repatriation period of 120 days. The CBC authorizes the commercial banks to issue credit cards, but card users must pay balances due for purchases abroad with their own resources. However, under the concept of extraordinary expenditures, each person may acquire foreign exchange in the formal market without declaring the purpose.

Proceeds from Invisible Transactions and Current Transfers

Repatriation requirements	Yes.

Surrender requirements	Proceeds from selected transactions (e.g., royalties and copyright fees, commissions, proceeds from insurance, and other benefits related to foreign trade) are subject to a 100% surrender requirement.

Capital Transactions

Controls on capital and money market instruments

On capital market securities

Purchase locally by nonresidents

Nonresidents can invest in domestic securities in 3 ways:

(1) Through acquisition by foreign investment funds (FICE). These are formed by foreign capital and administered by an open society established in Chile. Investments cannot exceed 5% of social capital in any 1 company and 10% of the funds' total assets. These funds cannot invest more than 40% of their portfolios in equities of the same holding period, and all FICEs as a group may not hold more than 25% of the equities of the same open society. Other requirements for FICEs are a 5-year minimum holding period, a profit tax of 10%, and some portfolio restrictions that vary with the duration of the holding period;

(2) Through a financial investment (purchase of fixed income securities and equities). These are, however, subject to a reserve requirement of 30% for 1 year, and a minimum holding period requirement of 1 year and to the general income tax law. Equities that have American Depository Receipts (ADRs) can be acquired in the country and converted into ADRs. These transactions are also subject to the 30% reserve requirement. The issuance of primary ADRs is exempt from the above restrictions, but the issuers are subject to minimum international rating requirements and there is a minimum amount to be issued;

(3) Through loans. These can also be used to finance the purchase of securities in the country. They are subject to a 1-year reserve requirement of 30%, a 4% tax on interest payments, and a 1.2% stamp tax.

Sale or issue locally by nonresidents

Proceeds from the sale of domestic securities by nonresidents are subject to the 1-year holding period requirement if the capital inflow entered as a financial investment. The sale of equities that are the property of foreigners due to the ADR mechanism is possible, since Chilean ADRs can be converted into domestic stock. However, the resources obtained through the sale must be repatriated. ADRs issued from equities directly acquired in the Chilean stock market (also called secondary ADRs) are tightly restricted, both for the authorized period for acquiring stocks domestically and for the authorized period for acquiring foreign exchange after a local stock sale. All the associated foreign exchange operations must be effected through the formal exchange market. Issuance of foreign securities by nonresidents is subject to the same procedures applied to domestic securities. In practice, no foreign securities are traded domestically. Once the respective taxes have been paid, profits may be transferred freely without delay.

Purchase abroad by residents

Except for banks and pension funds, there are no restrictions on the acquisition of international fixed-income assets and current account deposits. The associated foreign exchange must be acquired in the informal market. Pension funds are authorized to hold up to 9% of their funds in foreign assets, including a variety of fixed-income assets and company shares up to 4.5% of the fund. Investments by life insurance companies are limited to 10% of their technical reserves and risk net worth.

Sale or issue abroad by residents

Residents can issue equities and bonds abroad, and the associated foreign exchange operations must be effected through the formal exchange market. Equities can be sold according to the rules that regulate capital inflows through the mechanism of ADRs. Primary ADR issues are only subject to minimum amounts (US$25 million the first time, and thereafter US$10 million), and to 2 minimum international risk-rating requirements, for long-term debt of BBB+ for banks and BBB for other firms.

On money market instruments

Purchase locally by nonresidents

In general, these acquisitions are authorized for nonresidents, but there are regulations governing the mode of inflow. The associated capital inflow liquidation and the subsequent repatriation of proceeds must be effected through the formal exchange market. Acquisition through external loans are subject to a reserve requirement of 30%, a tax on interest of 4%, and a stamp tax of 1.2%. Acquisition through FICEs is subject to a minimum holding period of 5 years in addition to a 10% profit tax. In the case of financial investments, there is a 30% 1-year reserve requirement and a minimum holding period of 1 year, and they are subject to the general income tax law.

Sale or issue locally by nonresidents

These transactions are not authorized and neither is the promotion of these or other financial services from abroad. To operate in the domestic financial market, the company must be registered and established, and must have brought in capital for operational purposes. The legal mechanism used is the creation of a Chilean agency of the foreign corporation.

Purchase abroad by residents

The acquisition of money market instruments by individuals and nonfinancial companies is not restricted. However, the formal exchange market is not available for these operations.

Sale or issue abroad by residents

These transactions are subject to a reserve requirement of 30%.

On collective investment securities

Purchase locally by nonresidents

These purchases are considered financial investments subject to a reserve requirement of 30% for a year and a minimum holding period of 1 year. Funds that enter Chile through an FICE are subject to a minimum holding period of 5 years.

Sale or issue locally by nonresidents

These transactions are not permitted. To operate in the domestic financial market, the company must be registered and established, and must have brought in capital for operational purposes. Once this has occurred, the sales of collective instrument securities are subject to the same domestic rules as any other investment, with no restrictions on the repatriation of profits.

Purchase abroad by residents

There are no restrictions for nonfinancial agents, but there is no access to the formal exchange market for these purposes. Pension funds are also restricted by the type of fund (mainly to avoid leveraged and hedged funds), country risk, regulation, liquidity, experience of the fund, and participant's concentration. Investments are also subject to certain limits: they should not exceed 4.5% of the pension fund, and variable income securities from any issuer should not exceed 2% of the fund.

Sale or issue abroad by residents

In practice, Chilean mutual funds (open funds) and investment funds (closed funds) are not offered directly abroad. To operate abroad, such funds must meet the existing regulations of the foreign country. Domestically issued instruments can be sold to nonresidents, but funds must be repatriated. These inflows are considered a financial investment subject to a reserve requirement of 30% annually and a 1-year holding requirement. FICEs that come into Chile under foreign ownership may be sold and traded in the New York or the London stock exchanges. The capital committed by the FICE must remain invested in Chile for 5 years.

Controls on derivatives and other instruments

Purchase locally by nonresidents

The market is not well developed. Nonresidents cannot participate in the local market for currency derivatives.

Sale or issue locally by nonresidents

To operate, foreign agents must have resident status.

Purchase abroad by residents

The CBC regulates currency and interest rate derivatives taking place in foreign markets. Interest rate derivatives do not exist in the local market and are not regulated. Speculative positions with derivatives abroad can be taken by nonfinancial institutions that acquire the foreign exchange in the informal market. Banks can cover themselves in currency derivatives up to the level of the underlying asset or liability position that needs to be covered. In the case of interest rate derivatives, banks are only allowed to cover mismatches between assets and liabilities. Pension funds and insurance companies are only allowed to cover themselves against currency volatility up to a maximum of their foreign financial investments on a currency-by-currency basis.

Sale or issue abroad by residents	Derivatives for currency and interest rates exist for operations with foreign agents in over-the-counter operations, with security dealers or brokers that are authorized by the foreign authorities, or with foreign banks. There is access to formal spot exchange markets for hedging purposes. Currency and interest rate options are allowed, except for banks. For residents, including banks, other derivative contracts (interest rates, currencies, and commodity prices) are permitted up to the amount of the underlying external asset or liability position that needs to be covered. However, these contracts cannot be effected on the formal market, except by banks and institutional investors.

Controls on credit operations

Commercial credits

By residents to nonresidents	All types of nonfinancial agents (except pension funds and insurance companies) are allowed to engage in international trade lending, but these operations must be effected through the informal exchange market.
To residents from nonresidents	Commercial credits can be contracted with foreign banks and financial entities under a 30% reserve requirement charged on an average balance and subject to a 4% tax on interest. Export advances and direct supplier credits to importers are exempted from the reserve requirement. Associated foreign exchange transactions must be effected through the formal exchange market.

Financial credits

By residents to nonresidents	Operations by insurance companies, pension funds, and institutional investors are restricted. Others must operate through the informal market. In April 1997, access to the formal market was extended to all credits.
To residents from nonresidents	Financial credits can be contracted with foreign banks and financial entities, subject to a 1-year 30% reserve requirement, a 4% tax on interest, and a stamp tax of 1.2%. Under Chapter XIV of the CEIR, debtors may use the formal market to prepay credits or to maintain the resources in an account abroad as a guarantee to creditors. Such funds are exempt from the 30% reserve requirement, provided the weighted average of the terms of each credit and the residual of the original credit are similar.

Guarantees, sureties, and financial backup facilities	
By residents to nonresidents	These transactions are not allowed except for banks, which have to be authorized by the CBC. Only the following operations can be guaranteed or backed up by banks: external credits received by domestic enterprises, financial credits, the issuance of documents abroad, and forward contracts with authorized agents abroad.
To residents from nonresidents	Yes.

Controls on direct investment

Outward direct investment	Restrictions exist in the case of ownership in a foreign company, investments in a project, or establishment of a company abroad. Investments may be made: (1) through the formal exchange market, in which case the CBC grants approval but the investment is subject to a 120-day profit repatriation while avoiding double taxation; or (2) through the informal exchange market, where the CBC must only be informed. There are also some limitations on the purchase of equities and foreign direct investment through the formal exchange market, in which case the CBC may give authorization to proceed, depending upon the specific information it is provided about the investment. There is a diversification requirement that allows a maximum investment in subsidiaries and branches in 1 foreign country of 20% of the capital and reserves of a local bank. Investment abroad in foreign subsidiaries and branches must be deducted from the local capital base.

Investment by commercial banks is limited to 25% of each bank's capital and reserves, and restricted to bills and bonds issued or guaranteed by foreign governments or central banks and private enterprises with a minimum long-term international debt risk rating (and its equivalent for short-term debt) of BBB.

Pension funds and insurance companies are subject to a minimum long-term international debt risk rating of BBB. In April 1997, the following transactions were permitted in the formal market: investments abroad, including acquisition of real or financial assets; and participation in companies and in contracts for the exploration and exploitation of domestic resources. There is, however, a reporting obligation to the CBC. Repatriation of investments, including profits, were exempted from the 30% reserve requirement.

Inward direct investment

Capital contributions to new establishments or shares in existing ones are subject to a 1-year minimum holding period and a minimum amount of US$10,000. Projects of significant size may be undertaken; there is a minimum holding period of 1 year, and the investor enjoys favorable taxation treatment with regard to the choice between the general income tax law or the guaranteed payment profit tax of 42%. There is also guaranteed access to the formal exchange market for repatriation.

Controls on liquidation of direct investment

Investments must be held in Chile for at least 1 year to qualify for repatriation. After that period, it must be demonstrated that the assets were sold and applicable taxes paid.

Controls on real estate transactions

Yes.

Purchase abroad by residents

Purchases are permitted through the informal market, but insurance companies can invest only 3% of their reserves and risk net worth.

Purchase locally by nonresidents

Purchases are treated as a financial investment and are subject to a minimum investment requirement of US$10,000, a reserve requirement of 30%, and a minimum holding period of 1 year.

Sale locally by nonresidents

The investment must have been held for 1 year in Chile and it must be demonstrated that the asset was sold and applicable taxes paid.

Provisions specific to commercial banks and other credit institutions

Borrowing abroad

Banks are permitted to obtain foreign trade credits subject to a reserve requirement of 30% against the average balance. They may also obtain financial credits with a reserve requirement of 30% for a year.

Maintenance of accounts abroad

Nonbank financial institutions are not allowed to maintain accounts abroad. Banks may hold foreign time deposits within the margin for financial investment abroad. External current accounts are not restricted.

Lending to nonresidents (financial or commercial credits)

Banks are only allowed to grant loans related to foreign trade. However, they can purchase debt instruments and sovereign bonds issued abroad. Time deposits are considered part of the margin for financial investments. Banks satisfying a capital adequacy ratio of at least 10% may acquire stocks of foreign banks or establish branches abroad. Deposits, loans, and other assets of Chilean banks with foreign banks of Chilean ownership cannot exceed 25% of the capital and reserves of the foreign bank.

Lending locally in foreign exchange

Banks are only permitted to grant foreign exchange credits associated with foreign trade. However, they may grant loans or acquire securities denominated or expressed in foreign exchange provided they remain within the open position limits.

Purchase of locally issued securities denominated in foreign exchange

These purchases are subject to open position limits.

Differential treatment of nonresident deposit accounts and/or deposit accounts in foreign exchange

Reserve requirements

The requirement for foreign currency deposits, for both time and current account deposits, is 30%. The requirement for domestic currency time deposits is 9%.

Liquid asset requirements	Yes.
Interest rate controls	By law there are ceilings on interest rates for both domestic and foreign currency loans. Those ceilings are defined as one-and-a-half times the average market interest rate.
Investment regulations	Foreign financial investments by commercial banks are limited to 25% of each bank's capital and reserves, and are restricted to bills and bonds issued or guaranteed by foreign governments or central banks and private enterprises. The general minimum long-term international debt risk rating (and its equivalent for short-term debt) for the financial instruments is BBB-, and up to 30% of the 25% margin can be invested in BB- instruments. The foreign exchange needed to invest abroad must be obtained in the formal exchange market.
Open foreign exchange position limits	The limit is 20% of capital and reserves. This margin includes derivative and spot instruments, foreign investment, assets and liabilities issued abroad or denominated in foreign exchange. Additionally, there is a foreign financial investment ceiling of 25% of the capital and reserves of each bank, a maximum investment in subsidiaries and branches abroad of 20% of the capital and reserves of domestic banks, and a requirement that the balance of all acquisitions and sales of foreign exchange for a bank be positive.
Provisions specific to institutional investors	Pension funds and insurance companies may hold only foreign instruments of a minimum international long-term risk rating requirement of BBB. These investors may also acquire foreign instruments guaranteed by the U.S. Treasury, such as Brady Bonds. Acquisition of equities and variable income assets by pension funds is restricted to instruments in some international markets. Specifically, there are rules on the transparency, regulation, and information of the stock exchange where these instruments can be acquired. However, for insurance companies, the possible stock exchange options are wider; insurance companies can invest in markets where there is a daily average of at least US$10 million of equity transactions. Mutual funds may use the formal exchange market to make investments abroad.
Limits (max.) on portfolio invested abroad	Pension funds may invest up to 9% of their resources abroad. Life insurance companies may invest their technical reserves and their risk net worth with global limits of 10% in financial investments and 3% in real estate. The limits for general insurance companies differ from those of the life insurance companies only in the case of financial investment abroad. The limit for the former is 15%. In April 1997, pension funds were permitted to invest up to 12% of their resources abroad.
Currency matching regulations on assets/liabilities composition	n.a.
Other controls imposed by securities laws	No.

Changes During 1996

Exports and export proceeds	*March 7.* Export payments in advance must be channeled through the formal exchange market.
	May 29. Any export credit must be related to a particular shipment and must be paid as soon as export proceeds are received.
	July 4. Debtors of external credits recorded under Chapter VI of Title II of the CEIR are authorized to settle amortization interest, commissions, and expenses corresponding to these operations directly abroad with export proceeds; the CBC must be informed of these settlements.
Payments for invisible transactions and current transfers	*April 17.* The CBC increased unrestricted access to the formal exchange market to individuals for documented travel, and medical and study expenses to US$15,000 a month from US$3,000 a month.

October 3. The CBC eliminated the restrictions on the share of mutual fund assets that can be invested abroad.

Proceeds from invisible transactions and current transfers

Capital transactions

January 29. Debtors of credits recorded in Chapter XIV of the CEIR may access in advance the formal market to prepay the credits or maintain the resources in an account abroad, which may be given in guarantee to the creditor.

March 22. External credits destined exclusively to prepay foreign credits that were previously authorized and recorded with the CBC were exempted from the 30% reserve requirement, provided the weighted average terms of each credit and the residual of the original credit are similar.

March 22. Mutual funds were permitted to use the formal exchange market to make investments abroad.

Changes During 1997

Exchange arrangements

January 20. The floating exchange rate band was widened to 12.5% above and below the reference exchange rate. The composition of the basket of currencies was modified to 0.8 U.S. dollar, 0.24435 deutsche mark, and 5.911 Japanese yen. The exchange rate arrangement was reclassified as managed floating.

Payments for invisible transactions and current transfers

April 16. The limit of US$15,000 for purchases of foreign exchange for these transactions in the formal exchange market was eliminated.

Capital transactions

March 27. Foreign financial investments of Chapter XIV of the CEIR for amounts of less than US$100,000 were exempted from the cash reserve requirement.

April 16. The repatriation of proceeds from investments abroad, including profits, made through the formal market was exempted from the 30% reserve requirement.

April 21. The limit on investments abroad by pension funds was increased to 12% from 9%.

April 26. Access to the formal exchange market was extended to allow for certain investments abroad, which include the acquisition of real or financial assets, participation in companies, contracts for the exploration and exploitation of natural resources abroad, deposits abroad, and the granting of foreign credits. The obligation to inform the CBC is maintained.

PEOPLE'S REPUBLIC OF CHINA

(Position as of December 31, 1996)

Status Under IMF Articles of Agreement

Article VIII	Date of acceptance: December 1, 1996.

Exchange Arrangement

Currency	The currency of the People's Republic of China is the renminbi (RMB). The currency unit is the yuan (100 fen = Y1 and 10 fen = 1 jiao).
Exchange rate structure	Unitary.
Classification	
Managed floating	The exchange rate of the renminbi is determined in the interbank foreign exchange market. The People's Bank of China (PBC) announces a reference rate for the renminbi against the U.S. dollar, the Hong Kong dollar, and the Japanese yen based on the weighted average price of foreign exchange transactions during the previous day's trading. Daily movement of the exchange rate of the renminbi against the U.S. dollar is limited to 0.3% on either side of the reference rate as announced by the PBC. The buying and selling rates of the renminbi against the Hong Kong dollar and the Japanese yen may not deviate more than 1% on either side of the reference rate; in the case of other currencies, the deviations should not exceed 0.5% on either side of their respective reference rates. The selling price for cash transactions is the same as the buying price for cash transactions for all quoted currencies. The buying price for cash should not exceed 2.5% of its spot rate.
	The Shanghai-based China Foreign Exchange Trading System (CFETS) is a nationally integrated electronic system for interbank foreign exchange trading. At present, it is electronically linked with 25 foreign exchange trading centers located in major cities. All foreign exchange transactions are conducted through the system. Financial institutions involved in foreign exchange transactions must become members of the CFETS.
Exchange tax	No.
Exchange subsidy	No.
Forward exchange market	No.

Arrangements for Payments and Receipts

Prescription of currency requirements	The currencies used in transactions are determined by the respective contracts.
Payment arrangements	
Bilateral arrangements	
Inoperative	China has terminated arrangements with Cuba, the Democratic People's Republic of Korea, Mongolia, Russia, and Vietnam. Cash settlements with these countries have been adopted.
Administration of control	
Exchange control authorities	The PBC has authority over control and the State Administration of Foreign Exchange (SAFE) is responsible for implementing regulations.
International security restrictions	No.
Payment arrears	No.

Controls on trade in gold (coins and/or bullion)

Controls on domestic ownership and/or trade	Trading of gold and silver is restricted to pharmaceutical, industrial, and other approved users. Private persons may hold gold but not trade it. Nonresidents can buy gold, gold products, silver, and silver products but must present the invoice to export them.
Controls on external trade	Unlimited amounts may be imported but must be declared. Exportation requires permits.

Controls on exports and imports of banknotes

On exports

Domestic currency	The exportation of domestic currency is limited to RMB 6,000.
Foreign currency	Travelers on official business can carry as much foreign currency as needed. Residents going abroad can carry foreign currency in cash up to the equivalent of $1,000. For amounts exceeding $1,000, approval of the SAFE is required. Banks will issue a "permit to carry foreign currency abroad" based on SAFE approval.

On imports

Domestic currency	n.a.
Foreign currency	The import of foreign currency must be declared to customs.

Resident Accounts

Eligibility to hold accounts

Juridical persons	Domestic establishments may maintain specified categories of foreign exchange accounts with permits issued by SAFE. Foreign-funded enterprises (FFEs) may open (1) foreign exchange settlement accounts for receipts and payments under the current account with a maximum amount stipulated by the SAFE for each enterprise; and (2) foreign exchange special accounts for receipts and payments under the capital account.
Natural persons	Foreign currency savings accounts may be opened with authorized banks.
Foreign exchange accounts permitted	Yes.
Held domestically	These accounts are permitted, but prior approval is required.
Held abroad	These accounts are permitted, but prior approval is required.
Accounts in domestic currency convertible into foreign currency	Domestic establishments in need of foreign exchange may convert domestic currency into foreign currency at authorized banks by presenting valid proof and commercial bills.

Nonresident Accounts

Eligibility to hold accounts

Juridical persons	FFEs and joint ventures can maintain foreign exchange accounts and use them to make authorized payments abroad.
Natural persons	Persons staying in China for a short time may open foreign currency savings accounts.
Foreign exchange accounts permitted	These accounts are permitted, but prior approval is required.
Domestic currency accounts	Yes.
Convertible into foreign currency	These accounts are permitted, but prior approval is required.

Blocked accounts	No.

Imports and Import Payments

Foreign exchange budget	No.
Financing requirements for imports	
Advance payment requirements	Importers may make advance payment of loans not exceeding $100,000 at the banks, by presenting valid proof and commercial bills. Prior SAFE approval is required for payment of loans exceeding 15% of the contract amount or the equivalent of $100,000.
Documentation requirements for release of foreign exchange for imports	Importers must provide valid proof and commercial bills, mainly import permits, automatic registration permits, proof of import, customs declarations, verification forms for foreign exchange payments, import contracts, and the like to obtain foreign exchange or pay directly from their foreign exchange accounts.
Preshipment inspection	All imports require prior inspection to their release by customs at the port of entry.
Letters of credit	n.a.
Import licenses and other nontariff measures	
Positive list	All enterprises other than registered foreign trade companies (FTCs) must obtain approval from local foreign trade bureau, in accordance with the Ministry of Foreign Trade and Economic Cooperation (MOFTEC) authorization, as well as a license from the local bureau for industry and commerce, to engage in foreign trade.
Negative list	Imports of all secondhand garments, poisons, narcotic drugs, diseased animals, and plants are prohibited. In addition, the importation of weapons, ammunition and explosives, radio receivers and transmitters, manuscripts, printed and recorded materials, and films that are deemed to be detrimental to Chinese political, economic, cultural, and moral interests is prohibited.
Licenses with quotas	Yes.
Import taxes and/or tariffs	Import tariff rates fall into 2 categories: general and preferential. Preferential rates are granted to imports from countries with which China has a trade treaty or agreement. Other imports are subject to the general rate of duty. The average unweighted tariff rate is 35.7%. China has a number of special economic zones where imports of inputs and capital goods are exempt from tariffs.
Taxes collected through the exchange system	No.
State import monopoly	FTCs conduct trade in specified products, including wheat, chemical fertilizers, crude oil and oil products, rubber, steel, timber, plywood, polyester fibers, tobacco and its products, cotton, and wool.

Exports and Export Proceeds

Repatriation requirements	Yes.
Surrender requirements	Domestic establishments must sell their export earnings to designated banks; FFEs may retain their export earnings, provided those earning do not exceed the maximum amount allowed for a foreign exchange surrender account as prescribed by the SAFE; otherwise the balance, if any, must be sold to authorized banks or sold through foreign exchange adjustment centers.
Financing requirements	No.
Documentation requirements	No.

Export licenses

Without quotas

Exports of specific machine tools require a license from the SAFE for the Inspection of Import and Export Commodities for purposes of quality control. Controls in the form of registration for surveillance purposes are exercised on the importation of machinery and electric equipment in order to monitor the supply and demand situation.

With quotas

Quotas for 24 product items are allocated through a bidding system under which successful bidders are required to guarantee maximum export value by offering higher benchmark export prices.

Export taxes

Export duties are levied on 47 products.

Taxes collected through the exchange system

No.

Payments for Invisible Transactions and Current Transfers

Controls on these payments

Nontrade payments by FFEs and public enterprises are subject to the same provisions. Resident individuals are subject to different regulations. Payments for freight and insurance, unloading and storage, administrative expenses, commissions, travel, medical treatment, study abroad, consulting and legal fees, as well as foreign workers' wages, gambling and prize earnings, family maintenance and alimony, and remittances of profits and dividends are subject to indicative limits and/or bona fide test.

Commissions

Quantitative limits

SAFE approval is required for amounts exceeding the prescribed limits (i.e., as a percentage of f.o.b. pricing. In the case of a hidden commission, the rebate should not exceed 2% of total contract amount and, in the case of a stated commission, the rebate should not exceed 5%. If rebates exceed those percentages, they should be below $10,000). Traders may pay directly at authorized banks by presenting valid proof and commercial bills.

Payments for travel

The foreign exchange requirements of companies within the budget are provided according to the prescribed limits. There are no restrictions on payments for travel of FFE staff.

"Interim Regulations on Nontrade and Nonbusiness Foreign Exchange Utilization," published by the Ministry of Finance, imposes a limit on the amount of foreign exchange utilized by persons traveling abroad on official business. Residents traveling to Hong Kong, China, and Macao for personal reasons may purchase up to $500 worth of foreign currencies; individuals traveling to other countries or regions (including Taiwan Province of China) may purchase up to $1,000 worth of foreign currencies.

Prior approval

Approval of the SAFE is required for amounts exceeding those limits.

Quantitative limits

Yes.

Medical costs

Quantitative limits

Residents may purchase foreign exchange up to $500 for payments of medicines and medical equipment abroad; for larger amounts, they must submit appropriate documentation for SAFE's verification.

Study abroad costs

Quantitative limits

Persons paying for their own studies abroad may be allowed a onetime purchase of foreign exchange of up to $1,000. Larger amounts require the approval of the SAFE.

Subscriptions and membership fees

Quantitative limits

Yes.

Consulting/legal fees

    Quantitative limits   Yes.

Pensions

    Quantitative limits   Pensions, including severance and separation payments, may be converted into foreign currency.

Family maintenance/alimony

    Quantitative limits   Yes.

Credit card use abroad   n.a.

Proceeds from Invisible Transactions and Current Transfers

Repatriation requirements   Yes.

Surrender requirements   Foreign grants and financial aid received by domestic establishments and foreign exchange earmarked for external payments as prescribed by aid contracts may be maintained with the approval of the SAFE; foreign embassies and consulates, representative offices of international organizations and affiliates of foreign juridical persons, resident persons and foreign expatriates may retain their foreign exchange; FFEs may retain foreign exchange earnings from current account transactions, provided the retained amount does not exceed the maximum limit allowed by the SAFE. Balances, if any, must be sold to authorized banks or through foreign exchange swap centers.

Capital Transactions

Controls on capital and money market instruments

On capital market securities

    Purchase locally by nonresidents   Nonresidents may only purchase B shares. The face value of B shares is denominated in renminbi, which are listed on the Chinese Securities Exchange and can only be bought by foreign investors.

    Sale or issue locally by nonresidents   These transactions are not permitted.

    Purchase abroad by residents   Residents, except financial institutions permitted to engage in foreign borrowing, and authorized industrial and trade enterprises or groups are not permitted to purchase securities abroad. A qualifications review by the SAFE is required for financial institutions to purchase securities abroad.

    Sale or issue abroad by residents   Prior approval by the PBC, the SAFE, or the Securities Supervisory Board is required. Issuing bonds abroad must be integrated within the state's plan for utilizing foreign capital. Bonds can only be issued by financial institutions approved by the PBC.

On money market instruments

    Purchase locally by nonresidents   Nonresidents are not allowed to purchase money market instruments.

    Sale or issue locally by nonresidents   Nonresidents are not allowed to sell or issue money market instruments.

    Purchase abroad by residents   Residents, except financial institutions permitted to engage in foreign borrowing, and authorized industrial and trade enterprises or groups are not allowed to purchase money market instruments. Financial institutions must undergo a review of qualifications by the SAFE before purchasing foreign money market instruments.

    Sale or issue abroad by residents   Sale or issue abroad of securities, other than stocks, requires PBC and SAFE approval.

On collective investment securities

Purchase locally by nonresidents These transactions are not allowed.

Sale or issue locally by nonresidents There are no regulations, and if these instruments are traded, they must be approved by the Securities Policy Commission.

Purchase abroad by residents Same regulations as for purchase of money market instruments apply.

Sale or issue abroad by residents Same regulations as for sale or issue of money market instruments apply.

Controls on derivatives and other instruments

Purchase locally by nonresidents These transactions are not allowed.

Sale or issue locally by nonresidents These transactions are not allowed.

Purchase abroad by residents Operations in such instruments by financial institutions are subject to prior review of qualifications and to limits on open foreign exchange positions.

Sale or issue abroad by residents Same regulations as for purchases apply.

Controls on credit operations

Commercial credits

By residents to nonresidents Industrial and commercial enterprises may not provide lending to nonresidents. Provision of loans to nonresidents by financial institutions is subject to review of qualifications by the SAFE and to a foreign exchange asset-liability ratio requirement.

To residents from nonresidents Only financial institutions permitted by the SAFE to engage in external borrowing and authorized industrial and commercial enterprises or groups can engage in external borrowing of commercial credit. For credit over 1-year maturity, the loan must be part of the state plan for utilizing foreign capital and must be approved by the SAFE. Short-term commercial credit (with a maturity of 1 year or less) is subject to foreign exchange balance requirements. Financial institutions permitted to engage in foreign borrowing are free to conduct short-term foreign borrowing within the target balance without obtaining approval, but must register the borrowing with the SAFE.

Short-term foreign financing with maturity of 3 months or less provided to enterprises (excluding FFEs) is not subject to limitations, but short-term financing of longer than 3 months is subject to short-term foreign exchange balance requirements, and the borrowing must be registered with the SAFE.

FFEs may borrow from nonresidents without obtaining approval, but must report the borrowing to SAFE.

Financial credits Same regulations as for commercial credits apply.

Guarantees, sureties, and financial backup facilities

By residents to nonresidents The regulation on External Guarantees Provided by Domestic Entities of September 1996 allows the provision of guarantees by authorized financial institutions and non-financial legal entities that have foreign exchange receipts. Government agencies or institutions cannot provide guarantees.

Controls on direct investment

Outward direct investment Foreign exchange is provided for the investment after a SAFE review of sources of foreign exchange assets and an assessment of the investment risk involved, approval by MOFTEC, and registration with the SAFE.

Inward direct investment As long as nonresidents meet requirements under Sino-foreign joint-venture laws and other relevant regulations, and are approved by MOFTEC, nonresidents are free to invest in China. There is no restriction on the inward remittance of funds as far as exchange control is concerned. For environmental and security reasons, inward direct investment in some industries is prohibited.

Controls on liquidation of direct investment	No.
Controls on real estate transactions	
Purchase abroad by residents	Same regulations as for direct investment apply.
Purchase locally by nonresidents	Same regulations as for direct investment apply.
Sale locally by nonresidents	n.a.
Provisions specific to commercial banks and other credit institutions	
Borrowing abroad	Same regulations as for commercial credits apply.
Maintenance of accounts abroad	Prior approval by the SAFE is required for domestic entities opening foreign exchange accounts abroad.
Lending to nonresidents (financial or commercial credits)	Lending is allowed subject to review of qualifications by the SAFE and to asset-liability ratio requirements.
Lending locally in foreign exchange	Lending is mainly subject to qualifications review by the SAFE and to asset-liability ratio requirements.
Purchase of locally issued securities denominated in foreign exchange	China does not issue securities denominated in foreign currency.
Differential treatment of nonresident deposit accounts and/or deposit accounts in foreign exchange	
Reserve requirements	There are different reserve requirements for deposits in renminbi and in foreign currency, and also between the latter in domestic banks and in FFEs (i.e., 13% for deposits in renminbi, 5% for any foreign currency deposit in domestic banks, and 3% for deposits in foreign currency for over 3 months and 5% for less than 3 months, in FFEs).
Liquid asset requirements	Bank foreign exchange liquid assets (1 year or less) should not be less than 60% of liquid liabilities (1 year or less) and 30% of total foreign exchange assets. Total deposits with 3-month maturities, deposits in both domestic and foreign banks, funds used for purchasing transferable foreign-currency-denominated securities, deposits with the central bank, and cash holdings should not be less than 15% of total foreign exchange assets. Nonbank foreign exchange liquid assets (1 year or less) should not be less than 60% of liquid liabilities (1 year or less) and 25% of total assets. Total deposits with 3-month maturities, deposits in both domestic and foreign banks, funds used for purchasing transferable foreign-currency-denominated securities, deposits with the central bank, and cash holdings should not be less than 10% of total assets.
Credit controls	Total loans, investment guarantees (calculated as 50% of the balance guaranteed), and other foreign exchange credits provided to a legal entity by banks or nonbank financial institutions should not exceed 30% of the foreign exchange capital owned by the banks or nonbank financial institutions.
Investment regulations	Bank equity investment should not exceed the difference between bank capital and mandatory paid-in capital. Nonbank financial institutions' total equity investment (excluding trust account) should not exceed the difference between their capital and mandatory paid-in capital.
Open foreign exchange position limits	For financial institutions trading foreign exchange on their own behalf, the daily total amount traded (total open foreign exchange position) should not exceed 20% of the foreign exchange working capital. As authorized by the highest level of management, financial institutions trading foreign exchange on their own behalf may retain a small amount of overnight open position, but this should not exceed 1% of the foreign exchange working capital.
Provisions specific to institutional investors	No.

Changes During 1996

Status under IMF Articles of Agreement

December 1. China accepted the obligations of Article VIII, Sections 2, 3, and 4 of the Fund Agreement.

Exchange arrangements

July 1. Foreign-funded banks were allowed to sell foreign exchange for bona fide transactions and become designated foreign exchange banks.

Resident accounts

July 1. FFEs foreign exchange accounts were distinguished into 2 types: the foreign exchange settlement account with a maximum amount stipulated by the SAFE for each enterprise for current account transactions; and the foreign exchange special account for receipts and payments for capital account transactions.

July 1. FFEs were allowed to conduct their foreign exchange transactions either with banks or in the swap center.

Payments for invisible transactions and current transfers

July 1. Limits on invisible transactions and current transfers by resident individuals were increased. Bona fide requests of foreign exchange above these limits are authorized by the SAFE, and provided by banks.

Capital transactions

September 25. The regulation on External Guarantees Provided by Domestic Entities was passed, allowing for the provision of guarantees by authorized financial institutions and nonfinancial legal entities that have foreign exchange receipts.

COLOMBIA

(Position as of December 31, 1996)

Status Under IMF Articles of Agreement

Article XIV	Yes.

Exchange Arrangement

Currency	The currency of Colombia is the Colombian peso.
Other legal tender	Various commemorative gold coins are also legal tender.
Exchange rate structure	Unitary.
Classification	
Managed floating	The Banco de la República (BR) conducts foreign exchange transactions with the Ministry of Finance (MOF) and authorized financial intermediaries. The BR announces the upper and lower limits of a 14 percentage point band 10 days in advance for indicative purposes. The BR quotes buying and selling rates for certain other currencies daily on the basis of the buying and selling rates for the U.S. dollar in markets abroad. All foreign exchange operations take place at a market-determined exchange rate. The Superintendency of Banks calculates a representative market exchange rate based on market rates (i.e., the weighted average of buying and selling effected by foreign exchange market intermediaries, excluding teller transactions). The government purchases foreign exchange for all public debt payments and other expenditures included in the national budget under the same conditions as other authorized intermediaries. The BR stands ready to sell foreign exchange warrants (*titulos canjeables por certificados de cambio*) to public enterprises in the electric sector and to the National Federation of Coffee Growers.
	These warrants, expressed in U.S. dollars, have a maturity of 12 months, and within their period of validity, may be sold to the BR for pesos at the reference market buying rate on the date of repurchase. Warrants bear interest at the rate equal to that of the external loan, but never higher than the average 30-day rate on primary certificates of deposit at the close of operations in the New York market for the day before the certificate is issued less 1 percentage point if held by public sector recipients of external loans. Warrants held longer than 12 months may be resold to the BR at the reference market rate on the last day of the twelfth month.
Exchange tax	Surtaxes include a 7% surtax on remittances of earnings on existing non-oil foreign investments, a 12% surtax on remittances of earnings on existing foreign investments in the oil sector, and a 12% surtax on remittances of earnings from foreign investments made after 1993. Also, a 10% withholding tax on foreign exchange receipts from personal services and other transfers is applied.
Exchange subsidy	Tax credit certificates for nontraditional exports (CERTs) are granted at different percentage rates.
Forward exchange market	Residents are permitted to buy forward cover against exchange rate risks with respect to foreign exchange debts in convertible currencies registered at the BR on international markets. Residents may also deal in over-the-counter forward swaps and options in U.S. dollars.
Official cover of forward operations	No.

Arrangements for Payments and Receipts

Prescription of currency requirements	Payments and receipts are normally effected in U.S. dollars, but residents and financial intermediaries are allowed to carry out operations in any currency.

Payment arrangements

Regional arrangements

Settlements with Argentina, Bolivia, Brazil, Chile, the Dominican Republic, Ecuador, Mexico, Paraguay, Peru, Uruguay, and Venezuela may be made through accounts maintained within the framework of the multilateral clearing system of the LAIA.

Clearing agreements

Colombia maintains reciprocal credit agreements with China.

Barter agreements and open accounts

n.a.

Administration of control

Exchange control authorities

The Customs and Taxes Directorate (DIAN) within the MOF enforces ex post control and supervision over trade transactions and is responsible for applying penalties for any violation of the trade regulations. The Superintendency of Trade and Industry and the Superintendency of Banks are also responsible for the enforcement of exchange regulations. The authorized foreign exchange intermediaries are commercial banks, financial corporations, the Financiera Energética Nacional (FEN), the Banco de Comercio Exterior de Colombia (BANCOLDEX), and savings and loans corporations. Exchange houses are authorized to carry out a range of foreign exchange activities. The BR keeps an accounting record both of foreign investment in Colombia and of debts abroad and controls the movement of foreign capital as well as the transfer of profits, dividends, and commissions.

International security restrictions

No.

Payment arrears

No.

Controls on trade in gold (coins and/or bullion)

Controls on domestic ownership and/or trade

The BR effects domestic sales of gold for industrial use directly at a price equivalent to the average quotation in the London gold market during the previous day; this price is converted into pesos at the representative market exchange rate.

Controls on exports and imports of banknotes

No.

Resident Accounts

Eligibility to hold accounts

Juridical and natural persons are eligible.

Foreign exchange accounts permitted

Held domestically

Accounts must be registered at the BR (compensation accounts) and may be used to pay for imports, to invest abroad in financial assets, or to carry out any other foreign exchange operation.

Approval required

n.a.

Held abroad

Proceeds from services (except interest and profits) and transfers may be used to maintain foreign accounts abroad; these accounts do not have to be registered at the BR.

Approval required

n.a.

Nonresident Accounts

Eligibility to hold accounts

Juridical and natural persons are eligible.

Foreign exchange accounts permitted

Credit institutions are authorized to receive short-term deposits in foreign currency from nonresident individuals or firms; these deposits are freely available to the holders, but banks must report transactions through these accounts to the BR.

Domestic currency accounts	Deposits in these accounts need not be registered at the BR; they may be used only for trade-related transactions. Banks must report transactions through these accounts to the BR.
Convertible into foreign currency	Yes.

Imports and Import Payments

Foreign exchange budget	No.
Financing requirements for imports	Importers may purchase foreign exchange directly from the exchange market. In addition, they may use the proceeds from deposits held abroad. However, foreign enterprises in the oil, coal, and natural gas sectors and firms in the free-trade areas are not permitted to purchase foreign exchange from financial intermediaries. Import payments must be made within 6 months of the due date of the bill of lading.
Documentation requirements for release of foreign exchange for imports	All imports must be registered at the Colombian Institute of Foreign Trade (INCOMEX).
Domiciliation requirements	n.a.
Preshipment inspection	Yes.
Letters of credit	Yes.
Import licenses and other nontariff measures	Most imports are free and require registration only with INCOMEX if the f.o.b. value exceeds $500. There is a global free list applicable to all countries, a national list applicable only to LAIA member countries, and special lists applicable only to LAIA member countries and those of the Andean Pact. Imports of medicines, chemical products, and weapons and munitions are subject to licensing requirements.
	Reimbursable imports involve purchases of official foreign exchange from a financial intermediary, including imports of machinery and equipment financed by international credit institutions. Nonreimbursable imports consist mainly of aid imports under grants and commodities constituting part of a direct investment. Import registrations are granted automatically. However, import registrations by some public sector agencies are screened by INCOMEX to determine whether local substitutes are available. Both import licenses and registrations are valid for 6 months, except those for agricultural and livestock products and for capital goods, which are valid for 3 months and for 12 months, respectively. Import licenses may be extended only once.
Positive list	n.a.
Negative list	n.a.
Import taxes and/or tariffs	With certain exceptions, imports are subject to the common external tariff of the Andean Pact.
Taxes collected through the exchange system	No.
State import monopoly	Imports of crude oil and petroleum products are effected by Empresa Colombiana de Petroleo (ECOPETROL).

Exports and Export Proceeds

Repatriation requirements	No.
Surrender requirements	All proceeds that are repatriated must be surrendered to authorized financial intermediaries within 6 months or must be maintained in foreign accounts registered at the BR. Foreign enterprises in the oil, coal, and natural gas sectors and firms in free-trade areas are not required to surrender their foreign exchange. On surrendering export proceeds in

the foreign exchange market, exporters of products other than coffee, petroleum and petroleum products, and exports effected through special arrangements (such as barter and compensation) may receive tax credit certificates at any of 3 rates—2.5%, 4%, and 5% of domestic value added—depending on the product and the country of destination. These certificates, which are freely negotiable and are quoted on the stock exchange, are accepted at par by tax offices for the payment of income tax, customs duties, and certain other taxes.

Exports of coffee are subject to the following regulations: (1) the minimum surrender price is the sales price shown on the export declaration; (2) exporters pay a coffee contribution on the basis of international market prices; (3) the National Coffee Committee (composed of the Ministers of Finance and Agriculture and the Managing Director of the Federation) may establish a physical coffee contingent on the basis of international coffee prices; and (4) the National Coffee Committee establishes a domestic price for export-type coffee expressed in pesos per cargo of 125 kilograms.

Foreign exchange proceeds earned by the public sector may be surrendered to financial intermediaries or to the BR.

Financing requirements	No.
Documentation requirements	
Domiciliation	n.a.
Preshipment inspection	Yes.
Export licenses	No.

Payments for Invisible Transactions and Current Transfers

Controls on these payments

There are no controls on payments for freight and insurance, unloading and storage costs, administrative expenses, travel, medical treatment, study abroad, subscriptions and membership fees, consulting and legal fees, foreign workers' wages, pensions, or family maintenance and alimony. Contracts involving royalties, commissions, trademarks, or patents should be registered with INCOMEX for statistical purposes only.

Interest payments

Quantitative limits

The limit on contractual interest rates of 2.5% over LIBOR remains in effect for the public sector, and there is a limit of 20% a year in U.S. dollar terms for the private sector.

Profit/dividends

Prior approval

Capital must be registered with the BR before profits can be repatriated. Annual transfers of profits abroad and repatriation of capital are not restricted, but they may be temporarily restricted if international reserve holdings of the BR fall below the equivalent of 3 months of imports.

Gambling/prize earnings

Indicative limits/bona fide test   n.a.

Credit card use abroad

Indicative limits/bona fide test   n.a.

Proceeds from Invisible Transactions and Current Transfers

Repatriation requirements	No.
Surrender requirements	No.

Capital Transactions

Controls on capital and money market instruments	Purchases of these instruments, whether locally by nonresidents or abroad by residents, must be registered with the BR.
On capital market securities	
Purchase locally by nonresidents	The purchase of 10% or more of the shares of a Colombian financial institution requires the prior approval of the Superintendency of Banks. Foreign investments in the form of placement of shares in a fund established to make investments in the stock exchange and in debt papers issued by the financial sector are permitted.
Sale or issue locally by nonresidents	n.a.
Purchase abroad by residents	Yes.
Sale or issue abroad by residents	Yes.
On money market instruments	
Purchase locally by nonresidents	Yes.
Sale or issue locally by nonresidents	Yes.
On collective investment securities	
Purchase locally by nonresidents	Yes.
Sale or issue locally by nonresidents	Yes.
Purchase abroad by residents	Yes.
Controls on derivatives and other instruments	
Sale or issue locally by nonresidents	Yes.
Controls on credit operations	
Commercial credits	
By residents to nonresidents	Yes.
To residents from nonresidents	Credits must be registered with the BR, but short-term foreign borrowing is permitted. Foreign loans with maturities ranging from 1 day to 3 years are subject to a nonremunerated deposit requirement of 50% of the loan. The deposits are held for a period corresponding to the loan maturities. Nonremunerated deposits are required for loans of over 6 months for imports; deposits are held for 18 months. Exempted from the deposit requirement are credits for imports of capital goods; short-term loans granted by BANCOLDEX to Colombian exporters for up to 12 months; credit card balances; loans destined for Colombian investments abroad; and green coffee, coal, and oil preshipment financing. There is a limit on contractual interest rates of 3% over LIBOR or the U.S. prime rate for the public sector. Foreign loans for government entities in excess of specified amounts require prior authorization from the MOF. For loans to the government, or guaranteed by the government, the following are also required: prior authorization from the National Council for Economic and Social Policy (CONPES) and from the BR, prior consultation with the Interparliamentary Committee on Public Credit, and ex post approval from the President of the Republic. Such loans are also subject to the executive decree that authorizes the initiation of negotiations.
Financial credits	Yes.
Guarantees, sureties, and financial backup facilities	n.a.

Controls on direct investment

Outward direct investment | Investments should be registered with the BR.

Inward direct investment | Up to 100% ownership in any sector of the economy, except in defense, waste disposal, and real estate, is allowed. Special regimes remain in effect in the financial, petroleum, and mining sectors.

Controls on liquidation of direct investment | Repatriation of proceeds must be registered with the BR.

Controls on real estate transactions

Purchase abroad by residents | Purchases should be registered with the BR.

Purchase locally by nonresidents | Yes.

Sale locally by nonresidents | Yes.

Provisions specific to commercial banks and other credit institutions

Borrowing abroad | n.a.

Maintenance of accounts abroad | n.a.

Lending to nonresidents (financial or commercial credits) | n.a.

Lending locally in foreign exchange | n.a.

Purchase of locally issued securities denominated in foreign exchange | n.a.

Differential treatment of nonresident deposit accounts and/or deposit accounts in foreign exchange | n.a.

Investment regulations | n.a.

Open foreign exchange position limits | The limit is 20% of net worth. There are no regulations governing the net foreign exchange positions of exchange houses; they may sell their excess foreign holdings to authorized financial intermediaries because they do not have access to the BR.

Provisions specific to institutional investors

Limits (min.) on portfolio invested locally | Yes.

Changes During 1996

Capital transactions

July 31. The prior authorization requirement for foreign direct investment was eliminated. The authorization requirement for supplementary foreign investment, which was previously applied only to mining, was extended to other sectors.

February 23. Foreign loans with maturities ranging from 1 day to 3 years were subject to a nonremunerated deposit requirement of 50% of the loan. Loans of over 6 months for imports are subject to a nonremunerated deposit requirement; these deposits are held for 18 months.

COMOROS

(Position as of December 31, 1996)

Status Under IMF Articles of Agreement

Article VIII	Date of acceptance: June 1, 1996.

Exchange Arrangement

Currency	The currency of Comoros is the Comorian franc.
Other legal tender	n.a.
Exchange rate structure	Unitary.
Classification	
Pegged	The Comorian franc is pegged to the French franc at CF 1 per F 0.0133. Exchange rates for currencies are officially quoted on the basis of the fixed rate of the Comorian franc for the French franc and the Paris exchange market rates for other currencies.
Exchange tax	No.
Exchange subsidy	No.
Forward exchange market	Forward cover against exchange rate risk is authorized by the Central Bank of the Comoros (CBC) and is provided to traders by the commercial bank (the only authorized dealer) for up to 3 months. In practice, this has not been effected.
Official cover of forward operations	No.

Arrangements for Payments and Receipts

Prescription of currency requirements	Settlements with France, Monaco, and the Operations Account countries are made in Comorian francs, French francs, or the currency of any other Operations Account country. Settlements with all other countries are usually made through correspondent banks in France in any of the currencies of those countries or in French francs through foreign accounts in francs.
Payment arrangements	Yes.
Bilateral arrangements	n.a.
Regional arrangements	n.a.
Clearing agreements	n.a.
Barter agreements and open accounts	n.a.
Administration of control	
Exchange control authorities	The Minister of Finance and Trade has sole authority in exchange control matters but has delegated certain exchange control powers to the BCEAO and to authorized banks. Exchange control is administered by the CBC. The Ministry of Finance and Budget supervises borrowing and lending abroad, inward direct investment, and all outward investment. With the exception of those relating to gold, the country's exchange control measures do not apply to (1) France (and its overseas departments and territories) and Monaco; and (2) all other countries whose bank of issue is linked with the French Treasury by an Operations Account (Benin, Burkina Faso, Cameroon, Central African Republic, Chad, Republic of Congo, Côte d'Ivoire, Equatorial Guinea, Gabon, Mali, Niger, Senegal, and Togo).
Payment arrears	
Official	Yes.

Private	n.a.
Controls on trade in gold (coins and/or bullion)	
Controls on domestic ownership and/or trade	Yes.
Controls on external trade	Imports and exports of monetary gold require prior authorization. Imports and exports of articles containing gold are subject to declaration, but personal jewelry within the limit of 500 grams a person are exempt from such declaration.
Controls on exports and imports of banknotes	
On exports	
Domestic currency	Yes.
Foreign currency	Residents traveling to France, Monaco, and the Operations Account countries may take out the equivalent of CF 500,000 in banknotes and any amount in other means of payment. Residents traveling to countries other than France, Monaco, and the other Operations Account countries may take out any means of payment up to the equivalent of CF 250,000 a person a trip. Any amount in excess of these limits is subject to CBC approval, which is granted if supportive documentation is provided. Nonresident travelers may export the equivalent of CF 500,000 in banknotes and any means of payment issued abroad in their name without providing documentary justification. Other cases are authorized pursuant to the exchange regulations when supporting documents can be produced.
On imports	
Domestic currency	Resident and nonresident travelers may bring in any amount of domestic banknotes and coins.
Foreign currency	Travelers may bring in any amount of foreign currency.

Resident Accounts

Eligibility to hold accounts	Yes.
Juridical persons	n.a.
Natural persons	n.a.
Foreign exchange accounts permitted	Opening of these accounts is permitted, but is not practiced.
Held domestically	n.a.
Held abroad	n.a.

Nonresident Accounts

Eligibility to hold accounts	Yes.
Juridical persons	n.a.
Natural persons	n.a.
Domestic currency accounts	Yes.
Convertible into foreign currency	n.a.

Imports and Import Payments

Foreign exchange budget	No.

Financing requirements for imports	No.
Documentation requirements for release of foreign exchange for imports	
Domiciliation requirements	All import transactions must be domiciled with the authorized bank if the value is CF 500,000 or more.
Preshipment inspection	Yes.
Letters of credit	Yes.
Import licenses used as exchange licenses	n.a.
Import licenses and other nontariff measures	The importation of most goods, except those originating from member countries of the EU, Monaco, and the Operations Account countries, is subject to individual licensing.
Negative list	The importation of certain goods is prohibited from all countries for health or security reasons.
Open general licenses	n.a.
Import taxes and/or tariffs	There are import duty rates of 20%, 30%, and 40%; a specific tax that varies by type of product; and an administrative fee of 3%.
Taxes collected through the exchange system	n.a.
State import monopoly	No.

Exports and Export Proceeds

Repatriation requirements	Proceeds from exports to foreign countries must be repatriated within 30 days of the expiration of the commercial contract.
Surrender requirements	Proceeds must be sold immediately after repatriation to the authorized bank.
Documentation requirements	With a few exceptions, exports to any destination are free of licensing requirements.
Letters of credit	Yes.
Guarantees	n.a.
Domiciliation	All export transactions must be domiciled with an authorized bank if the value is CF 500,000 or more.
Export licenses	Yes.
Without quotas	n.a.
With quotas	n.a.

Payments for Invisible Transactions and Current Transfers

Controls on these payments	Payments for invisibles to France, Monaco, and the Operations Account countries are permitted freely. Invisible payments to other countries are subject to approval, which is granted when supporting documents are produced. Payments for invisibles related to authorized imports are not restricted. Payments for study abroad, subscriptions and membership fees, consulting and legal feels, foreign workers' wages, pensions, gambling and prize earnings, and family maintenance and alimony are subject to indicative limits and/or bona fide tests.
Freight/insurance	n.a.
Unloading/storage costs	n.a.
Administrative expenses	n.a.

Commissions	n.a.
Interest payments	n.a.
Profit/dividends	Repatriation of dividends and other earnings from nonresidents' direct investments is authorized and guaranteed under the Investment Code.
Quantitative limits	n.a.
Indicative limits/bona fide test	n.a.
Payments for travel	
Quantitative limits	Yes.
Indicative limits/bona fide test	Residents traveling to countries other than France, Monaco, and the other Operations Account countries may take out any means of payment up to the equivalent of CF 500,000 a person a trip. Any amount in excess of these limits is subject to the prior approval of the CBC, which is granted if supporting documentation is provided.
Medical costs	n.a.
Credit card use abroad	
Prior approval	n.a.
Quantitative limits	The same limits as for tourist and business travel apply.
Indicative limits/bona fide test	n.a.

Proceeds from Invisible Transactions and Current Transfers

Repatriation requirements	Proceeds from transactions with France, Monaco, and the Operations Account countries may be retained. All amounts due from residents of other countries with respect to services and all income earned in those countries from foreign assets must be repatriated within 1 month of the due date or date of receipt.
Surrender requirements	Export proceeds in foreign currency must be sold immediately to an authorized bank.
Restrictions on use of funds	The use of proceeds is limited to Operations Account countries.

Capital Transactions

Controls on capital and money market instruments	Capital flows between the Comoros and France, Monaco, and the Operations Account countries are, in principle, free of exchange control. Capital transfers to all other countries require exchange control approval, but capital receipts from such countries are normally permitted freely.
On capital market securities	Yes.
Purchase locally by nonresidents	n.a.
Sale or issue locally by nonresidents	n.a.
Purchase abroad by residents	n.a.
Sale or issue abroad by residents	n.a.
On money market instruments	Yes.
Purchase locally by nonresidents	n.a.
Sale or issue locally by nonresidents	n.a.
Purchase abroad by residents	n.a.
Sale or issue abroad by residents	n.a.
On collective investment securities	Yes.

Purchase locally by nonresidents	n.a.
Sale or issue locally by nonresidents	n.a.
Purchase abroad by residents	n.a.
Sale or issue abroad by residents	n.a.

Controls on derivatives and other instruments   Yes.

Purchase locally by nonresidents	There is no local market in these instruments.
Sale or issue locally by nonresidents	n.a.
Purchase abroad by residents	n.a.
Sale or issue abroad by residents	n.a.

Controls on credit operations

Commercial credits

By residents to nonresidents	Credits must have a minimum maturity of 90 days.
To residents from nonresidents	Yes.

Financial credits

By residents to nonresidents	n.a.
To residents from nonresidents	Yes.

Guarantees, sureties, and financial backup facilities

By residents to nonresidents	n.a.
To residents from nonresidents	Yes.

Controls on direct investment

Outward direct investment	Controls relate to the approval of the underlying transactions, not to payments or receipts.
Inward direct investment	Yes.

Provisions specific to commercial banks and other credit institutions

Borrowing abroad	Yes.
Maintenance of accounts abroad	n.a.
Lending to nonresidents (financial or commercial credits)	Yes.
Lending locally in foreign exchange	Lending does not take place in practice.
Purchase of locally issued securities denominated in foreign exchange	There is no local market in these securities.
Differential treatment of nonresident deposit accounts and/or deposit accounts in foreign exchange	n.a.
Investment regulations	n.a.
Open foreign exchange position limits	n.a.

Changes During 1996

Status under IMF Articles of Agreement	*June 1.* Comoros accepted the obligations of Article VIII, Sections 2, 3, and 4 of the Fund Agreement.

DEMOCRATIC REPUBLIC OF THE CONGO[1]

(Position as of December 31, 1996)

Status Under IMF Articles of Agreement

Article XIV	Yes.

Exchange Arrangement

Currency	The currency of the Democratic Republic of the Congo is the new zaïre.
Exchange rate structure	Unitary.
Classification	
Independent floating	The external value of the new zaïre is determined in daily fixing sessions, in which all financial institutions and the Banque Nationale du Congo (BNC) participate. The rate emerging from the fixing session is based on the rate prevailing in the unofficial exchange market. All commercial banks and financial institutions (including 91 bureaus) are permitted to trade in foreign exchange. Banks determine daily the value in new zaïres of the transactions in Belgian francs, French francs, and U.S. dollars and report to the BNC the calculated average effective buying and selling rates of the 3 currencies as well as the highest and lowest rates quoted in these transactions. The BNC uses the fixing date to arrive at the average effective exchange rate of the new zaïre against 23 other currencies and units, based on the rates provided by the IMF between the U.S. dollar and the other currencies. The fixing rate is used as an indicative rate at the opening of trading on the day of their publication and is applied to all government operations, including debt-service payments and the transactions of government-owned enterprises. On December 31, 1995, the rate published by the BNC was NZ 14,830.5 per $1, while the parallel rate was NZ 15,800 per $1.
	Charges or commissions are not assessed on interbank market transactions. In their transactions with customers, commercial banks and financial institutions may charge an exchange commission not exceeding 1%. The spread between the buying and selling rates for foreign banknotes set by the commercial banks and financial institutions in the foreign exchange market must not exceed 5%.
Exchange tax	Effective December 27, 1996, a charge of 2% is levied on any exchange operation of authorized banks.
Exchange subsidy	No.
Forward exchange market	Yes.
Official cover of forward operations	n.a.

Arrangements for Payments and Receipts

Prescription of currency requirements	Payments from nonresidents to residents must be made in 1 of the 23 convertible currencies whose rates are published daily by the BNC. Residents must make payments to nonresidents in 1 of the listed convertible currencies or by crediting nonresident accounts in new zaïres or in foreign currency. Settlements with the member countries of the CEPGL and the CEEAC are made through SDR and Central African Unit of Account (UCAC) accounts established under arrangements concluded by the BNC with the central banks of the countries concerned. Balances in these convertible accounts at the end of a settlement period—each quarter for CEPGL countries and each month for CEEAC countries—are transferable into the currency stipulated by the creditor. Virtually all settlements (other than for reexports) with member countries of the CEEAC are effected through accounts with foreign correspondent banks after clearing through the Central African Clearing House through its account with the BNC.

---

[1] Formerly known as Zaïre.

Payment arrangements

Bilateral arrangements

   Inoperative — Yes.

Regional arrangements — Yes.

Clearing agreements — There are arrangements with Burundi and Rwanda. Payments are made through the SDR accounts of the BNC and the central banks of the other 2 countries.

Administration of control

Exchange control authorities — The BNC regulates exchange transactions, supervises authorized banks and dealers, and regulates open foreign exchange positions.

International security restrictions — No.

Payment arrears

Official — Yes.

Private — Yes.

Controls on trade in gold (coins and/or bullion)

Controls on domestic ownership and/or trade — Only nationals of the Democratic Republic of the Congo are allowed to purchase, transport, sell, or hold gold within the country outside the boundaries of areas covered by exclusive mining concessions. Foreign individuals or corporate persons and corporate persons by law may do so only on behalf of and for the account of authorized marketing agencies.

Controls on external trade — Exports of gold and diamonds by authorized marketing agencies do not require prior authorization from the BNC.

Controls on exports and imports of banknotes

On exports

   Domestic currency — The exportation of banknotes and coins of the Democratic Republic of the Congo is permitted only up to the equivalent of $100. However, the exportation of these banknotes and coins by travelers from Burundi and Rwanda is authorized within the limits of the agreements concluded between the members of the CEPGL.

   Foreign currency — Yes.

On imports

   Domestic currency — The importation of banknotes of the Democratic Republic of the Congo is permitted up to the equivalent of $100.

   Foreign currency — An unlimited amount of banknotes and other means of payment in foreign currency may be brought into the country.

Resident Accounts

Eligibility to hold accounts — Juridical and natural persons are eligible.

Foreign exchange accounts permitted — Effective December 27, 1997, these accounts are permitted. These accounts, which may be credited or debited without restrictions, may be sight or term accounts, may bear interest, and may be denominated in any currency for which the BNC publishes exchange rates.

Held domestically — Yes.

Held abroad — Public and/or semipublic enterprises may open foreign bank accounts with prior authorization from the BNC.

Accounts in domestic currency convertible into foreign currency	Yes.

Nonresident Accounts

Eligibility to hold accounts	Juridical and natural persons are eligible.
Foreign exchange accounts permitted	These accounts may be credited or debited without restriction, effective from December 27, 1996.
Domestic currency accounts	These accounts may be credited or debited without restriction. Prior approval is required.
Convertible into foreign currency	No.
Blocked accounts	No.

Imports and Import Payments

Foreign exchange budget	There is a budget for imports by the government and the BNC.
Financing requirements for imports	No.
Documentation requirements for release of foreign exchange for imports	
Preshipment inspection	With a few exceptions, imports are subject to a preshipment inspection. The amount, the invoice price, and the quality of imports must be verified and found acceptable by the foreign agents of the Zaïrian Control Office (OZAC); however, in special cases, verification may be effected upon arrival, subject to a waiver from the BNC. Verification certificates are not required for import values (f.o.b.) of up to SDR 1,000 a tariff item, or up to SDR 5,000 a shipment.
Letters of credit	Yes.
Import licenses used as exchange licenses	All importers are required to first obtain an Import License and Authorization to Purchase Foreign Currency.
Import licenses and other nontariff measures	Prior approval from the BNC is required for (1) imports in the form of foreign contributions to capital intended for resale; (2) imports financed by suppliers' credits or other interest-bearing foreign financing with a maturity of more than 1 year, except imports contracted or guaranteed by the government; (3) imports requiring a down payment in foreign currency before shipment; and (4) imports requiring special authorization from the government and imports of currency, coins, and articles imitating or bearing monetary symbols of the Democratic Republic of the Congo's currency. Import licensing requirements were eliminated on December 27, 1996.
	All goods shipped by sea must be transported on vessels belonging to shipowners that are bonded with the Office zaïrois de gestion des frets maritimes and whose freight charges have been negotiated with that office.
Positive list	Yes.
Negative list	Certain imports, including arms, explosives and ammunition, narcotics, materials contrary to public morals, and certain alcoholic beverages, are prohibited or require special authorization from the government.
Open general licenses	Most imports are subject only to an import declaration at the authorized banks. In general, import declarations remain valid for 12 months; an importer wishing to extend the validity period must so indicate in the import documents accompanying the declaration. The validity may be extended for the first time by the authorized banks if shipment has begun; if shipment has not begun, extension of the validity period requires authorization

from the BNC. Imports of goods intended for expansion of a capital base or for the importer's own use may be effected without a declaration to an authorized bank, provided that the value does not exceed SDR 1,000 for each tariff item and SDR 5,000 a shipment, and that the shipments are financed from the importer's own resources.

Import taxes and/or tariffs	The customs tariff rates range from 15% to 50%, with a special rate of 5% for some equipment. The rate of the turnover tax ranges up to 20%.
Taxes collected through the exchange system	No.
State import monopoly	No.

Exports and Export Proceeds

Repatriation requirements	Export or reexport proceeds must be repatriated within 30 calendar days from the date of shipment. Proceeds from exports of gold and diamonds must be received at the bank within 10 days after the date of shipment. With exports on consignment, export proceeds shall be repatriated as soon as the merchandise has been sold.
Surrender requirements	Surrender requirements were eliminated on December 27, 1996.
Financing requirements	No.
Documentation requirements	
Letters of credit	Yes.
Guarantees	Yes.
Domiciliation	Yes.
Preshipment inspection	All exports require an inspection certificate issued by the OZAC; coffee exports also require a quality certificate from the Zaïrian office for coffee (OZACAF).
Export licenses	Licensing requirements for exports were lifted on December 27, 1996.
Without quotas	Exporters must file an exchange document (declaration of foreign exchange commitment), which banks are normally authorized to validate, for all exports. These declarations must specify the type of merchandise to be exported, its price, and the currency in which payment is to be received. Declarations of foreign exchange commitment are normally valid for 90 days.
Export taxes	Export, turnover, and statistical taxes have been suspended.

Payments for Invisible Transactions and Current Transfers

Controls on these payments	There are no controls on payments for unloading and storage costs, administrative expenses, and the use of credit cards abroad. Payments for freight and insurance, commissions, profits and dividends, travel, medical treatment, study abroad, subscriptions and membership fees, consulting and legal fees, foreign workers' wages, pensions, gambling and prize earnings, family maintenance and alimony, and remittances of profits and dividends are subject to indicative limits and/or bona fide tests.
Commissions	Payment of commissions for representing foreign brand names is regulated.
Interest payments	
Prior approval	Prior approval for this type of transaction was required up to December 27, 1996.
Profit/dividends	
Prior approval	Prior approval for this type of transaction was required up to December 27, 1996.
Consulting/legal fees	
Prior approval	Prior approval for this type of transaction was required up to December 27, 1996.

Foreign workers' wages

Prior approval	Prior approval for this type of transaction was required up to December 27, 1996.
Quantitative limits	Transfer abroad of foreigners' wages for the preceding year is limited. Transfer abroad of expatriates' wages is limited to 50% of net wages in the case of new employees, provided that the remaining 50% is adequate to cover local needs.

Pensions

Prior approval	Prior approval for this type of transaction was required up to December 27, 1996.
Quantitative limits	Up to December 27, 1996, the amount transferable had to be justified.

Gambling/prize earnings

Prior approval	Yes.

Family maintenance/alimony

Prior approval	Yes.

Proceeds from Invisible Transactions and Current Transfers

Repatriation requirements	Yes.
Surrender requirements	Proceeds must be surrendered to authorized banks. A declaration must be made for each transaction. For some operations, proceeds may be credited to a resident foreign currency account.
Restrictions on use of funds	Receipts credited to a resident's account in foreign exchange are conveyed to the authorized banks as needed by the account holders.

Capital Transactions

Controls on capital and money market instruments	There are controls on treasury bill transactions.
Controls on derivatives and other instruments	No.
Controls on credit operations	Residents may borrow abroad to invest in the Democratic Republic of the Congo.
Commercial credits	
To residents from nonresidents	Yes.
Financial credits	
To residents from nonresidents	Yes.
Guarantees, sureties, and financial backup facilities	
To residents from nonresidents	Yes.
Controls on direct investment	Equity contributions are authorized, and transfers abroad of such contributions made under the Investment Code are guaranteed.
Outward direct investment	Approval was required up to December 27, 1996.
Controls on liquidation of direct investment	The repatriation of foreign capital brought in under the provisions of the Investment Code is permitted only at the time of liquidation, nationalization, or partial or total transfers of shares.
Controls on real estate transactions	
Purchase locally by nonresidents	Yes.

Sale locally by nonresidents	Up to December 27, 1996, the proceeds were required to be paid into special accounts of nonresidents.
Provisions specific to commercial banks and other credit institutions	
Borrowing abroad	Yes.
Maintenance of accounts abroad	Yes.
Lending to nonresidents (financial or commercial credits)	Bridge loans require prior consent of the BNC.
Differential treatment of nonresident deposit accounts and/or deposit accounts in foreign exchange	
Reserve requirements	n.a.
Liquid asset requirements	n.a.
Interest rate controls	n.a.
Credit controls	Yes.
Open foreign exchange position limits	The ceiling on the foreign exchange position of each bank is authorized by the BNC.
Provisions specific to institutional investors	No.
Other controls imposed by securities laws	No.

Changes During 1996

Exchange arrangements	*December 27.* Authorized banks were required to assess a charge of 2% on any exchange operation.
Resident accounts	*December 27.* All restrictions on opening and operating these accounts were lifted.
Nonresident accounts	*December 27.* All restrictions on opening and operating these accounts were lifted.
Imports and import payments	*December 27.* The import licensing requirement was abolished.
Exports and export proceeds	*December 27.* All surrender requirements and the licensing requirement for exports were eliminated.
Payments for invisible transactions and current transfers	*December 27.* All transactions were further liberalized.
Capital transactions	*December 27.* Residents were allowed to borrow abroad for investment in the Democratic Republic of the Congo.
	December 27. Proceeds from sales of real estate by nonresidents were required to be paid into special accounts.

REPUBLIC OF CONGO

(Position as of December 31, 1996)

Status Under IMF Articles of Agreement

Article VIII   Date of acceptance: June 1, 1996.

Exchange Arrangement

Currency

The currency of the Republic of Congo is the CFA franc. The CFA franc is issued by the BEAC and is legal tender also in Cameroon, the Central African Republic, Chad, Equatorial Guinea, and Gabon.

Exchange rate structure   Unitary.

Classification

Pegged

The CFA franc is pegged to the French franc, the intervention currency, at the fixed rate of CFAF 1 per F 0.01. The official buying and selling rate is CFAF 100 per F 1. Exchange transactions in French francs between the BEAC and commercial banks take place at the same rate. Buying and selling rates for certain other foreign currencies are also officially posted, with quotations based on the fixed rate for the French franc and the rate for the currency concerned in the Paris exchange market. Payments to all countries are subject to a commission of 0.75%, with a minimum charge of CFAF 75; exempt from this commission are payments of the state, the Postal Administration, the BEAC, salaries of Congolese diplomats abroad, expenditures of official missions abroad, scholarships of persons studying or training abroad, and debt-service payments due from companies that have entered into an agreement with the Republic of Congo. Foreign exchange purchased by the Diamond Purchase Office is subject to a commission of 0.5%, with a minimum charge of CFAF 100. An additional commission of 0.25% is levied on all payments to countries that are not members of the BEAC.

Exchange tax   No.

Exchange subsidy   No.

Forward exchange market

There are no spot or forward exchange markets for the CFA franc. However, exporters and importers can always cover their position on the Paris foreign exchange market.

Official cover of forward operations   No.

Arrangements for Payments and Receipts

Prescription of currency requirements

Since the Republic of Congo is an Operations Account country, settlements with France, Monaco, and the Operations Account countries are made in CFA francs, French francs, or the currency of any other institute of issue that maintains an Operations Account with the French Treasury. Settlements with all other countries are usually made in any of the currencies of those countries or in French francs through foreign accounts in francs.

Payment arrangements

Regional arrangements

An Operations Account is maintained with the French Treasury. All purchases or sales of foreign currencies or French francs against CFA francs are ultimately settled through a debit or credit to the Operations Account.

Clearing agreements   Yes.

Barter agreements and open accounts   n.a.

Administration of control

Exchange control authorities

Payments to the following countries, although subject to declaration, are unrestricted: (1) France (and its overseas departments and territories) and Monaco; and (2) all other countries whose bank of issue is linked with the French Treasury by an Operations

221

Account (Benin, Burkina Faso, Cameroon, Central African Republic, Chad, Comoros, Côte d'Ivoire, Equatorial Guinea, Gabon, Mali, Niger, Senegal, and Togo). Settlements and investment transactions with all foreign countries, however, are subject to control.

The General Directorate of Credit and Financial Relations in the Ministry of Finance and the Budget supervises borrowing and lending abroad. Exchange control is administered by the Ministry of Economy, Planning, and Finance (MEPF), which has delegated approval authority to the General Directorate. All exchange transactions relating to foreign countries must be effected through authorized intermediaries—that is, the Postal Administration and authorized banks.

Payment arrears	
Official	Yes.
Private	n.a.
Controls on trade in gold (coins and/or bullion)	
Controls on domestic ownership and/or trade	Residents are free to hold gold in the form of coins, art objects, or jewelry; however, to hold gold in any other form, the prior authorization of the MEPF is required.
Controls on external trade	The prior authorization of the MEPF is required to import or export gold in any form. Exempt from the authorization requirement are (1) imports and exports by or on behalf of the Treasury or the BEAC and (2) imports and exports of manufactured articles containing a small quantity of gold (such as gold-filled or gold-plated articles). Both licensed and exempt imports of gold are subject to customs declaration. There are no official exports of gold.
Controls on exports and imports of banknotes	
On exports	
Domestic currency	n.a.
Foreign currency	Residents traveling for tourist or business purposes to countries in the franc zone are allowed to take out an unlimited amount in banknotes or other payment instruments in French francs. The reexportation of foreign banknotes is allowed up to the equivalent of CFAF 250,000; the reexportation of foreign banknotes above these ceilings requires documentation demonstrating either the importation of foreign banknotes or their purchase against other means of payment registered in the name of the traveler or through the use of nonresident deposits lodged in local banks. The reexportation by nonresident travelers of means of payments other than banknotes issued abroad and registered in the name of the nonresident traveler is not restricted, subject to documentation that they had been purchased with funds drawn from a foreign account in CFA francs or with other foreign exchange.
On imports	
Domestic currency	n.a.

Resident Accounts

n.a.

Nonresident Accounts

Domestic currency accounts	The regulations pertaining to nonresident accounts are based on regulations that were applied in France before the abolition of all capital controls in 1989. Because the BEAC has suspended the repurchase of BEAC banknotes circulating outside the territories of its member countries, BEAC banknotes received by foreign correspondents' authorized banks mailed to the BEAC agency in Brazzaville may not be credited to foreign accounts in francs.

| Convertible into foreign currency | n.a. |
| Approval required | n.a. |

Imports and Import Payments

Documentation requirements for release of foreign exchange for imports

Domiciliation requirements

All imports from countries other than France (as defined above), Monaco, and the Operations Account countries must be domiciled with an authorized bank. Licenses for imports from countries other than France (as defined above), Monaco, and the Operations Account countries must be domiciled with an authorized bank and require a visa from the Foreign Trade Directorate and the General Directorate of Credit and Financial Relations.

| Preshipment inspection | n.a. |
| Letters of credit | n.a. |

Import licenses used as exchange licenses

The approved import license entitles importers to purchase the necessary exchange, provided that the shipping documents are submitted to an authorized bank.

Import licenses and other nontariff measures

An annual import program classifies imports by zones: (1) the countries of the UDEAC; (2) France; (3) other Operations Account countries; (4) EU countries other than France; and (5) all remaining countries. Thirteen product items under this program require licenses, and others are subject to ex post declaration.

Open general licenses

Except for cement, goods from all countries may be imported freely and without licenses following the implementation of the 1994 UDEAC customs and tax reforms. All imports, however, are subject to declaration.

Licenses with quotas

Imports of cement are subject to quotas.

Other nontariff measures

All imports of commercial goods must be insured through authorized insurance companies in the Republic of Congo.

Import taxes and/or tariffs

The common duty rates of the UDEAC member countries are 5% for basic necessities, 10% for raw materials and capital goods, 20% for intermediate and miscellaneous goods, and 30% for consumer goods products requiring special protection. Intra-UDEAC customs duties are 20% of the common external rates.

Import surcharges of 30% have been introduced on imports of goods previously subject to quantitative restrictions. These surcharges are to be eliminated in 3 to 6 years, with the longer period applying to certain agricultural and textile products.

Taxes collected through the exchange system

No.

State import monopoly

No.

Exports and Export Proceeds

Repatriation requirements

Proceeds from exports to countries outside the BEAC zone must be collected and repatriated within 180 days of arrival of the commodities at their destination.

Surrender requirements

Export proceeds must be surrendered within 8 days of the due date.

Documentation requirements

| Letters of credit | n.a. |
| Guarantees | n.a. |

Domiciliation

All export transactions relating to countries other than France, Monaco, and the Operations Account countries must be domiciled with an authorized bank.

Preshipment inspection	n.a.
Export licenses	In principle, all exports require an exchange commitment. But most exports to France, Monaco, and the Operations Account countries may be made freely.
Without quotas	Yes.
With quotas	n.a.
Export taxes	Export taxes of up to 13% apply to certain goods.
Taxes collected through the exchange system	No.

Payments for Invisible Transactions and Current Transfers

Controls on these payments	Payments for invisibles to France, Monaco, and the Operations Account countries are permitted freely; payments to other countries are only subject to declaration and presentation of appropriate documents to the MEPF for approval, which is granted when the appropriate documents are submitted. For many types of payment, the monitoring function of the MEPF has been delegated to authorized banks and the Postal Administration. Payments for invisibles related to trade are permitted freely when the basic trade transaction has been approved or does not require authorization.
Interest payments	
Prior approval	Yes.
Indicative limits/bona fide test	n.a.
Profit/dividends	
Prior approval	Transfers of income are permitted with the authorization of the General Directorate of Credit and Financial Relations.
Indicative limits/bona fide test	n.a.
Payments for travel	
Prior approval	Allowances in excess of the limits are subject to the authorization of the MEPF.
Quantitative limits	Residents traveling for tourist or business purposes to countries in the franc zone are allowed to take out an unlimited amount in banknotes or other payment instruments in French francs. The allowances for travel to countries outside the franc zone are subject to the following regulations: (1) for tourist travel, CFAF 100,000 a day, with a maximum of CFAF 2 million a trip; (2) for business travel, CFAF 250,000 a day, with a maximum of CFAF 5 million a trip; and (3) for official travel, the equivalent of expenses paid and CFAF 100,000 a day, with a maximum of CFAF 2 million a trip. All resident travelers, regardless of destination, must declare in writing all means of payment at their disposal at the time of departure and to surrender within 8 days all means of payment exceeding the equivalent of CFAF 25,000.
Indicative limits/bona fide test	Yes.
Medical costs	
Prior approval	Yes.
Quantitative limits	There is a limit of CFAF 100,000 a day, with a maximum of CFAF 2.5 million a trip.
Indicative limits/bona fide test	Yes.
Study abroad costs	
Quantitative limits	Yes.
Indicative limits/bona fide test	Yes.
Foreign workers' wages	
Prior approval	Yes.

Quantitative limits	The transfer of the entire net salary of a foreigner working in the Republic of Congo is permitted upon presentation of the appropriate pay voucher, provided that the transfer takes place within 3 months of the pay period. Transfers by residents of amounts smaller than CFAF 500,000 to nonmember countries of the franc zone are subject to simple declaration, and those exceeding CFAF 500,000 require prior authorization. Transfers to nonmember countries by nonresidents living in the Republic of Congo for less than 1 year are subject to authorization. Members of diplomatic missions, employees of international organizations, employees of companies operating in the Republic of Congo, government employees, and members of liberal professions are exempt from this regulation.
Indicative limits/bona fide test	Yes.
Credit card use abroad	
Prior approval	Yes.
Quantitative limits	The use of credit cards, which must be issued by resident financial intermediaries and approved by the MEPF, is limited to the ceilings applied for tourist and business travel.
Indicative limits/bona fide test	Yes.

Proceeds from Invisible Transactions and Current Transfers

Repatriation requirements	All amounts due from residents of foreign countries with respect to services and all income earned in those countries from foreign assets must be collected when due.
Surrender requirements	Proceeds should be surrendered within 1 month of the due date.
Restrictions on use of funds	No.

Capital Transactions

Controls on capital and money market instruments	Capital movements between the Republic of Congo and France (as defined above), Monaco, and the Operations Account countries are free, although ex post declarations are required. Such movements to countries that are not members of the BEAC are subject to a commission of 0.25% in addition to the 0.75% commission. Most international capital transactions are subject to prior authorization. Capital transfers abroad require exchange control approval and are restricted, but capital receipts from abroad are generally permitted freely.
	All foreign securities, foreign currency, and titles embodying claims on foreign countries or nonresidents that are held in the Republic of Congo by residents or nonresidents must be deposited with authorized banks in the Republic of Congo.
On capital market securities	
Purchase locally by nonresidents	n.a.
Sale or issue locally by nonresidents	The issuing, advertising, or offering for sale of foreign securities in the Republic of Congo requires prior authorization from the MEPF. Exempt from authorization, however, are operations in connection with (1) loans backed by a guarantee from the Congolese government; and (2) shares similar to securities whose issuing, advertising, or offering for sale in the Republic of Congo has previously been authorized.
Purchase abroad by residents	Yes.
Sale or issue abroad by residents	n.a.
On money market instruments	
Purchase locally by nonresidents	n.a.
Sale or issue locally by nonresidents	n.a.
Purchase abroad by residents	Yes.

Sale or issue abroad by residents	n.a.
On collective investment securities	
Purchase locally by nonresidents	n.a.
Sale or issue locally by nonresidents	n.a.
Purchase abroad by residents	Yes.
Sale or issue abroad by residents	n.a.
Controls on derivatives and other instruments	
Purchase locally by nonresidents	n.a.
Sale or issue locally by nonresidents	n.a.
Purchase abroad by residents	Yes.
Sale or issue abroad by residents	n.a.
Controls on credit operations	
Commercial credits	Special controls (in addition to any exchange control requirement that may apply) are maintained over borrowing and lending abroad.
By residents to nonresidents	All lending in CFA francs to nonresidents is prohibited unless special authorization is obtained from the MEPF. The following are, however, exempt from this authorization: (1) loans in foreign currency granted by registered banks and (2) other loans whose total amount outstanding does not exceed the equivalent of CFAF 5 million for any 1 lender. The making of loans that are free of authorization, and each repayment, must be reported to the General Directorate of Credit and Financial Relations within 20 days.
To residents from nonresidents	Borrowing requires prior authorization from the MEPF. However, loans contracted by registered banks and small loans, where the total amount outstanding does not exceed CFAF 10 million for any 1 borrower, the interest is no higher than 5%, and the term is at least 2 years, are exempt from this requirement. The contracting of loans that are free of authorization, and each repayment, must be reported to the General Directorate of Credit and Financial Relations within 20 days of the operation. Borrowing backed by a guarantee from the government is exempt from authorization.
Financial credits	Yes.
Guarantees, sureties, and financial backup facilities	Yes.
Controls on direct investment	
Outward direct investment	The prior approval of the MEPF is required.
Inward direct investment	Investments (including those made through foreign companies that are directly or indirectly controlled by persons in the Republic of Congo and those made by overseas branches or subsidiaries of companies in the Republic of Congo) require the prior approval of the MEPF, unless they involve the creation of a mixed-economy enterprise. The new Investment Code adopted on March 6, 1996, simplifies procedures relating to private, domestic, and foreign investment.
Controls on liquidation of direct investment	The full or partial liquidation of direct investments must be declared to the MEPF within 20 days.

Changes During 1996

Status under IMF Articles of Agreement	*June 1.* The Republic of Congo accepted the obligations of Article VIII, Sections 2, 3, and 4 of the Fund Agreement.
Capital transactions	*March 6.* A new Investment Code came into effect.

COSTA RICA

(Position as of March 31, 1997)

Status Under IMF Articles of Agreement

Article VIII	Date of acceptance: February 1, 1965.

Exchange Arrangement

Currency	The currency of Costa Rica is the Costa Rican colón.
Exchange rate structure	Unitary.
Classification	
Managed floating	The external value of the colón is determined in the interbank market. Foreign exchange trading occurs in the organized electronic foreign exchange market (MONED) among authorized traders, which is where the Central Bank (CB) carries out its intervention operations. Foreign exchange trading also takes place directly between authorized institutions outside the MONED. The government and public sector institutions conduct foreign exchange transactions with the state commercial banks and the CB at the official reference exchange rate, which is calculated at the close of each business day as the weighted average of the exchange rates used in the market during the day.
Exchange tax	A tax of 15% calculated on the average daily spread between buying and selling rates applies to all foreign exchange transactions in the interbank market.
Forward exchange market	No.

Arrangements for Payments and Receipts

Prescription of currency requirements	Nearly all payments for exchange transactions are made in U.S. dollars. Trade payments to Central America may be made in U.S. dollars or in local currencies.
Payment arrangements	No.
Administration of control	
Exchange control authorities	Regulations are issued by the CB's Superintendency of Banks and Financial Institutions (SUGEF).
International security restrictions	No.
Payment arrears	No.
Controls on trade in gold (coins and/or bullion)	
Controls on domestic ownership and/or trade	Natural and juridical persons may buy or sell domestically produced gold (except national archaeological treasures).
Controls on external trade	Licenses from the CB are required for exports of gold.
Controls on exports and imports of banknotes	No.

Resident Accounts

Eligibility to hold accounts	Juridical and natural persons are eligible.

Foreign exchange accounts permitted	Yes.
Held domestically	Yes.
Held abroad	Yes.
Accounts in domestic currency convertible into foreign currency	Yes.

Nonresident Accounts

Eligibility to hold accounts	Juridical and natural persons are eligible.
Foreign exchange accounts permitted	No.
Domestic currency accounts	No.

Imports and Import Payments

Financing requirements for imports	No.
Documentation requirements for release of foreign exchange for imports	No.
Import licenses and other nontariff measures	Imports made on a barter basis require a barter license issued by the Ministry of Economy and Commerce.
Import taxes and/or tariffs	Customs tariffs on most goods range from 5% to 20%. In addition, the following taxes are levied on imports: (1) a sales tax of 13%, from which certain essential items are exempt; and (2) selective consumption taxes at rates ranging from zero to 75%.
Taxes collected through the exchange system	No.
State import monopoly	Imports of fuels are made by the Costa Rican Oil Refinery and imports of grains by the National Production Council.

Exports and Export Proceeds

Repatriation requirements	Proceeds must be repatriated within 90 days before the end of the fiscal year.
Surrender requirements	No.
Documentation requirements	An export form (*formulario único de exportación*) must be filed.
Export licenses	
Without quotas	Licenses are required for the following: armaments, munitions, scrap iron, and scrap of nonferrous base metals from the Ministry of Economy and Commerce; sugar from the Agricultural Industrial Board for Sugarcane; beans, rice, ipecacuanha root, onions, cotton, meat, and thoroughbred cattle from the National Council of Production; airplanes from the Civil Aviation Board and the Ministry of Economy and Commerce; Indian art objects made of gold, stone, or clay from the National Museum; tobacco from the Tobacco Defense Board; textiles, flowers, lumber, certain livestock, and wild animals and plants of the forest from the Ministry of Agriculture and Livestock; and coffee from the Coffee Institute. In addition, when there is a lien on coffee in favor of a bank, that bank's approval is required before the CB grants an export license.
Export taxes	Taxes are levied on traditional exports and, in some cases, are graduated in line with international prices. There are no taxes on nontraditional exports to countries outside

Central America, and exporters of these products are entitled to receive freely negotiable tax credit certificates at the following rates based on f.o.b. value: 15% for exports to the United States, Puerto Rico, and Europe; and 20% for exports to Canada. These certificates ceased to be issued to new exporters after 1992, but exporters existing at that time benefit from them consistent with previous contractual arrangements.

Taxes collected through the exchange system	n.a.

Payments for Invisible Transactions and Current Transfers

Controls on these payments

There are no controls on these payments, but a 15% withholding tax is levied on profits, dividends, and remittances of interest abroad, except for remittances to foreign banks or their financial entities recognized by the CB as institutions normally engaged in international transactions, and for interest payments on government borrowing abroad.

Proceeds from Invisible Transactions and Current Transfers

Repatriation requirements

Repatriation must take place within 90 days of the end of the fiscal year.

Surrender requirements

No.

Capital Transactions

Controls on capital and money market instruments

There are no controls on transactions on these instruments.

Controls on derivatives and other instruments

No.

Controls on credit operations

Commercial credits

The National Budget Authority (composed of the Minister of Finance, the Minister of Planning, and the President of the CB) is in charge of authorizing the negotiation of new external credits contemplated by the central government, decentralized agencies, and state enterprises.

Financial credits

By residents to nonresidents

Private commercial banks, finance companies, and cooperatives must inform the CB when contracting credits abroad.

Controls on direct investment

No.

Controls on liquidation of direct investment

No.

Controls on real estate transactions

No.

Changes During 1996

No significant changes occurred in the exchange and trade system.

Changes During 1997

Imports and import payments

March 19. The sales tax was reduced to 13% from 15%.

CÔTE D'IVOIRE

(Position as of December 31, 1996)

Status Under IMF Articles of Agreement

Article VIII	Date of acceptance: June 1, 1996.

Exchange Arrangement

Currency

The currency of Côte d'Ivoire is the CFA franc.

Exchange rate structure

Unitary.

Classification

Pegged

The CFA franc is pegged to the French franc, the intervention currency, at the fixed rate of CFAF 1 per F 0.01. Exchange rates for other currencies are derived from the rate for the currency concerned in the Paris exchange market and the fixed rate between the French franc and the CFA franc. BCEAO levies no commission on transfers to or from all countries outside the WAEMU. However, banks and the postal system levy a commission on transfers to all countries outside the WAEMU, which must be surrendered to the Treasury.

Exchange tax

No.

Exchange subsidy

No.

Forward exchange market

Forward exchange cover for eligible imports must not extend beyond 1 month for certain specified goods and 3 months for goods designated essential commodities with no renewal of cover possible. Forward cover against exchange rate risk is permitted with prior authorization from the Directorate of the Treasury, Monetary, and Banking Affairs in the Ministry of Economics, Finance, and Planning (MEFP), only for payments for imports of goods and only for the currency stipulated in the commercial contract.

Official cover of forward operations

No.

Arrangements for Payments and Receipts

Prescription of currency requirements

Because Côte d'Ivoire is linked to the French Treasury through an Operations Account, settlements with France, Monaco, and other countries linked to the French Treasury through an Operations Account are made in CFA francs, French francs, or the currency of any other Operations Account country.

Payment arrangements

Clearing agreements

Current payments to or from The Gambia, Ghana, Guinea, Guinea-Bissau, Liberia, Mauritania, Nigeria, and Sierra Leone are normally made through the WACH.

Administration of control

Exchange control authorities

Exchange control is administered by the Directorate of the Treasury, Monetary, and Banking Affairs in the MEFP.

International security restrictions

No.

Payment arrears

Official

Yes.

Controls on trade in gold (coins and/or bullion)

Controls on external trade

Imports and exports of gold from or to any other country require prior authorization from the MEFP, which is seldom granted.

Controls on exports and imports of banknotes

On exports

Foreign currency

The reexportation of foreign banknotes is allowed up to the equivalent of CFAF 250,000; the reexportation of foreign banknotes above these ceilings requires documentation demonstrating either the importation of the foreign banknotes or their purchase against other means of payment registered in the name of the traveler or through the use of nonresident deposits at local banks.

On imports

Foreign currency

Residents and nonresidents may bring in any amount of foreign banknotes and coins (except gold coins) of countries outside the Operations Account area. Residents bringing in foreign banknotes and foreign currency traveler's checks exceeding the equivalent of CFAF 5,000 must declare them to customs upon entry and sell them to an authorized intermediary bank within 8 days.

Resident Accounts

Eligibility to hold accounts

Juridical and natural persons are eligible.

Foreign exchange accounts permitted

Yes.

Held domestically

These accounts are permitted, but prior approval is required.

Held abroad

These accounts are permitted, but prior approval is required.

Accounts in domestic currency convertible into foreign currency

Yes.

Nonresident Accounts

Eligibility to hold accounts

Juridical and natural persons are eligible.

Foreign exchange accounts permitted

These accounts are permitted, but prior approval is required.

Domestic currency accounts

Because the BCEAO has suspended the repurchase of banknotes circulating outside the territories of the CFA franc zone, nonresident accounts may not be credited or debited with BCEAO banknotes. These accounts may not be overdrawn without the prior authorization of the MEFP. Transfers of funds between nonresident accounts are not restricted.

Convertible into foreign currency

Yes.

Blocked accounts

No.

Imports and Import Payments

Foreign exchange budget

No.

Financing requirements for imports

No.

Documentation requirements for release of foreign exchange for imports

Domiciliation requirements

All imports exceeding CFAF 500,000 are subject to this requirement.

Preshipment inspection	Inspection for quality and price is required for imports exceeding CFAF 3 million; imports valued between CFAF 1.5 million and CFAF 3 million may be subject to random inspection.
Letters of credit	Letters of credit are required for goods imported from outside EU, Operations Account countries, and ACP countries.

Import licenses and other nontariff measures

Positive list	Imports are classified into three categories: (1) goods requiring prior authorization or the approval of ministries; (2) goods subject to quantitative or other restrictions requiring licenses issued by the Directorate of External Trade Promotions; and (3) freely importable goods.
Open general licenses	Import licenses for a short list of controlled products are issued by the Directorate of External Trade Promotions in the Ministry of Commerce.

Import taxes and/or tariffs	A maximum tariff rate of 35% is in effect. A statistical tax of 2.5% is levied on the c.i.f. value of all imports. Imports from members of the WAEMU and the ECOWAS are exempt from the surcharges.
Taxes collected through the exchange system	No.
State import monopoly	No.

Exports and Export Proceeds

Repatriation requirements	Proceeds from exports, including to countries in the Operations Account area, must be received within 120 days of the arrival of the goods at their destination.
Surrender requirements	Export receipts must be collected through authorized intermediary banks within 1 month of the due date.
Financing requirements	No.
Documentation requirements	Exports require a customs declaration. Exports of cocoa and coffee are subject to a specific unitary export tax and can be effected only by exporters authorized by the Price Stabilization Fund.
Letters of credit	Yes.
Guarantees	n.a.
Domiciliation	All exports valued at more than CFAF 500,000 must be domiciled with an authorized bank.
Export licenses	Exports of lumber are subject to quantitative quotas allocated through an auction.
Export taxes	Yes.
Taxes collected through the exchange system	No.

Payments for Invisible Transactions and Current Transfers

Controls on these payments	Payments to France, Monaco, and the Operations Account countries are permitted freely; those to other countries must be approved. Payments for invisibles related to trade are permitted freely.
Payments for travel	
Prior approval	Allowances in excess of these limits are subject to authorization from the MEFP.

Quantitative limits	The limits are CFAF 500,000 a trip for tourism and CFAF 75,000 a day up to 1 month for business travel.
Indicative limits/bona fide test	n.a.

Medical costs

Quantitative limits	The limits are the same as for tourist travel.
Indicative limits/bona fide test	n.a.

Study abroad costs

Quantitative limits	The limits are the same as for tourist travel.
Indicative limits/bona fide test	n.a.

Subscriptions and membership fees

Indicative limits/bona fide test	Yes.

Consulting/legal fees

Indicative limits/bona fide test	Yes.

Credit card use abroad

Quantitative limits	Credit cards can be used up to the ceilings for tourist and business travel.
Indicative limits/bona fide test	n.a.

Proceeds from Invisible Transactions and Current Transfers

Repatriation requirements	All proceeds must be collected and repatriated in full from transactions with non-Operations Account countries.
Surrender requirements	All proceeds from transactions with non-Operations Account countries must be surrendered.
Restrictions on use of funds	No.

Capital Transactions

Controls on capital and money market instruments	Capital movements to foreign countries are restricted. Capital may freely enter the member countries of the WAEMU, except with respect to direct investment subject to prior declaration and certain loan operations requiring advance authorization. Exempt from authorization, however, are operations in connection with: (1) loans backed by a guarantee from the government of Côte d'Ivoire; and (2) foreign shares similar to securities whose issuing, advertising, or offering for sale in Côte d'Ivoire has already been authorized. With the exception of controls relating to foreign securities, these measures do not apply to relations with France, Monaco, member countries of the WAEMU, and the Operations Account countries. Special controls are also maintained over the soliciting of funds for deposit with foreign natural persons and foreign firms and institutions, and over publicity aimed at placing funds abroad or at subscribing to real estate and building operations abroad; these special controls also apply to France, Monaco, and the Operations Account countries.

On capital market securities

Sale or issue locally by nonresidents	These transactions are subject to the prior authorization of the MEFP. The issue or sale of securities that have been authorized in advance may be purchased by a resident only after the latter has obtained prior approval of the MEFP. Securities sales consisting of the liquidation of an investment by means of a transfer between a nonresident and a resident may be freely executed, subject to the prescriptions concerning the financial settlement of the operation. Settlement of the operation on securities by transfer abroad

or by crediting a nonresident account requires the preparation of an exchange authorization submitted for the approval of the MEFP in support of documents attesting to the validity of the operation.

Purchase abroad by residents	These purchases and the transfer abroad of funds associated with them require the prior authorization of the MEFP.
Sale or issue abroad by residents	Residents are free to sell the securities of resident corporations abroad. If these operations result in the foreign control of establishments resident in Côte d'Ivoire, the foreign investors are required to file a declaration in advance with the MEFP. Securities sales involving the liquidation of an investment abroad are subject to prior declaration to the MEFP. The proceeds in foreign exchange from the sale or liquidation must be surrendered to an authorized intermediary bank.

On money market instruments

Sale or issue locally by nonresidents	These sales are subject to the prior authorization of the MEFP (except sales involving the liquidation of an investment, which are restricted). Transfer of the proceeds of these operations requires the preparation of an exchange authorization submitted for the approval of the MEFP in support of documents attesting to the validity of the operation.
Purchase abroad by residents	These purchases are subject to the prior authorization of the MEFP.
Sale or issue abroad by residents	Residents may freely sell money market instruments abroad. Sales involving the liquidation of an investment are subject to prior declaration. The proceeds in foreign exchange from the sale or liquidation must be surrendered to an authorization intermediary bank. The issue of money market instruments abroad by residents is governed by the provisions applicable to loans.

On collective investment securities

Sale or issue locally by nonresidents	Yes.
Purchase abroad by residents	Yes.
Sale or issue abroad by residents	Yes.

Controls on derivatives and other instruments	These instruments, which are almost nonexistent in Côte d'Ivoire, fall within the scope of the regulatory framework generally applicable to securities and investments.
Purchase locally by nonresidents	n.a.
Sale or issue locally by nonresidents	n.a.
Purchase abroad by residents	n.a.
Sale or issue abroad by residents	n.a.

Controls on credit operations

Commercial credits	For the issue of securities constituting a loan, the borrower must request advance authorization from the MEFP. However, this authorization is not required for loans contracted by authorized intermediaries or that comply with specific conditions as to amount and interest rate.
By residents to nonresidents	These credits may be granted subject to the following provisions: (1) Debts arising from exports of goods must be collected and the corresponding amounts repatriated through the BCEAO within 30 days of the payment due date. The payment due date is the date specified in the commercial contract. It must in any case be no more than 120 days after the shipment of the goods. (2) Debts arising from payment for services must also be collected and surrendered on the exchange market no later than 2 months after the payment due date. No administrative limit is set for this due date.
To residents from nonresidents	These credits may be freely granted. Their repayment is generally authorized, subject to the presentation of documents attesting to the validity of the commercial transaction or the provision of the service, as well as the payment due date.

Financial credits

By residents to nonresidents

The granting of financial credits requires the prior authorization of the MEFP. In order to transfer funds abroad to service these facilities, an exchange authorization is prepared and submitted with the required vouchers to the MEFP.

To residents from nonresidents

These facilities may be freely granted and the funds to service them must be transferred from abroad by an authorization intermediary. However, if these operations are carried out between a direct investment company established in Côte d'Ivoire and its parent company abroad, they are considered to be direct investments and are therefore subject to prior declaration to the MEFP.

The transfer abroad of the funds necessary to service a loan is subject to authorization if the loan itself required prior authorization. Requests for authorization must be accompanied by all supporting documents necessary to ensure the validity of the operation: authorization to borrow, references from the report prepared in connection with disbursement of the proceeds of the loan, and the like.

Guarantees, sureties, and financial backup facilities

By residents to nonresidents

The granting of these facilities requires the prior authorization of the MEFP. In order to transfer funds abroad to service these facilities, an exchange authorization is prepared and submitted, with the required vouchers, to the MEFP.

To residents from nonresidents

These facilities may be freely granted and the funds to service them must be transferred from abroad by an authorization intermediary. However, if these operations are carried out between a direct investment company established in Côte d'Ivoire and its parent company abroad, they are considered to be direct investments and are therefore subject to prior declaration to the MEFP.

Controls on direct investment

Outward direct investment

Investment abroad (including purchases of real estate) by a resident is subject to prior authorization by the MEFP, which must be requested by the party concerned in a letter designating the authorized intermediary that will execute payment. This payment, by transferring funds abroad or by crediting a foreign account in francs, may not be made before the end of the time period agreed by the parties.

Inward direct investment

Investments are subject to prior declaration to the MEFP, which has a period of 2 months in which to request the suspension of the operation. The transfer of a direct investment by a nonresident to another nonresident is also subject to prior declaration. Special incentives are provided for foreign and domestic investments in certain priority sectors and priority geographical areas. The incentives include exemption from customs duties and tariffs on all imported capital equipment and spare parts for investment projects, provided that no equivalent item is produced in Côte d'Ivoire. In addition, all such investments are exempt for a specified period, depending on the investment sector or area, from corporate profit taxes, patent contributions, and capital assets taxes. In general, the exemption covers 100% of applicable tax up to the fourth-to-last year of the exemption period and is reduced progressively to 75% of the tax in the third-to-last year, 50% in the second-to-last year, and 25% in the last year. Imports of raw materials for which no equivalents are produced locally are not exempt from import duties and taxes.

Controls on liquidation of direct investment

Proceeds may be freely transferred abroad or credited to a foreign account in francs after presentation of the requisite vouchers to the MEFP and the ministry's response. The liquidation of investments, whether Ivoirien investments abroad or foreign investments in Côte d'Ivoire, must be reported to the ministry within 20 days of the operation.

Controls on real estate transactions

Purchase abroad by residents

Purchases are subject to prior authorization by the MEFP, which must be requested by the party concerned in a letter designating the authorized intermediary that will execute payment. This payment, by transferring funds abroad or by crediting a foreign account in francs, may not be made before the end of the time period agreed by the parties.

| Purchase locally by nonresidents | Purchases can be freely made if they are not direct investments in a business, branch, or corporation. |
| Sale locally by nonresidents | Proceeds may be freely transferred abroad or credited to a foreign account in francs after presentation of the requisite vouchers to the MEFP and the ministry's response. |

Provisions specific to commercial banks and other credit institutions

Maintenance of accounts abroad	Banks and financial institutions are not permitted to hold liquid assets outside the WAEMU, except to cover the requirements of their current operations.
Lending to nonresidents (financial or commercial credits)	These operations can be freely executed in the case of commercial credits or are subject to the prior authorization of the MEFP in the case of loans, financial credits, or the purchase of securities issued abroad.
Lending locally in foreign exchange	General regulations on lending locally in foreign currency or purchasing locally issued securities denominated in foreign exchange apply.

Differential treatment of nonresident deposit accounts and/or deposit accounts in foreign exchange

| *Credit controls* | Yes. |

Provisions specific to institutional investors

Limits (max.) on portfolio invested abroad	Yes.
Limits (min.) on portfolio invested locally	Yes.
Currency matching regulations on assets/liabilities composition	Yes.

| **Other controls imposed by securities laws** | No. |

Changes During 1996

| **Status under IMF Articles of Agreement** | *June 1.* Côte d'Ivoire accepted the obligations of Article VIII, Sections 2, 3, and 4 of the Fund Agreement. |

CROATIA

(Position as of March 31, 1997)

Status Under IMF Articles of Agreement

Article VIII   Date of acceptance: May 29, 1995.

Exchange Arrangement

Currency   The currency of Croatia is the kuna.

Exchange rate structure   Unitary.

Classification

Managed floating   The exchange rate of the kuna is determined in the interbank foreign exchange market. The National Bank of Croatia (NBC) may set intervention exchange rates, which it applies in transactions with banks outside the interbank market for leveling undue fluctuations in the exchange rate.

Exchange tax   No.

Exchange subsidy   No.

Forward exchange market

Official cover of forward operations   The NBC has provided, on occasion, swap facilities at par for banks in a very limited forward market.

Arrangements for Payments and Receipts

Prescription of currency requirements   No.

Payment arrangements

Bilateral arrangements

  Operative   There is an arrangement with Italy.

Administration of control

Exchange control authorities   The NBC formulates and administers exchange rate policy and may issue foreign exchange regulations. A trade law was enacted on February 17, 1996. Companies wishing to engage in foreign trade must register with the commercial courts. The representative offices of foreign companies must be registered with the Ministry of Economy (MOE).

International security restrictions

In accordance with IMF Executive Board Decision No. 144-(52/51)   Yes.

In accordance with UN sanctions   Yes.

Payment arrears

Official   Yes.

Controls on trade in gold (coins and/or bullion)

Controls on external trade   The exportation of unprocessed gold and gold coins by producers of gold or by authorized commercial banks is subject to the approval of the NBC. Importation of gold is subject to the approval of the MOE.

Controls on exports and imports of banknotes

On exports

Domestic currency	The exportation of Croatian currency by both residents and nonresidents is limited to HRK 2,000 a person.
Foreign currency	Resident natural persons may take abroad up to the equivalent of DM 1,000. An additional amount equivalent up to DM 2,000 may be taken out, provided that it is withdrawn from foreign currency accounts or purchased from banks for travel expenses. In both cases, the NBC may allow higher amounts to be taken out on a case-by-case basis.

On imports

Domestic currency	The importation of Croatian currency by both residents and nonresidents is limited to HRK 2,000 a person.

Resident Accounts

Eligibility to hold accounts	Resident natural and juridical persons may, in principle, open and operate foreign exchange accounts only in Croatia. However, the NBC has the authority to allow resident juridical persons to keep foreign exchange in accounts with foreign banks in order to cover the costs of business operations and to meet the requirement of regular foreign trade activities abroad. The law also makes specific provisions for resident juridical persons engaged in capital project construction abroad to maintain accounts with foreign banks, subject to a license issued by the NBC.
Foreign exchange accounts permitted	
Held domestically	Yes.
Held abroad	Yes.
Accounts in domestic currency convertible into foreign currency	Yes.

Nonresident Accounts

Eligibility to hold accounts	Nonresident natural and juridical persons may open foreign exchange accounts with fully licensed banks in Croatia.
Foreign exchange accounts permitted	These accounts may be credited freely with foreign exchange and debited for payments abroad for conversion into domestic currency; reconversion of domestic currency into a foreign currency is permitted. As a measure against money laundering, juridical persons may not credit these accounts with foreign banknotes exceeding $20,000, without special permission from the NBC. Effective March 12, 1997, nonresident juridical persons can withdraw up to the equivalent of HRK 15,000 each month from their deposit accounts.
Domestic currency accounts	These accounts may be opened with the proceeds from sales of goods and services or with foreign exchange transferred from abroad.
Convertible into foreign currency	Foreign exchange may be purchased with funds held in these accounts without restriction.
Blocked accounts	Balances in foreign exchange accounts held by residents (natural persons) of the former Yugoslavia (Serbia/Montenegro) were blocked and have been replaced by claims on the Croatian government.

Imports and Import Payments

Foreign exchange budget

No.

Financing requirements for imports

Advance payment requirements

Advance payments for imports are permitted, except where down payments are required by suppliers in accordance with customary international practices.

Documentation requirements for release of foreign exchange for imports

Invoice of agreement is required for transfers.

Import licenses and other nontariff measures

Import quotas were abolished by the decree of July 12, 1996, although such quotas are, in principle, allowed for under the trade law, under conditions similar to WTO rules. All imports are free from licensing requirements except for a list of products whose importation is controlled by international agreement for noneconomic reasons (such as arms, gold, illegal drugs and narcotics, and artistic and historic work), and a small number of other products (notably iron tubes in bars). The importation of these items is allowed on a case-by-case basis.

Negative list

Yes.

Import taxes and/or tariffs

Imports are subject to customs tariffs of up to 25%, with a few exceptions. The exemption for duty-free imports by travelers is $100. Goods imported by travelers and postal shipments up to the value of $500 are subject to a simplified customs procedure with a unified tariff rate of 8%. For imports exceeding that value, the regular import tariffs and taxes are applied. Returning citizens may bring into the country household effects duty free in an amount that is relative to the period spent abroad for household effects and for private business purposes without restrictions, but are subject to the approval of the Ministry of Finance on a case-by-case basis. Under certain conditions, goods imported by nonresidents for investment purposes are exempt from import duties. Also, raw materials and intermediate products used in the production of exports are exempt from all import duties and taxes, provided that the value added of the export product is at least 30% of the value of the imported items and that export proceeds are received in convertible currency.

Taxes collected through the exchange system

No.

State import monopoly

No.

Exports and Export Proceeds

Repatriation requirements

Export proceeds must be collected and repatriated in full within 90 days of date of exportation. This period may be extended up to 150 days with permission from the NBC. If payment terms in excess of 90 days have been agreed to with foreign importers, the credit arrangement must be registered with the NBC.

Surrender requirements

No.

Financing requirements

No.

Documentation requirements

Guarantees

Yes.

Export licenses

Exports are free of restrictions except for certain products for which permits must be obtained (e.g., weapons, drugs, and art objects); several basic foodstuffs to ensure adequate domestic supplies; unrenewable resources (oil and natural gas); and hides and wood.

Export taxes

No.

Payments for Invisible Transactions and Current Transfers

Controls on these payments	No.

Proceeds from Invisible Transactions and Current Transfers

Repatriation requirements	Proceeds from services are, in principle, subject to the same regulations as those applying to exports.
Surrender requirements	No.
Restrictions on use of funds	No.

Capital Transactions

Controls on capital and money market instruments	Inward portfolio investment is not restricted, except in central bank short-term securities in the primary market. In general, outward portfolio investment is restricted.
On capital market securities	
Purchase abroad by residents	The restriction applies to natural persons only.
On money market instruments	
Purchase locally by nonresidents	Only purchases on the primary market are permitted.
Sale or issue locally by nonresidents	Yes.
Purchase abroad by residents	The restriction applies to natural persons only.
Sale or issue abroad by residents	Yes.
On collective investment securities	
Sale or issue locally by nonresidents	Yes.
Purchase abroad by residents	Purchases by juridical persons are free but those by natural persons require approval from the NBC.
Controls on derivatives and other instruments	
Sale or issue locally by nonresidents	Yes.
Purchase abroad by residents	The restriction applies to natural persons only.
Controls on credit operations	
Commercial credits	
To residents from nonresidents	Resident juridical persons, including commercial banks, may borrow abroad but are required to register the loans contracted with the NBC.
Financial credits	
By residents to nonresidents	Resident juridical persons may extend financial credits to nonresidents if the credit represents shares.
Guarantees, sureties, and financial backup facilities	
By residents to nonresidents	Yes.

Controls on direct investment

Outward direct investment

Such investments must generally be undertaken through loans abroad or through reinvestment of profits. Foreign direct investment abroad by residents must be registered with the MOE within 30 days from the signature of the contract.

Inward direct investment

Investments must be registered with the commercial courts only.

Controls on liquidation of direct investment

Proceeds may be transferred after settlement of legal obligations, including tax payments.

Controls on real estate transactions

Purchase abroad by residents

Residents may acquire real estate abroad on the basis of reciprocity of treatment, but in practice, they are not permitted to purchase foreign exchange in the exchange market for this purpose; the use of balances in foreign exchange accounts for this purpose is also prohibited.

Purchase locally by nonresidents

Nonresident natural persons may acquire real estate in Croatia through inheritance as long as their country of residence extends reciprocal treatment to residents of Croatia. Nonresident natural persons not engaged in economic activities in Croatia may purchase real estate only under the same conditions. Nonresident natural or juridical persons engaged in economic activities in Croatia may also purchase real estate under these conditions and may sell it to resident or nonresident juridical persons.

Provisions specific to commercial banks and other credit institutions

Differential treatment of nonresident deposit accounts and/or deposit accounts in foreign exchange

No.

Open foreign exchange position limits

The limit is 30% of the bank's Tier 1 capital.

Provisions specific to institutional investors

Limits (max.) on portfolio invested abroad

Investment funds may not invest more than 5% of the value of the fund in the securities of a single issuer. However, this limit may increase to 10% provided that not more than 40% of the assets of the fund are invested in securities of other issuers. In addition, investment funds may acquire bonds of one issuer only if the total face value of these bonds does not exceed 10% of the total face value of all the bonds of the same issuer, if they are in circulation. For purposes of determining this limit, bonds of the Croatian state, member states of the EU, and other member states of the OECD are valued at one-half their face value.

Other controls imposed by securities laws

No.

Changes During 1996

Imports and import payments

February 17. A trade law was enacted.

July 12. Import quotas were removed.

Capital transactions

February 17. Domestic juridical persons were permitted to invest abroad in the form of foreign direct investment (on the basis of the new trade law).

Changes During 1997

Nonresident accounts

March 12. Foreign juridical persons were permitted to withdraw up to the foreign currency equivalent of HRK 15,000 each month from their deposit accounts at authorized banks.

CYPRUS

(Position as of March 31, 1997)

Status Under IMF Articles of Agreement

Article VIII	Date of acceptance: January 9, 1991.

Exchange Arrangement

Currency	The currency of Cyprus is the Cyprus pound.
Exchange rate structure	Unitary.

Classification

Pegged	The Cyprus pound is pegged to a basket based on the ECU at ECU 1.7086 per £C 1, within margins of 2.25% around the ECU central rate. Subject to certain limitations, including a limit on spreads between buying and selling rates, authorized dealers (banks) are free to determine and quote their own buying and selling rates.
Exchange tax	No.
Exchange subsidy	No.
Forward exchange market	Authorized dealers may trade in the forward market at rates freely negotiated with their customers. For U.S. dollars and pounds sterling, however, forward margins may not be larger than those applied by the Central Bank of Cyprus (CBC) for cover for a similar period. Authorized dealers are allowed to purchase forward cover from the CBC at prevailing rates or to conduct forward operations between 2 foreign currencies for cover in 1 of the 2 currencies.
Official cover of forward operations	The CBC offers authorized dealers facilities for forward purchases of U.S. dollars and pounds sterling for exports for periods of up to 24 months and for imports normally for up to 9 months.

Arrangements for Payments and Receipts

Prescription of currency requirements	No.
Payment arrangements	No.

Administration of control

Exchange control authorities	Exchange controls are administered by the CBC in cooperation with authorized dealers to whom authority has been delegated to approve applications for the allocation of foreign exchange for a number of bona fide transactions.

International security restrictions

In accordance with IMF Executive Board Decision No. 144-(52/51)	On October 7, 1993, the CBC notified the IMF of restrictions imposed previously against the Federal Republic of Yugoslavia (Serbia/Montenegro) pursuant to relevant UN Security Council resolutions. These restrictions were terminated on October 16, 1996, but bank balances belonging to the National Bank of Yugoslavia remain frozen.
In accordance with UN sanctions	Economic sanctions against Iraq, Libya and the UNITA organization pursuant to UN Security Council resolutions are administered by the CBC and relevant government departments.
Payment arrears	No.

Controls on trade in gold (coins and/or bullion)

Controls on domestic ownership and/or trade

Residents may hold and acquire gold coins in Cyprus for numismatic collection purposes. Residents other than the monetary authorities, authorized dealers in gold, and industrial users are not allowed to hold or acquire gold bullion at home or abroad.

Controls on external trade

The exportation of gold coins or bullion requires the permission of the CBC. Authorized dealers in gold are permitted to import gold bullion only for the purpose of disposing of it to industrial users.

Controls on exports and imports of banknotes

On exports

Domestic currency

Resident travelers may take out up to £C 100. Nonresident travelers may take out any amount of Cypriot banknotes that they imported and declared on arrival. In the case of failure to declare the banknotes imported on arrival, nonresidents may export up to the equivalent of $1,000 in Cypriot or foreign banknotes.

Authorized dealers may dispatch any amount of Cypriot banknotes to foreign banks in exchange for foreign currency.

Foreign currency

Resident travelers may take out any amount of foreign banknotes purchased from authorized dealers as part of their foreign currency allowances. Nonresident travelers may take out any amount of foreign banknotes that they imported and declared on arrival, as well as any amount purchased from banks in Cyprus against external funds. In addition, departing nonresidents may convert, through authorized dealers, domestic currency up to £C 100 into foreign banknotes, which they can export.

On imports

Foreign currency

Nonresidents entering Cyprus should declare to customs any Cypriot or foreign banknotes that they plan to reexport, deposit with authorized dealers, or use to purchase immovable property or goods to export.

Resident Accounts

Eligibility to hold accounts

Juridical and natural persons are eligible.

Foreign exchange accounts permitted

Yes.

Held domestically

Residents dealing with transit trade may deposit up to 97.5% of sale proceeds in these accounts and use balances to pay for the value of traded goods. Residents engaged in manufacturer-exporter activities may deposit up to 50% of export proceeds in these accounts and use balances to pay for imports of raw materials used in production.

Both transit traders and manufacturers-exporters are, however, required to convert into Cyprus pounds at the end of each year any balances in excess of the amount that is necessary for payments of traded goods or raw materials during the following 3 months. Resident hoteliers may deposit in such accounts part of their receipts in foreign currency that they need to make imminent installment payments on foreign currency loans. Approval of the CBC is required for residents other than those referred to above and below.

Held abroad

Cypriot repatriates may keep in foreign currency accounts, external accounts with banks in Cyprus, or accounts with banks abroad all of their foreign currency holdings and earnings accruing from properties they own abroad. Resident individuals temporarily working abroad may maintain their foreign currency earnings in foreign currency accounts, external accounts with banks in Cyprus, or accounts with banks abroad. Approval of the CBC is required for residents other than those referred to in the preceding paragraph. Such approval, however, is granted only in exceptional circumstances.

Accounts in domestic currency convertible into foreign currency	These accounts are designated as external accounts.

Nonresident Accounts

Eligibility to hold accounts	Juridical and natural persons are eligible.
Foreign exchange accounts permitted	Nonresidents may open and maintain accounts with authorized dealers, which may be credited freely with payments from nonresidents (such as transfers from other external accounts or foreign currency accounts), with proceeds from sales of any foreign currency by nonresidents (including declared banknotes), and with authorized payments from residents in Cyprus pounds.
	The accounts may be debited for payments to residents and nonresidents, for remittances abroad, for transfers to other external accounts or foreign currency accounts, and for payments in cash (Cyprus pounds) in Cyprus. Companies registered or incorporated in Cyprus that are accorded nonresident status (generally designated as offshore companies) by the CBC as well as their nonresident employees may maintain foreign currency accounts in Cyprus or abroad, as well as local disbursement accounts for meeting their payments in Cyprus.
Domestic currency accounts	Yes.
Convertible into foreign currency	These accounts are designated as external accounts, and the same regulations as for foreign currency accounts apply.
Blocked accounts	Blocked accounts are maintained in the name of nonresidents for funds that may not immediately be transferred outside of Cyprus. Blocked funds may either be held as deposits or be invested in government securities or government-guaranteed securities. Income earned on blocked funds is freely transferable to the nonresident beneficiary or may be credited to an external account or foreign currency account.
	In addition to income, up to £C 50,000 in principal may be released annually from blocked funds for transfer outside Cyprus. Funds can also be released from blocked accounts to meet reasonable expenses in Cyprus of the account holder and his or her family, including educational expenses, donations to charitable institutions in Cyprus, payments for the acquisition of immovable property in Cyprus, and any other amounts authorized by the CBC.

Imports and Import Payments

Foreign exchange budget	No.
Financing requirements for imports	
Advance payment requirements	Prior approval of the CBC is required for amounts exceeding £C 50,000. Authorized dealers are allowed to sell to departing residents foreign exchange up to £C 20,000 for purchases and for the importation of goods into Cyprus; for larger amounts, approval by the CBC is required.
Documentation requirements for release of foreign exchange for imports	
Domiciliation requirements	Yes.
Import licenses used as exchange licenses	Yes.
Import licenses and other nontariff measures	Most imports are free of licensing requirements. A license is required for a small number of commodities prescribed by the Minister of Commerce, Industry, and Tourism.

Nonresidents may not import commodities into Cyprus unless they are granted a special import license by the Minister of Commerce, Industry, and Tourism. The importation of goods such as motor vehicles to be used temporarily by visitors, goods to be exhibited in Cyprus and reexported, etc. is not subject to this requirement.

Positive list	The import of goods originating in Turkey is prohibited.
Import taxes and/or tariffs	Yes.
Taxes collected through the exchange system	No.
State import monopoly	No.

Exports and Export Proceeds

Repatriation requirements	All exports whose value exceeds £C 1,000 are subject to exchange control monitoring to ensure the repatriation of the sale proceeds.
Surrender requirements	Export proceeds must be surrendered to authorized dealers without delay.
Financing requirements	No.
Documentation requirements	
Domiciliation	Yes.
Export licenses	There are no licensing requirements, but the Minister of Commerce, Industry, and Tourism may restrict certain exports or exports to a specific destination when deemed necessary on the grounds of public interest or to comply with Cyprus's international obligations.
Without quotas	n.a.
With quotas	n.a.
Export taxes	No.

Payments for Invisible Transactions and Current Transfers

Controls on these payments	Payments for invisibles abroad require the approval of the CBC, but approval for certain types of payments has been delegated to authorized dealers.
Freight/insurance	If the payment exceeds £C 5,000, documentary evidence must be subsequently submitted to the CBC. The CBC approves applications for the remittance of insurance premiums owed to foreign insurance companies.
Indicative limits/bona fide test	n.a.
Unloading/storage costs	
Prior approval	Yes.
Administrative expenses	
Prior approval	Yes.
Commissions	
Prior approval	Payments in excess of 5% of the price of exported goods require prior approval of the CBC.
Quantitative limits	Yes.
Indicative limits/bona fide test	Yes.
Interest payments	
Prior approval	Yes.

Profit/dividends	Profits and dividends from approved foreign investments may be transferred abroad without limitation after payment of due taxes and charges.
Payments for travel	
Quantitative limits	Authorized dealers are allowed, without reference to the CBC, to sell to resident travelers foreign exchange up to £C 1,000 a person a trip for tourist travel. Moreover, payments for travel may be made through credit cards issued by authorized dealers. The allowance for business travel is £C 150 a day with a maximum of £C 1,500 a trip, or £C 80 a day with a maximum of £C 800 a trip if the traveler holds an international business credit card. Authorized dealers may approve, without reference to the CBC, applications by resident travel agents to pay foreign travel agents and hotels up to £C 10,000 for each organized trip.
Indicative limits/bona fide test	The CBC approves applications for higher amounts to cover bona fide expenses without limitation.
Medical costs	
Quantitative limits	The limit is £C 5,000 for medical expenses abroad.
Indicative limits/bona fide test	Unlimited additional amounts are provided with the approval of the CBC.
Study abroad costs	
Quantitative limits	Exchange allowances are based on the cost of living, which is reviewed yearly. The current annual allowance for living expenses for studies in Greece is £C 4,000; for other western European countries, £C 5,800; for North America, £C 7,200; for Australia, £C 4,300; and for all other countries, £C 4,000. There is no limit on the remittance of foreign exchange for payment of tuition fees.
Indicative limits/bona fide test	Greater amounts may be allowed with the approval of the CBC.
Subscriptions and membership fees	
Prior approval	Prior approval of the CBC is required for amounts higher than £C 300.
Quantitative limits	Authorized dealers may carry out payments for subscription to professional bodies or societies up to £C 300 a transaction.
Indicative limits/bona fide test	n.a.
Consulting/legal fees	
Prior approval	Yes.
Foreign workers' wages	
Prior approval	Yes.
Quantitative limits	Nonresidents who are temporarily employed in Cyprus by resident firms or individuals and are paid in local currency may deposit with authorized dealers up to £C 500 of their monthly remuneration in external or foreign currency accounts, the balance of which may be freely transferred abroad without reference to the CBC.
Indicative limits/bona fide test	Deposits or transfers of amounts greater than £C 500 need approval of the CBC.
Pensions	
Prior approval	Yes.
Gambling/prize earnings	
Prior approval	Yes.
Family maintenance/alimony	
Prior approval	Yes.
Quantitative limits	Residents may remit, through authorized dealers, up to £C 200 every 6 months to relatives or other persons who reside abroad without reference to the CBC.

Indicative limits/bona fide test	Prior approval of the CBC is required for greater amounts.
Credit card use abroad	Authorized dealers may issue personal credit cards valid abroad to any resident, except for residents studying abroad or temporarily living abroad. These cards, which are designated as international personal cards, may be used abroad for payments to hotels and restaurants; transportation expenses; doctors, clinics, or hospitals; international telephone calls; cash withdrawals up to £C 100 a trip; and any other payments of a total value not exceeding £C 300 a trip. In addition, international personal cards may be used for payments abroad or from Cyprus up to £C 300 for each transaction for the following purposes: examination fees, application fees for admission to foreign educational institutions, subscriptions to professional bodies or societies, fees for enrollment in professional or educational seminars or conferences, and hotel reservation fees. International personal cards may also be used for mail orders of books up to £C 300.
	Authorized dealers may also issue company cards valid abroad (designated as international business cards) to resident businessmen and professionals who are involved in the international trade of goods or services and travel abroad on business. Holders of international business cards may charge mail orders of books or equipment for the company up to £C 1,000, as well as the payments allowed for holders of international personal cards.
Quantitative limits	Yes.
Indicative limits/bona fide test	n.a.

Proceeds from Invisible Transactions and Current Transfers

Repatriation requirements	Yes.
Surrender requirements	Receipts from invisibles must be sold to an authorized dealer.
Restrictions on use of funds	Yes.

Capital Transactions

Controls on capital and money market instruments	Capital transfers abroad require authorization from the CBC.
On capital market securities	
Purchase locally by nonresidents	Nonresident aliens may own up to 49% of the issued capital of public companies (i.e., companies whose shares are admitted to the Cyprus Stock Exchange) other than banks, while there is no limit on the total percentage of the capital of such companies owned by nonresidents of Cypriot origin, provided each nonresident (Cypriot or alien) person's shareholding does not exceed 5% of the company's issued capital.
	For public companies in the banking sector, the limit on total nonresident (Cypriot and alien) participation is 15% of the company's issued capital, of which not more than 6% may be owned by nonresident aliens, provided each nonresident person's shareholding does not exceed 0.5% of the company's issued capital.
	Public companies and stockbrokers are authorized to carry out the relevant transactions with nonresidents without reference to the CBC, subject to the limits described above. Applications over these limits may be approved by the CBC.
Sale or issue locally by nonresidents	Securities issued by nonresidents may be admitted to the Cyprus Stock Exchange, but residents are not generally permitted to purchase them.
Purchase abroad by residents	Outward portfolio investment is permitted only for Cypriot repatriates and residents temporarily working abroad, who may freely use their balances in foreign currency or external accounts to purchase securities abroad, and for resident employees of multinational enterprises who participate in the employee stock purchase plan offered to them by their employer.

Sale or issue abroad by residents	Prior approval of the CBC is required.
On money market instruments	
Purchase locally by nonresidents	Nonresidents may purchase treasury bills denominated in Cyprus pounds.
Sale or issue locally by nonresidents	Issuance requires prior approval of the CBC.
Purchase abroad by residents	Except for banks and institutional investors, only Cypriot repatriates and residents temporarily working abroad may purchase money market instruments abroad by using their balances in foreign currency or external accounts.
Sale or issue abroad by residents	Prior approval of the CBC is required.
On collective investment securities	
Purchase locally by nonresidents	The purchase of securities issued by public investment companies in Cyprus is permitted within the limits applied to capital market securities.
Sale or issue locally by nonresidents	Securities issued by nonresidents may be admitted to the Cyprus Stock Exchange, but residents are not generally permitted to purchase them.
Purchase abroad by residents	Except for institutional investors, only Cypriot repatriates and residents temporarily working abroad may purchase such securities abroad by using their balances in foreign currency or external accounts.
Sale or issue abroad by residents	Prior approval of the CBC is required.
Controls on derivatives and other instruments	Yes.
Controls on credit operations	
Commercial credits	
By residents to nonresidents	Credits with a maturity of up to 180 days for the export of goods from Cyprus may be freely granted. Other credits require approval of the CBC.
To residents from nonresidents	Commercial credits with a maturity of up to 200 days for imports of goods to Cyprus may be negotiated freely. Other credits are subject to approval of the CBC.
Financial credits	
By residents to nonresidents	Residents other than authorized dealers are not allowed to grant these credits without the approval of the CBC.
To residents from nonresidents	These credits are subject to approval by the CBC, which is usually granted for productive projects.
Guarantees, sureties, and financial backup facilities	
By residents to nonresidents	Authorized dealers may issue these guarantees without reference to the CBC in several cases including tender guarantees up to 5% of the tender price, performance bonds up to 10% of the contract price, guarantees for the refund of advance payments, and guarantees in respect of any other transactions where an immediate payment to the nonresident beneficiary could be made under the existing exchange control rules. In other cases, prior approval of the CBC is required.
Controls on direct investment	
Outward direct investment	Approval of the CBC is required. The amount of capital that can be directly transferred abroad is limited to £C 0.5 million. If only the issue of a guarantee is required, the amount of the guarantee should not exceed £C 1 million. In cases where direct transfer of capital as well as a guarantee is required, the total amount should not exceed £C 1 million, provided the amount of capital to be directly transferred does not exceed £C 0.5 million. In exceptional cases where it appears certain that a large part of the investment will be repatriated in a short time, the governor of the CBC may approve larger amounts.

Inward direct investment	Investments require prior approval of the CBC. In most cases, foreign participation of up to 100% is permitted. An application may be rejected if the proposed investment will affect national security, have adverse environmental effects, is deemed harmful for the Cypriot economy, or if the amount to be invested is lower than indicative minimum limits.
	In the primary sector, foreign participation of up to 49% is allowed. Applications are examined by the CBC in consultation with the Ministry of Agriculture, Natural Resources, and Environment.
	There is no limit on the percentage of foreign participation in the manufacturing sector, or in wholesale and retail trade. The CBC handles the applications if the foreign participation does not exceed 49% and the amount to be invested is lower than £C 750,000. Otherwise, applications are considered jointly by the CBC and the Ministry of Commerce, Industry, and Tourism.
	For most other activities, foreign participation of up to 100% is permitted. Over 70 types of services have been classified into 2 categories for which the indicative minimum limits of investment are £C 50,000 and £C 100,000.
	Investors in the tourism sector are subject to the government tourism policy applicable at the time. The current policy, which was introduced in 1995, provides for up to 49% of foreign participation in hotels and other tourism establishments. However, up to 100% of foreign participation may be allowed for supplementary tourism projects such as golf courses, marinas, etc.
	Applications for the establishment of new banks, insurance or financial companies, newspaper and magazine publishing houses, and new airlines are considered on a case-by-case basis, and the extent of allowable foreign participation is decided on the merits of each individual case.
	For a small number of activities that are considered saturated, no foreign participation is allowed. These activities include land development and education and public utility services governed by specific legislation, such as distribution of electricity, telecommunications, etc.
Controls on liquidation of direct investment	Proceeds may be repatriated in full at any time after payment of taxes.
Controls on real estate transactions	
Purchase abroad by residents	Residents are generally not allowed to purchase real estate abroad, except when the real estate is part of an authorized direct investment project.
Purchase locally by nonresidents	Nonresidents cannot acquire immovable property in Cyprus other than by inheritance, except with the approval of the Council of Ministers, and they are required to pay the purchase price with foreign exchange. Nonresidents of Cypriot origin do not need approval of the Council of Ministers. Foreign investments in real estate for speculative purposes are not approved.
Sale locally by nonresidents	Proceeds are transferable abroad after payment of taxes, provided the seller acquired the property by paying with foreign exchange; otherwise, proceeds are transferable abroad at the rate of £C 50,000 a year through a blocked account.
Provisions specific to commercial banks and other credit institutions	
Borrowing abroad	Prior approval of the CBC is required.
Maintenance of accounts abroad	Authorized dealers are allowed to maintain working balances with foreign banks within limits prescribed by the CBC, as well as deposits abroad held as cover for their deposit liabilities in foreign currencies.
Lending to nonresidents (financial or commercial credits)	Authorized dealers are allowed to grant medium- and long-term loans in foreign currencies to nonresidents of up to 20% of their deposit liabilities in foreign currencies. They are also allowed to grant loans and credits to offshore companies registered in Cyprus of up to 10% of their deposit liabilities in foreign currencies.

	In addition, authorized dealers are allowed to lend Cyprus pounds up to a maximum of £C 3,000 to nonresident individuals temporarily living in Cyprus.
Lending locally in foreign exchange	Authorized dealers may grant short-term credit facilities in foreign currency (e.g., discounting bills of exchange) to residents without reference to the CBC. For other lending to residents in foreign currency, prior approval of the CBC is required. Such approval is usually granted for the following purposes: to finance transit trade, to provide working capital for resident oil companies or for industries operating in the industrial free zone, to meet the financial needs of Cyprus Airways, and to finance other desirable productive projects.
Purchase of locally issued securities denominated in foreign exchange	Yes.
Differential treatment of nonresident deposit accounts and/or deposit accounts in foreign exchange	The monetary regulations applied to accounts in foreign currencies (held either by nonresidents or by residents) are different from those applied to accounts in Cyprus pounds.
Reserve requirements	Yes.
Liquid asset requirements	Liquid assets in foreign currencies equal to at least 60% of deposit liabilities in foreign currencies must be maintained. For deposits in Cyprus pounds, there is no prescribed liquidity ratio since January 1, 1996. However, the liquidity positions of banks are monitored by the CBC for prudential purposes.
Interest rate controls	Accounts in Cyprus pounds are subject to an interest rate ceiling of 9%, whereas accounts in foreign currencies are not subject to interest rate ceilings.
Credit controls	Yes.
Investment regulations	There are prescribed assets that may be held with respect to accounts in foreign currencies. Authorized dealers can purchase securities issued abroad, such as securities issued by solvent foreign governments and traded in recognized stock exchanges abroad, within certain limits prescribed by the CBC.
Open foreign exchange position limits	The net open/uncovered position in any one foreign currency and the overall aggregate net position in all foreign currencies may not exceed 10% and 15%, respectively, of the authorized dealer's capital base, except with the prior approval of the CBC.
Provisions specific to institutional investors	
Limits (max.) on portfolio invested abroad	Insurance companies and public investment companies may invest abroad a maximum of 20% of their portfolio. Other institutional investors are not allowed to invest abroad.
Limits (min.) on portfolio invested locally	Yes.
Other controls imposed by securities laws	Yes.

Changes During 1996

Arrangements for payments and receipts	*July 5.* The prohibition of transactions associated with deliveries of weapons and military equipment to the constituent republics of the former Socialist Republic of Yugoslavia was terminated in accordance with the relevant UN Security Council decision of June 18, 1996.
	October 16. Sanctions against the Federal Republic of Yugoslavia were terminated, but bank balances belonging to the National Bank of Yugoslavia remain frozen.
Imports and import payments	*January 1.* Most quantitative import restrictions were abolished, and the number of commodities for which an import license is required was reduced.

Capital transactions

March 29. Investment companies admitted to the Cyprus Stock Exchange were allowed to invest abroad up to 20% of their portfolio.

June 18. The rules governing portfolio investment in Cyprus by nonresidents were liberalized. The limit on total nonresident Cypriot participation in the issued capital of public companies (i.e., companies whose shares are admitted to the Cyprus Stock Exchange) other than banks was abolished. The limit on total nonresident participation in the issued capital of each such company was increased to a maximum of 49% from 25%, provided each nonresident person's shareholding does not exceed 5% of the company's issued capital.

June 18. For public companies in the banking sector, the limit on total nonresident participation was raised to 15% of the company's issued capital from 8%, while the nonresident alien participation within this limit was raised to 6% from 3%, provided each nonresident person's shareholding does not exceed 0.5% of the company's issued capital.

June 18. The CBC authorized public companies to carry out transactions with nonresidents without reference to the CBC, subject to the limits described above. The CBC may grant approval for nonresident participation in public companies over these limits.

Changes During 1997

Imports and import payments

February 11. The requirement of deposits with the CBC for advance import payments was abolished.

Payments for invisible transactions and current transfers

January 29. Authorized dealers were empowered to approve, without reference to the CBC, applications by residents for transactions concerning triangular trade, i.e., payments through Cyprus for goods transported from one foreign country to another.

March 1. The use of personal international credit cards was expanded so as to cover cash withdrawals up to £C 100 a trip, additional payments for any purpose up to £C 300 a trip, and mail orders of books up to £C 300.

Capital transactions

January 30. Nonresidents who acquired real estate in Cyprus by paying with foreign exchange were granted the right to transfer abroad in a lump sum the entire proceeds from the sale of such property, after payment of taxes. Previously, they were allowed to transfer abroad up to £C 50,000 or the original acquisition cost paid with foreign exchange, whatever was higher. The remainder was deposited in a blocked account and released at the rate of £C 50,000 a year following the year of sale.

February 5. The policy was liberalized in regard to direct investments in Cyprus by nonresidents. Under the new policy, administrative procedures have become simpler and, in most cases, foreign participation of up to 100% was permitted. Previously 100% of nonresident participation was allowed only for the manufacture of products new to Cyprus or products exclusively for export, as well as selected tourist projects. The list of saturated activities where no foreign participation is allowed was substantially reduced; it includes land development; education; and public utility services that are governed by specific legislation, such as distribution of electricity, telecommunications, etc. In particular, wholesale trade and retail trade are no longer considered saturated sectors.

March 3. Cypriot repatriates (i.e., residents of Cyprus who were previously resident in other countries) who decide to emigrate again were granted the right to transfer abroad in a lump sum all the funds they previously imported in Cyprus and converted to local funds, in addition to the emigration allowance granted to any emigrant.

CZECH REPUBLIC

(Position as of May 31, 1997)

Status Under IMF Articles of Agreement

Article VIII	Date of acceptance: October 1, 1995.

Exchange Arrangement

Currency	The currency of the Czech Republic is the Czech koruna.
Exchange rate structure	Unitary.

Classification

Managed floating — Throughout 1996 and early 1997, the external value of the Czech koruna was determined on the basis of a basket consisting of the deutsche mark (65%) and the U.S. dollar (35%). The Czech National Bank (CNB) quoted daily buying and selling rates for 23 convertible currencies, the ECU, and the SDR. Commercial banks set their own foreign exchange rates of the Czech koruna against other currencies, which were applied to the transactions with their clients. Since February 28, 1996, the exchange rate of the Czech koruna quoted by the CNB was allowed to fluctuate within band limits of ±7.5% against the central rate. Since May 27, 1997, the external value of the Czech koruna has been determined by supply and demand conditions in the foreign exchange market. The CNB manages the rate with a view to maintaining a stable relationship against the deutsche mark. The CNB may intervene in the foreign exchange market and may signal a desired exchange rate band.

Exchange tax	There is no exchange tax; however, on the occasion of fixing, the CNB collects a fee of 0.25% on its foreign exchange transactions with commercial banks.
Exchange subsidy	No.
Forward exchange market	Yes.
Official cover of forward operations	No.

Arrangements for Payments and Receipts

Prescription of currency requirements	No.
Payment arrangements	No.

Administration of control

Exchange control authorities	The Ministry of Finance and the CNB are responsible for the administration of exchange controls and regulations in accordance with the Foreign Exchange Act. In general, the Ministry of Finance exercises authority over governmental credits, central and local authorities, budgetary organizations, and state funds. The CNB exercises authority over the activities of all other agents.
International security restrictions	No.
Payment arrears	No.

Controls on trade in gold (coins and/or bullion)

Controls on domestic ownership and/or trade	Gold bullion may, with some exceptions, be traded only with authorized agents (generally banks).
Controls on external trade	The export and import of gold bullion and/or more than 10 gold coins must be reported.

Controls on exports and imports of banknotes

There are reporting obligations on exports and imports exceeding KC 200,000.

Resident Accounts

Eligibility to hold accounts

Juridical and natural persons are eligible.

Foreign exchange accounts permitted

Yes.

Held domestically

Yes.

Held abroad

These accounts are permitted, but prior approval is required, with some exceptions.

Accounts in domestic currency convertible into foreign currency

Yes.

Nonresident Accounts

Eligibility to hold accounts

Juridical and natural persons are eligible.

Foreign exchange accounts permitted

Foreign exchange may be deposited freely and payments may be made in the Czech Republic or abroad without restriction from these accounts.

Domestic currency accounts

Domestic currency accounts may be opened with commercial banks in koruny. Balances on these accounts may be used freely to make payments in the Czech Republic. All transfers abroad from these accounts can be made freely.

Convertible into foreign currency

Yes.

Blocked accounts

No.

Imports and Import Payments

Foreign exchange budget

No.

Financing requirements for imports

Foreign invoices may be settled only through bank transfers.

Documentation requirements for release of foreign exchange for imports

No.

Import licenses and other nontariff measures

Negative list

Yes.

Open general licenses

Import licenses are required for a few strategic items, such as uranic ore, its concentrates, coal, natural gas, poisons, military materials, firearms and ammunition, narcotics, and clothing (excluding imports from the EU and EFTA). In addition, an automatic licensing system accompanied by levies applies to some agricultural products, mineral fuel and oils, iron and steel and their products, and some chemical products.

Licenses with quotas

Imports of hard coal, lignite, uranium ore and its derivatives, and technological components containing uranium are subject to licenses with quotas.

Import taxes and/or tariffs

All imports are subject to an ad valorem customs duty of up to 45% for industrial goods and up to 233% for agricultural goods. Imports are also subject to a value-added tax of 5% or 22%. Imports from the Slovak Republic are exempt from customs duties under a customs union. Imports from developing countries are granted preferences.

Taxes collected through the exchange system

No.

State import monopoly	No.

Exports and Export Proceeds

Repatriation requirements	Yes.
Surrender requirements	No.
Documentation requirements	No.
Export licenses	
Without quotas	The Ministry of Defense grants export licenses for armaments. The Ministry of Culture grants export licenses for items of cultural/artistic value. A limited number of products require export licenses for purposes of health control (including livestock and plants), facilitating voluntary restraints on products on which partner countries have imposed import quotas (such as textiles and steel products), or preserving for the internal market natural resources or imported raw materials (such as energy, metallurgical materials, wood, foodstuffs, pharmaceutical products, and construction materials). For the two latter groups of products, neither quantitative nor value limits are in force.
Export taxes	No.

Payments for Invisible Transactions and Current Transfers

Controls on these payments	Remittance of profits and dividends is permitted, once tax obligations have been met.

Proceeds from Invisible Transactions and Current Transfers

Repatriation requirements	Yes.
Surrender requirements	No.
Restrictions on use of funds	No.

Capital Transactions

Controls on capital and money market instruments	
On capital market securities	
Sale or issue locally by nonresidents	The issue of foreign securities in the Czech Republic or their introduction on the domestic market is allowed only with a foreign exchange permit from the CNB.
Purchase abroad by residents	The purchase of foreign securities by residents requires a foreign exchange permit granted by foreign exchange authorities, except in the following cases:
	(1) A purchase within the framework of a direct investment;
	(2) A purchase from the account of a foreign exchange entity having a banking license with a required scope of activities;
	(3) A purchase through a foreign exchange entity having a banking license with a required scope of activities;
	(4) A purchase of publicly tradable foreign bonds denominated in Czech currency issued in the Czech Republic only with a foreign exchange permit;
	(5) A purchase of employee shares and other financially preferred shares issued by a nonresident, his domestic employees, or the domestic employees of a resident in whose enterprise the issuer has an ownership participation; and

(6) A purchase of foreign securities acquired from another resident pursuant to a separate act.

Sale or issue abroad by residents   The yield is subject to the transfer obligation.

On money market instruments

   Sale or issue locally by   The issue of foreign securities in the Czech Republic or their introduction on the do-
   nonresidents   mestic market is allowed only with a foreign exchange permit from the CNB.

   Purchase abroad by residents   Yes.

On collective investment securities

   Sale or issue locally by   The issue of foreign securities in the Czech Republic or their introduction on the do-
   nonresidents   mestic market is allowed only with a foreign exchange permit from the CNB.

   Purchase abroad by residents   Yes.

Controls on derivatives and other   Pursuant to the Foreign Exchange Act, the regulation includes only those derivatives
instruments   whose assets are built up through financial measures in foreign currency, gold, and foreign securities.

Sale or issue locally by nonresidents   The issue of foreign securities in the Czech Republic or their introduction on the domestic market is allowed only with a foreign exchange permit from the CNB.

Purchase abroad by residents   Yes.

Sale or issue abroad by residents   These transactions are permitted if a participant in the transaction is a foreign exchange
   entity having a banking license with a required scope of activities; otherwise, a CNB
   foreign exchange permit is required.

Controls on credit operations

Financial credits

   By residents to nonresidents   Financial credits can be extended by residents to nonresidents only based on a foreign
   exchange permit from the foreign exchange authorities. The following operations are
   exceptions:

   (1) The credit is extended by a bank having a banking license with a required scope of
   activities;

   (2) The extended credit is a direct investment; and

   (3) The credit is granted between natural persons and is not intended for business
   activities.

Guarantees, sureties, and financial
backup facilities

   By residents to nonresidents   A nonresident's obligation can be secured only with a foreign exchange permit from
   foreign exchange authorities. However, there are exceptions where the guarantee is
   provided by a foreign exchange entity having a license with a required scope of
   activities.

Controls on direct investment   No.

Controls on liquidation of direct   No.
investment

Controls on real estate transactions

Purchase locally by nonresidents   A nonresident who is not a citizen of the Czech Republic can acquire real estate only in
   those cases specified by the act:

   (1) By heritage;

   (2) For the diplomatic representation of a foreign country under the terms of reciprocity;

(3) If it is real estate acquired in an unapportioned co-ownership of a married couple of which only one is a nonresident, or where a nonresident acquires property from a husband, wife, parents, or grandparents.

(4) Through the exchange of domestic real estate owned by the nonresident for other domestic real estate the usual price of which does not exceed the usual price of the former real estate;

(5) If the nonresident has a preemption by reason of a proportioned co-ownership of real estate;

(6) If the real estate is a construction built by a nonresident on his or her own land; and

(7) Under the terms explicitly stipulated by the Act on Mitigating the Consequences of Some Property Injustice.

Sale locally by nonresidents	No.
Provisions specific to commercial banks and other credit institutions	
Lending locally in foreign exchange	The range is determined by the banking license granted.
Purchase of locally issued securities denominated in foreign exchange	The range is determined by the banking license granted.
Open foreign exchange position limits	Both as a monetary regulation limiting open short position vis-à-vis nonresidents and as a prudential regulation limiting commercial banks' open positions in foreign currency.
Provisions specific to institutional investors	Investments in an entity cannot exceed 20% of its equity.
Limits (min.) on portfolio invested locally	Yes.
Other controls imposed by securities laws	The Act on Bonds establishes that the introduction of bonds by residents on the foreign exchange market and by nonresidents on the domestic market is allowed only with a permit from the Ministry of Finance.

The Act on Securities establishes that the introduction of foreign securities denominated in koruny on the domestic market is allowed only if these securities are traded on the public market in the issuer's country.

In addition, there are special regulations on acquiring the capital participation of nonresidents in selected institutions or economic areas—banking (a CNB permit required), audit institutions (to a maximum of 10%), and the Securities Stock Exchange (to a maximum of 33%).

Changes During 1996

Exchange arrangements	*February 28.* The foreign exchange band within which the Czech koruna is allowed to fluctuate was widened from ±0.5% to ±7.5% against the central rate.

Changes During 1997

Exchange arrangements	*May 27.* The foreign exchange rate band was canceled and a new exchange arrangement introduced based on a managed floating system aimed at the stability of the Czech koruna against the deutsche mark.

DENMARK

(Position as of December 31, 1996)

Status Under IMF Articles of Agreement

Article VIII   Date of acceptance: May 1, 1967.

Exchange Arrangement

Currency   The currency of Denmark is the Danish krone.

Exchange rate structure   Unitary.

Classification

Cooperative arrangement   Denmark participates in the ERM of the EMS. In accordance with this agreement, Denmark maintains the spot exchange rates between the Danish krone and the currencies of the other participants within margins of 15% above or below the cross rates based on the central rates expressed in ECUs.

Exchange tax   No.

Exchange subsidy   No.

Forward exchange market   Yes.

Official cover of forward operations   Yes.

Arrangements for Payments and Receipts

Prescription of currency requirements   No.

Payment arrangements   No.

Administration of control   No.

International security restrictions

In accordance with IMF Executive Board Decision No. 144-(52/51)   Yes.

In accordance with UN sanctions   Denmark maintains exchange restrictions against Iraq in accordance with UN Security Council Resolution No. 661, and against Libya in accordance with UN Security Council Resolution No. 833.

Payment arrears   No.

Controls on trade in gold (coins and/or bullion)   No.

Controls on exports and imports of banknotes   No.

Resident Accounts

Eligibility to hold accounts   Juridical and natural persons are eligible.

Foreign exchange accounts permitted   Yes.

Held domestically   Yes.

Held abroad	Yes.
Accounts in domestic currency convertible into foreign currency	No.

Nonresident Accounts

Eligibility to hold accounts	Juridical and natural persons are eligible.
Foreign exchange accounts permitted	Yes.
Domestic currency accounts	No.
Blocked accounts	No.

Imports and Import Payments

Foreign exchange budget	No.
Financing requirements for imports	No.
Documentation requirements for release of foreign exchange for imports	No.
Import licenses and other nontariff measures	
Open general licenses	A few items require a license when originating in Japan, the Republic of Korea, or any other country outside the EU that is not a state trading country. A larger number of items require a license when originating in or purchased from Albania, Bulgaria, China, the Czech Republic, Hungary, the Democratic People's Republic of Korea, Mongolia, Poland, Romania, the Slovak Republic, the Baltic countries, Russia, and the other countries of the FSU, and Vietnam.
Licenses with quotas	They are required for imports of textiles, toys, and footwear.
Import taxes and/or tariffs	No.
State import monopoly	No.

Exports and Export Proceeds

Repatriation requirements	No.
Surrender requirements	No.
Financing requirements	No.
Documentation requirements	No.
Export licenses	
Without quotas	Except for certain items subject to strategic controls, licenses are required only for exports of waste and scrap of certain metals.
Export taxes	No.

Payments for Invisible Transactions and Current Transfers

Controls on these payments	No.

Proceeds from Invisible Transactions and Current Transfers

Repatriation requirements	No.
Surrender requirements	No.
Restrictions on use of funds	No.

Capital Transactions

Controls on capital and money market instruments	No.
Controls on derivatives and other instruments	No.
Controls on credit operations	No.
Controls on direct investment	No.
Controls on liquidation of direct investment	No.
Controls on real estate transactions	
Purchase abroad by residents	Yes.
Purchase locally by nonresidents	Purchases are prohibited, except in the case of acquisitions by:

(1) Persons who have formerly been residents of Denmark for at least five years;

(2) EU nationals working in Denmark and EU-based companies operating in Denmark for residential or business purposes; and

(3) Non-EU nationals who either are in possession of a valid residence permit or are entitled to stay in Denmark without such a permit for residential or active business purposes.

Provisions specific to commercial banks and other credit institutions	No.
Provisions specific to institutional investors	No.
Other controls imposed by securities laws	No.

Changes During 1996

No significant changes occurred in the exchange and trade system.

DJIBOUTI

(Position as of December 31, 1996)

Status Under IMF Articles of Agreement

Article VIII   Date of acceptance: September 19, 1980.

Exchange Arrangement

Currency	The currency of Djibouti is the Djibouti franc.
Exchange rate structure	Unitary.
Classification	
Pegged	The Djibouti franc is pegged to the U.S. dollar, the intervention currency, at DF 177.721 per $1. The official buying and selling rates for currencies other than the U.S. dollar are set by local banks on the basis of the cross rates for the U.S. dollar in international markets.
Exchange tax	No.
Exchange subsidy	No.
Forward exchange market	No.

Arrangements for Payments and Receipts

Prescription of currency requirements	No.
Payment arrangements	No.
Administration of control	No.
International security restrictions	
In accordance with UN sanctions	Yes.
Payment arrears	No.
Controls on trade in gold (coins and/or bullion)	No.
Controls on exports and imports of banknotes	No.

Resident Accounts

Eligibility to hold accounts	Juridical and natural persons are eligible.
Foreign exchange accounts permitted	Yes.
Held domestically	Yes.
Held abroad	Yes.
Accounts in domestic currency convertible into foreign currency	Yes.

Nonresident Accounts

Eligibility to hold accounts	Juridical and natural persons are eligible.
Foreign exchange accounts permitted	Yes.
Domestic currency accounts	Yes.
Convertible into foreign currency	Yes.
Blocked accounts	Yes.

Imports and Import Payments

Foreign exchange budget	No.
Financing requirements for imports	No.
Documentation requirements for release of foreign exchange for imports	No.
Import licenses and other nontariff measures	No.
Import taxes and/or tariffs	Formally, customs duties are not charged on imports, but, in practice, fiscal duties are levied by means of the general consumption tax, at rates ranging from 3% to 40%. Certain commodities, including alcoholic beverages, noncarbonated mineral water, petroleum products, khat, and tobacco, are subject to a surtax of various rates. Additional taxes are levied on imported milk products and fruit juice.
Taxes collected through the exchange system	No.
State import monopoly	No.

Exports and Export Proceeds

Repatriation requirements	No.
Surrender requirements	No.
Financing requirements	Yes.
Documentation requirements	
Letters of credit	Yes.
Export licenses	No.
Export taxes	No.

Payments for Invisible Transactions and Current Transfers

Controls on these payments	No.

Proceeds from Invisible Transactions and Current Transfers

Repatriation requirements	No.
Surrender requirements	No.

Restrictions on use of funds	No.

Capital Transactions

Controls on capital and money market instruments	No.
Controls on derivatives and other instruments	No.
Controls on credit operations	No.
Controls on direct investment	No.
Controls on liquidation of direct investment	No.
Controls on real estate transactions	No.
Provisions specific to commercial banks and other credit institutions	
Lending to nonresidents (financial or commercial credits)	Yes.
Lending locally in foreign exchange	Yes.
Purchase of locally issued securities denominated in foreign exchange	Yes.
Differential treatment of nonresident deposit accounts and/or deposit accounts in foreign exchange	
Liquid asset requirements	Yes.
Provisions specific to institutional investors	
Currency matching regulations on assets/liabilities composition	There is a matching requirement with respect to both the amount of transaction and the intervention currency, and also with respect to maturities and interest rates.
Other controls imposed by securities laws	No.

Changes During 1996

No significant changes occurred in the exchange and trade system.

DOMINICA

(Position as of December 31, 1996)

Status Under IMF Articles of Agreement

Article VIII   Date of acceptance: December 13, 1979.

Exchange Arrangement

Currency   The currency of Dominica is the Eastern Caribbean dollar, issued by the ECCB.

Exchange rate structure   Unitary.

Classification

Pegged   The Eastern Caribbean dollar is pegged to the U.S. dollar, the intervention currency.

Exchange tax   No.

Exchange subsidy   No.

Forward exchange market   No.

Arrangements for Payments and Receipts

Prescription of currency
requirements   Settlements with residents of the territories participating in the ECCB Agreement must
                                                  be made in Eastern Caribbean dollars; those with member countries of the CARICOM
                                                  must be made in the currency of the CARICOM country concerned. Settlements with
                                                  residents of other countries may be made in any foreign currency that is acceptable to
                                                  the country where the settlement is being made.

Payment arrangements

Regional arrangements   As a member of the CARICOM, Dominica participates in the CMCF.

Clearing agreements   Dominica is a member of the OECS.

Administration of control

Exchange control authorities   Exchange control is administered by the Ministry of Finance (MOF) and applies to all
                                                  countries outside the ECCB area. The MOF has delegated to commercial banks certain
                                                  powers to approve sales of foreign currencies within specified limits. The Ministry of
                                                  Trade administers import and export arrangements and controls.

International security restrictions   Trade with Iraq is prohibited.

In accordance with IMF Executive   n.a.
Board Decision No. 144-(52/51)

Payment arrears

Official   Yes.

Private   n.a.

Controls on trade in gold (coins
and/or bullion)

Controls on domestic ownership and/or   Residents are permitted to acquire and hold gold coins for numismatic purposes only.
trade

Controls on external trade   Small quantities of gold may be imported for industrial purposes only with the approval
                                                  of the MOF.

Controls on exports and imports of banknotes

On exports

Domestic currency   The exportation of Eastern Caribbean banknotes and coins (other than numismatic coins) outside the ECCB area is limited to amounts prescribed by the ECCB.

Resident Accounts

Eligibility to hold accounts   Juridical persons are eligible.

Foreign exchange accounts permitted   Yes.

Held domestically   These accounts are normally confined to major exporters, and can only be credited with foreign currencies obtained abroad. Payments from these accounts do not require approval.

Accounts in domestic currency convertible into foreign currency   n.a.

Nonresident Accounts

Foreign exchange accounts permitted   These accounts are permitted; prior approval is required.

Imports and Import Payments

Financing requirements for imports   No.

Documentation requirements for release of foreign exchange for imports   Payments for authorized imports are permitted upon presentation to a commercial bank of documentary evidence of purchase.

Domiciliation requirements   n.a.

Preshipment inspection   n.a.

Letters of credit   n.a.

Import licenses used as exchange licenses   n.a.

Import licenses and other nontariff measures   All imports from Iraq are prohibited, and all imports from the member countries of the former CMEA require a license.

Negative list   Imports of specified goods originating outside the OECS, Belize, and CARICOM require a license. Imports of a subset of these goods from the more developed countries of CARICOM (Barbados, Jamaica, Guyana, and Trinidad and Tobago) also require a license.

Licenses with quotas   There are certain quantitative restrictions on imports of beverages, flour, and margarine; quotas are allocated to traditional importers based on their historical market shares.

Import taxes and/or tariffs   Dominica applies the CET of CARICOM. Most rates are ad valorem ranging from zero to 45%. Lower rates apply to machinery (zero to 15%) and some essential foodstuffs (10% to 15%), while higher rates apply to domestic appliances (25% to 40%) and motor vehicles (25% to 45%). Specific duties are applied to some goods. Imports are also subject to a 1% customs service charge.

Taxes collected through the exchange system   No.

State import monopoly	Imports of sugar and rice are conducted by a state agency.

Exports and Export Proceeds

Repatriation requirements	Yes.
Surrender requirements	The conversion of export proceeds to an ECCB currency account is mandatory, unless the exporter has a foreign currency account into which the proceeds may be paid.
Documentation requirements	No.
Export licenses	Exports to Iraq are prohibited, and specific licenses are required for the exportation of certain goods to any destination.
Without quotas	Yes.
Export taxes	Banana exported by the Dominica Banana Marketing Corporation are subject to a levy of 1% if the export price is between $0.55 and $0.60 a pound; if the export price exceeds $0.60 a pound, an additional levy equivalent to 25% of the excess is imposed.
Taxes collected through the exchange system	n.a.

Payments for Invisible Transactions and Current Transfers

Controls on these payments	All settlements overseas require exchange control approval. In January 1996 commercial banks were authorized to sell foreign currency in amounts up to EC$100,000. Amounts over this limit require approval by the MOF, but are generally granted.
Freight/insurance	
Prior approval	Yes.
Quantitative limits	n.a.
Indicative limits/bona fide test	n.a.
Unloading/storage costs	
Prior approval	Yes.
Quantitative limits	n.a.
Indicative limits/bona fide test	n.a.
Administrative expenses	
Prior approval	Yes.
Quantitative limits	n.a.
Indicative limits/bona fide test	n.a.
Commissions	
Prior approval	Yes.
Quantitative limits	n.a.
Indicative limits/bona fide test	n.a.
Interest payments	
Prior approval	Yes.
Quantitative limits	n.a.
Indicative limits/bona fide test	n.a.

Profit/dividends

   Prior approval   Yes.

   Quantitative limits   n.a.

   Indicative limits/bona fide test   n.a.

Payments for travel

   Prior approval   Amounts in excess of the limits require MOF approval.

   Quantitative limits   The limit is EC$3,000 for each trip outside the ECCB area, subject to a maximum of 2 trips in any 12-month period and upon presentation of travel documents. For bona fide business travelers, the limit is EC$1,000 for each day outside Dominica, provided the total does not exceed EC$30,000 in any 12-month period and subject to presentation of travel documents.

   Indicative limits/bona fide test   Yes.

Medical costs

   Prior approval   Amounts in excess of the limits require MOF approval.

   Quantitative limits   The limit is EC$1,000 a day up to a maximum of EC$30,000 in any 12-month period, subject to presentation of travel documents and a medical certificate.

   Indicative limits/bona fide test   Yes.

Study abroad costs

   Prior approval   Amounts in excess of the limits require MOF approval.

   Quantitative limits   The limit is EC$15,000 a student in each academic year for educational expenses, including accommodation.

   Indicative limits/bona fide test   Yes.

Subscriptions and membership fees

   Prior approval   Yes.

   Quantitative limits   n.a.

   Indicative limits/bona fide test   n.a.

Consulting/legal fees

   Prior approval   Yes.

   Quantitative limits   n.a.

   Indicative limits/bona fide test   n.a.

Foreign workers' wages

   Prior approval   Earnings of foreign workers may be remitted after settlement of all taxes or other public liabilities.

   Quantitative limits   n.a.

   Indicative limits/bona fide test   n.a.

Pensions

   Prior approval   Yes.

   Quantitative limits   n.a.

   Indicative limits/bona fide test   n.a.

Family maintenance/alimony

   Prior approval   Amounts in excess of the limits require MOF approval.

Quantitative limits	The limits are EC$2,400 in any 12-month period and EC$3,600 for minors or incapacitated dependents.
Indicative limits/bona fide test	Yes.
Credit card use abroad	
Prior approval	Yes.
Quantitative limits	n.a.
Indicative limits/bona fide test	n.a.

Proceeds from Invisible Transactions and Current Transfers

Repatriation requirements	Yes.
Surrender requirements	Foreign currency proceeds from these transactions must be sold to a bank or deposited into a foreign currency account.

Capital Transactions

Controls on capital and money market instruments	All outward transfers of capital require exchange control approval.
On capital market securities	
Purchase locally by nonresidents	n.a.
Sale or issue locally by nonresidents	n.a.
Purchase abroad by residents	These purchases are normally permitted.
Sale or issue abroad by residents	n.a.
On money market instruments	
Purchase locally by nonresidents	n.a.
Sale or issue locally by nonresidents	n.a.
Purchase abroad by residents	Yes.
Sale or issue abroad by residents	n.a.
On collective investment securities	
Purchase locally by nonresidents	n.a.
Sale or issue locally by nonresidents	n.a.
Purchase abroad by residents	Yes.
Sale or issue abroad by residents	n.a.
Controls on derivatives and other instruments	n.a.
Controls on credit operations	
Commercial credits	
By residents to nonresidents	MOF approval is required.
To residents from nonresidents	n.a.

Financial credits

    By residents to nonresidents   Yes.

    To residents from nonresidents   n.a.

Guarantees, sureties, and financial
backup facilities

    By residents to nonresidents   Yes.

    To residents from nonresidents   n.a.

Controls on direct investment

Outward direct investment   Yes.

Inward direct investment   Investments require exchange control approval.

Controls on liquidation of direct investment   Proceeds may be remitted after the discharge of any related liabilities.

Controls on real estate transactions

Purchase abroad by residents   Yes.

Purchase locally by nonresidents   n.a.

Sale locally by nonresidents   n.a.

Changes During 1996

Payments for invisible transactions and current transfers   *January 1.* Regulations on sales of foreign currency were liberalized and simplified. Commercial banks were allowed to sell up to EC$100,000 in foreign currency without prior approval of the MOF.

DOMINICAN REPUBLIC

(Position as of February 28, 1997)

Status Under IMF Articles of Agreement

Article VIII   Date of acceptance: August 1, 1953.

Exchange Arrangement

Currency   The currency of the Dominican Republic is the Dominican peso.

Exchange rate structure

Dual   There are 2 exchange rates: the official rate and the interbank rate.

Classification

Managed floating   The official exchange rate is adjusted each week based on the buying rate in the inter-bank market, which is determined by supply and demand. The Central Bank (CB) occasionally intervenes in the market.

Exchange tax   A commission of 1.5% is charged on sales of foreign exchange in both the interbank market and the official market.

Exchange subsidy   No.

Forward exchange market   No.

Arrangements for Payments and Receipts

Prescription of currency requirements   Settlements with Bolivia, Brazil, Chile, Colombia, Ecuador, Mexico, Peru, and Uruguay may be made through special accounts established under reciprocal credit agreements within the framework of the LAIA. All payments must be invoiced in U.S. dollars; otherwise, no obligations are imposed on importers, exporters, or other residents regarding the currency to be used for payments to or from nonresidents. Service payments on the external public debt are executed in the same currency in which the loan is denominated.

Payment arrangements

Bilateral arrangements

  Operative   Yes.

Regional arrangements   The Dominican Republic is a member of LAIA.

Clearing agreements   Yes.

Barter agreements and open accounts   Settlements under the reciprocal credit agreement with Argentina and Venezuela, which had been suspended, were restarted when credit lines were reestablished on February 15, and October 24, 1996, respectively.

Administration of control

Exchange control authorities   Exchange control policy is determined by the Monetary Board and administered by the CB.

International security restrictions   No.

Payment arrears

Official   Some public sector debt-service payments are in arrears, mostly arising from conciliation problems.

Private   Some private sector debt-service payments are in arrears, mostly arising from contract negotiations.

Controls on trade in gold (coins and/or bullion)

Controls on domestic ownership and/or trade

Residents may purchase, hold, and sell gold coins for numismatic purposes only. Residents (other than the monetary authorities and authorized industrial users) are not allowed to hold or acquire gold in any other form except jewelry.

Controls on external trade

Imports and exports of gold in any form other than jewelry, constituting the personal effects of a traveler, require licenses issued by the CB.

Controls on exports and imports of banknotes

On exports

   Domestic currency

Travelers are allowed to export up to RD$20,000 in domestic banknotes and RD$100 in coins.

   Foreign currency

Travelers are allowed to export up to US$10,000.

On imports

   Domestic currency

Travelers are allowed to import up to RD$20,000 in domestic banknotes and up to RD$100 in coins.

Resident Accounts

Eligibility to hold accounts

Juridical and natural persons are eligible.

Foreign exchange accounts permitted

Yes.

Held domestically

Yes.

Held abroad

No.

Accounts in domestic currency convertible into foreign currency

These accounts are not permitted, but domestic currency can readily be converted to foreign currency in a separate transaction.

Nonresident Accounts

Eligibility to hold accounts

Juridical and natural persons are eligible.

Foreign exchange accounts permitted

The same regulations as for residents apply.

Domestic currency accounts

Yes.

Convertible into foreign currency

These accounts are not permitted, but domestic currency can readily be converted to foreign currency in a separate transaction.

Blocked accounts

No.

Imports and Import Payments

Foreign exchange budget

No.

Financing requirements for imports

No.

Documentation requirements for release of foreign exchange for imports

Payments for oil are transacted through the CB at the official exchange rate, and these imports require certification of the use of foreign currency for customs clearance. All other imports are transacted through the interbank market and are only subject to verification of appropriate documentation, except for the industrial free-trade zones.

Import licenses and other nontariff measures

Negative list

The list includes mainly agricultural products.

Licenses with quotas

Imports of refined sugar require licenses.

Import taxes and/or tariffs

Most tariff rates range from 5% to 35% with certain imported luxury goods subject to an excise tax ranging from 5% to 80%. Duties are waived for any imports used in the manufacture of nontraditional products to be exported within a year.

Taxes collected through the exchange system

Yes.

State import monopoly

The state refinery has exclusive rights to import certain petroleum products for resale.

Exports and Export Proceeds

Repatriation requirements

Yes.

Surrender requirements

A 100% requirement applies to all traditional exports (i.e., cocoa, sugar, coffee, tobacco, and mineral products).

Financing requirements

Exporters may not extend credit to foreign buyers with a maturity of more than 30 days from the date of shipment without authorization from the CB.

Documentation requirements

Export documentation is required. A single export documentation form was introduced on February 3, 1997.

Export licenses

Certain exports are prohibited for environmental protection purposes.

With quotas

Licenses are required for preferential sugar exports, particularly to the United States.

Export taxes

No.

Payments for Invisible Transactions and Current Transfers

Controls on these payments

All invisible payments may be made freely through commercial banks, subject to documentation requirements. However, quantitative limits apply to payments for travel, medical costs, study abroad, and subscriptions and membership fees. There are no controls on payments for pensions, gambling and prize earnings, family maintenance and alimony, the use of credit cards abroad, and on remittances of profits and dividends. Payments for freight and insurance, unloading and storage costs, administrative expenses, commissions, interest, travel, medical treatment, study abroad, and subscriptions and membership fees require prior approval and are subject to indicative limits and/or bona fide tests.

Consulting/legal fees

Prior approval

Technical assistance fees must be registered with the CB.

Foreign workers' wages

Prior approval

Prior approval of the president of the Republic is required for the hiring of Haitian workers to harvest sugarcane.

Proceeds from Invisible Transactions and Current Transfers

Repatriation requirements

Yes.

Surrender requirements

While most exchange proceeds from invisibles may be sold in the interbank market, certain receipts (e.g., for international phone calls, international credit card transactions, jet fuel, foreign embassies' operations, among others) must be surrendered to the CB.

Restrictions on use of funds	No.

Capital Transactions

Controls on capital and money market instruments	There are controls on external debt contracted by the public sector. There are no restrictions on capital inflows to the private sector, but such investments must be registered with the CB.
Controls on derivatives and other instruments	No.
Controls on credit operations	
Commercial credits	
To residents from nonresidents	Prior CB approval is required.
Financial credits	
To residents from nonresidents	External debt can be contracted directly by the central government, subject to congressional authorization. New loans by other public entities require authorization from the president of the Republic for their subsequent registration by the Monetary Board. Private external debt must be registered with the CB, except for foreign exchange advances on future traditional exports, which require approval from the CB.
Guarantees, sureties, and financial backup facilities	
To residents from nonresidents	There are no controls on these facilities if guarantees are related to financial credits.
Controls on direct investment	
Inward direct investment	Investments must be registered with the CB. Investment in the following sectors is prohibited: (1) disposal of toxic waste and of dangerous or radioactive substances not produced in the country; (2) activities that affect public health and the environment; and (3) production of materials and equipment that affect defense and national security.
Controls on liquidation of direct investment	No.
Controls on real estate transactions	
Purchase locally by nonresidents	Certain restrictions apply to purchases of real estate by nonresidents.
Provisions specific to commercial banks and other credit institutions	
Lending locally in foreign exchange	Yes.
Differential treatment of nonresident deposit accounts and/or deposit accounts in foreign exchange	
Reserve requirements	Foreign currency deposits are not subject to reserve requirements up to an amount equivalent in U.S. dollars to 3 times the bank's capital and reserves, valued at the official exchange rate. Since January 25, 1996, deposits in national currency are subject to a 20% reserve requirement.
Investment regulations	Yes.
Open foreign exchange position limits	Banks' foreign exchange positions must be fully covered.
Provisions specific to institutional investors	No.
Other controls imposed by securities laws	No.

Changes During 1996

Exchange arrangements

December 20. The official exchange rate (previously fixed) was based on the buying rate in the interbank foreign exchange market.

Arrangements for payments and receipts

February 15. The line of credit with Argentina was reestablished under a reciprocal credit agreement.

October 24. The line of credit with Venezuela was reestablished under a reciprocal credit agreement.

Capital transactions

January 25. Deposits in domestic currency were subjected to a 20% reserve requirement.

Changes During 1997

Exports and export proceeds

February 3. A single export documentation form was introduced.

ECUADOR

(Position as of December 31, 1996)

Status Under IMF Articles of Agreement

Article VIII   Date of acceptance: August 31, 1970.

Exchange Arrangement

Currency   The currency of Ecuador is the Ecuadoran sucre.

Exchange rate structure

Dual   There are two exchange rates: the free market rate and the Central Bank of Ecuador (CBE) official exchange rate. All legally permitted foreign exchange transactions, other than those conducted through the CBE, may be conducted in the free market.

Classification

Managed floating   The market rate of the sucre against the U.S. dollar moves within a band of ±5% around the midpoint preannounced by the CBE; the midpoint depreciates at an annual rate of 21%. The selling rate of the CBE is established weekly at a level equal to the average selling rate in the free market of the previous week. The buying rate of the CBE is set 2% lower than its selling rate. The CBE's selling rate is applied to all external payments of the public sector.

Exchange tax   No.

Exchange subsidy   No.

Forward exchange market   Banks and other financial institutions authorized to conduct foreign exchange transactions are permitted to conduct forward swaps and options and transactions in other financial derivative instruments, subject to the supervision and control of the Superintendency of Banks.

Official cover of forward operations   No.

Arrangements for Payments and Receipts

Prescription of currency requirements   Exchange proceeds from all countries, except for LAIA members, must be received in convertible currencies. Whenever possible, import payments must be made in the currency stipulated in the import license. Some settlements with Cuba and Hungary take place through bilateral accounts.

Payment arrangements

Bilateral arrangements

Operative   There are arrangements with Cuba and Hungary.

Regional arrangements   Yes.

Clearing agreements   Payments between Ecuador and Argentina, Bolivia, Brazil, Chile, Colombia, the Dominican Republic, Mexico, Paraguay, Peru, Uruguay, and Venezuela may be made within the framework of the multilateral clearing system of the LAIA.

Administration of control

Exchange control authorities   Public sector foreign exchange transactions are carried out exclusively through the CBE. Exports must be registered with the CBE to guarantee repatriation of any foreign exchange proceeds from the transaction. Private sector foreign exchange transactions related to the exportation for, and production, transportation, and commercialization of oil and its derivatives may be carried out through the free market or through the CBE.

Private sector foreign exchange transactions may be effected through banks and exchange houses authorized by the Monetary Board.

International security restrictions	No.
Payments arrears	
Official	Arrears are maintained with respect to public and publicly guaranteed debt-service payments to official and private creditors.
Controls on trade in gold (coins and/or bullion)	No.
Controls on external trade	No.
Controls on exports and imports of banknotes	No.

Resident Accounts

Eligibility to hold accounts	Juridical and natural persons are eligible.
Foreign exchange accounts permitted	Yes.
Held domestically	Yes.
Held abroad	Yes.
Accounts in domestic currency convertible into foreign currency	No.

Nonresident Accounts

Eligibility to hold accounts	Juridical and natural persons are eligible.
Foreign exchange accounts permitted	Yes.
Domestic currency accounts	Yes.
Convertible into foreign currency	Yes.
Blocked accounts	No.

Imports and Import Payments

Foreign exchange budget	No.
Financing requirements for imports	No.
Advance payment requirements	Prepayments for imports by the private sector are permitted.
Documentation requirements for release of foreign exchange for imports	No.
Import licenses and other nontariff measures	Prior import licenses are required for all permitted imports. In addition, Petroecuador may, without a license, import supplies, materials, and equipment during emergencies.
Negative list	Imports of psychotropics, used vehicles, and parts and pieces are prohibited primarily to protect the environment and health. Imports of antiques and certain items related to health and national security are also prohibited. Certain imports require prior authorization from government ministries or agencies for ecological, health, and national security reasons.

Import taxes and/or tariffs	Most goods are subject to import tariff rates of 5%, 10%, 15%, 20%, or 35%. Automobiles are subject to a 40% rate calculated on the basis of a set of reference prices. For certain agricultural goods, tariffs are imposed on goods with prices below a certain lower benchmark and rebates are granted on goods with prices above an upper benchmark. Under provisions of the WTO, Ecuador has agreed to eliminate price bands of imports of 130 farm products over a 7-year period. All private sector imports are subject to the 10% value-added tax.
Taxes collected through the exchange system	No.
State import monopoly	No.

Exports and Export Proceeds

Repatriation requirements	Yes.
Surrender requirements	All export proceeds must be surrendered to authorized financial entities, but exporters may deduct up to 15% from their surrender requirement to cover the actual cost of consular fees and commissions paid abroad. The surrender requirement does not apply to exports effected under authorized barter transactions. The surrender requirement does not apply to exports to countries with which Ecuador has bilateral payments agreements. In such cases, exporters are required to provide official documentation from the recipient country establishing the applicable forms of payment. Exporters of marine products are permitted to retain up to 30% of the f.o.b. value of their shipments to cover the actual cost of leasing foreign ships. Minimum reference prices are established for exports of bananas, coffee, fish products, cocoa, and semifinished products of cocoa to help ensure that exchange proceeds are fully surrendered. Payment of foreign exchange for petroleum exports is made on the basis of the sale prices stated in the sales contracts and must be surrendered within 30 days of the date of shipment.
Financing requirements	No.
Documentation requirements	Barter transactions require the prior approval of the Ministry of Industry, Commerce, and Fisheries, and must be registered with the CBE.
Export licenses	Exports do not require licenses but must be registered for statistical purposes.
Without quotas	The export prices of bananas, cocoa, coffee, fish, and semifinished cocoa products are subject to minimum reference prices.
Export taxes	All crude oil exports are subject to a tax of S/.5 a barrel. A further tax of $1.02 a barrel is applied to crude oil exported through the pipeline.
Taxes collected through the exchange system	No.

Payments for Invisible Transactions and Current Transfers

Controls on these payments	All public sector payments for invisibles, including interest on public debt, are transacted at the central bank rate. Other payments for current invisibles must be settled in the free market. Residents and nonresidents traveling abroad by air must pay a tax of $25 a person. Airline tickets for foreign travel are taxed at 10%, and tickets for travel by ship are taxed at 8% for departure from Ecuador and 4% for the return trip.

Proceeds from Invisible Transactions and Current Transfers

Repatriation requirements	Yes.

Surrender requirements	All receipts from invisibles must be sold in the free market, except for interest income on exchange reserves of the CBE and all invisible receipts of the public sector, which are transacted at the central bank rate.
Restrictions on use of funds	Yes.

Capital Transactions

Controls on capital and money market instruments	Capital may freely enter or leave the country through the free market.
On money market instruments	
Sale or issue locally by nonresidents	There are controls on the issue of these instruments.
On collective investment securities	
Sale or issue locally by nonresidents	There are controls on the issue of these instruments.
Controls on derivatives and other instruments	No.
Controls on credit operations	All foreign loans granted to or guaranteed by the government or official entities, whether or not they involve the disbursement of foreign exchange, are subject to prior approval from the Monetary Board. A request for such approval must be submitted by the Minister of Finance and Public Credit to the Monetary Board, accompanied by detailed information on the loan contract and the investment projects it is intended to finance. In examining the request, the Monetary Board considers the effects that the loan and the related investment may have on the balance of payments and on monetary aggregates. For public sector entities, the projects to be financed must be included in the General Development Plan.
	New external credits with a maturity of over 1 year that are contracted by the private sector, either directly or through the domestic financial system, must be registered with the CBE within 45 days of disbursement. Nonregistered credits are subject to a service charge equivalent to 0.25% of the credit amount. Lending by residents to nonresidents is also restricted.
Controls on direct investment	No.
Controls on liquidation of direct investment	No.
Controls on real estate transactions	No.
Provisions specific to commercial banks and other credit institutions	No.
Provisions specific to institutional investors	No.
Other controls imposed by securities laws	No.

Changes During 1996

Exchange arrangements	*August 12.* The midpoint of the exchange rate band was devalued by 8.4% and the annual rate of depreciation of the midpoint rate was increased from 16.5% to 18.5% in local currency terms.
Resident accounts	*May 9.* The regulations on commercial banks' correspondent accounts abroad were applied to nonbank financial institutions as well.

Imports and import payments

January 19. Prior authorization from the Ministry of Defense was required for the importation of fishing vessels up to 250 metric tons.

February 27. In accordance with the law on controlled substances, permission for imports of certain drugs and substances was required from the National Council of Controlled Substances (Consejo Nacional de Control de Sustancias Estupefacientes y Psicotropicas).

March 31. The regulatory framework for the importation of automobiles and automobile parts was liberalized further.

May 9. The import nomenclature was amended in order to bring the import tariff schedule into conformity with the Cartagena Agreement.

July 2. For environmental reasons, 13 tariff lines were added to the list of products requiring prior import authorization and 4 tariff lines were placed on the list of prohibited products. For 63 other tariff lines, the approval process was streamlined by replacing authorization by several ministries with a single interministerial approval process.

Capital transactions

June 5. The process for approving public sector external loans was amended to exclude prior approval by the Planning Office (CONADE). However, public sector enterprises were required to present to the Monetary Board more stringent financial statements to ensure that the entities can service the debt in a timely manner. The regulatory framework for registering private sector capital inflows was widened to include all types of extended credits. Furthermore, private agents were also required to register changes in repayment schedules, including rollovers of credit.

EGYPT

(Position as of December 31, 1996)

Status Under IMF Articles of Agreement

Article XIV   Yes.

Exchange Arrangement

Currency   The currency of Egypt is the Egyptian pound.

Exchange rate structure

Multiple   In addition to the market exchange rate there is a special rate of LE 1.30 per $1 that is applied to transactions effected under the bilateral payments agreement with Sudan, and a rate of LE 0.3913 per $1 that is used for the liquidation of minimal balances related to terminated bilateral payments agreements.

Classification

Managed floating   The external value of the Egyptian pound is determined in the foreign exchange market. The U.S. dollar is used as the intervention currency by the Central Bank of Egypt (CBE). Nonbank foreign exchange dealers are permitted to operate in the free market. They may buy and sell domestic and foreign means of payment (banknotes, coins, and traveler's checks) on their own account. These transactions may be conducted either in cash or through their accounts maintained with authorized banks in Egypt. In addition, authorized nonbank dealers may broker any foreign exchange operation and transaction except transfers to and from the country, on the accounts of their bank or nonbank customers.

Exchange tax   No.

Exchange subsidy   No.

Forward exchange market   Authorized commercial banks are permitted to conduct forward foreign exchange transactions for their own account. No prior approval by the CBE is required, and the banks are free to determine the rates applied for forward transactions.

Official cover of forward operations   No.

Arrangements for Payments and Receipts

Prescription of currency requirements   Certain settlements with countries with which indemnity agreements concerning compensation for nationalized property are in force are made through special accounts in Egyptian pounds with the CBE. The balances of these accounts are very minimal. Suez Canal dues are expressed in SDRs and are paid by debiting free accounts in foreign currency. Settlements with Sudan are made in accordance with the terms of the bilateral agreement.

Payment arrangements

Bilateral arrangements

   Operative   There is an agreement with Sudan.

   Inoperative   There is an agreement with Russia to settle debts between Egypt and the Baltic countries and other countries of the FSU. The agreement, signed on November 10, 1994, has been operative since April 25, 1995.

Barter agreements and open accounts   Yes.

279

Administration of control

Exchange control authorities | Banks are authorized to execute foreign exchange transactions within the framework of a general authorization without obtaining specific exchange control approval.

International security restrictions

In accordance with UN sanctions | Restrictions exist against Libya.

Payments arrears | There are payment arrears with certain non-Paris club creditors.

Official | Yes.

Private | Yes.

Controls on trade in gold (coins and/or bullion)

Controls on domestic ownership and/or trade | Banks are not authorized to deal or speculate, on their own or customers' accounts, in precious metals.

Controls on exports and imports of banknotes

On exports

Domestic currency | Travelers may take out up to LE 1,000.

On imports

Domestic currency | Persons arriving in Egypt may import up to LE 1,000.

Resident Accounts

Eligibility to hold accounts | Juridical and natural persons are eligible.

Foreign exchange accounts permitted | Yes.

Held domestically | "D" accounts may be opened in relation with payments agreements (most of these accounts were opened a long time ago). These accounts are usually credited with transfers under the respective agreement. Balances are used for settlement of local payments allowed under the bilateral agreement, including for imports from Egypt. Currently, outstanding balances on these accounts are minimal.

Held abroad | No.

Accounts in domestic currency convertible into foreign currency | Balances can be converted through the foreign exchange market.

Nonresident Accounts

Eligibility to hold accounts | Juridical and natural persons are eligible.

Foreign exchange accounts permitted | "Free accounts" may be opened in the name of any entity. These accounts may be credited with transfers of convertible currencies from abroad and transfers from other similar accounts, foreign banknotes (convertible currencies), and interest earned on these accounts. These accounts may be debited for transfers abroad, transfers to other similar accounts, withdrawals in foreign banknotes by the owner or others, and for payments in Egypt.

Domestic currency accounts | "Special capital accounts" may be credited with proceeds from sales of real estate owned by foreigners residing abroad. Authorized banks may transfer funds abroad from these accounts up to the amount in foreign exchange previously transferred and surrendered for Egyptian pounds at the time of the acquisition of the property, plus 5% of the value of the property for each year following the first 5 years of ownership until

the property is sold. The remainder may be paid and/or transferred in 5 equal installments. As of July 15, 1996, these accounts were canceled and changed into convertible
current accounts.

"Capital and operations accounts" may be opened by companies covered by Law
No. 230 (July 1989). These accounts may be credited with transfers from abroad, advance payments and long-term rents in foreign exchange, loans, funds purchased from
the free market, and funds purchased from the free accounts to meet the project requirement; they may be debited for payments by the account holder (e.g., imports, profit
remittances, interest, other invisibles, and financing of local expenditures).

Convertible into foreign currency	Yes.
Blocked accounts	No.

Imports and Import Payments

Foreign exchange budget	No.
Financing requirements for imports	No.
Documentation requirements for release of foreign exchange for imports	No.
Import licenses and other nontariff measures	
Negative list	Most items can be imported freely.
Import taxes and/or tariffs	From September 1996, products are classified into 7 groups for customs purposes with tariff rates ranging from 5% to 55% (with several exceptions). Surcharges at rates of 2% and 4% apply to most imports.
Taxes collected through the exchange system	No.
State import monopoly	No.

Exports and Export Proceeds

Repatriation requirements	No.
Surrender requirements	No.
Financing requirements	No.
Documentation requirements	No.
Export licenses	
Without quotas	Exports of raw hides are restricted.
Export taxes	No.

Payments for Invisible Transactions and Current Transfers

Controls on these payments	No.

Proceeds from Invisible Transactions and Current Transfers

Repatriation requirements	Foreign exchange earned abroad may be held indefinitely abroad or in local free accounts.

Surrender requirements	No.
Restrictions on use of funds	No.

Capital Transactions

Controls on capital and money market instruments

On capital market securities

Sale or issue locally by nonresidents — There are no restrictions under the Foreign Exchange Law and Regulations on the issue of securities in the country by nonresidents. Trading in securities denominated in foreign currencies must be settled in foreign currencies. The foreign exchange market could be mediated for transferring proceeds associated with the sale of both Egyptian securities and foreign securities.

Controls on derivatives and other instruments — Derivatives do not exist in the Egyptian market.

Controls on credit operations

Commercial credits

To residents from nonresidents — No restrictions are applied if the maturity of the commercial credits is up to 1 year or if these credits are received by the private sector. With regard to ministries, governmental administrations, public authorities, and public sector companies, they are all required to refer to the CBE when borrowing from abroad in convertible currencies, in order to register loans of more than a 1-year term. If external loans are used to finance capital goods or projects, such a transaction falls under the state investment plan.

Controls on direct investment

Inward direct investment — There are no general restrictions, but nonbank companies of foreign exchange dealers should be owned entirely by Egyptians.

Controls on liquidation of direct investment — Upon the request by foreign investors, and subject to approval of the board of the General Investment Authority, repatriation of the invested capital will be within the limits of its value calculated on the basis of the announced exchange rate at the time of liquidation or disposition. This should be in 5 equal annual installments, provided that the Authority approves the result of the liquidation. Exceptionally, the invested capital could be transferred in full, if the balance of the foreign currency account held by the investor with one of the authorized bank permits, or if the Authority's board approved making the transfer in full under certain conditions. If the invested capital is provided in kind, it may be repatriated in kind.

Controls on real estate transactions

Purchase locally by nonresidents — Yes.

Sale locally by nonresidents — Yes.

Provisions specific to commercial banks and other credit institutions

Differential treatment of nonresident deposit accounts and/or deposit accounts in foreign exchange

Reserve requirements — Deposits in foreign currency held by either nationals or foreigners are subject to a 10% requirement (the interest-free reserve ratio requirement of deposits in Egyptian pounds is 15%), which must be deposited with the CBE at LIBOR.

Liquid asset requirements — The requirement for assets in foreign currency is 25%, while it is 20% with regard to assets in Egyptian pounds.

Open foreign exchange position limits	The limits are: (1) for each currency (local or foreign): 10% of Tier 1 and Tier 2 capital; (2) for total long or short positions: 20% of Tier 1 and Tier 2 capital; and (3) total foreign assets to total foreign liabilities, or vice versa, should not exceed 105%.
Provisions specific to institutional investors	No.
Other controls imposed by securities laws	The sale or issue of securities or collective instrument securities on local markets by nonresidents should be in accordance with Law No. 95 (1992) requiring, inter alia, the preparation of a prospectus to be approved by the Capital Market Authority (CMA) in which case Law No. 95 does not provide any restriction on the transfer abroad of the proceeds associated with these sales or issues.

Changes During 1996

Imports and import payments	*September 30.* Import tariffs and import surcharges were reduced: the maximum tariff was reduced to 55% from 70%, and all tariff rates above 30% were reduced by 10–15 percentage points. The higher rate of import surcharge was reduced to 4% from 5%.
Capital transactions	*July 15.* Restrictions affecting the timing of the transfer abroad by nonresidents of the proceeds of sales of Egyptian real estate were eliminated.

EL SALVADOR

(Position as of May 31, 1997)

Status Under IMF Articles of Agreement

Article VIII

Date of acceptance: November 6, 1946.

Exchange Arrangement

Currency

The currency of El Salvador is the Salvadoran colón.

Other legal tender

Gold coins in denominations of C 25, C 50, C 100, C 200, and C 2,500 are legal tender, but do not circulate.

Exchange rate structure

Unitary.

Classification

Managed floating

The Central Reserve Bank (CRB) publishes the daily exchange rates, which are applied to its transactions with the public sector, and the calculation of tax obligations. These exchange rates are the simple average of the exchange rates set by commercial banks and exchange houses on the previous working day. Since January 1, 1994, the CRB has intervened in the foreign exchange market to maintain the exchange rate at C 8.75 per $1.

Exchange tax

No.

Exchange subsidy

No.

Forward exchange market

No.

Arrangements for Payments and Receipts

Prescription of currency requirements

No.

Payment arrangements

No.

Administration of control

Exchange control authorities

The CRB administers exchange regulations. All private sector foreign exchange transactions are delegated to the commercial banks and exchange houses. The Centro de Trámites de Exportación (CENTREX) issues certificates of origin and health when foreign importers require them. The Salvadoran Coffee Council issues permits freely to private sector traders to conduct external or domestic trade in coffee.

International security restrictions

No.

Payment arrears

No.

Controls on trade in gold (coins and/or bullion)

No.

Controls on exports and imports of banknotes

No.

Resident Accounts

Eligibility to hold accounts

Juridical and natural persons are eligible.

Foreign exchange accounts permitted

Yes.

Held domestically	Balances on these accounts may be sold to the commercial banks or used to make payments abroad without restriction. Transfers of funds between these accounts are not restricted, but the commercial banks are required to submit periodic reports to the CRB on the use of such accounts.
Held abroad	Yes.
Accounts in domestic currency convertible into foreign currency	Yes.

Nonresident Accounts

Eligibility to hold accounts	Juridical and natural persons are eligible.
Foreign exchange accounts permitted	Yes.
Domestic currency accounts	Yes.
Convertible into foreign currency	Yes.
Blocked accounts	No.

Imports and Import Payments

Foreign exchange budget	No.
Financing requirements for imports	No.
Documentation requirements for release of foreign exchange for imports	No.
Import licenses and other nontariff measures	
Positive list	Import permits issued by the Ministry of Economy are required for gasoline, kerosene, fuel oil, asphalt, propane and butane gas, cloth and jute sacks, sugar, and molasses.
Import taxes and/or tariffs	Most import tariffs range up to 20%, although some products, such as automobiles, alcoholic beverages, textiles, and luxury goods, are subject to an import tariff of 30%. There are no tariffs on capital goods and selected inputs. Exporters of nontraditional products to markets outside Central America receive duty drawbacks on imported raw materials equivalent to 6% of f.o.b. value of exports.
Taxes collected through the exchange system	No.
State import monopoly	No.

Exports and Export Proceeds

Repatriation requirements	No.
Surrender requirements	No.
Financing requirements	No.
Documentation requirements	No.
Export licenses	All exports must be registered, with the exception of exports amounting to less than $5,000, unless the product specifications call for such certification. Export permits, issued by the Ministry of Finance, are required for diesel fuel, liquefied petroleum gas, and gray cement.

Without quotas	Yes.
Export taxes	No.

Payments for Invisible Transactions and Current Transfers

Controls on these payments	No.

Capital Transactions

Controls on capital and money market instruments	No.
Controls on derivatives and other instruments	No.
Controls on credit operations	No.
Controls on direct investment	
Inward direct investment	Foreign direct investments and inflows of capital with a maturity of more than 1 year must be registered with the Ministry of the Economy but are not restricted. Certain minimum capital requirements exist for businesses owned by foreign residents and those having foreign resident shareholders.
Controls on liquidation of direct investment	No.
Controls on real estate transactions	No.
Provisions specific to commercial banks and other credit institutions	
Borrowing abroad	External borrowing by financial institutions is subject to a reserve requirement of 10%. The CBS started remunerating reserves on short-term financial system external borrowing on November 1, 1996.
Open foreign exchange position limits	The limit on the net foreign asset position of commercial banks has been gradually reduced to 20% of capital on November 1, 1996, and then to 10% on May 1, 1997.
Provisions specific to institutional investors	No.
Other controls imposed by securities laws	No.

Changes During 1996

Capital transactions	*November 1.* The CBS started remunerating reserves held on short-term financial system external borrowing.

Changes During 1997

Capital transactions	*April 1.* Reserve requirements on all deposits, including those in foreign exchange, and on short-term financial system external borrowing may be partially held in authorized central bank securities.
	May 1. The limit on the net foreign asset position of commercial banks was reduced to 10%.

EQUATORIAL GUINEA

(Position as of December 31, 1996)

Status Under IMF Articles of Agreement

Article VIII	Date of acceptance: June 1, 1996.

Exchange Arrangement

Currency

The currency of Equatorial Guinea is the CFA franc, issued by the BEAC.

Exchange rate structure

Unitary.

Classification

Pegged

The CFA franc is pegged to the French franc, the intervention currency, at the fixed rate of CFAF 1 per F 0.01. Exchange transactions in French francs between the BEAC and commercial banks take place at the same rate. Buying and selling rates for certain other foreign currencies are also officially posted, with quotations based on the fixed rate for the French franc and the rates in the Paris exchange market for the currencies concerned. A commission of 0.5% is levied on transfers to countries that are not members of the BEAC, except transfers in respect of central and local government operations, payments for imports covered by a duly-issued license domiciled with a bank, scheduled repayments on loans properly obtained abroad, travel allowances paid by the government and its agencies for official missions, and payments of insurance premiums.

Exchange tax

No.

Exchange subsidy

No.

Forward exchange market

No.

Arrangements for Payments and Receipts

Prescription of currency requirements

Because Equatorial Guinea is an Operations Account country, settlements with France, Monaco, and the other Operations Account countries are made in CFA francs, French francs, or the currency of any other institute of issue that maintains an Operations Account with the French Treasury. Settlements with all other countries are usually made through correspondent banks in France in the currencies of those countries or in French francs through foreign accounts.

Payment arrangements

Bilateral arrangements

n.a.

Regional arrangements

An Operations Account is maintained at the French Treasury.

Clearing agreements

n.a.

Barter agreements and open accounts

n.a.

Administration of control

Exchange control authorities

Exchange control is administered by the Directorate General of Exchange Control (DNCC) of the Ministry of Finance (MOF). Exchange transactions relating to all countries must be effected through authorized banks. Import licenses for goods other than gold are issued by the Ministry of Commerce and Industry, and those for gold by the Ministry of Mines. Export licenses are issued by the MOF.

Payment arrears

Official

Yes.

Private   n.a.

Controls on trade in gold (coins and/or bullion)

Controls on domestic ownership and/or trade

Residents are free to hold, acquire, and dispose of gold jewelry. They must have the approval of the Directorate of Mines to hold gold in any other form. Approval is not normally given because there are no industrial users in Equatorial Guinea. Newly mined gold must be declared to the Directorate of Mines, which authorizes either its exportation or its sale in the domestic market.

Controls on external trade

Exports are allowed only to France. Imports and exports of gold require prior authorization from the Directorate of Mines and the MOF; authorization is seldom granted for imports. Exempt from this requirement are (1) imports and exports by or on behalf of the monetary authorities, and (2) imports and exports of manufactured articles containing a small quantity of gold (such as gold-filled or gold-plated articles). Both licensed and exempt imports of gold are subject to customs declaration.

Controls on exports and imports of banknotes

On exports

   Domestic currency

Residents traveling for tourism or business purposes to countries in the franc zone are allowed to take out BEAC banknotes up to CFAF 2 million; amounts in excess of this limit may be taken out in other means of payment.

   Foreign currency

All resident travelers, regardless of destination, must declare in writing all means of payment at their disposal at the time of departure. The reexportation of foreign banknotes is allowed up to the equivalent of CFAF 250,000; the reexportation of foreign banknotes above this ceiling requires documentation demonstrating either the importation of foreign banknotes or their purchase against other means of payment registered in the name of the traveler or through the use of nonresident deposits lodged in local banks.

On imports

   Foreign currency

Resident and nonresident travelers may bring in any amount of banknotes and coins issued by the BEAC, the Bank of France, or a bank of issue maintaining an Operations Account with the French Treasury, as well as any amount of foreign banknotes and coins (except gold coins) of countries outside the Operations Account Area.

Resident Accounts

n.a.

Nonresident Accounts

Eligibility to hold accounts

The regulations pertaining to nonresident accounts are based on regulations applied in France. Juridical and natural persons are eligible.

Foreign exchange accounts permitted

The principal nonresident accounts are foreign accounts in French francs.

Approval required   n.a.

Domestic currency accounts

Because the BEAC suspended in 1993 the repurchase of BEAC banknotes circulating outside the territories of the CFA franc zone, BEAC banknotes received by the foreign correspondents of authorized banks and mailed to the BEAC agency in Equatorial Guinea by the Bank of France or the BCEAO may not be credited to foreign accounts in francs.

Convertible into foreign currency — These accounts are permitted, but prior approval is required.

Imports and Import Payments

Financing requirements for imports

Minimum financing requirements — n.a.

Documentation requirements for release of foreign exchange for imports

Domiciliation requirements — All import transactions of which the value exceeds CFAF 50,000 must be domiciled with an authorized bank. Import transactions by residents involving goods for use outside Equatorial Guinea must be domiciled with a bank in the country of final destination.

Preshipment inspection — n.a.

Letters of credit — n.a.

Import licenses used as exchange licenses — n.a.

Import licenses and other nontariff measures — Imports valued at more than CFAF 50,000 are subject to licensing, but licenses are issued freely.

Positive list — n.a.

Negative list — n.a.

Open general licenses — n.a.

Licenses with quotas — n.a.

Import taxes and/or tariffs — Equatorial Guinea applies the common duty rates of the UDEAC on imports from nonmembers (5% for basic necessities, 10% for raw materials and capital goods, 20% for intermediate and miscellaneous goods, and 30% for consumer goods), except for higher rates imposed on a limited number of luxury goods (15% to 40%). Duties on imports from other UDEAC members are set at 20% of those for imports from nonmembers. Fiscal duties and turnover taxes are also applied to imports.

Taxes collected through the exchange system — n.a.

Exports and Export Proceeds

Repatriation requirements — Proceeds from exports to all countries must be repatriated within 30 days of the payment date stipulated in the sales contract. Payments for exports must be made within 30 days of the arrival date of the merchandise at its destination.

Documentation requirements

Letters of credit — n.a.

Guarantees — n.a.

Domiciliation — Export transactions valued at CFAF 50,000 or more must be domiciled with an authorized bank. Exports to all countries are subject to domiciliation requirements for the appropriate documents.

Preshipment inspection — n.a.

Export taxes — n.a.

Taxes collected through the exchange system — No.

Payments for Invisible Transactions and Current Transfers

Controls on these payments

Payments in excess of CFAF 500,000 for invisibles to France, Monaco, and the Operations Account countries require prior declaration but are permitted freely; those to other countries are subject to the approval of the MOF. Payments for invisibles related to trade are permitted freely when the basic trade transaction has been approved or does not require authorization. Transfers of income accruing to nonresidents in the form of profits, dividends, and royalties are also permitted freely when the basic transaction has been approved. Payments for freight and insurance, unloading and storage costs, administrative expenses, commissions, travel expenses, medical treatment, study abroad, subscriptions and membership fees, consulting and legal fees, pensions, gambling and prizes earnings, family maintenance and alimony, interest, the remittances of profits and dividends, and the use of credit cards abroad are subject to prior approval, indicative limits, and/or bona fide tests.

Freight/insurance

Quantitative limits

Except in the case of expatriates working in Equatorial Guinea on a temporary basis, payments of insurance premiums of up to CFAF 50,000 to foreign countries are permitted; larger amounts may be authorized by the DNCC.

Profit/dividends

Quantitative limits

The transfer of rent from real property owned in Equatorial Guinea by foreign nationals is permitted up to 50% of the income declared for taxation purposes, net of tax. Remittances for current repair and management of real property abroad are limited to the equivalent of CFAF 200,000 every 2 years.

Payments for travel

Quantitative limits

Residents traveling for tourism or business purposes to countries in the franc zone are allowed to take out BEAC banknotes up to CFAF 2 million; amounts in excess of this limit may be taken out in other means of payment. The allowances for travel to countries outside the franc zone are subject to the following regulations: (1) for tourist travel, CFAF 100,000 a day, up to CFAF 2 million a trip; (2) for business travel, CFAF 250,000 a day, up to CFAF 5 million a trip; (3) allowances in excess of these limits are subject to the authorization of the MOF or, by delegation, the BEAC; and (4) the use of credit cards, which must be issued by resident financial intermediaries and approved by the MOF, is limited to the ceilings indicated above for tourist and business travel. Returning resident travelers are required to declare all means of payment in their possession upon arrival at customs and to surrender within 8 days all means of payment exceeding the equivalent of CFAF 25,000. All resident travelers, regardless of destination, must declare in writing all means of payment at their disposal at the time of departure. The reexportation by nonresident travelers of means of payment other than banknotes issued abroad and registered in the name of the nonresident traveler is not restricted, subject to documentation that it has been purchased with funds drawn from a foreign account in CFA francs or with other foreign exchange.

Foreign workers' wages

Transfers are permitted upon presentation of the appropriate pay voucher as well as justification of expenses, provided that transfers take place within 3 months of the pay period concerned.

Credit card use abroad

The use of credit cards, which must be issued by resident financial intermediaries and approved by the MOF, is limited to the ceilings for tourist and business travel.

Proceeds from Invisible Transactions and Current Transfers

Repatriation requirements

Proceeds from transactions in invisibles with France, Monaco, and the Operations Account countries may be retained. All amounts due from residents of other countries in respect of services, and all income earned in those countries from foreign assets, must be collected within 1 month of the due date.

Surrender requirements	Proceeds earned in countries outside the franc zone must be surrendered within 1 month of collection if received in foreign currency.

Capital Transactions

Controls on capital and money market instruments	Capital movements between Equatorial Guinea and France, Monaco, and the Operations Account countries are free of exchange control. Capital transfers to all other countries require exchange control approval and are restricted, but capital receipts from such countries are freely permitted.
On capital market securities	
Sale or issue locally by nonresidents	n.a.
Purchase abroad by residents	Yes.
Sale or issue abroad by residents	Yes.
On money market instruments	
Sale or issue locally by nonresidents	n.a.
Purchase abroad by residents	Yes.
Sale or issue abroad by residents	Yes.
On collective investment securities	
Purchase locally by nonresidents	n.a.
Sale or issue locally by nonresidents	n.a.
Purchase abroad by residents	Yes.
Sale or issue abroad by residents	Yes.
Controls on credit operations	
Commercial credits	
By residents to nonresidents	n.a.
To residents from nonresidents	Yes.
Financial credits	
By residents to nonresidents	n.a.
To residents from nonresidents	Yes.
Guarantees, sureties, and financial backup facilities	
By residents to nonresidents	n.a.
To residents from nonresidents	Yes.
Controls on direct investment	
Outward direct investment	Yes.
Inward direct investment	Yes.

Changes During 1996

Status under IMF Articles of Agreement	*June 1.* Equatorial Guinea accepted the obligations of Article VIII, Sections 2, 3, and 4 of the Fund Agreement.

ERITREA

(Position as of December 31, 1996)

Status Under IMF Articles of Agreement

Article XIV	Yes.

Exchange Arrangement

Currency
The Ethiopian birr is the provisional legal tender.

Exchange rate structure

Dual
The official exchange rate is the marginal auction rate that applies to transactions between Eritrea and Ethiopia concerning oil refinery services, all aid-funded imports, and most service transactions. There is also a more depreciated preferential exchange rate that is used for most private imports and exports and the conversion of foreign exchange remittances by Eritreans living abroad.

Classification

Managed floating
The official exchange rate of Eritrea is the marginal auction exchange rate of Ethiopia's birr, determined in the weekly foreign exchange auction conducted by the National Bank of Ethiopia (NBE). The preferential rate is fixed by the authorities at Br 7.20 to the U.S. dollar.

Exchange tax
The NBE prescribes a commission of 0.25% for purchases of foreign exchange and 0.75% for sales of foreign exchange, except for banknote transactions. The authorized dealers are permitted, but not required, to levy a service charge of up to 0.25% for buying and 0.75% for selling for their own account.

Exchange subsidy
No.

Forward exchange market
No.

Arrangements for Payments and Receipts

Prescription of currency requirements
All transactions with Ethiopia, except those related to the imports of spare parts for the refinery in Assab and the purchase of certain Ethiopian exports, are settled in Ethiopian birr.

Payment arrangements
No.

Administration of control

Exchange control authorities
The NBE oversees all foreign exchange transactions of the authorized dealers and issues dealers' licenses. It may from time to time issue regulations, directives, and instructions on foreign exchange matters. The Exchange Control Department of the NBE issues permits only for those imports that require foreign exchange from the banking system. The National Licensing Office issues licenses for importers, exporters, and commercial agents, and the Ministry of Trade and Industry regulates foreign investments. The Asmara Chamber of Commerce issues certificates of origin for exports.

International security restrictions
No.

Payment arrears
No.

Controls on trade in gold (coins and/or bullion)

Controls on domestic ownership and/or trade
Authorization from the Ministry of Energy, Mines, and Water Resources is required for ownership or possession of gold or other precious metals or ores. Residents may own gold jewelry without restrictions.

Controls on external trade	Yes.
Controls on exports and imports of banknotes	Travelers are not required to declare their foreign currency holdings upon departure.
On exports	
Domestic currency	Currently, Eritrea does not have its own national currency.
Foreign currency	Travelers are allowed to reconvert their balances in Ethiopian birr into foreign currencies upon departure.
On imports	
Domestic currency	Currently, Eritrea does not have its own national currency.
Foreign currency	Travelers are not required to declare their foreign currency holdings upon entry into Eritrea.

Resident Accounts

Eligibility to hold accounts	Juridical and natural persons are eligible. Only investors and individuals earning foreign exchange in connection with foreign trade are allowed to open accounts.
Foreign exchange accounts permitted	Yes.
Held domestically	Only investors and individuals earning foreign exchange in connection with foreign trade are allowed to open accounts.
Held abroad	These accounts are restricted to resident banks. Nonbank residents may not open accounts abroad, except if specifically authorized by the NBE.
Accounts in domestic currency convertible into foreign currency	No.

Nonresident Accounts

Eligibility to hold accounts	Juridical and natural persons are eligible.
Foreign exchange accounts permitted	Resident Eritreans working temporarily abroad may be permitted to maintain nonresident U.S. dollar accounts in Eritrea. NBE approval is required.
Domestic currency accounts	Available only to members of the diplomatic community, welfare organizations, nongovernmental organizations and their personnel, as well as joint ventures and other business firms that invest their capital, wholly or partially, in foreign exchange.
Convertible into foreign currency	Yes.
Blocked accounts	No.

Imports and Import Payments

Foreign exchange budget	No.
Financing requirements for imports	Most imports financed with official foreign exchange are effected under letters of credit (LCs) or on a cash-against-documents basis. Suppliers' credits must be registered with the NBE.
Advance import deposits	Only for LC type of imports.
Documentation requirements for release of foreign exchange for imports	Suppliers' credits must be registered with the NBE.

| Import licenses used as exchange licenses | Import payments made through the banking system require a permit issued by the NBE upon presentation of pro forma invoices providing information as to type, quantity, unit price, and freight cost (where applicable). |

Import licenses and other nontariff measures

| Open general licenses | All importers must have a valid trade license issued by the National Licensing Office. These licenses must be renewed each year at a fee of Br 200. Imports of cars and other motor vehicles require prior permission from the Ministry of Transportation. |

Import taxes and/or tariffs

| Taxes collected through the exchange system | A commission of 2% is collected on imports that do not require official foreign exchange and are not aid funded (franco valuta imports). |
| **State import monopoly** | The company that produces tobacco and matches holds the monopoly over the imports of these products. |

Exports and Export Proceeds

Repatriation requirements	All export proceeds must be repatriated within 90 days of shipment; where justified, this deadline can be extended by another 90 days.
Surrender requirements	No.
Financing requirements	Exports may be made under LCs, on an advance payment basis, or on a consignment basis.
Documentation requirements	All exports require documentation by the NBE. Certain commodities require clearance from specific government bodies (e.g., the Eritrean Institute of Standards). In particular, livestock and cereals require permission from the Ministry of Agriculture, and marine products require permission from the Ministry of Marine Resources.
Export licenses	Exporters must be licensed by the National Licensing Office. The annual licensing fee is Br 200.
Without quotas	Yes.
Export taxes	No.

Payments for Invisible Transactions and Current Transfers

Controls on these payments	There are no controls on foreign workers' wages, pensions, or family maintenance and alimony. Payments for freight and insurance, unloading and storage costs, administrative expenses, commissions, subscriptions and membership fees, consulting and legal fees, and interest require prior approval.
Profit/dividends	For investments certified under the Investment Proclamation No. 59 (1994), foreign investors may freely remit proceeds received from the liquidation of investment and/or expansion, and payments received from the sale or transfer of shares. Petroleum contractors and subcontractors may freely transfer abroad funds accruing from petroleum operations and may pay subcontractors and expatriate staff abroad.
Payments for travel	
Quantitative limits	For business trips, $250 a person a day for up to 30 days a trip. Exporters may use freely their retention balances for travel purposes. For personal travel, the allowance is $100 a person (adult or minor) a trip. Eritrean nationals can purchase air travel tickets in local and foreign currency.
Medical costs	
Prior approval	Recommendation of the Medical Board of the Ministry of Health is required.

Quantitative limits	Up to $10,000 for treatment abroad, other than in Ethiopia. The limit may be exceeded in special circumstances.
Study abroad costs	
Prior approval	Approval is granted for higher education expenses only.

Proceeds from Invisible Transactions and Current Transfers

Repatriation requirements	No.
Surrender requirements	No.
Restrictions on use of funds	No.

Capital Transactions

Controls on capital and money market instruments	
On capital market securities	
Purchase locally by nonresidents	Yes.
Sale or issue locally by nonresidents	n.a.
Purchase abroad by residents	Authorized banks may acquire securities with the approval of the NBE.
Sale or issue abroad by residents	n.a.
On money market instruments	
Purchase locally by nonresidents	n.a.
Sale or issue locally by nonresidents	n.a.
Purchase abroad by residents	Yes.
Sale or issue abroad by residents	n.a.
On collective investment securities	n.a.
Controls on credit operations	
Commercial credits	
By residents to nonresidents	n.a.
To residents from nonresidents	Foreign borrowing by residents must be registered with the NBE.
Financial credits	
By residents to nonresidents	n.a.
To residents from nonresidents	Authorized banks may borrow abroad or overdraw their correspondent accounts abroad with the approval of the NBE.
Guarantees, sureties, and financial backup facilities	n.a.
Controls on direct investment	
Outward direct investment	n.a.
Inward direct investment	Foreign direct investment is permitted in all sectors. However, domestic retail and wholesale trade, and import and commission agencies are open to foreign investors only when Eritrea has a bilateral agreement of reciprocity with the country of the investor;

the latter condition may be waived by the government. Approved investments and their subsequent expansion enjoy exemption from customs duties and sales tax for capital goods and spare parts associated with the investment. There are no exemptions from income tax.

Controls on liquidation of direct investment	No.
Controls on real estate transactions	
Purchase abroad by residents	Yes.
Purchase locally by nonresidents	Yes.
Provisions specific to commercial banks and other credit institutions	
Borrowing abroad	Borrowing is subject to prior approval of the NBE.
Lending to nonresidents (financial or commercial credits)	Yes.
Lending locally in foreign exchange	Yes.
Purchase of locally issued securities denominated in foreign exchange	n.a.

Changes During 1996

Imports and import payments	*March 30.* The NBE ceased to provide foreign exchange for imports of certain goods.

ESTONIA

(Position as of December 31, 1996)

Status Under IMF Articles of Agreement

Article VIII

Date of acceptance: August 15, 1994.

Exchange Arrangement

Currency

The currency of Estonia is the kroon.

Exchange rate structure

Unitary.

Classification

Pegged

The exchange rate of the kroon is pegged to the deutsche mark at the rate of EEK 8 per DM 1. The Bank of Estonia (BOE) exchanges kroon banknotes and reserve deposits of commercial banks with the BOE into deutsche mark and vice versa at that exchange rate. Transactions in convertible currencies are freely handled by commercial banks that can freely quote their own exchange rates.

Exchange tax

No.

Exchange subsidy

No.

Forward exchange market

Yes.

Official cover of forward operations

No.

Arrangements for Payments and Receipts

Prescription of currency requirements

Settlements with the Baltic countries, Russia, and the other countries of the FSU can be effected through a system of correspondent accounts maintained by the BOE with the respective central banks. Balances accrued in these accounts may in most cases be used freely by their holders to purchase either goods or services in the country concerned. In operating these accounts, the BOE acts as an intermediary only and does not convert any balances to krooni. Kroon balances held by the central banks of the Baltic countries, Russia, and the other countries of the FSU on their correspondent accounts are fully convertible without delay. These agreements also allow for separate decentralized payment arrangements between commercial banks in the respective countries and do not provide for swing credits or overdraft facilities. Commercial banks in Estonia are permitted and encouraged to open their own correspondent accounts with commercial banks in the Baltic countries, Russia, and the other countries of the FSU.

Payment arrangements

Bilateral arrangements

Operative

At the beginning of 1996, Estonia had bilateral agreements with Armenia, Azerbaijan, Belarus, Kazakhstan, Kyrgyz Republic, Latvia, Lithuania, Moldova, Russia, Tajikistan, Turkmenistan, Ukraine, and Uzbekistan.

Inoperative

Some accounts with a number of countries of the FSU are inoperative.

Regional arrangements

n.a.

Clearing agreements

n.a.

Barter agreements and open accounts

n.a.

Administration of control

Exchange control authorities

The BOE issues and enforces foreign exchange regulations.
The Ministry of Finance (MOF) controls and monitors import and exports, and licenses gold trading.

International security restrictions	No.
Payment arrears	Some external debt issues with Russia and the other countries of the FSU are not yet settled.
Official	All external debt with Russia is official.

Controls on trade in gold (coins and/or bullion)

Controls on domestic ownership and/or trade	Domestic trade in gold is subject to licensing requirements administered by the MOF.
Controls on external trade	International trade in gold is subject to licensing requirements administered by the MOF.

Controls on exports and imports of banknotes

On exports

Domestic currency	There is a limit on exports of the 1-kroon coin of 20 a person.

Resident Accounts

Eligibility to hold accounts	Juridical and natural persons are eligible.
Foreign exchange accounts permitted	Yes.
Held domestically	Yes.
Held abroad	Yes.
Accounts in domestic currency convertible into foreign currency	Yes.

Nonresident Accounts

Eligibility to hold accounts	Juridical and natural persons are eligible.
Foreign exchange accounts permitted	Yes.
Domestic currency accounts	Yes.
Convertible into foreign currency	Yes.
Blocked accounts	No.

Imports and Import Payments

Foreign exchange budget	No.
Financing requirements for imports	No.
Documentation requirements for release of foreign exchange for imports	No.
Import licenses and other nontariff measures	
Negative list	Yes.

Import taxes and/or tariffs	Customs duties are levied on fur, fur goods, launches, yachts, and motorized water skis. Imports are also subject to a state duty and a value-added tax of 18%, which is also levied on domestically produced goods.
Taxes collected through the exchange system	No.
State import monopoly	No.

Exports and Export Proceeds

Repatriation requirements	No.
Surrender requirements	No.
Financing requirements	No.
Documentation requirements	No.
Export licenses	
Without quotas	Licenses are required for metals, spirits, tobacco and tobacco goods, drugs, cars, weapons, ammunition, explosives, fuel, motor oil, and lottery tickets.
Export taxes	The MOF collects a specific fee in line with WTO principles to cover the cost of administrative processing, and an export duty of 100% is levied on items of cultural value.
Taxes collected through the exchange system	No.

Payments for Invisible Transactions and Current Transfers

Controls on these payments	No.

Proceeds from Invisible Transactions and Current Transfers

Repatriation requirements	No.
Surrender requirements	No.
Restrictions on use of funds	No.

Capital Transactions

Controls on direct investment	No.

Changes During 1996

Arrangements for payments and receipts	*December 6.* The exportation of the 1-kroon coin was limited to 20 a person.

ETHIOPIA

(Position as of December 31, 1996)

Status Under IMF Articles of Agreement

Article XIV	Yes.

Exchange Arrangement

Currency	The currency of Ethiopia is the Ethiopian birr.
Exchange rate structure	Unitary.
Classification	
Independent floating	The official exchange rate of the birr against the U.S. dollar is the marginal rate (i.e., the lowest successful bid) determined in weekly auctions for announced quantities of foreign exchange, as determined by the National Bank of Ethiopia (NBE).
Exchange tax	Authorized dealers must observe a prescribed commission of 0.5% on buying and 1.5% on selling, which accrues to the NBE, and they may levy service charges of up to 0.25% on buying and 0.75% on selling for their own accounts.
Exchange subsidy	No.
Forward exchange market	No.

Arrangements for Payments and Receipts

Prescription of currency requirements	Settlements with Eritrea, except those related to imports of spare parts for the refinery in Assab, Eritrea, are made in birr.
Payment arrangements	No.
Administration of control	
Exchange control authorities	All foreign exchange transactions must be carried out through authorized dealers under the control of the NBE. The Exchange Controller of the NBE issues exchange licenses for all exports and payments abroad and issues permits for all shipments. The Ministry of Trade formulates external trade policy.
Controls on trade in gold (coins and/or bullion)	Import and export exchange licenses are required by the NBE.
Controls on domestic ownership and/or trade	The ownership of personal jewelry is permitted. However, unless authorized by the Ministry of Mines and Energy, the possession or custody of 50 ounces or more of raw or refined gold or platinum, or gold or platinum in the form of nuggets, ore, or bullion, is not permitted. Newly mined gold is sold by the Ethiopian Mineral Resources Development Corporation to the NBE.
Controls on external trade	Licenses to import or export gold in any form are issued by the NBE.
Controls on exports and imports of banknotes	
On exports	
Domestic currency	Travelers may take out Br 10 in Ethiopian banknotes.
Foreign currency	Except for short-term visitors, travelers must have an authorization to reexport foreign exchange. Reconversion of birr to foreign exchange must be supported by documentary evidence of prior exchange of foreign currency.

On imports

Domestic currency	Travelers may bring in Br 10 in Ethiopian currency.
Foreign currency	Travelers must declare any foreign currency in their possession when entering Ethiopia.

Resident Accounts

Eligibility to hold accounts

Juridical and natural persons are eligible. Exporters and recipients of remittances are allowed to open foreign exchange accounts but cannot use the funds to acquire shares, stocks, bonds, or any other security denominated in foreign exchange without the prior approval of the NBE.

Foreign exchange accounts permitted

Yes.

Held domestically

These accounts are permitted, but exporters must have the NBE's approval.

Held abroad

No.

Accounts in domestic currency convertible into foreign currency

No.

Nonresident Accounts

Eligibility to hold accounts

Juridical and natural persons are eligible.

Foreign exchange accounts permitted

Approval from the Exchange Control Department of the NBE is required to open these accounts. Deposits to these accounts must be made in foreign exchange. Balances may be transferred freely abroad, and transfers between nonresident accounts do not require prior approval. Members of the diplomatic community must use transferable or non-transferable birr accounts for payment of local expenses. Joint ventures are permitted to open foreign currency accounts or transferable or nontransferable birr accounts to purchase raw materials, equipment, and spare parts not available in Ethiopia. Once documentary evidence of the entry of the goods purchased with such funds is submitted to the Exchange Control Department, funds from these accounts may be freed. Ethiopian nonresidents can maintain interest-bearing accounts, but non-Ethiopians may hold only current accounts.

Domestic currency accounts

Yes.

Convertible into foreign currency

These accounts are permitted, but prior approval is required.

Blocked accounts

Blocked accounts of nonresidents are maintained to retain funds in excess of Br 20,000 arising from disinvestments in Ethiopia.

Imports and Import Payments

Foreign exchange budget

No.

Financing requirements for imports

Imports of goods on the negative list (i.e., used clothing) are ineligible for the foreign exchange auctions. Importation under suppliers' credits requires prior approval of the terms and conditions of the credit, and such imports are limited to raw and intermediate materials, pharmaceuticals, and machinery and transport equipment. Payments by letter of credit (LC), mail transfer, telegraphic transfer, or cash-against-documents at sight are normally accepted, but the NBE must be consulted regarding imports on a cash-against-documents basis.

Advance import deposits

If the importer is successful, an LC is opened by the NBE, while foreign exchange is freed once the imports have arrived.

Documentation requirements for release of foreign exchange for imports	Final invoices separately showing f.o.b. cost and freight charges and nonnegotiable bills of lading. Exchange licenses may be obtained when a valid importer's license is presented. Applications for exchange licenses must be accompanied by information on costs and payment terms, and evidence that adequate insurance has been arranged with the Ethiopian Insurance Corporation.
Preshipment inspection	n.a.
Letters of credit	n.a.
Import licenses and other nontariff measures	
Positive list	n.a.
Negative list	Includes used clothing and items restricted for reasons of health and security. Imports of cars and other vehicles require prior authorization from the Ministry of Transport and Communications.
Import taxes and/or tariffs	Yes.
Taxes collected through the exchange system	No.
State import monopoly	No.

Exports and Export Proceeds

Repatriation requirements	Yes.
Surrender requirements	Ninety percent of the net proceeds from exports must be surrendered in freely convertible currencies or in any other acceptable foreign currency.
Export licenses	
Without quotas	All exports are licensed through the Exchange Controller, and all shipments require a permit from that office; some commodities also require approval from specific government bodies.
With quotas	Exports of raw hides and skins are regulated or prohibited until the needs of local factories are met.
Export taxes	The exportation of coffee is subject to a coffee export duty at the rate of Br 15 a quintal, a coffee export cess at the rate of Br 5 a quintal, and a coffee surtax.
Taxes collected through the exchange system	n.a.

Payments for Invisible Transactions and Current Transfers

Controls on these payments	Payments for invisibles require exchange licenses.
Freight/insurance	Residents may remit premiums on insurance policies purchased before April 1962.
Prior approval	Yes.
Quantitative limits	Invisibles connected with trade transactions are treated on the same basis as the goods to which they relate.
Unloading/storage costs	
Prior approval	Yes.
Administrative expenses	
Prior approval	Yes.

Commissions	n.a.
Interest payments	n.a.
Profit/dividends	After paying local taxes, foreign companies may remit dividends on their invested and reinvested capital in any currency.
Indicative limits/bona fide test	n.a.
Payments for travel	
Prior approval	Yes.
Quantitative limits	Persons traveling abroad for business purposes related to imports or exports are granted foreign exchange up to $10,000 a year. For other business travel, the limits for tourism are applied. Tourists 18 years or older are allowed up to $300 a trip. For government travel, the allowance rates vary by country and foreign currency based on the cost of living.
Medical costs	
Prior approval	Verification by a medical board and the Ministry of Health is required.
Indicative limits/bona fide test	n.a.
Study abroad costs	
Prior approval	Yes.
Quantitative limits	The limit is $2,000 a student, a year. Foreign nationals who are not entitled to remittance facilities may, however, remit up to 30% of their net earnings for the education of their children.
Subscriptions and membership fees	
Prior approval	Yes.
Quantitative limits	n.a.
Indicative limits/bona fide test	n.a.
Consulting/legal fees	n.a.
Foreign workers' wages	
Prior approval	Yes.
Quantitative limits	Foreign contractual employees can take out foreign exchange during the terms of their service and upon final departure, not to exceed their earnings. However, the value of fee accommodation gratuity, accumulated leave pay, and similar benefits may not be included for remittance purposes. Other expatriate employees may take out the same amount on final departure, but not more than Br 20,000 in any 1 year.
	Foreign employees of foreign embassies, legations, consulates, and international organizations whose salaries are fully paid in foreign currency from sources outside Ethiopia can take out and/or transfer their net earnings to the extent of the balance in their nonresident foreign currency account, nonresident transferable birr account, and/or nontransferable birr accounts.
Pensions	n.a.
Gambling/prize earnings	n.a.
Family maintenance/alimony	n.a.
Credit card use abroad	n.a.

Proceeds from Invisible Transactions and Current Transfers

Repatriation requirements   Yes.

Surrender requirements	Ninety percent of proceeds must be surrendered, of which 40% should be surrendered at negotiable rates within 21 days of receipt.

Capital Transactions

Controls on capital and money market instruments	
On capital market securities	
Purchase locally by nonresidents	n.a.
Sale or issue locally by nonresidents	n.a.
Purchase abroad by residents	Banks may not acquire securities denominated in foreign currencies without the permission of the NBE.
On money market instruments	
Purchase locally by nonresidents	n.a.
Sale or issue locally by nonresidents	The NBE is the only issuer of treasury bills.
Purchase abroad by residents	n.a.
Sale or issue abroad by residents	Authorized banks may place their funds abroad freely, except on fixed-term deposits.
On collective investment securities	There is no market in these instruments.
Controls on derivatives and other instruments	There is no market in these instruments.
Controls on credit operations	
Commercial credits	
By residents to nonresidents	n.a.
To residents from nonresidents	Yes.
Financial credits	
By residents to nonresidents	n.a.
To residents from nonresidents	Banks need prior approval from the NBE to overdraw their accounts with foreign correspondents, borrow funds abroad, or accept deposits in foreign currency.
Guarantees, sureties, and financial backup facilities	These instruments are not available.
Controls on direct investment	
Outward direct investment	n.a.
Inward direct investment	Foreign investors are permitted to hold a majority share in a joint venture, except in the following sectors: public utilities, telecommunications, banking and insurance, transport, and trade in selected products deemed essential to the economy by law. All applications for joint ventures must be approved by the Investment Office; a minimum of 25% of share capital must be paid before registration. Investments were allowed in large-scale engineering and metallurgical industries, capital and technology-intensive large-scale pharmaceutical and fertilizer production, and in activities that supply strategic raw materials to the chemical industry, as well as in real estate developments and smaller hotels. Exemptions from income taxes are granted for up to 5 years for new projects and for up to 3 years for major extensions to existing projects. Imports of investment goods and spare parts for such ventures are also eligible for exemption from customs duties and other specified import levies.

Controls on liquidation of direct investment	Authorization of the Exchange Controller is required for repatriation of capital, and registration of capital inflows with the exchange control authorities establishes the evidence of inflows that is required for authorization. All recognized and registered foreign investments may be terminated on presentation of documents regarding liquidation and on payment of all taxes and other liabilities. Subject to appropriate documentation, foreign businessmen with nonregistered investments may transfer their capital abroad on liquidation and final departure from Ethiopia but may not transfer more than Br 20,000 in any 1 calendar year; funds in excess of this amount must be deposited in a blocked account with an authorized bank. This regulation does not apply to joint ventures established under Council of State Special Decree No. 11/1989 (of July 5, 1989) and investments made under Proclamation No. 15/1992 (of May 25, 1992). Transfers by emigrants who have operated their own businesses are restricted to Br 20,000 in any 1 calendar year. Proceeds from the liquidation of a joint venture (as well as dividends received from the activities of a joint venture and payments received from the sale or transfer of shares) may be remitted abroad in convertible currency without restriction. A joint venture may also transfer abroad in convertible currency payments for debts, fees, or royalties in respect of technology transfer agreements.
Controls on real estate transactions	
Purchase abroad by residents	Yes.
Purchase locally by nonresidents	An investment license is required for these purchases.
Sale locally by nonresidents	n.a.
Provisions specific to commercial banks and other credit institutions	
Borrowing abroad	Banks may not borrow from, or enter into a guarantee agreement with banks abroad, unless authorized by the NBE.
Lending locally in foreign exchange	Domestic banks may grant personal loans to staff members of international institutions.
Purchase of locally issued securities denominated in foreign exchange	n.a.
Differential treatment of nonresident deposit accounts and/or deposit accounts in foreign exchange	
Reserve requirements	n.a.
Liquid asset requirements	n.a.
Interest rate controls	Yes.
Credit controls	n.a.
Investment regulations	n.a.
Open foreign exchange position limits	n.a.

Changes During 1996

Exchange arrangements	*July 27.* The frequency of foreign exchange auctions was increased to weekly trading from biweekly trading.
Resident accounts	*October 1.* Resident foreign exchange accounts were permitted for recipients of export earnings and remittances.
Imports and import payments	*July 20.* The franco valuta mechanism was phased out.
	July 20. The negative list was narrowed to used clothing and items restricted for health and security reasons.

July 27. The 25% foreign exchange cover requirement for the foreign exchange auction was eliminated.

Exports and export proceeds

October 1. The surrender requirement was reduced to 90% from 100%; 50% to be surrendered to the NBE and 40% to the foreign exchange market within 3 weeks. The remaining 10% may be held in foreign exchange deposits.

Proceeds from invisible transactions and current transfers

October 1. The surrender requirement was reduced to 90% from 100%; 50% to be surrendered to the NBE and 40% to the foreign exchange market within 3 weeks. The remaining 10% may be held in foreign exchange deposits.

Capital transactions

June 18. Joint ventures of foreign investments with Ethiopian private partners was allowed in large-scale engineering and metallurgical industries, capital- and technology-intensive large-scale pharmaceutical and fertilizer production, and in activities that supply strategic raw materials to the chemical industry. Foreign direct investment was allowed in real estate developments and smaller hotels.

FIJI

(Position as of December 31, 1996)

Status Under IMF Articles of Agreement

Article VIII

Date of acceptance: August 4, 1972.

Exchange Arrangement

Currency

The currency of Fiji is the Fiji dollar.

Exchange rate structure

Unitary.

Classification

Pegged

The external value of the Fiji dollar is determined on the basis of a weighted basket of currencies, comprising the Australian dollar, the Japanese yen, the New Zealand dollar, the pound sterling, and the U.S. dollar. The exchange rate of the Fiji dollar in terms of the U.S. dollar, the intervention currency, is fixed daily by the Reserve Bank of Fiji (RBF) on the basis of quotations for the U.S. dollar and other currencies included in the basket.

Exchange tax

No.

Exchange subsidy

No.

Forward exchange market

Forward exchange facilities are provided by authorized dealers for trade transactions for periods of up to 6 months for exports and 9 months for imports, up to a ratio of their capital.

Official cover of forward operations

No.

Arrangements for Payments and Receipts

Prescription of currency requirements

Although no specific requirements exist, settlements must be made in convertible currencies acceptable to either country as directed by the Exchange Control Act.

Administration of control

Exchange control authorities

Exchange control is administered by the RBF acting as agent of the government; the RBF delegates to authorized dealers the authority to approve normal import payments and other current payments and transfers up to specified limits or full amounts in some cases.

Controls on trade in gold (coins and/or bullion)

Controls on domestic ownership and/or trade

Residents may freely purchase, hold, and sell gold coins, but not gold bullion.

Controls on external trade

The exportation of gold coins, except numismatic coins and collectors' pieces, requires specific permission from the RBF. The importation of gold, other than gold coins, from all sources requires a specific import license issued by the Ministry of Finance and Economic Planning; these are restricted to authorized gold dealers. Gold coins and gold bullion are exempt from fiscal duty but are subject to a 10% value-added tax (VAT). Gold jewelry is also exempt from fiscal duty but subject to a 10% VAT and is not under licensing control. Samples of gold and gold jewelry sent by foreign manufacturers require import licenses if their value exceeds F$200. Exports of gold jewelry are free of export duty but require licenses if their value exceeds F$1,000. Exports of gold bullion are subject to an export duty of 3%.

Controls on exports and imports of banknotes

On exports

    Domestic currency — Exports are allowed up to F$500 a trip.

    Foreign currency — Exports are allowed up to the amount declared at the time of arrival.

On imports

    Domestic currency — Travelers may bring in freely Fijian banknotes, but must declare them to customs or immigration officials on arrival.

    Foreign currency — Travelers may bring in freely foreign currency banknotes, but must declare them to customs or immigration officials on arrival in order to export the unused balance on departure.

Resident Accounts

Eligibility to hold accounts — Juridical and natural persons are eligible.

Foreign exchange accounts permitted — Yes.

Held domestically — These accounts are permitted, but prior approval is required.

Held abroad — These accounts are permitted, but prior approval is required.

Accounts in domestic currency convertible into foreign currency — Yes.

Nonresident Accounts

Eligibility to hold accounts — Juridical and natural persons are eligible.

Foreign exchange accounts permitted — These accounts may be credited freely with the account holders' salaries (net of tax), with interest payable on the account, and with payments from other external accounts.

Domestic currency accounts — These accounts may be credited freely with the account holders' salaries (net of tax), with interest payable on the account, with payments from other external accounts, with the proceeds of sales of foreign currency or foreign coins by the account holder, and with Fiji banknotes that the account holder brought into Fiji or acquired by debit to an external account or by the sale of foreign currency in the country during a temporary visit. External accounts may also be credited with payments by residents for which either general or specific authority has been given. External accounts may be debited for payments to residents of Fiji, transfers to other external accounts, payments in cash in Fiji, and purchases of foreign exchange.

Convertible into foreign currency — These accounts are permitted, but prior approval is required.

Imports and Import Payments

Foreign exchange budget — No.

Financing requirements for imports

Minimum financing requirements — n.a.

Advance payment requirements — Authorized banks may approve advance payments for imports of up to F$100,000 an application without specific approval from the RBF if such payments are required by the supplier.

Advance import deposits	n.a.
Documentation requirements for release of foreign exchange for imports	Payments for authorized imports are permitted upon application and submission of documentary evidence to authorized dealers, who may allow payments for goods that have been imported under either a specific import license or an open general license.
Domiciliation requirements	n.a.
Preshipment inspection	n.a.
Letters of credit	n.a.
Import licenses used as exchange licenses	n.a.
Import licenses and other nontariff measures	Imports of frozen chicken and lubrication oil products in any form from the United States require a specific import license. The Ministry of Trade and Commerce is responsible for issuing import licenses, with the exception of those for gold and timber. Import licenses and other nontariff measures for gold are issued by the Ministry of Finance and Economic Planning; for timber, by the Ministry of Forestry. A wide range of consumer goods are imported by national cooperative societies under a joint arrangement with 6 other Pacific Island countries. All imports must meet required technical standards on labeling, packaging, and expiration date requirements. All agricultural and forestry products are subject to quarantine clearance.
Negative list	The importation of a few commodities is prohibited for security, health, or public policy reasons.
Licenses with quotas	Import licenses for frozen chicken from the United States are issued on a quota basis.
Import taxes and/or tariffs	Import tariffs range from 5% to 22.5%. A 10% VAT is also levied.
Taxes collected through the exchange system	n.a.
State import monopoly	No.

Exports and Export Proceeds

Repatriation requirements	Exporters are required to collect the proceeds from exports within 6 months of the date of shipment of the goods from Fiji and may not, without specific permission, grant more than 6 months' credit to a nonresident buyer.
Surrender requirements	Exporters may retain, with prior approval of the RBF, up to 20% of export proceeds in foreign currency accounts maintained with an authorized dealer or a foreign bank abroad; the rate of retention from each export receipt is not subject to control.
Export licenses	Export licenses are issued by various government departments and monitored by the Comptroller of Customs. Specific licenses are required only for exports of sugar, wheat bran, copra meal, certain lumber, certain animals, and a few other items. Irrespective of export-licensing requirements, however, exporters are required to produce an export permit for commercial consignment of all goods with an f.o.b. value of more than F$1,000; this permit is required for exchange control purposes.
Without quotas	n.a.
With quotas	n.a.
Export taxes	A 3% export duty is levied on exports of sugar, gold, and silver.
Taxes collected through the exchange system	n.a.

Payments for Invisible Transactions and Current Transfers

Controls on these payments	Controls are mostly in the form of documentation requirements. Most payments have been fully delegated to authorized banks without any restrictions or limits. All payments are subject to indicative limits and/or bona fide tests.

Commissions

Quantitative limits The limit is F$100,000 an application.

Interest payments

Prior approval These payments may be effected provided that prior specific approval for the loan was granted by the RBF.

Profit/dividends Emigrants are allowed to transfer, after 1 year abroad, the full amount of the current year's dividends or profits earned on assets left in Fiji.

Prior approval Nonresident-owned companies must obtain permission from the RBF to transfer dividends abroad. Under the present policy, remittance of the current year's profits and 4 years' retained earnings that have not previously been remitted is allowed.

Quantitative limits Yes.

Payments for travel

Prior approval Approval is required for amounts above F$8,000 a trip.

Quantitative limits Yes.

Medical costs

Prior approval No approval is required, provided that payment is made directly to the institution.

Quantitative limits Foreign exchange provided is restricted to amounts due.

Study abroad costs

Prior approval Approval is required for living allowances above F$20,000 a beneficiary, a year, in addition to tuition fees paid directly to the institution.

Quantitative limits Yes.

Subscriptions and membership fees

Prior approval Approval is required for payments above F$15,000 an applicant.

Consulting/legal fees

Prior approval Approval is required for payments above F$200,000.

Foreign workers' wages

Prior approval Approval is required for payments above F$100,000.

Gambling/prize earnings

Prior approval Yes.

Family maintenance/alimony

Prior approval Approval is required for amounts above F$15,000 a year.

Quantitative limits Gift payments are limited to F$2,500 an applicant a year.

Credit card use abroad

Prior approval Yes.

Quantitative limits The use of credit cards for travel-related expenses is not restricted, except for a F$5,000 limit on their use for shopping on each trip; in addition, F$500 a month may be withdrawn in cash.

Proceeds from Invisible Transactions and Current Transfers

Repatriation requirements	Yes.
Surrender requirements	Residents are required to sell all their foreign currency receipts to an authorized dealer within 1 month of their return. Receipts of interest, dividends, and amortization must be surrendered semiannually unless approval for reinvestment abroad has been granted by the RBF.
Restrictions on use of funds	No.

Capital Transactions

Controls on capital and money market instruments	
On capital market securities	Prior approval by the RBF is required.
Purchase locally by nonresidents	Yes.
Sale or issue locally by nonresidents	Yes.
Purchase abroad by residents	Yes.
Sale or issue abroad by residents	Yes.
On money market instruments	Yes.
On collective investment securities	Yes.
Controls on derivatives and other instruments	
Purchase locally by nonresidents	Yes.
Sale or issue locally by nonresidents	Yes.
Purchase abroad by residents	Yes.
Sale or issue abroad by residents	Yes.
Controls on credit operations	
Commercial credits	Residents must obtain prior permission from the RBF to borrow foreign currency in Fiji or abroad.
By residents to nonresidents	Yes.
To residents from nonresidents	Yes.
Financial credits	Yes.
Guarantees, sureties, and financial backup facilities	Yes.
Controls on direct investment	
Outward direct investment	Yes.
Inward direct investment	Foreign investment in Fiji is normally expected to be financed from a nonresident source. Such foreign investment may be given "approved status," which guarantees the right to repatriate dividends and capital.
Controls on liquidation of direct investment	Requires specific permission from the RBF, which is readily granted with evidence that the investment funds originated offshore. Nonresident-owned companies are permitted to repatriate in full the proceeds from sales of assets and capital gains on investments of up to F$15 million a year.

Controls on real estate transactions

Purchase abroad by residents

The purchase of personal property abroad is not permitted.

Purchase locally by nonresidents

Approval by the Ministry of Land is required for purchases of state-owned property. Settlements require RBF approval to ensure proceeds are received in Fiji and that funds are sourced from abroad.

Sale locally by nonresidents

Controls on settlements are to safeguard local interest, before proceeds from sales are remitted abroad.

Provisions specific to commercial banks and other credit institutions

Borrowing abroad

Authorized dealers must obtain permission from the RBF to borrow abroad.

Lending to nonresidents (financial or commercial credits)

Authorized dealers may lend up to F$200,000 to a newly established company or a branch of a company in Fiji (other than a bank) that is controlled directly or indirectly by persons who reside outside Fiji and up to F$30,000 to individual nonresident customers; individual nonresident borrowers must repay their loans before leaving Fiji. Any amounts in excess of these limits require prior approval from the RBF.

Lending locally in foreign exchange

The banks and nonbank financial institutions may not lend foreign currency to any resident of Fiji without the specific permission of the RBF.

Purchase of locally issued securities denominated in foreign exchange

Yes.

Differential treatment of nonresident deposit accounts and/or deposit accounts in foreign exchange

n.a.

Investment regulations

n.a.

Open foreign exchange position limits

Commercial banks are allowed to maintain specific net open positions based on their actual capital holdings in Fiji.

Provisions specific to institutional investors

Limits (max.) on portfolio invested abroad

Yes.

Limits (min.) on portfolio invested locally

n.a.

Currency matching regulations on assets/liabilities composition

n.a.

Changes During 1996

Payments for invisible transactions and current transfers

January 1. Current limits on remittances for commissions, subscriptions and membership fees, and family maintenance; on payments for travel and studies abroad; and on the use of credit cards abroad were adopted.

FINLAND

(Position as of December 31, 1996)

Status Under IMF Articles of Agreement

Article VIII   Date of acceptance: September 25, 1979.

Exchange Arrangement

Currency   The currency of Finland is the markka (100 penni = Fmk 1).

Exchange rate structure   Unitary.

Classification

Cooperative arrangement   Finland joined the ERM of the EMS on October 14, 1996. In accordance with this mechanism, Finland maintains spot exchange rates between the markka and the currencies of the other participants within margins of 15% above or below the cross rates based on the central rates expressed in ECUs.

Exchange tax   No.

Exchange subsidy   No.

Forward exchange market   Yes.

Official cover of forward operations   No.

Arrangements for Payments and Receipts

Prescription of currency requirements   No.

Payment arrangements   No.

Administration of control

Exchange control authorities   There are no exchange controls. Import licensing is administered by the National Board of Customs. Export licensing relating to international export control regimes is administered by the trade department/foreign trade division of the Ministry of Trade and Industry.

International security restrictions

In accordance with IMF Executive Board Decision No. 144-(52/51)   Finland maintains exchange restrictions pursuant to UN Security Council resolutions against Iraq and Libya. Exchange restrictions on the Federal Republic of Yugoslavia (Serbia/Montenegro), and certain areas of the Republic of Bosnia and Herzegovina were terminated in October 1996, with the exception of certain claims. A UN Security Council resolution on food for oil (Iraq) was implemented in December 1996.

In accordance with UN sanctions   Yes.

Payments arrears   No.

Controls on trade in gold (coins and/or bullion)   No.

Controls on exports and imports of banknotes   No.

Resident Accounts

Eligibility to hold accounts   Juridical and natural persons are eligible.

Foreign exchange accounts permitted   Yes.

Held domestically	Yes.
Held abroad	Yes.
Accounts in domestic currency convertible into foreign currency	Yes.

Nonresident Accounts

Eligibility to hold accounts	Juridical and natural persons are eligible.
Foreign exchange accounts permitted	Yes.
Domestic currency accounts	Yes.
Convertible into foreign currency	Yes.
Blocked accounts	No.

Imports and Import Payments

Foreign exchange budget	No.
Financing requirements for imports	No.
Documentation requirements for release of foreign exchange for imports	No.
Import licenses and other nontariff measures	
Negative list	Yes.
Licenses with quotas	The following products are subject to quantitative import restrictions and require an import license when imported into the EU: certain steel products subject to bilateral agreements with Russia and Ukraine, certain steel products subject to autonomous community quotas for Kazakhstan, specific textile products subject to bilateral agreements with third countries, particular third-country textile products subject to autonomous community quotas, and certain Chinese industrial products subject to autonomous community quotas.
Import taxes and/or tariffs	No.
State import monopoly	No.

Exports and Export Proceeds

Repatriation requirements	No.
Surrender requirements	No.
Financing requirements	No.
Documentation requirements	No.
Export licenses	Export licenses are required only for exports of goods related to international export control regimes and are administered by the Ministry of Trade and Industry. The sale of arms is strictly controlled by the Ministry of Defense.
Without quotas	Yes.
Export taxes	No.

Payments for Invisible Transactions and Current Transfers

Controls on these payments   There are no controls on these payments.

Proceeds from Invisible Transactions and Current Transfers

Repatriation requirements   No.

Surrender requirements   No.

Restrictions on use of funds   No.

Capital Transactions

Controls on capital and money market instruments

On capital market securities

Purchase locally by nonresidents   The control applies only to the purchase of shares and other securities of a participatory nature, which may be affected by laws on inward direct investment and establishment.

Controls on derivatives and other instruments   No.

Controls on credit operations   No.

Controls on direct investment

Inward direct investment   Acquisition of shares giving at least one-third of the voting rights in a Finnish defense enterprise to a single foreign owner requires prior confirmation by the Ministry of Defense; approval can be denied only if the safeguarding of the public defense is jeopardized.

Controls on liquidation of direct investment   No.

Controls on real estate transactions

Purchase locally by nonresidents   The controls apply only to the acquisition of real estate (1) for recreational purposes or secondary residences by nonresidents who have not previously been residents of Finland for at least 5 years; and (2) in the Aaland Islands.

Provisions specific to commercial banks and other credit institutions

Open foreign exchange position limits   Prudential regulation harmonized with EU directives is applied.

Provisions specific to institutional investors

Limits (max.) on portfolio invested abroad   Yes.

Limits (min.) on portfolio invested locally   Yes.

Currency matching regulations on assets/liabilities composition   Yes.

Other controls imposed by securities laws   Yes.

Changes During 1996

Exchange arrangements   *October 14.* Finland joined the ERM of the EMS.

FRANCE

(Position as of December 31, 1996)

Status Under IMF Articles of Agreement

Article VIII	Date of acceptance: February 15, 1961.

Exchange Arrangement

Currency	The currency of France is the French franc.
Exchange rate structure	Unitary.
Classification	
Cooperative arrangement	France participates in the ERM of the EMS. In accordance with this agreement, France maintains the spot exchange rates between the franc and the currencies of the other participants within margins of 15% above and below the cross rates based on the central rates expressed in ECUs.
	Fixed conversion rates in terms of the franc apply to the CFP franc, which is the currency of the overseas territories of French Polynesia, New Caledonia, and Wallis and Futuna Islands, and the two groups of African countries that are linked to the French Treasury through an Operations Account: Benin, Burkina Faso, Côte d'Ivoire, Mali, Niger, Senegal, and Togo (*franc de la Communauté financière africaine*, issued by the BCEAO); and Cameroon, Central African Republic, Chad, Republic of Congo, Equatorial Guinea, and Gabon (*franc de la Coopération financière en Afrique centrale*, issued by the BEAC). These fixed parities are CFPF 1 per F 0.055 and CFPF 1 per F 0.01, respectively.
	The Comorian franc, issued by the Central Bank of the Comoros, which holds an Operations Account with the French Treasury, is linked to the French franc by a fixed parity of FC 1 to F 0.0133.
Exchange tax	No.
Exchange subsidy	No.
Forward exchange market	Registered banks in France and Monaco, which may also act on behalf of banks established abroad or in Operations Account countries, are permitted to deal spot or forward in the exchange market in France. Registered banks may also deal spot and forward with their correspondents in foreign markets in all currencies. Nonbank residents may purchase foreign exchange forward in respect of specified transactions. All residents, including nonenterprise individuals, may purchase or sell foreign exchange forward without restriction. Forward sales of foreign currency are not restricted, whether or not they are for hedging purposes.
Official cover of forward operations	No.

Arrangements for Payments and Receipts

Prescription of currency requirements	No.
Payment arrangements	No.
Administration of control	
Exchange control authorities	The Directorate of the Treasury in the Ministry of the Economy is the coordinating agency for financial relations with foreign countries. It is responsible for all matters relating to inward and outward direct investment and has certain powers over matters relating to insurance, reinsurance, annuities, and the like. The execution of all transfers

has been delegated to registered banks and stockbrokers and to the Postal Administration.

International security restrictions

In accordance with UN sanctions

Restrictions on payments have been imposed on Iraq in accordance with the UN Security Council Resolution No. 986 (1995).

Controls on trade in gold (coins and/or bullion)

No.

Controls on exports and imports of banknotes

Amounts exceeding the equivalent of F 50,000 must be declared to customs upon arrival or departure. At the request of Algeria, Morocco, and Tunisia, banknotes issued by these countries may not be exchanged in France.

Resident Accounts

Eligibility to hold accounts

Juridical and natural persons are eligible.

Foreign exchange accounts permitted

Yes.

Held domestically

Yes.

Held abroad

Yes.

Accounts in domestic currency convertible into foreign currency

Yes.

Nonresident Accounts

Eligibility to hold accounts

Juridical and natural persons are eligible.

Foreign exchange accounts permitted

Yes.

Domestic currency accounts

Yes.

Convertible into foreign currency

Yes.

Blocked accounts

No.

Imports and Import Payments

Foreign exchange budget

No.

Financing requirements for imports

No.

Documentation requirements for release of foreign exchange for imports

A customs declaration is required.

Import licenses and other nontariff measures

Some imports from non-EU countries are subject to minimum prices; these require an administrative visa issued by the Central Customs Administration or the appropriate ministry and sometimes, exceptionally, an import license. Imports of products of the ECSC require such administrative visas when originating in non-ECSC countries. Imports from non-EU countries of most products covered by the CAP of the EU are subject to variable import levies that have replaced previous barriers. Common EU regulations are also applied to imports from non-EU countries of most other agricultural and livestock products. Quantitative restrictions consist of EU-wide and national restrictions. The former include textile and apparel limits under the MFA and voluntary export restraints. National measures are authorized under Article 115 of the EU Treaty.

For some commodities, such as petroleum and petroleum products, global quotas are allocated annually. In other cases, quotas are allocated semiannually and apply to all countries (other than those that have bilaterally negotiated quotas or receive privileged treatment).

Licenses with quotas	Licenses are required for some countries and some products. Imports of goods that originate outside of the EU and are subject to quantitative restrictions require individual licenses. Common EU regulations are also applied to imports from non-EU countries.
Import taxes and/or tariffs	Duties are collected at the time of entry into the EU in relation to the origin of the products and a tariff nomenclature. An agricultural levy (within the CAP) and, if necessary, an antidumping levy can be added.
Taxes collected through the exchange system	No.
State import monopoly	No.

Exports and Export Proceeds

Repatriation requirements	No.
Surrender requirements	No.
Financing requirements	No.
Documentation requirements	A customs declaration is required.
Export licenses	
Without quotas	Certain prohibited goods may be exported only under a special license.
Export taxes	Exports are not taxed, except for works of art, which are subject to the value-added tax.

Payments for Invisible Transactions and Current Transfers

Controls on these payments	No.

Proceeds from Invisible Transactions and Current Transfers

Repatriation requirements	No.
Surrender requirements	No.
Restrictions on use of funds	No.

Capital Transactions

Controls on capital and money market instruments	Capital movements between France and Monaco and the Operations Account countries are free of exchange control. The French capital market is based on the principle of freedom of access and operation. The only restrictions apply to the issuance of certificates of deposit by nonresident banks and to Eurofranc issues, which are subject to rules set by the Eurofranc Committee that establishes that the majority of Eurofranc issues must be sold abroad.
On capital market securities	
Purchase locally by nonresidents	Yes.
Sale or issue locally by nonresidents	Yes.

Sale or issue abroad by residents	Yes.
On money market instruments	
Sale or issue locally by nonresidents	Nonresidents can only issue commercial papers.
Sale or issue abroad by residents	Yes.
On collective investment securities	
Sale or issue locally by nonresidents	The restriction does not apply to collective investment securities that are of EU origin and comply with EC Directive 85/611/EC.
Purchase abroad by residents	French mutual funds can acquire securities only in the EU-regulated market or in markets admitted by the Securities Exchange Commission.
Controls on derivatives and other instruments	No.
Controls on credit operations	No.
Controls on direct investment	Direct investments are defined as those where foreign investors hold more than one-third of the capital. In the case of firms whose shares are quoted on the stock exchange, the threshold is reduced to 20% of the capital and applies to each individual foreign participation but not to the total of foreign participation. To determine whether a company is under foreign control, the Ministry of Economy and Finance may also take into account any special relationships resulting from stock options, loans, patents and licenses, and commercial contracts.
Inward direct investment	Investments are prohibited in areas pertaining to public order and defense.
Controls on liquidation of direct investment	The liquidation proceeds of foreign direct investment in France may be freely transferred abroad; the liquidation must be reported to the Ministry within 20 days of its occurrence. The liquidation of direct investments abroad is free from any prior application, provided that the corresponding funds had been reported to the Bank of France.
Controls on real estate transactions	No.
Provisions specific to commercial banks and other credit institutions	No.
Provisions specific to institutional investors	
Currency matching regulations on assets/liabilities composition	European insurance companies are required to cover their technical reserves with assets expressed in the same currency.
Other controls imposed by securities laws	No.

Changes During 1996

No significant changes occurred in the exchange and trade system.

GABON

(Position as of December 31, 1996)

Status Under IMF Articles of Agreement

Article VIII	Date of acceptance: June 1, 1996.

Exchange Arrangement

Currency	The currency of Gabon is the CFA franc.
Exchange rate structure	Unitary.
Classification	
Pegged	The CFA franc is pegged to the French franc, the intervention currency, at the fixed rate of CFAF 1 per F 0.01. Exchange transactions in French francs between the BEAC and commercial banks take place at the same rate. Buying and selling rates for certain foreign currencies are also officially posted, with quotations based on the fixed rate for the French franc and the rate for the currency concerned in the Paris exchange market, and include a commission. Commissions are levied at the rate of 0.25% on transfers made by the banks for their own accounts and on all private capital transfers to countries that are not members of the BEAC, except those made for the account of the Treasury, national accounting offices, national and international public agencies, and private entities granted exemption by the Ministry of Finance, Budget, and Participations (MOFBP) because of the nature of their activities.
Exchange tax	No.
Exchange subsidy	No.
Forward exchange market	There are no forward exchange markets for the CFA franc. However, exporters and importers can always cover their position on the Paris foreign exchange market.

Arrangements for Payments and Receipts

Prescription of currency requirements	Since Gabon is an Operations Account country, settlements with France, Monaco, and the other Operations Account countries are made in CFA francs, French francs, or the currency of any other institute of issue that maintains an Operations Account with the French Treasury. Settlements with all other countries are usually made through correspondent banks in France in the currencies of those countries or in French francs through foreign accounts in francs.
Payment arrangements	
Regional arrangements	An Operations Account is maintained with the French Treasury that links Operations Account countries. All purchases or sales of foreign currencies or French francs against CFA francs are ultimately settled through a debit or credit to the Operations Account.
Administration of control	
Exchange control authorities	The Directorate of Financial Institutions of the MOFBP supervises borrowing and lending abroad. Exchange control is administered by the MOFBP, which has partly delegated approval authority to the authorized banks for current payments and to the BEAC for issues related to the external position of the banks. All exchange transactions relating to foreign countries must be effected through authorized intermediaries—that is, the Postal Administration and authorized banks. Import and export authorizations, where necessary, are issued by the Directorate of External Trade of the Ministry of Commerce and Industry.
Payment arrears	No.

Controls on trade in gold (coins and/or bullion)

Controls on domestic ownership and/or trade

Residents are free to hold, acquire, and dispose of gold in any form in Gabon.

Controls on external trade

Imports and exports of gold require the authorization of the MOFBP. Exempt from this requirement are (1) imports and exports by or on behalf of the monetary authorities, and (2) imports and exports of manufactured articles containing a small quantity of gold (such as gold-filled or gold-plated articles). The exportation of gold is the monopoly of the Société gabonaise de recherches et d'exploitation minières. Imports of gold exempted from licensing and authorization requirements are subject to customs declaration.

Controls on exports and imports of banknotes

On exports

Domestic currency

There is no limit on the amount of banknotes that residents and nonresidents can export from one BEAC country to another, but exports of banknotes outside the BEAC zone are prohibited.

Foreign currency

Residents traveling outside the BEAC zone are subject to the various limits imposed on foreign exchange allowances allocated for each trip, depending on the nature of the travel. Nonresident travelers may take with them foreign currency or other foreign means of payment equivalent to the maximum amount declared upon entry into the BEAC zone. Above this ceiling or in the absence of declaration, nonresidents must provide supporting documents explaining the origin of such amounts.

On imports

Domestic currency

There is no limit on the amount of banknotes that residents and nonresidents can import into one BEAC country from another, but imports of banknotes from outside the BEAC zone, both by residents and nonresidents, are prohibited.

Foreign currency

Resident and nonresident travelers may bring in any amount of banknotes and coins issued by the Bank of France or any other bank of issue maintaining an Operations Account with the French Treasury, as well as any amount of foreign banknotes and coins (except gold coins) of countries outside the Operations Account area.

Resident Accounts

Eligibility to hold accounts

Juridical and natural persons are eligible.

Foreign exchange accounts permitted

Yes.

Held domestically

No.

Held abroad

These accounts are permitted, but prior approval is required.

Nonresident Accounts

Eligibility to hold accounts

Juridical and natural persons are eligible.

Foreign exchange accounts permitted

These accounts are permitted, but prior approval is required.

Domestic currency accounts

The regulations pertaining to nonresident accounts are based on regulations that were applied in France before the abolition of all capital controls in 1989. Because the BEAC has suspended the repurchase of BEAC banknotes circulating outside the territories of its member countries, BEAC banknotes received by foreign correspondents' authorized banks and mailed to the BEAC agency in Libreville may not be credited to foreign accounts in francs.

Convertible into foreign currency	Yes.

Imports and Import Payments

Foreign exchange budget	No.
Financing requirements for imports	No.
Documentation requirements for release of foreign exchange for imports	
Domiciliation requirements	All import transactions relating to foreign countries must be domiciled with an authorized bank.
Preshipment inspection	n.a.
Letters of credit	n.a.
Import licenses used as exchange licenses	Import declarations to or licenses approved by the Ministry of Foreign Trade and the MOFBP (Directorate of Financial Institutions) entitle importers to purchase the necessary foreign exchange, provided that the shipping documents are submitted to the authorized bank.
Import licenses and other nontariff measures	All imports of commercial goods must be insured through authorized insurance companies in Gabon.
Negative list	Some imports are prohibited for security and health reasons.
Open general licenses	Except for sugar, imports from all countries are free and do not require licenses. All imports, however, are subject to declaration.
Licenses with quotas	Importation of sugar is subject to quotas.
Import taxes and/or tariffs	The common duty rates of the UDEAC member countries of 5% for basic necessities, 10% for raw materials and capital goods, 20% for intermediate goods, and 30% for consumer goods are applied.
Taxes collected through the exchange system	No.
State import monopoly	No.

Exports and Export Proceeds

Repatriation requirements	Proceeds from exports to countries outside the BEAC zone must be collected and repatriated within 30 days of the payment date stipulated in the contract, unless a special waiver is granted by the MOFBP.
Surrender requirements	Export proceeds received in currencies other than those of France or an Operations Account country must be surrendered within 1 month of collection.
Documentation requirements	
Letters of credit	n.a.
Guarantees	n.a.
Domiciliation	Export transactions relating to foreign countries must be domiciled with an authorized bank.
Preshipment inspection	n.a.

Export licenses	Exports are subject to declaration to the Ministry of Foreign Trade.
Without quotas	n.a.
With quotas	n.a.
Export taxes	Export taxes are levied on mining products (0.5%) and forest products (5% to 11%).
Taxes collected through the exchange system	No.

Payments for Invisible Transactions and Current Transfers

Controls on these payments	Payments for invisibles to France, Monaco, and the Operations Account countries are permitted freely; payments to other countries are subject to declaration and presentation of appropriate documents to the MOFBP. For many types of payments, the monitoring function of the MOFBP has been delegated to authorized banks and the Postal Administration. Payments for invisibles related to trade are permitted freely when the basic trade transaction has been approved or does not require authorization. There are no controls on payments for freight and insurance, unloading and storage costs, administrative expenses, commissions, subscriptions and membership fees, and consulting and legal fees, or on interest payments and remittances of profits and dividends.
Payments for travel	
Quantitative limits	Residents traveling to other countries of the franc zone may obtain an unlimited allocation in French francs. Within the BEAC zone, BEAC banknotes can be exported without limits. Residents traveling outside the BEAC zone are allowed to take out foreign banknotes and other means of payment up to a limit of CFAF 2 million and CFAF 5 million for tourism and business purposes, respectively.
Indicative limits/bona fide test	Yes.
Medical costs	
Quantitative limits	Persons traveling to countries outside the franc zone for medical reasons may obtain an exchange allocation of up to CFAF 2,500,000.
Indicative limits/bona fide test	Yes.
Study abroad costs	
Quantitative limits	Students or trainees leaving Gabon for the first time or returning to their normal place of study in countries outside the BEAC zone may obtain an exchange allowance equivalent to CFAF 1 million.
Indicative limits/bona fide test	Yes.
Foreign workers' wages	
Quantitative limits	Foreign workers are allowed to transfer 50% of their net salary upon presentation of their pay vouchers, provided that the transfers take place within 3 months of the pay period concerned.
Credit card use abroad	
Prior approval	Yes.
Quantitative limits	The use of credit cards, which must be issued by resident financial intermediaries and approved by the MOFBP, is limited to the ceilings indicated above for tourism and business travel.
Indicative limits/bona fide test	Yes.

Proceeds from Invisible Transactions and Current Transfers

Repatriation requirements	Proceeds from transactions in invisibles with France, Monaco, and the Operations Account countries may be retained.

Surrender requirements	All amounts due from residents of other countries in respect of services and all income earned in those countries from foreign assets must be collected and, if received in foreign currency, surrendered within a month of the due date. Returning resident travelers are required to declare all means of payment in their possession upon arrival at customs and surrender within 8 days all means of payment exceeding the equivalent of CFAF 25,000.
Restrictions on use of funds	No.

Capital Transactions

Controls on capital and money market instruments	Capital movements between Gabon and France, Monaco, and the Operations Account countries are free of exchange control, except for the sale or introduction of foreign securities. Capital transfers to all other countries are restricted and require the approval of the Directorate of Financial Institutions, but capital receipts from these countries are permitted freely. All foreign securities, foreign currency, and titles embodying claims on foreign countries or nonresidents that are held in Gabon by residents or nonresidents must be deposited with authorized banks in Gabon.
On capital market securities	
Purchase locally by nonresidents	n.a.
Sale or issue locally by nonresidents	The issuing, advertising, or offering for sale of foreign securities in Gabon requires prior authorization from the MOFBP. Exempt from authorization, however, are operations in connection with (1) loans backed by a guarantee from the Gabonese government, and (2) shares similar to securities whose issuing, advertising, or offering for sale in Gabon has previously been authorized.
Purchase abroad by residents	Yes.
Sale or issue abroad by residents	n.a.
On money market instruments	Yes.
Purchase locally by nonresidents	n.a.
Sale or issue locally by nonresidents	n.a.
Purchase abroad by residents	n.a.
Sale or issue abroad by residents	n.a.
On collective investment securities	Yes.
Purchase locally by nonresidents	n.a.
Sale or issue locally by nonresidents	n.a.
Purchase abroad by residents	n.a.
Sale or issue abroad by residents	n.a.
Controls on derivatives and other instruments	Yes.
Purchase locally by nonresidents	n.a.
Sale or issue locally by nonresidents	n.a.
Purchase abroad by residents	n.a.
Sale or issue abroad by residents	n.a.

Controls on credit operations

Commercial credits

By residents to nonresidents

Lending by residents or by branches or subsidiaries in Gabon of juridical persons whose registered office is abroad requires prior authorization from the MOFBP. The following are, however, exempt from this authorization: (1) loans granted by registered banks and (2) other loans, of which the total amount outstanding does not exceed CFAF 50 million for any one lender. However, for loans that are free of authorization, each repayment must be declared to the Directorate of Financial Institutions within 20 days of the operation except when the total outstanding amount of all loans granted abroad by the lender does not exceed CFAF 5 million.

To residents from nonresidents

Borrowing by residents or by branches or subsidiaries in Gabon of juridical persons whose registered office is abroad requires prior authorization from the MOFBP. The following are, however, exempt from this authorization: (1) loans constituting a direct investment abroad for which prior approval has been obtained; (2) loans directly connected with the rendering of services abroad by the persons or firms mentioned above, or with the financing of commercial transactions either between Gabon and countries abroad or between foreign countries in which these persons or firms take part; (3) loans contracted by registered banks; and (4) loans other than those mentioned above, of which the total amount outstanding does not exceed CFAF 50 million for any one borrower. However, for the contracting of loans referred to under (4) that are free of authorization, each repayment must be declared to the Directorate of Financial Institutions within 20 days of the operation unless the total outstanding amount of all loans contracted abroad by the borrower is CFAF 5 million or less.

Financial credits

Yes.

Guarantees, sureties, and financial backup facilities

Yes.

By residents to nonresidents

n.a.

To residents from nonresidents

n.a.

Controls on direct investment

Outward direct investment

Investments, including those made by companies in Gabon that are directly or indirectly under foreign control and those made by branches or subsidiaries of foreign companies in Gabon, must be declared to the MOFBP unless they take the form of a capital increase resulting from reinvestment of undistributed profits.

Inward direct investment

Investments must be declared to the MOFBP within 20 days of the operation unless they take the form of a capital increase resulting from the reinvestment of undistributed profits; within 2 months of receipt of the declaration, the MOFBP may request the postponement of the project. Foreign companies investing in Gabon must offer shares for purchase by Gabonese nationals for an amount equivalent to at least 10% of the company's capital.

Controls on liquidation of direct investment

The full or partial liquidation of direct investments in Gabon must be declared to the MOFBP within 20 days of the operation unless the operation involves the relinquishing of a shareholding that had previously been approved as constituting a direct investment in Gabon.

Controls on real estate transactions

Purchase abroad by residents

n.a.

Purchase locally by nonresidents

Purchases are not permitted.

Sale locally by nonresidents

n.a.

Changes During 1996

Status under IMF Articles of Agreement

June 1. Gabon accepted the obligations of Article VIII, Sections 2, 3, and 4 of the Fund Articles of Agreement.

THE GAMBIA

(Position as of December 31, 1996)

Status Under IMF Articles of Agreement

Article VIII	Date of acceptance: January 21, 1993.

Exchange Arrangement

Currency	The currency of The Gambia is the Gambian dalasi.
Exchange rate structure	Unitary.
Classification	
Independent floating	The exchange rate of the dalasi is determined in the foreign exchange market. Commercial banks and foreign exchange bureaus are free to transact among themselves, with the Central Bank of The Gambia (CBG), or with customers at exchange rates agreed on by the parties to these transactions. The CBG conducts a foreign exchange market review session on the last working day of each week with the participation of the commercial banks and foreign exchange bureaus. During this session, the average market rate during the week is announced as the rate for customs valuation purposes for the following week.
Exchange tax	No.
Exchange subsidy	No.
Forward exchange market	No.

Arrangements for Payments and Receipts

Prescription of currency requirements	No.
Payment arrangements	
Clearing agreements	Settlements with the BCEAO, Ghana, Guinea, Guinea-Bissau, Liberia, Mali, Mauritania, Nigeria, and Sierra Leone are normally made through the WAEMU.
Administration of control	No.
International security restrictions	No.
Payment arrears	No.
Controls on trade in gold (coins and/or bullion)	No.
Controls on exports and imports of banknotes	No.

Resident Accounts

Eligibility to hold accounts	Juridical and natural persons are eligible.
Foreign exchange accounts permitted	Yes.
Held abroad	Yes.
Approval required	n.a.

Nonresident Accounts

Eligibility to hold accounts	Juridical and natural persons are eligible.
Foreign exchange accounts permitted	No.
Domestic currency accounts	Yes.
Convertible into foreign currency	Accounts denominated in dalasis are designated external accounts, and may be opened without reference to the CBG when commercial banks are satisfied that the account holder's source of funds is from abroad in convertible foreign currency. Designated external accounts may be credited with payments from residents of other countries, with transfers from other external accounts, and with the proceeds of sales through the banking system of other convertible currencies. They may be debited for payments to residents of other countries, for transfers to other external accounts, and for purchases of other convertible currencies.
Blocked accounts	No.

Imports and Import Payments

Foreign exchange budget	No.
Financing requirements for imports	No.
Documentation requirements for release of foreign exchange for imports	No.
Import licenses and other nontariff measures	
Negative list	Imports of certain goods are prohibited for social, health, or security reasons.
Open general licenses	Yes.
Import taxes and/or tariffs	Customs duty rates range from 4% to 60% with a few goods subject to higher rates. All merchandise imports are subject to a national sales tax of 10% calculated on the c.i.f. value. Imports by the government, diplomatic missions, and charitable organizations are exempt from this tax.
Taxes collected through the exchange system	No.
State import monopoly	No.

Exports and Export Proceeds

Repatriation requirements	No.
Surrender requirements	No.
Financing requirements	No.
Documentation requirements	No.
Export licenses	
Without quotas	The exportation of forestry products is subject to prior authorization from the Forestry Department.
Export taxes	No.

Payments for Invisible Transactions and Current Transfers

Controls on these payments	No.

Proceeds from Invisible Transactions and Current Transfers

Repatriation requirements	No.
Surrender requirements	No.
Restrictions on use of funds	No.

Capital Transactions

Controls on capital and money market instruments

On capital market securities

Sale or issue locally by nonresidents — There are no capital markets or stock exchange markets in The Gambia.

Sale or issue abroad by residents — These transactions are allowed if residents have the means to conduct them.

On money market instruments — There is no market in these instruments.

On collective investment securities — There is no market in these instruments.

Controls on derivatives and other instruments — These instruments do not exist.

Controls on credit operations — Commercial banks may provide overdraft facilities to members of diplomatic and international missions in The Gambia.

Financial credits

To residents from nonresidents — Yes.

Guarantees, sureties, and financial backup facilities

To residents from nonresidents — Very few big investors enjoy these facilities.

Controls on direct investment

Inward direct investment — Inward transfers for purposes of direct equity investment are not restricted but must be reported to the CBG for statistical purposes.

Controls on liquidation of direct investment — Transfers of proceeds may be made after all taxes are paid.

Controls on real estate transactions

Purchase abroad by residents — Yes.

Purchase locally by nonresidents — Yes.

Sale locally by nonresidents — Yes.

Provisions specific to commercial banks and other credit institutions

Maintenance of accounts abroad — The Social Security and Finance Holding Company is not allowed to maintain these accounts.

Investment regulations — Inward investors are expected to bring in their own foreign funds.

Open foreign exchange position limits	The limits set by the CBG must be observed on a weekly basis and transactions must be reported daily to the CBG.
Provisions specific to institutional investors	No.
Other controls imposed by securities laws	No.

Changes During 1996

No significant changes occurred in the exchange and trade system.

GEORGIA

(Position as of January 31, 1997)

Status Under IMF Articles of Agreement

Article VIII	Date of acceptance: December 20, 1996.

Exchange Arrangement

Currency
The currency of Georgia is the lari.

Exchange rate structure
Unitary.

Classification

Managed floating
Between January and August 1996, the official exchange rates for the U.S. dollar and the Russian ruble were based on the rates at the fixing sessions at the Tbilisi Interbank Currency Exchange (TICEX) the previous Friday. Since August 12, 1996, the official exchange rate for the U.S. dollar is determined daily. The official rates for other currencies are determined on the basis of the cross rates for the U.S. dollar and the currencies concerned in the international market. The official exchange rates are used for budget and tax accounting purposes, as well as for all payments between the government and enterprises and other legal entities. The National Bank of Georgia (NBG) and the major commercial banks participate in the fixing sessions at the TICEX for all commercial transactions; the exchange rate of the lari is negotiated freely between the banks and foreign exchange bureaus that are licensed by the NBG and their customers. Foreign exchange bureaus are permitted to buy and sell foreign currency notes.

Exchange tax
No.

Exchange subsidy
No.

Forward exchange market
No.

Arrangements for Payments and Receipts

Prescription of currency requirements
Settlements for transactions between the governments of Kazakhstan, Latvia, Lithuania, Russia, and Uzbekistan can be made through a system of correspondent accounts in convertible currency. Correspondent accounts with the Baltic countries and the other countries of the FSU are either inoperative or no longer exist.

Payment arrangements
No.

Administration of control

Exchange control authorities
The NBG is responsible for administering exchange control regulations, which are formulated in collaboration with the Ministry of Finance (MOF). The NBG has the authority to issue general foreign exchange licenses to banks that permit them to engage in foreign exchange transactions with residents and nonresidents and to open correspondent accounts with banks outside Georgia. The NBG also has the authority to issue internal licenses to banks that permit them to engage in the same range of foreign exchange transactions as general license holders, except the opening of correspondent accounts with banks abroad. All transfers of foreign exchange by holders of internal licenses must be carried out through correspondent accounts held either with the NBG or with a bank that holds a general license. The NBG also has the authority to issue licenses for the establishment of exchange bureaus to engage in cash transactions.

International security restrictions
No.

Controls on trade in gold (coins and/or bullion)
A license is required to trade in gold.

Controls on domestic ownership and/or trade	Yes.
Controls on external trade	Yes.

Controls on exports and imports of banknotes

On exports

Domestic currency — Since July 15, 1996, up to 4 units of each currency denomination may be taken out without permission.

Foreign currency — The exportation of foreign currency notes by nonresidents is permitted up to the amount originally imported. Residents may export up to the equivalent of $500 without restriction. Amounts in excess of $500 are subject to a "special fee" ranging from 2% for amounts up to the equivalent of $10,000 to 3% for amounts above $10,000.

On imports — A declaration is required.

Resident Accounts

Eligibility to hold accounts	Juridical and natural persons are eligible.
Foreign exchange accounts permitted	Yes.
Held domestically	There are no restrictions on the opening and use of these accounts, and the balances may be used for all authorized transactions.
Held abroad	Yes.
Accounts in domestic currency convertible into foreign currency	Yes.

Nonresident Accounts

Eligibility to hold accounts	Juridical and natural persons are eligible.
Foreign exchange accounts permitted	Yes.
Domestic currency accounts	Yes.
Convertible into foreign currency	Yes.
Blocked accounts	No.

Imports and Import Payments

Foreign exchange budget	No.
Financing requirements for imports	No.
Documentation requirements for release of foreign exchange for imports	No.
Import licenses and other nontariff measures	
Negative list	Licenses are required for imports of weapons, narcotics, industrial equipment, pharmaceuticals, and agricultural pesticides; licenses are issued by the State Committee on Foreign Economic Relations (SCFER).

Import taxes and/or tariffs	A customs duty of 12% is levied on most non-CIS imports as well as imports of fuels from CIS countries; from January 1, 1997, certain goods are subject to a 5% customs duty, including specific capital goods, medical goods and equipment, and certain raw materials. All imports are subject to a 0.2% customs processing fee.
Taxes collected through the exchange system	No.

Exports and Export Proceeds

Repatriation requirements	No.
Surrender requirements	No.
Financing requirements	No.
Documentation requirements	The export contract registration requirement applicable to exports of steel and metals, manganese and copper concentrates, wine and liquor, and mineral water was abolished in December 1996.
Letters of credit	n.a.
Guarantees	n.a.
Domiciliation	n.a.
Preshipment inspection	n.a.
Export licenses	Licensing is administered by the SCFER. Licenses are required for logs; pine seeds; numismatic collections considered national treasures; certain biological, paleontological, archeological, and ethnographic goods; and raw materials for production of medicine. Exports of scrap metal are prohibited. Exports of arms and narcotics are subject, in practice, to prohibitions.
Without quotas	Yes.
Export taxes	All exports are subject to a general customs processing fee of 0.2%.
Taxes collected through the exchange system	n.a.

Payments for Invisible Transactions and Current Transfers

Controls on these payments	All payments are subject to indicative limits/bona fide tests.
Consulting/legal fees	
Prior approval	n.a.
Quantitative limits	n.a.
Foreign workers' wages	
Prior approval	n.a.
Quantitative limits	n.a.
Pensions	
Prior approval	n.a.
Quantitative limits	n.a.
Gambling/prize earnings	n.a.

Family maintenance/alimony

Prior approval	n.a.
Quantitative limits	n.a.
Credit card use abroad	n.a.

Proceeds from Invisible Transactions and Current Transfers

Repatriation requirements	No.
Surrender requirements	No.
Restrictions on use of funds	No.

Capital Transactions

Controls on capital and money market instruments	Inward and outward capital operations are not restricted but are subject to registration requirements for monitoring purposes.
Controls on derivatives and other instruments	No.
Controls on credit operations	No.
Controls on direct investment	A new Foreign Investment Law became effective on December 6, 1996. Under this law, the taxation and promotion of investment activities by joint ventures and foreign enterprises are regulated by the current tax legislation. Foreign investment enterprises that received licenses before this law came into effect will continue to enjoy all rights and benefits granted under the previous law for a period of 5 years from the date of issuance of those licenses.
Controls on liquidation of direct investment	No.

Changes During 1996

Status under IMF Articles of Agreement	*December 20.* Georgia accepted the obligations of Article VIII, Sections 2, 3, and 4 of the Fund Agreement.
Exchange arrangements	*August 12.* The official exchange rate is determined at daily auctions.
Arrangements for payments and receipts	*July 15.* Exportation of lari banknotes was limited to 4 units of each currency denomination, unless permission is obtained.
Exports and export proceeds	*December 6.* The export contract registration requirement was abolished.
Capital transactions	*December 6.* A new Foreign Investment Law became effective.

Changes During 1997

Imports and import payments	*January 1.* The customs duty applied to barter operations was unified with the one applied to certain nonbarter operations at 12%. In addition, a 5% customs duty on imports of certain capital goods, medical goods and equipment, and certain raw materials was introduced.

GERMANY

(Position as of December 31, 1996)

Status Under IMF Articles of Agreement

Article VIII   Date of acceptance: February 15, 1961.

Exchange Arrangement

Currency   The currency of Germany is the deutsche mark (DM).

Exchange rate structure   Unitary.

Classification

Cooperative arrangement   Germany participates in the ERM of the EMS within margins of ±15%, except for the
                                Netherlands guilders for which the band fluctuation is ±2.25%. The arrangements imply
                                that the Deutsche Bundesbank (the central bank) stands ready to buy or sell the curren-
                                cies of the other participating states in unlimited amounts at specified intervention rates.
                                In principle, interventions within the EMS are made in participating currencies but may
                                also take place in third currencies, such as the U.S. dollar. Participants in the EMS do
                                not maintain exchange rates for other currencies within fixed limits but do intervene
                                from time to time to smooth out erratic fluctuations in exchange rates.

Exchange tax   No.

Exchange subsidy   No.

Forward exchange market   Residents and nonresidents may freely negotiate forward exchange contracts for both
                                commercial and financial transactions in all leading convertible currencies in the do-
                                mestic exchange market and at major international foreign exchange markets. Germany
                                has no officially fixed rates in the forward exchange market. All transactions are nego-
                                tiated at free market rates.

Official cover of forward operations   No.

Arrangements for Payments and Receipts

**Prescription of currency
requirements**   No.

Payment arrangements   No.

Administration of control

Exchange control authorities   All banks in Germany are permitted to carry out foreign exchange transactions.

International security restrictions

In accordance with IMF Executive   Restrictions imposed on payments and transfers for current international transactions
Board Decision No. 144-(52/51)   regarding the Federal Republic of Yugoslavia (Serbia/Montenegro) were lifted in accor-
                                    dance with UN Security Council Resolution No. 1074 (1996).

In accordance with UN sanctions   In compliance with UN Security Council resolutions, restrictions have been imposed on
                                    the making of payments and transfers for current international transactions regarding
                                    Iraq and Libya.

Payment arrears   No.

**Controls on trade in gold (coins
and/or bullion)**   No.

**Controls on exports and imports of
banknotes**   No.

Resident Accounts

Eligibility to hold accounts	Juridical and natural persons are eligible.
Foreign exchange accounts permitted	Yes.
Held domestically	Yes.
Held abroad	Yes.
Accounts in domestic currency convertible into foreign currency	Yes.

Nonresident Accounts

Eligibility to hold accounts	Juridical and natural persons are eligible.
Foreign exchange accounts permitted	Yes.
Domestic currency accounts	Yes.
Convertible into foreign currency	Yes.
Blocked accounts	Yes.

Imports and Import Payments

Foreign exchange budget	No.
Financing requirements for imports	No.
Documentation requirements for release of foreign exchange for imports	No.
Import licenses and other nontariff measures	Imports of numerous textile products are subject to bilateral agreements and regulations of the EU with various supplier countries. Most goods covered by the CAP are subject to variable import levies. Imports of rolled steel products from Russia and Ukraine are subject to an annual quota under a voluntary restrictions agreement.
Negative list	Yes.
Licenses with quotas	The importation of certain nontextile goods from China is subject to the EU's annual global quota.
Import taxes and/or tariffs	No.
State import monopoly	No.

Exports and Export Proceeds

Repatriation requirements	No.
Surrender requirements	No.
Financing requirements	No.
Documentation requirements	For statistical purposes, an export notification is required for all goods.
Export licenses	
Without quotas	Certain exports (mostly strategic goods) are subject to individual or general licensing. The customs authorities exercise control over export declarations.

Export taxes   No.

Payments for Invisible Transactions and Current Transfers

Controls on these payments   No.

Proceeds from Invisible Transactions and Current Transfers

Repatriation requirements   No.

Surrender requirements   No.

Restrictions on use of funds   No.

Capital Transactions

Controls on capital and money market instruments

On capital market securities

Purchase locally by nonresidents   The purchase of federal savings bonds by nonresident entities is not allowed.

Sale or issue locally by nonresidents   The sale or issue of bonds denominated in deutsche mark issued by banks with a maturity of less than 2 years is prohibited.

Sale or issue abroad by residents   Securities denominated in deutsche mark should only be issued under the lead management of credit institutions domiciled in Germany.

On money market instruments

Purchase locally by nonresidents   The sale or issue of money market securities and instruments denominated in deutsche mark issued by banks with a maturity of less than 2 years is prohibited.

Sale or issue locally by nonresidents   The sale or issue of money market securities and instruments denominated in deutsche mark issued by banks by both residents and nonresidents is prohibited.

Sale or issue abroad by residents

Controls on derivatives and other instruments   No.

Controls on credit operations   No.

Controls on direct investment   No.

Controls on liquidation of direct investment   No.

Controls on real estate transactions   No.

Provisions specific to commercial banks and other credit institutions

Differential treatment of nonresident deposit accounts and/or deposit accounts in foreign exchange

Reserve requirements   Banks are subject to minimum reserve requirements on the level of their foreign liabilities with maturities of less than 4 years of 2% on sight deposits and time deposits and 1.6% on savings deposits; the requirements in principle are the same as those applied to domestic liabilities. Book liabilities to nonresidents in foreign currency are exempt from reserve requirements to the extent of the book claims on nonresidents in foreign currency with maturities of less than 4 years.

Open foreign exchange position limits	Yes.
Provisions specific to institutional investors	No.
Other controls imposed by securities laws	Yes.

Changes During 1996

No significant changes occurred in the exchange and trade system.

GHANA

(Position as of December 31, 1996)

Status Under IMF Articles of Agreement

Article VIII	Date of acceptance: February 2, 1994.

Exchange Arrangement

Currency	The currency of Ghana is the cedi.
Exchange rate structure	Unitary.
Classification	
Independent floating	The exchange rate of the cedi is determined in the interbank foreign exchange market. The average exchange rate in the interbank market is used for official valuation purposes but is not always applied by authorized banks in their transactions with each other or with their customers. Rates are quoted by authorized dealers for certain other currencies, with daily quotations based on the buying and selling rates for the U.S. dollar in markets abroad.
Exchange tax	No.
Exchange subsidy	No.
Forward exchange market	No.

Arrangements for Payments and Receipts

Prescription of currency requirements	Settlements related to transactions covered by bilateral payment agreements are made through clearing accounts maintained by the Bank of Ghana (BOG) and the central banks of the countries concerned. Proceeds from exports to countries with which Ghana does not have bilateral payment agreements must be received in the currency of the importing country (if that currency is quoted by the BOG) or debited for authorized inward payments to residents of Ghana, for transfers to other official accounts related to the same country, and for transfers to the related clearing account at the BOG.
Payment arrangements	
Bilateral arrangements	
Inoperative	Ghana has agreements with Bulgaria, China, Cuba, the Czech Republic, Poland, Romania, and the Slovak Republic. The clearing balances on these agreements are being settled.
Administration of control	
Exchange control authorities	The Foreign Transactions Examinations Office (FTEO) of the BOG records and confirms foreign capital inflows and administers foreign exchange for official payments and travel. All foreign exchange transactions by the private sector are approved and transacted by authorized banks without reference to the BOG.
International security restrictions	No.
Payment arrears	No.
Controls on trade in gold (coins and/or bullion)	
Controls on domestic ownership and/or trade	Domestic transactions in gold may be authorized by the State Gold Mining Corporation in collaboration with the BOG, and certain domestic sales may be carried out by permit under the Gold Mining Products Protection Ordinance.

Controls on external trade	Ghanaian residents may not buy or borrow any gold from, or sell or lend any gold to, any person other than an authorized dealer. Imports of gold other than those by or on behalf of the monetary authorities are not normally licensed. The import duty on gold, including bullion and partly worked gold, is levied at a uniform rate of 30%. The gold mines export their output in semirefined form.

Controls on exports and imports of banknotes

On exports

Domestic currency — The exportation of Ghanaian banknotes is permitted up to $5,000.

Foreign currency — Residents traveling abroad are permitted to carry up to the equivalent of $3,000.

On imports

Domestic currency — Travelers may reimport up to the $5,000 they were allowed to export.

Resident Accounts

Eligibility to hold accounts	Juridical and natural persons are eligible.
Foreign exchange accounts permitted	Yes.
Held domestically	Yes.
Held abroad	No.
Accounts in domestic currency convertible into foreign currency	No.

Nonresident Accounts

Eligibility to hold accounts	Juridical and natural persons are eligible. Nonresident account status is granted to embassies, delegations, consulates, and offices of high commissioners in Ghana and to the non-Ghanaian members of their staffs. It is also available to international institutions and foreign-registered companies operating in Ghana, and to nonresident Ghanaians.
Foreign exchange accounts permitted	Prior approval is required. The accounts may be credited with authorized outward payments, with transfers from other foreign accounts, and with the proceeds from sales of convertible currency. They may be debited for inward payments, for transfers to other foreign accounts, and for purchases of external currencies.
Domestic currency accounts	These accounts are permitted, but prior approval is required.
Convertible into foreign currency	Yes.
Blocked accounts	Funds not placed at the free disposal of nonresidents—for example, certain types of capital proceeds—may be deposited in blocked accounts, which may be debited for authorized payments, including for purchases of approved securities.

Imports and Import Payments

Foreign exchange budget	No.
Financing requirements for imports	No.
Documentation requirements for release of foreign exchange for imports	
Preshipment inspection	Yes.

Letters of credit	Most imports are effected with confirmed letters of credit established through authorized banks on a sight basis.
Import licenses and other nontariff measures	
Negative list	Imports of narcotics and firearms are not permitted.
Import taxes and/or tariffs	Tariffs range from zero to 25% of the c.i.f. value of imports. A significant portion of imports, mostly for investment, is exempted.
Taxes collected through the exchange system	No.
State import monopoly	No.

Exports and Export Proceeds

Repatriation requirements	Exporters are required to collect and repatriate in full the proceeds from their exports within 60 days of shipment; proceeds from exports of nontraditional products may be sold in a foreign exchange bureau upon receipt.
Surrender requirements	Exporters are generally allowed to retain up to 35% of their export proceeds in foreign exchange accounts. However, the retention ratio is 60% for the Ashanti Gold Mining Company, 20% for log exporters, and 2% for the Cocoa Board. The retention ratio for nontraditional exports is 100%, and proceeds are generally channeled through banks other than the BOG.
Financing requirements	No.
Documentation requirements	
Letters of credit	Letters of credit are required, except for nontraditional exports.
Guarantees	Yes.
Domiciliation	Yes.
Preshipment inspection	An inspection is required, except for nontraditional exports.
Export licenses	No.
Export taxes	Cocoa exports are subject to an export tax that is calculated as the difference between export proceeds and payments to farmers, together with the Cocoa Board's costs if proceeds exceed payments.
Taxes collected through the exchange system	No.

Payments for Invisible Transactions and Current Transfers

Controls on these payments	There are no controls on payments for insurance and interest, on remittances of profits and dividends, or on the use of credit cards abroad. Freight charges may be paid to the local shipping agents; the transfer of funds to cover such charges is normally permitted, provided that the application is properly documented.
Payments for travel	
Quantitative limits	Residents traveling abroad are permitted to carry up to the equivalent of $3,000. In addition, resident travelers are permitted to carry up to the equivalent of $5,000 for direct purchases abroad.
Indicative limits/bona fide test	Yes.

Proceeds from Invisible Transactions and Current Transfers

Repatriation requirements	Yes.
Surrender requirements	All receipts from invisibles must be sold to authorized dealers.
Restrictions on use of funds	Yes.

Capital Transactions

Controls on capital and money market instruments

On capital market securities

Purchase locally by nonresidents

Nonresidents may purchase securities listed on the Ghana Stock Exchange (GSE); individual holdings and total holdings of all nonresidents in one security listed on the GSE may not exceed 10% and 74%, respectively. For companies not listed on the GSE, non-resident participation requires the following minimum equity injections to acquire shares: (1) $10,000 or its equivalent in capital goods when the enterprise is a joint venture; (2) $50,000 or its equivalent in capital goods when the enterprise is wholly owned by a non-Ghanaian; and (3) $300,000 or its equivalent in capital goods in the case of a trading enterprise involved only in the purchasing and selling of goods that is either wholly or partly owned by a non-Ghanaian and that employs at least 10 Ghanaians.

Sale or issue locally by nonresidents

These transactions require prior approval from the BOG and the Ministry of Finance (MOF). The transfer or repatriation of proceeds from sales must be reported to the BOG.

Purchase abroad by residents

There are no restrictions on these purchases, but the transfer of funds for the purchase of securities requires the prior approval of the BOG.

Sale or issue abroad by residents

These transactions require the prior approval of the BOG.

On money market instruments

Purchase locally by nonresidents

Current regulations do not allow nonresidents to bring in foreign exchange for the purpose of investing in local money market instruments (BOG and government securities). However, nonresidents holding local currencies can invest in these instruments.

Sale or issue locally by nonresidents

These transactions are not allowed.

Purchase abroad by residents

No restrictions apply to these purchases, but the transfer of funds for purchases of these instruments is not allowed.

Sale or issue abroad by residents

These transactions are not allowed.

On collective investment securities

Purchase locally by nonresidents

These purchases require prior approval of the BOG.

Sale or issue locally by nonresidents

These transactions, as well as the transfer abroad of proceeds associated with these sales, require BOG approval.

Purchase abroad by residents

There are no restrictions on these purchases, but the transfer of funds needs prior approval from the BOG.

Sale or issue abroad by residents

These transactions require the consent of the MOF.

Controls on derivatives and other instruments

Currently, a local market in derivatives and other instruments does not exist. No restrictions apply, but the transfer of funds abroad requires BOG approval.

Controls on credit operations

Commercial credits

To residents from nonresidents

Prior approval is required for the credits, which must be channeled through the banking system. Transactions must be supported by relevant documents.

Financial credits

   To residents from nonresidents   These credits require BOG approval.

Controls on direct investment

Outward direct investment   All capital outflows must be approved by the BOG; applications for such transfers must be supported by documentary evidence and are considered on their merits.

Inward direct investment   Certain areas of economic activity are not open to foreigners. Foreign investments in Ghana require the prior approval of the Ghana Investment Center if they are to benefit from the facilities available under the Investment Code (1981), under which approved investments are guaranteed, in principle, the right to transfer profits and, in the event of sale or liquidation, capital proceeds. Tax holidays and initial capital allowances are also available for such investments. The code stipulates that the assets of foreign investors may not be expropriated. Disputes over the amount of compensation are settled in accordance with the established procedure for conciliation—for example, through arbitration by the International Center for Settlements of Investment Disputes or the United Nations Commission on International Trade and Law.

The minimum qualifying amounts of investment by a non-Ghanaian are as follows: (1) $10,000 or its equivalent in capital goods by way of equity participation in a joint-venture enterprise with a Ghanaian partner; (2) $450,000 or its equivalent in capital goods by way of equity when the enterprise is wholly owned by a non-Ghanaian; and (3) $300,000 or its equivalent in goods by way of equity capital when the enterprise is either wholly or partly owned by a non-Ghanaian, employs at least 10 Ghanaians, and is involved in the purchasing and selling of goods.

Controls on liquidation of direct investment   No.

Controls on real estate transactions

Purchase abroad by residents   Individuals are not normally granted foreign exchange for these purchases.

Purchase locally by nonresidents   These purchases required the prior approval of an Implementing Committee through the Minister of Foreign Affairs until August 1996, when Parliament repealed this requirement.

Sale locally by nonresidents   Yes.

Provisions specific to commercial banks and other credit institutions

Borrowing abroad   Central bank notification is required.

Maintenance of accounts abroad   Central bank notification is required.

Lending to nonresidents (financial or commercial credits)   Yes.

Lending locally in foreign exchange   Yes.

Purchase of locally issued securities denominated in foreign exchange   These purchases are allowed within reasonable or acceptable limits.

Differential treatment of nonresident deposit accounts and/or deposit accounts in foreign exchange

   Reserve requirements   Yes.

   Liquid asset requirements   Yes.

Open foreign exchange position limits   Based on the volume of foreign exchange transactions of dealer banks. This is subject to periodic review.

Provisions specific to institutional investors

Limits (min.) on portfolio invested locally

Nonresidents cannot buy more than 74% of shares in companies registered on the GSE.

Other controls imposed by securities laws

No.

Changes During 1996

Capital transactions

August 8. The prior approval of an Implementing Committee through the Minister of Foreign Affairs is no longer required for the purchase of local real estate by nonresidents.

GREECE

(Position as of December 31, 1996)

Status Under IMF Articles of Agreement

Article VIII Date of acceptance: July 22, 1992.

Exchange Arrangement

Currency The currency of Greece is the drachma.

Exchange rate structure Unitary.

Classification

Managed floating The exchange rate for the drachma is determined in daily fixing sessions in which the Bank of Greece (BOG) and authorized commercial banks participate. Greece is a member of the EMS. The drachma is included in the ECU basket, but Greece does not participate in the ERM of the EMS.

Exchange tax No.

Exchange subsidy No.

Forward exchange market

Official cover of forward operations The BOG provides credit institutions forward foreign exchange transactions including currency swaps and options.

Arrangements for Payments and Receipts

Prescription of currency requirements Settlements with all countries may be made in any convertible foreign currency or through nonresident deposit accounts in drachmas.

Payment arrangements No.

Administration of control

Exchange control authorities There are no exchange controls. Resident credit institutions are authorized to carry out all the necessary formalities for the settlement of all transactions with nonresidents and are obliged to provide to the BOG all the information necessary to compile the balance of payments. In addition, natural and juridical persons must inform the BOG, for statistical purposes, of transactions with nonresidents of sums greater than ECU 2,000 if a domestic banking institution is not involved.

International security restrictions

In accordance with IMF Executive Board Decision No. 144-(52/51) n.a.

In accordance with UN sanctions Yes.

Payments arrears No.

Controls on trade in gold (coins and/or bullion)

Controls on domestic ownership and/or trade Residents may freely purchase new gold sovereigns from the BOG through licensed stockbrokers at a price set by the BOG. These gold coins may be resold only to the BOG or to the Athens Stock Exchange. Holders of gold coins acquired in the free market that existed before December 22, 1965, may sell them without any formality to the BOG or to an authorized bank at the official price.

Controls on external trade Gold bars or coins brought in by travelers and declared upon entry may be reexported after approval by the BOG.

344

Controls on exports and imports of banknotes

On exports

Residents and nonresidents leaving Greece should declare amounts of banknotes and personal checks in domestic and foreign currency exceeding the equivalent of ECU 2,000. For amounts up to the equivalent of ECU 10,000, they must provide in the declaration their fiscal number and the purpose of the transfer. If the amount is up to ECU 20,000, they must also provide a copy of their tax certificate. Exports of larger amounts must be carried out through resident credit institutions.

Domestic currency

Yes.

Foreign currency

Nonresidents leaving Greece within a year of their arrival may take out foreign banknotes up to the equivalent of $1,000, as well as traveler's checks and other means of payment in their name, irrespective of amount. Larger amounts can be taken out no later than December 31 of the calendar year following the year in which the nonresident entered Greece, provided that they were declared upon entry.

On imports

Residents and nonresidents entering Greece should declare the imported banknotes and personal checks in domestic and foreign currency, if the total amount exceeds the equivalent of ECU 10,000.

Resident Accounts

Eligibility to hold accounts

Juridical and natural persons are eligible.

Foreign exchange accounts permitted

Yes.

Held domestically

These accounts may be credited with foreign exchange and foreign banknotes brought into Greece and declared upon entry. Principal and interest on these accounts are freely transferable abroad. Residents may also open accounts in foreign exchange with undeclared foreign banknotes; principal and interest on these accounts may be withdrawn in drachmas and in foreign exchange but may not be transferred abroad.

Held abroad

Yes.

Accounts in domestic currency convertible into foreign currency

No.

Nonresident Accounts

Eligibility to hold accounts

Juridical and natural persons are eligible.

Foreign exchange accounts permitted

Yes.

Domestic currency accounts

Yes.

Convertible into foreign currency

Yes.

Blocked accounts

No.

Imports and Import Payments

Foreign exchange budget

No.

Financing requirements for imports

No.

Documentation requirements for release of foreign exchange for imports

No.

Import licenses and other nontariff measures	Special import licenses are required for some specific products from certain low-cost countries under EU surveillance. Special regulations govern imports of certain items such as medicines, narcotics, and motion picture films.
Licenses with quotas	Yes.
Other nontariff measures	Yes.
Import taxes and/or tariffs	No.
State import monopoly	No.

Exports and Export Proceeds

Repatriation requirements	No.
Surrender requirements	No.
Financing requirements	No.
Documentation requirements	No.
Export licenses	No.
Export taxes	No.

Payments for Invisible Transactions and Current Transfers

Controls on these payments	There are no controls on payments for freight and insurance, unloading and storage, administrative expenses, commissions, interest, medical treatment, subscription and membership fees, consulting and legal fees, pensions, family maintenance and alimony, or on the remittances of profits and dividends.
Payments for travel	
Quantitative limits	Yes.
Indicative limits/bona fide test	The limit is ECU 2,000 a trip a person in banknotes; additional amounts are permitted upon presentation of the relevant documentation.
Study abroad costs	
Quantitative limits	Yes.
Indicative limits/bona fide test	The limit is ECU 2,000 a trip a person in banknotes; additional amounts are permitted upon presentation of the relevant documentation.
Foreign workers' wages	
Prior approval	Remittances of earnings by foreign workers are permitted, with the provision of the relevant documentation.
Gambling/prize earnings	
Prior approval	Approval is subject to relevant documentation.
Credit card use abroad	
Quantitative limits	The limit on withdrawal in foreign banknotes is the equivalent of ECU 1,000 a month.
Indicative limits/bona fide test	Yes.

Proceeds from Invisible Transactions and Current Transfers

Repatriation requirements	No.

Surrender requirements	No.
Restrictions on use of funds	No.

Capital Transactions

Controls on capital and money market instruments

On capital market securities

   Purchase locally by nonresidents — The purchase of shares and other securities of a participatory nature in the broadcasting and maritime sectors, which may be affected by the laws on inward direct investment and establishment, is prohibited.

On money market instruments	No.
On collective investment securities	No.
Controls on derivatives and other instruments	No.
Controls on credit operations	No.

Controls on direct investment

Inward direct investment — Investments in border regions by non-EU residents require approval for reasons of national security. There are also restrictions on the acquisition of mining rights and participation in new or existing enterprises if these are engaged in radio and television broadcasting or maritime and air transport.

Controls on liquidation of direct investment	No.
Controls on real estate transactions	No.
Provisions specific to commercial banks and other credit institutions	No.
Provisions specific to institutional investors	No.

Other controls imposed by securities laws — Transactions in nonorganized capital markets are not allowed.

Changes During 1996

No significant changes occurred in the exchange and trade system.

GRENADA

(Position as of December 31, 1996)

Status Under IMF Articles of Agreement

Article VIII   Date of acceptance: January 24, 1994.

Exchange Arrangement

Currency   The currency of Grenada is the Eastern Caribbean dollar, which is issued by the ECCB.

Exchange rate structure   Unitary.

Classification

Pegged   The Eastern Caribbean dollar is pegged to the U.S. dollar, the intervention currency, at EC$2.70 per US$1.

Exchange tax   No.

Exchange subsidy   No.

Forward exchange market   No.

Arrangements for Payments and Receipts

Prescription of currency requirements   Settlements with residents of member countries of the CARICOM must be made either through external accounts in Eastern Caribbean dollars, in the currency of the CARICOM country concerned, or in U.S. dollars. Settlements with residents of the former Sterling Area, other than CARICOM countries, may be made in pounds sterling, in any other former Sterling Area currency, or in Eastern Caribbean dollars to and from external accounts. Settlements with residents of other countries are made in any foreign currency or through an external account in Eastern Caribbean dollars.

Payment arrangements   No.

Administration of control

Exchange control authorities   Exchange control is administered by the Ministry of Finance (MOF) and applies to all countries. The MOF delegates to authorized dealers the authority to approve some import payments and certain other outward payments. The Trade Division of the MOF administers trade control.

International security restrictions   No.

Payment arrears   No.

Controls on trade in gold (coins and/or bullion)

Controls on domestic ownership and/or trade   Residents other than the monetary authorities, authorized dealers, and industrial users are not permitted to hold or acquire gold in any form other than jewelry or coins for numismatic purposes.

Controls on external trade   Imports of gold are permitted for industrial purposes only and are subject to customs duties and charges. The MOF issues licenses to import gold. The exportation of gold is not normally permitted.

Controls on exports and imports of banknotes

On exports

  Domestic currency   n.a.

Foreign currency	Nonresident travelers may export, with the approval of the MOF, any foreign currency they previously brought into Grenada.

Resident Accounts

Eligibility to hold accounts	Juridical and natural persons are eligible.
Foreign exchange accounts permitted	These accounts may be freely debited but can be credited only with foreign exchange earned or received from outside the ECCB area. Holder of these accounts must submit regular statements of debits and credits to the MOF.
Held domestically	Yes.
Held abroad	n.a.

Nonresident Accounts

Eligibility to hold accounts	Juridical and natural persons are eligible.
Foreign exchange accounts permitted	The same regulations as for resident accounts apply.
Domestic currency accounts	These accounts must be credited with funds from an external source, and a statement of debits and credits must be submitted to the MOF every month for each external account.
Convertible into foreign currency	Yes.
Blocked accounts	No.

Imports and Import Payments

Foreign exchange budget	No.
Financing requirements for imports	No.
Documentation requirements for release of foreign exchange for imports	Payments for documented imports are free of restrictions. Payments for restricted imports and any goods (and services) in excess of the limits of authorized dealers require permission from the MOF.
Letters of credit	Yes.
Import licenses and other nontariff measures	Ceiling prices on garments, handbags, refrigerators, and stoves are set.
Negative list	Prohibited goods include whole chickens, chicken eggs, live breeding poultry, war toys, animal skins, and various drugs deemed to be dangerous.
Licenses with quotas	There are quantitative restrictions on certain items from non-CARICOM sources, including milk, sugar, rice, a variety of tropical fruits and vegetables, carbonated beverages, arms and ammunition, industrial gas, paints, and miscellaneous items associated with furniture, clothing, and the construction industry. Items from the CARICOM area that require licenses include curry products, cigarettes, industrial gas, furniture, exotic birds, solar water heaters, and various tropical fruits and vegetables.
Import taxes and/or tariffs	Imports from non-CARICOM countries are subject to a CET of 30%–35%. All imports are subject to a 5% customs service charge, and imports not exempt from customs duties are subject to a consumption tax of 15%, 20%, or 55%. Imports of capital equipment and imports by domestic associations involved in major crop production (provided they are for improvements in the growing or packaging of bananas, maize, or nutmeg) are exempt from import duties.
Taxes collected through the exchange system	No.

| **State import monopoly** | The Marketing and National Importing Board (MNIB) is the sole authorized importer of bulk purchases of milk, flour, and sugar. |

Exports and Export Proceeds

| **Repatriation requirements** | Yes. |
| **Surrender requirements** | Proceeds must be surrendered to authorized dealers in foreign exchange (commercial banks). |

Documentation requirements

Letters of credit	n.a.
Preshipment inspection	n.a.
Export licenses	Specific licenses are required for the exportation of exotic birds, coral, mineral products, and live sheep and goats to any destination.
Without quotas	Yes.
Export taxes	No.

Payments for Invisible Transactions and Current Transfers

| **Controls on these payments** | Payments for invisibles related to authorized imports for subscriptions and membership fees, interest payments, and the use of credit cards abroad are not restricted. |

Profit/dividends

Prior approval	Approval is granted if all related liabilities have been discharged and the investment was registered with the MOF.
Quantitative limits	n.a.
Indicative limits/bona fide test	n.a.

Payments for travel

| *Quantitative limits* | The limits are EC$100,000 a person a year for personal and business travel. |
| *Indicative limits/bona fide test* | Yes. |

Medical costs

| *Quantitative limits* | The limit is EC$100,000. |
| *Indicative limits/bona fide test* | Yes. |

Study abroad costs

| *Prior approval* | MOF approval is required, and permission is usually granted on presentation of documentation of registration and the costs of tuition and other expenses. |

Consulting/legal fees

| *Prior approval* | MOF approval, which is granted on the basis of agreements incorporating payment for such services, is required. Payments may be made up to the amount approved, subject where applicable to withholding on income tax. |

Foreign workers' wages

| *Prior approval* | Yes. |

Pensions

| *Prior approval* | Approval is granted upon proof of immigrant status. |

Indicative limits/bona fide test	n.a.
Family maintenance/alimony	
Prior approval	Approval is granted upon proof of established liabilities.
Indicative limits/bona fide test	n.a.

Proceeds from Invisible Transactions and Current Transfers

Repatriation requirements	Yes.
Surrender requirements	The surrender of foreign currency proceeds from invisibles is mandatory.

Capital Transactions

Controls on capital and money market instruments	All outward capital transfers require exchange control approval.
On capital market securities	
Sale or issue locally by nonresidents	n.a.
Purchase abroad by residents	Residents may not purchase foreign currency securities abroad for private purposes. Certificates of title to foreign currency securities held by residents must be lodged with an authorized depository in Grenada, and earnings on these securities must be repatriated.
Sale or issue abroad by residents	n.a.
On money market instruments	
Sale or issue locally by nonresidents	n.a.
Purchase abroad by residents	MOF approval is required.
Sale or issue abroad by residents	n.a.
On collective investment securities	
Purchase locally by nonresidents	n.a.
Sale or issue locally by nonresidents	Yes.
Purchase abroad by residents	MOF approval is required.
Sale or issue abroad by residents	n.a.
Controls on derivatives and other instruments	
Purchase locally by nonresidents	n.a.
Sale or issue locally by nonresidents	n.a.
Purchase abroad by residents	MOF approval is required.
Sale or issue abroad by residents	n.a.
Controls on credit operations	
Commercial credits	MOF approval is required.
By residents to nonresidents	Local currency financing is not ordinarily permitted and requires the approval of the MOF.

To residents from nonresidents	Yes.
Financial credits	
To residents from nonresidents	MOF approval is required.
Guarantees, sureties, and financial backup facilities	
By residents to nonresidents	Yes.
To residents from nonresidents	MOF approval is required.
Controls on direct investment	
Outward direct investment	MOF approval is required.
Inward direct investment	Exchange control approval is required.
Controls on liquidation of direct investment	Remittances of proceeds are permitted, provided that all related liabilities have been discharged and that the original investment was registered with the MOF.
Controls on real estate transactions	An alien landholding license must be issued by the Office of the Prime Minister.
Purchase abroad by residents	Yes.
Provisions specific to commercial banks and other credit institutions	
Borrowing abroad	Authorized dealers may freely assume short-term liability positions in foreign currencies to finance approved transfers for both trade and nontrade transactions. Any borrowing abroad by authorized dealers to finance their domestic operations requires the approval of the MOF.
Maintenance of accounts abroad	n.a.
Lending to nonresidents (financial or commercial credits)	Local currency financing requires the approval of the MOF and is not ordinarily permitted.
Purchase of locally issued securities denominated in foreign exchange	n.a.
Differential treatment of nonresident deposit accounts and/or deposit accounts in foreign exchange	
Liquid asset requirements	n.a.
Interest rate controls	n.a.
Provisions specific to institutional investors	No.

Changes During 1996

Payments for invisible transactions and current transfers	*February 1.* The limit on foreign exchange a person may purchase from authorized dealers without obtaining exchange control approval was increased to EC$100,000 from EC$10,000.

GUATEMALA

(Position as of December 31, 1996)

Status Under IMF Articles of Agreement

Article VIII   Date of acceptance: January 27, 1947.

Exchange Arrangement

Currency   The currency of Guatemala is the quetzal.

Exchange rate structure   Unitary.

Classification

Independent floating   The exchange rate is determined in the interbank market where the Bank of Guatemala (BOG) intervenes to moderate undue fluctuations, to purchase foreign exchange on behalf of the public sector, and to service its own external debt. All foreign exchange transactions of the public sector must take place through the BOG at a reference rate that is equivalent to the weighted average of the buying and selling rates in the interbank market during the day before the previous business day.

Exchange tax   No.

Exchange subsidy   No.

Forward exchange market   No.

Arrangements for Payments and Receipts

**Prescription of currency
requirements**   In practice, most transactions in foreign exchange are denominated in U.S. dollars, domestic currency, or other means of payment, in accordance with special payment agreements.

Payment arrangements

Regional arrangements   Guatemala is a member of the CACM.

Administration of control

Exchange control authorities   The BOG administers exchange controls. Foreign exchange transactions in the public sector are carried out exclusively through the BOG; those in the private sector are made through banks and foreign exchange houses authorized by the Monetary Board.

International security restrictions   No.

Payment arrears

Official   Arrears are maintained with respect to certain external payments related to official debt, mostly with Paris Club creditors.

Private   n.a.

**Controls on trade in gold (coins
and/or bullion)**

Controls on domestic ownership and/or
trade   The BOG may buy and sell gold coins and bullion either directly or through authorized banks and is entitled to buy gold holdings surrendered by any resident. The BOG sells gold to domestic artistic or industrial users in accordance with guidelines from the Monetary Board with the government's approval.

Controls on external trade   The exportation of gold is prohibited except when the BOG issues a special export license. Gold is imported only by the BOG.

Controls on exports and imports of banknotes	No.

Resident Accounts

n.a.

Nonresident Accounts

Eligibility to hold accounts	Yes.
Juridical persons	n.a.
Natural persons	n.a.
Foreign exchange accounts permitted	Members of embassies and staff of international institutions are allowed to hold these accounts, but approval is required.
Domestic currency accounts	Yes.
Convertible into foreign currency	No.

Imports and Import Payments

Foreign exchange budget	No.
Financing requirements for imports	No.
Documentation requirements for release of foreign exchange for imports	No.
Import licenses and other nontariff measures	Imports of most goods are unrestricted and require neither registration nor a license.
Open general licenses	Licenses are required for imports of coffee beans and coffee plants, lead, poultry, milk, eggs, sugar, wheat flour, and cottonseed.
Import taxes and/or tariffs	Guatemala applies the common external tariff of the CACM, which ranges from 5% to 20% with virtually all intra-CACM trade exempt from tariffs. Some products, such as coffee, sugar, oil, wheat, and alcohol, which are traded with the CACM, are subject to tariffs ranging from 5% to 20%. The weighted-average tariff is 8%. Tariffs are 20% on textiles and footwear, 15% on tires, and 25% on clothing. There are a number of exceptions and special tariff regimes, and about 3% of imported items are subject to tariffs independently of the CACM. Some agricultural products are subject to variable levies between 5% and 45%. Imports of chicken are subject to tariffs of 20% up to a monthly quota of 300 tons and 45% for imports exceeding this quota.
Taxes collected through the exchange system	No.
State import monopoly	No.

Exports and Export Proceeds

Repatriation requirements	Yes.
Surrender requirements	Foreign exchange proceeds must be sold to an authorized participant in the interbank market other than the BOG. The granting of export licenses is contingent upon the agreement to sell export proceeds to any authorized participant in the interbank market other than the BOG within 90 days of the date of issue (this period may be extended to 180 days).

Financing requirements	No.
Documentation requirements	No.
Export licenses	Exporters must obtain an export license issued by the BOG before the Guatemalan customs can authorize shipment of the merchandise. A few other items, including gold (unless the BOG issues a special export license) and silver, may not be exported in any form.
With quotas	Exports of wheat flour, ethyl alcohol, roasted coffee, and tobacco and cigarettes to Central American countries are temporarily restricted.
Export taxes	No.

Payments for Invisible Transactions and Current Transfers

Controls on these payments	No.

Proceeds from Invisible Transactions and Current Transfers

Repatriation requirements	Yes.
Surrender requirements	Proceeds for invisibles must be sold to an authorized financial institution at the market rate.
Restrictions on use of funds	No.

Capital Transactions

Controls on capital and money market instruments	No.
Controls on derivatives and other instruments	No.
Guarantees, sureties, and financial backup facilities	
To residents from nonresidents	Yes.
Controls on direct investment	
Inward direct investment	Foreign direct investment in the petroleum sector is regulated by special legislation.
Controls on liquidation of direct investment	No.
Controls on real estate transactions	
Sale locally by nonresidents	n.a.
Provisions specific to commercial banks and other credit institutions	
Borrowing abroad	n.a.
Maintenance of accounts abroad	n.a.
Lending to nonresidents (financial or commercial credits)	n.a.
Lending locally in foreign exchange	n.a.
Purchase of locally issued securities denominated in foreign exchange	n.a.

Differential treatment of nonresident deposit accounts and/or deposit accounts in foreign exchange

n.a.

Investment regulations

n.a.

Open foreign exchange position limits

The limit for banks and finance companies is 25% of the value of their paid-up capital and reserves; for exchange houses, it is 100%. Foreign exchange exceeding these limits at the end of each day must be negotiated in the interbank market or sold to the BOG.

Changes During 1996

No significant changes occurred in the exchange and trade system.

GUINEA

(Position as of December 31, 1996)

Status Under IMF Articles of Agreement

Article VIII

Date of acceptance: November 17, 1995.

Exchange Arrangement

Currency

The currency of Guinea is the Guinean franc.

Other legal tender

Silver commemorative coins are also legal tender.

Exchange rate structure

Unitary.

Classification

Independent floating

The exchange rate of the Guinean franc is determined by supply and demand for foreign exchange between authorized dealers and their clients, or among dealers themselves.

Exchange tax

No.

Exchange subsidy

No.

Forward exchange market

No.

Arrangements for Payments and Receipts

Prescription of currency requirements

All current transactions effected in Guinea must be settled in Guinean francs. Settlements on account of transactions covered by bilateral payment agreements are made in currencies prescribed by, and through accounts established under, the provisions of the agreements. Settlements with countries other than members of the WACH are made in designated convertible currencies quoted by the Central Bank of the Republic of Guinea (CBRG).

Payment arrangements

Bilateral arrangements

Inoperative

Guinea maintains bilateral payment agreements with Bulgaria, China, the Czech Republic, Egypt, Romania, Russia, and the Slovak Republic.

Clearing agreements

Settlements with the BCEAO, and The Gambia, Ghana, Guinea-Bissau, Liberia, Mauritania, Nigeria, and Sierra Leone are normally made through the WACH.

Barter agreements and open accounts

n.a.

Administration of control

Exchange control authorities

Exchange control authority is vested in the CBRG, which has delegated to the commercial banks authority to (1) approve import and import application forms; (2) allocate foreign exchange to travelers holding foreign airline tickets; and (3) manage foreign currency accounts. All settlements with foreign countries, including payments for imports, may be effected by the commercial banks.

International security restrictions

No.

Payment arrears

Official

Yes.

Private

Yes.

Controls on trade in gold (coins and/or bullion)

The CBRG purchases gold in Guinean francs at international prices. At the seller's request, the CBRG may purchase 50% of output in foreign currency.

Controls on domestic ownership and/or trade	Transactions in nonmonetary gold are not subject to restrictions.
Controls on external trade	The exportation of gold is subject to prior authorization by the CBRG.

Controls on exports and imports of banknotes

On exports

Domestic currency	Exportation is limited to GF 5,000 a person a trip.
Foreign currency	Exportation of foreign currency is made through the CBRG.

On imports

Domestic currency	Importation is limited to GF 5,000 a person a trip.
Foreign currency	The importation of foreign banknotes and traveler's checks is permitted, subject to declaration on entry. Residents, however, must surrender both to commercial banks within 15 days of their return.

Resident Accounts

Eligibility to hold accounts	Juridical and natural persons are eligible.
Foreign exchange accounts permitted	Yes.
Held domestically	Exporters may hold all of their earnings in foreign currency in local bank accounts.
Approval required	n.a.
Held abroad	These accounts are permitted, but prior approval is required.
Accounts in domestic currency convertible into foreign currency	Accounts in convertible Guinean francs may be credited with deposits in foreign exchange, irrespective of its origin. The accounts may be debited freely and converted by commercial banks into foreign currencies without prior authorization from the CBRG. Interest rates on these accounts are negotiated between the account holder and the bank.

Nonresident Accounts

Eligibility to hold accounts	Juridical and natural persons are eligible.
Foreign exchange accounts permitted	Yes.
Domestic currency accounts	The same regulations as for resident accounts apply.
Convertible into foreign currency	Yes.
Blocked accounts	No.

Imports and Import Payments

Foreign exchange budget	Yes.
Financing requirements for imports	
Minimum financing requirements	The minimum financing requirement must be at least $2,000.
Advance payment requirements	Advance payments may be established by the commercial agreement.
Documentation requirements for release of foreign exchange for imports	All imports of up to $200,000 require authorization, which is granted by the commercial banks on behalf of the CBRG. Authorization is given for 2 types of imports: (1) imports for which importers have access to foreign exchange provided at rates determined

during weekly fixing sessions; and (2) imports financed with importers' own foreign exchange resources. To obtain authorization, importers are required to fill out either an import form for imports of up to $5,000 f.o.b., or an import application request form for imports of more than $5,000 f.o.b. For imports financed with foreign exchange obtained from the interbank foreign exchange market, authorization is given only after price, quality, and terms of financing (for import credits) are verified. Requests for foreign exchange must be submitted through commercial banks at the daily fixing sessions. Imports financed with importers' own foreign exchange resources comprise goods for which foreign exchange is derived from sources other than the official foreign exchange resources of Guinea and mainly cover imports by 3 "mixed-economy" companies (the Friguia Company; the Guinea Bauxite Company; and AREDOR, the diamond company) and foreign embassies.

Domiciliation requirements	Yes.
Preshipment inspection	Yes.
Letters of credit	Yes.

Import licenses and other nontariff measures

Negative list	Imports of armaments, ammunitions, and narcotics are prohibited.
Import taxes and/or tariffs	All imports are subject to an 18% VAT, custom duties of 8%, and customs charges of 7%, with the following exceptions: animals, flour, sugar, pharmaceutical products, and fertilizers are subject to a 6% duty and a 2% charge; and food industry imports, cement, and agricultural machinery are subject to an 8% duty and a 2% charge. In addition, a surtax of 20% or 30% is imposed on all luxury goods, and a surtax of 30% to 60% is levied on nonalcoholic beverages, certain wines, and spirits. Imports of the 3 mixed enterprises in the mining sector are regulated by special agreements and are subject to a 5.6% levy.
Taxes collected through the exchange system	No.
State import monopoly	No.

Exports and Export Proceeds

Repatriation requirements	Yes.
Surrender requirements	Private traders may retain all of their proceeds to finance authorized imports. Gold exporters and vendors may retain all of their proceeds. Mixed enterprises may retain abroad all their proceeds and may use them for import payments, operating costs, and external debt service.
Financing requirements	No.

Documentation requirements

Letters of credit	Yes.
Guarantees	Yes.
Domiciliation	All private sector exports require domiciliation with a commercial bank and submission of an export description to help prevent shortages of goods needed for domestic consumption and to identify capital outflows. Exports of the mining sector are exempt from this requirement.
Preshipment inspection	Yes.
Export licenses	The exportation of wild animals (dead or alive), meats, articles of historic or ethnographic interest, jewelry, articles made of precious metals, and plants and seeds require special authorization from designated agencies. Planters may be granted special authorization to export specific quantities of pineapples, bananas, or citrus fruits.

Without quotas	Yes.
With quotas	Yes.
Export taxes	Exports of diamonds are subject to a tax of 3%, and exports of gold and other precious metals to a 5% tax.
Taxes collected through the exchange system	No.

Payments for Invisible Transactions and Current Transfers

Controls on these payments

Freight/insurance

    Indicative limits/bona fide test Yes.

Administrative expenses

    Indicative limits/bona fide test Yes.

Commissions

    Indicative limits/bona fide test Yes.

Interest payments

    Indicative limits/bona fide test Yes.

Profit/dividends

    Indicative limits/bona fide test Yes.

Payments for travel

    Quantitative limits Yes.

    Indicative limits/bona fide test Yes.

Medical costs

    Indicative limits/bona fide test Yes.

Study abroad costs

    Prior approval Yes.

    Indicative limits/bona fide test Yes.

Subscriptions and membership fees

    Indicative limits/bona fide test Yes.

Consulting/legal fees

    Indicative limits/bona fide test Yes.

Foreign workers' wages

    Prior approval Approval is granted only for contracts approved by the Ministry of Labor.

    Quantitative limits Yes.

    Indicative limits/bona fide test Yes.

Family maintenance/alimony

    Indicative limits/bona fide test Yes.

Credit card use abroad

    Prior approval Yes.

Proceeds from Invisible Transactions and Current Transfers

Repatriation requirements	Yes.
Surrender requirements	No.
Restrictions on use of funds	No.

Capital Transactions

Controls on capital and money market instruments	All capital transfers through the official exchange market require authorization from the CBRG. Outward capital transfers by Guinean nationals through the official market are prohibited.
On capital market securities	
Purchase locally by nonresidents	Yes.
Sale or issue locally by nonresidents	Yes.
On money market instruments	
Purchase locally by nonresidents	n.a.
Sale or issue locally by nonresidents	Yes.
On collective investment securities	
Purchase abroad by residents	n.a.
Sale or issue abroad by residents	n.a.
Controls on direct investment	
Outward direct investment	n.a.
Inward direct investment	The minimum investment is GF 10 million. Guinean nationals must have controlling interests in enterprises requiring foreign investment of GF 10 million to GF 50 million.
Controls on liquidation of direct investment	No.

Changes During 1996

Imports and import payments	*July 1.* A VAT with a rate of 18% was introduced, replacing the turnover tax.

GUINEA-BISSAU

(Position as of March 31, 1997)

Status Under IMF Articles of Agreement

Article VIII   Date of acceptance: January 1, 1997.

Exchange Arrangement

Currency   The currency of Guinea-Bissau is the Guinea-Bissau peso.

Exchange rate structure

Dual   There are 2 exchange rates: (1) the official rate set by the Central Bank of Guinea-Bissau (CBGB) for its transactions and for those of government agencies, and (2) the commercial rate.

Classification

Pegged   Up to March 1997, Guinea-Bissau maintained a managed float system. The official buying rate against the U.S. dollar, which served as the intervention currency, was adjusted as necessary and maintained within a 2% average of the commercial rate. The commercial rate is freely determined in the foreign exchange market consisting of 2 commercial banks and exchange bureaus. The CBGB regularly intervenes in the market through sales of foreign exchange. Effective from March 13, 1997, Guinea-Bissau pegged the peso to the CFA franc. The currency conversion lasted 3 months and was effected at the rate of PG 65 per CFAF 1 on the basis of the December 31, 1996 market exchange rates.

Exchange tax   No.

Exchange subsidy   No.

Forward exchange market   No.

Arrangements for Payments and Receipts

Prescription of currency requirements   No.

Payment arrangements

Regional arrangements   Guinea-Bissau participates in the WACH, which includes member countries of the BCEAO, as well as The Gambia, Ghana, Guinea, Liberia, Mauritania, Nigeria, and Sierra Leone. On May 2, 1997, Guinea-Bissau joined the WAEMU.

Administration of control

Exchange control authorities   The CBGB exercises control over foreign exchange transactions involving the use of foreign exchange belonging to or administered by it. Foreign exchange transactions effected by commercial banks with resources derived from sources other than those of the CBGB are, in general, not controlled by the CBGB.

Payment arrears

Official   Yes.

Private   n.a.

Controls on trade in gold (coins and/or bullion)

Controls on domestic ownership and/or trade   The CBGB may engage in gold purchases and sales transactions with the public.

Controls on external trade	Exports and imports of gold are prohibited unless expressly authorized.
Controls on exports and imports of banknotes	
On exports	
Domestic currency	n.a.
Foreign currency	Foreign travelers may take out on departure any unspent foreign exchange they have declared on entry.
On imports	n.a.

Resident Accounts

Eligibility to hold accounts	Juridical and natural persons are eligible.
Foreign exchange accounts permitted	Yes.
Held domestically	Residents may maintain foreign exchange accounts if they are authorized to engage in foreign currency transactions or if they receive income in foreign currency under contracts with nonresidents. Prior approval is required.
Held abroad	n.a.

Nonresident Accounts

Eligibility to hold accounts	Juridical and natural persons are eligible.
Foreign exchange accounts permitted	Demand and time accounts with commercial banks. Balances on these accounts may be used without restriction, except for the requirement of prior notice for withdrawals above certain preestablished limits. Banks may pay interest up to 4% a year on demand accounts, whereas interest rates on time deposits may be negotiated freely. Prior approval is required.

Imports and Import Payments

Foreign exchange budget	No.
Financing requirements for imports	No.
Documentation requirements for release of foreign exchange for imports	
Preshipment inspection	Yes.
Import licenses and other nontariff measures	All imports, regardless of whether they involve the use of official or free market foreign exchange, require a prior import license issued by the Ministry of Commerce and Tourism, primarily for statistical purposes. Except for a short negative list, licenses are issued automatically after verification of invoice prices for goods to be taxed. Since the official availability of foreign exchange in the country is not considered when licenses are issued, import licenses are not a foreign exchange allocation instrument, and their possession does not guarantee the importers access to the official exchange market. However, importers are free to arrange for payment through the banking system with their own foreign exchange or foreign exchange purchased on the parallel market. Payments for imports with foreign exchange purchased from, or administered by, the CBGB require authorization from the CBGB, which is granted on the basis of the priority of the products involved and the availability of foreign exchange.

Negative list	Yes.
Other nontariff measures	n.a.
Import taxes and/or tariffs	Imports are subject to tariffs up to 70%, a customs service tax of 6% to 10%, and a 3% surcharge.
Taxes collected through the exchange system	n.a.
State import monopoly	No.

Exports and Export Proceeds

Repatriation requirements	Yes.
Surrender requirements	Exporters must surrender all receipts to the banking system; the intermediary banks purchase for their own account 70% at a rate freely agreed with the exporter and the remaining 30% for the account of the CBGB at the official rate on the date of settlement of the export transaction.
Financing requirements	No.
Export licenses	All exports require a prior export license. Only exporters registered with the Ministry of Commerce and Tourism may obtain these licenses, which are granted automatically in most cases. Prior licenses are intended primarily for statistical purposes, although they are also used to check the prices of exports. There are no products of which the exportation is reserved solely for the public sector.
Without quotas	Yes.
Export taxes	Exports, except those to ECOWAS countries, are subject to a customs service tax of 5%, with cashew nut exports also subject to a special tax of 13%. Agricultural exports are also subject to a rural property tax of 2% if they are processed and 1% if unprocessed.
Taxes collected through the exchange system	No.

Payments for Invisible Transactions and Current Transfers

Controls on these payments	There are no controls on payments for freight and insurance, unloading and storage costs, administrative expenses, commissions, interest payments, profits and dividends, medical costs, study abroad costs, subscriptions and membership fees, and consulting and legal fees.
Payments for travel	
Quantitative limits	The limit is the equivalent of $5,000.
Indicative limits/bona fide test	Yes.
Foreign workers' wages	n.a.
Pensions	n.a.
Gambling/prize earnings	n.a.
Family maintenance/alimony	n.a.
Credit card use abroad	n.a.

Proceeds from Invisible Transactions and Current Transfers

Surrender requirements	No.

Restrictions on use of funds	No.

Capital Transactions

Controls on direct investment

Inward direct investment — The Investment Code provides incentives to inward direct investments and protection against the nationalization and expropriation of assets.

Controls on liquidation of direct investment — No.

Changes During 1996

No significant changes occurred in the exchange and trade system.

Changes During 1997

Status under IMF Articles of Agreement — *January 1.* Guinea-Bissau accepted the obligations of Article VIII, Sections 2, 3, and 4 of the Fund Agreement.

Exchange arrangements — *March 3.* The exchange rate of the Guinea-Bissau peso was pegged to the CFA franc.

Arrangements for payments and receipts — *March 13.* The agreement to admit Guinea-Bissau into the WAEMU on May 2, 1997 was ratified.

GUYANA

(Position as of January 31, 1997)

Status Under IMF Articles of Agreement

Article VIII   Date of acceptance: December 27, 1966.

Exchange Arrangement

Currency   The currency of Guyana is the Guyana dollar.

Exchange rate structure   Unitary.

Classification

Independent floating   The exchange rate of the Guyana dollar is determined freely in the cambio market. The Bank of Guyana (BOG) conducts certain transactions on the basis of the cambio rate by averaging quotations of the 3 largest dealers on the date the transaction takes place. In accordance with the bilateral agreements with the central banks of the CARICOM, the BOG quotes weekly rates for certain CARICOM currencies.

Exchange tax   No.

Exchange subsidy   No.

Forward exchange market   The only arrangement for forward cover against exchange rate risk operates in the official sector in respect of exchange rate guarantees that are provided to certain deposits in dormant accounts. However, no exchange rate guarantee has been given for deposits made after end-March 1989.

Official cover of forward operations   Yes.

Arrangements for Payments and Receipts

Prescription of currency   No.
requirements

Payment arrangements

Bilateral arrangements

Operative   There are arrangements with all CARICOM central banks.

Administration of control

Exchange control authorities   The Exchange Control Act was repealed in May 1996.

International security restrictions   No.

Payment arrears

Official   Arrears exist with Argentina, China, India, Kuwait, Libya, OPEC Fund, Russia, Venezuela, and Yugoslavia.

Private   Arrears exist on certain dormant accounts holding domestic currency deposits equivalent in value to pending applications for foreign exchange.

Controls on trade in gold (coins and/or bullion)

Controls on domestic ownership and/or trade   Residents other than the monetary authorities, authorized dealers, producers of gold, and authorized industrial users are not allowed to hold or acquire gold in any form except for numismatic purposes, and jewelry, at home or abroad, without special permission.

Controls on external trade   Imports and exports of gold in any form by or on behalf of the monetary authorities, authorized dealers, producers of gold, and industrial users require permits issued by the Guyana Gold Board.

Controls on exports and imports of banknotes

On imports

Foreign currency

Travelers entering Guyana with foreign currency in excess of the equivalent of $10,000 must declare the amount.

Resident Accounts

Eligibility to hold accounts

Juridical and natural persons are eligible.

Foreign exchange accounts permitted

Yes.

Held domestically

Exporters are allowed to maintain and operate foreign exchange accounts. These accounts are approved on merit but are generally granted to bona fide exporters who require imported inputs for production and/or have external loan obligations. These accounts may be credited with all or a portion of retained export proceeds and proceeds of foreign currency loans. They may be debited freely for any payments at the discretion of the account holder.

Held abroad

Yes.

Accounts in domestic currency convertible into foreign currency

These accounts may be convertible at the prevailing cambio exchange rate.

Nonresident Accounts

Eligibility to hold accounts

Juridical and natural persons are eligible.

Foreign exchange accounts permitted

External accounts may be opened by commercial banks without the prior approval of the central bank for citizens of Guyana residing permanently abroad; citizens of other countries temporarily residing in Guyana; nonresidents attached to diplomatic missions or international organizations; branches of companies incorporated outside of Guyana; and companies incorporated in Guyana but controlled by nonresidents abroad. These accounts may be maintained in U.S. dollars, pounds sterling, or Canadian dollars, and may be credited with noncash instruments of convertible foreign currencies transferred through the banking system. These accounts may also be credited freely with all authorized payments by residents of Guyana to nonresidents; other credits require approval. They may be debited freely for payments for any purpose to residents of any country, for transfers to other external accounts, for withdrawals by the account holder in Guyana, and for transfers to nonresident accounts.

Domestic currency accounts

External accounts opened by persons who temporarily resided in Guyana and who enjoyed diplomatic privileges and immunities were discontinued on January 2, 1997. The BOG guaranteed foreign exchange to cover these accounts upon request by the commercial bank where they were held.

Convertible into foreign currency

Yes.

Blocked accounts

No.

Imports and Import Payments

Foreign exchange budget

The BOG prepares a hard currency receipts and payments statement to monitor projected flows.

Financing requirements for imports

Import transactions effected through the cambio exchange market are permitted without restriction. Most imports of consumer goods take place on this basis. Certain payments for official imports effected by commercial banks on behalf of the BOG require the Bank's prior approval.

Documentation requirements for release of foreign exchange for imports	Requirements are related mainly to petroleum products.
Other	Documents required include invoices, bills of lading, and certificates of origin.
Import licenses and other nontariff measures	There are no licensing requirements for permissible imports, except for petroleum products and some 20 items affecting national security, health, public safety, and the environment.
Negative list	Imports of unprocessed meat, poultry, fruit, and processed fruit items are restricted, subject to import-licensing controls, from all non-CARICOM sources.
Import taxes and/or tariffs	The CET of CARICOM is applied to all imports from outside the market. Tariffs range from 5% to 25%. Intra-CARICOM trade is free of import duties.
Taxes collected through the exchange system	No.
State import monopoly	No.

Exports and Export Proceeds

Repatriation requirements	No.
Surrender requirements	The requirement was eliminated on December 31, 1996.
Financing requirements	No.
Documentation requirements	No.
Export licenses	Licenses are required for exports of gold and wildlife.
Without quotas	Gold exports are not subject to quotas.
With quotas	There are quotas for the supply of some commodities to preferential markets, and for wildlife exports.
Export taxes	There are levies on exports of rice and sugar. For exports of timber, bauxite, sugar, live birds, and aquarium fish, an export duty is applied.
Taxes collected through the exchange system	No.

Payments for Invisible Transactions and Current Transfers

Controls on these payments	Payments for invisibles to all countries may be freely effected through the cambio exchange market.

Proceeds from Invisible Transactions and Current Transfers

Repatriation requirements	No.
Surrender requirements	No.
Restrictions on use of funds	No.

Capital Transactions

Controls on capital and money market instruments	There are no securities in Guyana.

Controls on derivatives and other instruments	No.
Controls on credit operations	No.
Commercial credits	
By residents to nonresidents	Yes.
To residents from nonresidents	Borrowing requires prior approval.
Financial credits	Same regulations as for commercial credits apply.
By residents to nonresidents	Yes.
To residents from nonresidents	Yes.
Guarantees, sureties, and financial backup facilities	
By residents to nonresidents	Yes.
To residents from nonresidents	Yes.
Controls on direct investment	No.
Controls on liquidation of direct investment	No.
Controls on real estate transactions	No.
Provisions specific to commercial banks and other credit institutions	
Lending to nonresidents (financial or commercial credits)	Yes.
Lending locally in foreign exchange	Yes.
Open foreign exchange position limits	Positions are presently being monitored. The setting of limits is under consideration.
Provisions specific to institutional investors	No.
Other controls imposed by securities laws	No.

Changes During 1996

Arrangements for payments and receipts	*May 6.* The Exchange Control Act was repealed.
Exports and export proceeds	*December 31.* The surrender requirement was eliminated.

Changes During 1997

Nonresident accounts	*January 2.* The system of external accounts for persons who temporarily resided in Guyana and who enjoyed diplomatic privileges and immunities was discontinued, and eligible customers were encouraged by commercial banks to open nonresident foreign currency accounts. While operative, these Guyana dollar-denominated accounts were provided foreign exchange guarantee by the BOG, upon request of the commercial banks where they were held.

HAITI

(Position as of December 31, 1996)

Status Under IMF Articles of Agreement

Article VIII   Date of acceptance: December 22, 1953.

Exchange Arrangement

Currency   The currency of Haiti is the gourde.

Other legal tender   The U.S. dollar circulates freely and is generally accepted in Haiti. Several gold coins have been issued that are legal tender but do not circulate.

Exchange rate structure   Unitary.

Classification

Independent floating   The exchange rate is determined in the exchange market. Since April 1995, the Bank of the Republic of Haiti (BRH), the central bank, has operated a dollar clearinghouse. Commercial banks quote buying and selling rates for certain other currencies based on the buying and selling rates of the U.S. dollar in exchange markets abroad. The market is dominated by money changers, with the banks following this market.

Exchange tax   No.

Exchange subsidy   No.

Forward exchange market   No.

Arrangements for Payments and Receipts

Prescription of currency   No.
requirements

Payment arrangements

Bilateral arrangements

   Operative   In December 1996, 85% of Haiti's debt toward Argentina was canceled, and the remaining 15% was rescheduled until 2001.

Administration of control

Exchange control authorities   The BRH administers the foreign exchange system together with the Ministry of Finance and Economic Affairs (MFEA) and the Ministry of Commerce and Industry (MCI).

International security restrictions

Payment arrears   No.

Controls on trade in gold (coins and/or bullion)

Controls on domestic ownership and/or trade   Residents may hold and acquire gold coins in Haiti for numismatic purposes. With this exception, residents other than the monetary authorities and authorized industrial users are not allowed to hold or acquire gold in any form other than jewelry, at home or abroad.

Controls on external trade   The BRH has the exclusive right to purchase gold domestically and to export gold in the form of coins, mineral dust, or bars. Gold in any form, other than jewelry carried as personal effects by travelers, may be imported and exported only by the BRH. Exports of gold require, in addition, prior authorization from the MCI and the MFEA, as well as

370

an endorsement from the MCI, before customs clearance. However, commercial imports of articles containing a small amount of gold, such as gold watches, are freely permitted and do not require an import license or other authorization.

Controls on exports and imports of banknotes	No.

Resident Accounts

Eligibility to hold accounts	Juridical and natural persons are eligible.
Foreign exchange accounts permitted	These accounts may be credited with export proceeds, with transfers from abroad received by exchange houses, or with receipts from maritime agencies and nongovernmental organizations.
Held domestically	Yes.
Held abroad	Yes.

Nonresident Accounts

Eligibility to hold accounts	Juridical and natural persons are eligible. Same regulations as for residents apply.
Foreign exchange accounts permitted	Yes.
Domestic currency accounts	Yes.
Convertible into foreign currency	n.a.

Imports and Import Payments

Foreign exchange budget	No.
Financing requirements for imports	No.
Documentation requirements for release of foreign exchange for imports	No.
Import licenses and other nontariff measures	No.
Import taxes and/or tariffs	There are 3 standard tariff rates, 5%, 10%, and 15%. Several goods have special tariff rates—gasoline, 25%; and cement, rice, and sugar, 3%. A domestic turnover tax is charged on the c.i.f. value plus import duties. All imports, except for inputs used by certain export industries, are subject to a 4% verification fee.
Taxes collected through the exchange system	No.
State import monopoly	No.

Exports and Export Proceeds

Repatriation requirements	No.
Surrender requirements	No.
Financing requirements	No.
Export licenses	Exports of agricultural products require prior authorization from the MCI. Authorization is usually granted freely but may be withheld when domestic supplies are low.

Without quotas   n.a.

With quotas   Exports of manufactured products to the United States, such as women's and girls' blouses and shirts of cotton and synthetic fibers, men's shirts of synthetic fibers and cotton, cotton gloves, cotton pants, and cotton housecoats are subject to quotas.

Export taxes   No.

Payments for Invisible Transactions and Current Transfers

Controls on these payments   No.

Proceeds from Invisible Transactions and Current Transfers

Repatriation requirements   No.

Surrender requirements   No.

Restrictions on use of funds   No.

Capital Transactions

Controls on direct investment

Outward direct investment   n.a.

Inward direct investment   Investments require prior government approval. Investments in handcraft industries are not normally approved.

Provisions specific to commercial banks and other credit institutions   Private banks are required to maintain at least 85% of their liabilities in domestic assets for local customers. This requirement, however, is not enforced.

Borrowing abroad   n.a.

Maintenance of accounts abroad   n.a.

Lending to nonresidents (financial or commercial credits)   n.a.

Lending locally in foreign exchange   n.a.

Purchase of locally issued securities denominated in foreign exchange   n.a.

Differential treatment of nonresident deposit accounts and/or deposit accounts in foreign exchange

Reserve requirements   Reserve requirements for local currency deposits are 48%. No reserve requirements apply to foreign currency deposits.

Liquid asset requirements   n.a.

Interest rate controls   n.a.

Credit controls   n.a.

Investment regulations   n.a.

Open foreign exchange position limits   n.a.

Changes During 1996

Imports and import payments   *June 10.* The 3% consular fee and the 1% administrative fee on all imports were replaced by a 4% verification fee.

HONDURAS

(Position as of December 31, 1996)

Status Under IMF Articles of Agreement

Article VIII

Date of acceptance: July 1, 1950.

Exchange Arrangement

Currency

The currency of Honduras is the Honduran lempira.

Exchange rate structure

Dual

There are two exchange rates: the rate resulting from the auctions and the rate used for debt conversion (L 2 = $1).

Classification

Managed floating

The exchange rate for the lempira is determined in foreign exchange auctions. Banks and exchange houses are required to sell all their daily foreign exchange purchases to the Central Bank of Honduras (CBH). Buyers (banks, exchange houses, or private individuals) bid at a price that cannot differ from the base price set by the authorities by more than 5% in either direction. The base exchange rate is adjusted every 5 auctions according to changes in the differential between domestic and international inflation and in the exchange rates of currencies of trading partners of Honduras with respect to the U.S. dollar. The amount of foreign exchange offered at each auction must be at least 60% of the CBH's purchase of foreign exchange from its agents. The minimum amount of foreign exchange to be offered and the base price are announced before the auction. Individuals willing to purchase foreign exchange must make offers in lempiras for amounts ranging between $5,000 and $300,000. Foreign exchange agents may purchase for their own account to satisfy private demands lower than $5,000. The maximum amount of foreign exchange that can be purchased for this purpose is $30,000 for commercial banks and $10,000 for foreign exchange houses. Foreign exchange agents may charge up to 1.5% commission on sales to the public lower than $5,000 and up to 1.2% for larger sales. Auction rates may deviate from the base rate by ±5%. Auctions are held once each working day and each bidder can make up to 3 offers in each auction.

Exchange tax

No.

Exchange subsidy

No.

Forward exchange market

No.

Arrangements for Payments and Receipts

Prescription of currency requirements

Trade transactions with the rest of Central America may be carried out in local currencies, barter and compensation mechanisms, or U.S. dollars.

Payment arrangements

No.

Administration of control

Exchange control authorities

The CBH exercises control.

International security restrictions

No.

Payment arrears

Yes.

Official

n.a.

Private

n.a.

Controls on trade in gold (coins and/or bullion)	
Controls on external trade	In general, imports and exports of gold require a license issued by the CBH; such licenses are not normally granted. Commercial imports and exports of jewelry and other articles that contain gold require a license issued by the Ministry of Economy; for most articles, licenses are granted freely. Exports of gold are subject to a tax of 5%.

Resident Accounts

Eligibility to hold accounts	Juridical and natural persons are eligible.
Foreign exchange accounts permitted	Banks are required to hold these deposits in (1) foreign currency notes in their vaults, (2) deposits in the CBH, (3) special accounts at correspondent banks abroad, (4) investments in high-liquidity foreign instruments, or (5) advance export- or import-financing instruments.
Held domestically	Yes.
Held abroad	n.a.
Accounts in domestic currency convertible into foreign currency	No.

Nonresident Accounts

Eligibility to hold accounts	Juridical and natural persons are eligible.
Foreign exchange accounts permitted	Same regulations as for resident accounts apply.
Domestic currency accounts	Yes.
Convertible into foreign currency	Yes.

Imports and Import Payments

Foreign exchange budget	No.
Financing requirements for imports	The financing of imports is channeled either through the banking system or through exchange houses, with foreign exchange purchased in the free market or with credits obtained abroad.
Documentation requirements for release of foreign exchange for imports	No.
Import licenses and other nontariff measures	Most imports do not require a license. However, imports exceeding $3,000 must be registered.
Positive list	Imports of arms and similar items require a license issued by the Ministry of Defense.
Import taxes and/or tariffs	Import duties range from zero to 20%. Over 1,600 items from other Central American countries are exempt from import duties, except for a 1.5% import surcharge. There are duty-free and industrial processing zones that benefit from tariff exemptions.
Taxes collected through the exchange system	No.
State import monopoly	No.

Exports and Export Proceeds

Repatriation requirements

Yes.

Surrender requirements

All export earnings, except those from trade with other Central American countries, must be surrendered to banks or exchange houses within a period of 20 to 85 days. Proceeds from coffee exports must be surrendered within 20 days. Exporters are allowed to retain 30% of their foreign exchange proceeds to finance their own imports, as well as to pay for their authorized external obligations. Commercial banks and exchange houses are required to sell all the purchased foreign exchange to the CBH.

Financing requirements

No.

Export licenses

No licenses are required, but exports must be registered for statistical purposes.

Export taxes

Bananas are subject to an export tax of $0.50 for a 40-pound box. However, production from newly planted areas is exempt, while production from rehabilitated areas is subject to a $0.25 tax for a box. Sugar is subject to an export tax when the export price exceeds a certain level.

Taxes collected through the exchange system

n.a.

Payments for Invisible Transactions and Current Transfers

Controls on these payments

There are no controls on these payments, but all buyers of foreign exchange are required to fill out a form stating the purpose for which the funds will be used. There are no limits on the amount purchased.

Proceeds from Invisible Transactions and Current Transfers

Repatriation requirements

No.

Surrender requirements

No.

Restrictions on use of funds

No.

Capital Transactions

Controls on capital and money market instruments

Purchases of capital shares in existing domestic firms are permitted with the exception of defense-related industries, hazardous industries, and small-scale industry and commerce.

On capital market securities

Sale or issue abroad by residents

n.a.

On money market instruments

Sale or issue locally by nonresidents

n.a.

Sale or issue abroad by residents

n.a.

On collective investment securities

Purchase locally by nonresidents

There are no restrictions on activities involving the receipt of foreign exchange and its transfer abroad for investment in mutual funds.

Sale or issue locally by nonresidents

Foreign mutual funds and similar financial institutions must have permission to collect funds in Honduras for deposit or investment abroad.

Sale or issue abroad by residents

n.a.

Controls on credit operations	The approval of congress is required for all public sector foreign borrowing. Private sector external debt contracts must be registered with the CBH for statistical purposes only.
Commercial credits	
By residents to nonresidents	n.a.
To residents from nonresidents	Yes.
Financial credits	
By residents to nonresidents	n.a.
To residents from nonresidents	Yes.
Guarantees, sureties, and financial backup facilities	
By residents to nonresidents	n.a.
To residents from nonresidents	Yes.
Controls on direct investment	
Outward direct investment	n.a.
Inward direct investment	Investments are permitted in all sectors without restriction, with the exception of defense-related industries, hazardous industries, and small-scale industry and commerce. Investments in hazardous industries require prior approval. All foreign investments must be registered with the Secretary of Economy and Trade.
Controls on liquidation of direct investment	No.
Controls on real estate transactions	
Purchase locally by nonresidents	n.a.
Sale locally by nonresidents	n.a.
Provisions specific to commercial banks and other credit institutions	
Borrowing abroad	Borrowing requires CBH approval.
Maintenance of accounts abroad	Commercial banks must deposit abroad 38% of foreign exchange deposits held by the private sector.
Lending to nonresidents (financial or commercial credits)	CBH authorization is required.
Lending locally in foreign exchange	Financial institutions may lend 50% of their foreign exchange deposits locally in foreign exchange.
Purchase of locally issued securities denominated in foreign exchange	n.a.
Differential treatment of nonresident deposit accounts and/or deposit accounts in foreign exchange	
Reserve requirements	All types of deposits are subject to a 12% requirement.
Liquid asset requirements	Foreign exchange deposits are subject to a 50% requirement.
Credit controls	Credit with funds from foreign exchange deposits must be granted to export-related industries.
Open foreign exchange position limits	n.a.

Changes During 1996

Exchange arrangements

April 19. The base exchange rate is to be modified after every 5 auctions according to changes in the differential between domestic and international inflation and in the exchange rates of the currencies of trading partners of Honduras with respect to the U.S. dollar. Auction rates cannot deviate from the base rate by more than 5% in either direction.

Imports and import payments

January 1. The customs service surcharge was lowered to 1.5%.

Exports and export proceeds

January 1. The 10% income tax for coffee with an f.o.b. value greater than $80 a quintal was eliminated retroactively.

HONG KONG, CHINA

(Position as of December 31, 1996)

Status Under IMF Articles of Agreement

Article VIII   Date of acceptance: February 15, 1961.

Exchange Arrangement

Currency   The currency of Hong Kong is the Hong Kong dollar.

Other legal tender   Commemorative gold coins of HK$1,000 are legal tender, but are mostly kept by collectors and seldom circulated.

Exchange rate structure

Unitary   The authorities do not maintain margins in respect of exchange transactions.

Classification

Pegged   The Hong Kong dollar is linked to the U.S. dollar, the intervention currency, at the rate of HK$7.80 per US$1. Under this linked exchange rate arrangement, the 3 note-issuing banks must deliver to the Exchange Fund an amount in U.S. dollars that is equivalent to the local currency issued at the linked exchange rate as backing for their Hong Kong dollar note issues. The Exchange Fund, in turn, issues to each note-issuing bank non-interest-bearing certificates of indebtedness denominated in Hong Kong dollars.

Conversely, the note-issuing banks may redeem U.S. dollars from the Exchange Fund by delivering certificates of indebtedness and withdrawing local banknotes from circulation at the same linked exchange rate. The amount of indebtedness of the Exchange Fund represented by the certificates of indebtedness will be reduced accordingly. Other banks may acquire local currency notes from the note-issuing banks against Hong Kong dollar deposits for Hong Kong dollar value. The exchange rate of the Hong Kong dollar is set in the exchange market at freely negotiated rates for all transactions except those that are conducted for note-issuing purposes between the Exchange Fund and the note-issuing banks.

Exchange tax   No.

Exchange subsidy   No.

Forward exchange market   The forward exchange markets are operated on private sector initiatives.

Official cover of forward operations   No.

Arrangements for Payments and Receipts

Prescription of currency requirements   No.

Payment arrangements   No.

Administration of control   No.

International security restrictions   Sanctions are implemented by the Hong Kong government in accordance with Orders in Council issued by the Hong Kong government, which has the status of law in Hong Kong.

In accordance with IMF Executive Board Decision No. 144-(52/51)   n.a.

In accordance with UN sanctions   n.a.

Payments arrears	No.
Controls on trade in gold (coins and/or bullion)	No.
Controls on exports and imports of banknotes	No.

Resident Accounts

Eligibility to hold accounts	Juridical and natural persons are eligible.
Foreign exchange accounts permitted	Yes.
Held domestically	Yes.
Held abroad	Yes.
Accounts in domestic currency convertible into foreign currency	Yes.

Nonresident Accounts

Eligibility to hold accounts	No distinction is made between resident and nonresident accounts. Juridical and natural persons are eligible.
Foreign exchange accounts permitted	Yes.
Domestic currency accounts	Yes.
Convertible into foreign currency	Yes.
Blocked accounts	No.

Imports and Import Payments

Foreign exchange budget	No.
Financing requirements for imports	No.
Documentation requirements for release of foreign exchange for imports	No.
Import licenses and other nontariff measures	
Negative list	Imports of certain articles are subject to licensing control by the Director-General of Trade. Import licenses are required for reasons of health, safety, environmental protection, or security, or for fulfillment of Hong Kong's international trade obligations.
Import taxes and/or tariffs	All imports are free of duties, although an excise tax for revenue and health purposes is levied on imported and domestically produced cigarettes and other tobacco products, liquors, methyl alcohol, and hydrocarbon oils.
State import monopoly	No.

Exports and Export Proceeds

Repatriation requirements	No.
Surrender requirements	No.

Financing requirements	No.
Documentation requirements	No.
Export licenses	
Without quotas	Exports of certain articles are subject to licensing control by the Director-General of Trade. Export licenses are required for reasons of health, safety, environmental protection, or security, or for fulfillment of Hong Kong's international trade obligations.
With quotas	Yes.
Export taxes	No.

Payments for Invisible Transactions and Current Transfers

Controls on these payments	No.

Proceeds from Invisible Transactions and Current Transfers

Repatriation requirements	No.
Surrender requirements	No.
Restrictions on use of funds	There are no limitations on receipts from invisibles. Income from foreign sources, capital gains, distribution from trusts, and dividends is not taxed in Hong Kong; interest income from domestic sources received by licensed banks and corporations carrying on business in Hong Kong is subject to a profits tax. Interest earned on bank deposits by individuals is not subject to the salaries tax.

Capital Transactions

Controls on capital and money market instruments	No exchange control requirements are imposed on capital receipts or payments by residents or nonresidents. A license or an authorization is required for companies, whether incorporated in Hong Kong or elsewhere, to conduct banking, insurance, securities, and futures dealings. Otherwise, all overseas companies are required only to register with the Companies Registry within 1 month of establishing a business in Hong Kong.
Controls on derivatives and other instruments	No.
Controls on credit operations	No.
Controls on direct investment	No.
Controls on liquidation of direct investment	No.
Controls on real estate transactions	No.
Provisions specific to commercial banks and other credit institutions	
Open foreign exchange position limits	All authorized institutions are required to report to the Hong Kong Monetary Authority (HKMA) their foreign currency positions (including options) monthly. Locally incorporated institutions are required to report their consolidated foreign currency positions. The aggregate net open position (calculated as the sum of net long/short positions of individual currencies) should normally not exceed 5% of the capital base of the institution and the net open position in any individual currency should not exceed 10% of the capital base. For subsidiaries of foreign banks, where the parent consolidates the foreign exchange risk on a global basis and there is adequate home supervision, the HKMA may accept higher limits. For branches of foreign banks, the HKMA reviews and monitors

their internal limits, which are usually set by their head offices and home supervisory authorities.

Provisions specific to institutional investors

No.

Other controls imposed by securities laws

No.

Changes During 1996

No significant changes occurred in the exchange and trade system.

HUNGARY

(Position as of January 31, 1997)

Status Under IMF Articles of Agreement

Article VIII	Date of acceptance: January 1, 1996.

Exchange Arrangement

Currency	The currency of Hungary is the Hungarian forint.
Exchange rate structure	Unitary.
Classification	
Managed floating	The National Bank of Hungary (NBH) adjusts the official exchange rate of the forint in accordance with a preannounced rate of crawl effected against a currency basket comprising the deutsche mark (70%) and the U.S. dollar (30%). The official exchange rate is fixed at 11:00 a.m. every day against the basket and is calculated for 20 convertible currencies and the ECU within margins of 2.25%, but licensed banks are free to determine their own margins within the band.
Exchange tax	No.
Exchange subsidy	No.
Forward exchange market	Commercial banks may engage in forward transactions at exchange rates negotiated freely between the banks and their customers.
Official cover of forward operations	No.

Arrangements for Payments and Receipts

Prescription of currency requirements	No.
Payment arrangements	
Bilateral arrangements	
Operative	There are agreements with Brazil and Ecuador, under which outstanding balances are settled every 90 days.
Inoperative	There are agreements with Albania, Bulgaria, Cambodia, the Lao People's Democratic Republic, Russia, and Vietnam for the settlement of outstanding transferable or clearing ruble balances with shipments of goods.
Administration of control	
Exchange control authorities	Authority for enforcing foreign exchange regulations is vested in the NBH.
International security restrictions	
In accordance with UN sanctions	In compliance with UN Security Council Resolution No. 661, Hungary continues to maintain payments restrictions against Iraq.
Payment arrears	No.
Controls on trade in gold (coins and/or bullion)	No.
Controls on exports and imports of banknotes	
On exports	
Domestic currency	Residents and nonresidents may, without a license, take out of the country up to Ft 300,000 a trip.

382

Foreign currency	Exports are limited to the equivalent of Ft 50,000 a person a trip, without a license.
On imports	
Domestic currency	Imports are limited to Ft 300,000 a person a trip.

Resident Accounts

Eligibility to hold accounts

Juridical and natural persons are eligible.

Foreign exchange accounts permitted

Yes.

Held domestically

Resident natural persons may freely maintain convertible currency accounts at authorized commercial banks. Resident juridical persons may open convertible currency accounts only with funds originating from specific sources, such as export proceeds, foreign borrowing, and capital paid in convertible currency by the foreign owners of joint-venture companies, inheritance, or donations paid in convertible currency for foundations, churches and social organizations, and budgetary institutions. Prior approval is required.

Held abroad

Yes.

Accounts in domestic currency convertible into foreign currency

Conversion is free in all liberalized items and in all authorized cases.

Nonresident Accounts

Eligibility to hold accounts

Juridical and natural persons are eligible.

Foreign exchange accounts permitted

Yes.

Domestic currency accounts

Yes.

Convertible into foreign currency

Convertible forint accounts may be credited with legally acquired forint; proceeds from the conversion of convertible currency or forint acquired from nonliberalized or unauthorized transactions can be placed in a nonconvertible forint account, which does not bear interest.

Blocked accounts

No.

Imports and Import Payments

Foreign exchange budget

No.

Financing requirements for imports

No.

Documentation requirements for release of foreign exchange for imports

A declaration stating the use of foreign exchange must be completed.

Import licenses and other nontariff measures

Licenses are required for imports that are destined for the settlement of outstanding balances in transferable or clearing rubles.

Negative list

Yes.

Licenses with quotas

Licenses are needed for products falling under the global quota on consumer goods.

Import taxes and/or tariffs

Goods for personal use brought in by returning Hungarian travelers are subject to a general import duty of 15%, based on the actual invoice price with a duty-free allowance of Ft 8,000. Residents, if they are employees of a domestic agency and if they are stationed abroad for more than one year, may import, free of customs duty, goods for personal use up to a value equivalent to 40% of their earnings. In addition to customs duties, imports are subject to an import surcharge. The surcharge was reduced from 8% to 7% on July 1, 1996; to 6% on October 1, 1996; and to 4% on March 10, 1997. It is to be reduced further to 3% on May 15, 1997, and eliminated by July 1, 1997.

Taxes collected through the exchange system	No.
State import monopoly	No.

Exports and Export Proceeds

Repatriation requirements	Export proceeds must be received in officially quoted convertible currencies, in Hungarian forint from convertible forint accounts of nonresidents, or in nonconvertible currency. Proceeds in convertible currencies must be repatriated to Hungary upon receipt of the foreign exchange. Certain exemptions are granted, stipulated in the law, or subject to specific approval by the NBH. In the case of nonconvertible currencies, the exporters are required to make a best effort to exchange those into convertible currency and repatriate the convertible currency.
Surrender requirements	Foreign exchange receipts may be deposited in a foreign exchange account at a domestic bank but can only be used for all liberalized transactions. Export proceeds received in forint by nonresidents may be deposited in convertible forint accounts with licensed banks, and nonresidents are allowed to convert balances in such accounts into foreign exchange for transfer abroad.
Financing requirements	No.
Documentation requirements	No.
Export licenses	Exports of items included in the negative list require a license.
Export taxes	No.

Payments for Invisible Transactions and Current Transfers

Controls on these payments	No.

Proceeds from Invisible Transactions and Current Transfers

Repatriation requirements	Proceeds are subject to the same requirement as export proceeds.
Surrender requirements	Resident natural persons are exempted. Resident juridical persons, except for transfers defined as international economic activities (including exports), are subject to the surrender requirement.
Restrictions on use of funds	No.

Capital Transactions

Controls on capital and money market instruments	
On capital market securities	
Sale or issue locally by nonresidents	Transactions in OECD central government bonds, bonds and shares of OECD-based enterprises with investment grade credit rating, and the sale of shares of parent companies to the employees of its subsidiary company are free. For transactions in other instruments, a foreign exchange license is required. The license is liberally granted, on a case-by-case basis, after submitting a request and its accompanying documents. All

proceeds associated with authorized transactions can be freely converted and transferred abroad by nonresidents.

Purchase abroad by residents

The same regulations as for sale or issue by nonresidents apply. Funds required for transactions can be freely converted and transferred abroad by residents. The transaction may be done through a resident brokerage company.

On money market instruments

These transactions require a foreign exchange license, which is granted in exceptional cases, on a case-by-case basis, after submitting a request and its accompanying documents. Proceeds associated with the transactions can be freely converted and transferred abroad.

Purchase locally by nonresidents

Yes.

Sale or issue locally by nonresidents

Yes.

Purchase abroad by residents

Yes.

Sale or issue abroad by residents

Yes.

On collective investment securities

Purchase locally by nonresidents

Transactions for closed-end funds are free, but those for open-end funds require a license, which is granted in exceptional cases.

Sale or issue locally by nonresidents

The same regulations as for transactions in money market instruments apply.

Purchase abroad by residents

The same regulations as for transactions in money market instruments apply.

Sale or issue abroad by residents

Transactions for closed-end funds are free, but those for open-end funds require a license, which is granted in exceptional cases.

Controls on derivatives and other instruments

These transactions require a foreign exchange authority license, which is granted in exceptional cases, on a case-by-case basis.

Purchase locally by nonresidents

Yes.

Sale or issue locally by nonresidents

Yes.

Purchase abroad by residents

Yes.

Sale or issue abroad by residents

Yes.

Controls on credit operations

Financial credits

By residents to nonresidents

Credits between close relatives are free; in all other cases, a foreign exchange authority license is needed, which is granted liberally in the case of long- and medium-term credits and granted exceptionally in the case of short-term credits.

To residents from nonresidents

Medium- and long-term financial credits for enterprises and private persons who borrow from their close relatives are allowed. All other credits require a foreign exchange authority license, which is granted liberally, on a case-by-case basis.

Guarantees, sureties, and financial backup facilities

By residents to nonresidents

These transactions are allowed if they are related to international commercial transactions or if the guarantee is related to a customs duty. In all other cases, a foreign exchange authority license is needed, which is granted liberally, on a case-by-case basis.

Controls on direct investment

Outward direct investment

Equity participation in a nonresident enterprise is considered as foreign direct investment and is free if the participation in the share or equity capital or the value of assets of the foreign enterprise is more than 10%. The following preconditions should also be met: (1) the law of the country of incorporation should allow the transfer to Hungary of profits and capital in convertible foreign exchange; (2) the resident's liability should not exceed (except in the case of a branch) its share in the enterprise; (3) the country of incorporation should be a member of the OECD, or there should be an investment protection agreement in place with the country; (4) the resident should have no custom duty, tax or pension, health insurance, or social security contribution liability outstanding; (5) the resident should not be in bankruptcy or under liquidation and no such action should have been initiated against it in the year of application or the previous 2 calendar years; (6) during the period stipulated above, there should be no negative decision against the investor made by the foreign exchange authority; and (7) during the same period, no senior employee of the applicant should have been a senior member of the supervisory committee of an enterprise against which the foreign exchange authority had made a negative decision. If the planned investment does not meet any of the listed criteria, the application will automatically fall under a foreign exchange authority licensing procedure.

Inward direct investment	Foreign investment in the form of joint ventures with Hungarian enterprises may be established without approval, but in the case of banks, foreign participation exceeding 10% of equity requires government approval. Joint ventures may also be established in duty-free zones. In both cases, the joint venture is considered as a Hungarian legal entity, but those in duty-free zones are exempted from several regulations. Machines and equipment, technical know-how, and patents may qualify as foreign investment.
Controls on liquidation of direct investment	Guarantee is given by law for the transfer of the foreign investors' share of profits, the invested capital, and capital gains.
Controls on real estate transactions	
Purchase abroad by residents	A foreign exchange authority license is required on a case-by-case basis, which is granted liberally after submitting a request and its accompanying documents.
Purchase locally by nonresidents	Approval of local municipal authorities is required.
Provisions specific to commercial banks and other credit institutions	
Borrowing abroad	Financial institutions must report all foreign borrowing to the NBH.
Lending to nonresidents (financial or commercial credits)	As of January 1, 1997, short-term lending is allowed within the following rules:

(1) Total outstanding lending to nonresidents should not exceed 50% of the total amount of convertible currency drawn from nonresidents or the amount stipulated in a foreign exchange authority license; and

(2) A bank may not have an aggregate lending with an individual borrower of more than 25% of its adjusted capital. In the case of medium- and long-term lending, a case-by-case foreign exchange authority license is needed, which is granted liberally after submitting a request and its accompanying documents. In the case of purchase of short-term securities with an original maturity of less than 1 year, their aggregate amount should not exceed 50% of the total amount of convertible currency liabilities. In that figure, short-term lending should also be included. In the case of purchase of medium- and long-term securities, the same rules apply as for residents.

Lending locally in foreign exchange	The granting of credits to foreigners by Hungarian financial institutions is, in most cases, limited to credits with maturities of up to 1 year. Short-term lending locally to nonresidents is allowed within the framework stipulated above. Lending to residents is liberalized. (The foreign exchange loan from the point of view of the resident borrower is practically an index loan, where the forint amount is indexed to the exchange rate of a convertible currency, since the borrower may get the loan only in domestic currency. From the point of view of the bank, its books contain a foreign exchange lending.)
Purchase of locally issued securities denominated in foreign exchange	Purchase of locally issued foreign exchange denominated securities is allowed, but a foreign exchange authority license is required to issue such securities; this license is granted in exceptional cases, on a case-by-case basis.

Differential treatment of nonresident deposit accounts and/or deposit accounts in foreign exchange	
Reserve requirements	As of January 1, 1997, the interest paid on obligatory reserves placed at the NBH on foreign exchange assets of the banks is 17%, and that paid on domestic currency assets is 12%.
Interest rate controls	n.a.
Open foreign exchange position limits	The gross aggregate position is limited to 30% of the bank's adjusted capital. Banks should adhere to the limit on a daily basis.
Provisions specific to institutional investors	In the case of insurance companies, these provisions are included in the Law on Insurance Companies and Insurance Activities (1995); in the case of pension funds, in a Government Decree (1994); and in the case of mutual funds, in a law (1991).
Limits (max.) on portfolio invested abroad	Yes.
Limits (min.) on portfolio invested locally	Yes.
Currency matching regulations on assets/liabilities composition	Investments abroad are not allowed.
Other controls imposed by securities laws	No.

Changes During 1996

Status under IMF Articles of Agreement	*January 1.* Hungary accepted the obligations of Article VIII, Sections 2, 3, and 4 of the Fund Agreement.
Arrangements for payments and receipts	*July 1.* Residents and nonresidents were permitted to bring into or take out of Hungary up to Ft 300,000 a person a trip.
Capital transactions	*March 20.* Government approval requirement was lifted for foreign participation exceeding 10% of the equity of a bank.
	July 1. The issue and private placement and introduction of (1) OECD government bonds and (2) bonds and shares of OECD-based enterprises with highest credit rating were liberalized. Residents may acquire these securities from abroad through resident brokerage firms.
	July 1. The law on foreign exchange provided for the liberalization of the acquisition by nonresidents of domestic securities with remaining maturities of 1 year or more. That provision was changed to encompass debt instruments with an original maturity of 1 year or more. Resident employees of subsidiaries of foreign enterprises may buy the shares of the parent enterprise, even if the latter is not OECD-based or does not have the highest credit rating.

Changes During 1997

Capital transactions	*January 1.* The issue and introduction of bonds with a maturity of 1 year or more and shares of OECD-based enterprises with investment grade credit rating as well as depository receipts issued thereof as negotiable instruments were liberalized. Residents may acquire the above securities through any resident brokerage firm. Short-term lending to nonresidents by banks was limited to 50% of total foreign exchange liabilities (previously limited to 50% of foreign exchange liabilities from foreigners). Futures and options transactions between 2 foreign currencies by banks were liberalized.

ICELAND

(Position as of December 31, 1996)

Status Under IMF Articles of Agreement

Article VIII   Date of acceptance: September 19, 1983.

Exchange Arrangement

Currency   The currency of Iceland is the Icelandic króna (plural: krónur).

Other legal tender   A commemorative gold coin with face value of ISK 100 is legal tender, but it does not circulate.

Exchange rate structure   Unitary.

Classification

Pegged   The external value of the króna is pegged to a basket of 16 currencies: Belgian franc, Canadian dollar, Danish krone, deutsche mark, Finnish markka, French franc, Italian lira, Japanese yen, Netherlands guilder, Norwegian krone, Portuguese escudo, the pound sterling, Spanish peseta, Swedish krona, Swiss franc, and the U.S. dollar. The Central Bank of Iceland (CBI) intervenes in the exchange market to keep the exchange rate within a margin of ± 6% around the central rate.

Exchange tax   No.

Exchange subsidy   No.

Forward exchange market   Iceland has no organized forward market and the króna has no quoted forward exchange rate. However, forward contracts can be freely negotiated in all currencies.

Official cover of forward operations   No.

Arrangements for Payments and Receipts

Prescription of currency requirements   No.

Payment arrangements   No.

Administration of control

Exchange control authorities   The Ministry of Industry and Commerce has ultimate responsibilities for imports and, in consultation with the CBI, for capital movements and foreign exchange regulation. The CBI licenses the foreign exchange dealers on a commercial basis and sets the reporting requirements for statistical purposes and for implementation of control on inward foreign direct investment.

International security restrictions

In accordance with IMF Executive Board Decision No. 144-(52/51)   Iceland notified the IMF on July 31, 1992, that, in compliance with UN Security Council Resolution No. 757 (1992), certain restrictions had been imposed on payments and transfers for current international transactions with respect to the Federal Republic of Yugoslavia (Serbia/Montenegro).

In accordance with UN sanctions   On December 1, 1995, Iceland notified the IMF that exchange restrictions against Libya had been imposed in accordance with UN Security Council Resolution No. 883 (1993).

Payments arrears   No.

Controls on trade in gold (coins and/or bullion)   No.

388

Controls on exports and imports of banknotes	No.

Resident Accounts

Eligibility to hold accounts	Juridical and natural persons are eligible.
Foreign exchange accounts permitted	Residents opening bank accounts abroad must provide the CBI with a notification of their opening.
Held domestically	n.a.
Held abroad	n.a.

Nonresident Accounts

Eligibility to hold accounts	Juridical and natural persons are eligible.
Foreign exchange accounts permitted	Banks must report to the CBI the monthly positions of nonresident accounts. All accounts in domestic banks must be identified by name and identification number.
Domestic currency accounts	Yes.
Convertible into foreign currency	n.a.
Blocked accounts	No.

Imports and Import Payments

Foreign exchange budget	No.
Financing requirements for imports	No.
Documentation requirements for release of foreign exchange for imports	No.
Import licenses and other nontariff measures	Imports of foods and services are free, except when international agreements provide otherwise.
Negative list	Live animals and certain other agricultural products require health certificates.
Open general licenses	Imports by tourists and foreign visitors require a license.
Import taxes and/or tariffs	Yes.
Taxes collected through the exchange system	n.a.
State import monopoly	Tobacco can only be imported under state trading arrangements.

Exports and Export Proceeds

Repatriation requirements	No.
Surrender requirements	No.
Financing requirements	No.
Documentation requirements	No.
Export licenses	
Without quotas	Exports of military, fisheries, and agricultural products require licenses from the Ministry of Foreign Affairs and Foreign Trade.

Export taxes	No.

Payments for Invisible Transactions and Current Transfers

Controls on these payments	No.

Proceeds from Invisible Transactions and Current Transfers

Repatriation requirements	No.
Surrender requirements	No.
Restrictions on use of funds	No.

Capital Transactions

Controls on capital and money market instruments

The purchase of shares or other equity capital may be affected by laws on inward direct investment.

On capital market securities

Purchase locally by nonresidents

Yes.

Sale or issue locally by nonresidents

Foreign governments and other authorities are prohibited from issuing debt instruments in Iceland unless permitted by the CBI.

On money market instruments

Sale or issue by nonresidents

Yes.

Controls on derivatives and other instruments

Sale or issue locally by nonresidents

Foreign governments and other authorities are prohibited from issuing debt instruments in Iceland unless permitted by the CBI.

Controls on credit operations

No.

Controls on direct investment

Inward direct investment

Foreign direct investments are regulated by the special law on foreign investment (No. 34/1991), as follows: (1) only resident Icelandic citizens or domestically registered companies wholly owned by resident Icelandic citizens may fish within the Icelandic fishing limit or operate primary fish processing facilities; (2) investments by foreign governments and public authorities are prohibited in Iceland; (3) only Icelandic state and local authorities, resident Icelandic citizens, or domestically registered Icelandic companies wholly owned by resident Icelandic citizens may acquire the right to harness waterfalls and geothermal energy; the restriction applies to power production and distribution companies; (4) investments by nonresidents in domestic airlines may not exceed 49%; (5) there are also restricted conditions for residency of managers and majority of voting power in holding companies; and (6) residents of the EEA are exempted from restriction (3), and the Minister of Commerce may grant exemptions from this and from requirement (2).

Until May 15, 1996, investments by nonresidents in commercial banks could not exceed 25%, although foreign banks were allowed to open branches in Iceland, while financial limits were put on any single investment in Iceland and the total foreign investments in any industry. On the same date, indirect investments in the fish industry were allowed.

Controls on real estate transactions

Purchase locally by nonresidents

The conditions to own real estate in Iceland are: (1) individual owners must be Icelandic citizens; (2) in the case of unlimited companies, all owners must be Icelandic citizens;

and (3) joint-stock companies must be registered in Iceland, with at least 80% owned by Icelandic citizens, and all of the members of the board of directors being Icelandic citizens. Icelandic citizens must control the majority of the voting power at annual meetings. The same conditions apply if the real estate is to be leased for more than 3 years or if the lease agreement cannot be terminated with less than 1 year's notice. However, a company that is granted an operating license in Iceland may acquire real estate for its own use as long as the license does not carry with it the right to exploit natural resources. Citizens of the EEA and other foreign citizens who have been domiciled in Iceland for at least 5 years are exempted from these restrictions. The Minister of Justice may grant others exemption from these requirements.

Sale locally by nonresidents	Yes.
Provisions specific to commercial banks and other credit institutions	No.
Provisions specific to institutional investors	No limits are imposed on portfolios invested locally or abroad.
Other controls imposed by securities laws	No.

Changes During 1996

Capital transactions

January 1. Restrictions on foreign inward direct investment in the sector of energy development were abolished in accordance with EEA requirements.

May 15. The special law on foreign investment (No. 34/1991) was amended, allowing foreign investment in the fish industry and abolishing restrictions in commercial banks and financial ceilings of individual investment and total investments in any industry.

INDIA

(Position as of December 31, 1996)

Status Under IMF Articles of Agreement

Article VIII   Date of acceptance: August 20, 1994.

Exchange Arrangement

Currency   The currency of India is the Indian rupee.

Exchange rate structure   Unitary.

Classification

Independent floating   The exchange rate of the rupee is determined in the interbank market. The Reserve Bank of India (RBI) purchases spot U.S. dollars from authorized persons at their designated offices or branches at the rate determined on the basis of the market exchange rate.

Exchange tax   No.

Exchange subsidy   No.

Forward exchange market   Authorized dealers are allowed to deal forward in any permitted currency. Forward purchases or sales of foreign currencies against rupees with banks abroad are prohibited. The RBI has on occasion purchased or sold forward U.S. dollars. The RBI may enter into swap transactions, under which it buys spot U.S. dollars and sells forward for up to 6 months.

Official cover of forward operations   The Export Credit Guarantee Corporation of India, Ltd. (ECGC) provides protection against exchange fluctuation with respect to deferred receivables from the date of a bid up to 15 years after the award of a contract; exchange cover is offered in Australian dollars, deutsche mark, French francs, Japanese yen, pounds sterling, Swiss francs, U.A.E. dirhams, and U.S. dollars. For payments specified in other convertible currencies, cover is provided at the discretion of the ECGC.

Arrangements for Payments and Receipts

Prescription of currency requirements   For prescription of currency purposes, countries are divided into 2 groups:

(1) Member countries of the ACU (except Nepal). All payments on account of eligible current international transactions must be settled through the ACU arrangement, as are transactions effected on a deferred basis with the ACU countries. However, settlement of payments toward imports of sugar, fertilizer, and pulses from any of the ACU countries may be made outside the ACU mechanism in any permitted currency. Indian exporters are also permitted to accept payment in free foreign exchange in respect of their exports to ACU countries, provided such payment is voluntarily offered by the importer in the ACU country.

(2) The external group (all other countries). Payments to these countries may be made in Indian rupees to the account of a resident of any of these countries or in any permitted currency, and receipts from these countries may be obtained in Indian rupees from accounts maintained with an authorized dealer or in banks situated in any of these countries or in any permitted currency. Payments relating to current transactions financed with loans from international institutions are settled outside the ACU mechanism. However, special rules may apply with respect to exports under lines of credit extended by the government of India to the governments of certain foreign countries.

Payment arrangements

Regional arrangements   Yes.

Clearing agreements	Nepal is a member of the ACU, but the RBI does not deal in Nepalese rupees. The RBI stands ready to purchase and sell spot and sell forward currencies of the member countries of the ACU.

Administration of control

Exchange control authorities	Exchange control is administered by the RBI in accordance with the general policy laid down by the government in consultation with the RBI. Much of the routine work of exchange control is delegated to authorized dealers. Import and export licenses, where necessary, are issued by the Director General of Foreign Trade.

International security restrictions

In accordance with IMF Executive Board Decision No. 144-(52/51)	Yes.
In accordance with UN sanctions	Yes.
Payment arrears	No.

Controls on trade in gold (coins and/or bullion)

Controls on domestic ownership and/or trade	There are no restrictions on internal trade in gold. However, gold mines continue to sell gold to industrial users through the distribution network of the State Bank of India (SBI) as well as through market sales. Forward trading in gold or silver is prohibited.
Controls on external trade	Exports of gold in any form other than jewelry produced in India for exportation with a gold value not exceeding 10% of the total value, and jewelry constituting the personal effects of a traveler, subject to certain monetary limits, are prohibited unless effected by or on behalf of the monetary authorities. The net exportation of gold from India is not permitted. Exporters of jewelry may import their essential inputs such as gold with import licenses granted by the licensing authority. Under this scheme, the foreign buyer may supply gold or silver in advance and free of charge for the manufacture and ultimate export of gold or silver jewelry and articles thereof.
	Under the Gold Jewelry and Articles Export Promotion and Replenishment Scheme, exporters of gold jewelry and articles are entitled to replenishment of gold through the designated branches of the SBI, or any other agency nominated by the Ministry of Commerce, at a price indicated in the certificate issued by the SBI after the purchase of the gold. The Scheme is limited to exports that are supported by an irrevocable letter of credit, payment of cash on a delivery basis, or advance payment in foreign exchange. Exports of gold jewelry may also be allowed on a collection basis (documents against acceptance [DA]). The exporter has the option to obtain gold from the SBI in advance. On presentation of the required documents, the appropriate release order and gem replenishment license may be issued by the licensing authority, provided that the exporters satisfy value-added and other requirements under the Scheme.
	Special permission for imports of gold and silver is granted only in exceptional cases where either no foreign exchange transaction is involved or the metals are needed for a particular purpose. Special permission is also granted when the gold or silver is imported for processing and reexportation, and provided that payments for the importation will not be required, the entire quantity of metal imported will be reexported in the form of jewelry, and the value added will be repatriated to India in foreign exchange through an authorized dealer.

Controls on exports and imports of banknotes

On exports

Domestic currency	In general, the exportation of Indian currency notes and coins, except to Bhutan and Nepal, is prohibited. The exportation to Nepal of Indian currency notes in denominations higher than Rs 100 is also prohibited. However, resident Indians may take with them Indian currency notes not exceeding Rs 1,000 a person at any one time to countries other than Nepal when going abroad on a temporary visit.

Foreign currency	Authorized dealers, exchange bureaus, and authorized money changers are permitted to sell foreign currency notes and coins, up to the equivalent of Rs 100 to travelers going to Bangladesh and up to $2,000 or its equivalent a year to those going to other countries except Bhutan and Nepal. Nonresidents may take out the foreign currency that they brought in (and declared on entry if it exceeded $2,500), less the amounts sold to authorized dealers and authorized money changers in India.

On imports

Domestic currency	The importation of Indian currency notes and coins is prohibited. However, any person may bring in Indian currency notes (other than notes of denominations larger than Rs 100) from Nepal. Indian travelers may bring in up to Rs 1,000 a person if they previously took out this amount when traveling abroad on a temporary visit.
Foreign currency	Foreign currency notes may be brought in without limit, provided that the total amount is declared to the customs authorities upon arrival if the value of foreign notes, coins, and traveler's checks exceeds $10,000 or its equivalent and/or if the aggregate value of foreign currency notes brought in at any one time exceeds $2,500 or its equivalent.

Resident Accounts

Eligibility to hold accounts	The accounts of Indians and of Bhutanese and Nepalese nationals residing in Bhutan and Nepal, as well as the accounts of offices and branches of Indian, Bhutanese, and Nepalese firms, companies, or other organizations in Bhutan and Nepal, are treated as resident accounts. However, residents of Nepal obtain their foreign exchange requirements from the Nepal Rastra Bank. Juridical and natural persons are eligible.
Foreign exchange accounts permitted	Yes.
Held domestically	Yes.
Held abroad	These accounts are permitted, but prior approval is required.

Nonresident Accounts

Eligibility to hold accounts	Accounts related to all foreign countries other than Bhutan and Nepal are treated as nonresident accounts. Juridical and natural persons are eligible.
Foreign exchange accounts permitted	(1) "Ordinary nonresident rupee accounts" of individuals or firms may be credited with: (i) the proceeds of remittances received in any permitted currency from abroad through normal banking channels, balances sold by the account holder in any permitted currency during his or her visit to India, or balances transferred from rupee accounts of nonresident banks; and (ii) legitimate dues paid in rupees by the account holder in India. For credits exceeding Rs 10,000, the authorized dealers are required to ascertain the bona fide nature of the transaction before crediting the account. Authorized dealers may debit the ordinary nonresident rupee accounts for all local disbursements, including investments in India that are covered by the general or special permission of the RBI.

(2) "Nonresident external rupee (NRER) accounts" may be opened for nonresidents of Indian nationality or origin or for overseas companies and partnership firms of which at least 60% is owned by nonresidents of Indian nationality or origin. In addition to authorized dealers holding licenses under the 1973 Foreign Exchange Regulation Act, some state cooperative banks and certain urban cooperative banks and scheduled commercial banks not holding such licenses have also been permitted by the RBI to open and maintain nonresident rupee accounts, subject to certain conditions. Such accounts may also be opened for eligible persons during temporary visits to India against the tender of foreign currency traveler's checks, notes, or coins. They may be credited with new funds remitted through banking channels from the country of residence of the account holder or from any country. They may also be credited with the proceeds of foreign currency traveler's checks, personal checks, and drafts in the name of the

account holder, as well as foreign currency notes and coins tendered by the account holder while in India and with income on authorized investments. The transfer of funds from other NRER accounts or the foreign currency nonresident (FCNR) accounts is also allowed for bona fide personal purposes. The accounts may be debited for disbursement in India and for transfers abroad. Debiting is also permitted for any other transaction if covered under general or special permission granted by the RBI. Balances may also be used to purchase foreign currency; rupee traveler's checks or traveler's letters of credit for the use of the account holder, his or her family and dependents; and, in the case of corporate entities, for the use of directors and employees. Investments in the shares of Indian companies, in partnership firms and the like, or in immovable property may be made with the approval of the RBI. Interest on deposits in nonresident external accounts in any bank in India is exempt from the personal income tax, although juridical persons are not entitled to this exemption. Interest earnings are transferable. The balances held in such accounts by natural and juridical persons are exempt from the wealth tax; gifts to close relatives in India from the balances in these accounts are exempt from the gift tax.

(3) "FCNR accounts" denominated in deutsche mark, Japanese yen, pounds sterling, or U.S. dollars may be held in the form of term deposits by persons of Indian nationality or origin and by overseas companies as specified above. These accounts may be credited with amounts received through normal banking channels, including interest earnings. Balances may be repatriated at any time without reference to the RBI. Balances may also be used for the purposes for which debits to NRER accounts are allowed. The exchange rate guarantees (issued by the RBI) on existing deposits under a previous FCNR scheme will remain in effect until the deposits mature. The current FCNR accounts operate in the same manner as the old FCNR accounts, except that the issuing bank (not the RBI) provides the exchange rate guarantee on deposit balances.

(4) "Nonresident (nonrepatriable) rupee deposit accounts" may be opened by nonresident Indian nationals, overseas corporate bodies predominantly owned by nonresident Indian nationals, and foreign citizens of non-Indian origin (except Pakistani and Bangladeshi nationals). These accounts may be opened with funds in freely convertible foreign exchange remitted from abroad or funds transferred from existing NRER or FCNR accounts. The funds in these accounts may not be repatriated abroad at any time. Since October 1994, the transfer abroad of accruing interest has been permitted.

(5) "Foreign currency ordinary (nonrepatriable) deposit accounts" may be maintained by nonresidents. These accounts may be denominated in U.S. dollars and credited with funds received from abroad in freely convertible foreign exchange, or transferred from existing NRER or FCNR accounts. On maturity of deposits, the rupee value of the principal and accrued interest may be credited to the ordinary nonresident rupee accounts of the depositor.

Domestic currency accounts	Nonresident (nonrepatriable) rupee deposit accounts may be opened with funds in freely convertible foreign exchange remitted from abroad or funds transferred from existing NRER or FCNR accounts. The funds in these accounts may not be repatriated abroad at any time. Since October 1994, the transfer abroad of accruing interest has been permitted.
Convertible into foreign currency	Yes.
Blocked accounts	No.

Imports and Import Payments

Foreign exchange budget	No.
Import licenses and other nontariff measures	
Positive list	The importation of certain specified precious, semiprecious, and other stones; safety, security, and related items; seeds, plants, and animals; insecticides and pesticides; drugs and pharmaceuticals; chemicals and allied items relating to the small-scale sector; most consumer goods and certain other items is restricted.

Negative list	Importation of tallow, fat and/or oils rendered or unrendered of any animal origin, animal rennet, wild animals (including their parts and products), and ivory is prohibited. Imports from Fiji and Iraq are also prohibited.
Import taxes and/or tariffs	No.
State import monopoly	Certain specified types of petroleum products, fertilizers, edible and nonedible oils, seeds, and cereals are canalized for import through the state trading enterprises, i.e., Indian Oil Corporation Ltd., Minerals and Metals Trading Corporation of India Ltd., State Trading Corporation of India Ltd., and the Food Corporation of India.

Exports and Export Proceeds

Repatriation requirements	Proceeds must be repatriated by the due date of receipt or within 6 months of shipment, whichever is earlier. Regarding exports made to Indian-owned warehouses abroad established with the permission of the RBI, a period of up to 15 months is allowed for the realization of export proceeds. Exporters are required to obtain permission from the RBI through authorized dealers in the event that the export value is not realized within the prescribed period. The RBI also administers a scheme under which engineering goods (capital goods and consumer durables) may be exported under deferred credit arrangements, so that the full export value is paid in installments over more than 6 months.
Surrender requirements	Exporters are permitted to retain up to 35% of foreign exchange receipts in foreign currency accounts with banks in India. In the case of 100% export-oriented units, units in export processing zones, and units in hardware/software technology parts, up to 50% of foreign exchange receipts may be retained.
Export licenses	Licenses are required for exports of mineral ores and concentrates and chemicals, including those specified in the UN Chemical Weapons Convention.
Without quotas	n.a.
With quotas	n.a.
Export taxes	Yes.
Taxes collected through the exchange system	No.

Payments for Invisible Transactions and Current Transfers

Controls on these payments	There are no controls on payments for freight and insurance and unloading and storage.
Administrative expenses	n.a.
Commissions	n.a.
Interest payments	Remittances are allowed after all taxes and other liabilities have been paid.
Prior approval	Yes.
Quantitative limits	Yes.
Indicative limits/bona fide test	Yes.
Profit/dividends	Remittances are allowed subject to certain conditions and provided that all current taxes and other liabilities have been cleared.
Prior approval	Yes.
Payments for travel	
Prior approval	Yes.
Quantitative limits	Up to $2,000 a person a year may be released by authorized dealers for 1 or more trips abroad, except visits to Bhutan and Nepal. The limits for various categories of business

travel are as follows: (1) the per diem for senior executives is $500 and for others, $350; (2) Indian firms participating in trade fairs/exhibitions and private printers and publishers wishing to participate in overseas book fairs and exhibitions abroad can obtain up to $20,000 or its equivalent; (3) the limit for remittances by Indian shipping companies toward fees for solicitors and adjusters is $10,000; and (4) the limit for remittances to foreign data service vendors for the use of international data bases is $10,000.

Indicative limits/bona fide test	Yes.
Medical costs	
Prior approval	n.a.
Quantitative limits	Yes.
Indicative limits/bona fide test	Yes.
Study abroad costs	n.a.
Subscriptions and membership fees	n.a.
Consulting/legal fees	n.a.
Foreign workers' wages	
Prior approval	Yes.
Quantitative limits	Foreign workers, except those from China, Pakistan, and South Africa, are permitted to make reasonable remittances to their own countries to pay insurance premiums, to support their families, and for other expenses. Authorized dealers may allow such remittances of up to 75% of the net income of foreign workers, provided that the workers hold valid employment visas.
Indicative limits/bona fide test	Yes.
Pensions	
Prior approval	Yes.
Quantitative limits	Yes.
Indicative limits/bona fide test	n.a.
Gambling/prize earnings	n.a.
Family maintenance/alimony	n.a.
Credit card use abroad	n.a.

Proceeds from Invisible Transactions and Current Transfers

Repatriation requirements	Proceeds must be repatriated.
Surrender requirements	Up to 25% of receipts may be retained.

Capital Transactions

Controls on capital and money market instruments

On capital market securities

Purchase locally by nonresidents — Foreign institutional investors (FIIs) are permitted to make investments in all securities traded on the primary and secondary markets, including equity and other securities, and instruments of companies listed on the stock exchange in India. FIIs are also allowed to invest in dated government securities, either on behalf of clients or using proprietary funds. FIIs are required to register initially with the Securities and Exchange Board of

India (SEBI) and with the RBI. There is no restriction on the value of investments by FIIs in the primary and secondary markets, but investment in debt instruments may not exceed 30% of total investment. Portfolio investments in primary or secondary markets are subject to a ceiling of 5% of the issued share capital for individual FII holdings and 24% of issued share capital for the total holdings of all registered FIIs in any one company, with the exception of: (1) foreign investments under financial collaboration, which are permitted up to 51%; and (2) investments through offshore single and regional funds, global depository receipts, and convertibles in the Euromarket.

Sale or issue locally by nonresidents

Nonresidents are not permitted to issue securities in the local market. In regard to securities of Indian companies held by nonresidents, transfer to a resident is required to be confirmed by the RBI. Transfer of sale proceeds is permitted subject to tax, provided no restrictions were imposed on the repatriation of sale proceeds while approving the original investment. Transfer between two nonresidents does not require such confirmation, but a nonresident transferee requires permission for the purchase of shares of an Indian company.

Purchase abroad by residents

RBI permission is required for acquiring, holding, or disposing of any foreign security. If the acquisition is permitted, transfer of the needed funds from India is also permitted. In the case of a sale of foreign securities, the repatriation of sale proceeds to India is required, unless otherwise specified. Indians who have returned to India after a minimum continuous stay of 1 year abroad have been exempted from the requirement of obtaining RBI permission for continuing to hold securities already purchased prior to their return to India out of incomes earned by them while abroad. They are also free to utilize sales proceeds of such securities for acquisition of further securities without permission of the RBI.

Sale or issue abroad by residents

The same regulations as for purchases abroad by residents apply.

On money market instruments

Purchase locally by nonresidents

These transactions require RBI approval.

Sale or issue locally by nonresidents

These transactions require RBI approval.

Purchase abroad by residents

Residents are not permitted to purchase such instruments abroad without authorization of the RBI.

Sale or issue abroad by residents

These transactions are not permitted.

On collective investment securities

Resident companies are not permitted to issue any security to nonresidents without approval of the RBI.

Purchase locally by nonresidents

These transactions require RBI prior approval.

Sale or issue locally by nonresidents

Issue of collective investment securities by nonresidents on local markets in India is not permitted. Nonresidents can also acquire any foreign security without authorization from the RBI.

Purchase abroad by residents

These transactions require RBI prior approval.

Sale or issue abroad by residents

These transactions require permission from the RBI; the Unit Trust of India has been granted permission for issuing certain securities abroad.

Controls on derivatives and other instruments

Purchase locally by nonresidents

Resident companies are not permitted to issue rupee-based derivatives and other instruments in India.

Sale or issue locally by nonresidents

These transactions are not allowed.

Purchase abroad by residents

Authorized dealers are allowed to purchase hedge instruments for corporate clients.

Sale or issue abroad by residents

These transactions require RBI permission.

Controls on credit operations

Commercial credits

By residents to nonresidents

A commercial credit of up to 6 months can be allowed regarding exports on DA terms. Contracts for exports involving payments to be realized beyond the normal period of 6 months are treated as deferred payment exports. Such exports are permitted keeping in mind the credit terms offered, commodity to be exported, and other related considerations. This applies to turnkey/construction/service contracts undertaken by Indian exporter on credit terms. Under the Buyer's Credit Scheme, the EXIM Bank offers credits to foreign buyers in connection with the export of capital goods and turnkey projects in India in participation with commercial banks in India. These are considered by EXIM Bank depending upon the creditworthiness, standing and financial position of the overseas borrower, economic viability of the project, standing of the Indian exporter, etc.

To residents from nonresidents

Short-term loans and credits maturing within 1 year are considered by RBI on their terms and conditions comparable with the terms offered in overseas markets. Proposals for raising foreign currency loans and credits, i.e., buyer's credits, supplier's credits, or lines of credit by firms, companies, or lending institutions, for financing the cost of goods, technology, or for any other purpose, require approval from the Ministry of Finance (MOF).

Financial credits

By residents to nonresidents

These transactions require prior permission from the RBI.

To residents from nonresidents

The contracting of all foreign currency loans and credits secured from nonresident persons and companies (including banks) as well as repayment of such loans and credits, and payments of interest and other charges on such loans require prior permission from the RBI. Borrowing proposals, except for loans less than 1 year, must be cleared by the MOF before they may be approved by the RBI.

Guarantees, sureties, and financial backup facilities

By residents to nonresidents

These transactions require authorization from the RBI.

To residents from nonresidents

The RBI has permitted authorized dealers to grant loans to residents against guarantees from nonresidents, subject, inter alia, to the condition that no direct or indirect payment abroad by way of guarantee commission or otherwise is made.

Controls on direct investment

Outward direct investment

Investments are subject to approval of the RBI. Proposals for participation in overseas joint ventures, the setting up of wholly owned subsidiaries or opening of offices abroad that involve remittance of cash, export of goods from India, etc., are considered in light of the financial position and track record of the applicant Indian company, the past export performance, and the benefits likely to accrue in terms of foreign exchange earnings by way of exports, technology transfer, profits, dividends, and so forth.

Inward direct investment

Foreign equity up to 74% is permitted by the RBI in specified high-priority industries on an automatic basis. The RBI also allows foreign equity holdings up to 51% in trading companies primarily engaged in export activities. Other applications require clearance from the government of India. A liberal policy is followed for investments in India by nonresidents of Indian origin or overseas corporate bodies predominantly owned by such persons. Foreign companies are also permitted to set up liaison offices in India for carrying on liaison activities, provided their entire expenses are remitted from abroad. Applications for investment in areas that do not fall within the authority of the RBI but that are covered by the foreign investment policy are approved by the Foreign Investment Promotion Board (FIPB). Such investments may be approved up to 100% of capital on a case-by-case basis. The Ministry of Industry is the relevant agency for all issues related to foreign direct investment, including approvals. In the case of coal, hydro, and nonconventional energy-based power projects, the Power Ministry may grant automatic approvals of up to 100% foreign equity under certain conditions. Nonresidents, noncitizens, and nonbank companies not incorporated under Indian law must have permission from the RBI to initiate, expand, or continue any business activity in India and to hold or acquire shares of any company carrying on a trading, commercial, or industrial activity in India.

Nonresidents of Indian nationality or origin may invest freely in any public or private limited company or in any partnership or proprietary concern engaged in any activity except agricultural or plantation activities and real estate business (excluding real estate development, such as construction of houses, etc.), provided that (1) funds for investment either are remitted from abroad through normal banking channels or are drawn from their nonresident accounts; (2) repatriation of the capital invested or the profits and dividends arising therefrom will not be requested; and (3) overall limits on holdings of shares and convertible debentures bought through the stock exchange by nonresident Indians (see below) are adhered to.

Overseas companies, societies, and partnership firms of which at least 60% is owned by nonresidents of Indian nationality or origin, and overseas trusts in which at least 60% of the beneficial interest is irrevocably held by nonresident Indians are also allowed to invest in any public or private limited company in accordance with the above provisions.

Nonresident Indians and overseas companies, as defined above, may use funds derived from fresh remittances or held in their nonresident (external) or foreign currency (nonresident) accounts to:

(1) make portfolio investments with repatriation benefits up to 1% of the capital, provided that their total holdings of shares and convertible debentures held on either a repatriable or nonrepatriable basis by all nonresident investors do not exceed 5%, or 24%, in the case a company so decides through a general body resolution, of the paid-up capital of the company concerned, or of the total paid-up value of each series of convertible debentures issued by the company concerned;

(2) invest freely in national savings certificates with full repatriation benefits;

(3) invest up to 40% of the new equity capital issued by a company setting up industrial manufacturing projects, hospitals (including diagnostic centers), hotels of at least 3-star category, and shipping, software, and oil exploration services with repatriation rights for capital and income, subject to deduction of applicable Indian taxes;

(4) place up to 100% in new investments, including expansion of existing industrial undertakings in specified priority industries with free repatriation of such investments. Foreign direct investment is permitted in trading companies. Trading companies must be registered with the Ministry of Commerce and must obtain a certificate of their status as either export, trading, star trading, or super star trading house before applying to the RBI for remittances or dividends. The RBI has the authority to permit foreign investment of up to 51% of the paid-up capital of such Indian companies. A higher percentage, up to 100%, is considered for approval by the FIPB, provided that the funding company is primarily engaged in exports. Existing joint-venture companies may raise the ratio of foreign equity shares to 51% of their capital through expansion of their capital base or through preferential allocation of shares to the foreign investor. Firms in certain manufacturing industries and tourist industries obtain RBI automatic approval for the expansion;

(5) invest on a nonrepatriable basis in money market mutual funds (only NRIs), subject to RBI approval; and

(6) invest up to 51% of equity on a repatriable basis in unlisted companies in all industries except those mentioned in Annex III of the Industrial Policy.

Controls on liquidation of direct investment

Sale of shares, securities, and immovable property requires approval of the RBI. Repatriation of after-tax sale proceeds is generally permitted, provided no condition about nonrepatriation was imposed when approving the original investment.

Controls on real estate transactions

These transactions require RBI permission.

Purchase abroad by residents	Indians who have returned to India after a minimum continuous stay of 1 year abroad are, however, permitted to hold immovable property acquired with funds earned while they were abroad. They are also free to dispose of such properties or acquire new properties from the sale proceeds of such properties.
Purchase locally by nonresidents	Nonresident Indians and overseas companies (predominantly owned by nonresident Indians) may invest in companies engaged in real estate development (e.g., construction of houses, etc.); up to 100% of new investments may have to be locked in for a period of 3 years for disinvestment. After 3 years, remittances of disinvestment will be allowed up to the original investment in foreign exchange. In case of overseas corporate bodies, profits may be repatriated up to 16%.
Sale locally by nonresidents	Repatriation of after-tax sale proceeds is generally permitted, provided no condition about nonrepatriation was imposed while approving the original investment.

Provisions specific to commercial banks and other credit institutions

Borrowing abroad	Borrowing is subject to approval by the government of India, the MOF, and the Department of Economic Affairs. Authorized dealers may avail themselves of loans, overdrafts, and other types of fund-based credit facilities from their overseas branches and correspondents up to $500,000 or its equivalent for meeting the requirements of normal exchange activities. Loans or overdrafts in excess of this limit may be obtained solely for the purpose of replenishing the dealers' rupee resources in India without prior approval from the RBI. Repayment of such borrowings requires prior approval from the RBI or may be accorded only when the debtor bank has no outstanding borrowings in India from the RBI or any other bank or financial institution and is clear of all money market borrowings for a period of at least 4 weeks before the repayment.
Maintenance of accounts abroad	Authorized dealers may maintain balances at levels that are commensurate with their normal business needs. In all other cases (e.g., airlines and shipping companies), specific permission by the RBI is required.
Lending to nonresidents (financial or commercial credits)	Lending is subject to individual RBI approval. However, authorized dealers have been permitted to invest their temporary surplus funds in foreign treasury bills and make deposits with banks abroad.
Lending locally in foreign exchange	Banks may lend to residents to meet genuine foreign exchange requirements toward preshipment credit in foreign currency for financing domestic inputs or for granting foreign currency loans to FCNR bank account holders.
Purchase of locally issued securities denominated in foreign exchange	No scheme is in place allowing for these transactions.
Differential treatment of nonresident deposit accounts and/or deposit accounts in foreign exchange	
Reserve requirements	While resident deposit liabilities are subject to statutory reserve requirements, nonresident deposits under FCNR (banks) and nonresident (nonrepatriable) rupee deposit schemes are completely exempted, and liabilities under the NRER scheme are subject to concessional reserve requirements.
Interest rate controls	While interest on resident deposits for maturities of over 2 years has been completely deregulated, interest rates on FCNR (banks), which need to be aligned to the international rates, are decided by the RBI. Interest rates on nonresident (nonrepatriable) rupee deposit schemes are, however, deregulated for all maturities.
Credit controls	n.a.
Open foreign exchange position limits	Banks are required to maintain on an ongoing basis tier I capital at 5% of the open position limit approved by the RBI, and the overall open position limit should have a reasonable relation to the capital of the bank.

Changes During 1996

Capital transactions

February 28. The RBI allowed nonresident Indians (NRIs) to invest on a nonrepatriable basis in money market mutual funds subject to RBI approval. NRIs and overseas corporate bodies are allowed to invest on a repatriable basis up to 51% of equity in unlisted companies in all industries except those mentioned in Annex III of the Industrial Policy.

April 3. The uniform limit on commercial banks' foreign exchange exposure was replaced by individual limits to be approved by the RBI.

August 5. Authorized dealers in foreign exchange were allowed to offer hedge instruments to Indian companies without prior approval.

August 21. The Power Ministry granted automatic approvals of up to 100% foreign equity to coal, hydro, and nonconventional energy-based power projects under certain conditions.

October 3. Authorized dealers were allowed to on-lend foreign currency funds obtained under the FCNR(B) scheme to the domestic market. They were also allowed to take cross-currency positions in their foreign exchange holdings, subject to certain conditions.

November 9. FIIs were allowed to invest up to 100% of their funds in corporate debt.

INDONESIA

(Position as of April 30, 1997)

Status Under IMF Articles of Agreement

Article VIII	Date of acceptance: May 7, 1988.

Exchange Arrangement

Currency	The currency of Indonesia is the rupiah.
Other legal tender	Two commemorative gold coins are also legal tender.
Exchange rate structure	Unitary.
Classification	
Managed floating	The exchange rate is determined by Bank Indonesia (BI) under a system of managed float, under which the bank announces a daily "conversion rate band" (for official transactions with foreign exchange banks, government, as well as with supranational institutions), and an "intervention band" consisting of buying and selling rates that are computed on the basis of a basket of currencies. The conversion rates are set so that the buying and selling rates are within 2% of the previous day's closing spot market rate. The spread of the intervention band was increased on June 13, 1996, to Rp 118 (5%) from Rp 66, and to Rp 192 (approximately 8%) on September 10, 1996. The U.S. dollar is the intervention currency.
Exchange tax	No.
Exchange subsidy	No.
Forward exchange market	Forward and swap transactions are conducted at rates fixed bilaterally between the BI and the banks concerned.
Official cover of forward operations	Yes.

Arrangements for Payments and Receipts

Prescription of currency requirements	No.
Payment arrangements	
Barter agreements and open accounts	There are countertrade arrangements as part of bids for government-sponsored construction or procurement projects, whose import component is valued at more than Rp 500 million.
Administration of control	
Exchange control authorities	In general, there are no restrictions on foreign exchange transactions. However, the Commercial Offshore Loan Team (COLT) has the authority to institute regulations regarding commercial offshore borrowing.
International security restrictions	Restrictions against Israel are in place.
In accordance with UN sanctions	Restrictions against countries on which the UN has imposed a trade embargo are in effect.
Payment arrears	
Controls on trade in gold (coins and/or bullion)	
Controls on external trade	Travelers may freely take out up to Rp 65,000 a person in Indonesian commemorative gold and silver coins issued in August 1970, and up to Rp 130,000 a person in gold and

silver coins issued in October 1974; amounts in excess of these limits require the prior approval of the BI. Gold may be imported freely. Imports are subject to a levy of Rp 25 per $1.

Controls on exports and imports of banknotes

On exports

Domestic currency

Travelers may take out Indonesian notes and coins up to Rp 50,000 a person; repatriation in excess of this amount requires prior approval from the BI or must be done through specified banks.

On imports

Domestic currency

Travelers may bring in Indonesian notes and coins up to Rp 50,000 a person; repatriation in excess of this amount requires prior approval from the BI or must be done through specified banks.

Resident Accounts

Eligibility to hold accounts

Juridical and natural persons are eligible.

Foreign exchange accounts permitted

Yes.

Held domestically

Only checking and time deposit accounts are permitted.

Held abroad

Yes.

Accounts in domestic currency convertible into foreign currency

No checks may be drawn on foreign currency accounts.

Nonresident Accounts

Eligibility to hold accounts

Juridical and natural persons are eligible.

Foreign exchange accounts permitted

Only checking and time deposit accounts are permitted. No checks may be drawn on foreign currency accounts.

Domestic currency accounts

Yes.

Convertible into foreign currency

Yes.

Blocked accounts

No.

Imports and Import Payments

Foreign exchange budget

No.

Financing requirements for imports

Requirements in general are set by commercial banks on the basis of their assessment. However, a 100% face value of red clause letters of credit (LCs) and advance payments should be guaranteed.

Documentation requirements for release of foreign exchange for imports

Domiciliation requirements

Cement-asbestos sheets, dry batteries, steel slabs, low-voltage electric cord, and electric light bulbs are subject to quality control.

Preshipment inspection

Imports are subject to preshipment inspection in the exporting country by agencies designated by the government that bears inspection expenses. Following inspection, the PT Surveyor Indonesia in Jakarta is required to issue on behalf of its agency in the exporting country a survey report (LPS) specifying the type, quality, quantity, and estimated cost of the goods; the applicable tariff code; freight charges; import duties; and value-added taxes. The LPS must be sent by the agency in Jakarta directly to the bank that has opened LCs or, for imports not covered by LCs, to the bank designated by the importer. In April 1997, the preshipment inspection was changed to inspection upon arrival, conducted by the customs. Customs is required to issue the LPS that was previously issued by Surveyor Indonesia.

Letters of credit

Rules for import payments were revised on June 14, 1996: payments may now be undertaken using LCs opened at foreign exchange banks, as well as by other standard methods. Payments must be due within 360 days.

Import licenses and other nontariff measures

Negative list

Imports from Israel and the countries against which the United Nations has imposed a trade embargo are prohibited, as are imports from all sources of most secondhand goods and of certain products. In addition, secondhand engines and their parts and other capital goods may be imported by industrial firms for their own use or for the reconditioning of their industry, in accordance with the guidelines of the Ministry of Trade (MOT) and of Industry. Certain categories of agricultural imports, including foodstuffs, beverages, and fruits, may be imported only by registered importers designated by the MOT. The procurement policies of companies approved for the importation of fruit, alcoholic beverages, and chickens are evaluated annually by the government, although explicit quantitative restrictions are not placed on these products.

Open general licenses

There is a registry of authorized importers that includes only Indonesian nationals, although foreign investors are permitted to import the items required for their own projects. Although all imports into Indonesia are subject to licensing requirements, most are classified under the nonresident license (also called general importer license).

Import taxes and/or tariffs

Certain products are granted preferential duties within the framework of the AFTA and the WTO.

Taxes collected through the exchange system

Import taxes are collected through foreign exchange banks authorized by the Ministry of Finance (MOF).

State import monopoly

Imports of certain goods remain restricted to approved importers, most of which are state enterprises. Petramina has a monopoly on the importation of lubricating oil and lubricating fats, and Dahana on the importation of ammunition and explosive gelatin. The Board of Logistics has the sole right to import rice, fertilizer, and sugar. The monopoly rights of approved importers (sole agents) also remain in effect for the importation of certain heavy equipment and motor vehicles, although this right may be transferred to general importers. The importation of trucks is subject to restriction.

Exports and Export Proceeds

Repatriation requirements

No.

Surrender requirements

No.

Financing requirements

Exporters (and export suppliers) may sell their export proceeds to the BI. Exporters may discount export drafts with a remaining maturity of between 30 and 720 days. The BI accepts 5 currencies for rediscount (U.S. dollars, Japanese yen, deutsche marks, Singapore dollars, and Netherlands guilders), and uses SIBOR as the floating reference rate. The discount rate for special exporters (textiles, textile products, shoes, electronics, timber, rattan products, and leather goods) was reduced from 1% above SIBOR to SIBOR, and for general exporters from SIBOR plus 2% to SIBOR plus 1%. Drafts can be rediscounted in rupiah or dollars. The discount facility for export drafts may be used by suppliers of export-related products. Based on local LCs, suppliers of export-related goods can seek bank drafts and sell them to the BI, provided their remaining maturity is between 30 and 90 days. The discount rate for bank drafts is the BI's 3-month money market securities' cut-off rate minus 0.5%.

Documentation requirements

Letters of credit
Exports with sight LC conditions must be settled not later than 30 days from the date the exports are registered with the foreign exchange bank.

Domiciliation
Yes.

Preshipment inspection
Exports of rattan, leather, wood, and wood products must be examined before shipment. Quality controls are also maintained on fish, manioc (cassava), shrimp, coffee, tea, pepper, spices, vegetable oil, and cocoa beans.

Export licenses
Exports to Israel and the countries against which the UN has imposed a trade embargo are prohibited, as are exports to all countries of certain categories of unprocessed or low-quality rubber, brass and copper scrap (except from the island of Irian Jaya), iron scrap, steel scrap, and antiques of cultural value. Exporters are required to possess trade permits issued by the MOT.

Without quotas
Exports of certain domestically produced commodities must have prior authorization from the MOT in order to meet domestic demand and to encourage domestic processing of certain raw materials. Items affected by such controls include clove seeds, logs, fertilizer, cement, construction reinforcements of iron, automobile tires, paper, asphalt, stearin, cattle, salt, wheat flour, maize, soybeans, rice, copra, olein, raw rattan, meat, and all goods produced from subsidized raw materials. Concern about domestic price stability sometimes leads to suspension of exports of various items in this category.

With quotas
Manioc may be exported only by approved exporters. Textiles and textile products subject to import quotas in the consumer countries may be exported only by approved textile exporters, who may transfer their allocated quotas to other approved exporters through the Commodity Exchange Board.

Export taxes
Export taxes ranging from $250 to $4,800 per cubic meter are applied to sawed and processed timber. Exports of logs are subject to taxes ranging from $500 to $4,800 per cubic meter. Certain processed wood products are not taxed. Certain other products are subject to export taxes ranging from 5% to 30%.

Taxes collected through the exchange system
Taxes are collected through foreign exchange banks authorized by the MOF.

Payments for Invisible Transactions and Current Transfers

Controls on these payments
No.

Proceeds from Invisible Transactions and Current Transfers

Repatriation requirements
No.

Surrender requirements
No.

Capital Transactions

Controls on capital and money market instruments

On capital market securities

Purchase locally by nonresidents
The purchase of shares is limited to a maximum of 49% of total shares issued by an individual company listed on the Indonesian Stock Exchange.

Sale or issue locally by nonresidents
The Capital Market Act (1995) does not differentiate issuers by nationality. Both resident or nonresident issuers have to comply with the public offering requirements, one of which is that issuers must be Indonesian legal entities. There is no explicit restriction on nonresidents on public offering of securities in the Indonesian market.

Sale or issue abroad by residents	No restriction applies as long as the shares are not listed on the Indonesian Stock Exchange. If those securities are listed on the Indonesian Stock Exchange, they initially should comply with the Capital Market Act and with the requirement on the maximum percentage of foreign ownership of shares. However, Indonesian companies do not issue shares but rather American depository receipts in the U.S. capital market and global depository receipts on the London Stock Exchange.

On money market instruments

Sale or issue locally by nonresidents	These transactions are prohibited.
Sale or issue abroad by residents	Banks require approval from the COLT for issuance of instruments with maturities over 2 years or for amounts exceeding $20 million a year a creditor; however, total issuances should not exceed 30% of the bank's capital.

On collective investment securities

Purchase locally by nonresidents	No person may purchase more than 1% of any fund.

Controls on derivatives and other instruments	Derivative transactions other than those associated with foreign exchange and interest rates are prohibited. However, derivative transactions in equities are only allowed with prior permission from the BI on a case-by-case basis.
Purchase abroad by residents	Banks are obliged to enter into a written agreement with their clients and explain the risks involved. Losses over 10% of banks' capital must be reported to the BI.
Sale or issue abroad by residents	Same regulations as for purchases abroad by residents apply.

Controls on credit operations

Commercial credits

By residents to nonresidents	In general, there are no restrictions on the granting of credit by residents (excluding banks) to nonresident entities.
To residents from nonresidents	Resident entities, especially nonbank private sectors, may borrow from nonresidents; however, they have to submit periodic reports to the COLT of the BI on their borrowing. The following are subject to authorization by the COLT: (1) borrowings related to development projects using nonrecourse, limited recourse, advance payment, trustee borrowing, leasing, and similar financing; (2) borrowings related to development projects with financing based on build-operate-transfer, build-and-transfer, and similar schemes; and (3) borrowings related to the government or a state company (including the State Bank of Pertamina), including in the form of government equity participation, guarantee for provision of feed stock supply, and guarantee for products offtaker.

Financial credits

By residents to nonresidents	In general, there are no restrictions on the granting of credit by residents (excluding banks) to nonresident entities.
To residents from nonresidents	Yes.

Guarantees, sureties, and financial backup facilities

By residents to nonresidents	Banks are allowed to provide sureties and guarantees to nonresident entities only under the following conditions: (1) when there is sufficient contraguarantee from bona fide overseas banks (excluding overseas branches from the relevant bank); and (2) when there is a cash deposit valued 100% of the guarantee granted.

Controls on direct investment

Inward direct investment	Several sectors are restricted: (1) foreign investment companies in infrastructure projects such as seaports, generation, transmission and distribution of electricity for public use,

telecommunications, shipping, airlines, potable water supply, public railways, and nuclear electric power generation should be established by way of joint venture between foreign and Indonesian partners, and the share of Indonesian partners should be at least 5% of the total capital issued at the outset of the company; and (2) a foreign investment company may be established as a straight investment, which means that 100% of the shares may be owned by a foreign citizen and/or entities. However, some of the company's shares must be sold to an Indonesian citizen and/or entities through direct placement and/or indirectly through the domestic capital market no later than 15 years after commencement of commercial operations.

Foreign ownership of direct investments must begin to be divested by the eleventh year of production. For investments above $50 million, divestment of 50% must be completed within 20 years. For smaller investments, the divestment requirement is less stringent.

All foreign enterprises are eligible to receive preferential customs duty treatment for imports of required raw materials for the first 2 years of production activity. Raw materials may be imported with no time limit. In addition, an enterprise exporting more than 65% of its production is free to hire foreign experts as needed to maintain its export commitments.

Controls on liquidation of direct investment

Investors are granted the right to repatriate capital, to transfer profits (after settlement of taxes and financial obligations in Indonesia), and to make transfers relating to expenses connected with the employment of foreign nationals in Indonesia and relating to depreciation allowances. The law provides that no transfer permit shall be issued for capital repatriation as long as investment benefits from tax relief are being received; at present, however, foreign payments do not require a transfer permit.

Controls on real estate transactions

Purchase locally by nonresidents

According to Agrarian Law (1960), nonresidents are only allowed to buy land with the land title status "the right to use of land (*Hak Pakai*)," but since the land title of real estate in Indonesia is "the right to build on land (HGB)," they are not allowed to buy real estate. Nonresidents, however, are permitted to engage in inward direct investment in local real estate.

Sale locally by nonresidents

Yes.

Provisions specific to commercial banks and other credit institutions

Borrowing abroad

The COLT supervises all foreign commercial loan transactions. COLT's prior approval is required before any public enterprise, commercial bank, or public sector body may accept a loan from abroad. Resident banks or credit institutions, specifically the ones that deal with international trade and finance activities, are allowed to borrow abroad within limits. An annual borrowing ceiling is imposed by the BI for foreign commercial borrowing of more than 2 years' maturity. In addition, the prospective borrowers obtain COLT decisions for queuing on the international capital market before soliciting for such borrowings. In addition, banks may receive foreign commercial borrowing with maturities of no more than 2 years on a bilateral basis without prior approval from the BI, but the banks should maintain the total amount of such borrowings to a maximum of 30% of their capital. Trade financing, such as issuance of LCs, red clause LCs, supplier's and buyer's credits with maturities not exceeding 1 year and amounts of less than $20 million, are not considered borrowings that require approval from the COLT. Foreign commercial borrowings received by financial institutions, such as leasing companies, factoring companies, and consumer financing companies, may not exceed 5 times the company's net worth less its equity share.

Lending to nonresidents (financial or commercial credits)

Banks are not allowed to grant loans, or financial or commercial credits, in either rupiah or foreign exchange, to nonresidents, including those with authorization from residents to obtain credit.

Lending locally in foreign exchange

Banks are permitted to lend locally in foreign exchange, subject to the requirement that 80% of the foreign exchange loans must be provided for export activity. Banks can also purchase locally issued securities denominated in foreign exchange, subject to the requirement that the securities must be investment grade and should not be issued by their groups. To do this, banks should take into account other exchange regulations, namely the regulation on net open position (NOP) aimed at prudential control, with the limits as follows: the average of total NOP, both on and off balance sheet, in a week must not exceed 25% of the bank's capital and the average NOP off balance sheet in a week must not exceed 25% of the bank's capital.

Purchase of locally issued securities denominated in foreign exchange

This is, however, limited by open position limits.

Differential treatment of nonresident deposit accounts and/or deposit accounts in foreign exchange

Interest rate controls

Banks are free to set their interest rates on both deposits and loans. In the case of taxes, revenues gained from interest of nonresident deposit accounts are taxed at 20% or at a percentage stipulated on the Tax Agreement between the government of Indonesia and the government of a nonresident entity, while the revenues gained from interest of resident deposit accounts are taxed at 15%.

Credit controls

Foreign exchange banks are required to allocate at least 50% of all foreign exchange credits to export-oriented businesses that earn foreign exchange.

Open foreign exchange position limits

The limits are:

(1) the average total NOP, both on and off balance sheet, in a week must not exceed 25% of the bank's capital; and

(2) the average NOP off balance sheet in a week must not exceed 25% of the bank's capital.

Provisions specific to institutional investors

Insurance and reinsurance companies licensed in Indonesia are not allowed to invest abroad except for private placement in companies conducting insurance business overseas, such as insurance companies, reinsurance companies, insurance brokers, loss adjusters, etc. Indonesian mutual funds are prohibited from investing abroad.

Limits (max.) on portfolio invested abroad

Liabilities denominated in foreign currency of insurance and reinsurance companies exceeding assets denominated in foreign currency shall not be more than 10% of shareholders' equity.

Currency matching regulations on assets/liabilities composition

n.a.

Other controls imposed by securities laws

Foreign investors as a group may purchase up to 49% of the authorized and outstanding shares of an Indonesian company that has had a public offering.

Changes During 1996

Exchange arrangements

June 13. The intervention band was widened to Rp 118 (5%).

September 10. The intervention band was widened to Rp 192 (8%).

Imports and import payments

June 14. Import payments were allowed using LCs opened in foreign exchange banks. Payments are due within 360 days.

Exports and export proceeds

December 31. The discount facility for export drafts was extended to suppliers of export-related products and the discount rate was reduced. Exporters (and export suppliers) may sell their export proceeds to the BI. Exporters may discount export drafts with a remaining maturity of between 30 and 720 days. The BI accepts 5 currencies for rediscount (U.S. dollars, Japanese yen, deutsche marks, Singapore dollars, and Netherlands guilders), and uses SIBOR as the floating reference rate. The discount rate for special exporters (textiles, textile products, shoes, electronics, timber, rattan products, and leather goods) was reduced from 1% above SIBOR to SIBOR, and for general exporters from SIBOR plus 2% to SIBOR plus 1%. Drafts can be rediscounted in rupiah or dollars. Based on local LCs, suppliers of export-related goods can seek bank drafts and sell them to the BI, provided their remaining maturity is between 30 and 90 days. The discount rate for bank drafts is BI's 3-month money market securities cut-off rate minus 0.5%.

Changes During 1997

Imports and import payments

April 30. Preshipment inspections were changed to inspections upon arrival to be conducted by customs. Customs is required to issue an LPS, which previously was done by Surveyor Indonesia.

ISLAMIC REPUBLIC OF IRAN

(Position as of December 31, 1996)

Status Under IMF Articles of Agreement

Article XIV	Yes.

Exchange Arrangement

Currency

The currency of the Islamic Republic of Iran is the Iranian rial.

Exchange rate structure

Dual

The exchange rate system consists of the following rates: (1) the official rate, which is fixed at Rls 1,750 per $1, applies mainly to the imports of essential goods; and (2) the export rate, which is fixed at Rls 3,000 per $1 and applies to all other transactions.

Classification

Managed floating

The exchange rates are set by Bank Markazi (BM).

Exchange tax

No.

Exchange subsidy

No.

Forward exchange market

No.

Arrangements for Payments and Receipts

Prescription of currency requirements

No.

Payment arrangements

Bilateral arrangements

All bilateral payment arrangements have been terminated, and the outstanding credit balances are in the process of being settled.

Regional arrangements

Settlements of current transactions with the member countries of the ACU, also including Bangladesh, India, Myanmar, Nepal, Pakistan, and Sri Lanka, are required to be effected in AMUs; settlements with these countries are made every 2 months.

Administration of control

Exchange control authorities

Exchange control authority is vested in the BM. Imports and exports are governed by regulations issued periodically by the Ministry of Commerce.

Payment arrears

External payments arrears have been reduced to about $200 million in December 1996 from $3.2 billion in March 1995, as a result of bilateral debt restructurings.

Official

n.a.

Private

n.a.

Controls on trade in gold (coins and/or bullion)

Controls on external trade

Authority to trade in gold for monetary purposes is reserved for the BM. Exports of gold ingots, coins, or semifinished products are prohibited. Exports of finished articles may be effected in accordance with relevant regulations. Natural and juridical persons, including authorized banks, may import gold, platinum, and silver bullion for commercial purposes, in accordance with the relevant regulations. Travelers may bring in jewelry up to a value equivalent to Rls 5 million and may take out the entire value, provided that it is recorded on their passport. The importation of personal jewelry with a value exceeding this amount requires approval from the BM. The exportation of Iranian gold coins for numismatic purposes requires prior approval from the BM.

411

Controls on exports and imports of banknotes

On exports

Domestic currency   Travelers leaving the Islamic Republic of Iran may take out with them up to Rls 200,000 in Iranian banknotes.

Foreign currency   Iranian nationals traveling abroad may export up to $1,000 for each individual passport or up to a maximum of $500 a person for group passports. Foreign exchange from foreign-currency-denominated accounts originating abroad and/or credit cards may be transferred by natural persons without any limitation.

On imports

Domestic currency   n.a.

Resident Accounts

Foreign exchange accounts permitted   Yes.

Held domestically   Yes.

Accounts in domestic currency convertible into foreign currency   No.

Nonresident Accounts

Eligibility to hold accounts   Foreign nationals may open these accounts.

Foreign exchange accounts permitted   Foreign exchange originating abroad and deposited in these accounts may be transferred abroad without limitations.

Domestic currency accounts   The balance of rial accounts may be used only in the Islamic Republic of Iran.

Convertible into foreign currency   No.

Imports and Import Payments

Foreign exchange budget   No.

Financing requirements for imports

Advance payment requirements   Requirements range from 15% to 100% depending on the creditworthiness of the customer and the type of goods.

Documentation requirements for release of foreign exchange for imports

Domiciliation requirements   Yes.

Preshipment inspection   Yes.

Letters of credit   Imports through letters of credit (LCs) and bills of exchange are permitted.

Import licenses used as exchange licenses   Yes.

Import licenses and other nontariff measures   Import regulations distinguish between authorized, conditional, and prohibited goods. Authorized goods can be imported without restriction. Conditional goods can be imported under certain conditions. Clearance through customs is authorized upon presentation of shipping documents endorsed by an authorized bank and of a permit issued by the Ministry of Commerce. Certain goods, such as pharmaceuticals and imports by the

	Ministry of the Post, Telegraph, and Telephone, must be accompanied by a special permit.
Negative list	Imports from Israel are prohibited.
Licenses with quotas	Yes.
Import taxes and/or tariffs	Most imports are subject to an ad valorem commercial benefit tax in addition to any applicable customs duties.
Taxes collected through the exchange system	Yes.
State import monopoly	No.

Exports and Export Proceeds

Repatriation requirements	Exporters of non-oil goods are required to repatriate to the banking system 100% of their foreign exchange earnings upon settlement; 50% of earnings from industrial goods and 30% of earnings from other goods may be allocated to exporters for their imports.
	In September 1996, the period between the date on which goods are exported and the date on which foreign exchange earnings are repatriated to the banking sector was extended to 8 months from 6 in the case of carpet exporters, and for other exporters it was increased to 5 months from 3 months. The list of import items that exporters could buy with the proportion of foreign exchange earnings that they are allowed to retain was expanded.
Surrender requirements	The ratios are the same as those for the repatriation requirement.
Documentation requirements	
Letters of credit	Export of goods and services through LCs and/or trustee transactions is permitted.
Guarantees	Yes.
Domiciliation	n.a.
Preshipment inspection	n.a.
Export licenses	The Ministry of Commerce issues an overall export license for some goods, while for other goods, licenses are issued on a case-by-case basis.
With quotas	Licenses are issued on a case-by-case basis.

Payments for Invisible Transactions and Current Transfers

Controls on these payments	
Freight/insurance	Freight charges may only be transferred through LCs up to a maximum of 30% of the f.o.b. value of goods. Only Iranian insurance companies may issue insurance policies for imports of goods.
Prior approval	n.a.
Quantitative limits	n.a.
Indicative limits/bona fide test	n.a.
Unloading/storage costs	n.a.
Administrative expenses	Payment of administration charges can be made with BM permission.
Prior approval	Yes.
Quantitative limits	n.a.
Indicative limits/bona fide test	n.a.

Interest payments	
Prior approval	Yes.
Payments for travel	The transfer of income in rials earned from ticket sales by foreign airline companies may be allowed at the official exchange rate by the BM.
Quantitative limits	The limits are $1,000 a year for a person with an individual passport and $500 a person for those traveling with a group passport. In the case of travel to neighboring countries, the limits are $300 a year a person for individual passports and $150 a person for group passports.
Indicative limits/bona fide test	n.a.
Medical costs	
Prior approval	Yes.
Quantitative limits	Limits are set on an ad hoc basis; foreign exchange may be obtained at the official rate up to the amount specified by the Ministry of Health.
Indicative limits/bona fide test	n.a.
Study abroad costs	
Prior approval	Yes.
Quantitative limits	The amount of allowances varies according to the cost of living in the country of study. The limits are $1,517 a month a student, plus 60% for a spouse and 30% for each child, at the official exchange rate. In certain cases when this amount is not sufficient to cover tuition, additional amounts to cover university fees and expenses may be allowed. Foreign exchange allowances at the official exchange rate are granted to students under scholarships in nonmedical fields with the approval of the Ministry of Culture and Higher Education, and to those in the medical field, with the approval of the Ministry of Health, Treatment, and Medical Education. Students without scholarships are allocated foreign exchange at the export rate upon evidence of acceptance by an institution and receipt of a tuition invoice.
Subscriptions and membership fees	
Prior approval	Yes.
Quantitative limits	Yes.
Consulting/legal fees	Payment of consulting/legal fees with the confirmation of the Bureau of Legal Services of Iran is permitted.
Prior approval	n.a.
Quantitative limits	n.a.
Indicative limits/bona fide test	n.a.
Foreign workers' wages	
Prior approval	Yes.
Quantitative limits	Foreign nationals working in the Islamic Republic of Iran (public sector) whose services are considered essential are allowed to remit up to 50% of their net salaries at the official export exchange rate, up to a maximum of $500 a month, with the prior approval of the BM.
Indicative limits/bona fide test	n.a.
Family maintenance/alimony	n.a.
Credit card use abroad	n.a.

Proceeds from Invisible Transactions and Current Transfers

Repatriation requirements	Yes.

Surrender requirements	Yes.

Capital Transactions

Controls on capital and money market instruments

On capital market securities

Purchase locally by nonresidents — Nonresidents may invest in instruments traded on the Teheran Stock Exchange, but the investment is not protected under the investment law.

Sale or issue locally by nonresidents — n.a.

Purchase abroad by residents — n.a.

Sale or issue abroad by residents — n.a.

On money market instruments — n.a.

On collective investment securities — n.a.

Controls on direct investment

Outward direct investment — Permitted with the confirmation of the High Council for Investment.

Inward direct investment — Controls are administered by the Organization for Investment and Economic and Technical Assistance of the Ministry of Economic Affairs and Finance if the investment took place in accordance with the Law Concerning Attraction and Protection of Foreign Capital Investment.

Controls on liquidation of direct investment — The repatriation of capital is guaranteed with the approval of the Organization for Investment and Economic and Technical Assistance of the Ministry of Economic Affairs and Finance and the BM.

Changes During 1996

Exports and export proceeds — *September 30.* The period between the date on which goods are exported and the date on which foreign exchange earnings are repatriated to the banking sector was extended to 8 months from 6 months in the case of carpet exporters, and for other exporters, it was increased to 5 months from 3 months.

September 30. The list of import items that exporters could buy with the proportion of foreign exchange earnings that they are allowed to retain was expanded.

IRAQ

(Position as of December 31, 1994)

Status Under IMF Articles of Agreement

Article XIV	Yes.

Exchange Arrangement

Currency

The currency of Iraq is the Iraqi dinar.

Exchange rate structure

Dual

The exchange rate system consists of 2 rates: (1) the official rate, which is fixed at ID 1,750 per $1, and applies mainly to the imports of essential goods; and (2) the export rate, which is fixed at ID 3,000 per $1 and applies to all other transactions.

Classification

Pegged

The Iraqi dinar is pegged to the U.S. dollar, the intervention currency. The exchange rates are set by the Central Bank of Iraq (CBI).

Exchange tax   No.

Exchange subsidy   No.

Forward exchange market   No.

Arrangements for Payments and Receipts

Prescription of currency requirements

Settlements with foreign countries normally must be made in any of the listed currencies or in Iraqi dinars from a nonresident account, provided that the funds in the account were obtained originally through credits in any one of the listed currencies. Payments to and receipts from Israel are prohibited.

Administration of control

Exchange control authorities

Exchange control authority is vested in the Board of Administration of the CBI. Certain approval authority has been delegated to the Department of Foreign Exchange and Banking Supervision of the CBI and to licensed dealers. Foreign exchange transactions must take place through a licensed dealer unless otherwise authorized by the governor of the CBI. Branches of the Rafidain Bank and the Rasheed Bank are licensed dealers. The Ministry of Trade (MOT) formulates import policy and the annual import program.

Controls on trade in gold (coins and/or bullion)

Controls on domestic ownership and/or trade

n.a.

Controls on external trade

Residents and nonresidents may bring into Iraq, free of customs duty, worked and unworked gold, regardless of its weight, provided that they declare it upon importation. Residents may take out with them worked gold not exceeding 5 grams a person, subject to declaration; such gold may be brought back on their return to the country. Nonresident Iraqis are allowed to take out worked gold that they brought with them for personal use.

Controls on exports and imports of banknotes

On exports

Domestic currency

ID 5 is the maximum amount allowed.

Foreign currency	n.a.
On imports	
Domestic currency	Amounts up to ID 1,000 are allowed.
Foreign currency	Travelers may bring in foreign exchange, including currency notes (other than Israeli currency), in unlimited amounts provided that they declare the funds on an exchange control form; amounts not intended to be taken out of the country are exempt from declaration.

Resident Accounts

Eligibility to hold accounts	Yes.
Juridical persons	n.a.
Natural persons	Yes.
Foreign exchange accounts permitted	Yes.
Held domestically	Resident Iraqis and resident nationals of other Arab countries are allowed to open foreign currency accounts at the commercial banks and to use the balances in these accounts without restriction, provided the accounts have been credited with foreign banknotes.
Approval required	n.a.
Held abroad	n.a.

Nonresident Accounts

Eligibility to hold accounts	Yes.
Juridical persons	n.a.
Natural persons	Yes.
Foreign exchange accounts permitted	Nonresident Iraqis and nonresident nationals of other Arab countries are allowed to open foreign currency accounts at the commercial banks and to use the balances in these accounts without restriction, provided the accounts have been credited with foreign banknotes. Nonresident accounts are divided into ordinary nonresident accounts, which involve current payment transactions, and special nonresident accounts, which involve capital transfer transactions. Balances on these accounts and any applicable interest are freely transferable abroad in foreign currencies, provided that the funds have been deposited with licensed dealers within 3 months of transfer. Iraqi nationals residing abroad (or their legal representatives) may withdraw from their nonresident accounts up to ID 100,000 a year in 3 installments to cover personal expenses in their country of residence.
Approval required	n.a.

Imports and Import Payments

Documentation requirements for release of foreign exchange for imports	
Domiciliation requirements	n.a.
Preshipment inspection	n.a.

Letters of credit	n.a.
Import licenses used as exchange licenses	The Rafidain Bank or the Rasheed Bank provides foreign exchange upon presentation of the exchange control copy of the import license except in some instances, when reference must be made to the CBI.
Import licenses and other nontariff measures	Licenses are issued in accordance with an annual import program. Imports of all goods from Israel are prohibited. All private imports are subject to licenses, except imports of materials constituting basic elements for development projects.
Positive list	n.a.
Negative list	Imports of some commodities on a protected list are, in principle, prohibited from all sources.
Open general licenses	n.a.
Licenses with quotas	n.a.
Import taxes and/or tariffs	To finance the Export Subsidy Fund, a tax of 0.5% is levied on imports of capital goods, and a tax of 0.75% is levied on imports of consumer goods. All imports subject to import duty are also subject to a customs surcharge. Foreign companies implementing development projects in Iraq are exempt from all import duties and domestic taxes accruing from the implementation of these projects, including income taxes due on the earnings of their non-Iraqi workers.
Taxes collected through the exchange system	n.a.
State import monopoly	Imports of commodities are normally handled by the public sector.

Exports and Export Proceeds

Repatriation requirements	Yes.
Surrender requirements	Exporters of 13 goods manufactured by firms in the public sector must repatriate 60% of their foreign exchange proceeds through the Rafidain Bank or the Rasheed Bank and surrender them within 2 months of shipment. Other exporters may retain their export proceeds in a foreign exchange account with the commercial banks for 3 years and use them to pay for licensed imports.
Export licenses	All exports to Israel and exports of certain goods to all other countries are prohibited. The MOT may prohibit the exportation of any commodity when supply falls short of domestic demand. All exports are licensed freely through the General Company for Exhibitions and Trading Services.
Without quotas	n.a.
With quotas	n.a.

Payments for Invisible Transactions and Current Transfers

Controls on these payments	All payments for invisibles require prior approval. Information on indicative limits and/or bona fide tests for all payments, as well as for quantitative limits for most transactions, is not available. Some limits are listed below.
Freight/insurance	Foreign exchange is not granted to merchants to purchase insurance abroad for their exports.
Payments for travel	
Quantitative limits	The basic allowance for travel to Arab and socialist countries, Cyprus, Greece, and Turkey is ID 300 a person a trip for travelers 18 years of age or over (ID 50 for persons under 18 years); the basic allowance for other countries is ID 500 a person a trip for travelers 18 years of age or over (ID 250 for persons under 18 years).

Study abroad costs

    Quantitative limits — Students abroad are allocated a fixed amount in Iraqi dinars to be transferred to the country of their residence, except for certain countries (such as India, the Baltic countries, Russia, and the other countries of the FSU, and countries in North Africa), where students are paid a fixed amount in U.S. dollars.

Foreign workers' wages — The Rafidain Bank and the Rasheed Bank are permitted to transfer salaries of teachers who are nationals of Arab countries employed by the Ministry of Higher Education, and of scientific researchers and medical doctors, in accordance with the terms of their contracts.

    Quantitative limits — Certain nonresident private sector workers who have contracts with public institutions in Iraq are permitted to transfer the amounts provided for in those contracts. Those not employed under contracts may transfer abroad a monthly amount of ID 10 a person if not insured and ID 20 a person if insured and working in the private sector. Skilled noncontractual workers employed in the nationalized sector by the government are entitled to ID 40 a person a month. Persons under 16 years and over 55 years of age, however, are not allowed to transfer their earnings abroad.

Proceeds from Invisible Transactions and Current Transfers

Repatriation requirements — Yes.

Surrender requirements — Foreign exchange receipts in excess of ID 100 must be surrendered to a licensed dealer within 3 months.

Capital Transactions

Controls on capital and money market instruments — All capital transactions effected abroad by residents, whether Iraqis or foreign nationals, require prior approval.

On capital market securities — Yes.

    Purchase locally by nonresidents — n.a.

    Sale or issue locally by nonresidents — n.a.

    Purchase abroad by residents — n.a.

    Sale or issue abroad by residents — n.a.

On money market instruments — Yes.

    Purchase locally by nonresidents — n.a.

    Sale or issue locally by nonresidents — n.a.

    Purchase abroad by residents — n.a.

    Sale or issue abroad by residents — n.a.

On collective investment securities — Yes.

    Purchase locally by nonresidents — n.a.

    Sale or issue locally by nonresidents — n.a.

    Purchase abroad by residents — n.a.

    Sale or issue abroad by residents — n.a.

Controls on derivatives and other instruments	Yes.
Purchase locally by nonresidents	n.a.
Sale or issue locally by nonresidents	n.a.
Purchase abroad by residents	n.a.
Sale or issue abroad by residents	n.a.
Controls on direct investment	
Outward direct investment	All investments effected abroad by residents, whether Iraqis or foreign nationals, require prior approval.
Inward direct investment	No foreign (defined as non-Arab) participation is allowed in the capital of private sector companies, but citizens of other Arab countries may participate with Iraqis in projects in the industrial, agricultural, and tourism sectors; participation is encouraged by the Arab Investment Law (1988). The law permits (1) Iraqi investors to hold up to 49% of an enterprise, provided that their contribution and profits to be paid in Iraqi dinars and the minimum capital of the enterprise is ID 0.5 million; (2) Arab investors to transfer annually up to 100% of the profits distributed to them, but not exceeding 20% of their paid-in capital; and (3) nationals of Arab countries to bring capital into Iraq in Iraqi currency for industrial and agricultural investments. Arab investors are allowed to transfer capital in a convertible currency through a licensed bank, or physical assets that will be used in the enterprises they are planning to establish, provided that used machinery and equipment have at least one-half of their productive life left.
Controls on liquidation of direct investment	Yes.

Changes During 1995–96

[The IMF has not received from the authorities the information required for a description of the exchange and trade system as of December 1995 and December 1996.]

IRELAND

(Position as of December 31, 1996)

Status Under IMF Articles of Agreement

Article VIII   Date of acceptance: February 15, 1961.

Exchange Arrangement

Currency   The currency of Ireland is the Irish pound.

Exchange rate structure   Unitary.

Classification

Cooperative arrangement   Ireland participates in the ERM of the EMS. In accordance with this mechanism, Ireland maintains spot exchange rates between the Irish pound and the currencies of the other participants within margins of 15% above or below the cross rates based on the central rates expressed in ECUs.

Exchange tax   No.

Exchange subsidy   No.

Forward exchange market   Banks are free to provide forward exchange facilities.

Official cover of forward operations No.

Arrangements for Payments and Receipts

Prescription of currency requirements   No.

Payment arrangements   No.

Administration of control   No.

International security restrictions

In accordance with IMF Executive Board Decision No. 144-(52/51)   Yes.

In accordance with UN sanctions   Restrictions were imposed on financial transfers in respect of Iraq in August 1990, and in respect of Libya in December 1993. Restrictions regarding Haiti were revoked in December 1994. Restrictions regarding the Federal Republic of Yugoslavia (Serbia/Montenegro) were suspended in accordance with EC Regulation No. 2382/96, following the passing of UN Security Council Resolution No. 1074 of October 1995.

Payment arrears   No.

Controls on trade in gold (coins and/or bullion)   No.

Controls on exports and imports of banknotes   No.

Resident Accounts

Eligibility to hold accounts   Juridical and natural persons are eligible.

Foreign exchange accounts permitted   Yes.

Held domestically	Yes.
Held abroad	Yes.
Accounts in domestic currency convertible into foreign currency	Yes.

Nonresident Accounts

Eligibility to hold accounts	Juridical and natural persons are eligible.
Foreign exchange accounts permitted	Yes.
Domestic currency accounts	Yes.
Convertible into foreign currency	Yes.
Blocked accounts	These are accounts blocked in accordance with UN sanctions.

Imports and Import Payments

Foreign exchange budget	No.
Financing requirements for imports	No.
Documentation requirements for release of foreign exchange for imports	No.
Import licenses and other nontariff measures	
Negative list	For reasons of national policy, imports of certain goods (e.g., specified drugs, explosives, and firearms and ammunition) are prohibited without special licenses.
Licenses with quotas	Imports of certain goods (including textiles, steel, footwear, and ceramic products) originating in certain non-EU countries are subject to either quantitative restrictions or surveillance measures. Imports from non-EU countries of products covered by the CAP are subject to a system of access quotas.
Import taxes and/or tariffs	The EU system of customs duties applies to imports.
Taxes collected through the exchange system	No.
State import monopoly	No.

Exports and Export Proceeds

Repatriation requirements	No.
Surrender requirements	No.
Financing requirements	No.
Documentation requirements	No.
Export licenses	Exports of dual-use goods to both EU and non-EU countries may require export licenses.
Without quotas	n.a.
With quotas	n.a.

Export taxes	No.

Payments for Invisible Transactions and Current Transfers

Controls on these payments	No.

Proceeds from Invisible Transactions and Current Transfers

Repatriation requirements	No.
Surrender requirements	No.
Restrictions on use of funds	No.

Capital Transactions

Controls on capital and money market instruments	No.
Controls on derivatives and other instruments	No.
Controls on credit operations	No.
Controls on direct investment	
Inward direct investment	Investment by foreign-controlled enterprises does not require authorization, except for some sectors subject to special conditions.
Controls on liquidation of direct investment	No.
Controls on real estate transactions	
Purchase locally by nonresidents	Persons, individuals, and companies whose principal place of residence/registered office is outside the territory of the EU/EEA must apply to the Land Commission for permission to purchase land. Such permission is rarely withheld.
Provisions specific to commercial banks and other credit institutions	No.
Provisions specific to institutional investors	No.
Other controls imposed by securities laws	No.

Changes During 1996

No significant changes occurred in the exchange and trade system.

ISRAEL

(Position as of February 28, 1997)

Status Under IMF Articles of Agreement

Article VIII   Date of acceptance: September 21, 1993.

Exchange Arrangement

Currency   The currency of Israel is the new sheqel (NIS) (plural new sheqalim).

Exchange rate structure   Unitary.

Classification

Managed floating   The exchange rate of the new sheqel is managed with regard to a basket of currencies comprising the deutsche mark, the French franc, the Japanese yen, the pound sterling, and the U.S. dollar. The market exchange rate fluctuates within margins of ± 7% around the midpoint rate in response to market forces and intervention policy. Since December 17, 1991, both the midpoint and the band have been adjusted daily, reflecting the annual difference between the domestic inflation target and the projected inflation of the main trading partners. The adjustment of the band has been 6% on an annual basis since July 26, 1993.

Exchange tax   No.

Exchange subsidy   No.

Forward exchange market   Forward exchange transactions between foreign currencies are permitted. Transactions in futures and options, including traded contracts on foreign currencies, foreign interest rates, commodities, and security prices by both resident companies and individuals, are allowed. However, resident firms may only enter into such contracts in order to cover commercial risks arising from permitted transactions. Transactions in commodities may only be entered into in order to cover risks, and transactions, other than in traded contracts, must be carried out in conjunction with an authorized dealer bank or, through it, against a foreign bank or broker. Forward transactions in new sheqalim may only be conducted for hedging purposes, provided that the transaction is carried out with an authorized dealer in foreign exchange and up to a period of 1 month.

Official cover of forward operations   n.a.

Arrangements for Payments and Receipts

Prescription of currency requirements   Yes.

Payment arrangements   No.

Administration of control

Exchange control authorities   Exchange control is the responsibility of the Controller of Foreign Exchange; it is administered by the Bank of Israel (BOI) in cooperation with other government agencies and is carried out through authorized banks that are permitted to deal in foreign exchange. Other institutions (e.g., security brokers and foreign exchange dealers) may obtain a limited license to deal in foreign exchange.

International security restrictions   No.

Payment arrears   No.

Controls on trade in gold (coins and/or bullion)

Controls on external trade

Residents are allowed to import and export gold, subject to the same regulations as those applied to merchandise trade, and to transact in gold bullion and coins. Gold certificates are treated as foreign securities.

Controls on exports and imports of banknotes

On exports

Domestic currency

Resident travelers may take out up to the equivalent of $200 a person a trip. Nonresident travelers leaving Israel are permitted to take out up to the equivalent of $100, and to repurchase through an authorized dealer at the port of departure foreign currency up to the equivalent of $500.

Foreign currency

Nonresidents may purchase foreign currency on presentation of documents showing the previous conversion of foreign currency into Israeli currency, with a limit for each visit of $5,000 a person over 18 years and $2,000 a person under 18 years (a temporary leave of less than 2 weeks during the visit does not affect the person's right). Only commercial banks are authorized to export foreign currency to foreign banks.

Resident Accounts

Eligibility to hold accounts

Juridical and natural persons are eligible.

Foreign exchange accounts permitted

Yes.

Held domestically

There are two main types of accounts:

(1) Foreign Currency Deposit Accounts (PAMAH). The period during which foreign currency may be held in a resident transferred position (PAMAH) is 30 days. Export proceeds and unilateral transfers directly received from abroad, as well as unused travel allowances, may be deposited in these accounts. The liquidity requirements are 6% for a current account and 3% for a time deposit account with a maturity of up to 1 year, and zero for a time deposit account with a maturity exceeding 1 year. Resident restitution deposit accounts may be maintained under PAMAH. These accounts may be held only by recipients of restitution payments or certain disability pensions. The liquidity requirement for these accounts is the same as the above. Funds deposited in these accounts are tax free and may be used up to a limit of $1,800 for additional travel allowances; and

(2) Exempt Resident Deposit Accounts. Certain residents (mostly immigrants) may deposit funds brought from abroad in these accounts. Balances on these accounts may be freely transferred abroad. In addition, a resident may open a deposit account linked to a foreign currency (PATZAM) with a maturity period of at least 1 month.

Held abroad

Certain residents (mostly immigrants) may hold accounts abroad. Prior approval is required.

Accounts in domestic currency convertible into foreign currency

No.

Nonresident Accounts

Eligibility to hold accounts

Juridical and natural persons are eligible.

Foreign exchange accounts permitted

Account holders may freely effect transfers from their foreign currency account and may also convert funds held in the account into local currency at the market exchange rate. There are no restrictions on the opening of convertible local currency accounts by nonresidents; funds in these accounts may be used in permitted transactions, including transfers between nonresidents.

Domestic currency accounts	Yes.
Convertible into foreign currency	Deposits linked to foreign currency or the CPI are not convertible. Prior approval is required.
Blocked accounts	No.

Imports and Import Payments

Foreign exchange budget	No.
Financing requirements for imports	
Advance payment requirements	Advance payments for imports of goods to be supplied within 1 year are allowed. On April 1, 1996, the reporting requirement for the advance payment for imports and for transit and brokerage transactions of up to $5,000 was eliminated. In addition, the amount that an authorized dealer may transfer abroad on the basis of a supplier's invoice or written quotation was raised to $5,000 from $3,000. On February 9, 1997, the follow-up and reporting requirements for sums of up to $10,000 were eliminated for advance payment of imports and for transit and brokerage transactions.
Documentation requirements for release of foreign exchange for imports	Banks automatically grant foreign exchange to pay for authorized imports when the relevant documents (import documents, bills of lading, and letters of credit) are presented. Foreign exchange is also provided automatically for repayment of suppliers' credits. Importers are allowed to use foreign currency proceeds of loans obtained abroad directly for import payments without first depositing the funds with an authorized Israeli bank.
Import licenses and other nontariff measures	With the exception of agricultural products, imports are free of quantitative restrictions. A special regime applies to imports from countries that restrict or prohibit imports from Israel.
Positive list	n.a.
Negative list	n.a.
Open general licenses	n.a.
Licenses with quotas	n.a.
Import taxes and/or tariffs	No.
State import monopoly	No.

Exports and Export Proceeds

Repatriation requirements	Proceeds in foreign currencies must be received within 12 months of the date of exportation.
Surrender requirements	Proceeds may be held in a PAMAH account or sold to authorized banks. However, exporters may retain in a bank account abroad up to 10% of export proceeds received over the previous 12-month period and use the funds to pay for imports and other authorized payments abroad. In cases where the exporter is a firm with limited liabilities, the amount allowed to be deposited in a bank account abroad is also part of the overall limit on the portfolio investment abroad of the firm. For inputs directly imported by an exporter, there is a system of rebates of customs duties, wharf charges, and other related charges. On February 9, 1997, exporters were permitted to deposit in a bank abroad proceeds received from a financial institution abroad against the discounting of notes.
Financing requirements	No.
Documentation requirements	No.
Export licenses	Most exports do not require licenses. Exports of oil and certain defense equipment require licensing.

Without quotas	Yes.
Export taxes	No.

Payments for Invisible Transactions and Current Transfers

Controls on these payments

There are no controls on payments for freight and insurance, unloading and storage costs, administrative expenses, commissions, subscriptions and membership fees, consulting and legal fees, pensions, or on interest, nor on remittances of profits and dividends or gambling and prize earnings.

Payments for travel

Quantitative limits

The limit is $7,000 a person a trip in cash, traveler's checks, and cash withdrawals on credit cards.

Indicative limits/bona fide test

Additional cash allowances may be granted on request. Residents holding PAMAH restitution accounts may withdraw an additional amount of $1,800.

Medical costs

Quantitative limits

A resident who requires hospitalization abroad is permitted to pay up to the equivalent of $30,000 in advance. While abroad, he or she is permitted to pay the remainder of expenses on submission of receipts.

Indicative limits/bona fide test

On February 9, 1997, documentation requirements to purchase foreign exchange were liberalized.

Study abroad costs

Quantitative limits

The exchange allowance for students studying at institutions of higher education abroad is $1,000 a month in addition to tuition expenses. On February 9, 1997, advance transfers of the exchange allowance for students were permitted for up to 1 year.

Indicative limits/bona fide test

Yes.

Foreign workers' wages

Indicative limits/bona fide test

Yes.

Family maintenance/alimony

Quantitative limits

Residents may make support or gift remittances of up to $2,000 a year.

Indicative limits/bona fide test

Yes.

Credit card use abroad

Prior approval

Approval is limited to the purchase of tourist services abroad.

Quantitative limits

Since April 1, 1996, the annual limit for credit card payments abroad for imports of goods and services was raised to $5,000 from $1,500. Residents, while in Israel, are permitted to make credit card payments abroad of up to $10,000 a year.

Indicative limits/bona fide test

The limit for cash withdrawals is $7,000 a trip.

Proceeds from Invisible Transactions and Current Transfers

Repatriation requirements

Yes.

Surrender requirements

Exchange proceeds from invisibles may, in general, be kept in foreign exchange in PAMAH accounts or sold to authorized banks. For 30 years after entering Israel, immigrants are exempt from the requirement to surrender their foreign exchange to authorized banks, and they may hold these foreign currencies freely with authorized banks in Israel or with banks abroad.

Restrictions on use of funds	Restrictions are in accordance with general rules pertaining to the use of foreign currency.

Capital Transactions

Controls on capital and money market instruments

On capital market securities

Purchase locally by nonresidents — Nonresidents may purchase any security traded on the stock exchange.

Sale or issue locally by nonresidents — Proceeds may be freely transferred.

Purchase abroad by residents — Households may purchase freely securities abroad, provided they are issued by a government. The business sector may purchase securities abroad under the same conditions as households but with a limit of up to 5% of sales or 10% of capital. All transactions and transfer of funds abroad should be conducted through an authorized dealer in foreign exchange (usually a bank).

Sale or issue abroad by residents — The proceeds of these issues must usually be transferred to Israel. Special permits are provided for holding the issues abroad. The transfer of funds required to service security issues is allowed.

On money market instruments

Purchase locally by nonresidents — Nonresidents may purchase money market instruments traded on the stock exchange (such as treasury bills).

Purchase abroad by residents — Households may purchase freely money market instruments that are traded on an exchange abroad. The business sector may purchase market instruments abroad with a limit set as a percentage of sales or capital.

Sale or issue abroad by residents — Residents may issue money market instruments that are traded on an exchange abroad. The proceeds of these issues must usually be transferred to Israel; however, special permits for holding these proceeds abroad are granted to all issuers. The transfer of funds required to service security issues is allowed.

On collective investment securities

Purchase locally by nonresidents — Nonresidents may purchase certificates of participation in mutual funds. Nonresidents are not allowed to purchase certificates of deposit in provident funds.

Sale or issue locally by nonresidents — The sale or issue of collective instrument securities on local markets is allowed, provided that the securities are traded on the stock market. However, the issue of such securities requires authorization from the authorities.

Purchase abroad by residents — Households may buy certificates of participation in mutual funds that are either traded on an exchange or authorized by the appropriate authority in the issuing country. The business sector may purchase such certificates with a limit.

Sale or issue abroad by residents — The sale or issue of collective instrument securities abroad by residents is not allowed.

Controls on derivatives and other instruments

Purchase abroad by residents — Residents may purchase derivatives and other securities abroad. However, the business sector is restricted to hedging, while households may purchase for both hedging and for speculation.

Sale or issue abroad by residents — Yes.

Controls on credit operations

Commercial credits

By residents to nonresidents — Credits may be granted up to a period of 1 year. In the case of capital goods, long-term credit may also be granted.

Financial credits

By residents to nonresidents

Nonbanks are generally not allowed to grant financial credit to nonresidents. However, an Israeli company may grant financial credit to its subsidiary abroad, provided the parent company holds at least 5% of the equity of its subsidiary. An Israeli company in which a nonresident holds at least 75% of the shares may grant credit to the nonresident, with a permit, up to the amount of the equity held by this nonresident.

To residents from nonresidents

Direct loans from nonresidents to Israeli residents are not restricted.

Guarantees, sureties, and financial backup facilities

By residents to nonresidents

A resident may provide sureties, guarantees, or financial backup facilities to a nonresident if they are related to a permitted transaction. Guarantees may also be granted to an agent in an export transaction.

Controls on direct investment

Outward direct investment

Only active incorporated Israeli companies are permitted to undertake direct investment abroad (e.g., in subsidiaries and real estate) without any quantitative limit on the size of the investment, provided that the investment does not amount to more than 10% of the company's equity or 5% of its sales turnover, whichever is larger. On April 1, 1996, direct investment abroad by foreign subsidiaries of Israeli companies was liberalized. On February 9, 1997, emigrants were permitted to transfer abroad up to 20% of their assets.

Inward direct investment

Foreign exchange brought into Israel for the purpose of investment in the form of equity capital or shareholders' loans may be granted preferential tax treatment.

Controls on liquidation of direct investment

Proceeds may be repatriated if the original source of the investment was foreign currency or a nonresident local currency account.

Controls on real estate transactions

Purchase abroad by residents

Only the business sector is permitted to conduct these transactions. Individuals are not allowed to make such investments, except for the purchase of a time-share unit not exceeding $15,000.

Sale locally by nonresidents

Proceeds may be repatriated if the original source of the investment was foreign currency or a nonresident local currency account.

Provisions specific to commercial banks and other credit institutions

Borrowing abroad

Resident "authorized dealer banks" are free to borrow abroad in the form of nonresident accounts or loans from foreign banks. In addition, they may issue securities abroad.

Lending to nonresidents (financial or commercial credits)

Authorized dealer banks are free to grant loans, including financial credits denominated in foreign or local currency. They may purchase fixed-income securities abroad.

Differential treatment of nonresident deposit accounts and/or deposit accounts in foreign exchange

Reserve requirements

The same reserve ratios apply to bank accounts held by both residents and nonresidents denominated in foreign or local currency. However, interest is paid only on reserve requirements that are due to nonresident foreign currency accounts. All foreign currency accounts are subject to additional secondary reserve ratios, half of which must be deposited with the BOI in an interest-generating account.

Open foreign exchange position limits

The size of the limit for each bank is a proportion of the bank's equity (with a minimum position size granted to small banks). The limits are applied on the basis of weekly averages.

Provisions specific to institutional investors

Limits (max.) on portfolio invested abroad

Regular mutual funds may invest up to 10% of their assets in securities abroad. Special mutual funds intended for investment abroad may invest up to 50% of their assets abroad. Mutual funds intended for nonresidents may invest up to 75% of their assets abroad. Provident funds may invest up to 2% of their assets abroad in recognized foreign securities. Pension funds and insurance companies are not allowed to invest abroad. Income and profits earned in foreign currency by institutional investors from these investments, including capital gains, are taxed at the rate of 35%.

Limits (min.) on portfolio invested locally

n.a.

Other controls imposed by securities laws

Foreign underwriters must comply with the same criteria as those that apply to domestic underwriters, as stated by the Securities Law.

Changes During 1996

Resident accounts

January 4. Incoming and outgoing tourist foreign currency deposits were consolidated as one "travel agent deposit." The regulations that applied to the separate deposits apply to the consolidated one.

Imports and import payments

April 1. The reporting requirement for advance payment of imports and for transit and brokerage transactions of up to $5,000 was eliminated.

April 1. The amount that an authorized dealer may transfer abroad on the basis of a supplier's invoice or written quotation was raised to $5,000 from $3,000.

July 7. Electronic payments in foreign currency for imports were liberalized.

Exports and export proceeds

Payments for invisible transactions and current transfers

April 1. The annual limit for credit card payments abroad for the import of goods or services was raised to $5,000 from $1,500.

Capital transactions

February 7. Uniform rules were set for the purchasing and selling of foreign securities traded abroad and on the Tel Aviv Securities Exchange (TASE). Foreign securities purchased with local currency are registered in the name of the authorized dealer and deposited in a custody deposit account in the name of the nonresident.

April 1. Individual residents were permitted to purchase a time-share unit abroad with a maximum limit of $15,000.

April 1. Nonresidents were permitted to repurchase foreign currency that was transferred for investment purposes (purchase of an asset in Israel) directly from abroad.

April 1. The definition of Israeli securities was expanded to include the redeemable shares of an Israeli company (e.g., a preference share that may be redeemed) and the right or warrant that grants the right to purchase such shares. Thus, nonresidents were permitted to purchase such securities and deposit the income from them and the proceeds from their sale in a nonresident deposit account, provided they are bought with funds from a nonresident deposit.

April 1. Direct investment abroad by foreign subsidiaries of Israeli companies was liberalized.

Changes During 1997

Imports and import payments

February 9. The follow-up and reporting requirements for sums of up to $10,000 were eliminated for advance payment of imports and for transit and brokerage transactions.

Exports and export proceeds

February 9. Exporters were permitted to deposit in a bank abroad proceeds received from a financial institution abroad against the discounting of notes.

Payments for invisible transactions and current transfers

February 9. Documentation requirements to obtain a travel allowance were liberalized. Advance transfers of the exchange allowance for students were permitted for up to 1 year.

Capital transactions

February 9. Emigrants were permitted to transfer abroad up to 20% of their assets.

February 9. Residents were permitted to deposit in a resident foreign currency deposit account a loan in foreign currency received from a nonresident or from an authorized dealer bank, as well as the proceeds from selling foreign securities or income from them, even if the security was purchased with local currency.

February 9. Residents were permitted to purchase abroad any security for which a price is published by an international quoting agency in accordance with the list determined by the Controller of Foreign Exchange (e.g., Reuter's, Bloomberg, etc.), irrespective of the stock market on which the security is traded. They may also purchase a new foreign security, at offering, if that agency has made information about the offering available.

February 9. A foreign company registered in Israel was permitted to export profits accrued from its activities in Israel upon termination of these activities, subject to the conditions set forth by the Comptroller of Foreign Currency.

ITALY

(Position as of December 31, 1996)

Status Under IMF Articles of Agreement

Article VIII   Date of acceptance: February 15, 1961.

Exchange Arrangement

Currency   The currency of Italy is the Italian lira.

Exchange rate structure   Unitary.

Classification

Cooperative arrangement   Italy rejoined the ERM of the EMS on November 25, 1996. The arrangement implies that the Bank of Italy (BOI) stands ready to buy or sell currencies of the other participating states in unlimited amounts at specified intervention rates. In principle, interventions within the EMS are made in participating currencies but may also take place in third currencies, such as the U.S. dollar. Participants in the EMS do not maintain exchange rates for other currencies within fixed limits but do intervene from time to time to smooth out erratic fluctuations in exchange rates.

Exchange tax   No.

Exchange subsidy   No.

Forward exchange market   Premiums and discounts in the forward exchange market are normally left to the interplay of market forces.

Official cover of forward operations No.

Arrangements for Payments and Receipts

Prescription of currency requirements   Settlements with foreign countries are normally made in quoted currencies or in lire on foreign accounts.

Payment arrangements

Clearing agreements   Italy maintains clearing accounts with Croatia and Slovenia. The accounts are used for trade in cross-border areas. The balances in these accounts may be used only to finance trade between certain districts of Croatia and Slovenia and the Italian provinces of Trieste and Gorizia. The balances are not transferable. There is no automatic mechanism through which outstanding balances are settled within 90 days. Only Italy is allowed to maintain a debit balance on these accounts.

Administration of control

Exchange control authorities   Residents are allowed to conduct foreign exchange transactions freely, with settlements to be effected either through authorized intermediaries (BOI, authorized banks, and the Postal Administration) or directly, by drawing on external accounts or by offsetting debts and credits vis-à-vis other residents or nonresidents. Operators and authorized intermediaries must, for statistical purposes, transmit data to the Italian Foreign Exchange Office on their foreign transactions that exceed the equivalent of Lit 20 million by filling out a foreign exchange statistical return.

International security restrictions

In accordance with IMF Executive Board Decision No. 144-(52/51)   Yes.

In accordance with UN sanctions   Certain restrictions are imposed on the making of payments and transfers for current international transactions in respect to Iraq, Libya, and the movement UNITA in Angola.

Payment arrears	No.
Controls on trade in gold (coins and/or bullion)	
Controls on external trade	Purchases and sales of gold abroad are legally reserved for the monetary authorities. Residents may purchase and import unrefined gold under ministerial license for industrial purposes. The exportation of unrefined gold is subject to licensing by the Ministry of Foreign Trade. The importation and exportation of gold coins, including coins that are legal tender in a foreign country, are unrestricted. Imports gold coins are subject to a value-added tax at 19%.
Controls on exports and imports of banknotes	Residents are allowed to take with them into or out of the country Italian or foreign banknotes and bearer securities of any denomination up to the equivalent of Lit 20 million. For fiscal and anti-money-laundering purposes, transfers exceeding this amount must be carried out through authorized intermediaries. Residents are allowed to enter and leave the country carrying securities denominated in lire or in foreign currencies worth Lit 20 million, provided that they are not bearer securities and that they are declared to customs.
	Nonresidents may take up to Lit 20 million in banknotes and securities of any denomination into and out of Italy without formalities. If they bring in banknotes and securities in an amount in excess of Lit 20 million, they must declare the excess amount to customs on a special form upon entering Italy. Nonresidents may reexport larger sums but only up to the amount in excess of Lit 20 million that they have imported and declared. No limit applies to exports of nonbearer securities; nonresidents need only submit the above-mentioned form to customs. The limitations described above do not apply to transfers effected by banks when they act as senders or beneficiaries.
On exports	
Domestic currency	Yes.
Foreign currency	Yes.
On imports	
Domestic currency	Yes.
Foreign currency	Yes.

Resident Accounts

Eligibility to hold accounts	Juridical and natural persons are eligible.
Foreign exchange accounts permitted	Yes.
Held domestically	Yes.
Held abroad	Yes.
Accounts in domestic currency convertible into foreign currency	Yes.

Nonresident Accounts

Eligibility to hold accounts	Juridical and natural persons are eligible.
Foreign exchange accounts permitted	Yes.
Domestic currency accounts	Yes.

Convertible into foreign currency	Yes.
Blocked accounts	These are accounts that have been blocked in compliance with UN Security Council resolutions.

Imports and Import Payments

Foreign exchange budget	No.
Financing requirements for imports	No.
Documentation requirements for release of foreign exchange for imports	No.
Import licenses and other nontariff measures	Imports are governed by EU regulations according to which imports of most products, except for textiles and some products originating from China, are free of licensing and quantitative restrictions. Imports from non-EU countries of most products covered by the CAP are subject to variable import levies, which have replaced all previous barriers to imports. Common EU regulations are also applied to imports of most other agricultural and livestock products from non-EU countries. Payments for imports are not regulated, without prejudice to the general rules cited in the section on Administration of Control.
Negative list	Yes.
Licenses with quotas	Yes.
Import taxes and/or tariffs	Yes.
Taxes collected through the exchange system	No.
State import monopoly	No.

Exports and Export Proceeds

Repatriation requirements	No.
Surrender requirements	No.
Financing requirements	No.
Documentation requirements	No.
Export licenses	
Without quotas	Exports to non-EU countries are free, with the exception of high-technology products included in EC Regulation No. 3381/94 and of oil extracted from the seabed, which are subject to ministerial authorization.
Export taxes	No.

Payments for Invisible Transactions and Current Transfers

Controls on these payments	No.

Proceeds from Invisible Transactions and Current Transfers

Repatriation requirements	No.
Surrender requirements	No.

Restrictions on use of funds   No.

Capital Transactions

Controls on capital and money market instruments

On collective investment securities

   Sale or issue locally by nonresidents   The public offering in Italy of securities issued by mutual funds that are not covered by EU directives is subject to authorization.

Controls on derivatives and other instruments   No.

Controls on credit operations   No.

Controls on direct investment   No.

Controls on liquidation of direct investment   No.

Controls on real estate transactions   No.

Provisions specific to commercial banks and other credit institutions

Open foreign exchange position limits   A capital ratio of 8% of the position applies.

Provisions specific to institutional investors

Currency matching regulations on assets/liabilities composition   At least 80% of liabilities in any currency must be matched with assets in the same currency, except if the assets to be held in that currency do not exceed 7% of total assets.

Other controls imposed by securities laws   No.

Changes During 1996

Exchange arrangements   *November 25.* Italy rejoined the ERM of the EMS with a central rate of Lit 1,906 to the ECU.

Arrangements for payments and receipts   *November 4.* According to UN Security Resolution No. 1074, Italy lifted restrictions imposed on the making of payments and transfers for current international transactions in respect of the Federal Republic of Yugoslavia (Serbia/Montenegro).

JAMAICA

(Position as of December 31, 1996)

Status Under IMF Articles of Agreement

Article VIII	Date of acceptance: February 22, 1963.

Exchange Arrangement

Currency
The currency of Jamaica is the Jamaica dollar.

Other legal tender
Commemorative gold coins in denominations of J$20, J$100, and J$250 are legal tender but do not circulate.

Exchange rate structure
Unitary.

Classification

Independent floating
The exchange rate of the Jamaica dollar is determined in the interbank market. The foreign exchange market is operated by the commercial banks, other authorized dealers, cambios, and the Bank of Jamaica (BJ). The commercial banks buy and sell for their own account. Cambios are required to sell to the BJ a prescribed minimum amount of foreign exchange that they have purchased. Excess foreign exchange may be sold without restrictions to the commercial banks, other authorized dealers, and the general public. Proceeds from official loans, divestment of government assets, and taxes on the bauxite sector payable in foreign currency are sold directly to the BJ. While there is no restriction on transactions in any currency, the principal foreign currencies accepted in the exchange market are the Canadian dollar, the pound sterling, and the U.S. dollar.

Exchange tax
No.

Exchange subsidy
No.

Forward exchange market
The market is currently inactive.

Official cover of forward operations
No.

Arrangements for Payments and Receipts

Prescription of currency requirements
Payments to all countries may be made by crediting Jamaica dollars to an external account or a foreign currency account. Receipts from all countries must be received by debit of an external account or in any foreign currency.

Payment arrangements

Regional arrangements
Jamaica is a member of CARICOM.

Clearing agreements
The clearing arrangements within the framework of CARICOM have been suspended since November 1, 1990. The BJ no longer intervenes in CARICOM private sector commercial transactions; settlements for such transactions are effected by the commercial banking sector in convertible currencies.

Barter agreements and open accounts
n.a.

Administration of control

Exchange control authorities
Trading in foreign exchange, except by and through an authorized dealer, is prohibited. The Minister of Finance (MOF) has the authority to issue directions to specified classes of persons regarding the acquisition of foreign assets.

Controls on trade in gold (coins and/or bullion)
There are no restrictions on the purchase, sale, or holding of gold for numismatic or industrial purposes.

Controls on exports and imports of banknotes	No.

Resident Accounts

Eligibility to hold accounts	Juridical and natural persons are eligible.
Foreign exchange accounts permitted	Funds on these accounts ("A" accounts) may be transferred freely between residents and nonresidents. In cases when the transferee is a bank, licensed deposit-taking institution, credit union, building society, cambio operator, unit trust, or pension fund, the acquisition of the foreign currency must be in accordance with directions issued by the MOF. External accounts may be credited with payments by residents of Jamaica, with transfers from other external accounts, and with the proceeds from the sale to an authorized dealer of gold or foreign currencies. They may be debited for payments to residents of Jamaica, for transfers to other external accounts, and for the purchase of foreign currencies.
Held domestically	Yes.
Held abroad	Yes.
Accounts in domestic currency convertible into foreign currency	These accounts ("B" accounts) are exempt from tax on interest earned, provided that deposits are held as certificates of deposit with at least a 1-year maturity. After September 22, 1991, new B accounts were not permitted to be opened.

Nonresident Accounts

Eligibility to hold accounts	Juridical and natural persons are eligible.
Foreign exchange accounts permitted	A accounts held by nonresidents are subject to the same regulations applied to those accounts held by residents, but nonresidents may open tax-free foreign currency A accounts. All credits to these accounts must originate directly from foreign remittances and not from the local purchase of foreign exchange.
Domestic currency accounts	Same regulations as for accounts held by residents apply.
Convertible into foreign currency	Yes.
Blocked accounts	No.

Imports and Import Payments

Foreign exchange budget	Yes.
Financing requirements for imports	No.
Documentation requirements for release of foreign exchange for imports	No.
Import licenses and other nontariff measures	Import licenses are required for pharmaceutical products and items that endanger public health or security; otherwise, goods may be imported freely without a license. Import licenses, when required, are issued by the Trade Board, which is responsible to the Minister of Industry and Commerce. Imports of motor vehicles require a permit for government statistical purposes. Payments for imports may be made by commercial banks without reference to the BJ.
Import taxes and/or tariffs	Imports are subject to customs tariffs of up to 25% in compliance with the CET arrangement of CARICOM. Some agricultural products are subject to stamp duties of up to 95%. Taxes are collected by customs at the port of entry.

Taxes collected through the exchange system	No.
State import monopoly	No.

Exports and Export Proceeds

Repatriation requirements	No.
Surrender requirements	No.
Financing requirements	No.
Documentation requirements	No.
Export licenses	Most goods may be exported without restriction. However, specific licenses are required for exports of certain agricultural products, ammunition, explosives, firearms, antique furniture, motor vehicles, mineral and metal ores, paintings, jewelry, and petroleum products.
Export taxes	No.

Payments for Invisible Transactions and Current Transfers

Controls on these payments	No.

Proceeds from Invisible Transactions and Current Transfers

Repatriation requirements	No.
Surrender requirements	No.
Restrictions on use of funds	No.

Capital Transactions

Controls on capital and money market instruments	
On money market instruments	
Sale or issue locally by nonresidents	These transactions are subject to ministerial approval; a prospectus is required under the Companies Act.
Purchase abroad by residents	For banks, licensed deposit-taking institutions, credit unions, building societies, cambio operators, unit trusts, and pension funds, the purchase must be in accordance with directions issued by the MOF.
Sale or issue abroad by residents	Same regulations as for purchases apply.
On collective investment securities	Ministerial approval is required for banks, licensed deposit-taking institutions, credit unions, building societies, cambio operators, unit trusts, and pension funds.
Purchase locally by nonresidents	Yes.
Sale or issue locally by nonresidents	Yes.
Purchase abroad by residents	Yes.
Sale or issue abroad by residents	Yes.

Controls on credit operations	No.
Controls on direct investment	No.
Controls on liquidation of direct investment	No.
Controls on real estate transactions	No.

Provisions specific to commercial banks and other credit institutions

Differential treatment of nonresident deposit accounts and/or deposit accounts in foreign exchange

    Reserve requirements — There is a cash reserve requirement of 20% for foreign currency deposits and of 25% for domestic currency deposits.

    Liquid asset requirements — The requirement is 40% for assets in foreign currency compared to 47% for domestic currency assets.

Provisions specific to institutional investors — Mutual funds schemes must be approved by the Securities Commission.

Limits (min.) on portfolio invested locally — The minimum to be specified by the Superintendent of Insurance shall not exceed 70% of the domestic liabilities of the company.

Currency matching regulations on assets/liabilities composition — Commercial banks and licensed deposit-taking institutions are liable to be required to match their Jamaica dollar liabilities to their clients with Jamaica dollar assets.

Other controls imposed by securities laws — Nonresident companies must be incorporated or registered in Jamaica or other CARICOM member states in order to obtain a license to deal in securities or give investment advice. The nonresident company must be owned, controlled, or supervised by persons who are citizens of, and are actually residents in, Jamaica or other CARICOM state as may be prescribed.

Changes During 1996

No significant changes occurred in the exchange and trade system.

JAPAN

(Position as of December 31, 1996)

Status Under IMF Articles of Agreement

Article VIII	Date of acceptance: April 1, 1964.

Exchange Arrangement

Currency	The currency of Japan is the Japanese yen.
Exchange rate structure	Unitary.

Classification

Independent floating — The exchange rate of the Japanese yen is determined on the basis of supply and demand. However, the authorities intervene when necessary in order to counter disorderly conditions in the markets. The principal intervention currency is the U.S. dollar.

Exchange tax	No.
Exchange subsidy	No.
Forward exchange market	Forward exchange contracts may be negotiated against foreign currencies quoted on the Tokyo exchange market and in other major international foreign exchange markets. There are no officially set rates in the forward market, and forward exchange transactions are based on free market rates.
Official cover of forward operations	No.

Arrangements for Payments and Receipts

Prescription of currency requirements	No.
Payment arrangements	No.

Administration of control

Exchange control authorities — The exchange and trade control system is operated mainly by the Ministry of Finance (MOF), the Ministry of International Trade and Industry (MITI), and the Bank of Japan (BOJ) acting as the government's agent. Most of the authority for verifying normal payments is, however, delegated to authorized banks, referred to as foreign exchange banks. Import- and export-reporting requirements are handled by the MITI.

International security restrictions

In accordance with UN sanctions — Imports from, and exports to, Iraq and Libya require permission from the MITI. For transactions that involve payments from Japan to residents of Iraq and Libya or by residents of these countries to foreign countries through Japan, permission from the MOF is required. Intermediary trade of petroleum and its products destined for Angola requires permission from the MITI. All other payments for invisibles from Japan to residents of Iraq and Libya require permission from the MITI.

Payment arrears	No.
Controls on trade in gold (coins and/or bullion)	No.

Controls on exports and imports of banknotes

On exports

   Domestic currency — The exportation of domestic banknotes exceeding ¥5 million requires ministerial approval.

Resident Accounts

Eligibility to hold accounts	Juridical and natural persons are eligible.
Foreign exchange accounts permitted	Yes.
Held domestically	No.
Held abroad	Overseas deposits by residents up to the equivalent of ¥200 million are not restricted. Qualified Japanese enterprises in insurance, transportation, and securities are permitted to maintain overseas deposits under blanket licensing.
Accounts in domestic currency convertible into foreign currency	Yes.

Nonresident Accounts

Eligibility to hold accounts	Juridical and natural persons are eligible.
Foreign exchange accounts permitted	No.
Domestic currency accounts	Yes.
Convertible into foreign currency	Payment of interest on balances in such accounts may be restricted when it is deemed necessary to prevent drastic fluctuations in the exchange rate of the yen.
Blocked accounts	No.

Imports and Import Payments

Foreign exchange budget	No.
Financing requirements for imports	No.
Documentation requirements for release of foreign exchange for imports	No.
Import licenses and other nontariff measures	The Import Restriction System covers 77 items (4-digit Harmonized Commodity Description and Coding System (HS) base), which are subject to import restrictions falling under the state trading, national security, public health, and moral protection provisions of the GATT. For the restricted items, once importers obtain authorization from the MITI, they receive an import quota certificate that entitles them to receive an import license from an authorized foreign exchange bank automatically upon application. For the importation of certain other goods from certain countries or shipping areas, individual authorization must be obtained from the MITI. Import settlements effected under the special methods (i.e., those effected by means of open accounts or those involving payments made more than 2 years before import declaration or after more than 2 years of shipment) require authorization from the MITI.
Negative list	Yes.
Open general licenses	Yes.
Licenses with quotas	Yes.
Import taxes and/or tariffs	No.
State import monopoly	No.

Exports and Export Proceeds

Repatriation requirements	No.
Surrender requirements	No.
Financing requirements	No.
Documentation requirements	No.
Export licenses	Export restraint may be applied either globally or to certain destinations, and it may cover export volume, export prices, or other conditions. At the end of 1995, 27 export cartels were operating under the provisions of the Export and Import Transactions Law. In addition, 228 items were subject to a license under the Foreign Exchange and Foreign Trade Control Law to control their exportation to specified destinations either because of short supply in the domestic market (e.g., nickel) or to forestall the imposition of import restrictions by other countries (e.g., certain textiles). Exports under processing contracts and exports for which settlements are effected under the special methods described above require authorization from the MITI. Exports of specified raw materials for foreign processing and reimportation require individual licenses.
Without quotas	Yes.
With quotas	Yes.
Export taxes	No.

Payments for Invisible Transactions and Current Transfers

Controls on these payments	No.

Proceeds from Invisible Transactions and Current Transfers

Repatriation requirements	No.
Surrender requirements	No.
Restrictions on use of funds	No.

Capital Transactions

Controls on capital and money market instruments	Capital transactions, in principle, can be conducted freely unless certain procedures are specifically required. Such procedures may take the form of requiring (1) prior approval; (2) prior notice with a waiting period, during which the MOF or the MITI may request or order that the transaction be suspended or modified on the basis of prescribed criteria; or (3) prior notice without a waiting period.
On capital market securities	Acquisition of securities for portfolios may be made freely through designated securities firms, and foreign exchange banks and designated institutional investors may freely acquire securities for portfolio investments. However, acquisition of such securities through securities firms other than the designated ones and borrowings by residents require prior notice without a waiting period.
Sale or issue locally by nonresidents	Yen-denominated securities and yen-related dual currency bonds issued abroad cannot be resold to Japanese residents until after the expiration of a 40-day waiting period.
Purchase abroad by residents	Prior notification is required.
Sale or issue abroad by residents	Issue of securities abroad by residents is subject to prior notification with a 20-day waiting period.
Controls on derivatives and other instruments	No.

Controls on credit operations

Financial credits

By residents to nonresidents

Loans are subject to prior notice with a 20-day waiting period. Transactions requiring prior notice with a 20-day waiting period may be subject to suspension or modification by the MOF if, in the Minister's opinion, the transaction might adversely affect (1) international financial markets or Japan's international credit standing; (2) domestic and financial capital markets; (3) business activities of a sector of Japanese industries or the smooth performance of the national economy; and (4) implementation of Japan's international agreements, international peace and security, or the maintenance of public order. The MOF may shorten the waiting period when the transaction under consideration is deemed without adverse consequences.

Controls on direct investment

Inward direct investment

The provisions apply to (1) majority equity ownership of enterprises or establishment of branch operations; (2) any acquisition of shares in unlisted companies; (3) acquisition by a foreign investor of the shares of a listed company (including individual companies for which the stock price in over-the-counter transactions is made public by the Securities Dealers Association) that reach 10% or more when added to those owned by related persons; and (4) acquisition of loans of more than 1-year maturity or securities privately placed in Japan, under certain circumstances.

Any change of business objectives of a company with one-third or more foreign ownership is also subject to the direct investment provisions. Foreign investors are required to report investments only after undertaking them unless concerns arise about adverse implications for national security, public order, public safety, the activities of Japanese enterprises in related lines of activities, the general performance of the economy, or the maintenance of mutual equality of treatment of direct investment with other countries, in which cases requests or orders for suspension or modification of specific aspects of the transaction may be made.

Controls on liquidation of direct investment

No.

Controls on real estate transactions

No.

Provisions specific to commercial banks and other credit institutions

Maintenance of accounts abroad

There is (1) a ceiling on the investment by credit cooperatives in foreign-currency-denominated bonds, excluding corporate bonds issued by nonresidents, equivalent to 30% of their net worth; and (2) a ceiling of 5% of assets for investment in foreign-currency-denominated securities by the loan trust accounts of trust banks.

Lending to nonresidents (financial or commercial credits)

Foreign loans by banks are legally subject to prior notice with a waiting period but, in most cases, may be made upon notification. The banks are free to lend yen on a long-term basis overseas.

Lending locally in foreign exchange

This lending requires permission, except when the lender is an authorized foreign exchange bank.

Purchase of locally issued securities denominated in foreign exchange

Purchase of these securities from a resident requires permission, but purchase from nonresidents is subject to prior notification.

Provisions specific to institutional investors

Limits (max.) on portfolio invested abroad

The limits are (1) 30% of total assets for insurance companies holding securities issued by nonresidents; (2) the same ratio applies to purchases of foreign-currency-denominated assets; (3) 20% of the reserve funds issued by nonresidents for holding by the Post Office Insurance Fund of bonds; and (4) 30% of pension trust assets for foreign-currency-denominated assets purchased by pension funds (for the new money deposited from April 1, 1990, effective December 27, 1991, the ceiling was raised to 50% on the basis of each institutional account, and the ceiling for foreign-affiliated companies was raised to 70%).

Other controls imposed by securities laws   Yes.

Changes During 1996

Arrangements for payments and receipts

November 1. Restrictions in accordance with UN Security Council sanctions were lifted with regard to imports from Croatia, Bosnia and Herzegovina, and the Federal Republic of Yugoslavia (Serbia/Montenegro); and for transactions that involve payments for invisibles to residents of, and exports to Croatia, Bosnia and Herzegovina, and the Federal Republic of Yugoslavia (Serbia/Montenegro).

Resident accounts

April 1. The amount of overseas deposits by residents, which are not restricted, was raised to ¥200 million.

JORDAN

(Position as of December 31, 1996)

Status Under IMF Articles of Agreement

Article VIII   Date of acceptance: February 20, 1995.

Exchange Arrangement

Currency   The currency of Jordan is the Jordan dinar.

Other legal tender   The Central Bank of Jordan (CBJ) issues commemorative gold coins, which, although legal tender, do not circulate but are available to residents, nonresidents, and domestic numismatists.

Exchange rate structure   Unitary.

Classification

Pegged   The Jordan dinar is officially pegged to the SDR, but in practice it has been pegged to the U.S. dollar since late 1995. A fee of 0.1% may be levied by the CBJ on foreign currency transfers. Amounts transferred from customers' deposits in foreign currency, as well as transfers made by governmental entities, diplomatic missions, and nonprofit and humanitarian organizations are exempt from this fee as are amounts less than JD 300.

Exchange subsidy   No.

Forward exchange market   Licensed banks may buy foreign currencies without limit against the Jordan dinar from their customers on a forward deal basis, and they may sell foreign currencies against the Jordan dinar to their customers on a forward deal basis to pay for imports into Jordan.

Official cover of forward operations   For corporations or projects considered to be of vital national interest, the CBJ may offer a forward exchange facility in respect of forward exchange cover provided by Jordanian banks.

Arrangements for Payments and Receipts

Prescription of currency requirements   No.

Payment arrangements

Bilateral arrangements

   Inoperative   There is an arrangement with the Republic of Yemen.

Administration of control

Exchange control authorities   Exchange control is administered by the Foreign Exchange Control Department of the CBJ. Import policy is determined by the Ministry of Industry and Trade in cooperation with the Ministries of Finance, Supply, Agriculture, and Health.

International security restrictions   No.

Payment arrears

Official   Yes.

Controls on trade in gold (coins and/or bullion)

Controls on external trade   Imports of gold in any form are permitted without the prior approval of the CBJ. Exports of gold are allowed, subject to repatriation requirements. Nonresidents are also permitted to take gold out of Jordan if they originally brought it into Jordan or its foreign currency equivalent.

Controls on exports and imports of banknotes

On exports

  Domestic currency   Exports of up to JD 5,000 are allowed.

  Foreign currency   Nonresidents may take out up to the amount they declared on entry.

Resident Accounts

Eligibility to hold accounts   Juridical and natural persons are eligible.

Foreign exchange accounts permitted   Yes.

Held domestically   Individuals may maintain foreign currency accounts at licensed banks. Juridical persons may also open foreign currency accounts, provided that outstanding balances (including interest earnings) in each account do not exceed JD 1 million. Excess amounts must be sold for Jordan dinars to licensed banks or the CBJ. Withdrawals and transfers from such accounts for current payments are free of restrictions.

Held abroad   No.

Accounts in domestic currency convertible into foreign currency   No.

Nonresident Accounts

Eligibility to hold accounts   Juridical and natural persons are eligible.

Foreign exchange accounts permitted   These accounts may be opened with proof of nonresidency. Withdrawals and transfers from these accounts are free of restrictions.

Domestic currency accounts   Withdrawals and transfers from these accounts are free of restrictions provided that deposits are made from the sources identified in the application approved by the CBJ.

Convertible into foreign currency   Yes.

Blocked accounts   No.

Imports and Import Payments

Foreign exchange budget   No.

Financing requirements for imports

Advance import deposits   There is no legal requirement for advance import deposits; banks are free to set the percentage of advance import deposits they collect from customers against letters of credit (LCs) for imports at their discretion.

Documentation requirements for release of foreign exchange for imports

Preshipment inspection   Yes.

Letters of credit   Yes.

Import licenses and other nontariff measures   Licenses are not required except for goods on the negative list.

Negative list   The list includes imports from countries that have bilateral agreements with Jordan and imports by certain institutions.

Import taxes and/or tariffs	Customs duties are levied at one single rate.
Taxes collected through the exchange system	No.
State import monopoly	Oil imports are conducted by a state agency.

Exports and Export Proceeds

Repatriation requirements	No.
Surrender requirements	No.
Financing requirements	No.
Documentation requirements	No.
Export licenses	
Without quotas	Licenses for exports are not required except for exports to countries that have banking arrangements with Jordan.
Export taxes	No.

Payments for Invisible Transactions and Current Transfers

Controls on these payments	There are no controls on payments for freight and insurance, unloading and storage costs, and administrative expenses, or on commissions, interest payments and remittances of profits and dividends.
	Payments for travel, medical treatment, study abroad, subscriptions and membership fees, family maintenance and alimony, and the use of credit cards abroad require prior approval and are subject to a limit of JD 35,000 a year; no limits are imposed if transfers are made from foreign currency accounts held by nonresidents.

Proceeds from Invisible Transactions and Current Transfers

Repatriation requirements	No.
Surrender requirements	No.
Restrictions on use of funds	No.

Capital Transactions

Controls on capital and money market instruments	Outward transfers of capital by residents require approval and are not normally permitted.
On capital market securities	
Purchase abroad by residents	Yes.
Sale or issue abroad by residents	n.a.
On money market instruments	
Purchase locally by nonresidents	Nonresidents may use convertible currencies to purchase Premium Development Bonds denominated in Jordan dinars. Proceeds from redemption at maturity, including interest, are transferable in any convertible currency.
Purchase abroad by residents	Yes.

Sale or issue abroad by residents	n.a.
On collective investment securities	
Purchase abroad by residents	Yes.
Sale or issue abroad by residents	n.a.
Controls on derivatives and other instruments	
Purchase abroad by residents	Yes.
Sale or issue abroad by residents	n.a.
Controls on credit operations	
Commercial credits	
By residents to nonresidents	Licensed banks and financial companies may extend credit facilities in Jordan dinars to residents and nonresidents against their foreign currency deposits. The amounts of credit facilities extended to nonresidents against their foreign currency deposits should not exceed 5% of total credit granted by a bank or a financial company. Furthermore, the balance of the foreign currency deposit used as collateral against the extended credit facilities should not, at any time, be less than the outstanding balance of credit facilities. Effective January 20, 1996, the CBJ excluded loans extended to finance the export sector from its prior approval requirements, leaving such loans to be decided upon freely by licensed banks, provided that banks continue to comply with CBJ prudential requirements.
To residents from nonresidents	n.a.
Financial credits	
By residents to nonresidents	Yes.
To residents from nonresidents	n.a.
Guarantees, sureties, and financial backup facilities	
By residents to nonresidents	Yes.
To residents from nonresidents	n.a.
Controls on direct investment	
Outward direct investment	The CBJ may grant permission to banks; insurance companies; contractors; and industrial, agricultural, trade, and tourist firms to transfer funds abroad for specified investments or operating purposes. The transfer of funds for purposes of investment in Arab countries is permitted only if mutual treatment or bilateral agreements exist between Jordan and the country. It is the investor's responsibility to provide foreign exchange to finance such investments.
Inward direct investment	n.a.
Provisions specific to commercial banks and other credit institutions	
Borrowing abroad	n.a.
Maintenance of accounts abroad	n.a.
Lending to nonresidents (financial or commercial credits)	Commercial banks are permitted to invest abroad up to 50% of their foreign exchange holdings.
Lending locally in foreign exchange	n.a.
Purchase of locally issued securities denominated in foreign exchange	n.a.

Differential treatment of nonresident deposit accounts and/or deposit accounts in foreign exchange

n.a.

Changes During 1996

Resident accounts

October 29. Resident Jordanians were allowed to maintain foreign currency deposits with licensed banks in Jordan without any limit.

October 29. Resident accounts in foreign currencies were treated on equal footing with nonresident accounts in foreign currencies with respect to current payments.

October 29. Banks were permitted to manage portfolios in foreign currencies for resident accounts on the same basis applied to nonresident accounts.

October 29. The rules governing foreign currency margin trading for nonresident accounts and resident accounts in foreign currencies were unified.

Imports and import payments

January 20. The CBJ excluded loans extended to finance the export sector from its prior approval requirements, leaving such loans to be decided upon freely by licensed banks, provided that the banks continue to comply with CBJ prudential requirements.

October 29. Restrictions were lifted on payments for invisibles (from accounts in foreign currencies) to residents who have resident accounts in foreign currencies.

October 29. The CBJ authorized licensed banks to conduct asset swap operations for holders of foreign currency accounts without the approval of the CBJ.

KAZAKHSTAN

(Position as of December 31, 1996)

Status Under IMF Articles of Agreement

Article VIII   Date of acceptance: July 16, 1996.

Exchange Arrangement

Currency   The currency of Kazakhstan is the tenge.

Exchange rate structure   Unitary.

Classification

Independent floating   The official exchange rates of the tenge against the U.S. dollar, the deutsche mark, and
                                    the Russian ruble are determined once a week on the basis of rates in the foreign ex-
                                    change interbank and exchange bureau markets, and are announced each Monday by the
                                    National Bank of Kazakhstan (NBK). Official rates for more than 30 other currencies
                                    are set on the basis of cross rates in international markets. The currency market includes
                                    the interbank currency exchange, which conducts daily trading in online mode using an
                                    electronic trading system, an over-the-counter interbank market, and a network of ex-
                                    change bureaus handling cash foreign exchange transactions. Banks may participate in
                                    auctions on their own account or on behalf of their clients. Banks can also trade in an
                                    over-the-counter interbank market at freely negotiated rates. There are more than
                                    2,000 exchange bureaus that conduct foreign exchange cash transactions.

Exchange tax   No.

Exchange subsidy   No.

Forward exchange market   Foreign exchange futures are quoted at the Kazakh Stock Exchange and the Interna-
                                    tional Kazakh Agroindustrial Exchange.

Official cover of forward operations   No.

Arrangements for Payments and Receipts

Prescription of currency   All transactions between residents must be effected in tenge, unless otherwise stipulated
requirements   by law. Transactions between residents and nonresidents can be made in any currency as
                                    long as they comply with the relevant foreign exchange regulations of the NBK. The
                                    NBK has the right to impose restrictions on the payment currency for a resident's export
                                    operations.

Payment arrangements

Bilateral arrangements

  Operative   Settlements with the Baltic countries, Russia, and the other countries of the FSU are
                                    made through a system of correspondent accounts of the NBK and commercial banks.

Administration of control

Exchange control authorities   The NBK controls exchange transactions, supervises authorized banks, regulates open
                                    foreign exchange positions, and has the authority to reintroduce surrender requirements.

                                    The Ministry of Finance (MOF) supervises licensing of a limited number of imports and
                                    exports, monitors transactions in precious metals and stones, monitors capital transac-
                                    tions (i.e., external debt), and supervises the payment of export and import duties.
                                    Authorized banks and nonbank financial institutions are agents for foreign exchange
                                    control.

International security restrictions   No.

Payments arrears   No.

Controls on trade in gold (coins and/or bullion)

Controls on domestic ownership and/or trade	All gold produced from Kazakh raw materials must first be offered on the primary market, where the NBK and the MOF have the first right to sell and buy. Thereafter, the gold can be sold on the secondary market, including international markets. Licensed banks and other juridical persons are allowed to participate in the primary market. Memorial and jubilee coins produced from precious metals are regulated by currency regulations.
Controls on external trade	Yes.

Controls on exports and imports of banknotes

On exports	A declaration is required upon exit.
Domestic currency	Yes.
Foreign currency	Documents certifying the legal origin of funds are required when exporting more than $10,000.
On imports	A declaration is required upon entry.
Domestic currency	Yes.
Foreign currency	Yes.

Resident Accounts

Eligibility to hold accounts	Juridical and natural persons are eligible.
Foreign exchange accounts permitted	Yes.
Held domestically	Yes.
Held abroad	A license from the NBK is required. Accounts may be denominated in foreign or domestic currency.
Accounts in domestic currency convertible into foreign currency	Yes.

Nonresident Accounts

Eligibility to hold accounts	Juridical and natural persons are eligible.
Foreign exchange accounts permitted	Yes.
Domestic currency accounts	Yes.
Convertible into foreign currency	Yes.
Blocked accounts	No.

Imports and Import Payments

Foreign exchange budget	No.
Financing requirements for imports	
Advance payment requirements	Prepayment before 180 days requires prior registration with the NBK.
Documentation requirements for release of foreign exchange for imports	Presentation to an authorized bank of the relevant contract, agreement, or accord is required.

Domiciliation requirements	Yes.
Preshipment inspection	Yes.
Letters of credit	Yes.
Import licenses used as exchange licenses	Yes.
Import licenses and other nontariff measures	Import licenses are required for 11 categories of goods.
Negative list	Two categories of goods are subject to restrictions for public health and security reasons.
Import taxes and/or tariffs	Customs duties and excises are levied on imported goods.
Taxes collected through the exchange system	No.
State import monopoly	No.

Exports and Export Proceeds

Repatriation requirements	All proceeds must be repatriated, unless a license is granted by the NBK. Transfers of foreign currency to accounts of authorized banks must be done within 10 days of the date payment is made.
Surrender requirements	The NBK has the right to introduce a surrender requirement at any time.
Financing requirements	No.
Documentation requirements	
Letters of credit	Yes.
Guarantees	Yes.
Domiciliation	Yes.
Preshipment inspection	There is selective independent inspection of exports.
Export licenses	
Without quotas	A negative list based on security reasons requires export licenses for 17 commodity groups.
With quotas	n.a.
Export taxes	No.

Payments for Invisible Transactions and Current Transfers

Controls on these payments	Bona fide tests are applied to all payments.
Freight/insurance	
Quantitative limits	A maximum of 95% of the amount of the transaction may be reinsured abroad.
Payments for travel	
Quantitative limits	There are country-specific limits for business travel.
Indicative limits/bona fide test	For amounts exceeding $10,000, a document certifying the legal origins of the funds is required.
Subscriptions and membership fees	
Prior approval	An NBK license is required.

Gambling/prize earnings

   Indicative limits/bona fide test   The legal origin of funds must be documented.

Proceeds from Invisible Transactions and Current Transfers

Repatriation requirements   All proceeds should be repatriated, unless the NBK grants a license.

Surrender requirements   No.

Restrictions on use of funds   Yes.

Capital Transactions

Controls on capital and money market instruments

On capital market securities   Yes.

On money market instruments   Yes.

On collective investment securities   Yes.

Controls on derivatives and other instruments

Purchase locally by nonresidents   Yes.

Sale or issue locally by nonresidents Yes.

Purchase abroad by residents   Yes.

Sale or issue abroad by residents   Yes.

Controls on credit operations

Commercial credits

   By residents to nonresidents   Registration with the NBK is required for credits with a maturity of more than 180 days.

   To residents from nonresidents   Yes.

Financial credits

   By residents to nonresidents   A license is required for operations with a maturity of more than 180 days involving foreign exchange values.

   To residents from nonresidents   Registration with the NBK is required for credits with a maturity of more than 180 days.

Guarantees, sureties, and financial   Yes.
backup facilities

Controls on direct investment

Outward direct investment   Residents must obtain a license from the NBK to invest abroad.

Inward direct investment   Prior registration with the NBK is required.

**Controls on liquidation of direct   Yes.
investment**

Controls on real estate transactions

Purchase abroad by residents   A license from the NBK is required.

Purchase locally by nonresidents   Registration with the NBK is required.

Sale locally by nonresidents   Registration with the NBK is required.

Provisions specific to commercial banks and other credit institutions

Borrowing abroad	Registration with the NBK is required to receive credits for a term of more than 180 days.
Maintenance of accounts abroad	Yes.
Lending to nonresidents (financial or commercial credits)	A license from the NBK is required when extending credits in foreign currency for a term of more than 180 days.
Lending locally in foreign exchange	Yes.
Purchase of locally issued securities denominated in foreign exchange	Yes.
Differential treatment of nonresident deposit accounts and/or deposit accounts in foreign exchange	
Reserve requirements	Yes.
Liquid asset requirements	Yes.
Interest rate controls	Yes.
Investment regulations	Yes.
Open foreign exchange position limits	The open position in any one currency is limited to 30% of a bank's capital, and the total open position is limited to 50% of a bank's capital.

Provisions specific to institutional investors

Limits (max.) on portfolio invested abroad	Yes.
Limits (min.) on portfolio invested locally	Yes.
Currency matching regulations on assets/liabilities composition	Yes.
Other controls imposed by securities laws	A license is required for professional activities on the securities market and stock exchanges.

Changes During 1996

Status under IMF Articles of Agreement	*July 16.* Kazakhstan accepted the obligations of Article VIII, Sections 2, 3, and 4 of the Fund Agreement.
Arrangements for payments and receipts	*July 3.* Precious metals offered for sale at primary market trading sessions that are not sold were permitted to be sold on the secondary market or exported abroad.
	December 24. The Law on Foreign Exchange Regulation was passed.
Nonresident accounts	*February 1.* Limitations imposed on the use of proceeds of current international transactions deposited in certain "T" accounts were removed.
	February 1. Transfer of funds from "I" accounts in bank deposits, deposit certificates of banks, bonds (including government bonds), and other types of debt obligations was permitted.
Imports and import payments	*February 1.* Limitations on the making of pre- and postdelivery import payments were removed.
Exports and export proceeds	*August 15.* Independent preshipment inspection of goods exported from the Republic of Kazakhstan was abolished, and selective independent inspection of export contracts was instituted.

KENYA

(Position as of December 31, 1996)

Status Under IMF Articles of Agreement

Article VIII	Date of acceptance: June 30, 1994.

Exchange Arrangement

Currency	The currency of Kenya is the Kenya shilling.
Exchange rate structure	Unitary.
Classification	
Independent floating	The exchange rate is determined in the interbank market. Foreign exchange bureaus are authorized to deal in cash and foreign traveler's checks. The official exchange rate is set at the previous day's average market rate. The U.S. dollar is the principal intervention currency. The official exchange rate applies only to government and government-guaranteed external debt-service payments and to government imports for which there is a specific budget allocation.
Exchange tax	No.
Exchange subsidy	No.
Forward exchange market	Commercial banks are authorized to enter into forward exchange contracts with their customers at market-determined exchange rates in currencies of their choice. There are no limits on the amount or period of cover.
Official cover of forward operations	No.

Arrangements for Payments and Receipts

Prescription of currency requirements	No.
Payment arrangements	No.
Administration of control	
Exchange control authorities	The Central Bank Act gives the Central Bank of Kenya (CBK) powers to license and regulate foreign exchange transactions.
International security restrictions	No.
Payment arrears	Kenya is negotiating to reschedule arrears amounting to $62 million that accrued to commercial banks prior to end-1993.
Official	Yes.
Controls on trade in gold (coins and/or bullion)	No.
Controls on exports and imports of banknotes	No.

Resident Accounts

Eligibility to hold accounts	Juridical and natural persons are eligible.
Foreign exchange accounts permitted	Yes.

455

Held domestically	Yes.
Held abroad	Yes.
Accounts in domestic currency convertible into foreign currency	Yes.

Nonresident Accounts

Eligibility to hold accounts	Juridical and natural persons are eligible.
Foreign exchange accounts permitted	Yes.
Domestic currency accounts	Yes.
Convertible into foreign currency	Yes.
Blocked accounts	No.

Imports and Import Payments

Foreign exchange budget	No.
Financing requirements for imports	No.
Documentation requirements for release of foreign exchange for imports	A copy of the import declaration, a final invoice, and a copy of the customs entry must be submitted.
Preshipment inspection	The inspection is required for all imports with an f.o.b. value of more than $1,000. These are subject to inspection for quality, quantity, and price, and require a clean report of findings. On August 19, 1996, banks were allowed to use their discretion to effect clean payments (for imports) provided they obtain an undertaking from the importer to submit the documents later.
Import licenses and other nontariff measures	
Negative list	The list includes a few items for health, security, and environmental reasons.
Import taxes and/or tariffs	Yes.
Taxes collected through the exchange system	No.
State import monopoly	No.

Exports and Export Proceeds

Repatriation requirements	No.
Surrender requirements	No.
Financing requirements	No.
Documentation requirements	No.
Export licenses	
Without quotas	Coffee, tea, and horticultural produce may be exported only if a sales contract is registered with the Coffee Board, Tea Board, and Horticultural Crops Development Authority, respectively. Exports of certain foods and agricultural products require special licenses to ensure adequate supplies in the domestic market. Exports of minerals, precious stones, and other essential strategic materials are also subject to special licensing.

Export taxes   No.

Payments for Invisible Transactions and Current Transfers

Controls on these payments   No.

Proceeds from Invisible Transactions and Current Transfers

Repatriation requirements   No.

Surrender requirements   No.

Restrictions on use of funds   No.

Capital Transactions

Controls on capital and money market instruments

On capital market securities

 Purchase locally by nonresidents   Nonresidents are allowed to purchase a maximum of 40% of shares of primary or secondary issues. A nonresident cannot purchase more than 5% of the total of secondary or primary issues.

 Sale or issue locally by nonresidents   There is no control on the sale of securities by nonresidents. However, issuance of securities by nonresidents requires prior approval from the Capital Markets Authority (CMA).

 Sale or issue abroad by residents   Sale or issue of securities abroad by residents requires prior approval from the CMA.

On money market instruments

 Sale or issue locally by nonresidents   There are no controls on sales, but the issuing requires prior approval from the CBK.

 Sale or issue abroad by residents   The sale or issuance of money market instruments abroad by residents requires prior approval by the CBK.

On collective investment securities   The same regulations as for capital market securities apply.

 Purchase locally by nonresidents   Yes.

 Sale or issue locally by nonresidents   Yes.

Controls on derivatives and other instruments

Sale or issue locally by nonresidents   CBK's approval is required for these transactions.

Sale or issue abroad by residents   CBK's approval is required for these transactions.

Controls on credit operations   No.

Controls on direct investment   No.

Controls on liquidation of direct investment   No.

Controls on real estate transactions

Purchase locally by nonresidents   Purchases of real estate are subject to government approval.

Provisions specific to commercial banks and other credit institutions

Differential treatment of nonresident deposit accounts and/or deposit accounts in foreign exchange

    Reserve requirements   Foreign currency deposits are not subject to reserve requirements.

Open foreign exchange position limits   Foreign exchange exposure is limited to a maximum of 20% of paid-up capital (assigned). Foreign exchange exposure is defined as net foreign assets reported on the balance sheet.

Provisions specific to institutional investors   No.

Other controls imposed by securities laws   No.

Changes During 1996

Arrangements for payments and receipts   *August 19.* Commercial banks were required to complete the CBK statistical forms for all foreign exchange transactions above $10,000 (or equivalent).

Resident accounts   *August 19.* Foreign currency accounts were permitted to be opened by residents.

Nonresident accounts   *August 19.* Nonresidents were allowed to open foreign currency accounts.

Imports and import payments   *July 1.* The minimum value of imports subject to preshipment inspection was raised to an f.o.b. value of $1,000 from $500.

    August 19. Banks were allowed to use their discretion to effect clean payments (for imports) provided they obtain an undertaking from the importer to submit the documents later.

    August 19. Goods purchased by importers in Kenya no longer need to be insured with companies licensed to conduct business in Kenya.

Proceeds from invisible transactions and current transfers   *June 19.* Exportation and importation of local and foreign currency notes exceeding $5,000 (K Sh 300,000) were required to be declared to customs for statistical purposes.

    August 19. Reporting requirements for exportation/importation of local and foreign currency notes were removed.

Capital transactions   *August 19.* Details of outward investment transactions in amounts of the equivalent of $500,000 and above were required to be reported to the CBK for statistical purposes.

KIRIBATI

(Position as of December 31, 1996)

Status Under IMF Articles of Agreement

Article VIII   Date of acceptance: August 22, 1986.

Exchange Arrangement

Currency   The currency of Kiribati is the Australian dollar.

Other legal tender   Kiribati coins are also in circulation.

Exchange rate structure   Unitary.

Classification

Pegged   There is no central monetary institution and the authorities do not buy or sell foreign exchange. The Bank of Kiribati (BOK), the only commercial bank, quotes daily rates for 15 currencies on the basis of their respective values against the Australian dollar.

Exchange tax   No.

Exchange subsidy   No.

Forward exchange market   No.

Arrangements for Payments and Receipts

Prescription of currency requirements   Outward and inward payments may be settled in Australian currency or in any other currency. Purchases and sales of foreign currencies in exchange for Australian dollars must be undertaken with the BOK, the only authorized foreign exchange dealer.

Payment arrangements   No.

Administration of control   No.

International security restrictions   No.

Payment arrears   No.

Controls on exports and imports of banknotes   No.

Resident Accounts

Foreign exchange accounts permitted   Yes.

Held domestically   Yes.

Held abroad   Yes.

Nonresident Accounts

Eligibility to hold accounts   Juridical and natural persons are eligible.

Foreign exchange accounts permitted   Yes.

Blocked accounts   No.

Imports and Import Payments

Foreign exchange budget	No.
Financing requirements for imports	No.
Import licenses and other nontariff measures	
Positive list	n.a.
Negative list	Imports of certain goods are prohibited for health, safety, or environmental reasons.
Open general licenses	n.a.
Licenses with quotas	n.a.
Import taxes and/or tariffs	Tariffs ranging from zero to 80% apply to most private imports. Specific duties apply to imports of rice, flour, petroleum products, alcoholic beverages, and tobacco products.
Taxes collected through the exchange system	n.a.
State import monopoly	No.

Exports and Export Proceeds

Repatriation requirements	No.
Surrender requirements	No.
Financing requirements	No.
Export licenses	Copra, a dried coconut meat that produces coconut oil, can be exported only through the Kiribati Copra Cooperative Society.
Export taxes	No.

Payments for Invisible Transactions and Current Transfers

Controls on these payments	No.

Proceeds from Invisible Transactions and Current Transfers

Surrender requirements	No.

Capital Transactions

Controls on direct investment	
Outward direct investment	n.a.
Inward direct investment	The authorities encourage investments in the export-promoting or import-substituting sectors. All applications for foreign investment up to $A 250,000 must be made to the Foreign Investment Commission for approval. Applications with a larger capital contribution are approved by the Cabinet.

Changes During 1996

No significant changes occurred in the exchange and trade system.

REPUBLIC OF KOREA

(Position as of March 31, 1997)

Status Under IMF Articles of Agreement

Article VIII   Date of acceptance: November 1, 1988.

Exchange Arrangement

Currency   The currency of Korea is the won.

Exchange rate structure   Unitary.

Classification

Managed floating   The exchange rate of the won against the U.S. dollar is determined on the basis of the weighted average of interbank rates for the won-dollar spot transactions of the previous day. During each business day, the won rate against the dollar in the interbank market is allowed to fluctuate within margins of ±2.25% against the market average rate of the previous day.

Exchange tax   No.

Exchange subsidy   No.

Forward exchange market   Foreign exchange banks may conduct forward transactions, futures transactions, swaps, and options between foreign currencies, as well as between the won and foreign currencies. There are no specific restrictions on the terms of forward contracts in respect of interbank transactions; however, the terms of forward contracts between foreign exchange banks and nonbank customers must be based on a bona fide transaction.

Official cover of forward operations   No.

Arrangements for Payments and Receipts

Prescription of currency requirements   All settlements with other countries may be made in any convertible currency except the won. Residents are permitted to carry out current transactions denominated in won, provided that remittances are made in foreign currencies. For this purpose, nonresidents are allowed to open settlement accounts in won (free won accounts) for current transactions as well as for reinsurance contracts and investments in domestic stocks.

Payment arrangements   No.

Bilateral arrangements   No.

Administration of control

Exchange control authorities   The Ministry of Finance and Economy (MOFE) initiates policy with respect to prescription of currency, method of settlement, foreign exchange operations, payments for current transactions, and capital transactions and transfers. The Bank of Korea (BOK) executes most of the above functions; it also regulates the operations of the exchange market and may intervene in it.

International security restrictions   No.

Payment arrears   No.

Controls on trade in gold (coins and/or bullion)

Controls on external trade   Residents are allowed to import and export gold other than gold coins in circulation, subject to the same regulations as those applied to merchandise trade (Foreign Trade Act).

461

Controls on exports and imports of banknotes

On exports

Domestic currency   Banknotes in excess of W 8 million may not be exported without permission from the BOK.

Foreign currency   Banknotes in excess of the equivalent of $10,000 may not be exported without specific permission. Upon leaving Korea, nonresidents may purchase foreign currency up to the amount they have sold during their stay in Korea.

On imports

Domestic currency   The importation of Korean currency in excess of W 8 million is restricted.

Foreign currency   Residents and nonresidents must register domestic or foreign currency they bring into Korea at a customs office if the amount exceeds the equivalent of $10,000.

Resident Accounts

Eligibility to hold accounts   Juridical and natural persons are eligible.

Foreign exchange accounts permitted   Yes.

Held domestically   The foreign currency composition of these accounts may be changed without restriction.

Held abroad   Institutional investors are permitted to hold deposits abroad for asset diversification purposes without a quantitative ceiling. General corporations and individuals are permitted to hold deposits abroad of up to $3 million and $50,000 a year, respectively.

Accounts in domestic currency convertible into foreign currency   No.

Nonresident Accounts

Eligibility to hold accounts   Juridical and natural persons are eligible.

Foreign exchange accounts permitted   Remittances from these accounts and withdrawals in foreign currency may be made freely. The approval of the bank where the account is held is not required for remittances abroad or transfers to other foreign currency accounts for purchases and withdrawals of foreign means of payment or for payments relating to approved transactions.

Domestic currency accounts   Yes.

Convertible into foreign currency   Yes.

Imports and Import Payments

Foreign exchange budget   No.

Financing requirements for imports   No.

Documentation requirements for release of foreign exchange for imports   No.

Import licenses and other nontariff measures   Under the Imports Diversification Program introduced to promote a geographically balanced import structure, there are 152 items for which imports are restricted; the program is to be abolished by the end of 1999.

Negative list   Yes.

Open general licenses   All imports require licenses, but for most imports licenses are issued upon application. Imports are divided into 2 categories: automatic approval items and restricted items. As of July 1, 1996, 81 of the 10,859 basic items on the Harmonized System were classified as restricted imports. Imports of raw materials for the production of exports are normally approved automatically, irrespective of their classification. Import licenses are granted only to registered traders, who are required to have exported and/or imported a minimum value of $500,000 in any 1 of the last 2 calendar years. Of the 81 items restricted under the GATT balance of payments provision, 73 items are scheduled to be liberalized by 1997. However, quantitative restrictions will be applied for rice, subject to Annex 5 of the WTO Agreement on Agriculture.

Licenses with quotas	A trade commission may recommend quotas and quality standards if it has determined that certain imports have harmed domestic industries.
Import taxes and/or tariffs	No.
State import monopoly	No.

Exports and Export Proceeds

Repatriation requirements	Export earnings exceeding $50,000 must be repatriated to Korea within 6 months, except in specific cases. However, general trading companies licensed under the Foreign Trade Act and enterprises whose trade value in the previous year exceeded $5 million are allowed to retain overseas deposits up to 50% of this value within the limit of $500 million.
Surrender requirements	No.
Financing requirements	No.
Documentation requirements	No.
Export licenses	
Without quotas	There are 2 agricultural and fishery products and 8 industrial products currently subject to voluntary export restraints.
With quotas	There are quotas under the ATC and other bilateral agreements.
Export taxes	No.

Payments for Invisible Transactions and Current Transfers

Controls on these payments	There are no controls on payments for freight and insurance, unloading and storage costs, administrative expenses, profits and dividends, medical costs, subscriptions and membership fees, pensions, or gambling and prize earnings.
Commissions	
Prior approval	Approval of the BOK is required for the remittance of commissions not directly linked with trade and for remittances exceeding the established limits.
Quantitative limits	The limits are $50,000 and 10% of the value of the underlying transactions.
Indicative limits/bona fide test	Yes.
Interest payments	
Prior approval	The transfer of income from securities acquired through inheritance is subject to prior approval.
Payments for travel	
Quantitative limits	The monthly allowance for residents staying abroad for over 30 days is $10,000. For those staying abroad over 1 year, a remittance of $50,000 (including basic travel allowances) is allowed within 2 weeks after the time of departure.

| *Indicative limits/bona fide test* | Residents traveling abroad may, in general, purchase foreign exchange up to the equivalent of $10,000 a trip as their basic travel allowance; additional foreign exchange may also be purchased for specified expenses, including transportation costs. |

Study abroad costs

| *Quantitative limits* | The basic monthly allowance for students under 20 years old is $3,000; for students with a dependent family, an additional allowance of $500 for a spouse and each child is allowed. |

| *Indicative limits/bona fide test* | Yes. |

Consulting/legal fees

| *Prior approval* | Fees related to financial or insurance businesses require MOFE approval, and other fees require BOK approval. |

Foreign workers' wages

| *Quantitative limits* | Salaries, except for basic living expenses and retirement allowances, may be remitted to the home countries. |

Family maintenance/alimony

| *Quantitative limits* | Residents are allowed to remit up to $5,000 a transaction to their parents and children living abroad for living expenses and to their relatives abroad for wedding gifts or funeral donations, with no restrictions on the number of remittances. |

| *Indicative limits/bona fide test* | Yes. |

Credit card use abroad

| *Quantitative limits* | Residents can make payments abroad by credit card for expenditures relating to travel and tourism; for amounts exceeding $5,000 a month, the foreign exchange authorities must verify the authenticity of the payments. |

| *Indicative limits/bona fide test* | Yes. |

Proceeds from Invisible Transactions and Current Transfers

| **Repatriation requirements** | Yes. |
| **Surrender requirements** | Residents are permitted to hold foreign currency earned from invisible transactions, but once converted into won, a limit applies to reconversion. Residents and nonresidents must register domestic and foreign exchange they bring into Korea at customs if the amount exceeds the equivalent of $10,000. The importation by travelers of Korean currency in excess of W 2 million is restricted. The proceeds received by construction companies from construction activity abroad must be deposited in foreign currency accounts at domestic foreign exchange banks, and profits may be converted into won following the completion of each project. Domestic firms engaged in international construction and service businesses may deposit abroad up to 30% of the balance of their overseas contracts or $3 million, whichever is greater. |

Capital Transactions

Controls on capital and money market instruments

On capital market securities

| *Purchase locally by nonresidents* | Nonresidents may freely acquire listed stocks up to 5% individually and 20% collectively of the local number of shares issued. For convertible bonds issued by small- and medium-sized enterprises (SMEs), they may acquire up to 5% individually and 30% collectively of the total value of convertible bonds. For other purchases, including public bonds designated by the Securities Exchange Commission, nonresidents require prior approval from the MOFE. |

Sale or issue locally by nonresidents	International organizations may issue won-denominated bonds in the domestic capital market; however, other nonresidents require prior approval from the MOFE in order to issue securities in the market. Nonresidents may sell those securities or the rights thereof that they were allowed to acquire.
Sale or issue abroad by residents	The issue of won-denominated securities abroad requires prior approval of the MOFE. Foreign-currency-denominated securities may be issued abroad by residents by submitting a report to the MOFE. The report of issuance is assumed to be accepted 7 days after submission unless notification to the contrary is made by the MOFE.

On money market instruments

Purchase locally by nonresidents	Foreign investment funds and international beneficiary certificates established with the approval of the MOFE can purchase domestic money market securities without approval of the authorities. For transactions of money market securities between residents and nonresidents other than those mentioned above, approval of the MOFE is required.
Sale or issue locally by nonresidents	These transactions require MOFE approval.
Sale or issue abroad by residents	Certificates of deposit and commercial paper may be regarded as securities like equities and bonds by the Foreign Exchange Management Act (FEMA), Decree (FEMD), and Regulation (FEMR). These money market securities may be issued in won or foreign currencies. The issue of foreign-currency-denominated securities on a foreign money market must be filed with the MOFE. Investors who have been approved to purchase foreign money market securities are allowed to sell such securities.

On collective investment securities

Purchase locally by nonresidents	The same controls as for capital market securities apply.
Sale or issue locally by nonresidents	The issuance of beneficiary certificates by trust companies, either in the domestic or the foreign market, is subject to MOFE approval. The approval system on the issuance of beneficiary certificates is designed especially to protect investors and may be regarded as a kind of prudential regulation. The size of the issuance of beneficiary certificates shall be established at an appropriate amount in consideration of the volume of the capital inflow resulting from the capital market opening.
Purchase abroad by residents	Such purchase is subject to approval by the MOFE.
Sale or issue abroad by residents	Issuance and sale of collective investment securities by foreign trust companies in the domestic market require MOFE approval. Although the purchase of domestic collective investment securities by nonresidents requires MOFE approval, nonresidents may sell domestic collective investment securities they have lawfully acquired.

Controls on derivatives and other instruments

Purchase locally by nonresidents	Foreign investment funds or international beneficiary certificates established with permission from the MOFE may purchase domestic instruments and claims without reporting. Also, foreign banks can purchase domestic instruments and claims from domestic foreign exchange banks. Other transactions require permission from the MOFE. Effective May 1996, stock index futures began to be traded on the existing stock exchange, and nonresidents' access to the market was allowed within certain limits.
Sale or issue locally by nonresidents	The issue of foreign instruments and claims on the domestic financial market requires MOFE approval. It is not necessary for nonresidents to obtain permission or submit a report when selling domestic instruments and claims once they are permitted to purchase them.
Purchase abroad by residents	Residents other than foreign exchange banks may trade through a foreign exchange bank within certain limits equivalent to actual demand.
Sale or issue abroad by residents	These transactions require approval by the MOFE.

Controls on credit operations

Commercial credits

By residents to nonresidents

SMEs, firms engaged in social overhead capital projects, foreign-financed firms with high technology, and domestic firms that wish to repay overseas borrowing earlier than contracted may borrow abroad. Foreign borrowing by these firms of more than $1 million and with maturities of more than 3 years is governed by the Foreign Capital Inducement Act. Foreign-financed companies are, in principle, subject to the same regulations governing foreign borrowing as other enterprises. Deferred receipt exports on a letter-of-credit basis, for which the settlement period is less than 3 years from the shipment of goods or signing of the export bill of exchange, are allowed without restriction. For settlement periods of more than 3 years, these exports are allowed in the following cases with validation from a foreign exchange bank: (1) when payment is guaranteed by the importing country's central government agency or central bank; (2) when they are covered by export insurance; and (3) when qualified foreign banking institutions, as designated by the BOK, open letters of credit and guarantee payment.

Imports exceeding 360 days are allowed with the validation of a foreign exchange bank in cases where refund guarantees must be provided by the exporting country's central government agency, central bank, or qualified banking institution.

Residents wishing to enter into lease contracts for assets other than real estate from nonresidents shall obtain validation from a foreign exchange bank.

To residents from nonresidents

All methods of settlement for trade in goods and services are free, except for those methods specified on the negative list under the FEMR.

Financial credits

By residents to nonresidents

These credits require prior approval from the MOFE.

To residents from nonresidents

Foreign exchange banks may borrow abroad. Borrowing by high-technology, foreign-financed manufacturing companies is allowed up to 100% of the foreign-invested capital. Also, maturity is limited to 3 years or less, and limitations are imposed on the use of funds. Foreign borrowing repayable within 3 years is governed by the Foreign Exchange Act. The maximum maturity period permitted for deferred payments is 180 days for imports of raw materials for export production.

Guarantees, sureties, and financial backup facilities

By residents to nonresidents

Residents, other than banks, must obtain approval from the BOK, except for the following cases: (1) when a foreign importer is granted an offshore loan by a foreign exchange bank to finance imports from a resident, and the said resident pledges a guarantee in foreign currency; (2) when a resident concludes a contract guaranteeing performance or bearing responsibility for the liabilities assumed by the nonresident, who in turn is providing a guarantee, such as bid bonds or other sureties, related to international bids or contracts entered into by a resident; and (3) when residents provide guarantees to serve as collateral for spot financing. There are no restrictions on the provision of underwritten backup facilities by the domestic institutional investors when they participate in an international underwriting syndicate.

To residents from nonresidents

Any resident may freely accept a guarantee relating to an overseas borrowing to finance an overseas investment from another resident, in which the surety for the guarantee is pledged by nonresidents. Other transactions related to the creation of credits arising from liability guarantee contracts between residents and nonresidents require approval from the BOK. Therefore, residents are free to take up financial backup facilities offered by nonresidents as long as the issuance of overseas securities has been properly reported.

Controls on direct investment

Outward direct investment

For investments of up to $10 million, validation of a foreign exchange bank is needed; for amounts between $10 million and $50 million, notification to the BOK is needed. If the amount exceeds $50 million, approval of the BOK is needed, and the Overseas Investment Advisory Committee examines the investment plan to analyze the effects of the investment on the domestic economy prior to issuing an approval.

Inward direct investment

Equity participation is possible by increasing the amount invested in newly established or existing enterprises. Direct investment by means of mergers and acquisitions is not allowed. For the establishment and extension of a domestic branch of a foreign enterprise, approval from the MOFE is required for financial institutions; approval of the BOK is required for nonfinancial institutions and notification to the BOK for establishment of an office. Investments in public utilities, radio, and television are restricted.

Direct investments are allowed in all industries, except those specified on a "negative" list, including about 5% of all industries listed in the Korean standard industrial classification and less than 1% of industries in the manufacturing sector.

In general, foreign-financed companies are no longer required to set up partnerships with local firms. There are no restrictions on the maximum value of foreign investment. Tax privileges may be granted to foreign-financed projects that involve advanced technology. Tax privileges have been continuously reduced, and postinvestment controls have also been relaxed to treat foreign and local companies equally.

All foreign direct investments, except those in industries on the negative list, are subject to a notification requirement. A notification is deemed accepted by a foreign exchange bank unless it advises to the contrary.

Controls on liquidation of direct investment

No.

Controls on real estate transactions

Purchase abroad by residents

Overseas direct investments in the fields of lease and sale of real estate, construction, and operation of golf courses are prohibited. No approvals or notifications are required for acquisition of overseas real estate by foreign exchange banks, government authorities, and residents if given as gifts or through inheritance from nonresidents. However, a notification to the BOK is required for the acquisition of real estate necessary for approved business activities costing up to $10 million. For real estate necessary for approved business activities exceeding $10 million, permission from the BOK is required.

Purchase locally by nonresidents

The following are not restricted: acquisition of domestic land or mortgages, leasing of domestic real estate by nonresidents, and acquisition of real estate or associated rights other than land by nonresidents from nonresidents. Notification to the BOK is required for the acquisition of real estate and its associated rights, including real estate acquired through inheritance or as a gift from nonresidents, and the establishment of fixed collateral not assuming the transfer of ownership. Approval of the MOFE is required for real estate acquisitions other than those specified above.

Sale locally by nonresidents

Approval from the BOK is required.

Provisions specific to commercial banks and other credit institutions

Borrowing abroad

For reference, the foreign exchange banks are required to report to the MOFE the funding of maturities of 1 year or more and for amounts exceeding $10 million.

Lending to nonresidents (financial or commercial credits)

Foreign exchange banks may extend credits without restriction to nonresidents in foreign currency. Other credit institutions that used to be able to extend credits up to $10 million were allowed to extend foreign currency credits to nonresidents without restriction in 1996. Foreign currency loans by resident banks to nonresidents of less than $2 million are permitted freely. Loans ranging from $2 million to $20 million require ex post notification to the MOFE, and loans exceeding $20 million require prior notification to the MOFE. Other credit institutions may extend credits up to $10 million.

Lending locally in foreign exchange

There are loan ceilings according to the economic sector.

Differential treatment of nonresident deposit accounts and/or deposit accounts in foreign exchange

Reserve requirements

Reserve requirements on foreign currency deposit accounts are 9% for resident accounts and 1% for nonresident accounts.

Open foreign exchange position limits

The limits are as follows: (1) overall overbought position, 15% of the total equity capital at the end of the previous month; (2) overall oversold position, 10% of the total equity capital at the end of the previous month or $20 million, whichever is greater; and (3) spot oversold position, 3% of the total equity capital or $5 million, whichever is greater.

Provisions specific to institutional investors

In addition to the foreign exchange laws or foreign exchange controls, all institutional investors have their own rules for asset operations. For example, securities companies must keep their proportion of the portfolio invested within 30% of their total assets. Insurance companies and securities investment trust companies can maintain their portfolio abroad within 10% and 30% of their total assets, respectively.

Limits (max.) on portfolio invested abroad

Institutional investors are permitted to hold deposits abroad for asset diversification purposes without a quantitative ceiling. General corporations and individuals are permitted to hold deposits abroad of up to $3 million and $50,000 a year, respectively.

Other controls imposed by securities laws

Restrictions imposed by the Securities Laws are as follows: (1) domestic securities investments by nonresident foreign nationals are regulated by "Rules on Sales and Purchases of Securities by Foreigners" established by the Securities Exchange Commission (SEC). The main contents of the Rules include investment ceilings, investment procedures, and the management of foreign investors, etc.; (2) overseas securities investments by residents are regulated by "Rules on Sales and Purchases of Overseas Securities" established by the SEC. The main contents of the Rules include securities' eligibility for investment and transaction procedures, etc.; (3) issuance of overseas securities by residents are regulated by "Rules on Issuance of Overseas Securities" and "Rules on Management of Listed Companies on Overseas Securities Markets" established by the SEC. The main contents of the Rules include the eligibility of issuers, the use of funds raised by issuance, and the obligations of issuers on reporting, etc.; and (4) international securities transactions by residents are regulated by "Rules on Securities Business by Domestic Branches of Foreign Securities Companies" established by the SEC. The main contents of the Rules include the accumulation of retained earnings and the obligation of submitting financial statements, etc. The main contents of "Rules on Overseas Securities Business by Domestic Securities Companies" include the restriction on the investment of domestic listed stocks by overseas branches of securities companies.

Changes During 1996

Arrangements for payments and receipts

June 1. The prescription of currency requirements applicable to foreign currencies were abolished.

June 1. Deposits overseas in won were allowed within the ceiling on the amount of won that can be carried out when traveling abroad. Also, residents were allowed to purchase and sell won, within the ceiling on the amount of won that can be carried out when traveling abroad, at both the domestic foreign exchange banks overseas and at branches and subsidiaries of foreign banks.

June 1. The limit on won that can be carried in and out when traveling abroad was raised to W 8 million from W 3 million.

Exports and export proceeds

June 1. The limit on the amount of foreign currency that can be held abroad by general trading companies was raised to 50% with the maximum of $500 million of the trading value from 30% with the maximum of $300 million.

Capital transactions

April 1. The ceilings on securities investments by residents were abolished.

May 1. The issuance of deferred receipts by foreign companies was allowed.

May 3. Stock index futures began to be traded on the existing stock exchange, and non-residents' access to the market was allowed within a limit of 15%.

June 1. The extension of foreign currency credits abroad by resident institutional investors was liberalized.

July 1. The ceiling on export advances for large enterprises was raised to 15% of the export value of the previous year from 10%.

October 31. The ceiling on stock investments by nonresidents was raised twice. The ceiling on aggregate purchases rose to 20% from 15%, and the ceiling on individual purchases rose to 5% from 3%.

October 31. Indirect investment in domestic bonds was allowed by means of the Country Fund.

November 1. The access of nonresidents to the stock index of the futures market was raised to 30% from 15%.

Changes During 1997

Capital transactions

March 31. The total quantitative ceilings on the issuance of foreign-currency-denominated securities abroad were raised.

KUWAIT

(Position as of December 31, 1996)

Status Under IMF Articles of Agreement

Article VIII   Date of acceptance: April 5, 1963.

Exchange Arrangement

Currency   The currency of Kuwait is the Kuwaiti dinar.

Exchange rate structure   Unitary.

Classification

Pegged   The external value of the Kuwaiti dinar is determined on the basis of a fixed but adjust-
                                                able relationship between the dinar and a weighted basket of currencies of Kuwait's
                                                trade and financial partners. The Central Bank of Kuwait (CBK) sets the exchange rate
                                                vis-à-vis the U.S. dollar on the basis of the latest market quotations in relation to the
                                                other currencies included in the basket.

Exchange tax   No.

Exchange subsidy   No.

Forward exchange market   Yes.

Official cover of forward operations   Official coverage is extended to forward contracts related to commercial transactions.

Arrangements for Payments and Receipts

Prescription of currency   No.
requirements

Payment arrangements

Regional arrangements   GCC central banks maintain a regional arrangement to exchange GCC banknotes.

Barter agreements and open accounts   Yes.

Administration of control

Exchange control authorities   There is no exchange control, and both residents and nonresidents may freely purchase
                                                and sell foreign exchange. All trade with Israel is prohibited. Payments may not be
                                                made to or received from Israel for any type of transaction.

International security restrictions   No.

Payment arrears   No.

Controls on trade in gold (coins
and/or bullion)

Controls on external trade   Monetary authorities and merchants registered with the Ministry of Commerce and In-
                                                dustry (MCI) may import and export gold in any form if such gold is at least 18-karat
                                                fine; gold jewelry may not be imported or sold unless it is properly hallmarked. Jewelry
                                                and precious metals in any form, manufactured or unmanufactured, are subject to an
                                                import duty of 4%.

Controls on exports and imports of   No.
banknotes

Resident Accounts

Eligibility to hold accounts	Juridical and natural persons are eligible.
Foreign exchange accounts permitted	Yes.
Held domestically	Yes.
Held abroad	Yes.
Accounts in domestic currency convertible into foreign currency	Yes.

Nonresident Accounts

Eligibility to hold accounts	Juridical and natural persons are eligible.
Foreign exchange accounts permitted	Yes.
Domestic currency accounts	Yes.
Convertible into foreign currency	Yes.
Blocked accounts	No.

Imports and Import Payments

Foreign exchange budget	No.
Financing requirements for imports	No.
Documentation requirements for release of foreign exchange for imports	No.

Import licenses and other nontariff measures

Import licenses are required for all commercial imports other than fresh fruits and vegetables. Licenses, except for wheat and flour, are issued freely to registered Kuwaiti merchants and companies. To be registered, the importer must be either a Kuwaiti citizen, a firm in which all partners are Kuwaiti nationals, or a shareholding or limited liability company in which Kuwaiti nationals own at least 51% of the stock.

Government procurement policies grant preferences to Kuwaiti-produced goods up to a price margin of 5% over goods produced in other GCC countries and 10% over goods produced in non-GCC countries.

Negative list

The importation of oxygen, certain steel and asbestos pipes, pork and foodstuffs containing pork, alcoholic beverages, used vehicles over 5 years old, portable telephones, chewing tobacco, and gas cylinders is prohibited.

Open general licenses

Imports of industrial equipment, machinery, and their spare parts require industrial licenses valid for one-time use only. Licenses are issued to registered and licensed industrial establishments with the approval of the Industrial Development Commission at the MCI. Private imports of personal objects may be permitted under individual or specific licenses. Registered importers handling a variety of commodities may obtain a general license valid for 1 year. Other importers must obtain specific licenses for individual commodities, which are also valid for 1 year.

Import taxes and/or tariffs

Kuwait applies the uniform tariff structure of the GCC. A minimum tariff of 4% applies to non-GCC imports, while no tariffs apply to imports with at least 40% local value added from other GCC members. Imports of foodstuffs, as well as some machinery and equipment, spare parts, and raw materials are exempt from import duties. Kuwait applies higher tariffs in industries where domestic producers cater to at least 40% of the local market. Tariff rates differ depending on the domestic value-added content of the products in question. If the domestically produced goods contain at least 20%, 30%, or 40% of domestic value added, protective duties of 15%, 20%, and 25%, respectively, may be applied to competing imports. The degree of protection given by the formula is reduced by 5% in the case of consumer goods. The maximum duty imposed on products that compete with locally manufactured goods is 100%.

Taxes collected through the exchange system	No.
State import monopoly	No.

Exports and Export Proceeds

Repatriation requirements	No.
Surrender requirements	No.
Financing requirements	No.
Documentation requirements	No.
Export licenses	Exports of live sheep and poultry, sugar, fats, rice, meat, eggs, milk, cheese, butter, olive oil, fresh fruits, vegetables in any form, beans, lentils, chickpeas, jams, and cement may be prohibited in time of emergency or shortage in Kuwait. These items may be exported in limited quantities only under a special license issued by the MCI. Exports of arms and ammunition also require licenses.
With quotas	Yes.
Export taxes	No.

Payments for Invisible Transactions and Current Transfers

Controls on these payments	No.

Proceeds from Invisible Transactions and Current Transfers

Repatriation requirements	No.
Surrender requirements	No.
Restrictions on use of funds	No.

Capital Transactions

Controls on capital and money market instruments	The listing of foreign stocks and bonds on the Kuwait Stock Exchange is subject to the approval of the Exchange Committee.
On capital market securities	
Purchase locally by nonresidents	GCC nationals are allowed to purchase local stocks up to a certain limit. Other nonresidents are not allowed to purchase capital market securities, namely, stocks. However, nonresidents can purchase local treasury bills and bonds through local banks and investment companies.
Sale or issue locally by nonresidents	Yes.

On money market instruments

   Sale or issue locally by   Yes.
   nonresidents

On collective investment securities

   Purchase locally by nonresidents   Yes.

   Sale or issue locally by   Yes.
   nonresidents

Controls on derivatives and other instruments

Purchase locally by nonresidents   Yes.

Sale or issue locally by nonresidents   Yes.

Controls on credit operations   No.

Controls on direct investment

Inward direct investment   Government agreement is necessary for the participation of nonresident capital in resident corporations in Kuwait; foreign participation in new Kuwaiti companies must be less than 49%. The participation of GCC nationals in companies established in Kuwait may reach up to 75% of the capital, and there are no restrictions on participation in retail trade enterprises by non-Kuwaiti GCC nationals.

Controls on liquidation of direct investment   No.

Controls on real estate transactions

Purchase locally by nonresidents   Only GCC nationals can purchase real estate for private residence purposes of up to 3,000 square meters.

Sale locally by nonresidents   Yes.

Provisions specific to commercial banks and other credit institutions

Lending to nonresidents (financial or commercial credits)   Yes.

Differential treatment of nonresident deposit accounts and/or deposit accounts in foreign exchange

   Liquid asset requirements   Yes.

   Interest rate controls   Yes.

Provisions specific to institutional investors   No.

Other controls imposed by securities laws   No.

Changes During 1996

No significant changes occurred in the exchange and trade system.

KYRGYZ REPUBLIC
(Position as of March 31, 1997)

Status Under IMF Articles of Agreement

Article VIII   Date of acceptance: March 29, 1995.

Exchange Arrangement

Currency   The currency of the Kyrgyz Republic is the som (100 tiyiyns = 1 som).

Exchange rate structure   Unitary.

Classification

Managed floating   The exchange rate of the som vis-à-vis the U.S. dollar is determined on the basis of auctions that are held twice a week at the National Bank of the Kyrgyz Republic (NBK) in which licensed commercial banks and foreign exchange bureaus participate. Exchange rates for other currencies are determined on the basis of cross-exchange rates. The NBK publishes the exchange rate of the som in terms of the U.S. dollar and 38 other currencies twice a week. In addition to the NBK, the commercial banks and the Settlement-and-Savings Company under the NBK are authorized to conduct foreign exchange transactions. Purchases and sales of foreign exchange are permitted without restriction.

Exchange tax   No.

Exchange subsidy   No.

Forward exchange market   No.

Arrangements for Payments and Receipts

Prescription of currency requirements   There are no prescription of currency requirements, and settlements may be made in any currency, including nonconvertible currencies (e.g., Russian rubles and Kazakh tenge).

Payment arrangements

Bilateral arrangements   There are agreements with the Baltic countries, Russia, and the other countries of the FSU except Georgia; there are credit agreements with Pakistan and Turkey.

  Operative   Yes.

Regional arrangements   There are agreements with the Interstate Bank and the Central Asian Bank for Cooperation and Development.

Administration of control

Exchange control authorities   The NBK has responsibility for managing its gold and foreign exchange reserves. The som is fully convertible with no restrictions on buying, selling, or holding foreign currencies. The NBK is also responsible for issuing foreign exchange licenses to commercial banks and to foreign exchange bureaus. Foreign trade is regulated by the Ministry of Foreign Trade and Industry, which issues import and export licenses when required. Licenses for foreign investment and registration of foreign investors are granted by the State Commission for Foreign Investments and Economic Aid in coordination with the Ministry of Finance.

International security restrictions   No.

Payment arrears   No.

Controls on trade in gold (coins and/or bullion)   All gold produced is sold at market prices. The government and the NBK have priority in purchasing at that price. If the government and the NBK do not exercise that right, the gold is sold either in the domestic market or abroad.

Controls on exports and imports of banknotes	No.

Resident Accounts

Eligibility to hold accounts	Juridical and natural persons are eligible.
Foreign exchange accounts permitted	These accounts must be registered with the NBK and account information must be transmitted to the tax authorities.
Held domestically	Yes.
Held abroad	Yes.
Accounts in domestic currency convertible into foreign currency	Yes.

Nonresident Accounts

Eligibility to hold accounts	Juridical and natural persons are eligible.
Foreign exchange accounts permitted	Yes.
Domestic currency accounts	Yes.
Convertible into foreign currency	Yes.
Blocked accounts	No.

Imports and Import Payments

Foreign exchange budget	No.
Financing requirements for imports	No.
Documentation requirements for release of foreign exchange for imports	No.
Import licenses and other nontariff measures	
Negative list	Imports of armaments, explosive materials, nuclear materials and equipment, poisons, narcotics, works of art, antiques, precious rare earth materials, and rare animal and vegetable matter used in pharmaceutical products are prohibited for reasons of national interest.
Import taxes and/or tariffs	Goods from the former CIS countries can be imported duty free. Imports from non-CIS countries are subject to a flat customs duty of 10%. The following goods were made subject to a special customs fee on imports from CIS and non-CIS countries in 1996: gasoline (25%), electronic goods (20%), furniture (10%), carpets (35%), and crystal (30%).
	At end-January 1997, the government converted the customs fees on gasoline, carpets, and crystal to excise fees and thus only electronic goods and furniture remain subject to higher customs fees.
Taxes collected through the exchange system	No.
State import monopoly	No.

Exports and Export Proceeds

Repatriation requirements	No.
Surrender requirements	No.
Financing requirements	No.
Documentation requirements	No.
Export licenses	Exports of weapons, explosives, nuclear materials, poisons, drugs, works of arts, antiques, precious rare earth materials, and rare animal and vegetable matter used in pharmaceutical products require licenses for reasons of national interest.
Without quotas	Yes.
Export taxes	No.

Payments for Invisible Transactions and Current Transfers

Controls on these payments	No.

Proceeds from Invisible Transactions and Current Transfers

Repatriation requirements	No.
Surrender requirements	No.
Restrictions on use of funds	No.

Capital Transactions

Controls on capital and money market instruments	
On capital market securities	
Sale or issue locally by nonresidents	Yes.
Sale or issue abroad by residents	Yes.
On money market instruments	
Sale or issue locally by nonresidents	Yes.
Sale or issue abroad by residents	Yes.
Controls on derivatives and other instruments	Currently these instruments are not regulated.
Controls on credit operations	No.
Controls on direct investment	
Inward direct investment	Yes.
Controls on liquidation of direct investment	No.
Controls on real estate transactions	
Purchase locally by nonresidents	Purchases are subject to approval by the government.

Provisions specific to commercial banks and other credit institutions

Maintenance of accounts abroad   After an account is opened, it must be registered.

Purchase of locally issued securities denominated in foreign exchange   Yes.

Open foreign exchange position limits   Yes.

Provisions specific to institutional investors

Limits (max.) on portfolio invested abroad   Investment funds are not permitted to invest, locally or abroad, more than 10% of their total assets in the securities of a single issuer, or to hold more than 25% of the common stock of an issuer.

Other controls imposed by securities laws   No.

Changes During 1996

Exchange arrangements   *July 10.* The mandatory purchase by the NBK of gold extracted and produced in the Kyrgyz Republic was abolished, and it was established that the government of the Kyrgyz Republic and the NBK have priority in purchasing gold extracted and produced in the Kyrgyz Republic.

December 2. The Ministry of Foreign Trade and Industry was established.

Exports and export proceeds   *February 27.* Export taxes were abolished for silk cocoons and hides.

August 25. Export taxes of 30% were introduced for grain.

October 17. Export taxes on grain were abolished.

Changes During 1997

Exchange arrangements   *March 27.* The Settlement and Savings Company under the NBK received a license to accept foreign currency deposits.

March 28. A general agreement on customary terms for effecting bilateral transactions on the interbank currency market and the state securities market, and an agreement on the establishment of a representative office were concluded with the Interstate Bank.

LAO PEOPLE'S DEMOCRATIC REPUBLIC

(Position as of March 31, 1997)

Status Under IMF Articles of Agreement

Article XIV	Yes.

Exchange Arrangement

Currency	The currency of the Lao People's Democratic Republic (Lao PDR) is the kip (KN).
Other legal tender	The Thai baht and U.S. dollar circulate freely and are used for payments.
Exchange rate structure	Unitary.
Classification	
Managed floating	The exchange rate is determined in the interbank market; commercial banks and foreign exchange bureaus are permitted to buy and sell foreign exchange at freely determined rates, provided the spread between buying and selling rates remains less than 2%. In practice, however, la Banque pour le commerce extérieur du Laos, the major state-owned commercial bank and the dominant transactor in the official exchange market, sets the exchange rate. Based on this information, the exchange arrangement has been reclassified as managed floating from March 31, 1997.
Exchange tax	No.
Exchange subsidy	No.
Forward exchange market	No.

Arrangements for Payments and Receipts

Prescription of currency requirements	No prescription of currency requirements are imposed on receipts or payments but, in principle, the central bank (CB) provides and accepts only deutsche mark, French francs, Japanese yen, pounds sterling, Swiss francs, Thai baht, and U.S. dollars.
Payment arrangements	Yes.
Bilateral arrangements	Yes.
Operative	n.a.
Inoperative	n.a.
Regional arrangements	n.a.
Clearing agreements	n.a.
Barter agreements and open accounts	Bilateral trading arrangements are maintained with China, Poland, Russia, Thailand, and Vietnam.
Administration of control	
Exchange control authorities	Official transactions are handled by the central bank. The Ministry of Commerce (MOC) grants import and export authorization to state trading companies, joint ventures between domestic enterprises and foreign investors, cooperatives, and other public and private enterprises.
Controls on trade in gold (coins and/or bullion)	
Controls on external trade	Imports and exports of gold and silver require CB authorization.

Resident Accounts

Eligibility to hold accounts

Juridical and natural persons are eligible.

Foreign exchange accounts permitted

Foreign exchange accounts may be credited with (1) proceeds from exports of goods and services; (2) other transfers from abroad; (3) transfers or payments from foreign currency accounts opened with commercial banks within the Lao PDR; and (4) foreign banknotes and coins. These accounts, which are interest bearing, may be debited for conversion into kip for domestic expenditure, or foreign exchange balances may be used for authorized external payments and transfers.

Held domestically

Yes.

Held abroad

n.a.

Nonresident Accounts

Eligibility to hold accounts

Juridical and natural persons are eligible.

Foreign exchange accounts permitted

These accounts may be credited with (1) remittances from abroad; (2) transfers from other nonresident and resident foreign currency accounts in Lao PDR; and (3) foreign currency brought into the country by the account holder and duly declared upon arrival. Nonresidents are not allowed to accept, for deposit to their accounts, foreign currency proceeds from exports of goods and services of residents without the approval of the CB. These accounts, which bear interest, may be debited for (1) conversion into kip; (2) transfers into residents' and nonresidents' foreign currency accounts maintained with an authorized commercial bank; (3) payments in kip to accounts of residents or nonresidents; and (4) payments and transfers abroad.

Domestic currency accounts

These accounts may be credited with (1) sales of foreign currencies and (2) transfers from other convertible kip accounts of holders of the same category. Nonresidents are not permitted to deposit kip belonging to residents to their convertible kip accounts. These accounts may be debited for (1) payments in kip and (2) conversion into foreign currency at the prevailing buying rate of the commercial bank concerned.

Convertible into foreign currency

Yes.

Imports and Import Payments

Foreign exchange budget

No.

Financing requirements for imports

Minimum financing requirements

n.a.

Advance payment requirements

n.a.

Advance import deposits

Margin deposits are required against letters of credit, and the rates are set by the Lao Bank for Foreign Trade (BCEL) and other commercial banks.

Documentation requirements for release of foreign exchange for imports

Domiciliation requirements

n.a.

Preshipment inspection

n.a.

Letters of credit

Yes.

Import licenses used as exchange licenses

n.a.

Import licenses and other nontariff measures

Import licenses issued by the MOC and provincial government authorities are required for all goods. Imports may be made by any registered export-import business. These consist of state trading companies, joint-venture trade companies, and private trade companies. These companies are categorized as enterprises producing either mainly for export, for import substitution only, for general multicommodity, for export-import, or for export promotion. Imports are classified into 9 categories. Enterprises that are producing import substitutes are allowed to import only materials for construction and electrical products and instruments; vehicles and spare parts; medicine, medical equipment, and chemical products for manufacturing; and fuel.

Negative list	Yes.
Licenses with quotas	Imports of vehicles, with the exception of imports for foreign investment projects, international organizations, diplomats and retirees, are subject to quotas set by the government.
Import taxes and/or tariffs	The tariff structure is composed of 6 rates (5%, 10%, 15%, 20%, 30%, and 40%). The lowest rates apply to imports of raw materials, certain inputs, and certain essential consumer goods. The highest rates of 30% and 40% apply to luxury consumer goods, certain beverages, and tobacco. Special tariff rates apply to vehicles (50%, 80%, 100%, and 150%), cigarettes (60%), and beer (80%).
Taxes collected through the exchange system	n.a.
State import monopoly	No.

Exports and Export Proceeds

Repatriation requirements	Yes.
Surrender requirements	No.
Export licenses	Export licenses, which are issued by the MOC and provincial government authorities, are required for all products.
With quotas	Quotas apply only to timber.
Export taxes	Export duties are levied on certain products at rates ranging from 3% to 30%.
Taxes collected through the exchange system	n.a.

Payments for Invisible Transactions and Current Transfers

Controls on these payments	No.

Proceeds from Invisible Transactions and Current Transfers

Repatriation requirements	Proceeds from invisibles are, in practice, treated in the same way as proceeds from merchandise exports.
Surrender requirements	No.
Restrictions on use of funds	No.

Capital Transactions

Controls on capital and money market instruments	Outward capital transfers by residents are not permitted.
On capital market securities	Yes.

Purchase locally by nonresidents	n.a.
Sale or issue locally by nonresidents	n.a.
Purchase abroad by residents	n.a.
Sale or issue abroad by residents	n.a.
On money market instruments	Yes.
Purchase locally by nonresidents	n.a.
Sale or issue locally by nonresidents	n.a.
Purchase abroad by residents	n.a.
Sale or issue abroad by residents	n.a.
On collective investment securities	Yes.
Purchase locally by nonresidents	n.a.
Sale or issue locally by nonresidents	n.a.
Purchase abroad by residents	n.a.
Sale or issue abroad by residents	n.a.
Controls on derivatives and other instruments	Yes.
Purchase locally by nonresidents	n.a.
Sale or issue locally by nonresidents	n.a.
Purchase abroad by residents	n.a.
Sale or issue abroad by residents	n.a.
Controls on direct investment	
Outward direct investment	Yes.
Inward direct investment	Yes.
Controls on liquidation of direct investment	No.
Provisions specific to commercial banks and other credit institutions	
Borrowing abroad	n.a.
Maintenance of accounts abroad	n.a.
Lending to nonresidents (financial or commercial credits)	n.a.
Lending locally in foreign exchange	n.a.
Purchase of locally issued securities denominated in foreign exchange	n.a.
Differential treatment of nonresident deposit accounts and/or deposit accounts in foreign exchange	
Reserve requirements	All kip and foreign currency deposits are subject to reserve requirements. Reserves on kip deposits are to be held in kip.

Liquid asset requirements	n.a.
Interest rate controls	n.a.
Credit controls	n.a.
Investment regulations	n.a.
Open foreign exchange position limits	n.a.

Changes During 1996

No significant changes occurred in the exchange and trade system.

Changes During 1997

Exchange arrangements   *March 31.* The exchange rate arrangement was reclassified as managed floating.

LATVIA

(Position as of January 31, 1997)

Status Under IMF Articles of Agreement

Article VIII   Date of acceptance: June 10, 1994.

Exchange Arrangement

Currency   The currency of Latvia is the lats.

Exchange rate structure   Unitary.

Classification

Managed floating   The lats is informally pegged to the SDR and, since February 1994, has maintained a constant exchange rate against the SDR of LVL 0.7997 per SDR 1. The Bank of Latvia (BOL) quotes fixing rates of the lats against 22 convertible currencies daily. These rates are used for accounting purposes, and are valid through the next day. The BOL also quotes in real time buying and selling rates for the currencies in the SDR basket (i.e., U.S. dollars, French francs, deutsche mark, Japanese yen, and pounds sterling). The spread between the buying and selling rates is 2%.

Exchange tax   No.

Exchange subsidy   No.

Forward exchange market   No.

Arrangements for Payments and Receipts

Prescription of currency requirements   Settlements with the Baltic countries, the Russian Federation, and the other countries of the former Soviet Union can be made through any means, including through a system of correspondent accounts. Settlements with countries with which the BOL maintains agreements on mutual settlement of accounts are effected in accordance with the terms of these agreements.

Payment arrangements

Bilateral arrangements

Inoperative   Inoperative bilateral payment agreements are maintained with Armenia, Azerbaijan, Estonia, Georgia, Kazakhstan, the Kyrgyz Republic, Lithuania, Moldova, the Russian Federation, Tajikistan, Ukraine, and Uzbekistan. Outstanding balances from similar accounts with Belarus and Turkmenistan have been cleared.

Regional arrangements   n.a.

Administration of control

Exchange control authorities Government decisions adopted by the cabinet of ministers and approved by parliament prevail in foreign exchange and trade matters, but the authority to issue regulations governing foreign exchange transactions has been delegated to the BOL. All foreign exchange transactions must be effected through authorized banks and enterprises licensed by the BOL.

International security restrictions   No.

Payment arrears   No.

Controls on trade in gold (coins and/or bullion)

Controls on domestic ownership and/or trade   A license is required.

Controls on exports and imports of banknotes	No.

Resident Accounts

Eligibility to hold accounts	Resident natural persons and enterprises are allowed to hold foreign currencies in domestic or foreign bank accounts and to use these funds for domestic payments.
Foreign exchange accounts permitted	Yes.
Held domestically	Yes.
Held abroad	Yes.
Accounts in domestic currency convertible into foreign currency	Yes.

Nonresident Accounts

Eligibility to hold accounts	Nonresident natural persons and enterprises are permitted to hold bank accounts in Latvia denominated in either foreign or domestic currency.
Foreign exchange accounts permitted	Yes.
Domestic currency accounts	Yes.
Convertible into foreign currency	Yes.

Imports and Import Payments

Foreign exchange budget	No.
Financing requirements for imports	No.
Documentation requirements for release of foreign exchange for imports	No.
Import licenses and other nontariff measures	
Positive list	n.a.
Negative list	There are virtually no licensing requirements for imports except on imports of sugar, cereals, tobacco and tobacco products, alcoholic beverages, and fuels, which are retained for statistical purposes. For national health and safety reasons, licenses are also required for pyrotechnic products, arms and ammunition, combat vehicles, and prepared explosives.
Import taxes and/or tariffs	The tariff system includes a basic tariff rate of 20% for final nonagricultural goods, with 15% applied to goods from countries with MFN status. In 1995, 39% of imports were assessed the 15% MFN duty rate or less. Another 57% of imports were subject to lower duties under free-trade agreements. Only 4% of imports were subject to the 20% rate. Estimated production-weighted average tariff rates of 53% (46% MFN rates) are applied to agricultural goods. Most raw materials, spare parts, fruit, nuts, coffee, and tea are assessed a 1% duty (0.5% when imported from MFN countries). Some final goods are exempt from customs duties. Specific duties apply to a few goods, such as certain grains, flour, sugar, certain confectionary products, alcohol, cigarettes, cars, and motorcycles.

At end-July 1996, Latvia maintained trade and economic cooperation agreements providing for MFN status with the following countries: Armenia, Australia, Azerbaijan, Belarus, Canada, Cyprus, China, Cuba, Hungary, Iceland, India, Kazakhstan, the Kyrgyz Republic, Moldova, Poland, Romania, Russia, Tajikistan, Turkmenistan, Ukraine, the United States, Uzbekistan, and Vietnam. Latvia has free-trade agreements with the other Baltic countries, the European Union, EFTA, the Czech Republic, the Slovak Republic, and Slovenia.

Taxes collected through the exchange system	No.
State import monopoly	No.

Exports and Export Proceeds

Repatriation requirements	No.
Surrender requirements	No.
Financing requirements	No.
Documentation requirements	No.
Export licenses	No.
Export taxes	Export duties are levied on waste and scrap metals, certain categories of round logs, certain mineral products, works of art, antiques, and certain books.
Taxes collected through the exchange system	No.

Payments for Invisible Transactions and Current Transfers

Controls on these payments	No.

Proceeds from Invisible Transactions and Current Transfers

Repatriation requirements	No.
Surrender requirements	No.
Restrictions on use of funds	No.

Capital Transactions

Controls on capital and money market instruments	No.
Controls on derivatives and other instruments	No.
Controls on credit operations	No.
Controls on direct investment	
Inward direct investment	Nonresidents are not allowed to hold more than 49% of shares in companies operating in the forestry sector and in lottery and gambling businesses.
Controls on liquidation of direct investment	No.

Controls on real estate transactions

Purchase locally by nonresidents

The purchase of buildings is permitted, but the purchase of land near borders and in environmentally protected areas is not allowed.

In October 1996, the law on land privatization in rural regions was passed, allowing juridical persons registered in Latvia to purchase rural land when more than one-half of the paid share capital of the company belongs (1) to citizens of Latvia or to citizens of countries with which Latvia has an agreement on promotion of foreign investment; (2) to a group of the previous categories; and (3) it is a public joint-stock company, shares of which are quoted on the stock exchange.

On January 13, 1997, the law on land reform in cities was passed, establishing that urban land can be purchased by foreign juridical persons registered in Latvia when more than one-half of the paid share capital of the company belongs to the citizens of Latvia or to natural or juridical persons of countries with which Latvia has an agreement on promotion of foreign investment.

Juridical persons registered in Latvia have the right to purchase land under buildings and constructions that have been acquired as a result of privatization and the land necessary for the maintenance of buildings and constructions.

Provisions specific to commercial banks and other credit institutions

Open foreign exchange position limits

The open foreign currency position is limited to 10% of capital for any single foreign currency and 20% of capital for all foreign currencies.

Provisions specific to institutional investors

No.

Other controls imposed by securities laws

No.

Changes During 1996

Capital transactions

April 9. The requirement of cabinet approval for foreign direct investment above $1 million was eliminated.

December 5. The law on land privatization in rural regions was passed, allowing juridical persons registered in Latvia to purchase rural land when more than one-half of the paid share capital of the company belongs (1) to citizens of Latvia or to citizens of countries with which Latvia has an agreement on promotion of foreign investment; (2) to a group of the previous categories; and (3) it is a public joint-stock company, shares of which are quoted on the stock exchange.

Changes During 1997

Capital transactions

January 13. Regulations of the cabinet of ministers with the power of the law on privatization and expropriation of urban land of Republic of Latvia were passed. The Regulations allow persons registered in Latvia to purchase urban land when more than one-half of the paid share capital of the company belongs (1) to the citizens of Latvia, (2) to the citizens of countries with which Latvia has an agreement to promote foreign investment, (3) a group of the previous categories, and (4) it is a public joint-stock company, quoting shares on the stock exchange.

LEBANON

(Position as of December 31, 1996)

Status Under IMF Articles of Agreement

Article VIII	Date of acceptance: July 1, 1993.

Exchange Arrangement

Currency	The currency of Lebanon is the Lebanese pound.
Exchange rate structure	Unitary.
Classification	
Independent floating	Exchange rates are market determined, but the authorities may announce buying or selling rates for certain currencies and intervene when necessary in order to maintain orderly conditions in the exchange market. Banks are allowed to engage in spot transactions in any currency except in Israeli new sheqalim.
Exchange tax	No.
Exchange subsidy	No.
Forward exchange market	Banks are prohibited from engaging in forward transactions unless the transactions are related to foreign trade.
Official cover of forward operations	No.

Arrangements for Payments and Receipts

Prescription of currency requirements	No.
Payment arrangements	
Barter agreements and open accounts	n.a.
Administration of control	No.
International security restrictions	No.
Controls on trade in gold (coins and/or bullion)	The importation, exportation, and domestic sale of foreign gold coins require a certificate, issued by the Office for the Protection of the Consumer, that indicates the gold content and weight.
Controls on domestic ownership and/or trade	Yes.
Controls on external trade	Yes.
Controls on exports and imports of banknotes	No.

Resident Accounts

Eligibility to hold accounts	Yes.
Juridical persons	n.a.
Natural persons	n.a.
Foreign exchange accounts permitted	Yes.

Held domestically	Yes.
Approval required	n.a.
Held abroad	n.a.

Nonresident Accounts

Eligibility to hold accounts	Yes.
Juridical persons	Yes.
Natural persons	n.a.
Foreign exchange accounts permitted	Yes.
Approval required	n.a.
Domestic currency accounts	Banks are prohibited from receiving deposits or opening accounts in Lebanese pounds for nonresident banks and financial institutions. Such accounts cannot be held at nonresident banks or financial institutions.
Convertible into foreign currency	Yes.
Blocked accounts	No.

Imports and Import Payments

Foreign exchange budget	No.
Financing requirements for imports	
Advance import deposits	Importers must place with banks a prior deposit of 15% of the value of the letter of credit (LC) in the same currency as the LC.
Documentation requirements for release of foreign exchange for imports	
Letters of credit	Banks must ensure that importers possess a valid import license, if required, before issuing LCs.
Import licenses and other nontariff measures	Import licenses are required for certain finished goods, insulated electric and telephone wires, and copper cables.
Positive list	n.a.
Negative list	All imports from Israel are prohibited. Imports prohibited year-round include citrus fruits, apples, and liquid milk. Imports prohibited during a specified period of the year include squash, eggplant, green beans, watermelons, peas, apricots, potatoes, onions, cucumbers, tomatoes, garlic, jew's mallow, okra, muskmelons, pears, peaches, green almonds, grapes, green peppers, pomegranates, and green plums. Imports of certain other agricultural products and all seeds require a license.
Import taxes and/or tariffs	The tariff regime is based on the Brussels Tariff Nomenclature. Ad valorem duty rates on most products range from zero to 20% and are applied on a most-favored-nation basis, except for certain imports from Arab countries, which are accorded a preferential rate. The tax on motor vehicles is levied at the rate of 20% of the first LL 25 million and 35% on the remaining value. The following rates apply to alcoholic beverages: beer, 35% of the value; champagne, wine, and vermouths, 80% of the value; and arak, 50% of the value.
Taxes collected through the exchange system	No.

State import monopoly	Imports of some goods are reserved for the government.

Exports and Export Proceeds

Repatriation requirements	No.
Surrender requirements	No.
Financing requirements	No.
Documentation requirements	No.
Export licenses	Exports of arms and ammunition, narcotics, and similar products are prohibited. Licenses are required for wheat and wheat derivatives to any country and for all exports to the Democratic People's Republic of Korea.
Without quotas	Yes.
Export taxes	No.

Payments for Invisible Transactions and Current Transfers

Controls on these payments	No.

Proceeds from Invisible Transactions and Current Transfers

Repatriation requirements	No.
Surrender requirements	No.
Restrictions on use of funds	No.

Capital Transactions

Controls on capital and money market instruments	No.
Controls on derivatives and other instruments	No.
Controls on credit operations	
Commercial credits	
By residents to nonresidents	Yes.
To residents from nonresidents	n.a.
Financial credits	
By residents to nonresidents	Yes.
To residents from nonresidents	n.a.
Guarantees, sureties, and financial backup facilities	
By residents to nonresidents	Yes.
To residents from nonresidents	n.a.
Controls on direct investment	No.

Controls on liquidation of direct investment	No.
Controls on real estate transactions	No.
Provisions specific to commercial banks and other credit institutions	
Borrowing abroad	n.a.
Maintenance of accounts abroad	n.a.
Lending to nonresidents (financial or commercial credits)	Banks are prohibited from receiving deposits, extending credits, or opening accounts in Lebanese pounds for nonresident banks and financial institutions. However, this restriction does not apply to guarantees issued by nonresident banks and financial institutions as collateral to loans in Lebanese pounds, provided that such loans are for commercial or investment activities in Lebanon.
Lending locally in foreign exchange	n.a.
Purchase of locally issued securities denominated in foreign exchange	n.a.
Differential treatment of nonresident deposit accounts and/or deposit accounts in foreign exchange	Under a "free zone" banking facility, the commercial banks are exempted from fees for deposit insurance in respect of foreign currency deposits by nonresidents. Income from all accounts with banks have been exempt from the income tax. Under the National Investment Insurance Scheme, new foreign investments are insured against losses arising from noncivil risks, including war. Compensation is paid on losses of more than 10% of the insured value.
Reserve requirements	n.a.
Liquid asset requirements	n.a.
Interest rate controls	n.a.
Credit controls	n.a.
Investment regulations	n.a.
Open foreign exchange position limits	Banks may maintain a trading position in foreign currency of up to 5% (short or long) of the core capital of banks, and a fixed position in foreign currency (long) of up to 60% of core capital in Lebanese pounds.

Changes During 1996

No significant changes occurred in the exchange and trade system.

LESOTHO

(Position as of December 31, 1996)

Status Under IMF Articles of Agreement

Article XIV	Yes.

Exchange Arrangement

Currency	The currency of Lesotho is the loti.
Other legal tender	The South African rand is also legal tender.
Exchange rate structure	Unitary.
Classification	
Pegged	The loti is pegged to the South African rand at M 1 per R 1.
Exchange tax	No.
Exchange subsidy	No.
Forward exchange market	Authorized dealers are permitted to conduct forward exchange operations through their correspondent banks abroad at rates quoted by the latter. Forward exchange cover, however, is not common in Lesotho.
Official cover of forward operations	n.a.

Arrangements for Payments and Receipts

Prescription of currency requirements	Settlements by or to residents of the CMA with all countries outside the CMA may be made in rand to and from a nonresident account and in any foreign currency.
Payment arrangements	
Regional arrangements	As Lesotho is part of the CMA, payments within the CMA are unrestricted and unrecorded except for statistical and customs purposes. In its relations with countries outside the CMA, Lesotho applies exchange controls that are largely similar to those applied by South Africa and Swaziland.
Administration of control	
Exchange control authorities	The Central Bank of Lesotho (CBL) controls foreign exchange transactions and delegates to commercial banks the authority to approve certain types of current payments up to established limits. Permits are issued by the Department of Customs and Excise on the recommendation of the Department of Trade and Industry. Licenses for financial institutions accepting deposits and insurance companies, brokers, and agents are issued by the CBL.
International security restrictions	
In accordance with UN sanctions	According to UN Security Council Resolutions No. 661 and No. 757 and in accordance with actions taken by other members of the CMA, Lesotho imposed restrictions on current payments and transfers to Iraq and to the Federal Republic of Yugoslavia (Serbia/Montenegro), respectively.
Payment arrears	No.
Controls on trade in gold (coins and/or bullion)	
Controls on domestic ownership and/or trade	Only authorized dealers may trade in gold, but anyone may hold gold.

Controls on external trade	Exports of gold from the CMA are prohibited.
Controls on exports and imports of banknotes	
On exports	
Domestic currency	Exports of currency from the CMA are prohibited.
Foreign currency	Exports of foreign currency from the CMA by residents are prohibited; visitors may re-export the unspent portion of foreign currency brought into the country.

Resident Accounts

Eligibility to hold accounts	Yes.
Juridical persons	Banks may hold foreign exchange accounts abroad.
Natural persons	n.a.
Foreign exchange accounts permitted	Yes.
Held domestically	No.
Held abroad	Only banks may hold these accounts.
Approval required	n.a.
Accounts in domestic currency convertible into foreign currency	These accounts are prohibited.

Nonresident Accounts

Eligibility to hold accounts	Yes.
Juridical persons	n.a.
Natural persons	n.a.
Foreign exchange accounts permitted	Yes.
Approval required	n.a.
Domestic currency accounts	Yes.
Convertible into foreign currency	These accounts are prohibited.
Blocked accounts	Funds in emigrant blocked loti accounts may be invested in quoted securities and other such investments approved by the CBL. The free transfer of income from an emigrant's blocked assets is limited to M 300,000 a family unit a year.

Imports and Import Payments

Foreign exchange budget	No.
Financing requirements for imports	
Advance payment requirements	Payments are not normally allowed before the date of shipment or dispatch, except with the prior approval or special authorization from the CBL. Authorized dealers can permit, without the CBL's approval, advance payment of up to 33.3% of the ex-factory cost of capital goods if suppliers require it or if it is normal in the trade concerned.
Documentation requirements for release of foreign exchange for imports	No.

Import licenses and other nontariff measures

Lesotho is a member of the SACU and all imports, except certain food imports, originating in any country of the SACU are unrestricted. Imports from countries outside the SACU are usually licensed in conformity with the import regulations of the SACU. Lesotho reserves the right to restrict certain imports. Import permits are valid for all countries and entitle the holder to buy the foreign exchange required to make payments for imports from outside the SACU.

Negative list

With certain exceptions, imports from outside the SACU must conform to a negative list and be licensed.

Licenses with quotas

Certain food imports from within the SACU are subject to import licensing.

Import taxes and/or tariffs

Lesotho applies the external customs tariffs of the SACU.

Taxes collected through the exchange system

No.

State import monopoly

No.

Exports and Export Proceeds

Repatriation requirements

All export proceeds must be repatriated.

Surrender requirements

Unless otherwise permitted, all export proceeds must be surrendered within 6 months of the date of the export transaction.

Financing requirements

A state-supported export credit scheme is in effect, involving credit guarantees, and pre- and post-shipment credits.

Export licenses

Without quotas

Certain exports are subject to licensing for revenue purposes; this requirement, in practice, is limited to the exportation of diamonds. Most exports are shipped without license to or through South Africa.

Export taxes

No.

Payments for Invisible Transactions and Current Transfers

Controls on these payments

There are no controls on payments for freight and insurance, unloading and storage costs, administrative expenses, commissions, foreign workers' wages, pensions, family maintenance and alimony, or the use of credit cards abroad. Authorized dealers are permitted to approve some types of current payments up to established limits.

Interest payments

Quantitative limits

Emigrants are allowed to transfer, through normal banking channels, up to M 300,000 of earnings on blocked assets.

Indicative limits/bona fide test

n.a.

Profit/dividends

These transfers are not restricted, provided the funds were not obtained through excessive use of local borrowing facilities.

Prior approval

Prior approval of the CBL is required.

Indicative limits/bona fide test

n.a.

Payments for travel

Prior approval

Yes.

Quantitative limits

There is an indicative limit of M 60,000 a year for adults and M 20,000 for children under 12 years of age, at an average daily rate of up to M 2,000 for the duration of the visit. The basic annual exchange allowance for travel to neighboring countries—Angola, Botswana, the Democratic Republic of the Congo, Malawi, Mozambique, Zambia, and

Zimbabwe—is M 20,000 an adult and M 5,000 a child under 12 years of age, at an average daily rate of up to M 1,000 for the duration of the visit. Emigrant allowances are up to M 200,000 a family or up to M 100,000 a person.

Indicative limits/bona fide test	Larger allowances may be obtained for business travel.
Medical costs	
Prior approval	Yes.
Quantitative limits	n.a.
Indicative limits/bona fide test	Yes.
Study abroad costs	
Prior approval	Yes.
Quantitative limits	The limits are M 4,000 a month for a single student or M 8,000 a month for a student accompanied by a spouse who is not studying.
Indicative limits/bona fide test	n.a.
Subscriptions and membership fees	n.a.
Consulting/legal fees	
Prior approval	Yes.
Quantitative limits	The limit for professional fees is M 10,000, and the limit for technical services is M 50,000.
Indicative limits/bona fide test	n.a.
Gambling/prize earnings	n.a.

Proceeds from Invisible Transactions and Current Transfers

Repatriation requirements	Yes.
Surrender requirements	Proceeds must be surrendered within 7 days of the date of accrual, unless an exemption is obtained.

Capital Transactions

Controls on capital and money market instruments	
On capital market securities	
Purchase locally by nonresidents	Prior approval is required.
Sale or issue locally by nonresidents	Quantitative limits exist.
Purchase abroad by residents	Yes.
On money market instruments	n.a.
On collective investment securities	
Sale or issue locally by nonresidents	Quantitative restrictions apply.
Controls on derivatives and other instruments	No legal or regulatory framework exists.

Controls on credit operations

Commercial credits

By residents to nonresidents

Export credits are available for up to 6 months; in certain circumstances, the maturity can be extended by 6 months. Longer-term credits require exchange control approval.

To residents from nonresidents

These credits require exchange control approval.

Financial credits

By residents to nonresidents

These credits require prior approval. However, nonresident, wholly owned subsidiaries may borrow locally up to 100% of the total shareholder's investment.

To residents from nonresidents

Prior approval is required to ensure that repayments and servicing of the loans do not disrupt the balance of payments and to ensure that the level of interest rates paid is reasonable in terms of prevailing international rates.

Guarantees, sureties, and financial backup facilities

By residents to nonresidents

Guarantees of up to M 25,000 in respect of overdraft facilities for residents of Botswana, Malawi, Zambia, and Zimbabwe for domestic, farming, and business purposes may be approved.

To residents from nonresidents

n.a.

Controls on direct investment

The rulings on applications for inward and outward capital transfers may depend on whether the applicant is a temporary resident foreign national, a nonresident, or a resident.

Outward direct investment

Outward direct investment is prohibited.

Inward direct investment

Inward capital transfers should be properly documented to facilitate the subsequent repatriation of interest, dividends, profits, and other income.

Controls on liquidation of direct investment

Yes.

Controls on real estate transactions

Purchase abroad by residents

These transactions are prohibited.

Provisions specific to commercial banks and other credit institutions

Borrowing abroad

Prior approval is required.

Maintenance of accounts abroad

n.a.

Lending to nonresidents (financial or commercial credits)

Authorized dealers may lend up to M 20,000, provided that the total available to the borrower from any source does not exceed this amount. Facilities in excess of such amount need prior approval.

Lending locally in foreign exchange

n.a.

Purchase of locally issued securities denominated in foreign exchange

n.a.

Differential treatment of nonresident deposit accounts and/or deposit accounts in foreign exchange

n.a.

Investment regulations

n.a.

Open foreign exchange position limits

n.a.

Changes During 1996

No significant changes occurred in the exchange and trade system.

LIBERIA

(Position as of December 31, 1996)

Status Under IMF Articles of Agreement

Article XIV	Yes.

Exchange Arrangement

Currency

The currency of Liberia is the Liberian dollar. There are 2 Liberian dollar notes, Liberty notes and J.J. Roberts notes. Although officially at par, the market assigns different values to Liberty notes and J.J. Roberts notes. The Roberts notes are traded at premium against Liberty notes.

Other legal tender

The U.S. dollar is also legal tender.

Exchange rate structure

Dual

There is an official exchange rate, which is limited to the settlement of tax obligations, compliance with reserve requirements, and data reporting and a parallel exchange rate that applies to most transactions, including government spending.

Classification

Pegged

The Liberian dollar is pegged to the U.S. dollar at Lib$1 per US$1. The U.S. dollar attracts a substantial premium in parallel market transactions, and commercial banks charge high commissions for sales of offshore funds. Foreign exchange dealers other than banks are permitted to buy and sell currencies other than the U.S. dollar at market-determined exchange rates.

Exchange tax	No.
Exchange subsidy	No.
Forward exchange market	No.

Arrangements for Payments and Receipts

Prescription of currency requirements	Some exporters must pay withholding taxes and corporate income taxes in U.S. dollars. Hotels are required to receive payments from foreign guests in foreign exchange.
Payment arrangements	
Bilateral arrangements	n.a.
Regional arrangements	n.a.
Clearing agreements	Settlements with the BCEAO and The Gambia, Ghana, Guinea, Guinea-Bissau, Mali, Mauritania, Nigeria, and Sierra Leone are normally made through the WACH.
Barter agreements and open accounts	n.a.
Administration of control	
Exchange control authorities	Export- and import-licensing regulations are administered by the Ministry of Commerce and Industry.
Payments arrears	
Official	Yes.
Private	n.a.
Controls on trade in gold (coins and/or bullion)	
Controls on domestic ownership and/or trade	n.a.

Controls on external trade	Imports and exports of gold in any form are subject to licenses issued by the Ministry of Land, Mines, and Energy; import licenses are issued freely, but export licenses are granted restrictively.

Resident Accounts

n.a.

Nonresident Accounts

n.a.

Imports and Import Payments

Foreign exchange budget	No.
Financing requirements for imports	No.
Documentation requirements for release of foreign exchange for imports	
Domiciliation requirements	n.a.
Preshipment inspection	Preshipment inspection is required to ascertain the country of origin, the quality, the quantity, and the value of all goods to be shipped. Both final and intermediate goods are subject to inspection, except for imports with an f.o.b. value of less than $3,000.
Letters of credit	n.a.
Import licenses used as exchange licenses	n.a.
Import licenses and other nontariff measures	
Negative list	There is no general system of import control, but the importation of some items, including safety matches, electrode welding rods, and liquefied petroleum gas, is subject to licensing and quantitative restrictions. Licensing requirements are liberally enforced. Imports of arms, ammunition, and explosives require prior licenses. In addition, imports of certain goods (for example, narcotics, other than for medicinal purposes) are prohibited. Licenses to import inexpensive, widely consumed varieties of rice are issued to private distributors by the Ministry of Commerce and Industry. The importation of more expensive rice is not subject to official controls.
Positive list	n.a.
Open general licenses	n.a.
Licenses with quotas	n.a.
Import taxes and/or tariffs	The nominal average tariff rate is 31%.
Taxes collected through the exchange system	No.
State import monopoly	No.

Exports and Export Proceeds

Repatriation requirements	Yes.
Surrender requirements	Exporters are required to surrender 25% of export proceeds to the National Bank of Liberia (NBL) through the commercial banks; this requirement is not strictly enforced.

The government and the NBL receive priority for the purchase of this foreign exchange. The portion of the foreign exchange surrender that is not purchased by the public sector is then made available to commercial banks at par.

Financing requirements	No.
Export licenses	Licenses are generally issued freely and serve mainly to enforce the 25% surrender of export proceeds and taxation or, for agricultural products, to assure certification of quality and origin.
Without quotas	Export licenses are required for elephant tusks and ivory; wild animals; cement; agricultural products other than rubber, flour, and sugar; and certain other items, such as arms, ammunition, and explosives.
With quotas	n.a.
Export taxes	An export tax of 15% is levied on diamonds.
Taxes collected through the exchange system	n.a.

Payments for Invisible Transactions and Current Transfers

Controls on these payments	No.

Proceeds from Invisible Transactions and Current Transfers

Repatriation requirements	No.
Surrender requirements	No.
Restrictions on use of funds	No.

Capital Transactions

Controls on capital and money market instruments	No exchange control requirements are imposed on capital receipts or payments by residents.
Controls on derivatives and other instruments	No.
Controls on credit operations	No.
Controls on direct investment	No.
Controls on liquidation of direct investment	No.
Controls on real estate transactions	No.

Changes During 1996

No significant changes occurred in the exchange and trade system.

SOCIALIST PEOPLE'S LIBYAN ARAB JAMAHIRIYA

(Position as of December 31, 1996)

Status Under IMF Articles of Agreement

Article XIV	Yes.

Exchange Arrangement

Currency	The currency of Libya is the Libyan dinar.
Exchange rate structure	Unitary.
Classification	
Pegged	The Libyan dinar is pegged to the SDR at the rate of LD 1 per SDR 2.80. Margins of up to 47% are allowed around this fixed relationship, and the dinar has been depreciated to the maximum extent permitted within those margins to LD 1 per SDR 1.905.
Exchange tax	Since 1985, fees have been levied on outward foreign exchange transfers for the purpose of financing the Great Man-Made River Project.
Exchange subsidy	No.
Forward exchange market	No.

Arrangements for Payments and Receipts

Prescription of currency requirements	All settlements with Israel are prohibited. Settlements with other countries are made in convertible currencies.
Payment arrangements	
Bilateral arrangements	
Operative	An agreement is maintained with Malta; outstanding balances are settled in convertible currencies every 90 days.
Inoperative	n.a.
Administration of control	
Exchange control authorities	The Central Bank of Libya (CBL) administers exchange control and has delegated some powers to authorized banks. The General People's Congress regulates policy on imports and exports, which is executed by the Secretariat of Planning, the Economy, and Trade.
International security restrictions	No.
Payment arrears	No.
Controls on trade in gold (coins and/or bullion)	
Controls on domestic ownership and/or trade	Residents may freely purchase, hold, and sell gold in any form other than bars.
Controls on external trade	The CBL imports processed and unprocessed gold and precious metals; it also sells gold bars to domestic goldsmiths for manufacture at prices announced from time to time. The gold must be processed before it may be sold to the public. Unworked gold is subject to an import duty of 15%.
Controls on exports and imports of banknotes	
On exports	
Domestic currency	Travelers may not take out Libyan currency.

Foreign currency	Notes up to LD 300 may be taken out in a calendar year as a basic travel allowance. Additional amounts may be granted in special circumstances. Pilgrims to Saudi Arabia are entitled to a special quota. Temporary residents may take out any foreign currency notes that they had previously brought in and declared to customs. Foreign exchange converted into Libyan dinars by visiting tourists may be reconverted upon departure, with the exception of a minimum local expenditure of $50 for each day spent in the country.

Resident Accounts

Eligibility to hold accounts	Juridical and natural persons are eligible.
Foreign exchange accounts permitted	Yes.
Held domestically	Individual residents are allowed to keep foreign currencies in domestic bank accounts and to transfer balances abroad without restriction. Exporters are allowed to retain foreign exchange earnings in a special account that may be used to finance imports of raw materials, spare parts, and machinery needed for export production. Approval of the CBL is required.
Held abroad	n.a.

Nonresident Accounts

Eligibility to hold accounts	Juridical and natural persons are eligible.
Domestic currency accounts	Nonresidents who are gainfully employed in the country are permitted to open these accounts, which may be credited with their legitimate earnings. All other credits to nonresident accounts require the prior approval of the CBL.
	Funds brought in by nonresident contractors undertaking contracts in their own names must be kept with an authorized bank. Payments received by contractors in respect of their contracts may also be credited to these accounts. Remittances from these accounts are subject to the prior approval of the CBL after submission of the prescribed evidence, but, in general, remittances are permitted up to the net-of-tax amount specified in the contract.
Convertible into foreign currency	These accounts are permitted, but prior approval is required.
Blocked accounts	Nonresident-owned capital that is not permitted to be transferred abroad is credited to blocked accounts. With the approval of the CBL, funds in blocked accounts (with certain exceptions) may be used for expenditures in Libya, up to LD 500 a year, to cover the cost of visits by the owner of the funds or a close relative; for payment of legal fees and taxes; for remittances to the owner of the funds in his country of permanent residence (up to LD 1,000 in a calendar year); and for remittances in cases of hardship. When the funds have been in a blocked account for 5 years, they qualify, upon payment of due taxes, for remittance in full to the owner in his country of permanent residence. The blocked accounts of persons (with certain exceptions) who have left the country permanently are being released in installments.

Imports and Import Payments

Foreign exchange budget	Yes.
Financing requirements for imports	
Advance import deposits	Authorized banks may not open a letter of credit (LC) without an advance import deposit equal to at least 20% of the value of the import.

Documentation requirements for release of foreign exchange for imports

Domiciliation requirements — n.a.

Preshipment inspection — n.a.

Letters of credit — Before a LC is established, a marine insurance policy from a local insurance company must be submitted.

Import licenses used as exchange licenses — Exchange permits required for imports are readily granted by the authorized banks following central bank approval, provided that a firm contract exists and an import license has been obtained from the Secretariat of Planning, the Economy, and Trade.

Import licenses and other nontariff measures — Imports undertaken by state-owned enterprises do not require licenses if they are authorized within the annual commodity budget; other imports are subject to licensing. Resident firms undertaking development projects may import needed items not included in the annual commodity budget if the items are not available locally. Imports by non-residents, however, must be financed with foreign exchange resources from abroad. With the exception of strategic goods (i.e., 9 essential food items, medicines, insecticides, petroleum products, tobacco, and gold) retained by public corporations, all other goods may be imported by either public or private entities within the provisions of the annual commodity budget.

All imports from Israel are prohibited. Importers are required to deal directly with producers abroad and not through intermediaries.

Negative list — Imports of mineral water, fruit juices, instant tea, certain types of coffee, green vegetables, poultry, preserved meats and vegetables, alcoholic beverages, peanuts, oriental rugs, soaps, envelopes, crystal chandeliers, toy guns, luxury cars, and furs are prohibited.

Open general licenses — n.a.

Licenses with quotas — n.a.

Import taxes and/or tariffs — Imports are subject to customs duties and surcharges, the latter being 10% of the applicable customs duties. All products from Arab countries are exempt from customs duties, provided domestic value added is at least 40%.

Taxes collected through the exchange system — n.a.

State import monopoly — A state-owned company controlled by the CBL has a monopoly over the importation of gold and precious metals.

Exports and Export Proceeds

Repatriation requirements — All proceeds must be repatriated within 6 months of shipment.

Surrender requirements — Exporters are allowed to retain up to 40% of earnings.

Documentation requirements

Letters of credit — All exports require the opening of LCs.

Guarantees — n.a.

Domiciliation — n.a.

Preshipment inspection — n.a.

Export licenses — In general, exporters do not need export licenses but must register with the Export Promotion Council and supply on a regular basis the relevant documentation on their exports. Exports of nonmonetary gold (other than for processing abroad), scrap metals, eggs, chicken, fish, olive oil, paint, tires, steel, and tractors are prohibited. Exports or reexports of wheat, wheat flour, crushed wheat, barley, rice, tea, sugar, tomato paste, and macaroni, which are subsidized commodities, are prohibited. All exports to Israel are prohibited.

Without quotas	Export licenses are required for raw wool, hides and skins, and agricultural products.
With quotas	n.a.

Payments for Invisible Transactions and Current Transfers

Controls on these payments	Payments for invisibles related to authorized imports and interest payments are not restricted. All other payments for invisibles, as well as payments in excess of the approval authority delegated to the banks, require the prior approval of the CBL.
Profit/dividends	Profits generated by foreign capital invested in projects deemed to contribute to the economic development of the country may be transferred freely to the country of origin, provided that the paid-up capital is not less than LD 200,000 and that at least 51% of the shares are held by foreign nationals.
Prior approval	n.a.
Quantitative limits	n.a.
Indicative limits/bona fide test	n.a.
Payments for travel	Foreign exchange allocations for travel were suspended in 1992.
Indicative limits/bona fide test	n.a.
Medical costs	
Quantitative limits	n.a.
Indicative limits/bona fide test	n.a.
Study abroad costs	
Quantitative limits	n.a.
Indicative limits/bona fide test	n.a.
Subscriptions and membership fees	
Quantitative limits	n.a.
Indicative limits/bona fide test	n.a.
Consulting/legal fees	
Quantitative limits	n.a.
Indicative limits/bona fide test	n.a.
Foreign workers' wages	
Prior approval	Nonresidents employed by the state, by state-owned enterprises, and by foreign companies may remit (1) up to 50% of their net salaries each month if their contracts do not specify that lodging, board, or both will be made available free of charge by the employer; or (2) up to 75% of their net salaries if their contracts specify that the employer will provide both lodging and board free of charge at work sites in remote areas. Staff of UN agencies, embassies, consulates, and medical institutions are exempt from these regulations.
Quantitative limits	Yes.
Indicative limits/bona fide test	n.a.
Pensions	
Quantitative limits	n.a.

Indicative limits/bona fide test	n.a.
Family maintenance/alimony	
Quantitative limits	n.a.
Indicative limits/bona fide test	n.a.

Proceeds from Invisible Transactions and Current Transfers

Repatriation requirements	Yes.
Surrender requirements	All foreign exchange receipts must be surrendered.

Capital Transactions

Controls on capital and money market instruments	Purchase abroad of these instruments by residents requires approval.
On capital market securities	
Purchase locally by nonresidents	n.a.
Sale or issue locally by nonresidents	n.a.
Purchase abroad by residents	Yes.
Sale or issue abroad by residents	n.a.
On money market instruments	
Purchase locally by nonresidents	n.a.
Sale or issue locally by nonresidents	n.a.
Purchase abroad by residents	Yes.
Sale or issue abroad by residents	n.a.
On collective investment securities	
Purchase locally by nonresidents	n.a.
Sale or issue locally by nonresidents	n.a.
Purchase abroad by residents	Yes.
Sale or issue abroad by residents	n.a.
Controls on credit operations	
Commercial credits	Residents must obtain prior CBL approval to borrow funds abroad.
By residents to nonresidents	Yes.
To residents from nonresidents	Yes.
Financial credits	
By residents to nonresidents	n.a.
To residents from nonresidents	Yes.

Guarantees, sureties, and financial
backup facilities

　　By residents to nonresidents　　　　n.a.

　　To residents from nonresidents　　　Yes.

Controls on direct investment

Outward direct investment　　　　　　Yes.

Inward direct investment　　　　　　　Foreign participation in industrial ventures set up after March 20, 1970, is permitted on a minority basis, but only if it leads to increased production in excess of local requirements, introduction of the latest technology, and cooperation with foreign firms in exporting the surplus production.

Controls on liquidation of direct investment　　Foreign capital invested in projects deemed to contribute to the economic development of the country may be transferred freely to the country of origin, provided that the paid-up capital is not less than LD 200,000 and that at least 51% of the shares are held by foreign nationals.

Controls on real estate transactions

Purchase abroad by residents　　　　　Residents must have prior permission from the Committee of the People's Bureau for Foreign Affairs and International Economic Cooperation to purchase real estate abroad.

Purchase locally by nonresidents　　　Yes.

Sale locally by nonresidents　　　　　n.a.

Changes During 1996

No significant changes occurred in the exchange and trade system.

LITHUANIA

(Position as of December 31, 1996)

Status Under IMF Articles of Agreement

Article VIII   Date of acceptance: May 3, 1994.

Exchange Arrangement

Currency   The currency of Lithuania is the litas.

Exchange rate structure   Unitary.

Classification

Pegged   The litas is pegged to the U.S. dollar at LTL 1 per U.S. dollar since April 1994 when the currency board arrangement was established.

Exchange tax   No.

Exchange subsidy   No.

Forward exchange market   No.

Arrangements for Payments and Receipts

Prescription of currency requirements   No.

Payment arrangements

Bilateral arrangements

Operative   Correspondent accounts exist between the Bank of Lithuania (BOL) and the central banks of the Baltic countries, Russia, and the other countries of the FSU. These accounts need not be used for payments originating after October 1992.

Inoperative   Ruble-denominated correspondent accounts maintained with the central banks of the Baltic countries, Russia, and the other countries of the FSU have been closed and are in the process of being settled.

Regional arrangements   n.a.

Clearing agreements   n.a.

Barter agreements and open accounts   n.a.

Administration of control

Exchange control authorities   Parliament has the legislative authority in foreign exchange and trade matters; it has adopted a banking law delegating to the BOL the authority to issue regulations governing foreign exchange transactions. All foreign exchange transactions must be effected through authorized banks licensed by the BOL. Authorized banks are allowed to transact among themselves, as well as with residents and nonresidents of Lithuania, and are divided into 4 categories, depending on the types of transactions they are permitted to conduct. The simplest type of license limits the operations to buying and selling foreign exchange (cash and traveler's checks). At present, several banks have been granted a general license that allows them to offer a full range of banking services (including issuing letters of credit) in foreign exchange operations, and they are permitted to open correspondent accounts with banks abroad.

Controls on trade in gold (coins and/or bullion)   No.

Controls on exports and imports of banknotes	No.

Resident Accounts

Eligibility to hold accounts	Juridical and natural persons are eligible.
Foreign exchange accounts permitted	Yes.
Held domestically	Yes.
Held abroad	n.a.

Nonresident Accounts

Eligibility to hold accounts	Juridical and natural persons are eligible.
Foreign exchange accounts permitted	Yes.
Domestic currency accounts	Yes.
Convertible into foreign currency	Yes.

Imports and Import Payments

Foreign exchange budget	No.
Financing requirements for imports	No.
Import licenses and other nontariff measures	There are no quantitative restrictions or licensing requirements on imports, except for health and national security reasons.
Positive list	n.a.
Negative list	n.a.
Open general licenses	n.a.
Licenses with quotas	n.a.
Other nontariff measures	Certain agricultural goods and alcoholic beverages are subject to duties, and certain quantitative restrictions are used to control trade in strategic goods and technology to protect Lithuania's cultural heritage and to prevent illegal trade in copper and other nonferrous metals, alloys, and scrap. Alcoholic beverages and tobacco can be imported only by traders registered with the government, but import quantities are unrestricted.
Import taxes and/or tariffs	A 3-tier tariff structure exists consisting of: (1) a "conventional" rate applied to countries granted MFN status; (2) a "preferential" rate applied to countries with which Lithuania has a foreign trade agreement; (3) an "autonomous" rate that is 5% to 10% greater than the MFN rate applied to all other countries. For most imports, a 10% tariff rate applies. Higher tariff rates are levied on certain products (such as live animals, agricultural products, alcohol and tobacco, and a few manufactured goods), some exceeding 30%. The majority of agricultural products (and certain other items such as alcohol) are subject to zero tariff rates.
	A tax at the uniform rate of 0.01% is imposed on imports (and exports) for the sole purpose of collecting statistical information on trade.
Taxes collected through the exchange system	No.

Exports and Export Proceeds

Repatriation requirements	No.
Surrender requirements	No.
Export licenses	Quantitative export restrictions have been almost eliminated. From November 1, 1994, to May 1, 1996, the following products were subject to temporary export prohibitions: red clover seeds, feathers and down used for stuffing, raw hides and skins, unprocessed pine and birch timber with a thin-end diameter of not less than 20 cm., unprocessed oak and ash timber, and glands and other organs used for pharmaceutical products and organotherapeutical uses without quotas issued by the Ministry of Health Care. This prohibition served to protect a small number of domestic processors of primary products. The export bans were not binding for countries that have signed a foreign trade agreement with Lithuania. In the case of products, banned exports account for only 20% of total exports, because wood is mostly exported to Finland, Switzerland, and Germany, all of which have foreign trade agreements with Lithuania. Regulations governing trade in strategic goods and technology, cultural objects, nonferrous scrap, and waste apply to exports as well as imports.
Export taxes	Export duties are levied on certain raw materials and selected products.
Taxes collected through the exchange system	No.

Payments for Invisible Transactions and Current Transfers

Controls on these payments	No.

Proceeds from Invisible Transactions and Current Transfers

Repatriation requirements	No.
Surrender requirements	No.
Restrictions on use of funds	No.

Capital Transactions

Controls on capital and money market instruments	No.
Controls on derivatives and other instruments	No.
Controls on credit operations	
Commercial credits	
To residents from nonresidents	Yes.
Financial credits	
To residents from nonresidents	Resident firms may borrow foreign exchange from authorized banks or borrow directly from banks abroad with the approval of the BOL.
Guarantees, sureties, and financial backup facilities	Yes.
By residents to nonresidents	n.a.
To residents from nonresidents	n.a.

Controls on direct investment

Inward direct investment

There are no restrictions, except in fields that are subject to prohibition under the Law on Foreign Capital Investments: state defense, production and sale of narcotic substances, and lottery business. The law permits the state to sell shares to nonresidents, guarantees nondiscriminatory national treatment to foreign investors, and protects investments against nationalization and expropriation. The purchase of state-owned enterprises is subject to authorization from the Central Privatization Committee. One of the main conditions in this process is that the company must remain involved in the same type of business for at least 1 year under the new ownership. While firms with 100% foreign capital ownership are allowed to operate in Lithuania, the government reserves the right to establish limits on foreign investment in Lithuanian enterprises. In joint ventures in the transportation and communication sectors, the domestic partner is required to hold the majority of shares. Wholly owned ventures in the alcoholic beverage or tobacco industries are prohibited. Enterprises with foreign investment must be insured by Lithuanian insurance companies, even if the company retains other insurance services outside Lithuania.

Controls on liquidation of direct investment

The Law of Foreign Investments guarantees the free repatriation of all after-tax profits as well as invested capital, with no limitation on timing or amount. It also provides for important tax incentives. If the foreign investment was made before the end of 1993, the profit tax is reduced by 70% (to a range of 8.7% to 29% for 5 years). For another 3 years, the profit tax is reduced by 50%. For investments made between January 1994 and December 1995, profits are taxed at a rate reduced by 50% for 6 years. For joint ventures, these reductions are proportional to the foreign capital invested.

Controls on real estate transactions

Purchase locally by nonresidents

The ownership of land by nonresidents in Lithuania is prohibited, but lease contracts with limits to 2 hectares of land in Vilnius and 10 hectares outside the capital are permitted for up to 99 years and may be renewed thereafter. In the near future, according to EU requirements, nonresidents of certain foreign countries will be allowed to purchase land.

Sale locally by nonresidents

Yes.

Provisions specific to commercial banks and other credit institutions

Maintenance of accounts abroad

Resident banks or other credit institutions must inform the BOL about their accounts with foreign banks.

Purchase of locally issued securities denominated in foreign exchange

Locally issued securities must be denominated in the national currency.

Open foreign exchange position limits

Banks' overall open positions may not exceed 30% of their capital, and the open position in individual currencies may not exceed 20% of the banks' capital. The open position limit does not apply to the U.S. dollar.

Provisions specific to institutional investors

No.

Other controls imposed by securities laws

No.

Changes During 1996

No significant changes occurred in the exchange and trade system.

LUXEMBOURG

(Position as of January 31, 1997)

Status Under IMF Articles of Agreement

Article VIII   Date of acceptance: February 15, 1961.

Exchange Arrangement

Currency   The currency of Luxembourg is the Luxembourg franc. Belgium and Luxembourg are linked in a monetary association, and the currencies are at par.

Other legal tender   The Belgian franc also circulates as legal tender.

Exchange rate structure   Unitary.

Classification

Cooperative arrangement   Luxembourg participates in the ERM of the EMS. In accordance with this agreement, Belgium and Luxembourg maintain spot exchange rates between their currencies and the currencies of the other participants within margins of 15% above or below the cross-rates derived from the central rates expressed in ECUs.

Exchange tax   No.

Exchange subsidy   No.

Forward exchange market   Yes.

Official cover of forward operations n.a.

Arrangements for Payments and Receipts

Prescription of currency requirements   No.

Payment arrangements   No.

Administration of control   No.

International security restrictions

In accordance with IMF Executive   Luxembourg applies exchange restrictions against Iraq.
Board Decision No. 144-(52/51)

In accordance with UN sanctions   Yes.

Payment arrears   No.

Controls on trade in gold (coins and/or bullion)   No.

Controls on exports and imports of banknotes   No.

Resident Accounts

Eligibility to hold accounts   Juridical and natural persons are eligible.

Foreign exchange accounts permitted   Yes.

Held domestically   Yes.

Held abroad	Yes.
Accounts in domestic currency convertible into foreign currency	Yes.

Nonresident Accounts

Eligibility to hold accounts	Juridical and natural persons are eligible.
Foreign exchange accounts permitted	Yes.
Domestic currency accounts	Yes.
Convertible into foreign currency	Yes.
Blocked accounts	These are accounts affected by international security restrictions.

Imports and Import Payments

Foreign exchange budget	No.
Financing requirements for imports	No.
Documentation requirements for release of foreign exchange for imports	No.
Import licenses and other nontariff measures	
Positive list	Payments for imports may be made freely. Individual licenses are required for certain specified imports from all countries (most imports do not require an import license when imported from the member countries of the EU), including many textile and steel products, diamonds, weapons, and nontextile products from China. All other commodities are free of license requirements.
Licenses with quotas	Along with EU countries, the BLEU applies quotas on a number of textile products from non-EU countries in the framework of the MFA and also applies a system of minimum import prices to foreign steel product quotas on a number of steel products from Russia and Ukraine, and quotas on a number of products from China (toys, shoes, ceramic, porcelain, and glassware). On January 1, 1997, the quota on imports of steel products from Kazakhstan was eliminated.
Import taxes and/or tariffs	Luxembourg applies the Common Import Regime of the EU to imports of most other agricultural and livestock products from non-EU countries.
Taxes collected through the exchange system	No.
State import monopoly	No.

Exports and Export Proceeds

Repatriation requirements	No.
Surrender requirements	No.
Financing requirements	No.
Documentation requirements	No.
Export licenses	Export licenses are required only for a few products, mostly of a strategic character, and for diamonds and for some iron and steel products.

Without quotas	Yes.
Export taxes	No.

Payments for Invisible Transactions and Current Transfers

Controls on these payments	No.

Proceeds from Invisible Transactions and Current Transfers

Repatriation requirements	No.
Surrender requirements	No.
Restrictions on use of funds	No.

Capital Transactions

There are no controls on capital transactions. A currency matching requirement on the composition of assets and liabilities applies to insurance companies only.

Changes During 1996

Arrangements for payments and receipts

October 2. Exchange restrictions against the Federal Republic of Yugoslavia (Serbia/Montenegro) and against the Republic of Bosnia and Herzegovina under the control of Serb forces were lifted.

Changes During 1997

Imports and import payments

January 1. Authorization for imports of certain preserved foodstuffs (tuna, bonito, and sardines) was abolished.

January 1. The quota on imports of steel products from Kazakhstan was lifted.

FORMER YUGOSLAV REPUBLIC OF MACEDONIA

(Position as of February 28, 1997)

Status Under IMF Articles of Agreement

Article XIV	Yes.

Exchange Arrangement

Currency	The currency of the former Yugoslav Republic of Macedonia is the denar.
Exchange rate structure	Unitary.
Classification	

Managed floating

The exchange market operates at two levels—wholesale (enterprises, commercial banks, and the National Bank of Macedonia (NBM)) and retail (households). The NBM participates in the wholesale market to maintain the value of the denar against the deutsche mark at a level that would meet balance of payments objectives. Buying and selling rates for transactions between authorized banks and enterprises have to be reported to the NBM, which calculates an average daily rate. Based on this rate and cross rates on the international market, the NBM publishes rates for 22 currencies. The NBM deals at the published midpoint rates plus or minus a margin of 0.3%.

The retail level of the foreign exchange market consists of foreign exchange bureaus, which are owned and operated by banks; enterprises; and natural persons. Foreign exchange bureaus may hold foreign exchange positions equivalent to 100% of the net foreign exchange purchases in the preceding 10 days.

Exchange tax	No.
Exchange subsidy	No.
Forward exchange market	Forward foreign exchange contracts for trade transactions are permitted.
Official cover of forward operations	The NBM may conclude forward foreign exchange contracts.

Arrangements for Payments and Receipts

Prescription of currency requirements	No.
Payment arrangements	No.
Administration of control	
Exchange control authorities	The parliament has the authority to legislate laws governing foreign exchange and trade transactions. Certain changes in the trade regime may be made through government regulations. The NBM is authorized to control foreign exchange operations of banks and other financial institutions. The Ministry of Finance is authorized to control foreign exchange and trade operations and the credit relations of enterprises abroad, as well as other forms of business activities abroad, encompassing all enterprises that operate internationally. Certain foreign exchange control activities have been delegated to the participants in the foreign exchange market and the customs office. The Ministry of Foreign Relations administers the Commercial Companies Act.
International security restrictions	No.
Payment arrears	
Official	Arrears are maintained with respect to debt with the European Investment Bank, which will be cleared during 1997.

Controls on trade in gold (coins and/or bullion)

Controls on domestic ownership and/or trade

Gold producers must report all production (including quality) and quantity sold. Processors are also required to report all quantities bought and processed.

Controls on external trade

The importation and exportation of gold require NBM approval.

Controls on exports and imports of banknotes

On exports

Domestic currency

A maximum of MDen 5,000 in denominations of 100-, 50-, 20-, and 10-denar banknotes may be exported.

Foreign currency

Up to DM 1,000 for private domestic travelers, and for business travelers up to the amount stated on the bank order form. Nonresidents may export foreign currency up to the amount declared upon arrival in the country.

On imports

Domestic currency

Same limits as in exportation apply.

Foreign currency

Foreign travelers must declare foreign currency over DM 300.

Resident Accounts

Eligibility to hold accounts

Juridical and natural persons are eligible.

Foreign exchange accounts permitted

Foreign exchange deposits made after April 26, 1991, are freely disposable, i.e., they can be withdrawn in foreign currency or converted into denars.

Held domestically

Yes.

Held abroad

Enterprises with foreign operations may hold these accounts, but prior approval is required.

Accounts in domestic currency convertible into foreign currency

No.

Nonresident Accounts

Eligibility to hold accounts

Juridical and natural persons are eligible.

Foreign exchange accounts permitted

These accounts may be credited freely with foreign exchange and debited for payments abroad or for conversion into denars.

Domestic currency accounts

Yes.

Convertible into foreign currency

Yes.

Blocked accounts

No.

Imports and Import Payments

Foreign exchange budget

No.

Financing requirements for imports

No.

Documentation requirements for release of foreign exchange for imports

A contract, invoice, or customs declaration should be submitted to the commercial bank effecting the payment. Generally, payments for imports are permitted after the importation of goods. Beginning February 28, 1997, imports of raw materials may not be paid in advance. Exceptionally, payments in advance are permitted for imports of equipment and spare parts, some essential consumer goods, and goods financed by foreign loans.

Import licenses and other nontariff measures	Imports of certain goods, such as weapons and medicines, are subject to licensing requirements for security or public health reasons.
Positive list	Yes.
Negative list	Yes.
Licenses with quotas	Quotas were eliminated on December 2, 1996.
Import taxes and/or tariffs	A new customs tariff schedule was introduced on July 31, 1996, eliminating most import surcharges and fees. Customs duties on most items range up to 35%; rates on raw materials range from zero to 8%; machinery and equipment from 5% to 20%; consumer goods from 15% to 35%; and agricultural goods from 20% to 60%. The number of bands were reduced to 7 and the average rate to about 15%. There is also a 1% documentation fee.
Taxes collected through the exchange system	No.
State import monopoly	No.

Exports and Export Proceeds

Repatriation requirements	All export proceeds from transactions that are not based on commodity credits have to be transferred by the exporters into the country within 90 days from the day the exportation was made.
Surrender requirements	Exporters must sell their proceeds to the foreign exchange market within 4 business days of transferring them into the country, use the proceeds for payments abroad, or deposit them in banks for a period of up to 90 days, after which they must sell their proceeds in the foreign exchange market.
Financing requirements	No.
Documentation requirements	No.
Export licenses	Generally, exports are liberal. However, in some exceptional cases the export of certain goods requires a license from the appropriate authorities.
Without quotas	Yes.
With quotas	Quotas were eliminated on December 2, 1996.
Export taxes	No.

Payments for Invisible Transactions and Current Transfers

Controls on these payments	No.

Proceeds from Invisible Transactions and Current Transfers

Repatriation requirements	Proceeds from invisibles are subject to the same regulations as those applicable to merchandise exports.
Surrender requirements	Yes.
Restrictions on use of funds	No.

Capital Transactions

Controls on capital and money market instruments	Outward portfolio investment by resident natural and juridical persons is not permitted. There are no regulations on inward portfolio investment.

On capital market securities

    Purchase locally by nonresidents — n.a.

    Sale or issue locally by nonresidents — Yes.

    Purchase abroad by residents — Yes.

    Sale or issue abroad by residents — n.a.

On money market instruments

    Purchase locally by nonresidents — n.a.

    Sale or issue locally by nonresidents — Yes.

    Purchase abroad by residents — Yes.

    Sale or issue abroad by residents — n.a.

On collective investment securities — n.a.

Controls on credit operations

Commercial credits — Short-term commercial banks' credit lines with a maturity from 90 days to 180 days should be registered.

    By residents to nonresidents — Only credits for the export of goods are permitted. Export credits exceeding 90 days and credits for import of goods exceeding 180 days should be registered with the NBM.

    To residents from nonresidents — Credits for the import of goods for consumption are not permitted.

Financial credits

    By residents to nonresidents — Only commercial banks are permitted to conclude financial credits involving promotion of export of goods and services.

    To residents from nonresidents — Yes.

Guarantees, sureties, and financial backup facilities

    By residents to nonresidents — Only commercial banks may effect these transactions, which should be registered with the NBM.

Controls on direct investment

Outward direct investment — Investments require approval from and registration with the Ministry of Foreign Affairs.

Inward direct investment — Nonresidents are allowed to invest in existing firms, establish their own firms, or establish joint ventures except in a few sectors (such as arms production). Imports of raw materials, spare parts, and equipment not produced domestically by joint-venture firms are exempt from customs duties if the foreign share in the investment is at least 20%.

Controls on liquidation of direct investment — All foreign investment registered with the Ministry of Foreign Affairs is protected from nationalization.

Controls on real estate transactions — Yes.

Provisions specific to commercial banks and other credit institutions

Borrowing abroad — Yes.

Maintenance of accounts abroad — Yes.

Lending to nonresidents (financial or commercial credits) — Yes.

Lending locally in foreign exchange — This lending is not permitted.

Differential treatment of nonresident
deposit accounts and/or deposit accounts in foreign exchange

   Reserve requirements   Nonresident deposits in denars are subject to requirements, but foreign exchange deposits are not.

   Credit controls   Credit controls apply only to domestic currency credits.

Open foreign exchange position limits   Yes.

Changes During 1996

Imports and import payments   *July 31.* A new customs tariff schedule following the harmonized system and eliminat-
ing most import surcharges and fees was introduced. The new tariffs range up to 35%
for the great majority of items. The number of bands was reduced to 7 from 18 and the
average rate (including additional import taxes) was reduced to about 15% from 28%.

August 9. After the new customs tariff schedule was introduced, a new list of all goods
by export and import regime was adopted. The trade regime consists of 3 categories:
(1) liberal exports/imports, (2) quantitative quotas for exports/imports, and (3) license
requirements.

December 2. The new list of all goods by trade regime was changed.

Exports and export proceeds   *December 2.* The quantitative quotas for exports were eliminated.

Changes During 1997

Imports and import payments   *February 28.* The NBM changed the regulation for payment of imports in advance,
allowing only imports of equipment and spare parts, some essential consumer goods,
and goods financed by foreign loans to be paid in advance.

February 28. Advance payments for raw materials were no longer allowed.

MADAGASCAR

(Position as of January 31, 1997)

Status Under IMF Articles of Agreement

Article VIII   Date of acceptance: September 18, 1996.

Exchange Arrangement

Currency   The currency of Madagascar is the Malagasy franc.

Exchange rate structure   Unitary.

Classification

Independent floating   The exchange rate is determined freely in the official interbank market. The French franc is the only currency quoted on this market, and the exchange rates of other currencies are determined on the basis of the cross-rate relationships of the currencies concerned in the Paris exchange market.

Exchange tax   No.

Exchange subsidy   No.

Forward exchange market   There are limited arrangements for forward cover against exchange rate risk.

Official cover of forward operations   Exporters can buy foreign currency 120 days prior to settlement from their bank.

Arrangements for Payments and Receipts

Prescription of currency requirements   No.

Payment arrangements

Bilateral arrangements

   Operative   n.a.

   Inoperative   There is an arrangement with Mauritius.

Barter agreements and open accounts   Regulations prohibit barter trade.

Administration of control

Exchange control authorities   Exchange control is administered by the Exchange Operations Monitoring Unit of the General Directorate of the Treasury, which also supervises borrowing and lending abroad by residents, and the issue, sale, or introduction of foreign securities in Madagascar. Approval authority for exchange control has been delegated to authorized intermediaries, and all exchange transactions relating to foreign countries must be effected through such intermediaries, except for capital operations.

Payment arrears

Official   Yes.

Private   Yes.

Controls on trade in gold (coins and/or bullion)

Controls on domestic ownership and/or trade   Approved collectors acting in their own name and on their own account may purchase gold within the country from holders of valid gold mining titles, from authorized holders of gold washing rights at the Gold Board, and from agencies for approved collectors.

Controls on external trade	Imports and exports of gold require prior authorization from the Ministry of Commerce after review by the Directorate of Energy and Mines, and by the Ministry of Mining. Exempt from this requirement are (1) imports and exports by or on behalf of the Central Bank of Madagascar (CBM), and (2) imports and exports of manufactured articles containing a minor quantity of gold (such as gold-filled or gold-plated articles). Travelers are authorized to export 50 grams or 250 carats of gold jewelry or gold articles a person, and 50 grams or 250 carats of numismatic items a person. Imports of gold, whether licensed or exempt from license, are subject to customs declaration. Holders of a valid gold mining title or a gold washing permit or rights thereto are free to sell the gold recovered to any approved collector. However, Malagasy authorities, represented by the CBM or its agents, have first rights to purchase gold produced in the country. The Gold Board and agencies authorized by the Ministry of Mining may export gold in all its forms.

Controls on exports and imports of banknotes

On exports

    Domestic currency — Resident and nonresident travelers may take abroad up to FMG 25,000 in Malagasy banknotes.

    Foreign currency — Residents and nonresident travelers may take abroad any amount of foreign currency, but a declaration is required if the amount is more than the equivalent of F 50,000.

On imports

    Domestic currency — Residents and nonresidents may bring in up to FMG 25,000.

    Foreign currency — Resident and nonresident travelers may bring in any amount of foreign currency, but a declaration is required if the amount is more than the equivalent of F 50,000.

Resident Accounts

Eligibility to hold accounts	Juridical and natural persons are eligible.
Foreign exchange accounts permitted	Yes.
Held domestically	Only transfers from abroad or from another foreign currency account, as well as foreign banknotes, or traveler's and bank checks may be deposited in these accounts without justification. These accounts may be freely debited either for conversion into Malagasy francs through a sale on the interbank market or by transfer to a foreign account in Madagascar or abroad. Conversion into foreign banknotes is allowed only within the limits stipulated under the applicable foreign exchange control regulation.
Held abroad	No.
Accounts in domestic currency convertible into foreign currency	No.

Nonresident Accounts

Eligibility to hold accounts	Juridical and natural persons are eligible.
Foreign exchange accounts permitted	Nonresidents are treated the same as residents for the purpose of opening these accounts.
Domestic currency accounts	Transactions between enterprises in the free trade zone and residents are conducted through the enterprises' foreign accounts in Malagasy francs.
Convertible into foreign currency	No.
Blocked accounts	No.

Imports and Import Payments

Foreign exchange budget	No.
Financing requirements for imports	No.
Documentation requirements for release of foreign exchange for imports	
Domiciliation requirements	The requirement applies to all imports.
Preshipment inspection	Yes.
Letters of credit	n.a.
Import licenses and other nontariff measures	There is a shortlist of imports subject to administrative control primarily for health and security reasons.
Positive list	n.a.
Negative list	n.a.
Open general licenses	n.a.
Licenses with quotas	n.a.
Import taxes and/or tariffs	Import tariffs range from 10% to 30%. Imports are also subject to customs duties ranging up to 20%, although the sum of the import tariff and customs duty may not exceed 30% for any item. Some imports, mostly luxury goods, are subject to excise import taxes of 10% to 120%. A pretax of 3% to 5%, deductible from the corporate tax, is paid on all imports.
Taxes collected through the exchange system	No.
State import monopoly	Petroleum products are imported by a state monopoly.

Exports and Export Proceeds

Repatriation requirements	All export proceeds should be repatriated within 90 days of the shipment date.
Surrender requirements	Yes.
Financing requirements	No.
Documentation requirements	
Letters of credit	Yes.
Guarantees	n.a.
Domiciliation	The requirement applies for exports exceeding FMG 1 million.
Preshipment inspection	Yes.
Export licenses	No.
Export taxes	Exports of vanilla are subject to an export tax of about $21 per kilogram.
Taxes collected through the exchange system	Yes.

Payments for Invisible Transactions and Current Transfers

Controls on these payments	Transfers of interest payments, profits and dividends, foreign workers' wages, and pensions must be effected through licensed intermediaries and have, since September 1996,

been subject to a simple declaration to the intermediaries. In January 1997, the payment of airfares in Malagasy francs was authorized. Payments for invisibles related to authorized imports are not restricted. Quantitative limits for allowances for travel and for study abroad were abolished on August 28, 1996 and November 28, 1996, respectively.

Proceeds from Invisible Transactions and Current Transfers

Repatriation requirements

Proceeds must be repatriated within 30 days of the due date.

Surrender requirements

Proceeds must be sold in the interbank market.

Capital Transactions

Controls on capital and money market instruments

Capital movements between Madagascar and foreign countries, and between residents and nonresidents are subject to prior authorization from the Ministry of Finance (MOF). There are no capital market regulations, due to the absence of a capital market.

On capital market securities

Purchase locally by nonresidents

Yes.

Sale or issue locally by nonresidents

Exempt from authorization are operations in connection with shares similar to securities whose issuing or offering for sale in Madagascar has previously been authorized.

Purchase abroad by residents

Yes.

Sale or issue abroad by residents

Yes.

Controls on credit operations

Commercial credits

By residents to nonresidents

These operations currently do not take place.

To residents from nonresidents

Credits for export prefinancing operations are permitted.

Financial credits

By residents to nonresidents

Borrowing abroad by natural or juridical persons, whether public or private, requires prior authorization from the MOF, although loans contracted by authorized banks or credit institutions with special legal status are exempt. Enterprises in the free trade zone are permitted to contract and service foreign loans freely, and interest and amortization payments on foreign loans contracted directly by these companies are not restricted.

To residents from nonresidents

Yes.

Controls on direct investment

Outward direct investment

Investments abroad by Malagasy nationals, including those made through foreign companies directly or indirectly controlled by persons resident in Madagascar and those made by overseas branches or subsidiaries of companies located in Madagascar, are subject to prior authorization from the MOF.

Inward direct investment

Investments, including those made by companies in Madagascar that are directly or indirectly under foreign control and those made by branches or subsidiaries of foreign companies in Madagascar, as well as corresponding transfers, may be freely conducted within Madagascar without authorization or investment approval, according to Law 96-015 of August 13, 1996.

Controls on liquidation of direct investment

The total or partial liquidation of these investments, whether Malagasy investments abroad or foreign investments in Madagascar, must be reported to the MOF. Proceeds from the liquidation of foreign investment may be repatriated with the prior authorization of the MOF.

Controls on real estate transactions

Purchase abroad by residents	These purchases are prohibited, unless otherwise approved by the MOF.
Purchase locally by nonresidents	n.a.
Sale locally by nonresidents	Transfer of proceeds of sale is subject to prior authorization by the MOF.

Provisions specific to commercial banks and other credit institutions

Controls are implemented through bank supervision.

Maintenance of accounts abroad	n.a.
Lending to nonresidents (financial or commercial credits)	n.a.
Lending locally in foreign exchange	n.a.
Purchase of locally issued securities denominated in foreign exchange	n.a.
Differential treatment of nonresident deposit accounts and/or deposit accounts in foreign exchange	n.a.
Investment regulations	n.a.
Open foreign exchange position limits	n.a.

Changes During 1996

Status under IMF Articles of Agreement

September 18. Madagascar accepted the obligations of Article VIII, Sections 2, 3, and 4 of the Fund Agreement.

Exchange arrangements

September 16. The Bank and Financial Institution Supervisory Commission authorized the opening of exchange bureaus.

Exports and export proceeds

December 30. The deadline for surrendering export proceeds to the interbank foreign exchange market was abolished.

Payments for invisible transactions and current transfers

August 28. The limit on the foreign exchange allowance for travel was eliminated.

November 28. The limit on the foreign exchange allowance for study abroad was eliminated.

Proceeds from invisible transactions and current transfers

September 12. Granting of foreign exchange for current payments was to be based on a simple declaration to authorized intermediaries.

December 30. The deadline for surrendering proceeds from these transactions was abolished.

Capital transactions

August 13. Foreign direct investment was no longer subject to prior authorization.

Changes During 1997

Payments for invisible transactions and current transfers

January 13. Payment of air transport in domestic currency by all persons traveling to Madagascar was authorized.

MALAWI

(Position as of December 31, 1996)

Status Under IMF Articles of Agreement

Article VIII

Date of acceptance: December 7, 1995.

Exchange Arrangement

Currency

The currency of Malawi is the Malawi kwacha.

Exchange rate structure

Unitary.

Classification

Independent floating

The exchange rate of the Malawi kwacha is determined on the basis of supply and demand. Authorized dealer banks (ADBs) may buy and sell foreign currencies at freely determined market exchange rates. Foreign exchange bureaus are authorized to conduct spot transactions with the general public on the basis of exchange rates negotiated with their clients.

Exchange tax

No.

Exchange subsidy

No.

Forward exchange market

No.

Arrangements for Payments and Receipts

Prescription of currency requirements

Payments to and receipts from nonresidents may be made in any convertible currency traded in Malawi or in Malawi kwacha through nonresident accounts.

Payment arrangements

No.

Administration of control

Exchange control authorities

Exchange control is administered by the Reserve Bank of Malawi (RBM) under the authority of the Ministry of Finance (MOF).

International security restrictions

No.

Payment arrears

No.

Controls on trade in gold (coins and/or bullion)

Controls on domestic ownership and/or trade

Residents may purchase, hold, and sell only gold coins for numismatic purposes. Only the monetary authorities can hold or acquire gold at home or abroad in any form other than jewelry.

Controls on external trade

Only the monetary authorities can conduct external trade in gold. Imports of gold in any form other than jewelry require licenses issued by the Ministry of Commerce and Industry (MCI) in consultation with the MOF; such licenses are not normally granted except for imports by or on behalf of the monetary authorities and industrial users.

Controls on exports and imports of banknotes

On exports

Domestic currency

Up to MK 200 may be exported.

Foreign currency

Approval for exports is granted subject to verification of need.

On imports

Domestic currency

Up to MK 200 may be imported.

Resident Accounts

Eligibility to hold accounts

Juridical and natural persons are eligible.

Foreign exchange accounts permitted

Yes.

Held domestically

Residents receiving foreign exchange regularly from abroad, including exporters, may maintain these accounts and use balances to make authorized payments and transfers without restriction. Prior approval is required.

Held abroad

No.

Accounts in domestic currency convertible into foreign currency

No.

Nonresident Accounts

Eligibility to hold accounts

Juridical and natural persons are eligible.

Domestic currency accounts

These accounts may be credited with proceeds of sales of any convertible currency, with authorized payments in Malawi kwacha from abroad, and with transfers from other nonresident accounts. These accounts may be debited to make payments to residents of Malawi for any purpose, transfer freely to other nonresident accounts, and make payments to account holders temporarily residing in Malawi. Prior approval is required.

Convertible into foreign currency

n.a.

Blocked accounts

Credits to and debits from these accounts do not require prior authorization, and authorization is normally given for balances to be invested in an approved manner. Interest earned on balances may be transferred to the account holder's country of residence.

Imports and Import Payments

Foreign exchange budget

No.

Financing requirements for imports

Importers are free to choose any method of payment, and import payments may be made to an appropriate local nonresident account in Malawi currency or in any convertible currency. When imports arrive in the country and payment is due, the importer must submit applications for foreign exchange. Such applications must be accompanied by relevant importation and customs documents. Depending on the means of payment (e.g., letters of credit), commercial banks may require counterpart deposits.

Minimum financing requirements

n.a.

Advance payment requirements

Prepayment for imports is not allowed.

Advance import deposits

Official regulations do not require these deposits; however, commercial banks do so as a banking practice.

Documentation requirements for release of foreign exchange for imports

No.

Import licenses and other nontariff measures

Imports of certain agricultural products and used clothing, as well as gold, fertilizers, switchblade knives, explosives, arms and ammunition, wild animals, live fish, and copyrighted articles require specific licenses from the MCI. Specific import licenses are usually issued within 1 week of application and are normally valid for 6 months.

Open general licenses

Most imports are subject to the open general license system, including imports from Commonwealth countries and from countries that are members of the GATT.

Import taxes and/or tariffs	Customs tariffs are ad valorem and range from zero to 45% of c.i.f. value with a weighted average of about 21%. Tariffs on textiles are 35% and the effective maximum rate is 40% on most items. Government imports are exempt from customs tariffs. Imports are also subject to a surtax ranging up to 20%.
Taxes collected through the exchange system	No.
State import monopoly	No.

Exports and Export Proceeds

Repatriation requirements	Yes.
Surrender requirements	ADBs are required to convert 60% of foreign exchange received from exports immediately upon receipt at the prevailing buying exchange rate and credit the Malawi kwacha proceeds to the customer's account. The remaining 40% may be credited to the exporter's foreign currency account. There are no restrictions on the time period over which such balances may be held. This 60% conversion is also applied to U.S. dollar proceeds from the tobacco and tea auctions. In the case of tobacco proceeds, the conversion is 100% until the seller has fully repaid his overdraft with his bankers. The exporter or recipient of the U.S. dollar proceeds from the auction may freely sell his or her foreign exchange to any authorized foreign exchange dealer.
Export licenses	
Without quotas	Imports of implements of war, petroleum products, nickel, atomic energy materials, and certain agricultural and animal products require licenses.
Export taxes	Specific duties, or cesses, are levied on exports of hides and skins, and tobacco. A duty drawback system exists for imports of certain inputs used in exported manufactured goods.
Taxes collected through the exchange system	No.

Payments for Invisible Transactions and Current Transfers

Controls on these payments	Commercial banks are authorized to provide foreign exchange, without reference to the exchange control authorities, for all current invisible payments, but certain invisible payments are subject to indicative limits. There are no controls on payments for the costs of study abroad, subscriptions and membership fees, and consulting and legal fees.
Freight/insurance	
Indicative limits/bona fide test	Yes.
Unloading/storage costs	
Indicative limits/bona fide test	Yes.
Administrative expenses	
Indicative limits/bona fide test	Yes.
Commissions	
Indicative limits/bona fide test	Yes.
Interest payments	
Indicative limits/bona fide test	Yes.

Profit/dividends

Prior approval	These transfers are not restricted, provided that no recourse is made to local borrowing to finance them.
Indicative limits/bona fide test	Yes.

Payments for travel

Quantitative limits	The limits are $3,000 a trip for tourist travel, and $5,000 a trip for business travel. There is no limit on the number of trips that may be taken.
Indicative limits/bona fide test	Foreign exchange in excess of these limits is granted upon proof of need.

Medical costs

Quantitative limits	The limit is $5,000.
Indicative limits/bona fide test	Yes.

Foreign workers' wages

Prior approval	Yes.
Quantitative limits	The limit is two-thirds of current net earnings.

Proceeds from Invisible Transactions and Current Transfers

Repatriation requirements	Yes.
Surrender requirements	Proceeds may be retained in full and held in foreign-currency-denominated accounts with ADBs.
Restrictions on use of funds	No.

Capital Transactions

Controls on capital and money market instruments	Inward transfers of non-debt-creating capital are not restricted. Outward transfers of capital are controlled mainly for residents.

On capital market securities

Purchase locally by nonresidents	n.a.
Sale or issue locally by nonresidents	n.a.
Purchase abroad by residents	Specific exchange control approval is required.
Sale or issue abroad by residents	n.a.

On money market instruments

Purchase locally by nonresidents	n.a.
Sale or issue locally by nonresidents	n.a.
Purchase abroad by residents	Yes.
Sale or issue abroad by residents	n.a.

On collective investment securities

Purchase locally by nonresidents	n.a.
Sale or issue locally by nonresidents	n.a.

Purchase abroad by residents	Yes.
Sale or issue abroad by residents	n.a.

Controls on credit operations

Commercial credits

By residents to nonresidents	n.a.
To residents from nonresidents	Borrowing abroad by residents requires prior exchange control approval, which is normally granted provided that the terms of repayment, including the servicing costs, are acceptable.

Financial credits

By residents to nonresidents	n.a.
To residents from nonresidents	Yes.

Controls on direct investment

Outward direct investment	Yes.

Controls on liquidation of direct investment | Repatriation of investments is permitted if the original investment was made with funds brought into the country.

Controls on real estate transactions

Purchase abroad by residents	Yes.
Purchase locally by nonresidents	n.a.
Sale locally by nonresidents	n.a.

Changes During 1996

No significant changes occurred in the exchange and trade system.

MALAYSIA

(Position as of December 31, 1996)

Status Under IMF Articles of Agreement

Article VIII   Date of acceptance: November 11, 1968.

Exchange Arrangement

Currency   The currency of Malaysia is the ringgit.

Exchange rate structure   Unitary.

Classification

Managed floating   The Malaysian ringgit is determined by supply and demand. The Bank Negara Malaysia (BNM) intervenes only to maintain orderly market conditions and to avoid excessive fluctuations in the value of the ringgit. The BNM also monitors the exchange rate against a weighted basket of currencies of Malaysia's major trading partners and the currencies of settlement. The commercial banks are free to determine and quote exchange rates, whether spot or forward, to all customers for all currencies other than those of Israel and the Federal Republic of Yugoslavia (Serbia/Montenegro).

Forward exchange market   Forward exchange contracts may be effected for both commercial and financial transactions. For financial transactions, prior approval is required. For commercial transactions, forward cover for imports is provided for up to 12 months from the intended date of import, while for export purposes, the forward cover would be up to 6 months from the export date.

Official cover of forward operations   No.

Arrangements for Payments and Receipts

Prescription of currency requirements   Special rules apply to settlements with Israel and the Federal Republic of Yugoslavia (Serbia/Montenegro).

Payment arrangements

Bilateral arrangements

Operative   There are 12 arrangements: 5 Palm Oil Credit and Payment Arrangements (POCPAs), 1 revolving credit, and 6 with the LAIA.

Inoperative   There are 10 arrangements: 1 POCPA and 9 with the LAIA.

Regional arrangements   n.a.

Clearing agreements   n.a.

Barter agreements and open accounts   n.a.

Administration of control

Exchange control authorities   The Controller of Foreign Exchange (COFE), who is also the Governor of the Bank of the BNM, administers exchange control.

International security restrictions

In accordance with IMF Executive Board Decision No. 144-(52/51)   On June 23, 1993, Malaysia notified the Fund that it had imposed certain restrictions on payments and transfers for current international transactions with respect to the Federal Republic of Yugoslavia (Serbia/Montenegro).

In accordance with UN sanctions   Yes.

Payment arrears	No.
Controls on trade in gold (coins and/or bullion)	No.
Controls on exports and imports of banknotes	
On exports	
Domestic currency	There is no restriction on the exportation of currency notes in a traveler's immediate possession. The exportation of ringgit currency by any other means requires prior approval from the COFE.
Foreign currency	Exportation of foreign currency notes, other than on the person or in the baggage of a traveler, requires prior approval.
On imports	
Domestic currency	No limitation is imposed on a traveler's importation of currency notes. The importation of ringgit banknotes by other than commercial banks, or by any other means, requires prior approval from the COFE.

Resident Accounts

Eligibility to hold accounts	Juridical and natural persons are eligible.
Foreign exchange accounts permitted	
Held domestically	Exporters are allowed to retain a portion of their export proceeds in foreign currency accounts with authorized banks in Malaysia up to $10 million. Thirty-five designated banks are permitted to offer foreign currency accounts to residents. All other domestic banks must obtain permission from the COFE before offering foreign currency accounts to residents. These accounts can be opened only with designated banks.
Held abroad	Residents with no domestic borrowing are allowed to open foreign currency accounts with an overseas branch of Malaysian-owned banks. Residents with domestic borrowing require prior approval.
Accounts in domestic currency convertible into foreign currency	Yes.

Nonresident Accounts

Eligibility to hold accounts	Juridical and natural persons are eligible.
Foreign exchange accounts permitted	All commercial and merchant banks are allowed to open these accounts.
Domestic currency accounts	Nonresident ringgit accounts in Malaysia are designated external accounts. There are no restrictions on debits to external accounts. Credits to these accounts are freely permitted, subject only to the completion of statistical forms for amounts exceeding RM 100,000, if residents make such payments. Proceeds from the sale of any foreign currency may be credited to external accounts, and the balances may be transferred to any other resident or nonresident account or converted into any currency, except those of Israel and the Federal Republic of Yugoslavia (Serbia/Montenegro). All debits and credits to the latter accounts require prior approval. Commercial banks are required to place domestic currency funds of foreign banking institutions held in non-interest-bearing vostro accounts with the BNM in designated non-interest-bearing current accounts.
Convertible into foreign currency	Yes.

Blocked accounts	All debits and credits to accounts of residents of Israel and the Federal Republic of Yugoslavia (Serbia/Montenegro) require prior approval.

Imports and Import Payments

Import licenses and other nontariff measures	The authority for import control rests with the Royal Customs and Excise Department of the Federal Ministry of Finance. Import licensing throughout Malaysia is administered daily by the Ministry of International Trade and Industry together with other specified authorities, such as the Ministry of Primary Industries, the Malaysian Timber Board, and the Veterinary Department, on behalf of the Royal Customs and Excise Department.
Positive list	n.a.
Negative list	Imports from Israel require licenses. Finished motor vehicle imports are subject to nonautomatic import licensing, which is administered by the Ministry of International Trade and Industry. The movement of live animals between peninsular Malaysia, Sabah, and Sarawak is subject to a permit issued by the Veterinary Department. Imports of the meat, bones, hides, hooves, horns, and offal of any animal or any portion of an animal from all countries require an import license. Imports of primates, whether dead or alive, require an import license, subject to approval from the Department of Wildlife and National Parks. Imports from Haiti are prohibited.
Open general licenses	n.a.
Licenses with quotas	Certain imports are subject to quantitative restrictions, which are reviewed periodically, to protect local industries temporarily when required.
Import taxes and/or tariffs	Yes.
Taxes collected through the exchange system	n.a.

Exports and Export Proceeds

Repatriation requirements	Proceeds from exports must be received and repatriated according to the payment schedule specified in the commercial contract, but no longer than 6 months after the date of exportation.
Surrender requirements	Exporters are allowed to retain a portion of their export proceeds in foreign currency accounts with designated banks up to $10 million.
Documentation requirements	Exports of rubber from peninsular Malaysia require a certificate issued by the Malaysian Rubber Exchange and Licensing Board.
Letters of credit	n.a.
Guarantees	n.a.
Domiciliation	n.a.
Preshipment inspection	n.a.
Export licenses	Exports to Israel and the Federal Republic of Yugoslavia (Serbia/Montenegro) require export licensing from the Ministry of International Trade and Industry. Exports of logs are restricted and require licensing from the Malaysian Timber Industries Board. Exports of petroleum and petroleum products, arms and related materials, military vehicles and equipment, and police equipment to Haiti are prohibited. Exports of roofing tiles, bricks, minerals, rice and paddy in any form, milk and specified milk products, textiles, and all other goods as specified in the second schedule of Customs (Prohibition of Exports) Order No. 1988 of the 1967 Customs Act are subject to permits.
Without quotas	n.a.

With quotas	n.a.

Export taxes Export incentives are provided to companies that export Malaysian products. The primary incentives include a double deduction of expenses incurred in overseas promotion, export credit refinancing, and duty drawbacks.

Taxes collected through the exchange system n.a.

Payments for Invisible Transactions and Current Transfers

Controls on these payments Payments for invisibles to all other countries other than Israel and the Federal Republic of Yugoslavia (Serbia/Montenego) may be made without restriction. Remittances to nonresidents of profits on all bona fide investments are permitted, subject only to the completion of statistical forms for amounts RM 100,000 and above. Remittances of interest payments do not require prior approval as long as such payments are in accordance with the terms of the loan obtained.

Proceeds from Invisible Transactions and Current Transfers

Repatriation requirements Proceeds from invisibles must be repatriated according to the proceeds schedule specified in the agreement.

Surrender requirements If received in foreign currency, proceeds may be retained in permitted foreign currency accounts.

Capital Transactions

Controls on capital and money market instruments

On capital market securities

Sale or issue locally by nonresidents Malaysia has no exchange control restrictions for nonresidents selling Malaysian securities in the country, nor does it require them to repatriate the proceeds of the sale. However, nonresidents must obtain approval to issue securities in the country.

Purchase abroad by residents No restrictions apply for transactions valued at less than RM 100,000; but for those amounting to RM 100,000 or more, the following requirements must be met: (1) the payment is made in foreign currency and (2) the resident has no domestic borrowing or for corporate residents with domestic credit facilities, the total payment to nonresidents for the purpose of investment abroad does not exceed the aggregate amount of RM 10 million in a calendar year. The prior approval of the COFE is required for transactions that do not comply with the above requirements. Effective November 15, 1996, investment abroad is considered on a corporate group basis.

Sale or issue abroad by residents No exchange controls apply to a resident for the sale of securities abroad. However, a resident must obtain approval to issue securities abroad. Approval is given if the proceeds associated with these issues are used to finance productive activities in Malaysia, particularly for projects that generate foreign exchange earnings or save on the future outflow of foreign exchange through the production of import substitution goods. The proceeds from the sale or permitted issuance of securities are required to be transferred to Malaysia.

On money market instruments

Sale or issue locally by nonresidents Same regulations as for securities apply.

Purchase abroad by residents Same regulations as for securities apply.

Sale or issue abroad by residents	When residents issue money market instruments abroad, it is considered obtaining credit facilities. Residents are freely permitted to obtain credit facilities in foreign currency only up to RM 5 million. For amounts exceeding this figure, prior approval of the COFE is required. Approval is given for foreign currency credit facilities raised on reasonable terms to finance productive activities in Malaysia, particularly for projects that generate sufficient foreign exchange to service the external debt so created.

On collective investment securities

Sale or issue locally by nonresidents	There is no exchange control on the sale of Malaysian securities in the country by nonresidents and for the latter to repatriate the proceeds of the sale. However, approval is required for nonresidents to issue securities in the country.
Purchase abroad by residents	Same regulations as for securities apply.
Sale or issue abroad by residents	Same regulations as for securities apply.

Controls on derivatives and other instruments

Purchase abroad by residents	A resident must obtain permission to make payments to a nonresident for any spot or forward contract or interest rate futures not transacted at a futures exchange in Malaysia.
Sale or issue abroad by residents	Residents must obtain permission to issue and to sell financial instruments abroad.

Controls on credit operations

Commercial credits

By residents to nonresidents	No controls apply to residents other than authorized dealers to extend credit to nonresidents for the export of goods from Malaysia up to a maximum period of 6 months from the date of export.
To residents from nonresidents	A resident is permitted to obtain credit facilities in foreign currency up to the equivalent of RM 5 million in the aggregate from licensed banks, licensed merchant banks, and nonresidents. Any larger amount would require the prior approval of the COFE. Residents are not allowed to obtain loans in ringgit from nonresidents. There is no restriction for residents to obtain commercial credits from nonresidents for the importation of capital goods for a period not exceeding 12 months.

Financial credits

By residents to nonresidents	No restrictions apply to credits granted by residents (other than authorized dealers) in foreign currency to nonresidents of less than RM 100,000. Larger credits are permitted, provided that (1) the payment is made in foreign currency and (2) the resident has no domestic borrowing or for corporate residents with domestic credit facilities, the total payment to nonresidents for the purpose of investment abroad does not exceed the aggregate amount of RM 10 million in a calendar year. The COFE's prior approval is required for any payments that do not comply with the above requirements. Effective November 15, 1996, loans to nonresidents by corporate residents are considered on a corporate group basis.
To residents from nonresidents	A resident is permitted to obtain total credit in foreign currency of up to RM 5 million from licensed banks, licensed merchant banks, and nonresidents. Any larger amount would require the prior approval of the COFE. Residents are not allowed to obtain loans in ringgit from nonresidents.

Guarantees, sureties, and financial backup facilities

By residents to nonresidents	These transactions are permitted. However, any payment to a nonresident in relation to or consequential to the guarantee must be made in foreign currency.
To residents from nonresidents	Residents are permitted to obtain financial guarantees of any amount in ringgit or foreign currency only from (1) a licensed offshore bank in the Labuan International Offshore Financial Center; or (2) nonresident individuals or nonresidents who are shareholders, subsidiaries, related or associate companies that are not financial institutions, provided all payments related to the guarantees are made in foreign currency. Otherwise, approval is required.

Controls on direct investment

Outward direct investment

Yes.

Inward direct investment

There are no exchange restrictions. However, the following inward investments require prior approval from the Foreign Investment Committee (FIC): (1) acquisition of any substantial fixed assets by foreign interests; (2) acquisition of assets or interests, mergers, and takeovers of companies and businesses in Malaysia by any means that will cause ownership or control to pass to foreign interests; (3) acquisition of 15% or more of the voting power (equity interests) by any foreign interest or associated group or by a foreign interest in the aggregate of 30% or more of the voting power of a Malaysian company or business; (4) control of Malaysian companies and businesses through any form of joint-venture agreement, management agreement, or technical assistance arrangement; (5) merger or takeover of any company or business in Malaysia; and (6) any other proposed acquisition of assets or interests exceeding RM 5 million in value.

Incorporation of a Malaysian company by a foreign entity does not require the approval of the FIC. However, increases in the paid-up capital of a Malaysian company that involve any foreign entity require the approval of the FIC under the following circumstances: (1) the total value of the foreign entity's new subscription exceeds RM 5 million; (2) the total of the foreign entity's new subscription exceeds 15% of the voting power in the relevant company; (3) as a result of the increase in paid-up capital, any foreign entity increases its voting power to more than 15% in the relevant company; (4) the total of the new subscription by several foreign entities increases their joint voting power to 30% or more of the voting power in the relevant company; (5) as a result of the increase in paid-up capital, the aggregate holding of several foreign entities increases to 30% or more of the voting power in the relevant company; and (6) an increase in the paid-up capital of any Malaysian company to more than RM 5 million on incorporation, the holdings of foreign entities constitute more than 15% of the voting power, or the joint holdings of several foreign entities constitute 30% or more of the voting power of the company concerned.

In addition, the permitted percentage of equity held by foreigners also depends on the percentage of production exported, whether high-technology products are purchased, or whether priority products are produced for the domestic market. For projects involving extracting, mining, and processing mineral ores, a majority foreign equity participation of up to 100% is permitted.

Controls on liquidation of direct investment

The proceeds of investments may be repatriated freely on resale, subject to the completion of a statistical form for amounts of RM 100,000 or more.

Controls on real estate transactions

Purchase abroad by residents

Same regulations as for purchases of securities abroad by residents apply.

Provisions specific to commercial banks and other credit institutions

Borrowing abroad

Only authorized dealers and tier 1 merchant banks are allowed to borrow freely in foreign currency from nonresidents. Other financial institutions are subject to controls.

Maintenance of accounts abroad

Only authorized dealers in foreign currencies are permitted to maintain accounts abroad. Other credit institutions are generally not permitted to maintain these accounts, except for licensed merchant banks and tier 1 merchant banks.

Lending to nonresidents (financial or commercial credits)

Authorized dealers are allowed to extend loans in foreign currency to nonresidents. A banking institution is, however, allowed to extend credit in ringgit to:

(1) individuals up to an aggregate of RM 200,000 for any purpose except to finance the acquisition or development of immovable property in Malaysia; and

(2) a bank or a stockbroking company that maintains an external account, provided that:

(a) the total credit facilities of the borrowers from all banking institutions do not exceed RM 5 million; and

(b) the credit facilities are used by (i) the nonresident stockbroker to finance funding gaps if there is a delay in receipt of funds from its nonresident clients for the payment of securities purchased on the Kuala Lumpur Stock Exchange; and (ii) the nonresident correspondent bank to finance unforeseen or inadvertent funding gaps arising from the mismatching of receipts and payments through the external account. The extension of loans in ringgit to nonresidents exceeding the amounts or for purposes other than those stipulated above requires the prior permission of the COFE.

Lending locally in foreign exchange	Authorized dealers and merchant banks are allowed to lend in foreign currency to residents.
Purchase of locally issued securities denominated in foreign exchange	Purchases are allowed, provided that the issuance of the securities has been approved.
Open foreign exchange position limits	The criteria in determining banks' net overnight foreign currency open position limits are based on a matrix that takes into account their shareholders' funds and dealing capacity.

Provisions specific to institutional investors

Limits (max.) on portfolio invested abroad

Insurance companies are prohibited from holding foreign assets except under the following circumstances: (1) such investment funds would be derived only from premiums received from the insurer's offshore business; (2) such foreign assets are maintained solely to meet foreign liabilities arising from an insurer's insurance or reinsurance business overseas; (3) the foreign assets should not be more than the amount reasonably required for meeting liabilities in foreign currency after taking into account expected cash flow; and (4) the COFE approves the transactions.

Limits (min.) on portfolio invested locally

Insurance companies are required to invest at least 80% of their insurance funds in authorized Malaysian assets as specified in the Second Schedule of the Insurance Act (1963).

Employee Provident Fund (EPF) investment in foreign securities is subject to the approval of the Minister of Finance. There are no specific regulations governing foreign investment of the EPF. However, the EPF is required to invest a minimum of 50% of its annual investible funds in securities issued or guaranteed by the federal government, provided that the total amount of funds invested in such securities is not less than 70% of its total investment.

Unit trust funds can invest up to 10% of the fund's net asset value in securities listed on foreign stock exchanges. Prior approval from the Securities Commission is required for such investment.

Other controls imposed by securities laws

There are no restrictions on foreign firms trading in the corporate debt, equity, and derivative market. However, the following transactions require approval of the FIC: (1) any proposed acquisition of 15% or more of the voting power by any one foreign interest or associated group, or foreign interests in the aggregate of 30% or more of the voting power of a Malaysian company or business; (2) company or business in any merger and takeover in Malaysia, whether by Malaysian or foreign interests; and (3) any other proposed acquisition of assets or interests exceeding in value RM 5 million, whether by Malaysians or foreign interests. Foreign companies with no substantial business operations in Malaysia are not normally granted listing on the local stock exchange.

Changes During 1996

Resident accounts

November 15. The maximum overnight limit for export accounts was increased to $10 million from $5 million.

Payments for invisible transactions and current transfers

February 1. The threshold for the completion of the statistical forms for each remittance to or receipt of funds from nonresidents was raised to RM 100,000 or its equivalent in foreign currency from amounts exceeding RM 50,000.

MALDIVES

(Position as of December 31, 1996)

Status Under IMF Articles of Agreement

Article XIV	Yes.

Exchange Arrangement

Currency	The currency of Maldives is the rufiyaa. (Rf 1 per 100 laari).
Exchange rate structure	Yes.
Classification	
Managed floating	The exchange rate is determined by demand and supply in the market, although the Maldives Monetary Authority (MMA) may intervene when appropriate.
Exchange tax	No.
Exchange subsidy	No.
Forward exchange market	No.

Arrangements for Payments and Receipts

Prescription of currency requirements	Foreign currency must be converted to rufiyaa through a bank or a licensed money changer authorized by the MMA.
Payment arrangements	No.
Administration of control	No.
International security restrictions	
In accordance with UN sanctions	Imports from Iraq and the Federal Republic of Yugoslavia (Serbia/Montenegro) are prohibited.
Payment arrears	No.
Controls on trade in gold (coins and/or bullion)	Transactions in gold are not subject to regulation.
Controls on exports and imports of banknotes	No.

Resident Accounts

Eligibility to hold accounts	Yes.
Juridical persons	n.a.
Natural persons	n.a.
Foreign exchange accounts permitted	Yes.
Held domestically	Yes.
Held abroad	Yes.
Accounts in domestic currency convertible into foreign currency	Yes.

Nonresident Accounts

Eligibility to hold accounts	Judicial and natural persons are eligible. No distinction is made between accounts held by residents and those held by nonresidents.
Foreign exchange accounts permitted	Yes.
Domestic currency accounts	No.
Convertible into foreign currency	No.
Blocked accounts	No.

Imports and Import Payments

Foreign exchange budget	No.
Financing requirements for imports	No.
Documentation requirements for release of foreign exchange for imports	No.
Import licenses and other nontariff measures	Import operations may only be conducted after being registered and licensed at the Ministry of Trade and Industries.
Open general licenses	All goods may be imported under an open general license (OGL) system. Licenses are issued on application. Imports from Iraq and the Federal Republic of Yugoslavia (Serbia/Montenegro) are prohibited.
Licenses with quotas	All private sector imports of rice, wheat flour, and sugar are subject to a quota.
Import taxes and/or tariffs	Duties are levied on all merchandise items other than rice, flour, and sugar.
Taxes collected through the exchange system	No.
State import monopoly	No.

Exports and Export Proceeds

Repatriation requirements	No.
Surrender requirements	No.
Financing requirements	No.
Documentation requirements	No.
Export licenses	Export licenses are issued by the Ministry of Trade and Industries. The private sector may export most items, with the exception of fresh and frozen tuna.
Without quotas	n.a.
With quotas	Quotas for exports of aquarium fish have been in effect since 1982.
Export taxes	Exports of fish and fish products and reexports are exempt from duties. However, a 50% tax is levied on the export of ambergris.
Taxes collected through the exchange system	No.

Payments for Invisible Transactions and Current Transfers

Controls on these payments	No.

Proceeds from Invisible Transactions and Current Transfers

Repatriation requirements	No.
Surrender requirements	No.
Restrictions on use of funds	No.

Capital Transactions

Controls on capital and money market instruments

On capital market securities

Purchase locally by nonresidents — Although no law prohibits these purchases, there is a restriction on the foreign purchase of shares placed by some companies that have floated their securities.

Sale or issue locally by nonresidents — There is a regulation that prevents raising capital through public offering; however, it does not discriminate against foreign participation, but requires majority government interest and control in operations.

On collective investment securities — n.a.

Controls on credit operations — No.

Controls on direct investment

Inward direct investment — Investments require prior approval from the government. Investors are required to provide at least 75% of their capital investment in cash or goods financed from outside Maldives.

Provisions specific to commercial banks and other credit institutions

Differential treatment of nonresident deposit accounts and/or deposit accounts in foreign exchange — n.a.

Investment regulations — n.a.

Open foreign exchange position limits — n.a.

Changes During 1996

No significant changes occurred in the exchange and trade system.

MALI

(Position as of December 31, 1996)

Status Under IMF Articles of Agreement

Article VIII	Date of acceptance: June 1, 1996.

Exchange Arrangement

Currency

The currency of Mali is the CFA franc.

Exchange rate structure

Unitary.

Classification

Pegged

The CFA franc is pegged to the French franc at the rate of CFAF 1 per F 0.01. Exchange rates for other currencies are derived from the rate for the currency concerned in the Paris exchange market and the fixed rate between the French franc and the CFA franc. They include a bank commission of 2.5‰ on transfers to all countries outside the WAEMU, which must be surrendered in its entirety to the Treasury.

Exchange tax

There is no exchange tax, but foreign exchange transfers are subject to a stamp tax.

Exchange subsidy

No.

Forward exchange market

Forward exchange contracts may be arranged with the prior authorization of the Ministry of Finance and Commerce (MFC). For certain products, the duration of forward exchange rate cover may be extended to 3 months but cannot be renewed. For exports, the duration of forward exchange contracts may not exceed 120 days after the arrival of the goods at their destination.

Official cover of forward operations

No.

Arrangements for Payments and Receipts

Prescription of currency requirements

Settlements with France, Monaco, and other countries linked to the French Treasury through an Operations Account are made in CFA francs, French francs, or the currency of any other Operations Account country. There are no prescription of currency requirements for transfers to non-WAEMU franc zone countries.

Payment arrangements

Regional arrangements

n.a.

Clearing agreements

Yes.

Administration of control

Exchange control authorities

The MFC has sole authority in exchange control matters but has delegated certain exchange control powers to the BCEAO and to authorized banks.

International security restrictions

No.

Payment arrears

No.

Controls on trade in gold (coins and/or bullion)

Authorization from the Directorate of External Commerce, issued after a favorable ruling by the Directorate of Monetary and Financial Affairs of the MFC, is required to hold, sell, import, export, or deal in raw diamonds and precious and semiprecious materials.

Controls on external trade

Commercial imports and exports of gold do not require authorization from the MFC but are subject to all foreign trade regulations, including bank domiciliation, customs declaration, and the obligation to repatriate export proceeds. Travelers may export gold jewelry and personal belongings, other than gold coins and ingots, up to a maximum weight of 500 grams.

Controls on exports and imports of banknotes

On exports

Domestic currency

Residents traveling to non-BCEAO countries are not allowed to take out BCEAO banknotes.

Foreign currency

The reexportation of foreign banknotes for amounts exceeding the equivalent of CFAF 250,000 requires documentation demonstrating the importation of the foreign banknotes, their purchase against other means of payment registered in the name of the traveler, or through the use of nonresident deposits in local banks.

On imports

Foreign currency

Nonresidents may bring in any amount of foreign banknotes and coins (except gold coins) of countries outside the Operations Account area. Residents bringing in foreign banknotes and foreign currency traveler's checks exceeding the equivalent of CFAF 25,000 must declare them to customs upon entry and sell them to an authorized intermediary bank within 8 days.

Resident Accounts

Eligibility to hold accounts

Juridical and natural persons are eligible.

Foreign exchange accounts permitted

No.

Accounts in domestic currency convertible into foreign currency

No.

Nonresident Accounts

Eligibility to hold accounts

Juridical and natural persons are eligible.

Foreign exchange accounts permitted

No.

Domestic currency accounts

Because the BCEAO has suspended the repurchase of banknotes circulating outside the territories of the CFA franc zone, nonresident accounts may not be credited or debited with BCEAO banknotes.

Convertible into foreign currency

These accounts are permitted, but prior approval is required.

Blocked accounts

Yes.

Imports and Import Payments

Foreign exchange budget

No.

Financing requirements for imports

No.

Documentation requirements for release of foreign exchange for imports

Domiciliation requirements

A domiciliation requirement exists for all imports exceeding CFAF 500,000.

Preshipment inspection

An inspection for quality and price is required.

Letters of credit

Letters of credit are required for imports of goods outside EU, Operations Account, and ACP countries.

Import licenses used as exchange licenses	n.a.

Import licenses and other nontariff measures

There are no import licensing requirements, but imports are required to be registered, and permits are issued automatically. Imports from Israel are prohibited.

Import taxes and/or tariffs

Imports are subject to a customs duty (up to 5%), a fiscal duty (up to 25%), and a customs service fee (5%). Some goods are exempt from these charges. Tariff rates are ad valorem (except for those on petroleum products) and based on c.i.f. values. Petroleum is subject to a variable levy. Imports are subject to additional taxes ranging from 7.5% to 55%, which were temporarily suspended in 1994.

Taxes collected through the exchange system

No.

Exports and Export Proceeds

Repatriation requirements

Exports to foreign countries must be recorded with an authorized bank, and all export proceeds, including those originating in France and other countries linked to the French Treasury by an Operations Account, must be repatriated through the BCEAO.

Surrender requirements

Proceeds must be surrendered within 30 days of the payment due date or within 120 days of shipment if no payment date is specified in the sales contract.

Financing requirements

No.

Documentation requirements

Domiciliation

Yes.

Export licenses

All exports require only a certificate of registration.

Export taxes

No.

Payments for Invisible Transactions and Current Transfers

Controls on these payments

Payments to France, Monaco, and the countries linked to the French Treasury by an Operations Account are permitted freely. Payments for invisibles related to trade are permitted freely when the basic trade transaction has been approved or does not require authorization. There are no controls on payments for freight and insurance, unloading and storage costs, administrative expenses, commissions, or interest. Payments for travel, medical treatment, study abroad, subscriptions and membership fees, consulting and legal fees, foreign workers' wages, pensions, gambling and prize earnings, family maintenance and alimony, and the use of credit cards abroad are subject to indicative limits and/or bona fide tests. Prior approval is required for payments for subscriptions and membership fees, consulting and legal fees, pensions, gambling and prize earnings, family maintenance and alimony, remittances of profits and dividends, and the use of credit cards abroad.

Profit/dividends

Quantitative limits

n.a.

Indicative limits/bona fide test

n.a.

Payments for travel

Prior approval

MFC approval is needed for travel outside the CFA franc zone and for allowances in excess of the limits.

Quantitative limits

CFA 500,000 a trip for tourist travel and CFAF 2,750,000 for business travel (includes allowance for tourist travel).

Medical costs

    Prior approval   n.a.

Foreign workers' wages   The transfer of salaries is permitted upon presentation of the appropriate pay voucher, provided that the transfer takes place within 3 months of the pay period or that there is a reciprocity agreement with the foreigner's country of nationality.

Credit card use abroad   Credit cards must be issued by resident financial intermediaries and authorized banks.

    Quantitative limits   Limits are the same as for tourist and business travel.

Proceeds from Invisible Transactions and Current Transfers

Repatriation requirements   Yes.

Surrender requirements   Proceeds, except those from transactions with France, Monaco, and the countries linked to the French Treasury by an Operations Account must be surrendered.

Restrictions on use of funds   No.

Capital Transactions

Controls on capital and money market instruments   Capital movements between Mali and France, Monaco, and the countries linked to the French Treasury by an Operations Account are free of restrictions. Capital transfers to all other countries require authorization from the MFC and are restricted, but capital receipts from these countries are permitted freely.

On capital market securities

    Sale or issue locally by nonresidents   n.a.

    Purchase abroad by residents   Yes.

    Sale or issue abroad by residents   n.a.

On money market instruments

    Sale or issue locally by nonresidents   n.a.

    Purchase abroad by residents   Yes.

    Sale or issue abroad by residents   n.a.

On collective investment securities

    Sale or issue locally by nonresidents   n.a.

    Purchase abroad by residents   Yes.

    Sale or issue abroad by residents   n.a.

Controls on derivatives and other instruments

Sale or issue locally by nonresidents   n.a.

Purchase abroad by residents   Yes.

Sale or issue abroad by residents   n.a.

Controls on credit operations

Commercial credits   Special controls apply for borrowing outside the region.

By residents to nonresidents	Yes.
To residents from nonresidents	Yes.
Financial credits	
By residents to nonresidents	These credits are allowed if the borrower has the financial capacity to contract them.
To residents from nonresidents	Yes.
Guarantees, sureties, and financial backup facilities	
By residents to nonresidents	n.a.
To residents from nonresidents	Yes.
Controls on direct investment	
Outward direct investment	Yes.
Controls on liquidation of direct investment	Yes.
Controls on real estate transactions	
Purchase abroad by residents	Yes.
Purchase locally by nonresidents	n.a.
Sale locally by nonresidents	Yes.
Provisions specific to commercial banks and other credit institutions	
Borrowing abroad	Yes.
Maintenance of accounts abroad	Yes.
Lending to nonresidents (financial or commercial credits)	Yes.
Differential treatment of nonresident deposit accounts and/or deposit accounts in foreign exchange	There are no regulations on opening foreign exchange accounts.
Credit controls	Yes.
Investment regulations	Yes.
Open foreign exchange position limits	Yes.
Provisions specific to institutional investors	
Limits (max.) on portfolio invested abroad	Yes.
Limits (min.) on portfolio invested locally	Yes.
Other controls imposed by securities laws	No.

Changes During 1996

Exchange arrangements	*June 1.* Mali accepted the obligations of Article VIII, Sections 2, 3, and 4 of the Fund Agreement.

MALTA

(Position as of February 28, 1997)

Status Under IMF Articles of Agreement

Article VIII   Date of acceptance: November 30, 1994.

Exchange Arrangement

Currency
The currency of the Malta is the Maltese lira.

Other legal tender
Malta has 23 denominations of gold coins, which are legal tender.

Exchange rate structure
Unitary.

Classification

Pegged
The exchange rate of the Maltese lira is determined on the basis of a weighted basket of currencies comprising the pound sterling, the U.S. dollar, and the ECU. Unless market conditions indicate otherwise, a spread of 0.25% is applied to the middle rate to compute the buying and selling rates for transactions between the Central Bank of Malta (CBM) and the credit institutions (authorized banks). These transactions may be conducted in deutsche mark, pounds sterling, or U.S. dollars in amounts of less than Lm 150,000. Transactions in smaller amounts are handled through the interbank market. There is no limit on the spread between the buying and selling rates the credit institutions may quote. Authorized banks may also establish rates for currencies not quoted by the CBM based on the latest international market rates.

Exchange tax
No.

Exchange subsidy
The subsidy is in the form of a guaranteed exchange rate of the pound sterling provided temporarily by the CBM to tour operators from the United Kingdom. This arrangement is to be terminated in May 1997.

Forward exchange market
Yes.

Official cover of forward operations
The CBM provides forward cover directly to government departments and public sector bodies in respect of such transactions. Forward rates are based on interest rate differentials between market rates and international money market rates.

Arrangements for Payments and Receipts

Prescription of currency requirements
Authorized payments to all countries may be made by crediting Maltese liri to an external account or in any foreign currency, while the proceeds of exports to all countries may be received in any foreign currency.

Payment arrangements

Bilateral arrangements

Operative
There is an agreement with Libya with outstanding balances being settled in convertible currencies within 90 days.

Administration of control

Exchange control authorities
The CBM, as agent for the Minister of Finance (MOF), administers exchange controls. Approval authority for the allocation of foreign exchange for certain purposes has been delegated to the credit institutions. Authority to approve specified foreign exchange payments has also been delegated to a number of foreign exchange bureaus. The CBM is responsible for issuing licenses to operators of such agencies.

542

International security restrictions

In accordance with IMF Executive Board Decision No. 144-(52/51)	Yes.
In accordance with UN sanctions	Certain restrictions on payments and transfers to Iraq and Libya remain in force in compliance with UN Security Council resolutions.
Other	Yes.

Payment arrears

No.

Controls on trade in gold (coins and/or bullion)

Controls on domestic ownership and/or trade

Residents are allowed to hold coins and acquire jewelry but must obtain permission from the CBM to purchase and sell any gold coins that are not legal tender.

Controls on external trade

Subject to exchange control permission, authorized importers may import gold bullion solely for the manufacture of gold articles. The importation of gold coins is controlled to ensure that such coins are used for genuine numismatic purposes. With the exception of gold and silver filigree, the importation of which is still restricted, the requirement of an import license has been removed as of February 1997 for gold coins, gold bullion, and manufactured and semimanufactured articles of gold and silver.

The exportation of nonmanufactured gold by residents other than the monetary authorities also requires exchange control permission.

Controls on exports and imports of banknotes

On exports

Domestic currency

Travelers may export up to Lm 25 a person.

Foreign currency

Nonresident travelers may export foreign currency up to the amount they bring in. Residents may export up to Lm 2,500 a trip.

On imports

Domestic currency

Without the authorization of the MOF, only Lm 50 in notes and coins that are or have been legal tender in Malta may be imported.

Foreign currency

Subject to the provisions of the Money Laundering Act (1994), any amount of foreign currency may be imported in connection with current capital transactions.

Resident Accounts

Eligibility to hold accounts

Juridical and natural persons are eligible.

Foreign exchange accounts permitted

Residents may invest up to Lm 5,000 a year in these accounts without prior approval.

Held domestically

Export companies may deposit export proceeds in these accounts for a maximum period of 4 months. Approval is not required if amounts do not exceed the portfolio investment limit or if the deposited funds are repatriated funds.

Held abroad

Subject to exchange control permission, juridical and natural persons may maintain savings and demand deposit accounts abroad.

Accounts in domestic currency convertible into foreign currency

No.

Nonresident Accounts

Eligibility to hold accounts

Juridical and natural persons are eligible.

Foreign exchange accounts permitted	These accounts may be credited with funds from overseas sources or with income earnings from permitted activities carried out in Malta.
Domestic currency accounts	The same criteria as for foreign exchange accounts apply.
Convertible into foreign currency	Yes.

Imports and Import Payments

Foreign exchange budget	No.
Financing requirements for imports	No.
Documentation requirements for release of foreign exchange for imports	Payments for all authorized imports may be made freely, provided that currency regulations are complied with and that supporting documents, including the customs entry form for imports over Lm 20,000 and related import license, where applicable, are submitted to the intermediary bank.
Import licenses and other nontariff measures	The Director of Imports and Internal Trade in the Ministry for Economic Services administrates trade controls.
Negative list	Imports of fresh and frozen fish are controlled. Licenses are required for the importation of items that need clearance for health, safety, security, and environmental reasons, as well as for particularly sensitive items, such as fresh and frozen fish, and lace.
Open general licenses	Other products may be imported without an import license.
Licenses with quotas	n.a.
Import taxes and/or tariffs	No.
State import monopoly	The importation of barley, maize, hard and soft wheat, and certain petroleum products is undertaken only by state-owned enterprises.

Exports and Export Proceeds

Repatriation requirements	Proceeds must be received within 6 months of shipment.
Surrender requirements	Proceeds must be surrendered to the authorized banks. However, exporters may retain export proceeds in foreign currency deposit accounts with authorized banks for up to 4 months to make import payments connected with their exporting business.
Financing requirements	No.
Documentation requirements	Exporters must submit customs documentation forms for exports over Lm 20,000.
Export licenses	With the exception of works of art and certain essential goods, all products can be exported freely.
Without quotas	Certain textile products for export to countries in the EU require licenses for monitoring purposes.
Export taxes	No.

Payments for Invisible Transactions and Current Transfers

Controls on these payments	There are no controls on payments for freight and insurance, unloading and storage costs, administrative expenses, interest, commissions, medical costs, study abroad, subscriptions and membership fees, consulting and legal fees, foreign workers' wages, pensions, gambling and prizes earnings, remittances of profits and dividends or for the use of credit cards abroad.
Payments for travel	There are no restrictions on payments for accommodation and transportation expenses, as long as they are paid for in Malta or abroad with credit cards.

Quantitative limits	Residents are entitled to a travel allowance equivalent to Lm 2,500 a trip.
Indicative limits/bona fide test	Amounts in excess of the above limit may be granted upon submission of documentary proof of need.

Family maintenance/alimony

Quantitative limits	The annual limit each resident may transfer abroad to other family members or as a cash gift is Lm 2,500. Remittances above this limit require exchange control approval.
Indicative limits/bona fide test	Yes.

Proceeds from Invisible Transactions and Current Transfers

Repatriation requirements	Proceeds must be received within 6 months of payments.
Surrender requirements	Receipts must be offered for sale to an authorized bank or, if permitted by the CBM, deposited in a foreign currency account under the same conditions as those stipulated for exporters.
Restrictions on use of funds	No.

Capital Transactions

Controls on capital and money market instruments

On capital market securities

Purchase locally by nonresidents	Approval from the CBM must be obtained to purchase or acquire securities that are not listed on the Malta Stock Exchange. Such approval is not required for portfolio investment undertaken by nonresidents in the form of bank deposits, government treasury bills, and securities listed on the Malta Stock Exchange.
Sale or issue locally by nonresidents	Securities may not be issued without the approval of the Malta Financial Services Centre (MFSC).
Purchase abroad by residents	Individuals and companies are permitted to invest up to Lm 5,000 a year. Any investment above that amount requires exchange control approval. Repatriated funds and insurance payments to residents received from nonresident sources are eligible for investment overseas.
Sale or issue abroad by residents	Residents are permitted to sell their approved holdings of foreign portfolio investments and acquire other such investments. However, they are not permitted to issue securities overseas without CBM approval.

On money market instruments

Sale or issue locally by nonresidents	Same regulations as for capital market securities apply.
Purchase abroad by residents	Same regulations as for capital market securities apply.
Sale or issue abroad by residents	Same regulations as for capital market securities apply.
On collective investment securities	Same regulations as for money market instruments apply.
Controls on derivatives and other instruments	Investments in these instruments are very limited. Same regulations as for money market instruments apply.

Controls on credit operations

Commercial credits	Exchange control approval is not required for commercial credits, but export proceeds must be received within 6 months of shipment, unless otherwise authorized.

Financial credits

    By residents to nonresidents   Loans require approval.

    To residents from nonresidents   Loans in excess of Lm 5,000 may be obtained from foreign sources, provided that the loan is for a period of over 3 years and related documentation is submitted for registration purposes. Borrowing in excess of Lm 5,000 for a period of less than 3 years' maturity is subject to CBM approval.

Guarantees, sureties, and financial
backup facilities

    By residents to nonresidents   These transactions are allowed if related to trade transactions.

Controls on direct investment

Outward direct investment   Residents, both individuals and companies, are allowed to remit up to Lm 150,000 a year for direct investment purposes. Investments in excess of that amount require CBM approval.

Inward direct investment   Prior CBM approval is required. Such authorization is denied only in exceptional cases. Direct investment is usually prohibited if the investment is in the real estate, wholesale, and retail trade sectors (particularly the importation of consumer goods for resale). Applications for direct investment in other activities may also be refused if the sectors involved are considered sensitive from a local economy perspective.

Controls on liquidation of direct
investment   The remittance of proceeds requires CBM approval, which is usually granted once documentary evidence of the original investment is submitted.

Controls on real estate transactions

Purchase abroad by residents   CBM approval is required; the CBM considers each case on its own merits. Residents are, however, allowed to purchase real estate overseas using funds already held in portfolio investments abroad.

Purchase locally by nonresidents   Nonresidents may acquire immovable property in Malta as their own residence, with the permission of the MOF, on the condition that the cost of property to be acquired exceeds Lm 15,000 and that funds originate from overseas.

Provisions specific to commercial
banks and other credit institutions   Credit institutions, other than offshore banks, as well as certain financial institutions, may hold foreign assets up to a limit specified by the CBM; this limit is exclusive of foreign assets held as a hedge against foreign currency liabilities.

Borrowing abroad   Such borrowings have to be registered with the CBM.

Maintenance of accounts abroad   Credit institutions may hold accounts subject to portfolio limits.

Lending to nonresidents (financial or
commercial credits)   Lending and purchases of securities abroad are permitted, subject to banking directives on large exposures and as long as foreign asset portfolio limits are not exceeded.

Lending locally in foreign exchange   Lending is permitted, subject to the foreign asset portfolio limits stipulated by the CBM.

Purchase of locally issued securities   n.a.
denominated in foreign exchange

Differential treatment of nonresident
deposit accounts and/or deposit accounts in foreign exchange

    Reserve requirements   Reserve requirements, however, are not applicable in the case of credit institutions carrying out the business of banking exclusively with nonresident customers (that is, offshore banks).

Open foreign exchange position limits   There are quantitative limits set by the CBM, which are revised from time to time. Different limits apply to individual banks.

Provisions specific to institutional
investors   Investments of funds that originate from overseas or from resident sources, as long as the latter do not exceed the yearly portfolio investment allowance, are permitted.

Resident insurance companies have limits imposed by the CBM on the size of their foreign asset portfolio. These limits are revised from time to time.

Limits (max.) on portfolio invested abroad

Same regulations as for portfolio investments abroad apply.

Changes During 1996

Capital transactions

January 1. The limit on direct investment abroad was raised to Lm 150,000 a year from Lm 50,000 a year.

March 29. Residents were allowed to take out life insurance policies in foreign currency with nonresidents lawfully carrying out in Malta the business of life insurance. Both the initial subscription and the annual premiums are not to exceed the portfolio investment limit of Lm 5,000 a year currently granted to residents over 18 years of age.

Changes During 1997

Imports and import payments

February 4. The requirement of a license for the importation of gold coins, gold bullion, and manufactured and semimanufactured articles of gold and silver was removed.

MARSHALL ISLANDS

(Position as of December 31, 1996)

Status Under IMF Articles of Agreement

Article VIII   Date of acceptance: May 21, 1992.

Exchange Arrangement

Currency   The currency of the Marshall Islands is the U.S. dollar.

Exchange rate structure   Unitary.

Classification

Pegged   The authorities do not buy or sell foreign exchange. Foreign exchange transactions are handled by 3 commercial banks, which are authorized foreign exchange dealers and are regulated by a statutory banking board. The banks buy and sell foreign exchange at the rates quoted in the international markets.

Exchange tax   No.

Exchange subsidy   No.

Forward exchange market   Forward transactions may be conducted through commercial banks without restrictions.

Official cover of forward operations No.

Arrangements for Payments and Receipts

Prescription of currency requirements   Outward and inward payments may be settled in U.S. currency or in any other convertible currency.

Payment arrangements   No.

Administration of control   There are no exchange control regulations.

International security restrictions No.

Payment arrears   No.

Controls on exports and imports of banknotes

On exports   n.a.

Resident Accounts

Eligibility to hold accounts   Juridical and natural persons are eligible.

Foreign exchange accounts permitted   Yes.

Held domestically   Yes.

Approval required   n.a.

Held abroad   Commercial banks are not permitted to transfer abroad more than 25% of deposits received from residents. In practice, this regulation is not strictly enforced and does not prevent a depositor from transferring deposits abroad.

Approval required   n.a.

Accounts in domestic currency convertible into foreign currency	Yes.

Nonresident Accounts

Eligibility to hold accounts	Juridical and natural persons are eligible.
Foreign exchange accounts permitted	Yes.
Approval required	n.a.
Domestic currency accounts	Yes.
Convertible into foreign currency	Yes.
Approval required	n.a.
Blocked accounts	No.

Imports and Import Payments

Foreign exchange budget	No.
Financing requirements for imports	No.
Documentation requirements for release of foreign exchange for imports	No.
Import licenses and other nontariff measures	
Negative list	Imports of certain products are prohibited for environmental, health, safety, or social reasons.
Open general licenses	Imports are not subject to import licensing requirements, but importers must obtain a business license.
Import taxes and/or tariffs	Specific and ad valorem duties are levied on imports. Ad valorem duties range from 5% to 75%. Most items are charged a 10% tariff rate, while a 5% rate is applied to food items, medicines, building materials, and heavy machinery. Specific duties are applied on cigarettes, certain beverages, and fuels.
Taxes collected through the exchange system	No.
State import monopoly	No.

Exports and Export Proceeds

Repatriation requirements	No.
Surrender requirements	No.
Financing requirements	No.
Documentation requirements	No.
Export licenses	Exports are not subject to licensing requirements, taxes, or quantitative restrictions. The exportation of copra and its by-products is conducted solely by the government-owned Tobolar Copra Processing Plant, Inc.
Export taxes	No.

Payments for Invisible Transactions and Current Transfers

Controls on these payments	No.

Proceeds from Invisible Transactions and Current Transfers

Repatriation requirements	No.
Surrender requirements	No.
Restrictions on use of funds	No.

Capital Transactions

Controls on direct investment

Outward direct investment   Foreign investors are required to submit applications to the Cabinet and obtain a license in order to engage in business or to acquire an interest in a business in the Marshall Islands.

Inward direct investment   Yes.

Controls on real estate transactions

Purchase abroad by residents   n.a.

Purchase locally by nonresidents   Foreigners are prohibited from owning land, but investors can obtain long-term leases for up to 50 years with an option to renew on land needed for their business.

Sale locally by nonresidents   n.a.

Changes During 1996

No significant changes occurred in the exchange and trade system.

MAURITANIA

(Position as of December 31, 1996)

Status Under IMF Articles of Agreement

Article XIV	Yes.

Exchange Arrangement

Currency
The currency of Mauritania is the ouguiya.

Exchange rate structure
Unitary.

Classification

Independent floating
The exchange rate for the ouguiya is market determined. The Central Bank of Mauritania (CBM) sells foreign currency notes and traveler's checks only for official travel and for other exceptional purposes at a commission of 1.75%. Only intermediary banks and foreign exchange bureaus licensed by the CBM are authorized to buy and sell foreign exchange. Authorized banks and exchange bureaus are free to set their commissions for foreign currency transactions. The source of foreign exchange need not be declared, and foreign exchange may be purchased anonymously. Hotels, shipping companies, travel agencies, and similar businesses may buy banknotes and traveler's checks in foreign currencies under the control of a licensed intermediary bank, but these entities are not authorized to sell such means of payments to the public and must surrender any foreign exchange they have purchased to the bank that granted them the "delegated" authorization.

The average exchange rate is applied to foreign clearing transactions of the Postal Administration. This exchange rate is also applied to remittances through the Postal Administration by Mauritanian workers residing abroad.

Exchange tax
No.

Exchange subsidy
No.

Forward exchange market
No.

Arrangements for Payments and Receipts

Prescription of currency requirements
All settlements with Israel are prohibited.

Administration of control

Exchange control authorities
Administration of control is vested in the CBM, the Ministry of Economy and Finance, and the Ministry of Commerce (MOC). Exchange control authority to approve current international transactions is delegated to authorized banks and foreign exchange bureaus. All imports require exchange control approval from the CBM.

Payment arrears

Official
n.a.

Private
n.a.

Controls on trade in gold (coins and/or bullion)

Controls on external trade
All imports and exports of gold, except manufactured articles containing a minor quantity of gold, require prior authorization from the CBM.

Controls on exports and imports of banknotes

On exports

Domestic currency

Travelers are not allowed to take out domestic banknotes and coins.

Foreign currency

Residents are authorized to export foreign exchange obtained legally and must provide documentation to prove the source. Nonresidents of foreign nationality may freely export payment instruments denominated in foreign currencies in amounts up to those declared upon entry, less amounts surrendered in exchange for ouguiya in the minimum lump sum of UM 10,000 a day. Prior to their departure, these nonresidents may repurchase foreign exchange from banks and bureaus if they have surrendered foreign exchange during their stay in amounts exceeding the minimum lump sum. Nonresident holders of foreign accounts denominated in a foreign currency or in convertible ouguiya may export any traveler's checks denominated in foreign currencies that have been purchased by debit to the aforementioned accounts.

On imports

Domestic currency

Imports are not allowed.

Foreign currency

Residents and nonresidents of Mauritania can freely import foreign banknotes but must exchange them at an authorized bank within 15 days of arrival. Nonresident foreign nationals must declare imported foreign banknotes in excess of $2,000; they can reexport the declared amount minus the equivalent of UM 10,000 for each day of their stay.

Resident Accounts

Eligibility to hold accounts

Juridical and natural persons are eligible.

Foreign exchange accounts permitted

Yes.

Held domestically

Exporters holding import-export permits may open these accounts to deposit the retained portion of their export proceeds in foreign exchange. These accounts may be debited for expenses relating to exporters' production activities or for surrender of foreign exchange to the market.

Held abroad

Licensed banks and foreign exchange bureaus may freely open accounts with banks abroad to accommodate foreign exchange market transactions. Other residents are not allowed to maintain accounts abroad.

Nonresident Accounts

Eligibility to hold accounts

Juridical and natural persons are eligible.

Foreign exchange accounts permitted

Licensed intermediary banks may open freely the following nonresident accounts: (1) nonresident convertible accounts, which may be denominated in foreign currencies or in convertible ouguiya, and transit accounts. Nonresident convertible accounts may be credited with transfers from abroad or from another foreign account; proceeds from the encashment of checks drawn on a foreign bank or on another foreign account opened in a Mauritanian bank to the order of the account holder; transfers issued by a licensed intermediary bank by order of a resident in payment of transactions authorized by the exchange control regulations; and proceeds from the surrender of foreign exchange on account on the foreign exchange market (however, banknotes, whether foreign or issued by the CBM, may not be deposited). These accounts may be debited for foreign exchange surrendered on the foreign exchange market, funds made available abroad, withdrawals of traveler's checks denominated in a foreign currency by the holder, transfers in favor of another foreign account or a resident, checks issued by the holder of the account in favor of another nonresident or a resident, and withdrawals of banknotes issued by the CBM; and (2) transit accounts, which may be opened freely by resident consignees on their books in the name of shipping companies.

Domestic currency accounts	Convertible ouguiya accounts may be credited in the same manner as foreign exchange accounts.
Convertible into foreign currency	Yes.
Blocked accounts	No.

Imports and Import Payments

Foreign exchange budget	No.
Financing requirements for imports	
Minimum financing requirements	n.a.
Advance payment requirements	Advance payments for imports require the prior approval of the CBM.
Advance import deposits	n.a.
Documentation requirements for release of foreign exchange for imports	All imports must be insured with the Mauritanian State Insurance and Reinsurance Company.
Domiciliation requirements	Holders of import-export permits are exempted from the domiciliation requirement. Imports by nonholders of import-export permits are subject to the approval of the MOC, and import transactions must be domiciled with an authorized bank.
Preshipment inspection	n.a.
Letters of credit	n.a.
Import licenses used as exchange licenses	Upon presentation of the import certificate approved by the CBM, the importer may purchase the foreign exchange from an authorized bank or an exchange bureau.
Import licenses and other nontariff measures	The holders of import-export permits must have a certificate that is endorsed by the CBM. Nonholders of import-export permits are subject to the authorization of the MOC.
Negative list	Imports of a few goods are prohibited for reasons of health or public policy.
Open general licenses	Yes.
Licenses with quotas	n.a.
Import taxes and/or tariffs	There is a general customs duty of 15% and a reduced rate of 5% on selected goods. Certain capital goods, various consumer goods (e.g., tea, salt, medicines) are exempt. All imports from the WAEC that are not subject to the regional cooperation tax are also exempt from customs duties, as are some imports from Algeria, Morocco, Tunisia, and the EU. In addition to the customs duty, import taxes are levied at rates ranging from 5% to 166%, with various exemptions. A turnover tax is levied at rates ranging from 10% to 20% (with exemptions). A regional cooperation tax is levied on certain industrial products imported from WAEC countries in lieu of customs duties.
Taxes collected through the exchange system	No.

Exports and Export Proceeds

Repatriation requirements	All export proceeds must be repatriated. Exports of iron ore, which are the monopoly of the National Industrial and Mining Company, enjoy a special exemption to the repatriation of export proceeds.
Surrender requirements	The surrender requirement is 70%: 30% to the CBM and 40% to the market. The remaining 30% may be retained in foreign currency accounts for up to 30 days, after which it must be converted in the market for ouguiya.

Documentation requirements	Export certificates submitted to the CBM for approval must specify the quantity, value, and destination of all goods.
Letters of credit	n.a.
Guarantees	n.a.
Domiciliation	Exports exceeding UM 20,000 must be domiciled.
Preshipment inspection	n.a.
Export licenses	Exports of goods by holders of import-export cards require only a certificate endorsed by the CBM. Exports by nonholders of this card are subject to the authorization of the MOC.
Without quotas	Yes.
With quotas	n.a.
Export taxes	A tax is levied on exports of fish and crustaceans at rates ranging from 8% to 20% for specialized catches, and at a rate of 5% for shrimp and crayfish.
Taxes collected through the exchange system	No.

Payments for Invisible Transactions and Current Transfers

Controls on these payments	The signing of a contract for services rendered by nonresidents to residents is subject to the CBM's endorsement; foreign exchange necessary to pay for their services may be acquired upon presentation of the endorsed contract and a bill of costs.
	Payments for freight and insurance, unloading and storage, administrative expenses, commissions, consulting and legal fees, family maintenance and alimony, interest payments, and remittances of profits and dividends require prior approval and are subject to indicative limits and/or bona fide tests.
Payments for travel	
Prior approval	Amounts in excess of the limit are subject to the prior approval of the CBM.
Quantitative limits	The limit is UM 15,000 a day for the duration of the stay abroad.
Indicative limits/bona fide test	For travel purposes, residents may freely purchase banknotes and traveler's checks denominated in foreign currencies upon presentation of their passport and a travel ticket.

Proceeds from Invisible Transactions and Current Transfers

Repatriation requirements	Proceeds must be repatriated within 4 months.
Surrender requirements	Earnings from services routinely rendered abroad by residents must be domiciled at a licensed intermediary bank. Proceeds must be surrendered in exchange for ouguiya under the same conditions as proceeds from exports of goods.

Capital Transactions

Controls on capital and money market instruments	Capital movements are subject to exchange control. Outward capital transfers require CBM approval and are restricted, but capital receipts are normally permitted freely, although the subsequent investment of the funds in Mauritania may require approval.
On capital market securities	
Purchase locally by nonresidents	n.a.
Sale or issue locally by nonresidents	n.a.

Purchase abroad by residents	Yes.
Sale or issue abroad by residents	n.a.
On money market instruments	
Purchase locally by nonresidents	n.a.
Sale or issue locally by nonresidents	n.a.
Purchase abroad by residents	Yes.
Sale or issue abroad by residents	n.a.
On collective investment securities	
Purchase locally by nonresidents	n.a.
Sale or issue locally by nonresidents	n.a.
Purchase abroad by residents	Yes.
Sale or issue abroad by residents	n.a.
Controls on credit operations	
Commercial credits	
By residents to nonresidents	Yes.
To residents from nonresidents	n.a.
Financial credits	
By residents to nonresidents	Yes.
To residents from nonresidents	n.a.
Guarantees, sureties, and financial backup facilities	
By residents to nonresidents	Yes.
To residents from nonresidents	n.a.
Controls on direct investment	Investments must be declared to the CBM before they are made.
Outward direct investment	Yes.
Inward direct investment	Yes.
Controls on real estate transactions	
Purchase abroad by residents	Yes.
Purchase locally by nonresidents	n.a.
Sale locally by nonresidents	n.a.

Changes During 1996

No significant changes occurred in the exchange and trade system.

MAURITIUS

(Position as of December 31, 1996)

Status Under IMF Articles of Agreement

Article VIII   Date of acceptance: September 29, 1993.

Exchange Arrangement

Currency   The currency of Mauritius is the Mauritian rupee.

Exchange rate structure   Unitary.

Classification

Managed floating   The rupee/U.S. dollar exchange rate is determined by the interbank market.

Exchange tax   No.

Exchange subsidy   No.

Forward exchange market   Commercial banks are free to provide forward exchange cover to their clients.

Official cover of forward operations   No.

Arrangements for Payments and Receipts

Prescription of currency requirements   No.

Payment arrangements

Bilateral arrangements

   Operative   Mauritius maintains a bilateral agreement with Madagascar.

   Inoperative   n.a.

Regional arrangements   Mauritius is a member of the PTA Clearing House.

Clearing agreements   Yes.

Barter agreements and open accounts   n.a.

Administration of control

Exchange control authorities   The Bank of Mauritius (BOM) issues foreign exchange dealing licenses to commercial banks who act as authorized dealers and money changer licenses. The Ministry of Trade and Shipping is responsible for issuing import permits where necessary.

Controls on trade in gold (coins and/or bullion)

Controls on domestic ownership and/or trade   Residents other than the monetary authorities are permitted to hold gold for numismatic purposes or as personal jewelry and ornaments.

Controls on external trade   The BOM is the sole importer of pure gold for sale to jewelers and industrialists.

Controls on exports and imports of banknotes   No.

Resident Accounts

Eligibility to hold accounts   Juridical and natural persons are eligible. There is no distinction between accounts of residents and nonresidents in Mauritius.

Foreign exchange accounts permitted	Yes.
Held domestically	Yes.
Held abroad	Yes.

Nonresident Accounts

Eligibility to hold accounts	Juridical and natural persons are eligible.
Foreign exchange accounts permitted	Yes.
Approval required	n.a.
Domestic currency accounts	Yes.
Convertible into foreign currency	n.a.
Approval required	n.a.
Blocked accounts	No.

Imports and Import Payments

Foreign exchange budget	No.
Financing requirements for imports	No.
Documentation requirements for release of foreign exchange for imports	No.
Import licenses and other nontariff measures	Importers must be licensed.
Positive list	n.a.
Negative list	Controlled goods require import permits from the Ministry of Trade and Shipping.
Open general licenses	Yes.
Licenses with quotas	n.a.
Import taxes and/or tariffs	Duty rates range up to 100%, with most items subject to rates up to 20%. Certain items are subject to import excise duties ranging from 15% to 400%.
Taxes collected through the exchange system	n.a.
State import monopoly	The State Trading Corporation has a monopoly on imports of petroleum products. The State Trading Corporation and a private company share the monopoly on imports of cement.

Exports and Export Proceeds

Repatriation requirements	Yes.
Surrender requirements	In August 1996, the percentage of sugar export proceeds that had to be sold to the BOM was reduced to 75% from 100%. The remaining 25% is sold by the Mauritius Sugar Syndicate at an auction, at which commercial banks and the BOM may participate.
Financing requirements	No.

Documentation requirements	No.
Export licenses	A permit is required for exports of textile products to the United States and Canada.
Without quotas	n.a.
With quotas	Mauritius maintains quotas on exports of textiles and clothing to the United States and Canada under bilateral export restraint agreements. Sugar exports to the EU are restricted under the Sugar Protocol of the Lome Convention. Sugar exports to the United States are also under quotas.
Export taxes	Yes.
Taxes collected through the exchange system	n.a.

Payments for Invisible Transactions and Current Transfers

Controls on these payments	No.

Proceeds from Invisible Transactions and Current Transfers

Repatriation requirements	No.
Surrender requirements	No.
Restrictions on use of funds	No.

Capital Transactions

Controls on capital and money market instruments	No.
Controls on derivatives and other instruments	No.
Controls on credit operations	No.
Controls on direct investment	No.
Controls on liquidation of direct investment	No.
Controls on real estate transactions	
Purchase locally by nonresidents	Noncitizens must obtain the permission of the Minister of Internal Affairs to acquire and hold property. The purchase must be financed by funds transferred from abroad through banks.
Provisions specific to commercial banks and other credit institutions	
Borrowing abroad	n.a.
Maintenance of accounts abroad	n.a.
Lending to nonresidents (financial or commercial credits)	n.a.
Lending locally in foreign exchange	Offshore banks may lend to both residents and nonresidents in foreign currencies.
Purchase of locally issued securities denominated in foreign exchange	n.a.

Differential treatment of nonresident deposit accounts and/or deposit accounts in foreign exchange	n.a.
Investment regulations	n.a.
Open foreign exchange position limits	n.a.
Provisions specific to institutional investors	No.

Changes During 1996

Exports and export proceeds
August 1. The 100% surrender requirement to the BOM for sugar export proceeds was changed to 75% surrender to the BOM and 25% surrender to the interbank auction.

MEXICO

(Position as of February 28, 1997)

Status Under IMF Articles of Agreement

Article VIII   Date of acceptance: November 12, 1946.

Exchange Arrangement

Currency   The currency of Mexico is the Mexican peso.

Exchange rate structure   Unitary.

Classification

Independent floating   The exchange rate of the Mexican peso is determined in the interbank foreign exchange
                                         market.

On August 7, 1996, the Bank of Mexico (BOM) introduced a scheme to purchase foreign exchange from the market without abandoning the commitment to the floating rate
system. Under the scheme, the BOM holds monthly auctions of options, giving financial
institutions the right to sell U.S. dollars to the BOM in exchange for Mexican pesos.
The options, which are valid for a 1-month period, can be exercised at the discretion of
the holders, provided that the rate of exchange is no more depreciated than the average
rate over the preceding 20 working days. The monthly auction amount was set at
$130 million; the amount was increased to $200 million on September 30, 1996, and to
$300 million on January 31, 1997.

The BOM doubled the potential amount of options auctioned each month to $600 mil-
lion on February 19, 1997. If 80% ($240 million out of $300 million maximum) of the
options to sell U.S. dollars to the BOM is exercised within the first 16 days of the
month, the BOM will conduct a second auction of options for up to another $300 mil-
lion. The BOM also announced that it would be prepared to auction (sell) up to
$200 million a day in the foreign market, but would accept only those bids that are at
least 2% more depreciated (in terms of Mexican pesos per U.S. dollar) than the fix of the
previous day.

Exchange tax   No.

Exchange subsidy   No.

Forward exchange market   Forward cover is available from authorized commercial banks. There is an over-the-
                                         counter market in forwards and options in foreign exchange. In addition, the Chicago
                                         Mercantile Exchange trades future contracts on the peso.

Official cover of forward operations   No.

Arrangements for Payments and Receipts

Prescription of currency   In accordance with payments agreements with the central banks of Argentina, Bolivia,
requirements   Brazil, Chile, Colombia, the Dominican Republic, Ecuador, Paraguay, Peru, Uruguay,
                                         and Venezuela, payments to these countries may be made through the BOM and the
                                         central bank of the country concerned within the framework of the multilateral clearing
                                         system of the LAIA. Similar payments arrangements exist with the central banks of
                                         Costa Rica, El Salvador, Guatemala, Honduras, and Nicaragua.

Payment arrangements

Bilateral arrangements

  Operative   There is an arrangement with the central bank of Malaysia.

Regional arrangements   Yes.

Administration of control	No.
International security restrictions	No.
Payment arrears	No.
Controls on trade in gold (coins and/or bullion)	No.
Controls on exports and imports of banknotes	No.

Resident Accounts

Eligibility to hold accounts	Juridical and natural persons are eligible.
Foreign exchange accounts permitted	Yes.
Held domestically	Commercial banks are permitted to open checking accounts denominated in U.S. dollars payable in Mexico only for (1) residents in the northern border area of Mexico, (2) firms domiciled in Mexico in any part of the country, and (3) official representatives of foreign governments and international organizations and foreigners working in these institutions. In case of time deposits denominated in U.S. dollars, commercial banks are permitted to open accounts for firms established in Mexico but are payable only abroad.
Held abroad	Yes.
Accounts in domestic currency convertible into foreign currency	No.

Nonresident Accounts

Eligibility to hold accounts	Juridical and natural persons are eligible.
Foreign exchange accounts permitted	No.
Domestic currency accounts	Yes.
Blocked accounts	No.

Imports and Import Payments

Foreign exchange budget	No.
Financing requirements for imports	No.
Documentation requirements for release of foreign exchange for imports	No.
Import licenses and other nontariff measures	Import licenses from the Secretariat of Commerce and Industrial Promotion (SECOFI) are required for only 179 of the 11,285 items on which Mexico's general import tariff is levied, except for temporary imports of raw materials and intermediate goods for export industries. On average, import licenses cover the applicant's import needs for 9 months and may be extended for 3 months. Import needs are estimated at 20% above the amount of previous actual imports but may be increased when justified. New licenses are issued only if the applicant can demonstrate that at least 70% of earlier licenses have been effectively used. For some commodities, "open-ended" import licenses may be granted, allowing imports to be effected during a period of 6 months to 1 year, subject to an overall limit. Depending on the importer's performance, the license may be

renewed repeatedly. Imports of new cars of a given manufacturer are limited to 143% of export levels of the same manufacturer. Imports of used cars are subject to the prior approval of the SECOFI.

Negative list	Yes.
Open general licenses	Yes.
Licenses with quotas	Yes.
Import taxes and/or tariffs	Import tariffs range from zero to 20%, with higher rates for some products (clothing, footwear, and leather goods are subject to a 35% tariff). Imports from members of LAIA are granted preferential duty treatment and there are free trade zones in place in certain regions. Free trade agreements exist with Bolivia, Chile, Colombia, Costa Rica, and Venezuela. Trade with the United States and Canada takes place under NAFTA. Mexico has applied antidumping duties on a variety of products: corrugated rod from Brazil; doorknobs, footwear, tools, chinaware, and chemical products from China; bicycle tires from India; beef from the EU; and metal sheets, steel sheets, metal plates, seamless tubes, and pipes from the United States.
Taxes collected through the exchange system	No.
State import monopoly	No.

Exports and Export Proceeds

Repatriation requirements	No.
Surrender requirements	No.
Financing requirements	No.
Documentation requirements	No.
Export licenses	Most exports do not require licenses. Exports of a few specified items related to endangered species and archaeological pieces are prohibited.
Export taxes	Export taxes are limited to only a few items such as sugar, corn flour, turtle oil, and electricity, among others.
Taxes collected through the exchange system	No.

Payments for Invisible Transactions and Current Transfers

Controls on these payments	There are no controls on these payments. The purchasing of personal insurance policies abroad is not restricted, but casualty insurance policies intended to cover events that will take place in Mexico may be contracted only with Mexican companies, including subsidiaries of foreign insurance companies established in Mexico. Reinsurance may be contracted with foreign reinsurance companies.

Proceeds from Invisible Transactions and Current Transfers

Repatriation requirements	No.
Surrender requirements	No.
Restrictions on use of funds	No.

Capital Transactions

Controls on capital and money market instruments

On capital market securities

Sale or issue locally by nonresidents

Yes.

Purchase abroad by residents

There are restrictions on the purchase by securities firms for their own account and by financial institutions.

On money market instruments

Sale or issue locally by nonresidents

Pursuant to the Securities Exchange Act, only documents registered in the National Registry of Securities and Intermediaries (NRSI) may be offered publicly.

Purchase abroad by residents

There are restrictions on purchases by securities firms for their own account and by financial institutions.

Sale or issue abroad by residents

These transactions are subject to registration with the NRSI.

On collective investment securities

Sale or issue locally by nonresidents

Only documents registered in the NRSI may be offered publicly.

Sale or issue abroad by residents

These transactions are subject to registration with the NRSI.

Controls on derivatives and other instruments

Purchase locally by nonresidents

The holder, who is the beneficiary of the right consigned in the document, may be foreign persons or corporations. In this case, the aforementioned persons may only acquire warrants when the underlying securities are of the free subscription type or related to a neutral investment trust authorized by the National Banking and Securities Commission (NBSC).

Sale or issue locally by nonresidents

The warrants should be issued with reference to shares registered on the Mexican Stock Exchange and portfolios of representatives; shares of the capital of corporations should be registered on the Mexican Stock Exchange. In addition, it is required that the issuer of the derivative be a corporation with shares registered at the NRSI.

Purchase abroad by residents

The Secretariat of Finance and Public Credit (SHCP) establishes a ceiling on the amount that credit institutions are allowed to lend to each borrower.

Sale or issue abroad by residents

These transactions are not permitted.

Controls on credit operations

Commercial credits

To residents from nonresidents

There are limits on credits denominated in foreign currency.

Financial credits

By residents to nonresidents

Yes.

To residents from nonresidents

There are limits on credits denominated in foreign currency.

Controls on direct investment

Outward direct investment

Although there exists no restriction in this respect, the Mexican government reserves the right to introduce foreign exchange control measures that may affect outward direct investment.

Inward direct investment

Investments are normally allowed up to 100% of equity without prior authorization, with certain exceptions:

(1) Investments in the following sectors are reserved for the state: oil and other hydrocarbons; basic petrochemicals; electricity; nuclear energy generation; radioactive

minerals; communication via satellite; telegraph; radiotelegraphy; postal service; railroads; issue of paper money; minting of coins; and the control and supervision of ports, airports, and heliports;

(2) Investments in the following sectors are reserved exclusively for Mexican nationals or Mexican corporations with a foreign exclusion clause: retail trade of gasoline and liquefied petroleum gas; radio and television broadcasting, with the exception of cable television; road transport (excluding courier and packaged goods transport services); credit unions and development banks; and certain professional and technical services. However, foreign investors wishing to invest in these activities may acquire shares in companies engaged in these sectors through the Neutral Investment Mechanism;

(3) Investments in the following sectors require prior authorization: acquisition of more than 49% of the equity in a Mexican corporation if the total value of assets exceeds $25 million; maritime transport and certain port services; administration of air terminals; cellular telephones; construction activities, including the construction of pipelines for oil and its derivatives; oil and gas drilling; legal services; private education; credit information; securities rating institutions; and insurance agents. In order to obtain prior authorization, investors must submit their proposals to the National Commission of Foreign Investment. Approval is automatic if a formal response is not made within 45 working days of the date of application. In reaching its decision, the commission takes into account the impact of investments on employment and training of workers, the technological contribution, compliance with environmental provisions in relevant laws, and the contribution to the economy; and

(4) Ceilings on foreign ownership are applied to the following sectors: financial institutions; air transportation; manufacturing of explosives and firearms; printing and publication of domestic newspapers; agricultural land; cable television and basic telephone services; video text and packet-switching services; and transportation by air and land, and certain activities related to maritime transport.

Controls on liquidation of direct investment

No.

Controls on real estate transactions

Purchase locally by nonresidents

The restrictions are the following: (1) the acquisition by foreign nonresidents of real estate outside a 100-kilometer strip alongside the Mexican land border and a 50-kilometer strip inland from the Mexican coast, provided the investor agrees to consider himself Mexican and to refrain from invoking the protection of the investor's government regarding the property thus acquired; and (2) the acquisition by foreign nonresidents of real estate through a real estate trust within the zone defined above.

Provisions specific to commercial banks and other credit institutions

Borrowing abroad

Borrowing abroad is permitted subject to open foreign exchange position limits.

Maintenance of accounts abroad

Resident banks can maintain accounts abroad but must maintain an equilibrium between their positions in foreign exchange and domestic currency.

Lending to nonresidents (financial or commercial credits)

The SHCP establishes a ceiling on the amount that credit institutions are allowed to lend to each borrower.

Lending locally in foreign exchange

Banks are permitted to lend locally in foreign currencies but the debt may be discharged by delivering the equivalent amount in accordance to the rate of exchange in domestic currency.

Open foreign exchange position limits

The liabilities of commercial banks denominated in foreign currency must not exceed the larger amount of either (1) 10% of the daily balances of their liabilities in the previous quarter plus an additional 4% of such liabilities if those resources are used to finance foreign trade transactions or capital goods purchases, or (2) 1.6 times the net capital of the institution. Commercial banks must balance their positions in foreign currency on a daily basis subject to covered exchange rate risk, irrespective of the residence of the lender. Short and long positions are acceptable as long as they do not exceed 15% of the bank's net capital.

Provisions specific to institutional investors	Insurance companies can operate with nonresidents including in the following areas: (1) administer the reserves retained from domestic or foreign insurance companies corresponding to reinsurance operations; (2) foreign investment of technical reserves corresponding to operations that take place abroad; and (3) constitute banking deposits abroad.
	There are 3 types of mutual funds: (1) variable-income mutual funds in which foreign persons and corporations can acquire representative shares of mutual funds as well as foreign financial entities and groups of foreign persons; (2) fixed-income mutual funds in which representative shares of this type of mutual funds can be acquired by foreign persons and corporations, foreign financial entities, and groups of foreign corporations; and (3) capital-risk mutual funds in which the representative shares of these kinds of funds may be acquired by foreigners, persons, and corporations, provided that this participation does not exceed 49% of the shares of the respective mutual fund.
Limits (max.) on portfolio invested abroad	Mutual funds portfolios may not be invested abroad.
Other controls imposed by securities laws	No.

Changes During 1996

Exchange arrangements	*August 7.* The BOM introduced a scheme to purchase foreign exchange from the market without abandoning the commitment to the floating rate system. Under the scheme, the BOM holds monthly auctions of options up to $130 million, giving financial institutions the right to sell U.S. dollars to the BOM in exchange for Mexican pesos. The options, which are valid for a 1-month period, can be exercised at the discretion of the holders, provided that the rate of exchange is no more depreciated than the average rate over the preceding 20 working days.
	September 30. The BOM increased the amount of options auctions to $200 million.
Imports and import payments	*August 13.* SECOFI imposed punitive import tariffs on chinaware from China.
	August 21. SECOFI imposed punitive import tariffs on metal sheets from the United States.
	August 28. SECOFI imposed punitive import tariffs on footwear from China.
	September 5. SECOFI imposed punitive import tariffs on beef from the European Union.
	October 17. SECOFI imposed punitive import tariffs on chemical products and tools from China.
	November 1. SECOFI imposed punitive import tariffs on bicycle tires from India.
	November 8. SECOFI imposed punitive import tariffs on metal plates from the United States.
Capital transactions	*October 7.* The BOM removed the prohibition on national credit institutions to carry passive operations in domestic currency with foreign financial institutions and foreign exchange houses.

Changes During 1997

Exchange arrangements	*January 31.* The BOM increased the amount of options auctions to $300 million a day.
	February 19. Two modifications to the exchange rate system were introduced. First, the BOM doubled the potential amount of options auctioned each month to $600 million. If 80% ($240 million out of $300 million maximum) of the options to sell U.S. dollars to the BOM is exercised within the first 16 days of the month, the BOM will conduct a second auction of options for up to another $300 million. Second, the BOM also announced that it would be prepared to auction (sell) up to $200 million a day in the foreign market, but would accept only those bids that are at least 2% more depreciated (in terms of Mexican pesos per U.S. dollar) than the fix of the previous day.

FEDERATED STATES OF MICRONESIA

(Position as of December 31, 1996)

Status Under IMF Articles of Agreement

Article VIII	Date of acceptance: June 24, 1993.

Exchange Arrangement

Currency	The currency of the Federated States of Micronesia is the U.S. dollar.
Exchange rate structure	Unitary.
Classification	
Independent floating	The authorities do not buy or sell foreign exchange. Foreign exchange transactions are handled by 3 commercial banks, which are authorized foreign exchange dealers and are regulated by a statutory banking board. The banks buy and sell foreign exchange at the rates quoted in international markets.
Exchange tax	No.
Exchange subsidy	No.
Forward exchange market	Forward transactions may be conducted through commercial banks without restriction.
Official cover of forward operations	No.

Arrangements for Payments and Receipts

Prescription of currency requirements	No.
Payment arrangements	No.
Administration of control	No.
International security restrictions	No.
Payment arrears	No.
Controls on trade in gold (coins and/or bullion)	No.
Controls on exports and imports of banknotes	No.

Resident Accounts

Eligibility to hold accounts	Juridical and natural persons are eligible.
Foreign exchange accounts permitted	Yes.
Held domestically	Yes.
Approval required	n.a.
Held abroad	Yes.
Approval required	n.a.
Accounts in domestic currency convertible into foreign currency	Yes.

Nonresident Accounts

Eligibility to hold accounts	Juridical and natural persons are eligible.
Foreign exchange accounts permitted	Yes.
Domestic currency accounts	Yes.
Convertible into foreign currency	Yes.
Approval required	n.a.
Blocked accounts	No.

Imports and Import Payments

Foreign exchange budget	No.
Financing requirements for imports	No.
Import licenses and other nontariff measures	Importers must obtain a business license.
Negative list	Imports of certain products are prohibited for environmental, health, safety, or social reasons.
Import taxes and/or tariffs	Import duties are levied on an ad valorem or specific basis as follows: cigarettes, carbonated nonalcoholic beverages, drink mixes and preparations, coffee, tea, beer, malt beverages, and wines, 25%; spirits and distilled alcoholic beverages, $10 per U.S. gallon; and gasoline and diesel fuel, 5¢ per U.S. gallon. Ad valorem duties are 3% on foodstuffs, 100% on laundry bar soap, and 4% on all other products.
Taxes collected through the exchange system	No.
State import monopoly	No.

Exports and Export Proceeds

Repatriation requirements	No.
Surrender requirements	No.
Financing requirements	No.
Export licenses	Exports are not subject to licensing requirements, taxes, or quantitative restrictions. The purchasing and exportation of copra and dried coconut meat yielding coconut oil are conducted solely by the Coconut Development Authority.
Export taxes	No.

Payments for Invisible Transactions and Current Transfers

Controls on these payments	No.

Proceeds from Invisible Transactions and Current Transfers

Repatriation requirements	No.
Surrender requirements	No.

Restrictions on use of funds	No.

Capital Transactions

Controls on credit operations	
Commercial credits	n.a.
Financial credits	
By residents to nonresidents	Banks are prohibited from lending more than the equivalent of 50% of their deposits to nonresidents.
Guarantees, sureties, and financial backup facilities	n.a.
Controls on direct investment	
Inward direct investment	Foreign investors must obtain an application from the federal government and submit it for review and action to the Foreign Investment Board of the state in which the business will be located. They must obtain a license from the federal government to engage in business or to acquire an interest in a business in the Federated States of Micronesia. If a foreign investor wishes to conduct business in more than one state, an application for each state must be obtained from the federal government and submitted to the Federal Investment Board of each of the states in which the business will be located and operated. Priorities for foreign investment are reviewed by the federal and state authorities from time to time.
Controls on liquidation of direct investment	No.
Controls on real estate transactions	
Purchase locally by nonresidents	Foreign investment in the real estate and construction sectors is prohibited in accordance with the laws prohibiting landownership by foreigners. Foreign investors normally obtain long-term leases (usually up to 25 years with an option to renew for another 25 years) for land needed for their business.
Sale locally by nonresidents	Yes.
Provisions specific to commercial banks and other credit institutions	
Lending to nonresidents (financial or commercial credits)	Commercial banks are not permitted to transfer abroad more than 50% of deposits received from residents. In practice, the regulation is not strictly enforced and does not prevent a depositor from transferring deposits abroad.
Lending locally in foreign exchange	n.a.
Purchase of locally issued securities denominated in foreign exchange	n.a.

Changes During 1996

No significant changes occurred in the exchange and trade system.

MOLDOVA

(Position as of February 28, 1997)

Status Under IMF Articles of Agreement

Article VIII	Date of acceptance: June 30, 1995.

Exchange Arrangement

Currency

The currency of Moldova is the Moldovan leu.

Exchange rate structure

Unitary.

Classification

Independent floating

Until November 28, 1996, the official exchange rates against the U.S. dollar and the Russian ruble were established in the daily fixing sessions at the Interbank Foreign Currency Exchange of Moldova (IFCEM). Effective November 29, 1996, only the rate against the U.S. dollar started to be quoted in the daily fixing sessions. The official exchange rate is used for accounting and tax valuation purposes. Institutions eligible to deal in foreign exchange are authorized banks and foreign exchange bureaus. The latter are authorized to purchase from and sell to residents and nonresidents foreign banknotes and traveler's checks in any currency. Authorized banks and foreign exchange bureaus may set their own buying and selling rates in their foreign exchange transactions.

Exchange tax

No.

Exchange subsidy

No.

Forward exchange market

No.

Arrangements for Payments and Receipts

Prescription of currency requirements

No.

Payment arrangements

Regional arrangements

Moldova is a member of the Payments Union within the CIS.

Administration of control

Exchange control authorities

The National Bank of Moldova (NBM) has the ultimate authority in the area of foreign exchange arrangements and is responsible for managing the country's foreign exchange reserves, regulating the currency market, and granting licenses to engage in foreign currency transactions.

International security restrictions

No.

In accordance with IMF Executive Board Decision No. 144-(52/51)

n.a.

Payment arrears

No.

Controls on trade in gold (coins and/or bullion)

Controls on domestic ownership and/or trade

The Ministry of Finance (MOF) establishes regulations governing domestic trade.

Controls on external trade

A license from the MOF is required to conduct international trade in gold.

Controls on exports and imports of banknotes

On exports

Domestic currency

The export limit is MDL 500; for exports to Romania the limit is MDL 2,500.

Foreign currency

For freely convertible currencies, the limit is $50,000 upon presentation of a customs declaration for the importation of the currency or approval of an authorized bank or the NBM. Without these documents, the limit is $5,000 for residents and as much as was imported or received from abroad for nonresidents. For nonconvertible currencies, there are no limits.

Resident Accounts

Eligibility to hold accounts

Juridical persons

Juridical persons may open 1 account in a freely convertible currency and 1 account each in nonconvertible currencies.

Natural persons

Natural persons may open an account only in a freely convertible currency.

Foreign exchange accounts permitted

Yes.

Held domestically

All foreign currency earnings of residents must be deposited in their accounts at authorized banks. Account holders may not use foreign exchange balances in their accounts to settle domestic transactions. Approval by the MOF is required only for organizations included in the budget.

Held abroad

These accounts are permitted, but approval from the NBM is required.

Accounts in domestic currency convertible into foreign currency

These accounts may be used for current international transactions and for capital transactions, in accordance with the law on Foreign Investment. Approval from the NBM is required for capital transactions.

Nonresident Accounts

Eligibility to hold accounts

Juridical and natural persons are eligible.

Foreign exchange accounts permitted

Nonresidents with foreign currency deposits at authorized banks in Moldova may freely transfer the balances abroad or sell them on the foreign exchange market through authorized banks.

Domestic currency accounts

Accounts in Moldovan lei may be opened by nonresidents from CIS countries with approval from the central bank of the relevant country. Other nonresidents may open accounts in Moldovan lei at authorized banks in Moldova if the funds were received from selling foreign exchange in the foreign exchange market in Moldova or as a result of selling goods, providing services, or other labor.

Convertible into foreign currency

Nonresidents may convert Moldovan lei into foreign exchange provided the lei were received as a result of a current international transaction, with the exception of Moldovan lei received from selling restricted currencies (for CIS countries and Romania). For nonresident natural persons, conversion into a freely convertible currency is allowed if the foreign currency was previously imported or transferred into Moldova and sold to a bank, and customs documents showing that the foreign currency had been imported into Moldova are submitted to the purchasing bank.

Blocked accounts

These are accounts of juridical persons blocked by the U.S.S.R. Vnesheconombank in 1992.

Imports and Import Payments

Foreign exchange budget	No.
Financing requirements for imports	No.
Advance payment requirements	If a contract is not executed, the amount of the advance payment must be repatriated into Moldova no later than 90 days after such advance payment was made.
Documentation requirements for release of foreign exchange for imports	A contract with a nonresident is required.
Import licenses and other nontariff measures	Imports of medicine, medical equipment, chemicals, and industrial waste are subject to licensing for the purpose of protecting the consumer and ensuring compliance with domestic standards.
Import taxes and/or tariffs	There are 6 tariff bands, with the maximum tariff applied to consumer electronics, cars, tobacco products, alcoholic beverages, cocoa products, jewelry, and luxury furniture. Energy, medicine, medical equipment, raw materials, cereals, and baby food are exempt from tariffs. Customs fees are also applied.
Taxes collected through the exchange system	No.
State import monopoly	No.

Exports and Export Proceeds

Repatriation requirements	Proceeds must be repatriated no later than 180 days from the issuance of the custom declaration or from the date of a bill, statement, or protocol confirming that services have been rendered or work done. However, the NBM can extend the period for a valid reason.
Surrender requirements	No.
Financing requirements	No.
Documentation requirements	A declaration on the repatriation of foreign exchange proceeds is required.
Export licenses	Exports of goods considered important are subject to licenses.
Without quotas	n.a.
With quotas	n.a.
Export taxes	There are no taxes on exports to non-CIS countries except for a customs fee of 0.25% of the value of the shipment. Exports to CIS countries are subject to excise taxes and VAT, as these taxes are assessed on the basis of the origin principle within the CIS.
Taxes collected through the exchange system	No.

Payments for Invisible Transactions and Current Transfers

Controls on these payments	In general, for payments in freely convertible currencies of up to $1,000, a natural person must show a supporting document. For payments for medical costs, study abroad, subscriptions and membership fees, consulting and legal fees, and family maintenance and alimony over $1,000, approval by the NBM is required. There are no controls on payments for freight and insurance, unloading and storage costs, interest payments, profits and dividends, foreign workers' wages, and pensions.
Administrative expenses	
Quantitative limits	Yes.

Commissions

    Quantitative limits   Yes.

    Indicative limits/bona fide test   n.a.

Payments for travel

    Prior approval   For amounts in freely convertible currencies in excess of $5,000 a trip, a resident unable to produce evidence of the currency's importation or receipt from abroad must obtain prior approval.

    Quantitative limits   Residents may export up to $5,000 of freely convertible currencies.

Medical costs

    Quantitative limits   Residents may transfer up to $1,000 in freely convertible currencies for treatment upon presentation of supporting documents.

Study abroad costs

    Quantitative limits   Residents may transfer up to $1,000 in freely convertible currencies for education costs upon presentation of supporting documents.

    Indicative limits/bona fide test   n.a.

Subscriptions and membership fees

    Quantitative limits   Residents may transfer up to $1,000 in freely convertible currencies.

    Indicative limits/bona fide test   n.a.

Consulting/legal fees

    Quantitative limits   Residents may transfer up to $1,000 in freely convertible currencies.

Gambling/prize earnings

    Prior approval   Yes.

    Quantitative limits   Residents may export up to $5,000. Nonresidents are not permitted to transfer prize earnings abroad.

Family maintenance/alimony

    Quantitative limits   Residents may transfer up to $1,000 of freely convertible currencies.

    Indicative limits/bona fide test   n.a.

Credit card use abroad   Issuance of credit cards against accounts of juridical persons is allowed, and issuance of debit cards against type "A" accounts of natural persons is allowed.

    Prior approval   Yes.

Proceeds from Invisible Transactions and Current Transfers

Repatriation requirements   All proceeds from invisibles, except the earnings of workers residing abroad, must be repatriated.

Surrender requirements   No.

Restrictions on use of funds   No.

Capital Transactions

Controls on capital and money market instruments   Registration of the importation of capital and licensing of its exportation are required.

On capital market securities

    Purchase locally by nonresidents   Registration with the NBM is required.

Sale or issue locally by nonresidents	Licensing by the NBM is required.
Purchase abroad by residents	Licensing by the NBM is required.
Sale or issue abroad by residents	Registration with the NBM is required.

On money market instruments

Purchase locally by nonresidents	The purchase of state securities is subject to licensing of the MOF.
Sale or issue locally by nonresidents	Licensing by the NBM is required.
Purchase abroad by residents	Licensing by the NBM is required.
Sale or issue abroad by residents	Registration with the NBM is required.

On collective investment securities

Purchase locally by nonresidents	Registration with the NBM is required.
Sale or issue locally by nonresidents	Licensing by the NBM is required.
Purchase abroad by residents	Licensing by the NBM is required.
Sale or issue abroad by residents	Registration with the NBM is required.

Controls on derivatives and other instruments

Purchase locally by nonresidents	Registration with the NBM is required.
Sale or issue locally by nonresidents	Licensing by the NBM is required.
Purchase abroad by residents	Licensing by the NBM is required.
Sale or issue abroad by residents	Registration with the NBM is required.

Controls on credit operations	Loan agreements with nonresidents are required to be registered with the NBM.

Commercial credits

By residents to nonresidents	Licensing by the NBM is required.
To residents from nonresidents	The agreement should be registered with the NBM.

Financial credits

By residents to nonresidents	Licensing by the NBM is required.
To residents from nonresidents	Contracts must be registered with the NBM.
Guarantees, sureties, and financial backup facilities	Contracts must be registered with the NBM.
By residents to nonresidents	Licensing by the NBM is required.
To residents from nonresidents	Contracts must be registered with the NBM.

Controls on direct investment

Outward direct investment	Licensing by the NBM is required.
Inward direct investment	Registration with the NBM is required.
Controls on liquidation of direct investment	Yes.

Controls on real estate transactions

Purchase abroad by residents	Licensing by the NBM is required.

Purchase locally by nonresidents	Registration is required.
Sale locally by nonresidents	n.a.

Provisions specific to commercial banks and other credit institutions

Borrowing abroad	Registration with the NBM is required.
Maintenance of accounts abroad	For type "B" and "C" banking licenses (with aggregate normative capital of more than MDL 8 million) no restriction applies to accounts in freely convertible currency, but approval of the NBM is required for accounts in nonconvertible currencies.
Lending to nonresidents (financial or commercial credits)	Licensing by the NBM is required.
Lending locally in foreign exchange	Authorized banks are permitted to lend in freely convertible currencies only to importers that are resident juridical persons.
Purchase of locally issued securities denominated in foreign exchange	Securities denominated in foreign exchange are not issued.

Differential treatment of nonresident deposit accounts and/or deposit accounts in foreign exchange

Reserve requirements	Uniform reserve requirements of 8% apply to local currency and foreign currency deposits.
Liquid asset requirements	The requirement is 30% of the bank's liabilities for demand deposits.
Credit controls	Yes.
Open foreign exchange position limits	For each type of currency, the limit is 10% of the aggregate normative capital, and the aggregate limit is 25% of the aggregate normative capital.

Provisions specific to institutional investors

Limits (max.) on portfolio invested abroad	Licensing by the NBM is required.
Limits (min.) on portfolio invested locally	Registration with the NBM is required.
Other controls imposed by securities laws	Investors and primary dealers are prohibited from purchasing more than 35% of a single issue of government securities.

Changes During 1996

Exchange arrangements	*November 28.* The mechanism for quoting the exchange rate of the Moldovan leu was changed; the official exchange rate against the U.S. dollar is set in the daily fixing sessions. Rates for other convertible currencies are determined on the basis of their U.S. dollar cross rates in the international market.
Capital transactions	*May 17.* Resident companies were required to obtain NBM permission for providing loans in foreign currency.

Changes During 1997

Capital transactions	*February 1.* Reserve requirements solely in Moldovan lei for liabilities of commercial banks in freely convertible currencies were introduced.

MONGOLIA

(Position as of December 31, 1996)

Status Under IMF Articles of Agreement

Article VIII   Date of acceptance: February 1, 1996.

Exchange Arrangement

Currency   The currency of Mongolia is the tugrik.

Exchange rate structure   Unitary.

Classification

Independent floating   In principle, the official exchange rate of the tugrik is set daily by the Bank of Mongolia (BoM) as the midpoint of the previous day's average buying and selling rates established by transactions among participants in the interbank foreign exchange market. However, the volume of trading is very low, and the BoM currently adjusts the official rate only once a week rather than once a day. The official exchange rate is applied to public sector import and service payments, including for debt service, and to trade and service transactions conducted under bilateral payments arrangements. All other transactions, including sales of retained foreign exchange by public sector enterprises, take place through the interbank market. Exchange rates for other convertible currencies are calculated on the basis of the cross rates against the U.S. dollar in international markets. The spread between commercial banks' buying and selling rates is limited to 1%.

Exchange tax   No.

Exchange subsidy   No.

Forward exchange market   No.

Arrangements for Payments and Receipts

Prescription of currency requirements   No.

Payment arrangements

Bilateral arrangements

   Operative   Trade with certain former members of the CMEA is conducted on an ad hoc basis under bilateral arrangements concluded before 1991.

   Inoperative   Some of the outstanding balances under the clearing arrangements of the former International Bank for Economic Cooperation (IBEC) are still under negotiation. Under inoperative bilateral trade arrangements, there are also outstanding balances with China, the Islamic State of Afghanistan, and the Federal Republic of Yugoslavia (Serbia/Montenegro).

Clearing agreements   Mongolia maintains a bilateral clearing agreement with the Democratic People's Republic of Korea.

Administration of control

Exchange control authorities International transactions are governed by the Foreign Exchange Law (1994).

International security restrictions

In accordance with IMF Executive Board Decision No. 144-(52/51)   Mongolia notified the IMF on November 4, 1994, that restrictions had been imposed on certain transactions with the Federal Republic of Yugoslavia (Serbia/Montenegro).

In accordance with UN sanctions   n.a.

Payment arrears	No.
Controls on trade in gold (coins and/or bullion)	
Controls on domestic ownership and/or trade	Producers of gold are required to sell all their output to the BoM.
Controls on external trade	The BoM has an exclusive right on external trade in gold.
Controls on exports and imports of banknotes	
On exports	
Domestic currency	Exportation of domestic banknotes is prohibited.
On imports	
Domestic currency	Importation of domestic banknotes is prohibited.

Resident Accounts

Eligibility to hold accounts	Juridical and natural persons are eligible.
Foreign exchange accounts permitted	Accounts may be held at authorized banks; they may be credited with retained export earnings and foreign exchange transferred from abroad and the balances may be used for any purpose without restriction.
Held domestically	Yes.
Held abroad	n.a.
Accounts in domestic currency convertible into foreign currency	Yes.

Nonresident Accounts

Eligibility to hold accounts	Juridical and natural persons are eligible. However, registration with the State Registry is required for juridical persons.
Foreign exchange accounts permitted	Yes.
Domestic currency accounts	Yes.
Convertible into foreign currency	Yes.

Imports and Import Payments

Foreign exchange budget	No.
Financing requirements for imports	No.
Documentation requirements for release of foreign exchange for imports	No.
Import licenses and other nontariff measures	An excise tax of 100% is levied on imports of alcohol and cigarettes.
Negative list	Imports of drugs, materials that encourage or depict violence or pornography, and items that could cause environmental damage are banned.
Open general licenses	Imports of historical artifacts, precious metals, weapons, radioactive materials, ferrous and nonferrous metals, and goods and services requiring licenses under international contracts and agreements require a special permit.

Import taxes and/or tariffs	There is a uniform customs duty of 15%; imports of machinery and equipment by joint ventures and equipment used by disabled people are exempt from the customs duty.
Taxes collected through the exchange system	No.
State import monopoly	No.

Exports and Export Proceeds

Repatriation requirements	No.
Surrender requirements	No.
Financing requirements	No.
Documentation requirements	No.
Export licenses	
Without quotas	Exports of historical artifacts, precious metals, weapons, radioactive materials, ferrous and nonferrous metals, and goods and services requiring licenses under international contracts and agreements require a special permit. The ban on exports of raw cashmere was lifted on July 1, 1996.
With quotas	Yes.
Export taxes	Export taxes apply to export of nonferrous and scrap metals.

Payments for Invisible Transactions and Current Transfers

Controls on these payments	No.

Proceeds from Invisible Transactions and Current Transfers

Repatriation requirements	No.
Surrender requirements	No.
Restrictions on use of funds	No.

Capital Transactions

Controls on capital and money market instruments	
On capital market securities	
Sale or issue locally by nonresidents	Issue is prohibited.
On money market instruments	
Sale or issue locally by nonresidents	Issue is prohibited.
On collective investment securities	
Sale or issue locally by nonresidents	Issue is prohibited.
Controls on derivatives and other instruments	
Sale or issue locally by nonresidents	Issue is prohibited.

Controls on credit operations

Commercial credits

   By residents to nonresidents   Registration with the Ministry of Finance (MOF) is required.

   To residents from nonresidents   Registration with the BoM is required.

Financial credits

   By residents to nonresidents   Registration with the MOF is required.

   To residents from nonresidents   Registration with the BoM is required.

Guarantees, sureties, and financial backup facilities   No.

Controls on direct investment

Inward direct investment   Investment by private corporations is encouraged particularly in export promotion, projects using advanced technology, and the exploitation of natural resources. The Law on Foreign Investment guarantees that foreign firms not be nationalized and that foreign investors will have the right to dispose of their assets. The maximum rate of profit tax is 40%, and foreign investors are exempt from the tax for 3 to 10 years, depending on the sector and export performance. In addition, the law stipulates that entities with foreign participation may export at world prices or other agreed prices, and they may import or export directly or in cooperation with foreign trade enterprises.

Controls on liquidation of direct investment   No.

Controls on real estate transactions

Purchase abroad by residents   Registration with the State Real Estate Registry is required.

Purchase locally by nonresidents   Registration with the State Real Estate Registry is required.

Provisions specific to commercial banks and other credit institutions

Borrowing abroad   Registration with the BoM is required.

Maintenance of accounts abroad   BoM permission is required.

Open foreign exchange position limits   The limit is 20% of capital, including a subceiling of 10% for any individual currency.

Provisions specific to institutional investors   No.

Other controls imposed by securities laws   Securities may be issued only by government institutions upon approval of the Great Hural or by companies registered in Mongolia.

It is prohibited to lend securities. Any person owing 5% and above of total shares of any company must report it to the Securities Committee of the Great Hural within 5 days after acquisition. Any person who intends to own directly or indirectly 20% and above of total shares of any company must make a tender offer in accordance with Article 8 of the Securities Law of Mongolia.

Changes During 1996

Status under IMF Articles of Agreement   *February 1.* Mongolia accepted the obligations of Article VIII, Sections 2, 3, and 4 of the Fund Agreement.

Exports and export proceeds   *January 1.* A tax on exports of nonferrous and scrap metals was introduced.

July 1. The ban on exports of raw cashmere was lifted.

MOROCCO

(Position as of January 31, 1997)

Status Under IMF Articles of Agreement

Article VIII	Date of acceptance: January 21, 1993.

Exchange Arrangement

Currency	The currency of Morocco is the Moroccan dirham.
Other legal tender	Commemorative gold coins with a face value of DH 250 and DH 500, and commemorative silver coins with a face value of DH 50, DH 100, DH 150, and DH 200 are also legal tender.
Exchange rate structure	Unitary.
Classification	
Pegged	Since June 1996, the exchange rate is determined freely in an interbank foreign exchange market. Bank Al-Maghrib (BAM) intervenes in the market to maintain rates within a spread around the central rate. The central exchange rate of the Moroccan dirham is pegged to a basket of currencies comprising Morocco's principal trading partners, and weighted in accordance with the geographic distribution of Morocco's foreign trade and the pattern of currencies of settlement. The BAM fixes daily rates for the rated currencies on the basis of variations in the value of the basket. Rates for most currencies quoted in Morocco are established on the basis of the daily dirham-French franc rate and the cross rates for those currencies in relation to the French franc in the international exchange markets.
Exchange tax	No.
Exchange subsidy	No.
Forward exchange market	Yes.
Official cover of forward operations	The official forward foreign exchange cover facility was suspended in June 1996 following the creation of the foreign exchange market.

Arrangements for Payments and Receipts

Prescription of currency requirements	No.
Payment arrangements	
Bilateral arrangements	
Inoperative	Arrangements with Mali and Guinea have been inoperative since the 1960s.
Regional arrangements	There is a regional payment arrangement operated by the central banks of Algeria, Libya, Mauritania, Morocco, and Tunisia.
Administration of control	
Exchange control authorities	Exchange control is administered by the Foreign Exchange Office (FEO), an agency under the Ministry of Finance and Foreign Investment. This office has delegated the execution of the main exchange control measures to authorized banks. Import and export licenses, when required, are issued by the Ministry of Foreign Trade.
International security restrictions	
In accordance with IMF Executive Board Decision No. 144-(52/51)	The restrictions have not been communicated to the Board.

In accordance with UN sanctions	Morocco maintains restrictions for security reasons against Iraq and the Federal Republic of Yugoslavia (Serbia/Montenegro) pursuant to UN Security Council resolutions.
Payment arrears	No.

Controls on trade in gold (coins and/or bullion)

Controls on domestic ownership and/or trade	Residents may purchase, hold, and sell gold coins in Morocco for numismatic or investment purposes. Ten different types of foreign gold coins are traded on the Casablanca Stock Exchange, which does not, however, deal in gold bars.
Controls on external trade	Imports of gold are subject to authorization from the Directorate of Customs and Indirect Taxes Administration. Each year, the Ministry of Finance fixes a quota for the importation of gold ingots. The quota is then allocated among jewelers and industrial users of precious metals. Exports of gold are prohibited.

Controls on exports and imports of banknotes

On exports

Domestic currency	The exportation of domestic banknotes is prohibited.
Foreign currency	Visitors to Morocco are permitted to repurchase foreign exchange against presentation of exchange certificates up to the amount of the original conversion of foreign exchange into dirhams. Residents may also export foreign banknotes following general or special approval by the Exchange Office.

On imports

Domestic currency	The importation of domestic banknotes is prohibited.
Foreign currency	Nonresident travelers may freely bring in foreign banknotes, traveler's checks, and other means of payment denominated in foreign currency. Resident travelers may also bring in foreign banknotes in any amount, as well as any other means of payment in foreign exchange but must surrender them within 30 days of their return to Morocco.

Resident Accounts

Eligibility to hold accounts	Juridical and natural persons are eligible.
Foreign exchange accounts permitted	Yes.
Held domestically	Any Moroccan exporter of goods or services already holding a convertible export promotion account (CCPEX) is allowed to open a foreign exchange account. Those without a CCPEX must receive prior approval from the Exchange Office. Up to 20% of foreign exchange receipts may be credited to these accounts simultaneously with the sale of the remaining 80% to domestic banks. There is no restriction on crediting foreign exchange accounts either with the proceeds from financial investments held in the accounts or with transfers from another of the holder's foreign exchange accounts. These accounts may be freely debited for payment of business expenses as provided for in the exchange regulations, for investing in authorized intermediary banks, for subscribing to bonds issued by the Moroccan Treasury, for crediting another foreign exchange account or a CCPEX held in the exporter's name, or for surrender of foreign currency to banks.
Held abroad	Approval is required, except for foreign nationals.
Accounts in domestic currency convertible into foreign currency	Exporters of goods and services may open accounts in convertible dirhams at Moroccan banks, which may be credited with the dirham equivalent of 20% of repatriated foreign currency sold to domestic banks. Funds in these accounts may be used to finance expenses incurred abroad and related to the holder's business activity. Fishing companies may place up to 100% of the dirham equivalent of their repatriated exchange receipts in these accounts. Exporters may choose either a foreign exchange account or a convertible

export promotion account, or may hold both kinds, provided the overall percentage of repatriated foreign exchange receipts placed in the accounts does not exceed the 20% limit.

Nonresident Accounts

Eligibility to hold accounts

Juridical and natural persons are eligible.

Foreign exchange accounts permitted

The following accounts may be opened:

(1) Foreign currency accounts in the names of foreign nationals may be maintained by natural or juridical persons of foreign nationality who are either residents or nonresidents. These accounts may be freely credited with transfers from abroad with foreign banknotes, checks, traveler's checks, or any other means of payment denominated in foreign currency; and with foreign currency withdrawn from domestic banks, following general or special authorization from the FEO. They may be freely debited for transfers abroad in favor of the account holder or to a foreign third party, for the surrender of foreign currency to domestic banks, and for the payment of checks denominated in foreign currency.

(2) Foreign currency accounts in the names of Moroccan residents living abroad may be opened by individuals of Moroccan nationality residing abroad. These accounts may be credited freely with transfers from abroad, checks or any other means of payment denominated in foreign currency, foreign currency withdrawn from domestic banks following general or special authorization from the FEO, the return on investments effected on the basis of these accounts, and transfers from another foreign currency account or from an account in convertible dirhams. They may be freely debited for transfers abroad, transfers to another account in foreign currency or in convertible dirhams, foreign currency subscriptions for notes issued by the Moroccan Treasury, and for surrender of foreign currency to domestic banks.

Domestic currency accounts

Yes.

Convertible into foreign currency

These are restricted to resident or nonresident natural and juridical persons of foreign nationality, and may be freely credited with generally or specifically authorized transfers, and with dirhams obtained from the sale to banks of foreign exchange, including banknotes. They may be freely debited for payments made in Morocco and for purchases of foreign exchange at banks. There are no restrictions on transfers between foreign accounts in convertible dirhams, or on transfers to replenish these accounts. Holders of these accounts may obtain international credit cards for settlement of all expenses in Morocco and abroad. Convertible dirham accounts may be freely opened in the name of nonresident Moroccans residing abroad. Overdrafts are not allowed, and there are no restrictions on the interest rate payable. These accounts may be credited freely with (1) dirhams from the sale of convertible currencies, including banknotes, to domestic banks; (2) transfers authorized by the FEO; (3) payments of interest accrued on these accounts; (4) transfers from foreign accounts in convertible dirhams; and (5) transfers from term deposits in convertible dirham accounts. They may be debited freely for (1) the purchase of foreign exchange from domestic banks; (2) dirham payments in Morocco; (3) transfers to foreign accounts in convertible dirhams; and (4) transfers to term deposits in convertible dirham accounts.

These accounts may also be debited freely, either for the benefit of the account holder or for other nonresidents, for the purchase of foreign banknotes, traveler's checks, or other foreign-currency-denominated means of payment. Convertible dirham accounts for exporters may be opened by exporters of goods or services with Moroccan banks. These accounts may be credited with the equivalent of 20% of the foreign currency repatriated and surrendered to domestic banks.

Balances on these accounts may be used to finance expenditures contracted abroad and linked to the professional activity of those concerned. Fishing companies may credit to these accounts up to 100% of the foreign currency repatriated. Exporters have the choice of maintaining either foreign currency accounts or convertible dirham accounts. They may also hold both accounts simultaneously, provided that the overall percentage of export earnings to be credited to both accounts does not exceed 20% of foreign exchange earnings. Convertible term accounts are designed to attract funds from nonresident foreigners who are not entitled to guaranteed transfers.

These funds may be transferred henceforth within a maximum period of 5 years. The holders of such accounts may use the available funds, without prior authorization from the FEO, to fund investments in Morocco; buy treasury bonds; purchase Moroccan marketable securities; settle expenses incurred in Morocco; and, in the case of foreign corporations, provide their Moroccan subsidiaries with current account advances. They may also freely transfer the balances to resident or nonresident foreigners or to Moroccan nationals residing abroad. The beneficiaries of the proceeds of these accounts may use them to cover expenses incurred by foreign companies shooting films in Morocco; to purchase secondary residences under certain conditions; and to finance up to 50% of an investor's participation in investments in Morocco (the remainder must be financed with funds transferred from abroad). Funds invested with the proceeds of convertible term accounts may be transferred abroad without restriction in the event of liquidation or transfer, except for certain categories that are subject to a 3-year waiting period.

Blocked accounts	No.

Imports and Import Payments

Foreign exchange budget	No.
Financing requirements for imports	
Minimum financing requirements	For all imports, an import certificate lodged with an authorized bank is required to make payments related to goods and incidental costs. Imports used for the production of export goods may be financed directly from the proceeds of foreign exchange claims of the same exporter within the framework of special lines of credit that Moroccan commercial banks are authorized to contract with their foreign correspondents. Moroccan commercial banks may make advance payments abroad for imports of capital goods up to 25% of their f.o.b. value.
Documentation requirements for release of foreign exchange for imports	Except for goods imported by air, insurance policies for imports must be taken out with insurance companies in Morocco. However, for a limited group of goods, insurance policies may be underwritten abroad. This group includes externally funded imports, if the financing terms include foreign insurance, capital goods and equipment under turnkey contracts, or duly authorized investment programs, in crude oil, gas, cattle, and wood. Imports are subject to a disembarkation inspection.
Domiciliation requirements	Yes.
Import licenses and other nontariff measures	Imports of items representing about 8% of industrial production are subject to minimum import prices (reference prices) for antidumping or safeguarding purposes.
Positive list	Imports of arms and explosives, as well as secondhand clothing and used tires, require licenses.
Negative list	Imports of products that affect public security, morale, and health may be prohibited. Secondhand clothing and used tires are also prohibited.
Open general licenses	Licensing requirements for imports of used cars were abolished in May 1996, and for imports of cereals, edible oils, sugar, and products derived from these licensing requirements were abolished in June.
Import taxes and/or tariffs	Customs duties are levied on an ad valorem basis, with rates ranging from 2.5% to 43.5% for industrial goods; tariffs on agricultural goods range up to 300%. Many consumer goods not produced in Morocco are subject to a 5% duty. In addition, imports are subject to levies of 12.5% or 15%. Imports used for the production of exports are exempt from customs duties and other restrictions.

| Taxes collected through the exchange system | No. |

| **State import monopoly** | No. |

Exports and Export Proceeds

| **Repatriation requirements** | All exporters must sign a guarantee to repatriate and surrender foreign exchange proceeds. Export proceeds collected abroad may be used directly abroad to finance imports of goods and raw materials of goods for export. |

| **Surrender requirements** | Foreign exchange must be surrendered within 1 month of the date of payment by foreign buyers specified in the commercial contract; in principle, this date must not be more than 150 days from the date of arrival of the merchandise. This deadline may be extended if warranted by business conditions and approved by the FEO. Residents of Moroccan nationality, including individuals and corporations, must repatriate foreign exchange receipts accruing from all their noncommercial claims and surrender them to an authorized bank. Other residents must surrender noncommercial receipts only if the receipts result from their activities in Morocco. Exporters are authorized to obtain up to 20% of export earnings in convertible dirham or foreign exchange accounts. |

| **Financing requirements** | No. |

| **Documentation requirements for release of foreign exchange for imports** | |

| Preshipment inspection | Yes. |

| **Export licenses** | |

| Without quotas | Exports of flour, charcoal, certain animals, plants, and archaeological items are subject to authorization. |

| **Export taxes** | Mineral products are subject to an ad valorem export tax of 0.5%, except for hydrocarbons, for which the tax is 5%, and phosphates, for which a tax on phosphate exploration equivalent to DH 34 per ton of gross phosphates has been levied since 1992. A 1% quality control tax is levied on exports of foodstuff. |

| Taxes collected through the exchange system | No. |

Payments for Invisible Transactions and Current Transfers

| **Controls on these payments** | Authorized banks are permitted to make payments and settle expenses incidental to commercial transactions covered by the relevant import or export documents and for travel and study abroad without authorization from the FEO. Moroccan enterprises are permitted to settle in dirhams the expenses incurred by their foreign managers and nonresident foreigners working for or on behalf of these enterprises. Foreign airlines operating in Morocco may transfer, without prior authorization from the FEO, any surplus revenue from the proceeds of ticket sales, excess baggage, and air freight. Transfers with respect to sea and road transportation may be made directly to authorized banks. There are no controls on payments for unloading and storage costs, administrative expenses, subscriptions and membership fees, or on the remittances of profits and dividends. All other payments and transfers, except for pensions, are subject to indicative limits and/or bona fide tests. |

| Payments for travel | |

| *Quantitative limits* | The maximum allowance is the equivalent of DH 5,000 a person a year. This allowance may be increased by DH 1,500 for a minor child on the passport of the beneficiary parent and accompanying said parent at the time of travel abroad. The same allocation may |

also be granted to Moroccan residents living abroad upon their return to their home country, provided they have not benefited from the 15% allocation on remittances within the previous 12 months up to a limit of DH 20,000. Residents of foreign nationality who wish to travel abroad may be granted foreign exchange equivalent to all of their savings from income. Business travel by exporters of goods and services may be financed without restriction by debiting convertible export promotion accounts or foreign currency accounts maintained with Moroccan banks. In the case of business travel allowances for others, annual foreign exchange allowances are approved by the Exchange Office on the basis of need, with a daily limit of DH 2,000. Banks have been empowered to provide advance allowances of up to DH 40,000 to small- and medium-size enterprises and of up to DH 20,000 a year for business travel by individuals not belonging to either of these categories. In all cases, business travel allowances cannot be added to allowances for tourist travel. The foreign exchange office grants exemptions as needed.

Medical costs

Prior approval

Approval by the Ministry of Health is required.

Quantitative limits

Commercial banks are authorized to sell foreign exchange for medical treatment abroad up to the equivalent of DH 20,000 and to make transfers on patients' behalf for treatment abroad in favor of hospitals and medical institutions concerned.

Study abroad costs

Quantitative limits

The limits are (1) an annual installation allowance equivalent to DH 10,000 and the same amount for a person accompanying a minor student leaving Morocco for the first time; (2) school fees to foreign academic institutions, upon submission of documentary evidence and without limit; and (3) a monthly allowance for living expenses amounting to the equivalent of DH 6,000 a month for nonscholarship holders and DH 4,000 for scholarship holders. In addition to these funds, banks are authorized to effect the transfer of rent and corresponding charges in favor of the foreign landlord once the student or his or her legal guardian has submitted a lease and a certificate of residence or any other equivalent document. The limit is DH 2,000 a month for foreign nationals residing in Morocco to cover the cost of higher education for a child studying abroad.

Indicative limits/bona fide test

Applications for additional amounts must be referred to the FEO for approval, which is granted on proof of need.

Foreign workers' wages

Quantitative limits

Foreigners residing in Morocco and employed in either the private or public sector or engaged in professions in industry, commerce, and agriculture may transfer up to 50% of their income, whether or not their spouses reside in Morocco.

Pensions

Commercial banks are authorized to transfer retirement pensions provided by public and private agencies in favor of Moroccans residing abroad permanently.

Quantitative limits

Foreign retired persons and foreign spouses of Moroccans may transfer up to 50% of their income. They may also freely contribute to their retirement or social security funds in their country of origin.

Gambling/prize earnings

Prior approval

Yes.

Quantitative limits

Yes.

Family maintenance/alimony

Transfers are approved upon presentation of documentary evidence.

Prior approval

Yes.

Quantitative limits

Yes.

Credit card use abroad

Quantitative limits

Yes.

Proceeds from Invisible Transactions and Current Transfers

Repatriation requirements

Residents of Moroccan nationality, including individuals and corporations, must repatriate foreign exchange receipts accruing from all their noncommercial claims and surrender them to an authorized bank. Other residents must surrender noncommercial receipts only if the receipts result from their activities in Morocco. Moroccans working abroad must surrender within 1 month all foreign exchange in their possession, but on departure from Morocco, they may export without restriction foreign banknotes obtained by debiting their accounts in convertible dirhams. If they do not have such an account, they may take out 15% of foreign exchange repatriated and surrendered 12 months before to Moroccan banks up to a limit of DH 20,000. If these facilities are not available, Moroccan residents living abroad may take advantage of the same DH 5,000 tourist allocation that applies to residents. Resident travelers may bring in foreign banknotes in any amount, as well as any other means of payment in foreign exchange but must surrender them within 30 days of their return to Morocco.

Surrender requirements

Exporters of services are required to obtain up to 20% of their export earnings in amounts denominated in foreign currency or convertible dirhams.

Restrictions on use of funds

No.

Capital Transactions

Controls on capital and money market instruments

On capital market securities

Sale or issue locally by nonresidents

The issuance of capital market securities by nonresidents is prohibited. There are, however, no restrictions on the sale of Moroccan securities by nonresidents. Proceeds from such sales may also be freely transferred, provided that the relevant purchases are financed by foreign exchange inflows or any comparable means.

Purchase abroad by residents

Purchases of foreign securities by residents of Moroccan nationality and transfers of the funds required for such purchases are subject to the prior approval of the FEO. Residents of foreign nationality are free to purchase securities abroad or, generally speaking, to constitute assets abroad.

Sale or issue abroad by residents

Yes.

On money market instruments

Purchase locally by nonresidents

Where the purchase of such instruments or securities is financed by a foreign exchange inflow or by the proceeds of the sale of other securities previously purchased through the surrender of foreign exchange, the transfer of disinvestment proceeds, including capital gains, and of income generated by such investment, is free.

Sale or issue locally by nonresidents

The issuance of these instruments by nonresidents is prohibited.

Purchase abroad by residents

Purchases require the prior authorization of the FEO, which is granted under certain conditions. On the other hand, residents of foreign nationality are free to engage in operations abroad financed with their foreign exchange holdings.

Sale or issue abroad by residents

Yes.

On collective investment securities

Same regulations as for money market instruments apply.

Purchase abroad by residents

Yes.

Sale or issue abroad by residents

Yes.

Controls on derivatives and other instruments

Purchase locally by nonresidents — These instruments have not been developed in Morocco.

Purchase abroad by residents — Residents of Moroccan nationality may subscribe to such instruments abroad only with the prior approval of the FEO.

Sale or issue abroad by residents — Yes.

Controls on credit operations

Commercial credits

By residents to nonresidents — Merchandise exporters are free to grant commercial credits to nonresidents for up to 150 days; longer terms may be granted with the approval of the FEO, as required for business purposes.

Financial credits

By residents to nonresidents — The granting of financial loans by residents to nonresidents is subject to the approval of the FEO.

To residents from nonresidents — Financial credits are limited to foreign loans for financing investment operations or foreign trade.

Guarantees, sureties, and financial backup facilities

By residents to nonresidents — Moroccan banks may issue or accept in favor of residents sureties issued on behalf of nonresidents in support of the participation of said nonresidents in public or private contracting, the supplying of goods or services, the refund of down payments, and the substitution of guarantee with holdings. Similarly, they may issue sureties on behalf of nonresidents in support of tax liabilities or financial obligations. A counter-guarantee from a foreign bank is required for sureties issued by Moroccan banks on behalf of nonresidents. Where claims are entered under sureties issued or accepted in favor of residents on behalf of nonresidents, the relevant amounts must be repatriated to Morocco.

To residents from nonresidents — Provisions of guarantees are allowed on the condition that they are contracted through resident Moroccan banks.

Controls on direct investment

Outward direct investment — Outward direct investments are subject to the prior approval of the FEO, but residents of foreign nationality are free to invest abroad.

Controls on liquidation of direct investment — There are no restrictions on transfers made directly with the banking system of the proceeds of the liquidation or sale of foreign investment, including capital gains. For the liquidation of any investment not falling under the convertibility arrangements, the relevant proceeds must be deposited in a convertible time deposit account denominated in dirhams. Funds placed therein may be transferred over a 5-year period in equal annuities.

Controls on real estate transactions

Purchase abroad by residents — Yes.

Purchase locally by nonresidents — Foreign nationals cannot purchase properties outside of urban limits.

Provisions specific to commercial banks and other credit institutions

Borrowing abroad — Commercial banks can only borrow abroad to finance foreign trade or investment operations.

Lending to nonresidents (financial or commercial credits) — The granting of loans abroad by Moroccan banks is subject to approval by the Exchange Office. However, banks may use cash held in foreign exchange accounts (by foreign nationals, Moroccan citizens residing abroad, and exporters) for granting buyer's credits to foreign, nonresident customers of Moroccan exporters.

Lending locally in foreign exchange	Moroccan banks may grant foreign exchange loans to residents for the financing of foreign trade operations and investment, within the limits of their respective foreign exchange positions as authorized by the rules of the foreign exchange market.
Purchase of locally issued securities denominated in foreign exchange	Purchases are subject to the prior approval of the FEO.
Differential treatment of nonresident deposit accounts and/or deposit accounts in foreign exchange	
Reserve requirements	Convertible dirham and foreign exchange accounts are excluded from reserve requirements.
Liquid asset requirements	All deposits are taken into account for the calculation of liquid asset requirements.
Open foreign exchange position limits	A limit of 20% of net equity (7% for the position in any single currency) was introduced in June 1996.
Provisions specific to institutional investors	
Limits (max.) on portfolio invested abroad	Prior approval by the FEO is required for portfolio investment abroad.

Changes During 1996

Exchange arrangements	*June 3.* An interbank foreign exchange market was established. Banks were allowed to freely trade foreign exchange against dirhams spot; forward operations are limited to transactions related to imports, exports, or foreign borrowing.
Imports and import payments	*January 1.* Licensing requirements for imports of cereals, edible oils, and sugar were abolished.
	February 1. Licensing requirements for imports of sugar products were abolished.
	March 1. Licensing requirements for imports of oilseed were abolished.
	May 1. Payment for imports in a currency other than the one stipulated in the commercial contract was allowed for cereals, cereal products, and edible oils.
	May 20. Licensing requirements for imports of used cars were abolished.
	June 1. Payment for imports for refined edible oils and products.
Capital transactions	*June 3.* Banks' open position was limited to 20% of net equity (7% for the position in any single currency).

Changes During 1997

Exchange arrangements	*January 31.* Banks were authorized to engage in foreign exchange operations with foreign banks using cash in a foreign currency.

MOZAMBIQUE

(Position as of January 31, 1997)

Status Under IMF Articles of Agreement

Article XIV	Yes.

Exchange Arrangement

Currency	The currency of Mozambique is the metical (plural meticais).
Exchange rate structure	Unitary.
Classification	
Independent floating	The external value of the metical is determined by supply and demand in the exchange market, where the Bank of Mozambique (BM), the commercial banks, and foreign exchange bureaus participate. The interbank market was established on July 16, 1996.
Exchange tax	No.
Exchange subsidy	No.
Forward exchange market	No.

Arrangements for Payments and Receipts

Prescription of currency requirements	No.
Payment arrangements	No.
Administration of control	
Exchange control authorities	The BM is responsible for foreign exchange policy and administers its control.
Controls on trade in gold (coins and/or bullion)	
Controls on domestic ownership and/or trade	Ownership of gold bullion is not allowed.
Controls on external trade	The importation and exportation of gold are governed by special regulations.
Controls on exports and imports of banknotes	
On exports	
Domestic currency	Exports of domestic currency are subject to a limit of Mt 500,000.
Foreign currency	Nonresidents may export foreign banknotes up to the amount they declared on entry.
On imports	
Domestic currency	Imports of domestic currency are subject to a limit of Mt 500,000, provided they have been previously exported.

Resident Accounts

Eligibility to hold accounts	Juridical and natural persons are eligible.
Foreign exchange accounts permitted	Yes.

Held domestically	Yes.
Held abroad	These accounts are permitted, but prior approval is required.
Accounts in domestic currency convertible into foreign currency	Yes.

Nonresident Accounts

Eligibility to hold accounts	Juridical and natural persons are eligible.
Foreign exchange accounts permitted	Yes.
Domestic currency accounts	These accounts may be opened with funds from the conversion of foreign currency or from employment and technical assistance contracts approved by competent institutions; transfers of such funds abroad are not permitted.
Convertible into foreign currency	No.

Imports and Import Payments

Foreign exchange budget	No.
Financing requirements for imports	Confirmation of the existence of sufficient funds in the bank is required.
Advance payment requirements	Documentary proof of the arrival of goods has to be presented within 90 days of payment.
Advance import deposits	Documentary proof of the arrival of goods has to be presented within 90 days of payment.
Documentation requirements for release of foreign exchange for imports	
Domiciliation requirements	Yes.
Preshipment inspection	Inspection is required for all imports in excess of $2,500, with the exception of perishable commodities and imports for the personal needs of diplomats.
Import licenses and other nontariff measures	
Negative list	A negative product list exists for imports financed by donors' funds. In order to ensure that donors' requirements are met, the Office for the Coordination of Import Programs reviews import requests. Tied import support funds are allocated by the BM to the commercial banks.
Open general licenses	All imports exceeding the equivalent of $500 are subject to registration by the Ministry of Commerce. Licenses specifying, among other things, the place of embarkation and disembarkation of the goods, the amount and currency of payment, and the source of financing are routinely granted. Individuals may import goods up to the equivalent of $500 without an import license if the goods are financed with their own foreign exchange resources and tied aid funds are not involved.
Import taxes and/or tariffs	Yes.
Taxes collected through the exchange system	No.
State import monopoly	No.

Exports and Export Proceeds

Repatriation requirements	All export proceeds, except in cases authorized by the BM, must be collected through the commercial banks.
Surrender requirements	The surrender requirement was eliminated on January 1, 1997. Companies that export more than 85% of their production qualify for the status of free trade zone.
Financing requirements	No.
Documentation requirements	Yes.
Export licenses	All exports are subject to registration.
Without quotas	n.a.
With quotas	n.a.
Export taxes	The general export duty of 0.5% was suspended for 5 years on December 31, 1994. A ban on exports of raw cashews was suspended in 1995 and replaced by an export duty. The duty was lowered to 14% in November 1996 from 20%.
Taxes collected through the exchange system	No.

Payments for Invisible Transactions and Current Transfers

Controls on these payments	Commercial banks and exchange bureaus are authorized to sell foreign exchange up to $5,000 to individuals to pay expenses associated with travel, study, or medical treatment abroad, as well as for film rental, expenses for fairs and exhibitions, contributions to international organizations, and subscriptions to publications. Operations exceeding this amount, or for other purposes, are subject to licensing by the BM. There are no controls on payments for freight and insurance, unloading and storage costs, administrative expenses, commissions, gambling and prize earnings, or family maintenance and alimony.
Profit/dividends	
Prior approval	Remittances of profit and dividends from foreign direct investment may be made in accordance with the specific project authorization.
Payments for travel	
Prior approval	Yes.
Quantitative limits	Yes.
Indicative limits/bona fide test	n.a.
Medical costs	
Prior approval	Yes.
Quantitative limits	Yes.
Indicative limits/bona fide test	n.a.
Study abroad costs	
Prior approval	Yes.
Quantitative limits	Yes.
Indicative limits/bona fide test	n.a.
Subscriptions and membership fees	
Prior approval	Yes.

Quantitative limits	Yes.
Indicative limits/bona fide test	n.a.
Foreign workers' wages	
Prior approval	Yes.
Quantitative limits	Foreign experts working in Mozambique may remit abroad all or part of their salaries, depending on the terms of their employment contracts.
Indicative limits/bona fide test	n.a.
Pensions	
Prior approval	Yes.

Proceeds from Invisible Transactions and Current Transfers

Repatriation requirements	Yes.
Surrender requirements	Certain Mozambican nationals working abroad under officially arranged contracts (specifically, miners in the Republic of South Africa) are obliged to remit 60% of their earnings through the BM and to convert them into meticais.
Restrictions on use of funds	No.

Capital Transactions

Controls on capital and money market instruments	BM approval is required for purchases or sales abroad by residents of capital and money market instruments in excess of $5,000.
On capital market securities	
Purchase locally by nonresidents	n.a.
Sale or issue locally by nonresidents	n.a.
Purchase abroad by residents	Yes.
Sale or issue abroad by residents	Yes.
On money market instruments	
Purchase locally by nonresidents	n.a.
Sale or issue locally by nonresidents	n.a.
Purchase abroad by residents	Yes.
Sale or issue abroad by residents	Yes.
On collective investment securities	
Purchase locally by nonresidents	n.a.
Sale or issue locally by nonresidents	n.a.
Purchase abroad by residents	Yes.
Sale or issue abroad by residents	Yes.
Controls on derivatives and other instruments	BM approval is required for purchases or sales abroad by residents of derivatives and other instruments in excess of $5,000.

Purchase locally by nonresidents	n.a.
Sale or issue locally by nonresidents	n.a.
Purchase abroad by residents	Yes.
Sale or issue abroad by residents	Yes.
Controls on credit operations	
Commercial credits	
By residents to nonresidents	Yes.
To residents from nonresidents	Public and private enterprises need BM approval to borrow abroad. All foreign borrowing must be registered with the BM. Borrowing by the government must be obtained on concessionary terms.
Financial credits	Yes.
Guarantees, sureties, and financial backup facilities	Yes.
Controls on direct investment	
Outward direct investment	Yes.
Inward direct investment	Foreign investors are guaranteed the right to repatriate their initial capital. The incentives for foreign investments include tax and customs exemptions for specified periods and for access to domestic credit. Foreign investment proposals are processed by the Foreign Investment Promotion Center.
Controls on liquidation of direct investment	Yes.
Controls on real estate transactions	Yes.
Provisions specific to commercial banks and other credit institutions	
Borrowing abroad	Yes.
Lending to nonresidents (financial or commercial credits)	Yes.
Purchase of locally issued securities denominated in foreign exchange	n.a.
Differential treatment of nonresident deposit accounts and/or deposit accounts in foreign exchange	
Reserve requirements	Yes.
Liquid asset requirements	Yes.
Credit controls	Yes.
Investment regulations	Yes.
Open foreign exchange position limits	Commercial banks and other financial institutions may hold a limited amount of foreign exchange.
Provisions specific to institutional investors	
Limits (max.) on portfolio invested abroad	Yes.
Currency matching regulations on assets/liabilities composition	n.a.

Changes During 1996

Exchange arrangements	*July 16.* An interbank foreign exchange market was established.
Arrangements for payments and receipts	*January 4.* A new Foreign Exchange Law was introduced.
	July 19. The regulations for the new Foreign Exchange Law were introduced.
Exports and export proceeds	*November 29.* The export duty for cashews was lowered to 14% from 20%.
	December 30. Exporters of goods were allowed to hold 100% of net earnings on foreign exchange accounts.
Payments for invisible transactions and current transfers	*December 30.* Exporters of services were allowed to hold 100% of net earnings on foreign exchange accounts.

Changes During 1997

Exports and export proceeds	*January 1.* The surrender requirement was abolished.

MYANMAR

(Position as of December 31, 1996)

Status Under IMF Articles of Agreement

Article XIV	Yes.

Exchange Arrangement

Currency	The currency of Myanmar is the kyat.

Exchange rate structure

Dual	In addition to the official exchange rate, foreign exchange certificates (FECs) are issued by the Central Bank of Myanmar (CBM) in denominations of 1, 5, 10, and 20 units, and exchangeable with 6 hard currencies or with acceptable traveler's checks. FECs are widely used and serve the needs of visitors and investors in Myanmar. FECs are available for kyats at the market-determined rate at a new exchange center in Yangon. Holders of FECs may deposit them into their foreign exchange accounts. An unofficial parallel market for foreign exchange also exists.

Classification

Pegged	The Myanmar kyat is officially pegged to the SDR at K 8.50847 per SDR 1. Myanmar applies margins of 2% to spot exchange transactions based on the fixed kyat-SDR rate. The buying and selling rates of the kyat for the deutsche mark, French franc, Japanese yen, pound sterling, Swiss franc, and U.S. dollar, quoted by the Myanma Foreign Trade Bank (MFTB), are determined on the basis of the daily calculations of the value of these currencies against the SDR, as are rates for the currencies of some member countries of the ACU (i.e., the Bangladesh taka, Indian rupee, Iranian rial, Nepalese rupee, Pakistan rupee, and Sri Lanka rupee). The buying and selling rates for the Belgian franc, Italian lira, Hong Kong dollar, Malaysian ringgit, Netherlands guilder, and Singapore dollar are determined daily on the basis of the appropriate cross rates in the Singapore market, and the buying and selling rates for other currencies are based on the appropriate cross rates published in the Asian *Wall Street Journal* or the London *Financial Times*.

Exchange tax	No.
Exchange subsidy	No.
Forward exchange market	No.

Arrangements for Payments and Receipts

Prescription of currency requirements	Settlements with member countries of the ACU are made in ACU dollars through the ACU mechanism. From January 1, 1996, 1 ACU dollar equals 1 U.S. dollar.

Payment arrangements

Regional arrangements	Myanmar is a member of the ACU.
Clearing agreements	Yes.
Barter agreements and open accounts	Bilateral trade arrangements with neighboring countries exist. These arrangements do not provide for the extension of credit.

Administration of control

Exchange control authorities	Exchange control is administered by the CBM in accordance with instructions from the Ministry of Finance and Revenue (MFR). A Foreign Exchange Control Board headed by the Deputy Prime Minister allocates foreign exchange for the public sector.

International security restrictions	No.
Payment arrears	
Official	Arrears are maintained with respect to debt-service payments of the central government.
Controls on trade in gold (coins and/or bullion)	
Controls on external trade	Imports and exports of gold are not allowed for the private sector. Jewelry for personal use may be brought into Myanmar, subject to customs declaration at the port of arrival. Personal jewelry of a prescribed value is permitted to be taken out, subject to the condition that the jewelry will be brought back into the country. No conditions are attached, however, to the taking out of personal jewelry that was declared to customs when it was brought into Myanmar. Gold bullion may not be imported from any source.
Controls on exports and imports of banknotes	
On exports	
Domestic currency	The exportation of Myanmar currency is prohibited.
Foreign currency	Residents who have been granted an official permit to travel abroad are allowed to buy $500 from the MFTB and the Myanmar Investment and Commercial Bank (MICB) on presentation of FEC 500 or from their own foreign currency accounts. Nonresidents leaving Myanmar within 6 months of arriving may take out any balance of foreign currency they brought in with them and may also reconvert the remaining balance of the FECs purchased in excess of the minimum required purchase of $300.
On imports	
Domestic currency	The importation of Myanmar currency is prohibited.
Foreign currency	Travelers may bring in up to $2,000 or its equivalent without any declaration. Tourists arriving in Myanmar are required to purchase FECs equivalent to a minimum value of $300, but amounts in excess of this minimum may be reconverted into foreign exchange on departure.

Resident Accounts

Eligibility to hold accounts	Juridical and natural persons are eligible.
Foreign exchange accounts permitted	Yes.
Held domestically	Foreign currency accounts of national firms may be kept with private domestic banks permitted to conduct foreign exchange transactions. Accounts may be opened in U.S. dollars only by Myanmar nationals who earn foreign exchange. Account holders are allowed to import under import licenses issued by the Ministry of Commerce (MOC) on the basis of letters of credit or on a collection basis. With prior approval, account holders may use funds from their accounts to purchase air tickets for family visits abroad and to make payments for personal imports, for examination fees for their children, and for medical treatment abroad. Transfers of funds between accounts are permitted.
Held abroad	Prior approval is required to open these accounts.
Accounts in domestic currency convertible into foreign currency	Conversion is permitted only for payments of official expenses.

Nonresident Accounts

Eligibility to hold accounts	Juridical and natural persons are eligible.

Foreign exchange accounts permitted	Foreign currency accounts of foreign diplomatic missions and international organizations and their home-based personnel may be kept with the MFTB only. Other foreign residents may open foreign currency accounts with any bank authorized to deal in foreign exchange. Prior authorization is required to open these accounts.
Domestic currency accounts	Yes.
Convertible into foreign currency	All debits and credits to these accounts require prior authorization.
Blocked accounts	No.

Imports and Import Payments

Foreign exchange budget	An import program for the public sector is prepared annually as part of the foreign exchange budget drawn up jointly by the Ministry of National Planning and Economic Development and the MFR.
Financing requirements for imports	All payments for imports not originating from border trade are made through private domestic banks permitted to conduct foreign exchange business. State economic enterprises obtain foreign exchange directly from the MFTB, within the approved foreign exchange budget, after receiving endorsement from the respective ministries. Payments for border imports may be effected directly from the proceeds of border exports. Myanmar nationals who have opened foreign currency accounts are allowed to make unlimited payments for personal imports with the funds from their accounts. Myanmar nationals working abroad under official permits who have not yet opened foreign currency accounts may make payments on their personal imports out of their accumulated savings of legitimate funds.
Advance payment requirements	The State Bank requires a 100% advance payment, while private bank requirements vary according to the credit standing of their customer.
Advance import deposits	Yes.
Documentation requirements for release of foreign exchange for imports	
Domiciliation requirements	n.a.
Preshipment inspection	Yes.
Letters of credit	Yes.
Import licenses used as exchange licenses	Yes.
Import licenses and other nontariff measures	Imports from any country are free, except with countries under UN embargo or with which Myanmar has severed diplomatic relations. With a few exceptions, private sector imports require import licenses for each transaction and are largely financed from the importer's foreign currency account. Import licenses may be obtained for priority items (List A), nonpriority items (List B), and "neutral" items. An importer wishing to import items from List B or neutral items is generally required to import goods on List A at a value equivalent to 50% and 25% of the values of goods on List B and of neutral items, respectively. Private importers must register at the MOC and renew their licenses annually. Border imports require permits. Exporters of agricultural, forestry, and fisheries products are encouraged to import up to the equivalent of 25% of the export value of selected items that will contribute to the production in these sectors.
Negative list	Certain items, such as opium and other narcotics, playing cards, and gold and silver bullion, may not be imported from any source.
Open general licenses	Joint ventures with private interests may be granted open general licenses on a case-by-case basis, and are exempt from List A requirements. State economic enterprises may import goods for their own use and for resale with open general licenses, whereas government departments may import only for their own use.

Import taxes and/or tariffs	Tariff rates range from zero to 40%. Agricultural implements, raw materials, and other essential imports are taxed at low rates, while the highest rates are applied to imports of luxury goods.
Taxes collected through the exchange system	No.
State import monopoly	No.

Exports and Export Proceeds

Repatriation requirements	Proceeds from exports must be fully repatriated.
Surrender requirements	No.
Financing requirements	No.
Documentation requirements	
Letters of credit	Yes.
Domiciliation	n.a.
Preshipment inspection	Yes.
Export licenses	Export trade may be conducted with any country without restriction, except those under UN embargo or with which Myanmar has severed diplomatic relations.
Without quotas	In practice, state agencies responsible for production may export any product in excess of what is needed for domestic consumption. Special permits are required for exports of antiques. State enterprises have a monopoly on the exportation of rice, teak, petroleum and natural gas, pearls, jade, and precious stones and metals. Rice is exported by the Myanma Agricultural Produce Trading through the Myanma Export-Import Services; private traders and cooperatives are also permitted to export a number of beans and pulses, rattan, flour, and cut flowers under valid export permits issued by the MOC. Border trade of certain products, including rice, teak, rubber, petroleum, hides, leather, some beans and pulses, maize, cotton, and groundnuts, is not permitted.
Export taxes	Excluding goods under the exemption list, commercial taxes are levied on all exports at 5%, provided the proceeds are received in foreign currency. A specific duty of 10 kyats per metric ton is levied on all varieties of rice. Customs duties are levied on rice, bamboo, cereal, raw hides, and cakes.
Taxes collected through the exchange system	No.

Payments for Invisible Transactions and Current Transfers

Controls on these payments	All payments for invisibles outside the public sector are subject to approval and are considered on a case-by-case basis. Information on indicative limits and/or bona fide tests is not available.
Freight/insurance	Remittances of insurance premium payments other than for Myanma Insurance are not permitted.
Payments for travel	
Quantitative limits	Yes.
Foreign workers' wages	
Quantitative limits	Balances of salary and lawful income earned that remain after payment of taxes and deduction of living expenses of the worker or his or her family may be transferred abroad through a bank with the approval of the CBM.

Pensions

   Quantitative limits   Remittance to retired government employees is permitted only if the persons concerned were nonnationals throughout their term of service and are now residing in their native countries.

Family maintenance/alimony

   Quantitative limits   Family remittances are permitted only for foreign technicians employed under contract by the government; the limit is one-half of the net salary if the spouse is living abroad and one-third of the net salary if the spouse is living in Myanmar.

Credit card use abroad   n.a.

Proceeds from Invisible Transactions and Current Transfers

Repatriation requirements   Yes.

Surrender requirements   Unless exchange control authorities grant a special waiver, 10% of proceeds must be paid as income tax. Myanmar nationals working abroad with permission from the government are required to pay an income tax at the rate of 10% of their gross earnings in foreign exchange. Myanmar seamen serving abroad and Myanmar nationals working abroad under their own arrangements must pay as income tax 10% of their gross earnings. Myanmar nationals working abroad in UN organizations are not required to pay income tax. Myanmar nationals working abroad in private organizations are required to transfer to Myanmar as tax 10% of their gross earnings in foreign exchange through embassies in their country of residence.

Restrictions on use of funds   Use is subject to exchange control approval.

Capital Transactions

Controls on capital and money market instruments   Yes.

On capital market securities   n.a.

On money market instruments   n.a.

On collective investment securities   n.a.

Controls on credit operations

Commercial credits

   To residents from nonresidents   Yes.

Financial credits

   To residents from nonresidents   Yes.

Guarantees, sureties, and financial backup facilities

   To residents from nonresidents   Yes.

Controls on direct investment

Outward direct investment   n.a.

Inward direct investment   The Myanmar Investment Commission may accept proposals for investment from foreigners for full ownership and under joint venture, with the share of foreign capital representing at least 35% of the total capital. To facilitate and promote foreign investment, the commission may grant exemption from customs duties and other internal taxes on machinery and equipment imported during construction of the project, spare parts used in business, and raw materials imported for the first 3 years of commercial production, as well as exemption from the income tax for a period of up to 3 consecutive years, including the year when production of goods and services began, or for longer than 3 years, depending upon the profitability of the enterprise. Furthermore, accelerated depreciation allowances may be granted. Types of economic activity and the sectors open to foreign investment are specified in a detailed positive list.

Controls on liquidation of direct investment	The government guarantees that an economic enterprise formed under a permit will not be nationalized during the term of the contract or during an extended term. Repatriation of capital and profits is allowed through banks after payment of taxes and prescribed funds.
Controls on real estate transactions	
Purchase abroad by residents	Yes.
Purchase locally by nonresidents	Yes.
Sale locally by nonresidents	Yes.
Provisions specific to commercial banks and other credit institutions	
Borrowing abroad	Yes.
Maintenance of accounts abroad	Yes.
Lending to nonresidents (financial or commercial credits)	Yes.
Lending locally in foreign exchange	n.a.
Purchase of locally issued securities denominated in foreign exchange	n.a.

Changes During 1996

Arrangements for payments and receipts	*January 1.* Settlement with ACU countries are to be made in ACU dollars, which are at par with the U.S. dollar.
	January 1. Residents who have been granted permission to travel abroad are allowed to obtain up to $500 from the MFTB or the MICB.
Resident accounts	*January 1.* The 10% bank charge on the opening of foreign currency accounts was abolished.

NAMIBIA

(Position as of April 30, 1997)

Status Under IMF Articles of Agreement

Article VIII   Date of acceptance: September 20, 1996.

Exchange Arrangement

Currency   The currency of Namibia is the Namibia dollar.

Other legal tender   The South African rand is also legal tender.

Exchange rate structure   Unitary.

Classification

Pegged   The Namibia dollar is pegged to the South African rand at par. The exchange rate of the Namibia dollar against other currencies is determined on the basis of cross rates of the South African rand against the currencies concerned in international markets. The exchange market in Namibia has developed as an extension of the exchange market in South Africa.

Exchange tax   No.

Exchange subsidy   No.

Forward exchange market   Authorized dealers are permitted to conduct forward exchange operations, including forward cover, with residents in any foreign currency in respect of authorized trade and nontrade transactions. Forward exchange contracts may cover the entire period of the outstanding commitments and accruals. Forward cover is also provided to nonresidents, subject to certain limitations. Gold mining companies and houses may sell forward anticipated receipts of their future gold sales. Forward cover is provided in U.S. dollars only and is available to authorized dealers for maturities not exceeding 12 months at a time in the form of swap transactions involving Namibia dollars (South African rand) and U.S. dollars with a margin based on the interest rate differential between the two currencies.

Official cover of forward operations   Special forward cover at preferential rates is provided in respect of import financing.

Arrangements for Payments and Receipts

Prescription of currency requirements   No.

Payment arrangements

Regional arrangements   Namibia is part of the CMA, and therefore no restrictions are applied to payments within the CMA. In principle, payments are not controlled.

Administration of control

Exchange control authorities   The Bank of Namibia (BON), on behalf of the Ministry of Finance, controls all external currency transactions. In its relations with countries outside the CMA, Namibia applies exchange controls that are almost identical to those applied by the other CMA members.

International security restrictions   No.

Payment arrears   No.

Controls on trade in gold (coins and/or bullion)

Controls on domestic ownership and/or trade   Residents are permitted to purchase, hold, and sell gold coins within the CMA for numismatic and investment purposes only.

| Controls on external trade | All exports and imports of gold require the prior approval of the monetary authorities. |

Controls on exports and imports of banknotes

On exports

| *Domestic currency* | An individual may export up to N$500. |
| *Foreign currency* | Export of foreign currency not authorized in terms of exchange control rulings requires prior BON approval. |

On imports

| *Domestic currency* | Upon entry from countries outside the CMA, residents and nonresidents may bring in a total of N$500 in Namibian banknotes or R 500 in South African banknotes. There are no limitations on the importation of domestic currency from Lesotho and Swaziland. |

Resident Accounts

Eligibility to hold accounts	Yes.
Juridical persons	n.a.
Natural persons	n.a.
Foreign exchange accounts permitted	Yes.
Held domestically	n.a.
Held abroad	These accounts may be permitted, particularly for import and export concerns.
Accounts in domestic currency convertible into foreign currency	Yes.

Nonresident Accounts

Eligibility to hold accounts	Juridical and natural persons are eligible.
Foreign exchange accounts permitted	On August 19, 1996, export processing zone (EPZ) customers were allowed foreign currency accounts. These accounts are kept offshore via a local authorized dealer and are set to facilitate the foreign currency disbursements of EPZ enterprises. Transactions through these accounts must conform to normal banking practices and must be carried out with the full cognizance and approval of the authorized dealer concerned.
Approval required	n.a.
Domestic currency accounts	The regulations that apply to these accounts in South Africa also apply in Namibia. On August 19, 1996, EPZ nonresident accounts were allowed. These are Namibia dollar accounts, funded with foreign currency and are used for the normal operational requirements and expenditures of EPZ enterprises and to facilitate local investments. Balances remaining in these accounts are freely convertible and remittable abroad.
Convertible into foreign currency	Yes.
Blocked accounts	There are emigrant blocked accounts in rand. The regulations applying to these accounts in South Africa also apply in Namibia. On December 31, 1996, a limit of N$50,000 a year on releases from these accounts in respect to gifts and donations to third-party residents in Namibia was set. On April 2, 1997, the limit on these releases was increased to N$100,000.

Imports and Import Payments

| **Foreign exchange budget** | No. |

Financing requirements for imports

Advance payment requirements

Advance payments for imports require the approval of the BON. Authorized dealers may authorize "cash with order" advance payments and approve up to 33.3% of the ex-factory cost of capital goods.

Documentation requirements for release of foreign exchange for imports

Documentation confirming receipts of the imported articles into Namibia, (e.g., bill of entry, local post receipts) is required.

Letters of credit

They can be established by authorized dealers locally.

Import licenses and other nontariff measures

There are no restrictions on imports originating in any country of the SACU. Imports from countries outside the SACU are usually licensed in conformity with South Africa's import regulations. Permits are valid for 1 year, are expressed in value terms, and are valid for imports from any country outside the SACU. At present, about 90% of imports require a permit.

Negative list

Namibia has the right to restrict certain imports (through customs duties or quantitative restrictions) from countries outside the SACU, and, under certain conditions, from countries within the SACU.

Licenses with quotas

n.a.

Import taxes and/or tariffs

Imports from countries outside the SACU are subject to surcharges ranging from 7.5% for foodstuffs to 40% for nonessential luxury goods.

Taxes collected through the exchange system

A general sales tax of 11% is levied on all imports as well as on locally produced goods.

State import monopoly

No.

Exports and Export Proceeds

Repatriation requirements

All export proceeds are normally required to be repatriated.

Surrender requirements

All export proceeds are normally required to be surrendered within 6 months of shipment or within 30 days of the date of accrual. Since July 4, 1996, corporate entities that operate in the export field and also import goods from abroad were allowed to offset the cost of imports against the proceeds of exports, provided the set-off takes place within 30 days.

Documentation requirements

Letters of credit

Yes.

Guarantees

Yes.

Export licenses

Most exports are permitted without a license.

Without quotas

Permits are required for exports of goods in short supply to non-SACU countries.

Export taxes

n.a.

Taxes collected through the exchange system

No.

Payments for Invisible Transactions and Current Transfers

Controls on these payments

Authorized dealers may approve trade-related invisible payments without limitation and other invisible payments up to established limits. Larger amounts may be granted on presentation of documentary proof of need. There are no controls on payments for freight and insurance, unloading and storage, administrative expenses, commissions, medical costs, subscriptions and membership fees, consulting and legal fees, and on interest payments. On April 21, 1997, virtually all remaining controls on current account transactions were abolished, except in cases where the limits were retained to make the remaining controls on capital outflows effective.

Profit/dividends

Prior approval

No prior approval is required, but if a local company is contracting any loans via a local source, an application should be lodged with the BON.

Payments for travel

Quantitative limits

On April 21, 1997, allowances were increased and the previously determined distinctions between neighboring and other countries were abolished. Residents may obtain up to N\$80,000 for a person 12 years or older, and N\$25,000 for a child under the age of 12 years each calendar year. Residents traveling to destinations outside the CMA are allowed to take out foreign exchange in any form.

Indicative limits/bona fide test

Yes.

Study abroad costs

Prior approval

Yes.

Quantitative limits

Since April 21, 1997, the annual allowance is N\$80,000 for a student or N\$160,000 for a student accompanied by a nonstudent spouse.

Indicative limits/bona fide test

Yes.

Foreign workers' wages

Prior approval

Yes.

Quantitative limits

Contract workers may transfer two-thirds of their monthly salary.

Pensions

Prior approval

Applications are considered on the merits of the particular case.

Indicative limits/bona fide test

Yes.

Gambling/prize earnings

Prior approval

Normally, Namibians are discouraged from participating in international lotteries. Most requests in this regard are declined.

Quantitative limits

n.a.

Family maintenance/alimony

Prior approval

Yes.

Quantitative limits

Maintenance transfers are limited to N\$2,000 for a receiving family unit a month. Alimony payments are not limited. Since December 31, 1996, upon emigration, emigrants may export motor vehicles within an overall insured value of N\$100,000 as well as personal effects and household goods of N\$100,000.

Credit card use abroad

Prior approval

Departing residents are required to complete the form MP928 prior to departure.

Quantitative limits

Limits must be in accordance with prescribed travel allowances.

Indicative limits/bona fide test

Yes.

Proceeds from Invisible Transactions and Current Transfers

Repatriation requirements

Yes.

Surrender requirements

Proceeds from invisibles must be surrendered within 30 days of the date of accrual unless exemption is obtained.

Restrictions on use of funds

Prior BON approval should be obtained to use such funds outside the CMA.

Capital Transactions

Controls on capital and money market instruments

Inward transfers of capital from non-CMA countries for equity investment are freely permitted, whereas applications by residents to retain funds in, or transfer them to, countries outside the CMA for bona fide long-term investments in specific development projects or for the expansion of existing projects owned or controlled by residents are considered on their own merits.

On capital market securities

Sale or issue locally by nonresidents

Proceeds from the sale of quoted or unquoted CMA securities, real estate, and other equity investments by nonresidents are freely transferable.

Purchase abroad by residents   Yes.

Sale or issue abroad by residents   Yes.

On money market instruments

Sale or issue locally by nonresidents   n.a.

Purchase abroad by residents   Yes.

Sale or issue abroad by residents   Yes.

On collective investment securities

Sale or issue locally by nonresidents   n.a.

Purchase abroad by residents   Yes.

Sale or issue abroad by residents   Yes.

Controls on derivatives and other instruments

Purchase locally by nonresidents   n.a.

Sale or issue locally by nonresidents   n.a.

Purchase abroad by residents   Namibian residents should obtain prior BON approval.

Sale or issue abroad by residents   Yes.

Controls on credit operations

Commercial credits

Credit operations outside the CMA are subject to specific approval from the BON, which is generally given for borrowings abroad with a maturity of at least 6 months by domestic entrepreneurs, except for speculative borrowings or consumer credit. Authorized dealers are generally permitted to raise funds abroad in their own names for the financing of Namibia's foreign trade and other approved purposes.

By residents to nonresidents   Yes.

To residents from nonresidents   Yes.

Financial credits

By residents to nonresidents

Since July 4, 1996, a wholly nonresident-owned company may borrow 100% of shareholder equity locally. On April 1, 1997, nonresident-owned local companies' access to domestic credit was increased, i.e., only companies that are 50% or more foreign owned will be subject to exchange controls.

To residents from nonresidents   Yes.

Guarantees, sureties, and financial backup facilities   Yes.

Controls on direct investment

Outward direct investment

Applications by residents to retain funds in, or transfer them to, countries outside the CMA for bona fide long-term investments in specific development projects or for the expansion of existing projects owned or controlled by residents are considered on their own merits. Since July 4, 1996, Namibian corporations may invest up to N$20 million abroad. If the investment exceeds N$20 million, the balance must be financed abroad by means of foreign borrowing without recourse to, or guarantee from, Namibia. Also, since that date, approved foreign subsidiaries may expand activities abroad without prior approval, provided such expansion is financed by foreign borrowings or by the employment of profits earned by the foreign subsidiary. On April 1, 1997, the limit on foreign investment was increased to N$30 million to countries other than SADC members, and a new facility of N$50 million in respect of investment in SADC member countries was established. Also, consideration was to be given to foreign borrowings to finance these investments being raised with recourse to or guarantee from Namibia, implying that the local corporations' balance sheets may be used in negotiating such a facility.

Inward direct investment

Inward transfers of capital from non-CMA countries for equity investment may be freely made.

Controls on liquidation of direct investment

Families emigrating outside the CMA are granted the normal tourist allowance and are permitted to remit up to N$250,000 (N$125,000 for single persons). Any balance exceeding this limit must be credited to an emigrant blocked account. The balance, including earned income, may be transferred under prescribed conditions. Immigrants are required to furnish the exchange control authorities with a complete return of their foreign assets and liabilities at the time of their arrival. Any foreign assets they transfer to Namibia may, through the same channel, be retransferred abroad within the first 5 years of their arrival.

Controls on real estate transactions

Purchase abroad by residents

Yes.

Provisions specific to commercial banks and other credit institutions

Borrowing abroad

Authorized dealers are generally permitted to raise funds abroad in their own names for the financing of Namibia's foreign trade and for other approved purposes.

Lending to nonresidents (financial or commercial credits)

Prior approval is needed for lending not related to trade transactions.

Lending locally in foreign exchange

Lending is prohibited.

Purchase of locally issued securities denominated in foreign exchange

n.a.

Provisions specific to institutional investors

Limits (max.) on portfolio invested abroad

Investments are allowed only by way of swaps. On July 4, 1996, the limit was increased to 10% of the total value of the local fund from 5%.

Institutional investors were allowed foreign currency transfers during 1996 of up to 3% of the net inflow of funds during their 1995 calendar year. Approval of these transfers is subject to the said overall limit of 10%.

On April 21, 1997, the foreign currency transfers allowed in 1996 were extended to 1997. Accordingly, transfers abroad of up to 3% of the net inflow of funds during the preceding year may be allowed. In addition, 2% of the net inflow of funds during a preceding year could be utilized for investment in the stock exchanges of SADC members, still subject to the overall limit of 10% of the total assets applicable to asset swaps.

The definition of institutional investor was expanded to include the unit trust management company itself. In the past, only the fund itself qualified for asset swap transactions.

| Limits (min.) on portfolio invested locally | The minimum is 35% of the total assets of pension funds and insurance companies. |

| Other controls imposed by securities laws | Yes. |

Changes During 1996

| Status under IMF Articles of Agreement | *September 20.* Namibia accepted the obligations of Article VIII, Sections 2, 3, and 4 of the Fund Agreement. |

| Nonresident accounts | *August 19.* EPZ customer foreign currency accounts were allowed; these accounts are kept offshore via a local authorized dealer and are set up to facilitate the foreign currency disbursements of EPZ enterprises. Transactions through these accounts must conform to normal banking practices and must be carried out with the full cognizance and approval of the authorized dealer concerned. |

| | *August 19.* EPZ nonresident accounts were allowed. Balances remaining in these accounts are freely convertible and remittable abroad. |

| | *December 31.* Up to N$50,000 a year may be released from these accounts in respect to gifts and donations to third-party residents in Namibia. |

| Imports and import payments | *December 31.* Upon emigration, emigrants may export motor vehicles within an overall insured value of N$100,000 as well as personal effects and household goods of N$100,000. |

| Capital transactions | *July 4.* Foreign investors' access to domestic credit was doubled; a wholly nonresident-owned company can borrow 100% of shareholders' equity locally. |

| | *July 4.* The limit in respect of asset swap transactions by institutional investors was increased to 10% of the total assets of the local fund from 5%. |

| | *July 4.* Institutional investors were allowed foreign currency transfers during 1996 of up to 3% of the net inflow of funds during their 1995 calendar year. Approval of such transfers is subject to the said overall limit of 10%. |

| | *July 4.* Corporate entities that operate in the export field and also import goods from abroad were allowed to offset the cost of imports against the proceeds of exports, provided the transaction takes place within 30 days. |

| | *July 4.* Namibian corporations may invest up to N$20 million abroad. If the investment exceeds N$20 million, the balance must be financed abroad by means of foreign borrowing without recourse to or guarantee from Namibia. |

| | *July 4.* Existing approved foreign subsidiaries may expand activities abroad without prior approval, provided such expansion is financed by foreign borrowings or by the employment of profits earned by the foreign subsidiary. |

Changes During 1997

| Arrangements for payments and receipts | *January 13.* Neighboring countries were redefined to include Mauritius and Tanzania, in addition to Angola, Botswana, the Democratic Republic of the Congo, Malawi, Mozambique, Zambia, and Zimbabwe. |

| Nonresident accounts | *April 21.* The allowed annual amount for release from the local blocked account in respect to gifts to third-party residents in Namibia was increased to N$100,000 from N$50,000. |

| Payments for invisible transactions and current transfers | *April 21.* Virtually all controls on current account transactions were abolished, except in cases where the limits were retained to make the remaining controls on capital outflows effective. |

April 21. Namibians traveling abroad were allowed a maximum of N$80,000 for a person of 12 years or older, and N$25,000 for a child under the age of 12 years for each calendar year (this limit was increased from the previous limit of N$60,000). The previous distinction between neighboring and other countries was dispensed with. Previously, allowances for travel to neighboring countries (Angola, Botswana, the Democratic Republic of the Congo, Malawi, Mozambique, Zambia, and Zimbabwe) were restricted to N$20,000 an adult a calendar year.

April 21. Namibian residents studying on a full-time basis abroad may obtain an annual study allowance of N$80,000 a student or N$160,000 for a student accompanied by a nonstudent spouse.

Capital transactions

April 1. Nonresident-owned local companies' access to domestic credit was increased, i.e., only companies that are 50% or more foreign owned are to be subject to exchange controls.

April 21. The limit on foreign investment by Namibian corporations was increased to N$30 million for countries other than SADC members, and a new facility of N$50 million in respect to investment in SADC member countries was established. Also, consideration was to be given to foreign borrowings to finance such investments being raised with recourse to or guarantee from Namibia, implying that the local corporations' balance sheets may be used in negotiating such a facility.

April 21. The foreign currency transfers allowed in 1996 were extended to 1997. Accordingly, transfers abroad up to 3% of the net inflow of funds during the preceding year were allowed. In addition, 2% of the net inflow of funds during a preceding year could be utilized for investment in the stock exchanges of SADC members, still subject to the overall limit of 10% of the total assets applicable to asset swaps. The definition of institutional investor was expanded to include the unit trust management company itself. In the past, only the fund itself qualified for asset swap transactions.

NEPAL

(Position as of December 31, 1996)

Status Under IMF Articles of Agreement

Article VIII   Date of acceptance: May 30, 1994.

Exchange Arrangement

Currency   The currency of Nepal is the Nepalese rupee.

Other legal tender   The Indian rupee may be used to effect all bona fide transactions.

Exchange rate structure   Unitary.

Classification

Pegged   The official exchange rate is determined by linking it closely to the Indian rupee with cross rates against other currencies determined by commercial banks on the basis of demand and supply. Buying and selling rates are quoted daily for certain other currencies with quotations based on the buying and selling rates for the U.S. dollar in markets abroad.

Exchange tax   No.

Exchange subsidy   No.

Forward exchange market   Banks provide forward exchange cover for trade transactions.

Official cover of forward operations   No.

Arrangements for Payments and Receipts

Prescription of currency requirements   Convertibility between the Indian rupee and the Nepalese rupee is unrestricted in Nepal, and the Indian rupee may be used to effect all bona fide transactions. All current transactions with member countries of the ACU other than India must be effected through the ACU. Payments for selected imports from India may be settled in U.S. dollars. Other imports and proceeds from exports to India must be settled in Indian rupees. Proceeds from exports to other countries must be received in convertible currencies.

Payment arrangements

Regional arrangements   Yes.

Clearing agreements   Nepal is a member of the ACU.

Administration of control

Exchange control authorities   Payments in convertible currencies may be made without permission, subject to the procedures prescribed by the Nepal Rastra Bank (NRB). All exchange transactions must be settled through authorized dealers. Nonbank authorized dealers are licensed to accept foreign currencies only for their services to foreign nationals.

Payment arrears   No.

Controls on trade in gold (coins and/or bullion)

Controls on external trade   Persons who have stayed abroad for more than 1 month and have an official source of foreign earnings may import up to 10 kilograms of gold.

Controls on exports and imports of banknotes

On exports

   Domestic currency   Nepalese currency may not be exported to countries other than India, and may be taken to India only by Nepalese and Indian nationals.

   Foreign currency   Foreign banknotes, other than Indian banknotes, may not be taken out by residents without permission. Nonresidents may take out the unchanged amount of any foreign banknotes they bring in.

On imports

   Domestic currency   Nepalese and Indian currencies may be brought in only from India and only by Nepalese and Indian nationals.

   Foreign currency   Residents and nonresidents may freely bring in foreign banknotes, but must declare amounts exceeding the equivalent of $2,000.

Resident Accounts

Eligibility to hold accounts   Juridical and natural persons are eligible.

Foreign exchange accounts permitted   Exporters are allowed to deposit up to 100% of export earnings in a foreign exchange account to cover trade-related expenses. Nepalese citizens earning foreign exchange from working abroad (except in Bhutan and India) for more than 3 months may open these accounts. Commercial banks may accept deposits denominated in Australian dollars, Canadian dollars, deutsche mark, French francs, Japanese yen, Netherlands guilders, pounds sterling, Singapore dollars, Swiss francs, and U.S. dollars and are free to determine the rate of interest paid on deposits. Current accounts may be opened with a minimum equivalent to $500, and time deposits with a minimum equivalent to $3,000.

Held domestically   These accounts are permitted, but prior approval is required.

Held abroad   n.a.

Nonresident Accounts

Eligibility to hold accounts   Juridical persons, foreign diplomats, foreign nationals working in projects financed with foreign aid funds under bilateral or multilateral agreements with the government, and nonresidents may freely open foreign currency accounts with Nepalese banks.

Foreign exchange accounts permitted   Accounts may be maintained in all specified convertible currencies, and balances on these accounts may be freely transferred abroad.

Domestic currency accounts   Yes.

Convertible into foreign currency   Prior approval is required to open these accounts. Nonresidents who receive or bring into Nepal foreign currencies, which they convert into Nepalese rupees and deposit with a Nepalese bank, may reconvert them for transfer out of the country, subject to the prior approval of the NRB.

Blocked accounts   No.

Imports and Import Payments

Foreign exchange budget   No.

Financing requirements for imports   No.

Documentation requirements for release of foreign exchange for imports   No.

Import licenses and other nontariff measures	Most imports are covered under OGL. Silver is mostly imported by the NRB and sold to silver jewelers and handicraft-exporting industries through the commercial banks. Imports of silver up to 150 kilograms are allowed for those who have stayed abroad more than 1 month and have an official source of foreign exchange.
Negative list	Imports of arms, ammunition, wireless transmitters, precious metals, and jewelry require special permission from the government.
Open general licenses	Yes.
Import taxes and/or tariffs	There are 5 tariff rates (5%, 10%, 20%, 40%, and 110%), with most goods subject to either the 20% or the 40% rate. Nepalese citizens returning from abroad who have spent at least 15 nights out of the country are permitted to bring in goods worth Nrs 1,000 free of customs duties and sales taxes. Those citizens with official sources of foreign exchange earnings and who have stayed abroad for 1 month or more are allowed additional imports without proper documentation.
Taxes collected through the exchange system	No.
State import monopoly	No.

Exports and Export Proceeds

Repatriation requirements	Proceeds from exports must be repatriated within 180 days of receipt. As of September 30, 1996, exporters are allowed to accept short payment in export proceeds, if it does not exceed either 1% of the export value or $500, whichever is higher.
Surrender requirements	Exporters may retain their export earnings on their foreign currency account with local banks. Ready-made garment exporters are allowed to import fabrics from India in convertible currencies not exceeding 50% of their export earnings.
Financing requirements	Commercial banks may grant preexport credit of up to 70% of the f.o.b. value of products specified by the government to all individuals and institutions holding irrevocable letters of credit (LCs) opened or endorsed by foreign banks acceptable to the Nepalese banks. Such credit may be provided for a maximum of 3 months; this period may be extended without penalty under special circumstances beyond the control of the exporter.
Documentation requirements	
Letters of credit	Exports valued at more than $1,000 to countries other than India are allowed only against irrevocable LCs or advance payments by foreign banks.
Domiciliation	Reexportation to India of non-Nepalese goods and reexportation to any destination of goods imported from India are prohibited.
Preshipment inspection	Yes.
Export licenses	Exports of items having archaeological and religious value, old coins, narcotics, and explosive materials are prohibited.
With quotas	The export volume of ready-made garments to the United States is restricted by a quota that increases annually by 6%.
Export taxes	n.a.
Taxes collected through the exchange system	No.

Payments for Invisible Transactions and Current Transfers

Controls on these payments	All payments are subject to indicative limits and/or bona fide tests. Information on quantitative limits for most payments is not available.

Payments for travel

    Quantitative limits   The limit ranges from $300 to $1,500, depending on the destination.

Foreign workers' wages

    Quantitative limits   Migrant workers are allowed to take out the equivalent of $1,500 annually.

Gambling/prize earnings   n.a.

Credit card use abroad   n.a.

Proceeds from Invisible Transactions and Current Transfers

n.a.

Capital Transactions

Controls on capital and money market instruments

On capital market securities

    Purchase locally by nonresidents   Nonresidents can invest in equity shares up to 25% of the capital of Nepalese companies.

    Sale or issue locally by nonresidents   n.a.

    Purchase abroad by residents   Yes.

    Sale or issue abroad by residents   n.a.

On money market instruments

    Purchase locally by nonresidents   n.a.

    Sale or issue locally by nonresidents   n.a.

    Purchase abroad by residents   Yes.

    Sale or issue abroad by residents   n.a.

On collective investment securities

    Purchase locally by nonresidents   Yes.

    Sale or issue locally by nonresidents   n.a.

    Purchase abroad by residents   Yes.

    Sale or issue abroad by residents   n.a.

Controls on credit operations

Commercial credits

    By residents to nonresidents   Yes.

    To residents from nonresidents   n.a.

Financial credits

    By residents to nonresidents   Yes.

    To residents from nonresidents   n.a.

Controls on direct investment

Outward direct investment

Nepalese citizens, whether residing in Nepal or not, are not allowed to make any type of investment in foreign countries, except as specifically exempted by government notice. The exemptions include the purchase and sale of insurance policies abroad, and investments abroad by any banking or financial institution incorporated in Nepal.

Inward direct investment

Investments require prior approval in the form of a guarantee from the Industrial Promotion Board. Foreign investment is not permitted in cottage, small-scale, or defense-related industries unless substantial transfers of technology are involved. Foreign investors can hold 100% equity in large- and medium-scale industries, i.e., those with fixed assets of more than Nrs 10 million. Foreign security firms are permitted to form joint ventures with local state exchange members, but their ownership is limited to 40%.

Controls on liquidation of direct investment

Approval from the NRB and the Industrial Promotion Board is required.

Controls on real estate transactions

Purchase abroad by residents   Yes.

Purchase locally by nonresidents   n.a.

Sale locally by nonresidents   n.a.

Provisions specific to commercial banks and other credit institutions

Borrowing abroad   n.a.

Lending locally in foreign exchange   n.a.

Purchase of locally issued securities   n.a.
denominated in foreign exchange

Provisions specific to institutional investors

Limits (max.) on portfolio invested   Yes.
abroad

Currency matching regulations on   n.a.
assets/liabilities composition

Changes During 1996

Exports and export proceeds

June 6. The proportion of export earnings that ready-made garment exporters were allowed to import from India in convertible currencies was increased to 50% from 30%.

September 30. Exporters were allowed to accept short payment in export proceeds if such payment does not exceed either 1% of the export value or $500, whichever is higher.

Payments for invisible transactions and current transfers

June 30. Indicative limits for travel were from $300 to $1,500, depending on destination.

Capital transactions

July 31. Foreign portfolio investment of up to 25% of the paid-up capital of a company was allowed. Foreign securities firms were permitted to form joint ventures with local stock exchange members. The portion of their ownership in such ventures was limited to 40%.

NETHERLANDS

(Position as of December 31, 1996)

Status Under IMF Articles of Agreement

Article VIII   Date of acceptance: February 15, 1961.

Exchange Arrangement

Currency   The currency of the Netherlands is the Netherlands guilder.

Exchange rate structure   Unitary.

Classification

Cooperative arrangement   The Netherlands participates in the ERM of the EMS. In accordance with this agreement, the Netherlands maintains the spot exchange rates between the Netherlands guilder and the currencies of the other participants within margins of 15% above and below the cross rates based on the central rates expressed in ECUs. Under a special bilateral agreement, the spot exchange rate of the Netherlands guilder and the deutsche mark is maintained within a fluctuation band of ±2.25%.

Exchange tax   No.

Exchange subsidy   No.

Forward exchange market   Forward exchange contracts are not limited as to delivery period nor is an underlying trade transaction required.

Official cover of forward operations   No.

Arrangements for Payments and Receipts

Prescription of currency requirements   No.

Payment arrangements   No.

Administration of control   No.

International security restrictions

In accordance with IMF Executive Board Decision No. 144-(52/51)   In compliance with the relevant UN Security Council resolutions, certain restrictions are imposed on financial transactions with Iraq and Libya.

In accordance with UN sanctions   Yes.

Payment arrears   No.

Controls on trade in gold (coins and/or bullion)   No.

Controls on exports and imports of banknotes   No.

Resident Accounts

Eligibility to hold accounts   Juridical and natural persons are eligible.

Foreign exchange accounts permitted   Yes.

Held domestically   Yes.

Held abroad   Yes.

Accounts in domestic currency convertible into foreign currency	Yes.

Nonresident Accounts

Eligibility to hold accounts	Juridical and natural persons are eligible.
Foreign exchange accounts permitted	Yes.
Domestic currency accounts	Yes.
Convertible into foreign currency	Yes.
Blocked accounts	In compliance with relevant UN Security Council resolutions, funds belonging to Iraq and Libya are blocked.

Imports and Import Payments

Foreign exchange budget	No.
Financing requirements for imports	No.
Documentation requirements for release of foreign exchange for imports	No.
Import licenses and other nontariff measures	Imports from Angola and Iraq are prohibited. Imports of most products covered by the CAP from non-EU countries are subject to import levies. Common EU regulations are applied to most agricultural and livestock products.
Negative list	Import licenses are required for imports originating in Hong Kong, Japan, and state trading countries (i.e., the People's Republic of China, the Democratic People's Republic of Korea, and Vietnam), as well as for the importation of goods of unknown origin. In addition, import licenses are required for a limited number of products, mainly those of the agricultural, steel, and textile sectors.
Licenses with quotas	Imports of textiles originating in the Far East and in state trading countries.
Import taxes and/or tariffs	Yes.
Taxes collected through the exchange system	No.
State import monopoly	No.

Exports and Export Proceeds

Repatriation requirements	No.
Surrender requirements	No.
Financing requirements	No.
Documentation requirements	No.
Export licenses	
Without quotas	Export licenses are required for only a few commodities, mostly of a strategic character, for some agricultural products, and for iron and steel scrap and related products.
Export taxes	No.

Payments for Invisible Transactions and Current Transfers

Controls on these payments	No.

Proceeds from Invisible Transactions and Current Transfers

Repatriation requirements	No.
Surrender requirements	No.
Restrictions on use of funds	No.

Capital Transactions

Controls on capital and money market instruments	Inward and outward capital transfers by residents and nonresidents are not restricted, but they are subject to reporting requirements based on the External Financial Relations Act (1994). Transactions between residents and nonresidents in all stocks and bonds listed on the Amsterdam Stock Exchange take place at official market exchange rates and are unrestricted. Residents may freely purchase officially listed securities abroad. Placement with residents of unlisted foreign debentures denominated in guilders (such as foreign Euroguilder notes) and transactions in unlisted stocks are free of license. Nonresidents may have their securities, domestic or foreign, exported to them; securities held in the Netherlands are not subject to deposit.
Controls on derivatives and other instruments	No.
Controls on credit operations	No.
Controls on direct investment	No.
Controls on liquidation of direct investment	No.
Controls on real estate transactions	Nonresidents may freely purchase real estate in the Netherlands for personal use or investment, and residents may freely purchase real estate abroad. Extension of payment and mortgage borrowing from nonresidents is free of license.
Provisions specific to commercial banks and other credit institutions	
Open foreign exchange position limits	Limits are imposed on banks' total position in foreign currency and precious metals. Banks are required to report to the Nederlandsche Bank their position in each foreign currency and precious metal (spot, forward, and option positions) at the end of each month.
Provisions specific to institutional investors	No.
Other controls imposed by securities laws	No.

Changes During 1996

Arrangements for payments and receipts	*February 27.* Restrictions against areas of Bosnia and Herzegovina under the control of Bosnian Serb forces were suspended and later lifted, in accordance with UN Security Council Resolution No. 1022.
Nonresident accounts	*February 27.* Blocked accounts related to funds belonging to designated persons in areas of Bosnia and Herzegovina under the control of Bosnian Serb forces were suspended and later eliminated, in accordance with UN Security Council Resolution No. 1022.
Imports and import payments	*February 27.* Nontariff measures against areas of Bosnia and Herzegovina under the control of Bosnian Serb forces were suspended and later lifted, in accordance with UN Security Council Resolution No. 1022.

NETHERLANDS ANTILLES

(Position as of December 31, 1996)

Status Under IMF Articles of Agreement

Article VIII   Date of acceptance: February 15, 1961.

Exchange Arrangement

Currency   The currency of the Netherlands Antilles is the Netherlands Antillean guilder.

Exchange rate structure   Unitary.

Classification

Pegged   The Netherlands Antillean guilder is pegged to the U.S. dollar at NA f. 1.7900 per $1. The U.S. dollar is the intervention currency. The official selling rate is NA f. 1.80 per $1. Official buying and selling rates for certain other currencies are set daily on the basis of rates of the U.S. dollar abroad.

Exchange tax   No.

Exchange subsidy   No.

Forward exchange market   No.

Arrangements for Payments and Receipts

Prescription of currency requirements   No.

Payment arrangements   No.

Administration of control

Exchange control authorities   The Central Bank (CB) issues exchange licenses where required. The Department of Finance issues import licenses where required, and authorized banks may provide foreign exchange for almost all current transactions without prior approval of the CB.

International security restrictions   No.

Payment arrears   No.

Controls on trade in gold (coins and/or bullion)   No.

Controls on exports and imports of banknotes

On exports

  Domestic currency   Exportation is prohibited except for traveling purposes.

  Foreign currency   Nonresidents may take with them on departure any foreign currency that they brought in.

Resident Accounts

Eligibility to hold accounts   Juridical and natural persons are eligible.

Foreign exchange accounts permitted   Resident individuals may hold these accounts without a special license.

Held domestically   Yes.

Held abroad	These accounts are permitted; transfers from a local bank account to foreign accounts are allowed up to NA f. 10,000 a quarter.
Accounts in domestic currency convertible into foreign currency	Yes.

Nonresident Accounts

Eligibility to hold accounts	Juridical and natural persons are eligible.
Foreign exchange accounts permitted	These accounts are permitted, but prior approval is required.
Domestic currency accounts	Yes.
Convertible into foreign currency	These accounts are permitted, but approval is required for accounts exceeding NA f. 200,000.
Blocked accounts	No.

Imports and Import Payments

Foreign exchange budget	No.
Financing requirements for imports	Imports with delivery dates exceeding payment dates by more than 12 months must be reported to the CB.
Documentation requirements for release of foreign exchange for imports	No.
Import licenses and other nontariff measures	No.
Import taxes and/or tariffs	Imported goods for which there are locally produced substitutes are subject to tariffs ranging from 25% to 90%. Certain commodities are subject to import surcharges in Bonaire and Curaçao.
Taxes collected through the exchange system	No.
State import monopoly	No.

Exports and Export Proceeds

Repatriation requirements	If export proceeds are not received within 12 months of shipment, the delay must be reported to the CB.
Surrender requirements	No.
Financing requirements	No.
Documentation requirements	No.
Export licenses	No.
Export taxes	No.

Payments for Invisible Transactions and Current Transfers

Controls on these payments	Most types of current invisible payments and remittances may be made freely. A license is required if the delivery and payment dates are more than 1 year apart. Companies

must submit their annual report to the CB for verification of the actual amount of profits and dividends recorded before they may remit them.

Proceeds from Invisible Transactions and Current Transfers

Repatriation requirements	No.
Surrender requirements	No.
Restrictions on use of funds	No.

Capital Transactions

Controls on capital and money market instruments	Investments by residents in officially listed foreign securities (and in mutual funds whose shares are listed) are permitted free of license up to NA f. 100,000 a year, provided that these payments occur through a local exchange bank. Reinvestment of proceeds from the sales of securities is also allowed.
On capital market securities	Yes.
On money market instruments	Yes.
On collective investment securities	Yes.
Controls on derivatives and other instruments	
Purchase locally by nonresidents	Yes.
Sale or issue locally by nonresidents	Yes.
Purchase abroad by residents	Yes.
Sale or issue abroad by residents	Yes.
Controls on credit operations	Credit operations require licenses, which are normally granted.
Commercial credits	Yes.
Financial credits	Yes.
Guarantees, sureties, and financial backup facilities	Yes.
Controls on direct investment	
Outward direct investment	Investments are subject to control.
Inward direct investment	Investments require licenses, which are normally granted.
Controls on liquidation of direct investment	No.
Controls on real estate transactions	
Purchase abroad by residents	A license is required for these purchases.
Provisions specific to commercial banks and other credit institutions	
Differential treatment of nonresident deposit accounts and/or deposit accounts in foreign exchange	
Reserve requirements	A 2% reserve requirement is applied to the adjusted domestic debt of commercial banks. Additionally, there are prudential regulations concerning the extension of credits (the large exposure requirement).

Liquid asset requirements	No deficit liquidity position is allowed.
Credit controls	There is a monetary cash reserve requirement. During 1996, net domestic credit to the private sector by commercial banks was allowed to grow by 3%; lending funded through foreign borrowing, given due proof and after CB approval, was exempted from this ceiling.
Investment regulations	CB approval is required for the acquisition of shares in other companies.
Open foreign exchange position limits	Authorized banks' overall positions must always be positive and in currencies considered "freely usable."

Provisions specific to institutional investors

Limits (max.) on portfolio invested abroad	The limits are 60% for the first NA f. 10 million, 50% for the next NA f. 10 million, and 40% for additional amounts.
Limits (min.) on portfolio invested locally	The limits are 40% for the first NA f. 10 million, 50% for the next NA f. 10 million, and 60% for additional amounts.
Currency matching regulations on assets/liabilities composition	n.a.

Other controls imposed by securities laws

There is no securities law.

Changes During 1996

No significant changes occurred in the exchange and trade system.

NEW ZEALAND

(Position as of December 31, 1996)

Status Under IMF Articles of Agreement

Article VIII   Date of acceptance: August 5, 1982.

Exchange Arrangement

Currency   The currency of New Zealand is the New Zealand dollar.

Exchange rate structure   Unitary.

Classification

Independent floating   The exchange rate of the New Zealand dollar is determined on the basis of supply and demand in the foreign exchange market.

Exchange tax   No.

Exchange subsidy   No.

Forward exchange market   Yes.

Official cover of forward operations   No.

Arrangements for Payments and Receipts

Prescription of currency requirements   No.

Payment arrangements   No.

Administration of control   No.

International security restrictions

In accordance with IMF Executive Board Decision No. 144-(52/51)   New Zealand notified the IMF on September 6, 1990, that, in compliance with UN Security Council Resolution No. 661 (1990), certain restrictions had been imposed on the making of payments and transfers for current international transactions with respect to Iraq, and similarly on September 30, 1992, with respect to the Federal Republic of Yugoslavia (Serbia/Montenegro) in compliance with UN Security Council Resolution No. 757 (1992). Since December 3, 1993, certain restrictions on the making of payments and transfers for current international transactions pursuant to the UN Security Council resolutions have been imposed with respect to Libya.

In accordance with UN sanctions   Yes.

Payment arrears   No.

Controls on trade in gold (coins and/or bullion)   No.

Controls on exports and imports of banknotes   The Financial Transactions Reporting Act that came into force on August 1, 1996, requires that imports and exports of banknotes be reported. A customs documentation form, required when entering or leaving the country, includes a requirement to declare amounts greater than $NZ 10,000 or its equivalent.

Resident Accounts

Eligibility to hold accounts   Juridical and natural persons are eligible.

Foreign exchange accounts permitted   Yes.

Held domestically	Yes.
Held abroad	Yes.
Accounts in domestic currency convertible into foreign currency	Yes.

Nonresident Accounts

Eligibility to hold accounts	Juridical and natural persons are eligible.
Foreign exchange accounts permitted	Yes.
Domestic currency accounts	Yes.
Convertible into foreign currency	Yes.
Blocked accounts	No.

Imports and Import Payments

Foreign exchange budget	No.
Financing requirements for imports	No.
Documentation requirements for release of foreign exchange for imports	No.
Negative list	Import prohibitions and restrictions affect some 70 products or classes of products—primarily plants, animals, and products considered dangerous to human health or not in the public interest.
Import taxes and/or tariffs	The only tariffs over 20% apply to motor vehicles and motor vehicle parts, and certain other products (including textiles, clothing, footwear, and carpeting). Most tariffs are ad valorem, but specific duties apply to some products. Under the terms of the ANZCERTA and the SPARTECA, imports of qualifying goods enter duty free from Australia and SPARTECA countries. Eligible imports from developing countries that have not graduated beyond a specified threshold are accorded tariff preferences under the GSP. In addition, duty free access is given to most imports from 36 least-developed countries.
Taxes collected through the exchange system	No.
State import monopoly	No.

Exports and Export Proceeds

Repatriation requirements	No.
Surrender requirements	No.
Financing requirements	No.
Documentation requirements	No.
Export licenses	
Without quotas	Certain items classified as strategic goods may be exported only when specific requirements have been met and an export permit has been issued.
With quotas	Many of New Zealand's exports are currently restricted by quotas and other quantitative restrictions imposed by its principal trading partners. For example, exports of lamb and butter to the EU and exports of beef and dairy products to the United States are subject to either quotas or voluntary export restraints.

Export taxes	No.

Payments for Invisible Transactions and Current Transfers

Controls on these payments	No.

Proceeds from Invisible Transactions and Current Transfers

Repatriation requirements	No.
Surrender requirements	No.
Restrictions on use of funds	No.

Capital Transactions

Controls on capital and money market instruments	No.
Controls on derivatives and other instruments	No.
Controls on credit operations	No.
Controls on direct investment	
Inward direct investment	Under the Overseas Investment Regulations of 1995, which took effect on January 15, 1996, there are separate authorization procedures for "nonland" and "land" investments, which apply both to new investors and to existing foreign-controlled firms.
	Nonland investments involving the acquisition of over 25% of the shares of a New Zealand company, and where the consideration exceeds $NZ 10 million or which involve the purchase of property in excess of $NZ 10 million used in carrying on a business, are subject to a bona fide investor test. Established foreign-controlled enterprises also need approval for investments exceeding $NZ 10 million in areas unrelated to that consented to originally. However, since these investors were screened when they first invested, the procedure is straightforward.
Controls on liquidation of direct investment	No.
Controls on real estate transactions	
Purchase locally by nonresidents	Foreign investment in certain types of land is subject to both a bona fide investor test and a "national interest" test. Land acquisitions that require authorization relate to any land exceeding 5 hectares in area or where the consideration exceeds $NZ 10 million, and islands or land containing or adjoining reserves, historic or heritage areas, and the foreshore or lakes in excess of 0.4 hectares.
Provisions specific to commercial banks and other credit institutions	No.
Provisions specific to institutional investors	No.
Other controls imposed by securities laws	No.

Changes During 1996

Capital transactions	*August 1*. The Overseas Investment Regulations became effective.

NICARAGUA

(Position as of March 31, 1997)

Status Under IMF Articles of Agreement

Article VIII   Date of acceptance: July 30, 1964.

Exchange Arrangement

Currency   The currency of Nicaragua is the córdoba.

Exchange rate structure   Unitary.

Classification

Managed floating   A crawling peg system in which the exchange rate is adjusted 1% a month is maintained. The central government and financial institutions are free to undertake purchases or sales of foreign exchange with the Central Bank of Nicaragua (CBN), and financial institutions and exchange houses are permitted to carry out transactions with the private sector. On March 31, 1997, Nicaragua's exchange arrangement was reclassified to managed floating from adjusted according to a set of indicators.

Exchange tax   There is no tax, but the CBN charges a commission of 1% on sales of foreign exchange.

Exchange subsidy   No.

Forward exchange market   No.

Arrangements for Payments and Receipts

Prescription of currency requirements   No.

Payment arrangements   No.

Administration of control

Exchange control authorities   The CBN administers the exchange control system, and allows authorized commercial banks and exchange houses to make foreign exchange transactions.

International security restrictions   No.

Payment arrears

Official   Payment arrears are maintained with the Central American Bank of Economic Integration.

Private   n.a.

Controls on trade in gold (coins and/or bullion)

Controls on domestic ownership and/or trade   The Nicaraguan Mining Institute manages the country's gold production. The CBN reserves the right to purchase up to 25% of gold production by private mines, at prices prevailing in international markets. However, the mines may export gold freely if the CBN does not purchase this amount during a certain period. Natural and juridical persons may trade gold coins (commemorative gold coins were issued in 1967, 1975, and 1980) for numismatic purposes only.

Controls on exports and imports of banknotes   No.

Resident Accounts

Eligibility to hold accounts	Juridical and natural persons are eligible.
Foreign exchange accounts permitted	Yes.
Held domestically	Yes.
Held abroad	Yes.
Accounts in domestic currency convertible into foreign currency	Yes.

Nonresident Accounts

Eligibility to hold accounts	Juridical and natural persons are eligible.
Foreign exchange accounts permitted	Yes.
Domestic currency accounts	Córdoba accounts with exchange guarantee (maintenance of value) contracts may be opened with commercial banks.
Convertible into foreign currency	Yes.
Blocked accounts	No.

Imports and Import Payments

Foreign exchange budget	No.
Financing requirements for imports	No.
Documentation requirements for release of foreign exchange for imports	All importers must submit an import declaration form either to commercial banks or to customs in case they are using their own resources.
Letters of credit	Some import payments are made with sight drafts, but almost all are made through letters of credit.
Import licenses and other nontariff measures	
Open general licenses	Yes.
Import taxes and/or tariffs	Imports of 746 items are subject to a temporary import tariff independent of their origin, and all imports are subject to a sales tax and the Central American Common Tariff.
Taxes collected through the exchange system	No.
State import monopoly	No.

Exports and Export Proceeds

Repatriation requirements	No.
Surrender requirements	Surrender requirements were abolished on January 1, 1996, but all exporters benefiting from the export promotion mechanism must deposit export proceeds in an account at commercial banks. Exporters may mobilize the account later without any restriction.
Financing requirements	No.

Documentation requirements	No.
Export licenses	Export licenses are not required, but all exports must be registered (*Registro Unico de Exportación*) with the Ministry of Economy.
Export taxes	No.

Payments for Invisible Transactions and Current Transfers

Controls on these payments	No.

Proceeds from Invisible Transactions and Current Transfers

Repatriation requirements	No.
Surrender requirements	No.
Restrictions on use of funds	No.

Capital Transactions

Controls on capital and money market instruments	No.
Controls on derivatives and other instruments	No.
Controls on credit operations	Credits to residents from nonresidents must be reported to the CBN, for statistical purposes, within 30 days after the credits have been granted.
Controls on direct investment	
Inward direct investment	Foreign exchange originating from new investments or additions to capital must be surrendered to the CBN through commercial banks.
Controls on liquidation of direct investment	No.
Controls on real estate transactions	No.
Provisions specific to commercial banks and other credit institutions	
Maintenance of accounts abroad	Individual limits apply depending on the type of credit institution. With regard to sight deposits, limits are imposed according to working capital requirements, and up to 100% of capital for certificate of deposits. Other prudential regulations, as established by the Superintendency of Financial Institutions, apply.
Differential treatment of nonresident deposit accounts and/or deposit accounts in foreign exchange	
Reserve requirements	The requirement is 15% for deposits in domestic currency, and 25% for foreign currency deposits.
Open foreign exchange position limits	There are prudential regulations established by the Superintendency of Financial Institutions.
Provisions specific to institutional investors	No.
Other controls imposed by securities laws	No.

Changes During 1996

Exchange arrangements

January 1. The dual exchange rate system was unified.

Exports and export proceeds

January 1. Surrender requirements were eliminated.

Changes During 1997

Exchange arrangements

March 31. Nicaragua's exchange arrangement was reclassified to managed floating from adjusted according to a set of indicators.

NIGER

(Position as of December 31, 1996)

Status Under IMF Articles of Agreement

Article VIII   Date of acceptance: June 1, 1996.

Exchange Arrangement

Currency   The currency of Niger is the CFA franc.

Exchange rate structure   Unitary.

Classification

Pegged   The CFA franc is pegged to the French franc, the intervention currency, at the fixed rate of CFAF 1 per F 0.01. Exchange rates for other currencies are derived from the rate for the currency concerned in the Paris exchange market and the fixed rate between the French franc and the CFA franc. They include a bank commission of 2.5‰ on transfers to all countries outside the WAEMU, which must be surrendered in its entirety to the Treasury.

Exchange tax   No.

Exchange subsidy   No.

Forward exchange market   Forward exchange contracts may be arranged with the prior authorization of the Ministry of Finance and Planning (MOFP). Such cover may be provided for payments for permitted imports and for the currency stipulated in the commercial contract. The maturity period must not exceed 1 or 3 months, depending on the nature of the goods involved, and is not renewable.

Official cover of forward operations   No.

Arrangements for Payments and Receipts

Prescription of currency requirements   Because Niger is linked to the French Treasury through an Operations Account, settlements with France, Monaco, and other countries linked to the French Treasury through an Operations Account are made in CFA francs, French francs, or the currency of any other Operations Account country.

Payment arrangements

Bilateral arrangements   n.a.

Clearing agreements   Current payments to or from The Gambia, Ghana, Guinea, Guinea-Bissau, Liberia, Mauritania, Nigeria, and Sierra Leone are normally made through the WACH. Settlements with all other countries are usually effected either in foreign currencies through correspondent banks in France or in French francs through foreign accounts in francs.

Administration of control

Exchange control authorities   Exchange control is administered by the Financial Relations Directorate of the MOFP.

International security restrictions   No.

Payment arrears   Yes.

Official   n.a.

Private   n.a.

Controls on trade in gold (coins and/or bullion)

Controls on external trade   Imports and exports of gold require prior authorization from the MOFP. Exempt from this requirement are (1) imports and exports by or on behalf of the Treasury or the

627

BCEAO; (2) imports and exports of manufactured articles containing a minor quantity of gold (such as gold-filled or gold-plated articles); and (3) articles of gold up to a combined weight of 500 grams when carried by a traveler. Both licensed and exempt imports of gold are subject to customs declaration.

Controls on exports and imports of banknotes

On exports

Domestic currency   n.a.

Foreign currency   The reexportation of foreign banknotes is allowed up to the equivalent of CFAF 250,000; for larger amounts, documentation demonstrating either the importation of the foreign banknotes or their purchase against other means of payment registered in the name of the traveler or through the use of nonresident deposits in local banks is required. Residents traveling for tourist or business purposes to countries in the franc zone that are not members of the WAEMU are allowed to take out the equivalent of up to CFAF 2 million in banknotes other than CFA franc banknotes; amounts in excess of this limit may be taken out in other means of payment.

On imports

Foreign currency   Nonresidents may bring in any amount of foreign banknotes and coins (except gold coins) of countries outside the Operations Account area. Residents bringing in foreign banknotes and foreign currency traveler's checks exceeding the equivalent of CFAF 25,000 must surrender them within 8 days of entry.

Resident Accounts

Eligibility to hold accounts   Juridical and natural persons are eligible.

Accounts in domestic currency convertible into foreign currency   These accounts are not provided for under the exchange regulations.

Nonresident Accounts

Eligibility to hold accounts   Juridical and natural persons are eligible.

Foreign exchange accounts permitted   These accounts are permitted, but prior authorization from the Minister of the MOFP is required.

Domestic currency accounts   These accounts are subject to strict regulations; they may not be credited with banknotes of the BCEAO, the Bank of France, or any other bank of issue with an Operations Account with the French Treasury.

Convertible into foreign currency   Nonresident accounts may be converted into any currency.

Blocked accounts   No.

Imports and Import Payments

Foreign exchange budget   No.

Financing requirements for imports   No.

Documentation requirements for release of foreign exchange for imports

Domiciliation requirements   All imports exceeding CFAF 25,000 must be domiciled with an authorized bank.

Import licenses and other nontariff measures

Positive list

A license is required for imports of petroleum products.

Import taxes and/or tariffs

The customs tariff regime consists of 3 ad valorem rates of 5%, 10%, and 30%. There is also a 5% processing fee levied on imports.

Taxes collected through the exchange system

No.

State import monopoly

Petroleum products and pharmaceuticals are imported by a state monopoly.

Exports and Export Proceeds

Repatriation requirements

Yes.

Surrender requirements

The due date of payment for exports cannot exceed 180 days after the goods arrive at their destination. Proceeds from exports, regardless of the purchasing country, must be repatriated in their entirety through an authorized intermediary bank no later than 15 days from the date of receipt.

Documentation requirements

Exports of livestock, leather and skins, onions, rice, and sugar are subject to the submission of a statistical registration certificate. Exports to France and the Operations Account countries may be made freely. Exports of domestic products and imported commodities to other countries require an exchange commitment.

Letters of credit

n.a.

Guarantees

n.a.

Domiciliation

All exports of more than CFAF 500,000 must be domiciled with an authorized intermediary bank.

Preshipment inspection

n.a.

Export licenses

No.

Export taxes

Exports and reexports are subject to a 5% statistical tax. Reexports are subject to a special tax of 10%.

Taxes collected through the exchange system

No.

Payments for Invisible Transactions and Current Transfers

Controls on these payments

Payments for invisible transactions with France, Monaco, and the countries linked to the French Treasury by an Operations Account are permitted freely. Payments for invisibles related to trade are permitted freely when the basic trade transaction has been approved or does not require authorization.

Profit/dividends

Transfers of profits are permitted freely when the basic transaction has been approved.

  Prior approval

Yes.

  Quantitative limits

Yes.

  Indicative limits/bona fide test

n.a.

Payments for travel

  Prior approval

Approval is required for travel outside the franc zone.

  Quantitative limits

The limits are the equivalent of CFAF 500,000 a trip for tourist travel and CFAF 75,000 a day for up to 1 month for business travel.

Indicative limits/bona fide test	Allowances in excess of the limits are subject to the authorization of the MOFP or, by delegation, the BCEAO.
Medical costs	n.a.
Study abroad costs	n.a.
Subscriptions and membership fees	n.a.
Consulting/legal fees	n.a.
Foreign workers' wages	
Prior approval	Approval of the Monetary and Financial Relations Directorate is required.
Quantitative limits	These transfers are normally limited to 70% of net pay.
Indicative limits/bona fide test	Larger transfers are permitted if supported by appropriate documentary evidence.
Pensions	n.a.
Gambling/prize earnings	n.a.
Family maintenance/alimony	n.a.
Credit card use abroad	
Prior approval	Yes.
Quantitative limits	Credit cards may be used up to the ceilings for tourist and business travel.
Indicative limits/bona fide test	n.a.

Proceeds from Invisible Transactions and Current Transfers

Repatriation requirements	Yes.
Surrender requirements	All amounts due, except for transactions with France, Monaco, and Operations Account countries, must be surrendered within 2 months of the due date or date of receipt.

Capital Transactions

Controls on capital and money market instruments	Capital transactions between Niger and France, Monaco, and the other countries linked with the French Treasury by Operations Accounts are free of exchange control. Capital transfers to all other countries require approval from the exchange control authority and are restricted.
On capital market securities	
Sale or issue locally by nonresidents	Yes.
Purchase abroad by residents	Yes.
Sale or issue abroad by residents	Yes.
On money market instruments	
Sale or issue locally by nonresidents	Yes.
Purchase abroad by residents	Yes.
Sale or issue abroad by residents	Yes.
On collective investment securities	
Sale or issue locally by nonresidents	Yes.

Purchase abroad by residents	Yes.
Sale or issue abroad by residents	Yes.

Controls on derivatives and other instruments

Sale or issue locally by nonresidents	Yes.
Purchase abroad by residents	Yes.
Sale or issue abroad by residents	Yes.

Controls on credit operations

Commercial credits	Special controls are maintained over borrowing abroad. Such operations require prior authorization from the MOFP, except in the cases of operations in connection with loans backed by a guarantee from the Nigerien government.
By residents to nonresidents	Lending abroad is subject to prior authorization from the MOFP.
To residents from nonresidents	Borrowing requires prior declaration to the MOFP when the outstanding amount for any 1 borrower exceeds CFAF 30 million. The repayment of a foreign loan constituting a direct investment is subject to the same formalities as the liquidation of a direct investment. The repayment of other loans requires authorization only if the loans were subject to prior authorization.
Financial credits	Yes.
Guarantees, sureties, and financial backup facilities	Yes.

Controls on direct investment

Outward direct investment	Investments require prior MOFP authorization, and 75% of it must be financed through foreign borrowing.
Inward direct investment	Investments must be declared to the MOFP before they are made, including those made by companies in Niger that are directly or indirectly under foreign control and those made by branches or subsidiaries of foreign companies in Niger. Direct investments are those implying control of a company or an enterprise. However, mere acquisition of interest in the company is not considered direct investment when it does not exceed 20% of the capital of a company whose shares are quoted on a stock exchange. The MOFP has a period of 2 months from the receipt of the declaration to request postponement of the project.
Controls on liquidation of direct investment	The liquidation of Nigerien investments abroad or foreign investments in Niger must be reported to the MOFP and the BCEAO within 20 days of each operation.

Controls on real estate transactions

Purchase abroad by residents	Yes.
Purchase locally by nonresidents	n.a.
Sale locally by nonresidents	n.a.

Provisions specific to commercial banks and other credit institutions

Borrowing abroad	Loans contracted by authorized banks are exempt from the requirement of prior authorization from the MOFP. Earnings from such arrangements must be sold immediately on the foreign exchange market or debited from a foreign account denominated in French francs.
Maintenance of accounts abroad	Restrictions apply to resident institutions.
Lending to nonresidents (financial or commercial credits)	Foreign lending is subject to prior authorization from the MOFP.

Lending locally in foreign exchange	n.a.
Purchase of locally issued securities denominated in foreign exchange	n.a.
Differential treatment of nonresident deposit accounts and/or deposit accounts in foreign exchange	n.a.
Investment regulations	n.a.
Open foreign exchange position limits	n.a.

Provisions specific to institutional investors

Limits (max.) on portfolio invested abroad	Dispensation from the MOFP for risks undertaken abroad is required.
Limits (min.) on portfolio invested locally	Yes.
Currency matching regulations on assets/liabilities composition	Yes.

Other controls imposed by securities laws   Restrictions are imposed by the Insurance Code—Inter-African Conference of Insurance Markets (CIMA).

Changes During 1996

Status under IMF Articles of Agreement   *June 1.* Niger accepted the obligations of Article VIII, Sections 2, 3, and 4 of the Fund Agreement.

NIGERIA
(Position as of December 31, 1996)

Status Under IMF Articles of Agreement

Article XIV	Yes.

Exchange Arrangement

Currency	The currency of Nigeria is the naira.
Exchange rate structure	Dual. There is an official exchange rate, at which all government transactions with the Central Bank of Nigeria (CBN) are conducted, and a market-determined exchange rate in the Autonomous Foreign Exchange Market (AFEM), at which all other transactions take place.
Classification	
Pegged	The official exchange rate is pegged to the U.S. dollar at ₦ 22 per $1.
Exchange tax	No.
Exchange subsidy	Yes.
Forward exchange market	Forward exchange transactions at the AFEM rate are permitted among the authorized foreign exchange dealers and between the dealers and their customers.
Official cover of forward operations	n.a.

Arrangements for Payments and Receipts

Prescription of currency requirements	No.
Payment arrangements	
Regional arrangements	n.a.
Clearing agreements	Settlements with the central banks of the member states of the WAEMU are normally made through the WACH in West African Units of Account.
Barter agreements and open accounts	Yes.
Administration of control	
Exchange control authorities	The Federal Ministry of Finance (FMF) formulates basic exchange control policy and issues directives as appropriate for the operation of the AFEM. The CBN appoints and revokes the appointments of authorized dealers or authorized buyers of foreign currency, and supervises and monitors the operation of the AFEM.
International security restrictions	No.
Payment arrears	External debt service payments are limited to 30% of oil proceeds after deductions for certain specified purposes. The Debt Conversion Program (DCP) regulates the purchase of selected Nigerian foreign debt instruments at a discount and the disposition of the naira proceeds from the conversion of such debt.
Official	The majority of arrears are to Paris Club bilateral creditors, but there are also small amounts of arrears to multilateral and non-Paris Club bilateral creditors.
Controls on trade in gold (coins and/or bullion)	
Controls on domestic ownership and/or trade	Residents other than the monetary authorities, producers of gold, and authorized industrial users are not allowed, without special permission, to hold or acquire gold in any form other than jewelry or coins, at home or abroad.

Controls on external trade	The importation and exportation of gold in any form other than jewelry require specific licenses issued by the FMF.
Controls on exports and imports of banknotes	
On exports	
Domestic currency	The exportation of domestic currency in excess of ₦1,000 is prohibited.
Foreign currency	n.a.
On imports	
Domestic currency	The importation of domestic currency in excess of ₦1,000 is prohibited.
Foreign currency	n.a.

Resident Accounts

Eligibility to hold accounts	Juridical and natural persons are eligible.
Foreign exchange accounts permitted	Yes.
Held domestically	Any person may open, maintain, and operate a domiciliary account designated in foreign currency with an authorized dealer.
Held abroad	n.a.
Accounts in domestic currency convertible into foreign currency	n.a.

Nonresident Accounts

Eligibility to hold accounts	Juridical and natural persons are eligible.
Foreign exchange accounts permitted	External accounts are maintained for diplomatic representatives of all countries and international organizations. They may be credited with authorized payments by residents of Nigeria to residents of foreign countries, with payments from other external accounts, and with proceeds from sales of foreign currencies. They may be debited for payments to residents of Nigeria, for payments to other external accounts, and for purchases of foreign currencies.
Approval required	n.a.
Domestic currency accounts	Funds derived from local sources may be deposited in nonresident accounts.
Convertible into foreign currency	Nonresident accounts may be credited with proceeds from services rendered locally, provided that the operation of such accounts has been reported to, and approval has been obtained from, the CBN before any foreign transfers are effected.
Blocked accounts	n.a.

Imports and Import Payments

Foreign exchange budget	No.
Financing requirements for imports	No.
Documentation requirements for release of foreign exchange for imports	Unless a "clean report of findings" on the goods to be imported has been issued, foreign exchange settlements for imports may not be effected.

Domiciliation requirements	n.a.
Preshipment inspection	All containerized imports, irrespective of their value, and uncontainerized imports valued at the equivalent of $1,000 or more are subject to preshipment inspection.
Letters of credit	Import payments covered by confirmed letters of credit are made, on presentation of the specified documents to the overseas correspondents, on the understanding that the goods paid for will arrive in Nigeria and that all shipping documents are lodged by importers with the authorized dealer as agents of the Nigerian government within 21 days of negotiation of the specified documents.

Import licenses and other nontariff measures

Negative list	The importation of poultry, eggs, mosquito repellant, coils, plastic domestic articles, beer, maize, sorghum, millet, wheat flour, vegetable oils, barytes and bentonites, retreaded or used tires, motor vehicles and motorcycles over 8 years old, and gaming machines is prohibited.
Import taxes and/or tariffs	Import duties range from zero to 100%, with most goods subject to rates between 10% and 40%. The unweighted average duty is about 35%. In addition, 3 import surcharges apply: a 5% port development surcharge, a 1% Raw Materials and Development Council surcharge, and a 0.02% freight rate stabilization surcharge earmarked for the Nigerian Shippers Council. An import duty rebate of 25% applies to most goods, and certain categories of imports are exempt from import taxes. There are also a 7% port development surcharge, a 5% levy on imported sugar, and a 2% surcharge on automobiles.
Taxes collected through the exchange system	No.

Exports and Export Proceeds

Repatriation requirements	Yes.
Surrender requirements	All oil exploration and producing companies, as well as oil services companies, must sell their foreign exchange earnings to the CBN at the prevailing AFEM rate. Non-oil exporters are permitted to sell their export proceeds to authorized dealer banks at autonomous foreign exchange market rates.

Documentation requirements

Letters of credit	Payment for exports should be made with letters of credit or any other approved international mode of payment.
Guarantees	n.a.
Domiciliation	Repatriated non-oil export proceeds and other inflows should be held in domiciliary accounts maintained with authorized dealers in Nigeria. Holders of the domiciliary accounts have easy access to their funds maintained therein, subject to the existing guidelines, and may sell their export proceeds to banks other than those where they maintain their domiciliary accounts.
Preshipment inspection	All exports, oil and non-oil, from Nigeria are subject to preshipment inspection by government-appointed inspection agents. All exporters are responsible for the payment of a service charge for the Nigerian Export Supervision Scheme (NESS) at rates determined and advised by the FMF.
Export licenses	Exports of unrefined gold and petroleum products are subject to licensing. The exportation of African antiques, works of art, and objects used in African ceremonies is prohibited, except under certain conditions. Exports of timber (processed and unprocessed), raw hides and skins, cassava, maize, rice, yam, beans, scrap metal, and unprocessed rubber latex and rubber lumps are prohibited. Exports of petroleum are handled by the Nigerian National Petroleum Corporation and are subject to special arrangements.

Without quotas	Yes.
Export taxes	No.

Payments for Invisible Transactions and Current Transfers

Controls on these payments	Applications for foreign exchange must be submitted to the CBN through designated banks; verification is on an ex post basis. Basic allowances are provided for some payments. There are no controls on payments for freight and insurance, unloading and storage costs, and administrative expenses.
Profit/dividends	
Prior approval	Remittances are approved by the FMF, subject to documentation requirements. Interest income, profits and dividends, patent license fees, and other invisibles connected with approved projects under the DCP may not be repatriated before 5 years from the date of release of redemption proceeds for actual investment, or before 5 years after such profits and dividends are made or paid, whichever is later.
Indicative limits/bona fide test	n.a.
Payments for travel	A personal travel allowance is allowed for all Nigerian citizens in the AFEM without any restriction as to the amount of entitlement and age limit. Nigerian children born abroad and holding foreign passports are also entitled to the allowances, provided their status as Nigerians is confirmed. Business trip allowances are permitted for registered companies without any limit placed on the amount that a company may enjoy in any calendar year.
Study abroad costs	Foreign exchange remittances in the AFEM are allowed for all levels of educational studies in overseas institutions.
Consulting/legal fees	Up to 20% of the fees for projects of very high technological content, for which indigenous expertise is not available, may be remitted.
Prior approval	n.a.
Quantitative limits	Yes.
Indicative limits/bona fide test	n.a.
Foreign workers' wages	
Quantitative limits	The limit is 75% of net salary after tax, subject to a documentation requirement.
Indicative limits/bona fide test	Evidence of income earned and taxes paid must be provided.

Proceeds from Invisible Transactions and Current Transfers

Repatriation requirements	All proceeds must be received through the CBN or designated banks.
Surrender requirements	All proceeds must be surrendered to the CBN.

Capital Transactions

Controls on capital and money market instruments	Applications for capital transfers abroad are approved by the FMF.
On capital market securities	
Purchase locally by nonresidents	n.a.
Sale or issue locally by nonresidents	These transactions may be conducted through authorized dealers, with prior permission of the FMF.

Purchase abroad by residents	Residents of Nigeria may not deal in foreign currency securities, or buy from or sell to nonresidents of Nigeria any security payable in naira without the permission of the FMF.
Sale or issue abroad by residents	Yes.

On money market instruments

Purchase locally by nonresidents	n.a.
Sale or issue locally by nonresidents	Yes.
Purchase abroad by residents	Yes.
Sale or issue abroad by residents	Yes.

On collective investment securities

Purchase locally by nonresidents	n.a.
Sale or issue locally by nonresidents	Yes.
Purchase abroad by residents	Yes.
Sale or issue abroad by residents	Yes.

Controls on derivatives and other instruments

Purchase locally by nonresidents	n.a.
Sale or issue locally by nonresidents	n.a.
Purchase abroad by residents	Yes.
Sale or issue abroad by residents	Yes.

Controls on credit operations

Commercial credits

By residents to nonresidents	The permission of the FMF is required for companies (other than banks) registered in Nigeria that are controlled directly or indirectly from outside Nigeria. However, to enable companies to meet temporary shortages of funds, licensed banks in Nigeria may grant loans or overdrafts for periods of up to 14 days, or may increase the amount of any advance or overdraft by the amount of loan interest or bank charges payable thereon. General permission is also given for any loan, bank overdraft, or other credit facility to be arranged to finance Nigerian imports or exports of goods.
To residents from nonresidents	Except for the purpose of financing imports or exports, permission is required from the FMF for any individual, firm, company, or branch resident in Nigeria to borrow abroad. In addition, official agencies and state-controlled corporations require the prior approval of the FMF for any foreign borrowing. The contracting of suppliers' credits abroad by state-controlled corporations or agencies is also subject to approval from the FMF.
Financial credits	Yes.
Guarantees, sureties, and financial backup facilities	n.a.

Controls on direct investment

Outward direct investment	n.a.
Inward direct investment	There are ceilings for foreign capital participation in the equity capital of enterprises in various sectors of the economy. Nonresident investors may apply to the FMF for approved status, the granting of which means that sympathetic consideration will be given to future requests to repatriate the capital and related profits and dividends. The Nigerian Investment Promotion Commission deals with all matters relating to approval

and the prescription of applicable incentives for direct capital investment in priority areas.

Controls on liquidation of direct investment

Approval of the FMF, which is subject to documentation requirements, is needed. Capital proceeds arising from subsequent disposal of the investment made under the DCP may be repatriated only 10 years after the effective investment of the proceeds, and is limited to 20% a year.

Controls on real estate transactions

Purchase abroad by residents — Yes.

Purchase locally by nonresidents — n.a.

Sale locally by nonresidents — n.a.

Changes During 1996

Imports and import payments

January 1. Importers were made responsible for the payment of the service charge for the Comprehensive Import Supervision Scheme (CISS) at rates to be determined and advised by the FMF.

Exports and export proceeds

January 1. All exports, oil and non-oil, became subject to preshipment inspection by government-appointed inspection agents.

January 1. The administration and disbursement of export incentives were entrusted to the Nigerian Export Promotion Council.

Payments for invisible transactions and current transfers

January 1. Payments in foreign exchange of hotel bills by foreign visitors, airport tax, fees for the renewal of resident permits and allied services rendered by the Immigration Service, port and allied charges, international ticket fares, etc., became optional. Such payments can now be made in naira.

NORWAY

(Position as of December 31, 1996)

Status Under IMF Articles of Agreement

Article VIII   Date of acceptance: May 11, 1967.

Exchange Arrangement

Currency   The currency of Norway is the Norwegian krone.

Exchange rate structure   Unitary.

Classification

Managed floating   The exchange rate of the Norwegian krone is determined by market forces; however, the Bank of Norway (BN) intervenes to maintain stability.

Exchange tax   No.

Exchange subsidy   No.

Forward exchange market   Yes.

Official cover of forward operations   No.

Arrangements for Payments and Receipts

Prescription of currency requirements   No.

Payment arrangements   No.

Administration of control   Yes.

Exchange control authorities   The BN, in cooperation with the Ministry of Finance and Customs, exercises control.

International security restrictions

In accordance with UN sanctions   Restrictions have been imposed on financial transactions with Libya and Iraq (in accordance with UN Security Council Resolutions Nos. 661/90, 686/91, and 670/90). Sanctions against the Republic of Bosnia and Herzegovina (in accordance with UN Security Council Resolution No. 1022/1995) were lifted in March 1996.

Payment arrears   No.

Controls on trade in gold (coins and/or bullion)   No.

Controls on exports and imports of banknotes   A resident or nonresident who on entry into or departure from Norway is carrying Norwegian and/or foreign banknotes and coins equivalent to an amount in excess of NKr 25,000 a person, a journey, is obliged to notify the Customs Administration on entry or departure on the prescribed form.

A resident or nonresident staying in Norway who receives a dispatch by post, courier, or other form of transport, containing Norwegian and/or foreign banknotes and coins from abroad, or who sends such a dispatch abroad, equivalent to an amount in excess of NKr 25,000, is obliged to notify the BN in writing.

Resident Accounts

Eligibility to hold accounts   Juridical and natural persons are eligible.

Foreign exchange accounts permitted	The existence of these accounts must be reported to the BN.
Held domestically	Yes.
Held abroad	Yes.
Accounts in domestic currency convertible into foreign currency	Yes.

Nonresident Accounts

Eligibility to hold accounts	Juridical and natural persons are eligible.
Foreign exchange accounts permitted	The existence of these accounts must be reported to the BN.
Domestic currency accounts	Yes.
Convertible into foreign currency	The existence of these accounts must be reported to the BN.
Blocked accounts	No.

Imports and Import Payments

Foreign exchange budget	No.
Financing requirements for imports	No.
Documentation requirements for release of foreign exchange for imports	No.
Import licenses and other nontariff measures	There are certain measures imposed for sanitary reasons.
Negative list	All imports from Iraq and Libya are prohibited. Certain textiles and garments are subject to import licensing for surveillance purposes. Footwear from Taiwan Province of China is subject to licensing requirements.
Open general licenses	Yes.
Licenses with quotas	These licenses are required for textiles.
Import taxes and/or tariffs	No.
State import monopoly	No.

Exports and Export Proceeds

Repatriation requirements	No.
Surrender requirements	No.
Financing requirements	No.
Documentation requirements	No.
Export licenses	
Without quotas	Exports subject to regulation are listed and require licenses. Exports to any country under NKr 2,000 are exempt; for arms and ammunition, this limit is NKr 500, and for fish and fish products, NKr 1,000.
Export taxes	Yes.

Taxes collected through the exchange system	No.

Payments for Invisible Transactions and Current Transfers

Controls on these payments
There are no controls on these payments. The regulation prohibiting residents from contracting for an insurance policy other than nonlife insurance with a foreign insurance company that is not established within the territory of the EEA was abolished on December 11, 1996.

Proceeds from Invisible Transactions and Current Transfers

Repatriation requirements	No.
Surrender requirements	No.
Restrictions on use of funds	No.

Capital Transactions

Controls on capital and money market instruments

On capital market securities
The rule that a resident intending to buy or sell foreign securities that are not normally bought or sold in an EEA country is obliged to trade through a Norwegian securities broker was abolished on December 11, 1996.

Purchase locally by nonresidents
The restriction applies only to the purchase of shares and other securities of a participating nature that may be affected by laws on inward direct investment and establishment.

Controls on derivatives and other instruments	No.
Controls on credit operations	No.
Controls on direct investment	No.
Controls on liquidation of direct investment	No.
Controls on real estate transactions	No.

Provisions specific to commercial banks and other credit institutions

Open foreign exchange position limits
Foreign exchange banks and financial institutions are subject to exposure regulation, and must submit reports on their net foreign currency position to the BN. Net positions of up to 10% of the financial institutions' equity and subordinated loan capital may be taken out in individual currencies and the aggregate position must be kept within 20% of the financial institutions' equity and subordinated loan capital.

Provisions specific to institutional investors

Currency matching regulations on assets/liabilities composition
There are no currency matching regulations on assets/liabilities composition for investment funds. However, such regulations exist for insurance and pension funds for which net financial assets in a currency have to be equivalent to at least 80% of technical provisions in the same currency at any time. An insurance company cannot have negative financial assets in a currency.

Other controls imposed by securities laws
Other restrictions are included in Act No. 52 (1981) on Securities Funds and Rules for Asset Management.

Changes During 1996

Arrangements for payments and receipts

March 8. Sanctions against the Republic of Bosnia and Herzegovina were lifted.

Payments for invisible transactions and current transfers

December 11. The regulation prohibiting residents from contracting for an insurance policy other than nonlife insurance with a foreign insurance company that is not established within the territory of the EEA was abolished.

Capital transactions

December 11. The rule that a resident intending to buy or sell foreign securities that are not normally bought or sold in an EEA country is obliged to trade through a Norwegian securities broker was abolished.

OMAN

(Position as of December 31, 1996)

Status Under IMF Articles of Agreement

Article VIII	Date of acceptance: June 19, 1974.

Exchange Arrangement

Currency	The currency of Oman is the rial Omani.
Exchange rate structure	Unitary.
Classification	
Pegged	The exchange rate of the rial Omani is pegged to the U.S. dollar at RO 1 per $2.6008. The commercial banks' rates for other currencies are based on market rates in London.
Exchange tax	No.
Exchange subsidy	No.
Forward exchange market	Yes.
Official cover of forward operations	Yes.

Arrangements for Payments and Receipts

Prescription of currency requirements	All settlements with Israel and the use of its currency are prohibited.
Payment arrangements	No.
Administration of control	
Exchange control authorities	The Central Bank of Oman (CBO) has exclusive exchange control authority; there is no exchange control legislation.
International security restrictions	
Other	Restrictions are imposed with respect to Israel.
Payment arrears	No.
Controls on trade in gold (coins and/or bullion)	
Controls on external trade	Gold transactions with Israel are prohibited.
Controls on exports and imports of banknotes	No.

Resident Accounts

Eligibility to hold accounts	No distinction is made between accounts held by residents and those held by nonresidents.
Foreign exchange accounts permitted	Yes.
Held domestically	Yes.
Held abroad	Yes.

Accounts in domestic currency convertible into foreign currency	Yes.

Nonresident Accounts

Foreign exchange accounts permitted	Yes.
Domestic currency accounts	Yes.
Convertible into foreign currency	Yes.
Blocked accounts	No.

Imports and Import Payments

Foreign exchange budget	No.
Financing requirements for imports	No.
Documentation requirements for release of foreign exchange for imports	No.
Import licenses and other nontariff measures	Licenses are required for imports.
Negative list	Companies operating in Oman and trading in manufactured oil products are prohibited from importing specified products as long as domestic production is deemed adequate to satisfy local demand.
Open general licenses	n.a.
Other nontariff measures	All imports from Israel are prohibited.
Import taxes and/or tariffs	Customs duties range from 5% for most goods to 100% for imports of alcoholic beverages and limes. Customs duties are not levied on government imports.
Taxes collected through the exchange system	Yes.
State import monopoly	No.

Exports and Export Proceeds

Repatriation requirements	No.
Surrender requirements	No.
Financing requirements	No.
Documentation requirements	No.
Export licenses	All exports to Israel are prohibited.
Export taxes	No.

Payments for Invisible Transactions and Current Transfers

Controls on these payments	Payments for invisibles are generally not restricted, except for payments to Israel. Remittances by commercial banks require prior approval from the CBO.

Proceeds from Invisible Transactions and Current Transfers

Repatriation requirements	No.
Surrender requirements	No.
Restrictions on use of funds	No.

Capital Transactions

Controls on capital and money market instruments

On capital market securities

   Purchase locally by nonresidents — Foreign share ownership in Omani companies is limited to 49%, but it could be raised to 100%.

Controls on derivatives and other instruments — No.

Controls on credit operations — No.

Commercial credits — The Oman Develpment Bank can provide medium- and long-term loans at preferential interest rates for project financing in the petroleum, agricultural, fishery, and mineral sectors; it can also give assistance in preinvestment research. In addition, the government provides loans at subsidized interest rates for those projects with a majority Omani shareholding that are used for industrial production for exportation, industrial production using indigenous raw materials or labor, or the development of tourism.

Controls on direct investment

Inward direct investment — Investment in business firms in Oman by nonresidents requires prior approval.

Controls on liquidation of direct investment — No.

Controls on real estate transactions — No.

Provisions specific to commercial banks and other credit institutions

Borrowing abroad — Yes.

Differential treatment of nonresident deposit accounts and/or deposit accounts in foreign exchange

   Credit controls — n.a.

Open foreign exchange position limits — The limit is 40% of banks' capital and reserves.

Changes During 1996

No significant changes occurred in the exchange and trade system.

PAKISTAN

(Position as of December 31, 1996)

Status Under IMF Articles of Agreement

Article VIII	Date of acceptance: July 1, 1994.

Exchange Arrangement

Currency	The currency of Pakistan is the Pakistan rupee.
Exchange rate structure	Unitary.
Classification	
Managed floating	The exchange rate of the Pakistan rupee is set by the State Bank of Pakistan (SBP).
Exchange tax	No.
Exchange subsidy	No.
Forward exchange market	Yes.
Official cover of forward operations	Forward exchange cover for private foreign currency deposits is provided by the SBP, which charges an annual fee of 6.66%, 9.13%, 4.04%, and 4.75%, respectively, on deposits in deutsche mark, Japanese yen, pounds sterling, and U.S. dollars.

Arrangements for Payments and Receipts

Prescription of currency requirements	No.
Payment arrangements	
Regional arrangements	Yes.
Clearing agreements	Payments to, and receipts from, member countries of the ACU with respect to current transactions are effected in AMUs, which is equal to $1.
Administration of control	
Exchange control authorities	The SBP has delegated authority to a number of banks and financial institutions to deal in all foreign currencies, to supervise surrender requirements, and to sell foreign exchange within limits prescribed by the SBP.
International security restrictions	No.
Payment arrears	No.
Controls on trade in gold (coins and/or bullion)	
Controls on external trade	The exportation of gold is prohibited unless authorized by the SBP; such permission is not usually granted. Imports are allowed through 3 dealers authorized by the government.
Controls on exports and imports of banknotes	
On exports	
Domestic currency	An individual may take out up to PRs 500 and PRs 3,000 to India and to other countries, respectively.

646

On imports

   Domestic currency

An individual may bring in up to PRs 500 from India and PRs 3,000 from other countries. Coins from India may be imported up to Indian Rs 5 a person each time.

Resident Accounts

Eligibility to hold accounts

Juridical and natural persons are eligible.

Foreign exchange accounts permitted

Yes.

Held domestically

These accounts may be credited with remittances from abroad, traveler's checks, foreign currency notes, proceeds from foreign exchange bearer certificates (FEBCs), foreign currency bearer certificates (FCBCs), and dollar bearer certificates (DBCs). Sources of acquisition of foreign exchange are not required to be revealed. However, receipts from exports of goods and services; earnings from services of residents; earnings and profits of overseas offices or branches of Pakistan firms or companies and banks; and foreign exchange released from Pakistan for any specified purpose may not be credited to these accounts. Balances held in these accounts are freely transferable abroad, and there are no limits on amounts of withdrawal. These accounts may be permanently retained, and the rate of interest on term deposits (of 3 months and up to 5 years) is fixed by the SBP with the approval of the government. The rates are based on the Eurodollar deposit bid rate of Barclays Bank, London. The margins over the Eurodollar deposit bid rates range from 0.75% for 3-month deposits to 2% for 5-year deposits.

Held abroad

Balances of up to $1,000 can be held abroad with the approval of the SBP. Prior approval is required.

Accounts in domestic currency convertible into foreign currency

Yes.

Nonresident Accounts

Eligibility to hold accounts

Juridical and natural persons are eligible.

Foreign exchange accounts permitted

Pakistan nationals residing abroad and foreign nationals, whether residing abroad or in Pakistan, and firms, companies, and charitable bodies owned by persons who are otherwise eligible to open foreign currency accounts (FCAs) may open FCAs with banks in Pakistan without the prior approval of the exchange control authorities. The accounts may be denominated in deutsche mark, French francs, Japanese yen, pounds sterling, and U.S. dollars; credit balances may be transferred abroad, and interest on such accounts is exempt from income tax. Deposit holders wishing to make payments in Pakistan must first convert the foreign exchange drawn from their accounts into Pakistan rupees. If Pakistan nationals holding such accounts return to Pakistan, they may retain the accounts permanently. Banks in Pakistan receiving such deposits must sell the foreign exchange to the SBP. Authorized dealers under the FCA facility may accept term deposits in foreign currency from their overseas branches and foreign banks operating abroad, including financial institutions owned by them; such term deposits must be at least $5 million (or the equivalent in other currencies) for a maturity period of at least 3 months. The rates of interest paid on these deposits may not exceed 0.5% above LIBOR.

Domestic currency accounts

The accounts of individuals, firms, or companies residing outside Pakistan are designated nonresident accounts. (Different rules apply to the nonresident rupee accounts of individuals, firms, or companies, on the one hand, and to the nonresident rupee accounts of banks, on the other hand.) Authorized banks are permitted to open nonresident accounts for nonbank nonresidents without prior SBP approval when the accounts are opened with funds received from abroad through banking channels or with rupee funds accepted for remittance abroad. Debits and credits to nonresident accounts for specified purposes may be made by authorized banks without prior approval.

Convertible into foreign currency	When opened as convertible rupee accounts with funds received from abroad.
Blocked accounts	Accounts of residents of India, other than the accounts of the Indian Embassy and its personnel, are blocked.

Imports and Import Payments

Foreign exchange budget	No.
Financing requirements for imports	No.
Documentation requirements for release of foreign exchange for imports	Clean-on-board shipped bill of lading and others as per contract or letters of credit are required.
Domiciliation requirements	Yes.
Preshipment inspection	Inspection on some items was required up to March 1997.
Letters of credit	Yes.
Import licenses and other nontariff measures	Import licenses are not required. Imports from Israel are prohibited. Imports of 34 items on the health and safety list are restricted. Importing of 16 items on the procedural list (e.g., petroleum) requires certain technical expertise.
Negative list	Many of the products on the negative list consist of products banned for religious and health reasons, or to discourage consumption of luxury items, or goods banned under international agreements.
Import taxes and/or tariffs	There are 13 import tariff rates ranging from 10% to 65%, and tariffs of 100% to 265% are levied on imports of automobiles and alcoholic beverages. In addition, a 10% regulatory duty is imposed on most imported goods.
Taxes collected through the exchange system	n.a.

Exports and Export Proceeds

Repatriation requirements	Proceeds must be repatriated within 4 months of shipment.
Surrender requirements	Proceeds must be surrendered within 4 months of shipment; in cases where exporters are not required to pay commission to the overseas buyers/agents, or they pay the commission at a rate lower than the permissible rate, they can keep the commission differential up to 5% of the f.o.b. value of the goods in foreign currency accounts and these funds can be used for specific purposes. The surrender of Afghanis accruing from exports to the Islamic State of Afghanistan is not required.
Financing requirements	No.
Documentation requirements	The documents required are a firm order and the exporter's registration with the Export Promotion Bureau.
Domiciliation	Yes.
Export licenses	Exports to Israel are not allowed.
With quotas	Export licenses are required for maize, cement, gram, split gram, and camels.
Export taxes	There are no export duties; however, a nominal fee of 0.5% is chargeable on exports of cotton, tea, lac, tobacco, wheat, hides, and skins. Regulatory duties are levied on exports of tomatoes and uncrushed/crushed bones at rates ranging from 15% to 25%, and on exports of wet blue tanned hides and skins, at a rate of 50%.
Taxes collected through the exchange system	No.

Other export taxes	The standard rate of income tax on export/import proceeds is 1%. It is reduced to 0.75% on exports of goods manufactured in Pakistan, and to 0.5% on exports of jewelry, ceramics, surgical equipment, and sporting goods.

Payments for Invisible Transactions and Current Transfers

Controls on these payments

Unloading/storage costs

Prior approval	Yes.

Administrative expenses

Quantitative limits	Yes.

Commissions

Quantitative limits	Commission, brokerage, and other charges are generally limited to 5% of invoice values, 1% for cotton and cement, and more for a few other goods.
Indicative limits/bona fide test	Yes.

Interest payments

Quantitative limits	Generally, the limits are set at 5% of the loan amount.
Indicative limits/bona fide test	n.a.

Profit/dividends	The remittance of dividends declared on current profits is allowed freely to foreign shareholders if the investment was made on a repatriable basis. The remittance of profits by branches of foreign companies other than banks and those engaged in insurance, shipping, and the airline business is permitted without restriction provided that the required documents are submitted to the SBP. The same regulation applies to head office expenses charged to a branch's profit-and-loss account and accepted for tax purposes by the Pakistan income tax authorities.
Prior approval	Yes.
Indicative limits/bona fide test	n.a.

Payments for travel

Quantitative limits	The allowance for private travel to countries other than the Islamic State of Afghanistan, Bangladesh, and India is $50 a day for up to 42 days during a calendar year on submission of travel documents to the authorized dealers. Requests for foreign exchange in excess of these amounts are to be referred by the authorized dealers to the SBP, giving justification for the additional amount. Unspent foreign exchange, however, must be surrendered to an authorized dealer. The entitlement can be used in installments.
	There are also specific allowances for pilgrims' travel to Saudi Arabia. Exporters of goods with annual export earnings of more than PRs 2.5 million and exporters of services with annual earnings of more than PRs 0.25 million are granted a renewable business travel allowance of $200 a day, up to $6,000 a business trip. In addition, business travelers may settle credit card charges of up to $100 a day, subject to a maximum of $3,000 for a 30-day visit, with the encashment of FCBCs.
Indicative limits/bona fide test	Yes.

Medical costs

Prior approval	Approval is required on a case-by-case basis.

Study abroad costs	Foreign exchange allowances for students' tuition fees and expenses as required by institutions may be obtained from authorized dealers without approval from the SBP.
Quantitative limits	Allowances for professional training abroad are granted at $1,200 a month.

Subscriptions and membership fees

   Quantitative limits — There is no limit for individuals. For professional and specialized organizations, the limit is PRs 20,000 a calendar year.

Consulting/legal fees

   Prior approval — Yes.

Pensions

   Prior approval — Yes.

Gambling/prize earnings — Remittance of earnings is not allowed.

Family maintenance/alimony

   Prior approval — Yes.

   Quantitative limits — Allowances are determined on a case-by-case basis.

Credit card use abroad

   Quantitative limits — There are no limits if the amount is charged to a foreign currency account of the card-holder.

   Indicative limits/bona fide test — n.a.

Proceeds from Invisible Transactions and Current Transfers

Repatriation requirements — Yes.

Surrender requirements — Proceeds must be surrendered within 3 months. Travel agents and tour agents are permitted to retain up to 5% of their foreign exchange earnings for marketing and related export promotion expenses.

Restrictions on use of funds — No.

Capital Transactions

Controls on capital and money market instruments

On capital market securities

   Sale or issue locally by nonresidents — There are no restrictions on the sale of securities purchased in Pakistan. Nonresidents, however, are not permitted to issue securities in Pakistan.

   Purchase abroad by residents — Residents are allowed to purchase shares abroad and transfer the required funds through the mechanism of FEBCs.

   Sale or issue abroad by residents — Residents can sell or issue securities after obtaining approval from the Corporate Law Authority. The proceeds associated with these issues are required to be transferred to Pakistan or used for purchase of plants and machinery abroad. Transfer of funds required to service these security issues is permitted.

On money market instruments

   Sale or issue locally by nonresidents — There are no restrictions on the sale of securities purchases in Pakistan. Nonresidents, however, are not permitted to issue securities in Pakistan.

   Purchase abroad by residents — These transactions are not permitted.

   Sale or issue abroad by residents — Residents can sell or issue money market instruments after obtaining approval from the Corporate Law Authority. The proceeds associated with these issues are required to be transferred to Pakistan or used for purchase of plants and machinery abroad. Transfer of funds required to service these security issues is permitted.

On collective investment securities

Sale or issue locally by nonresidents

There are no restrictions on the sale of securities purchased in Pakistan. Nonresidents, however, are not permitted to issue securities in Pakistan.

Sale or issue abroad by residents

Residents can sell or issue securities after obtaining approval from the Corporate Law Authority. The proceeds associated with these issues are required to be transferred to Pakistan or used for purchase of plants and machinery abroad. Transfer of funds required to service these security issues is permissible.

Controls on derivatives and other instruments

Purchase locally by nonresidents

Only rights shares exist.

Sale or issue locally by nonresidents

Yes.

Purchase abroad by residents

Yes.

Sale or issue abroad by residents

Yes.

Controls on credit operations

Commercial credits

By residents to nonresidents

Credits of up to 4 months with respect to exported goods, and up to 12 1/2 years with respect to the export of plants and machinery are permitted.

To residents from nonresidents

Credit with respect to imports of goods is permitted.

Financial credits

By residents to nonresidents

These credits are not allowed.

Guarantees, sureties, and financial backup facilities

By residents to nonresidents

There are no restrictions if the transaction relates to imports.

Controls on direct investment

Outward direct investment

Direct investment abroad requires prior approval under foreign exchange laws. Resident Pakistan nationals require prior approval from the SBP to sell movable or immovable assets held abroad, and liquidation proceeds must be repatriated to Pakistan through normal banking channels.

Inward direct investment

Investment in the following specified industries is not allowed: alcohol, specified industries of arms and ammunitions, security printing, currency and mint, and high explosives and radioactive substances.

Controls on liquidation of direct investment

No.

Controls on real estate transactions

Purchase abroad by residents

Residents are not permitted to purchase real estate abroad.

Purchase locally by nonresidents

Purchases for business purposes are not restricted.

Sale locally by nonresidents

Disinvestment proceeds should not exceed original investment.

Provisions specific to commercial banks and other credit institutions

Borrowing abroad

Transactions are not allowed for temporary periods, and only if they become necessary for the normal course of business.

Maintenance of accounts abroad

Commercial banks and other credit institutions are allowed to maintain foreign accounts; limits for balances are fixed by the SBP in relation to the foreign exchange business handled by each bank.

Lending to nonresidents (financial or commercial credits)	Lending is not permitted.
Lending locally in foreign exchange	Lending is not permitted.
Purchase of locally issued securities denominated in foreign exchange	Yes.
Differential treatment of nonresident deposit accounts and/or deposit accounts in foreign exchange	
Reserve requirements	Yes.
Liquid asset requirements	Yes.
Credit controls	Credit limits apply to granting loans in domestic currency to companies controlled by nonresidents. The overall limits range from 25% to 100% of paid-up capital of a company depending on the sector of activity. No such limits apply to companies exporting at least 50% of their products. With the specific approval of the SBP, companies controlled by nonresidents and branches of foreign companies can contract foreign currency loans for meeting their working capital requirements. Additional rupee loans on a matching basis are also permitted by the SBP against such foreign currency loans.
Investment regulations	Yes.
Open foreign exchange position limits	Open position balances in Nostro Accounts are regulated by the Foreign Exchange Department.
Provisions specific to institutional investors	No.
Other controls imposed by securities laws	No.

Changes During 1996

No significant changes occurred in the exchange and trade system.

PANAMA

(Position as of December 31, 1996)

Status Under IMF Articles of Agreement

Article VIII
Date of acceptance: November 26, 1946.

Exchange Arrangement

Currency
The currency of Panama is the balboa. Locally issued currency is limited to coins, including several commemorative coins in small denominations.

Other legal tender
The U.S. dollar is legal tender and circulates freely in Panama. Panama has issued 2 commemorative gold coins with face values of B 100 and B 500, which are legal tender but do not circulate.

Exchange rate structure
Unitary.

Classification

Pegged
The currency of Panama is pegged to the U.S. dollar at the rate of B 1 per $1. Commercial banks quote buying and selling rates for certain other currencies based on the buying and selling rates for the U.S. dollar in markets abroad.

Exchange tax
No.

Exchange subsidy
No.

Forward exchange market
No.

Arrangements for Payments and Receipts

Prescription of currency requirements
No.

Payment arrangements
No.

Administration of control

Exchange control authorities
The Ministry of Commerce and Industry issues import licenses when required, and, through the Panama Trade Development Institute, determines all aspects of agreements on free trade and bilateral preferential treatment with countries in the region. The Ministry of Finance and Treasury issues export licenses when required. The Ministry of Planning and Economic Policy, the Ministry of Agriculture and Livestock Development, and the Agricultural Marketing Institute, through various product-specific commissions, determine the import quotas for certain agricultural commodities.

Payment arrears
Panama reached an agreement with its creditor banks on a debt and debt-service reduction operation and cleared oil debt obligations vis-à-vis Mexico and Venezuela.

Official
n.a.

Private
n.a.

Controls on trade in gold (coins and/or bullion)

Controls on external trade
Imports and exports of gold in any form other than jewelry carried as personal effects by travelers require a license if effected by residents other than the monetary authorities. Exports of unworked gold produced in Panama are subject to an export duty of 1% ad valorem, and exports of gold coins (other than U.S. coins, which are exempt) are subject to a duty of 0.5%.

Resident Accounts

Eligibility to hold accounts	Juridical and natural persons are eligible.
Foreign exchange accounts permitted	Yes.
Held domestically	Yes.
Held abroad	Yes.
Accounts in domestic currency convertible into foreign currency	n.a.

Nonresident Accounts

Eligibility to hold accounts	Juridical and natural persons are eligible.
Foreign exchange accounts permitted	Yes.

Imports and Import Payments

Foreign exchange budget	No.
Financing requirements for imports	No.
Documentation requirements for release of foreign exchange for imports	No.
Import licenses and other nontariff measures	In general, import licenses are not required, but individuals or companies engaged in import activities require a commercial or industrial license.
Negative list	Only a few products are banned or require special import permits. Imports by the public sector are subject to special requirements.
Open general licenses	n.a.
Licenses with quotas	Import quotas are maintained on some products in the agricultural sector and agro-industries, including timber, salt, fishmeal, milk, and sugar. Contingent mechanisms of quotas for imports of agricultural goods are to be implemented in the second quarter of 1997.
Import taxes and/or tariffs	Most tariff rates are on an ad valorem basis and are assessed on the c.i.f. value of imports. For some products, the tax is specific. In cases where both tax rates are stated, the applicable rate is the one that produces the higher tax revenue. If the tax is specific, an additional tax of 7.5% on the c.i.f. value is charged, except for (1) specified pharmaceutical products and foodstuffs, for which the additional tax rates are 2.5% and 3.5%, respectively; (2) books and certain agricultural inputs, which are duty free; and (3) specified raw materials for manufacturing, for which the tax is 5%.
	The range of tariffs for the main agricultural products is between 15% and 60%; the tariff rate on raw materials for the manufacturing sector is 3%. The maximum tariff for agro-industrial products is 40% and for industrial products 50%, with the exception of certain products. All imports into the city of Colón designated as the Colón Free Zone and the newly established export-processing zones are exempt from duties.
Taxes collected through the exchange system	No.
State import monopoly	No.

Exports and Export Proceeds

Repatriation requirements	No.
Surrender requirements	No.
Financing requirements	No.
Documentation requirements	No.
Export licenses	Specific export licenses are required for products that are subject to export taxes and for certain other goods. Exports of firearms and ammunition are prohibited. Any product (including raw materials and machinery) may be imported into the Colón Free Zone and stored, modified, processed, assembled, repacked, and reexported without being subject to customs procedures.
Without quotas	n.a.
With quotas	n.a.
Export taxes	Export taxes are levied on gold, silver, platinum, manganese, other minerals, unrefined sugar, coconuts, scrap metal, pearls, animal wax, nispero gum, ipecac root, and rubber. Certain nontraditional exports (with a minimum local cost-of-production content of 20%) are eligible for tax credit certificates equivalent to 20% of value added. Export processing zones are exempt from all taxes.
Taxes collected through the exchange system	No.

Payments for Invisible Transactions and Current Transfers

Controls on these payments	No.

Proceeds from Invisible Transactions and Current Transfers

Repatriation requirements	No.
Surrender requirements	No.
Restrictions on use of funds	No.

Capital Transactions

Controls on capital and money market instruments	No.
Controls on derivatives and other instruments	No.
Controls on credit operations	No.
Controls on direct investment	No.
Controls on liquidation of direct investment	No.
Controls on real estate transactions	No.
Provisions specific to commercial banks and other credit institutions	Some foreign-controlled banks are authorized to conduct business only with nonresidents.
Borrowing abroad	n.a.

Maintenance of accounts abroad	n.a.
Lending to nonresidents (financial or commercial credits)	n.a.
Lending locally in foreign exchange	n.a.
Purchase of locally issued securities denominated in foreign exchange	n.a.
Differential treatment of nonresident deposit accounts and/or deposit accounts in foreign exchange	n.a.
Investment regulations	n.a.
Open foreign exchange position limits	n.a.

Changes During 1996

Imports and import payments

October 2. The General Council of the WTO approved Panama's Protocol of Accession. (The ratification of this Protocol by the Assembly will take place in the second quarter of 1997, and the Assembly will have to approve a number of laws to bring Panamanian regulations in line with the Protocol.)

December 26. Import tariffs were reduced to a maximum of 50% for industrial products and to 40% for agro-industrial products; specific taxes on imports were transformed into ad valorem taxes; quotas, restrictive import permit requirements, bans, and reference prices were eliminated, except for those explicitly permitted under the WTO agreement.

PAPUA NEW GUINEA

(Position as of December 31, 1996)

Status Under IMF Articles of Agreement

Article VIII   Date of acceptance: December 4, 1975.

Exchange Arrangement

Currency   The currency of Papua New Guinea is the kina.

Exchange rate structure   Unitary.

Classification

Independent floating   The exchange rate of the kina is determined freely in the interbank market in which authorized dealer banks participate with the Bank of Papua New Guinea (BPNG) acting as broker. The commercial banks, the only authorized foreign exchange dealers, publish rates for all current transactions with their customers within a maximum spread between the buying and selling rates of 2%.

Exchange tax   No.

Exchange subsidy   No.

Forward exchange market   Exporters and importers are free to take out forward cover with the commercial banks at market-determined rates. Each commercial bank is subject to a prudential limit on its uncovered forward position.

Official cover of forward operations   At its discretion, the BPNG may intervene in the forward exchange market.

Arrangements for Payments and Receipts

Prescription of currency requirements   Contractual commitments to persons residing outside Papua New Guinea and expressed in a foreign currency must be paid in foreign currency. Export proceeds may be received in any foreign currency.

Payment arrangements   No.

Administration of control

Exchange control authorities   Foreign exchange control is administered by the BPNG under the Central Banking Act. Overall policy is determined by the government with the advice of the BPNG. The BPNG has delegated considerable powers to the commercial banks operating in Papua New Guinea, which have been appointed authorized dealers in foreign exchange.

International security restrictions

In accordance with IMF Executive Board Decision No. 144-(52/51)   Papua New Guinea notified the IMF on July 22, 1992, that, in compliance with UN Security Council Resolution No. 757 (1992), certain restrictions had been imposed on the making of payments and transfers for current international transactions in respect of the Federal Republic of Yugoslavia (Serbia/Montenegro).

In accordance with UN sanctions   n.a.

Payment arrears   No.

Controls on trade in gold (coins and/or bullion)

Controls on external trade   The exportation of gold is restricted to licensed gold exporters. For the large mines, the licenses are contained in their respective mining agreements. For exports of alluvial gold, specific export licenses are required from the BPNG.

Controls on exports and imports of banknotes

On exports

Domestic currency

Travelers wishing to take or send out domestic currency in excess of K 200 in notes and K 5 in coins must obtain approval from the BPNG. Domestic coins issued for numismatic purposes may be taken out freely.

Foreign currency

Overseas visitors are free to take out any currency they brought in and declared on arrival.

On imports

Domestic currency

n.a.

Resident Accounts

Eligibility to hold accounts

Juridical and natural persons are eligible.

Foreign exchange accounts permitted

Yes.

Held domestically

These accounts are permitted; resident business entities are required to obtain BPNG approval, except for term deposits placed for a minimum of 90 days.

Held abroad

n.a.

Nonresident Accounts

Eligibility to hold accounts

Juridical and natural persons are eligible.

Foreign exchange accounts permitted

Yes.

Imports and Import Payments

Foreign exchange budget

No.

Financing requirements for imports

No.

Documentation requirements for release of foreign exchange for imports

Authorized dealers may, without referring to the BPNG, approve applications for import transactions that are not subject to quotas or licensing requirements. Authorized dealers may make payments up to K 5,000 upon presentation of commercial invoices. Payments in excess of K 5,000 require a set of shipping documents and a copy of the customs forms, as well as commercial invoices.

Letters of credit

Yes.

Import licenses and other nontariff measures

Negative list

Imports of a limited number of goods are restricted for reasons of health and security, while others are prohibited to protect domestic markets, including sugar, poultry, and pork. The importation of most fresh fruits and vegetables is banned (except for apples, onions, and potatoes for processing). In the event of shortages on the domestic market, special import licenses are issued and imports are subject to a 50% tariff.

Licenses with quotas

Yes.

Import taxes and/or tariffs

The import tariff regime consists of the following rates: (1) zero rate for essential items (including food staples such as rice and meat not produced domestically); (2) 8% or 11% for basic goods (including some consumer goods and raw materials); (3) 40% for intermediate goods; (4) 55% for luxury goods; and (5) 15% or 100% for selected goods that have domestic substitutes, such as tinned mackerel and citrus fruits. On December 31, 1996, the import ban on sugar was replaced with an 85% tariff.

Taxes collected through the exchange system	No.
State import monopoly	No.

Exports and Export Proceeds

Repatriation requirements	Export proceeds must be received within 6 months of the date of export.
Surrender requirements	Export proceeds must be sold to an authorized dealer.
Financing requirements	No.
Documentation requirements	No.
Export licenses	When exporters are not in a position to comply with the conditions of the general authority, they must apply to the BPNG for specific authorization.
Without quotas	Licenses are required for exports of logs, pearls, fishery and marine products, wood-chips, sandalwood, rattan, coffee, cocoa, and copra. Log export licenses are issued subject to minimum export price guidelines.
With quotas	n.a.
Export taxes	Although exports of unprocessed products are subject to export levies, these have been temporarily waived, except for those on fish (10%) and logs (15% to 70%).
Taxes collected through the exchange system	No.

Payments for Invisible Transactions and Current Transfers

Controls on these payments	There are controls on these payments, but approval is readily granted for most, provided that supporting documentation is submitted. Authorized foreign exchange dealers may approve payments and transfers up to the equivalent of K 500,000 a year for all adult individuals and corporations. Payments and transfers in excess of this amount, except trade-related and debt-service payments, must be referred to the BPNG. For payments or transfers exceeding the equivalent of K 50,000 a year, a certificate of tax payment is required. Payments for the servicing of foreign debt may be approved without a fixed limit by authorized dealers.

Proceeds from Invisible Transactions and Current Transfers

Repatriation requirements	Yes.
Surrender requirements	Residents are not permitted to retain foreign exchange earnings from any source without the approval of the BPNG.
Restrictions on use of funds	Approval is required for the disposal of foreign currency proceeds, other than by sale to an authorized dealer in Papua New Guinea, or for its retention.

Capital Transactions

Controls on capital and money market instruments	There are no restrictions for inward portfolio investment. Authorized dealers may approve outward investments by resident individuals and corporations up to the equivalent of K 500,000 a year; investment in excess of the equivalent of K 500,000 requires the

approval of the BPNG. Income from the investment must be returned to Papua New Guinea as received. Prior clearance from the tax authorities is required for these transactions if the amount exceeds K 50,000 in any calendar year.

On capital market securities

Sale or issue locally by nonresidents	n.a.
Purchase abroad by residents	Yes.
Sale or issue abroad by residents	n.a.

On money market instruments

Sale or issue locally by nonresidents	n.a.
Purchase abroad by residents	Yes.
Sale or issue abroad by residents	n.a.

On collective investment securities

Sale or issue locally by nonresidents	n.a.
Purchase abroad by residents	Yes.
Sale or issue abroad by residents	n.a.

Controls on derivatives and other instruments

Purchase locally by nonresidents	n.a.
Sale or issue locally by nonresidents	n.a.
Purchase abroad by residents	Yes.
Sale or issue abroad by residents	n.a.

Controls on credit operations

Commercial credits

By residents to nonresidents	n.a.
To residents from nonresidents	Permission is required for these credits; however, authorized foreign exchange dealers may approve offshore foreign currency borrowing by residents, other than businesses involved in the forestry sector or mineral resources exploration, without limit, provided that the term is for not less than 1 year and that interest rates and fees do not exceed the levels specified by the BPNG. Repayment of principal is subject to a 6-month moratorium, commencing on the date of disbursements. A maximum debt-to-equity ratio of 5:1 applies to net outstanding borrowing. In the case of a business involved in mineral resource exploration activities, inward investment is considered non-interest-bearing equity or loan funds (including preference shares) until the business is successful, at which point any excess above the minimum equity-to-debt ratio specified for that operation can be converted into an interest-bearing loan.

Financial credits

By residents to nonresidents	n.a.
To residents from nonresidents	Yes.

Guarantees, sureties, and financial backup facilities

By residents to nonresidents	n.a.

To residents from nonresidents	Yes.
Controls on direct investment	
Outward direct investment	Yes.
Controls on liquidation of direct investment	Proceeds may be transferred, provided that tax clearance certificates are produced.
Controls on real estate transactions	
Purchase abroad by residents	Yes.
Sale locally by nonresidents	n.a.
Provisions specific to commercial banks and other credit institutions	
Borrowing abroad	n.a.
Maintenance of accounts abroad	n.a.
Lending to nonresidents (financial or commercial credits)	n.a.
Lending locally in foreign exchange	n.a.
Purchase of locally issued securities denominated in foreign exchange	n.a.
Investment regulations	n.a.
Open foreign exchange position limits	Yes.

Changes During 1996

Imports and import payments	*December 31.* The import ban on sugar was replaced with an 85% tariff.

PARAGUAY

(Position as of December 31, 1996)

Status Under IMF Articles of Agreement

Article VIII   Date of acceptance: August 23, 1994.

Exchange Arrangement

Currency   The currency of Paraguay is the Paraguayan guaraní.

Exchange rate structure   Unitary.

Classification

Independent floating   The authorities do not maintain margins with respect to foreign exchange transactions, and exchange rates are determined in the exchange market. The Central Bank of Paraguay (CBP) intervenes in the market to smooth out any sharp fluctuations in the exchange rate of the guaraní due to seasonal changes in demand and supply conditions as well as to speculative capital flows. The intervention currency is the U.S. dollar.

Exchange tax   No.

Exchange subsidy   No.

Forward exchange market   Commercial banks are permitted to enter into forward transactions with respect to trade transactions and on terms that may be negotiated freely with customers.

Official cover of forward operations   No.

Arrangements for Payments and Receipts

Prescription of currency requirements   No.

Payment arrangements

Clearing agreements   Payments between Paraguay and Argentina, Bolivia, Brazil, Chile, Colombia, the Dominican Republic, Ecuador, Mexico, Peru, Uruguay, and Venezuela are made through accounts maintained with the CBP and other central banks participating in the multilateral clearing arrangements of the LAIA. Clearing takes place every 4 months.

Administration of control

Exchange control authorities   The CBP has the authority to determine foreign exchange policy in consultation with other agencies of the government. In practice, decisions are taken by the Economic Cabinet on the advice of CBP, which is responsible for implementing its decisions. The CBP supervises through the Superintendency of Banks, foreign exchange transactions carried out by banks and exchange houses. The CBP regulates open foreign exchange positions.

International security restrictions   No.

Payment arrears   No.

Controls on trade in gold (coins and/or bullion)

Controls on external trade   The exportation and importation of gold by nonbank residents and industrial users in any form other than jewelry require the prior authorization of the CBP. Payments for gold imports by industrial users must be made through commercial banks.

Controls on exports and imports of banknotes

On imports   n.a.

Eligibility to hold accounts

Juridical persons   Yes.

Natural persons   n.a.

Foreign exchange accounts permitted   Yes.

Held domestically   Yes.

Held abroad   Yes.

Nonresident Accounts

Eligibility to hold accounts   Juridical and natural persons are eligible.

Foreign exchange accounts permitted   Yes.

Domestic currency accounts   Yes.

Convertible into foreign currency   Yes.

Imports and Import Payments

Foreign exchange budget   No.

Financing requirements for imports   No.

Documentation requirements for release of foreign exchange for imports

Preshipment inspection   All products must be inspected.

Import licenses and other nontariff measures

Negative list   Imports of certain products that may be harmful to public health, national security, or animal or plant health are prohibited. However, these restrictions may be waived to ensure adequate domestic supplies.

Import taxes and/or tariffs   Paraguay, as a member of the MERCOSUR, applies its common external tariff, which is composed of 11 rates ranging up to 20%. Paraguay was allowed to exempt 399 items from the CET—these exemptions are to be phased out by 2006 by gradually raising tariff rates to 14% on most capital goods and to 20% for telecommunications. Typical rates on goods exempt from the CET are zero for raw materials and intermediate goods; 5% for capital goods; 6% for items for tourism; 10% for consumer goods; 15% for vehicles whose c.i.f. value exceeds $10,000; and 20% for vehicles whose c.i.f. value exceeds $20,000. Similarly, on intra-MERCOSUR trade, Paraguay was allowed 427 exceptions to free trade with tariff rates ranging from 6% to 30% to be phased out by 2001. The CBP levies a commission of 0.125% on all import payments made under the LAIA Reciprocal Payments Agreement.

Taxes collected through the exchange system   No.

State import monopoly	No.

Exports and Export Proceeds

Repatriation requirements	The proceeds of exports must be collected through the financial system within 120 days of completion of the banking formalities related to the shipping documents. This requirement was eliminated on October 1, 1996.
Surrender requirements	No.
Financing requirements	No.
Documentation requirements	No.
Export licenses	
Without quotas	Exports of logs and unprocessed forest products, rawhides, and wild animals are prohibited. Certain other exports require prior authorization from the appropriate agency. All other exports are not restricted, except with regard to technical standards imposed by the National Institute of Technology and Standardization, the Ministry of Industry and Commerce, the Ministry of Public Health, or the Ministry of Agriculture and Livestock, depending on the product exported.
With quotas	n.a.
Export taxes	No.

Payments for Invisible Transactions and Current Transfers

Controls on these payments	There are no controls on payments for freight and insurance, unloading and storage costs, administrative expenses, interest, commissions, travel, medical treatment, study abroad, subscriptions and membership fees, consulting and legal fees, foreign workers' wages, pensions, gambling and prize earnings, family maintenance, or the use of credit cards abroad.
Profit/dividends	
Prior approval	Only financial enterprises require authorization of the CBP to transfer earnings. The government may grant exemptions from taxes, customs, and import surcharges on proposed investments that are duly registered and approved.

Proceeds from Invisible Transactions and Current Transfers

Repatriation requirements	No.
Surrender requirements	There are no surrender requirements for proceeds from invisibles, except for royalties and remuneration from the binational entities administering the ITAIPU and YACERITA dams, which are transferred in full to the CBP for the account of the Ministry of Finance.
Restrictions on use of funds	No.

Capital Transactions

Controls on capital and money market instruments	No.
Controls on credit operations	No.
Controls on direct investment	No.

Controls on liquidation of direct investment	No.
Controls on real estate transactions	No.
Provisions specific to commercial banks and other credit institutions	
Borrowing abroad	n.a.
Maintenance of accounts abroad	n.a.
Lending to nonresidents (financial or commercial credits)	n.a.
Lending locally in foreign exchange	n.a.
Purchase of locally issued securities denominated in foreign exchange	n.a.
Differential treatment of nonresident deposit accounts and/or deposit accounts in foreign exchange	
Reserve requirements	Reserves should be constituted in foreign currency.
Liquid asset requirements	n.a.
Open foreign exchange position limits	Commercial banks may maintain a daily foreign exchange overbought position not exceeding 100% of their capital and reserves, or an oversold position of up to 50% of their capital and reserves. Exchange houses may maintain a daily overbought position of up to $250,000.
Provisions specific to institutional investors	No.

Changes During 1996

Imports and import payments	*January 1.* External tariffs started to be reduced gradually under the MERCOSUR agreement.
Exports and export proceeds	*October 1.* The repatriation requirement was eliminated.

PERU

(Position as of December 31, 1996)

Status Under IMF Articles of Agreement

Article VIII   Date of acceptance: February 15, 1961.

Exchange Arrangement

Currency   The currency of Peru is the nuevo sol.

Exchange rate structure   Unitary.

Classification

Independent floating   The exchange rate of the nuevo sol is determined freely by supply and demand. Cross rates with nondollar currencies are determined against the U.S. dollar.

Exchange tax   No.

Exchange subsidy   No.

Forward exchange market   Forward transactions take place only in the commercial banking sector.

Official cover of forward operations   No.

Arrangements for Payments and Receipts

Prescription of currency requirements   No.

Payment arrangements

Regional arrangements   Payments between Peru and Argentina, Bolivia, Brazil, Chile, Colombia, the Dominican Republic, Ecuador, Malaysia, Mexico, Paraguay, Uruguay, and Venezuela may be made through accounts maintained with each other by the Central Reserve Bank of Peru (CRBP) and the other central banks concerned within the framework of the multilateral clearing system of the LAIA.

Clearing agreements   Yes.

Administration of control

Exchange control authorities   Exchange houses are authorized to purchase foreign exchange and traveler's checks from residents and nonresidents and to sell foreign exchange for tourism abroad and for purchases by nonresidents. Borrowing abroad by the public sector and by the private sector with government guarantee is subject to prior approval by supreme decree within the limits established by the Financing Requirement Law of the public sector.

International security restrictions   No.

Payment arrears   Arrears are maintained on nonguaranteed credits of suppliers, commercial banks, and official loans obtained from Eastern European countries.

Official   Yes.

Controls on trade in gold (coins and/or bullion)   No.

Controls on exports and imports of banknotes   No.

Resident Accounts

Eligibility to hold accounts	Juridical and natural persons are eligible.
Foreign exchange accounts permitted	Yes.
Held domestically	Yes.
Held abroad	Yes.
Accounts in domestic currency convertible into foreign currency	Yes.

Nonresident Accounts

Eligibility to hold accounts	Juridical and natural persons are eligible.
Foreign exchange accounts permitted	Yes.
Domestic currency accounts	Yes.
Convertible into foreign currency	Yes.
Blocked accounts	No.

Imports and Import Payments

Foreign exchange budget	No.
Financing requirements for imports	No.
Documentation requirements for release of foreign exchange for imports	
Preshipment inspection	Preinspection at the port of embarkation by international firms for imports exceeding $2,000 is required. However, this is not a requirement for the release of foreign exchange.
Import licenses and other nontariff measures	
Positive list	n.a.
Negative list	Imports may be prohibited for social, health, or security reasons.
Import taxes and/or tariffs	Imported goods are subject to a uniform value-added tax of 18% of their c.i.f. value in addition to the import duty. Some agricultural products are exempted from the value-added tax. The tariff rate on about 13% of import items is 25%, and the remaining products are subject to a 15% rate, excluding imports subject to trade agreements. Raw materials and intermediate goods imported under the Temporary Admission Regime are exempt from import duties.
Taxes collected through the exchange system	No.
State import monopoly	No.

Exports and Export Proceeds

Repatriation requirements	No.

Surrender requirements	No.
Financing requirements	No.
Documentation requirements	No.
Export licenses	No.
Export taxes	No.

Payments for Invisible Transactions and Current Transfers

Controls on these payments	These payments are free except for public debt-service payments, which are subject to payment authorization.

Proceeds from Invisible Transactions and Current Transfers

Repatriation requirements	No.
Surrender requirements	No.
Restrictions on use of funds	No.

Capital Transactions

Controls on capital and money market instruments

On capital market securities

Sale or issue abroad by residents — The issue of bonds in foreign currency by a domestic bank of maturity larger than 1 year average, and placed in a foreign country, is subject to the minimum reserve requirement ranging from 9% to 30% of the issuing entity's capital. These issues must be followed by a first-class foreign underwriter or arranger. The placement of amounts above the 30% limit is subject to the general reserve requirements.

Controls on derivatives and other instruments	No.
Controls on credit operations	No.
Controls on direct investment	
Inward direct investment	Foreign investment by petroleum companies is subject to special contracts with the government.
Controls on liquidation of direct investment	No.
Controls on real estate transactions	No.
Provisions specific to commercial banks and other credit institutions	
Lending to nonresidents (financial or commercial credits)	Credits and credits contingent granted by resident banks to nonresident banks or other financial institutions, plus deposit accounts held in these nonresident institutions cannot exceed the following limits relative to the bank's effective capital: (1) 5% if the financial institution is not supervised by an entity similar to the "Superintendencia de Banca y Seguros de Peru"; (2) 10% if the nonresident financial institution is supervised by an entity similar to the "Superintendencia de Banca y Seguros de Peru"; (3) 30% if the financial institution is a first-class bank; and (4) 50% if the excess in each of the preceding cases corresponds to letters of credit, excluding those corresponding to the payment agreement and reciprocal credits.

Also, contingent credits and leasing granted by resident banks to nonresident individuals or institutions, excluding nonresident banks or other financial institutions covered by Article 211 (Law No. 26702 of December 9, 1996), cannot exceed 5% of their effective capital. The above limits can be raised to 10% if the following guarantees are provided for the excess over the limit: (1) mortgages; and (2) securities issued by an institution listed in the stock market and whose quality is guaranteed by the specialized institution in that country. On a very limited basis, the limits of 5% and 10% can be raised to 40% of the effective equity if the following guarantees are provided for the excess over the limit: (1) deposits in the bank; and (2) securities, guarantees, and other liabilities of a bank with an arrangement under the payment agreement and reciprocal credits or with a first-class nonresident bank.

Reserve requirements

The deposit accounts in foreign currency are subject to a marginal reserve requirement of 45%. However, the CRBP remunerates the 36% additional reserve requirement with the 3-month LIBOR rate. The other 9 percentage points of the obligatory reserve requirement are not remunerated. This requirement is applied to all deposit accounts and does not discriminate between residents and nonresidents. Also, domestic currency obligations of financial institutions linked to changes in the exchange rate and domestic currency deposits related to swap operations are subject to 45% of the reserve requirement.

Provisions specific to institutional investors

Limits (max.) on portfolio invested abroad

The limit for pension funds is 5% of the fund.

Limits (min.) on portfolio invested locally

A maximum of 40% in government and central bank securities jointly or a maximum of 30% for each; 40% in deposits in or financial system bonds jointly (or 30% and 25% individually, respectively); 40% in other mortgage securities; 10% in short-term financial instruments; 35% in private enterprise bonds; 30% jointly (or 30% respectively) in mutual funds, derivatives, and representative stocks of social capital; 35% in variable rent instruments; and among the latter, 35% in convertible stocks and labor stocks.

Other controls imposed by securities laws

No.

Changes During 1996

Capital transactions

November 23. The maximum level of participation of variable rent instruments in institutional investors' portfolio was raised from 30% to 35%. Among those instruments, the maximum level for convertible stocks and labor stocks was raised from 30% to 35%.

PHILIPPINES

(Position as of March 31, 1997)

Status Under IMF Articles of Agreement

Article VIII   Date of acceptance: September 8, 1995.

Exchange Arrangement

Currency

The currency of the Philippines is the Philippine peso.

Other legal tender

Various denominations of gold coins are also legal tender.

Exchange rate structure

Unitary.

Classification

Independent floating

Exchange rates are determined on the basis of demand and supply in the foreign exchange market. However, the Bangko Sentral ng Pilipinas (BSP) intervenes when necessary to limit sharp fluctuations in the exchange rate and to maintain orderly conditions in the market. Commercial banks trade in foreign exchange through the Philippine Dealing System (PDS), an electronic screen-based network. The PDS allows trading between 8:30 a.m. and 5:30 p.m. daily among authorized agent banks and the BSP. The exchange rate of the peso vis-à-vis the U.S. dollar at the beginning of the trading day is the weighted average of all transactions in the PDS during the preceding day.

Exchange tax

No.

Exchange subsidy

No.

Forward exchange market

All forward transactions to purchase foreign exchange from nonresidents, including renewals thereof, require prior clearance by the BSP.

Official cover of forward operations

The cover facility for oil import financing was discontinued in February 1997.

Arrangements for Payments and Receipts

Prescription of currency requirements

There are no prescription of currency requirements for outgoing payments, but all foreign exchange proceeds from exports and invisibles must be obtained in the following acceptable currencies: Australian dollars, Austrian schillings, Bahrain dinars, Belgian francs, Brunei dollars, Canadian dollars, deutsche mark, French francs, Hong Kong dollars, Indonesian rupiahs, Italian lire, Japanese yen, Kuwaiti dinars, Malaysian ringgit, Netherlands guilders, pounds sterling, Saudi Arabian riyals, Singapore dollars, Swiss francs, Thai baht, U.A.E. dirhams, U.S. dollars, and other such currencies that may be declared acceptable by the BSP. Payments may be made in pesos for exports to ASEAN countries, provided that the BSP is not asked to intervene in the clearing of any balances from this payment scheme. Authorized agent banks may accept notes denominated in the prescribed currencies for conversion into pesos.

Payment arrangements

No.

Administration of control

Exchange control authorities

Foreign exchange regulations are administered by the BSP on the basis of policy decisions adopted by the Monetary Board.

International security restrictions

No.

Payment arrears

No.

Controls on trade in gold (coins and/or bullion)

Controls on domestic ownership and/or trade

Small-scale miners are required to sell all of their production to the BSP. All forms or types of gold may be bought and sold without specific approval of the BSP. Producers selling gold to the BSP are paid in Philippine pesos on the basis of the latest London fixing price and the prevailing Philippine peso-U.S. dollar exchange rate. The gold so acquired is deemed to be part of the official international reserves. The BSP may sell gold grains, pellets, bars, and sheets to local jewelry manufacturers and other industrial users upon application or to banks only for resale to jewelry manufacturers and industrial users, at the BSP's gold-selling price plus a service fee to cover costs, including the costs of conversion and packaging.

Controls on external trade

Gold produced by small-scale miners must be sold to the BSP; all other forms of gold may be exported. There are no restrictions on the importation of any form of gold except coin blanks essentially of gold, gold coins, and coins without any indication of actual fineness of gold content.

Controls on exports and imports of banknotes

On exports

Domestic currency

Resident and nonresident travelers must obtain prior authorization from the BSP to take out more than ₱ 10,000 in domestic banknotes and coins or checks, money orders, and other bills of exchange drawn in pesos.

Foreign currency

Departing nonresidents are allowed to reconvert at airports or other ports of exit unspent pesos up to a maximum of $200 or an equivalent amount in other foreign exchange without proof of sales of foreign exchange to authorized agent banks.

On imports

Domestic currency

Travelers may bring in freely up to ₱ 10,000 in domestic banknotes and coins and checks, money orders, and other bills of exchange drawn in pesos. The importation exceeding that amount requires prior authorization from the BSP.

Foreign currency

Travelers may bring in freely any amount of foreign currency.

Resident Accounts

Eligibility to hold accounts

Juridical and natural persons are eligible.

Foreign exchange accounts permitted

Yes.

Held domestically

Yes.

Held abroad

Yes.

Accounts in domestic currency convertible into foreign currency

No.

Nonresident Accounts

Eligibility to hold accounts

Juridical and natural persons are eligible.

Foreign exchange accounts permitted

Nonresident accounts may be credited only with the proceeds from inward remittances of foreign exchange or convertible foreign currencies and with peso income earned by nonresidents from the Philippines.

Domestic currency accounts

Nonresident peso deposit accounts may be freely withdrawn.

Convertible into foreign currency

Conversion of domestic currency accounts is allowed only up to the equivalent amount of foreign exchange remitted to the Philippines as well as to the equivalent amount of peso income earned by nonresidents.

Blocked accounts	No.

Imports and Import Payments

Foreign exchange budget	No.
Financing requirements for imports	No.
Documentation requirements for release of foreign exchange for imports	Commercial banks may sell foreign exchange for payments of imports under letters of credit (LCs), documents against acceptance (D/A), documents against payments (D/P), open account (OA) arrangement, and direct remittance. Registration of D/A and OA imports with the BSP for monitoring purposes is needed only if payments are to be made from the banking system; prior approval of the BSP, regardless of maturity, is not required. Any extension of maturities must be reported to the BSP 30 days before the effective date. Import arrangements not involving payments using foreign exchange purchased from the banking system, such as self-funded no-dollar imports and importation on a consignment basis, are allowed without prior approval from the BSP.
Preshipment inspection	Under the Comprehensive Imports Supervision Scheme (CISS), preshipment inspection is required for imports valued at more than $500 from all countries. Imports declared in the shipping documents as off quality, used, secondhand, scraps, off grade, or a similar term indicating that the article is not brand new are subject to CISS inspection even if the value of the imports is less than $500.
Letters of credit	LCs must be opened on or before the date of shipment with a validity period of up to 1 year. Only 1 LC may be opened for each import transaction; amendments to such an arrangement need not be referred to the BSP for prior approval except when amendment shall extend the total validity of the LC beyond 1 year.
Import licenses and other nontariff measures	Generally, all merchandise imports are allowed without a license.
Positive list	Yes.
Negative list	The importation of certain products is regulated or restricted for reasons of public health and safety, national security, international commitments, and development and rationalization of local industries.
Open general licenses	Commodity imports are classified into 3 categories: freely importable, regulated, and prohibited. To import regulated products, a clearance or permit is required from the appropriate government agency (including the BSP).
Licenses with quotas	Quantitative restrictions are imposed on imports of rice.
Import taxes and/or tariffs	The import tariff structure consists of 4 rates: 3%, 10%, 20%, and 30%. Rates on imported capital goods are 3% and 10%, with the former applying to goods without domestic substitutes. Deviations from the standard rates include (1) up to double the applicable standard rate for imports of final goods in industries that have "pioneer" status at the Board of Investment (BOI), and imports of agricultural products for which quantitative restrictions are being removed under the WTO agreement; and (2) duty exemptions for certain imported capital goods registered with the BOI prior to January 1, 1995 or subject to provisions of RA 7369 and RA 7844 of the Export Development Act. Some 300 products under RA 7369 are duty exempt, as are imports of machinery, equipment, and accompanying spare parts used in export manufacturing. The BOI no longer offers tax and duty exemptions on imports of capital equipment and spare parts. Instead, newly registered firms may only obtain duty reductions on eligible imports to 3%. Tariff rates in the textile and apparel sectors are 3% for inputs and 30% for final products.
Taxes collected through the exchange system	No.
State import monopoly	No.

Exports and Export Proceeds

Repatriation requirements	No.
Surrender requirements	No.
Financing requirements	Payments for exports may be made in acceptable currencies in the following forms without prior BSP approval: LCs, D/Ps, D/As, OA arrangements, cash against documents arrangements, consignment, export advance, and prepayment.
Documentation requirements	All exports must be covered by an export declaration issued by the Department of Trade and Industry duly prepared by the exporter.
Export licenses	Exports of selected seeds and shoots of native plants, endangered fish and wildlife (including selected marine species), and stalactites and stalagmites are prohibited.
Without quotas	Yes.
Export taxes	No.

Payments for Invisible Transactions and Current Transfers

Controls on these payments	All payments are subject to indicative limits and/or bona fide tests. Authorized banks may sell foreign exchange to residents for nontrade payments, except obligations related to foreign loans or foreign investments up to $25,000, without written application or supporting documents from the buyer. For amounts exceeding $25,000, the banks require a written application and supporting documents from the buyer. On January 15, 1997, the ceiling was raised to $50,000 for sales with no written application and supporting documents required. The implementing guidelines on this amendment, however, have not yet been issued.
Interest payments	
Prior approval	Service payments on foreign loans effected by purchases of foreign exchange through authorized agent banks are limited to those transactions whose original capital transfer has previously been registered with the BSP. Unregistered loans can be serviced also through transactions in the nonbank market.
Profit/dividends	Service payments relating to foreign direct investments effected by purchases of foreign exchange through authorized agent banks are limited to those transactions whose original capital transfer has previously been registered with the BSP. Unregistered investments can also be serviced through transactions in the nonbank market.

Proceeds from Invisible Transactions and Current Transfers

Repatriation requirements	No.
Surrender requirements	No.
Restrictions on use of funds	No.

Capital Transactions

Controls on capital and money market instruments	
On capital market securities	
Purchase locally by nonresidents	Registration with the BSP or designated custodian bank is required. As a general rule, registration with the BSP of foreign investments in the form of government securities, securities listed in the Philippine Stock Exchange, money market instruments, or bank deposits is not mandatory. Said registration is necessary only if the source of the foreign

exchange needed for capital repatriation and remittance of dividends, profits and earnings which accrue thereon is purchased from the banking system.

Sale or issue locally by nonresidents

Sale or issue of securities in the Philippines is allowed only after the proper license to do business in the country is secured by the nonresident from the appropriate government agency(ies).

Purchase abroad by residents

Residents may invest abroad without registering their investments with the BSP only if (1) the investment is funded by withdrawals from Foreign Currency Deposit Units (FCDUs); (2) the funds to be invested are not among those required to be sold to authorized agent banks (AABs) for pesos; or (3) the sources of funds are from the banking system but in amounts less than $6 million for an investor a year. For amounts above $6 million (an investor a year), prior approval and registration with the BSP is required.

Sale or issue abroad by residents

Registration with the BSP or designated custodian bank is required. In addition, sales proceeds from international allocations of initial public offerings and shares of domestic companies listed in foreign stock exchanges must also be reported to the BSP within 5 days of receipt and remitted inwardly to the country. The servicing or transfer of funds pertaining to registered investments using foreign exchange from the banking system in this category is allowed without BSP approval.

On money market instruments

The same regulations apply as for capital market securities.

On collective investment securities

The same regulations apply as for capital market securities.

Controls on derivatives and other instruments

Prior BSP approval is required for transactions in these instruments. Only banks and nonbank financial intermediaries performing quasibanking functions and their affiliates/subsidiaries duly authorized by the BSP are allowed to deal in derivative transactions.

Purchase locally by nonresidents

Yes.

Sale or issue locally by nonresidents

Yes.

Purchase abroad by residents

Yes.

Sale or issue abroad by residents

Yes.

Controls on credit operations

Commercial credits

To residents from nonresidents

Prior BSP approval and registration are required for guaranteed, short-term trade-related loans contracted by nonbank residents. For those not covered by public sector guarantees, prior authority to incur the obligation is not required. They are still, however, subject to the registration requirement for debt servicing using foreign exchange from the banking system.

Financial credits

By residents to nonresidents

Credits require prior BSP approval. The usual restrictions on outward remittances and registration requirements apply.

To residents from nonresidents

As a general rule, all foreign loans contracted by nonbank residents with guarantees from the public sector or from local commercial banks require prior BSP approval or registration. Those not covered by guarantees are required to be registered only to make them eligible for subsequent debt servicing using foreign exchange from the banking system.

Guarantees, sureties, and financial backup facilities

By residents to nonresidents

Guarantees for the account of the public sector, as well as those issued by government-owned and controlled corporations in favor of nonresidents, require prior BSP approval. Specific guarantees for the account of the private sector do not require prior approval but must be reported to the BSP for registration purposes to be eligible for debt servicing using foreign exchange.

To residents from nonresidents	Guarantees issued by foreign banks and financial institutions to secure obligations of residents involved in foreign lending operations require prior BSP approval. Those issued to secure authorized peso loans or FCDU loans, as well as foreign obligations (which do not involve foreign lending) of local firms, do not require prior approval but must be reported to the BSP for registration purposes to be eligible for debt servicing using foreign exchange to be purchased from the banking system in the event of a default by the principal debtor.
Controls on direct investment	The same regulations apply as for investments in money market instruments.
Outward direct investment	Yes.
Controls on liquidation of direct investment	BSP-registered foreign investments enjoy full and immediate repatriation of capital and remittance of profits, dividends, and other earnings.
Controls on real estate transactions	The same regulations apply as for investments in money market instruments.
Purchase abroad by residents	Yes.
Purchase locally by nonresidents	Ownership of land by nonresidents as well as the exploration, development, and utilization of natural resources is limited to 40% equity and is subject to the provisions of the Philippines Constitution.
Sale locally by nonresidents	For sale of real estate by nonresidents not pertaining to BSP-registered investments, they may purchase only as much foreign exchange as they sold to AABs for pesos.
Provisions specific to commercial banks and other credit institutions	
Borrowing abroad	Commercial banks authorized to operate under the expanded foreign currency deposit system may borrow from other FCDUs, nonresidents, and offshore banking units, subject to existing rules on foreign borrowings.
Lending to nonresidents (financial or commercial credits)	Banks may grant commercial credit to nonresidents under any of the following modes of payment without prior BSP approval: LCs, D/Ps or cash against payment, D/As, OA arrangements, intercompany open account offset, consignments, and export advances. Commercial banks, which are authorized to operate under the expanded foreign currency deposit system, may grant foreign currency loans as may be allowed by the BSP.
Lending locally in foreign exchange	The following foreign currency loans may be granted by FCDUs of commercial banks without prior BSP approval: (1) private sector loans, if they are to be serviced using foreign exchange to be obtained outside the banking system; (2) short-term loans to financial institutions for normal interbank transactions; and (3) short-term loans to commodity and service exporters, and producers/manufacturers, provided that the loan proceeds are to be used to finance the import costs of goods and services necessary in the production of goods. Regular units of commercial banks may also grant foreign currency loans to residents involving trade transactions.
Purchase of locally issued securities denominated in foreign exchange	An Expanded Foreign Currency Deposit Unit (EFCDU) of commercial banks may invest in foreign-currency-denominated securities.
Open foreign exchange position limits	Depository banks operating FCDUs or EFCDUs need to maintain full cover for their foreign currency liabilities at all times. For FCDUs, at least 70% of the said cover must be maintained in the same currency of the liability and up to 30% may be denominated in other acceptable foreign currencies. Long and short foreign exchange positions of banks must not exceed 20% and 10%, respectively, of their total unimpaired capital. Any excess beyond the limit must be settled daily.
Provisions specific to institutional investors	
Limits (max.) on portfolio invested abroad	Except as may be authorized by the Monetary Board, the total equity investments in and/or loans to any single enterprise abroad by any investment house with quasi-banking functions shall not at any time exceed 15% of their net worth. Outward investments by residents in amounts exceeding $6 million require prior approval and registration by the BSP. For amounts not exceeding $6 million, the funds to be invested may be purchased from authorized agent banks.

Other controls imposed by securities laws	As a general rule, no securities may be sold or offered for sale to the public within the country unless such securities have been registered and permitted to be sold by the Securities Exchange Commission (SEC). A foreign corporation whose securities are listed and traded in a local stock exchange must designate a transfer agent and registrar in the Philippines. As a general rule, a broker, dealer, or salesman must register with the SEC to do business in the country.

Changes During 1996

Exchange arrangements	*March 1.* The PDS mechanism to limit volatility in the exchange rate (by halting trading for 2 hours) was eliminated.
Imports and import payments	*May 16.* Certain quantitative restrictions on specified agricultural products were lifted.
	June 16. The requirement of prior clearance from the Department of Energy or the Energy Regulatory Board for importation of refined petroleum products and exportation of oil and petroleum products was abolished.
Exports and export proceeds	*April 17.* The authority to issue export declarations was transferred from the BSP to the Department of Trade and Industry, and the delegated authority of commercial banks and offshore banking units to issue and register export declarations was withdrawn.
Proceeds from invisible transactions and current transfers	*December 31.* The requirement to present a valid certification from the Inter-Agency Committee on Domestic Borrowings of Foreign Firms that the applicant foreign firm meets the guidelines prescribed by the Monetary Board on such domestic borrowings was eliminated.
Capital transactions	*August 1.* The functioning of the Inter-Agency Committee created to administer peso borrowings of foreign companies was discontinued effective January 1997.

Changes During 1997

Exchange arrangements	*February 8.* All forward transactions, including renewals thereof, from nonresidents require prior approval of the BSP. Official forward exchange cover for oil import financing was discontinued.
Payments for invisible transactions and current transfers	*January 15.* The Monetary Board Resolution No. 40 raised the ceiling for authorized banks to provide foreign exchange for these payments to $50,000 from $25,000.
Capital transactions	*February 6.* The issuance of peso-denominated instruments in the international capital markets, as well as inward remittances of foreign exchange to the Philippines and sale thereof for pesos to the local banking system and resident enterprises participating in such activity, require prior BSP approval.
	March 15. Loans of resident private sector borrowers from FCDUs and offshore sources, and nonresident loans serviced by foreign exchange purchased outside the banking system no longer require prior BSP approval. Foreign currency deposits are eligible as collateral for peso loans or foreign currency loans to residents and nonresidents.

POLAND

(Position as of March 31, 1997)

Status Under IMF Articles of Agreement

Article VIII   Date of acceptance: June 1, 1995.

Exchange Arrangement

Currency

The currency of Poland is the zloty, with 100 groszy per one zloty. New currency notes and coins were issued on January 1, 1995, replacing the old currency at a rate of 1 to 10,000. (Old currency remained in circulation until the end of 1996.)

Other legal tender

Coins made from precious metals are also legal tender.

Exchange rate structure

Unitary.

Classification

Managed floating

The central exchange rate of the zloty is pegged to a basket of 5 currencies. The central rate is adjusted under a crawling peg policy at a preannounced rate. Since May 16, 1995, the National Bank of Poland (NBP) has allowed the exchange rate of the zloty at the interbank market to fluctuate within margins of ±7% around the central rate. Once a day, the NBP quotes fixing rates (i.e., official market rates) for U.S. dollars and deutsche mark, with fixing rates for other convertible currencies determined on the basis of cross-exchange rates on international markets; fixing rates fluctuate within a ±7% margin around the central parity. The NBP quotes exchange rates daily for 20 convertible currencies, the ECU, and the SDR. Outside the interbank market, banks are permitted to set freely their buying and selling rates in transactions with their clients.

The exchange rate on the foreign exchange bureau market (kantors), in which natural persons are allowed to transact freely, provided that the transaction is not a commercial one, is determined by market forces.

Exchange tax

No.

Exchange subsidy

No.

Forward exchange market

There are no formal forward exchange market arrangements, but a forward market exists for the stock market. However, large commercial banks provide forward contracts if requested.

Arrangements for Payments and Receipts

Prescription of currency requirements

Outstanding balances under the inoperative bilateral payments agreements are being settled in accordance with the terms of the agreements. Balances outstanding under the arrangements of the International Bank for Economic Cooperation are still being settled in transferable rubles. Settlements with all other countries may be made in any convertible currency.

Payment arrangements

Bilateral arrangements

Inoperative

There are agreements with Bangladesh, Brazil, China, Egypt, India, Iraq, Russia, Syria, Tunisia, and Turkey.

Clearing agreements

There are inoperative agreements with members of the former CMEA.

Administration of control

Exchange control authorities

The authority to make basic changes in the Foreign Exchange Law rests with parliament. Regulations are promulgated by the Ministry of Finance (MOF), in cooperation with the president of the NBP, in the form of general foreign exchange permits, or by the president of the NBP in the form of individual permits. General permits are issued for all residents and nonresidents, and for specified groups. The procedures for issuing individual permits are established by the president of the NBP in cooperation with the MOF. Decisions concerning individual foreign exchange permits are subject to appeal to the Supreme Administrative Court. Foreign exchange control is exercised by the MOF, the NBP, foreign exchange banks, border guards, and post offices.

International security restrictions

In accordance with IMF Executive Board Decision No. 144-(52/51)	Poland notified the IMF that, in compliance with UN Security Council resolutions, it had imposed and maintained a ban on trade with Iraq and on exports of certain products to Libya and that licenses are required for trade (and transit through Poland) with Bosnia and Herzegovina.
In accordance with UN sanctions	There is a ban on the supply of weapons and military equipment to Liberia, Somalia, Angola (also for crude oil, the ban is applicable only to UNITA rebel forces), and Rwanda (the ban is applicable only to rebel forces).

Payment arrears   No.

Controls on trade in gold (coins and/or bullion)

Controls on domestic ownership and/or trade	Resident individuals may hold gold in any form; trading in gold, other than in jewelry form, is subject to permission from the NBP.
Controls on external trade	Polish and foreign nationals may take abroad gold coins that bear value in foreign exchange. They may also bring into Poland coins made from precious metals that are legal tender in Poland.

Controls on exports and imports of banknotes

On exports

   Foreign currency

Under the general foreign exchange permit, Polish nationals may take abroad up to ECU 5,000 or its equivalent in foreign currencies, checks, and traveler's checks. Documentary proof of origin is necessary for amounts exceeding this limit. Residents must repatriate foreign exchange within 2 months of returning to Poland. For official and business travel, allowances are based on separate regulations on business travel and on collective wage agreements. Nonresidents are free to take out of Poland up to ECU 2,000 or its equivalent; higher amounts are allowed up to the amount declared upon entry into the country.

On imports

   Foreign currency

Nonresidents entering Poland are permitted to have up to ECU 2,000 or its equivalent in convertible currencies; higher amounts must be declared upon entry into the country.

Resident Accounts

Eligibility to hold accounts	Juridical and natural persons are eligible.
Foreign exchange accounts permitted	Residents who are natural persons may maintain foreign currency accounts ("A" accounts), and these accounts may be freely credited with convertible currency brought in or transferred from abroad and/or deposited without declaring the sources of funds. Balances in these accounts can be sold in foreign bureau markets; withdrawals in zlotys, converted at the prevailing exchange rate, are freely permitted. Funds in A accounts cannot be used for business activities. When leaving the country permanently, individuals are allowed, under the general foreign exchange permit, to transfer all funds from this account.
Held domestically	These accounts are permitted, but prior approval is required.

Held abroad	Residents (individuals and enterprises) carrying out economic activity abroad may hold foreign exchange accounts abroad to cover costs of such activity. The NBP must be notified about accounts opened abroad, and quarterly balances in these accounts must be reported to the NBP.
Accounts in domestic currency convertible into foreign currency	No.

Nonresident Accounts

Eligibility to hold accounts	Juridical and natural persons are eligible. The same regulations apply to both.
Foreign exchange accounts permitted	There are two types of convertible currency accounts for nonresidents, natural, and juridical persons: (1) unrestricted accounts ("rachunek wolny") that may be opened in any licensed foreign exchange bank; they may or may not pay interest, depending on an agreement with the bank. Unrestricted accounts may be credited only with funds that are freely transferable abroad. These accounts may also be credited with domestic currency that could be converted into foreign currencies and transferred abroad. The following sources of funds allow later transfer abroad: (a) transfers from abroad or foreign currencies declared at the border; (b) claims on residents resulting from foreign transactions in goods, services, or intellectual property; (c) inheritances and bequests for foreign persons; (d) remuneration for legal work for residents; (e) documented income from securities legally acquired in Poland; (f) reimbursements for overpaid taxes; and (g) receivables resulting from court, administrative, or arbitrage rulings; and (2) "C" accounts that may be maintained only in convertible currencies; these accounts may or may not pay interest, depending on an agreement with the bank. There is no control on sources of funds deposited at C accounts. However, there are limitations on transfers abroad from C accounts, and the limitations are the same as for unrestricted accounts.
Domestic currency accounts	These accounts may or may not pay interest, depending on an agreement with the bank, and they can be credited with funds from any title, but conversion into foreign currency and/or transfer abroad is subject to authorization, except for funds freely transferable abroad (see unrestricted accounts above).
Convertible into foreign currency	These accounts are permitted, but prior approval is required.
Blocked accounts	No.

Imports and Import Payments

Foreign exchange budget	No.
Financing requirements for imports	No.
Documentation requirements for release of foreign exchange for imports	No.
Import licenses and other nontariff measures	Licenses are not required for imports from the convertible currency area, with the exception of imports of radioactive materials and military equipment; alcoholic beverages other than beer; tobacco products; crude oil and oils obtained from bituminous minerals; gasoline and light oils; natural gas and other gaseous hydrocarbons; and goods for industrial assembly of motor vehicles.
Negative list	The importation of passenger cars and other passenger vehicles older than 10 years; trucks, vans, other utility cars, and passenger vehicles older than 3 years for transportation of more than 10 persons; cars with 2-cycle engines; and combine harvesters is prohibited.
Licenses with quotas	The importation of petroleum oils and oils obtained from bituminous minerals is subject to quantitative quotas.

Import taxes and/or tariffs	All commercial imports, regardless of country of origin or provenance, are subject to an ad valorem import tariff. As of January 1, 1996, new import tariffs based on the Harmonized System (HS 1996) and the Combined Nomenclature of the EU (CN 1996) were introduced, with 6 basic rates: zero on equipment for the disabled, mineral resources, textiles, and cattle hides; up to 3.6% on other raw materials; 7.4% to 11% on basic parts of semifinished and finished goods; 14.6% to 27.4% on industrial goods; 26.6% to 40% on agriculture and textile products; and 30% on luxury goods. Imports from developing countries are granted preferential treatment under the GSP. Also, imports from 42 developing countries, tropical products from chapters 6 to 24 of the HS, and many goods from chapters 32 and 94 of the HS that are of interest to developing countries enter Poland duty free. For the remaining goods imported from non-European developing countries whose per capita GDP is lower than Poland's, duties are reduced by 20% to 30% of the MFN rate. Imports are subject to an import surcharge of 3%; duties and taxes on imports for export production are refunded.
Taxes collected through the exchange system	No.
State import monopoly	No.

Exports and Export Proceeds

Repatriation requirements	Proceeds should be repatriated immediately.
Surrender requirements	No.
Financing requirements	No.
Export licenses	Licenses are required for exports carried out within the framework of international agreements that stipulate bilateral settlements and for temporary exports of capital goods and transport equipment for leasing.
Without quotas	Exports of raw hides and skins of bovine or equine animals, pickled or otherwise preserved; raw skins of sheep and lambs; leather of bovine or equine animals, and other animals without fur; ferrous waste and scrap; remelting scrap ingots of iron and steel; and waste and scrap of copper, nickel, aluminum, lead, zinc, and tin are subject to quota restrictions.
With quotas	Licenses are required for exports of coal, petroleum oils, and oils obtained from bituminous minerals; crude petroleum gases and other gaseous hydrocarbons; radioactive materials; and military equipment. Export licenses are required for goods subject to export quotas. Exports that are prohibited include (1) live poultry, i.e., fowls of the species *Gallus Domesticus*, ducks, geese, turkeys, and guinea fowls; (2) goose eggs fresh, preserved, or cooked; and (3) trade with Libya with respect to chemical catalyzers, pipes and tubes, steel chains, hydraulic and gas pumps, chemical installations, laboratory equipment, and automation equipment. All trade with Iraq is prohibited.
Export taxes	No.

Payments for Invisible Transactions and Current Transfers

Controls on these payments	There are no controls on payments for freight and insurance, unloading and storage costs, administrative expenses, interest, commissions, medical treatment, study abroad, subscriptions and membership fees, consulting and legal fees, foreign workers' wages, the use of credit cards abroad, or on remittances of profits and dividends.
Payments for travel	
Quantitative limits	There is no specific limit for official and business travel. Official and business travelers are allowed to take out foreign currency bought in banks up to the amounts on separate regulations on business travel and on collective wage agreements.

Indicative limits/bona fide test	Yes.
Pensions	
Prior approval	Domestic individuals who wish to transfer their pension abroad have to apply for an individual foreign exchange permit.
Quantitative limits	Yes.
Indicative limits/bona fide test	Yes.
Gambling/prize earnings	
Prior approval	Yes.
Quantitative limits	Yes.
Family maintenance/alimony	No restrictions apply to alimony benefits granted to foreign nationals.
Prior approval	Yes.
Indicative limits/bona fide test	Yes.

Proceeds from Invisible Transactions and Current Transfers

Repatriation requirements	Proceeds must be repatriated immediately. Natural persons receiving proceeds while they are abroad must repatriate the proceeds within 2 months after returning to Poland.
Surrender requirements	No.
Restrictions on use of funds	No.

Capital Transactions

Controls on capital and money market instruments	
On capital market securities	
Purchase locally by nonresidents	Purchase of Polish securities by nonresidents is free, except for shares of which the freedom to purchase can be limited by Poland's restrictions of foreign direct investment.
Sale or issue locally by nonresidents	Nonresidents are permitted to issue securities with maturities of 1 year or longer; these securities must be approved by the Security and Exchange Commission, and the overall limit on purchase of such securities is set at ECU 200 million a year.
Purchase abroad by residents	In OECD countries and countries having agreements on investment protection with Poland, residents are permitted to (1) acquire stakes in foreign companies if the stake gives at least 10% of votes, and (2) purchase securities issued with maturity not less than 1 year up to the amount of ECU 1,000 or its equivalent.
Sale or issue abroad by residents	Residents are permitted to issue securities with maturity of 1 year and longer on foreign markets. Residents issuing securities abroad must notify the NBP within 20 days from the transaction.
On money market instruments	
Purchase locally by nonresidents	Yes.
Sale or issue locally by nonresidents	NBP approval is required.
Purchase abroad by residents	NBP approval is required.
Sale or issue abroad by residents	NBP approval is required.

On collective investment securities

    Purchase locally by nonresidents   n.a.

    Sale or issue locally by nonresidents   n.a.

    Purchase abroad by residents   Yes.

    Sale or issue abroad by residents   Yes.

Controls on derivatives and other instruments   Yes.

Controls on credit operations

Commercial credits   The NBP must be notified within 20 days of granting the credits.

Financial credits

    By residents to nonresidents   Financial credits with maturities of 1 year or more were liberalized by the general foreign exchange permit effective April 1996. Financial credits with maturities below 1 year continue to need a permit with the exception of authorized banks.

    To residents from nonresidents   An NBP's foreign exchange permit is required for residents contracting financial credits with nonresidents, with the exception of (1) credits granted by authorized banks; (2) credits granted to residents by international banks guaranteed by the Council of Ministers or the NBP for financing investments in the country; and (3) credits contracted by residents abroad with the maturity of 1 year or more from the date of contracting the credit.

Guarantees, sureties, and financial backup facilities

    By residents to nonresidents   An NBP's foreign exchange permit is required, with the exception of (1) guarantees or sureties provided by the authorized banks; (2) guarantees and sureties provided by residents to nonresidents for performing financial obligations under the purchase of goods, services, and incorporeal rights; and (3) guarantees and sureties for performing financial obligations of residents under foreign contracts for goods, services, and incorporeal rights.

    To residents from nonresidents   n.a.

Controls on direct investment

Outward direct investment   An NBP's foreign exchange permit is required, with the exception of (1) purchasing shares and interests of companies based in OECD countries and in the countries with which Poland has ratified agreements on the mutual safeguard of investments with the total value of investment up to the equivalent of ECU 1 million with shares comprising at least 10% of the total votes at respective shareholders' meetings, and (2) purchasing or opening a branch or company in OECD countries.

Inward direct investment   New businesses need to register only with local courts, with the exception of (1) mergers with state-owned companies if state assets are to be utilized for more than 6 months or if state assets will become part of the capital, and (2) investments in the areas of air transport, broadcasting, insurance, domestic long distance or mobile telecommunications, and gambling and betting. Imports of capital goods for new joint ventures are exempt from customs duties. Although the law does not stipulate a minimum amount of capital that foreign nationals must invest in Poland, the minimum capital requirement set forth in the Polish commercial code for a limited liability or equity company is in effect and is applied to foreign investment.

Controls on liquidation of direct investment   The transfer of profits from joint ventures and from investments in shares of Polish companies is not restricted, and invested capital may be repatriated once outstanding obligations to creditors are discharged.

Controls on real estate transactions

Purchase abroad by residents

An NBP's foreign exchange permit is required for the purchase abroad by residents (natural persons) of real estate located abroad at the price on the day of such purchase totaling in excess of the equivalent of ECU 50,000, and for the transfer abroad of the foreign currency required for the purchase of such real estate.

Purchase locally by nonresidents

Until recently, nonresidents could acquire real estate or other immovable property in Poland only with permission from the Ministry of the Interior, except in the form of an inheritance. The amended Law on Acquisition of Real Estate by Foreigners, which went into effect on May 4, 1996, maintained this general rule, but introduced several important exemptions. Foreigners may acquire real estate without permit if (1) it is a separate apartment; (2) they have lived in Poland for at least 5 years after getting a permanent residence visa; (3) they are married to a Polish citizen for at least 2 years (purchased real estate must form a part of matrimonial community of property); or (4) real estate is purchased by nonresident legal persons for statutory purposes, and the area of real estate does not exceed 4,000 square meters in urban areas. The Council of Ministers may issue a regulation defining other cases where a permit is not required, providing that the area of acquired real estate does not exceed 4,000 square meters in urban and 10,000 square meters in rural areas. The Council of Ministers may also extend the area to be acquired without permit to 12,000 square meters in urban and 30,000 square meters in rural areas.

Sale locally by nonresidents

An NBP foreign exchange permit is required for the transfer abroad by nonresidents of the proceeds associated with the sale of real estate converted into foreign currency.

Provisions specific to commercial banks and other credit institutions

Lending to nonresidents (financial or commercial credits)

Banks are permitted to purchase securities abroad within the limits specified in the regulation by the president of the NBP on the kinds of securities issued abroad to be purchased by authorized banks.

Open foreign exchange position limits

A bank's open (net) foreign currency position (long or short) in relation to a single foreign currency may not exceed 15% of the bank's capital. The president of the NBP, on the bank's motion, may consent to a foreign currency paid in consideration for equity to be included in computation of the bank's foreign currency position.

Provisions specific to institutional investors

There are no pension funds in Poland.

Insurance companies are not affected by the foreign exchange operations in the country, and a MOF permit is required to commence insurance business. The MOF permit is required for investments by nonresidents in insurance companies through shares allowing for 25%, 33%, 50%, 60%, and 75% of votes, respectively, at general shareholders' meetings. Currently, there are restrictions on start-up of foreign insurance companies operation in the country (they will be permitted to operate as of January 1999 under the MOF permit). Prudential regulations establishing limits for investment of insurance funds in the country and abroad are provided by the act on insurance operating activity.

Nonresidents are allowed to invest in participating units issued by trust funds. There are no foreign exchange restrictions on the transfer abroad by nonresidents of foreign currency purchase against Polish currency associated with remission of participating units in trust funds.

Limits (max.) on portfolio invested abroad

n.a.

Limits (min.) on portfolio invested locally

n.a.

Currency matching regulations on assets/liabilities composition

n.a.

Other controls imposed by securities laws

No.

Changes During 1996

Exchange arrangements

January 8. Rate of crawl was reduced by 1% a month.

Arrangements for payments and receipts

January 3. The ban on trade with the Federal Republic of Yugoslavia (Serbia/Montenegro), imposed in line with UN Security Council resolutions, was lifted.

Imports and import payments

January 1. Import tariffs were lowered to zero to 3.6% for raw materials; 7.4% to 11% for basic parts of semifinished and finished goods; 14.6% to 27.4% for industrial goods; 26.6% to 40% for agriculture and textile products; and 30% for luxury goods.

January 1. The import surcharge was lowered to 3% from 5%.

Capital transactions

February 1. Direct investments of the Polish residents in the OECD countries and countries that concluded bilateral agreements on investment protection with Poland were allowed up to the limit of ECU 1 million. Transfer of gifts and inheritance for family members, purchase of real estate abroad and purchase of publicly traded securities (with maturity not less than 1 year) issued in OECD countries, and borrowing and lending activities were also liberalized.

May 4. The amended Law on Acquisition of Real Estate by Foreigners became effective.

Changes During 1997

Payments for invisible transactions and current transfers

February 1. Residents were allowed to transfer abroad funds to meet their liabilities to foreign entities incurred before changing their status (in terms of foreign exchange regulations) to that of resident.

February 1. Residents were allowed to transfer deposits or surety deposits related to tender procedures abroad.

February 1. Foreign nationals acting as members of supervisory boards or boards of directors of corporations were permitted to transfer abroad their salaries.

Capital transactions

February 1. The limit for investment in securities issued in Poland by foreign entities and allowed for public trading by the Polish Security and Exchange Commission was raised to ECU 300,000,000. Residents were allowed to purchase publicly traded securities in OECD countries or in the countries that concluded bilateral agreements on investment protection with Poland. Purchases higher than ECU 50,000 require 3 months' notice to the NBP.

March 18. Insurers were permitted to purchase long-term securities traded in OECD countries or in the countries that concluded bilateral agreements on investment protection with Poland rated Aaa-Baa3 by Moody's or AAA-BBB by S&P. In case of short-term securities, the minimum ratings required are: Prime 1–3 (Moody's) or A1–A3 (S&P). Insurers may invest abroad no more than 5% of the funds covering their insurance fund.

PORTUGAL

(Position as of December 31, 1996)

Status Under IMF Articles of Agreement

Article VIII   Date of acceptance: September 12, 1988.

Exchange Arrangement

Currency   The currency of Portugal is the Portuguese escudo.

Exchange rate structure   Unitary.

Classification

Cooperative arrangement   Portugal participates in the ERM of the EMS.

Exchange tax   No.

Exchange subsidy   No.

Forward exchange market   Yes.

Official cover of forward operations   No.

Arrangements for Payments and Receipts

Prescription of currency   No.
requirements

Payment arrangements   No.

Administration of control

Exchange control authorities   There are no exchange controls. Foreign trade policy is implemented by the Ministry of Economy. The Direção-Geral do Comércio in this ministry is responsible for administering trade controls and for issuing import and export licenses, declarations, and certificates.

International security restrictions

In accordance with IMF Executive   Portugal notified the IMF on September 12, 1990, that certain restrictions were imposed
Board Decision No. 144-(52/51)   on payments and transfers for current international transactions to residents or nationals of Iraq. In addition, the movements of any funds in Portugal that are controlled by public authorities or companies of Libya are prohibited.

In accordance with UN sanctions   Yes.

Payment arrears   No.

Controls on trade in gold (coins   A customs declaration is required for amounts exceeding Esc 2.5 million.
and/or bullion)

Controls on exports and imports of   The exportation or importation by residents or nonresidents of banknotes or coins and
banknotes   traveler's checks exceeding the equivalent of Esc 2.5 million must be declared to customs.

Resident Accounts

Eligibility to hold accounts   Juridical and natural persons are eligible.

Foreign exchange accounts   Yes.
permitted

Held domestically   Yes.

Held abroad	Yes.
Accounts in domestic currency convertible into foreign currency	Yes.

Nonresident Accounts

Eligibility to hold accounts	Juridical and natural persons are eligible.
Foreign exchange accounts permitted	Yes.
Domestic currency accounts	Yes.
Convertible into foreign currency	Yes.
Blocked accounts	No.

Imports and Import Payments

Foreign exchange budget	No.
Financing requirements for imports	No.
Documentation requirements for release of foreign exchange for imports	No.
Import licenses and other nontariff measures	For products under EU surveillance, the appropriate import documents, when required, are issued for statistical purposes and are granted automatically in 4 or 5 days.
Negative list	Imports of certain products are subject to an import license and are allowed under specific conditions, or are prohibited for reasons of health, public order, or the prevention of commercial fraud. For agricultural products covered by the CAP, an import certificate may be required. A few industrial products, such as steel products and some textiles and clothing, are subject to EU import restrictions when they originate in certain third countries. A more extensive restricted list applying to China includes some textiles and a small number of finished products.
Licenses with quotas	Imports subject to quantitative restrictions require an import license. Generally, licenses are valid for 6 months for customs clearance purposes.
Import taxes and/or tariffs	Yes.
Taxes collected through the exchange system	No.
State import monopoly	No.

Exports and Export Proceeds

Repatriation requirements	No.
Surrender requirements	No.
Financing requirements	No.
Documentation requirements	No.
Export licenses	No.
Export taxes	n.a.
Taxes collected through the exchange system	No.

Payments for Invisible Transactions and Current Transfers

Controls on these payments   No.

Proceeds from Invisible Transactions and Current Transfers

Repatriation requirements   No.

Surrender requirements   No.

Restrictions on use of funds   No.

Capital Transactions

Controls on capital and money market instruments

On capital market securities

Sale or issue locally by nonresidents   Restrictions apply in the case of the introduction of foreign securities issued by residents of a non-EU member country and which are not quoted on a recognized market of the issuer's country or of the country in which they are issued.

Controls on derivatives and other instruments   No.

Controls on credit operations   No.

Controls on direct investment

Inward direct investment   Investments are permitted in all sectors except those that, under general law, are closed to private enterprise corporations. Foreign investments should be registered within 30 days after the operation has been made. Projects of special interest to the Portuguese economy are covered by a separate and contractual regime.

Controls on liquidation of direct investment   No.

Controls on real estate transactions   No.

Provisions specific to commercial banks and other credit institutions

Differential treatment of nonresident deposit accounts and/or deposit accounts in foreign exchange

Reserve requirements   Yes.

Provisions specific to institutional investors

Limits (max.) on portfolio invested abroad   Yes.

Currency matching regulations on assets/liabilities composition   There is a requirement of 80% of currency matching of assets owned by insurance companies and pension funds.

Other controls imposed by securities laws   The Ministry of Finance issues regulations on the eligible assets of insurance companies and pension funds and of securities investment funds.

Changes During 1996

No significant changes occurred in the exchange and trade system.

QATAR

(Position as of December 31, 1996)

Status Under IMF Articles of Agreement

Article VIII	Date of acceptance: June 4, 1973.

Exchange Arrangement

Currency	The currency of Qatar is the Qatar riyal.
Exchange rate structure	Unitary.
Classification	
Limited flexibility with respect to a single currency	The official exchange rate for the Qatar riyal is pegged to the SDR at QR 4.7619 per SDR 1, within margins of ±7.25% around this rate. The Qatar Central Bank (QCB) sets daily rates for the U.S. dollar, the intervention currency. Exchange rates of commercial banks for transactions in U.S. dollars are based on the QCB's buying and selling rates. A spread of QR 0.0087 is applied to exchange transactions with the public. The buying and selling rates of commercial banks for other currencies are based on the QCB's rates for the U.S. dollar and on market rates for the currency concerned against the U.S. dollar.
Exchange tax	No.
Exchange subsidy	No.
Forward exchange market	In the commercial banking sector, importers may purchase foreign exchange in the forward market.
Official cover of forward operations	No.

Arrangements for Payments and Receipts

Prescription of currency requirements	All settlements with Iraq and Israel are prohibited, as are all financial transactions with the Federal Republic of Yugoslavia (Serbia/Montenegro). No other prescription of currency requirements are in force.
Payment arrangements	No.
Administration of control	
Exchange control authorities	The QCB is the exchange control authority, but, at present, there is no exchange control legislation. Import licenses are issued by the Ministry of Finance, Economy, and Commerce.
International security restrictions	Financial transactions with the Federal Republic of Yugoslavia (Serbia/Montenegro) are prohibited.
In accordance with IMF Executive Board Decision No. 144-(52/51)	n.a.
In accordance with UN sanctions	n.a.
Payment arrears	No.
Controls on trade in gold (coins and/or bullion)	
Controls on external trade	For trading purposes, the buying and selling of gold and precious metals require import licenses and are subject to customs duty. Transactions involving Iraq and Israel are prohibited.
Controls on exports and imports of banknotes	No.

Resident Accounts

Eligibility to hold accounts	Yes.
Juridical persons	n.a.
Natural persons	n.a.
Foreign exchange accounts permitted	Yes.
Held domestically	Yes.
Held abroad	Yes.
Accounts in domestic currency convertible into foreign currency	Yes.

Nonresident Accounts

Eligibility to hold accounts	No distinction is made between accounts held by residents and those held by nonresidents.
Juridical persons	n.a.
Natural persons	n.a.
Foreign exchange accounts permitted	Yes.
Domestic currency accounts	Yes.
Convertible into foreign currency	These accounts are permitted, but prior approval is required.

Imports and Import Payments

Foreign exchange budget	No.
Financing requirements for imports	No.
Documentation requirements for release of foreign exchange for imports	No.
Import licenses and other nontariff measures	Imports of alcoholic beverages, firearms, ammunition, and certain drugs are subject to licensing for reasons of health or public policy.
Negative list	All imports from Iraq and Israel are prohibited, as are imports of pork and its derivatives.
Open general licenses	n.a.
Import taxes and/or tariffs	Imports are generally subject to a customs tariff of 4%, which is the minimum rate applied by members of the GCC. The customs tariff on steel is 20%; on tobacco, 50%; and on alcohol, 100%. Imports from GCC member countries are exempt from tariffs.
Taxes collected through the exchange system	No.
State import monopoly	No.

Exports and Export Proceeds

Repatriation requirements	No.

Surrender requirements	No.
Financing requirements	No.
Documentation requirements	No.
Export licenses	No.
Export taxes	No.

Payments for Invisible Transactions and Current Transfers

Controls on these payments	There are no limitations on these payments, but payments to Iraq and Israel are prohibited.

Proceeds from Invisible Transactions and Current Transfers

Repatriation requirements	No.
Surrender requirements	No.
Restrictions on use of funds	No.

Capital Transactions

Controls on capital and money market instruments	No.
Controls on derivatives and other instruments	No.
Controls on credit operations	No.
Controls on direct investment	
Inward direct investment	Noncitizens may engage in simple crafts as well as in commerce, industry, agriculture, and services jointly with Qatari partners, who must hold at least 51% of the capital. Noncitizens may also establish companies specializing in contracting business with Qatari partners, subject to the above conditions, if it is determined that there is a need to establish such companies, or if there is a need for the experience and technology they provide.
Controls on liquidation of direct investment	No.
Controls on real estate transactions	No.
Provisions specific to commercial banks and other credit institutions	
Lending locally in foreign exchange	n.a.
Purchase of locally issued securities denominated in foreign exchange	n.a.
Provisions specific to institutional investors	No.
Other controls imposed by securities laws	No.

Changes During 1996

No significant changes occurred in the exchange and trade system.

ROMANIA

(Position as of May 31, 1997)

Status Under IMF Articles of Agreement

Article XIV	Yes.

Exchange Arrangement

Currency	The currency of Romania is the Romanian leu (plural lei).
Other legal tender	The convertible ruble continues to be used as a unit of account for outstanding CMEA balances.
Exchange rate structure	Unitary.

Classification

Independent floating

The exchange rate against the U.S. dollar (the reference exchange rate) is determined in the interbank foreign exchange market. The National Bank of Romania (NBR) intervenes in the exchange market to smooth out fluctuations in exchange rates and to build up foreign exchange reserves. Only 4 commercial banks authorized by the NBR could participate in the exchange market during most of 1996. In early 1997, the NBR reinstated dealer licenses to all commercial banks. Juridical persons other than authorized commercial banks may purchase or sell foreign exchange through authorized banks. The NBR quotes rates for 23 other currencies based on the rates for these currencies against the U.S. dollar in the countries concerned, and for the ECU. Foreign exchange bureaus conduct transactions only in foreign currency banknotes and traveler's checks and only with natural persons, and are free to set their exchange rates.

Forward exchange market	Yes.
Official cover of forward operations	n.a.

Arrangements for Payments and Receipts

Prescription of currency requirements	Payments to and from countries with which Romania has bilateral payments arrangements are made only in the currency and in accordance with the procedures set forth in those arrangements.

Payment arrangements

Bilateral arrangements

Operative	There are arrangements with China, the Democratic People's Republic of Korea, Pakistan, and some CMEA countries.
Inoperative	There are arrangements with Albania, Algeria, Costa Rica, Egypt, Greece, India, and the Islamic Republic of Iran.
Regional arrangements	n.a.
Clearing agreements	There are clearing arrangements with Bangladesh and CMEA countries, but they are only used to settle previous balances.
Barter agreements and open accounts	n.a.

Administration of control

Exchange control authorities	The NBR issues rules and regulations related to the control of foreign exchange transactions, and authorizes all capital transfers, including those connected with inheritances and the liquidation of capital assets owned by foreign natural persons.

The Ministry of Finance (MOF) grants visas for certain payments abroad. Domestic commercial banks are authorized by the NBR to conduct foreign exchange transactions abroad for current international transactions.

Payment arrears

Private   Yes.

Controls on trade in gold (coins and/or bullion)

Controls on domestic ownership and/or trade

The NBR has sole authority to purchase or to sell gold in any manner. It may grant permission to certain juridical persons for such purposes.

Controls on external trade   There are no actual authorizations for conducting external trade.

Controls on exports and imports of banknotes

On exports

   Domestic currency   Until April 21, 1997, resident natural persons could take out up to Lei 100,000 a person a trip in denominations no larger than Lei 5,000; on that date, the limits were changed to Lei 500,000 a person a trip and in denominations no larger than Lei 10,000.

   Foreign currency   Foreign nationals may take out their foreign currency deposited with authorized commercial banks or an amount equivalent to that which they brought into Romania. Residents may take out $5,000 a trip.

On imports

   Domestic currency   Until April 21, 1997, up to Lei 100,000 a person a trip in denominations no larger than Lei 5,000 could be brought in; on that date, the limit was raised to Lei 500,000 a person a trip in denominations no larger than Lei 10,000.

   Foreign currency   Natural persons may bring into Romania up to the equivalent of $10,000 a person a trip.

Resident Accounts

Eligibility to hold accounts

Juridical persons   These accounts may be held by (1) juridical persons who are registered in Romania (i.e., public institutions, embassies, consulates, other Romanian representatives abroad); (2) autonomous state agencies, commercial companies, associations, clubs, leagues, and any other profit or nonprofit juridical persons authorized to carry on activities within the Romanian territory; and (3) foreign branches, subsidiaries, representatives, and agencies.

Natural persons   These accounts may be held by (1) Romanian citizens, (2) natural persons with foreign citizenship, and (3) stateless persons living in Romania.

Foreign exchange accounts permitted

Yes.

Held domestically   Resident companies that are not exporters of goods and services may receive payment in foreign exchange from other resident companies if authorized by the NBR.

Held abroad   Resident persons need NBR approval.

Accounts in domestic currency convertible into foreign currency

Full convertibility is permitted for current account transactions. Convertibility for capital account transactions is limited and requires prior approval of the NBR.

Nonresident Accounts

Eligibility to hold accounts

Juridical persons | These accounts may be held by (1) juridical persons that are not registered and authorized to function within the Romanian territory; (2) foreign embassies, consulates, or other representatives, as well as international organizations or representatives of international organizations functioning within the Romanian territory; and (3) Romanian branches, subsidiaries, representatives, and agencies that carry out their activities and are registered abroad.

Natural persons | These accounts may be held by (1) foreign citizens working for embassies, consulates, or other representatives, as well as international organizations; (2) representatives of international organizations operating in Romania; (3) other foreign citizens; and (4) stateless persons.

Foreign exchange accounts permitted | Yes.

Domestic currency accounts | Applies to domestic currency obtained from legal activities in Romania.

Convertible into foreign currency | Convertibility is permitted, provided that the accounts are established under the provisions of the Foreign Investment Law (1991).

Blocked accounts | No.

Imports and Import Payments

Foreign exchange budget | No.

Financing requirements for imports

Advance payment requirements | A bank guarantee is required before an advance payment is made whenever there is a previous advance payment outstanding (i.e., goods not yet delivered).

Documentation requirements for release of foreign exchange for imports | Documents establishing that goods have been delivered must be presented to commercial banks.

Import licenses and other nontariff measures | Imports, in general, are not subject to licensing. The government may restrict imports for reasons of public health, national defense, and state security, in accordance with the provisions of the WTO.

Negative list | Yes.

Open general licenses | n.a.

Licenses with quotas | n.a.

Import taxes and/or tariffs | Tariff rates range between 2% and 35%, averaging about 17% for all goods on a trade-weighted basis. Tariffs ranging from zero to 40% are being applied in 1997 to cover at least 70% of all agricultural tariff positions.

Taxes collected through the exchange system | No.

State import monopoly | No.

Exports and Export Proceeds

Repatriation requirements | Resident juridical persons must maintain foreign exchange export proceeds in accounts opened at domestic commercial banks or foreign commercial banks authorized to operate in Romania but are free to use the balances in these accounts.

Surrender requirements	No.
Documentation requirements	No.
Export licenses	
Without quotas	n.a.
With quotas	Exports of timber, livestock, sunflower seeds, maize, certain mineral oils, chemical fertilizers, and copper alloys are subject to quotas. Exports of wheat, butter, a few hydrocarbon products, certain minerals, blood-based products, logs and wood products, and scrap metals were suspended, in some cases, on a temporary basis in 1996. Export restrictions on livestock, sunflower seeds, maize, and wheat were eliminated on May 1, 1997.

Payments for Invisible Transactions and Current Transfers

Controls on these payments	All payments and transfers must be documented. There are no controls on payments for freight and insurance, unloading and storage costs, administrative expenses, commissions, medical costs, study abroad, subscriptions and membership fees, consulting and legal fees, foreign workers' wages, family maintenance and alimony, interest, and credit card use abroad. Loans and credits from nonresidents abroad must be authorized by the NBR. Nonresidents may remit earnings from gambling and prizes freely.
Profit/dividends	
Quantitative limits	Only foreign investors holding an investor's certificate issued by the Romanian Development Agency may repatriate profits and dividends.
Indicative limits/bona fide test	Yes.
Payments for travel	
Quantitative limits	The limit is $5,000 a person a trip.
Pensions	
Prior approval	n.a.

Proceeds from Invisible Transactions and Current Transfers

Repatriation requirements	Yes.
Surrender requirements	No.
Restrictions on use of funds	No.

Capital Transactions

Controls on capital and money market instruments	
On capital market securities	
Sale or issue locally by nonresidents	Requires NBR approval and MOF endorsement.
Purchase abroad by residents	Requires NBR approval and MOF endorsement.
Sale or issue abroad by residents	Requires NBR approval and MOF endorsement.
On money market instruments	
Sale or issue locally by nonresidents	Requires NBR approval and MOF endorsement.

Purchase abroad by residents	Requires NBR approval and MOF endorsement.
Sale or issue abroad by residents	Requires NBR approval and MOF endorsement.

On collective investment securities

Sale or issue locally by nonresidents	Requires NBR approval and MOF endorsement.
Purchase abroad by residents	Requires NBR approval and MOF endorsement.
Sale or issue abroad by residents	Requires NBR approval and MOF endorsement.

Controls on derivatives and other instruments

Sale or issue locally by nonresidents	Requires NBR approval and MOF endorsement.
Purchase abroad by residents	Requires NBR approval and MOF endorsement.
Sale or issue abroad by residents	Requires NBR approval and MOF endorsement.

Controls on credit operations

Commercial credits	All commercial credits are subject to authorization. NBR approval is required for credits of over 1-year maturity, and commercial bank approval for credits of 1 year or less.
By residents to nonresidents	Yes.
To residents from nonresidents	Yes.
Financial credits	Yes.
Guarantees, sureties, and financial backup facilities	n.a.

Controls on direct investment

Outward direct investment	Requires NBR approval and MOF endorsement.
Controls on liquidation of direct investment	No.

Controls on real estate transactions

Purchase abroad by residents	NBR authorization is required.
Purchase locally by nonresidents	Nonresidents cannot purchase real estate.

Provisions specific to commercial banks and other credit institutions

Borrowing abroad	Resident banks are allowed to borrow abroad, but only with the authorization of the NBR.
Lending to nonresidents (financial or commercial credits)	NBR authorization is required.
Lending locally in foreign exchange	Banking companies are permitted to lend locally in foreign currency only for current foreign exchange operations.
Purchase of locally issued securities denominated in foreign exchange	Yes.
Differential treatment of nonresident deposit accounts and/or deposit accounts in foreign exchange	n.a.
Investment regulations	n.a.
Open foreign exchange position limits	n.a.

Changes During 1996

Exports and export proceeds

June 6. Exports of wheat, butter, a few hydrocarbon products, certain minerals, blood products, logs and wood products, and scrap metals were suspended.

Changes During 1997

Exports and export proceeds

May 1. Export restrictions on livestock, sunflower seeds, maize, and wheat were eliminated.

RUSSIAN FEDERATION

(Position as of December 31, 1996)

Status Under IMF Articles of Agreement

Article VIII   Date of acceptance: June 1, 1996.

Exchange Arrangement

Currency   The currency of Russia is the Russian ruble.

Exchange rate structure   Unitary.

Classification

Managed floating   The Central Bank of Russia (CBR) announces an official exchange rate each day along with rates at which it is willing to buy and sell. The official exchange rate is based on interbank market exchange rates and is used for accounting and taxation purposes, and for operations with the Ministry of Finance (MOF). An exchange rate band of Rub 5,000–Rub 5,600 per $1, was applied in the first half of 1996, while a corridor was applied in the second half, starting at Rub 5,000–Rub 5,600 and sliding on a daily basis at a rate of 1.5% per month to Rub 5,500–Rub 6,100 per $1 at end-December 1996. For 1997, the band that began at Rub 5,500–Rub 6,100 is to slide smoothly to Rub 5,750–Rub 6,350 at the end of the year. In addition to an active interbank market, auction markets are also organized in Moscow and other major cities. The U.S. dollar is the intervention currency of the CBR in the Moscow Interbank Currency Exchange (MICEX) and on other exchanges where the CBR operates. The CBR participates in the MICEX as a net buyer and seller of the U.S. dollar to smooth out short-term fluctuations in the exchange rate; it occasionally trades in foreign exchange through direct dealing on the interbank market outside the auctions.

Exchange tax   No.

Exchange subsidy   No.

Forward exchange market   A futures trading market has developed in Moscow and is regulated as part of the CBR exposure limits, and forward contracts are sold by authorized banks.

Official cover of forward operations   The CBR provides forward contracts to authorized commercial banks in conjunction with the "S" account scheme for nonresidents to repatriate the proceeds of their investment in government securities.

Arrangements for Payments and Receipts

Prescription of currency requirements   Yes.

Payment arrangements

Bilateral arrangements

   Operative   An agreement is maintained with India.

   Inoperative   Agreements are maintained with Bulgaria, China, Cuba, the Czech Republic, Egypt, Hungary, India, the Islamic State of Afghanistan, Mongolia, Poland, the Slovak Republic, Slovenia, and the Syrian Arab Republic.

Clearing agreements   Yes.

Administration of control

Exchange control authorities   The CBR is responsible for administering exchange control regulations, supervising and monitoring transactions of authorized banks, and regulating banks' open foreign exchange positions.

International security restrictions

In accordance with IMF Executive Board Decision No. 144-(52/51)	Certain restrictions against the Federal Republic of Yugoslavia (Serbia/Montenegro) apply.
In accordance with UN sanctions	Yes.

Payment arrears

Official	Yes.

Controls on trade in gold (coins and/or bullion)

Controls on domestic ownership and/or trade	Domestic trade in gold is not permitted. Monetary gold intended to be part of the country's foreign exchange reserves is purchased by the CBR and the government at world prices quoted on the London market and converted at the market exchange rate.
Controls on external trade	Transactions in precious metals (gold and silver bullion) require authorization, and transactions must be made through authorized banks possessing a special license issued by the CBR.

Controls on exports and imports of banknotes

On exports

Domestic currency	Residents and nonresidents traveling to areas where the Russian ruble is sole legal tender are allowed to take out a maximum of Rub 500,000 in banknotes.
Foreign currency	There are no limits on the amount of foreign banknotes a person may take out of the country, provided that a certificate from an authorized bank on the origin of the funds is presented to customs.

On imports

Domestic currency	n.a.

Resident Accounts

Eligibility to hold accounts	Juridical and natural persons are eligible.

Foreign exchange accounts permitted

Held domestically	Balances on these accounts may be used for effecting current foreign exchange transactions. The use of foreign exchange proceeds for capital transactions, with the exception of certain specific individual transactions, requires a CBR license.
Held abroad	Resident natural persons may maintain bank accounts abroad only during their stay outside Russia for the purpose of education, employment, medical treatment, or visiting. Upon return to Russia, bank accounts abroad must be closed, and balances must be credited to the accounts held in authorized banks operating in the territory of Russia. Resident juridical persons, including branches of Russian banks, may not maintain accounts abroad without special permission from the CBR. Resident banks may open correspondent accounts abroad in accordance with the procedures set out in the CBR's foreign exchange licenses. Authorized Russian banks are allowed to open correspondent accounts in the Baltic countries and the other countries of the FSU without restriction, provided that they comply with the regulation on exposure limits. Prior approval is required.
Accounts in domestic currency convertible into foreign currency	Yes.

Nonresident Accounts

Eligibility to hold accounts

Juridical and natural persons are eligible.

Foreign exchange accounts permitted

Yes.

Domestic currency accounts

Nonresidents may maintain 5 types of ruble accounts: (1) "T" accounts, which may be credited with proceeds from current international transactions (including proceeds from sales of goods and services to residents of Russia and interest earnings on the account itself), and debited for the servicing of export-import operations by their representative offices in Russia; (2) correspondent ruble accounts for nonresident banks under the same regime applicable to T accounts; (3) "I" accounts, which can be used for investment activities (including privatization operations); (4) nonresident accounts for natural persons; and (5) "S" accounts for transactions involving government securities. The transfer abroad of balances in T accounts and correspondent ruble accounts accumulated after June 1, 1996, is not restricted. The use of balances accumulated up to May 31, 1996, is limited to domestic transactions. I accounts may be used for a wide range of investment activities, including profit and dividend transfers. Balances maintained on I accounts may be transferred abroad without restriction after payment of applicable taxes. Nonresident natural and juridical persons may purchase foreign exchange only with ruble balances held in I accounts.

Convertible into foreign currency

These accounts are permitted, but prior approval is required.

Blocked accounts

No.

Imports and Import Payments

Foreign exchange budget

No.

Financing requirements for imports

No.

Documentation requirements for release of foreign exchange for imports

Domiciliation requirements

n.a.

Preshipment inspection

n.a.

Letters of credit

n.a.

Import licenses and other nontariff measures

Imports are generally free of quotas and licenses. Licenses are required for imports of medicine, raw materials for the production of medicine and pesticides, vodka and ethyl alcohol, and industrial waste.

Negative list

n.a.

Import taxes and/or tariffs

Most customs duties range from 5% to 15%; but some tariffs may attain 150%. The following imports are exempt from duties: foodstuffs, medicine, medical supplies and equipment, printed materials, children's articles, accompanied baggage up to $2,000 in value, equipment for the oil and gas industries, and ships and boats. Customs duties on imports from CIS countries and from developing countries are half the normal rates.

Taxes collected through the exchange system

No.

Exports and Export Proceeds

Repatriation requirements

The repatriation ratio is 100%.

Surrender requirements

Residents must sell 50% of export earnings through authorized banks.

Financing requirements	CBR permission is required for foreign exchange transactions associated with deferred payments for exports of goods exceeding 180 days and deferrals granted to residents for making advance payments against deliveries of imported goods exceeding 180 days.
Export licenses	Export licensing is limited to a small group of products (e.g., military equipment and arms, gold, diamonds, other precious metals and stones, certain food products, wildlife medicine, chemical raw materials for the production of medicine, and minerals). Export licenses are issued in accordance with application procedures established by the Ministry of Foreign Economic Relations. A limited number of goods determined by the Ministry of Environment may be exported only under a licensing regime.
With quotas	Yes.
Export taxes	Export duties are levied on about 100 product groups. Specific duties are denominated in ECU while ad valorem rates range up to 30%. There are numerous exemptions granted on a case-by-case basis.
Taxes collected through the exchange system	No.

Payments for Invisible Transactions and Current Transfers

Controls on these payments	Payments for invisibles are not restricted. Purchase of foreign exchange for all bona fide invisible transactions from authorized banks are allowed with proper documentation.

Proceeds from Invisible Transactions and Current Transfers

Repatriation requirements	Yes.
Surrender requirements	Proceeds from invisibles, except those from banking services, are subject to the surrender requirement.
Restrictions on use of funds	No.

Capital Transactions

Controls on capital and money market instruments

On capital market securities

Purchase locally by nonresidents	Nonresidents can purchase from residents securities denominated in foreign exchange or rubles with foreign exchange, as well as securities denominated in foreign exchange with rubles. Residents need prior authorization from the CBR for these transactions.
	No prior authorization is required to purchase securities denominated in rubles with rubles. Securities denominated in rubles or in foreign exchange may be purchased with funds from type T ruble accounts. Securities denominated in foreign exchange or in rubles with maturity over 1 year may be purchased with funds from type I accounts as well as from ruble correspondent accounts of nonresident banks.
	The parties shall notify the Federal Securities Market Commission (FKRTsB) of transactions involving the purchase by nonresidents of securities issued by residents.
Sale or issue locally by nonresidents	Nonresidents can sell to residents securities denominated in foreign exchange or in rubles with foreign exchange, as well as securities denominated in foreign exchange with rubles, provided residents have authorization from the CBR. The sale by nonresidents of securities denominated in rubles with rubles requires prior authorization. The parties to transactions shall notify the FKRTsB of concluded transactions for the purchase by residents of securities issued by nonresidents.

Securities issued by nonresidents are permitted to circulate or be initially placed in the securities market after registration of their prospectus with the FKRTsB. The face value of these securities should be denominated in rubles.

Foreign exchange proceeds from the sale of securities are credited to foreign exchange accounts opened by nonresidents in authorized banks, from which they may be freely transferred abroad. Ruble proceeds from the sale of securities and from securities issues may be credited to type T ruble accounts of nonresidents opened in authorized banks, or to ruble correspondent accounts of nonresident banks.

Purchase abroad by residents

Prior CBR approval is required.

Sale or issue abroad by residents

CBR approval is required. Proceeds from the sale are credited to current foreign exchange accounts of residents. Exports of securities by residents require prior authorization from the MOF and the State Customs Committee.

On money market instruments

Purchase locally by nonresidents

For nongovernment instruments, the same regulations as for capital markets apply.

The purchase by nonresidents of government short-term bonds (GKOs) and federal bonds (OFZs) is carried out from type S accounts. Nonresidents may not purchase more than 20% of an issue and may not invest funds for a term of fewer than 2 months. The export of profits is restricted by the size of compensation transactions.

Sale or issue locally by nonresidents

The same regulations as for capital market securities apply.

Purchase abroad by residents

The same regulations as for capital market securities apply.

Sale or issue abroad by residents

The same regulations as for capital market securities apply.

On collective investment securities

Transactions with nonresidents in foreign exchange may be carried out only if residents have authorization from the CBR to conclude such transactions. The parties should notify the FKRTsB of concluded transactions.

Purchase locally by nonresidents

The FKRTsB should be notified on purchases by nonresidents of collective investment securities issued by residents.

Sale or issue locally by nonresidents

Collective investment securities issued by nonresidents require registration of the prospectus for the securities with the FKRTsB. The face value of these securities must be denominated in rubles.

Foreign exchange proceeds from the sale of these securities must be credited to foreign exchange accounts and may be freely transferred abroad.

Purchase abroad by residents

Residents need prior authorization from the CBR to transfer foreign exchange in order to purchase these securities abroad. Funds for these purchases may be transferred from current foreign exchange accounts.

Residents need prior authorization from the CBR to purchase securities denominated in foreign exchange in Russia.

Sale or issue abroad by residents

The sale abroad by residents of collective investment securities for foreign exchange of prior authorization from the CBR and the transfer of proceeds from the sale requires prior authorization from the CBR. Proceeds from the sale are credited to current foreign exchange accounts.

Collective investment securities issued by a resident may circulate abroad, provided FKRTsB approval is granted. Residents may issue collective investment securities abroad with prior authorization from the CBR. The export by residents of collective investment securities requires prior authorization from the CBR and the State Customs Committee.

Controls on derivatives and other instruments

Purchase locally by nonresidents	Purchases in foreign exchange are permitted, provided residents have prior authorization from the CBR. The purchase of derivatives with rubles may be carried out freely from type T ruble accounts.
Sale or issue locally by nonresidents	Proceeds from sales of foreign exchange are allowed, provided the residents have prior authorization from the CBR. Foreign exchange proceeds may be freely transferred abroad.
	Ruble proceeds from sales may be used only within the territory of Russia or may be credited to ruble correspondent accounts of nonresident banks.
Purchase abroad by residents	Purchases are permitted, provided prior authorization from the CBR to transfer foreign exchange is granted. The transfer of funds to purchase derivatives abroad must be carried out from foreign exchange accounts.
Sale or issue abroad by residents	Sales are permitted with prior authorization from the CBR. The transfer of proceeds from the sales requires prior authorization from the CBR. Proceeds must be credited to current foreign exchange accounts.

Controls on credit operations

Commercial credits

    By residents to nonresidents — Credits in the form of prepayment for imported commodities with delivery within 180 days may be extended only after prior authorization from the CBR.

    To residents from nonresidents — Resident legal entities may borrow in the form of deferred payment for commodities exported by the resident for a period of more than 180 days only after prior authorization from the CBR.

Financial credits

    By residents to nonresidents — Credits for a term of more than 180 days may be extended only after prior authorization from the CBR.

    To residents from nonresidents — Residents may borrow for a term of more than 180 days only after prior authorization from the CBR.

Guarantees, sureties, and financial backup facilities

    By residents to nonresidents — Guarantees in foreign exchange are freely extended to residents by authorized banks that have the requisite banking license from the CBR. The performance of obligations under bank guarantees, as well as under surety agreements in which the party extending the surety is a resident that is not an authorized bank, may be carried out only after prior authorization from the CBR.

Controls on direct investment

Outward direct investment	Investments must be authorized by the CBR.
Inward direct investment	Investment through joint ventures or through outright ownership is not restricted, except in banking, where it is limited to 12% of aggregate authorized capital; exploration of natural resources, where a special license is required; and landownership, where it is prohibited. Enterprises with foreign capital shares must register with the Ministry of Economy. Investments exceeding Rub 100 million require a permit from the Council of Ministers. Foreign direct investments are accorded the same rules and privileges with regard to property ownership and economic activities as those accorded to residents. Foreign direct investments may be nationalized or expropriated only in exceptional cases in accordance with legislation, and, in such cases, the investor is entitled to compensation. Provisions protecting foreign investment, including a "grandfather" clause that protects foreign investment for a 3-year period from regulatory acts that would adversely affect their activities and a provision that any restrictions on activities of foreign investor can be introduced only by Russian law or by presidential decree.
Controls on liquidation of direct investment	Liquidation requires prior authorization from the CBR. The transfer abroad of proceeds is carried out by selling ruble funds credited to type I ruble accounts for foreign exchange, which may be freely exported.

Controls on real estate transactions

Purchase abroad by residents — CBR approval is required.

Purchase locally by nonresidents — Landownership is prohibited.

Provisions specific to commercial banks and other credit institutions

Borrowing abroad — Borrowing by banks possessing a general foreign exchange license does not require a special license.

Maintenance of accounts abroad — Authorized banks may open correspondent accounts in banks abroad pursuant to the terms specified in the banking license issued by the CBR (restrictions may be imposed on the number of banks that may open correspondent accounts). The opening of other types of accounts in banks abroad requires the prior authorization of the CBR.

Lending to nonresidents (financial or commercial credits) — Yes.

Lending locally in foreign exchange — A CBR license is required.

Purchase of locally issued securities denominated in foreign exchange — A CBR license is required.

Differential treatment of nonresident deposit accounts and/or deposit accounts in foreign exchange

  Reserve requirements — Different reserve requirements apply to deposits in local and foreign currency, but no distinction is made between resident and nonresident holders.

  Liquid asset requirements — n.a.

  Interest rate controls — n.a.

  Credit controls — n.a.

Investment regulations — n.a.

Open foreign exchange position limits — The limits are set in absolute amounts and differ according to the banks' capital as follows: (1) for capital up to Rub 1 billion, the limit is $100,000, while the limit/capital ratio may not be less than 33%; (2) for capital of Rub 1 to Rub 5 billion, the limit is $500,000, while the limit/capital ratio is in the range of 33% to 165%; (3) for capital of Rub 5 to Rub 10 billion, the limit is $1 million, while the limit/capital ratio is in the range of 33% to 66%; and (4) for banks with capital above Rub 10 billion, individual limits are set by the CBR.

Provisions specific to institutional investors — Investment by institutional investors in securities denominated in foreign exchange requires the prior authorization of the CBR.

Limits (max.) on portfolio invested abroad — Resident insurance companies may invest up to 20% abroad.

Limits (min.) on portfolio invested locally — Resident insurance companies must invest at least 80% locally.

Currency matching regulations on assets/liabilities composition — n.a.

Other controls imposed by securities laws — The federal law on the securities market states that the prohibition against giving preference to 1 potential owner over another in the purchase of securities does not apply to nonresidents.

Changes During 1996

Status under IMF Articles of Agreement — *June 1.* Russia accepted the obligations of Article VIII, Sections 2, 3, and 4 of the Fund Agreement.

Exchange arrangements

January 1. The band for the official exchange rate was set between Rub 4,550 and Rub 5,150.

May 17. The daily official exchange rate is to be determined on the basis of rates of major commercial banks in the interbank market. The CBR also announces rates on either side of the official rate at which they are willing to buy and sell foreign exchange.

July 1. A sliding corridor for the exchange rate was introduced beginning at Rub 5,000 to Rub 5,600 per dollar and sliding on a daily basis at a rate of 1.5% a month to Rub 5,500 to Rub 6,100 per dollar as of end-December.

Nonresident accounts

August 15. The CBR introduced a revised scheme to allow nonresidents greater access to the government securities market through S accounts. Under this scheme, nonresidents may participate in the market on the same basis as residents. The only proviso is that a nonresident must enter into a forward contract before repatriating balances from these accounts. An exchange rate guarantee is extended by the CBR through the quotation of forward exchange rates on a proportion of the amount to be repatriated. The proportion covered by the CBR, the guaranteed return, and the minimum contract maturity period were lowered in several steps in late 1996 to 50%, 12.5%, and 2 months respectively at end-1996 from 90%, 19%, and 3 months in August 1996.

RWANDA

(Position as of December 31, 1996)

Status Under IMF Articles of Agreement

Article XIV	Yes.

Exchange Arrangement

Currency	The currency of Rwanda is the Rwanda franc.
Exchange rate structure	Unitary.
Classification	
Independent floating	The exchange rate of the Rwanda franc is determined freely in the exchange market in which commercial banks and foreign exchange bureaus operate. Banks may apply a variable commission to these operations. Outward and inward transfers are subject to a commission of 4‰; as from July 17, 1996, the commission ceased to be applied to export financing loans. Export financing loans and loan servicing (repayment of principal and interest) are exempted from this commission. The National Bank of Rwanda (NBR) does not announce official exchange rates, but it calculates and publishes daily the average market exchange rate for reference purposes.
Exchange tax	No.
Exchange subsidy	No.
Forward exchange market	No.

Arrangements for Payments and Receipts

Prescription of currency requirements	No.
Payment arrangements	
Regional arrangements	The NBR maintains agreements with the central banks of the CEPGL, Burundi, and the Democratic Republic of the Congo. Under these arrangements, settlements are made through reciprocal accounts in convertible domestic currency. Payments to and from other member countries of the COMESA are made through the COMESA's clearinghouse.
Clearing agreements	Yes.
Barter agreements and open accounts	An arrangement exists with Uganda, but is not operational.
Administration of control	
Exchange control authorities	Foreign exchange control is vested in the NBR, which has delegated authority to authorized banks to carry out some of the controls.
International security restrictions	No.
Payment arrears	
Official	Yes.
Private	Yes.
Controls on trade in gold (coins and/or bullion)	
Controls on domestic ownership and/or trade	Trade is restricted to dealers approved by the relevant ministry.

Controls on external trade	Imports and exports of gold require a declaration.
Controls on exports and imports of banknotes	
On exports	
Domestic currency	A declaration is required for exports of banknotes exceeding the equivalent of $100.
Foreign currency	Only foreign exchange purchased from an authorized dealer may be exported freely. Foreign exchange declared to customs on entry in the country or in amounts not exceeding the equivalent of $10,000 may be reexported.
On imports	
Domestic currency	Declaration is required for import of banknotes exceeding the equivalent of $100.

Resident Accounts

Eligibility to hold accounts	Juridical and natural persons are eligible.
Foreign exchange accounts permitted	Yes.
Held domestically	Yes.
Held abroad	These accounts are permitted, but prior approval is required.
Accounts in domestic currency convertible into foreign currency	No.

Nonresident Accounts

Eligibility to hold accounts	Juridical and natural persons are eligible.
Foreign exchange accounts permitted	Yes.
Domestic currency accounts	Yes.
Convertible into foreign currency	No.
Blocked accounts	No.

Imports and Import Payments

Foreign exchange budget	No.
Financing requirements for imports	No.
Documentation requirements for release of foreign exchange for imports	Imports must be accompanied by a pro forma invoice stating the f.o.b. value.
Preshipment inspection	Imports with f.o.b. value of $10,000 or more and any partial deliveries of these goods must be inspected by an international agency with regard to the quality, quantity, price, and customs tariff of the goods before being shipped to Rwanda, unless otherwise provided by the NBR.
Import licenses used as exchange licenses	Yes.

Import licenses and other nontariff measures

Negative list

All imports of narcotics are prohibited. Certain categories of imports, such as explosives and weapons, require prior approval from the relevant authorities, regardless of origin and value. For reasons of health, the importation of human or veterinary medicines, disinfectants, insecticides, rodent poisons, fungicides, herbicides, and other toxic or potentially toxic chemicals is subject to approval of the pro forma invoices by the Ministry of Health.

Open general licenses

Yes.

Import taxes and/or tariffs

In addition to customs duties, a file processing charge equal to 1% of f.o.b. value is levied on imports at the time of declaration to cover the costs of the preshipment inspection agency.

Taxes collected through the exchange system

No.

State import monopoly

No.

Exports and Export Proceeds

Repatriation requirements

Proceeds must be repatriated within 7 days from the date of payment.

Surrender requirements

On December 26, 1996, the ratio of earnings from coffee and tea exports that must be sold to commercial banks at a freely negotiated exchange rate was reduced to 50% from 90%.

Financing requirements

No.

Documentation requirements

All exports, except trade samples and personal and household effects of travelers, are subject to prior declaration to the authorized banks.

Export licenses

Without quotas

Yes.

Export taxes

A tax on coffee exports is levied on the tonnage ranging from $101/ton to $1,650/ton. This taxation procedure varies depending on the harvest.

Taxes collected through the exchange system

No.

Payments for Invisible Transactions and Current Transfers

Controls on these payments

There are no controls on payments for freight and insurance, unloading and storage costs, administrative expenses, commissions, subscriptions and membership fees, consulting and legal fees, pensions, gambling and prize earnings, and the use of credit cards abroad.

Interest payments

Payments are permitted on loans for which the NBR was given prior notification of the loan contract and for which the funds were initially received by a local commercial bank.

Profit/dividends

Prior approval

Approval by authorized banks is required. Approval is subject to appropriate auditing of the accounts and a decision by the board of directors of the company.

Payments for travel

Quantitative limits

Official travel requires a travel authorization by the government or by an authorized agency. Daily allowances are granted for such travel. Businessmen may purchase up to $10,000 in payment instruments for each trip, but the number of business trips is not restricted. A maximum allowance of $4,000 a trip is granted for tourism.

Medical costs

   Quantitative limits — Residents may purchase up to $20,000 without supporting documents, unless provided by the NBR; prior authorization by the NBR is required for transfers of $20,000 or more.

Study abroad costs

   Quantitative limits — There is a limit of $25,000 a year, on presentation of supporting documents.

   Indicative limits/bona fide test — Yes.

Foreign workers' wages — Salaries and wages earned by foreign nationals employed in Rwanda under contract, net of taxes and employee's share of social security contributions, may be transferred abroad. The net earned income of self-employed foreign nationals, whether engaged in a profession or established as independent traders, may also be transferred abroad after payment of taxes. A fee of 0.4% is levied on transfers abroad. Payment of the employee's share of social security contributions and taxes is required.

   Prior approval — Prior authorization from the NBR is required for amounts exceeding $20,000 a year.

   Indicative limits/bona fide test — Yes.

Family maintenance/alimony

   Quantitative limits — The annual limit for expenses for a resident's family members living abroad is $1,000.

   Indicative limits/bona fide test — Yes.

Proceeds from Invisible Transactions and Current Transfers

Repatriation requirements — Yes.

Surrender requirements — Proceeds may be sold in the domestic foreign exchange market or may be held in foreign exchange accounts with banks located in the country.

Restrictions on use of funds — No.

Capital Transactions

Controls on capital and money market instruments — All outward transfers of capital require the prior approval of the NBR.

On capital market securities

   Purchase locally by nonresidents — n.a.

   Sale or issue locally by nonresidents — n.a.

   Purchase abroad by residents — Yes.

   Sale or issue abroad by residents — n.a.

On money market instruments

   Purchase locally by nonresidents — n.a.

   Sale or issue locally by nonresidents — n.a.

   Purchase abroad by residents — Yes.

   Sale or issue abroad by residents — n.a.

On collective investment securities

   Purchase locally by nonresidents — n.a.

Sale or issue locally by nonresidents	n.a.
Purchase abroad by residents	Yes.
Sale or issue abroad by residents	n.a.
Controls on derivatives and other instruments	Yes.
Purchase locally by nonresidents	n.a.
Sale or issue locally by nonresidents	n.a.
Purchase abroad by residents	Yes.
Sale or issue abroad by residents	n.a.
Controls on credit operations	
Commercial credits	
By residents to nonresidents	Credits are subject to NBR approval.
To residents from nonresidents	n.a.
Financial credits	
By residents to nonresidents	Credits are subject to NBR approval.
To residents from nonresidents	n.a.
Guarantees, sureties, and financial backup facilities	
By residents to nonresidents	These transactions are subject to NBR approval.
To residents from nonresidents	n.a.
Controls on direct investment	
Outward direct investment	Investments are subject to NBR approval.
Inward direct investment	n.a.
Controls on liquidation of direct investment	Repatriation of investments by nonresidents must be registered by authorized banks.
Controls on real estate transactions	
Purchase abroad by residents	Yes.
Purchase locally by nonresidents	n.a.
Sale locally by nonresidents	n.a.
Provisions specific to commercial banks and other credit institutions	
Borrowing abroad	Borrowing is allowed under certain conditions.
Lending to nonresidents (financial or commercial credits)	Lending is allowed under certain conditions.
Lending locally in foreign exchange	n.a.
Purchase of locally issued securities denominated in foreign exchange	n.a.
Differential treatment of nonresident deposit accounts and/or deposit accounts in foreign exchange	
Reserve requirements	Yes.

Liquid asset requirements	Yes.
Interest rate controls	The NBR sets the refinancing rate from time to time. Banks freely set their borrowing rates.
Credit controls	A 25% ceiling is applied to banks' own funds. Beyond this level, authorization from the NBR is required within the limit of 20% of banks' own funds. Foreign exchange amounts in excess of these limits must be sold on the market.
Investment regulations	Yes.
Open foreign exchange position limits	A prudential limit of 20% of banks' own funds is applied.
Provisions specific to institutional investors	No.

Changes During 1996

Exchange arrangements	*July 17.* Export financing loans were exempted from the 0.4‰ commission applied to outward and inward transfers.
Exports and export proceeds	*December 26.* The surrender requirement for coffee and tea export proceeds was reduced to 50% from 90%.

ST. KITTS AND NEVIS

(Position as of December 31, 1996)

Status Under IMF Articles of Agreement

Article VIII   Date of acceptance: December 3, 1984.

Exchange Arrangement

Currency

The currency of St. Kitts and Nevis is the Eastern Caribbean dollar, issued by the ECCB.

Exchange rate structure   Unitary.

Classification

Pegged

The Eastern Caribbean dollar is pegged to the U.S. dollar, the intervention currency, at EC$2.70 per US$1. The ECCB also quotes daily rates for the Canadian dollar and the pound sterling.

Exchange tax   No.

Exchange subsidy   No.

Forward exchange market   No.

Arrangements for Payments and Receipts

Prescription of currency requirements

Settlements with residents of ECCB countries must be effected in Eastern Caribbean dollars.

Payment arrangements   No.

Administration of control

Exchange control authorities

Exchange control is administered by the Ministry of Finance (MOF) and applies to all countries.

Payment arrears   No.

Controls on trade in gold (coins and/or bullion)   No.

Controls on exports and imports of banknotes   No.

Resident Accounts

Eligibility to hold accounts

Juridical persons   Yes.

Natural persons   n.a.

Foreign exchange accounts permitted

U.S. dollar accounts may be operated freely, but permission of the MOF is required to operate other foreign currency accounts.

Held domestically

Permission to open these accounts is normally confined to major exporters. These accounts may be credited only with foreign currency earned or received from abroad and may be freely debited. A minimum balance of US$1,000 must be maintained at all times to operate a U.S. dollar account.

Held abroad   n.a.

Nonresident Accounts

Eligibility to hold accounts	Juridical and natural persons are eligible.
Foreign exchange accounts permitted	Permission to open foreign currency accounts is normally confined to foreign nationals not ordinarily residing in St. Kitts and Nevis. The same regulations for credits and debits as for resident accounts held domestically apply.

Imports and Import Payments

Foreign exchange budget	No.
Financing requirements for imports	
Minimum financing requirements	n.a.
Advance payment requirements	Advance payments for imports in currencies other than U.S. dollars require prior approval from the MOF.
Advance import deposits	n.a.
Documentation requirements for release of foreign exchange for imports	Payments for authorized imports payable in U.S. dollars are permitted on presentation of documentary evidence of purchase to a bank, but payments in currencies other than the U.S. dollar need the approval of the MOF.
Domiciliation requirements	n.a.
Preshipment inspection	n.a.
Letters of credit	n.a.
Import licenses used as exchange licenses	n.a.
Import licenses and other nontariff measures	Individual licenses are required for imports that compete with local products unless they come from another member country of the CARICOM.
Positive list	n.a.
Negative list	n.a.
Open general licenses	Most goods are imported under open general licenses.
Licenses with quotas	n.a.
Import taxes and/or tariffs	St. Kitts and Nevis applies the common external tariff of CARICOM, which ranges up to 30%.
Taxes collected through the exchange system	No.

Exports and Export Proceeds

Repatriation requirements	Yes.
Surrender requirements	Export proceeds must be deposited into an ECCB currency account or an approved U.S. dollar account.
Export licenses	Specific licenses are required for the exportation of certain goods to any destination. However, the regulations governing export licenses are not formally adhered to.
Without quotas	n.a.
Export taxes	Export duties are levied on a few products.
Taxes collected through the exchange system	No.

Payments for Invisible Transactions and Current Transfers

Controls on these payments

All settlements overseas require exchange control approval, except when the currency involved is the U.S. dollar, in which case commercial banks are authorized to pay on presentation of documentary evidence. Where the currency involved is not the U.S. dollar, application must be made directly to the MOF; authorization is normally granted for certain specific purposes and services. As of January 26, 1996, individuals are permitted to purchase up to EC$100,000 without exchange control approval. Profits and dividends may be remitted in full, subject to confirmation of registration by the Commissioner of Inland Revenue for income tax purposes.

Specific information on the application of quantitative limits, indicative limits, and bona fide tests is not available.

Payments for travel

Quantitative limits

Residents may purchase foreign exchange from authorized banks up to the equivalent of EC$100,000 a year without authorization from the MOF.

Indicative limits/bona fide test

Travel allocations can be increased in bona fide cases with the authorization of the MOF.

Proceeds from Invisible Transactions and Current Transfers

Repatriation requirements

Yes.

Surrender requirements

Proceeds must be sold to a bank or deposited into an approved U.S. dollar account if the proceeds are in U.S. dollars.

Capital Transactions

Controls on capital and money market instruments

All outward capital transfers require exchange control approval.

On capital market securities

Purchase locally by nonresidents

For purchases of equity shares, an Aliens Land Holding license is required.

Sale or issue locally by nonresidents

Foreign exchange approval from the MOF is required for amounts exceeding EC$100,000.

Purchase abroad by residents

Same regulations apply as for sale or issue by nonresidents of capital market securities.

On money market instruments

Sale or issue locally by nonresidents

Same regulations apply as for sale or issue by nonresidents of capital market securities.

Purchase abroad by residents

Same regulations apply as for sale or issue by nonresidents of capital market securities.

On collective investment securities

Purchase locally by nonresidents

Same regulations apply as for sale or issue by nonresidents of capital market securities.

Sale or issue locally by nonresidents

Same regulations apply as for sale or issue by nonresidents of capital market securities.

Sale or issue abroad by residents

The seller of the instruments has to be licensed under the Banking Act, and transfers abroad in excess of EC$100,000 require approval from the MOF.

Controls on derivatives and other instruments

Presently, there is no market in derivatives and other instruments.

Controls on credit operations

Financial credits

  By residents to nonresidents   MOF approval and payment of a 2.5% Aliens Loan Levy is required for these transactions.

  To residents from nonresidents Foreign exchange approval from the MOF is required for amounts exceeding EC$100,000.

Guarantees, sureties, and financial backup facilities Foreign exchange approval from the MOF is required for amounts exceeding EC$100,000.

Controls on direct investment

Outward direct investment Foreign exchange approval from the MOF is required for amounts exceeding EC$100,000.

Inward direct investment Investments in equity require an Aliens Land Holding license.

Controls on liquidation of direct investment The remittance of proceeds of the liquidation of direct investments is permitted, subject to the discharge of any liabilities related to the investment. Transfer of proceeds exceeding EC$100,000 requires MOF approval.

Controls on real estate transactions

Purchase abroad by residents Purchasing real estate abroad for private purposes is not normally permitted.

Purchase locally by nonresidents n.a.

Sale locally by nonresidents n.a.

Provisions specific to commercial banks and other credit institutions

Lending to nonresidents (financial or commercial credits) MOF approval and payment of a 2.5% Aliens Loan Levy are required.

Lending locally in foreign exchange MOF approval is required, which is granted only in the case of projects generating foreign exchange to service the loan. The purchase of locally issued securities denominated in foreign currencies requires MOF approval.

Purchase of locally issued securities denominated in foreign exchange n.a.

Provisions specific to institutional investors No regulations exist.

Other controls imposed by securities laws No.

Changes During 1996

Payments for invisible transactions and current transfers *January 26.* Individuals were allowed to purchase up to EC$100,000 to effect any foreign exchange transaction.

ST. LUCIA

(Position as of December 31, 1996)

Status Under IMF Articles of Agreement

Article VIII   Date of acceptance: May 30, 1980.

Exchange Arrangement

Currency   The currency of St. Lucia is the Eastern Caribbean dollar issued by the ECCB.

Exchange rate structure   Unitary.

Classification

Pegged   The Eastern Caribbean dollar is pegged to the U.S. dollar, the intervention currency, at EC$2.70 per US$1. The ECCB also quotes daily rates for the Canadian dollar and the pound sterling.

Exchange tax   No.

Exchange subsidy   No.

Forward exchange market   No.

Arrangements for Payments and Receipts

Prescription of currency requirements   Settlements with residents of member countries of the CARICOM, except for Guyana, Jamaica, and Trinidad and Tobago, must be made either in the currency of the CARICOM country concerned or in Eastern Caribbean dollars. Settlements with residents of other countries may be made either in any foreign currency or in Eastern Caribbean dollars. When justified by the nature of the transaction, approval may be given to make payments for goods and services in a currency other than that of the country to which payment is to be made.

Payment arrangements   No.

Administration of control

Exchange control authorities   The Ministry of Finance, Statistics, and Negotiating (MFSN) applies exchange control to all currencies other than the Eastern Caribbean dollar.

International security restrictions   No.

Payment arrears   No.

Controls on trade in gold (coins and/or bullion)   No.

Controls on exports and imports of banknotes   No.

Resident Accounts

Eligibility to hold accounts   Juridical and natural persons are eligible.

Foreign exchange accounts permitted   Yes.

Held domestically   Since March 1, 1996, approval is no longer required.

Held abroad   Permission is granted in special cases where the applicant earns foreign exchange and has to make frequent payments abroad. Prior approval is required.

Accounts in domestic currency convertible into foreign currency	No.

Nonresident Accounts

Eligibility to hold accounts	Juridical and natural persons are eligible.
Foreign exchange accounts permitted	These accounts are permitted, but prior approval is required.
Domestic currency accounts	External accounts in Eastern Caribbean dollars may be opened for nonresident individuals and companies with the approval of the MFSN. These accounts may be credited only with foreign drafts or checks, but hotels may also deposit currency notes in them. Such accounts may be debited for payments to residents payable in Eastern Caribbean dollars and, after approval by the MFP, for the cost of foreign exchange required for travel or business purposes.
Convertible into foreign currency	These accounts are permitted, but approval is required is required for transactions exceeding EC$100,000.
Blocked accounts	No.

Imports and Import Payments

Foreign exchange budget	No.
Financing requirements for imports	
Minimum financing requirements	n.a.
Advance payment requirements	Advance payments require prior approval from the MFSN, for amounts exceeding EC$100,000.
Advance import deposits	n.a.
Documentation requirements for release of foreign exchange for imports	Payments in foreign currency for authorized imports are permitted upon application to a local bank and submission of certified customs entry.
Domiciliation requirements	n.a.
Preshipment inspection	n.a.
Letters of credit	n.a.
Import licenses used as exchange licenses	n.a.
Import licenses and other nontariff measures	
Negative list	Certain agricultural and manufactured products require individual licenses, unless they are imported from CARICOM countries.
Licenses with quotas	n.a.
Import taxes and/or tariffs	St. Lucia applies the Common External Tariff (CET) of up to 35% (except for certain agricultural goods). A customs service charge of 2% of the c.i.f. value is levied on all imports except for fertilizers, for which the rate is 0.2%. Exempt from import duties are live animals, milk, meat, fish, eggs, fertilizers, and most agricultural and manufacturing machinery. Goods produced in CARICOM countries may enter duty free.
Taxes collected through the exchange system	No.
State import monopoly	The importation of selected consumer items (e.g., rice, flour, and sugar) in bulk form is a state monopoly.

Exports and Export Proceeds

Repatriation requirements	Requirements were abolished on March 1, 1996.
Surrender requirements	Requirements were abolished on March 1, 1996.
Export licenses	Export licensing is required for certain primary products.
Without quotas	n.a.
With quotas	n.a.
Export taxes	A duty of 2.5% is levied on the f.o.b. value of banana exports. A special fee of US$0.02 per barrel is applied to reexports of petroleum.
Taxes collected through the exchange system	n.a.

Payments for Invisible Transactions and Current Transfers

Controls on these payments	Approval is required for transactions exceeding EC$100,000. There are no controls on payments for travel and for subscriptions and membership fees.
Freight/insurance	
Prior approval	Yes.
Indicative limits/bona fide test	Yes.
Unloading/storage costs	
Prior approval	Yes.
Indicative limits/bona fide test	Yes.
Administrative expenses	
Prior approval	Yes.
Indicative limits/bona fide test	Yes.
Commissions	
Prior approval	Yes.
Quantitative limits	Yes.
Indicative limits/bona fide test	Yes.
Interest payments	
Prior approval	Yes.
Quantitative limits	Yes.
Indicative limits/bona fide test	Yes.
Profit/dividends	
Prior approval	Yes.
Quantitative limits	With the approval of the MFSN, profits may be remitted in full, subject to confirmation by the Comptroller of Inland Revenue that local tax liabilities have been discharged. However, in cases where profits are deemed to be high, the MFSN reserves the right to phase remittances over a reasonable period.
Indicative limits/bona fide test	n.a.

Proceeds from Invisible Transactions and Current Transfers

Repatriation requirements   Requirements on proceeds of up to EC$100,000 were abolished on March 1, 1996.

Surrender requirements   No.

Capital Transactions

Controls on capital and money market instruments   Outward transfers exceeding EC$100,000 require exchange control approval.

On capital market securities

    Purchase locally by nonresidents   n.a.

    Sale or issue locally by nonresidents   n.a.

    Purchase abroad by residents   Yes.

    Sale or issue abroad by residents   n.a.

On money market instruments

    Purchase locally by nonresidents   n.a.

    Sale or issue locally by nonresidents   n.a.

    Purchase abroad by residents   Yes.

    Sale or issue abroad by residents   n.a.

On collective investment securities

    Purchase locally by nonresidents   n.a.

    Sale or issue locally by nonresidents   n.a.

    Purchase abroad by residents   Yes.

    Sale or issue abroad by residents   n.a.

Controls on derivatives and other instruments

Purchase locally by nonresidents   These transactions require approval from the MFSN (a person who has not resided in St. Lucia for 3 consecutive years is declared a nonresident).

Sale or issue locally by nonresidents   n.a.

Purchase abroad by residents   n.a.

Sale or issue abroad by residents   n.a.

Controls on credit operations

Commercial credits

    By residents to nonresidents   These credits require approval of the MFSN. Applications for nonresident loans are submitted by the authorized dealer (or other financial intermediary) to the MFSN on behalf of the applicant.

    To residents from nonresidents   Yes.

Financial credits   Yes.

Guarantees, sureties, and financial backup facilities   Yes.

Controls on direct investment

Outward direct investment	Yes.
Inward direct investment	Yes.

Controls on real estate transactions

Purchase abroad by residents	Yes.
Purchase locally by nonresidents	Nonresidents who purchase property are taxed at a higher rate than residents.
Sale locally by nonresidents	Amounts exceeding EC$100,000 require approval for repatriation of estate proceeds.

Provisions specific to commercial banks and other credit institutions

Borrowing abroad	Yes.
Maintenance of accounts abroad	Yes.
Lending to nonresidents (financial or commercial credits)	There are controls on loans exceeding EC$100,000.
Lending locally in foreign exchange	n.a.
Purchase of locally issued securities denominated in foreign exchange	n.a.
Differential treatment of nonresident deposit accounts and/or deposit accounts in foreign exchange	n.a.
Investment regulations	n.a.
Open foreign exchange position limits	n.a.

Changes During 1996

Arrangements for payments and receipts	*March 1.* Amounts exceeding EC$100,000 for current and capital transactions require MFSN approval.
Resident accounts	*March 1.* Foreign currency accounts may be maintained without prior approval from the MFSN.
Exports and export proceeds	*March 1.* Repatriation and surrender requirements were abolished.
Payments for invisible transactions and current transfers	*March 1.* Payments in excess of EC$100,000 require MFSN approval.
Proceeds from invisible transactions and current transfers	*March 1.* Repatriation and surrender requirements were abolished.
Capital transactions	*March 1.* Transfers abroad in excess of EC$100,000 require MFSN approval.

ST. VINCENT AND THE GRENADINES

(Position as of January 31, 1997)

Status Under IMF Articles of Agreement

Article VIII	Date of acceptance: August 24, 1981.

Exchange Arrangement

Currency	The currency of St. Vincent and the Grenadines is the Eastern Caribbean dollar, which is issued by the ECCB.
Exchange rate structure	Unitary.
Classification	
Pegged	The Eastern Caribbean dollar is pegged to the U.S. dollar, the intervention currency, at EC$2.70 per US$1.
Forward exchange market	No.
Official cover of forward operations	No.

Arrangements for Payments and Receipts

Prescription of currency requirements	Settlements with residents of member countries of the CARICOM can be made in any currency. Settlements with residents of other countries may be made in any foreign currency or through an external account in Eastern Caribbean dollars.
Payment arrangements	No.
Administration of control	
Exchange control authorities	Exchange control is administered by the Ministry of Finance (MOF), and applies to all countries outside the ECCB area. The MOF delegates to authorized dealers the authority to approve some import payments and certain other payments.
Payment arrears	No.
Controls on trade in gold (coins and/or bullion)	
Controls on domestic ownership and/or trade	Residents are permitted to acquire and hold gold coins for numismatic purposes only.
Controls on external trade	Imports of gold are permitted under license by the MOF for industrial purposes only.
Controls on exports and imports of banknotes	
On exports	n.a.

Resident Accounts

n.a.

Nonresident Accounts

Eligibility to hold accounts	Yes.
Juridical persons	n.a.

Natural persons	n.a.
Foreign exchange accounts permitted	These accounts may be opened by nonresidents with the authorization of the MOF and credited only with funds in the form of remittances from overseas. Except with the prior permission of the MOF, remittances in Eastern Caribbean currency, foreign currency notes and coins, and payments by residents may not be credited to a foreign currency account. These accounts may be debited for payments abroad without prior authorization from the MOF. The operating banks must submit quarterly statements of the accounts to the MOF.
Domestic currency accounts	External accounts may be opened for nonresidents with the authorization of the MOF. They are maintained in Eastern Caribbean dollars and may be credited with inward remittances in foreign currency and with transfers from other external accounts. Credits and debits to these accounts are subject to the same regulations as for foreign exchange accounts.
Convertible into foreign currency	n.a.

Imports and Import Payments

Foreign exchange budget	No.
Financing requirements for imports	
Minimum financing requirements	n.a.
Advance payment requirements	Advance payments for imports over EC$100,000 require prior approval from the MOF.
Advance import deposits	n.a.
Documentation requirements for release of foreign exchange for imports	Payments for authorized imports are permitted upon application and submission of documentary evidence and, where required, of the license.
Domiciliation requirements	n.a.
Preshipment inspection	n.a.
Letters of credit	n.a.
Import licenses used as exchange licenses	n.a.
Import licenses and other nontariff measures	Most goods may be freely imported. Imports of some goods that compete with typical exports of other member countries of the CARICOM and the OECS are subject to licenses.
Positive list	n.a.
Negative list	Imports of goods that compete with locally made products are prohibited in some cases.
Open general licenses	n.a.
Licenses with quotas	n.a.
Other nontariff measures	n.a.
Import taxes and/or tariffs	Effective January 1997, the import tariff rates range from zero to 25%. In addition, imports are subject to a consumption tax, ranging from 5% to 50% and levied on the tariff-inclusive value of imports. Goods imported from the member countries of the CARICOM are exempt from import tariffs and are subject only to the consumption tax. A customs service charge of 2.5% is imposed on the c.i.f. value of all imported goods with certain exceptions.
Taxes collected through the exchange system	n.a.

Exports and Export Proceeds

Repatriation requirements	Yes.
Surrender requirements	All export proceeds must be surrendered within 6 months.
Export licenses	Specific licenses are required for the exportation to any destination of some agricultural goods included in the CARICOM marketing protocol and in the CARICOM Oils and Fats Agreement. The licenses are issued by the Ministry of Trade, which, in some cases, has delegated its authority to the St. Vincent Central Marketing Corporation. Exports of goats, sheep, and lobsters are subject to licensing to prevent depletion of stocks.
Without quotas	n.a.
With quotas	n.a.
Export taxes	A 2% export duty is levied on bananas.
Taxes collected through the exchange system	n.a.

Payments for Invisible Transactions and Current Transfers

Controls on these payments	Payments for invisibles related to authorized imports (i.e., freight and insurance, unloading and storage, administrative expenses, commissions), for medical costs, expenses for study abroad, subscriptions and membership fees, consulting and legal fees, interest payments, and remittances of profits and dividends are not restricted. Other payments exceeding EC$100,000 must be approved by the MOF; approval is routinely granted.
Payments for travel	A 5% tax is levied on the value of all tickets for travel originating in St. Vincent and the Grenadines, whether or not they are purchased in the country.
Quantitative limits	The limits are the equivalent of EC$2,500 a year for travel outside the ECCB area, and EC$6,000 a year for business travel.
Indicative limits/bona fide test	These allocations may be increased with the authorization of the MOF.

Proceeds from Invisible Transactions and Current Transfers

Repatriation requirements	Yes.
Surrender requirements	Yes.

Capital Transactions

Controls on capital and money market instruments	All outward capital transfers require exchange control approval.
On capital market securities	
Purchase locally by nonresidents	n.a.
Sale or issue locally by nonresidents	n.a.
Purchase abroad by residents	Residents are normally not permitted to purchase foreign currency securities abroad for private purposes.
Sale or issue abroad by residents	n.a.
On money market instruments	
Purchase locally by nonresidents	n.a.

Sale or issue locally by nonresidents	n.a.
Purchase abroad by residents	Yes.
Sale or issue abroad by residents	n.a.
On collective investment securities	
Purchase locally by nonresidents	n.a.
Sale or issue locally by nonresidents	n.a.
Purchase abroad by residents	Yes.
Sale or issue abroad by residents	n.a.

Controls on credit operations

Commercial credits

By residents to nonresidents	MOF approval is required.
To residents from nonresidents	n.a.

Financial credits

By residents to nonresidents	Yes.
To residents from nonresidents	n.a.
Guarantees, sureties, and financial backup facilities	n.a.

Controls on direct investment

Outward direct investment	Yes.

Controls on liquidation of direct investment	The remittance of proceeds is permitted, subject to the discharge of any liabilities related to the investment.

Controls on real estate transactions

Purchase abroad by residents	Yes.
Purchase locally by nonresidents	Yes.
Sale locally by nonresidents	n.a.

Provisions specific to commercial banks and other credit institutions

Borrowing abroad	Any borrowing abroad by authorized dealers to finance their domestic operations requires the approval of the MOF.
Maintenance of accounts abroad	n.a.
Lending to nonresidents (financial or commercial credits)	n.a.
Lending locally in foreign exchange	n.a.
Purchase of locally issued securities denominated in foreign exchange	n.a.
Differential treatment of nonresident deposit accounts and/or deposit accounts in foreign exchange	n.a.
Investment regulations	n.a.
Open foreign exchange position limits	n.a.

Changes During 1996

Imports and import payments

January 1. The maximum import tariff was reduced to 30% from 35%.

January 1. The custom service charge was increased to 2.5% from 2%.

March 31. Advance payment for imports requires prior approval from the MOF only if the amount exceeds EC$100,000.

Payments for invisible transactions and current transfers

March 31. Current account transactions were liberalized for amounts below EC$100,000. Prior approval, quantitative limits, and indicative limits/bona fide tests were eliminated for (1) medical costs, (2) expenses for study abroad, (3) subscriptions and membership fees, and (4) consulting/legal fees that do not exceed EC$100,000.

Changes During 1997

Imports and import payments

January 1. The import tariff rate range was narrowed to zero to 25% from zero to 35%.

SAN MARINO

(Position as of December 31, 1996)

Status Under IMF Articles of Agreement

Article VIII	Date of acceptance: September 23, 1992.

Exchange Arrangement

Currency	The currency of San Marino is the Italian lira.
Other legal tender	The monetary agreement between San Marino and Italy, renewed on December 21, 1991, provides for San Marino to issue annually agreed amounts of San Marino lira coins equivalent in form to Italian coinage; these coins will be legal tender in both countries. The San Marino gold scudo is also issued, but is legal tender only in San Marino. It is not generally used in transactions because its numismatic value exceeds its defined legal value (Lit 50,000 per 1 scudo).
Exchange rate structure	Unitary.
Classification	Pegged.
Exchange tax	No.
Exchange subsidy	No.
Forward exchange market	Forward transactions may be conducted through commercial banks without restriction at rates quoted in Italian markets.
Official cover of forward operations	No.

Arrangements for Payments and Receipts

Prescription of currency requirements	Settlements with foreign countries are made in convertible currencies or in lire on foreign accounts.
Payment arrangements	No.
Administration of control	
Exchange control authorities	The Central Bank of San Marino (CBSM) may grant foreign exchange dealer status to Sammarinese financial institutions; currently, Sammarinese banks may maintain accounts only with financial institutions in Italy. As a result, foreign exchange transactions of domestic banks are effectively limited to buying foreign exchange at rates similar to those quoted in Italy and to conducting third-country transactions through Italian correspondents.
	Residents of San Marino are allowed to conduct foreign exchange transactions freely, with settlement effected through authorized Italian intermediaries (the Bank of Italy, the Italian Foreign Exchange Office, authorized banks, and the Postal Administration). Direct settlements (with residents drawing on their own external accounts) authorized under Italian Exchange Control Regulations in 1990 have not yet been utilized.
International security restrictions	No.
Payment arrears	No.
Controls on trade in gold (coins and/or bullion)	
Controls on domestic ownership and/or trade	n.a.
Controls on external trade	International trade in gold is governed by the Italy-San Marino Agreement on Financial and Exchange Relations.

725

Resident Accounts

Eligibility to hold accounts   Juridical and natural residents are free to maintain any type of deposit accounts; in practice, deposit accounts other than in lire are not offered by domestic banks.

Foreign exchange accounts permitted   Yes.

Held domestically   Yes.

Held abroad   Yes.

Accounts in domestic currency convertible into foreign currency   Yes.

Nonresident Accounts

Eligibility to hold accounts   Juridical and natural nonresidents are free to maintain any type of deposit accounts; in practice, deposit accounts other than in lire are not offered by domestic banks.

Foreign exchange accounts permitted   Yes.

Domestic currency accounts   Yes.

Convertible into foreign currency   Yes.

Blocked accounts   No.

Imports and Import Payments

Foreign exchange budget   No.

Financing requirements for imports   No.

Import licenses and other nontariff measures   No license, other than the general business license, is required to engage in trade transactions. Imports from Italy are not subject to restriction, whereas imports from third countries are subject to control under the relevant EU regulations.

Import taxes and/or tariffs   Customs duties on imports from outside the EU are collected by EU customs authorities on behalf of San Marino. A sales tax is levied on all imports at the time of entry. The structure of this tax corresponds closely to the Italian value-added tax, but the average effective rate is about 4% lower. Sale taxes levied on imports are rebated when the goods are reexported.

Taxes collected through the exchange system   No.

State import monopoly   The importation of electricity, gas, and water is reserved for the public sector.

Exports and Export Proceeds

Repatriation requirements   No.

Surrender requirements   No.

Financing requirements   No.

Export licenses   Exports to Italy are not regulated, while exports to third countries are governed by relevant Italian regulations.

Without quotas   Exports to any country of products listed in Decree No. 68 require licenses, while other exports do not require authorization.

Export taxes   n.a.

Taxes collected through the exchange system   No.

Payments for Invisible Transactions and Current Transfers

Controls on these payments   No.

Proceeds from Invisible Transactions and Current Transfers

Repatriation requirements   No.

Surrender requirements   No.

Restrictions on use of funds   No.

Capital Transactions

Controls on capital and money market instruments   Inward and outward capital transfers, with few exceptions, are not restricted.

Controls on derivatives and other instruments   No.

Controls on direct investment

Outward direct investment   n.a.

Inward direct investment   Investments require government approval, which is based on conformity with long-term developmental and environmental policy considerations. Foreign investors are accorded equal treatment with national firms.

Controls on liquidation of direct investment   No.

Controls on real estate transactions

Purchase abroad by residents   Yes.

Purchase locally by nonresidents   Purchases require approval from the Council of Twelve. Approval is granted on a case-by-case basis.

Sale locally by nonresidents   n.a.

Provisions specific to commercial banks and other credit institutions

Lending locally in foreign exchange   n.a.

Purchase of locally issued securities denominated in foreign exchange   n.a.

Differential treatment of nonresident deposit accounts and/or deposit accounts in foreign exchange   n.a.

Investment regulations   n.a.

Open foreign exchange position limits   n.a.

Provisions specific to institutional investors

Currency matching regulations on assets/liabilities composition   n.a.

Other controls imposed by securities laws   No.

Changes During 1996

No significant changes occurred in the exchange and trade system.

SÃO TOMÉ AND PRÍNCIPE

(Position as of December 31, 1996)

Status Under IMF Articles of Agreement

Article XIV	Yes.

Exchange Arrangement

Currency	The currency of São Tomé and Príncipe is the dobra.
Exchange rate structure	
Multiple	There are 4 exchange rates: the official, the exchange bureau, the commercial market, and the parallel market rates. Occasional spreads of more than 2% result between these rates.
Classification	
Independent floating	The indicative exchange rate of the dobra is determined daily as a weighted average of the exchange rates of the exchange bureaus, commercial banks, and the parallel market of the previous day. The intervention currency is the U.S. dollar. Rates for certain other currencies are determined on the basis of exchange rates of the U.S. dollar for the currencies concerned.
Exchange tax	The taxation system differs for import payments, transactions in foreign checks, and collection of export proceeds. On import-related exchange transactions, the arrangements are as follows: when a letter of credit (LC) is opened, a quarterly rate equivalent to 0.5% (minimum of $25 and maximum of $500) of the import value is charged and is payable with an additional commission of 0.5% to the Central Bank of São Tomé and Príncipe (CB). A stamp of duty of 0.25% is also payable, as well as a postage levy of $2. On foreign checks for collection, commercial banks charge a commission of $2 a transaction. For the collection of export proceeds, a commission of 0.125% (a minimum of $25 and a maximum of $300) is charged when the LC is opened and an additional fee of 0.125% when the funds are received. A postage levy of Db 39,000 is also charged.
Exchange subsidy	No.
Forward exchange market	No.

Arrangements for Payments and Receipts

Prescription of currency requirements	The CB may prescribe the currency in which foreign exchange transactions are to be made.
Payment arrangements	No.
Administration of control	
Exchange control authorities	All foreign exchange transactions are controlled by the CB, which applies the exchange controls flexibly. All exchange payments must be made through the CB, with the exception of 50% of earnings retained by producer-exporters for import payments. Import and export licenses are freely granted by the Directorate of External Commerce for statistical purposes.
International security restrictions	No.
Payment arrears	
Official	Yes.
Private	n.a.

Controls on trade in gold (coins and/or bullion)

Controls on domestic ownership and/or trade

n.a.

Controls on external trade

The export and import of gold require CB authorization.

Controls on exports and imports of banknotes

On exports

Foreign currency

The CB establishes the maximum amount that may be exported.

Resident Accounts

Eligibility to hold accounts

Juridical persons

Domestic accounts in foreign currency, other than those of credit institutions, may be freely opened only by export enterprises that are also producers, but the utilization of such accounts for making transfers abroad needs authorization on a case-by-case basis from the CB.

Natural persons

Individuals are not allowed to hold foreign currency deposits.

Foreign exchange accounts permitted

Yes.

Held domestically

Producers of exported goods may retain 50% of their export proceeds in accounts with banks, including those abroad (if they are correspondent banks of the CB). The utilization of such amounts of currency are confined to the importation of products and equipment necessary for productive activities.

Held abroad

Without the authorization of the CB, residents may not make foreign currency deposits or open or utilize bank accounts outside the country.

Nonresident Accounts

Eligibility to hold accounts

Juridical and natural persons are eligible.

Foreign exchange accounts permitted

These accounts may be freely opened and credited or debited, including for transfers abroad, as long as they are demand accounts or have a term of up to 1 year.

Approval required

n.a.

Imports and Import Payments

Foreign exchange budget

No.

Financing requirements for imports

Minimum financing requirements

n.a.

Advance payment requirements

Prepayment for imports is permitted only through the opening of LCs or through advance transfer when agreed upon by the CB.

Advance import deposits

When importers open LCs, the International Bank requires them to lodge a non-interest-bearing deposit in domestic currency of up to 100% of the value of the LCs, depending on the creditworthiness of the operator.

Documentation requirements for release of foreign exchange for imports

Domiciliation requirements | n.a.

Letters of credit | Yes.

Import licenses and other nontariff measures | Import licenses are automatically granted by the Directorate of External Commerce. All individuals and productive entities are permitted to engage in import activity. Medicines may be imported by the public pharmaceutical enterprise and the private pharmaceutical sector.

Positive list | n.a.

Negative list | n.a.

Open general licenses | n.a.

Import taxes and/or tariffs | Yes.

Taxes collected through the exchange system | Yes.

State import monopoly | Fuels and lubricants are imported by the public fuel enterprise.

Exports and Export Proceeds

Repatriation requirements | All export proceeds must be repatriated. However, producer-exporters may retain 50% of export proceeds in foreign exchange in bank accounts, including those abroad with correspondent banks of the CB, to meet their import requirements.

Surrender requirements | Exporters may retain 50% of export proceeds and must surrender the other 50% to the CB.

Export licenses | All exports require an export license specifying the quantity and c.i.f. or f.o.b. value of the export.

Without quotas | n.a.

With quotas | n.a.

Export taxes

Taxes collected through the exchange system | A commission of 0.125% is charged on the collection of export proceeds, with a minimum of $25 and a maximum of $300 when the LC is opened, and an additional commission of 0.125% when funds are received. A postage levy of $7.50 is also charged.

Other export taxes | Yes.

Payments for Invisible Transactions and Current Transfers

Controls on these payments | Payments for invisibles related to authorized imports, i.e., freight and insurance, unloading and storage costs, administrative expenses, commissions and interest payments, as well as subscriptions and membership fees, and consulting and legal fees are not restricted. Payments for other invisibles are approved within limits established by the CB. All payments related to invisibles are subject to a stamp tax of 0.5%. In addition, commercial banks charge a postage levy of $2 for clients (and $4 for others) on all transactions.

Profit/dividends | Transfers of profits by foreign companies established before independence have been suspended.

Prior approval | n.a.

Quantitative limits	Repatriation of profits of up to 15% a year of the investment value is permitted.
Indicative limits/bona fide test	n.a.
Payments for travel	
Prior approval	Yes.
Quantitative limits	Purchases of foreign exchange by residents for purposes of tourism are limited, although air fares may be paid in domestic currency.
Indicative limits/bona fide test	Yes.
Medical costs	
Prior approval	Yes.
Indicative limits/bona fide test	Transfers in excess of limits set by the CB for medical treatment abroad when local facilities are inadequate are approved in bona fide cases.
Study abroad costs	
Prior approval	Yes.
Indicative limits/bona fide test	At the beginning of the school year, a student is granted permission to transfer a variable amount to pay for expenses related to courses taken abroad; additional transfers may be granted if approved by the Ministry of Education and Culture.
Foreign workers' wages	
Prior approval	Personnel under technical assistance programs are allowed to transfer their savings in accordance with the terms of their contracts.
Quantitative limits	n.a.
Indicative limits/bona fide test	n.a.
Pensions	n.a.
Gambling/prize earnings	n.a.
Family maintenance/alimony	n.a.
Credit card use abroad	n.a.

Proceeds from Invisible Transactions and Current Transfers

n.a.

Capital Transactions

Controls on direct investment

Outward direct investment	n.a.
Inward direct investment	Investments, excluding those related to the extraction of hydrocarbons and other mining industries, are permitted on the same basis as domestic investments.

Provisions specific to commercial banks and other credit institutions

Borrowing abroad	n.a.
Lending to nonresidents (financial or commercial credits)	n.a.
Lending locally in foreign exchange	n.a.

Purchase of locally issued securities denominated in foreign exchange	n.a.
Differential treatment of nonresident deposit accounts and/or deposit accounts in foreign exchange	
Reserve requirements	The requirements are 30% on foreign exchange deposits (the requirement was reduced from 50% on May 1, 1996), and 15% on dobra deposits.
Liquid asset requirements	n.a.
Credit controls	n.a.
Investment regulations	n.a.
Open foreign exchange position limits	n.a.

Changes During 1996

Exports and export proceeds	*May 1.* The surrender requirement was reduced to 50% from 70%.
Capital transactions	*April 4.* The reserve requirement on foreign exchange deposits was reduced to 30% from 50%.

SAUDI ARABIA

(Position as of December 31, 1996)

Status Under IMF Articles of Agreement

Article VIII	Date of acceptance: March 22, 1961.

Exchange Arrangement

Currency	The currency of Saudia Arabia is the Saudi Arabian riyal.
Exchange rate structure	Unitary.
Classification	
Limited flexibility with respect to a single currency	The exchange rate of the Saudi Arabian riyal is pegged to the SDR at SRls 4.28255 per SDR 1. The intervention currency is the U.S. dollar, to which a close relationship is maintained. The Saudi Arabian riyal rate against the U.S. dollar is determined by the Saudi Arabian Monetary Agency (SAMA). The SAMA's middle rate, which has been stable since June 1986 at SRls 3.745 per $1, serves—together with the SAMA's selling and buying rates—as the basis for exchange quotations in the market, the banks being permitted to charge up to 0.125% above and below the SAMA's buying and selling rates.
Exchange tax	No.
Exchange subsidy	No.
Forward exchange market	The commercial banking sector has an active forward market to cover exchange risks for up to 12 months.
Official cover of forward operations	No.

Arrangements for Payments and Receipts

Prescription of currency requirements	Transactions with (and the use of the currency of) Israel are prohibited.
Payment arrangements	No.
Administration of control	
Exchange control authorities	Foreign exchange controls are administered by the SAMA.
International security restrictions	
In accordance with IMF Executive Board Decision No. 144-(52/51)	There have been restrictions on transactions with Iraq since September 1990.
In accordance with UN sanctions	In compliance with UN Security Council Resolution No. 757 (1992), certain restrictions have been imposed on the making of payments and transfers for current international transactions with respect to the former Federal Republic of Yugoslavia (Serbia/Montenegro), effective September 15, 1992.
Payment arrears	No.
Controls on trade in gold (coins and/or bullion)	
Controls on domestic ownership and/or trade	Residents may import and export gold in any form, except manufactured gold and jewelry, which are subject to a 12% customs duty. Gold of 14 karats or less may not be imported.

Controls on exports and imports of banknotes	No.

Resident Accounts

Eligibility to hold accounts	Juridical and natural persons are eligible.
Foreign exchange accounts permitted	Yes.
Held domestically	Yes.
Held abroad	Yes.
Accounts in domestic currency convertible into foreign currency	Yes.

Nonresident Accounts

Eligibility to hold accounts	Juridical and natural persons may open these accounts with permission of the SAMA.
Foreign exchange accounts permitted	These accounts are permitted, but prior approval is required.
Domestic currency accounts	Yes.
Convertible into foreign currency	These accounts are permitted, but prior approval is required.
Blocked accounts	No.

Imports and Import Payments

Foreign exchange budget	No.
Financing requirements for imports	No.
Documentation requirements for release of foreign exchange for imports	No.
Import licenses and other nontariff measures	
Negative list	Limited import restrictions on a few commodities are maintained for religious, health, and security reasons.
Open general licenses	Yes.
Import taxes and/or tariffs	Most imports are subject to customs duties at rates ranging from zero to 12%. For a few goods, the rate is 20% and for tobacco products, 50%. Imports from members of the GCC are exempt from duties, provided that at least 40% of value added is effected in GCC countries and that at least 51% of the capital of the producing firm is owned by citizens of GCC members.
Taxes collected through the exchange system	No.
State import monopoly	No.

Exports and Export Proceeds

Repatriation requirements	No.

Surrender requirements	No.
Financing requirements	No.
Documentation requirements	No.
Export licenses	Reexport of certain imported items benefiting from government subsidies is prohibited.
Export taxes	No.

Payments for Invisible Transactions and Current Transfers

Controls on these payments	No.

Proceeds from Invisible Transactions and Current Transfers

Repatriation requirements	No.
Surrender requirements	No.
Restrictions on use of funds	No.

Capital Transactions

Controls on capital and money market instruments

On capital market securities

Purchase locally by nonresidents — Portfolio investment in shares of listed Saudi Arabian joint-stock companies is restricted to Saudi Arabian nationals, Saudi Arabian corporations and institutions, and citizens of the GCC. Indirect portfolio investment in shares issued by Saudi Arabian joint-stock companies is allowed via special purpose vehicles (country fund), authorized by the SAMA; the fund will be established on July 26, 1997 and will be managed by Saudi American banks. There are no restrictions on portfolio investment in government securities.

Sale or issue locally by nonresidents — Nonresidents must seek permission of the Minister of Commerce to sell or issue securities within the Kingdom. There are no restrictions on the repatriation of the proceeds from the sale of securities issued by nonresidents. Residents may purchase or sell nonresident securities via brokerage services offered by domestic banks.

On money market instruments

Sale or issue locally by nonresidents — Same regulations as for capital market securities apply.

On collective investment securities

Purchase locally by nonresidents — Same regulations as for capital market securities apply.

Sale or issue locally by nonresidents — Same regulations as for capital market securities apply.

Controls on derivatives and other instruments

Sale or issue locally by nonresidents — Same regulations as for capital market securities apply.

Controls on credit operations

Commercial credits

By residents to nonresidents — Saudi Arabian banks must seek permission from the SAMA.

To residents from nonresidents — The SAMA's permission is required for Saudi Arabian riyal-denominated loans made through Saudi Arabian banks.

Guarantees, sureties, and financial
backup facilities

By residents to nonresidents   The SAMA's permission is required, except for Saudi Arabian banks.

To residents from nonresidents   Financial institutions that give guarantees to government projects must appear on the
                                         SAMA-approved list.

Controls on direct investment

Inward direct investment   Approved foreign investments in Saudi Arabia enjoy the same privileges as domestic
                                         capital. Foreign capital invested in industrial or agricultural projects with at least 25%
                                         Saudi Arabian participation is exempt from income and corporate tax for 10 years after
                                         production has begun.

Controls on liquidation of direct   No.
investment

Controls on real estate transactions

Purchase locally by nonresidents   Purchase of real estate is restricted to Saudi Arabian citizens, Saudi Arabian corpora-
                                         tions, Saudi Arabian institutions, and citizens of the GCC.

Provisions specific to commercial   The SAMA's approval is required by Saudi Arabian banks before acquiring shares in a
banks and other credit institutions company established outside the Kingdom.

Lending to nonresidents (financial or   The SAMA requires local banks to obtain its approval before inviting foreign banks to
commercial credits)   participate in Saudi Arabian riyal-denominated syndicated transactions inside or outside
                                         Saudi Arabia. Prior approval from the SAMA is also required for Saudi Arabian banks
                                         to participate in riyal-standard transactions arranged abroad.

Reserve requirements   For interbank deposits originating from foreign banks, only domestic currency deposits
                                         are subject to the SAMA's reserve requirements.

Open foreign exchange position limits   Open positions are monitored via prudential reports.

Provisions specific to institutional No.
investors

Other controls imposed by securities No.
laws

Changes During 1996

No significant changes occurred in the exchange and trade system.

SENEGAL

(Position as of May 31, 1997)

Status Under IMF Articles of Agreement

Article VIII   Date of acceptance: June 6, 1996.

Exchange Arrangement

Currency   The currency of Senegal is the CFA franc.

Exchange rate structure   Unitary.

Classification

Pegged   The CFA franc is pegged to the French franc at the rate of CFAF 100 per F 0.01. Exchange rates for other currencies are derived from the rate for the currency concerned in the Paris exchange market and the fixed rate between the French franc and the CFA franc. Authorized banks charge an exchange commission of 2% on purchases and sales of French francs and an exchange commission of 0.125 to 1‰ on purchases and sales of foreign exchange other than those directly related to external transactions. In addition, they levy a commission of 2.5‰ on transfers to all countries outside the WAEMU, all of which must be surrendered to the Treasury.

Exchange tax   No.

Exchange subsidy   No.

Forward exchange market   Forward cover against exchange rate risk is available to residents only for imports of a specified category of goods. All forward cover against exchange rate risk must be authorized by the Ministry of Economy, Finance, and Planning (MEFP). Forward cover may be provided only in the currency of settlement stipulated in the commercial contract. Maturities must correspond to the due date of foreign exchange settlement stipulated in the commercial contract and must not exceed 1 month. For some specified products, the maturity of forward cover may be extended 1 time for up to 3 months.

Official cover of forward operations   n.a.

Arrangements for Payments and Receipts

Prescription of currency requirements   Settlements with France, Monaco, and other countries linked to the French Treasury through an Operations Account are made in CFA francs, French francs, or the currency of any other Operations Account country.

Payment arrangements

Bilateral arrangements   n.a.

Regional arrangements   Yes.

Clearing agreements   Current transactions with The Gambia, Ghana, Guinea, Guinea-Bissau, Liberia, Mauritania, Nigeria, and Sierra Leone are normally made through the WACH.

Administration of control

Exchange control authorities   Exchange control is administered by the MEFP, which has delegated a part of the approval authority for exchange control to the BCEAO and to authorized banks. The Directorate of Money and Credit examines each request. Customs officers monitor outflows of foreign exchange and confirm imports and exports of goods effected through authorized banks, the Postal Administration, or the BCEAO. The BCEAO exercises exchange controls ex post.

737

International security restrictions

In accordance with IMF Executive Board Decision No. 144-(52/51)

Yes.

In accordance with UN sanctions

Payments to Iraq are prohibited.

Payment arrears

No.

Controls on trade in gold (coins and/or bullion)

Controls on external trade

Imports and exports of gold (gold jewelry and gold materials) require prior authorization from the MEFP. Exempt from this requirement are (1) imports and exports by the Treasury or the BCEAO; (2) imports and exports of manufactured articles containing a minor quantity of gold (such as gold-filled or gold-plated articles); and (3) imports and exports by travelers of gold articles up to a combined weight of 200 grams.

Controls on exports and imports of banknotes

On exports

Domestic currency

Travelers may export CFA franc banknotes. However, the suspension of BCEAO repurchases of exported banknotes continues. In addition, shipments of BCEAO notes between authorized intermediaries and their correspondent banks outside the WAEMU are strictly prohibited.

Foreign currency

The reexportation of foreign banknotes for amounts exceeding the equivalent of CFAF 50,000 by nonresidents requires documentation demonstrating either the importation of the foreign banknotes or their purchase against other means of payment registered in the name of the traveler or through the use of nonresident deposits in local banks.

On imports

Foreign currency

Nonresidents and residents may bring in any amount of foreign banknotes and coins (except gold coins) of countries outside the Operations Account area. Residents bringing in foreign banknotes and foreign currency traveler's checks exceeding the equivalent of CFAF 50,000 must declare them to customs upon entry and sell them to an authorized intermediary bank within 8 days.

Resident Accounts

Eligibility to hold accounts

Juridical and natural persons are eligible.

Foreign exchange accounts permitted

The opening of these accounts is subject to prior approval by the MEFP. The practice is generally not allowed because it is not covered by existing legislation.

Held domestically

These accounts are permitted, but prior approval is required.

Held abroad

The holding of accounts with banks abroad is not expressly prohibited. However, transfers for the accumulation of asset holdings abroad (i.e., outside the franc zone) by a resident must be approved by the MEFP.

Accounts in domestic currency convertible into foreign currency

No.

Nonresident Accounts

Eligibility to hold accounts

Juridical and natural persons are eligible.

Foreign exchange accounts permitted

The holding of accounts with banks located abroad must have prior approval from the MEFP.

Domestic currency accounts	These accounts may not be credited with BCEAO banknotes, French franc notes, or banknotes issued by central banks that maintain an Operations Account with the French Treasury. They may not be overdrawn without prior authorization of the MEFP. Funds may be transferred freely between nonresident accounts.
Convertible into foreign currency	Foreign accounts in francs may be freely debited for the purchase by nonresidents of foreign currencies on the official exchange market.
Blocked accounts	No.

Imports and Import Payments

Foreign exchange budget	No.
Financing requirements for imports	
Advance payment requirements	Advance payments for imports require authorization, and importers may not acquire foreign exchange until the contractual date of the payments.
Documentation requirements for release of foreign exchange for imports	Exchange authorization and invoices are required.
Domiciliation requirements	All import transactions exceeding CFAF 500,000 must be domiciled with authorized banks.
Preshipment inspection	An inspection is required for quality and price for goods exceeding CFAF 3 million f.o.b.
Import licenses and other nontariff measures	Quantitative restrictions may be applied on products for public health and security reasons.
Positive list	Used cars and secondhand clothing may be freely imported. The marketing of these articles requires mechanical inspection or a health clearance, respectively.
Negative list	Narcotics and firearms are prohibited.
Import taxes and/or tariffs	Import duties range between 5% and 45% (including a service fee of 5%).
Taxes collected through the exchange system	No.
State import monopoly	No.

Exports and Export Proceeds

Repatriation requirements	Proceeds from exports, including those to members of WAEMU and Operations Account countries, must normally be collected within 120 days of the arrival of the goods at their destination and repatriated through BCEAO not later than 1 month after the due date.
Surrender requirements	Yes.
Financing requirements	No.
Documentation requirements	A customs declaration is required.
Domiciliation	Exports of more than CFAF 500,000 must be domiciled with an authorized bank.
Export licenses	Licenses are required, except for unworked gold.
Without quotas	Yes.
Export taxes	No.

Payments for Invisible Transactions and Current Transfers

Controls on these payments
Payments for invisible transactions to France, Monaco, and Operations Account countries may be freely made. All other payments are subject to indicative limits and/or bona fide test. Payments for medical treatment, study abroad, subscriptions and membership fees, consulting and legal fees, gambling and prize earnings, family maintenance and alimony, and the use of credit cards abroad, as well as interest payments and remittances of profits and dividends are subject to prior approval.

Payments for travel

Quantitative limits
Residents traveling for tourism or business purposes to countries in the franc zone that are not members of the WAEMU are allowed to take out banknotes other than CFA franc notes up to the equivalent of CFAF 2 million; amounts in excess of this limit may be taken out in other means of payment. The allowances for travel to countries outside the franc zone are (1) for tourist travel, the equivalent of CFAF 1 million without limit on the number of trips or differentiation by the age of the traveler; and (2) for business travel, CFAF 200,000 a day for up to 1 month, corresponding to a maximum of CFAF 6 million (business travel allowances may be combined with tourism allowances). Allowances in excess of these limits are subject to the authorization of the MEFP.

Foreign workers' wages
Total net wages may be transferred upon presentation of pay slips, provided the transfer is made within 3 months following the pay period.

Credit card use abroad

Quantitative limits
Credit cards issued by resident financial intermediaries and specifically authorized by the MEFP may be used up to the ceilings for tourist and business travel.

Proceeds from Invisible Transactions and Current Transfers

Repatriation requirements
Yes.

Surrender requirements
Proceeds from transactions in invisibles with France, Monaco, and the Operations Account countries may be retained. All amounts due from residents of other countries for services and all income earned in those countries from foreign assets must be collected and surrendered, if received in foreign currency, within 1 month of due date or the date of receipt.

Restrictions on use of funds
No.

Capital Transactions

Controls on capital and money market instruments
Capital movements between Senegal and France, Monaco, and the Operations Account countries are free of exchange control. Capital transfers to all other countries require the approval of the MEFP, but capital receipts from such countries are permitted freely. All investments abroad by residents of Senegal require prior authorization from the MEFP; 75% of such investments must be financed with borrowing from abroad.

On capital market securities
Yes.

On money market instruments
Yes.

On collective investment securities

Sale or issue locally by nonresidents
n.a.

Purchase abroad by residents
Yes.

Sale or issue abroad by residents
Prior authorization is required.

Controls on derivatives and other instruments

Sale or issue locally by nonresidents	n.a.
Purchase abroad by residents	Yes.
Sale or issue abroad by residents	Yes.

Controls on credit operations

Commercial credits

By residents to nonresidents

Commercial credits may be freely granted in connection with merchandise exports if the due date of the payment is within 120 days of the shipment of the merchandise. Commercial credits in connection with the provision of services may be freely granted by residents; no limit is set for the payment due date.

To residents from nonresidents

Nonresidents may freely grant commercial credits to resident institutions. Repayments of commercial credits are generally authorized, subject to the submission of supporting documents.

Financial credits

By residents to nonresidents

These credits require the prior authorization of the MEFP. Transfer abroad of the funds necessary to service these facilities gives rise to the establishment of an "exchange authorization," subject to the approval of the MEFP and the submission of supporting documents.

To residents from nonresidents

There are no restrictions on the granting of these loans, provided the loan amount is under CFAF 70 million. The funds required for servicing these facilities must be transferred abroad by an authorized intermediary bank.

Guarantees, sureties, and financial backup facilities

By residents to nonresidents

The granting of guarantees and sureties is subject to prior approval by the MEFP. Transfer abroad of the funds required to service these facilities requires issuance of an "exchange permit" bearing the signature of the MEFP to accompany the supporting documents.

To residents from nonresidents

These facilities may be freely granted for amounts under CFAF 70 million. Transfer abroad of the funds required to service these facilities must be made by an authorized intermediary bank. If, however, these transactions take place between a direct investment company resident in Senegal and its parent company located abroad, they are considered to be direct investments and therefore require a prior declaration to the MEFP.

Controls on direct investment

Outward direct investment

All investments, including those made through foreign companies that are directly or indirectly controlled by persons in Senegal and those made by overseas branches or subsidiaries of companies in Senegal, require prior authorization from the MEFP; 75% of such investments must be financed with borrowing from abroad. Direct investments constitute investments implying control of a company or enterprise. Mere participation is not considered direct investment, unless it exceeds 20% of the capital of a company whose shares are quoted on a stock exchange.

Inward direct investment

Foreign direct investments in Senegal, including those made by companies in Senegal that are directly or indirectly under foreign control and those made by branches or subsidiaries of foreign companies in Senegal, must be reported to the MEFP before they are made.

Controls on liquidation of direct investment

The liquidation of direct and other investments, whether Senegalese investments abroad or foreign investments in Senegal, must be reported to the MEFP and the BCEAO within 20 days of each operation.

Controls on real estate transactions

Purchase abroad by residents

These purchases require prior authorization of the MEFP.

Purchase locally by nonresidents

Purchases for purposes other than direct investment in a business, branch, or company are allowed. They require a declaration to the MEFP for statistical purposes.

Sale locally by nonresidents

Sales must be declared to the MEFP. Operations may be settled only after approval of the MEFP. Following settlement, the liquidation or sale must be reported to the MEFP and to the BCEAO within 20 days of each operation.

Provisions specific to commercial banks and other credit institutions

Borrowing abroad

Borrowing requires a prior declaration to the MEFP when the contract exceeds CFAF 70 million. Borrowing requires prior authorization from the MEFP, except in the cases of (1) loans constituting a direct investment that are subject to prior declaration; (2) loans taken up by industrial firms to finance operations abroad, by international merchanting and export-import firms (approved by the MEFP) to finance transit trade, or by any type of firm to finance imports and exports; (3) loans contracted by authorized intermediary banks; and (4) subject to certain conditions, loans other than those mentioned above when the total outstanding amount of these loans, including the new borrowing, does not exceed CFAF 50 million for any one borrower. The repayment of loans not constituting a direct investment requires the special authorization of the MEFP if the loan itself was subject to such approval.

Maintenance of accounts abroad

Prior MEFP authorization is required.

Lending to nonresidents (financial or commercial credits)

Prior MEFP authorization is required.

Lending locally in foreign exchange

n.a.

Purchase of locally issued securities denominated in foreign exchange

Yes.

Differential treatment of nonresident deposit accounts and/or deposit accounts in foreign exchange

Reserve requirements

Yes.

Liquid asset requirements

Yes.

Interest rate controls

Interest rates are free, except for time deposits of CFAF 5 million or higher held for 1 year or more, and savings accounts, provided the usury law is observed.

Credit controls

Any overdraft or any advance granted to a nonresident requires the prior authorization of the MEFP. These claims are included in the international position of banks and financial institutions subject to special supervision.

Investment regulations

Yes.

Open foreign exchange position limits

Yes.

Provisions specific to institutional investors

No.

Other controls imposed by securities laws

No.

Changes During 1996

Status under IMF Articles of Agreement

June 6. Senegal accepted the obligations of Article VIII, Sections 2, 3, and 4 of the Fund Agreement.

Imports and import payments

July 9. Trade in secondhand clothing and used cars was liberalized.

Proceeds from invisible transactions and current transfers

August 18. Limits for travel allowances were increased.

Changes During 1997

Imports and import payments

May 2. The ceiling for preshipment inspection of merchandise was raised to CFAF 3 million, except for certain cases mandated specifically by the Customs Administration.

SEYCHELLES

(Position as of January 31, 1997)

Status Under IMF Articles of Agreement

Article VIII   Date of acceptance: January 3, 1978.

Exchange Arrangement

Currency   The currency of Seychelles is the Seychelles rupee.

Other legal tender   Various commemorative gold coins issued on several occasions since 1976 are also legal tender.

Exchange rate structure   Unitary.

Classification

Pegged   Since May 13, 1996, the Seychelles rupee has been pegged to a weighted basket of currencies of Seychelles' main trading and tourism partners: the U.S. dollar (22.4), the pound sterling (19.6), the French franc (16.1), the South African rand (11.5), the Singapore dollar (10.0), the deutsche mark (8.8), the Italian lira (7.8), and the Japanese yen (3.8). Exchange rates for various currencies are quoted on the basis of their New York closing rates for the U.S. dollar on the previous day, using the U.S. dollar rate for the Seychelles rupee, as derived from the fixed parity to the currency basket. The Central Bank of Seychelles (CBS) circulates these rates daily to the commercial banks. The CBS charges a commission of 0.125% on purchases and 0.875% on sales of pounds sterling, U.S. dollars, and French francs.

The commercial banks are authorized to deal in pounds sterling and other currencies at rates based on the exchange rates circulated daily by the CBS for the respective currencies. Other authorized dealers include casinos, guesthouses, hotels, restaurants, self-catering establishments, tour operators, travel agents, shipping agents, and ship chandlers. These dealers are restricted to buying only in the course of their licensed activity. They must sell all their foreign currency proceeds to the 5 commercial banks. All other transactions in foreign exchange are prohibited.

Exchange tax   No.

Exchange subsidy   No.

Forward exchange market   No.

Arrangements for Payments and Receipts

Prescription of currency requirements   No.

Administration of control

Exchange control authorities   The exchange control authorities are the CBS and the Ministry of Finance (MOF). The MOF partially controls foreign trade and domestic marketing through a mechanism of import and price controls.

International security restrictions   No.

Payment arrears

Private   Yes.

Controls on trade in gold (coins and/or bullion)

Controls on domestic ownership and/or trade | Residents may freely purchase, hold, and sell gold in any form, except for dealings in gold bullion, which are restricted to authorized dealers.

Controls on exports and imports of banknotes

On exports

Domestic currency | Travelers may take out up to SR 100 of domestic currency.

Foreign currency | Travelers may take out any amount of foreign currency.

On imports

Foreign currency | Overseas visitors may bring in any amount of currency for travel expenses.

Resident Accounts

n.a.

Nonresident Accounts

Eligibility to hold accounts | Juridical and natural persons are eligible.

Foreign exchange accounts permitted | Yes.

Approval required | n.a.

Domestic currency accounts | No.

Imports and Import Payments

Foreign exchange budget | No.

Financing requirements for imports | No.

Import licenses and other nontariff measures | Importers other than individuals are required to obtain import licenses from the Seychelles Licensing Authority, in accordance with objective criteria. In addition, for each shipment of commodities, an importer must apply to the Trade and Commerce Division of the Ministry of Finance for a permit, the granting of which is discretionary. Permits are normally not granted for cars older than 3 years and some nonessential commodities.

Effective January 1, 1996, an import quota system applicable to most imports was introduced. The quota allocation system is based on 75% of importers' 1995 imports. Imports related to the tourist industry are granted a higher percentage of their 1995 imports, and new importers are allocated SR 50,000.

Import taxes and/or tariffs | Imports are subject to taxes of up to 600%, with most goods subject to rates ranging between 5% and 30%.

Taxes collected through the exchange system | n.a.

State import monopoly | The Seychelles Marketing Board has the monopoly on imports of all foodstuffs.

Exports and Export Proceeds

Repatriation requirements | Yes.

Surrender requirements	All export proceeds must be converted through domestic commercial banks, who are the only authorized sellers of foreign exchange. During 1996, banks allocated 64.8% of their foreign exchange inflows to the Foreign Exchange Payments Scheme. Under the 7 categories of payments to which certain percentages of foreign exchange inflows are allocated, customers deposit the Seychelles rupee equivalent of their foreign exchange requirements in a special account. The system operates on a first-come, first-served basis for each category at banks. In addition, commercial banks surrendered 19% of their foreign exchange inflows to the government for purchases of essential imports by the Seychelles Marketing Board, loan repayments, and requirements of a utility company. The remaining 16.2% of inflows was used at the discretion of the banks.
	With a view to the eventual dismantling of the pipeline, surrender requirements were modified on January 1, 1997, to 20% to the pipeline; 30% to finance essential government imports; and the remaining 50% to be used at the discretion of banks.
Preshipment inspection	Residents may export to any country, but a permit is required for each shipment of commodities. These permits are granted on a routine basis by the Trade and Commerce Division of the MOF.

Payments for Invisible Transactions and Current Transfers

Controls on these payments	There are no controls on these payments. Restrictions on remittances of profits and dividends, and consulting and legal fees were lifted on January 1, 1997.

Proceeds from Invisible Transactions and Current Transfers

Repatriation requirements	Yes.
Surrender requirements	Residents must surrender the proceeds to a commercial bank within 21 days of the transaction.
Restrictions on use of funds	Receipts, with the exception of dividend remittances and transfers of management fees, may be disposed of freely.

Capital Transactions

Controls on capital and money market instruments	
On capital market securities	
Purchase locally by nonresidents	Yes.
Sale or issue locally by nonresidents	Yes.
On money market instruments	
Purchase locally by nonresidents	Yes.
On collective investment securities	
Purchase locally by nonresidents	Yes.
Controls on credit operations	
Financial credits	
By residents to nonresidents	Yes.
Controls on direct investment	
Inward direct investment	Foreign investment is freely permitted, provided that such investment does not involve ownership of land.

Controls on liquidation of direct investment	Restrictions on the transfers of proceeds were lifted on January 1, 1997.
Controls on real estate transactions	
Purchase locally by nonresidents	Yes.
Sale locally by nonresidents	Yes.

Changes During 1996

Exchange arrangements	*May 13.* The Seychelles rupee ceased to be pegged to the SDR and was pegged to a weighted basket of currencies of Seychelles' main trading and tourism partners.
Imports and import payments	*January 1.* An import quota system for most importers was introduced.
Capital transactions	*March 11.* Restrictions on commercial credits by residents to nonresidents were abolished.

Changes During 1997

Exchange arrangements	*January 1.* A new Foreign Exchange Regulations Act became effective.
Exports and export proceeds	*January 1.* Surrender requirements were modified.
Payments for invisible transactions and current transfers	*January 1.* Restrictions on remittances for profits and dividends and management fees were removed.
Capital transactions	*January 1.* Restrictions on remittances of proceeds from sale of assets were removed.

SIERRA LEONE

(Position as of December 31, 1996)

Status Under IMF Articles of Agreement

Article VIII   Date of acceptance: December 14, 1995.

Exchange Arrangement

Currency   The currency of Sierra Leone is the leone.

Exchange rate structure   Unitary.

Classification

Independent floating   Exchange rates are freely determined in the interbank market. Commercial banks and licensed foreign exchange bureaus may buy and sell foreign exchange with customers and trade among themselves or with the Bank of Sierra Leone (BSL), the central bank, freely. The BSL determines the exchange rate to be used in official transactions, including for customs valuation purposes, which is based on the weighted average rate of commercial bank and foreign exchange bureau transactions in the previous week. Foreign exchange bureaus are limited to spot transactions and are not allowed to sell traveler's checks.

Exchange tax   No.

Exchange subsidy   No.

Forward exchange market   No.

Arrangements for Payments and Receipts

Prescription of currency requirements   Payments for imports may be made in leones to the credit of an external account in the currency of the exporting country, in pounds sterling, or in U.S. dollars. Receipts from exports to countries other than China may be obtained in leones from an external account in the currency of the importing country or in any specified convertible currency.

Payment arrangements

Bilateral arrangements

 Inoperative   Yes.

Regional arrangements   n.a.

Clearing agreements   The WAEMU provides for settlements with the BSL by West African states (for Benin, Burkina Faso, Côte d'Ivoire, Mali, Niger, Senegal, and Togo) as well as with The Gambia, Ghana, Guinea, Guinea-Bissau, Liberia, Mali, Mauritania, and Nigeria.

Administration of control

Exchange control authorities   The Ministry of Finance (MOF) formulates exchange control policy in consultation with the BSL, but the day-to-day administration of exchange control is carried out by the BSL with the assistance of the commercial banks.

International security restrictions   No.

Payment arrears   Yes.

Official   n.a.

Private   n.a.

Controls on trade in gold (coins and/or bullion)

Controls on domestic ownership and/or trade	Residents may freely purchase, hold, and sell gold coins in Sierra Leone for numismatic purposes. Also, residents and nonresidents may freely purchase, hold, or sell certain Sierra Leonean commemorative gold coins. Residents are not allowed to hold gold in the form of bars or dust without a valid miner's or dealer's license.
Controls on external trade	Exports of gold require a license. Imports of gold in any form other than jewelry constituting the personal effects of a traveler require an individual import license.

Controls on exports and imports of banknotes

On exports

Domestic currency	On leaving Sierra Leone, travelers may take out up to Le 50,000.
Foreign currency	Nonresident travelers may take out any amount of foreign currency notes they declared on arrival. Employees on official business may take out up to the amount of the per diem allowance provided for that purpose. Travelers can take out up to $5,000 without restriction. Residents should declare on departure foreign exchange in excess of $5,000 with supporting documents.

On imports

Domestic currency	The importation of domestic banknotes is limited to Le 50,000 for each traveler.
Foreign currency	Commercial banks (authorized dealers) are allowed to import foreign currency to meet their operational requirements.

Resident Accounts

Eligibility to hold accounts	Juridical and natural persons are eligible.
Foreign exchange accounts permitted	Residents are permitted to maintain foreign currency accounts denominated in any convertible currency. These accounts, for which minimum balances vary from bank to bank, earn interest at a rate determined by the commercial banks. They may be credited with funds transferred from abroad, and balances on these accounts may be converted into leones to meet the account holder's local expenditures. Transfers abroad of balances in foreign currency accounts are permitted for current international transactions without prior approval from the BSL, subject to fulfilling the regulation governing the transactions.
Held domestically	Yes.
Held abroad	No.

Nonresident Accounts

Eligibility to hold accounts	Juridical and natural persons are eligible.
Foreign exchange accounts permitted	The same regulations as for resident accounts apply. All documented inward remittances can also be externalized without reference to the BSL.
Domestic currency accounts	Accounts in leones held on behalf of diplomatic missions, UN agencies, and their accredited staff are designated as external accounts. Leone deposits with external accounts are netted by the BSL, and balances standing to the credit of the account can be externalized without reference to the BSL.
Convertible into foreign currency	These accounts are permitted, but prior approval is required.
Blocked accounts	Yes.

Imports and Import Payments

Foreign exchange budget	No.
Documentation requirements for release of foreign exchange for imports	All applications for purchases of foreign exchange to pay for imported goods must be submitted to a commercial bank in Sierra Leone, supported by the following documents: completed exchange control form A1, original proforma invoice, final invoice, original bill of lading/airway bill, tax clearance certificate, and preshipment inspection certificate.
Domiciliation requirements	n.a.
Preshipment inspection	All goods imported into Sierra Leone, except petroleum and goods specifically exempted by the MOF, are subject to preshipment inspection and price verification by an international company appointed by the government.
Letters of credit	Goods to be financed with importers' own foreign exchange resources are permitted without letters of credit established with a local commercial bank.
Import licenses and other nontariff measures	
Negative list	All goods, except military goods, may be imported freely without a license.
Import taxes and/or tariffs	A sales tax of 20% of the landed value is levied on all imports except for capital goods and their spare parts, petroleum products, and baby food. All imports by unincorporated businesses are subject to a 2% tax as advance payment of income taxes.
Taxes collected through the exchange system	No.

Exports and Export Proceeds

Repatriation requirements	Exporters must repatriate export proceeds within 90 days of the date of export (approval of the BSL is required for an extension beyond 90 days). Proceeds from exports of diamonds that were prefinanced from external sources are not subject to the repatriation requirement.
Surrender requirements	No.
Documentation requirements	All exporters of commercial goods are required to complete export forms that must be endorsed by the exporter's commercial bank.
Letters of credit	n.a.
Guarantees	n.a.
Domiciliation	n.a.
Preshipment inspection	All exports, except for those exempted by the MOF, are subject to preshipment inspection and price verification, which is undertaken by an inspection company appointed by the government. Exporters who are subject to inspection must pay an export inspection fee of 1% before clearing their goods through customs.
Export licenses	Licenses are required only for exports of gold and diamonds; these export licenses, valid for 1 year or 6 months, are issued by the Department of Mines. Exports of the following articles are prohibited: those containing more than 25% silver; those manufactured or produced more than 75 years before the date of exportation; those mounted or set with diamonds, precious stones, and pearls (excluding personal jewelry or ornaments up to a value not exceeding the leone equivalent of $1,000); postage stamps of philatelic interest; and works of art.
Without quotas	Yes.
Export taxes	Licensed exporters of diamonds are subject to an administrative fee of 1% and an income tax of 1.5% based on the value in U.S. dollars of diamonds exported. Licensed exporters of gold must pay a 2.5% royalty.

Taxes collected through the exchange system

No.

Payments for Invisible Transactions and Current Transfers

Controls on these payments

Authority to provide foreign exchange for legitimate expenses is delegated to the commercial banks. There are no controls on payments for freight and insurance, unloading and storage costs, administrative expenses, interest, commissions, medical treatment, study abroad, subscriptions and membership fees, consulting and legal fees, family maintenance and alimony, or on remittances of profits and dividends.

Payments for travel

Quantitative limits

The limit is $5,000.

Indicative limits/bona fide test

Applications for travel allowances in excess of the limit must be supported by travel documents such as a ticket or passport.

Foreign workers' wages

Prior approval

Commercial banks can make remittances in favor of nonresident employees of international institutions, agencies, or foreign nongovernmental organizations only up to the remuneration package and in favor of other nonresidents when requests for such payment are supported by a valid work permit, a remuneration package agreement, and a tax clearance certificate.

Proceeds from Invisible Transactions and Current Transfers

Repatriation requirements

No.

Surrender requirements

No.

Restrictions on use of funds

No.

Capital Transactions

Controls on capital and money market instruments

Capital payments to nonresidents are subject to exchange control.

On capital market securities

Purchase locally by nonresidents

BSL approval is required before a security registered in or outside of Sierra Leone may be transferred to (or purchased by) a nonresident.

Sale or issue locally by nonresidents

These transactions are not permitted.

Purchase abroad by residents

Permission of the BSL is required both to purchase securities abroad and to transfer funds abroad to effect the purchase.

All funds accruing on such investment, as well as the capital upon termination of the investment, must be repatriated to Sierra Leone.

Sale or issue abroad by residents

Capital in respect of securities registered in Sierra Leone may not be transferred abroad without permission; for permission to be given, the company is usually required to obtain bank certification of the funds brought into Sierra Leone.

On money market instruments

Sale or issue locally by nonresidents

These transactions are not permitted.

Purchase abroad by residents

Purchases funded with domestic resources are not permitted.

Sale or issue abroad by residents	These transactions require BSL approval.
On collective investment securities	
Purchase locally by nonresidents	Yes.
Sale or issue locally by nonresidents	Yes.
Purchase abroad by residents	Purchases with funds brought from abroad are allowed. BSL certification is required.
Sale or issue abroad by residents	Yes.
Controls on derivatives and other instruments	These instruments are not available in Sierra Leone.
Purchase locally by nonresidents	Yes.
Sale or issue locally by nonresidents	Yes.
Purchase abroad by residents	Yes.
Sale or issue abroad by residents	Yes.
Controls on credit operations	
Financial credits	
By residents to nonresidents	Generally, permission of the BSL is required for the granting of any loan, whether by way of advance or bank overdraft, in Sierra Leone to nonresident entities. Permission of the BSL is also required for nonresident entities to borrow outside Sierra Leone. In addition to the above documentation, the proposed arrangement for repayment should be provided.
To residents from nonresidents	Prior approval of the BSL is required.
Guarantees, sureties, and financial backup facilities	
By residents to nonresidents	Prior approval of the BSL should be obtained for the giving or renewal of any guarantee or similar undertaking, and the resident's exposure must be 100% covered by the nonresident.
To residents from nonresidents	Prior approval of the BSL is required for these transactions and for the transfer of funds to service the facilities.
Controls on direct investment	
Outward direct investment	Investments are not allowed.
Inward direct investment	Noncitizens are prohibited from owning or controlling certain types of business. Income tax and customs duty concessions are granted to foreign and domestic companies undertaking industrial or agricultural activities that are needed for the development of the country.
Controls on liquidation of direct investment	No.
Controls on real estate transactions	
Purchase abroad by residents	Permission from the BSL is required.
Purchase locally by nonresidents	n.a.
Sale locally by nonresidents	n.a.
Provisions specific to commercial banks and other credit institutions	Commercial banks should not hold more than 25% of their deposit liabilities in foreign currency.
Borrowing abroad	n.a.

Maintenance of accounts abroad	Yes.
Lending to nonresidents (financial or commercial credits)	Banks are not engaged in foreign lending, and there are no regulations in this respect.
Lending locally in foreign exchange	Banks are not engaged in this lending.
Differential treatment of nonresident deposit accounts and/or deposit accounts in foreign exchange	
Reserve requirements	n.a.
Liquid asset requirements	n.a.
Credit controls	n.a.
Provisions specific to institutional investors	There are no regulations governing operations of foreign investors.

Changes During 1996

No significant changes occurred in the exchange and trade system.

SINGAPORE

(Position as of December 31, 1996)

Status Under IMF Articles of Agreement

Article VIII   Date of acceptance: November 9, 1968.

Exchange Arrangement

Currency	The currency of Singapore is the Singapore dollar.
Other legal tender	Singapore and Brunei currency notes and coins are freely interchangeable at par without charge in Singapore and Brunei.
Exchange rate structure	Unitary.
Classification	
Managed floating	The exchange rate of the Singapore dollar is determined freely in the foreign exchange market. However, the Monetary Authority of Singapore (MAS) monitors the external value of the Singapore dollar against a trade-weighted basket of currencies.
Exchange tax	No.
Exchange subsidy	No.
Forward exchange market	Foreign currency futures are traded at the Singapore International Monetary Exchange. Banks can hedge their exchange risk through a forward foreign exchange transaction.
Official cover of forward operations	n.a.

Arrangements for Payments and Receipts

Prescription of currency requirements	No.
Payment arrangements	Yes.
Regional arrangements	Yes.
Barter agreements and open accounts	n.a.
Administration of control	
Exchange control authorities	The MAS retains responsibility for exchange control matters. The Trade Development Board under the Ministry of Trade and Industry administers import and export licensing requirements for a very small number of products.
International security restrictions	
In accordance with IMF Executive Board Decision No. 144-(52/51)	n.a.
In accordance with UN sanctions	Financial assets owned by residents of Iraq and Libya are blocked. Singapore observes the import and export prohibitions covered by the UN Security Council resolutions.
Other	Yes.
Payment arrears	No.
Controls on trade in gold (coins and/or bullion)	
Controls on domestic ownership and/or trade	In the spot market, most of the trading is done on a "loco-London" basis for delivery of 995 fine gold. Kilobars of 999.9 fineness are most commonly traded, while 10-tola bars are also becoming popular. Spot gold prices for settlement in Singapore are derived by

adjusting the loco-London price with the location premium, which takes into account the cost of transportation and insurance. A gold futures contract is also available on the Singapore International Monetary Exchange.

Controls on exports and imports of banknotes	No.

Resident Accounts

Eligibility to hold accounts	Juridical and natural persons are eligible.
Foreign exchange accounts permitted	Yes.
Held domestically	Yes.
Held abroad	Yes.
Accounts in domestic currency convertible into foreign currency	Yes.

Nonresident Accounts

Eligibility to hold accounts	Juridical and natural persons are eligible.
Foreign exchange accounts permitted	Yes.
Domestic currency accounts	Yes.
Convertible into foreign currency	n.a.
Approval required	n.a.

Imports and Import Payments

Financing requirements for imports	No.
Documentation requirements for release of foreign exchange for imports	No.
Import licenses and other nontariff measures	Licenses are required for imports of rice. A few imports are controlled for health, safety, or security reasons.
Open general licenses	n.a.
Licenses with quotas	n.a.
Import taxes and/or tariffs	Very few imports are dutiable. Singapore is a party to the Common Effective Preferential Tariff (CEPT) Scheme for the AFTA. Customs duties are levied on imports of liquor, tobacco, petroleum, and motor cars.
Taxes collected through the exchange system	No.
State import monopoly	No.

Exports and Export Proceeds

Repatriation requirements	No.

Surrender requirements	No.
Financing requirements	No.
Documentation requirements	No.
Export licenses	
Without quotas	Export licenses are required for substances that deplete the stratospheric ozone layer, timber, and rubber.
With quotas	Certain exports (e.g., textiles and clothing) are subject to quantitative restrictions and other nontariff barriers in importing countries.
Export taxes	n.a.
Taxes collected through the exchange system	No.

Payments for Invisible Transactions and Current Transfers

Controls on these payments	No.

Proceeds from Invisible Transactions and Current Transfers

Repatriation requirements	No.
Surrender requirements	No.
Restrictions on use of funds	No.

Capital Transactions

Controls on capital and money market instruments	No.
Controls on derivatives and other instruments	No.
Controls on credit operations	No.
Controls on direct investment	No.
Controls on liquidation of direct investment	No.
Controls on real estate transactions	
Purchase abroad by residents	Yes.
Purchase locally by nonresidents	Foreign investment in residential and other properties (including vacant land) that have been zoned or approved for industrial or commercial use requires government approval. Foreigners may, however, freely purchase residential units in buildings of 6 or more stories and in approved condominium developments. Foreigners who make an economic contribution to Singapore will be given favorable consideration to purchase other residential properties for their own use and, in the case of foreign companies, to accommodate their senior personnel.
Provisions specific to commercial banks and other credit institutions	
Lending to nonresidents (financial or commercial credits)	Banks, merchant banks, and finance and insurance companies must consult the MAS if they intend to grant loans in Singapore dollars in excess of S$5 million to nonresidents. Non-Singapore citizens (excluding permanent residents of Singapore) and

non-Singapore companies are not to be granted Singapore dollar loans for the purchase of residential properties in Singapore.

Lending locally in foreign exchange	n.a.
Purchase of locally issued securities denominated in foreign exchange	n.a.
Differential treatment of nonresident deposit accounts and/or deposit accounts in foreign exchange	
Reserve requirements	Foreign currency deposits accepted under the Asian currency units of banks are not subject to reserve requirements.
Liquid asset requirements	Foreign currency deposits accepted under the Asian currency units of banks are not subject to the liquid asset requirement.
Credit controls	Banks, merchant banks, and finance companies may only grant unsecured credit facilities to individuals with a minimum income of S$30,000 a year. The quantum of such credit facilities may not exceed twice the monthly income of the borrower. For finance companies, the quantum of such credit facilities may not exceed the lesser of twice the monthly income of the borrower or S$5,000.
Open foreign exchange position limits	n.a.

Changes During 1996

Capital transactions

September 30. Nonresident firms were permitted to list on the stock market and to issue bonds in domestic currency, provided that 35% of their revenue is locally generated and their regional headquarters and senior management are based in Singapore.

SLOVAK REPUBLIC

(Position as of January 31, 1997)

Status Under IMF Articles of Agreement

Article VIII	Date of acceptance: October 1, 1995.

Exchange Arrangement

Currency	The currency of the Slovak Republic is the Slovak koruna. 100 haliere = 1 koruna.
Exchange rate structure	Unitary.
Classification	
Pegged	The Slovak koruna is pegged to a basket comprising the deutsche mark (weight of 60%) and the U.S. dollar (weight of 40%), within margins of ±7%, and the official exchange rate is determined in fixing sessions conducted daily by the National Bank of Slovakia (NBS).
Exchange tax	No.
Exchange subsidy	No.
Forward exchange market	n.a.
Official cover of forward operations	No.

Arrangements for Payments and Receipts

Prescription of currency requirements	No.
Payment arrangements	No.
Administration of control	
Exchange control authorities	The NBS is responsible for the administration of exchange controls and regulations in coordination with the Ministry of Finance (MOF). The NBS has authority over the activities of all registered enterprises and entrepreneurs. The MOF exercises jurisdiction in credits granted or accepted by the Slovak Republic as well as in exchange control matters relating to other ministries and central bodies of the state administration, budgetary and subsidized state organizations, special-purpose state funds, juridical persons established by separate law who are connected through financial ties to the state budget, and local communities and their budgetary and subsidized organizations.
	The MOF maintains foreign exchange records and documents pertaining to interstate negotiations on property claims, and implements the results of these negotiations within the country.
Payment arrears	No.
Controls on trade in gold (coins and/or bullion)	
Controls on domestic ownership and/or trade	Trade in gold is conducted exclusively by banks to the extent stipulated in the banking license.
Controls on exports and imports of banknotes	The prohibition on exports and imports of banknotes exceeding Sk 100,000 was eliminated on December 1, 1996; currently, a declaration is required if the amount exceeds a certain volume.

Resident Accounts

Eligibility to hold accounts   Juridical and natural persons are eligible.

Foreign exchange accounts   Yes.
permitted

Held domestically   Resident individuals, including unregistered entrepreneurs, may open foreign exchange accounts without specific permission and without revealing the source of their funds. The balances may be used without restrictions. Juridical persons need the approval of the NBS or the MOF to open these accounts.

Held abroad   These accounts are permitted. A resident may open an account abroad in foreign or Slovak currency, or enter into a contract for the safe custody or deposit of funds in foreign or Slovak currency in an account maintained abroad, only after obtaining a foreign exchange permit from the NBS or the MOF. However, a foreign exchange permit is not required: (1) when the resident has a banking or foreign exchange license; (2) in connection with a private individual's stay abroad; (3) to cover the documented operating costs of the resident's local representation or agency abroad; (4) for the purpose of depositing the resident's foreign exchange instruments if foreign legislation forbids the transfer of such funds to the country; or (5) for the payment of fees, taxes, and other documented expenses related to the administration and maintenance of real estate owned by the resident abroad.

Nonresident Accounts

Eligibility to hold accounts   Juridical and natural persons are eligible.

Foreign exchange accounts   Foreign exchange may be deposited freely into these accounts, and payments may be
permitted   made freely, locally or abroad.

Domestic currency accounts   Yes.

Convertible into foreign currency   Yes.

Blocked accounts   No.

Imports and Import Payments

Foreign exchange budget   No.

Financing requirements for imports   No.

Documentation requirements for   No.
release of foreign exchange for
imports

Import licenses and other nontariff   A system of variable levies accompanies import licensing.
measures

Negative list   Import licenses are required for some agricultural goods and a few strategic items, such as crude oil, natural gas, firearms and munitions, dual-use goods, and narcotics.

Open general licenses   An automatic licensing system applies to imports of several agricultural and industrial products and raw materials.

Licenses with quotas   From January 1, 1997, a nonautomatic licensing system was applied to coal.

Import taxes and/or tariffs   All imports, except those from the Czech Republic and from countries with whom the Slovak Republic has a customs union, are subject to an ad valorem tariff. Imports from developing countries are granted preferential treatment under the GSP: 42 least-developed countries, and 100 developing countries are granted 50% and 100% reductions from applicable duties, respectively. An import surcharge of 7.5% is imposed on certain goods, with the exception of inputs for the production of consumer goods.

Imported goods are taxed with a VAT, and there are excise duties on mineral oils, spirits, wine, beer, and tobacco.

Taxes collected through the exchange system	No.
State import monopoly	No.

Exports and Export Proceeds

Repatriation requirements	In general, a 100% repatriation requirement applies, but in the case of resident individuals the requirement applies to sums exceeding the equivalent of Sk 5,000.
Surrender requirements	Resident juridical persons are required to sell to a bank any foreign exchange receipts exceeding Sk 100,000.
Financing requirements	No.
Documentation requirements	No.
Export licenses	
Without quotas	Export licenses are required for narcotics, poisons, firearms and ammunition, and all dual-use goods and technologies.
With quotas	A limited number of products require export licenses for purposes of health control (including livestock and plants) to facilitate voluntary restraints on products on which partner countries have imposed import quotas (such as textiles and some agricultural products), or to preserve natural resources or imported raw materials (such as energy, metallurgical materials, wood, foodstuffs, pharmaceutical products, and construction materials) for the domestic market.
Export taxes	No.

Payments for Invisible Transactions and Current Transfers

Controls on these payments	There are no controls on these payments except for those set on allowances for travel expenses. Residents may use balances in foreign currency accounts and in domestic currency accounts for purposes of tourism without limit; additional purchases of cash in foreign currency for tourist travel abroad are subject to a $3,000 annual indicative limit. Official travel by employees of budgetary and subsidized organizations is subject to different allowances, depending on the country of destination.

Proceeds from Invisible Transactions and Current Transfers

Repatriation requirements	Residents must repatriate all proceeds without delay, net of fees, taxes, and other expenses incurred abroad in connection with the acquisition of such funds, but no later than 30 days from the date of acquisition, or the date of learning of such acquisition, or from the date of becoming a resident in the country.
Surrender requirements	Resident juridical persons must sell to a bank any foreign exchange they obtain exceeding Sk 100,000.
Restrictions on use of funds	No.

Capital Transactions

Controls on capital and money market instruments

On capital market securities

    Sale or issue locally by nonresidents — These transactions require a permit from the MOF and the NBS.

    Purchase abroad by residents — These transactions require a foreign exchange permit.

    Sale or issue abroad by residents — These transactions require permission from the MOF.

On money market instruments — The NBS regulates these transactions. Same regulations as for capital market securities apply.

On collective investment securities — Same regulations as for capital market securities apply.

Controls on derivatives and other instruments

Sale or issue locally by nonresidents — A permit from the MOF is required.

Purchase abroad by residents — A resident who is an authorized foreign exchange dealer and is not a bank or a securities trader may enter into contracts for dealing in financial derivatives solely on the basis of a foreign exchange permit. A foreign exchange permit is not required when the contract or business is effected with an authorized foreign exchange dealer within the range allowed by the banking or foreign exchange license.

Sale or issue abroad by residents — Same regulations as for purchases abroad by residents apply.

Controls on credit operations

Commercial credits

    By residents to nonresidents — n.a.

    To residents from nonresidents — Registered enterprises may freely obtain credits.

Financial credits — Credits require a special permit from the NBS.

    By residents to nonresidents — Financial credits with a maturity of 5 years or more provided by Slovak residents to residents of OECD countries were liberalized.

    To residents from nonresidents — n.a.

Guarantees, sureties, and financial backup facilities — These transactions require a foreign exchange permit.

    By residents to nonresidents — n.a.

    To residents from nonresidents — n.a.

Controls on direct investment

Outward direct investment — NBS approval is required except when the investment is made in an OECD country; normally, approval is granted if the investment is considered to facilitate exports from the Slovak Republic.

Inward direct investment — There is no limit on equity participation by nonresidents. Foreign exchange equity participation can be deposited in a foreign exchange account with a local bank.

Controls on liquidation of direct investment — No.

Controls on real estate transactions

Purchase abroad by residents — A foreign exchange permit is required, except for OECD countries.

Purchase locally by nonresidents	Nonresidents, with the exception of Slovak citizens, may acquire real estate in the country solely in the following cases: (1) by inheritance; (2) for the purpose of establishing diplomatic representation of a foreign country under conditions of mutuality; (3) when the real estate acquired is co-owned by a married couple, and when one of the partners is a nonresident, or when a nonresident acquires real estate from a spouse, sibling, parent, or grandparent; (4) when there is an exchange of domestic real estate owned by a nonresident for other domestic fixed assets, the price of which, pursuant to separate regulations, does not exceed the price of the original real estate as determined in accordance with separate regulations; (5) when the nonresident has preemptive purchase rights based on share ownership of the real estate; (6) when the real estate was built by the nonresident on his or her own land; and (7) when expressly permitted under separate legislation.
Sale locally by nonresidents	n.a.

Provisions specific to commercial banks and other credit institutions

Borrowing abroad	A banking license is required.
Maintenance of accounts abroad	n.a.
Lending to nonresidents (financial or commercial credits)	n.a.
Lending locally in foreign exchange	Lending is allowed within the extent of the banking license.
Purchase of locally issued securities denominated in foreign exchange	n.a.
Differential treatment of nonresident deposit accounts and/or deposit accounts in foreign exchange	n.a.
Investment regulations	n.a.
Open foreign exchange position limits	Banks are required to keep the ratio of foreign currency assets to liabilities below 1.05; their access to the exchange rate fixing sessions is subject to compliance with this requirement.

Provisions specific to institutional investors

Limits (max.) on portfolio invested abroad	n.a.
Currency matching regulations on assets/liabilities composition	n.a.
Other controls imposed by securities laws	n.a.

Changes During 1996

Exchange arrangements	*July 31.* The margins of the exchange rate band were widened to ±5%.
Arrangements for payments and receipts	*December 1.* The limit on the exporting and importing of Slovak or foreign currency (banknotes and coins) was abolished and replaced with a requirement to declare the exported or imported amount if it exceeds Sk 150,000.
Capital transactions	*December 1.* (1) Financial credits with a maturity of 5 years or more provided by Slovak residents to residents of OECD countries were liberalized.

December 1. (2) The receipt and provision of international trade credits for trade in goods and services with OECD members were liberalized on the condition that the creditor is a third party between the customer and the supplier.

December 1. (3) Foreign borrowings by residents with a maturity of 3 years or more were liberalized.

December 1. (4) The acquisition of real estate by Slovak residents in OECD member countries was liberalized.

December 1. (5) Direct investment by Slovak residents in OECD member countries was liberalized.

Changes During 1997

Exchange arrangements   *January 1.* The margins of the exchange rate band were widened to ±7%.

Imports and import payments   *January 1.* A nonautomatic licensing system was established for imports of coal.

SLOVENIA

(Position as of February 28, 1997)

Status Under IMF Articles of Agreement

Article VIII Date of acceptance: September 1, 1995.

Exchange Arrangement

Currency The currency of Slovenia is the tolar.

Exchange rate structure Unitary.

Classification

Managed floating The external value of the tolar is determined in the interbank exchange market, where the Bank of Slovenia (BOS) may participate. The BOS also may buy and sell foreign exchange in transactions with the government and commercial banks. Natural persons may conduct foreign exchange transactions with banks or foreign exchange offices at freely negotiated rates. Licensed banks may conduct foreign exchange transactions among themselves. Juridical persons may conduct foreign exchange transactions with banks or between themselves. The BOS publishes daily a moving 2-month average exchange rate for customs valuation and accounting purposes, as well as for government transactions.

Exchange tax No.

Exchange subsidy No.

Forward exchange market There is a forward exchange market, but the volume of trading is not significant.

Official cover of forward operations No.

Arrangements for Payments and Receipts

Prescription of currency requirements No.

Payment arrangements Yes.

Bilateral arrangements

Operative Slovenia maintains a payment agreement with the former Yugoslav Republic of Macedonia. The agreement allows juridical persons to conduct transactions through nonresidents' accounts held with banks. Provisions relating to the special clearing settlement are inoperative. Also, there is an agreement with Italy related to trade between the 2 border regions.

Administration of control

Exchange control authorities The Law on Foreign Exchange Business (1991) introduced a free foreign exchange market operated by banks and exchange offices, the BOS, and juridical and natural persons. The Law on Foreign Trade Transactions (1993) sets out the rules and regulations governing foreign trade activities. Cash transactions in foreign currencies are restricted; residents are required, in accordance with the Law on Foreign Exchange Business, to obtain permission from the BOS.

International security restrictions

In accordance with IMF Executive Board Decision No. 144-(52/51) Yes.

| In accordance with UN sanctions | A special law adopted in 1992 in accordance with UN sanctions, amended on May 16, 1996, maintains certain restrictions with regard to assets pertaining to the Federal Republic of Yugoslavia (Serbia/Montenegro). |

Payment arrears

No.

Controls on trade in gold (coins and/or bullion)

No.

Controls on exports and imports of banknotes

On exports

Domestic currency

Natural persons may take abroad up to SIT 300,000 a person. Banks are allowed to take abroad cash exceeding that amount with prior approval of the BOS for each operation.

Foreign currency

Residents may take abroad up to the equivalent of DM 3,000; amounts exceeding DM 3,000 require prior approval from the BOS.

On imports

Domestic currency

Natural persons may bring into the country up to SIT 300,000 a person. Banks are allowed to bring into the country cash exceeding that amount with prior approval of the BOS.

Foreign currency

There are reporting requirements for cash and checks exceeding the equivalent of SIT 2.2 million for natural persons according to regulations on money-laundering prevention.

Resident Accounts

Eligibility to hold accounts

Juridical persons

Resident juridical persons are, in principle, not allowed to maintain foreign currency accounts, with certain exceptions.

Natural persons

Yes.

Foreign exchange accounts permitted

Yes.

Held domestically

Resident natural persons are allowed to open and operate foreign currency accounts without restriction. Resident juridical persons are allowed to maintain accounts in connection with payments provided under the Law on Foreign Exchange Business.

Held abroad

Resident juridical persons may maintain accounts abroad only in specific cases. Only banks licensed for foreign payments may maintain accounts abroad; resident natural persons are not allowed to do so. Approval of the BOS is required.

Accounts in domestic currency convertible into foreign currency

Yes.

Nonresident Accounts

Eligibility to hold accounts

Juridical and natural persons are eligible.

Foreign exchange accounts permitted

Withdrawals in cash from these accounts are limited to the equivalent of SIT 250,000 a month; amounts exceeding this limit are subject to BOS approval.

Domestic currency accounts

Nonresidents may open local currency accounts and conduct tolar-denominated operations. These accounts may be "by name" only. Tolar cash withdrawals are limited to SIT 250,000 a month; withdrawals exceeding this amount are subject to prior approval of the BOS. Balances in these accounts may be converted into convertible currencies and repatriated.

Convertible into foreign currency	Yes.
Blocked accounts	These accounts are blocked as per implementation of UN resolutions.

Imports and Import Payments

Foreign exchange budget	No.
Financing requirements for imports	No.
Documentation requirements for release of foreign exchange for imports	Commercial banks effect payments upon the presentation of documents reflecting the purpose of the transaction.
Import licenses and other nontariff measures	Licensing requirements in the form of permits, for the purpose of control only, have been retained for specific groups of goods (e.g., drugs, explosives, precious metals, and arms and ammunition), and for security and public health reasons, in accordance with international conventions and codes.
Licenses with quotas	Slovenia maintains a system of import quotas applicable only to certain textile products. There are annual import quotas, which are allocated to relevant associations of the Chamber of Commerce of Slovenia. Quotas are not applied to imports from countries with which Slovenia has free trade agreements.
Import taxes and/or tariffs	There are customs and specific duties that are in accordance with the range accepted in the WTO. Customs duties range up to 27% for individual products, and certain agricultural products are subject to a 57.5% rate.
Taxes collected through the exchange system	No.
State import monopoly	No.

Exports and Export Proceeds

Repatriation requirements	Exporters are free to agree on payment terms with foreign importers. However, if the collection of export proceeds is delayed by more than 1 year, the transactions must be registered with the BOS as credit arrangements. Once received, export proceeds must be repatriated.
Surrender requirements	Exporters have 2 business days to sell their proceeds to importers at a freely negotiated exchange rate or to use the proceeds for payments abroad. After that term, they must sell their proceeds to an authorized bank.
Financing requirements	No.
Documentation requirements	No.
Export licenses	Except for certain items that are subject to licensing for security or health reasons in accordance with the international conventions and codes, exports are not restricted.
Without quotas	Yes.
Export taxes	A tax is levied on unworked wood (4%); the tax is not paid for exports to countries with which Slovenia has a free trade agreement.
Taxes collected through the exchange system	No.

Payments for Invisible Transactions and Current Transfers

Controls on these payments	Residents are not allowed to purchase insurance abroad, except in the case of reinsurance by insurance companies.

Proceeds from Invisible Transactions and Current Transfers

Repatriation requirements	Yes.
Surrender requirements	Yes.
Restrictions on use of funds	No.

Capital Transactions

Controls on capital and money market instruments

On capital market securities

Purchase locally by nonresidents

Nonresidents are obliged to conduct their portfolio investments in the secondary market-traded securities and derivatives through the custody accounts established with the licensed domestic banks, and held either in tolars or in foreign currency. Nonresidents may authorize either the licensed domestic bank or a proxy to effect transactions. The custody accounts representing a bank's foreign exchange liability need to be balanced with the equivalent foreign exchange assets.

Sale or issue locally by nonresidents

Nonresidents are not allowed to undertake such activities in the country. Foreign securities may be offered in Slovenia only with the prior approval of the Agency for Securities Market, by domestic brokerage companies, and licensed banks.

Purchase abroad by residents

Banks are allowed to purchase securities abroad. Provisions regulating direct investments and credit operations are applied in case of portfolio investments abroad.

Sale or issue abroad by residents

Same regulations as for purchase locally by nonresidents apply.

On money market instruments

Same regulations as for capital market securities apply.

On collective investment securities

Same regulations as for capital market securities apply.

Controls on derivatives and other instruments

Same regulations as for capital market securities apply.

Controls on credit operations

Commercial credits

Commercial credits are subject to registration with the BOS, provided the payment for goods and services is deferred for more than 12 months.

By residents to nonresidents

Yes.

To residents from nonresidents

Yes.

Financial credits

By residents to nonresidents

Domestic banks may extend financial credits to nonresidents in accordance with their policy. Domestic companies, other than banks, may extend financial credits to companies they control.

To residents from nonresidents

There are interest-free deposit requirements: 40% for loans with maturities of up to 7 years (up to 5 years until end-July 1996) and 10% for loans with maturities of more than 7 years (for credits concluded after December 28, 1996), except for loans issued by commercial banks or the Republic of Slovenia.

Controls on direct investment

Outward direct investment

Domestic legal entities (companies) must obtain permission of the Ministry of Finance. The permission is granted provided that (1) the domestic company has been operating with the profit, and the funds used do not exceed the amount of the latter; and (2) the taxes and the customs have been paid in the country.

Inward direct investment

Registration of foreign direct investments or establishment of (wholly or partially) foreign-owned companies is subject to the same conditions as those of domestic entities. Companies must be registered at the local Court of Justice, which is deemed to have informed the Ministry of Economic Cooperation and Development accordingly. Wholly foreign-owned companies are not allowed in the military equipment field, rail and air transport, communications and telecommunications, insurance, publishing, and mass media. Furthermore, in the following sectors, foreign participation is limited: auditing companies, stockbroking companies, management companies for investment funds, and authorized management companies. Foreign banks may not open branches in Slovenia, while the foreign participation in banks or the establishment of subsidiaries of foreign banks is subject to the prior approval of the BOS. Foreign acquisition of more than 25% of shares of newly privatized companies is subject to governmental approval.

Controls on liquidation of direct investment	Transfer of proceeds is free of any restrictions after all obligations in Slovenia have been met. Transfer of proceeds from realization of inheritance is free if the principle of reciprocity is guaranteed between Slovenia and the country of the recipient.
Controls on real estate transactions	
Purchase abroad by residents	Purchases that do not constitute a part of outward direct investments are, in principle, free.
Purchase locally by nonresidents	Foreigners may not own land and other real estate. Foreign states, however, may acquire rights to own property affixed to land used by them for diplomatic and consular purposes. Furthermore, foreigners may acquire a title to land only by inheritance, provided that reciprocity of such right of acquisition is recognized.
Provisions specific to commercial banks and other credit institutions	
Borrowing abroad	Banks are not allowed to raise short-term loans abroad. There is an interest-free deposit requirement for loans with maturities of up to 7 years (up to 5 years until end-July 1996) of 40%.
Maintenance of accounts abroad	Authorized domestic banks are permitted to hold accounts with foreign banks, provided that they meet credit solvency requirements of the country in which the foreign bank has its headquarters. Domestic banks must report these accounts to the BOS.
Lending locally in foreign exchange	Domestic authorized banks are allowed to extend credits in foreign currency to domestic persons, other than natural persons, provided they exceed in the moment when the credit is approved their minimum foreign exchange requirement, set by the BOS, by at least 10% and that the terms of the credit are not less favorable for the client than those prevailing on the international capital market. The funds so obtained may be used for payments abroad or for refinancing of the existing obligations from previously extended credits pursuant to this regulation.
Purchase of locally issued securities denominated in foreign exchange	Yes.
Differential treatment of nonresident deposit accounts and/or deposit accounts in foreign exchange	
Reserve requirements	There is an interest-free deposit requirement on tolar and foreign exchange deposit accounts of foreign banks and financial institutions as applied for purely financial loans; no restrictions apply to the transaction accounts of foreign banks and financial institutions. There is no difference in treatment of tolar deposits owned by residents or nonresidents.
Liquid asset requirements	Banks are prescribed to hold minimum required assets in foreign currencies. The amount is determined for each bank on a monthly basis with regard to its foreign payments operations (35% of the average monthly foreign payments over the last 3 months) and its foreign currency liabilities to households (for sight deposits 100%, time deposits up to 3 months 75%, time deposits over 3 months and up to 1 year 35%, and time deposits over 1 year 5%) and nonresidents (for sight deposits 90%, time deposits up to 3 months 75%, time deposits over 3 months and up to 1 year 35%, and time deposits over 1 year 5%).
Open foreign exchange position limits	From July 1996, commercial banks are obligated to match the net increase of certain foreign exchange obligations (and since December 1996, those of the companies they control) with certain foreign exchange claims.

Provisions specific to institutional investors

The Law on Insurance Companies (1994) and the Law on Investment Funds and Management Companies (1994) establish that:

(1) Insurance stock companies may not be owned only by nonresidents;

(2) Nonresidents can become stockholders of insurance companies only with the approval of the Ministry of Finance;

(3) If the majority of shares are owned by nonresidents, insurance companies cannot provide reinsurance;

(4) Mutual insurance funds should be owned only by residents;

(5) Management companies may be owned by nonresidents by more than 20% of shares only with the approval of the Agency of Securities Market;

(6) Authorized management companies (i.e., those authorized to manage investment companies that collect vouchers in the privatization process) may be owned by more than 10% of shares only with the approval of the Agency for Securities Market and the Ministry for Economic Affairs and Development; and

(7) Investment stock companies (closed investment fund) may invest in foreign securities up to 10% of total investments. Only foreign securities of explicitly stated stock exchanges by the Agency for Securities Market are eligible.

The Law on Pension Insurance establishes that the capital fund of the Pension Insurance Stock Company is owned by the Republic of Slovenia. Voluntary pension funds for extra pension rights are subject to rules for insurance stock companies.

Limits (max.) on portfolio invested abroad

Yes.

Limits (min.) on portfolio invested locally

Yes.

Other controls imposed by securities laws

The Law on Securities Market (1994) imposes restrictions on ownership by nonresidents of licensed market participants-brokers. Nonresidents may own up to 24% of the capital of a broker's company only with the approval of the Agency for Securities Market.

Changes During 1996

Arrangements for payments and receipts

May 16. The special law with regard to UN sanctions was amended, maintaining certain restrictions with regard to assets pertaining to the Federal Republic of Yugoslavia (Serbia/Montenegro).

Capital transactions

July 31. The maturity of loans borrowed abroad by residents subject to 40% interest-free deposit requirements was extended to 7 years from 5 years.

December 28. A 10% interest-free deposit requirement was introduced applicable to loans borrowed abroad by residents with maturities of more than 7 years.

Changes During 1997

Nonresident accounts

February 4. Cash withdrawals from foreign exchange accounts were limited to SIT 250,000 a month, or its equivalent. Amounts exceeding this limit are subject to BOS approval.

Capital transactions

January 21. Domestic banks were allowed to extend financial credits to nonresidents in accordance with their policy. Domestic companies, other than banks, may extend financial credits to companies they control.

February 4. Nonresidents are required to conduct their portfolio investments in the secondary market-traded securities and derivatives through custody accounts established with licensed domestic banks.

SOLOMON ISLANDS

(Position as of December 31, 1996)

Status Under IMF Articles of Agreement

Article VIII	Date of acceptance: July 24, 1979.

Exchange Arrangement

Currency	The currency of the Solomon Islands is the Solomon Islands dollar.
Exchange rate structure	Unitary.
Classification	
Pegged	The exchange rate for the Solomon Islands dollar is pegged to a trade-weighted basket of the currencies of the Solomon Islands' 4 major trading partners. The Central Bank of the Solomon Islands (CBSI) may make discretionary adjustments in the exchange value of the Solomon Islands dollar against the U.S. dollar each month within margins of 0.4% above or below the middle rate prevailing at the end of the previous month. The CBSI provides the commercial banks with daily limits on the buying and selling rates for the U.S. dollar in transactions with the CBSI and the public. The commercial banks in the Solomon Islands are free to determine their exchange rates for all other foreign currencies.
Exchange tax	A tax of SI$3 is levied on sales of foreign exchange exceeding SI$3,000.
Forward exchange market	Commercial banks may enter into forward contracts with residents of the Solomon Islands in any currency.
Official cover of forward operations	No.

Arrangements for Payments and Receipts

Prescription of currency requirements	Contractual commitments in a foreign currency to nonresidents may be met only by payments in the currency specified in the contract. Export proceeds may be received in any foreign currency or in Solomon Islands dollars from an account of an overseas bank with a bank in the Solomon Islands.
Payment arrangements	n.a.
Administration of control	
Exchange control authorities	Exchange control is administered by the CBSI through the Foreign Exchange Control Regulations (1977). The CBSI delegates extensive powers to commercial banks, which have been appointed authorized dealers in foreign exchange and may approve certain transactions up to specified limits.
International security restrictions	
In accordance with IMF Executive Board Decision No. 144-(52/51)	Certain restrictions have been imposed on the making of payments and transfers for current international transactions in respect of the Federal Republic of Yugoslavia (Serbia/Montenegro).
In accordance with UN sanctions	Yes.
Controls on trade in gold (coins and/or bullion)	
Controls on domestic ownership and/or trade	Only Solomon Islands nationals may be granted a license to pan for alluvial gold. The CBSI is authorized to buy, sell, and hold gold but has not yet undertaken any such transactions. Commercial mining companies require a license from the Ministry of Natural Resources to mine gold.

Controls on external trade	Commercial banks and all other residents are required to obtain a permit issued by the Ministry of Natural Resources to mine, buy, or export gold.

Controls on exports and imports of banknotes

On exports

Domestic currency	Travelers may not take out amounts in excess of SI$250 without the approval of the CBSI, which is not normally given.
Foreign currency	n.a.

On imports

Domestic currency	n.a.
Foreign currency	Nonresidents visiting the Solomon Islands may bring in any amount of currency for travel expenditures.

Resident Accounts

Eligibility to hold accounts

Juridical persons	Yes.
Natural persons	n.a.
Foreign exchange accounts permitted	Resident companies may obtain CBSI approval to hold these accounts in cases where there is a genuine need.
Held domestically	n.a.
Held abroad	n.a.

Nonresident Accounts

Eligibility to hold accounts	Juridical and natural persons are eligible.
Foreign exchange accounts permitted	Foreign exchange accounts may be held, but proof of bona fide need is required. Approval is required.
Domestic currency accounts	These accounts can be held only at authorized foreign exchange dealers.
Convertible into foreign currency	Balances may be transferred abroad with the approval of the CBSI or authorized dealers. CBSI approval is required for these accounts to be credited from Solomon Islands sources.

Imports and Import Payments

Documentation requirements for release of foreign exchange for imports	Authorized dealers are permitted to approve most transactions up to SI$25,000 without reference to the CBSI.
Domiciliation requirements	n.a.
Preshipment inspection	n.a.
Letters of credit	n.a.
Import licenses used as exchange licenses	n.a.
Import taxes and/or tariffs	The rate of import levy is 8%.

Taxes collected through the exchange system	A tax of SI$3 is levied on sales of foreign exchange exceeding SI$3,000.

Exports and Export Proceeds

Repatriation requirements	Proceeds must be received within 3 months of the date of exportation.
Surrender requirements	Export proceeds must be sold promptly to an authorized dealer.
Export licenses	Residents may export goods other than round logs without exchange control formalities, but they must comply with the terms of a general authorization issued by the CBSI. Exports of round logs require specific authority from the CBSI upon presentation of a market price certificate issued by the Ministry of Forestry, Conservation, and Environment.
Without quotas	If exporters cannot meet the conditions of a general authorization (repatriation, surrender, or market level price requirements), they must apply to the CBSI for a specific authorization. Authorization is not needed for goods valued under SI$250 in any one consignment or for certain exempt categories of goods, including most personal effects of passengers.
With quotas	n.a.
Export taxes	Exports of logs are subject to an export duty of 35% if valued up to SI$250 per cubic meter and 38% if of greater value.
Taxes collected through the exchange system	n.a.

Payments for Invisible Transactions and Current Transfers

Controls on these payments	There are no controls on payments for freight and insurance, unloading and storage costs, administrative expenses, commissions, and family maintenance and alimony. Transfers by postal order to persons residing permanently abroad are permitted up to SI$100 a week.
Interest payments	
Prior approval	Approval is readily granted for the repayment of loans contracted overseas.
Profit/dividends	
Prior approval	Approval is readily granted for payments of services and remittances of dividends, profits, and other earnings accruing to nonresidents from companies in the Solomon Islands, provided it can be shown they are properly due.
Quantitative limits	n.a.
Indicative limits/bona fide test	n.a.
Payments for travel	
Prior approval	Approval is normally given for the purchase of foreign currency for travel. Applications for travel funds must be submitted to an authorized dealer, and presentation of passports and airline tickets is required.
Quantitative limits	n.a.
Indicative limits/bona fide test	n.a.
Medical costs	n.a.
Study abroad costs	n.a.
Subscriptions and membership fees	n.a.

Consulting/legal fees	n.a.
Foreign workers' wages	
Prior approval	Approval is readily granted for the remittance of funds of temporary residents.
Credit card use abroad	n.a.

Proceeds from Invisible Transactions and Current Transfers

Repatriation requirements	Yes.
Surrender requirements	Approval is required for the disposal of proceeds other than by sale to an authorized dealer.

Capital Transactions

Controls on capital and money market instruments	All outward transfers of capital require exchange control approval by the CBSI.
On capital market securities	CBSI approval is required for transactions with these securities.
Purchase locally by nonresidents	Yes.
Sale or issue locally by nonresidents	Yes.
Purchase abroad by residents	Yes.
Sale or issue abroad by residents	Controls are not normally imposed on the sale of foreign securities acquired before March 1, 1997.
On money market instruments	n.a.
On collective investment securities	
Purchase locally by nonresidents	n.a.
Sale or issue locally by nonresidents	n.a.
Purchase abroad by residents	CBSI approval is required.
Sale or issue abroad by residents	CBSI approval is required.
Controls on derivatives and other instruments	
Controls on credit operations	
Commercial credits	
By residents to nonresidents	n.a.
To residents from nonresidents	CBSI approval is required to borrow funds from or to issue equity capital to a nonresident.
Financial credits	
By residents to nonresidents	n.a.
To residents from nonresidents	The Solomon Islands branch of a company incorporated overseas must have CBSI approval for borrowing funds from a nonresident, including the branch's overseas head office.
Controls on direct investment	
Outward direct investment	Investment by resident individuals or by companies and other organizations operating in the Solomon Islands is subject to certain limitations and when it is likely to be of benefit to the Solomon Islands.

Inward direct investment	Approval by the Foreign Investment Board is required for initial or increased foreign investment.
Controls on liquidation of direct investment	Approval is readily given for the transfer of proceeds.
Provisions specific to commercial banks and other credit institutions	
Borrowing abroad	n.a.
Maintenance of accounts abroad	n.a.
Lending to nonresidents (financial or commercial credits)	n.a.
Lending locally in foreign exchange	n.a.
Purchase of locally issued securities denominated in foreign exchange	n.a.
Differential treatment of nonresident deposit accounts and/or deposit accounts in foreign exchange	
Reserve requirements	n.a.
Liquid asset requirements	There is a 40% requirement.
Interest rate controls	n.a.
Credit controls	n.a.
Investment regulations	n.a.
Open foreign exchange position limits	Limits are set for each commercial bank.

Changes During 1996

No significant changes occurred in the exchange and trade system.

SOMALIA

(Position as of December 31, 1994)

Status Under IMF Articles of Agreement

Article XIV	Yes.

Exchange Arrangement

Currency

The currency of Somalia is the Somali shilling.

Exchange rate structure

Dual

There are two exchange markets: (1) the official market comprising the Central Bank of Somalia (CBS) and the 2 commercial banks operating as authorized dealers; the official rate applies to imports of goods and services and debt-service payments of the government; and (2) a free market, in which the exchange rate is freely negotiated between resident holders of foreign exchange accounts, that is, export/import accounts and external accounts.

Classification

Independent floating

The exchange rate of the Somali shilling is determined in the free market by supply and demand.

Exchange tax

No.

Exchange subsidy

No.

Forward exchange market

No.

Arrangements for Payments and Receipts

Prescription of currency requirements

Settlements with other countries must be made in Somali shillings or in specified currencies (deutsche mark, Djibouti francs, French francs, Italian lire, Kuwaiti dinars, pounds sterling, Saudi Arabian riyals, Swiss francs, U.A.E. dirhams, and U.S. dollars); however, residents are not permitted to make settlements with Israel or South Africa.

Administration of control

Exchange control authorities

Exchange licensing is the responsibility of the CBS.

Payment arrears

Yes.

Official

n.a.

Private

n.a.

Controls on trade in gold (coins and/or bullion)

Controls on domestic ownership and/or trade

Residents may hold and acquire, for numismatic purposes only, gold coins that are not legal tender in any country. With this exception, residents other than the monetary authorities and authorized industrial users are not allowed to hold or acquire gold in any form other than jewelry.

Controls on external trade

Imports and exports of gold in any form other than jewelry require the permission of the CBS; permission is not normally granted except for imports and exports by or on behalf of the monetary authorities and industrial users. Gold imported by jewelers must be melted down within 1 month to a fineness of not more than 22 karats. Imports of gold that originate in member countries of the EU are exempt from customs duty; imports from elsewhere are subject to a 10% duty.

Controls on exports and imports of banknotes

On exports

    Domestic currency   n.a.

On imports

    Domestic currency   Nonresidents may bring in with them up to So. Sh. 1,000. Nonresident Somalis and foreign national travelers without diplomatic status are required, upon their arrival in Somalia, to convert at least $100 or its equivalent to Somali shillings at the airport branch of the Commercial and Savings Bank, which acts on behalf of the CBS.

Resident Accounts

Eligibility to hold accounts   Juridical and natural persons are eligible.

Foreign exchange accounts permitted   These accounts may be credited with foreign exchange transferred from abroad and may be debited for any external payment. Residents may transfer funds to other external accounts. Funds in these accounts may be used for invisible payments as well as for merchandise import payments. All transactions between residents and nonresidents taking place through external accounts are effected at the official exchange rate.

Exporters of goods and services may deposit 40% of their foreign exchange proceeds from exports into export/import accounts. Funds in these accounts may be sold to importers holding export/import accounts and may be used only for merchandise import payments.

Held domestically   Yes.

Held abroad   No.

Nonresident Accounts

Eligibility to hold accounts   Juridical and natural persons are eligible.

Foreign exchange accounts permitted   Nonresident accounts in foreign currency and external accounts in U.S. dollars may be opened with the CBS by foreign embassies, international institutions, and nonresidents.

Imports and Import Payments

Foreign exchange budget   No.

Financing requirements for imports   All payments for private imports must be effected through letters of credit (LCs). Private importers may open LCs for imports at a commercial bank on the basis of foreign exchange made available for that purpose through a foreign currency account with the commercial bank; in such a case, the foreign exchange involved is kept in a suspense account until the time of settlement of the LCs.

Advance payment requirements   Yes.

Advance import deposits   A non-interest-bearing cash advance deposit of 100% is required to open LCs for private sector imports; the deposit is retained until the LCs are settled.

Documentation requirements for release of foreign exchange for imports

Letters of credit   Yes.

Import licenses used as exchange licenses   n.a.

Import licenses and other nontariff measures	Imports of alcohol, tobacco and tobacco products, crude oil and petroleum products, medical and pharmaceutical products, explosives, precious metals, jewelry, and minerals are subject to prior approval. All other items, except those prohibited for reasons of public safety and social policy, may be imported freely. Imports of goods originating in or shipped from Israel and South Africa are prohibited.
Negative list	Yes.
Open general licenses	n.a.
Licenses with quotas	n.a.
Import taxes and/or tariffs	n.a.
Taxes collected through the exchange system	n.a.
State import monopoly	No.

Exports and Export Proceeds

Repatriation requirements	All proceeds must be repatriated.
Surrender requirements	Exporters of bananas and livestock may retain 40% of their foreign exchange receipts in export/import accounts and must surrender the remainder to the CBS or to authorized dealers. Exporters of nontraditional goods may retain 70% of their export earnings.
Documentation requirements	For exports other than those made under LC arrangements, an advance payment deposit of 100% of the value of exports is required.
Letters of credit	n.a.
Guarantees	n.a.
Domiciliation	n.a.
Preshipment inspection	n.a.
Export licenses	Exports and reexports to Israel are prohibited. Bananas are exported only by SOMALFRUIT (previously, the National Banana Board). The exportation of various types of ivory, hides and skins, and minerals is subject to prior approval.
Without quotas	Yes.
With quotas	n.a.
Export taxes	A tax of 25% is levied on exports of livestock on the basis of minimum export prices used for purposes of duty collection.
Taxes collected through the exchange system	n.a.

Payments for Invisible Transactions and Current Transfers

Controls on these payments	All payments and transfers are subject to prior approval. Payments to Israel are prohibited. To prevent unauthorized capital transfers, payments for current invisibles through external accounts, as well as through the commercial banks selling foreign exchange on their own account, are subject to licensing.
Payments for travel	The CBS provides foreign exchange only for official travel expenses. Foreign exchange for private travel expenses may be purchased only from holders of external accounts with the approval of the CBS.
Quantitative limits	There is a limit of $200 a person a trip for business and tourist travel.
Indicative limits/bona fide test	The CBS may approve applications for larger amounts in exceptional cases.

Medical costs

    Quantitative limits   The limit is $3,000 a year for medical costs.

    Indicative limits/bona fide test   The CBS may approve applications for larger amounts in exceptional cases.

Study abroad costs

    Quantitative limits   The limit is $1,000 a year.

    Indicative limits/bona fide test   The CBS may approve applications for larger amounts in exceptional cases.

Subscriptions and membership fees

    Quantitative limits   n.a.

    Indicative limits/bona fide test   n.a.

Foreign workers' wages   Transfers of salaries, wages, gratuities, and allowances paid in Somalia to foreign personnel by enterprises registered under the Foreign Investment Law are allowed up to 50%.

Proceeds from Invisible Transactions and Current Transfers

Repatriation requirements   Proceeds from invisibles must be repatriated and declared.

Surrender requirements   Exporters of services may retain up to 40% of their foreign exchange receipts in external accounts; they must surrender the remainder to the CBS or to authorized dealers within 5 business days of their receipts.

Capital Transactions

Controls on capital and money market instruments   Capital transactions are subject to licensing unless they are authorized by the Foreign Investment Law.

On capital market securities

    Sale or issue locally by nonresidents   n.a.

    Purchase abroad by residents   Yes.

    Sale or issue abroad by residents   Yes.

On money market instruments

    Sale or issue locally by nonresidents   n.a.

    Purchase abroad by residents   Yes.

    Sale or issue abroad by residents   Yes.

On collective investment securities

    Sale or issue locally by nonresidents   n.a.

    Purchase abroad by residents   Yes.

    Sale or issue abroad by residents   Yes.

Controls on credit operations

Commercial credits   Yes.

Financial credits   Yes.

Guarantees, sureties, and financial backup facilities	Yes.

Controls on direct investment

Outward direct investment	Yes.
Inward direct investment	Investments must obtain approval from the Foreign Investment Board, which reviews proposals on a case-by-case basis, within a 60-day period.

Controls on liquidation of direct investment

Foreign investment (original investment plus any profit reinvested) may be freely repatriated 5 years from the date of the registration of the original investment. Repatriation may be effected in convertible currency or, at the investor's option, in the form of physical assets. The Foreign Investment Board may reduce the above-mentioned 5-year period. Capital gains resulting from the sale of shares or liquidation of assets are freely transferable after taxes are paid.

Controls on real estate transactions

Purchase abroad by residents	Yes.

Changes During 1995–96

[The IMF has not received from the authorities the information required for a description of the exchange and trade system as of December 1995 and December 1996.]

SOUTH AFRICA

(Position as of March 31, 1997)

Status Under IMF Articles of Agreement

Article VIII   Date of acceptance: September 15, 1973.

Exchange Arrangement

Currency   The currency of South Africa is the rand.

Exchange rate structure   Unitary.

Classification

Independent floating   The exchange rate of the rand is determined in the foreign exchange market. The authorities of South Africa do not maintain margins with respect to exchange transactions, but intervene in the exchange market to affect rates quoted by the commercial banks. The principal intervention currency is the U.S. dollar.

Exchange tax   No.

Exchange subsidy   No.

Forward exchange market   Subject to certain limitations, authorized dealers are permitted to conduct forward exchange operations, including cover for transactions by nonresidents. They are also permitted to provide forward exchange cover in any foreign currency to residents for any firm and to ascertain foreign exchange commitments and accruals due to or by nonresidents arising from authorized trade and nontrade transactions. Forward exchange contracts may cover the entire period of the outstanding commitments or accruals. Subject to certain limitations, forward exchange cover may also be provided to nonresidents. Gold mining companies and houses may sell forward anticipated receipts of their future gold sales.

Official cover of forward operations   The South African Reserve Bank (SARB) provides forward cover only against U.S. dollars. Such cover is given only against documentary evidence of foreign financing transactions to authorized dealers for maturities not exceeding 12 months in the form of rand-dollar swap transactions, with the margin based on an interest rate differential between the dollar and the rand. Forward cover for periods in excess of 12 months is available from authorized dealers only.

Arrangements for Payments and Receipts

Prescription of currency requirements   All countries outside the CMA constitute the nonresident area. The rand is legal tender in Lesotho and Namibia but not in Swaziland. Settlements by or to residents of the CMA with the nonresident area may be made in rand to and from a nonresident account and in any foreign currency (except the currencies of Lesotho, Namibia, and Swaziland). Lilangeni banknotes issued by Swaziland, loti banknotes issued by Lesotho, and Namibia dollar notes issued by Namibia are freely convertible into rand at par, but they are not legal tender in South Africa.

Payment arrangements

Regional arrangements   South Africa is part of the CMA. Payments within the CMA are unrestricted.

Administration of control

Exchange control authorities   Exchange licensing is the responsibility of the Treasury, which has delegated this authority to the SARB; in turn, the SARB has delegated many of its powers to the authorized dealers.

International security restrictions

In accordance with UN sanctions | According to UN Security Council Resolution No. 661, South Africa imposed restrictions on current payments and transfers to Iraq.

Payment arrears | No.

Controls on trade in gold (coins and/or bullion)

Controls on domestic ownership and/or trade | Residents of South Africa may purchase, hold, and sell gold coins in South Africa for numismatic purposes and investment, but only monetary authorities, authorized dealers, registered gold producers, and authorized industrial and professional users are allowed to purchase, hold, or sell gold in any form other than jewelry. The gold mining industry must sell its output to the SARB, as agent for the Treasury, within 1 month of production. The SARB pays the gold mines in U.S. dollars for their sales of production. As a special concession, the Chamber of Mines may sell or market one-third of South Africa's annual production of gold in the form of value-added gold products not exceeding 1 kilogram each. The mint strikes gold coins and the Krugerrand, which are legal tender, without a face value, and these are made available in limited numbers to the local market.

Controls on external trade | All exports of gold must be approved in advance by the SARB. Approval authority has been delegated to authorized dealers for exports of jewelry constituting the personal effects of a traveler, up to a value of R 50,000 (subject to a written declaration that the jewelry will be brought back to South Africa on the traveler's return); and for exports of gold jewelry by manufacturing jewelers subject to a written declaration that the articles are in fully manufactured form and that the gold content of each does not exceed 85% of the selling price to the ultimate consignee. Furthermore, after approval by the SARB, residents are allowed to export currency coins, including certain gold coins, for sale to numismatists.

Controls on exports and imports of banknotes

On exports

Domestic currency | Notes up to R 2,000 may be exported, but this amount is not regarded as part of the basic travel allowance. The limitation does not apply to migrant workers returning to neighboring countries, who are permitted to take with them reasonable amounts in banknotes. There are no limitations on the exportation of domestic currency to Lesotho, Namibia, and Swaziland. Foreign visitors leaving South Africa may take with them up to R 2,000 in SARB notes.

Foreign currency | Residents and contract workers leaving South Africa for destinations outside the CMA may take out their allowance in foreign banknotes. Foreign visitors leaving South Africa may take with them any amount of foreign notes brought into the country or obtained through the disposal of instruments of exchange brought into and converted in South Africa.

On imports

Domestic currency | Residents and nonresidents entering from countries outside the CMA may bring in up to R 2,000 in SARB notes. There are no limitations on the importation of domestic currency from Lesotho, Namibia, and Swaziland.

Resident Accounts

Eligibility to hold accounts | Juridical and natural persons are eligible.

Foreign exchange accounts permitted | Yes.

Held domestically | No.

Held abroad	These accounts are permitted, but approval is granted based on the merit of the application, and in most circumstances only if it can be demonstrated that the management of trade receipts and payments can be facilitated.
Accounts in domestic currency convertible into foreign currency	No.

Nonresident Accounts

Eligibility to hold accounts	Juridical and natural persons are eligible.
Foreign exchange accounts permitted	No.
Domestic currency accounts	These accounts may be credited with all authorized payments by residents, with the proceeds of sales of foreign currency to authorized dealers, and with payments from other nonresident accounts. They may be debited for payments to CMA residents for any purpose (other than loans); for payments to nonresidents for any purpose, by transfer to a local nonresident account or for remittance to any country outside the CMA; for the cost of purchases of any foreign currency; and for payments to account holders residing in South Africa for short periods.
Convertible into foreign currency	Yes.
Blocked accounts	These accounts are opened for emigrants from the CMA and are subject to exchange control restrictions. Any cash or proceeds from any other South African asset held at the time of departure and subsequently sold must be credited to this type of account. These funds may not be transferred abroad or to another emigrant blocked account in South Africa but must be retained on deposit with an authorized dealer, used within certain limits for the holder's living expenses while visiting South Africa, for other specified payments to residents, or for investment in any locally quoted securities (such securities may not, however, be exported and sold abroad).

Imports and Import Payments

Foreign exchange budget	No.
Financing requirements for imports	Yes.
Advance payment requirements	Payments are allowed before the date of shipment or dispatch, except for capital goods imports. Authorized dealers can permit, without the SARB's approval, advance payment of up to 33.3% of the ex-factory cost of capital goods if suppliers require it or if it is normal in the trade concerned.
Documentation requirements for release of foreign exchange for imports	Importers are automatically granted foreign exchange to pay for current imports upon presenting to their bank the necessary transport and consignment documents (proof of importation) and an import permit when required.
Import licenses and other nontariff measures	
Positive list	Imports that do not require a permit include all goods from Botswana, Lesotho, Malawi, Namibia, Swaziland, and Zimbabwe that are grown, produced, or manufactured in these countries, with the exception of a limited range of agricultural products from Malawi and Zimbabwe.
Negative list	The negative list includes all used goods; waste and scrap; fish, crustaceans, and mollusks; dairy products; dried fruit; black tea; certain vegetables and agricultural products; wines; mineral fuels; radioactive chemicals; new pneumatic tires; gold and coins; certain minerals and firearms; gambling machines; and ozone-depleting substances. All importers requiring import permits for trade or manufacturing purposes must be registered with

the Sub-directorate of Import and Export Control. The permits are valid for imports from any country.

Licenses with quotas	Import quotas apply to certain agricultural and a number of manufactured products.
Import taxes and/or tariffs	Tariff rates range up to 40%, except for motor vehicles, the rate for which is set at 57%.
Taxes collected through the exchange system	No.
State import monopoly	No.

Exports and Export Proceeds

Repatriation requirements	Unless otherwise permitted, all export proceeds must be remitted to South Africa.
Surrender requirements	Unless otherwise permitted, all export proceeds must be received within 6 months of the date of shipment or 7 days of the date of accrual. Except for exports made on a cash-on-delivery basis or those for which the full proceeds are received in advance, exporters are permitted to cover forward their export proceeds within 7 days of shipment.
Financing requirements	Authorized dealers may permit exporters to grant credit for up to 12 months, provided the credit is necessary in that particular trade or needed to protect an existing export market or capture a new one.
Documentation requirements	No.
Export licenses	
Without quotas	Exports outside the SACU of a limited number of products considered to be in relatively short supply or controlled for strategic reasons require export permits.
Export taxes	No.

Payments for Invisible Transactions and Current Transfers

Controls on these payments	Payments for freight and insurance, unloading and storage costs, administrative expenses, interest, commissions, medical treatment, study abroad, subscriptions and membership fees, consulting and legal fees, foreign workers' wages, gambling and prize earnings, and the remittances of profits and dividends are subject to indicative limits and/or bona fide tests.
Freight/insurance	
Prior approval	For trade-related payments, documentary evidence or declaration must be produced at the time of applying for foreign currency.
Profit/dividends	
Prior approval	Authorized dealers may grant approval provided that (1) the Department of Trade and Industry and the SARB have approved the relevant royalty agreement, and (2) the remittance of profits and dividends does not involve excessive use of local credit facilities. Income earned from securities held by nonresidents is freely transferable to their country of residence.
Payments for travel	
Quantitative limits	In June 1996, a single limit was set for tourist and business travel allowance at R 60,000 a year for an adult (R 20,000 for a child under 12) at an average daily rate not to exceed R 2,000 a day for the duration of the visit. Separately, an annual basic exchange allocation of R 20,000 an adult (R 5,000 for a child under 12) was set for travel to neighboring countries (Angola, Botswana, the Democratic Republic of the Congo, Malawi, Mozambique, Zambia, and Zimbabwe) at an average daily rate not exceeding R 1,000 a day for the duration of the visit. From July 1, 1997, South African residents traveling abroad will be allowed a maximum of R 80,000 for each person 12 years and older, and

R 25,000 for a child under 12, a calendar year, without any daily limit, irrespective of the country of destination.

Indicative limits/bona fide test	Exchange allowances in excess of the above limits may be provided with the approval of the SARB.

Study abroad costs

Quantitative limits	Approval is required for amounts exceeding R 80,000 a year, or R 160,000 if the student is accompanied by a spouse.

Foreign workers' wages — Amounts remitted must be the worker's own funds.

Family maintenance/alimony

Prior approval	Prior approval is required for amounts exceeding R 2,000 a month for a receiving family. There are no limits set for alimony payments, but a court order is required.
Quantitative limits	Approval is required for amounts exceeding R 2,000 a receiving family a month.

Credit card use abroad

Prior approval	Authorization is given only for use when traveling (an undertaking has to be signed to that effect).
Quantitative limits	Expenditure may not exceed 100% of the corresponding allowance.

Proceeds from Invisible Transactions and Current Transfers

Repatriation requirements	Yes.
Surrender requirements	Proceeds from invisibles must be surrendered within 30 days of the date of accrual, unless an exemption is obtained.
Restrictions on use of funds	Yes.

Capital Transactions

Controls on capital and money market instruments

On capital market securities

Sale or issue locally by nonresidents	The issue of securities by nonresidents requires prior exchange control approval, which is not normally granted.
Purchase abroad by residents	Approval is required. Institutions may obtain portfolio investments abroad under approval (asset swaps).
Sale or issue abroad by residents	Approval is required. Servicing should be undertaken from foreign sources if the funds are employed abroad, or from domestic sources if the funds were transferred to South Africa.

On money market instruments — The same regulations as for capital market securities apply.

Sale or issue locally by nonresidents	These transactions are not allowed.
Purchase abroad by residents	Yes.
Sale or issue abroad by residents	Yes.

On collective investment securities

Purchase abroad by residents	Such purchases by resident individuals are not allowed. Resident institutions may acquire investments as part of their approved portfolio investments abroad.

Controls on derivatives and other instruments

Purchase locally by nonresidents

Nonresidents may freely purchase derivative instruments, options, and futures on the local formal market (SAFEX), but over-the-counter (OTC) transactions require prior approval.

Sale or issue locally by nonresidents

Yes.

Purchase abroad by residents

Yes.

Sale or issue abroad by residents

Yes.

Controls on credit operations

Commercial credits

By residents to nonresidents

Export credits may be granted for up to 6 months. Banks may in certain circumstances allow a further extension of 6 months. Longer-term credit requires exchange control approval. In respect of services, payment has to be received in terms of the contract between the parties within a reasonable period after rendering the service.

Financial credits

By residents to nonresidents

Financial credits, such as loans, may not be extended without prior approval. However, nonresident wholly owned subsidiaries may borrow locally up to 100% of the total shareholders' investment (i.e., the paid-up equity capital, preference shares, undistributed profits, shareholders' loans from abroad, and, in certain instances, the hard core of shareholders' trade credit). The ability to borrow locally increases with the size of local participation by a set formula, which is generally granted.

To residents from nonresidents

Prior approval, which is generally granted, is required to ensure that the repayment and servicing of loans do not disrupt the balance of payments, and that the level of interest rates paid is reasonable in terms of prevailing international rates.

Guarantees, sureties, and financial backup facilities

By residents to nonresidents

Guarantees or sureties for financial loans require approval but not for trade transactions. Performance bonds may be issued.

Controls on direct investment

Outward direct investment

Exchange control approval is required. Investments by individuals are not permitted. Request by companies are considered in light of national interest, such as the benefit to South Africa's international reserves by, for example, generating exports of goods and services. Companies may be allowed to transfer up to R 30 million to finance approved investments abroad, and up to R 50 million for approved new investment in SADC countries other than Namibia, Swaziland, and Lesotho, where funds already flow freely.

Controls on liquidation of direct investment

No.

Controls on real estate transactions

Purchase abroad by residents

A South African may not purchase real estate outside South Africa/CMA without exchange control approval.

Provisions specific to commercial banks and other credit institutions

Borrowing abroad

All borrowings abroad by residents require exchange control approval. Banks may contract short-term working capital loans and short-term trade finance, but all medium-term and long-term commitments require exchange control approval.

Maintenance of accounts abroad

Banks may open Nostro accounts at their discretion.

Lending to nonresidents (financial or commercial credits)

Banks may lend up to R 20,000 provided that the total credit made available to a certain person from any source does not exceed this amount. Facilities exceeding this amount must obtain exchange control approval.

Lending locally in foreign exchange	Yes.
Purchase of locally issued securities denominated in foreign exchange	There are no securities denominated in foreign exchange in South Africa.
Differential treatment of nonresident deposit accounts and/or deposit accounts in foreign exchange	
Reserve requirements	Reserve requirements on all deposit accounts, held by residents or nonresidents and denominated in either rand or foreign exchange, are 2% of the amount of the deposit plus a further 1% on short-term liabilities (under 31 days).
Liquid asset requirements	The requirement is 5% of adjusted total liabilities.
Investment regulations	Investment in equity is limited to 100% of capital plus reserves.
Open foreign exchange position limits	The limit is 15% of qualifying capital plus reserves.
Provisions specific to institutional investors	
Limits (max.) on portfolio invested abroad	There are no exchange control restrictions on inward portfolio investment. On outward portfolio investment, the exchange control may authorize up to 10% of total assets for each qualifying institution (i.e., insurance companies, pension funds, and unit trusts) to be invested abroad by way of an asset swap. Subject to the overall limit of 10% of total assets, these institutions can invest up to 3% of the net inflow of funds for the calendar year 1996 in 1997, and an additional 2% in securities listed on stock exchanges in SADC countries.
Other controls imposed by securities laws	No.

Changes During 1996

Arrangements for payments and receipts	*June 24.* The limit on rand banknotes that may be imported or exported was increased to R 1,000 from R 500.
	July 30. Sanctions against the Federal Republic of Yugoslavia (Serbia/Montenegro) were lifted.
Payments for invisible transactions and current transfers	*June 24.* The separate limits for leisure and business travel were dispensed with and the limit for "neighboring countries" was set at R 20,000 for adults and R 5,000 for children with a daily limit of R 1,000. For other countries, the limit was set at R 60,000 for adults and R 20,000 for children at a daily limit of R 2,000. Virtually all quantitative limits on current payments and transfers doubled.
	June 24. The limit on rand banknotes that may be imported or exported was increased to R 1,000 from R 500.
Proceeds from invisible transactions and current transfers	*March 25.* Cash cover in foreign currency was permitted as security for securities lending transactions, provided the amount is held in a Nostro account of a South African authorized dealer.
Capital transactions	*June 24.* Access to domestic credit by foreign controlled entities was relaxed and the local financial assistance ratio doubled to 100% from 50%.
	June 24. The limit to enter into asset swaps by institutional investors was increased to 10% from 5% of local assets. They were also permitted to make foreign currency transfers during 1996 of up to 3% of the net inflow of funds generated during the 1995 calendar year within the overall 10% of total asset limit.
	June 24. Offshore investment expansion by corporations was permitted, provided it is financed by profits generated offshore from existing assets or financed abroad without recourse to South Africa.

June 24. Direct investment by corporations in countries outside the CMA will only be required to demonstrate a longer-term benefit to the country as opposed to an immediate benefit.

September 20. South Africans temporarily residing abroad were permitted to enjoy the same settling-in allowance as emigrants.

September 20. The ratio of 1:3 shareholders equity to shareholders loan funds of an affected person was eliminated.

November 21. Quoted securities may be exported as part or in lieu of the emigration facilities.

Changes During 1997

Arrangements for payments and receipts

March 13. The limit on banknotes that may be imported or exported was increased to R 2,000 from R 1,000.

Exports and export proceeds

March 13. The 7-day requirement within which foreign currency proceeds must be offered for sale was increased to 30 days.

Payments for invisible transactions and current transfers

March 13. All quantitative limits on current payments and transfers were abolished with the exception of the limits applicable to travel, study abroad, gifts, and maintenance payments. The limit on allowances for study abroad was increased to R 80,000 a year (R 5,000 a month), and if the student is accompanied by a spouse, to R 160,000 a year (R 10,000 a month). The student holiday allowance was increased to R 20,000 (R 10,000), and if the student is accompanied by a spouse, to R 40,000 (R 20,000). Travel allowance limits were amended by amalgamating the travel facilities applicable to neighboring and other countries as well as dispensing with the daily limit restriction. The limit was set at R 80,000 an adult and R 25,000 a child under 12 for a calendar year. The full travel facility may be taken in foreign banknotes. A traveler may now purchase the required foreign currency up to 60 days (28 days for travel to neighboring countries) prior to departure. The limit for family maintenance transfers was increased to R 2,000 a month from R 200 a month for a receiving family unit.

Capital transactions

March 13. Direct investment by corporations in countries outside of the CMA of up to R 30 million was permitted. In respect of investment into SADC countries, an amount of up to R 50 million may be allowed. Where the cost of investment exceeds the aforementioned amounts, the balance has to be financed abroad. As opposed to previous policy, consideration will now be given to such foreign borrowing being raised with recourse to or a guarantee from South Africa implying that the local corporate's balance sheet may be used in negotiating such a facility.

March 13. Institutional investors may avail themselves of foreign currency transfers during 1997 of up to 3% of the net inflow of funds during the 1996 calendar year, subject to an overall limit of 10% of their total assets. Additionally, transfers during 1997 of up to 2% of the net inflow of funds during the 1996 calendar year may be allowed to be invested on registered stock exchanges in any SADC member country. This dispensation is also subject to the overall limit of 10% of total assets applicable to asset swaps. Unit trust management companies may acquire foreign portfolio investments by way of asset swaps for up to 10% of total assets under management.

March 13. The definition of an "affected person" is amended by substituting the figure 50 for the figure 25.

March 13. Authorized dealers may grant facilities to nonaffected and affected persons with reliance on guarantees from abroad, provided the local financial assistance accorded the affected person does not exceed the limit calculated in terms of the formula ratio.

SPAIN

Status Under IMF Articles of Agreement

Article VIII	Date of acceptance: July 15, 1986.

Exchange Arrangement

Currency	The currency of Spain is the peseta.
Exchange rate structure	Unitary.
Classification	
Cooperative arrangement	Spain participates in the ERM of the EMS. In accordance with this agreement, Spain maintains the spot exchange rates between the peseta and the currencies of the other participants within margins of 15% above or below the cross rates based on the central rates expressed in ECUs. The agreement implies that the Bank of Spain (BOS), the central bank, stands ready to buy or sell the currencies of the other participating states in unlimited amounts at specified intervention rates.
Exchange tax	No.
Exchange subsidy	No.
Forward exchange market	Options and futures on the peseta are traded in major financial markets.
Official cover of forward operations	No.

Arrangements for Payments and Receipts

Prescription of currency requirements	No.
Payment arrangements	No.
Administration of control	The Peninsular Territories of the Spanish State, the Canary Islands, the Balearic Islands, Ceuta, and Melilla constitute a single exchange control territory.
Exchange control authorities	The Directorate-General of Foreign Investment and Commercial Policy has the power to authorize, verify, control, and monitor foreign investments and economic transactions, collections, payments, and transfers with the rest of the world. The Directorate-General of the Treasury and Financial Policy has authority to conduct the investigations and inspections required to prepare or change the policy applied in matters concerning exchange control as well as to initiate, address, and rule on penalties applied with regard to exchange control. In addition, the BOS has authority in a number of areas such as the following:
	(1) granting authorization to banks, savings and loans, and other financial institutions, when required, to transact business on the foreign exchange market, and registering institutions open to the public to engage in foreign exchange activities;
	(2) receiving information on collections, payments, and transfers abroad in which registered institutions are involved, and issuing instructions pertaining to the content, procedures, and frequency for such reporting; and
	(3) receiving information on financial and commercial credits and loans, accounts abroad held by residents in Spain, and netting operations.
International security restrictions	Specific financial transactions with Iraq and Libya are subject to authorization. On March 6, 1997, trade with Iraq was prohibited with the following exceptions: imports of petroleum and petroleum products and exports (or transit through Spanish territory),

items of basic necessity, medical products, and items that were approved by the committee established in UN Security Council Resolution No. 661 (1990).

In accordance with IMF Executive Board Decision No. 144-(52/51)

Spain notified the Fund on September 21, 1992, that, in compliance with UN Security Council Resolution No. 757 (1992), certain restrictions had been imposed on the making of payments and transfers for current international transactions in respect of the Federal Republic of Yugoslavia (Serbia/Montenegro). On April 26, 1996, these restrictions were lifted.

Payment arrears

No.

Controls on trade in gold (coins and/or bullion)

Controls on domestic ownership and/or trade

The acquisition of gold must be authorized by the Directorate-General of Foreign Trade.

Controls on external trade

Imports of bullion are permitted if they are used as raw materials for manufactured goods. Imports of gold in manufactured form (e.g., coins, medals, and the like) may be subject to quantitative restrictions, depending on the country of origin. Purchases of gold, silver, and platinum ingots are subject to a value-added tax at the rate of 33%.

Controls on exports and imports of banknotes

On exports

Domestic currency

The exportation of banknotes, coins, or bearer checks in excess of the equivalent of Ptas 1 million must be declared.

Foreign currency

Yes.

On imports

Domestic currency

The importation of more than the equivalent of Ptas 1 million in banknotes, coins, or bearer checks must be declared by nonresidents in certain cases.

Foreign currency

Yes.

Resident Accounts

Eligibility to hold accounts

Juridical and natural persons are eligible.

Foreign exchange accounts permitted

Yes.

Held domestically

Yes.

Held abroad

Collections and payments between residents and nonresidents through credits or debits to these accounts may be freely made. However, account holders are required to report the opening of such accounts and to provide information pertaining to credit and debit activities occurring in the accounts.

Accounts in domestic currency convertible into foreign currency

Yes.

Nonresident Accounts

Eligibility to hold accounts

Juridical and natural persons are eligible.

Foreign exchange accounts permitted

Yes.

Domestic currency accounts

Yes.

Convertible into foreign currency

Yes.

Blocked accounts   No.

Imports and Import Payments

Foreign exchange budget   No.

Financing requirements for imports   No.

Documentation requirements for   No.
release of foreign exchange for
imports

Import licenses and other nontariff
measures

Open general licenses   Imports of tractors, explosives, seed oil, and gold must be authorized by the Directorate-
                                              General of Foreign Trade, irrespective of the country of origin, or when imported from
                                              specific geographical areas (with distinctions being made among the members of the
                                              EU, those of the EFTA and the Mediterranean and ACP member countries of the WTO,
                                              and state trading countries).

Import taxes and/or tariffs   No.

State import monopoly   No.

Exports and Export Proceeds

Repatriation requirements   No.

Surrender requirements   No.

Financing requirements   No.

Documentation requirements   No.

Export licenses

Without quotas   Exports of textiles, steel, and some copper by-products require prior authorization from
                                              the Directorate-General of Foreign Trade.

Export taxes   No.

Payments for Invisible Transactions and Current Transfers

Controls on these payments   No.

Proceeds from Invisible Transactions and Current Transfers

Repatriation requirements   No.

Surrender requirements   No.

Restrictions on use of funds   No.

Capital Transactions

Controls on capital and money mar-
ket instruments

On capital market securities   Residents may purchase securities issued by nonresidents or by residents in a foreign
                                              market.

Purchase locally by nonresidents	The restriction applies only to the purchase of shares and other securities of a participating nature that may be affected by laws on inward direct investment and establishment.
Controls on derivatives and other instruments	No.

Controls on credit operations

Commercial credits

By residents to nonresidents	Residents (individuals or legal entities other than registered institutions) are required to file reports to the BOS of loans with a maturity of more than 1 year granted to nonresidents.
To residents from nonresidents	Residents other than registered institutions are required to file reports to the BOS for credits with a maturity of more than 1 year.

Financial credits

By residents to nonresidents	Residents are required to file a declaration with the BOS.
To residents from nonresidents	Residents are required to file a declaration with the BOS.

Controls on direct investment

Outward direct investment	Prior administrative verification is required in the following cases: (1) when the investment amounts to at least Ptas 250 million; (2) when the activity of the entity receiving the investment is the direct or indirect holding of share capital of other entities, irrespective of the amount of the investment; and (3) when the investment is made in a tax haven country.
Inward direct investment	Foreign direct investments in Spain are defined in accordance with guidelines established by the OECD that take into account whether effective control over the company has been obtained. Effective control is deemed to exist if the share of the investment is at least 10% of the company's capital. Prior verification is required only when foreign participation exceeds 50% and at least one of the following conditions applies: (1) foreign participation exceeds Ptas 500 million; and (2) foreign investors are residents of tax haven countries. Special authorization is required for non-EU foreign investment in television, radio, air transport, gambling, and defense-related industries. Special authorization is also required for a foreign government's participation in Spanish companies (other than governments of EU countries), unless otherwise regulated by international treaties.
Controls on liquidation of direct investment	No.

Controls on real estate transactions

Purchase abroad by residents	Purchases that exceed Ptas 250 million require prior verification.
Purchase locally by nonresidents	Prior verification is required for amounts exceeding Ptas 500 million or if investors are residents of tax haven countries.

Provisions specific to commercial banks and other credit institutions

Borrowing abroad	Financial credits obtained should be reported to the BOS.
Maintenance of accounts abroad	Yes.
Lending to nonresidents (financial or commercial credits)	Residents must report loans granted to nonresidents to the BOS.
Lending locally in foreign exchange	This type of operation is subject to the rules and regulations governing interest rates and commissions, rules of procedure, customer information, and publication applicable to credit institutions.
Differential treatment of nonresident deposit accounts and/or deposit accounts in foreign exchange	Nonresident deposit accounts may be opened and mobilized without restriction, with the exception of collections and payments from residents to nonresidents effected by account debits or credits. In such cases, information pertaining to the operation,

including whether the operation involves credits to accounts of nonresidents by nonresidents, must be declared, in which case certification of origin must be provided. For nonresident accounts, this status must be indicated. Accordingly, the holder must provide documentation attesting to nonresidency, and this status must be confirmed every year. Regular foreign peseta accounts and convertible foreign peseta accounts are governed by the provisions for nonresident deposits.

Reserve requirements   Yes.

**Provisions specific to institutional
investors**

Currency matching regulations on   Regulations differ according to the type of institutional investor.
assets/liabilities composition

**Other controls imposed by securities   Yes.
laws**

Changes During 1996

**Arrangements for payments and   *April 26.* Security restrictions with respect to the Federal Republic of Yugoslavia
receipts**   (Serbia/Montenegro) were lifted.

Changes During 1997

**Arrangements for payments and   *March 6.* Trade with Iraq was prohibited with the following exceptions: imports of pe-
receipts**   troleum and petroleum products and exports (or transit through Spanish territory), items
                                            of basic necessity, medical products, and items that were approved by the committee
                                            established in UN Security Council Resolution No. 661 (1990).

SRI LANKA

(Position as of January 31, 1997)

Status Under IMF Articles of Agreement

Article VIII	Date of acceptance: March 15, 1994.

Exchange Arrangement

Currency	The currency of Sri Lanka is the Sri Lanka rupee.
Exchange rate structure	Unitary.
Classification	
Managed floating	The Central Bank of Sri Lanka (CBSL) announces the daily spot buying and selling rates of the U.S. dollar against the Sri Lanka rupee for transactions with commercial banks within margins of 2%, and buys and sells the U.S. dollar on a spot basis at those rates.
Exchange tax	No.
Exchange subsidy	No.
Forward exchange market	Forward sales are permitted except for capital transfers and amortization of loans, up to a period of 360 days. The commercial banks provide a forward exchange market in which rates for current transactions are freely determined. They may cover such purchases by selling forward to their clients (that is, importers and shipping agents) or to other authorized dealers.
Official cover of forward operations	n.a.

Arrangements for Payments and Receipts

Prescription of currency requirements	Payments to and receipts from the member countries of the ACU with respect to current transactions and settlements are effected in U.S. dollars. For settlements with all other countries, payments for imports may be made in any foreign currency or in Sri Lanka rupees provided that the supplier maintains a nonresident account in Sri Lanka. Other payments may be made either in the currency of the country to which the payment is due or by crediting Sri Lanka rupees to a nonresident rupee account with the prior approval of the CBSL. Proceeds from exports must be received either in designated foreign currencies, in Sri Lanka rupees from a nonresident account that a foreign bank maintains with an authorized dealer, or in any other nonresident account that a person maintains with an authorized dealer, as approved by the CBSL.
Payment arrangements	No.
Administration of control	
Exchange control authorities	Exchange control is administered by the CBSL's Department of Exchange Control. All remittances of foreign exchange in Sri Lanka must normally be made through authorized commercial banks in accordance with procedures prescribed by the Controller of Exchange (CoE). Remittances may also be made through post offices under permits issued by the CoE. The Board of Investments (BOI) handles all applications relating to foreign investments in Sri Lanka.
Payment arrears	No.
Controls on trade in gold (coins and/or bullion)	
Controls on external trade	The importation of gold for domestic, industrial, or commercial purpose is permitted without restrictions. Commercial banks may import gold on a consignment basis for

793

duty-free sale to passengers at the Colombo International Airport. Reexportation of nonmonetary gold is allowed only in special circumstances. The exportation of gold coins and bullion requires licenses issued by the Controller of Imports and Exports with the approval of the CoE.

Controls on exports and imports of banknotes

On exports

   Domestic currency   Sri Lanka nationals may each take out of Sri Lanka up to SL Rs 1,000.

   Foreign currency   Unspent rupee balances from foreign exchange sold by foreign passport holders may be reconverted into foreign currency notes only at exit points, with original encashment documents issued by the authorized dealers or money changers. Individuals may take out foreign currency for travel purposes and are required to declare to customs if the amount exceeds $10,000 or its equivalent. Diplomats and non-Sri Lanka staff of foreign missions traveling abroad can take foreign currency notes in reasonable quantities for travel expenses.

On imports

   Domestic currency   Sri Lanka nationals may each bring into Sri Lanka up to SL Rs 1,000.

   Foreign currency   Travelers must declare at entry foreign exchange holdings exceeding $10,000 or its equivalent.

Resident Accounts

Eligibility to hold accounts   Juridical and natural persons are eligible.

Foreign exchange accounts permitted   Yes.

Held domestically   Residents may open and operate resident foreign currency accounts with a minimum balance equivalent to $500 in designated currencies and up to $10,000 without prior approval or with documentary evidence of receipt of funds through customs declarations.

Held abroad   These accounts are permitted; prior approval is required.

Accounts in domestic currency convertible into foreign currency   No.

Nonresident Accounts

Eligibility to hold accounts   Juridical and natural persons are eligible.

Foreign exchange accounts permitted   Sri Lankans employed abroad and nonnationals of Sri Lanka who are employed and reside abroad may maintain nonresident foreign currency (NRFC) accounts in designated foreign currencies. Credits to the accounts are limited to remittances from employment earnings abroad, foreign exchange earnings brought into the country by individuals, and interest payments in designated currencies. These accounts may be freely debited for payments abroad, with the exception of payments for the sale of movable or immovable property in Sri Lanka, purchase of capital assets abroad by residents, or for payments within Sri Lanka. Balances on NRFC accounts may be invested in enterprises approved by the BOI, with exemptions granted under Section 17 of the BOI Act. Dividends and profits earned and sales proceeds of such investments received in foreign currency may be credited to the NRFC accounts without the prior approval of the CoE. Resident foreigners may maintain foreign currency accounts with domestic commercial banks in any of 10 designated currencies without prior exchange control approval. These accounts must be operated by the domestic unit of the bank and not by its foreign currency banking unit. The accounts may be current, savings, or deposit accounts, but withdrawal of funds by check is not permitted. Credits to these accounts are limited to inward remittances and to amounts in Sri Lanka rupees authorized by the CoE for remittance abroad. Debits to these accounts are limited to outward remittances and to payments after converting into Sri Lanka rupees. Prior approval is not required.

Domestic currency accounts

These accounts may be held by (1) nonnationals residing outside Sri Lanka; (2) firms and companies registered outside Sri Lanka; (3) Sri Lanka nationals residing outside Sri Lanka; (4) emigrants; and (5) foreign banks. The opening of these accounts for categories (1)–(4), credits from inward remittances, and debits for local disbursements or outward remittances may be effected freely; however, local credits to these require prior approval. Accounts in category (4) are designated as nonresident blocked accounts only when instructions to that effect are received from the Department of Exchange Control. Local debits to such accounts may be freely effected, without prior approval; however, local credits to them and debits for outward remittances require prior approval. In category (5), foreign banks may open and operate nonresident accounts with local commercial banks without prior approval of the Department of Exchange Control.

Convertible into foreign currency

Yes.

Approval required

Yes.

Blocked accounts

These accounts are used to hold funds, usually of nonresidents, repatriates, and emigrants, that have not been accepted for transfer abroad. Authorized dealers may debit these accounts for local disbursements and credit them on account of pensions and income tax refunds. Balances of nonresident foreign citizens and foreign companies in approved blocked accounts outstanding on March 25, 1991, excluding Sri Lankan citizens who have emigrated or acquired foreign citizenship and Indian and Pakistani expatriates, may be remitted abroad. Sri Lankans who have emigrated and acquired foreign citizenship, and Sri Lankan citizens who have acquired permanent resident status abroad and whose accounts have been blocked for more than 5 years as of June 30, 1995, are also permitted to remit their account balances abroad. Except in the specified cases, remittances of up to SL Rs 350,000 are also allowed from these accounts without prior approval.

Imports and Import Payments

Foreign exchange budget

No.

Financing requirements for imports

Minimum financing requirements

Authorized dealers may approve applications to remit foreign exchange or to credit nonresident accounts against applications for the opening of a letter of credit (LC) and against proof of a valid import license, when applicable. These requirements do not apply if the value of a consignment does not exceed $3,000 (c.i.f.), consists of raw materials and spare parts for industries, and is for the direct use of the importer.

Advance payment requirements

Advance payments for personal imports are limited to $3,000.

Documentation requirements for release of foreign exchange for imports

Imports could be made on documents against payments (D/P) and documents on acceptance (D/A) terms without LCs being established, provided the shipping documents are routed through the supplier's bank to the importer's bank in Sri Lanka.

Preshipment inspection

Inspection is required for certain consumer goods.

Letters of credit

The requirement of establishing LCs for imports was lifted on March 21, 1996.

Import licenses and other nontariff measures

Most items do not require licenses, except imports of wheat, meslin, and wheat and meslin flour. Licensing requirements for imports of potatoes and big onions were eliminated on March 21, 1996. Certain machinery imports relating to foreign investment require the approval of the BOI.

Import taxes and/or tariffs

The tariff structure consists of 3 band rates: 35%, 20%, and 10%. A few categories of products (e.g., tobacco, liquor, crude oil, and some categories of motor vehicles) remain outside this tariff structure. A stamp duty of 2% is levied on LCs for certain imports.

Taxes collected through the exchange system	No.
State import monopoly	Imports of certain items, including wheat, guns and explosives, and certain chemicals and petroleum products, are restricted to government or state corporations.

Exports and Export Proceeds

Repatriation requirements	Special arrangements apply to exports made under trade and payments agreements and to exports made to a member country of the ACU.
Surrender requirements	No.
Financing requirements	Commercial banks may grant foreign currency loans from their foreign currency banking units to exporters for the financing of the importation of inputs required for the purpose of executing export orders. Since January 3, 1997, banks may grant these loans also from their domestic banking units. This facility is limited to 70% of the total value of the confirmed export order. The period of repayment of these loans is 8 months.
	Companies engaged in indirect exports may obtain foreign currency loans for the importation of raw materials on the basis of back-to-back LCs opened in foreign currency for receipt of payment in foreign currency, including payments from BOI enterprises.
Documentation requirements	No.
Export licenses	Licenses are required for exports of coral shanks and shells, timber, ivory and ivory products, and passenger vehicles registered in Sri Lanka prior to 1945.
Without quotas	Yes.
Export taxes	No.

Payments for Invisible Transactions and Current Transfers

Controls on these payments	Payments for unloading and storage costs and administrative expenses are free. All other payments and transfers are subject to indicative limits and/or bona fide tests.
Freight/insurance	Remittances of premium for insurance on exports are not permitted. Remittances of premium to foreign reinsurers for reinsurance are permitted.
Commissions	Reasonable amounts are allowed on export orders secured through agents abroad, provided that export proceeds have been repatriated to Sri Lanka.
Quantitative limits	n.a.
Interest payments	
Quantitative limits	n.a.
Profit/dividends	Profit remittances of nonresident partners and remittances of dividends to nonresident shareholders of companies whose financial assets are in rupees may be effected through commercial banks without prior approval if they relate to the year of application and do not include undistributed profits of the previous years or reserves of the company. However, considerable documentation is required to remit interim profits or dividends, or final profits or dividends.
Foreign workers' wages	
Quantitative limits	Technical employees of approved enterprises may remit their entire savings after meeting expenses and paying taxes and levies.
Gambling/prize earnings	
Prior approval	Yes.

Quantitative limits	Yes.
Credit card use abroad	Credit card use is allowed only for travel-related purposes.

Proceeds from Invisible Transactions and Current Transfers

Repatriation requirements	No.
Surrender requirements	No.
Restrictions on use of funds	Funds held abroad with CoE permission should not be used for the acquisition of property or other capital assets outside Sri Lanka.

Capital Transactions

Controls on capital and money market instruments	
On capital market securities	
Purchase locally by nonresidents	Investments in shares by nonresidents, up to 100% of the equity capital of existing listed and unlisted public companies, are permitted, subject to certain exclusions and limitations, without prior approval from the CoE through a Share Investment External Rupee Account maintained at a commercial bank. Companies incorporated abroad are permitted to invest in securities traded at the Colombo Stock Exchange, subject to the same terms and conditions as those applicable to such investments by approved country funds, approved regional funds, and nonresident individuals.
Sale or issue locally by nonresidents	Yes.
Purchase abroad by residents	Investments abroad by residents are not generally permitted unless there is evidence that they will promote the country's exports and generate reasonable profits.
Sale or issue abroad by residents	Yes.
On money market instruments	Yes.
On collective investment securities	Yes.
Controls on derivatives and other instruments	
Purchase locally by nonresidents	Yes.
Sale or issue locally by nonresidents	Yes.
Purchase abroad by residents	Yes.
Sale or issue abroad by residents	Yes.
Controls on credit operations	
Commercial credits	Yes.
Financial credits	Yes.
Guarantees, sureties, and financial backup facilities	Yes.
Controls on direct investment	
Outward direct investment	Investments abroad by residents are not generally permitted unless there is evidence that they will promote the country's exports and generate reasonable profits.
Inward direct investment	Approval for foreign investment is granted on the basis of the type of activity and the proportion of foreign capital ownership. Approval is automatically granted for foreign investment with equity capital ownership of up to 40%, except for certain activities restricted by special law or specific organizations.

Controls on liquidation of direct investment

Proceeds from the sale or liquidation of approved investments, along with the capital appreciation, may be remitted in full. Expatriates leaving Sri Lanka for residence in the country of their permanent domicile are permitted to transfer in full assets representing their retirement funds and savings. Persons who have had small businesses in Sri Lanka are allowed to transfer the capital they originally brought into the country, plus a reasonable amount of savings, subject to certain limits.

Authorized dealers may grant foreign exchange allocations to emigrants upon presentation of appropriate documentation. At the time of departure, emigrants may be granted foreign exchange to cover passage to the country of migration by normal direct route plus 20% of the passage fare to cover excess baggage expenses. Foreign exchange equivalent up to $2,000 an adult and $1,000 a child under 12 years of age can also be purchased at the time of departure. Personal effects of reasonable amounts plus jewelry up to SL Rs 150,000 for each married female, SL Rs 60,000 for unmarried females, SL Rs 30,000 for female emigrants under 12 years of age, and SL Rs 37,500 for male emigrants can be exported. Emigrants have also been permitted to effect capital transfers of up to SL Rs 750,000 an individual, up to a maximum limit of SL Rs 1 million a family unit.

Special provisions, governed by an agreement between Sri Lanka and India, apply to Indian families returning to India.

Controls on real estate transactions

Purchase abroad by residents	Yes.
Purchase locally by nonresidents	Yes.
Sale locally by nonresidents	Yes.

Provisions specific to commercial banks and other credit institutions

Borrowing abroad	Yes.
Maintenance of accounts abroad	n.a.
Lending to nonresidents (financial or commercial credits)	Yes.
Lending locally in foreign exchange	Yes.
Purchase of locally issued securities denominated in foreign exchange	Yes.
Open foreign exchange position limits	n.a.

Changes During 1996

Exchange arrangements

January 1. All transactions among ACU member countries take place in U.S. dollars.

Imports and import payments

March 21. The requirement of establishing LCs for imports was lifted.

July 26. Import licensing requirements for potatoes and big onions were eliminated.

Changes During 1997

Exports and export proceeds

January 3. Commercial banks were permitted to lend in foreign currency from the resources available in the foreign currency banking units in addition to domestic banking units.

SUDAN

(Position as of March 31, 1997)

Status Under IMF Articles of Agreement

Article XIV	Yes.

Exchange Arrangement

Currency	The currency of Sudan is the Sudanese dinar.
Other legal tender	The Sudanese pound (LSd) also circulates and has a fixed relationship to the Sudanese dinar (Sd) of LSd 10 = Sd 1.
Exchange rate structure	Unitary.

Classification

Independent floating	The exchange rate for the Sudanese dinar is determined in the market. Both commercial banks and licensed foreign exchange bureaus are authorized to freely quote buying and selling exchange rates to be applied to all transactions, other than certain compulsory sales of foreign exchange by commercial banks to the Bank of Sudan (BOS). The spread between commercial banks' buying and selling rates was changed from LSd 7 per U.S. dollar to 1.5% of each bank's buying price.
Exchange tax	No.
Exchange subsidy	No.
Forward exchange market	No.

Arrangements for Payments and Receipts

Prescription of currency requirements	Payments to all countries, except Egypt, and all monetary areas (the "convertible area") may be made in foreign currency from any free currency account or special foreign currency account, while receipts from the convertible area may be accepted in any convertible currency.

Payment arrangements

Bilateral arrangements

Inoperative	There is an agreement with Egypt, which has been suspended since 1992.

Administration of control

Exchange control authorities	Exchange control is administered by the BOS with the assistance of the authorized dealers, that is, commercial and specialized banks as well as nonbanks acting as exchange houses.
International security restrictions	No.

Payment arrears

Official	Yes.

Controls on trade in gold (coins and/or bullion)

Controls on domestic ownership and/or trade	With certain exceptions, only monetary authorities and authorized industrial users of gold are allowed to hold or acquire gold in any form other than jewelry. Residents may purchase, hold, and sell gold for numismatic purposes.
Controls on external trade	Imports and exports of gold in any form other than jewelry require a license issued by the Ministry of Commerce, Cooperation, and Supply; such licenses are not normally granted except for industrial users and for monetary authorities.

Controls on exports and imports of banknotes

On exports

    Domestic currency   Travelers may export up to LSd 5,000.

    Foreign currency   Up to $5,000 can be taken out of the country.

On imports

    Domestic currency   Travelers may import up to LSd 5,000.

    Foreign currency   Travelers may bring in any amount, but it must be declared and within 3 months either deposited in a foreign currency account, sold to an authorized dealer, or retransferred abroad.

Resident Accounts

Eligibility to hold accounts   Juridical and natural persons are eligible.

Foreign exchange accounts permitted

Held domestically   All residents, except the government, public institutions, and public sector enterprises are allowed to keep foreign exchange in free accounts. These accounts may be credited with any means of payment without restrictions, other than a customs declaration for cash deposits. Withdrawals from these accounts may be used to make transfers abroad; to make transfers to other free accounts; to purchase domestic currency; to make payments in foreign exchange to domestic institutions authorized to sell goods and services for foreign exchange; and for any other purpose.

Held abroad   No.

Accounts in domestic currency convertible into foreign currency   Yes.

Nonresident Accounts

Eligibility to hold accounts   Juridical and natural persons are eligible.

Foreign exchange accounts permitted   Diplomatic, foreign, international, and regional missions and organizations; foreign charities and aid organizations; foreign companies, foreign contractors, and the foreign personnel of these organizations are allowed to open special foreign accounts with authorized banks. These accounts may be credited with transfers from abroad. Special foreign currency accounts may be debited for transfers abroad, to finance foreign travel, to purchase local currency in order to finance local payments, to make foreign currency payments to local institutions authorized to sell goods and services for foreign currency, and to finance imports. Withdrawals can be made for the purpose of travel by the account holder or his or her family, and local payments in Sudanese pounds, requiring conversion to Sudanese currency at the commercial bank rate.

Except for airline companies, approval is required to open these accounts. These accounts may be credited with payments by their passengers, consignors, and agents, who are allowed to buy travel tickets in foreign currency.

Domestic currency accounts   These accounts may be opened by the same individuals and organizations as those allowed to open foreign exchange accounts.

Convertible into foreign currency   Balances may be converted subject to the purpose for conversion and if supported with documentary evidence.

Blocked accounts   No.

Imports and Import Payments

Foreign exchange budget	No.
Financing requirements for imports	
Advance import deposits	Authorized banks are free to obtain a deposit of any amount in foreign currency from the importer at least 1 month before the importer receives the shipping documents. Imports financed at the commercial market rate, including those financed with letters of credit, could be subject to an advance deposit of up to the full c.i.f. value.
Documentation requirements for release of foreign exchange for imports	Imports must be accompanied by a pro forma invoice, a valid commercial registration certificate, a valid tax clearance certificate, and a written consent of the authorized bodies for certain categories of imports.
Letters of credit	n.a.
Import licenses used as exchange licenses	n.a.
Import licenses and other nontariff measures	Licenses are required for imports through bilateral and preferential trade arrangements.
Negative list	Certain imports are prohibited for reasons of religion, health, and national security.
Other nontariff measures	Imports from Israel are prohibited.
Import taxes and/or tariffs	Yes.
Taxes collected through the exchange system	Yes.
State import monopoly	No.

Exports and Export Proceeds

Repatriation requirements	All export proceeds must be repatriated within 45 days of the date of the bill of lading.
Surrender requirements	As of August 12, 1996, exporters must surrender 30% and 70% to the BOS and the commercial banks, respectively. Until June 12, 1996, these ratios were 50% and 50%, respectively; at that time, they were changed to 40% and 60%, respectively. Exporters of winter cotton must surrender 100% of their proceeds to the BOS; exporters of gum arabic must surrender 95% to the BOS and 5% to the commercial banks; while exporters of cattle and meat, sunflower seeds, fruits and vegetables, and manufactured goods may retain 50% of their proceeds and surrender 15% to the BOS and the remaining 35% to the commercial banks.
Export licenses	Licenses are required for exports under bilateral protocol arrangements and under barter trade.
Without quotas	All exports to Israel are prohibited, as is the exportation of hides and skins, and charcoal and firewood.
With quotas	n.a.
Export taxes	Taxes are levied on all goods, except those that are exported under bilateral protocol arrangements and under barter agreements. The tax rate is 5%, except for cotton and gum arabic, which are taxed at 10%.
Taxes collected through the exchange system	No.

Payments for Invisible Transactions and Current Transfers

Controls on these payments	There are no controls on payments for unloading and storage, administrative expenses, commissions, travel, consulting and legal fees, pensions, gambling and prize earnings,

family maintenance and alimony, and credit card use abroad. Insurance for imports must normally be taken out with local companies.

Interest payments

    Prior approval   Amortization payments on loans to residents are subject to certification from the BOS regarding the original amount of the foreign loans.

    Indicative limits/bona fide test   Yes.

Profit/dividends

    Indicative limits/bona fide test   Yes.

Medical costs

    Indicative limits/bona fide test   Yes.

Study abroad costs

    Indicative limits/bona fide test   Yes.

Subscriptions and membership fees

    Indicative limits/bona fide test   Yes.

Foreign workers' wages

    Quantitative limits   Up to 50% of earnings can be transferred abroad, provided that certain documents are presented.

Proceeds from Invisible Transactions and Current Transfers

Repatriation requirements   Sudanese nationals working abroad are required to remit annually to domestic residents a minimum amount of foreign exchange, ranging from $300 to $5,000. Exceptions are allowed.

Surrender requirements   During 1996, proceeds were to be surrendered in the following ratios: from February 25 to April 9, 70% to the BOS and 30% to commercial banks; from April 10 to June 11, 50% to the BOS and 50% to commercial banks; from June 12 to August 11, 40% to the BOS and 60% to commercial banks; and from August 12 to November 13, 30% to the BOS and 70% to commercial banks. From November 14, 1996, to March 12, 1997, 85% was surrendered to the BOS and 15% to commercial banks. Since March 13, 1997, all proceeds may be surrendered to commercial banks. Shipping agencies are required to sell all foreign exchange proceeds to authorized dealers.

Restrictions on use of funds   Yes.

Capital Transactions

Controls on capital and money market instruments

On capital market securities

    Purchase abroad by residents   Yes.

    Sale or issue abroad by residents   Yes.

On money market instruments   Yes.

On collective investment securities   Yes.

Controls on derivatives and other instruments

Purchase locally by nonresidents   Yes.

Sale or issue locally by nonresidents   Yes.

Purchase abroad by residents   Yes.

Sale or issue abroad by residents	Yes.
Controls on credit operations	
Financial credits	
To residents from nonresidents	Yes.
Guarantees, sureties, and financial backup facilities	Yes.
Controls on direct investment	
Outward direct investment	Yes.
Inward direct investment	Investments are subject to the approval of the investment authority.
Controls on liquidation of direct investment	Repatriation must be approved by the BOS after submission of audited balance sheets and tax clearance certificates.
Provisions specific to commercial banks and other credit institutions	
Borrowing abroad	Yes.
Maintenance of accounts abroad	Yes.
Lending to nonresidents (financial or commercial credits)	Yes.
Lending locally in foreign exchange	Yes.
Purchase of locally issued securities denominated in foreign exchange	Yes.
Provisions specific to institutional investors	No.
Other controls imposed by securities laws	No.

Changes During 1996

Exports and export proceeds	*April 13.* General surrender requirements were set at 50% to the BOS and 50% to commercial banks.
	June 12. General surrender requirements were set at 40% to the BOS and 60% to commercial banks.
	August 12. General surrender requirements were set at 30% to the BOS and 70% to commercial banks.
Proceeds from invisible transactions and current transfers	*February 25.* Surrender requirements were set at 70% to the BOS and 30% to commercial banks.
	April 10. Surrender requirements were set at 50% to the BOS and 50% to commercial banks.
	June 12. Surrender requirements were set at 40% to the BOS and 60% to commercial banks.
	August 12. Surrender requirements were set at 30% to the BOS and 70% to commercial banks.
	November 14. Surrender requirements were set at 85% to the BOS and 15% to commercial banks.

Changes During 1997

Proceeds from invisible transactions and current transfers	*March 13.* All proceeds were allowed to be surrendered to commercial banks.

SURINAME

(Position as of December 31, 1996)

Status Under IMF Articles of Agreement

Article VIII   Date of acceptance: June 29, 1978.

Exchange Arrangement

Currency   The currency of Suriname is the Suriname guilder.

Other legal tender   Three gold coins are legal tender.

Exchange rate structure   Unitary.

Classification

Managed floating   Exchange rates are freely determined in the interbank market. Commercial banks and licensed foreign exchange houses may trade foreign exchange with customers, among themselves, or with the Central Bank of Suriname (CBS) on a freely negotiable basis. The CBS also trades foreign exchange with the government, but not with importers. The CBS determines the exchange rate to be used in official transactions, which is based on the weighted-average rate of commercial bank transactions over the last 5 days.

Exchange tax   Commercial banks charge commissions of 2% on sales of foreign exchange and 9.25% on transfers.

Forward exchange market   No.

Arrangements for Payments and Receipts

Prescription of currency requirements   Settlements in Suriname guilders between Suriname and foreign countries are not permitted; they must, in general, be made in specified convertible currencies (Australian dollars, Austrian schillings, Barbados dollars, Belgian francs, Canadian dollars, Danish kroner, deutsche mark, Eastern Caribbean dollars, French francs, Guyana dollars, Italian lire, Japanese yen, Netherlands guilders, Norwegian kroner, Portuguese escudos, pounds sterling, Swedish kronor, Swiss francs, Trinidad and Tobago dollars, and U.S. dollars).

Administration of control

Exchange control authorities   The CBS (1) is empowered to provide foreign exchange for import payments (subject to presentation of an import license, which serves as a general authorization for payment), this power has been delegated to commercial banks; and (2) approves import licenses if imports are paid with a letter of credit (LC).

Commercial banks (1) provide foreign exchange for imports. Except for limited amounts of foreign exchange for invisible payments not requiring an exchange license, banks are not permitted to sell foreign exchange unless the remitter submits an exchange license; and (2) may accept free of license those inward transfers of foreign exchange that do not result from borrowing abroad.

The Ministry of Trade and Industry (MTI) grants export and import licenses. However, 2 specified mining companies do not need licenses for their own import requirements. Similar exemptions may be granted to foreign companies for their industrial activities in Suriname, provided that they pay for imports from their own foreign exchange holdings.

The Federal Exchange Commission (FEC) (1) grants licenses for external payments other than imports of goods; (2) approves foreign loans; and (3) appoints authorized banks.

Payment arrears

Official

These arrears are owed largely to Brazil.

Private

n.a.

Controls on trade in gold (coins and/or bullion)

Controls on domestic ownership and/or trade

Producers of gold may sell only to the authorized gold buyers (the CBS and Grassalco). Locally produced gold must be surrendered to the FEC by sale to the CBS. The authorized gold buyers are permitted, however, to sell nuggets at freely agreed prices for industrial and artistic purposes. Dealings between residents in gold bars and other forms of unworked gold, with the exception of nuggets, are prohibited. As local production does not meet the demand for industrial purposes, the CBS may import some gold. Three kinds of gold coins with face values of Sf 100, Sf 200, and Sf 250 are legal tender. Residents may hold and acquire gold coins in Suriname for numismatic and investment purposes; authorized banks may freely negotiate gold coins among themselves and with other residents. Residents other than the monetary authorities, producers of gold, and authorized industrial and dental users are not allowed to hold or acquire gold in any form other than nuggets, jewelry, or coins, at home or abroad without special permission.

Controls on external trade

Imports and exports of gold in any form other than jewelry require exchange licenses issued by the FEC. Licenses are not normally granted except for imports and exports of coins by authorized banks, and for imports and exports by or on behalf of the monetary authorities, producers of gold, and industrial users. Residents arriving from abroad, however, may freely bring in gold, subject to declaration and provided that they surrender it to the CBS within 20 days. Nonresident travelers may also freely bring in gold, subject to declaration; they may reexport the declared amount freely. Imports of gold coins are duty free and those of unworked gold are subject to a duty of Sf 1.00 a gram, irrespective of origin. The general tariff for gold ornaments is 60% ad valorem. Imports and exports of all forms of gold are subject to a statistical fee of 0.5%; in addition, imports are subject to a licensing fee of 1.5%.

Controls on exports and imports of banknotes

On exports

Domestic currency

Both resident and nonresident travelers may take out up to Sf 100.

Foreign currency

Exports in excess of $10,000 require a written declaration.

On imports

Domestic currency

Travelers may bring in up to Sf 100.

Foreign currency

Travelers may bring in up to $10,000. Larger amounts must be declared. Nonresidents may take out of the country up to the amount they brought in and declared on entry.

Resident Accounts

Eligibility to hold accounts

Natural persons are eligible.

Foreign exchange accounts permitted

Resident nonbanks are allowed to open foreign currency accounts with domestic and foreign banks and to hold foreign securities, provided that the funds have not been acquired from sales of real estate in Suriname or from exports. Balances in these accounts and holdings of foreign assets may be used freely, except for travel, for which there is a limit of Sf 1,500 a person a year.

Held domestically

Yes.

Held abroad

Yes.

Nonresident Accounts

Eligibility to hold accounts	Juridical and natural persons are eligible.
Foreign exchange accounts permitted	Nonresidents, whether banks or nonbanks, may open accounts in U.S. dollars with domestic banks with prior permission from the FEC; no overdrafts are permitted. These accounts may not be credited with Surinamese tender.
Domestic currency accounts	Nonresidents other than banks may freely open accounts in Suriname guilders with domestic banks. Certain debits and credits are covered by a general license, and all others are subject to a specific license. These accounts must not be overdrawn, and, except for certain specified purposes, debits must not exceed a total of Sf 3,000 a month. Authorized banks may open nonresident accounts in Suriname guilders in the name of nonresident banks; these accounts also must not be overdrawn. Authorized banks may open nonresident accounts on behalf of nonresidents drawing pensions from the government or under company plans. A special permit is required to transfer pensions abroad. Nonresident accounts in guilders may not be credited with Suriname banknotes mailed from abroad.
Convertible into foreign currency	n.a.

Imports and Import Payments

Foreign exchange budget	No.
Financing requirements for imports	No.
Documentation requirements for release of foreign exchange for imports	
Domiciliation requirements	n.a.
Preshipment inspection	n.a.
Letters of credit	n.a.
Import licenses used as exchange licenses	Import licenses serve as a general authorization for payment. In case of payment by LC, the import license must be approved by the CBS.
Import licenses and other nontariff measures	Import licenses are required for all imports and are valid for 6 months, during which period the goods must be landed and paid for.
Positive list	n.a.
Negative list	Imports of some commodities are prohibited: pigs (excluding those for breeding); chicken, duck, and turkey meat; pork; fish (excluding kwie kwie fish and smoked herring), shrimp, and crab (fresh, cooled, frozen, salted, dried, or precooked); vegetables (excluding potatoes, onions, and garlic); edible roots and tubers; citrus fruits; bananas and plantains; coconuts; green and roasted coffee (excluding decaffeinated); rice and rice products (excluding baby food); sugar (excluding cubes and tablets weighing 5 grams or less a cube or tablet); aromatized or colored sugar or sugar syrup; noodles and macaroni; jam, jelly, and marmalade (excluding those for diabetics); peanut butter; syrups and concentrates for nonalcoholic beverages in packages of less than 5 kilograms (excluding those for diabetics); firewood and other nonprocessed wood; railroad ties; shingles; wooden structures for construction; wooden tiles and panels; wooden tools, handles, and coat hangers; men's and boys' shoes (excluding rubber and plastic boots and sport shoes); and sand, gravel, sidewalk tiles, and road bricks. Imports of some other items, such as explosives and narcotics, are prohibited for reasons of public policy or health.
Open general licenses	Yes.
Licenses with quotas	Commodities subject to quotas include kwie kwie fish, milk powder, potatoes, onions, garlic, fruits and nuts (other than citrus fruits, bananas, plantains, and coconuts), decaffeinated coffee, peanuts, baby food, tomato paste, certain preserved vegetables, matches,

furnishings, ready-made clothing, and furniture (excluding that for business establishments, such as offices, theaters, clinics, hotels, restaurants, and libraries).

Import taxes and/or tariffs	In addition to customs duties, a license fee of 1.5% is levied on the c.i.f. value of all imports. A statistical fee of 2.0% is levied on the c.i.f. value of imports of bauxite companies, and 0.5% of the c.i.f. value of other imports, including imports of gold.
Taxes collected through the exchange system	No.

Exports and Export Proceeds

Repatriation requirements	Certain export companies have received special permission from the FEC to maintain current accounts in foreign currency with their parent companies abroad and to use these for specified payments and receipts (including export proceeds).
Surrender requirements	Exporters of bauxite and bananas must surrender foreign exchange proceeds to the CBS at the official exchange rate. Bauxite companies are not subject to export surrender requirements but must sell foreign exchange to the CBS to pay for their local expenditures. Other exporters must surrender their proceeds to authorized commercial banks and are allowed to buy back up to 85% of the amount surrendered.
Financing requirements	No.
Documentation requirements	
Letters of credit	Licenses are issued if the exports are covered by LCs opened by buyers abroad. To verify prices, the MTI ascertains with the relevant government agency whether the export price as reported by the exporter is in accordance with world market prices.
Guarantees	n.a.
Domiciliation	n.a.
Preshipment inspection	n.a.
Export licenses	Exports require licenses issued by the MTI. Export licenses for cattle, pigs, fresh beef and pork, and planting materials are granted only on the advice of the Director of Agriculture, Animal Husbandry, and Fisheries. The export of baboon wood is prohibited and that of rice is subject to special regulations.
Without quotas	n.a.
With quotas	n.a.
Export taxes	Exports of processed and semiprocessed wood are subject to a tax of 100% of the f.o.b. value. Exports of bauxite are subject to a statistical fee of 2.0% of their f.o.b. value, and other exports are subject to a statistical fee of 0.5% of their f.o.b. value.
Taxes collected through the exchange system	n.a.

Payments for Invisible Transactions and Current Transfers

Controls on these payments	Transactions involving outward remittances of foreign exchange are subject to licensing. Application for a license must be submitted to the FEC at least 1 month before the intended date for effecting such a transaction.
Interest payments	License applications must be supported by an auditor's report and presented to the FEC for verification.
Profit/dividends	Transfers of profits from investments made after July 31, 1953, are permitted. License application must be supported by an auditor's report and presented to the FEC for verification. Profits must be transferred within 3 years; otherwise, they are considered to

have become part of the firm's working capital and may be transferred only in annual installments of 20%. Transfers in accordance with these decisions have been temporarily suspended.

Payments for travel	Travel allowances for residents are subject to licensing and are limited to the equivalent of $1,500 a person a calendar year.
Prior approval	Yes.
Quantitative limits	Yes.
Indicative limits/bona fide test	Yes.
Subscriptions and membership fees	
Prior approval	n.a.
Quantitative limits	Authorized banks and the General Post Office have authority to provide foreign exchange up to Sf 150 a month for payment of certain services (bank charges, legal fees, membership dues, copy and patent rights, etc.) as well as for advertising expenses and payments for books.
Indicative limits/bona fide test	n.a.
Foreign workers' wages	
Prior approval	Yes.
Quantitative limits	The head of a repatriating family may transfer the equivalent of Sf 10,000 plus 10% of his or her total taxable earnings in Suriname accrued during the period of residence. If his or her Surinamese assets exceed the sum thus calculated, the excess may be transferred at a rate of Sf 10,000 a year. Transfers abroad in excess of Sf 10,000 a year may be authorized under exceptional circumstances. Outward transfers for these purposes have been temporarily reduced.
Indicative limits/bona fide test	n.a.

Proceeds from Invisible Transactions and Current Transfers

Repatriation requirements	Yes.
Surrender requirements	Foreign exchange receipts from invisibles must be surrendered to an authorized bank.
Restrictions on use of funds	Yes.

Capital Transactions

Controls on capital and money market instruments	Subject to certain requirements, residents may purchase or sell in specified countries Surinamese corporate shares that have been designated as negotiable by the FEC.
On capital market securities	n.a.
On money market instruments	n.a.
On collective investment securities	n.a.
Controls on credit operations	
Commercial credits	
By residents to nonresidents	n.a.
To residents from nonresidents	Borrowing by nonbanks requires the prior approval of the FEC.
Financial credits	The foreign transactions of authorized banks are restricted, in principle, to those undertaken for the account of their customers. Banks are required, in principle, to surrender to the CBS any excess of foreign currency purchased.
By residents to nonresidents	Authorized banks may place abroad in short-term U.S. dollar assets the amounts corresponding to balances in their nonresident U.S. dollar accounts.

To residents from nonresidents	n.a.
Controls on direct investment	
Outward direct investment	Investments are not permitted, but exceptions may be made when it is considered that Surinamese interests will benefit. The FEC may, at its discretion, grant licenses for transfers abroad from the estate of a deceased person up to a maximum of Sf 10,000. For estates valued at more than Sf 10,000, further annual transfers are permitted so as to spread them over a period of up to 10 years. The FEC may allow emigrants (heads of family) to transfer in foreign exchange the equivalent of Sf 5,000 in a lump sum, and subsequently Sf 5,000 a year.
Inward direct investment	Yes.
Controls on liquidation of direct investment	Transfers are permitted at any time of the foreign exchange (including loans) imported by a nonresident entrepreneur for the company's use. Also permitted are transfers of capital proceeds from the sale to residents, or the liquidation of fully or partly foreign-owned companies or other forms of enterprise established by nonresidents with foreign capital after July 31, 1953.
Controls on real estate transactions	
Purchase abroad by residents	Residents may not purchase real estate abroad.
Purchase locally by nonresidents	n.a.
Sale locally by nonresidents	n.a.
Provisions specific to commercial banks and other credit institutions	
Borrowing abroad	n.a.
Maintenance of accounts abroad	Authorized banks are permitted to place part of their liquid funds abroad and to use the short-term credit lines extended by their foreign correspondent banks as a source of operating funds. The CBS guarantees the LCs issued by the authorized banks by pledging its balances up to a specified ceiling, while the authorized banks keep their balances abroad at a minimum level. This arrangement applies to the state-controlled Landbouw Bank, De Surinaamsche Bank, and Hakrinbank, but not to the Dutch-owned Algemene Bank Nederland. Authorized banks may place abroad in short-term U.S. dollar assets the amounts corresponding to balances in their nonresident U.S. dollar accounts.
Lending to nonresidents (financial or commercial credits)	n.a.
Lending locally in foreign exchange	n.a.
Purchase of locally issued securities denominated in foreign exchange	n.a.
Differential treatment of nonresident deposit accounts and/or deposit accounts in foreign exchange	n.a.
Investment regulations	n.a.
Open foreign exchange position limits	The foreign transactions of authorized banks are restricted, in principle, to those undertaken for the account of their customers, and banks are required, in principle, to surrender to the CBS any excess of foreign currency purchased.
Other controls imposed by securities laws	No.

Changes During 1996

Arrangements for payments and receipts	*December 16.* Surinamese traveling abroad and foreign tourists were allowed to take both in and out of the country $10,000 or the equivalent thereof in other convertible currencies. For amounts above the limit, border points must be notified in writing.

SWAZILAND

(Position as of December 31, 1996)

Status Under IMF Articles of Agreement

Article VIII	Date of acceptance: December 11, 1989.

Exchange Arrangement

Currency	The currency of Swaziland is the lilangeni (plural emalangeni).
Exchange rate structure	Unitary.

Classification

Pegged

The lilangeni is pegged to the South African rand at E 1 per R 1. Exchange rates for the U.S. dollar quoted by the Central Bank of Swaziland (CBS) are based on the exchange rate of the South African rand against the U.S. dollar. Rates are also quoted for the Canadian dollar, the deutsche mark, the French franc, the Japanese yen, the pound sterling, and the Swiss franc, based on the London and New York market quotations for these currencies against the U.S. dollar and for the ECU. The CBS also quotes rates for the currencies of the member states of the PTA (Kenya, Malawi, Zambia, and Zimbabwe) based on their relationship with the SDR as reported by the PTA clearinghouse.

Exchange tax	No.
Exchange subsidy	No.
Forward exchange market	The CBS permits authorized dealers to engage in forward exchange operations. The forward exchange rates are market determined.
Official cover of forward operations	No.

Arrangements for Payments and Receipts

Prescription of currency requirements	No.

Payment arrangements

Regional arrangements

Swaziland is part of the CMA; no restrictions are applied to payments within the CMA, and, in principle, payments are not controlled. Residents of Swaziland have access to the Johannesburg market, in accordance with the terms and conditions applied in that market.

Administration of control

Exchange control authorities

The CBS, on behalf of the Ministry of Finance, controls all external currency transactions. In relations with countries outside the CMA, Swaziland applies exchange controls that are generally similar to those of South Africa.

International security restrictions	No.
Payment arrears	No.

Controls on exports and imports of banknotes

On exports

Domestic currency	Exports of up to E 500 are allowed.
Foreign currency	Exports of up to one-half of the applicable travel entitlement are allowed.

On imports

Domestic currency

Exports of up to E 500 are allowed; however, no control applies to the residents of CMA countries.

Resident Accounts

Eligibility to hold accounts

Juridical and natural persons are eligible.

Foreign exchange accounts permitted

Yes.

Held domestically

Approval to open these accounts is rarely granted.

Held abroad

No.

Nonresident Accounts

Eligibility to hold accounts

Juridical and natural persons are eligible.

Foreign exchange accounts permitted

These accounts are permitted, but prior approval is required.

Domestic currency accounts

Yes.

Convertible into foreign currency

These accounts are permitted, but prior approval is required.

Blocked accounts

Balances in these accounts may be invested in quoted securities and other such investments as may be approved by the CBS.

Imports and Import Payments

Foreign exchange budget

No.

Financing requirements for imports

Minimum financing requirements

Yes.

Advance payment requirements

Yes.

Advance import deposits

Yes.

Documentation requirements for release of foreign exchange for imports

Import licenses used as exchange licenses

Import licenses entitle the holders to buy the foreign exchange required to make import payments.

Import licenses and other nontariff measures

Open general licenses

Swaziland is a member of the SACU with Botswana, Lesotho, Namibia, and South Africa, and no import restrictions are imposed on goods originating in any country of the customs union. Imports from South Africa, including goods originating outside the customs union, do not require licenses. Imports from countries outside the customs union require licenses. Ports of entry outside Swaziland may be used, but the Swazi authorities are responsible for controlling import licenses and payment procedures.

Import taxes and/or tariffs

Swaziland applies the customs tariff system of SACU on imports from outside the customs union.

Taxes collected through the exchange system

No.

State import monopoly	No.

Exports and Export Proceeds

Repatriation requirements	For goods shipped to countries outside the customs area, licensing is administered to ensure that export proceeds are repatriated in the prescribed manner and within the stipulated period.
Documentation requirements	Contract notes are required.
Export licenses	
Without quotas	All exports are subject to licensing. For those goods that are shipped to members of the customs area, licenses are used mainly for tax levy purposes.
With quotas	n.a.
Export taxes	A sugar export levy applies to export proceeds from the EU market.
Taxes collected through the exchange system	No.

Payments for Invisible Transactions and Current Transfers

Controls on these payments	Payments to nonresidents for current transactions, while subject to control, are not normally restricted. Authority to approve some types of current payments up to established limits is delegated to authorized dealers. Payments for freight and insurance, unloading and storage costs, interest, commissions, travel, medical treatment, study abroad, subscriptions and membership fees, consulting and legal fees, pensions, family maintenance and alimony, and the use of credit cards abroad, as well as remittances of profits and dividends are subject to indicative limits and/or bona fide tests.
Administrative expenses	
Prior approval	Yes.
Interest payments	
Prior approval	Yes.
Profit/dividends	
Prior approval	Yes.
Payments for travel	
Quantitative limits	The basic exchange allowance for business and holiday travel to neighboring countries other than those in the CMA is E 1,000 a day, not to exceed E 20,000 a calendar year, for an adult. The allowance for business and holiday visits to all other countries is E 60,000 for an adult and E 20,000 for a child. Residents traveling to the member countries of the PTA must use traveler's checks denominated in the units of account of the PTA.
Medical costs	
Quantitative limits	The limit is E 4,000.
Study abroad costs	
Quantitative limits	Travel allowances for students studying in non-CMA countries during vacation periods were increased to E 10,000 from E 6,000 for single students, and to E 20,000 from E 12,000 for married students, a calendar year. Study allowances for students in non-CMA countries were increased to E 5,000 a month for single students and E 10,000 a month for married students, from E 4,000 and E 8,000, respectively.

Subscriptions and membership fees

    Quantitative limits   The limit is E 10,000 an applicant a year.

Consulting/legal fees

    Quantitative limits   The limit is E 20,000 a case.

Foreign workers' wages

    Quantitative limits   The limit varies from one-third up to one-half of the gross monthly income.

    Indicative limits/bona fide test   n.a.

Pensions

    Prior approval   Yes.

Gambling/prize earnings

    Prior approval   n.a.

    Indicative limits/bona fide test   n.a.

Family maintenance/alimony

    Quantitative limits   The limit for alimony payments is E 3,500 a month, and the beneficiary must be a nonresident.

Credit card use abroad

    Prior approval   To use credit cards outside the CMA, a resident cardholder must complete a letter of undertaking before departure.

Proceeds from Invisible Transactions and Current Transfers

n.a.

Capital Transactions

Controls on capital and money market instruments   All inward capital transfers require the prior approval of the CBS and must be properly documented in order to facilitate the subsequent repatriation of interest, dividends, profits, and other income.

On capital market securities

    Purchase locally by nonresidents   Yes.

    Sale or issue locally by nonresidents   Balances in blocked accounts may be invested in quoted securities and other such investments as may be approved by the CBS.

    Purchase abroad by residents   Applications for most outward transfers of capital are considered on their merits.

    Sale or issue abroad by residents   Yes.

On money market instruments   Yes.

On collective investment securities   Yes.

Controls on derivatives and other instruments

Purchase locally by nonresidents   Yes.

Sale or issue locally by nonresidents   Yes.

Purchase abroad by residents   Yes.

Sale or issue abroad by residents   Yes.

Controls on credit operations

Commercial credits

    By residents to nonresidents   Yes.

    To residents from nonresidents   Borrowing in foreign currency is not allowed.

Financial credits   Yes.

Guarantees, sureties, and financial   Yes.
backup facilities

Controls on direct investment

Outward direct investment   Applications for most outward transfers of capital are considered on their merits.

Inward direct investment   Yes.

Controls on liquidation of direct   No.
investment

Controls on real estate transactions

Sale locally by nonresidents   n.a.

Provisions specific to commercial
banks and other credit institutions

Borrowing abroad   Residents are not permitted to borrow funds from abroad without prior approval.

Lending locally in foreign exchange   Yes.

Purchase of locally issued securities   n.a.
denominated in foreign exchange

Differential treatment of nonresident
deposit accounts and/or deposit accounts in foreign exchange

    Reserve requirements   Yes.

    Liquid asset requirements   Yes.

    Interest rate controls   Yes.

Investment regulations   The requirement that commercial banks invest 95% of their domestic liabilities in domestic assets was abolished on May 1, 1996.

Open foreign exchange position limits   n.a.

Other controls imposed by securities   No.
laws

Changes During 1996

Payments for invisible transactions   *June 1.* Allowances for business and holiday travel to neighboring countries other than
and current transfers   those in the CMA were increased to E 1,000 a day, not to exceed E 20,000 a calendar
year for an adult from E 900 a day, not to exceed E 12,000 a calendar year. The allow-
ance for business and holiday visits to all other countries was changed to E 60,000 an
adult and E 20,000 a child from E 25,000 an adult and E 12,500 a child.

June 1. Travel allowances for students studying in non-CMA countries during vacation
periods were increased to E 10,000 from E 6,000 for single students, and to E 20,000
from E 12,000 for married students a calendar year.

June 1. Study allowances for students in non-CMA countries were increased to E 5,000
a month for single students and E 10,000 a month for married students, from E 4,000
and E 8,000, respectively.

Capital transactions   *May 1.* The minimum local asset requirement, which had required commercial banks to
invest 95% of their domestic liabilities in domestic assets, was abolished.

SWEDEN

(Position as of December 31, 1996)

Status Under IMF Articles of Agreement

Article VIII   Date of acceptance: February 15, 1961.

Exchange Arrangement

Currency   The currency of Sweden is the Swedish krona.

Exchange rate structure   Unitary.

Classification

Independent floating   The exchange rate of the Swedish krona is determined on the basis of supply and demand.

Exchange tax   No.

Exchange subsidy   No.

Forward exchange market   Yes.

Official cover of forward operations   The Sveriges Riksbank, the central bank, and certain government agencies participate in the forward exchange rate market.

Arrangements for Payments and Receipts

Prescription of currency requirements   No.

Payment arrangements   No.

Administration of control No.

International security restrictions

In accordance with IMF Executive Board Decision No. 144-(52/51)   Sweden notified the IMF on August 7, 1992, that, in compliance with UN Security Council Resolution No. 757 (1992), certain restrictions with regard to payments and transfers in respect of the Federal Republic of Yugoslavia (Serbia/Montenegro) were imposed; these restrictions were extended in 1994 to areas of Bosnia and Herzegovina under the control of Bosnian Serb forces.

In accordance with UN sanctions   Financial transactions with Iraq are prohibited in accordance with UN Security Council Resolution No. 661 (1990) and other relevant resolutions. Certain restrictions were imposed on Libya and Angola (UN Security Resolutions No. 748 (1992) and No. 864 (1993)).

Payment arrears   No.

Controls on trade in gold (coins and/or bullion)   No.

Controls on exports and imports of banknotes   No.

Resident Accounts

Eligibility to hold accounts   Juridical and natural persons are eligible.

Foreign exchange accounts permitted   Yes.

Held domestically	Yes.
Held abroad	Residents may open accounts, provided that the amounts are reported to the Swedish National Tax Board for tax control and to the Riksbank for statistical purposes.
Accounts in domestic currency convertible into foreign currency	Yes.

Nonresident Accounts

Eligibility to hold accounts	Juridical and natural persons are eligible.
Foreign exchange accounts permitted	Yes.
Domestic currency accounts	External krona accounts may be held by nonresidents domiciled abroad, including persons who have become nonresidents after emigrating. They may be used for payments and transfers and may be converted into any foreign currency.
Convertible into foreign currency	Yes.
Blocked accounts	No.

Imports and Import Payments

Foreign exchange budget	No.
Financing requirements for imports	No.
Documentation requirements for release of foreign exchange for imports	No.
Import licenses and other nontariff measures	Imports on most iron and steel products from all countries outside the EU, other than countries of the EFTA or countries that are parties to the EEA, are subject to import licensing for surveillance purposes. Certain goods (such as fireworks, gloves, bicycles, brushes, etc.) from China are also subject to licensing for surveillance purposes. Imports from Iraq are prohibited due to UN sanctions. Import restrictions apply to certain categories of food as well as narcotic drugs, weapons, live animals, radioactive materials, and others.
Licenses with quotas	As a result of Sweden's membership in the EU, as of January 1, 1995, the importation of textiles and clothing from more than 50 countries has been subject to restrictions or licensing for surveillance purposes. Agricultural and fishery products have also been subject to import licensing. Some iron and steel products from Russia, Ukraine, and Kazakhstan are also subject to restrictions. Certain imports from China (shoes, porcelain, toys, etc.) are subject to restrictions.
Import taxes and/or tariffs	Alcohol, tobacco, and mineral oils are subject to import taxes and customs duty.
Taxes collected through the exchange system	No.
State import monopoly	No.

Exports and Export Proceeds

Repatriation requirements	No.
Surrender requirements	No.
Financing requirements	No.
Documentation requirements	No.
Export licenses	Exports to Iraq are prohibited due to UN sanctions.

Without quotas	Yes.
Export taxes	No.

Payments for Invisible Transactions and Current Transfers

Controls on these payments	No.

Proceeds from Invisible Transactions and Current Transfers

Repatriation requirements	No.
Surrender requirements	No.
Restrictions on use of funds	No.

Capital Transactions

Controls on capital and money market instruments

The restriction applies only to shares and other securities of a participatory nature that may be affected by laws on inward direct investment in fishing and civil aviation.

On capital market securities

   Purchase locally by nonresidents — Yes.

On money market instruments

   Purchase locally by nonresidents — Yes.

Controls on derivatives and other instruments — No.

Controls on credit operations — No.

Controls on direct investment — No.

Controls on liquidation of direct investment — No.

Controls on real estate transactions

Purchase locally by nonresidents — A permit may be required.

Provisions specific to commercial banks and other credit institutions

Open foreign exchange position limits — For prudential purposes, limits are placed on the net foreign positions (spot, forward, options) in individual foreign currencies and on the total net position in all currencies. The limit for each foreign currency and for the total net position is equivalent to 10% of a bank's capital base, unless the bank is recognized as a market maker, in which case the limit is equivalent to 15% of its capital base. A limit also exists on a bank's total net position calculated as the sum of all liability positions. This limit is equal to 30% of the bank's capital base and 30% for recognized market makers.

Provisions specific to institutional investors

Currency matching regulations on assets/liabilities composition — Same provisions as for banks exist.

Other controls imposed by securities laws — No.

Changes During 1996

No significant changes occurred in the exchange and trade system.

SWITZERLAND

(Position as of December 31, 1996)

Status Under IMF Articles of Agreement

Article VIII   Date of acceptance: May 29, 1992.

Exchange Arrangement

Currency   The currency of Switzerland is the Swiss franc.

Exchange rate structure   Unitary.

Classification

Independent floating   The exchange rate of the Swiss franc is determined by supply and demand. However, the Swiss National Bank (SNB) reserves the right to intervene in the foreign exchange market. All settlements are made at free market rates. The principal intervention currency is the U.S. dollar.

Exchange tax   No.

Exchange subsidy   No.

Forward exchange market   No officially fixed premiums and discount rates apply to forward exchange contracts, all of which are negotiated at free market rates.

Official cover of forward operations No.

Arrangements for Payments and Receipts

Prescription of currency requirements   No.

Payment arrangements   No.

Administration of control   No.

International security restrictions

In accordance with IMF Executive Board Decision No. 144-(52/51)   Certain restrictions have been imposed in respect of Iraq and Libya.

In accordance with UN sanctions   On the basis of UN sanctions, restrictions have been imposed on the making of payments and transfers for current international transactions regarding Iraq and Libya.

Payment arrears   No.

Controls on trade in gold (coins and/or bullion)

Controls on external trade   Import and export licenses, which are issued freely, are required for commercial imports and exports of certain articles containing gold.

Controls on exports and imports of banknotes   No.

Resident Accounts

Eligibility to hold accounts   Juridical and natural persons are eligible.

Foreign exchange accounts permitted   Yes.

818

Held domestically	Yes.
Held abroad	Yes.
Accounts in domestic currency convertible into foreign currency	Yes.

Nonresident Accounts

Eligibility to hold accounts	Juridical and natural persons are eligible.
Foreign exchange accounts permitted	Yes.
Domestic currency accounts	Yes.
Convertible into foreign currency	Yes.
Blocked accounts	No.

Imports and Import Payments

Foreign exchange budget	No.
Financing requirements for imports	No.
Documentation requirements for release of foreign exchange for imports	No.
Import licenses and other nontariff measures	Import controls apply only for defense-sensitive products.
Open general licenses	Licenses are required mostly for agricultural products.
Import taxes and/or tariffs	No.
State import monopoly	The importation of alcohol, butter, and wheat grain is a partial state monopoly.

Exports and Export Proceeds

Repatriation requirements	No.
Surrender requirements	No.
Financing requirements	No.
Documentation requirements	No.
Export licenses	The system is operated in part with the assistance of semiofficial or private organizations.
Without quotas	Exports of weapons, dual-use goods for the production of conventional weapons and weapons of mass destruction are restricted (approval is required).
Export taxes	No.

Payments for Invisible Transactions and Current Transfers

Controls on these payments	No.

Proceeds from Invisible Transactions and Current Transfers

Repatriation requirements	No.
Surrender requirements	No.
Restrictions on use of funds	No.

Capital Transactions

Controls on capital and money market instruments	No.
On capital market securities	Foreign and domestic bond issues denominated in Swiss francs must be reported to the SNB. The physical importation and exportation of Swiss and foreign securities are unrestricted. In case of any disturbances in the capital markets, the federal government may introduce a permit requirement for certain outward capital transfers (e.g., bond issues).
Controls on derivatives and other instruments	No.
Controls on credit operations	No.
Controls on direct investment	No.
Controls on liquidation of direct investment	No.
Controls on real estate transactions	
Purchase locally by nonresidents	Purchases by nonresidents require approval by the canton in which the property is situated. The approval of the canton is subject to supervision and appeal by the federal government.
Provisions specific to commercial banks and other credit institutions	No.
Provisions specific to institutional investors	For insurance companies, the overall limit is 30% if invested in bonds denominated in Swiss francs and 20% if invested in bonds denominated in foreign currencies.
	For life insurance the overall limit is 30% with limits for equities, bonds, and real estate of 25%, 20%, and 5% of the total portfolio, respectively.
Limits (max.) on portfolio invested abroad	Yes.
Other controls imposed by securities laws	No.

Changes During 1996

No significant changes occurred in the exchange and trade system.

SYRIAN ARAB REPUBLIC

(Position as of December 31, 1996)

Status Under IMF Articles of Agreement

Article XIV

Yes.

Exchange Arrangement

Currency

The currency of the Syrian Arab Republic is the Syrian pound.

Exchange rate structure

Multiple

The exchange rate system consists of 5 official rates and 2 unofficial rates. The official rates are (1) the official rate of LS 11.20/11.25 per $1 applies to the repayment of loans and interests arising from bilateral payments agreements; (2) the budget accounting rate, introduced on January 2, 1996, applies to public sector exports of petroleum, all government imports (including essential subsidized commodities and invisibles), and repayment of loans and interest not related to bilateral payments agreements; (3) the "rate in neighboring countries" of LS 43.5/44 per $1 applies to all public and private capital inflows, the 25% of export proceeds surrendered by the private sector, and that part of the 75% of export proceeds retained by private sector exporters that is not used to finance their own or others' imports; to travel allowances; to tourism and medical expenses; to student allowances; to remittances abroad and payments by the public sector approved by the Committee for Foreign Exchange; to all public sector enterprises' foreign exchange transactions; to earnings of staff of UN and diplomatic missions in the Syrian Arab Republic; and to domestic expenses of foreign oil companies; (4) the promotion rate of LS 20.22 per $1, which is used only for payments of allowances to students who started overseas study before January 1, 1991; and (5) the "government fee rate" (LS 42.95/43.00 per $1), which applies to a number of fees, including those on transit and port services, and for customs valuation of some imports.

The unofficial rates are (1) the free market rate, which stood at LS 50.9 per $1 on December 31, 1996, and (2) the "export proceeds" rate in which a market-determined rate applies to goods that may be imported only with foreign exchange earned through exports. Exporters who do not use all of their export earnings to import goods may sell their retained foreign exchange earnings to importers in this market. In December 1996, the exchange rate in this market stood at LS 55 per $1.

Classification

Pegged

The official rate is pegged to the U.S. dollar at LS 11.20/11.25 per $1.

Exchange tax

No.

Exchange subsidy

No.

Forward exchange market

No.

Arrangements for Payments and Receipts

Prescription of currency requirements

The Exchange Office prescribes the currencies that can be obtained for exports. Proceeds from exports to all countries may be obtained in any convertible currency. Prescription of currency requirements are not applied to outgoing payments. All payments to, and receipts from, Israel are prohibited. With few exceptions, non-Syrians visiting the Syrian Arab Republic are required to settle their bills in foreign exchange.

Payment arrangements

Bilateral arrangements

Operative

There is an agreement with the Islamic Republic of Iran.

Inoperative	There is an agreement with Russia and Sri Lanka.
Regional arrangements	n.a.
Clearing agreements	n.a.
Barter agreements and open accounts	n.a.

Administration of control

Exchange control authorities	The Ministry of Economy and Foreign Trade (MOEFT) determines policy with regard to imports and exports and issues import licenses. The Exchange Office issues exchange licenses for invisibles and capital transactions.

Controls on trade in gold (coins and/or bullion)

Controls on external trade	Temporary imports of gold are exempt from import licensing, but exports are subject to licensing.

Controls on exports and imports of banknotes

On exports

Domestic currency	Syrian banknotes may not be exported. However, travelers to Jordan and Lebanon who are not eligible for a foreign exchange allowance may take with them up to LS 5,000 a trip. Nonresidents leaving the Syrian Arab Republic are not allowed to reconvert Syrian currency into foreign exchange.
Foreign currency	Residents traveling abroad may take with them foreign exchange up to $2,000 a trip to all countries except Jordan and Lebanon.

On imports

Domestic currency	Nonresidents are permitted to bring unlimited amounts of Syrian currency without declaration.
Foreign currency	Nonresidents are permitted to bring up to $5,000 without declaration.

Resident Accounts

Eligibility to hold accounts	Juridical and natural persons are eligible.
Foreign exchange accounts permitted	Residents were permitted to open foreign exchange accounts on September 26, 1996. Deposits may not be transferred to other residents and deposits in the form of banknotes may only be withdrawn in that form, unless transferred abroad for medical treatment, education, newspaper subscriptions, and other similar noncommercial purposes. Deposits for a term of 90 days or more accrue a competitive rate of interest.
Held domestically	Residents not involved in export activities and wishing to open transferable foreign currency accounts are required to present written evidence that they have sources of income from abroad.
Held abroad	n.a.

Nonresident Accounts

Eligibility to hold accounts	Juridical and natural persons are eligible.
Foreign exchange accounts permitted	Nonresidents may open accounts in convertible foreign currencies at the CBS for the deposit of funds from abroad. Balances in such accounts may be sold to local banks, transferred abroad without restriction, or used to pay for authorized imports. Temporary nonresident accounts may be opened in the name of nonresidents temporarily residing in the Syrian Arab Republic. These accounts may not be used, however, for funds received in settlement currencies, through payment conventions.

Approval required	n.a.
Domestic currency accounts	These accounts may be credited with the proceeds in foreign currencies sold to the authorized banks and with other receipts in foreign currencies; they may be debited without prior approval to pay for Syrian exports to the country of the account holder and for expenses in the Syrian Arab Republic.
Convertible into foreign currency	No.

Imports and Import Payments

Foreign exchange budget	The foreign exchange requirements of the state trading agencies are met from the annual foreign exchange budget; these agencies automatically receive import licenses upon submission of documentation of their import requirements.
Financing requirements for imports	When foreign exchange is not made available, private imports must be financed with the importers' own resources through external credit arrangements, foreign currency deposits maintained in the Syrian Arab Republic by nonresidents, or foreign exchange purchased from other private or mixed enterprises through the intermediary of the Commercial Bank of Syria (ComBS) at the rate in neighboring countries. Imports of many goods are restricted to specific methods of financing. A number of imports may only be imported using foreign exchange generated through exports.
Minimum financing requirements	n.a.
Advance payment requirements	n.a.
Advance import deposits	A non-interest-bearing advance deposit is required for public sector imports for an amount equal to 100% of the value of the imports. For several categories of goods, an advance import deposit equal to 100% of the value of the import, plus a 3% fee, is required.
Documentation requirements for release of foreign exchange for imports	
Domiciliation requirements	n.a.
Preshipment inspection	n.a.
Letters of credit	Private importers are authorized to import products specified on the permitted list by opening letters of credit at the ComBS.
Import licenses used as exchange licenses	n.a.
Import licenses and other nontariff measures	All imports valued at more than LS 2,000 (LS 500 for imports from Lebanon) require licensing. A fee ranging from LS 25 to LS 200 is charged upon the issuance of an import license.
Positive list	The list of items that the private sector is permitted to import include certain agricultural goods, industrial goods, and raw materials. Imports of goods not on the permitted list are prohibited, with certain exceptions. Imports must come directly from the country of origin, but the MOEFT has the authority to permit certain goods to be imported from countries other than the country of origin.
	Imports from the Syrian free zones are allowed for certain industrial goods and for goods with a free-zone value added of at least 40%. Imports of commodities originating in Israel are prohibited.
Open general licenses	n.a.
Licenses with quotas	n.a.
Import taxes and/or tariffs	An import surcharge of 2% is charged on all imports; government imports and imports of certain essential items are exempted. Imports for customs duty purposes are valued at

different exchange rates (11.25, 23, and 43), according to the categories of goods, while import tariffs range up to 200%. All previous special levies on imports have been replaced by a unified import surcharge ranging from 6% to 35%.

Taxes collected through the exchange system	n.a.
State import monopoly	Many basic commodities (such as paper, salt, tobacco, wheat, iron and steel, and certain agricultural machinery) are imported only by state trading agencies or, for their own account, by certain private sector importers.

Exports and Export Proceeds

Repatriation requirements	Yes.
Surrender requirements	Exporters are required to repatriate and surrender the proceeds to the ComBS within 60 days of the date of shipment to Lebanon, within 4 months of the date of export shipment to other Arab countries, and within 6 months of the date of shipment to any other country. The public sector enterprises may retain 100% of their export proceeds in special foreign currency accounts. In the case of fruits and vegetables, public and private sector exporters may convert 100% of the proceeds at the rate in neighboring countries.
Financing requirements	The ComBS may accept prepayments for exports of Syrian products.
Documentation requirements	Exports of a few goods to all countries and all exports to Israel are prohibited.
Letters of credit	n.a.
Guarantees	n.a.
Domiciliation	n.a.
Preshipment inspection	n.a.
Export licenses	Exports of wheat, barley, cotton, cotton yarn, and their derivatives are made by the government organizations dealing in cereals and cotton. Petroleum products are handled by the Petroleum Marketing Office. Exports of certain other commodities are also reserved for government agencies, state trading agencies, or specified companies.
Without quotas	Yes.
With quotas	n.a.
Export taxes	Exports of cotton are subject to a 12.5% tax applied to the value of the exports (f.o.b.), less the cost of transportation within the Syrian Arab Republic. Exports of other agricultural commodities (processed foods and, most importantly, textiles) were abolished.
Taxes collected through the exchange system	n.a.

Payments for Invisible Transactions and Current Transfers

Controls on these payments	Most payments for invisibles must be made at the rate in neighboring countries.
Freight/insurance	
Prior approval	Yes.
Quantitative limits	n.a.
Indicative limits/bona fide test	n.a.
Unloading/storage costs	
Prior approval	Yes.

Quantitative limits	n.a.
Indicative limits/bona fide test	n.a.
Administrative expenses	
Prior approval	Yes.
Quantitative limits	n.a.
Indicative limits/bona fide test	n.a.
Commissions	
Prior approval	Yes.
Quantitative limits	n.a.
Indicative limits/bona fide test	n.a.
Interest payments	
Prior approval	Yes.
Quantitative limits	n.a.
Indicative limits/bona fide test	n.a.
Profit/dividends	Remittances must be authorized by the Exchange Office upon proof of payment of income tax. Profits from projects approved by the Higher Committee for Investment under the new investment law can be repatriated freely.
Prior approval	Yes.
Quantitative limits	n.a.
Indicative limits/bona fide test	n.a.
Payments for travel	Residents traveling abroad may take with them foreign exchange up to $2,000 a trip to all countries except Jordan and Lebanon. Of this amount, up to the equivalent of LS 5,000 a trip may be purchased at the rate in neighboring countries for travel to Arab countries (except Jordan and Lebanon), and up to the equivalent of LS 7,500 a trip for travel to non-Arab countries. Travelers to Jordan and Lebanon are not eligible for a foreign exchange allowance, but may take with them up to LS 5,000 a trip in Syrian banknotes. For children 10 years and younger, the allowances are 50% of the above amounts. For travel to countries with which payments arrangements are maintained, 50% of the travel allocation must be handled through the clearing account concerned (30% for business travelers). On departure, residents of Syrian nationality must pay an exit tax of LS 600 a person if traveling to Arab countries and LS 1,500 a person for other destinations. An airport stamp tax of LS 200 is added to this tax. Workers on secondments to a foreign country may take with them the entire amount of the allocation on producing proof that they have transferred foreign exchange from abroad; otherwise, they may take with them only foreign exchange equivalent to 25% of the above-mentioned allocations.
Prior approval	n.a.
Quantitative limits	Yes.
Medical costs	
Prior approval	The allowance for medical treatment must be authorized by the Ministry of Health.
Quantitative limits	n.a.
Indicative limits/bona fide test	n.a.
Study abroad costs	
Prior approval	The allowance for education is subject to prior approval from the Ministry of Higher Education.

Quantitative limits	n.a.
Subscriptions and membership fees	
Prior approval	Yes.
Quantitative limits	n.a.
Indicative limits/bona fide test	n.a.
Consulting/legal fees	
Prior approval	Yes.
Quantitative limits	n.a.
Indicative limits/bona fide test	n.a.
Foreign workers' wages	
Prior approval	Yes.
Quantitative limits	Up to 60% of the salaries received by foreign technicians and experts employed in the Syrian Arab Republic, and 50% of the salaries of personnel of foreign diplomatic and international missions in the Syrian Arab Republic may be transferred. Foreign staff connected with foreign direct investments are allowed to transfer 100% of severance pay.
Indicative limits/bona fide test	n.a.
Pensions	
Prior approval	Yes.
Quantitative limits	n.a.
Indicative limits/bona fide test	n.a.
Gambling/prize earnings	n.a.
Family maintenance/alimony	
Prior approval	Yes.
Quantitative limits	The limit is LS 250 for each transfer, and is effected upon presentation of proof of need.
Indicative limits/bona fide test	n.a.
Credit card use abroad	n.a.

Proceeds from Invisible Transactions and Current Transfers

Repatriation requirements	Yes.
Surrender requirements	Proceeds from transactions by the public sector must be sold at the official rate and those from transactions by the private sector must be sold at the rate in neighboring countries. All Syrian employees working abroad are subject to an annual tax of $50–$700, depending on their profession, and are allowed import tax exemptions on luxury items (valued between $500 and $7,000) if the equivalent funds are surrendered at the rate in neighboring countries. Syrian government employees who are on leave and working abroad are required to repatriate and convert a minimum of 25% of each year's earnings received in foreign exchange at the rate in neighboring countries.
Restrictions on use of funds	Yes.

Capital Transactions

Controls on capital and money market instruments	All capital transfers to and from the Syrian Arab Republic take place at the rate in neighboring countries. Exports of capital require the approval of the Exchange Office.

On capital market securities	There is no market in medium- and long-term government bonds in the Syrian Arab Republic. Bonds are issued on an as-needed basis to government-owned banks to supplement their capital base.
Purchase locally by nonresidents	n.a.
Sale or issue locally by nonresidents	n.a.
Purchase abroad by residents	Yes.
Sale or issue abroad by residents	n.a.
On money market instruments	The only instruments available in the Syrian Arab Republic are investment bonds issued by the Popular Credit Bank as agent of the government. The bonds, which carry an interest rate of 9% a year, have 10-year maturity but have a short-term effective holding period as they are redeemable after 3 to 6 months. They may only be purchased by nonbank Syrian residents and by the Popular Credit Bank itself.
Purchase locally by nonresidents	n.a.
Sale or issue locally by nonresidents	n.a.
Purchase abroad by residents	Yes.
Sale or issue abroad by residents	n.a.
On collective investment securities	
Purchase locally by nonresidents	There is no collective investment institution in the Syrian Arab Republic.
Sale or issue locally by nonresidents	n.a.
Purchase abroad by residents	Yes.
Sale or issue abroad by residents	n.a.

Controls on credit operations

Commercial credits

By residents to nonresidents	Yes.
To residents from nonresidents	n.a.

Financial credits

By residents to nonresidents	Yes.
To residents from nonresidents	n.a.

Guarantees, sureties, and financial backup facilities

By residents to nonresidents	Yes.
To residents from nonresidents	n.a.

Controls on direct investment

Outward direct investment	Yes.
Inward direct investment	The Syrian Arab Republic provides special facilities for the investment of funds of immigrants and of nationals of Arab states, including a 7-year tax exemption from all taxes in the tourism and agricultural industries. Projects with minimum fixed assets of LS 10 million approved by the government benefit from a number of exemptions from exchange and trade regulations, including exemption from customs duties of imports of required machinery, equipment, and vehicles. Mixed companies with at least 25% public participation are exempted from all taxes for 7 years and private companies are exempted for 5 years; exemption periods may be extended by an additional 2 years if the

company exports at least 50% of its output. Investors are permitted to hold foreign currency accounts to finance convertible currency requirements. These accounts comprise all capital and loans secured in foreign currency and 75% of foreign currency exports. All profits may be transferred freely. The Syrian Arab Republic has investment guarantee agreements with France, Germany, Switzerland, and the United States.

Controls on liquidation of direct investment	Investors are free to repatriate foreign exchange capital after 5 years from the date of investment. Capital may be repatriated after 6 months if the project suffers from events beyond the control of the investor.
Controls on real estate transactions	
Purchase abroad by residents	Yes.
Purchase locally by nonresidents	Nonresidents and foreign nationals may acquire immovable property only after presenting evidence that they have converted into Syrian pounds the foreign exchange equivalent of the price of property at the authorized local bank.
Sale locally by nonresidents	n.a.
Provisions specific to commercial banks and other credit institutions	
Borrowing abroad	n.a.
Maintenance of accounts abroad	n.a.
Lending to nonresidents (financial or commercial credits)	n.a.
Lending locally in foreign exchange	n.a.
Purchase of locally issued securities denominated in foreign exchange	n.a.
Differential treatment of nonresident deposit accounts and/or deposit accounts in foreign exchange	
Reserve requirements	Foreign currency deposits are not subject to reserve requirements.
Liquid asset requirements	n.a.
Interest rate controls	Yes.
Credit controls	There is an annual credit plan.
Investment regulations	n.a.
Open foreign exchange position limits	n.a.

Changes During 1996

Exchange arrangements	*January 2.* A new budget accounting rate was introduced. The CBS and the ComBS were allowed to buy public sector foreign currency receipts from exports of crude oil and petroleum products at the rate of LS 22.95 per $1 and to sell foreign currency for the import of petroleum products, most government imports of goods and services, including essential subsidized commodities, and debt service payments not related to bilateral payments agreements at the rate of LS 23 per $1.
	January 8. The ComBS was allowed to buy foreign currency from grants at the rate in neighboring countries.
	September 26. The neighboring countries' rate was devalued from LS 42/43 per $1 to LS 43.5/44 per $1.
Resident accounts	*September 26.* Residents were permitted to open foreign exchange accounts at the ComBS with no questions asked as to the source of the deposit. The deposits may not be

transferred to other residents, and if made in the form of banknotes, may only be withdrawn as banknotes unless transferred abroad for medical treatment, education, newspaper subscriptions, and other similar noncommercial purposes.

Nonresident accounts

January 8. Diplomatic and UN missions and their staffs were allowed to exchange all their transfers to the Syrian Arab Republic at the rate in neighboring countries.

Exports and export proceeds

April 16. Exporters were required to repatriate and surrender the proceeds to the CBS within 60 days of the date of shipment to Lebanon, within 4 months of the date of shipment to other Arab countries, and within 6 months of the date of shipment to any other country.

TAJIKISTAN

(Position as of December 31, 1996)

Status Under IMF Articles of Agreement

Article XIV	Yes.

Exchange Arrangement

Currency	The currency of Tajikistan is the Tajik ruble.
Exchange rate structure	Unitary.
Classification	
Independent floating	Buying and selling exchange rates of the National Bank of Tajikistan (NBT) are set on auctions held at the Tajik Interbank Foreign Currency Exchange (TICEX) in Dushanbe. The interbank and retail markets transact at freely determined rates, but these rates are generally based on, and close to, the TICEX rate.
Exchange tax	No.
Exchange subsidy	No.
Forward exchange market	No.

Arrangements for Payments and Receipts

Prescription of currency requirements	Residents of Tajikistan may make and receive payments and transfers in any convertible currency as well as in Tajik rubles. Residents and nonresidents may use foreign exchange for domestic transactions, except for special cases as defined by the authorities. Commercial transactions with nonresidents must be conducted via correspondent accounts maintained either by authorized commercial banks or by the NBT. The NBT has correspondent accounts with the Baltic countries, Russia, and the other countries of the FSU, but these accounts are effectively inoperative.
Payment arrangements	
Bilateral arrangements	
Inoperative	There are inoperative agreements with the CIS countries.
Regional arrangements	n.a.
Clearing agreements	n.a.
Barter agreements and open accounts	Barter trade is prohibited, except for aluminum trade. However, in practice, it still takes place, including bartering as part of debt deals negotiated by the government.
Administration of control	
Exchange control authorities	The NBT (1) acts as nonexclusive agent for the Republic of Tajikistan in the administration of foreign exchange controls; (2) issues licenses to commercial banks to conduct banking operations and foreign currency operations; (3) is exclusively responsible for the supervision and regulation of financial institutions; (4) manages official foreign exchange reserves; and (5) formulates basic foreign exchange policy. The Ministry of Finance (MOF) registers foreign investors for inward direct investment.
Payment arrears	
Official	Yes.
Private	Yes.
Controls on exports and imports of banknotes	Importation and exportation of foreign currency banknotes and Tajik ruble banknotes are freely permitted, subject only to declaration of amounts over $500.

On exports

    Domestic currency   Yes.

    Foreign currency   Yes.

On imports

    Domestic currency   Yes.

    Foreign currency   Yes.

Resident Accounts

Eligibility to hold accounts	Juridical and natural persons are eligible.
Foreign exchange accounts permitted	Yes.
Held domestically	Yes.
Held abroad	These accounts are permitted under the Law on Foreign Currency Control, but they are prohibited under the Monetary Law. In practice, however, these accounts may be opened with prior authorization from the NBT.
Accounts in domestic currency convertible into foreign currency	Yes.

Nonresident Accounts

Eligibility to hold accounts	Juridical and natural persons are eligible.
Foreign exchange accounts permitted	Yes.
Domestic currency accounts	Yes.
Convertible into foreign currency	Yes.
Blocked accounts	No.

Imports and Import Payments

Foreign exchange budget	No.
Financing requirements for imports	No.
Documentation requirements for release of foreign exchange for imports	
Domiciliation requirements	n.a.
Preshipment inspection	n.a.
Letters of credit	Yes.
Import licenses used as exchange licenses	n.a.
Import licenses and other nontariff measures	The importation of firearms, narcotics, poisons, chemical weapons, and nuclear materials is prohibited.
Open general licenses	n.a.
Licenses with quotas	n.a.
Import taxes and/or tariffs	A uniform 10% import tariff is imposed on all imports.

Taxes collected through the exchange system	No.
State import monopoly	No.

Exports and Export Proceeds

Repatriation requirements	The requirement became effective on March 1, 1996.
Surrender requirements	The surrender requirement was abolished on February 24, 1996. Foreign exchange proceeds may be either held by exporters in foreign currency accounts with domestic banks or sold in the interbank market.
Financing requirements	Yes.
Documentation requirements	For exports of cotton, a 100% advance payment and approval are required.
Letters of credit	Yes.
Guarantees	Yes.
Domiciliation	n.a.
Preshipment inspection	n.a.
Export licenses	No.
Export taxes	Customs duties on exports were abolished on March 1, 1996.

Payments for Invisible Transactions and Current Transfers

Controls on these payments	No.

Proceeds from Invisible Transactions and Current Transfers

Repatriation requirements	No.
Surrender requirements	No.
Restrictions on use of funds	No.

Capital Transactions

Controls on capital and money market instruments	
On capital market securities	
Sale or issue locally by nonresidents	Yes.
Purchase abroad by residents	n.a.
Sale or issue abroad by residents	Registration with the MOF and NBT approval are required.
On money market instruments	
Purchase abroad by residents	NBT approval is required.
Sale or issue abroad by residents	NBT approval is required.
On collective investment securities	
Purchase abroad by residents	NBT approval is required.
Sale or issue abroad by residents	NBT approval is required.

Controls on derivatives and other instruments

Purchase abroad by residents | NBT approval is required.

Sale or issue abroad by residents | NBT approval is required.

Controls on credit operations

Commercial credits

By residents to nonresidents | There are no restrictions for loans of up to 90 days maturity.

To residents from nonresidents | There are no restrictions for loans of up to 180 days maturity.

Financial credits

By residents to nonresidents | There are no restrictions for loans of up to 180 days maturity.

To residents from nonresidents | There are no restrictions for loans of up to 180 days maturity. For loans over 180 days, NBT approval is required.

Guarantees, sureties, and financial backup facilities

By residents to nonresidents | There are no restrictions for loans of up to 180 days maturity. For loans over 180 days, NBT approval is required.

Controls on direct investment | Foreign investors are required to register with the MOF.

Outward direct investment | NBT approval is required.

Controls on liquidation of direct investment | No.

Controls on real estate transactions

Purchase abroad by residents | NBT approval is required.

Provisions specific to commercial banks and other credit institutions

Differential treatment of nonresident deposit accounts and/or deposit accounts in foreign exchange

Reserve requirements | Yes.

Liquid asset requirements | Yes.

Credit controls | Yes.

Open foreign exchange position limits | Individual and overall net positions must not exceed 5% and 20%, respectively, of unimpaired capital at the end of each banking day.

Provisions specific to institutional investors | No.

Other controls imposed by securities laws | No.

Changes During 1996

Imports and import payments | *March 1.* A uniform 10% import duty was introduced.

Exports and export proceeds | *February 24.* Export duties, export licenses, and surrender requirements were abolished, and a repatriation requirement was imposed, effective March 1, 1996.

February 24. Restrictions related to prepayment, tax clearance, and other documentary requirements were introduced for exports of cotton, and the monopoly on exports of cotton was lifted.

TANZANIA

(Position as of December 31, 1996)

Status Under IMF Articles of Agreement

Article VIII   Date of acceptance: July 15, 1996.

Exchange Arrangement

Currency   The currency of Tanzania is the Tanzania shilling.

Exchange rate structure   Unitary.

Classification

Independent floating   The external value of the Tanzania shilling is determined in the interbank market. The Bank of Tanzania (BOT) intervenes in the interbank market only to smooth movements that are caused by transitory factors. The official exchange rate is based on the interbank market rate and remains within a 2% band around the current day's market rate. The official exchange rate is used for accounting, taxation, and settlement of government obligations. During the first half of 1996, only a few foreign exchange bureaus that met new capital requirements were allowed to participate in the interbank market. As of July 1, 1996, all bureaus were prohibited from participating in the market.

Exchange tax   No.

Exchange subsidy   No.

Forward exchange market   Authorized dealers may enter into forward contracts for purchases and sales of foreign currencies with their customers in export and import transactions.

Official cover of forward operations   The BOT does not offer forward cover against exchange rate risk.

Arrangements for Payments and Receipts

Prescription of currency requirements   No.

Payment arrangements

Bilateral arrangements

 Inoperative   There is an agreement with Mozambique.

Regional arrangements   Tanzania participates in the PTA.

Clearing agreements   There are agreements with Kenya and Uganda.

Administration of control

Exchange control authorities   The Minister of Finance (MOF) has delegated authority to administer exchange control, including in Zanzibar, to customs and the BOT. The BOT delegates authority to make payments abroad to all licensed banks.

Payment arrears

Official   Yes.

Private   n.a.

Controls on trade in gold (coins and/or bullion)   No.

Controls on exports and imports of banknotes

On exports

Domestic currency — Travelers may take out of the country up to the equivalent of $100.

Foreign currency — Nonresident travelers may take out of the country foreign currency notes and traveler's checks of any remaining amount of the foreign exchange brought into Tanzania.

On imports

Domestic currency — Returning travelers may bring in up to T Sh 1,000 in banknotes.

Resident Accounts

Eligibility to hold accounts — Juridical and natural persons are eligible.

Foreign exchange accounts permitted — Yes.

Held domestically — Yes.

Held abroad — No.

Nonresident Accounts

Eligibility to hold accounts — Juridical and natural persons are eligible.

Foreign exchange accounts permitted — These accounts are permitted, but prior approval is required.

Domestic currency accounts — Nonresident accounts are maintained by foreign nationals temporarily residing in Tanzania; by firms, companies, or other organizations registered or incorporated outside Tanzania; and by foreign diplomatic missions, the United Nations, or other international organizations and their officials in Tanzania. The balances of nonconvertible accounts may be transferred from Tanzania after approval is obtained from the BOT. There are 6 subcategories of nonresident accounts: external, shipping/airline, special, ordinary, expatriate, and unspecified.

Convertible into foreign currency — Yes.

Blocked accounts — No.

Imports and Import Payments

Foreign exchange budget — No.

Financing requirements for imports — No.

Documentation requirements for release of foreign exchange for imports — The release of foreign exchange in excess of $5,000 requires an import declaration form.

Domiciliation requirements — n.a.

Preshipment inspection — Imports of goods exceeding $5,000 require a preshipment inspection document.

Letters of credit — n.a.

Import licenses and other nontariff measures

Negative list — Certain imports to the mainland from any source may be prohibited for reasons of health or security.

Import taxes and/or tariffs	Customs tariffs are levied on the c.i.f. value of imports. There are 4 rates: 10%, 20%, 30%, and 40%. A minimum rate of 5% is granted by the MOF for imports considered to be in the public interest. Low tariffs are also charged on imports of machinery. Specific duties are levied on alcoholic beverages, tobacco, and petroleum products. Statutory exemptions are granted to the diplomatic corps, as well as to religious, educational, and welfare institutions. Discretionary full or partial exemptions may be allowed by the MOF if the imports are deemed to be in the public interest.
Taxes collected through the exchange system	No.
State import monopoly	No.

Exports and Export Proceeds

Repatriation requirements	Proceeds from exports from the mainland must be repatriated within 2 months of the date of exportation unless justification for nonrepatriation can be made. Proceeds from exports of traditional goods from Zanzibar must be repatriated.
Surrender requirements	No.
Export licenses	Licenses for exportation from the mainland are required for only a few items for health, sanitary, or national heritage reasons.
Without quotas	Yes.
Export taxes	A tax of 2% is levied on traditional exports.
Taxes collected through the exchange system	No.

Payments for Invisible Transactions and Current Transfers

Controls on these payments	There are no controls on payments for freight and insurance, unloading and storage costs, administrative expenses, commissions, study abroad, subscriptions and membership fees, consulting and legal fees, or on the use of credit cards abroad.
Interest payments	The transfer of income from investments by nonresidents is not restricted, provided all tax obligations have been met.
Profit/dividends	The transfer of income from investments by nonresidents is not restricted, provided all tax obligations have been met.
Payments for travel	
Indicative limits/bona fide test	Yes.
Medical costs	
Indicative limits/bona fide test	Yes.
Foreign workers' wages	
Quantitative limits	Commercial banks and certain other institutions have the authority to approve remittances abroad of up to one-third of the salary, throughout the period of employment, of foreigners temporarily working in Tanzania under contract and having a firm commitment to leaving the country.
Indicative limits/bona fide test	Yes.

Proceeds from Invisible Transactions and Current Transfers

Surrender requirements	No.

Capital Transactions

Controls on capital and money market instruments

Capital transfers to all countries are subject to approval by commercial banks. All transfers of foreign currency funds from residents to nonresidents or to foreign-controlled resident bodies require specific approval from the BOT. Similarly, transfers of funds from nonresidents to residents require BOT approval.

On capital market securities

Purchase locally by nonresidents — Yes.

Sale or issue locally by nonresidents — Yes.

Purchase abroad by residents — Bonds/shares issued abroad can be freely held and transferred by residents provided that such securities were acquired with externally generated funds. These purchases have to be reported to the BOT.

Sale or issue abroad by residents — Yes.

On money market instruments — Yes.

On collective investment securities — Yes.

Controls on derivatives and other instruments — Yes.

Controls on credit operations

All loans or overdrafts from residents to nonresidents or to foreign-controlled resident bodies require approval from the BOT. Credits to residents from nonresidents are subject to external debt management regulations. For deferred payments not exceeding 365 days, authorized dealers may give approval subject to guidelines of terms of such payments issued by the BOT.

Controls on direct investment

Outward direct investment — Investments require BOT approval.

Inward direct investment — All foreign direct investment must be approved by the Investment Promotion Center; some areas are reserved for investment by the public sector, and certain other areas are reserved exclusively for Tanzanian citizens.

Controls on liquidation of direct investment

Repatriation of capital and associated income is done through commercial banks upon presentation of audited accounts indicating declared dividends, profits, or capital to be repatriated, plus authenticated documents confirming payment of all taxes, based on the delegated authority from the BOT.

Controls on real estate transactions

Purchase abroad by residents — Purchases require BOT approval.

Purchase locally by nonresidents — Yes.

Sale locally by nonresidents — Yes.

Provisions specific to commercial banks and other credit institutions

Borrowing abroad — Borrowing is subject to external debt-management regulations. Otherwise, banks and financial institutions are allowed to operate credit lines with correspondents.

Lending to nonresidents (financial or commercial credits) — Yes.

Purchase of locally issued securities denominated in foreign exchange — Yes.

Open foreign exchange position limits — The limit is 20% of core capital.

Changes During 1996

Status under IMF Articles of Agreement	*July 15.* Tanzania accepted the obligations of Article VIII, Sections 2, 3, and 4 of the Fund Agreement.
Exchange arrangements	*January 1.* Foreign exchange bureaus not meeting new capital requirements were no longer permitted to maintain accounts with domestic banks and thereby prohibited from providing trade finance. They were also prohibited from participating in the interbank foreign exchange market.
	July 1. All foreign exchange bureaus were prohibited from participating in the interbank market. Bureaus' activities were limited to money-changing transactions for travel purposes only.
Nonresident accounts	*January 1.* Restrictions on nonresident accounts were removed.
Exports and export proceeds	*January 1.* The requirement on delays in repatriation of proceeds was removed and replaced by a requirement that reasonable efforts to repatriate be made.
Payments for invisible transactions and current transfers	*January 1.* All limits on the purchase of foreign exchange for invisibles were replaced by automatic sale for all bona fide requests. The limit on the amount of domestic currency that can be taken out of the country was raised.
Proceeds from invisible transactions and current transfers	*January 1.* Receipts from invisibles were no longer required to be sold to an authorized dealer.
Capital transactions	*July 1.* Commercial banks were permitted to have a foreign currency asset-liability mismatch of up to 20% of core capital.

THAILAND

(Position as of December 31, 1996)

Status Under IMF Articles of Agreement

Article VIII	Date of acceptance: May 4, 1990.

Exchange Arrangement

Currency	The currency of Thailand is the baht.
Exchange rate structure	Unitary.
Classification	
Pegged	The external value of the baht is determined on the basis of an undisclosed, weighted basket of currencies of Thailand's major trading partners.
Exchange tax	No.
Exchange subsidy	No.
Forward exchange market	Forward exchange transactions are carried out between commercial banks and customers and among the commercial banks. All forward transactions must be related to underlying trade and financial transactions. The forward premium in the baht-U.S. dollar rate is freely determined and usually reflects interest rate differentials.
Official cover of forward operations	No.

Arrangements for Payments and Receipts

Prescription of currency requirements	No.
Payment arrangements	No.
Administration of control	
Exchange control authorities	The Bank of Thailand (BOT) on behalf of the Ministry of Finance (MOF) administers exchange controls, but it delegates responsibility to authorized banks for approving most transactions. Import and export licenses are issued by the Ministry of Commerce.
International security restrictions	
In accordance with UN sanctions	Yes.
Payment arrears	No.
Controls on trade in gold (coins and/or bullion)	
Controls on domestic ownership and/or trade	Residents may hold and negotiate domestically gold jewelry, gold coins, and unworked gold. Purchases or sales of gold on commodity futures exchanges are prohibited.
Controls on external trade	Imports and exports of gold other than gold jewelry are prohibited, unless a license has been obtained from the MOF or the transaction is made on behalf of the monetary authorities. Foreign tourists may take out precious stones, gold or platinum ornaments, and other articles without restriction. Exports of gold bullion are prohibited. Exporters and importers of gold ornaments exceeding B 500,000 in value must complete foreign exchange transaction forms at customs when submitting import or export entry forms. Gold ornaments are not subject to export duty or taxes.

Controls on exports and imports of banknotes

On exports

   Domestic currency   Travelers may take out domestic currency up to B 50,000; those traveling to Vietnam and the countries bordering Thailand are allowed to take out a maximum of B 500,000.

Resident Accounts

Eligibility to hold accounts	Juridical and natural persons are eligible.
Foreign exchange accounts permitted	Yes.
Held domestically	These accounts are permitted, and no approval is required if funds originate from abroad and the total outstanding balances in all accounts do not exceed $5 million for a juridical person and $500,000 for a natural person.
Held abroad	These accounts are permitted, but approval is required if deposits are made with funds of domestic origin.
Accounts in domestic currency convertible into foreign currency	No.

Nonresident Accounts

Eligibility to hold accounts	Juridical and natural persons are eligible.
Foreign exchange accounts permitted	These accounts are permitted; approval is not required if funds originate from abroad.
Domestic currency accounts	Yes.
Convertible into foreign currency	These accounts are permitted; approval is not required if funds originate from abroad, if they are transferred from other nonresidents' baht accounts, or if baht proceeds are borrowed from authorized banks.
Blocked accounts	No.

Imports and Import Payments

Foreign exchange budget	No.
Financing requirements for imports	No.
Documentation requirements for release of foreign exchange for imports	Importers are required to complete foreign exchange transaction forms for transactions whose value exceeds B 500,000 when submitting import entry forms to customs, except for certain goods, such as military equipment imported by the Ministry of Defense, donated goods, and samples.
Import licenses and other nontariff measures	Most commodities may be freely imported, but import licenses are required for certain goods. Milk producers are required to purchase locally produced milk in some quantity when they import skimmed milk into Thailand.
Negative list	Imports of some goods are prohibited for protective or social reasons.
Import taxes and/or tariffs	Ad valorem and/or specific duties are imposed on imports. In addition, special duties are levied on certain commodities, and surcharges are levied on imports that compete with the output of promoted domestic firms.
Taxes collected through the exchange system	No.

| State import monopoly | No. |

Exports and Export Proceeds

Repatriation requirements — Export proceeds exceeding B 500,000 must be received within 180 days from the date of exportation.

Surrender requirements — Foreign exchange proceeds must be surrendered to authorized banks or deposited in foreign currency accounts with authorized banks in Thailand within 15 days of receipt, except for proceeds used to service external obligations.

Financing requirements — No.

Documentation requirements — Exporters are required to complete a foreign exchange transaction form for transactions exceeding B 500,000 when submitting the export entry form at customs.

Export licenses — Exports of rice, canned tuna, sugar, certain types of coal and charcoal, and textile products are subject to licensing and quantitative restrictions and, in a few cases, to prior approval, irrespective of destination. All other products may be exported freely.

Without quotas — Yes.

With quotas — Yes.

Export taxes — Exports of wood, wood articles, and hides are subject to higher ad valorem or specific duties.

Taxes collected through the exchange system — No.

Payments for Invisible Transactions and Current Transfers

Controls on these payments — Foreign exchange transaction forms must be completed for transactions of more than $5,000.

Proceeds from Invisible Transactions and Current Transfers

Repatriation requirements — Yes.

Surrender requirements — Proceeds must be surrendered to authorized banks or retained in foreign currency accounts with authorized banks in Thailand within 15 days of receipt. Travelers passing through Thailand, foreign embassies, and international organizations are exempted from this requirement.

Restrictions on use of funds — No.

Capital Transactions

Controls on capital and money market instruments — The sale or issue of securities is under the jurisdiction of the Securities Exchange Commission (SEC). Under the securities law, the same rules and regulations apply to both capital market securities (those with a maturity over 1 year) and short-term money market securities (those debt securities with maturity of not more than 1 year). Foreign issuers must comply with the same rules and regulations as local issuers. Under those regulations, any companies wishing to issue securities to the public need to be approved by the SEC and file the disclosure documents with the SEC for public access.

On capital market securities

Purchase locally by nonresidents — Foreign equity participation is limited to 25% of the paid-up registered capital of locally incorporated banks, finance companies, credit finance companies, and asset

management companies. The combined shareholdings of an individual and his/her related family members must not exceed 5% of a bank's paid-up registered capital and
10% of that of finance companies and credit foncier companies. Foreign equity participation is limited to 49% for other Thai corporations.

Purchase abroad by residents	Purchases require approval of the BOT.
Sale or issue abroad by residents	The potential issuer must submit an application for approval to the SEC, and permission will be granted if the issuer can prove that the issue will only be traded overseas, both in the primary or secondary market. There are no restrictions associated with the transfer of proceeds on funds to service debt abroad. All debt-service payments can be made freely.

On money market instruments

Sale or issue locally by nonresidents	Yes.
Purchase abroad by residents	These transactions require approval from the BOT.
Sale or issue abroad by residents	These transactions are not allowed. However, finance companies are allowed to issue negotiable certificate of deposit (NCDs) and bills of exchange in foreign currency with more than a 1-year maturity for sale to the public abroad or for sale to institutions that are authorized to operate in foreign exchange. The transfer of proceeds associated with these issues or the transfer of funds required to service these instruments can be made freely.

On collective investment securities

Purchase locally by nonresidents	There are no restrictions on the purchase of securities offered by local fund management companies.
Sale or issue locally by nonresidents	The same regulations apply as for money market instruments.
Purchase abroad by residents	These transactions require approval of the BOT.
Sale or issue abroad by residents	The launching of funds requires approval from the SEC, both locally and abroad, and only local fund management companies are allowed to issue this instrument. In addition, funds managed by local firms will be deemed to have Thai nationality regardless of the nationality of the majority of the unit holders. The transfer of proceeds and the transfer of funds required to service these instruments may be made freely.

Controls on derivatives and other instruments	A securities company is not permitted to purchase or sell futures or options on securities either in its own name or for customers, or to engage in any business that is not a li-censed securities business, unless the SEC issues a notification or grants an approval allowing such transactions or business.
Sale or issue locally by nonresidents	The issuance of warrants or equity-related instruments and bonds by nonresidents in the local market is subject to approval by the SEC. The approval criteria is based on the soundness of the underlying stock. There is no discriminatory practice against nonresi-dents for participating in the financial market.
Purchase abroad by residents	The purchase of derivative instruments by residents and the transfer of funds require approval by the BOT.
Controls on credit operations	
Commercial credits	Credits may be contracted in the form of deferred payments, bilateral netting, or open accounts. Most payments are settled within 180 days of the exportation of goods.
Financial credits	
By residents to nonresidents	Only authorized banks are allowed to grant financial credits subject to the rule of net foreign exchange position. Residents may only grant loans to their affiliated companies if they own at least 25% of total shares in the company and up to $10 million a year without approval from the BOT.

To residents from nonresidents	There is no restriction on these credits. Repayment of financial credits to nonresidents can be made freely as long as residents have an obligation to pay to nonresidents in foreign currency.

Controls on direct investment

Outward direct investment	Investments exceeding $10 million a year require approval from the BOT.
Inward direct investment	Foreign capital may be brought into the country without restriction, but proceeds must be surrendered to authorized banks or deposited in foreign currency accounts with authorized banks in Thailand within 15 days of receipt.

Controls on liquidation of direct investment	All proceeds can be repatriated without restriction upon submission of supporting evidence.

Controls on real estate transactions

Purchase abroad by residents	Yes.
Purchase locally by nonresidents	These purchases, except those of condominiums, are not allowed with money that originates from abroad.
Sale locally by nonresidents	Yes.

Provisions specific to commercial banks and other credit institutions

Lending to nonresidents (financial or commercial credits)	Government financial institutions, except the Export-Import Bank of Thailand, are not allowed to practice foreign lending activities. Authorized banks in Thailand may lend to nonresidents in foreign currency without restriction.
Lending locally in foreign exchange	Commercial lending to particular industries denominated in foreign currencies can be partially (50%) included as foreign assets in order to recognize the potential risk that banks may not be fully repaid as exchange rate risk is heightened.

Differential treatment of nonresident deposit accounts and/or deposit accounts in foreign exchange

Liquid asset requirements	Overall, commercial banks are required to hold liquid assets of at least 7% of their deposit base. The liquid assets comprise at least 2% in nonremunerated balance at the BOT, at most 2.5% in vault cash, and the rest in government and other eligible securities. Finance companies are also required to hold a 7% liquid asset ratio: 0.5% in nonremunerated balances at the BOT, and the rest in the form of deposits at banks located in Thailand, lending on demand to banks in Thailand, and eligible securities. For the nonresident baht accounts with a maturity of less than 1 year, commercial banks, finance companies, and finance and security companies are required to maintain 7% of their deposits at the BOT.
Investment regulations	Commercial banks are allowed to buy or hold shares in a limited company (including public companies) in an amount not exceeding 10% of the total shares sold and 20% of their capital fund. Banks can seek approval to hold shares above the 10% limit in the following cases: (1) companies set up for supporting functions; (2) companies that operate as financial arms, such as leasing companies and factoring companies; (3) companies set up to manage foreclosed properties; and (4) companies set up to manage projects that are beneficial to the economy, especially infrastructure projects.
Open foreign exchange position limits	The limit imposed is between −15% (for a negative balance) and 20% (for a positive balance).

Provisions specific to institutional investors

Limits (max.) on portfolio invested abroad	Mutual funds and provident funds have to invest their total portfolio in the domestic market. The criteria for insurance companies to invest abroad are as follows: (1) the fund can be invested in equity and debenture issued by juridical persons incorporated under the ASEAN Agreement or the United Nation's Economic and Social Commission

for Asia and the Pacific (ESCAP) Agreement to specifically operate reinsurance business; and (2) the funds may be invested in equity issued by nonresident juridical persons other than specified in (1) with approval from the authorities, and by using the surplus funds. Total investments under (1) and (2) must not exceed 5% of total assets.

Other controls imposed by securities laws

Under the Securities Act, there are no restrictions for nonresidents to have equity participation in Thai security companies. However, National Executive Decree No. 281 imposes a 50% limit on nonresident's equity participation in any company. Foreign security companies are permitted access to the Thai securities market in the form of representative offices whose roles are limited to providing research material for their parent companies. In addition, they are allowed to enter into joint partnership with Thai security companies and to provide professional consultancy services.

Changes During 1996

No significant changes occurred in the exchange and trade system.

TOGO

(Position as of December 31, 1996)

Status Under IMF Articles of Agreement

Article VIII   Date of acceptance: June 1, 1996.

Exchange Arrangement

Currency   The currency of Togo is the CFA franc.

Exchange rate structure   Unitary.

Classification

Pegged   The CFA franc is pegged to the French franc, the intervention currency, at the fixed rate of CFAF 1 per F 0.01. The official buying and selling rate is CFAF 100 per F 1. Exchange rates for other currencies are derived from the rate for the currency concerned in the Paris exchange market and the fixed rate between the French franc and the CFA franc. There is a bank commission of 2.5‰ on transfers to all countries outside the WAEMU, which must be surrendered to the Treasury.

Exchange tax   No.

Exchange subsidy   No.

Forward exchange market   Forward exchange contracts may be arranged with the prior authorization of the Ministry of Economy and Finance (MEF). Permission may be granted only in respect of the importation of certain clearly specified goods. The maturity of exchange contracts can be no more than 3 months for essential or strategic goods and 1 month for all other goods.

Official cover of forward operations   No.

Arrangements for Payments and Receipts

Prescription of currency requirements   Because Togo is linked to the French Treasury through an Operations Account, settlements with France, Monaco, and other countries linked to the French Treasury through an Operations Account are made in CFA francs, French francs, or the currency of any other Operations Account country.

Payment arrangements

Clearing agreements   Current payments to or from The Gambia, Ghana, Guinea, Guinea-Bissau, Liberia, Mauritania, Nigeria, and Sierra Leone are normally made through the WACH.

Administration of control

Exchange control authorities Exchange control is administered by the MEF, which also supervises the following: borrowing abroad; the issuing, advertising, or offering for sale of foreign securities in Togo; inward direct investment and all outward investment; and the soliciting of funds in Togo for placement in foreign countries.

International security restrictions   No.

Payment arrears

Official   Yes.

Controls on trade in gold (coins and/or bullion)

Controls on external trade   Import and exports of gold from or to any other country require prior authorization from the MEF.

Controls on exports and imports of banknotes

On exports

   Foreign currency   The reexportation of foreign banknotes by nonresidents is allowed up to the equivalent of CFAF 250,000; the reexportation of foreign banknotes above these ceilings requires documentation demonstrating either the importation of the foreign banknotes or their purchase against other means of payment registered in the name of the traveler or through the use of nonresident deposits in local banks.

On imports

   Domestic currency   Residents and nonresidents may bring in any amount of banknotes and coins issued by the BCEAO, the Bank of France, or any institute of issue maintaining an Operations Account with the French Treasury, as well as any amount of foreign banknote operations and coins (except gold coins) of countries outside that account area.

   Foreign currency   Residents and nonresidents may bring in any amount of foreign banknotes and coins (except gold coins) of countries outside the Operations Account area. Residents bringing in foreign banknotes and foreign currency traveler's checks exceeding the equivalent of CFAF 25,000 must declare them to customs upon entry and sell them to an authorized intermediary bank within 8 days.

Resident Accounts

Eligibility to hold accounts   Juridical and natural persons are eligible.

Foreign exchange accounts permitted   Only diamond-processing companies are free to open these accounts; all others must obtain a special authorization from the MEF.

Held domestically   These accounts are permitted, but prior approval is required.

Held abroad   These accounts are permitted, but prior approval is required.

Accounts in domestic currency convertible into foreign currency   Yes.

Nonresident Accounts

Eligibility to hold accounts   Juridical and natural persons are eligible.

Foreign exchange accounts permitted   These accounts are subject to authorization from the MEF.

Domestic currency accounts   Because the BCEAO has suspended the repurchase of banknotes circulating outside the territories of the CFA franc zone, nonresident accounts may not be credited or debited with BCEAO banknotes without prior authorization.

Convertible into foreign currency   Yes.

Blocked accounts   No.

Imports and Import Payments

Foreign exchange budget   No.

Financing requirements for imports   No.

Documentation requirements for release of foreign exchange for imports   Importers may purchase foreign exchange for import payments after establishing bank payment order accounts (*dossiers de domiciliation*) and submitting supporting documents, but not earlier than 8 days before shipment if a documentary credit is opened, or on the due date of payment if the products have already been imported.

Domiciliation requirements	All imports exceeding CFAF 500,000 must be domiciled at an authorized bank.
Letters of credit	Required for goods outside the EU, Operations Account countries, and ACP countries.
Import licenses and other nontariff measures	
Positive list	Yes.
Open general licenses	Licenses are issued for imports of pharmaceuticals, explosives, and firearms. Imports of potatoes may be prohibited during the period when local production is adequate to meet local demand (between August and February).
Import taxes and/or tariffs	The following taxes are imposed on all imports: a statistical tax of 3%; fiscal import duties of 5%, 10%, and 20%; a value-added tax of 7% or 18%. With the exception of the value-added tax, which is assessed on the basis of the c.i.f. value of imports inclusive of fiscal import duties, all other taxes are levied on c.i.f. values.
Taxes collected through the exchange system	No.
State import monopoly	No.

Exports and Export Proceeds

Repatriation requirements	The due date for payment for exports to foreign countries, including the Operations Account area, may not be later than 180 days after the arrival of the goods at their destination.
Surrender requirements	The proceeds must be surrendered within 1 month of the due date to authorized intermediaries; authorized diamond-purchasing officers, however, may retain foreign currency proceeds in foreign currency accounts with authorized banks in Togo.
Financing requirements	No.
Documentation requirements	Phosphate rock is subject to a specific export tax.
Letters of credit	Yes.
Guarantees	n.a.
Domiciliation	All export transactions over CFAF 500,000 must be domiciled with an authorized bank.
Export licenses	Gold, diamonds, and all other precious metals are subject to MEF authorization. Exports to all countries require licenses in certain cases.
Without quotas	Yes.
Export taxes	
Taxes collected through the exchange system	No.
Other export taxes	Yes.

Payments for Invisible Transactions and Current Transfers

Controls on these payments	Payments for invisibles to France, Monaco, and the Operations Account countries are permitted freely; those to other countries are subject to approval. Payments for invisibles related to trade are permitted by a general authorization when the basic trade transaction has been approved or does not require authorization.
	There are no controls on payments for freight and insurance, unloading and storage, administrative expenses, commissions, or interest, nor on remittances of profits and dividends.

Payments for travel

    Prior approval   Yes.

    Quantitative limits   Residents traveling for tourism or business purposes to countries in the franc zone that are not members of the WAEMU are allowed to take out up to the equivalent of CFAF 2 million in banknotes other than CFA banknotes; amounts in excess of this limit may be taken out in the form of other means of payment. The allowances for travel to countries outside the franc zone are (1) for tourist travel, CFAF 500,000 without limit on the number of trips or differentiation by the age of the traveler; and (2) for business travel, CFAF 75,000 a day for up to 1 month, corresponding to a maximum of CFAF 2.25 million (business travel allowances may be combined with tourist allowances).

    Indicative limits/bona fide test   Allowances in excess of these limits must be authorized by the MEF or, by delegation, the BCEAO.

Medical costs

    Quantitative limits   The limits are the same as for tourist travel.

    Indicative limits/bona fide test   Yes.

Study abroad costs

    Quantitative limits   The limits are the same as for tourist travel.

    Indicative limits/bona fide test   Yes.

Subscriptions and membership fees

    Indicative limits/bona fide test   Yes.

Consulting/legal fees

    Indicative limits/bona fide test   Yes.

Foreign workers' wages   The transfer of the entire net salary of a foreign national working in Togo is permitted upon presentation of the appropriate pay voucher, residence permit, or work permit, provided that the transfer takes place within 3 months of the pay period.

    Prior approval   Yes.

Pensions

    Indicative limits/bona fide test   Yes.

Gambling/prize earnings

    Indicative limits/bona fide test   Yes.

Family maintenance/alimony

    Indicative limits/bona fide test   Yes.

Credit card use abroad

    Quantitative limits   The limits are the same as for tourist and business travel.

Proceeds from Invisible Transactions and Current Transfers

Repatriation requirements   Yes.

Surrender requirements   Proceeds from transactions with France, Monaco, and the Operations Account countries may be retained. All amounts due from residents of other countries in respect of services, and all income earned in those countries from foreign assets must be collected and surrendered within 1 month of the due date or the date of receipt.

Restrictions on use of funds   No.

Capital Transactions

Controls on capital and money market instruments

Capital movements between Togo and France, Monaco, and the other countries of the Operations Account area are free of exchange control; capital transfers to all other countries require exchange control approval from the MEF and are restricted, but capital receipts from such countries are permitted freely. Exempt from authorization are transactions with shares that are identical to, or can be substituted for, securities whose issuing, advertising, or offering for sale in Togo has already been authorized.

On capital market securities

Sale or issue locally by nonresidents	Yes.
Purchase abroad by residents	Yes.
Sale or issue abroad by residents	Yes.

On money market instruments

Sale or issue locally by nonresidents	Yes.
Purchase abroad by residents	Yes.
Sale or issue abroad by residents	Yes.

On collective investment securities

Sale or issue locally by nonresidents	Yes.
Purchase abroad by residents	Yes.
Sale or issue abroad by residents	Yes.

Controls on derivatives and other instruments

Purchase locally by nonresidents	n.a.
Sale or issue locally by nonresidents	Yes.
Purchase abroad by residents	Yes.
Sale or issue abroad by residents	n.a.

Controls on credit operations

Commercial credits

Borrowing by residents from nonresidents requires prior authorization from the MEF. The following are, however, exempt from this authorization: (1) loans constituting a direct investment, which are subject to prior declaration; (2) borrowing by industrial firms to finance operations abroad or by international merchanting and export-import firms to finance imports and exports; (3) loans contracted by authorized intermediary banks; and (4) subject to certain conditions, loans other than those mentioned above, when the total amount outstanding of these loans does not exceed CFAF 100 million for any one borrower. The repayment of loans not constituting a direct investment requires the special authorization of the MEF, if the loan itself was subject to such approval, but is exempt if the loan was exempt from special authorization. Lending abroad is subject to prior authorization from the MEF.

By residents to nonresidents	Yes.
To residents from nonresidents	Yes.
Financial credits	Yes.
Guarantees, sureties, and financial backup facilities	Yes.

Controls on liquidation of direct investment	The liquidation of investment must be reported to the MEF and to the BCEAO within 20 days of each operation.
Controls on real estate transactions	
Purchase abroad by residents	Yes.
Purchase locally by nonresidents	Yes.
Sale locally by nonresidents	Yes.
Provisions specific to commercial banks and other credit institutions	
Lending to nonresidents (financial or commercial credits)	MEF authorization is required.
Lending locally in foreign exchange	Yes.
Purchase of locally issued securities denominated in foreign exchange	Yes.
Differential treatment of nonresident deposit accounts and/or deposit accounts in foreign exchange	
Credit controls	Yes.
Provisions specific to institutional investors	
Limits (max.) on portfolio invested abroad	Yes.
Limits (min.) on portfolio invested locally	Yes.
Currency matching regulations on assets/liabilities composition	Yes.
Other controls imposed by securities laws	No.

Changes During 1996

Status under IMF Articles of Agreement	*June 1.* Togo accepted the obligations of Article VIII, Sections 2, 3, and 4 of the Fund Agreement.

TONGA

(Position as of December 31, 1996)

Status Under IMF Articles of Agreement

Article VIII   Date of acceptance: March 22, 1991.

Exchange Arrangement

Currency   The currency of Tonga is the pa'anga.

Exchange rate structure   Unitary.

Classification

Pegged   The external value of the pa'anga is determined on the basis of a weighted basket of currencies comprising the U.S. dollar, the Australian dollar, and the New Zealand dollar.

Exchange tax   No.

Exchange subsidy   No.

Forward exchange market   Commercial banks are allowed to provide forward exchange cover, but their gross foreign exchange liabilities must not exceed T$1 million. Provision of forward exchange cover for squash exporters requires the approval of the Ministry of Finance (MOF).

Official cover of forward operations   No.

Arrangements for Payments and Receipts

Prescription of currency requirements   No.

Payment arrangements   No.

Bilateral arrangements   No.

Administration of control

Exchange control authorities   Foreign exchange transactions are regulated by the MOF.

International security restrictions   No.

Payment arrears   No.

Resident Accounts

n.a.

Nonresident Accounts

n.a.

Imports and Import Payments

Foreign exchange budget   No.

Import licenses and other nontariff measures   Licenses are required for all imports, but they are issued freely.

Positive list	n.a.
Negative list	n.a.
Open general licenses	n.a.
Licenses with quotas	Import quotas apply only to fresh eggs and are intended to protect domestic producers, but the restriction is not enforced. The importation of certain items is restricted for cultural or environmental reasons or to protect the health and safety of residents.
Import taxes and/or tariffs	Import tariffs of up to 35% are levied on an ad valorem basis. Imports of a few items (petroleum, tobacco, and alcoholic beverages) are subject to either specific tariffs or ad valorem rates of up to 300%. The tariff rates on motor vehicles is 45%. Imports by the reigning monarch, by the government and the public sector, by diplomatic missions, under certain technical assistance agreements, and imports of personal effects are exempt from tariffs. Imports are also subject to a 20% port and services tax, except for items under the Industrial Development Incentives Act, which qualify for concessional rates, and imports of government and quasi-government organizations, which are exempt.
Taxes collected through the exchange system	No.
State import monopoly	No.

Exports and Export Proceeds

Repatriation requirements	Yes.
Surrender requirements	All export proceeds must be repatriated within 12 months, but this regulation is not enforced.
Export licenses	Licenses are required for all exports weighing more than 10 kilograms. Licenses are granted liberally except for squash.
Without quotas	Yes.
Export taxes	No.

Payments for Invisible Transactions and Current Transfers

Controls on these payments	All payments are subject to prior approval, indicative limits, and/or bona fide tests. Commercial banks are authorized to provide foreign exchange for invisible payments. Shipping and airline agencies may remit income earned from activities in Tonga upon producing income statements relating to local business activities that have been submitted to their respective head offices.

Proceeds from Invisible Transactions and Current Transfers

n.a.

Capital Transactions

Controls on capital and money market instruments	
On capital market securities	
Purchase locally by nonresidents	n.a.

Sale or issue locally by nonresidents	n.a.
Purchase abroad by residents	The acquisition of foreign financial assets is, in principle, prohibited, but in practice the restriction is not strictly enforced because the repatriation requirement is not enforced.
Sale or issue abroad by residents	n.a.

On money market instruments

Purchase locally by nonresidents	n.a.
Sale or issue locally by nonresidents	n.a.
Purchase abroad by residents	Yes.
Sale or issue abroad by residents	n.a.

On collective investment securities

Purchase locally by nonresidents	n.a.
Sale or issue locally by nonresidents	n.a.
Purchase abroad by residents	Yes.
Sale or issue abroad by residents	n.a.

Controls on derivatives and other instruments

Purchase locally by nonresidents	n.a.
Sale or issue locally by nonresidents	n.a.
Purchase abroad by residents	Yes.
Sale or issue abroad by residents	n.a.

Controls on credit operations

Commercial credits

By residents to nonresidents	Yes.
To residents from nonresidents	n.a.

Financial credits

By residents to nonresidents	Yes.
To residents from nonresidents	n.a.

Controls on direct investment

Outward direct investment	Investments require a license, which is usually given if the transaction is considered beneficial to Tongan exports.
Inward direct investment	Licenses are required for direct foreign investment. High-technology projects are readily approved. Intermediate projects are accepted if there is a local partner, and simple projects that can be undertaken by locals are likely to be rejected. Investment in certain sectors, including wholesale and retail, transportation and some tourism-related activities, and all resource-based activities such as fishing are prohibited. However, joint ventures may be allowed if the project is deemed beneficial to the country. No time period has been specified for the approval process, which can be quite lengthy, but once licensed, foreign projects in manufacturing and tourism are fully eligible for incentives.

Controls on real estate transactions

Purchase abroad by residents	Yes.

Purchase locally by nonresidents	n.a.
Sale locally by nonresidents	n.a.
Provisions specific to commercial banks and other credit institutions	
Borrowing abroad	n.a.
Maintenance of accounts abroad	n.a.
Lending to nonresidents (financial or commercial credits)	n.a.
Lending locally in foreign exchange	n.a.
Purchase of locally issued securities denominated in foreign exchange	n.a.
Differential treatment of nonresident deposit accounts and/or deposit accounts in foreign exchange	n.a.
Investment regulations	n.a.
Open foreign exchange position limits	The limit is T$1 million. Commercial banks must surrender all of their foreign exchange, apart from small working balances to the central bank.

Changes During 1996

No significant changes occurred in the exchange and trade system.

TRINIDAD AND TOBAGO

(Position as of January 31, 1997)

Status Under IMF Articles of Agreement

Article VIII	Date of acceptance: December 13, 1993.

Exchange Arrangement

Currency	The currency of Trinidad and Tobago is the Trinidad and Tobago dollar.
Exchange rate structure	Unitary.
Classification	
Independent floating	The exchange rate of the Trinidad and Tobago dollar is determined in the interbank market on the basis of supply and demand.
Exchange tax	No.
Exchange subsidy	No.
Forward exchange market	Banks are allowed to conduct foreign exchange transactions, both spot and forward, with the public without limitation.
Official cover of forward operations	No.

Arrangements for Payments and Receipts

Prescription of currency requirements	Settlements may be made in Austrian schillings, Belgian francs, Canadian dollars, Danish kroner, deutsche mark, French francs, Italian lire, Japanese yen, Myanmar kyats, Netherlands guilders, Norwegian kroner, Portuguese escudos, Spanish pesetas, Swedish kronor, Swiss francs, pounds sterling, and U.S. dollars.
Payment arrangements	
Regional arrangements	Trinidad and Tobago is a member of CARICOM.
Administration of control	
Exchange control authorities	Authority to administer exchange control is vested in the Central Bank of Trinidad and Tobago (CBTT) acting under the authority of the Ministry of Finance (MOF).
International security restrictions	No.
Payment arrears	No.
Controls on trade in gold (coins and/or bullion)	
Controls on domestic ownership and/or trade	Residents are permitted to purchase, hold, or sell gold coins for numismatic purposes. Unless specifically permitted by the MOF, one party to transactions in gold between residents must be an authorized bank.
Controls on external trade	Exports of gold are controlled by the Ministry of Trade and Industry and are subject to specific export licenses, which are normally issued only to monetary authorities.
Controls on exports and imports of banknotes	
On exports	
Domestic currency	For amounts exceeding TT$20,000, a customs declaration is required.

On imports

   Domestic currency   Residents and nonresidents may bring in up to TT$20,000 freely, but for larger amounts, a customs declaration is required.

   Foreign currency   Resident and nonresident travelers may bring in notes up to the equivalent of US$5,000 freely, but for larger amounts, a customs declaration is required.

Resident Accounts

Eligibility to hold accounts   Juridical and natural persons are eligible.

Foreign exchange accounts permitted   Yes.

Held domestically   Yes.

Held abroad   Yes.

Accounts in domestic currency convertible into foreign currency   Yes.

Nonresident Accounts

Eligibility to hold accounts   Juridical and natural persons are eligible.

Foreign exchange accounts permitted   Yes.

Domestic currency accounts   Yes.

Convertible into foreign currency   These accounts are permitted, but prior approval is required.

Blocked accounts   No.

Imports and Import Payments

Foreign exchange budget   No.

Financing requirements for imports   No.

Documentation requirements for release of foreign exchange for imports   No.

Import licenses and other nontariff measures   Duty-free licenses are granted to local concessionary manufacturers for imports of certain inputs for manufacturing.

All imports of food and drugs must satisfy prescribed standards. Imports of meat, live animals, plants, and mining materials are subject to specific regulations.

Negative list   Imports of firearms, ammunition, and narcotics are tightly controlled.

Open general licenses   All goods, unless excepted for reasons of health and security, may be imported under OGL arrangements.

Import taxes and/or tariffs   On January 1, 1996, the customs duty rates on most goods were reduced to a range of 5% to 25%. The rate on agricultural produce is 40%. Duty rates on consumer goods, such as perfumes, cosmetics, jewelry, clothing, and cotton and silk fabrics, range from 20% to 25%. The duty rates on motor vehicles range from 20% to 30%. On January 1, 1997, the maximum rate for most goods was reduced to 20%. All goods originating from CARICOM countries are exempt from duties, as are imports of some foodstuffs, fertilizers, and raw materials. Local enterprises producing import substitutes or export goods may be granted exemptions from customs duties by the Ministry of Trade and Industry and the Tourism Industrial Development Company, Ltd.

Taxes collected through the exchange system	No.
State import monopoly	Imports of animal feed, flour, rice, petroleum, and edible oil are effected principally by state companies.

Exports and Export Proceeds

Repatriation requirements	In practice, the foreign-owned petroleum company operating in Trinidad and Tobago repatriates all foreign exchange after providing for the equivalent of its local currency needs.
Surrender requirements	No.
Financing requirements	No.
Documentation requirements	No.
Export licenses	Individual licenses are required for some foodstuffs, firearms and explosives, animals, gold, petroleum and petroleum products, and certain products not produced locally. Export licenses for all other commodities are granted under OGLs. General licenses may also be issued at the discretion of the Ministry of Trade and Industry.
Without quotas	Yes.
Export taxes	No.

Payments for Invisible Transactions and Current Transfers

Controls on these payments	No.

Proceeds from Invisible Transactions and Current Transfers

Repatriation requirements	No.
Surrender requirements	No.
Restrictions on use of funds	No.

Capital Transactions

Controls on capital and money market instruments	Cross-border trading of shares of companies listed on the respective stock exchanges is permitted among the residents of Barbados, Jamaica, and Trinidad and Tobago; residents and companies of the other 2 countries are designated as residents of Trinidad and Tobago for exchange control purposes in cross-border trading.
Controls on derivatives and other instruments	No.
Controls on credit operations	No.
Controls on direct investment	
Inward direct investment	Holding shares in local companies is subject to compliance with the provisions of the Foreign Investment Act (1990).
Controls on liquidation of direct investment	No.
Controls on real estate transactions	
Purchase locally by nonresidents	Holding interest in real estate is subject to compliance with the provisions of the Foreign Investment Act (1990).

Provisions specific to commercial banks and other credit institutions

Differential treatment of nonresident deposit accounts and/or deposit accounts in foreign exchange

   Liquid asset requirements   A liquid asset ratio of 25% on foreign currency deposits is required.

Open foreign exchange position limits   A liquid asset ratio of 25% on foreign currency deposits is required.

Provisions specific to institutional investors

Limits (min.) on portfolio invested locally   Insurance companies are required to hold at least 80% of their investment assets locally.

Other controls imposed by securities laws   The Insurance Act (1980) imposes other controls.

Changes During 1996

No significant changes occurred in the exchange and trade system.

Changes During 1997

Imports and import payments   *January 1.* Custom duties were reduced to a range between 5% and 25% in compliance with the reduction schedule of the CET of the CARICOM.

TUNISIA

(Position as of May 31, 1997)

Status Under IMF Articles of Agreement

Article VIII
Date of acceptance: January 6, 1993.

Exchange Arrangement

Currency
The currency of Tunisia is the Tunisian dinar.

Exchange rate structure
Unitary.

Classification

Managed floating
The exchange rate of the Tunisian dinar is determined in the interbank market in which commercial banks, including offshore banks acting on behalf of their resident customers, conduct transactions at freely negotiated rates, but there is no limit on the spread between the buying and selling rates. The Central Bank of Tunisia (CBT) intervenes in the market and publishes an indicative interbank exchange rate for foreign currencies and banknotes by the following day, at the latest.

Exchange tax
No.

Exchange subsidy
No.

Forward exchange market
Importers and exporters are authorized to obtain forward exchange cover on the interbank market as of the date the contract is signed or the date on which the foreign commercial paper is domiciled, depending on the arrangements for the product concerned. Forward rates are freely negotiated by the transactor of the authorized counterpart bank. Forward cover may be established for up to 12 months for imports and up to 9 months for exports. Persons who provide services are eligible for exchange cover for up to 12 months, to be provided within 30 days of the date on which the claim originated. Trading on 3-month, 6-month, and 12-month foreign currency options in French francs, deutsche mark, and U.S. dollars is available to resident borrowers of foreign exchange.

Official cover of forward operations
The CBT extends exchange rate guarantees to certain officially guaranteed loans, with risk premiums based on domestic and international interest rates.

Arrangements for Payments and Receipts

Prescription of currency requirements
Settlements between Tunisia and other countries may be in any convertible currency (traded in the interbank market) or in convertible Tunisian dinars through foreign accounts. Payments to Israel are prohibited.

Settlements between Tunisia and Algeria, Libya, Mauritania, and Morocco may be effected through convertible accounts in the national currencies concerned at the respective central banks.

Payment arrangements
No.

Administration of control

Exchange control authorities
Exchange control is administered by the CBT and the Ministry of Trade (MOT). The CBT delegates authority over payments for imports and most invisibles to the authorized banks, whereas the MOT administers foreign trade control, which issues import and export authorization for products when required.

International security restrictions

In accordance with UN sanctions
Yes.

Payment arrears	No.
Controls on trade in gold (coins and/or bullion)	
Controls on domestic ownership and/or trade	Yes.
Controls on external trade	The CBT has a monopoly over the importation and exportation of monetary gold. Imports and exports of gold in other forms require joint approval from the CBT and the MOT.
Controls on exports and imports of banknotes	
On exports	
Domestic currency	Exports of banknotes and coins are prohibited.
Foreign currency	Nonresident travelers wishing to reexport the foreign exchange equivalent of amounts exceeding D 1,000 must declare to customs the foreign currencies they are importing upon their entry into Tunisia. There is no ceiling on the reconversion of Tunisian banknotes by nonresident travelers. Foreign exchange from dinar reconversion may be reexported upon presentation of a foreign exchange voucher or receipt if the amount to be reexported is less than D 1,000 or if the foreign exchange used in the purchase of the dinars was received abroad in the form of a check, draft, money order, or any other evidence of a claim or by debiting a foreign account in foreign currency or convertible dinars. The foreign exchange import declaration approved by customs is also required if the amount of foreign exchange from dinar reconversion exceeds the equivalent of D 1,000 derived from the surrender of foreign currencies physically imported from abroad.
On imports	
Domestic currency	Imports of banknotes and coins are prohibited.

Resident Accounts

Eligibility to hold accounts	Juridical and natural persons are eligible.
Foreign exchange accounts permitted	Yes.
Held domestically	(1) Professional accounts in foreign currency may be opened by (i) any resident natural person, (ii) any Tunisian juridical person, and (iii) any foreign juridical person in Tunisia with the foreign currency assets in connection with their activities. The accounts may be debited for (i) payment of any current operation pertaining to the activity for which they were opened, and (ii) any other transaction with general or specific authorization. Balances may also be placed on the foreign exchange market.
	(2) Special accounts in foreign currency may be opened by (i) natural persons of Tunisian nationality changing their normal residence to Tunisia from abroad, (ii) resident natural persons of Tunisian nationality or Tunisian juridical persons for their nontransferable assets legitimately acquired abroad, (iii) natural persons of foreign nationality residing in Tunisia, (iv) foreign juridical persons with branches in Tunisia, and (v) Tunisian diplomats and civil servants stationed abroad. Funds legitimately acquired abroad, not from the exportation of goods or services from Tunisia, may be credited to these accounts. They may be debited for (i) foreign exchange sold on the interbank market, (ii) foreign exchange remitted to the account holder, his or her spouse, parents, and offspring to undertake foreign travel, (iii) amounts credited to another special account in foreign currency or convertible dinars, and (iv) any payments abroad, including those for the acquisition of movable or real estate property located abroad or ownership rights abroad, for foreign claims, and for payments for imports subject to applicable foreign trade formalities. No approval is required, but a declaration of holding is requested.

Held abroad

No.

Accounts in domestic currency convertible into foreign currency

(1) Professional accounts in convertible dinars may be opened by resident natural or juridical persons with resources in foreign exchange, subject to CBT authorization. These accounts may be credited and debited under the terms laid down by the CBT in the authorization to open such accounts.

Special accounts in convertible dinars may be opened by the same natural and juridical persons that may open foreign exchange accounts. These special accounts may be credited with the dinar proceeds from sales on the interbank market of funds legitimately acquired abroad, but not from the exportation of goods or services from Tunisia. They may be debited for (i) payments of any kind in Tunisia; (ii) the acquisition of foreign currencies either for remittance to the account holder, his or her spouse, parents, and offspring, or for making payments abroad, particularly for the acquisition of movable or real estate property located abroad, or ownership rights abroad, for foreign claims and for payments for imports subject to applicable foreign trade formalities; and (iii) amounts credited to another special account in foreign currency or convertible dinars.

(2) Special export earnings accounts in convertible dinars may be opened by Tunisian or foreign natural persons residing in Tunisia who earn profits from the exportation of goods or services and/or who are shareholders or partners in a resident company earning profits from the exportation of goods or services. These accounts may be freely credited with (i) 5% of the export earnings realized by the account holder or received from companies in which he or she is a shareholder, (ii) proceeds from sales on the interbank market of foreign exchange representing income or revenue from assets acquired abroad by debiting the account, and (iii) interest on balances in the account.

They may be freely debited for (i) payments of any kind in Tunisia; (ii) purchases on the interbank market of foreign exchange to be used for foreign travel by the account holder, his or her spouse, parents, or offspring; and (iii) payments in connection with a current operation or to acquire rights and interests abroad not involving real property.

Nonresident Accounts

Eligibility to hold accounts

Juridical and natural persons are eligible.

Foreign exchange accounts permitted

Foreign accounts in convertible currencies may be opened freely by all nonresidents regardless of nationality. These accounts may be credited with (1) receipts in convertible foreign currencies or the dinar proceeds from sales of convertible currencies on the interbank market; banknotes must be declared to customs; (2) foreign exchange remitted to the account holder by a nonresident; (3) foreign currency purchased from the CBT through the debiting of a foreign account in convertible dinars; (4) authorized payments by residents in favor of the account holder; (5) interest payable by the authorized intermediaries on foreign exchange deposits in the accounts whenever they can use the funds thus deposited at remunerative rates; (6) transfers from other foreign accounts; and (7) the amount of cashed checks, traveler's checks, or drafts expressed in convertible currencies and made out by a nonresident to the order of the account holder. All other crediting requires prior authorization from the CBT, either directly or by delegation.

These accounts may be debited freely for (1) payments of any kind in Tunisia (irrespective of the payer's country of residence); (2) transfers abroad or delivery of foreign currency to the account holder, to any other nonresident beneficiary, or to residents with the status of permanent representatives or salaried employees of the account holder; and (3) transfers to other foreign accounts.

Domestic currency accounts

(1) Domestic nonresident accounts may be opened freely by authorized intermediaries in the name of foreigners residing temporarily in Tunisia. These accounts may be credited without authorization from the CBT with the following: (i) transfers of funds carried out in convertible currencies from a foreign country, (ii) revenue of any kind accruing in Tunisia to the holder of the account (in particular the nontransferable part of remuneration for services rendered by that person in Tunisia), (iii) liquid assets from

estates opened in Tunisia, (iv) proceeds from the repayment of loans previously granted in dinars with funds from the account holder's internal nonresident account, and (v) transfers from another internal nonresident account opened in the name of the account holder.

These accounts may be debited for (i) support of the account holder and his or her family in Tunisia, (ii) payment of costs of managing property in Tunisia, (iii) lending to residents, and (iv) transfers to another internal nonresident account opened in the name of the account holder.

(2) Special dinar accounts may be freely opened by foreign enterprises holding contracts in Tunisia approved by the CBT. Such enterprises are authorized to open for each contract a single special account in dinars, in which they may deposit the portion of the contract price payable in dinars to cover their local expenses. Such accounts may also be credited with funds from a foreign account in convertible foreign currency, the dinar equivalent of any transfer in convertible foreign currency from abroad, and interest accruing on funds deposited in the account. The account may be freely debited for the enterprise's contract-related expenses in Tunisia. Any transfer operations from such accounts must be authorized by the CBT. Interest is paid at rates comparable to those applied to resident accounts in dinars.

(3) Capital accounts may be opened in the name of a nonresident natural person of foreign nationality or by a nonresident juridical person. Subject to certain conditions, capital accounts may be credited, without the prior approval of the CBT, with the proceeds of sales on the stock exchange, or the contractual or advance redemption of transferable Tunisian securities; the sales proceeds of real estate through an attorney at the Supreme Court, or of rights to real estate situated in Tunisia; and with funds from another capital account.

Irrespective of the account holder's country of residence, capital accounts may be freely debited for the living expenses in Tunisia of the account holder and his or her family up to D 100 a person a week, provided that total withdrawals from 1 or more capital accounts in a calendar year do not exceed D 2,000 a family for trips to Tunisia between November 1 and March 31 of the subsequent year. In addition, a capital account holder traveling in Tunisia between November 1 and March 31 may withdraw from the account an amount equal to the foreign exchange imported for the trip and surrendered to the CBT, an authorized intermediary, or a subagency, provided that total withdrawals for the living expenses of the account holder and his or her family do not exceed D 2,000 a year. Such accounts may also be debited, subject to certain conditions, for expenses connected with the management of Tunisian securities; for the maintenance, repair, and insurance of real estate and all taxes; and for transfer to the credit of another capital account. Balances on capital accounts are freely transferable between nonresidents of foreign nationality, with the exception of juridical persons governed by public law. Subject to certain conditions, they may also be debited to assist the account holder's parents and offspring residing in Tunisia, at a maximum rate of D 50 a person a month. These accounts do not pay interest and may not be overdrawn. Natural and juridical persons of French or Italian nationality holding capital accounts may transfer all funds in their accounts regardless of the date of deposit.

(4) Suspense accounts may be opened by all nonresidents regardless of nationality and may be used for crediting all proceeds accruing to nonresidents and awaiting utilization. These proceeds may, upon general or specific approval, be used in Tunisia for specific purposes, transferred abroad, or transferred to other nonresident accounts. Subject to certain conditions, suspense accounts may be debited, without the prior authorization of the CBT, for purchases of Tunisian securities, subscriptions to issues of short-term debentures or bonds, portfolio management expenses in respect of certain securities, payments to the Tunisian government or public institutions, or payment of the expenses of managing securities deposited in a suspense file opened in the name of the account holder.

They may also be debited for settlement of living expenses incurred in Tunisia by the account holder and his or her family up to D 100 a person a week, provided that the total withdrawals in any calendar year from 1 or more accounts do not exceed D 2,000 a family. In addition, a suspense account holder traveling in Tunisia between November 1 and March 31 of the next year may withdraw from the account an amount equal to the foreign exchange imported for the trip and surrendered to the CBT, an authorized intermediary, or a subagency, provided that total withdrawals for the living expenses of the account holder and his or her family do not exceed D 2,000 a year. Up to D 50 a person a month may be debited to assist the offspring or parents of the resident account holder. Natural and juridical persons of French or Italian nationality holding suspense accounts may transfer all funds in their accounts regardless of the date of deposit. These accounts do not pay interest.

Convertible into foreign currency	Foreign accounts in convertible dinars may be opened freely by all nonresidents regardless of nationality. These accounts may be credited freely with (1) the dinar proceeds from sales of foreign currency on the interbank market; banknotes must be declared to customs; (2) foreign currency proceeds remitted to the account holder by a nonresident; (3) proceeds from authorized payments by residents in favor of the account holder; (4) proceeds from the conversion of the amount of cashed checks, traveler's checks, or drafts expressed in foreign currency and made out by a nonresident to the order of the account holder; (5) transfers from other foreign accounts; and (6) interest on balances in these accounts. No other amount may be credited to these accounts without authorization from the CBT, granted either directly or by delegation.
	These accounts may be freely debited for (1) payments of any kind in Tunisia, and (2) purchases on the interbank market of foreign currency either for transfers abroad or for delivery to the account holder, to any other nonresident beneficiary, or to residents with the status of representatives or salaried employees of the account holder.
Blocked accounts	No.

Imports and Import Payments

Foreign exchange budget	No.
Financing requirements for imports	No.
Documentation requirements for release of foreign exchange for imports	An import certificate is required; importers must receive a customs code number to obtain it.
Domiciliation requirements	Yes.
Import licenses and other nontariff measures	All imports are free except those that have an impact on law and order, hygiene, health, morals, protection of fauna and flora, and cultural heritage, and are effected by an import certificate upon presentation of a contract domiciled with an authorized intermediary. Goods not liberalized may be given import authorization by the MOT. Imports of raw materials, semifinished products, spare parts, and equipment that are paid from sources outside Tunisia may be effected without foreign trade formalities by enterprises for their own use up to a value of D 100,000. Furthermore, companies exclusively engaged in exporting goods or services and companies established in a free trade zone may import freely, without foreign trade formalities, any goods required for their production process, subject only to customs declaration. All imports from Israel are prohibited. Some items, a list of which is drawn up by the MOT, are subject to technical import controls.
Negative list	Goods not covered by the liberalization of foreign trade and those that have an impact on law and order, hygiene, health, morals, protection of flora and fauna, and cultural heritage are included in a list issued by decree. Cars remain temporarily subject to import licenses.
Import taxes and/or tariffs	In addition to customs duties, imports are subject to the value-added tax and, in some cases, to the consumption tax. Certain imports destined for domestic investment projects are eligible for full or partial exemption from import duties.

Taxes collected through the exchange system	No.
State import monopoly	No.

Exports and Export Proceeds

Repatriation requirements	Proceeds must be repatriated within 10 days of the payment due date. If no credit is extended, payment is due within 30 days of the date of shipment. Nonresident companies exclusively engaged in exporting goods or services and covered by the Investment Incentives Code as well as nonresident international trading companies and nonresident enterprises constituted in a free trade zone are not required to repatriate or surrender their export proceeds.
Surrender requirements	Resident exporters may credit up to 40% of their foreign exchange proceeds to their professional accounts.
Financing requirements	No.
Documentation requirements	
Domiciliation	Exports must be domiciled within 8 days of the date of shipment.
Preshipment inspection	Some products listed by the MOT are subject to export controls.
Export licenses	Most exports are free, and certain goods may be exported with an authorization issued by the MOT.
Without quotas	Yes.
Export taxes	No.

Payments for Invisible Transactions and Current Transfers

Controls on these payments	There are no controls on payments for freight and insurance, unloading and storage, administrative expenses, commissions, subscriptions and membership fees, consulting and legal fees, pensions, interest, or on remittances of profits and dividends.
Payments for travel	
Quantitative limits	The annual limits for tourist travel are D 500 an adult and D 250 a child under the age of 10. The business allowance for exporters is 10% of export proceeds for the current year, with an annual limit of D 80,000. The annual limit for business travel by importers ranges from D 5,000 to D 30,000, depending on turnover, and the annual limit for business travel by other professions ranges from D 2,000 to D 20,000, depending on turnover declared to the tax authorities. The allowance for promoters of new projects is up to D 5,000 and is granted only once for the duration of the project.
Indicative limits/bona fide test	The limit of D 750 for travel abroad for reasons of health may be exceeded if the patient's condition requires several trips abroad during the same year.
Medical costs	
Quantitative limits	The annual allowance for travel abroad for reasons of health is D 750. Persons accompanying patients may transfer up to D 250 a trip in the case of medical or paramedical staff and D 500 in all other cases.
Indicative limits/bona fide test	Yes.
Study abroad costs	
Quantitative limits	The annual settlement and the monthly educational expense allowances for a student are D 1,000 and D 600, respectively.
Indicative limits/bona fide test	Yes.

Foreign workers' wages

Quantitative limits	Contractually employed foreign nationals and foreign experts employed by the public sector may transfer up to 50% of their earnings; for technical assistants, limits on transfers are specified in their contracts.
Indicative limits/bona fide test	Yes.

Gambling/prize earnings

Prior approval	Yes.
Quantitative limits	Yes.
Indicative limits/bona fide test	Yes.

Family maintenance/alimony

Prior approval	Yes.
Quantitative limits	Yes.
Indicative limits/bona fide test	Yes.

Proceeds from Invisible Transactions and Current Transfers

Repatriation requirements	Yes.
Surrender requirements	The facilities associated with professional accounts in foreign exchange apply to proceeds from services to nonresidents.
Restrictions on use of funds	Foreign exchange deposited in professional accounts must be used in accordance with the rules governing the operation of accounts of this type.

Capital Transactions

Controls on capital and money market instruments

On capital market securities

Purchase locally by nonresidents	Stock may be freely acquired with foreign exchange transferred from abroad by foreign nonresidents in companies established in Tunisia. However, for stock with voting rights and for acquisitions that result in foreign ownership exceeding 50% of capital shares listed in the stock exchange and for unlisted shares, the approval of the High Investment Commission (HIC) is required. The subscription by nonresident foreigners of debt securities issued by the government or by resident companies is subject to approval by the CBT.
Sale or issue locally by nonresidents	Nonresidents may freely transfer net real proceeds from the sale of shares of companies established in Tunisia that were purchased with foreign exchange transferred from abroad for an investment made in accordance with the legislation in force. The issue by nonresidents of debentures in foreign exchange is subject to authorization.
Purchase abroad by residents	The accumulation of assets abroad by residents is subject to authorization. However, resident exporters may transfer D 20,000 to D 100,000 annually to finance equity participation in companies located abroad. The holders of special accounts in foreign currency or convertible dinars, or special export earnings accounts may purchase securities abroad by debiting these accounts.
Sale or issue abroad by residents	Yes.
On money market instruments	Yes.

On collective investment securities

   Purchase locally by nonresidents — Nonresidents may freely acquire shares of Tunisian mutual funds with foreign exchange transferred from abroad. However, the approval of the HIC is required if the acquisition raises the foreign ownership to more than 50% of the mutual fund's capital.

   Sale or issue locally by nonresidents — Nonresidents may freely transfer net real proceeds from sales of Tunisian mutual fund shares acquired with foreign exchange transferred from abroad.

   Purchase abroad by residents — Yes.

   Sale or issue abroad by residents — Yes.

Controls on derivatives and other instruments

Purchase locally by nonresidents — Yes.

Sale or issue locally by nonresidents — Yes.

Purchase abroad by residents — Yes.

Sale or issue abroad by residents — Yes.

Controls on credit operations

Commercial credits

   By residents to nonresidents — These credits require approval from the CBT, except for credits in foreign currency granted on the money market to refinance import or export operations of nonresident industrial enterprises established in Tunisia.

   To residents from nonresidents — Resident financial institutions and other resident enterprises may freely contract foreign currency loans from nonresidents up to an annual limit of D 10 million and D 3 million, respectively.

Financial credits — Resident financial institutions and other resident enterprises may freely contract foreign currency financial loans from nonresidents up to an annual limit of D 10 million and D 3 million, respectively; all other loans require approval from the CBT.

   By residents to nonresidents — Yes.

   To residents from nonresidents — Yes.

Guarantees, sureties, and financial backup facilities

   By residents to nonresidents — Resident banks may freely grant bid bonds, performance bonds, advance payment bonds, contract holdback bonds, or any other bonds to resident exporters of goods or services to guarantee their obligations to nonresidents. They may also freely grant guarantees for the payment by resident importers of their purchases from nonresident suppliers. The issue and establishment of repayment guarantees for foreign currency loans freely contracted by residents are not subject to approval.

   To residents from nonresidents — At the request, and with the counterguarantee, of a nonresident bank, resident banks may freely grant the usual bank guarantees required of nonresident service providers by resident transactors in connection with business contracts, work contracts, service contracts, etc.

Controls on direct investment

Outward direct investment — To transfer capital abroad, residents must obtain approval from the CBT; however, to support their export activities, exporters may freely transfer amounts ranging from D 20,000 to D 100,000 a calendar year to cover the installation, maintenance, and operating costs of branches and subsidiaries or to finance equity participation, and D 10,000 to D 50,000 to cover installation, maintenance, and operating costs of liaison or representative offices.

Inward direct investment	Foreigners may invest freely in most economic sectors. However, the participation of foreigners in certain service industries not exclusively engaged in export activities requires the approval of the HIC if such participation exceeds 50% of the capital stock.
Controls on liquidation of direct investment	All foreign direct investments carried out legitimately in Tunisia with foreign exchange transferred from abroad are guaranteed the right to repatriate the net proceeds from the sale or liquidation of the invested capital, even if the net proceeds exceed the initial value of foreign exchange invested.
Controls on real estate transactions	
Purchase abroad by residents	Yes.
Purchase locally by nonresidents	Purchases require approval from the CBT.
Sale locally by nonresidents	Yes.
Provisions specific to commercial banks and other credit institutions	
Borrowing abroad	Resident financial institutions may freely contract foreign currency loans from nonresidents up to an annual limit of D 10 million and D 3 million, respectively.
Maintenance of accounts abroad	Resident banks may freely open "correspondent" accounts with foreign banks of their choice.
Lending to nonresidents (financial or commercial credits)	The approval of the CBT is required, except for investment, commercial, and operating loans granted by resident banks to nonresident industrial enterprises established in Tunisia.
Lending locally in foreign exchange	Resident banks may freely extend credit to finance import and export operations.
Purchase of locally issued securities denominated in foreign exchange	Yes.
Differential treatment of nonresident deposit accounts and/or deposit accounts in foreign exchange	n.a.
Investment regulations	n.a.
Open foreign exchange position limits	Yes.
Provisions specific to institutional investors	
Limits (max.) on portfolio invested abroad	Yes.
Limits (min.) on portfolio invested locally	Yes.
Currency matching regulations on assets/liabilities composition	Yes.

Changes During 1996

Resident accounts	*July 5.* A special export earning account in convertible dinars was created.
Imports and import payments	*June 10.* Agricultural products were removed from the negative list.

Changes During 1997

Exchange arrangements	*May 9.* The interbank market was opened to forward exchange operations; and the spread between the buying and selling exchange rate on the interbank spot market was liberalized.

TURKEY

(Position as of March 31, 1997)

Status Under IMF Articles of Agreement

Article VIII	Date of acceptance: March 22, 1990.

Exchange Arrangement

Currency

The currency of Turkey is the Turkish lira.

Exchange rate structure

Unitary.

Classification

Managed floating

The exchange rate for the Turkish lira is market determined. Commercial banks, special financial institutions, authorized institutions, post, telephone, and telegraphic offices (PTT), and precious metal intermediary institutions are free to set their exchange rates according to market conditions. The lowest and highest rates applied in these transactions are to be reported daily to the Central Bank of Turkey (CBT). On each business day, the CBT announces an indicative exchange rate that is determined as the average of buying and selling rates of the 10 banks with the largest involvement in foreign exchange trading.

Exchange tax

No.

Exchange subsidy

No.

Forward exchange market

Banks and precious metal brokerage institutions may deal with forward transactions within the framework of the open position limits determined by the CBT. Forward exchange rates are freely established between the banks and their customers in accordance with international practices.

Official cover of forward operations

Banks may enter into swap transactions with the CBT with terms of quarterly periods up to 12 months; however, the CBT has not conducted forward transactions with banks since the first quarter of 1996.

Arrangements for Payments and Receipts

Prescription of currency requirements

Certain commercial transactions with the Czech Republic and Poland are made through special accounts denominated in U.S. dollars.

Payment arrangements

Clearing agreements

There are agreements with the Czech Republic, Poland, Russia, and the Slovak Republic.

Barter agreements and open accounts

There are banking agreements with the Czech Republic and Poland.

Administration of control

Exchange control authorities

The undersecretariat of the Treasury and the CBT administer the exchange controls; the undersecretariat of the Treasury authorizes banks to engage in foreign exchange operations, and regulates and supervises banks' open foreign exchange position limits together with the CBT.

International security restrictions

In accordance with IMF Executive Board Decision No. 144-(52/51)

Turkey notified the Fund, on September 12, 1990, that certain restrictions were imposed on the making of payments and transfers for current international transactions to the government of Iraq. Turkey notified the Fund on August 5, 1992, that, in compliance with UN Security Council Resolution No. 757 (1992), certain restrictions had been imposed on the making of payments and transfers for current international transactions in

868

respect of the Federal Republic of Yugoslavia (Serbia/Montenegro). However, effective May 2, 1996, restrictions that had been imposed on foreign trade, transfers of foreign exchange, and credit letters in respect of the Federal Republic of Yugoslavia were abolished.

In accordance with UN sanctions	Yes.
Payment arrears	No.

Controls on trade in gold (coins and/or bullion)

Controls on domestic ownership and/or trade

Domestic purchases and sales in Turkey of unprocessed gold imported by the CBT and by precious metals intermediary institutions can only be conducted at the Istanbul Gold Exchange. The purchase and sale of precious metals, stones, and articles are free within the country.

Controls on external trade

Exports and imports of precious metals, stones, and articles are free. Unprocessed gold may be imported by the CBT and by precious metals intermediary institutions that are members of the Precious Metals Exchange without being subject to the provisions of the Foreign Trade Regime, but the gold must be surrendered to the Istanbul Gold Exchange within 3 days.

Banks may open gold deposit accounts in the name of legal and real entities residing in Turkey and abroad. The account holders may freely use balances on their accounts.

Within the framework of the banking regulations, banks may extend gold credits to juridical and natural persons involved in the jewelry business, upon the physical delivery of the gold purchased by their institutions, and against the gold held in the gold deposit accounts. The buying and selling prices of gold are freely determined by banks.

Passengers may bring into and take out of the country ornamental articles made from precious metals and stones of which the value does not exceed $15,000. The taking out of ornamental articles exceeding this value is dependent on their declaration upon arrival or proof that they have been purchased in Turkey.

Controls on exports and imports of banknotes

On exports

Domestic currency

Travelers may freely take abroad up to the equivalent of $5,000.

Foreign currency

Travelers may freely take up to $5,000 or its equivalent out of the country. To take out more than this amount, nonresidents must declare banknotes upon arrival, and residents must present a document confirming that the foreign banknotes were purchased for invisible transactions.

Resident Accounts

Eligibility to hold accounts	Juridical and natural persons are eligible.
Foreign exchange accounts permitted	Yes.
Held domestically	Yes.
Held abroad	Yes.
Accounts in domestic currency convertible into foreign currency	No.

Nonresident Accounts

Eligibility to hold accounts	Juridical and natural persons are eligible.

Foreign exchange accounts permitted	Yes.
Domestic currency accounts	Yes.
Convertible into foreign currency	No.
Blocked accounts	No.

Imports and Import Payments

Foreign exchange budget	No.
Financing requirements for imports	No.
Documentation requirements for release of foreign exchange for imports	No.
Import licenses and other nontariff measures	The import license requirement was abolished on December 31, 1995.
Negative list	The importation of goods prohibited by law, such as narcotics, weapons, foreign coins made of metals other than gold, and ammunition, is allowed only with a special permit. Old, used, reconditioned, defective, substandard, soiled, or poor-quality goods may be imported only with special permission from the undersecretariat of the Treasury. But certain used goods that are not older than 5 years may be imported freely.
Licenses with quotas	Quotas are implemented as a requirement for the harmonization of the import policy of Turkey with that of the EU.
Import taxes and/or tariffs	No.
State import monopoly	No.

Exports and Export Proceeds

Repatriation requirements	Foreign exchange receipts must be repatriated within 180 days of the date of shipment. Exporters are allowed to use those proceeds for payments on imports and invisible transactions.
Surrender requirements	Receipts must be surrendered within 180 days of the date of repatriation. If exchange receipts are surrendered within 90 days, exporters are entitled to retain 30% of proceeds, which they may deposit in foreign exchange accounts with commercial banks, keep abroad, or dispose of freely. Exporters may retain export proceeds abroad up to $50,000. Effective June 1996, banks, special financial institutions, and the post, telephone, and telegraphic offices are required to sell to the foreign currency notes market and the CBT 4% and 10%, respectively, of all foreign exchange they obtain from exports, invisible transactions, and gold accounts within a period agreed with the CBT.
Financing requirements	No.
Documentation requirements	A new export credit program was introduced on January 15, 1996, by the Turkish Eximbank whereby different interest rates (i.e., OECD commercial interest reference rates, government bond yields, and SDR basket rates) are applied to these loans, depending on the importing country.
Letters of credit	Yes.
Guarantees	Yes.
Preshipment inspection	Yes.

Export licenses

Without quotas
Exports are generally free, but for the exportation of a few goods, permission from authorized institutions is required in advance. Exportation of certain goods requires registration for purposes of information on the importing country, price, quantity, and the method of payment, etc.

With quotas
A few products are subject to quotas.

Export taxes

Taxes collected through the exchange system
Export taxes on nuts, olive oil, rye, and unprocessed leather are collected through the exchange system.

Payments for Invisible Transactions and Current Transfers

Controls on these payments
There are no controls on these payments. Residents are allowed to use credit cards on a revolving basis up to $10,000 for travel and expenses abroad; balances exceeding $10,000 must be settled within 30 days.

Proceeds from Invisible Transactions and Current Transfers

Repatriation requirements
No.

Surrender requirements
No.

Restrictions on use of funds
No.

Capital Transactions

Controls on capital and money market instruments
Sales or issue of these instruments by nonresidents are subject to the permission of the Capital Market Board.

On capital market securities

Sale or issue locally by nonresidents
Sales by nonresidents (including investments, partnerships, and mutual funds abroad) of all kinds of securities and other capital instruments through the banks and intermediary institutions authorized according to the capital legislation may be made freely. The transfer of the income from such securities and instruments as well as the proceeds from their sale may be effected freely through banks and special finance institutions.

Purchase abroad by residents
Purchases and sales by residents of the securities traded in foreign financial markets are free, provided that the transactions are carried out by banks, special finance institutions, and intermediary institutions authorized according to the capital market legislation and that the transfer of their purchase value abroad is made through banks and special financial institutions.

On money market instruments

Sale or issue locally by nonresidents
Yes.

On collective investment securities

Sale or issue locally by nonresidents
Yes.

Controls on derivatives and other instruments
No.

Controls on credit operations

Commercial credits

To residents from nonresidents
Residents may freely obtain credits from abroad provided that they channel such credits through the banks or special finance institutions. However, the maturity of prefinancing

credits is 1 year. On July 22, the Resource Utilization Support Fund (RUSF) fee on loans to importers was reintroduced at 6%. Imports by exporters and importers for investment purposes remain exempt.

Financial credits

To residents from nonresidents | Credits with a maturity of over 1 year must be registered at the debt log maintained by the undersecretariat of the Treasury. On March 11, 1997, a RUSF fee of 6% was set for loans by residents other than banks.

Controls on direct investment

Outward direct investment | Residents may freely export capital in cash up to $5 million or its equivalent in other foreign currencies through banks or special financial institutions and capital in kind within the framework of the provisions of the customs legislation, with the purpose of investment, incorporating companies for commercial purposes, participating in an enterprise, or opening branches abroad. The permission to export capital in cash and/or in kind exceeding $5 million is given by the ministry to which the undersecretariat of the Treasury is attached.

Inward direct investment | Permission from the undersecretariat of the Treasury within the framework of the Encouragement of Foreign Capital Law is required. In establishing partnership or joint companies in the Turkish private sector, foreign investors must bring at least $50,000 of capital.

Controls on liquidation of direct investment | Proceeds may be transferred abroad, but must be reported to the CBT.

Controls on real estate transactions

Purchase locally by nonresidents | Nonresidents can acquire real estate in Turkey for tourism, petroleum, and banking activities if approved by the Council of Ministers. The acquisition of real estate in villages of Turkey by nonresidents is prohibited. If nonresidents acquire real estate via inheritance in villages of Turkey, it must be liquidated. For nonresidents to acquire real estate exceeding 30 hectares in independent rural areas not belonging to a village, a decision of the Council of Ministers is required. Nonresidents cannot acquire real estate in forbidden military and security areas.

Provisions specific to commercial banks and other credit institutions

Borrowing abroad | Credits obtained by banks from abroad are subject to a 4% tax, which is earmarked for the RUSF.

Lending to nonresidents (financial or commercial credits) | Resident banks and special finance institutions can extend credits to nonresidents in foreign exchange and in Turkish liras up to the total amount of the foreign exchange credits they have obtained and their foreign exchange deposit accounts, provided that the amount of the credits is within the limits determined in the Banking Law.

Lending locally in foreign exchange

Differential treatment of nonresident deposit accounts and/or deposit accounts in foreign exchange

Reserve requirements | Reserve requirement ratios are set at 8% for deposits in local currency and at 11% for foreign currency deposits. While different ratios are applied to domestic and foreign currency deposits, there is no difference between the ratios applied to the deposit accounts of nonresidents and residents.

Liquid asset requirements | Domestic deposits and other domestic liabilities are subject to a 6% liquidity ratio. Foreign deposits and other foreign liabilities are subject to a 3% liquidity ratio. The liquid assets must consist of government bonds, T-bills, and borrowing instruments issued by the Collective Housing Fund and Privatization Administration. Other domestic liabilities and the exceeding part of the short or long position are subject to an 8% liquidity ratio and other foreign exchange liabilities are subject to an 11% liquidity ratio. The amount pertaining to these ratios is held in cash. There is no difference between the ratios applied to the deposit accounts of nonresidents and residents.

Credit controls	There are some restrictions for banks granting credits to natural and juridical persons and for those connected with them.
Investment regulations	For banks, investment in real estate and in the companies that are not financial institutions is limited to a proportion of a bank's own funds. Banks may not engage in purchase and sale of commodities for commercial purposes, excluding, however, the trade of minted and ingot gold.
Open foreign exchange position limits	The limit is 50% of the capital base.
Provisions specific to institutional investors	
Limits (max.) on portfolio invested abroad	Only for investment trusts that invest the maximum of 25% of their capital and reserve funds on securities in their portfolios.
Other controls imposed by securities laws	No.

Changes During 1996

Arrangements for payments and receipts	*May 2.* Restrictions on foreign trade, transfers of foreign exchange, and letters of credit in respect to the Federal Republic of Yugoslavia (Serbia/Montenegro) were lifted.
Resident accounts	*August 2.* The limits for "super" foreign currency accounts, which may be denominated in deutsche mark and U.S. dollars, were reduced from DM 50,000 to DM 30,000 and $25,000 to $15,000, respectively. The terms of the accounts were also changed: in addition to 3-year terms, 2-year terms can also be applied.
	November 7. Individuals were permitted to open foreign currency deposit accounts against a letter of credit, and a super foreign currency account with the CBT. These accounts cannot be opened by individuals under the age of 18 and those going abroad for tourism, commercial, or other reasons. Individuals who have permanently returned to Turkey can open these accounts against the over-the-limit transfers sent to them by private or public social security institutions abroad.
Imports and import payments	*January 1.* An RUSF fee applied for credits obtained by banks from abroad was reduced from 6% to 4%. The fee on loans to importers was eliminated.
	July 22. The RUSF fee on loans to importers was reintroduced at 6%. Imports by exporters and importers for investment purposes remain exempt.
	October 24. A special advance import deposit scheme was introduced, under which Turkish citizens can import secondhand machinery and used automobiles when they deposit DM 50,000 at the CBT for 1 year.
Exports and export proceeds	*January 15.* A new export credit program was introduced by the Turkish Eximbank whereby different interest rates (i.e., OECD commercial interest reference rates, government bond yields, and SDR basket rates) are applied to these loans, depending on the importing country.
	May 7. Banks, special financial institutions, and the post, telephone, and telegraphic offices were required to sell to the foreign currency notes market and the CBT 4% and 10%, respectively, of all foreign exchange they obtain from exports, invisible transactions, and gold accounts within a period agreed with the CBT.
Payments for invisible transactions and current transfers	*April 1.* Obligatory payments to the Mass Housing Fund by Turkish citizens traveling abroad were abolished.
Capital transactions	*January 2.* The maturity restriction for keeping government securities issued in or indexed to foreign currencies was lifted for the liquidity requirement.

July 22. A 4% tax, earmarked for the RUSF, was levied on credits obtained by banks from abroad.

July 22. The reserve requirement ratios were set at 8% for domestic currency and at 11% for foreign currency deposits. Deposits and other liabilities in domestic currency were subject to a 6% liquidity ratio. Deposits and other liabilities in foreign currency were subject to a 3% liquidity ratio. These 2 ratios should be maintained in government bonds, T-bills, and borrowing instruments issued by the Collective Housing Fund and the Privatization Administration.

August 2. Securities denominated in or indexed to foreign currencies that have been issued directly by or under the guarantee of the undersecretariat of the Treasury or by the Privatization Administration in the domestic markets were subject to the liquidity and foreign exchange position ratios applied to the banks and special finance institutions.

August 7. The share of foreign exchange indexed asset liabilities regarding the securities defined in the preceding paragraph in total foreign exchange asset/liabilities was increased from 50% to 100%.

Changes During 1997

Capital transactions

March 11. The RUSF fee was amended. A rate of 4% was set for loans obtained by banks and financial institutions from abroad, and a 6% fee was set for loans obtained by other residents from abroad.

TURKMENISTAN

(Position as of April 30, 1997)

Status Under IMF Articles of Agreement

Article XIV	Yes.

Exchange Arrangement

Currency

The currency of Turkmenistan is the Turkmen manat.

Exchange rate structure

Dual

There are two exchange rates: (1) the official (non-cash) rate determined at a weekly auction in which commercial banks participate, and (2) the commercial bank cash rate determined by the banks within guidelines given by the Central Bank of Turkmenistan (CBT) and by parallel market rates.

Classification

Managed floating

Prior to the auction, the CBT issues an indicative rate, and adjusts the auction rate taking the bids into account. The auction and commercial bank cash rates are allowed to deviate substantially.

Exchange tax

No.

Exchange subsidy

No.

Forward exchange market

No.

Arrangements for Payments and Receipts

Prescription of currency requirements

Settlements with the Baltic countries, Russia, and a few other FSU countries are made through a system of correspondent accounts. Settlements with countries with which Turkmenistan has bilateral payments arrangements are effected in accordance with these agreements. Barter transactions, except gas exports, must take place through the State Commodity Exchange. All other transactions are made in convertible currencies.

Payment arrangements

Yes.

Bilateral arrangements

Operative

There is a bilateral arrangement with the Islamic Republic of Iran.

Inoperative

The bilateral agreement with Malaysia is inoperative.

Regional arrangements

n.a.

Clearing agreements

Trilateral agreements are maintained with Armenia and the Islamic Republic of Iran, and with Ukraine and the Islamic Republic of Iran.

Barter agreements and open accounts

There are barter trade agreements, primarily for gas exports, and there is an agreement with Kazakhstan for the export of electricity.

Administration of control

Exchange control authorities

The CBT, along with the Ministry of Economy and Finance (MEF) and the Tax Authority, depending on the type of operation involved, is empowered to issue exchange control regulations. The use of official foreign exchange reserves is controlled by the president of Turkmenistan.

International security restrictions

No.

Payment arrears

Official

Yes.

Private	Yes.
Controls on trade in gold (coins and/or bullion)	
Controls on domestic ownership and/or trade	Yes.
Controls on external trade	A license is required to engage in international trade in gold.
Controls on exports and imports of banknotes	Local and foreign banknotes may be freely exported and imported provided funds are declared on arrival and departure.

Resident Accounts

Eligibility to hold accounts	Juridical and natural persons are eligible.
Foreign exchange accounts permitted	Residents may hold foreign exchange accounts with local commercial banks.
Held domestically	These accounts may be opened if the holder possesses a certificate of registration issued by the Ministry of Foreign Economic Relations (MFER); the amount and currency of denomination of interest payable on these accounts is determined by the authorized bank. All external payments made using balances on these accounts must be approved by the CBT; however, cash withdrawals from the accounts in foreign currency may be made without the approval of the CBT.
Held abroad	Turkmen citizens residing overseas may open foreign exchange accounts abroad for the duration of their residence abroad, with permission from the CBT. Prior approval is required.

Nonresident Accounts

Eligibility to hold accounts	Juridical and natural persons are eligible.
Foreign exchange accounts permitted	Yes.

Imports and Import Payments

Foreign exchange budget	No.
Import licenses and other nontariff measures	
Negative list	Imports of goods on the negative list (arms, narcotics, antiques) are prohibited for national security reasons. An approval of the president or the Cabinet of Ministers (CM) is required to import these goods.
Import taxes and/or tariffs	Excise taxes are levied on alcoholic beverages, cigarettes, jewelry, and cars. Goods in transit are exempt.
Taxes collected through the exchange system	No.
State import monopoly	No.

Exports and Export Proceeds

Repatriation requirements	Yes.
Surrender requirements	From January 2, 1996, to April 1, 1997, there was a 70% surrender requirement for export earnings received by the oil and gas industry: 40% was to be surrendered to the Foreign Exchange Reserve Fund (FERF) and 30% to the CBT for use in the auctions. Other public sector organizations had a 50% surrender requirement: 20% to the auctions

and 30% to the FERF. All surrenders were made at the official exchange rate. Retained earnings could be exchanged at the auction rate or the cash rate.

On April 1, 1997, the surrender requirements on state sector export earnings were unified at 50%; surrenders are made at the auction rate. Retained earnings may be exchanged at the auction or the cash rates.

Joint ventures and private sector firms are not subject to the surrender requirement. Private sector foreign exchange earnings may be exchanged for Turkmen manat at the commercial bank cash rate.

Export licenses	All exports require a special license.
With quotas	Quantitative and price restrictions are imposed on exports of cotton and other raw materials to protect domestic supplies.
Export taxes	Yes.
Taxes collected through the exchange system	A fee is collected at the rate of 0.01% of the value of the licensed product that is sold in convertible currencies; the fee on exports to the Baltic countries, Russia, and other countries of the FSU is 0.1% of the ruble value of the licensed product. The customs department charges an administration fee of 0.2%.

Payments for Invisible Transactions and Current Transfers

Controls on these payments	All payments require prior approval.
Profit/dividends	
Quantitative limits	After the payment of taxes, profits may be reinvested in Turkmenistan, held in bank accounts in national or other currencies, or transferred abroad.
Indicative limits/bona fide test	n.a.

Proceeds from Invisible Transactions and Current Transfers

Repatriation requirements	Yes.
Surrender requirements	Proceeds must be sold to commercial banks, except the retained portion in the case of enterprises.

Capital Transactions

Controls on capital and money market instruments	Both inward and outward capital transfers are subject to CBT approval.
On capital market securities	
Purchase locally by nonresidents	Nonresidents' share in stocks of a resident company is limited to 49%. Nonresidents can purchase only registered shares.
Sale or issue locally by nonresidents	Approval of the CM is required. Annual quotas apply.
Purchase abroad by residents	Subject to quota and licensing by the CM.
Sale or issue abroad by residents	Subject to quota and licensing by the CM.
On money market instruments	All transactions in those instruments are subject to a CM license and quota.
On collective investment securities	No regulations exist on these securities.
Controls on derivatives and other instruments	There are no transactions in derivatives in Turkmenistan.
Controls on credit operations	A CBT license or approval is required for residents. Nonresidents need CBT approval.
Controls on direct investment	

Outward direct investment	Yes.
Inward direct investment	Investments by juridical persons are permitted, in principle, in all sectors. Investors are required to obtain an authorization from the MFER; if the amount exceeds $500,000, the approval of the CM of Turkmenistan is required. Foreign participation in joint-stock companies is limited to 49%.
Controls on liquidation of direct investment	Foreign investors have the right to recover investments within 6 months of liquidation.

Controls on real estate transactions

Purchase abroad by residents	Yes.
Purchase locally by nonresidents	n.a.
Sale locally by nonresidents	n.a.
Provisions specific to commercial banks and other credit institutions	A CBT license is required. Provided the license is granted, no controls apply to individual transactions.
Borrowing abroad	Yes.
Maintenance of accounts abroad	Yes.
Lending to nonresidents (financial or commercial credits)	Yes.
Lending locally in foreign exchange	Yes.
Purchase of locally issued securities denominated in foreign exchange	Yes.
Provisions specific to institutional investors	A CBT and/or an MEF license is required, depending on the type of institutional investors.
Limits (max.) on portfolio invested abroad	n.a.
Limits (min.) on portfolio invested locally	n.a.
Currency matching regulations on assets/liabilities composition	n.a.
Other controls imposed by securities laws	Institutional investors are required to meet minimum capital requirements. Responsibility rests with the CM, the CBT, and/or the MEF, depending on the type of investors.

Changes During 1996

Exchange arrangements	*January 1*. The foreign exchange auction was introduced.
	January 2. Official and commercial exchange rates were unified at manat 2,400 per $1.
	April 10. Official and commercial exchange rates were reunified at manat 3,000 per $1.
	May 2. Regular foreign exchange auctions commenced.
	September 25. Access to the auction was disallowed for importers of consumer goods.
Exports and export proceeds	*January 2*. The surrender requirement was set at 70% for gas exports and at 50% for other exports; surrenders were to be made at the official rate.

Changes During 1997

Exports and export proceeds	*April 1*. A 50% surrender requirement is applied only to state enterprises.

UGANDA

(Position as of December 31, 1996)

Status Under IMF Articles of Agreement

Article VIII	Date of acceptance: April 5, 1994.

Exchange Arrangement

Currency	The currency of Uganda is the Uganda shilling.
Exchange rate structure	Unitary.
Classification	
Independent floating	The external value of the Uganda shilling is determined in the interbank foreign exchange market. Certain transactions may be effected in foreign exchange bureaus that are licensed to buy and sell foreign exchange at freely negotiated rates.
Exchange tax	No.
Exchange subsidy	No.
Forward exchange market	Authorized banks may deal in the forward exchange market with customers in pounds sterling, U.S. dollars, and certain other convertible currencies, provided that there is an underlying approved import or export contract. Authorized foreign exchange dealers may impose a service charge of up to 1%.
Official cover of forward operations	No.

Arrangements for Payments and Receipts

Prescription of currency requirements	Authorized payments, including for imports to nonresidents, may be made in Uganda shillings to the credit of an external account in Uganda or in any other currency that is appropriate to the country of residence of the payee.
Payment arrangements	
Bilateral arrangements	
Inoperative	Uganda maintains clearing arrangements with Burundi, Rwanda, and the Democratic Republic of the Congo. Trade and payments agreements exist with Algeria, Cuba, Egypt, the Democratic People's Republic of Korea, and Libya.
Regional arrangements	Following the East African Cooperation Agreement, the Ugandan, Kenyan, and Tanzanian shillings are now freely convertible in the 3 countries. Excess holdings of Kenyan and/or Tanzanian shillings are repatriated to the respective central banks for immediate credit in U.S. dollars.
Clearing agreements	The Bank of Uganda (BOU) settles accounts in U.S. dollars with the member countries of the COMESA through the COMESA clearinghouse; residents of member countries may use national currencies in day-to-day payments during a transaction period of 2 calendar months; the monetary authorities settle net balances at the end of this period in convertible currencies.
Administration of control	
Exchange control authorities	The BOU administers exchange controls on behalf of the Minister of Finance (MOF), but has delegated a broad range of responsibilities to authorized banks and exchange bureaus. Import and export control regulations are administered by the Ministry of Commerce and Trade (MCT), which has powers to prohibit imports and exports.
International security restrictions	No.

Payment arrears

Official	Yes.
Private	Yes.

Controls on trade in gold (coins and/or bullion)

Controls on domestic ownership and/or trade	Residents may hold and acquire gold coins for numismatic purposes. Only monetary authorities and licensed dealers are allowed to hold or acquire gold in any form other than jewelry.
Controls on external trade	Imports and exports of gold in any form other than jewelry constituting the personal effects of a traveler require licenses issued by the Ministry of Mines.
Controls on exports and imports of banknotes	No.

Resident Accounts

Eligibility to hold accounts

Juridical persons	n.a.
Natural persons	Yes.
Foreign exchange accounts permitted	Resident exporters of goods who are earning commissions, consulting fees, rent, and other incomes in foreign exchange may operate foreign exchange accounts with commercial banks in Uganda. Payments made from these accounts are subject to the same regulations as those governing sales of foreign exchange in the foreign exchange bureaus.
Held domestically	Yes.
Held abroad	Yes.
Accounts in domestic currency convertible into foreign currency	Yes.

Nonresident Accounts

Eligibility to hold accounts

Juridical persons	n.a.
Natural persons	Yes.
Foreign exchange accounts permitted	Accounts held by diplomats may be credited with authorized payments by residents of Uganda and with transfers from other external accounts or any other external source. They may be debited freely for payments to nonresidents, for transfers to other external accounts in Uganda, and for purchases of foreign currencies from authorized dealers.
Domestic currency accounts	Yes.
Convertible into foreign currency	Yes.
Blocked accounts	n.a.

Imports and Import Payments

Foreign exchange budget	No.
Financing requirements for imports	No.

Documentation requirements for release of foreign exchange for imports	Importers should submit a form to obtain foreign exchange.
Import licenses and other nontariff measures	Most imports require licenses. Foreign exchange sales to various ministries and departments must be backed by documents showing the approval of the Central Tender Board. Importers are provided with a renewable certificate, which is valid for 6 months and which permits them to import a broad range of goods not on the negative list. The certificate does not prescribe the importation of a specific good.
Negative list	The importation of pornographic materials, beer, and soft drinks is prohibited. Imports of firearms and ammunition require special permission.
Other nontariff measures	There is a time-specific ban on importation of certain commodities.
Import taxes and/or tariffs	Customs duties are applied at 1 of 4 rates of up to 30%. Duties for intermediate goods, raw materials, and machinery range up to 8%.
Taxes collected through the exchange system	No.
State import monopoly	No.

Exports and Export Proceeds

Repatriation requirements	Yes.
Surrender requirements	No.
Financing requirements	No.
Documentation requirements	All exports require certificates from the MCT, which are valid for 6 months and are renewable; they may be restricted to ensure domestic supply.
Export licenses	
With quotas	Exports of coffee are subject to a quota under the International Coffee Organization (ICO).
Export taxes	The stabilization tax on coffee exports was abolished in June 1996.

Payments for Invisible Transactions and Current Transfers

Controls on these payments	No.

Proceeds from Invisible Transactions and Current Transfers

Repatriation requirements	No.
Surrender requirements	Proceeds may be sold in the foreign exchange interbank market.
Restrictions on use of funds	No.

Capital Transactions

Controls on capital and money market instruments	Capital transfers to all countries require individual exchange control approval.
On capital market securities	All imports and exports of securities require approval.
Purchase locally by nonresidents	Approval is freely granted for the purchase by nonresidents of Ugandan securities, provided that payment is received in an appropriate manner.

Sale or issue locally by nonresidents	These transactions are prohibited.
Purchase abroad by residents	These transactions are prohibited, except when permission of the MOF is granted.
Sale or issue abroad by residents	The transfer of proceeds associated with the sale or issue of securities abroad by residents of Uganda and the transfer of funds required to service these security issues require the approval of the MOF.

On money market instruments

Purchase locally by nonresidents	These purchases are prohibited.
Sale or issue locally by nonresidents	Yes.
Purchase abroad by residents	These transactions are prohibited, unless permitted by the MOF.
Sale or issue abroad by residents	These transactions are prohibited, unless permitted by the MOF.

On collective investment securities

Purchase locally by nonresidents	Requires prior approval from the BOU.
Sale or issue locally by nonresidents	Requires prior approval from the BOU.
Purchase abroad by residents	Requires prior approval from the BOU.
Sale or issue abroad by residents	Requires prior approval from the BOU.

Controls on derivatives and other instruments	
Purchase locally by nonresidents	Yes.
Sale or issue locally by nonresidents	Yes.
Purchase abroad by residents	Yes.
Sale or issue abroad by residents	Yes.
Controls on credit operations	No.
Controls on direct investment	
Outward direct investment	Requires prior approval from the BOU.
Inward direct investment	Investments are permitted with or without government participation. To secure a guarantee of repatriation, it is necessary to obtain "approved status" for the investment in terms of the Investment Code (1991). In normal circumstances, approval is given freely.
Controls on liquidation of direct investment	Requires prior approval from the BOU.
Controls on real estate transactions	
Purchase abroad by residents	Requires prior approval from the BOU.
Purchase locally by nonresidents	With the exception of agricultural land, nonresidents can purchase local real estate.
Sale locally by nonresidents	Requires prior approval from the BOU.
Provisions specific to commercial banks and other credit institutions	
Borrowing abroad	Commercial banks must seek BOU approval.
Lending to nonresidents (financial or commercial credits)	Banks can lend to nonresidents but are required to report to the BOU. Banks are free to purchase securities issued abroad.
Lending locally in foreign exchange	Banks are permitted to lend locally up to 80% of their total foreign liabilities in foreign currency.

Differential treatment of nonresident deposit accounts and/or deposit accounts in foreign exchange

Reserve requirements	Banks must hold 20% of foreign liabilities in reserve.
Credit controls	Commercial banks are subject to a limit only on lending in foreign currency.

Open foreign exchange position limits — Commercial banks are allowed to have an open position equivalent to 20% of core capital.

Provisions specific to institutional investors — No.

Other controls imposed by securities laws — No.

Changes During 1996

Exports and export proceeds — *June 12.* The stabilization tax on coffee exports was abolished.

UKRAINE

(Position as of December 31, 1996)

Status Under IMF Articles of Agreement

Article VIII   Date of acceptance: September 23, 1996.

Exchange Arrangement

Currency   The currency of Ukraine is the hryvnia.

Exchange rate structure   Unitary.

Classification

Managed floating   There are 2 foreign exchange markets. The National Bank of Ukraine (NBU) conducts daily foreign exchange auctions (the Birzha auctions), in which the official exchange rate of the hryvnia is determined. The official exchange rate applies to transactions of the NBU with the government. The interbank rate may not differ by more than 0.6% from the official rate.

Exchange tax   No.

Exchange subsidy   No.

Forward exchange market   No.

Arrangements for Payments and Receipts

Prescription of currency requirements   Payments to and receipts from all countries, other than those with which Ukraine has a bilateral payment agreement and which are made in the currencies and in accordance with the procedures set forth in those agreements, are settled in convertible currencies. Nonbarter trade with the Baltic countries, Russia, and the other countries of the FSU is now settled mainly in convertible currencies, especially the U.S. dollar.

Payment arrangements

Bilateral arrangements

　Operative   Yes.

　Inoperative   There are arrangements with the Baltic countries, Russia, and the other countries of the FSU.

Regional arrangements   Yes.

Barter agreements and open accounts Barter continues to be a major form of trade for Ukrainian companies in their transactions both with the Baltic countries, Russia, and the other countries of the FSU and with non-FSU countries.

Administration of control

Exchange control authorities   The NBU administers exchange controls.

International security restrictions

In accordance with IMF Executive Board Decision No. 144-(52/51)   n.a.

In accordance with UN sanctions   Restrictions on payments and the provision of financial services to Iraq are maintained.

Payment arrears

Private   n.a.

Controls on trade in gold (coins and/or bullion)

Controls on domestic ownership and/or trade

Residents are required to obtain a license from the Ministry of Finance to deal in precious stones and metals.

Controls on external trade

Permission for residents to export precious metals and precious stones is granted by the Cabinet of Ministers of Ukraine.

Controls on exports and imports of banknotes

On exports

Domestic currency

Residents may export up to the equivalent of 10 times the minimum wage. The limit for nonresidents is 5 times the minimum wage.

Foreign currency

Resident natural persons may export $1,000 in cash and $1,000 in traveler's checks without permission, and $4,000 in cash and $5,000 in traveler's checks with permission from an authorized bank. The total limit is set at $10,000 a person a trip. Nonresident natural persons may export $1,000 in cash and $1,000 in traveler's checks without permission, and $1,000 in cash and $5,000 in traveler's checks with permission, for a total limit of $7,000. The exportation of currency by residents and nonresidents in excess of established norms requires a license from the NBU.

On imports

Domestic currency

Resident and nonresident natural persons are permitted to import domestic currency up to the amounts declared in a customs declaration upon exit from Ukraine. Juridical persons must obtain a license from the NBU to import domestic currency.

Foreign currency

Resident and nonresident natural persons are permitted to import up to $50,000 in cash; for amounts in excess of this limit, permission from the NBU is required.

Resident Accounts

Eligibility to hold accounts

Juridical and natural persons are eligible.

Foreign exchange accounts permitted

Yes.

Held domestically

Certain conditions apply to these accounts.

Held abroad

These accounts are permitted, but a license from the NBU is required, except when the account is opened during a temporary stay abroad.

Accounts in domestic currency convertible into foreign currency

Yes.

Nonresident Accounts

Eligibility to hold accounts

Juridical and natural persons are eligible.

Foreign exchange accounts permitted

Residents of Kazakhstan, Russia, and Uzbekistan must submit a certified copy of the NBU approval to open a settlement account in foreign currency to the bank where the account is to be opened.

Domestic currency accounts

"P" accounts may be opened for the permanent representative office of a foreign company, firm, or international organization established without the status of a legal entity, through which a nonresident conducts all or part of his or her entrepreneurial activities in Ukraine. P accounts may be credited with the proceeds of transactions from any economic activity, including payments for current international transactions.

"N" accounts may be opened by a representative office of a nonresident legal entity, an institution, or a person who represents its interests in Ukraine and does not engage in entrepreneurial activities in the territory of Ukraine. The holders of N accounts are regarded as nonresidents for exchange control purposes, although they are treated as residents for tax purposes. N accounts may be credited with funds by selling foreign exchange to the servicing bank in order to effect settlement associated solely with the maintenance of the representative office, or with funds received by embassies and consulates for providing consular services. All N account holders may purchase foreign exchange on the interbank currency market to transfer funds abroad, including interest accrued on the balance in the account.

Convertible into foreign currency	P account holders may convert and transfer to their parent company or head office abroad proceeds of current international transactions, provided the balances in question derive from transactions connected with their economic activity. N account holders other than foreign diplomatic, consular, commercial, and other official missions and their offices may not purchase foreign exchange on the interbank market to transfer funds abroad from their N account. Nonresident natural persons may convert and transfer abroad funds from settlement accounts in hryvnias. Prior approval is required.
Blocked accounts	No.

Imports and Import Payments

Foreign exchange budget	No.
Financing requirements for imports	
Advance payment requirements	Yes.
Documentation requirements for release of foreign exchange for imports	Import contracts are required for banks to bid in foreign exchange auctions.
Domiciliation requirements	Yes.
Preshipment inspection	n.a.
Letters of credit	Yes.
Import licenses and other nontariff measures	Nontariff measures are limited to those for national safety and environmental reasons.
Negative list	Yes.
Open general licenses	n.a.
Import taxes and/or tariffs	There are 3 customs duty rates with a trade-weighted average rate of about 5%. The first category (preferred duty rate) applies to goods from countries with which Ukraine has a free trade agreement, imports from developing countries, and imports from countries that have a preferential agreement with Ukraine. The second category (concessional duty rate) applies to imports from countries that have entered into MFN agreements with Ukraine. The third category applies to imports from other sources.
	A value-added tax of 20% is levied on most imports.
Taxes collected through the exchange system	No.
State import monopoly	No.

Exports and Export Proceeds

Repatriation requirements	Exporters must repatriate all foreign exchange proceeds through domestic commercial banks within 90 days of shipment.
Surrender requirements	Within 5 days of repatriation, 50% of proceeds must be surrendered, all of which may be sold at the auctions. Exports by foreign firms are exempt from the surrender requirement.

Export licenses

Without quotas · n.a.

With quotas · Goods subject to voluntary export restraints or other international agreements and those falling under the "special export regime"—coal, precious metal scrap, and alcoholic spirits—are also subject to export quotas and licenses. The licenses required for these goods are, however, freely provided, except in the case of precious metal scrap. For grain exports, it is required that sales for the export market be undertaken through the agricultural commodity exchange. Access to the commodity exchange is restricted to those farmers who have fulfilled their obligations under the prepaid portion of the state contract. Export contract preregistration is limited to goods subject to voluntary export restraints or antidumping actions.

Export taxes · Taxes are applied to exports of animals and skins.

Taxes collected through the exchange system · No.

Payments for Invisible Transactions and Current Transfers

Controls on these payments · There are no controls on payments for freight and insurance, unloading and storage, administrative expenses, commissions, subscriptions and membership fees, consulting and legal fees, foreign workers' wages, pensions, or interest, as well as on remittances of profits and dividends and on the use of credit cards abroad.

Payments for travel

Quantitative limits · The limit for tourists is $8,000 a person a trip and for business travel 7$10,000 a trip, not to exceed $300 a day.

Indicative limits/bona fide test · Yes.

Medical costs

Prior approval · Yes.

Indicative limits/bona fide test · Yes.

Study abroad costs

Prior approval · Yes.

Indicative limits/bona fide test · Yes.

Proceeds from Invisible Transactions and Current Transfers

Repatriation requirements · Proceeds, except those of a few organizations with international operations such as the national airlines, are subject to repatriation requirements.

Surrender requirements · Individuals who provide services to nonresidents and exporters who need to service external debt obligations of over a 90-day maturity approved by the NBU are exempted from the surrender requirement. Intermediary firms in the foreign trade sector are required to surrender 50% of their profits in foreign exchange, rather than 50% of foreign exchange revenues.

Capital Transactions

Controls on capital and money market instruments

On capital market securities

Sale or issue locally by nonresidents · An NBU license is required.

Sale or issue locally by nonresidents	n.a.
Purchase abroad by residents	Yes.
Sale or issue abroad by residents	n.a.
On collective investment securities	An individual NBU license is required.
Purchase locally by nonresidents	Yes.
Sale or issue locally by nonresidents	Yes.
Purchase abroad by residents	Yes.
Sale or issue abroad by residents	Yes.

Controls on credit operations

Commercial credits

By residents to nonresidents	NBU approval is required.
To residents from nonresidents	External loans with maturities exceeding 90 days must be approved by the NBU.

Financial credits

By residents to nonresidents	Only authorized commercial banks have the right to extend financial credits to nonresident juridical persons.
To residents from nonresidents	These credits must be licensed by or registered with the NBU.
Guarantees, sureties, and financial backup facilities	n.a.

Controls on direct investment

Outward direct investment	Investments require an individual NBU license.
Inward direct investment	Foreign investments in most types of businesses are permitted, although licenses are required in some cases. Investments in insurance and businesses engaged in intermediation activities require a license from the Ministry of Finance, and investments in the banking sector require a license from the NBU. In addition, concessions from the Council of Ministers are required for investments in the mining sector; such concessions may be for a maximum of 49 years.
	Foreign investment in Ukraine must be made in convertible currency or in kind. The Russian ruble is not regarded as convertible currency for this purpose. Tax relief is granted to enterprises established with foreign funds.
Controls on liquidation of direct investment	The transfer of proceeds, after payment of taxes due, is guaranteed.

Changes During 1996

Status under IMF Articles of Agreement	*September 23.* Ukraine accepted the obligations of Article VIII, Sections 2, 3, and 4 of the Fund Agreement.

UNITED ARAB EMIRATES

(Position as of December 31, 1996)

Status Under IMF Articles of Agreement

Article VIII	Date of acceptance: February 13, 1974.

Exchange Arrangement

Currency	The currency of the United Arab Emirates is the U.A.E. dirham.
Exchange rate structure	Unitary.
Classification	
Limited flexibility with respect to a single currency	The exchange rate of the U.A.E. dirham is pegged to the SDR at Dh 4.76190 per SDR 1 within margins of ±7.25%. The U.A.E. dirham has maintained a stable relationship with the U.S. dollar, the intervention currency, since November 1980.
Exchange tax	No.
Exchange subsidy	No.
Forward exchange market	The United Arab Emirates Central Bank (UAECB) maintains a swap facility, which the commercial banks may use to purchase dirhams spot and sell dirhams forward for periods of 1 week, 1 month, and 3 months. For each bank, maximum limits of $20 million outstanding for 1-month and 3-month swaps and $10 million outstanding for 1-week swaps are in effect. There is also a limit of $3 million a day on purchases by each bank for 1-month and 3-month swaps. This facility is designed to provide temporary dirham liquidity to commercial banks. Swap facilities are not available to banks having a short position in dirhams, except for the covering of forward transactions for commercial purposes.
Official cover of forward operations	Yes.

Arrangements for Payments and Receipts

Prescription of currency requirements	There are no prescription requirements, but settlements with Israel are prohibited.
Payment arrangements	No.
Administration of control	No.
International security restrictions	No.
Payment arrears	No.
Controls on trade in gold (coins and/or bullion)	No.
Controls on exports and imports of banknotes	No.

Resident Accounts

Eligibility to hold accounts	Juridical and natural persons are eligible.
Foreign exchange accounts permitted	Yes.
Held domestically	Yes.

Held abroad	Yes.
Accounts in domestic currency convertible into foreign currency	Yes.

Nonresident Accounts

Eligibility to hold accounts

Juridical persons	These accounts may be opened by banks and by trade, financial, and industrial companies incorporated outside the United Arab Emirates that have no local branches; by branches of local institutions in foreign countries; and by embassies and diplomatic agencies.
Natural persons	These accounts may be opened by U.A.E. citizens working abroad and by foreigners working in the United Arab Emirates who have no residency.
Foreign exchange accounts permitted	Yes.
Domestic currency accounts	Yes.
Convertible into foreign currency	Yes.
Blocked accounts	No.

Imports and Import Payments

Foreign exchange budget	No.
Financing requirements for imports	No.
Documentation requirements for release of foreign exchange for imports	No.
Import licenses and other nontariff measures	Only licensed parties can enter the import trade. Importers can import only the commodities specified in their licenses.
Negative list	Imports of a few commodities are prohibited for health, security, or moral reasons.
Other nontariff measures	Imports from Israel are prohibited, as are imports of products manufactured by foreign companies blacklisted by the Arab League.
Import taxes and/or tariffs	Most imports are subject to a customs duty of 4% of the c.i.f. value. Imports of alcohol and tobacco are subject to higher rates. Imports originating from members of the GCC are exempt from duties.
Taxes collected through the exchange system	No.
State import monopoly	No.

Exports and Export Proceeds

Repatriation requirements	No.
Surrender requirements	No.
Financing requirements	No.
Documentation requirements	No.
Export licenses	No.

Export taxes	No.

Payments for Invisible Transactions and Current Transfers

Controls on these payments	No.

Proceeds from Invisible Transactions and Current Transfers

Repatriation requirements	No.
Surrender requirements	No.
Restrictions on use of funds	No.

Capital Transactions

Controls on capital and money market instruments

On capital market securities

Purchase locally by nonresidents	At least 70% of the shares of U.A.E. corporations must be held by U.A.E. nationals or organizations.
Sale or issue locally by nonresidents	Yes.

On collective investment securities

Purchase locally by nonresidents	Yes.
Sale or issue locally by nonresidents	Yes.
Controls on derivatives and other instruments	No.
Controls on credit operations	No.

Controls on direct investment

Inward direct investment	At least 51% of the equity of companies, other than branches of foreign companies, must be held by nationals of the United Arab Emirates. Nationals of the other member countries of the GCC are permitted to hold (1) up to 75% of the equity of companies in the industrial, agricultural, fisheries, and construction sectors, and in the consultancy areas; and (2) up to 100% of the equity of companies in the hotel industry. Furthermore, nationals of the other member countries of the GCC are permitted to engage in wholesale and retail trade activities, except in the form of companies, in which case they are subject to the Company Law of 1984.
Controls on liquidation of direct investment	No.

Controls on real estate transactions

Purchase locally by nonresidents	Yes.
Provisions specific to commercial banks and other credit institutions	Commercial banks operating in the United Arab Emirates are prohibited from engaging in nonbanking operations.
Lending to nonresidents (financial or commercial credits)	Banks operating in the United Arab Emirates are required to maintain special deposits with the UAECB equal to 30% of their placements with, or lending to, nonresident banks in dirhams with a remaining life of 1 year or less. The profits of certain banks are subject to a fee levied by local authorities at an annual rate of 20%.

Provisions specific to institutional   No.
investors

Other controls imposed by securities   No.
laws

Changes During 1996

No significant changes occurred in the exchange and trade system.

UNITED KINGDOM

(Position as of December 31, 1996)

Status Under IMF Articles of Agreement

Article VIII	Date of acceptance: February 15, 1961.

Exchange Arrangement

Currency	The currency of the United Kingdom is the pound sterling.
Other legal tender	Gold sovereigns and britannias are legal tender, but do not circulate.
Exchange rate structure	
Unitary	The U.K. authorities do not maintain margins in respect of exchange transactions.
Classification	
Independent floating	The exchange rate of the pound sterling is determined on the basis of supply and demand. However, the authorities may intervene at their discretion to moderate undue fluctuations in the exchange rate. (The United Kingdom suspended intervention obligations with respect to the exchange rate and intervention mechanism of the EMS on September 16, 1992.)
Exchange tax	No.
Exchange subsidy	No.
Forward exchange market	Banks are allowed to engage in forward exchange transactions in any currency, and they may deal among themselves and with residents and nonresidents in foreign notes and coins at free market exchange rates.
Official cover of forward operations	No.

Arrangements for Payments and Receipts

Prescription of currency requirements	No.
Payment arrangements	No.
Administration of control	No.
International security restrictions	
In accordance with IMF Executive Board Decision No. 144-(52/51)	The United Kingdom notified the IMF on September 22, 1994, that, in compliance with UN Security Council Resolution Nos. 883 and 841 (1993), certain restrictions had been imposed on the making of payments and transfers for current international transactions in respect of Libya and Haiti. Sanctions against the latter were lifted in October 1994. Restrictions against Iraq, as reported to the IMF on August 13, 1990, continue to be enforced. Sanctions against the Federal Republic of Yugoslavia (Serbia/Montenegro) and the Serbian-held areas of Bosnia and Herzegovina were lifted in accordance with UN Security Council Resolution No. 1074 with immediate effect on the adoption of the resolution by the UN Security Council on October 1, 1996. In the case of the former, paragraph 5 of UN Security Council Resolution No. 1022 (1995) concerning, inter alia, funds frozen pursuant to UN Security Council Resolution Nos. 757 (1992) and 820 (1993) remains in force.
In accordance with UN sanctions	Yes.
Payment arrears	No.

Controls on trade in gold (coins and/or bullion)

Controls on domestic ownership and/or trade

Gold bullion and gold coins are not subject to controls. Gold coins have also been issued in Jersey and the Isle of Man and are legal tender there. Except under license granted by the Treasury, it is an offense to melt down or break up any metal coin that is for the time being current in the United Kingdom or that, having been current there, has at any time after May 16, 1969, ceased to be so. There is a gold market in London in which gold bars are freely traded.

Controls on external trade

The exportation of gold in manufactured form more than 50 years old and valued at £8,000 and over for each item, or matching set of items, also requires a license from the Department of National Heritage.

Controls on exports and imports of banknotes

No.

Resident Accounts

Eligibility to hold accounts

Juridical and natural persons are eligible.

Foreign exchange accounts permitted

Yes.

Held domestically

Yes.

Held abroad

Yes.

Accounts in domestic currency convertible into foreign currency

Yes.

Nonresident Accounts

Eligibility to hold accounts

Juridical and natural persons are eligible.

Foreign exchange accounts permitted

Yes.

Domestic currency accounts

Yes.

Convertible into foreign currency

Yes.

Blocked accounts

No.

Imports and Import Payments

Foreign exchange budget

No.

Financing requirements for imports

No.

Documentation requirements for release of foreign exchange for imports

No.

Import licenses and other nontariff measures

Negative list

Yes.

Open general licenses

Most imports are admitted to the United Kingdom under an open general import license.

Licenses with quotas

The remaining restrictions concern textiles and clothing under the MFA and are maintained under various EU bilateral agreements with third countries that are not members of the MFA, certain steel products from Russia and Ukraine that are subject to the EU bilateral agreements, autonomous EU-wide restrictions on imports of certain steel products from Kazakhstan, EU-wide tariff quotas on certain products produced in the Czech Republic and the Slovak Republic, and EU-wide quotas on 7 categories of goods originating in China. Imports of cars from Japan are also subject to restraint under a separate agreement (the Elements of Consensus) between the EU and the Japanese government. A few articles may be imported under open individual licenses (i.e., without limit as to quantity or value).

Other nontariff measures	Imports of cereals and cereal products, beef and veal, mutton and lamb, poultry meat, and dairy products other than butter and cheese are subject to minimum import prices enforced through autonomously imposed variable import levies. Imports of many other agricultural, horticultural, and livestock products are subject to EU regulations.
Import taxes and/or tariffs	Yes.
Taxes collected through the exchange system	No.
State import monopoly	No.

Exports and Export Proceeds

Repatriation requirements	No.
Surrender requirements	No.
Financing requirements	No.
Documentation requirements	No.
Export licenses	Exports of certain products are controlled for reasons of national security, animal welfare, national heritage, and in accordance with international agreements.
Without quotas	Yes.
Export taxes	No.

Payments for Invisible Transactions and Current Transfers

Controls on these payments	No.

Proceeds from Invisible Transactions and Current Transfers

Repatriation requirements	No.
Surrender requirements	No.
Restrictions on use of funds	No.

Capital Transactions

Controls on capital and money market instruments	No.
Controls on derivatives and other instruments	No.
Controls on credit operations	No.
Controls on direct investment	
Inward direct investment	The Secretary of State for Trade and Industry may prohibit a proposed transfer of control of an important U.K. manufacturing undertaking to a nonresident where the

transfer is considered contrary to the interests of the United Kingdom or a substantial part of it. If it is considered that the national interest cannot appropriately be protected in any other way, property in such a proposal or completed transfer may be compulsorily acquired against compensation. Both prohibition and vesting orders are subject to parliamentary approval. These powers have not been used to date.

Controls on liquidation of direct investment

No.

Controls on real estate transactions

No.

Provisions specific to commercial banks and other credit institutions

Open foreign exchange position limits

Net spot liabilities in foreign currencies (i.e., the net amount of foreign currency resources funding sterling assets) form part of a bank's eligible liabilities that are subject to a 0.35% noninterest-bearing deposit requirement with the Bank of England and may also be subject to calls for special deposits to be placed with the bank. There is currently no special deposit call.

Provisions specific to institutional investors

No.

Other controls imposed by securities laws

No.

Changes During 1996

No significant changes occurred in the exchange and trade system.

UNITED STATES

(Position as of December 31, 1996)

Status Under IMF Articles of Agreement

Article VIII   Date of acceptance: December 10, 1946.

Exchange Arrangement

Currency   The currency of the United States is the U.S. dollar.

Exchange rate structure   Unitary.

Classification

Independent floating   The exchange rate of the U.S. dollar is determined freely in the foreign exchange market.

Exchange tax   No.

Exchange subsidy   No.

Forward exchange market   Yes.

Official cover of forward operations   No.

Arrangements for Payments and Receipts

Prescription of currency requirements   No.

Payment arrangements

Barter agreements and open accounts   n.a.

Administration of control   No.

International security restrictions The Department of the Treasury administers economic sanction programs involving direct or indirect financial or commercial transactions with Cuba, the Democratic People's Republic of Korea, Iraq, Libya, foreign terrorists who disrupt the Middle East peace process, and significant narcotics traffickers centered in Colombia, as specified under the Cuban Assets Control Regulations, the Foreign Assets Control Regulations, the Iraqi Sanctions Regulations, the Libyan Sanctions Regulations, the Middle East Terrorism Regulations, and the Narcotics Trafficking Sanctions Regulations, respectively. It also has administrative responsibility for blocked accounts of the above countries and groups of persons. Sanctions against the Bosnian Serbs and the Federal Republic of Yugoslavia (Serbia/Montenegro) were suspended in 1996, although funds blocked prior to May 10, 1996, and December 27, 1995, respectively, remain blocked until released in accordance with applicable law and without prejudice to the claims of the successor states to the former Yugoslavia. The Treasury Department also restricts certain offshore transactions involving strategic merchandise to certain countries, under the Transaction Control Regulations, and donative transfers to the United States, or that pose a risk of furthering terrorist acts in the United States by the governments of Syria and Sudan, under the Terrorist List Government Sanctions Regulations.

Payment arrears   No.

Controls on trade in gold (coins and/or bullion)

Controls on external trade   No controls are imposed, except for the countries and groups of persons to which international security restrictions apply.

Controls on exports and imports of banknotes	Individuals leaving or entering the United States with more than $10,000 in domestic or foreign currency, traveler's checks, money orders, or bearer-form negotiable securities must declare these to customs at the point of exit or entry.

Resident Accounts

Eligibility to hold accounts	Juridical and natural persons are eligible.
Foreign exchange accounts permitted	Yes.
Held domestically	Yes.
Held abroad	Yes.
Accounts in domestic currency convertible into foreign currency	Yes.

Nonresident Accounts

Eligibility to hold accounts	Juridical and natural persons are eligible.
Foreign exchange accounts permitted	Yes.
Domestic currency accounts	Yes.
Convertible into foreign currency	Yes.
Blocked accounts	Accounts blocked are those of Cuba, the Democratic People's Republic of Korea, Iraq, Libya, Middle East terrorists, and significant narcotics traffickers centered in Colombia; and residual accounts are blocked under sanctions against Serbia, Montenegro, and the Bosnian Serbs.

Imports and Import Payments

Foreign exchange budget	No.
Financing requirements for imports	No.
Documentation requirements for release of foreign exchange for imports	No.
Import licenses and other nontariff measures	
Negative list	The importation of goods and services that originate in Cuba, the Islamic Republic of Iran, Iraq, the Democratic People's Republic of Korea, and Libya are prohibited unless specifically authorized by the Treasury.
Open general licenses	n.a.
Licenses with quotas	Import quotas are in effect for certain agricultural products, including cotton of specified staple lengths, some cotton waste and products, certain dairy products, peanuts, and various products containing sugar. Import quotas, except those for peanuts, certain cotton products, butter, certain other dairy products, and specific products containing sugar, are on a country-of-origin basis. Quotas may be imposed on certain types of meat under conditions set forth in the Meat Import Act of 1979. Most dairy products that are subject to quotas are also subject to import licensing. Bilateral import quota agreements on textiles and clothing exist with numerous countries, which are to be phased out over 10 years beginning in 1995 under the ATC, negotiated in the Uruguay Round of Multilateral Trade Negotiations.

The ATC provided for the gradual and complete integration of apparel and textile products into the WTO regime over a 10-year transition period, and the gradual phasing out of quantitative restrictions on textile and apparel exports to the United States. "Integrated products" have been removed from the scope of the ATC's special safeguard mechanism, and any applicable quotas have been eliminated. Integration is taking place in 4 stages: in 1995, 16% of the volume of textile and apparel trade was integrated; at the beginning of year 4 and year 7, an additional 17% and 18%, respectively, will be integrated; and after year 10, all remaining products will be integrated. With regard to the phasing out of quotas, the vast majority of quotas affecting imports to the United States will be subject to automatic "growth-on-growth" liberalization each year of the transition period.

Import taxes and/or tariffs	Import tariffs are generally low, with higher-than-average rates for imports of beverages and tobacco, textiles and clothing, and leather and footwear. As a result of the Uruguay Round, all tariff lines are bound.
Taxes collected through the exchange system	No.
State import monopoly	No.

Exports and Export Proceeds

Repatriation requirements	No.
Surrender requirements	No.
Financing requirements	No.
Documentation requirements	No.
Export licenses	Exports of goods and services to the countries on the negative list are prohibited unless specifically authorized by the Treasury Department, or, in the cases of Cuba and the Democratic People's Republic of Korea, the Department of Commerce.
Without quotas	Ammunition may be exported only under license issued by the Office of Defense Trade Controls in the Department of State. The Department of Commerce administers controls directly on exports of crime control and detection equipment, as well as on instruments and related technical data, to all countries except other members of NATO, Australia, Japan, and New Zealand. The Department of Commerce administers controls directly on exports of other goods from the United States and on reexports of goods of U.S. origin from any area.
Export taxes	n.a.
Taxes collected through the exchange system	No.

Payments for Invisible Transactions and Current Transfers

Controls on these payments	No.

Proceeds from Invisible Transactions and Current Transfers

Repatriation requirements	No.
Surrender requirements	No.
Restrictions on use of funds	No.

Capital Transactions

Controls on capital and money market instruments

On capital market securities

Purchase locally by nonresidents — Laws on inward direct investment apply to purchases in the United States by nonresidents. The restriction applies only to the purchases by nonresidents of securities that may be restricted by laws on inward direct investment and establishment in the nuclear energy, maritime, communications, and air transport industries.

Sale or issue locally by nonresidents — Foreign mutual funds are restricted. This restriction applies only to (1) nonresident issuers that are defined as investment companies under the Investment Company Act of 1940, and (2) the use of small business registration forms and a small-issues exemption by nonresident issuers.

On money market instruments

Sale or issue locally by nonresidents — Foreign mutual funds are restricted. The restriction applies only to nonresident issuers that are defined as investment companies under the Investment Company Act of 1940.

Controls on derivatives and other instruments — No.

Controls on credit operations — No.

Financial credits

By residents to nonresidents — The Johnson Act prohibits, with certain exceptions, persons within the United States from dealing in financial obligations or extending loans to foreign governments that have defaulted on payments of their obligations to the U.S. government. The Act does not apply to those foreign governments that are members of both the IMF and the World Bank.

Controls on direct investment

Inward direct investment — Foreign acquisitions that threaten to impair national security may be suspended or prohibited. Investments involving ownership interest in banks are subject to federal and state banking laws and regulations. However, as noted above, there are restrictions on certain transactions with or involving Cuba, Iraq, the Democratic People's Republic of Korea, Libya, foreign terrorists who disrupt the Middle East peace process, significant narcotics traffickers centered in Colombia, and certain foreign terrorist governments. The Omnibus Trade Act (1988) contained a provision, the Exxon-Florio Amendment, authorizing the president to suspend or prohibit foreign acquisitions, mergers, and takeovers in the United States if he determines that the foreign investor might take action that would threaten to impair national security and if existing laws, other than the International Emergency Powers Act and the Exxon-Florio Amendment itself, are not, in the president's judgment, adequate or appropriate to protect national security.

Controls on liquidation of direct investment — No.

Controls on real estate transactions — No.

Purchase locally by nonresidents — Ownership of agricultural land by foreign nationals or by corporations in which foreign owners have an interest of at least 10% or substantial control must be reported to the Department of Agriculture. Certain states in the United States impose various restrictions on foreign nationals' purchases of land within their borders.

Provisions specific to commercial banks and other credit institutions — No.

Provisions specific to institutional investors — No.

Other controls imposed by securities laws	No.

Changes During 1996

Arrangements for payments and receipts	*January 16.* Sanctions against the Federal Republic of Yugoslavia (Serbia/Montenegro) were suspended, effective retroactively on December 27, 1995.
	May 10. Sanctions against the Bosnian Serbs were suspended.
Resident accounts	*August 22.* Donative transfers or transfers that pose a risk of furthering terrorist acts in the United States from the governments of Syria and Sudan were prohibited.

URUGUAY

(Position as of January 31, 1997)

Status Under IMF Articles of Agreement

Article VIII	Date of acceptance: May 2, 1980.

Exchange Arrangement

Currency

The currency of Uruguay is the Uruguayan peso.

Exchange rate structure

Unitary.

Classification

Managed floating

The exchange rate for the Uruguayan peso is determined in the exchange market, where the Central Bank of Uruguay (CBU) intervenes to ensure that the rate remains within a 7% band. The exchange rate band is depreciated monthly at a predetermined rate; the rate was lowered to 1.8% from 2% in April 1996 and to 1.4% in September 1996. The CBU announces its intervention buying and selling rates daily.

Exchange tax

Purchases of foreign exchange by public sector institutions are subject to a tax of 2%, with the exception of those by the CBU and official banks, which are exempt from the tax.

Exchange subsidy

No.

Forward exchange market

No.

Arrangements for Payments and Receipts

Prescription of currency requirements

All settlements of balances under the multilateral clearing system are made in U.S. dollars.

Payment arrangements

Bilateral arrangements

Operative

An arrangement with the Islamic Republic of Iran was effective until January 1997.

Inoperative

Bilateral arrangements with Cuba are inoperative.

Regional arrangements

Payments between Uruguay and the countries with which Uruguay has concluded reciprocal credit arrangements (i.e., Argentina, Bolivia, Brazil, Chile, Colombia, the Dominican Republic, Ecuador, Mexico, Paraguay, Peru, and Venezuela) may be made through accounts maintained with each other by the central banks within the framework of the multilateral clearing system of the LAIA.

Administration of control

Exchange control authorities

Exchange transactions are carried out through authorized banks, finance houses, exchange houses, and the Bank of the Republic. Exchange houses must be authorized by the CBU.

International security restrictions

No.

Payment arrears

No.

Controls on trade in gold (coins and/or bullion)

Controls on domestic ownership and/or trade

Residents and nonresidents may freely purchase, hold, and sell financial gold with a fineness of not less than 0.9.

Controls on external trade	Residents may freely import and export gold with a fineness of not less than 0.9. Gold for industrial purposes is subject to the general policy that governs the exportation, importation, and trading of goods.
Controls on exports and imports of banknotes	No.

Resident Accounts

Eligibility to hold accounts	Juridical and natural persons are eligible.
Foreign exchange accounts permitted	Yes.
Held domestically	Yes.
Held abroad	Yes.
Accounts in domestic currency convertible into foreign currency	Yes.

Nonresident Accounts

Eligibility to hold accounts	Juridical and natural persons are eligible.
Foreign exchange accounts permitted	Yes.
Domestic currency accounts	Yes.
Convertible into foreign currency	Yes.
Blocked accounts	No.

Imports and Import Payments

Foreign exchange budget	No.
Financing requirements for imports	No.
Documentation requirements for release of foreign exchange for imports	No.
Import licenses and other nontariff measures	
Negative list	Imports of used cars are prohibited.
Open general licenses	All imports are subject to registration that is generally valid for 180 days; goods must be cleared through customs during that period.
Import taxes and/or tariffs	Under MERCOSUR, a common external tariff (CET) exists among Argentina, Brazil, Paraguay, and Uruguay. It consists of 11 rates of up to 20%. Regionally produced capital and telecommunications goods are subject to tariffs of 14% and 16%, respectively. Parties to MERCOSUR are permitted to exempt up to 300 goods from the CET until the year 2001, at which time they are to converge to the CET. In addition, for Uruguay tariffs on capital goods, telecommunications, buses, and trucks will not converge until 2006.
	Import duties among MERCOSUR countries were generally eliminated, with certain exceptions. In Uruguay's case, exemptions on pharmaceuticals, plastics, automobile parts, textiles, and dairy products may remain in place through 1999. Duties on wheat,

tires, paper, glass, sugar, textiles, and apparel are computed on the basis of "minimum export prices," which provide a basis for a sliding surcharge on these goods depending on the difference between the minimum prices and declared c.i.f. import prices.

Taxes collected through the exchange system	No.
State import monopoly	No.

Exports and Export Proceeds

Repatriation requirements	No.
Surrender requirements	No.
Financing requirements	No.
Documentation requirements	No.
Export licenses	
Without quotas	Occasionally, and for special reasons (for example, stock position, protection, or sanitary considerations), certain exports are prohibited or are subject to special requirements.
Export taxes	Exports of dry, salted, and pickled hides are subject to a 5% tax.
Taxes collected through the exchange system	No.

Payments for Invisible Transactions and Current Transfers

Controls on these payments	No.

Proceeds from Invisible Transactions and Current Transfers

Repatriation requirements	No.
Surrender requirements	No.
Restrictions on use of funds	No.

Capital Transactions

Controls on capital and money market instruments	Uruguayan security market legislation allows for autoregulation in the stock markets, under the supervision of the CBU. The establishments that are regulated are financial intermediaries, insurance companies, and pension fund managers, which have their own regime. In the public sector, the type of operations permitted depends on the type of institution. Government agencies are covered by their own bylaws, and the central government and departmental governments are covered by their own procedures, which are more restrictive.
Controls on derivatives and other instruments	There are no regulations on derivative operations on the security market, as these instruments, even for commodities, do not exist in Uruguay.
Controls on credit operations	No.
Controls on direct investment	No.
Controls on liquidation of direct investment	No.

Controls on real estate transactions No.

Provisions specific to commercial banks and other credit institutions

Differential treatment of nonresident deposit accounts and/or deposit accounts in foreign exchange

    Reserve requirements There is a minimum mandatory reserve requirement (10%) for local currency and another for foreign currency, except for 30- to 180-day deposits, on which the local currency reserve requirement is 4% and the foreign currency reserve requirement is 10%. These reserve requirements are for currency holdings and notes, and demand deposits at the CBU in their respective currencies. Nonresident deposits placed with nonresidents are exempt from the foreign currency reserve requirement. Also, when establishing such reserves, the deposit at the CBU should be in an amount of not less than 50% of the minimum mandatory reserve requirement. There is a minimum interest-bearing mandatory reserve requirement of 10% in local currency on total deposits and other obligations covered by the non-interest-bearing reserve requirement regime. This reserve requirement can be established by a deposit at the CBU. There is also an 11.5% mandatory holding in dollar-denominated treasury notes on foreign currency deposits and liabilities under the reserve requirement regime, excluding those of nonresidents applying to placements with nonresidents.

Open foreign exchange position limits There is a ceiling on local and foreign currency-holding positions of 150% of the book value of equity less administrative fixed assets. There is also a ceiling on the asset or liability position of foreign-currency-denominated "operations to be settled" (i.e., future contracts and sales of securities subject to repurchase agreements) of 20% of the book value equity (i.e., fixed assets, investments, and deferred charges) less administrative fixed assets.

Provisions specific to institutional investors No.

Other controls imposed by securities laws No.

Changes During 1996

Exchange arrangements *April 1.* The monthly rate of depreciation of the exchange rate band was lowered to 1.8% from 2%.

September 1. The monthly rate of depreciation of the exchange rate band was lowered to 1.4% from 1.8%.

Capital transactions *May 30.* A new legal framework regulating the public offering of private securities was approved.

September 27. A law regulating investment funds was approved.

Changes During 1997

Arrangements for payments and receipts *January 31.* The bilateral payments agreement with the Islamic Republic of Iran ceased.

UZBEKISTAN

(Position as of January 31, 1997)

Status Under IMF Articles of Agreement

Article XIV	Yes.

Exchange Arrangement

Currency

The currency of Uzbekistan is the Uzbek sum.

Exchange rate structure

Multiple

There is an official exchange rate, established by the Central Bank of Uzbekistan (CBU), a rate freely established by authorized banks incorporating commissions (the spread (i.e., the commission) between the official rate and the exchange rate of authorized banks is currently set at 12%), and a cash rate resulting from cash transactions by natural persons at exchange bureaus. On January 1, 1997, the interbank rate became the rate that is applied to purchases of foreign exchange for payments of imports of most goods and other current transactions.

Classification

Managed floating

Since January 1, 1997, the official exchange rate of the sum vis-à-vis foreign currencies has been determined weekly taking into account current rates and transaction volumes on the currency exchange and in the over-the-counter market as well as changes in the most important macroeconomic indicators. Exchange rates for currencies that are not traded are determined from cross rates in the international market.

Exchange tax

No.

Exchange subsidy

No.

Forward exchange market

No.

Arrangements for Payments and Receipts

Prescription of currency requirements

Settlements with countries with which Uzbekistan maintains bilateral payment agreements are effected in accordance with the terms of the agreements. Under agreements with Belarus, Kazakhstan, Russia, and Ukraine, trade in local currency is permitted. Transactions with other countries are settled in convertible currencies.

Payment arrangements

Bilateral arrangements

Operative

Uzbekistan maintains agreements with Belarus, Kazakhstan, Latvia, Moldova, Russia, and Ukraine.

Inoperative

Agreements with Indonesia, the Islamic Republic of Iran, and Malaysia are inoperative.

Administration of control

Exchange control authorities

The CBU is responsible for foreign exchange regulations and the supervision of authorized banks. The Ministry of Foreign Economic Relations (MFER) is responsible for negotiating trade agreements with nontraditional trading partners, as well as those agreements denominated in hard currency with traditional trading partners. It is also responsible for implementing foreign trade agreements and external trade policy through the issuance of export licenses and quotas. The Ministry of Justice is responsible for approving foreign direct investment in the form of joint ventures.

International security restrictions

No.

Payment arrears	No.
Controls on trade in gold (coins and/or bullion)	
Controls on domestic ownership and/or trade	Yes.
Controls on external trade	With the exception of jewelry and collectibles, trade in gold is prohibited. However, joint ventures operating in the precious metals sector are free to export a portion of their output, corresponding to the share of profits of the foreign participant. Emigrants are allowed to take out of the country 100 grams of gold and 200 grams of silver in the form of jewelry or personal effects.
Controls on exports and imports of banknotes	
On exports	
Foreign currency	Nonresident individuals taking out foreign currency in excess of $2,000 of what they declared upon entering the country, with no receipts to show that the money was legally converted or how the money was spent, are subject to a 30% fee on the undocumented amount. Residents are limited to exporting $500 unless permission is granted by the CBU or the National Bank for Foreign Economic Activity. Legal entities are not allowed to export foreign banknotes.
On imports	
Foreign currency	Individuals importing more than $5,000 in banknotes are subject to a fee of 2% of the amount of foreign exchange imported. Legal entities are not allowed to import foreign banknotes.

Resident Accounts

Eligibility to hold accounts	Juridical and natural persons are eligible.
Foreign exchange accounts permitted	Yes.
Held domestically	Yes.
Held abroad	The CBU may approve accounts abroad on a case-by-case basis.
Accounts in domestic currency convertible into foreign currency	Yes.

Nonresident Accounts

Eligibility to hold accounts	Juridical and natural persons are eligible.
Foreign exchange accounts permitted	These accounts are permitted, but evidence must be furnished that the amounts involved were lawfully obtained.
Domestic currency accounts	Yes.
Convertible into foreign currency	Importers must present a preregistered contract before they can purchase foreign exchange.
Blocked accounts	De facto, local currency accounts of importers may be blocked (with the consent of the latter) by the banks while awaiting conversion.

Imports and Import Payments

Foreign exchange budget	No.

Financing requirements for imports	No.
Documentation requirements for release of foreign exchange for imports	There is a central bank licensing system whereby a $100 registration fee is paid by previous license holders and a $2,000 fee is paid by new importers for access to the foreign exchange auction to purchase foreign exchange for payment of consumer goods imports and related services. As of November 1, 1996, all import contracts are subject to preregistration with the MFER.
Import licenses and other nontariff measures	Imports of medicines, weapons, precious metals, uranium and other radioactive substances, foreign motion pictures and videos, and research data require import licenses from the MFER.
Negative list	The importation of publications, manuscripts, video and audio equipment, and photographs aimed at undermining state and social order are prohibited.
Import taxes and/or tariffs	Until end-March 1996, import tariffs ranged from 5% to 100% on 91 products, with 73 items being levied rates of 5%, 10%, or 20%. A 100% rate applies to used motor vehicles. On April 1, 1996, a new tariff schedule was introduced that reduced to 56 the number of items subject to tariffs ranging from 5% to 100% and to 47 the items subject to tariffs ranging from 5% to 20%. On November 1, 1996, new import duties established rates of 5% to 100% on 91 commodities or groups of commodities; additionally, a 1% duty was established on all imports not covered by another import duty. Effective September 23, 1996, excise taxes of 20% to 35% were imposed on 6 categories of consumer goods imports.
Taxes collected through the exchange system	No.
State import monopoly	No.

Exports and Export Proceeds

Repatriation requirements	Yes.
Surrender requirements	Proceeds in convertible currencies are subject to a 30% requirement. Receipts from transactions with the Baltic countries, Russia, and other countries of the FSU were subject to a 15% requirement until January 1, 1997, when requirements were unified at 30%.
Financing requirements	No.
Documentation requirements	
Letters of credit	Yes.
Guarantees	Yes.
Export licenses	Exports of medicines, weapons, precious metals, uranium and other radioactive substances, foreign motion pictures and videos, and research data require licenses from the MFER.
Without quotas	A system of automatic licensing exists for cotton exports.
With quotas	Exportation of nonferrous metals, crude oil, gas condensate, gasoline, diesel fuel, lint and cotton fiber, and ferrous metals is subject to export licensing in the amount of established quotas.
Export taxes	Export tariffs range from 5% to 100% on 73 products, with 66 items in the 10% to 50% range. On April 1, 1996, a new schedule of export tariffs established rates of 5% to 100% for 83 commodities or groups of commodities, the majority of which (59 items) are in the 5%, 10%, 15%, 20%, or 30% categories. The 100% rate applies only to exports of art objects and antiques.
Taxes collected through the exchange system	No.

Other export taxes	An excise tax of 50% is imposed on exports of 11 electronic consumer goods, and a tax of 25% is imposed on reexports.

Payments for Invisible Transactions and Current Transfers

Controls on these payments	No.

Proceeds from Invisible Transactions and Current Transfers

Repatriation requirements	Yes.
Surrender requirements	Proceeds earned by juridical entities are subject to the same requirements as those applicable to proceeds from exports.
Restrictions on use of funds	No.

Capital Transactions

Controls on capital and money market instruments	
On capital market securities	Yes.
On money market instruments	Yes.
On collective investment securities	Yes.
Controls on derivatives and other instruments	
Purchase locally by nonresidents	Yes.
Sale or issue locally by nonresidents	Yes.
Purchase abroad by residents	Yes.
Sale or issue abroad by residents	Yes.
Controls on credit operations	
Commercial credits	Yes.
Financial credits	Yes.
Guarantees, sureties, and financial backup facilities	Yes.
Controls on direct investment	
Outward direct investment	Yes.
Inward direct investment	Enterprises may establish joint ventures as foreign direct investment with the approval of the Ministry of Justice. Foreign equity capital participation is allowed up to 100%.
Controls on liquidation of direct investment	No.
Controls on real estate transactions	
Purchase locally by nonresidents	Yes.
Sale locally by nonresidents	Yes.
Provisions specific to commercial banks and other credit institutions	
Borrowing abroad	Yes.

Maintenance of accounts abroad	Permission from the CBU is required.
Lending to nonresidents (financial or commercial credits)	Yes.
Lending locally in foreign exchange	Since December 1996, banks have been allowed to make loans in foreign currencies, subject to the limit on the foreign currency open position.
Differential treatment of nonresident deposit accounts and/or deposit accounts in foreign exchange	
Reserve requirements	Yes.
Liquid asset requirements	Yes.
Interest rate controls	Yes.
Investment regulations	Yes.
Open foreign exchange position limits	Yes.
Provisions specific to institutional investors	
Limits (min.) on portfolio invested locally	Yes.
Other controls imposed by securities laws	No.

Changes During 1996

Imports and import payments	*April 1.* A new schedule of import tariffs established rates of 5% to 100% for 56 commodities or groups of commodities, the majority of which (47 items) are in the 5%, 10%, and 20% categories. The 100% rate applies solely to used vehicles.
	September 23. Excise taxes ranging from 20% to 35% were imposed on 6 categories of consumer goods imports.
	November 1. All import contracts were subject to preregistration with the MFER, and registration was required to obtain foreign exchange.
	November 1. New import duties established rates of 5% to 100% on 91 commodities or groups of commodities; additionally, a 1% duty was established on all imports not covered by another import duty.
Exports and export proceeds	*April 1.* A new schedule of export tariffs established rates of 5% to 100% for 83 commodities or groups of commodities, the majority of which (59 items) are in the 5%, 10%, 15%, 20%, or 30% categories. The 100% rate applies only to the exportation of art objects and antiques (with the authorization of the Ministry for Cultural Affairs).
Capital transactions	*December 13.* Banks were allowed to lend locally in foreign currencies to enterprises with foreign participation for project financing, subject to the limit on the foreign currency open position.

Changes During 1997

Exchange arrangements	*January 1.* The interbank rate became the rate applied to purchases of foreign exchange for payments of imports of most goods and for other current transactions.
Exports and export proceeds	*January 1.* Surrender requirements were unified at 30% for all receipts, including those from exports in convertible currencies and those to the Baltic countries, Russia, and the other FSU countries. Proceeds should be surrendered to authorized banks (on the over-the-counter market).

VANUATU

(Position as of December 31, 1996)

Status Under IMF Articles of Agreement

Article VIII   Date of acceptance: December 11, 1982.

Exchange Arrangement

Currency	The currency of Vanuatu is the vatu.
Exchange rate structure	Unitary.
Classification	
Pegged	The external value of the vatu is determined on the basis of an undisclosed transactions-weighted (trade and tourism receipts) basket of currencies of Vanuatu's major trading partners. The Reserve Bank of Vanuatu (RBV) buys from and sells to commercial banks U.S. dollars only. However, it also deals in pounds sterling, French francs, Australian dollars, deutsche mark, New Zealand dollars, and Japanese yen with other customers. The RBV quotes rates daily for the vatu against the above currencies. Buying and selling rates of the vatu against the currencies in the basket are quoted twice a day within margins ranging between 0.25% and 0.30% around the middle rate.
Exchange tax	No.
Exchange subsidy	No.
Forward exchange market	Commercial banks provide forward exchange rate cover facilities.
Official cover of forward operations	No.

Arrangements for Payments and Receipts

Prescription of currency requirements	No.
Payment arrangements	No.
Administration of control	No.
Payment arrears	No.
Controls on trade in gold (coins and/or bullion)	No.
Controls on exports and imports of banknotes	No.

Resident Accounts

Eligibility to hold accounts	Juridical and natural persons are eligible.
Foreign exchange accounts permitted	Yes.
Held domestically	Yes.
Held abroad	Yes.
Accounts in domestic currency convertible into foreign currency	Yes.

Nonresident Accounts

Eligibility to hold accounts — Juridical and natural persons are eligible.

Foreign exchange accounts permitted — Yes.

Domestic currency accounts — Yes.

Convertible into foreign currency — Yes.

Blocked accounts — No.

Imports and Import Payments

Foreign exchange budget — No.

Financing requirements for imports — No.

Documentation requirements for release of foreign exchange for imports — No.

Import licenses and other nontariff measures — The importation of frozen chicken, chicken pieces, T-shirts bearing a Vanuatu motif, firearms and ammunition, animals and plants, and transistor and telephone equipment is restricted through import-licensing arrangements. A similar restriction is applied to the importation of five basic products—rice, sugar, flour, canned fish, and tobacco products.

Positive list — Yes.

Import taxes and/or tariffs — Customs duties are levied mainly on an ad valorem basis on c.i.f. values, but alcoholic beverages, tobacco products, and petroleum products are subject to specific duties. Higher duty rates apply to goods that compete with domestically produced goods. A customs service charge of 5% is applied to most imports, based on duty-inclusive values.

Under an agreement amended in December 1995, certain products (frozen beef, canned tuna, tea, coffee, yogurt, cheese and curd, wooden furniture, kava, jam, fruit jellies, portland cement, matches, fiberglass boats, toilet paper, iron and steel nails, and plastic shopping bags) may be shipped duty free between Vanuatu, Solomon Islands, and Papua New Guinea.

Goods imported by the government and funded by external aid, goods imported for sale to and exported by tourists, ships' stores, goods imported for processing and reexportation, and goods imported for investment projects are exempt from duties.

Taxes collected through the exchange system — No.

State import monopoly — No.

Exports and Export Proceeds

Repatriation requirements — No.

Surrender requirements — No.

Financing requirements — No.

Documentation requirements — No.

Export licenses — The exportation of logs has been banned for environmental reasons.

Without quotas — Exports of certain products, such as trochus, green snails, bêches-de-mer, mother-of-pearl, aquarium fish, and crustaceans, as well as coconut crops for conservation purposes, are subject to authorization. Exports of copra, cocoa, and kava are channeled through the Vanuatu Commodities Marketing Board (VCMB); however, exports of kava can be undertaken by individuals subject to authorization from the VCMB. Artifacts having a special value, either as a result of ceremonial use or because they are more than 10 years old, are subject to authorization from the Cultural Center.

Export taxes

Most exports are subject to export duties, mainly on an ad valorem basis. Specific duties are levied on exports of timber products and a few other items.

Taxes collected through the exchange system

No.

Payments for Invisible Transactions and Current Transfers

Controls on these payments   No.

Proceeds from Invisible Transactions and Current Transfers

Repatriation requirements   No.

Surrender requirements   No.

Restrictions on use of funds   No.

Capital Transactions

Controls on capital and money market instruments   No.

Controls on derivatives and other instruments   No.

Controls on credit operations   No.

Controls on direct investment   No.

Controls on liquidation of direct investment   No.

Controls on real estate transactions   No.

Provisions specific to commercial banks and other credit institutions   No.

Provisions specific to institutional investors   No.

Other controls imposed by securities laws   No.

Changes During 1996

No significant changes occurred in the exchange and trade system.

VENEZUELA

(Position as of January 31, 1997)

Status Under IMF Articles of Agreement

Article VIII	Date of acceptance: July 1, 1976.

Exchange Arrangement

Currency	The currency of Venezuela is the bolívar.
Other legal tender	Venezuelan gold coins are legal tender, but they do not circulate.
Exchange rate structure	
Unitary	On April 22, 1996, the existing exchange rates—a legal parallel market rate for trading on local securities exchanges of foreign-currency-denominated government bonds trading on the secondary market ("Brady bonds"), and an exchange rate applicable to tourism, and credit card transactions temporarily introduced in October 1995—were unified.
Classification	
Managed floating	On July 8, 1996, an exchange rate band of ±7.5% around the central rate was introduced with an initial rate of Bs 470 per $1. During the remainder of 1996, the central rate was adjusted in line with the inflation target for the first quarter of 1996, i.e., 1.5% a month. On January 2, 1997, the central rate of the band of ±7.5% was set at Bs 472 per $1. During the rest of 1997, the central rate will be adjusted in line with the inflation target for 1997, i.e., 1.32% a month. The exchange rate is determined by supply and demand, but the Central Bank of Venezuela (CBV) intervenes in the market. The CBV determines the reference exchange rate daily.
Exchange tax	No.
Exchange subsidy	No.

Arrangements for Payments and Receipts

Prescription of currency requirements	No.
Payment arrangements	
Regional arrangements	Yes.
Clearing agreements	Payments between Venezuela and Argentina, Bolivia, Brazil, Chile, Colombia, Cuba, the Dominican Republic, Ecuador, Jamaica, Malaysia, Mexico, Peru, and Uruguay may be settled through the accounts maintained with each other at the CBV.
Administration of control	The Exchange Administration Board (EAB) and the associated Technical Administration Office were responsible for the administration of exchange transactions until April 22, 1996, when the EAB was closed with the elimination of exchange controls.
International security restrictions	No.
Payment arrears	Arrears are maintained on interest payments related to external debt.
Official	Yes.
Private	Yes.
Controls on trade in gold (coins and/or bullion)	
Controls on external trade	The exportation of nonmonetary gold (other than jewelry for personal use) and gold coins is subject to prior authorization from the CBV.

914

Controls on exports and imports of banknotes	Exports and imports of banknotes were subject to declaration to customs, before the elimination of exchange controls.

Resident Accounts

Eligibility to hold accounts	Juridical and natural persons are eligible.
Foreign exchange accounts permitted	Yes.
Held domestically	Yes.
Held abroad	Yes.
Accounts in domestic currency convertible into foreign currency	No.

Nonresident Accounts

Eligibility to hold accounts	Juridical and natural persons are eligible.
Foreign exchange accounts permitted	Yes.
Domestic currency accounts	Yes.
Convertible into foreign currency	No.
Blocked accounts	No.

Imports and Import Payments

Foreign exchange budget	No.
Financing requirements for imports	On April 22, 1996, when exchange rates were unified under a managed floating system, all import requirements were abolished.
Documentation requirements for release of foreign exchange for imports	Until April 22, 1996, applications for the purchase of foreign exchange for all imports in excess of $5,000 were approved by the EAB.
Letters of credit	Letters of credit were required for importers using the LAIA facility until April 22, 1996.
Import licenses and other nontariff measures	Some imports are subject to licensing for environmental, health, or security reasons.
Positive list	Imports of military arms must be authorized by the Defense Ministry. Imports of nonmilitary weapons must be authorized by the Ministry of Domestic Affairs. Some 24 tariff items, of which 7 are chemicals and about 17 are agro-industrial products, require approval from the import office.
Negative list	Importation of used motor vehicles is prohibited, except for hearses, prison vans, and ambulances.
Licenses with quotas	A very small number of agricultural products are subject to quantitative restrictions.
Import taxes and/or tariffs	There are 4 basic ad valorem tariff rates on manufactured goods (5%, 10%, 15%, and 20%), except for motor vehicles, which are subject to a special regime under the Andean Pact. The common external tariff on motor vehicles is 35% for passenger cars, 15% for cargo and commercial vehicles (except for vehicles under 4,500 kg, such as pickup trucks, for which the rate is 25%), and 3% for vehicle components and parts manufactured in member countries. Specific duties apply to agricultural products and certain other products (e.g., mineral fuels, oil, mineral wax, distilled products, and bituminous

substances). The industrial free zone of Paraguana and the free port of Margarita Island enjoy a special customs regime that includes exemptions from customs tariffs. Duty-free access is granted to imports from Colombia, Ecuador, and CARICOM countries under trade agreements.

Taxes collected through the exchange system	No.
State import monopoly	No.

Exports and Export Proceeds

Repatriation requirements	No.
Surrender requirements	Requirements were abolished on April 22, 1996. The state petroleum company (PDVSA) is required to surrender its export proceeds to the CBV.
Financing requirements	No.
Documentation requirements	No.
Export licenses	For certain products, licenses are required.
Without quotas	Yes.
Export taxes	Exports of agricultural commodities (except those destined to Andean Pact countries) are entitled to a fiscal credit of 10% of f.o.b. value in the form of a negotiable bond used for tax payments that is issued by the Ministry of Finance. There is a duty drawback system for manufactured products. There is an export tax on hydrocarbons.
Taxes collected through the exchange system	Export proceeds of PDVSA, the state petroleum company, were subject to a surtax of 4% until the end of 1996.

Payments for Invisible Transactions and Current Transfers

Controls on these payments	Until April 22, 1996, when controls on these payments were eliminated, all transfers for invisibles had to be authorized by the EAB, except for purchases of foreign exchange for travel and remittances abroad, which were subject to annual limits.

Proceeds from Invisible Transactions and Current Transfers

Repatriation requirements	Yes.
Surrender requirements	Requirements were abolished on April 22, 1996.
Restrictions on use of funds	No.

Capital Transactions

Controls on capital and money market instruments	
On capital market securities	
Purchase locally by nonresidents	Foreign investors are allowed to purchase corporate stocks in the Caracas Stock Exchange but must inform the Superintendency of Foreign Investment (SIEX) of such purchases at the end of each calendar year.
Sale or issue locally by nonresidents	These transactions must be authorized by the Comisión Nacional de Valores (CNV), taking into account the government's opinion.

Sale or issue abroad by residents	Authorization by the CNV is required.
On collective investment securities	
Sale or issue locally by nonresidents	Authorization by the CNV is required.
Controls on derivatives and other instruments	There are no regulations concerning derivatives, options, and futures.
Controls on credit operations	No.
Controls on direct investment	
Inward direct investment	Mass media, communications, newspapers in Spanish, and security services are reserved for national ownership. New investments do not require prior authorization from the SIEX but must be registered with the SIEX after the fact, and approval is automatically granted if the new investment is consistent with national legislation. Foreign enterprises may establish subsidiaries in Venezuela without prior authorization as long as they are consistent with the Commercial Code. The SIEX must, however, be notified within 60 working days about newly established subsidiaries. Investment in the petroleum and iron sectors is subject to specific regulations.
Controls on liquidation of direct investment	No.
Controls on real estate transactions	No.
Provisions specific to commercial banks and other credit institutions	
Lending locally in foreign exchange	Local banks can make loans denominated in foreign exchange.
Purchase of locally issued securities denominated in foreign exchange	There are limits regulated by the CBV in relation to foreign exchange position limits.
Differential treatment of nonresident deposit accounts and/or deposit accounts in foreign exchange	
Reserve requirements	Reserve requirements of 12% apply to all deposits.
Investment regulations	Commercial banks are not allowed to invest in stocks in excess of 20% of paid-in capital.
Open foreign exchange position limits	The net position cannot exceed 25% of banks' capital.
Provisions specific to institutional investors	No.
Other controls imposed by securities laws	No.

Changes During 1996

Exchange arrangements	*April 22.* The exchange rates were unified and exchange controls were eliminated.
	July 8. An exchange rate band of ±7.50% around the rate of Bs 470 per $1 was introduced.
Arrangements for payments and receipts	*April 22.* The Exchange Administration Board (EAB) and the associated Technical Administration Office, which were responsible for the administration of the exchange controls, were closed.
Resident accounts	*April 22.* Foreign exchange accounts were permitted to be held domestically.
Imports and import payments	*April 22.* All import requirements were abolished.

Exports and export proceeds	*April 22.* Repatriation requirements, except for PDVSA, were abolished.
	December 31. The 4% surtax on PDVSA export proceeds was eliminated.
Payments for invisible transactions and current transfers	*April 22.* Controls on these transactions were eliminated.
Capital transactions	*April 22.* Lending locally in foreign exchange was permitted.

Changes During 1997

Exchange arrangements	*January 2.* The central rate of the band of ±7.5% was set at Bs 472 per $1. During the rest of 1997, the central rate will be adjusted in line with the inflation target for 1997, i.e., 1.32% a month.

VIETNAM

(Position as of December 31, 1996)

Status Under IMF Articles of Agreement

Article XIV	Yes.

Exchange Arrangement

Currency	The currency of Vietnam is the dong.
Exchange rate structure	Unitary.
Classification	
Managed floating	Trading in the interbank market must take place at exchange rates within ranges stipulated daily by the State Bank of Vietnam (SBV). Only the SBV, state-owned banks, such as the Bank of Investment and Development, joint-stock banks, joint-venture banks, and branches of foreign banks may participate in the exchange market.
Exchange tax	No.
Exchange subsidy	No.
Forward exchange market	Yes.
Official cover of forward operations	No.

Arrangements for Payments and Receipts

Prescription of currency requirements	No.
Payment arrangements	
Clearing agreements	There is an agreement with Cambodia.
Administration of control	
Exchange control authorities	Exchange control is administered by the SBV.
Payment arrears	
Official	Yes.
Private	n.a.
Controls on trade in gold (coins and/or bullion)	
Controls on domestic ownership and/or trade	n.a.
Controls on external trade	Gold may be brought into the country, provided that required customs declarations are made and a customs tariff is paid; nonresidents are entitled to export gold up to the amount they brought in. The importation of gold by residents requires a license from the SBV.

Resident Accounts

Eligibility to hold accounts	Juridical and natural persons are eligible.
Foreign exchange accounts permitted	Organizations and enterprises must deposit all foreign exchange proceeds in foreign exchange accounts at domestic commercial banks that are licensed to conduct foreign

exchange business. Limits on foreign exchange holdings in such accounts are set by the commercial banks applying rules set by the SBV. Deposits in excess of those limits must be sold to the commercial banks.

Held domestically	Yes.
Held abroad	Firms in the aviation, shipping, postal, and insurance sectors, as well as commercial banks, finance companies, and other firms permitted to open branches abroad, may be granted permission to deposit foreign currency receipts from invisible transactions in foreign accounts. Prior approval is required.
Accounts in domestic currency convertible into foreign currency	These accounts may be maintained by Vietnamese enterprises that import goods and make payments for foreign services, and by foreign enterprises that produce import substitutes and build infrastructure.

Nonresident Accounts

Eligibility to hold accounts	Juridical and natural persons are eligible.
Foreign exchange accounts permitted	Yes.
Domestic currency accounts	No.
Blocked accounts	No.

Imports and Import Payments

Foreign exchange budget	The budget is indicative only and therefore, not binding.
Financing requirements for imports	No.
Documentation requirements for release of foreign exchange for imports	No.
Import licenses and other nontariff measures	Foreign trade enterprises require only a trading license. Some imports require a license issued by the Ministry of Trade.
Negative list	Imports of weapons, ammunition and explosives, and military equipment; drugs and toxic chemicals; dangerous and unhealthy cultural products; "reactionary and depraved" cultural products; fireworks and children's toys that detrimentally influence personality, education, social order, and safety; most used consumer goods; most used equipment operating at less than 80% of original specifications or over 10 years old; and most left-hand driven cars are prohibited.
Open general licenses	Yes.
Licenses with quotas	All import quotas are formally approved by the government. The Ministry of Planning and Investment, in coordination with the Ministry of Trade, may also impose ad hoc temporary quantity controls. Imports of steel, cement, fertilizer, passenger cars with less than 12 seats, motorcycles, and petroleum products and sugar are subject to quantitative controls.
Import taxes and/or tariffs	Import tariffs range up to 80%. Most imports of machinery, equipment, and medicine are exempt from tariffs. Certain imports of foreign enterprises, incorporated under the Law on Foreign Investment, are also exempt from tariffs. Tariff rates of 50% to 60% are applied to imports of garments and footwear, soft drinks, cosmetics, and automobiles.
Taxes collected through the exchange system	No.
State import monopoly	No.

Exports and Export Proceeds

Repatriation requirements All receipts must be repatriated, but no deadline is specified.

Surrender requirements Export earnings are subject to surrender requirements of up to 30%, but are not strictly enforced.

Financing requirements No.

Export licenses Export licenses for each shipment of rice, crude oil, products made of wool and rattan, and reexported goods are not required.

Without quotas State-owned firms with an annual export turnover of more than $5 million may obtain permanent direct foreign trading rights, whereas those with an annual export turnover in the range of $2 million to $5 million may obtain temporary direct foreign trading rights.

With quotas Exports of rice are subject to quota.

Export taxes n.a.

Taxes collected through the exchange system No.

Payments for Invisible Transactions and Current Transfers

Controls on these payments Payments for invisibles related to authorized imports are not restricted. All other transactions require individual authorization from the Ministry of Finance; information on application of quantitative limits or indicative limits and/or bona fide test on these transactions was not available at the time of publication.

Profit/dividends

Prior approval Remittances are subject to a tax of 5% to 10%.

Quantitative limits In principle, there are no limits, but in fact they are governed by the prevailing foreign exchange regulations.

Payments for travel

Prior approval Allocations exceeding the limits require SBV permission.

Quantitative limits The limit is $5,000 a trip, but the allocation can be raised to $10,000, if a traveler is using foreign exchange drawn from his/her own foreign currency accounts.

Indicative limits/bona fide test n.a.

Proceeds from Invisible Transactions and Current Transfers

Repatriation requirements All proceeds must be repatriated, but no deadline is specified.

Surrender requirements Yes.

Restrictions on use of funds Restrictions are the same as with other foreign exchange holdings.

Capital Transactions

Controls on capital and money market instruments No.

Controls on credit operations State-owned enterprises are subject to external borrowing ceilings.

Commercial credits

By residents to nonresidents No specific regulations exist.

To residents from nonresidents	Vietnamese organizations and citizens who need foreign currency for production and business purposes have been permitted, upon verification by competent agencies, to borrow foreign currency or obtain a bank guarantee for loans in foreign currency. If allowed to borrow directly from foreign countries, the borrower must report periodically to the SBV the expenditures in foreign currency from funds deposited abroad, including loan repayments.

Financial credits

By residents to nonresidents	No specific regulations exist.
To residents from nonresidents	These transactions are subject to prior approval by the SBV.

Controls on direct investment

Outward direct investment	Investments require special permission of the SBV and are not normally permitted.
Inward direct investment	Regulations provide for 3 forms of foreign investment: (1) contracted business cooperation, such as product-sharing arrangements; (2) joint ventures between a foreign investor and a Vietnamese private enterprise or state economic organization; and (3) firms wholly owned by foreign investors. The permitted share of foreign capital is at least 30%. There is a limit of 50 years to 70 years on the duration of the enterprise with foreign capital. The authority to grant foreign investment licenses is entrusted to the Ministry of Planning and Investment for projects under $1 million; for projects over $1 million, the provincial authorities concerned are consulted.

Controls on real estate transactions

Purchase abroad by residents	n.a.
Purchase locally by nonresidents	Land cannot be owned by foreign investors, but must be leased from the state.
Sale locally by nonresidents	n.a.

Provisions specific to commercial banks and other credit institutions

Borrowing abroad	SBV approval is required.
Maintenance of accounts abroad	SBV approval is required.
Lending to nonresidents (financial or commercial credits)	SBV approval is required.
Lending locally in foreign exchange	n.a.
Purchase of locally issued securities denominated in foreign exchange	n.a.
Differential treatment of nonresident deposit accounts and/or deposit accounts in foreign exchange	n.a.
Investment regulations	n.a.
Open foreign exchange position limits	The limit on the total open position is 30% of capital.

Changes During 1996

No significant changes occurred in the exchange and trade system.

WESTERN SAMOA

(Position as of December 31, 1996)

Status Under IMF Articles of Agreement

Article VIII   Date of acceptance: October 6, 1994.

Exchange Arrangement

Currency   The currency of Western Samoa is the tala.

Exchange rate structure   Unitary.

Classification

Pegged   The exchange rate is determined on the basis of a fixed relationship with a weighted basket of currencies of Western Samoa's main trading partners. The Central Bank of Samoa (CBS) has the authority to make discretionary exchange rate adjustments against the currency basket within a margin of up to 2%.

Exchange tax   An exchange levy of 1% is charged on gross sales of foreign exchange.

Forward exchange market   No.

Arrangements for Payments and Receipts

Prescription of currency requirements   No.

Payment arrangements   No.

Administration of control

Exchange control authorities   Overall responsibility for the administration of exchange control rests with the CBS, which delegates part of its powers to authorized banks. In principle, all payments to nonresidents require the CBS's approval. However, the Bank of Western Samoa and the Pacific Commercial Bank—the only authorized banks—are empowered to approve certain payments without limits and others up to specified amounts.

International security restrictions   No.

Payment arrears   No.

Controls on trade in gold (coins and/or bullion)   No.

Controls on exports and imports of banknotes

On exports

   Domestic currency   Exports are prohibited.

   Foreign currency   As part of their foreign currency allowance, resident travelers may take out foreign banknotes equivalent to WS$1,000 a person a trip.

On imports

   Domestic currency   Imports are prohibited, except for resident travelers who may take out foreign banknotes equivalent to WS$2,000 a person a trip as part of their foreign currency allowance.

Resident Accounts

Eligibility to hold accounts   Juridical and natural persons are eligible.

Foreign exchange accounts permitted	Residents who earn foreign exchange in the normal course of their business may open, with the approval of the CBS, external or foreign currency accounts with 1 of the 2 commercial banks.
Held domestically	Approval is required to open these accounts.
Held abroad	Yes.
Approval required	n.a.
Accounts in domestic currency convertible into foreign currency	Yes.

Nonresident Accounts

Eligibility to hold accounts	Juridical and natural persons are eligible.
Foreign exchange accounts permitted	Nonresidents who earn foreign exchange may open a foreign currency deposit account if there is a need to settle overseas commitments. Approval is required.
Domestic currency accounts	Yes.
Convertible into foreign currency	n.a.
Blocked accounts	No.

Imports and Import Payments

Foreign exchange budget	No.
Financing requirements for imports	
Advance payment requirements	The limit for advance payments is WS$3,000.
Advance import deposits	n.a.
Documentation requirements for release of foreign exchange for imports	Imports with a c.i.f. value of between WS$5,000 and WS$15,000 must be settled with a sight draft. Imports with a c.i.f. value of less than WS$5,000 may be imported under an open account, provided that payments are effected within 30 days of their arrival in Western Samoa.
Letters of credit	Imports with a c.i.f. value of more than WS$15,000 must be financed with a letter of credit.
Import licenses and other nontariff measures	
Negative list	The importation of a few products is prohibited for reasons of security or health. The importation of used cars requires prior approval of the CBS, which for safety reasons does not grant approval if vehicles are more than 5 years old.
Import taxes and/or tariffs	Import duties are applied on an ad valorem basis on c.i.f. values. Most products are subject to a tariff of 35%. Rates on machinery and agricultural inputs are generally levied at 20% or lower, while those on motor vehicles are levied at 50%.
	In addition, an import excise tax is levied on the value of certain imports, inclusive of import duties. For passenger cars, the excise is either 50%, 60%, or 70%, depending on engine size. Approved enterprises producing for export may receive full or partial exemption from duties and excise taxes on inputs and capital equipment.
Taxes collected through the exchange system	No.
State import monopoly	No.

Exports and Export Proceeds

Repatriation requirements

Yes.

Surrender requirements

Export proceeds must be surrendered to the authorized banks within 3 months of the date of shipment, except for export proceeds from goods shipped to American Samoa, which must be surrendered to the authorized bank within 4 weeks of the date of shipment.

Documentation requirements

Certificates validated by an authorized bank are required for exports in excess of WS$250.

Export licenses

Without quotas

All exports require export licenses issued by the Customs Department. Exports may be prohibited by the Director of Agriculture on grounds of low quality, or by order of the head of state to alleviate domestic shortages.

Export taxes

No.

Payments for Invisible Transactions and Current Transfers

Controls on these payments

All payments are subject to prior approval. Payments for certain invisibles may be approved by the authorized banks up to specified limits. Payments in excess of these limits, as well as payments for all other invisibles, require the prior approval of the CBS, which is granted when applications are supported by documentary proof that capital transactions are not involved. The CBS's approval process governing the remittance of invisible payments is concerned only with whether a transaction is bona fide. Payments other than those for medical treatment, study abroad, subscriptions and membership fees, and gambling and prizes earnings, are subject to quantitative limits and to indicative limits and/or bona fide tests.

Interest payments

A 15% withholding tax is levied on remittances of interest payments on overseas loans.

Prior approval

CBS approval is required.

Profit/dividends

A 15% withholding tax is levied on remittances of dividends at the source.

Prior approval

Remittances must be approved by the CBS.

Payments for travel

Quantitative limits

Residents and expatriates traveling overseas for private purposes are entitled to a foreign currency allowance equivalent to WS$400 a person a day, subject to a limit of WS$5,000 a person a trip; children under 15 years of age are entitled to 50% of the adult allowances. A daily allowance of WS$500 a person is allotted for business travel, with a limit of WS$6,000 a trip.

Medical costs

Indicative limits/bona fide test

Although no limit is set on remittances to cover expenses for medical treatment abroad, documentary evidence must be provided to support requests for such remittances.

Study abroad costs

Indicative limits/bona fide test

There is no specific limit for these remittances, but the amount requested must be supported by documentary evidence confirming that the beneficiary is enrolled at an educational institution abroad and costs are in line with the prevailing costs in the country of study.

Subscriptions and membership fees

Indicative limits/bona fide test

No specific limit exists, but amounts requested must be supported by documentary evidence.

Foreign workers' wages

Prior approval	Expatriate workers with local contracts of 1 year and longer are considered residents and need CBS approval if they wish to repatriate funds in excess of 80% of their net earnings on a fortnightly or monthly basis. Earnings not repatriated during the contract may be repatriated at the end of the contract.

Pensions

Indicative limits/bona fide test	Yes.

Gambling/prize earnings

Indicative limits/bona fide test	There are no restrictions for nonresidents, but residents require approval from CBS.

Family maintenance/alimony

Quantitative limits	Authorized banks may approve transfers of gifts to relatives and dependents, either for special family occasions or for maintenance, up to WS$500 a person a year.
Indicative limits/bona fide test	Requests for larger amounts may be approved by the CBS on a case-by-case basis.
Credit card use abroad	Credit cards may be used outside Western Samoa only for obtaining transport and other travel services. Applicants are required to submit charge vouchers when applying for approval to remit funds in reimbursement of charges incurred outside Western Samoa.

Proceeds from Invisible Transactions and Current Transfers

Repatriation requirements	Yes.
Surrender requirements	All proceeds must be surrendered to the authorized banks. Resident travelers must, on their return, sell to the banks all unused foreign exchange brought in.

Capital Transactions

Controls on capital and money market instruments	All outward capital transfers by residents require approval of the CBS.

On capital market securities

Purchase locally by nonresidents	n.a.
Sale or issue locally by nonresidents	n.a.
Purchase abroad by residents	Yes.
Sale or issue abroad by residents	n.a.

On money market instruments

Purchase locally by nonresidents	n.a.
Sale or issue locally by nonresidents	n.a.
Purchase abroad by residents	Yes.
Sale or issue abroad by residents	n.a.

On collective investment securities

Purchase locally by nonresidents	n.a.
Sale or issue locally by nonresidents	n.a.

Purchase abroad by residents	Yes.
Sale or issue abroad by residents	n.a.
Controls on credit operations	Credits to residents require CBS approval.
Commercial credits	
By residents to nonresidents	n.a.
To residents from nonresidents	Yes.
Financial credits	
By residents to nonresidents	n.a.
To residents from nonresidents	Yes.
Controls on direct investment	
Outward direct investment	Investments require CBS approval.
Inward direct investment	Yes.
Controls on liquidation of direct investment	Repatriation of investments require CBS approval.
Controls on real estate transactions	
Purchase abroad by residents	Purchases require CBS approval.
Purchase locally by nonresidents	n.a.
Sale locally by nonresidents	n.a.
Provisions specific to commercial banks and other credit institutions	
Borrowing abroad	Borrowing requires CBS approval.
Maintenance of accounts abroad	n.a.
Lending to nonresidents (financial or commercial credits)	n.a.
Lending locally in foreign exchange	n.a.
Purchase of locally issued securities denominated in foreign exchange	n.a.
Differential treatment of nonresident deposit accounts and/or deposit accounts in foreign exchange	n.a.
Investment regulations	n.a.
Open foreign exchange position limits	n.a.
Other controls imposed by securities laws	All outward capital transfers by residents require the specific approval of the CBS.

Changes During 1996

No significant changes occurred in the exchange and trade system.

REPUBLIC OF YEMEN

(Position as of December 31, 1996)

Status Under IMF Articles of Agreement

Article VIII	Date of acceptance: December 10, 1996.

Exchange Arrangement

Currency

The currency of the Republic of Yemen is the Yemeni rial.

Exchange rate structure

Unitary. On January 15, 1996, a special exchange rate for imports of wheat and flour was abolished. Until July 1, 1996, when the exchange system was unified, there were 2 exchange rates—the official rate, which applied only to transactions between the Central Bank of Yemen (CBY) and the Ministry of Finance, as well as for budget accounting and custom valuation purposes; and a floating market rate.

Classification

Independent floating

The exchange rate of the Yemeni rial is determined by supply and demand.

Exchange tax

No.

Exchange subsidy

No.

Forward exchange market

No.

Arrangements for Payments and Receipts

Prescription of currency requirements

No.

Payment arrangements

No.

Administration of control

Exchange control authorities

Exchange control authority is vested with the CBY.

International security restrictions

No.

Payment arrears

Official

Yes.

Private

Yes.

Controls on trade in gold (coins and/or bullion)

No.

Controls on exports and imports of banknotes

On exports

Domestic currency

Exports of Yemeni rial banknotes are prohibited.

On imports

Domestic currency

Imports of Yemeni rial banknotes are prohibited.

Resident Accounts

Eligibility to hold accounts

Juridical and natural persons are eligible.

Foreign exchange accounts permitted	Yes.
Held domestically	Yes.
Held abroad	Yes.
Accounts in domestic currency convertible into foreign currency	Yes.

Nonresident Accounts

Eligibility to hold accounts	Juridical and natural persons are eligible.
Foreign exchange accounts permitted	Yes.
Domestic currency accounts	Yes.
Convertible into foreign currency	Yes.
Blocked accounts	Yes.

Imports and Import Payments

Foreign exchange budget	No.
Financing requirements for imports	No.
Documentation requirements for release of foreign exchange for imports	
Letters of credit	Yes.
Import licenses used as exchange licenses	All importers holding an import license for wheat or flour may obtain the necessary foreign exchange from the CBY.
Import licenses and other nontariff measures	Imports are registered for statistical purposes.
Negative list	Some imports are banned for security and religious reasons, and 3 categories of goods are banned for economic reasons. Imports from Israel are prohibited, as well as certain types of used machinery.
Open general licenses	Yes.
Import taxes and/or tariffs	Yes.
Taxes collected through the exchange system	No.
State import monopoly	Imports of petroleum products are reserved for the Yemen Petroleum Company.

Exports and Export Proceeds

Repatriation requirements	No.
Surrender requirements	No.
Financing requirements	No.
Documentation requirements	No.
Export licenses	Exports are registered for statistical purposes. Exports to Israel are prohibited.

Export taxes	No.

Payments for Invisible Transactions and Current Transfers

Controls on these payments	No.

Proceeds from Invisible Transactions and Current Transfers

Repatriation requirements	No.
Surrender requirements	No.
Restrictions on use of funds	No.

Capital Transactions

Controls on capital and money market instruments	No.
Controls on derivatives and other instruments	No.
Controls on credit operations	
Commercial credits	
To residents from nonresidents	Yes.
Financial credits	
To residents from nonresidents	Effective January 15, 1996, contracting short-term foreign loans by the public sector was prohibited. Approval by the Council of Ministers is required for contracting medium- and long-term foreign loans by the public sector.
Guarantees, sureties, and financial backup facilities	
To residents from nonresidents	Yes.
Controls on direct investment	No.
Controls on liquidation of direct investment	Liquidation is free for approved and registered projects.
Controls on real estate transactions	No.
Provisions specific to commercial banks and other credit institutions	
Borrowing abroad	Yes.
Lending locally in foreign exchange	The CBY prohibits commercial and specialized banks from granting foreign currency loans to residents (except when a foreign donor provides concessional resources to specialized bankers and requires foreign currency onlending).
Differential treatment of nonresident deposit accounts and/or deposit accounts in foreign exchange	
Open foreign exchange position limits	Effective January 18, 1996, commercial and specialized banks are required to observe prudential regulations regarding currency exposure and to begin reporting their positions.
Provisions specific to institutional investors	No.

Other controls imposed by securities laws	No.

Changes During 1996

Status under IMF Articles of Agreement

December 10. The Republic of Yemen accepted the obligations of Article VIII, Sections 2, 3, and 4 of the Fund Agreement.

Exchange arrangements

January 15. The official exchange rate was depreciated from RYls 50 to RYls 100 per $1, and the special rate used for imports of wheat and flour was eliminated.

January 15. The multiple currency practice related to subsidy payments for wheat and flour imports was eliminated as the payment of the subsidy was clearly delinked from the foreign exchange transaction.

February 17. The law governing the operations of moneychangers was amended to eliminate provisions inconsistent with free-market operations.

July 1. The exchange system was unified by canceling the official exchange rate and adopting the floating free market rate for the purposes of budget accounting, transactions between the Ministry of Finance and the CBY, and customs valuation. The official rate was temporarily retained for customs valuation purposes on 8 items, but was subsequently eliminated on August 31, 1996.

Arrangements for payments and receipts

January 1. Hotels, airline companies, and agencies were required to collect all their bills in local currency and convert the balances to foreign exchange using the market exchange rate.

Resident accounts

January 1. The distinction between transferable and nontransferable accounts was eliminated, and these accounts became freely transferable.

Nonresident accounts

January 1. The distinction between transferable and nontransferable accounts was eliminated, and these accounts became freely transferable.

Imports and import payments

January 15. The restriction relating to the opening of import letters of credit by banks was abolished.

Capital transactions

January 1. Commercial and specialized banks were required to observe prudential regulations regarding foreign currency exposure and to begin reporting their positions.

January 15. Contracting short-term foreign loans by the public sector was prohibited and approval by the Council of Ministers was required for contracting medium- and long-term foreign loans by the public sector.

December 14. Commercial and specialized banks were prohibited from granting new foreign currency loans to residents (except when a foreign donor provides concessional resources to specialized banks and requires foreign currency onlending).

ZAMBIA

(Position as of December 31, 1996)

Status Under IMF Articles of Agreement

Article XIV	Yes.

Exchange Arrangement

Currency The currency of Zambia is the Zambian kwacha.

Exchange rate structure

Multiple There are 4 exchange rates: (1) the official exchange rate, which is applied to all government transactions (including debt service), the purchase of proceeds from external borrowing, and donor assistance by the Bank of Zambia (BOZ); (2) the commercial banks' corporate rate; (3) the commercial banks' retail rate; and (4) the interbank rate.

Classification

Independent floating The official rate is market determined, and the spread between the BOZ's buying and selling rates is fixed at 1.6%. On the basis of the bids and offers received, as well as other budgetary considerations (such as government and BOZ requirements, donor assistance funds, and export earnings), the BOZ determines the amount of foreign exchange to be sold to or purchased from the market through the dealing window. The exchange rates prevailing in the interbank market follow closely those established at the BOZ's dealing window.

Exchange tax No.

Exchange subsidy No.

Forward exchange market No.

Arrangements for Payments and Receipts

Prescription of currency requirements No.

Payment arrangements No.

Administration of control

Exchange control authorities All exchange controls have been abolished with the following exception: prior approval of the BOZ must be obtained for servicing of private debt incurred prior to January 28, 1994. The Ministry of Commerce, Trade, and Industry is responsible for trade control.

International security restrictions No.

Payment arrears Yes.

Official n.a.

Private n.a.

Controls on trade in gold (coins and/or bullion)

Controls on external trade Imports and exports of gold in any form other than jewelry require approval from the Ministry of Mines.

Controls on exports and imports of banknotes Amounts exceeding $5,000 must be declared.

Resident Accounts

Eligibility to hold accounts	Juridical and natural persons are eligible.
Foreign exchange accounts permitted	Yes.
Held domestically	Yes.
Held abroad	Yes.
Accounts in domestic currency convertible into foreign currency	Yes.

Nonresident Accounts

Eligibility to hold accounts	Juridical and natural persons are eligible.
Foreign exchange accounts permitted	Yes.
Domestic currency accounts	Yes.
Convertible into foreign currency	Yes.
Blocked accounts	No.

Imports and Import Payments

Foreign exchange budget	No.
Financing requirements for imports	No.
Documentation requirements for release of foreign exchange for imports	
Preshipment inspection	Imports are subject to preshipment inspection, except when the f.o.b. value of each import consignment is less than $10,000.
Letters of credit	n.a.
Import licenses used as exchange licenses	Yes.
Import licenses and other nontariff measures	Licenses for statistical purposes are required, but they are granted automatically by commercial banks. Personal and household effects, trade samples, diplomatic shipments, and vehicles brought in temporarily are exempted from this requirement.
Positive list	Yes.
Import taxes and/or tariffs	Tariff rates range from 20% to 50% (except for a few luxury goods, which are taxed at higher rates). Some imports are exempt under the provisions of bilateral agreements, and nontraditional exporters and certain import-competing firms are exempt under the Investment Act (1991). In addition, imported goods are subject to an "uplift factor" in computing domestic sales taxes.
Taxes collected through the exchange system	No.
State import monopoly	No.

Exports and Export Proceeds

Repatriation requirements	No.

Surrender requirements	The requirement on export proceeds of the Zambia Consolidated Copper Mines (ZCCM) of 45% was abolished on April 16, 1996.
Financing requirements	No.
Documentation requirements	All exports must be declared on the prescribed export declaration form for statistical purposes.
Export licenses	
Without quotas	Export licenses are required for most goods, although they are administered routinely by commercial banks under authority delegated by the Ministry of Commerce, Trade, and Industry. Exports of ivory are prohibited.
With quotas	White maize and fertilizers may be subject to a quota if domestic supply is short.

Payments for Invisible Transactions and Current Transfers

Controls on these payments	All payments for invisibles, except external debt-service payments, may be effected through banks and foreign exchange bureaus without the prior approval of the BOZ, subject to the requirement that no taxes are due.

Proceeds from Invisible Transactions and Current Transfers

Repatriation requirements	No.
Surrender requirements	No.
Restrictions on use of funds	No.

Capital Transactions

Controls on capital and money market instruments	Outward transfers are free of controls. No controls apply to the sale of assets between nonresidents and between residents and nonresidents.
Controls on derivatives and other instruments	No.
Controls on credit operations	All borrowings must be registered with the BOZ for statistical purposes.
Controls on direct investment	No.
Controls on liquidation of direct investment	No.
Controls on real estate transactions	No.
Provisions specific to commercial banks and other credit institutions	
Borrowing abroad	BOZ approval is required.
Lending locally in foreign exchange	n.a.
Purchase of locally issued securities denominated in foreign exchange	n.a.
Differential treatment of nonresident deposit accounts and/or deposit accounts in foreign exchange	
Reserve requirements	The statutory reserve ratio on foreign currency deposits is 5%.
Liquid asset requirements	The liquid asset reserve ratio is 40%.

Open foreign exchange position limits	The limit is 25% of regulatory capital.
Provisions specific to institutional investors	No.
Other controls imposed by securities laws	No.

Changes During 1996

Exchange arrangements

January 12. The basis for determining the BOZ official rate was changed from the weighted average commercial banks' rate to the BOZ dealing rate determined by demand and supply.

October 2. The BOZ spread, which had been fixed at 2%, became adjustable on a daily basis.

November 26. The spread between the BOZ buying and selling rates was fixed at 1.6%.

Exports and export proceeds

April 16. The surrender requirement of 45% applied to ZCCM was abolished.

Capital transactions

April 3. A statutory reserve ratio of 3% on foreign currency deposits was introduced.

July 20. The statutory reserve ratio on foreign currency deposits was raised to 5% from 3%.

July 29. The liquid asset requirement was increased to 35% from 30%.

September 20. The liquid asset requirement was increased to 40% from 35%.

ZIMBABWE

(Position as of December 31, 1996)

Status Under IMF Articles of Agreement

Article VIII   Date of acceptance: February 5, 1995.

Exchange Arrangement

Currency   The currency of Zimbabwe is the Zimbabwe dollar.

Exchange rate structure   Unitary.

Classification

Independent floating   The external value of the Zimbabwe dollar is determined in the exchange market. The U.S. dollar is the intervention currency. Authorized dealers and foreign exchange bureaus base their rates for foreign currencies on current international market rates. The spread applied by the Reserve Bank of Zimbabwe (RBZ) between the buying and selling rates is 0.8% for all currencies. Authorized dealers (authorized commercial and merchant banks) may charge an additional 0.25% on either side of the quoted rates of major currencies.

Exchange tax   No.

Exchange subsidy   No.

Forward exchange market   Forward exchange contracts are permitted only for trade transactions. There is no limit on the size of such contracts, but their duration must be at least 1 year, depending on the currencies involved and the type of coverage. Forward sales of foreign exchange take place at the spot preferential telex transfer rate plus a premium loading for 6 months, depending on the currencies involved and type of coverage. Authorized dealers are expected to quote to their customers the dealers' own telex transfer rates.

Official cover of forward operations   No.

Arrangements for Payments and Receipts

Prescription of currency requirements   All payments by nonresidents to residents must be effected in any of 17 currencies freely convertible through authorized dealers, with the exception of payments otherwise specified or effected through nonresident accounts.

Payment arrangements

Bilateral arrangements

Operative   There is an arrangement with Malaysia.

Clearing agreements   Under the Clearing House Agreement, within the PTA, residents of member countries may use national currencies in day-to-day payments during a transaction period of 2 calendar months; the monetary authorities settle net balances at the end of this period in convertible currencies.

Administration of control

Exchange control authorities   Exchange control is administered by the RBZ under powers delegated to it by the Minister of Finance. Authorized dealers have been empowered to approve certain foreign exchange transactions.

International security restrictions   No.

Payment arrears   No.

Controls on trade in gold (coins and/or bullion)

Controls on domestic ownership and/or trade

No person, either as principal or agent, may deal in or possess gold unless that person is (1) the holder of a license or permit; (2) the holder or distributor of a registered mining location from which gold is being produced; or (3) the employee or agent of any of the persons mentioned in (1) and (2) above and authorized by an employer or principal to deal in or possess gold that is already in the lawful possession of such employer or principal. A mining commissioner may issue to any person a permit authorizing the acquisition, possession, or disposal of any gold, provided the quantity does not exceed 1 troy ounce. In all other cases, permission can be issued only by the Secretary for Mines.

Three types of licenses may be issued under the terms of the Gold Trade Act: a gold dealing license, a gold recovery works license, and a gold assaying license. Barclays Bank of Zimbabwe, Ltd. is the only authorized dealer under the terms of the act. Each holder or distributor of a registered mining location is required to lodge with this bank all gold acquired each month by the tenth day of the following month. Any person intending to smelt gold or any article containing gold must first obtain a license issued by a district commissioner under the terms of the Secondhand Goods Act that authorizes the possession of smelting equipment.

Controls on external trade

The exportation of gold in unmanufactured form is controlled and licensed by the Ministry of Mines; these controls do not apply to the RBZ. No export licenses for gold are issued. The importation of gold is controlled by the Gold Trade Act, which requires those intending to import gold into Zimbabwe to meet certain requirements.

Controls on exports and imports of banknotes

On exports

  Domestic currency

Travelers may take out, as part of their travel allowance, up to Z$250.

  Foreign currency

Travelers may take out, as part of their travel allowance, up to the equivalent of US$500. Nonresident travelers may take out the traveler's checks they brought in, less the amount they sold to authorized dealers. Upon departure, nonresident travelers may reconvert unspent Zimbabwean currency into foreign currencies on presentation of exchange certificates.

On imports

  Domestic currency

A traveler may bring in up to Z$250.

  Foreign currency

Foreign currency and traveler's checks may be imported without restriction but must be sold or exchanged in Zimbabwe only through authorized dealers or foreign exchange bureaus.

Resident Accounts

Eligibility to hold accounts

Juridical and natural persons are eligible.

Foreign exchange accounts permitted

Resident exporters and individuals may open foreign currency accounts in 1 of the denominated currencies in local branches of authorized dealers. Funds in these accounts are traded at market-determined exchange rates. Funds withdrawn from these accounts and converted into local currency, however, may not be redeposited in the account, except in the case of the amount of the initial investment and income or capital gains from investments in listed companies on the stock exchange, unlisted companies, or money market accounts.

Held domestically

Yes.

Held abroad

n.a.

Accounts in domestic currency convertible into foreign currency

n.a.

Nonresident Accounts

Eligibility to hold accounts   Juridical and natural persons are eligible.

Foreign exchange accounts permitted   These accounts may be credited with foreign currencies, with payments from other non-resident accounts, or with payments by residents that would be eligible for transfer outside Zimbabwe. Nonresident accounts may be debited for payments to residents, for payments to other nonresident accounts, or for payments abroad. Nonresident individuals may open foreign currency accounts in 1 of the denominated currencies in local branches of authorized dealers. Funds in these accounts are traded at market-determined exchange rates. Funds withdrawn from these accounts and converted into local currency, however, may not be redeposited in the account, except in the case of the initial investment, and income or capital gains from investments in the stock exchange, unlisted companies, or money markets. Prior approval required.

Domestic currency accounts   Yes.

Convertible into foreign currency   n.a.

Blocked accounts   Only former residents residing outside Zimbabwe may maintain emigrants' accounts in Zimbabwe. Cash assets held in Zimbabwe in the names of emigrants must be blocked in these accounts, and all payments to and from these accounts are subject to various exchange restrictions.

Imports and Import Payments

Foreign exchange budget   No.

Financing requirements for imports

Minimum financing requirements   n.a.

Advance payment requirements   Authorized dealers may approve advance payments for imports up to US$50,000.

Advance import deposits   n.a.

Documentation requirements for release of foreign exchange for imports   Authorized dealers may approve applications to effect payments for authorized imports, provided the necessary documentation is submitted. Payments for imports into Zimbabwe from all countries may be made in Zimbabwean currency to a local nonresident account or in any foreign currency.

Domiciliation requirements   n.a.

Letters of credit   n.a.

Import licenses and other nontariff measures   There are no import-licensing requirements.

Negative list   The negative list for imports includes, besides items restricted for health or security reasons, textiles and apparel, alcoholic beverages, canned beverages, nonmonetary gold, pearls, precious and semiprecious stones, and some jewelry items.

Open general licenses   n.a.

Licenses with quotas   No quotas are in force, but seasonal restrictions are applied to certain agricultural products.

Other nontariff measures   Imports of certain goods (mostly agricultural and processed food products) require a special permit issued by the Ministry of Lands and Agriculture.

Import taxes and/or tariffs   The customs duty regime consists mainly of ad valorem duties, which range up to a maximum of 35% of the c.i.f. value for most consumer goods (up to 60% to 75% for vehicles) with a surtax of 10%, and specific duties on a number of products. Generally, imports are subject to an additional tax (between 12.5% and 20%) equivalent to the sales taxes imposed on goods sold domestically. Government imports and capital goods for statutory bodies are exempt from customs duties.

Taxes collected through the exchange system	No.
State import monopoly	Coffee, maize, sorghum, soybeans, and wheat may be imported only by the Grain Marketing and Cotton Marketing Boards or by others with the permission of the boards.

Exports and Export Proceeds

Repatriation requirements	Yes.
Surrender requirements	Exporters are permitted to retain 100% of export proceeds in foreign exchange. Marketing boards, however, are required to sell 100% of export proceeds to authorized dealers.
Financing requirements	Goods may not be exported without permission unless the customs authorities are satisfied that payment has been made in an approved manner or will be made within 3 months of the date of shipment (or a longer period if permitted by the RBZ).
	Payments for exports must be received in 1 of the following ways: (1) in a denominated currency; (2) in Zimbabwean currency from a nonresident account; and (3) in the case of Malawi and Botswana, by checks drawn in Malawi kwacha or Botswana pula, respectively. Under the PTA arrangement, member countries may use national currencies in the settlement of payments during a transaction period of 2 months, with net balances at the end of this period to be settled in convertible currencies. Exports to some 50 countries are approved only upon advance payment of export proceeds or if payment is covered by an irrevocable letter of credit issued or confirmed before exportation by a reputable overseas bank.
Documentation requirements	
Letters of credit	n.a.
Guarantees	n.a.
Domiciliation	n.a.
Export licenses	
Without quotas	Export licenses are required for the following: (1) any ore, concentrate, or other manufactured product of chrome, copper, lithium, nickel, tin, or tungsten; (2) petroleum products; (3) jute and hessian bags; (4) road or rail tankers for carrying liquids or semiliquids; (5) bitumen, asphalt, and tar; (6) wild animals and wild animal products; (7) certain wood products; (8) ammonium nitrate; and (9) implements of war. Export-licensing requirements are imposed for reasons of health and social welfare, as well as to ensure an adequate domestic supply of essential products. Export permits are required from the Ministry of Lands and Agriculture for some basic agricultural commodities, including maize, oilseeds, cheese, skim milk, seeds, potatoes, citrus fruits, apples, bananas, and tomatoes.
Export taxes	No.

Payments for Invisible Transactions and Current Transfers

Controls on these payments	Foreign exchange to pay for invisibles related to imports and, within certain limits, for other purposes is provided by commercial banks under delegated authority. Applications for foreign exchange exceeding the limits established for commercial banks are approved by the RBZ, which deals with each case on its merits.
Freight/insurance	
Quantitative limits	The limits are 30% of f.o.b. value of goods transported, but for goods that are of exceptional mass in relation to value, up to 80% of the f.o.b. value may be approved.
Indicative limits/bona fide test	Yes.

Unloading/storage costs

    Indicative limits/bona fide test   Yes.

Administrative expenses

    Indicative limits/bona fide test   Yes.

Commissions

    Prior approval   Yes.

    Quantitative limits   The following limits apply: (1) conforming commission—up to 2.5% of c.i.f. value; (2) buying commission—up to 5% of f.o.b. value; (3) foreign travel agents—up to 10% of sales; and (4) selling commission—up to 7.5% of f.o.b. value.

    Indicative limits/bona fide test   Yes.

Interest payments

    Indicative limits/bona fide test   Yes.

Profit/dividends

    Prior approval   Yes.

    Quantitative limits   All dividends declared by foreign investors in the export sector after January 1, 1995, may be remitted to foreign shareholders without restriction after payment of applicable taxes. Blocked funds relating to profits and dividends earned on foreign investments made prior to May 1993 may be externalized over a 3-year period starting July 1, 1995. Foreign companies established prior to September 1979 are permitted to remit 50% of net after-tax profits if exports comprise more than 25% of total sales.

        If direct foreign exchange allocation was used, the following rules apply: (1) a wholly foreign-owned company that meets the criteria to qualify as an export firm and funds its projects through a combination of foreign exchange or surplus funds is permitted to remit the declared dividends from net after-tax profits on a basis proportionate to the level of foreign exchange invested but limited to a maximum of 50% for 5 years from the beginning of operations, after which the company will qualify for 100% remittance of dividends; (2) a wholly foreign-owned company with its own blocked funds is permitted to repatriate 100% of its declared dividends, provided it meets all its foreign exchange requirements from external sources; and (3) in the case of a new joint venture that meets the criteria to qualify as an export firm and has at least 30% local participation, the foreign partner is allowed to remit 100% of its share of declared dividends, provided that it meets its share of foreign exchange requirements from external sources (blocked and surplus funds are assets held by foreigners as a result of the limited remittance of dividends).

        The following regulations apply to investments in the mining sector: (1) a wholly foreign-owned company that funds its projects through foreign funds is allowed to repatriate 100% of its net after-tax profits, provided that it qualifies as an export-oriented project; (2) a wholly foreign-owned company that funds its projects through a combination of foreign funds and either its own blocked funds, switched blocked funds, or surplus funds (subject to a minimum matching formula of 50–50) is allowed to remit dividends of up to 50% in proportion to the matching ratio; and (3) the level of dividend remittance for joint ventures subject to the minimum 30% local participation criterion is also determined by the matching formula used by the foreign shareholder. After 5 years, the company can remit 100% of its dividends to the foreign shareholder.

    Indicative limits/bona fide test   Yes.

Payments for travel

    Prior approval   Applications for emigrant status must be submitted to the RBZ; the settling-in allowance that emigrants may remit abroad is limited to Z$1,000 a family unit. In exceptional cases, the exchange control authorities will consider applications exceeding this maximum. All those applying for emigrant status are required to liquidate their assets within

6 months and to invest the total proceeds, less any settling-in allowance granted, in 4%, 12-year Zimbabwean government external bonds. If emigrants are unable to comply with the 6-month limit, the matter may be referred to the RBZ. Transferable allowances at the time of emigration are as follows: (1) per person under the age of 40 years, Z$500; (2) per person aged 40–59 years, Z$1,000; (3) family units and single persons (under 60 years of age) with dependents, Z$1,000; (4) family units (husband over 60 years of age) and single persons over 60, Z$7,000; (5) persons over 80 years of age, Z$10,000; and (6) handicapped or disabled persons, Z$10,000. A further release of capital is authorized as an annual allowance on each anniversary of the emigrant's departure, as follows: persons over 65 years of age, Z$2,000; and persons over 70 years of age, Z$3,000.

Quantitative limits

The basic foreign exchange allowance for holiday travel is US$5,000 a year. Children under 10 years are entitled to half this amount. The basic foreign exchange allowance for business travel is up to US$600 a day.

Indicative limits/bona fide test

Yes.

Medical costs

Quantitative limits

The limit is US$20,000 a trip for the patient and 1 companion. A travel allowance up to US$250 a day a person may be allowed.

Indicative limits/bona fide test

Applications for additional amounts must be submitted to the RBZ for approval.

Study abroad costs

Prior approval

Foreign exchange is provided for education abroad beyond the secondary school level for certain diploma and degree courses with RBZ approval.

Quantitative limits

The limit is US$50,000 a year.

Indicative limits/bona fide test

Yes.

Subscriptions and membership fees

Prior approval

Yes.

Quantitative limits

The annual limit for a company is US$20,000. The limit for an initial membership fee is US$250.

Indicative limits/bona fide test

Yes.

Consulting/legal fees

Prior approval

Yes.

Quantitative limits

The annual limit is US$5,000 an individual.

Indicative limits/bona fide test

Yes.

Foreign workers' wages

n.a.

Pensions

Remittance of pensions of former residents is guaranteed under the constitution.

Prior approval

n.a.

Quantitative limits

n.a.

Indicative limits/bona fide test

n.a.

Gambling/prize earnings

Prior approval

Yes.

Quantitative limits

Lottery prizes due to nonresidents may be transferred with the exception of the first prize.

Indicative limits/bona fide test

n.a.

Family maintenance/alimony

Prior approval

Yes.

Quantitative limits	The annual limit is US$2,000 for alimony and child support payments.
Indicative limits/bona fide test	Yes.
Credit card use abroad	
Prior approval	Yes.
Quantitative limits	Credit cards may be used abroad up to the limits set for invisible transactions.
Indicative limits/bona fide test	Yes.

Proceeds from Invisible Transactions and Current Transfers

Repatriation requirements	Yes.
Surrender requirements	Receipts from invisibles must be sold to authorized banks within a reasonable period of time. Residents performing services abroad may retain a portion of their earnings.

Capital Transactions

Controls on capital and money market instruments	Inward transfers of capital through normal banking channels are not restricted. Outward transfers of capital are controlled.
On capital market securities	
Purchase locally by nonresidents	Foreign investors are permitted to participate in the Zimbabwe Stock Exchange Market using currency received in Zimbabwe through normal banking channels. The initial investment plus any capital gains and dividend income may be remitted without restriction. Foreign investors may also invest up to a maximum of 15% of the assets brought to Zimbabwe in primary issues of bonds and stocks.
Purchase abroad by residents	Yes.
Sale or issue abroad by residents	Yes.
On money market instruments	
Purchase locally by nonresidents	Former residents holding blocked assets and new emigrants are allowed to invest their funds in government external bonds with a maturity of 12 years and an annual interest rate of 4%.
Purchase abroad by residents	Yes.
Sale or issue abroad by residents	Yes.
On collective investment securities	
Purchase abroad by residents	Yes.
Sale or issue abroad by residents	Yes.
Controls on credit operations	
Commercial credits	
By residents to nonresidents	n.a.
To residents from nonresidents	The limit on foreign borrowing without prior approval of the External Loans Coordinating Committee is US$5 million. Gold producers undertaking new expansion projects are permitted access to offshore financing in the form of gold loans.
Financial credits	
By residents to nonresidents	n.a.
To residents from nonresidents	Yes.

| Guarantees, sureties, and financial backup facilities | n.a. |

Controls on direct investment

| Outward direct investment | Yes. |

Inward direct investment — Direct foreign investments up to US$40 million in the preferred areas (mining, agro-industry, manufacturing, tourism, and high-technology services) are approved by the Zimbabwe Investment Centre. In the preferred areas, 100% foreign ownership is permitted; it is restricted to 25% in other areas. Previously blocked funds, whether already converted into government bonds or not, can qualify as new venture capital if they are reinvested in Zimbabwe in an approved project and matched by an inflow of investment funds of up to 50% of the reinvested blocked funds, as determined by the RBZ. Blocked funds can be used by third parties, foreign as well as domestic, for investment on freely negotiated terms; as new venture capital, the total investment is eligible to be remitted as dividends for up to 50% of after-tax profits. However, the "blocked" portion of the new investment, unlike new venture capital, must be reinvested in Zimbabwe for at least 5 years.

Controls on liquidation of direct investment — All foreign investments, irrespective of their source, that have been undertaken through normal banking channels since September 1, 1979, may be considered for repatriation up to the value of capital invested less dividends transferred abroad. The balance may be transferred only through the established medium of 6-year external government bonds bearing interest at the rate of 4% a year. Repatriation may be permitted without restriction if funds are used to acquire foreign exchange and if dividends were not remitted with such funds. The repatriation of capital invested before September 1, 1979, is prohibited. However, shareholders are allowed, within limits, to apply to the RBZ for the remittance of such capital upon the sale of shares to local residents, and if such application is approved, the capital is invested in external government bonds bearing interest at the rate of 4% a year and carrying a maturity of 12 years (for individuals) or 20 years (for firms). Repatriation at accelerated rates that depend on discounted sale prices of net equity is allowed.

Controls on real estate transactions

Purchase abroad by residents	Yes.
Purchase locally by nonresidents	n.a.
Sale locally by nonresidents	n.a.

Provisions specific to commercial banks and other credit institutions

Borrowing abroad	n.a.
Maintenance of accounts abroad	n.a.
Lending to nonresidents (financial or commercial credits)	n.a.
Lending locally in foreign exchange	n.a.
Purchase of locally issued securities denominated in foreign exchange	n.a.
Differential treatment of nonresident deposit accounts and/or deposit accounts in foreign exchange	n.a.
Investment regulations	n.a.
Open foreign exchange position limits	Authorized dealers are subject to overnight net foreign currency exposure limits.

Provisions specific to institutional investors

Limits (max.) on portfolio invested abroad

n.a.

Limits (min.) on portfolio invested locally

Purchase of shares by foreign investors is limited to 25% of the total equity of the company, with a limit of 5% for 1 investor. These limits are in addition to any existing foreign shareholdings in the companies.

Currency matching regulations on assets/liabilities composition

n.a.

Changes During 1996

No significant changes occurred in the exchange and trade system.

APPENDICES

	Total number of countries with this feature	Afghanistan, Islamic State of	Albania	Algeria	Angola	Antigua and Barbuda	Argentina	Armenia	Aruba	Australia	Austria	Azerbaijan	Bahamas, The	Bahrain	Bangladesh	Barbados	Belarus	Belgium	Belize	Benin	Bhutan	Bolivia	Bosnia and Herzegovina
Status under IMF Articles of Agreement																							
Article VIII	143					●	●	●	●	●	●		●	●	●	●			●	●	●	●	
Article XIV	42	●	●	●	●							●					●					●	●
Exchange rate arrangements																							
Pegged to:																							
Single currency	47					■	■	■		■				■		■			■	♦	◊		◊
Composite of currencies	22														⊕								
Flexibility limited	16										▼				+			▼					
More flexible arrangements																							
Managed floating	48				●												●						
Independent floating	51	●	●					●		●		●										●	
Exchange rate structure																							
Dual exchange rates	17											●											
Multiple exchange rates	6	●																					
Arrangements for payments and receipts																							
Bilateral payment arrangements	51	●	●			—								●		—	●			●	—		—
Payment arrears	54	—	●		●	●	●					—					●				—		—
Control on payments for invisible transactions and current transfers	105	●		●	●	●			●				●	●		●	●	●	●	●	●	●	●
Proceeds from exports and/or invisible transactions																							
Repatriation requirements	115	●	●	●	●	—	●	●					●	●		●	●	●	●	●	●	●	●
Surrender requirements	92	●		●	●				●				●	●		●	●		●	●	●	●	●
Capital transactions																							
Controls on:																							
Capital market securities	128	—	●	●	●		●		●	●			●	●	●	●	●	●	●	●	●		●
Money market instruments	112	—	●	●	●				●	●			●	●	●	●	●	●	●	●	●		●
Collective investment securities	107	—	●	●	●		●		●				—	●		●	●	—	●	●	●		●
Derivatives and other instruments	78	—	—	●	—				●	●				●		●	—	—	●	●	●		●
Commercial credits	103	—	●	●	●				●				—	●		●	●	●	●	●	●	●	●
Financial credits	76	—	●	●	●				●				—	●		●	●		●	●	●		●
Guarantees, sureties, and financial backup facilities	82	—	●	●	—				●				—	●		●	●	—	●	●	●		●
Direct investment	144	●	●	●	●		●		●	●				●		●	●	●	●	●	●		●
Liquidation of direct investment	54	●			●				●				—			●			●	●	●		
Real estate transactions	119	—	●	●	●		●		●	●	●		—	●		●	●	—	●	●	●		
Provisions specific to:																							
Commercial banks and other credit institutions	131	—	●	●	●	—	●		●					●		●	●		●	●	—		●
Institutional investors	60	—	—		—	—	●		●	—	●	—	—	●	●	—	●			●	—		—

For key and footnotes, see page 952.

	Botswana	Brazil	Brunei Darussalam	Bulgaria	Burkina Faso	Burundi	Cambodia	Cameroon	Canada	Cape Verde	Central African Republic	Chad	Chile	China	Colombia	Comoros	Congo, Dem. Rep. of	Congo, Rep. of	Costa Rica	Côte d'Ivoire	Croatia	Cyprus	Czech Republic	Denmark	Djibouti	Dominica	Dominican Republic	Ecuador	Egypt	El Salvador	Equatorial Guinea	Eritrea	Estonia	Ethiopia	Fiji
	●		●		●			●	●		●	●	●	●		●		●	●	●		●	●	●	●	●	●	●		●				●	●
		●		●		●	●			●					●			●							■	■				●		●	●	●	
			◇		◆			◆				◆	◆			◆			◆		◆				■	■						◆		◇	
	⊕					⊕				⊕											⊕	⊕													⊕
																								▼											
		●					●					●	●	●				●			●					●	●	●	●		●				
				●					●							●																		●	
	●	●				●					●																●	●			●				
																												●							
	●	●		●	●	●	—		●				●		—	●					●					●	●	●		—			●		—
		●			●	●	—		●	●	●				●	●			●	●						●	●	●	●	●			●	—	—
	●	●	●	●	●						●					●			●			●				●	●								
	●	●		●	●	●	●		●	●	●		●	●	●	●	●		●	●	●	●				●	●		●				●	●
	●	●		●	●	●	●		●	●	●		●	●		●	●		●			●				●	●	●		●			●	●
	●		●	●	●	●	●		●	●	●		●	●	●				●	●	●	●	●			●				●	●	—	●	●
			●	●	●	●		●			●	●		●			●		●	●	●	●	●			●		●		●	●	—	●	●
	●	●		●	●	●			●					●		●			●		●	●			●			●		●	—	—	—	●
	—	●		●	●	●	—		●					●		●			●	●	●	●			—					—	—	—	●	●
	●	●		●		●			●				●	●		●	●		●		●				●	●	●	●		—		—	●	●
	●	●		●	●	●		●		●		●	●	—	●		●		●	●	●	●			●	●	●			—		●	●
	●	●		●	●	●						—	●		●		●		●						●	●	●	●		—		—	●	●
	●	●	●	●	●	●				●	—	●	●		●	—	●	●							●			●	●	—		—	●	●
	●	●	●	●	●	●	●		●		●	—	●	●	●			●	—		●	●			●		●		●	—		—	●	●
	●	●		●	●	●	●		●		—	●	●	●	●	●	—	—	●	●		●		●	—	●		●	●	—	●	—	●	●
	●	●			—		—	—	—	—	—		●			●	—		—	—	●	●		●	—				—	—	—	—		●

	Finland	France	Gabon	Gambia, The	Georgia	Germany	Ghana	Greece	Grenada	Guatemala	Guinea	Guinea-Bissau	Guyana	Haiti	Honduras	Hong Kong, China	Hungary	Iceland	India	Indonesia	Iran, Islamic Rep. of	Iraq	Ireland	Israel	Italy
Status under IMF Articles of Agreement																									
Article VIII	•	•	•	•	•	•	•	•	•	•	•	•	•	•	•	•	•	•	•	•			•	•	•
Article XIV																					•	•			
Exchange rate arrangements																									
Pegged to:																									
Single currency			♦						■			♦												■	
Composite of currencies																		⊕							
Flexibility limited	▼	▼				▼																	▼		▼
More flexible arrangements																									
Managed floating				•				•							•	•	•			•				•	
Independent floating					•		•			•	•		•	•					•						
Exchange rate structure																									
Dual exchange rates											•				•						•	•			
Multiple exchange rates																									
Arrangements for payments and receipts																									
Bilateral payment arrangements							•				•		•	•			•					—			
Payment arrears				—							•	•	•	•	•						•	—			
Control on payments for invisible transactions and current transfers			•				•	•	•		•	•								•				•	•
Proceeds from exports and/or invisible transactions																									
Repatriation requirements			•				•		•	•	•	•			•		•			•				•	•
Surrender requirements			•				•		•	•	•				•		•			•				•	
Capital transactions																									
Controls on:																									
Capital market securities	•	•	•	•		•	•	•	•		•	—		—	—		•	•	•	•	—	—		•	
Money market instruments		•	•			•	•		•		•						•	•	•	•	—	•		•	
Collective investment securities		•	•			•			•			—	—		•		•		•	•	—	•		•	•
Derivatives and other instruments		•	•			•			•		—	—		—	—		•		•	•	—	•			
Commercial credits		•	•			•			•		—	—	•		•		•		•	•	—	—		•	
Financial credits		•	•			•			•		—	—	•		•		•		•	•	—			•	
Guarantees, sureties, and financial backup facilities			•						•	•	—	—			—		•		•	•				•	
Direct investment	•	•	•					•	•	•	•	—		•	•		•		•	•	•	•	•	•	•
Liquidation of direct investment			•						•								—		•		•	•			
Real estate transactions	•		•	—					•	—	—	—		—	—		•		•	•	—		•	•	•
Provisions specific to:																									
Commercial banks and other credit institutions	•	—	•	—	•	•			•		•				•	•	•		•	•	—			•	•
Institutional investors	•	•	—	—		•					—	—		—	—				•	•	—			•	•

For key and footnotes, see page 952.

Frameworks for Current and Capital Transactions in Member Countries[1]

first country page)[2]

	Jamaica	Japan	Jordan	Kazakhstan	Kenya	Kiribati	Korea	Kuwait	Kyrgyz Republic	Lao People's Dem. Rep.	Latvia	Lebanon	Lesotho	Liberia	Libyan Arab Jamahiriya	Lithuania	Luxembourg	Macedonia, fmr. Yugoslav Rep.	Madagascar	Malawi	Malaysia	Maldives	Mali	Malta	Marshall Islands	Mauritania	Mauritius	Mexico	Micronesia, Fed. States of	Moldova	Mongolia	Morocco	Mozambique	Myanmar	Namibia

	Nepal	Netherlands	Netherlands Antilles	New Zealand	Nicaragua	Niger	Nigeria	Norway	Oman	Pakistan	Panama	Papua New Guinea	Paraguay	Peru	Philippines	Poland	Portugal	Qatar	Romania	Russian Federation	Rwanda	St. Kitts and Nevis	St. Lucia	St. Vincent and the Grenadines	San Marino
Status under IMF Articles of Agreement																									
Article VIII	●	●	●	●	●	●		●	●	●	●	●	●	●	●	●	●	●		●		●	●	●	●
Article XIV							●												●		●				
Exchange rate arrangements																									
Pegged to:																									
Single currency			■			◆	■		■		■											■	■	■	◇
Composite of currencies	⊕																								
Flexibility limited		▼															▼	✚							
More flexible arrangements *Managed floating*					●			●		●						●				●					
Independent floating				●								●	●	●	●				●		●				
Exchange rate structure																									
Dual exchange rates							●																		
Multiple exchange rates																									
Arrangements for payments and receipts Bilateral payment arrangements						—											●		●	●					
Payment arrears					●	●	●				●		●						●	●					
Control on payments for invisible transactions and current transfers	●		●			●	●		●	●		●	●	●	●				●			●	●	●	
Proceeds from exports and/or invisible transactions *Repatriation requirements*	●					●	●		●			●	●			●			●	●	●			●	
Surrender requirements						●	●		●				●						●	●	●			●	
Capital transactions Controls on: *Capital market securities*	●		●			●	●	●	●	●	●		●	●	●	●			●	●	●	●	●	●	—
Money market instruments	●		●			●	●		●		●					●	●		●	●	●	●		●	—
Collective investment securities	●		●			●	●		●		●					●	●		●	●	●	●			
Derivatives and other instruments	—		●			●	●		●		—					●			●	●	●			●	—
Commercial credits	●		●			●	●		●		●					●	●		●	●	●			●	—
Financial credits	●		●			●	●		●							●	●		●		●				—
Guarantees, sureties, and financial backup facilities	—		●			●	—		●							●	●		—	—	●	●		—	—
Direct investment	●		●	●	●	●	●		●	●	●		●	●	●	●	●	●	●	●	●	●	●	●	●
Liquidation of direct investment	●					●	●												●				—		
Real estate transactions	●		●			●	●		●		●					●	●		●	●	●	●		●	●
Provisions specific to: *Commercial banks and other credit institutions*	●	●	●		●	●	—	●	●	●	●	●	●	●	●	●	●		●	●	●	●		●	—
Institutional investors	●		●			●	—	●	—	●	—	—		●	●	●			—	●				—	—

For key and footnotes, see page 952.

Frameworks for Current and Capital Transactions in Member Countries[1]
first country page)[2]

	São Tomé and Príncipe	Saudi Arabia	Senegal	Seychelles	Sierra Leone	Singapore	Slovak Republic	Slovenia	Solomon Islands	Somalia	South Africa	Spain	Sri Lanka	Sudan	Suriname	Swaziland	Sweden	Switzerland	Syrian Arab Republic	Tajikistan	Tanzania	Thailand	Togo	Tonga	Trinidad and Tobago	Tunisia	Turkey	Turkmenistan	Uganda	Ukraine	United Arab Emirates	United Kingdom	United States	Uruguay	Uzbekistan
		●	●	●	●	●	●	●	●		●	●	●		●	●	●	●			●	●	●	●	●	●	●		●	●	●	●	●	●	
	●									●				●					●	●								●							●
				◆												◇			■				◆												
				⊕			⊕		⊕													⊕		⊕											
		✚										▼																			✚				
							●		●						●	●	●									●	●	●		●				●	●
	●								●	●							●	●	●			●		●					●			●	●		
										●																		●							
	●																		●																●
			—		●			●	—	—				●	—				●	●		●							●	●				●	●
	●			●	●				—	●				●	●				—	●	●		●						●	●	—				
	●		●		●		●	●	●	●		●	●	●				●		●		●	●		●	●	●		●						
	●		●	●	●		●	●	●	●			●	●				●	●	●	●	●		●	●	●	●		●					●	
	●		●	●			●	●	●	●			●	●	—				●	●	●	●		●	●	●	●		●						●
	—	●	●	●	●		●	●	●	●	●	●	●	—	●	●		●	●	●	●		●	●	●	●	●		●			●		
	—	●	●	●	●		●	●	—	●		—	●	●				●	●	●	●		●	●	●	●	●		●			●		
	—	●	●		●		●	●	●	●			●	●				●	●	●	●		●	●	●	—	●	●						
	—	●	●	—	●		●	●	●	●		●	●				—	●	●	●	●		●		—	●	—						●
	—	●	●	—			—	●	●	●	●		●				—	●	●	●	●		●	●	●	●		●						●
	—	●		●				●	●	●	●							●	●	●	●		●		●	●		●						●
	—	●	●					—	●	●								●	●	●	●	—	●		●	●		—						
	●	●	●		●		●	●	●	●	●	●	●	●				●	●	●	●		●	●	●	●	●	●	●		●	●		●
	—		●	●				●	●			●						●		●		●	—			●								●
	—	●	●	●	●		●	●	●	—	●		—	●	●			●	●	●	●		●	●	●	●	●	—	●					●
	●	●	●	●	●		●	●	●	●	●	●	●	●	●		●	●	●		●	●	●	●	●	●	●	●	●		●			
	—			—	—	●	—	●	—			●	●			—		●	—		—	●	●	●	●	●		—						●

	Vanuatu	Venezuela	Vietnam	Western Samoa	Yemen, Republic of	Zambia	Zimbabwe
Status under IMF Articles of Agreement							
Article VIII	•	•		•	•		•
Article XIV			•			•	
Exchange rate arrangements							
Pegged to:							
Single currency							
Composite of currencies	⊕			⊕			
Flexibility limited							
More flexible arrangements							
Managed floating		•	•				
Independent floating					•	•	•
Exchange rate structure							
Dual exchange rates							
Multiple exchange rates							
Arrangements for payments and receipts							
Bilateral payment arrangements							•
Payment arrears		•	•		•	•	
Control on payments for invisible transactions and current transfers			•	•			•
Proceeds from exports and/or invisible transactions							
Repatriation requirements		•	•	•			•
Surrender requirements			•	•			•
Capital transactions							
Controls on:							
Capital market securities		•		•			•
Money market instruments				•			•
Collective investment securities		•		•			•
Derivatives and other instruments			—	—			—
Commercial credits			•	•	•		•
Financial credits			•	•	•		•
Guarantees, sureties, and financial backup facilities			—	—	•		—
Direct investment		•	•	•			•
Liquidation of direct investment			—	•			•
Real estate transactions			•	•			•
Provisions specific to:							
Commercial banks and other credit institutions		•	•	•	•	•	•
Institutional investors			—	—			•

Key and Footnotes

• indicates that the specified practice is a feature of the exchange system.

– indicates that data were not available at time of publication.

■ indicates that the arrangement is pegged to the U.S. dollar.

♦ indicates that the arrangement is pegged to the French franc.

◊ indicates that arrangements are pegged either to the Australian dollar, deutsche mark, Indian rupee, Italian lira, Singapore dollar, or South African rand.

▲ indicates that the composite is the SDR.

⊕ indicates that the composite is a basket of other currencies.

✦ indicates that flexibility is limited to a single currency.

▼ indicates that the country participates in the ERM of the EMS.

[1] The listing includes Hong Kong, China; Aruba; and the Netherlands Antilles.

[2] Usually December 31, 1996.

APPENDIX II: COUNTRY TABLE MATRIX

Status Under IMF Articles of Agreement

Article VIII

Article XIV

Exchange Arrangement

Currency

Other legal tender

Exchange rate structure

Unitary

Dual

Multiple

Classification

Pegged

Limited flexibility with respect to a
single currency

Cooperative arrangement

Adjusted according to a set of
indicators

Managed floating

Independent floating

Exchange tax

Exchange subsidy

Forward exchange market

Official cover of forward operations

Arrangements for Payments and Receipts

**Prescription of currency
requirements**

Payment arrangements

Bilateral arrangements

  Operative

  Inoperative

Regional arrangements

Clearing agreements

Barter agreements and open accounts

Administration of control

Exchange control authorities

International security restrictions

In accordance with IMF Executive
Board Decision No. 144-(52/51)

In accordance with UN sanctions

Other

Payment arrears

Official

Private

**Controls on trade in gold (coins
and/or bullion)**

Controls on domestic ownership and/or
trade

Controls on external trade

**Controls on exports and imports of
banknotes**

On exports

  Domestic currency

  Foreign currency

On imports

  Domestic currency

  Foreign currency

Resident Accounts

Eligibility to hold accounts

Juridical persons

Natural persons

**Foreign exchange accounts
permitted**

Held domestically

  Approval required

Held abroad

  Approval required

**Accounts in domestic currency con-
vertible into foreign currency**

Nonresident Accounts

Eligibility to hold accounts

Juridical persons

Natural persons

Foreign exchange accounts permitted

Approval required

Domestic currency accounts

Convertible into foreign currency

Approval required

Blocked accounts

Imports and Import Payments

Foreign exchange budget

Financing requirements for imports

Minimum financing requirements

Advance payment requirements

Advance import deposits

Documentation requirements for release of foreign exchange for imports

Domiciliation requirements

Preshipment inspection

Letters of credit

Import licenses used as exchange licenses

Import licenses and other nontariff measures

Positive list

Negative list

Open general licenses

Licenses with quotas

Import taxes and/or tariffs

Taxes collected through the exchange system

State import monopoly

Exports and Export Proceeds

Repatriation requirements

Surrender requirements

Financing requirements

Documentation requirements

Letters of credit

Guarantees

Domiciliation

Preshipment inspection

Export licenses

Without quotas

With quotas

Export taxes

Taxes collected through the exchange system

Payments for Invisible Transactions and Current Transfers

Controls on these payments

Freight/insurance

    Prior approval

    Quantitative limits

    Indicative limits/bona fide test

Unloading/storage costs

    Prior approval

    Quantitative limits

    Indicative limits/bona fide test

Administrative expenses

    Prior approval

    Quantitative limits

    Indicative limits/bona fide test

Commissions

    Prior approval

    Quantitative limits

    Indicative limits/bona fide test

Interest payments

    Prior approval

    Quantitative limits

    Indicative limits/bona fide test

Profit/dividends

    Prior approval

    Quantitative limits

    Indicative limits/bona fide test

Payments for travel

    Prior approval

    Quantitative limits

Indicative limits/bona fide test

Medical costs

    Prior approval

    Quantitative limits

    Indicative limits/bona fide test

Study abroad costs

    Prior approval

    Quantitative limits

    Indicative limits/bona fide test

Subscriptions and membership fees

    Prior approval

    Quantitative limits

    Indicative limits/bona fide test

Consulting/legal fees

    Prior approval

    Quantitative limits

    Indicative limits/bona fide test

Foreign workers' wages

    Prior approval

    Quantitative limits

    Indicative limits/bona fide test

Pensions

    Prior approval

    Quantitative limits

    Indicative limits/bona fide test

Gambling/prize earnings

    Prior approval

    Quantitative limits

    Indicative limits/bona fide test

Family maintenance/alimony

    Prior approval

    Quantitative limits

    Indicative limits/bona fide test

Credit card use abroad

    Prior approval

    Quantitative limits

    Indicative limits/bona fide test

Proceeds from Invisible Transactions and Current Transfers

Repatriation requirements

Surrender requirements

Restrictions on use of funds

Capital Transactions

Controls on capital and money market instruments

On capital market securities

Purchase locally by nonresidents

Sale or issue locally by nonresidents

Purchase abroad by residents

Sale or issue abroad by residents

On money market instruments

Purchase locally by nonresidents

Sale or issue locally by nonresidents

Purchase abroad by residents

Sale or issue abroad by residents

On collective investment securities

Purchase locally by nonresidents

Sale or issue locally by nonresidents

Purchase abroad by residents

Sale or issue abroad by residents

Controls on derivatives and other instruments

Purchase locally by nonresidents

Sale or issue locally by nonresidents

Purchase abroad by residents

Sale or issue abroad by residents

Controls on credit operations

Commercial credits

By residents to nonresidents

To residents from nonresidents

Financial credits

By residents to nonresidents

To residents from nonresidents

Guarantees, sureties, and financial backup facilities

By residents to nonresidents

To residents from nonresidents

Controls on direct investment

Outward direct investment

Inward direct investment

Controls on liquidation of direct investment

Controls on real estate transactions

Purchase abroad by residents

Purchase locally by nonresidents

Sale locally by nonresidents

Provisions specific to commercial banks and other credit institutions

Borrowing abroad

Maintenance of accounts abroad

Lending to nonresidents (financial or commercial credits)

Lending locally in foreign exchange

Purchase of locally issued securities denominated in foreign exchange

Differential treatment of nonresident deposit accounts and/or deposit accounts in foreign exchange

Reserve requirements

Liquid asset requirements

Interest rate controls

Credit controls

Investment regulations

Open foreign exchange position limits

Provisions specific to institutional investors

Limits (max.) on portfolio invested abroad

Limits (min.) on portfolio invested locally

Currency matching regulations on assets/liabilities composition

Other controls imposed by securities laws

Changes During 1996

**Status under IMF Articles of
Agreement**

Exchange arrangements

**Arrangements for payments and
receipts**

Resident accounts

Nonresident accounts

Imports and import payments

Exports and export proceeds

**Payments for invisible transactions
and current transfers**

**Proceeds from invisible transactions
and current transfers**

Capital transactions

Changes During 1997

**Status under IMF Articles of
Agreement**

Exchange arrangements

**Arrangements for payments and
receipts**

Resident accounts

Nonresident accounts

Imports and import payments

Exports and export proceeds

**Payments for invisible transactions
and current transfers**

**Proceeds from invisible transactions
and current transfers**

Capital transactions